KENTUCKY
RULES OF COURT

VOLUME I – STATE

2013

Mat #41258975

ISBN: 978–0–314–65407–6

PREFACE

———

This edition of the *Kentucky Rules of Court, Volume I – State, 2013* replaces the 2012 Edition, and any accompanying supplement(s). This volume provides in convenient form the text of court rules governing state practice in Kentucky, with amendments received through January 1, 2013.

THE PUBLISHER

February 2013

ADDITIONAL INFORMATION OR RESEARCH ASSISTANCE

For additional information or research assistance call the West reference attorneys at 1-800-REF-ATTY (1-800-733-2889). Contact West's editorial department directly with your questions and suggestions by e-mail at west.editor@thomson.com.

Visit West's home page at west.thomson.com.

WestlawNext™

THE NEXT GENERATION OF ONLINE RESEARCH

WestlawNext is the world's most advanced legal research system. By leveraging more than a century of information and legal analysis from Westlaw, this easy-to-use system not only helps you find the information you need quickly, but offers time-saving tools to organize and annotate your research online. As with Westlaw.com, WestlawNext includes the editorial enhancements (e.g., case headnotes, topics, key numbers) that make it a perfect complement to West print resources.

- FIND ANYTHING by entering citations, descriptive terms, or Boolean terms and connectors into the WestSearch™ box at the top of every page.

- USE KEYCITE® to determine whether a case, statute, regulation, or administrative decision is good law.

- BROWSE DATABASES right from the home page.

- SAVE DOCUMENTS to folders and add notes and highlighting online.

SIGN ON: next.westlaw.com
LEARN MORE: West.Thomson.com/WestlawNext
FOR HELP: 1–800–WESTLAW (1–800–937–8529)

TABLE OF CONTENTS

*

CONSTITUTIONAL JUDICIAL ARTICLE

Ratified November, 1975
Effective January 1, 1976
Including Amendments Received Through January 1, 2013

THE JUDICIAL DEPARTMENT

Ky Const § 109 The judicial power; unified system; impeachment

The judicial power of the Commonwealth shall be vested exclusively in one Court of Justice which shall be divided into a Supreme Court, a Court of Appeals, a trial court of general jurisdiction known as the Circuit Court and a trial court of limited jurisdiction known as the District Court. The court shall constitute a unified judicial system for operation and administration. The impeachment powers of the General Assembly shall remain inviolate.

HISTORY: 1974 c 84, § 1, adopted eff. 1–1–76

THE SUPREME COURT

Ky Const § 110 Composition; jurisdiction; quorum; special justices; districts; Chief Justice

(1) The Supreme Court shall consist of the Chief Justice of the Commonwealth and six associate Justices.

(2) (a) The Supreme Court shall have appellate jurisdiction only, except it shall have the power to issue all writs necessary in aid of its appellate jurisdiction, or the complete determination of any cause, or as may be required to exercise control of the Court of Justice.

(b) Appeals from a judgment of the Circuit Court imposing a sentence of death or life imprisonment or imprisonment for twenty years or more shall be taken directly to the Supreme Court. In all other cases, criminal and civil, the Supreme Court shall exercise appellate jurisdiction as provided by its rules.

(3) A majority of the Justices of the Supreme Court shall constitute a quorum for the transaction of business. If as many as two Justices decline or are unable to sit in the trial of any cause, the Chief Justice shall certify that fact to the Governor, who shall appoint to try the particular cause a sufficient number of Justices to constitute a full court for the trial of the cause.

(4) The Court of Appeals districts existing on the effective date of this amendment to the Constitution shall constitute the initial Supreme Court districts. The General Assembly thereafter may redistrict the Commonwealth, by counties, into seven Supreme Court districts as nearly equal in population and as compact in form as possible. There shall be one Justice from each Supreme Court district.

(5) (a) The Justices of the Supreme Court shall elect one of their number to serve as Chief Justice for a term of four years.

(b) The Chief Justice of the Commonwealth shall be the executive head of the Court of Justice and he shall appoint such administrative assistants as he deems necessary. He shall assign temporarily any justice or judge of the Commonwealth, active or retired, to sit in any court other than the Supreme Court when he deems such assignment necessary for the prompt disposition of causes. The Chief Justice shall submit the budget for the Court of Justice and perform all other necessary administrative functions relating to the court.

HISTORY: 1974 c 84, § 1, adopted eff. 1–1–76

THE COURT OF APPEALS

Ky Const § 111 Composition; jurisdiction; administration; panels

(1) The Court of Appeals shall consist initially of fourteen judges, an equal number to be selected from each Supreme Court district. The number of judges thereafter shall be determined from time to time by the General Assembly upon certification of necessity by the Supreme Court.

(2) The Court of Appeals shall have appellate jurisdiction only, except that it may be authorized by rules of the Supreme Court to review directly decisions of administrative agencies of the Commonwealth, and it may issue all writs necessary in aid of its appellate jurisdiction, or the complete determination of any cause within its appellate jurisdiction. In all other cases, it shall exercise appellate jurisdiction as provided by law.

(3) The judges of the Court of Appeals shall elect one of their number to serve as Chief Judge for a term of four years. The Chief Judge shall exercise such authority and perform such duties in the administration of the Court of Appeals as are prescribed in this section or as may be prescribed by the Supreme Court.

(4) The Court of Appeals shall divide itself into panels of not less than three judges. A panel may decide a cause by the concurring vote of a majority of its judges. The Chief Judge shall make assignments of judges to panels. The Court of Appeals shall prescribe the times and places in the Commonwealth at which each panel shall sit.

HISTORY: 1974 c 84, § 1, adopted eff. 1–1–76

THE CIRCUIT COURT

Ky Const § 112 Location; circuits; composition; administration; jurisdiction

(1) Circuit Court shall be held in each county.

(2) The Circuit Court districts existing on the effective date of this amendment to the Constitution shall continue under the name "Judicial Circuits," the General Assembly having power upon certification of the necessity therefor by the Supreme Court to reduce, increase or rearrange the judicial districts. A judicial circuit composed of more than one county shall be as compact in form as possible and of contiguous counties. No county shall be divided in creating a judicial circuit.

(3) The number of circuit judges in each district existing on the effective date of this amendment shall continue, the General Assembly having power upon certification of the necessity therefor by the Supreme Court, to change the number of circuit judges in any judicial circuit.

(4) In a judicial circuit having only one judge, he shall be the chief judge. In judicial circuits having two or more judges, they shall select biennially a chief judge, and if they fail to do so within a reasonable time, the Supreme Court shall designate the chief judge. The chief judge shall exercise such authority and perform such duties in the administration of his judicial circuit as may be prescribed by the Supreme Court. The Supreme Court may provide by rules for administration of judicial circuits by regions designated by it.

(5) The Circuit Court shall have original jurisdiction of all justiciable causes not vested in some other court. It shall have such appellate jurisdiction as may be provided by law.

(6) The Supreme Court may designate one or more divisions of Circuit Court within a judicial circuit as a family court division. A Circuit Court division so designated shall retain the general jurisdiction of the Circuit Court and shall have additional jurisdiction as may be provided by the General Assembly.

HISTORY: 2001 c 163, § 1, amendment approved 11–5–02; 1974 c 84, § 1, adopted eff. 1–1–76

Legislative Research Commission Note (11–15–02): 2001 Ky. Acts ch. 163, which contained the text of the amendment to this section that was ratified on November 5, 2002, also contained sec. 2, which reads as follows:

"District judges elected for the term beginning on the first Monday in January of 2003, who possess the qualifications of a Circuit Judge and who are assigned by the Chief Justice to serve as family court judges on or before the commencement of the term, shall on that date become Circuit Judges with terms of office coinciding with the terms of Circuit Judges generally, and another numbered division or divisions of that judicial circuit shall be created. When a District Judge becomes a Circuit Judge pursuant to this provision, that District Judgeship shall be abolished and there shall be no vacancy to fill. The General Assembly, upon the ratification of this amendment, shall enact legislation to implement the provisions of this amendment in a manner consistent with the Supreme Court's adjustment of any Circuit Court division as a family court division."

THE DISTRICT COURT

Ky Const § 113 Location; districts; composition; administration; trial commissioners; jurisdiction

(1) District Court shall be held in each county.

(2) The Circuit Court districts existing on the effective date of this amendment shall continue for District Court purposes under the name "Judicial Districts," the General Assembly having power upon certification of the necessity therefor by the Supreme Court to reduce, increase or rearrange the districts. A judicial district composed of more than one county shall be as compact in form as possible and of contiguous counties. No county shall be divided in creating a judicial district.

(3) Each judicial district created by this amendment initially shall have at least one district judge who shall serve as chief judge and there shall be such other district judges as the General Assembly shall determine. The number of district judges in each judicial district thereafter shall be determined by the General Assembly upon certification of necessity therefor by the Supreme Court.

(4) In a judicial district having only one judge he shall be the chief judge. In those districts having two or more judges they shall select biennially a chief judge and if they fail to do so within a reasonable time, the Supreme Court shall designate the chief judge. The chief judge shall exercise such authority and perform such duties in the administration of his district as may be prescribed by the Supreme Court.

(5) In any county in which no district judge resides the chief judge of the district shall appoint a trial commissioner who shall be a resident of such county and who shall be an attorney if one is qualified and available. Other trial commissioners with like qualifications may be appointed by the chief judge in any judicial district upon certification of the necessity therefor by the Supreme Court. All trial commissioners shall have power to perform such duties of the district court as may be prescribed by the Supreme Court.

(6) The district court shall be a court of limited jurisdiction and shall exercise original jurisdiction as may be provided by the General Assembly.

HISTORY: 1974 c 84, § 1, adopted eff. 1-1-76

CLERKS OF COURTS

Ky Const § 114   Selection; removal

(1) The Supreme Court shall appoint a clerk to serve as it shall determine.

(2) The Court of Appeals shall appoint a clerk to serve as it shall determine.

(3) The clerks of the Circuit Court shall be elected in the manner provided elsewhere in this Constitution. The clerks of the Circuit Court shall serve as the clerks of the District Court. The clerks of the Circuit Court shall be removable from office by the Supreme Court upon good cause shown.

HISTORY: 1974 c 84, § 1, adopted eff. 1-1-76

APPELLATE POLICY; RULE-MAKING POWER

Ky Const § 115   Right of appeal; procedure

In all cases, civil and criminal, there shall be allowed as a matter of right at least one appeal to another court, except that the Commonwealth may not appeal from a judgment of acquittal in a criminal case, other than for the purpose of securing a certification of law, and the General Assembly may prescribe that there shall be no appeal from that portion of a judgment dissolving a marriage. Procedural rules shall provide for expeditious and inexpensive appeals. Appeals shall be upon the record and not by trial de novo.

HISTORY: 1974 c 84, § 1, adopted eff. 1-1-76

Ky Const § 116   Rules governing jurisdiction, personnel, procedure, bar membership

The Supreme Court shall have the power to prescribe rules governing its appellate jurisdiction, rules for the appointment of commissioners and other court personnel, and rules of practice and procedure for the Court of Justice. The Supreme Court shall, by rule, govern admission to the bar and the discipline of members of the bar.

HISTORY: 1974 c 84, § 1, adopted eff. 1-1-76

OFFICES OF JUSTICES AND JUDGES

Ky Const § 117   Election

Justices of the Supreme Court and judges of the Court of Appeals, Circuit and District Court shall be elected from their respective districts or circuits on a nonpartisan basis as provided by law.

HISTORY: 1974 c 84, § 1, adopted eff. 1-1-76

Ky Const § 118   Vacancies

(1) A vacancy in the office of a justice of the Supreme Court, or of a judge of the Court of Appeals, circuit or district court which under Section 152 of this Constitution is to be filled by appointment by the Governor shall be filled by the Governor from a list of three names presented to him by the appropriate judicial nominating commission. If the Governor fails to make an appointment from the list within sixty days from the date it is presented to him, the appointment shall be made from the same list by the chief justice of the Supreme Court.

(2) There shall be one judicial nominating commission for the Supreme Court and the Court of Appeals, one for each judicial circuit, and one for each judicial district, except that a circuit and district having the same boundary shall have but one judicial nominating commission. Each commission shall consist of seven members, one of whom shall be the chief justice of the Supreme Court, who shall be chairman. Two mem-

bers of each commission shall be members of the bar, who shall be elected by their fellow members. The other four members shall be appointed by the Governor from among persons not members of the bar, and these four shall include at least two members of each of the two political parties of the Commonwealth having the largest number of voters. Members of a judicial circuit or judicial district nominating commission must be residents of the circuit or district, respectively, and the lawyer members of the commission shall be elected by the members of the bar residing in the circuit or district, respectively. The terms of office of members of judicial nominating commissions shall be fixed by the General Assembly. No person shall be elected or appointed a member of a judicial nominating commission who holds any other public office or any office in a political party or organization.

HISTORY: 1974 c 84, § 1, adopted eff. 1–1–76

Ky Const § 119   Terms of office

Justices of the Supreme Court and judges of the Court of Appeals and circuit court shall severally hold their offices for terms of eight years, and judges of the district court for terms of four years. All terms commence on the first Monday in January next succeeding the regular election for the office. No justice or judge may be deprived of his term of office by redistricting, or by a reduction in the number of justices or judges.

HISTORY: 1974 c 84, § 1, adopted eff. 1–1–76

Ky Const § 120   Compensation; expenses

All justices and judges shall be paid adequate compensation which shall be fixed by the General Assembly. All compensation and necessary expenses of the Court of Justice shall be paid out of the State Treasury. The compensation of a justice or judge shall not be reduced during his term.

HISTORY: 1974 c 84, § 1, adopted eff. 1–1–76

Ky Const § 121   Retirement and removal

Subject to rules of procedure to be established by the Supreme Court, and after notice and hearing, any justice of the Supreme Court or judge of the Court of Appeals, Circuit Court or District Court may be retired for disability or suspended without pay or removed for good cause by a commission composed of one judge of the Court of Appeals, selected by that court, one circuit judge and one district judge selected by a majority vote of the circuit judges and district judges, respectively, one member of the bar appointed

by its governing body, and two persons, not members of the bench or bar, appointed by the Governor. The commission shall be a state body whose members shall hold office for four-year terms. Its actions shall be subject to judicial review by the Supreme Court.

HISTORY: 1974 c 84, § 1, adopted eff. 1–1–76

Ky Const § 122   Eligibility

To be eligible to serve as a justice of the Supreme Court or a judge of the Court of Appeals, Circuit Court or District Court a person must be a citizen of the United States, licensed to practice law in the courts of this Commonwealth, and have been a resident of this Commonwealth and of the district from which he is elected for two years next preceding his taking office. In addition, to be eligible to serve as a justice of the Supreme Court or judge of the Court of Appeals or Circuit Court a person must have been a licensed attorney for at least eight years. No district judge shall serve who has not been a licensed attorney for at least two years.

HISTORY: 1974 c 84, § 1, adopted eff. 1–1–76

Ky Const § 123   Prohibited activities

During his term of office, no justice of the Supreme Court or judge of the Court of Appeals, Circuit Court or District Court shall engage in the practice of law, or run for elective office other than judicial office, or hold any office in a political party or organization.

HISTORY: 1974 c 84, § 1, adopted eff. 1–1–76

Ky Const § 124   Conflicting provisions

Any remaining sections of the Constitution of Kentucky as it existed prior to the effective date of this amendment which are in conflict with the provisions of amended Sections 110 through 125 are repealed to the extent of the conflict, but such amended sections are not intended to repeal those parts of Sections 140 and 142 conferring nonjudicial powers and duties upon county judges and justices of the peace. Nothing in such amended sections shall be construed to limit the powers otherwise granted by this Constitution to the county judge as the chief executive, administrative and fiscal officer of the county, or to limit the powers otherwise granted by the Constitution to the justices of the peace or county commissioners as executive, administrative and fiscal officers of a county, or of the fiscal court as a governing body of a county.

HISTORY: 1974 c 84, § 1, adopted eff. 1–1–76

RULES OF CIVIL PROCEDURE

Effective July 1, 1953
Including Amendments Received Through January 1, 2013

8

I TITLE AND SCOPE OF RULES; ONE FORM OF ACTION

CR 1 Title and scope of Rules

(1) The title of these Rules is Kentucky Rules of Civil Procedure. They may be cited as such, or as the "Civil Rules," or by the abbreviation "CR."

(2) These Rules govern procedure and practice in all actions of a civil nature in the Court of Justice except for special statutory proceedings, in which the procedural requirements of the statute shall prevail over any inconsistent procedures set forth in the Rules. Regulations and manuals published by the Administrative Office of the Courts upon authorization of the Supreme Court relating to internal policy and administration within the Court of Justice shall have the same effect as if incorporated in the Rules.

HISTORY: Amended eff. 1–1–78; prior amendment eff. 7–1–76; adopted eff. 7–1–53

CR 2 One form of action

There shall be one form of action to be known as "civil action."

HISTORY: Adopted eff. 7–1–53

II COMMENCEMENT OF ACTION; SERVICE OF PROCESS, PLEADINGS, MOTIONS AND ORDERS

CR 3 [Commencement of action; fees and costs]

CR 3.01 Commencement of action

A civil action is commenced by the filing of a complaint with the court and the issuance of a summons or warning order thereon in good faith.

HISTORY: Adopted eff. 7–1–53

CR 3.02 Circuit civil fees and costs

(1) The filing fees for a civil case in Circuit Court (including original actions of administrative agencies, special districts or boards) shall be paid to the circuit clerk at the time the case is filed and shall be $115.00, except as provided below:

(a) There shall be no filing fees for proceedings for a writ of habeas corpus, proceedings under RCr 11.42, and mental health proceedings under KRS Chapters 202A, 202B and 387.

(b) Fees required by KRS 453.060 and KRS 27A.630 and any other required fees (e.g., court facility fee, library fee) shall be paid in addition to the fees required by this rule.

(2) Additional costs, payable to the circuit clerk at the time the service is requested, shall be charged in Circuit Court civil cases as follows:

(a)	For a jury of six persons	$30.00
(b)	For a jury of more than six	$60.00
(c)	Filing a third party complaint	$30.00
(d)	Preparing a certification, including Act of Congress	$ 5.00
(e)	Providing a copy of a document (per page)	$ .25
(f)	Providing a copy of a video recording (per individual tape, disk or other media)	$20.00
(g)	Providing a copy of an audio recording (per individual tape, disk or other media)	$10.00
(h)	Issuing orders of attachment; executions, writ of possession after judgment	$20.00
(i)	Issuing garnishments	$10.00
(j)	Publishing a notice	As set by Newspaper
(k)	Certified mail fees	As set by Postal Service
(l)	Original deposition, including appearance fees and mileage	Assessed as Costs
(m)	Library fees	As set by KRS 172.180 and KRS 453.060

(3) The court, in its discretion, may provide for the payment of additional costs in cases requiring extraordinary services. If the circuit judge assesses additional costs, the circuit clerk shall collect as ordered including:

(a) A fee of $50.00 in domestic relations cases reopened after six months from the entry of the decree for the purpose of modifying the decree, to be collected from the movant at the filing of the motion;

(b) A fee of $50.00 in civil cases in each instance in which the number of items filed surpasses 50 in number or a multiple thereof (the 51st item, 101st item, etc.), to be collected following entry of the judgment;

(c) A fee of $100.00 per day for each day of a civil jury trial in excess of four (4) days, to be collected following entry of the judgment.

HISTORY: Amended by Order 2008–01, eff. 7–1–08; prior amendments eff. 1–1–07 (Order 2006–09), 1–1–05 (Orders 2005–1, 2004–5), 7–1–02, 3–15–97 (Order 97–2), 3–15–97; adopted eff. 1–1–97.

CR 3.03   District civil fees and costs

(1) The filing fee for a civil case in District Court shall be paid to the clerk at the time the case is filed and shall be $55.00, except as provided below:

(a) Where the case or controversy does not exceed $1500.00, exclusive of interests and costs (Small Claims), shall be $20.00;

(b) Where the amount in controversy is $500.00 or less and is not filed in small claims court, the fees shall be $30.00;

(c) Where the case involves the probate of an estate, the fees shall be $20.00;

(d) Where the case involves the appointment of guardians, conservators, and curators and is not related to a pending probate proceeding, the fees shall be $20.00 for each application;

(e) Where the matter involves a name change for a natural person, the fees shall be $20.00;

(f) Where the case involves a paternity determination under KRS Chapter 406, the fees shall be $20.00;

(g) Where the case involves mental health proceedings under KRS Chapter 202A, 202B or 387, there shall be no fees except as provided in paragraph (d) of this subsection;

(h) Where the case involves a hearing for a student pursuant to KRS 159.051, there shall be no fees;

(i) Where the case involves filing forcible detainer actions, the fees shall be $20.00; and

(j) Where the case involves filing a petition to marry under KRS 402.020, the fees shall be $5.00.

(k) Fees required by KRS 453.060 and KRS 27A.630 and any other required fees (e.g., court facility fee, library fee) shall be paid in addition to the fee required by this rule.

(2) Appeals to Circuit Court.

(a) The filing fees for an appeal from a district court civil matter to the circuit court shall be $60.00.

(b) In the case of a counterclaim or cross-claim that exceeds the jurisdictional amount of district court requiring transfer to circuit court, additional fees of $60.00 shall be paid by the party filing the counterclaim or cross-claim.

(c) In the case of a counterclaim or cross-claim that exceeds the jurisdictional amount for which the lessened fee is provided in subsection (1)(b) above, but which is not greater than the jurisdiction of District Court, additional fees of $15.00 shall be paid by the party filing such counterclaim or cross-claim.

(d) The fees required by KRS 453.060 shall be paid in addition to the fee required by this rule.

(3) Additional costs, payable to the circuit clerk at the time the service is requested, shall be charged in District Court civil cases as follows:

(a)	For a jury of six persons including paternity cases	$30.00
(b)	Filing a third party complaint	$30.00
(c)	Preparing a certification, including Act of Congress	$ 5.00
(d)	Providing a copy of a document (per page)	$ .25
(e)	Providing a copy of a video recording (per individual tape, disk or other media)	$20.00
(f)	Providing a copy of an audio recording (per individual tape, disk or other media)	$10.00
(g)	Issuing orders of attachment; executions, writ of possession after judgment	$20.00
(h)	Issuing garnishments	$10.00
(i)	Publishing a notice	As set by Newspaper

(j)	Certified mail fee	As set by Postal Service	
(k)	Original deposition, including appearance fees and mileage	Assessed as Costs	
(l)	Library fees	As set by KRS 172.180 and KRS 453.060	

(4) The court, in its discretion, may provide for the payment of additional costs in cases requiring extraordinary services.

HISTORY: Amended by Order 2008–01, eff. 7–1–08; prior amendments eff. 1–1–07 (Order 2006–09), 1–1–05 (Orders 2005–1, 2004–5), 7–1–02, 3–15–97 (Order 97–2), 3–15–97; adopted eff. 1–1–97

CR 4 Process

CR 4.01 Summons; issuance; by whom served

(1) Upon the filing of the complaint (or other initiating document) the clerk shall forthwith issue the required summons and, at the direction of the initiating party, either:

(a) Place a copy of the summons and complaint (or other initiating document) to be served in an envelope, address the envelope to the person to be served at the address set forth in the caption or at the address set forth in written instructions furnished by the initiating party, affix adequate postage, and place the sealed envelope in the United States mail as registered mail or certified mail return receipt requested with instructions to the delivering postal employee to deliver to the addressee only and show the address where delivered and the date of delivery. The clerk shall forthwith enter the facts of mailing on the docket and make a similar entry when the return receipt is received by him or her. If the envelope is returned with an endorsement showing failure of delivery, the clerk shall enter that fact on the docket. The clerk shall file the return receipt or returned envelope in the record. Service by registered mail or certified mail is complete only upon delivery of the envelope. The return receipt shall be proof of the time, place and manner of service. To the extent that the United States postal regulations permit authorized representatives of local, state, or federal governmental offices to accept and sign for "addressee only" mail, signature by such authorized representative shall constitute service on the officer. All postage shall be advanced by the initiating party and be recoverable as costs; or

(b) Cause the summons and complaint (or other initiating document), with necessary copies, to be transferred for service to any person authorized, other than by paragraph (1) of this Rule, to deliver them, who shall serve the summons and accompanying documents, and his return endorsed thereon shall be proof of the time and manner of service.

(2) A summons may be issued for service in any county, against any person to be served, and separate or additional summons may be issued against any

person to be served at the request of the initiating party.

HISTORY: Amended by Order 94–1, eff. 10–1–94; prior amendments eff. 6–1–78, 1–1–78, 6–1–60; adopted eff. 7–1–53

CR 4.02 Summons; form

The summons shall be issued in the name of the Commonwealth, be dated and signed by the clerk, contain the name of the court and the style and number of the action, and be directed to each defendant, notifying him that a legal action has been filed against him and that unless a written defense is made by him or by an attorney in his behalf within 20 days following the day on which the summons is served on him a judgment may issue against him for the relief demanded.

HISTORY: Amended eff. 7–1–75; prior amendment eff. 6–7–74; adopted eff. 7–1–53

CR 4.03 Summons; return

The person serving the summons shall make proof thereof to the court promptly, and in any event within the time during which the person served must respond.

HISTORY: Amended eff. 6–1–60; adopted eff. 7–1–53

CR 4.04 Personal service; summons and initiating document

(1) The summons and complaint (or other initiating document) shall be served together. The initiating party shall furnish the person making service with such copies as may be necessary.

(2) Service shall be made upon an individual within this Commonwealth, other than an unmarried infant or person of unsound mind, by delivering a copy of the summons and of the complaint (or other initiating document) to him personally or, if acceptance is refused by offering personal delivery to such person, or by delivering a copy of the summons and of the complaint (or other initiating document) to an agent authorized by appointment or by law to receive service of process for such individual.

(3) Service shall be made upon an unmarried infant or a person of unsound mind by serving his resident guardian or committee if there is one known to the plaintiff or, if none, by serving either his father or mother within this state or, if none, by serving the person within this state having control of such individual. If there are no such persons enumerated above, the clerk shall appoint a practicing attorney as guardian ad litem who shall be served. If any of the persons directed by this section to be served is a plaintiff, the person who stands first in the order named who is not a plaintiff shall be served.

(4) Service shall be made upon a partnership or unincorporated association subject to suit under a common name by serving a partner or managing

agent of the partnership or an officer or managing agent of the association, or an agent authorized by appointment or by law to receive service on its behalf.

(5) Service shall be made upon a corporation by serving an officer or managing agent thereof, or the chief agent in the county wherein the action is brought, or any other agent authorized by appointment or by law to receive service on its behalf.

(6) Service shall be made upon the Commonwealth or any agency thereof by serving the attorney general or any assistant attorney general.

(7) Service shall be made upon a county by serving the county judge or, if he is absent from the county, the county attorney. Service shall be made upon a city by serving the chief executive officer thereof or an official attorney thereof. Service on any public board or other such body, except state agencies, shall be made by serving a member thereof.

(8) Service may be made upon an individual out of this state, other than an unmarried infant, a person of unsound mind or a prisoner, either by certified mail in the manner prescribed in Rule 4.01(1)(a) or by personal delivery of a copy of the summons and of the complaint (or other initiating document) by a person over 18 years of age. Proof of service shall be made either by the return receipt mentioned in Rule 4.01(1)(a) or by affidavit of the person making such service, upon or appended to the summons, stating the time and place of service and the fact that the individual served was personally known to him. Such service without an appearance shall not authorize a personal judgment, but for all other purposes the individual summoned shall be before the courts as in other cases of personal service.

(9) Service may be made upon a nonresident individual who transacts business through an office or agency in this state, or a resident individual who transacts business through an office or agency in any action growing out of or connected with the business of such office or agency, by serving the person in charge thereof.

HISTORY: Amended eff. 7–1–79; prior amendments eff. 1–1–78, 7–1–75, 6–7–74, 7–1–69, 4–1–63, 6–1–60; adopted eff. 7–1–53

CR 4.05 Parties who may be constructively served

If a party sought to be summoned is: (a) An individual who is a nonresident of this state and known or believed to be absent therefrom, or (b) a corporation, or a partnership or unincorporated association which is subject to suit under a common name, having no agent in this state known to the plaintiff upon whom a summons may be lawfully served, or (c) an individual who has been absent from the state for four months or who has departed therefrom with the intent to delay or defraud his creditors, or (d) an individual who has left the county of his residence to avoid the service of a summons or has so concealed

himself that a summons cannot be served upon him, or (e) an individual whose name or place of residence is unknown to the plaintiff; the clerk shall forthwith, subject to the provisions of Rule 4.06, make an order upon the complaint warning the party to appear and defend the action within 50 days.

HISTORY: Amended eff. 1–1–78; prior amendment eff. 4–1–63; adopted eff. 7–1–53

CR 4.06 Warning order; affidavit

(1) The warning order provided in Rule 4.05 shall be made by the clerk only upon an affidavit of the plaintiff or his attorney, or if the plaintiff is under disability, of the party suing in his behalf or his attorney, stating the ground of the application for such order. The affiant shall state the last known address of the defendant, or, if the defendant is one designated in Rule 4.05(b) and its address is unknown, the last known address of one upon whom service may be had in its behalf, or shall state his ignorance of such of those facts as he does not know. If the affidavit is made by one other than the plaintiff, stating any grounds mentioned in Rule 4.05, the affidavit shall state the affiant's connection with the plaintiff and the affiant's belief that the plaintiff is ignorant of such facts as are unknown to the affiant.

(2) An affidavit made pursuant to the provisions of Rule 4.06(1), unless it is controverted by the defendant's affidavit, shall be sufficient evidence of the facts therein stated for the support of the action as well as of the warning order.

HISTORY: Amended eff. 1–1–78; prior amendment eff. 4–1–63; adopted eff. 7–1–53

CR 4.07 Warning order attorney

(1) The clerk at the time of making a warning order shall appoint, as attorney for the defendant, a practicing attorney of the court. The court may appoint another attorney as a substitute for the attorney appointed by the clerk. Neither the plaintiff nor his attorney shall be appointed, or be permitted to suggest the name of the defendant's attorney. Such attorney must make diligent efforts to inform the defendant, by mail, concerning the pendency and nature of the action against him, and must report the result of his efforts to the court within 50 days after his appointment.

(2) If the warning order attorney cannot inform the defendant concerning the action, he shall so report to the court and shall then make a defense by answer if he can. If unable to make defense, he shall so report.

(3) If the warning order attorney knows or learns that the defendant is an unmarried infant or of unsound mind he shall include such information in the report required by paragraph (1) of this rule, and upon the filing of such report he shall become the guardian ad litem for such defendant as if appointed under Rule 17.03.

(4) Nothing done by the warning order attorney acting in such capacity or as guardian ad litem under paragraph (3) of this rule shall be treated as an appearance by the defendant.

(5) No judgment shall be rendered against a defendant for whom a warning order is made until a report required by this rule has been filed. Failure to file a report required by this rule without good cause may be punished as a contempt of court.

(6) The court shall allow the warning order attorney a reasonable fee for his services, to be taxed as costs.

HISTORY: Amended eff. 1–1–78; prior amendment eff. 4–1–63; adopted eff. 7–1–53

CR 4.08   Constructive service; when effective

A defendant constructively summoned shall be deemed to have been summoned on the 30th day after the entry of a warning order and the action may proceed accordingly.

HISTORY: Adopted eff. 7–1–53

CR 4.09   Personal service in addition to constructive service

The plaintiff (or other initiating party) may at any time before judgment have the summons and the copy of the complaint (or other initiating document) served on the defendant (or other respondent) if found in this state though a warning order may have been entered against him, and after such service the case shall proceed as in other cases of actual service.

HISTORY: Amended eff. 7–1–75; prior amendment eff. 6–7–74; adopted eff. 7–1–53

CR 4.10   Defense by party constructively served

A party before the court by constructive service alone, which shall not include a party served as provided by Rule 4.04(2), shall be permitted to defend at any time before judgment even though in default. Such party may obtain any relief after judgment available to a party personally served.

HISTORY: Amended eff. 6–1–60; adopted eff. 7–1–53

CR 4.11   Court control of property; bond

In an action involving the property of a party before the court by constructive service alone, the court shall adjudicate the rights of the parties in the judgment and shall retain control over and preserve, for one year after the entry of the judgment, any property of which the constructively summoned party has been deprived thereby, or the proceeds thereof, unless prior to the expiration of that period the successful party executes a bond in a penal sum fixed by the court at not less than the fair market value of such property, with surety approved by the court. The condition of the bond shall be that if the constructively summoned party institutes a proceeding to obtain relief from the judgment within one year after its entry, the principal will comply with any new judgment concerning such property entered in such proceeding. If a bond is executed, or in the absence of a bond if no such proceeding is brought within the one year period, the property or its proceeds shall be disposed of in accordance with the judgment. If the original action involves persons having distinct interests, the bond may be executed for each according to his interest.

HISTORY: Amended eff. 6–1–60; adopted eff. 7–1–53

CR 4.12   Exemption of Commonwealth and political subdivisions—Repealed

HISTORY: Repealed eff. 4–1–63; amended eff. 6–1–60; adopted eff. 7–1–53

CR 4.13   Plaintiff may be examined touching his claim

Before rendering judgment against a defendant constructively summoned and who has not appeared, the court may cause the plaintiff to appear personally in court, or before a commissioner, and answer under oath concerning the statements of the complaint, or any defense thereto, including counterclaims, and may order the examination reduced to writing and filed with the papers of the action.

HISTORY: Adopted eff. 7–1–53

CR 4.14   Counterclaim disclosed allowed

If upon the examination allowed by Rule 4.13 any counterclaim is disclosed, it may be adjusted and allowed in the judgment.

HISTORY: Adopted eff. 7–1–53

CR 4.15   Unknown defendant

In an action against a person whose name is unknown to the plaintiff: (a) He shall be described in the complaint and process as unknown defendant, (b) if his name and place of residence, or either, be discovered by the plaintiff pending the action, the complaint shall be amended accordingly.

HISTORY: Amended eff. 1–1–78; prior amendment eff. 4–1–63; adopted eff. 7–1–53

CR 4.16   Summons; amendment

The court in its sound discretion and on such terms as it deems just may at any time allow any summons or other process or proof of service thereof to be amended, unless it clearly appears that the substantial rights of the party against whom it was issued would thereby be prejudiced.

HISTORY: Amended eff. 1–1–78; adopted eff. 7–1–53

CR 5   Service and filing of pleadings and other papers

CR 5.01   Service; when required

Every order required by its terms to be served, every pleading subsequent to the original complaint unless the court otherwise orders because of numerous defendants, every paper relating to discovery required to be served upon a party unless the court otherwise orders, every written motion other than one which may be heard ex parte, and every written notice, appearance, demand, offer of judgment, designation of record on appeal, and similar papers shall be served upon each party except those in default for failure to appear. Parties so in default shall be given notice of pleadings asserting new or additional claims for relief against them by summons or warning order issued thereon as provided in Rule 4.

HISTORY: Amended eff. 10–1–71; prior amendment eff. 4–1–63; adopted eff. 7–1–53

CR 5.02 Service; how made

Whenever under these rules service is required or permitted to be made upon a party represented by an attorney, which shall not include a warning order attorney, the service shall be made upon the attorney unless service upon the party is ordered by the court. Service upon the attorney or upon a party shall be made by delivering a copy to the attorney or party or by mailing it to the attorney or party at the last known address of such person; or, if no address is known, by leaving it with the clerk of the court. Delivery of a copy within this rule means handing it to the attorney or to a party; or leaving it at the office of the attorney or party with the person in charge thereof; or, if there is no one in charge, leaving it in a conspicuous place therein; or, if the office is closed or the person to be served has no office, leaving it at his dwelling house or usual place of abode with some person of suitable age and discretion then residing therein; or sending it by electronic means if the attorney or a party consents in writing. The attorney or a party consents to accept electronic service by filing and serving a notice that the attorney or party accepts electronic service. The notice must include the electronic notification address at which the attorney or party agrees to accept service. Service is complete upon mailing or electronic transmission, but electronic transmission is not effective if the serving party learns that it did not reach the person to be served.

HISTORY: Amended by Order 2010–09, eff. 1–1–11; adopted eff. 7–1–53

CR 5.03 Service; proof of

Whenever any pleading or other paper is served under Rules 5.01 and 5.02, proof of the time and manner of such service shall be filed before action is to be taken thereon by the court or the parties. Proof may be by certificate of a member of the bar of the court or by affidavit of the person who served the papers, or by any other proof satisfactory to the court. Such certificate or affidavit shall identify by name the persons so served. Proof of electronic service must state the electronic notification address of the person

served and that the document was served electronically.

HISTORY: Amended by Order 2010–09, eff. 1–1–11; prior amendment eff. 7–1–79; adopted eff. 7–1–53

CR 5.04 Service; numerous defendants

If the defendants are numerous, the court upon motion or of its initiative, may order that service of the pleadings of the defendants and replies thereto need not be made as between the defendants and that any cross-claim, counterclaim, or matter constituting an avoidance or affirmative defense contained therein shall be deemed to be denied or avoided by all other parties and that the filing of any such pleading with the court and service thereof upon the plaintiff constitutes due notice of it to the parties. A copy of every such order shall be served upon the parties in such manner and form as the court directs.

HISTORY: Adopted eff. 7–1–53

CR 5.05 Filing

(1) All papers after the complaint required to be served upon a party shall be filed with the court either before service or within a reasonable time thereafter.

(2) The filing of pleadings and other papers with the court as required by these rules shall be made by filing them with the clerk of the court, except that the judge may permit the papers to be filed with him, in which event he shall note thereon the filing date and forthwith transmit them to the office of the clerk.

(3) The clerk shall endorse upon every pleading and other paper filed with him in an action the date of its filing. Such endorsement shall constitute the filing of the pleading or other paper and no order of court shall be required.

(4) If accompanied by a motion for leave to proceed in forma pauperis and a supporting affidavit, and made in good faith, any matter to be filed under these rules, including appeals, shall be considered filed on the date it is tendered. If the motion to proceed in forma pauperis is denied, the moving party shall then have thirty (30) days to pay any required fees or costs or to appeal the decision. If the moving party fails to pay the required fees or costs, or to seek review, the matter shall be treated as though not timely filed. The time for certifying the record on appeal under CR 73.08 shall run from the date the motion to proceed in forma pauperis is granted.

HISTORY: Amended by Order 2010–09, eff. 1–1–11; prior amendments eff. 7–14–88 (Order 88–4), 1–1–86; adopted eff. 7–1–53

CR 5.06 Filing—discovery material

(1) Except as provided in paragraphs (2) and (3) of this rule, the following documents shall not be filed with the Court unless the Court orders otherwise:

(a) Interrogatories propounded under Rule 33,

(b) Requests for Production or Inspection made under Rule 34,

(c) Requests for Admission under Rule 36, and

(d) Subpoenas issued pursuant to Rule 45.

The party responsible for service of the document shall retain the original and become the custodian. The custodian shall provide access to all parties of record during the pendency of the action. Subpoenas shall be returned to the party requesting issuance.

(2) If a document not filed pursuant to Rule 5.06(1) is to be used at trial or is necessary to a pre-trial motion, the portion of the document to be used shall be filed with the Clerk of the Court at the outset of the trial or at the filing of the motion insofar as its use can be reasonably anticipated.

(3) When a document not filed pursuant to Rule 5.06(1) is needed for appeal purposes, post-trial motions, or any other purpose, the court before which the case is pending shall, upon motion of any party, order the necessary document be filed with the Clerk and it shall become part of the record. The parties may, at any time by stipulation, file documents not filed pursuant to Rule 5.06(1).

HISTORY: Amended by Order 91–2, eff. 11–15–91; prior amendment eff. 8–28–89; adopted eff. 1–1–85

CR 6   Time

CR 6.01   Computation

In computing any period of time prescribed or allowed by these rules, by order of court, or by any applicable statute, the day of the act, event or default after which the designated period of time begins to run is not to be included. The last day of the period so computed is to be included, unless it is a Saturday, a Sunday or a legal holiday, in which event the period runs until the end of the next day which is not a Saturday, a Sunday or a legal holiday. When the period of time prescribed or allowed is less than seven days, intermediate Saturdays, Sundays and legal holidays shall be excluded in the computation.

HISTORY: Amended eff. 7–1–69; adopted eff. 7–1–53

CR 6.02   Enlargement

When by statute or by these Rules or by a notice given thereunder or by order of court an act is required or allowed to be done at or within a specified time, the court for cause shown may, at any time in its discretion, (a) with or without motion or notice order the period enlarged if request therefor is made before the expiration of the period originally prescribed or as extended by a previous order or (b) upon motion made after the expiration of the specified period permit the act to be done where the failure to act was the result of excusable neglect; but it may not extend the time for taking any action under Rules 50.02, 52.02, 59.02, 59.04, 59.05, 60.02, 72.02, 73.02 and 74 except to the extent and under the conditions stated in them.

HISTORY: Amended by Order 85–2, eff. 1–1–86; prior amendments eff. 1–1–78, 7–1–69, 6–1–60; adopted eff. 7–1–53

CR 6.03   Unaffected by expiration of term

(1) The period of time provided for the doing of any act or the taking of any proceeding is not affected or limited by the continued existence or expiration of a term of court. The continued existence or expiration of a term of court in no way affects the power of a court to do any act or take any proceeding in any civil action which has been pending before it.

(2) The judge of each trial court may make or direct in vacation any order, rule, judgment or decree in any civil action, except the conducting of a trial when a jury is required under these rules.

HISTORY: Amended eff. 7–1–76; prior amendment eff. 4–1–63; adopted eff. 7–1–53

CR 6.04   For motions; affidavits

(1) A written motion, other than one which may be heard ex parte, and notice of the hearing thereof shall be served a reasonable time before the time specified for the hearing, unless a specific period is fixed by these rules or by order of the court. Such an order may for cause shown be made on ex parte application.

(2) When a motion is supported by affidavit, the affidavit shall be served with the motion; and, except as otherwise provided in Rule 59.03, opposing affidavits may be served not later than one day before the hearing, unless the court permits them to be served at some other time.

HISTORY: Adopted eff. 7–1–53

CR 6.05   Additional time after service by mail

Whenever a party has the right or is required to do some act or take some proceedings within a prescribed period after the service of a notice or other paper upon him and the notice or paper is served upon him by mail, 3 days shall be added to the prescribed period. This provision shall not apply to the service of summons by mail under Rule 4.01(1)(a).

HISTORY: Amended by Order 80–1, eff. 5–1–80; adopted eff. 7–1–53

III PLEADINGS AND MOTIONS

CR 7 Pleadings allowed; form of motions

CR 7.01 Pleadings

There shall be a complaint and an answer; a reply to counterclaim denominated as such; an answer to a cross-claim, if the answer contains a cross-claim; a third-party complaint, if leave is given under Rule 14 to summon a person who was not an original party; and a third-party answer, if a third-party complaint is served. No other pleading shall be allowed, except that the court may order a reply to an answer or a third-party answer.

HISTORY: Adopted eff. 7–1–53

CR 7.02 Motions and other papers

(1) An application to the court for an order shall be by motion which, unless made during a hearing or trial, shall be made in writing, shall state with particularity the grounds therefor, and shall set forth the relief or order sought. The requirement of writing is fulfilled if the motion is stated in a written notice of the hearing of the motion.

(2) The rules applicable to captions, signing, and other matters of form of pleadings apply to all motions and other papers provided for by these rules.

(3) Demurrers, pleas and exceptions for insufficiency of a pleading shall not be used.

(4) Except for exhibits and printed briefs, all pleadings and papers filed in the courts shall be typewritten in black type no smaller than 12 point on unglazed white paper 8 1/2 by 11 inches in dimension, leaving at least a double space between lines, a 1 1/2 inch margin on the left side, and shall be clearly readable. This requirement shall not apply to computer printouts or similar reproductions prescribed by the Administrative Office of the Courts for use in the district court or to orders, judgments and other papers routinely prepared by the circuit and district courts.

HISTORY: Amended by Order 95–1, eff. 11–1–95; prior amendments eff. 1–1–89, 10–1–82, 7–1–81, 9–1–80, 6–1–78, 1–1–78; adopted eff. 7–1–53

CR 7.03 Privacy protection for filings made with the court

(1) Unless the court orders otherwise, in a civil filing with the court, excluding domestic violence matters, that contains certain personal data, including an individual's social-security number or taxpayer-identification number, or birth date, or a financial-account number, an attorney or party making the filing must redact the document so the following information cannot be read:

(a) the digits of the social-security number or taxpayer-identification number;

(b) the month and day of the individual's birth; and

(c) the digits of the financial-account number.

Redaction may be made by any method, including but not limited to replacing the identifiers with neutral placeholders or covering the identifiers with an indelible mark, that so obscures the identifiers that they cannot be read.

(2) An attorney or party making a filing under part (1) above shall keep an unredacted, original copy of the filing. The attorney and party shall be custodians of the original or unredacted copy of the filing and shall present it upon order of the court.

(3) The court may order that a filing be made under seal without redaction. If the court orders an unredacted copy of the filing under seal, a copy redacted in compliance with part (1) of this rule may also be filed.

(4) For good cause, the court may by order in a case:

(a) require redaction of additional information; or

(b) limit or prohibit a nonparty's access to a document filed with the court.

(5) The clerk is not required to review filings with the court for compliance with this rule. The responsibility to redact filings rests with counsel and the party making the filing.

(6) A person waives the protection of this rule as to the person's own information by including it in a filing without redaction.

(7) An attorney or party failing to comply with this rule will be subject to the sanction powers of the court, including having the relevant filing stricken from the record. A conforming copy of a filing previously stricken from the record for failure to comply with this rule may be refiled unless otherwise ordered by the court.

HISTORY: Amended by Order 2010–09, eff. 1–1–11; adopted by Order 2009–01, eff. 4–1–09

CR 8 General rules of pleading

CR 8.01 Claims for relief

(1) A pleading which sets forth a claim for relief, whether an original claim, counterclaim, cross-claim, or third-party claim, shall contain (a) a short and plain statement of the claim showing that the pleader is entitled to relief and (b) a demand for judgment for the relief to which he deems himself entitled. Relief in the alternative or of several different types may be demanded.

(2) In any action for unliquidated damages the prayer for damages in any pleading shall not recite any sum as alleged damages other than an allegation that damages are in excess of any minimum dollar

amount necessary to establish the jurisdiction of the court; provided, however, that all parties shall have the right to advise the trier of fact as to what amounts are fair and reasonable as shown by the evidence. When a claim is made against a party for unliquidated damages, that party may obtain information as to the amount claimed by interrogatories. If this is done, the amount claimed shall not exceed the last amount stated in answer to interrogatories; provided, however, that the trial court has discretion to allow a supplement to the answer to interrogatories at any time where there has been no prejudice to the defendant.

HISTORY: Amended by Order 2006–09, eff. 1–1–07; prior amendments eff. 1–1–87 (Order 86–3), 1–1–85, 1–1–78; adopted eff. 7–1–53

CR 8.02 Defenses; form of denials

A party shall state in short and plain terms his defenses to each claim asserted and shall admit or deny the averments upon which the adverse party relies. If he is without knowledge or information sufficient to form a belief as to the truth of an averment, he shall so state and this has the effect of a denial. Denials shall fairly meet the substance of the averments denied. When a pleader intends in good faith to deny only a part or a qualification of an averment, he shall specify so much of it as is true and material and shall deny only the remainder. Unless the pleader intends in good faith to controvert all the averments of the preceding pleading, he may make his denials as specific denials of designated averments or paragraphs, or he may generally deny all the averments except such designated averments or paragraphs as he expressly admits; but, when he does so intend to controvert all its averments, he may do so by general denial subject to the obligations set forth in Rule 11.

HISTORY: Adopted eff. 7–1–53

CR 8.03 Affirmative defenses

In pleading to a preceding pleading, a party shall set forth affirmatively accord and satisfaction, arbitration and award, assumption of risk, contributory negligence, discharge in bankruptcy, duress, estoppel, failure of consideration, fraud, illegality, injury by fellow servant, laches, license, payment, release, res judicata, statute of frauds, statute of limitations, waiver, and any other matter constituting an avoidance or affirmative defense. When a party has mistakenly designated a defense as a counterclaim or a counterclaim as a defense, the court on terms, if justice so requires, shall treat the pleading as if there had been a proper designation.

HISTORY: Adopted eff. 7–1–53

CR 8.04 Effect of failure to deny

Averments in a pleading to which no responsive pleading is required or permitted shall be taken as denied or avoided. Averments in a pleading to which a responsive pleading is required are admitted when not denied in the responsive pleading, except that the following allegations must be proved:

(a) Those against a person under any disability.

(b) Those necessary to sustain an action for divorce.

(c) Those concerning value or amount of damages which are not for a sum certain or for a sum which may by computation be made certain.

HISTORY: Amended eff. 1–1–78; prior amendment eff. 4–1–63; adopted eff. 7–1–53

CR 8.05 Pleading to be concise and direct; consistency

(1) Each averment of a pleading shall be simple, concise, and direct. No technical forms of pleadings or motions are required.

(2) A party may set forth two or more statements of a claim or defense alternately or hypothetically, either in one count or defense or in separate counts or defenses. When two or more statements are made in the alternative and one of them if made independently would be sufficient, the pleading is not made insufficient by the insufficiency of one or more of the alternative statements. A party may also state as many separate claims or defenses as he has regardless of consistency and whether based on legal or on equitable grounds or on both. All statements shall be made subject to the obligations set forth in Rule 11.

HISTORY: Adopted eff. 7–1–53

CR 8.06 Construction of pleadings

All pleadings shall be so construed as to do substantial justice.

HISTORY: Adopted eff. 7–1–53

CR 9 Pleading special matters

CR 9.01 Capacity

It is not necessary to aver the capacity of a party to sue or be sued or the authority of a party to sue or be sued in a representative capacity or the legal existence of a partnership or an organized association of persons that is made a party. When a party desires to raise an issue as to the legal existence of any party or the capacity of any party to sue or be sued or the authority of a party to sue or be sued in a representative capacity, he shall do so by specific negative averment, which shall include such supporting particulars as are peculiarly within the pleader's knowledge.

HISTORY: Adopted eff. 7–1–53

CR 9.02   Fraud, mistake, condition of mind

In all averments of fraud or mistake, the circumstances constituting fraud or mistake shall be stated with particularity.   Malice, intent, knowledge, and other condition of mind of a person may be averred generally.

HISTORY: Adopted eff. 7–1–53

CR 9.03   Conditions precedent

In pleading the performance or occurrence of conditions precedent, it is sufficient to aver generally that all conditions precedent have been performed or have occurred.   A denial of performance or occurrence shall be made specifically and with particularity.

HISTORY: Adopted eff. 7–1–53

CR 9.04   Official document or act

In pleading an official document or official act, it is sufficient to aver that the document was issued or the act done in compliance with law.

HISTORY: Adopted eff. 7–1–53

CR 9.05   Judgment

In pleading a judgment or decision of a domestic or foreign court, judicial or quasi-judicial tribunal, or of a board or officer, it is sufficient to aver the judgment or decision without setting forth matter showing jurisdiction to render it.

HISTORY: Adopted eff. 7–1–53

CR 9.06   Special damages

When items of special damage are claimed, they shall be specifically stated.

HISTORY: Adopted eff. 7–1–53

CR 10   Form of pleadings

CR 10.01   Caption; names of parties

Every pleading shall have a caption setting forth the name of the court, the style of the action, the file number, and a designation as in Rule 7.01.   In the complaint the style of the action shall include the names of all the parties, but in other pleadings it is sufficient to state the name of the first party on each side with an appropriate indication of other parties.

HISTORY: Adopted eff. 7–1–53

CR 10.02   Paragraphs; separate statements

All averments of claim or defense shall be made in numbered paragraphs, the contents of each of which shall be limited as far as practicable to a statement of a single set of circumstances; and a paragraph may be referred to by number in all succeeding pleadings. Each claim founded upon a separate transaction or occurrence and each defense other than denials shall be stated in a separate count or defense whenever a separation facilitates the clear presentation of the matters set forth.

HISTORY: Adopted eff. 7–1–53

CR 10.03   Adoption by reference; exhibits

Statements in a pleading may be adopted by reference in a different part of the same pleading or in another pleading or in any motion.   A copy of any written instrument which is an exhibit to a pleading is a part thereof for all purposes.

HISTORY: Adopted eff. 7–1–53

CR 11   Signing of pleadings, motions, and other papers; sanctions

Every pleading, motion and other paper of a party represented by an attorney shall be signed by at least one attorney of record in his individual name, whose address shall be stated.   A party who is not represented by an attorney shall sign his pleading, motion, or other paper and state his address.   Except when otherwise specifically provided by Rule or statute, pleadings need not be verified or accompanied by affidavit.   The rule in equity that the averments of an answer under oath must be overcome by the testimony of two witnesses or of one witness sustained by corroborating circumstances is abolished.   The signature of an attorney or party constitutes a certification by him that he has read the pleading, motion or other paper;   that to the best of his knowledge, information, and belief formed after reasonable inquiry it is well grounded in fact and is warranted by existing law or a good faith argument for the extension, modification or reversal of existing law, and that it is not interposed for any improper purpose, such as to harass or to cause unnecessary delay or needless increase in the cost of litigation.   If a pleading, motion or other paper is not signed, it shall be stricken unless it is signed promptly after the omission is called to the attention of the pleader or movant.   If a pleading, motion, or other paper is signed in violation of this rule, the court, upon motion or upon its own initiative, shall impose upon the person who signed it, a represented party, or both, an appropriate sanction, which may include an order to pay to the other party or parties the amount of the reasonable expenses incurred because of the filing of the pleading, motion, or other paper, including a reasonable attorney's fee.   The Court shall postpone ruling on any Rule 11 motions filed in the litigation until after entry of a final judgment.

HISTORY: Amended by Order 89–1, eff. 8–28–89; prior amendments eff. 1–1–84, 4–1–63; adopted eff. 7–1–53

CR 12   Defenses and objections; when and how presented; motion for judgment on pleadings

CR 12.01   When presented

A defendant shall serve his/her answer within 20 days after service of the summons upon him/her.   A party served with a pleading stating a cross claim against him/her shall serve an answer thereto within 20 days after the service upon him/her. The plaintiff shall serve his/her reply to a counterclaim in the answer within 20 days after service of the answer or, if a reply is ordered by the court, within 20 days after service of the order, unless the order otherwise directs. The service of a motion permitted under Rule 12 alters these periods of time as follows unless a different time is fixed by order of the court: (1) if the court denies the motion or postpones its disposition until the trial on the merits, the responsive pleading shall be served within ten (10) days after entry of the court's order; (2) if the court grants a motion for a more definite statement, the responsive pleading shall be served within 10 days after the service of the more definite statement.

HISTORY: Amended by Order 98–2, eff. 1–1–99; prior amendment eff. 4–1–63; adopted eff. 7–1–53

CR 12.02 How presented

Every defense, in law or fact, to a claim for relief in any pleading, whether a claim, counterclaim, crossclaim, or third-party claim shall be asserted in the responsive pleading thereto if one is required, except that the following defenses may at the option of the pleader be made by motion: (a) lack of jurisdiction over the subject matter, (b) lack of jurisdiction over the person, (c) improper venue, (d) insufficiency of process, (e) insufficiency of service of process, (f) failure to state a claim upon which relief can be granted, and (g) failure to join a party under Rule 19. A motion making any of these defenses shall be made before pleading if a further pleading is permitted. No defense or objection is waived by being joined with one or more defenses or objections in a responsive pleading or motion. If a pleading sets forth a claim for relief to which the adverse party is not required to serve a responsive pleading, he may assert at the trial any defense in law or fact to that claim for relief. If, on a motion asserting the defense that the pleading fails to state a claim upon which relief can be granted, matters outside the pleading are presented to and not excluded by the court, the motion shall be treated as one for summary judgment and disposed of as provided in Rule 56, and all parties shall be given reasonable opportunity to present all material made pertinent to such a motion by Rule 56.

HISTORY: Amended eff. 1–1–78; prior amendment eff. 7–1–69; adopted eff. 7–1–53

CR 12.03 Motion for judgment on the pleadings

After the pleadings are closed but within such time as not to delay the trial, any party may move for judgment on the pleadings. If, on such motion, matters outside the pleading are presented to and not excluded by the court, the motion shall be treated as one for summary judgment and disposed of as provided for in Rule 56, and all parties shall be given reasonable opportunity to present all materials made pertinent to such a motion by Rule 56.

HISTORY: Adopted eff. 7–1–53

CR 12.04 Preliminary hearing

The defenses and relief enumerated in Rules 12.02 and 12.03, whether made in a pleading or by motion, shall be heard and determined before trial on application of any party unless the court orders that the hearing and determination thereof be deferred until the trial.

HISTORY: Adopted eff. 7–1–53

CR 12.05 Motion for more definite statement

If a pleading to which a responsive pleading is permitted is so vague or ambiguous that a party cannot reasonably be required to frame a responsive pleading, he may move for a more definite statement before interposing his responsive pleading. The motion shall point out the defects complained of and the details desired. If the motion is granted and the order of the court is not obeyed within 10 days after service of notice of the order or within such time as the court may fix, the court may strike the pleading to which the motion was directed or make such order as it deems just.

HISTORY: Adopted eff. 7–1–53

CR 12.06 Motion to strike

Upon motion made by a party before responding to a pleading or, if no responsive pleading is permitted by these rules, upon motion made by a party within 20 days after the service of the pleading upon him, or upon the court's own initiative at any time, the court may order stricken from any pleading any insufficient defense or any sham, redundant, immaterial, impertinent or scandalous matter.

HISTORY: Adopted eff. 7–1–53

CR 12.07 Consolidation of defenses in motion

A party who makes a motion under Rule 12 may join with it the other motions herein provided for and then available to him. If a party makes a motion under Rule 12 but omits therefrom any defense or objection then available to him which Rule 12 permits to be raised by motion, he shall not thereafter make a motion based on the defense or objection so omitted, except a motion as provided in paragraph (2) of Rule 12.08 on any of the grounds there stated.

HISTORY: Amended eff. 1–1–78; prior amendments eff. 7–1–69, 4–1–63; adopted eff. 7–1–53

CR 12.08 Waiver or preservation of certain defenses

(1) A defense of lack of jurisdiction over the person, improper venue, insufficiency of process, or insufficiency of service of process is waived (a) if omitted

from a motion in the circumstances described in Rule 12.07, or (b) if it is neither made by motion under Rule 12 nor included in a responsive pleading or an amendment thereof permitted by Rule 15.01 to be made as a matter of course.

(2) A defense of failure to state a claim upon which relief can be granted, a defense of failure to join a party indispensable under Rule 19, and an objection of failure to state a legal defense to a claim may be made in any pleading permitted or ordered under Rule 7.01, or by motion for judgment on the pleadings, or at the trial on the merits.

(3) Whenever it appears that the court lacks jurisdiction of the subject matter, the court shall dismiss the action.

HISTORY: Amended eff. 7–1–69; adopted eff. 7–1–53

CR 13   Counterclaims and cross-claims

CR 13.01   Compulsory counterclaims

A pleading shall state as a counterclaim any claim which at the time of serving the pleading the pleader has against any opposing party, if it arises out of the transaction or occurrence that is the subject matter of the opposing party's claim and does not require for its adjudication the presence of third parties of whom the court cannot acquire jurisdiction. The pleader need not state the claim if (a) at the time the action was commenced the claim was the subject of another pending action, or (b) the opposing party brought suit upon his claim by attachment or other process by which the court did not acquire jurisdiction to render a personal judgment on that claim, and the pleader is not stating any counterclaim under Rule 13. Any counterclaim against the Commonwealth, or any agency or political subdivision thereof, may be stated at the pleader's option.

HISTORY: Amended eff. 1–1–78; prior amendment eff. 7–1–69; adopted eff. 7–1–53

CR 13.02   Permissive counterclaims

A pleading, other than a reply, may state as a counterclaim any claim against an opposing party not arising out of the transaction or occurrence that is the subject matter of the opposing party's claim. In an action by more than one plaintiff, a claim that a plaintiff is or may be liable to the claimant for all or part of the claim asserted against him by another plaintiff in the action may be stated as a counterclaim.

HISTORY: Amended eff. 7–1–69; adopted eff. 7–1–53

CR 13.03   Counterclaim exceeding opposing claim

A counterclaim may or may not diminish or defeat the recovery sought by the opposing party. It may claim relief exceeding in amount or different in kind

from that sought in the pleading of the opposing party.

HISTORY: Adopted eff. 7–1–53

CR 13.04   Counterclaims against the Commonwealth

These rules shall not be construed to enlarge beyond the limits fixed by law the right to assert counterclaims or to claim credits against the Commonwealth or an officer or agency thereof.

HISTORY: Amended eff. 1–1–78; adopted eff. 7–1–53

CR 13.05   Counterclaim maturing or acquired after pleading

A claim which either matured or was acquired by the pleader after serving his pleading may, with the permission of the court, be presented as a counterclaim by supplemental pleading.

HISTORY: Adopted eff. 7–1–53

CR 13.06   Omitted counterclaim

When a pleader fails to set up a counterclaim through oversight, inadvertence, or excusable neglect, or when justice requires, he may by leave of court set up the counterclaim by amendment.

HISTORY: Adopted eff. 7–1–53

CR 13.07   Cross-claim against co-party

A pleading may state as a cross-claim any claim by one party against a co-party arising out of the transaction or occurrence that is the subject matter either of the original action or of a counterclaim therein or relating to any property that is the subject matter of the original action. Such cross-claim may include a claim that the party against whom it is asserted is or may be liable to the cross-claimant for all or part of a claim asserted in the action against the cross-claimant.

HISTORY: Adopted eff. 7–1–53

CR 13.08   Additional parties may be brought in

When the presence of parties other than those to the original action is required for the granting of complete relief in the determination of a counterclaim or cross-claim, the court shall order them to be brought in as defendants as provided in these rules.

HISTORY: Adopted eff. 7–1–53

CR 13.09   Separate trials; separate judgment

If the court orders separate trials as provided in Rule 42.02, judgment on a counterclaim or cross-claim may be rendered in accordance with the terms of Rule 54.02 even if the claims of the opposing party have been dismissed or otherwise disposed of.

HISTORY: Adopted eff. 7–1–53

CR 14   Third-party practice

CR 14.01   When defendant may bring in third party

A defendant may move for leave as a third-party plaintiff to assert a claim against a person not a party to the action who is or may be liable to him for all or part of the plaintiff's claim against him. If the motion is granted, summons and a copy of the third-party complaint, with a copy of the original complaint attached as an exhibit, shall be served on such a person, who shall be called the third-party defendant. He shall make his defenses to the third-party plaintiff's claim as provided in Rule 12 and his counterclaims against the third-party plaintiff and cross-claims against other third-party defendants as provided in Rule 13. The third-party defendant may assert against the plaintiff any defenses which the third-party plaintiff has to the plaintiff's claim. The third-party defendant may also assert any claim against the plaintiff arising out of the transaction or occurrence that is the subject matter of the plaintiff's claim against the third-party plaintiff. The plaintiff may assert any claim against the third-party defendant arising out of the transaction or occurrence that is the subject matter of the plaintiff's claim against the third-party plaintiff, and the third-party defendant thereupon shall assert his defenses as provided in Rule 12 and his counterclaims and cross-claims as provided in Rule 13. A third-party defendant may proceed under this rule against any person not a party to the action who is or may be liable to him for all or part of the claim made in the action against the third-party defendant.

HISTORY: Amended eff. 6–1–60; prior amendment eff. 3–1–55; adopted eff. 7–1–53

CR 14.02   When plaintiff may bring in third party

When a counterclaim is asserted against a plaintiff, he may cause a third party to be brought in under circumstances which under this rule would entitle defendant to do so.

HISTORY: Adopted eff. 7–1–53

CR 14.03   Special amici curiae in bond-issue proceedings

In every proceeding filed or pending in the circuit court calling for an adjudication concerning the validity of an issue or proposed issue of tax-exempt bonds the plaintiff shall file with the clerk of the Supreme Court a copy of the complaint accompanied by a letter stating that it is being furnished pursuant to this Rule 14.03. The Supreme Court shall thereupon appoint a practicing attorney as special amicus curiae to participate in the proceeding the same as if he or she were a party opposing the legality of the bond issue, with the right of appeal from any adverse judgment. The trial court shall allow the special amicus curiae a reasonable fee for his or her services, including such as have been performed incident to an appeal, to be taxed as a part of the costs of the proceeding.

HISTORY: Adopted by Order 80–3, eff. 12–31–80

CR 15   Amended and supplemental pleadings

CR 15.01   Amendments

A party may amend his pleading once as a matter of course at any time before a responsive pleading is served or, if the pleading is one to which no responsive pleading is permitted and the action has not been placed upon the trial calendar, he may so amend it at any time within 20 days after it is served. Otherwise a party may amend his pleading only by leave of court or by written consent of the adverse party; and leave shall be freely given when justice so requires. A party shall plead in response to an amended pleading within the time remaining for response to the original pleading or within 10 days after service of the amended pleading, whichever period may be longer, unless the court otherwise orders.

HISTORY: Adopted eff. 7–1–53

CR 15.02   Amendments to conform to the evidence

When issues not raised by the pleadings are tried by express or implied consent of the parties, they shall be treated in all respects as if they had been raised in the pleadings. Such amendment of the pleading as may be necessary to cause them to conform to the evidence and to raise these issues may be made upon motion of any party at any time, even after judgment; but failure so to amend does not affect the result of the trial of these issues. If evidence is objected to at the trial on the ground that it is not within the issues made by the pleadings, the court may allow the pleadings to be amended and shall do so freely when the presentation of the merits of the action will be subserved thereby and the objecting party fails to satisfy the court that admission of such evidence would prejudice him in maintaining his action or defense upon the merits. The court may grant a continuance to enable the objecting party to meet such evidence.

HISTORY: Adopted eff. 7–1–53

CR 15.03   Relation back of amendments

(1) Whenever the claim or defense asserted in the amended pleading arose out of the conduct, transaction, or occurrence set forth or attempted to be set forth in the original pleading, the amendment relates back to the date of the original pleading.

(2) An amendment changing the party against whom a claim is asserted relates back if the condition of paragraph (1) is satisfied and, within the period provided by law for commencing the action against him, the party to be brought in by amendment (a) has

received such notice of the institution of the action that he will not be prejudiced in maintaining his defense on the merits, and (b) knew or should have known that, but for a mistake concerning the identity of the proper party, the action would have been brought against him.

(3) The delivery or mailing of process to the attorney general of the Commonwealth, or an agency or officer who would have been a proper defendant if named, satisfies the requirement of paragraph (2) with respect to the Commonwealth or any agency or officer thereof to be brought into the action as a defendant.

HISTORY: Amended eff. 1–1–78; prior amendment eff. 7–1–69; adopted eff. 7–1–53

CR 15.04 Supplemental pleadings

Upon motion of a party the court may, upon reasonable notice and upon such terms as are just, permit him to serve a supplemental pleading setting forth transactions or occurrences or events which have happened since the date of the pleading sought to be supplemented. Permission may granted, even though the original pleading is defective in its statement of a claim for relief or defense. If the court deems it advisable that the adverse party plead to the supplemental pleading, it shall so order, specifying the time therefor.

HISTORY: Amended eff. 7–1–69; adopted eff. 7–1–53

CR 16 Pretrial procedure; formulating issues

CR 17 Parties plaintiff and defendant; capacity

CR 17.01 Real party in interest

Every action shall be prosecuted in the name of the real party in interest, but a personal representative, guardian, curator, committee of a person of unsound mind, trustee of an express trust, a person with whom or in whose name a contract is made for the benefit of another, a county, municipal corporation, public board or other such body, a receiver appointed by a court, the assignee or trustee of a bankrupt, an assignee for the benefit of creditors, or a person expressly authorized by statute to do so, may bring an action without joining the party or parties for whose benefit it is prosecuted. Nothing herein, however, shall abrogate or take away an individual's right to sue.

HISTORY: Adopted eff. 7–1–53

CR 17.02 Married persons

A married man or a married woman, regardless of age, may sue or be sued as a single person who has reached majority.

HISTORY: Adopted eff. 7–1–53

(1) In any action, the court may in its discretion direct the attorneys for the parties to appear before it for a conference to consider:

(a) The simplification of the issues;

(b) The necessity or desirability of amendments to the pleadings;

(c) The possibility of obtaining admissions of fact and documents which will avoid unnecessary proof;

(d) The limitation of the number of expert witnesses;

(e) The advisability of a preliminary reference of issues to a commissioner;

(f) Such other matters as may aid in the disposition of the action.

(2) The court shall make an order which recites the action taken at the conference, the amendments allowed to the pleadings, and the agreements made by the parties as to any of the matters considered, and which limits the issues for trial to those not disposed of by admissions or agreements of counsel; and such order when entered controls the subsequent course of the action, unless modified at or before the trial to prevent manifest injustice. The court in its discretion may establish by rule a pretrial calendar on which actions may be placed for consideration as above provided and may either confine the calendar to jury actions or to nonjury actions or extend it to all actions.

HISTORY: Amended eff. 1–1–78; prior amendment eff. 7–1–69; adopted eff. 7–1–53

IV PARTIES

CR 17.03 Infants and persons of unsound mind

(1) Actions involving unmarried infants or persons of unsound mind shall be brought by the party's guardian or committee, but if there is none, or such guardian or committee is unwilling or unable to act, a next friend may bring the action.

(2) Actions involving unmarried infants or persons of unsound mind shall be defended by the party's guardian or committee. If there is no guardian or committee or he is unable or unwilling to act or is a plaintiff, the court, or the clerk thereof if its judge or judges are not present in the county, shall appoint a guardian ad litem to defend unless one has been previously appointed under Rule 4.04(3) or the warning order attorney has become such guardian under Rule 4.07(3).

(3) No judgment shall be rendered against an unmarried infant or person of unsound mind until the party's guardian or committee or the guardian ad litem shall have made defense or filed a report stating that after careful examination of the case he is unable to make defense.

(4) Papers required to be served on a party under Rule 5.01 shall be served on the person bringing or defending an action under this rule.

(5) The court shall allow the guardian ad litem a reasonable fee for services, to be taxed as costs. Fees allowed to counsel for children, indigent parents or non-parental custodians of children in dependency, abuse or neglect cases, and to counsel for children or indigent parents in parental rights termination cases, under the Juvenile Code, shall not exceed the amounts specified in KRS 620.100 or KRS 625.080. Counsel fee awards shall not exceed the statutory maximum, regardless of the number of persons represented in a proceeding by the counsel.

HISTORY: Amended by Order 91–2, eff. 11–15–91; prior amendments eff. 5–1–80, 1–1–78, 4–1–63, 3–1–55; adopted eff. 7–1–53

CR 17.04 Prisoners

(1) Actions involving adult prisoners confined either within or without the State may be brought or defended by the prisoner. If for any reason the prisoner fails or is unable to defend an action, the court shall appoint a practicing attorney as guardian ad litem, and no judgment shall be rendered against the prisoner until the guardian ad litem shall have made defense or filed a report stating that after careful examination of the case he or she is unable to make defense.

(2) Fees allowed to counsel appointed to represent prisoners as respondents in dependency, abuse or neglect cases, or in parental rights termination cases, under the Juvenile Code, shall not exceed the amounts specified in KRS 620.100 or KRS 625.080. Counsel fee awards shall not exceed the statutory maximum, regardless of the number of persons represented in a proceeding by the counsel.

HISTORY: Amended by Order 95–1, eff. 11–1–95; adopted eff. 7–1–53

CR 18 Joinder of claims

CR 18.01 Independent or alternative claims

A party asserting a claim to relief as an original claim, counterclaim, cross-claim, or third-party claim, may join, either as independent or as alternate claims, as many claims, either legal or equitable, as he has against an opposing party.

HISTORY: Amended eff. 7–1–69; adopted eff. 7–1–53

CR 18.02 Dependent claims

Whenever a claim is one heretofore cognizable only after another claim has been prosecuted to a conclusion, the two claims may be joined in a single action; but the court shall grant relief in that action only in accordance with the relative substantive rights of the parties. In particular, a plaintiff may state a claim for money and a claim to have set aside a conveyance fraudulent as to him, without first having obtained a judgment establishing the claim for money.

HISTORY: Adopted eff. 7–1–53

CR 19 Joinder of persons needed for just adjudication

CR 19.01 Persons to be joined if feasible

A person who is subject to service of process, either personal or constructive, shall be joined as a party in the action if (a) in his absence complete relief cannot be accorded among those already parties, or (b) he claims an interest relating to the subject of the action and is so situated that the disposition of the action in his absence may (i) as a practical matter impair or impede his ability to protect that interest or (ii) leave any of the persons already parties subject to a substantial risk of incurring double, multiple, or otherwise inconsistent obligations by reason of his claimed interest. If he has not been so joined, the court shall order that he be made a party. If he should join as a plaintiff but refuses to do so, he may be made a defendant, or, in a proper case an involuntary plaintiff. If the joined party objects to venue and his joinder would render the venue of the action improper, he shall be dismissed from the action.

HISTORY: Amended eff. 1–1–78; prior amendment eff. 7–1–69; adopted eff. 7–1–53

CR 19.02 Determination by court whenever joinder not feasible

If a person as described in Rule 19.01 cannot be made a party, the court shall determine whether in equity and good conscience the action should proceed among the parties before it, or should be dismissed, the absent person being thus regarded as indispensible. The factors to be considered by the court include: (a) to what extent a judgment rendered in the person's absence might be prejudicial to him or those already parties; (b) the extent to which, by protective provisions in the judgment, by the shaping of relief, or other measures, the prejudice can be lessened or avoided; (c) whether a judgment rendered in the person's absence will be adequate; (d) whether the plaintiff will have an adequate remedy if the action is dismissed for nonjoinder.

HISTORY: Amended eff. 1–1–78; prior amendment eff. 7–1–69; adopted eff. 7–1–53

CR 19.03 Pleading reasons for nonjoinder

A pleading asserting a claim for relief shall state the names, if known to the pleader, of any persons as described in Rule 19.01 who are not joined, and the reasons why they are not joined.

HISTORY: Amended eff. 7–1–69; adopted eff. 7–1–53

CR 19.04   Exception of class actions

Rule 19 is subject to the provisions of Rule 23.

HISTORY: Adopted eff. 7–1–69

CR 20   Permissive joinder of parties

CR 20.01   Permissive joinder

All persons may join in one action as plaintiffs if they assert any right to relief jointly, severally, or in the alternative in respect of or arising out of the same transaction, occurrence, or series of transactions or occurrences and if any question of law or fact common to all these persons will arise in the action. All persons may be joined in one action as defendants if there is asserted against them jointly, severally, or in the alternative, any right to relief in respect of or arising out of the same transaction, occurrence, or series of transactions or occurrences and if any question of law or fact common to all defendants will arise in the action. A plaintiff or defendant need not be interested in obtaining or defending against all the relief demanded. Judgment may be given for one or more of the plaintiffs according to their respective rights to relief, and against one or more defendants according to their respective liabilities.

HISTORY: Amended eff. 7–1–69; adopted eff. 7–1–53

CR 20.02   Separate trials

The court may make such orders as will prevent a party from being embarrassed, delayed, or put to expense by the inclusion of a party against whom he asserts no claim and who asserts no claim against him, and may order separate trials or make other orders to prevent delay or prejudice.

HISTORY: Adopted eff. 7–1–53

CR 21   Misjoinder and nonjoinder of parties

Misjoinder of parties is not ground for dismissal of an action. Parties may be dropped or added by order of the court on motion of any party or of its own initiative at any stage of the action and on such terms as are just. Any claim against a party may be severed and proceeded with separately, in the discretion of the court.

HISTORY: Adopted eff. 7–1–53

CR 22   Interpleader

Persons having claims against the plaintiff may be joined as defendants and required to interplead when their claims are such that the plaintiff is or may be exposed to double or multiple liability. It is not ground for objection to the joinder that the claims of the several claimants or the titles on which their claims depend do not have a common origin or are not identical but are adverse to and independent of one another, or that the plaintiff avers that he is not liable in whole or in part to any or all of the claimants. A defendant exposed to similar liability may obtain such interpleader by way of cross-claim or counterclaim. The provisions of this section supplement and do not in any way limit the joinder of parties permitted in Rule 20.

HISTORY: Adopted eff. 7–1–53

CR 23   Class actions

CR 23.01   Prerequisites to class action

Subject to the provisions of Rule 23.02, one or more members of a class may sue or be sued as representative parties on behalf of all only if (a) the class is so numerous that joinder of all members is impracticable, (b) there are questions of law or fact common to the class, (c) the claims or defenses of the representative parties are typical of the claims or defenses of the class, and (d) the representative parties will fairly and adequately protect the interests of the class.

HISTORY: Amended eff. 1–1–78; prior amendment eff. 7–1–69; adopted eff. 7–1–53

CR 23.02   Class actions maintainable

An action may be maintained as a class action if the prerequisites of Rule 23.01 are satisfied, and in addition:

(a) The prosecution of separate actions by or against individual members of the class would create a risk of

(i) inconsistent or varying adjudications with respect to individual members of the class which would establish incompatible standards of conduct for the party opposing the class, or,

(ii) adjudications with respect to individual members of the class which would as a practical matter be dispositive of the interests of the other members not parties to the adjudications or substantially impair or impede their ability to protect their interests; or

(b) the party opposing the class has acted or refused to act on grounds generally applicable to the class, thereby making appropriate final injunctive relief or corresponding declaratory relief with respect to the class as a whole; or

(c) the court finds that the questions of law or fact common to the members of the class predominate over any questions affecting only individual members, and that a class action is superior to other available methods for the fair and efficient adjudication of the controversy. The matters pertinent to the findings include: (i) the interest of members of the class in individually controlling the prosecution or defense of separate actions; (ii) the extent and nature of any litigation concerning the controversy already commenced by or against members of the class; (iii) the desirability or undesirability of concentrating the litigation of the claims in the particular forum; (iv) the difficulties likely to be encountered in the management of a class action.

HISTORY: Amended eff. 1–1–78; adopted eff. 7–1–69

CR 23.03 Determination by order whether class action to be maintained; notice; judgment; actions conducted partially as class actions

(1) At an early practicable time after a person sues or is sued as a class representative, the court must determine by order whether to certify the action as a class action.

(2) An order that certifies a class action must define the class and the class claims, issues, or defenses, and must appoint class counsel under CR 23.07.

(3) An order that grants or denies class certification may be altered or amended before final judgment.

(4) If an appeal is taken from the Certification Order, as authorized by CR 23.06, notice shall not be given until a final non-appealable order has decided the issue. If no appeal is taken the court, after 11 days from the entry of its Certification Order, shall give notice as follows:

(a) For any class certified under CR 23.02(a) or 23.02(b), the court may direct appropriate notice to the class.

(b) For any class certified under CR 23.02(c), the court must direct to class members the best notice that is practicable under the circumstances, including individual notice to all members who can be identified through reasonable effort. The notice must clearly and concisely state in plain, easily understood language:

(i) the nature of the action;

(ii) the definition of the class certified;

(iii) the class claims, issues, or defenses;

(iv) that a class member may enter an appearance through an attorney if the member so desires;

(v) that the court will exclude from the class any member who requests exclusion by a specified date;

(vi) the time and manner for requesting exclusion; and

(vii) the binding effect of a class judgment, whether favorable or not, on members under CR 23.03.

(5) Whether or not favorable to the class, the judgment in a class action must:

(a) for any class certified under CR 23.02(a) or (b) include and describe those whom the court finds to be class members; and

(b) for any class certified under CR 23.02(c) include and specify or describe those to whom the CR 23.02(c) notice was directed, who have not requested exclusion, and whom the court finds to be class members.

(6) When appropriate, an action may be brought or maintained as a class action with respect to particular issues.

(7) When appropriate, a class may be divided into subclasses that are each treated as a class under this rule.

HISTORY: Amended by Order 2010–09, eff. 1–1–11; prior amendment eff. 1–1–78; adopted eff. 7–1–69

CR 23.04 Orders in conduct of actions

(1) In conducting an action under CR 23.03, the court may issue orders that:

(a) determine the course of proceedings or prescribe measures to prevent undue repetition or complication in presenting evidence or argument;

(b) require—to protect certified class members and fairly conduct the action—giving appropriate notice to some or all class members of:

(i) any step in the action

(ii) the proposed extent of the judgment; or

(iii) the members' opportunity to signify whether they consider the representation fair and adequate, to intervene and present claims or defenses, or to otherwise come into this action.

(c) impose conditions on the representative parties or on intervenors;

(d) require that the pleadings be amended to eliminate allegations about representation of absent persons and that the action proceed accordingly; or

(e) deal with similar procedural matters.

(2) An order under CR 23.04(1) may be altered or amended from time to time and may be combined with an order under Rule 16.

HISTORY: Amended by Order 2010–09, eff. 1–1–11; prior amendment eff. 1–1–78; adopted eff. 7–1–69

CR 23.05 Dismissal or compromise

The claims, issues, or defenses of a certified class may be settled, or defenses of a certified class may be settled, voluntarily dismissed, or compromised only with the court's approval. The following procedures apply to a proposed settlement, voluntary dismissal, or compromise:

(1) The court must direct notice in a reasonable manner to all class members who would be bound by the proposal.

(2) If the proposal would bind class members, the court may approve it only after a hearing and on finding that it is fair, reasonable, and adequate.

(3) The parties seeking approval must file a statement identifying any agreement made in connection with the proposal.

(4) If the class action was previously certified under CR 23.02(c), the court may refuse to approve a settlement unless it affords a new opportunity to request

exclusion to individual class members who had an earlier opportunity to request exclusion but did not do so.

(5) Any class member may object to the proposal if it requires court approval under this subdivision (5); the objection may be withdrawn only with the court's approval upon a showing of good cause.

HISTORY: Amended by Order 2010–09, eff. 1–1–11; adopted eff. 7–1–69

CR 23.06 Appeals

An order granting or denying class action certification is appealable within 10 days after the order is entered. An appeal does not stay proceedings in the circuit court unless the circuit judge or the Court of Appeals so orders. The matter shall be expedited in the appellate courts.

HISTORY: Adopted by Order 2010–09, eff. 1–1–11

CR 23.07 Class counsel

(1) Appointing Class Counsel. Unless a statute provides otherwise, a court that certifies a class must appoint class counsel. In appointing class counsel, the court:

(a) must consider:

(i) the work counsel has done in identifying or investigating potential claims in the action;

(ii) counsel's experience in handling class actions, other complex litigation, and the types of claims asserted in the action;

(iii) counsel's knowledge of the applicable law; and

(iv) the resources that counsel will commit to representing the class;

(b) may consider any other matter pertinent to counsel's ability to fairly and adequately represent the interests of the class;

(c) may order potential class counsel to provide information on any subject pertinent to the appointment and to propose terms for attorney's fees and nontaxable costs;

(d) may include in the appointing order provisions about the award of attorney's fees or nontaxable costs under CR 23.08; and

(e) may make further orders in connection with the appointment.

(2) When one applicant seeks appointment as class counsel, the court may appoint that applicant only if the applicant is adequate under CR 23.07(1) and (4). If more than one adequate applicant seeks appointment, the court must appoint the applicant best able to represent the interests of the class.

(3) The court may designate interim counsel to act on behalf of a putative class before determining whether to certify the action as a class action.

(4) Class counsel must fairly and adequately represent the interests of the class.

HISTORY: Adopted by Order 2010–09, eff. 1–1–11

CR 23.08 Attorney's fees and nontaxable costs

In a certified class action the court shall approve or award reasonable attorney's fees and nontaxable costs that are authorized by law or by the parties' agreement. The following procedures apply:

(1) A claim for an award must be made by motion to be heard at a time the court sets. Notice of the motion must be served on all parties and, for motions by class counsel, directed to class members in a reasonable manner.

(2) A class member, or a party from whom payment is sought, may object to the motion.

(3) The court may hold a hearing and must find the facts and state its legal conclusions under CR 52.01.

(4) The court may refer issues related to the amount of the award to a Commissioner, as provided in CR 53.

HISTORY: Adopted by Order 2010–09, eff. 1–1–11

CR 24   Intervention

CR 24.01   Intervention of right

(1) Upon timely application anyone shall be permitted to intervene in an action (a) when a statute confers an unconditional right to intervene, or (b) when the applicant claims an interest relating to the property or transaction which is the subject of the action and is so situated that the disposition of the action may as a practical matter impair or impede the applicant's ability to protect that interest, unless that interest is adequately represented by existing parties.

(2) Anyone possessing a statutory right of intervention under (1)(a) above, may move the court to intervene in a pending action and, on failure of a party to file an objection within ten (10) days to the intervention and a notice of hearing on the objection, have an order allowing the intervention without appearing in court for a hearing.

HISTORY: Amended by Order 93–1, eff. 9–1–93; prior amendments eff. 1–1–78, 7–1–69; adopted eff. 7–1–53

CR 24.02   Permissive intervention

Upon timely application anyone may be permitted to intervene in an action: (a) when a statute confers a conditional right to intervene or (b) when an applicant's claim or defense and the main action have a question of law or fact in common. When a party to an action relies for ground of claim or defense upon any statute or executive order administered by a governmental officer or agency or upon any regulation, order, requirement, or agreement issued or made pursuant to the statute or executive order, the officer or agency upon timely application may be permitted to intervene in the action. In exercising its discretion the court shall consider whether the intervention will unduly delay or prejudice the adjudication of the rights of the original parties.

HISTORY: Amended eff. 1–1–78; adopted eff. 7–1–53

CR 24.03   Procedure

A person desiring to intervene shall serve a motion to intervene upon the parties as provided in Rule 5. The motion shall state the grounds therefor and shall be accompanied by a pleading setting forth the claim or defense for which intervention is sought. The same procedure shall be followed when a statute gives a right to intervene. When the constitutionality of an act of the General Assembly affecting the public interest is drawn into question in any action, the movant shall serve a copy of the pleading, motion or other paper first raising the challenge upon the Attorney General.

HISTORY: Amended by Order 98–2, eff. 1–1–99; prior amendments eff. 1–1–78, 7–1–69; adopted eff. 7–1–53

CR 25   Substitution of parties

CR 25.01   Death

(1) If a party dies during the pendency of an action and the claim is not thereby extinguished, the court, within the period allowed by law, may order substitution of the proper parties. If substitution is not so made the action may be dismissed as to the deceased party. The motion for substitution may be made by the successors or representatives of the deceased party or by any party, and, together with the notice of hearing, shall be served on the parties as provided in Rule 5, and upon persons not parties as provided in Rule 4 for the service of summons. Upon becoming aware of a party's death, the attorney(s) of record for that party, as soon as practicable, shall file a notice of such death on the record and serve a copy of such notice in the same manner provided herein for service of the motion for substitution.

(2) In the event of the death of one or more of the plaintiffs or one or more of the defendants in an action in which the right sought to be enforced survives only to the surviving plaintiffs or only against the surviving defendants, the action does not abate. In the event the right of action does not survive to or against the remaining parties, the court may render judgment as between them if it can do so without prejudice to others. In either case the death shall be noted of record and the action shall proceed in favor of or against the surviving parties.

HISTORY: Amended by Order 2006–09, eff. 1–1–07; adopted eff. 7–1–53

CR 25.02   Incompetency

If a party becomes incompetent, the court upon motion served as provided in Rule 25.01 may allow the action to be continued by or against his representative.

HISTORY: Adopted eff. 7–1–53

CR 25.03   Transfer of interest

In case of any transfer of interest, the action may be continued by or against the original party, unless the court upon motion directs the person to whom the interest is transferred to be substituted in the action or joined with the original party. Service of the motion shall be made as provided in Rule 25.01.

HISTORY: Adopted eff. 7–1–53

CR 25.04   Public officers; death or separation from office

When an officer of the state, a county, city, or other governmental agency is a party to an action and during its pendency dies, resigns, or otherwise ceases to hold office, the action may be continued and maintained by or against his successor. Substitution may be made upon written motion of the successor or any party.

HISTORY: Amended eff. 1–1–78; adopted eff. 7–1–53

V   DEPOSITIONS AND DISCOVERY

CR 26   General provisions governing discovery

CR 26.01   Discovery methods

(1) Parties may obtain discovery by one or more of the following methods: depositions upon oral examination or written questions; written interrogatories; production of documents or things or permission to enter upon land or other property, for inspection and other purposes; physical and mental examinations; and requests for admission. Unless the court orders otherwise under Rule 26.03, the frequency of use of these methods is not limited.

(2) Electronic Format. In addition to serving a hard copy, a party propounding or responding to interrogatories, requests for production, or requests for admission is encouraged to serve the discovery request or response in an electronic format (either on a disk or as an electronic document attachment) in any commercially available word processing software system. If transmitted on disk, each disk shall be labeled, identifying the caption of the case, the document, and the word processing version in which it is being submitted. If more than one disk is used for the same document, each disk shall be in the same word processing version, shall be similarly labeled and

also shall be sequentially numbered. If transmitted by electronic mail, the document must be accompanied by electronic memorandum providing the forgoing identifying information.

HISTORY: Amended by Order 2004–5, eff. 1–1–05; adopted eff. 10–1–71

CR 26.02   Scope of discovery
(1) In general.

Parties may obtain discovery regarding any matter, not privileged, which is relevant to the subject matter involved in the pending action, whether it relates to the claim or defense of the party seeking discovery or to the claim or defense of any other party, including the existence, description, nature, custody, condition and location of any books, documents, or other tangible things and the identity and location of persons having knowledge of any discoverable matter. It is not ground for objection that the information sought will be inadmissible at the trial if the information sought appears reasonably calculated to lead to the discovery of admissible evidence.

(2) Insurance agreements.

A party may obtain discovery of the existence and contents of any insurance agreement under which any person carrying on an insurance business may be liable to satisfy part or all of a judgment which may be entered in the action or to indemnify or reimburse for payments made to satisfy the judgment. Information concerning the insurance agreement is not by reason of disclosure admissible in evidence at trial. For purposes of this Section, an application for insurance shall not be treated as part of an insurance agreement.

(3) Trial preparation: materials.

(a) Subject to the provisions of paragraph (4) of this rule, a party may obtain discovery of documents and tangible things otherwise discoverable under paragraph (1) of this rule and prepared in anticipation of litigation or for trial by or for another party or by or for that other party's representative (including his attorney, consultant, surety, indemnitor, insurer, or agent) only upon a showing that the party seeking discovery has substantial need of the materials in the preparation of his case and that he is unable without undue hardship to obtain the substantial equivalent of the materials by other means. In ordering discovery of such materials when the required showing has been made, the court shall protect against disclosure of the mental impressions, conclusions, opinions, or legal theories of an attorney or other representative of a party concerning the litigation.

(b) A party may obtain without the required showing a statement concerning the action or its subject matter previously made by that party. Upon request, a person not a party may obtain without the required showing a statement concerning the action or its subject matter previously made by that person. If the request is refused, the person may move for a court order. The provisions of Rule 37.01(4)[1] apply to the award of expenses incurred in relation to the motion. For purposes of this subparagraph (b), a statement previously made is (i) a written statement signed or otherwise adopted or approved by the person making it, or (ii) a stenographic, mechanical, electrical, or other recording, or a transcription thereof, which is a substantially verbatim recital of an oral statement by the person making it and contemporaneously recorded.

(4) Trial preparation: experts.

Discovery of facts known and opinions held by experts, otherwise discoverable under the provisions of paragraph (1) of this rule and acquired or developed in anticipation of litigation or for trial, may be obtained only as follows:

(a) (i) A party may through interrogatories require any other party to identify each person whom the other party expects to call as an expert witness at trial, to state the subject matter on which the expert is expected to testify, and to state the substance of the facts and opinions to which the expert is expected to testify and a summary of the grounds for each opinion. (ii) After a party has identified an expert witness in accordance with paragraph (4)(a)(i) of this rule or otherwise, any other party may obtain further discovery of the expert witness by deposition upon oral examination or written questions pursuant to Rules 30 and 31. The court may order that the deposition be taken, subject to such restrictions as to scope and such provisions, pursuant to paragraph (4)(c) of this rule, concerning fees and expenses as the court may deem appropriate.

(b) A party may discover facts known or opinions held by an expert who has been retained or specially employed by another party in anticipation of litigation or preparation for trial and who is not expected to be called as a witness at trial, only as provided in Rule 35.02 or upon a showing of exceptional circumstances under which it is impracticable for the party seeking discovery to obtain facts or opinions on the same subject by other means.

(c) Unless manifest injustice would result, (i) the court shall require that the party seeking discovery pay the expert a reasonable fee for time spent in responding to discovery under paragraphs (4)(a)(ii) and (4)(b) of this rule; and (ii) with respect to discovery obtained under paragraph (4)(a)(ii) of this rule the court may require, and with respect to discovery obtained under paragraph (4)(b) of this rule the court shall require, the party seeking discovery to pay the other party a fair portion of the fees and expenses reasonably incurred by the latter party in obtaining facts and opinions from the expert.

HISTORY: Amended by Order 2004–5, eff. 1–1–05; prior amendments eff. 1–1–78, 10–1–71; adopted eff. 7–1–53

[1] So in original.

CR 26.03 Protective orders

(1) Upon motion by a party or by the person from whom discovery is sought, and for good cause shown, the court in which the action is pending or alternatively, on matters relating to a deposition, the court in the judicial district where the deposition is to be taken may make any order which justice requires to protect a party or person from annoyance, embarrassment, oppression, or undue burden or expense, including one or more of the following: (a) that the discovery not be had; (b) that the discovery may be had only on specified terms and conditions, including a designation of the time or place; (c) that the discovery may be had only by a method of discovery other than that selected by the party seeking discovery; (d) that certain matters not be inquired into, or that the scope of the discovery be limited to certain matters; (e) that discovery be conducted with no one present except persons designated by the court; (f) that a deposition after being sealed be opened only by order of the court; (g) that a trade secret or other confidential research, development, or commercial information not be disclosed or be disclosed only in a designated way; (h) that the parties simultaneously file specified documents or information enclosed in sealed envelopes to be opened as directed by the court.

(2) If the motion for a protective order is denied in whole or in part, the court may, on such terms and conditions as are just, order that any party or person provide or permit discovery. The provisions of Rule 37.01(d) apply to the award of expenses incurred in relation to the motion.

HISTORY: Amended by Order 2010–09, eff. 1–1–11; prior amendment eff. 10–1–71; adopted eff. 7–1–53

CR 26.04 Sequence and timing of discovery

Unless the court upon motion, for the convenience of parties and witnesses and in the interests of justice, orders otherwise, methods of discovery may be used in any sequence and the fact that a party is conducting discovery, whether by deposition or otherwise, shall not operate to delay any other party's discovery.

HISTORY: Adopted eff. 10–1–71

CR 26.05 Supplementation of responses

A party who has responded to a request for discovery with a response that was complete when made is under no duty to supplement his response to include information thereafter acquired, except as follows:

(a) A party is under a duty seasonably to supplement his response with respect to any question directly addressed to (i) the identity and location of persons having knowledge of discoverable matters, and (ii) the identity of each person expected to be called as an expert witness at trial, the subject matter on which he is expected to testify, and the substance of his testimony.

(b) A party is under a duty seasonably to amend a prior response if he obtains information upon the basis of which (i) he knows that the response was incorrect when made, or (ii) he knows that the response though correct when made is no longer true and the circumstances are such that a failure to amend the response is in substance a knowing concealment.

(c) A duty to supplement responses may be imposed by order of the court, agreement of the parties, or at any time prior to trial through new requests for supplementation of prior responses.

HISTORY: Amended eff. 1–1–78; adopted eff. 10–1–71

CR 26.06 Effect of taking deposition or questioning deponent

The taking of a deposition or the questioning of a deponent shall not make evidence admissible which is otherwise incompetent or constitute a waiver of objections to its admissibility.

HISTORY: Amended eff. 10–1–71

CR 27 Depositions before action or pending appeal

CR 27.01 Before action
(1) Petition.

A person who resides in this state and expects to be a party to an action in a court hereof; or who, being a nonresident of this state, has an interest in real property herein, concerning which he expects to be a party to an action in a court hereof; and who desires to perpetuate the testimony of witnesses, may file in the circuit court of the county of the residence of any expected adverse party, or in which the real property is situated, a verified petition, entitled in the name of the petitioner, showing: (a) that the petitioner expects to be a party to an action cognizable in a court of this state but is presently unable to bring it or cause it to be brought; (b) the subject matter of the expected action and his interest therein; (c) the facts which he desires to establish by the proposed testimony and his reasons for desiring to perpetuate it; (d) the names or a description of the persons he expects will be adverse parties and their addresses so far as known; and (e) the names and addresses of the persons to be examined and the substance of the testimony which he expects to elicit from each, and shall ask for an order authorizing the petitioner to take the depositions of the persons to be examined named in the petition, for the purpose of perpetuating their testimony.

(2) Notice and service.

The petitioner shall thereafter serve a notice upon each person named in the petition as an expected adverse party, together with a copy of the petition, stating that the petitioner will apply to the court, at a time and place named therein, for an order described in the petition. At least 20 days before the date of hearing the notice shall be served either within or without the county in the manner provided in Rule 4 for service of summons; but if such service cannot be made upon any expected adverse party named in the petition, the procedure provided in Rule 4 for constructive service shall apply. If any expected adverse party is a person under disability the provisions of Rule 17 shall apply.

(3) Order and examination.

If the court is satisfied that the perpetuation of the testimony may prevent a failure or delay of justice, it shall make an order designating or describing the persons whose depositions may be taken and specifying the subject matter of the examination and whether the depositions shall be taken upon oral examination or written interrogatories. The depositions may then be taken in accordance with these rules; and the court may make orders of the character provided for by Rules 34 and 37. For perpetuating testimony, each reference therein to the court in which the action is pending shall be deemed to refer to the court in which the petition for such deposition was filed.

(4) Use of deposition.

If a deposition to perpetuate testimony is taken under these rules or if, although not so taken, it would be admissible in evidence in the courts of the state in which it is taken, or in any United States court sitting in this state, it may be used in any action involving the same subject matter subsequently brought in a court of this state in accordance with the provisions of Rule 32.01.

HISTORY: Amended eff. 1–1–78; prior amendment eff. 10–1–71; adopted eff. 7–1–53

CR 27.02   Pending appeal

If an appeal has been taken from a judgment of a trial court or before the taking of an appeal if the time therefor has not expired, the trial court in which the judgment was rendered may allow the taking of the depositions of witnesses to perpetuate their testimony for use in the event of further proceedings in the trial court. In such case the party who desires to perpetuate the testimony may make a motion in the trial court for leave to take the depositions, upon the same notice and service thereof as if the action was pending in the trial court. The motion shall show (a) the names and addresses of the persons to be examined and the substance of the testimony which he expects to elicit from each; (b) the reasons for perpetuating their testimony. If the court finds that the perpetuation of the testimony is proper to avoid a failure or delay of justice, it may make an order allowing the depositions to be taken and may make orders of the character provided for by Rules 34 and 35, and thereupon the depositions may be taken and used in the same manner and under the same conditions as are

prescribed in these rules for depositions taken in actions pending in the trial court.

HISTORY: Amended eff. 1–1–78; prior amendment eff. 7–1–76; adopted eff. 7–1–53

CR 27.03   Perpetuation by action

Rule 27 does not limit the power of a court to entertain an action to perpetuate testimony.

HISTORY: Amended eff. 4–1–63; adopted eff. 7–1–53

CR 28   Persons before whom depositions may be taken

CR 28.01   Within the state

Depositions taken in this state, to be used in its courts, shall be taken before an examiner; a judge, clerk, commissioner or official reporter of a court; a notary public; or before such other persons and under such other circumstances as shall be authorized by law.

HISTORY: Amended eff. 2–22–78; prior amendment eff. 1–1–78; adopted eff. 7–1–53

CR 28.02   Without the state

Depositions may be taken out of this state before a commissioner appointed by the governor of the state where taken; or before any person empowered by a commission directed to him by consent of the parties or by order of the court; or before a judge of a court, a justice of the peace, mayor of a city, or notary public; or before such persons and under such other circumstances as shall be authorized by the law of this state or the place where the deposition is taken.

HISTORY: Amended eff. 1–1–78; prior amendment eff. 4–1–63; adopted eff. 7–1–53

CR 28.03   Depositions to be used in other states

A party desiring to take depositions in this state to be used in proceedings outside this state, may produce to a judge of the district court of the district in which the witness resides a commission authorizing the taking of such depositions or proof of notice duly served; whereupon it shall be the duty of the judge to issue, pursuant to Rule 45, the necessary subpoenas. Orders of the character provided in Rule 45.02 may be made upon proper application therefor by the person to whom such a subpoena is directed. Failure by any person without adequate excuse to obey a subpoena served upon him pursuant to this rule may be deemed a contempt of the court from which the subpoena issued.

HISTORY: Amended eff. 6–1–78; prior amendments eff. 2–22–78, 1–1–78; adopted eff. 7–1–53

CR 29   Stipulations regarding discovery procedure

Unless the court orders otherwise, the parties may by written stipulation (a) provide that depositions may be taken before any person, at any time or place, upon any notice, and in any manner and when so taken may be used like other depositions, and (b) modify the procedures provided by these Rules for other methods of discovery, except that stipulations extending the time provided in Rules 33.01, 34.02 and 36.01 for responses to discovery may be made only with the approval of the court.

HISTORY: Amended eff. 10–1–71; adopted eff. 7–1–53

CR 30   Depositions upon oral examination

CR 30.01   When depositions may be taken

After commencement of the action, any party may take the testimony of any person, including a party, by deposition upon oral examination. Leave of court, granted with or without notice, must be obtained only if the plaintiff seeks to take a deposition prior to the expiration of 30 days after service of the summons upon any defendant, except that leave is not required (a) if a defendant has served a notice of taking deposition or otherwise sought discovery, or (b) if special notice is given as provided in Rule 30.02(2). The attendance of witnesses may be compelled by subpoena as provided in Rule 45. The deposition of a person confined in prison may be taken only by leave of court on such terms as the court prescribes.

HISTORY: Amended eff. 10–1–71; adopted eff. 7–1–53

CR 30.02   Notice of examination: general requirements; special notice; nonstenographic recording; production of documents and things; deposition of organization

(1) A party desiring to take the deposition of any person upon oral examination shall give reasonable notice in writing to every other party to the action. The notice shall state the time and place for taking the deposition and the name and address of each person to be examined, if known, and, if the name is not known, a general description sufficient to identify him or the particular class or group to which he belongs. If a subpoena duces tecum is to be served on the person to be examined, the designation of the materials to be produced as set forth in the subpoena shall be attached to or included in the notice.

(2) (a) Leave of court is not required for the taking of a deposition by plaintiff if the notice (i) states that the person to be examined is about to go out of the state and will be unavailable for examination unless his deposition is taken before expiration of the 30–day period, and (ii) sets forth facts to support the statement. The plaintiff's attorney shall sign the notice, and his signature constitutes a certification by him that to the best of his knowledge, information, and belief the statement and supporting facts are true. The sanctions provided by Rule 11 are applicable to the certification.

(b) If a party shows that when he was served with notice under subparagraph (a) of this paragraph (2) he was unable through the exercise of diligence to obtain counsel to represent him at the taking of the deposition, the deposition may not be used against him.

(3) The court may for cause shown enlarge or shorten the time for taking the deposition.

(4) Video recorded depositions may be taken in pending actions and shall be taxed as costs. Notice to take depositions shall be in accordance with the Rules of Civil Procedure. At the deposition the video recording equipment shall be operated by a person qualified to operate such recording equipment, who is to mark the recording with the style and number of the action and the name of the witness and to file a certificate which identifies the said recording.

Video recorded depositions shall be taken under the following conditions:

(a) The party noticing the deposition shall provide the operator with a copy of this rule. At the beginning of the recording of the deposition, the operator of the video recording equipment will focus on each attorney, party and witness present at the taking of the deposition, and such person shall be identified; or the operator may read a statement introducing by name parties to the litigation and the attorneys present without focusing on each person, at the election of the noticing party.

(b) The video recording equipment will remain stationary at all times during the deposition and will not "zoom" in or out on the witness excepting those times during the deposition when the witness is displaying, for the jury's viewing, exhibits or other pieces of demonstrative proof that can only be fairly and reasonably seen on the video recording by use of the equipment "zooming" in on said evidence. The purpose of this clause is so that the video recording equipment will not "zoom" in on a witness solely to give unfair or undue influence upon the words of the witness, and does not apply to the "zooming" in for other purposes described above.

(c) A stenographic transcript, in addition to the video recording, will not be necessary. Any party desiring such a transcript may obtain it at that party's cost.

(d) The video recording shall be kept in the possession of the attorney taking the deposition and will be available for the Court and any and all counsel to view, copy, or compare with a stenographic transcript, if any. If discrepancies appear between the stenographic transcript and the video recording, the discrepancies will be resolved by agreement of counsel or ruling of the Court if counsel cannot agree. The decision on the manner in which to handle the discrepancies, insofar as the video recording is concerned, will be included in the agreement of counsel or ruling of the Court.

(e) All objections will be reserved and shall not be stated on the video recording except for objections relating to the form of the question. Objections to testimony on the video recording will be resolved by agreement of counsel or ruling of the Court if counsel cannot agree. All objections relating to said depositions must be made at least 10 days before trial. An edited version shall be presented at trial.

(f) Admissibility of the video recording may be objected to by counsel if a review of the finished video recording reveals any technical errors giving undue influence to the testimony of the witness which would unfairly prejudice the side objecting, or if the general technical quality of the video recording is so poor that its being viewed by the jury would be unfairly prejudicial to the side so objecting.

(5) The notice to a party deponent may be accompanied by a request made in compliance with Rule 34 for the production of documents and tangible things at the taking of the deposition. The procedure of Rule 34.02 shall apply to the request.

(6) A party may in his notice and in a subpoena name as the deponent a public or private corporation or a partnership or association or governmental agency and describe with reasonable particularity the matters on which examination is requested. In that event, the organization so named shall designate one or more officers, directors, or managing agents, or other persons who consent to testify on its behalf, and may set forth, for each person designated, the matters on which he will testify. A subpoena shall advise a non-party organization of its duty to make such a designation. The persons so designated shall testify as to matters known or reasonably available to the organization. This paragraph (6) does not preclude taking a deposition by any other procedure authorized in these rules.

HISTORY: Amended by Order 2006–09, eff. 1–1–07; prior amendments eff. 10–1–94 (Order 94–1), 1–1–87, 1–1–78, 10–1–71, 7–1–69; adopted eff. 7–1–53

CR 30.03 Examination and cross-examination; record of examination; oath; objections

(1) Examination and cross-examination of witnesses may proceed as permitted at the trial under the provisions of Rules 43.05 and 43.06. The officer before whom the deposition is to be taken shall put the witness on oath and shall personally, or by someone acting under his or her direction and in his or her presence, record the testimony of the witness. The testimony shall be taken stenographically or recorded by any other means ordered in accordance with Rule 30.02(4). If requested by one of the parties, the testimony shall be transcribed at that party's expense.

(2) All objections made at the time of the examination to the qualifications of the officer taking the

deposition, or to the manner of taking it, or to the evidence presented, or to the conduct of any party, and any other objection to the proceeding, shall be noted by the officer upon the deposition. Evidence objected to shall be taken subject to the objections. In lieu of participating in the oral examination, parties may serve written questions in a sealed envelope on the party taking the deposition and he shall transmit them to the officer, who shall propound them to the witness and record the answers verbatim.

(3) Any objection to evidence during a deposition shall be stated concisely and in a nonargumentative and nonsuggestive manner. An attorney may instruct his or her client not to answer only when necessary to preserve a privilege, to enforce a limitation on evidence directed by the court, or to present a motion under CR 30.04.

(4) If the court finds such an impediment, delay, or other conduct has frustrated the fair examination of the deponent, it may impose upon the persons responsible an appropriate sanction, including the reasonable costs and attorney's fees incurred by any parties as a result thereof.

HISTORY: Amended by Order 95–1, eff. 11–1–95; prior amendments eff. 8–1–92, 10–1–71; adopted eff. 7–1–53

CR 30.04 Motion to terminate or limit examination

At any time during the taking of the deposition, on motion of a party or of the deponent and upon a showing that the examination is being conducted in bad faith or in such manner as unreasonably to annoy, embarrass, or oppress the deponent or party, the court in which the action is pending or the court in the judicial district where the deposition is being taken may order the officer conducting the examination to cease forthwith from taking the deposition, or may limit the scope and manner of the taking of the deposition as provided in Rule 26.03. If the order made terminates the examination, it shall be resumed thereafter only upon the order of the court in which the action is pending. Upon demand of the objecting party or deponent, the taking of the deposition shall be suspended for the time necessary to make a motion for an order. The provisions of Rule 37.01(4)[1] apply to the award of expenses incurred in relation to the motion.

HISTORY: Amended eff. 10–1–71; adopted eff. 7–1–53

1 So in original.

CR 30.05 Submission to witness; changes; signing

Any party to an action may make written request before the officer taking a deposition therein that it be submitted to the witness. In such event, and when the testimony is fully transcribed, the deposition shall be submitted to the witness for examination and shall be read to or by him. Any changes in form or substance which the witness desires to make shall be entered upon the deposition by the officer with a statement of the reasons given by the witness for making them. The deposition shall then be signed by the witness unless the witness is ill or cannot be found or refuses to sign. If the deposition is not signed by the witness, the officer shall sign it and state on the record the fact of the illness or absence of the witness or the fact of the refusal to sign together with the reason, if any, given therefor; and the deposition may then be used as fully as though signed, unless on a motion to suppress under Rule 32.04 the court holds that the reasons given for the refusal to sign require rejection of the deposition in whole or in part.

HISTORY: Adopted eff. 7–1–53

CR 30.06 Certification and filing by officer; copies; exhibits

(1) The officer shall certify on the deposition that the witness was duly sworn by him and that the deposition is a true record of the testimony given by the witness. He promptly shall deliver the deposition to the clerk of the court in which the action is pending, or send it by registered mail to the clerk for filing.

(2) Documents and things produced for inspection during the examination of the witness, shall, upon the request of a party, be marked for identification and annexed to and returned with the deposition, and may be inspected and copied by any party, except that (a) the person producing the materials may substitute copies to be marked for identification, if he affords to all parties fair opportunity to verify the copies by comparison with the originals, and (b) if the person producing the materials requests their return, the officer shall mark them, give each party an opportunity to inspect and copy them, and return them to the person producing them, and the materials may then be used in the same manner as if annexed to and returned with the deposition. Any party may move for an order that the original be annexed to and returned with the deposition to the court, pending final disposition of the case.

(3) Upon payment of reasonable charges therefor, not to exceed those fixed by statute, the officer shall furnish a copy of the deposition to any party or to the deponent.

HISTORY: Amended eff. 10–1–71; adopted eff. 7–1–53

CR 30.07 Failure to attend or to serve subpoena; expenses

(1) If the party giving the notice of the taking of a deposition fails to attend and proceed therewith and another party attends in person or by attorney pursuant to the notice, the court may order the party giving the notice to pay to such other party the amount of the reasonable expenses incurred by him and his attorney in so attending, including reasonable attorney's fees.

(2) If the party giving the notice of the taking of a deposition of a witness fails to serve a subpoena upon him and the witness because of such failure does not attend, and if another party attends in person or by attorney because he expects the deposition of that witness to be taken, the court may order the party giving the notice to pay to such other party the amount of the reasonable expenses incurred by him and his attorney in so attending, including reasonable attorney's fees.

HISTORY: Adopted eff. 7–1–53

CR 31 Depositions upon written questions

CR 31.01 Serving questions; notice

(1) After commencement of the action, any party may take the testimony of any person, including a party, by deposition upon written questions. The attendance of witnesses may be compelled by the use of subpoena as provided in Rule 45. The deposition of a person confined in prison may be taken only by leave of court on such terms as the court prescribes.

(2) A party desiring to take a deposition upon written questions shall serve them upon every other party with a notice stating (a) the name and address of the person who is to answer them, if known, and if the name is not known, a general description sufficient to identify him or the particular class or group to which he belongs, and (b) the name or descriptive title and address of the officer before whom the deposition is to be taken. A deposition upon written questions may be taken of a public or private corporation or a partnership or association or governmental agency in accordance with the provisions of Rule 30.02(6).

(3) Within 30 days after the notice and written questions are served, a party may serve cross questions upon all other parties. Within 10 days after being served with cross questions, a party may serve redirect questions upon all other parties. Within ten days after being served with redirect questions, a party may serve recross questions upon all other parties. The court may for cause shown enlarge or shorten the time.

HISTORY: Amended eff. 10–1–71; adopted eff. 7–1–53

CR 31.02 Officer to take responses and prepare record

A copy of the notice and copies of all questions served shall be delivered by the party taking the deposition to the officer designated in the notice, who shall proceed promptly, in the manner provided by Rules 30.03, 30.05 and 30.06, to take the testimony of the witness in response to the questions and to prepare, certify, and file or mail the deposition, attaching thereto the copy of the notice and the questions received by him. Neither party or his agent or attorney shall be present at the examination of the witness.

HISTORY: Amended eff. 10–1–71; adopted eff. 7–1–53

CR 31.03   Orders for the protection of parties and deponents—Deleted

HISTORY: Deleted by Order of Supreme Court, eff. 1–1–78; adopted eff. 7–1–53

CR 32   Use of depositions in court proceedings

CR 32.01   Use of depositions

At the trial or upon the hearing of a motion or an interlocutory proceeding, any part or all of a deposition, so far as admissible under the rules of evidence applied as though the witness were then present and testifying, may be used against any party who was present or represented at the taking of the deposition or who had reasonable notice thereof, in accordance with any of the following provisions:

(a) Any deposition may be used by any party for the purpose of contradicting or impeaching the testimony of deponent as a witness.

(b) The deposition of a party or of anyone who at the time of taking the deposition was an officer, director, or managing agent, or a person designated under Rule 30.02(6) or 31.01(2) to testify on behalf of a public or private corporation, partnership or association or governmental agency which is a party may be used by an adverse party for any purpose.

(c) The deposition of a witness, whether or not a party, may be used by any party for any purpose if the court finds the witness: (i) is at a greater distance than 100 miles from the place where the court sits in which the action is pending or out of the State, unless it appears that the absence of the witness was procured by the party offering the deposition; or (ii) is the Governor, Secretary, Auditor or Treasurer of the State; or (iii) is a judge or clerk of a court; or (iv) is a postmaster; or (v) is a president, cashier, teller or clerk of a bank; or (vi) is a practicing physician, dentist, chiropractor, osteopath, podiatrist or lawyer; or (vii) is a keeper, officer or guard of a penitentiary; or (viii) is dead; or (ix) is of unsound mind, having been of sound mind when his deposition was taken; or (x) is prevented from attending the trial by illness, infirmity, or imprisonment; or (xi) is in the military service of the United States or of this State; or (xii) if the court finds that such exceptional circumstances exist as to make it desirable, in the interest of justice and with due regard to the importance of presenting the testimony of witnesses orally in open court, to allow the deposition to be used.

(d) If only part of a deposition is offered in evidence by a party, an adverse party may require him to introduce any other part which ought in fairness to be considered with the part introduced, and any party may introduce any other parts.

(e) Depositions may be used in the trial of actions as provided in Rule 43.04.

(f) Substitution of parties does not affect the right to use depositions previously taken; and when an action in any court of this state or any United States court sitting in this state, has been dismissed and another action involving the same subject matter is afterward brought between the same parties or their representatives or successors in interest, all depositions lawfully taken and duly filed in the former action may be used in the latter as if originally taken therefor.

HISTORY: Amended by Order 92–1, eff. 8–1–92; prior amendments eff. 1–1–78, 10–1–71

CR 32.02   Objections to admissibility

Subject to the provisions of Rules 32.04(3) and 43.04(3), objection may be made at the trial or hearing to receiving in evidence any deposition or part thereof for any reason which would require the exclusion of the evidence if the witness were then present and testifying.

HISTORY: Amended eff. 10–1–71

CR 32.03   Effect of taking or using depositions

The taking of a deposition or the questioning of a deponent shall not make evidence admissible which is otherwise incompetent or constitute a waiver of objections to its admissibility.

HISTORY: Amended eff. 10–1–71

CR 32.04   Effect of errors and irregularities

(1) As to notice.

All errors and irregularities in the notice for taking a deposition are waived unless written objection is promptly served upon the party giving the notice.

(2) As to disqualification of officer.

Objection to taking a deposition because of disqualification of the officer before whom it is to be taken is waived unless made before the taking of the deposition begins or as soon thereafter as the disqualification becomes known or could be discovered with reasonable diligence.

(3) As to taking of deposition.

(a) Objections to the competency of a witness or to the competency, relevancy, or materiality of testimony are not waived by failure to make them before or during the taking of the deposition, unless the ground of the objection is one which might have been obviated or removed if presented at that time.

(b) Errors and irregularities occurring at the oral examination in the manner of taking the deposition, in the form of the questions or answers, in the oath or affirmation, or in the conduct of parties and errors of any kind which might be obviated, removed, or cured if promptly presented, are waived unless seasonable objection thereto is made at the taking of the deposition.

(c) Objections to the form of written questions submitted under Rule 31 are waived unless served in writing upon the party propounding them within the time allowed for serving the succeeding cross or other questions and within 3 days after service of the last questions authorized.

(4) As to completion and return of deposition.

Errors and irregularities in the manner in which the testimony is transcribed or the deposition is prepared, signed, certified, sealed, indorsed, transmitted, filed, or otherwise dealt with by the officer under Rules 30 and 31 are waived unless a motion to suppress the deposition or some part thereof is made with reasonable promptness after such defect is, or with due diligence might have been, ascertained.

HISTORY: Amended eff. 1–1–78; prior amendment eff. 10–1–71

CR 33   Interrogatories to parties

CR 33.01   Availability; procedures for use

(1) Any party may serve upon any other party written interrogatories to be answered by the party served or, if the party served is a public or private corporation or a partnership or association or governmental agency, by any officer or agent, who shall furnish such information as is available to the party. Interrogatories may, without leave of court, be served upon the plaintiff after commencement of the action and upon any other party with or after service of the summons upon that party.

(2) Each interrogatory shall be answered separately and fully in writing under oath, unless it is objected to, in which event the reasons for objection shall be stated in lieu of an answer. The answers are to be signed by the person making them, and the objections signed by the attorney making them. The party upon whom the interrogatories have been served shall serve a copy of the answers, and objections if any, within 30 days after the service of the interrogatories, except that a defendant may serve answers or objections within 45 days after service of the summons upon that defendant. The court may allow a shorter or longer time. The party submitting the interrogatories may move for an order under Rule 37.01 with respect to any objection to or other failure to answer an interrogatory.

(3) Each party may propound a maximum of thirty (30) interrogatories and thirty (30) requests for admission to each other party; for purposes of this Rule, each subpart of an interrogatory or request shall be counted as a separate interrogatory or request. The following shall not be included in the maximum allowed: interrogatories requesting (a) the name and address of the person answering; (b) the names and addresses of the witnesses; and (c) whether the person answering is willing to supplement his answers if information subsequently becomes available. Any party may move the court for permission to propound either interrogatories or requests for admission in excess of the limit of thirty (30).

HISTORY: Amended by Order 83–4, eff. 1–1–84; prior amendment eff. 10–1–71; adopted eff. 7–1–53

CR 33.02   Scope; use at trial

(1) Interrogatories may relate to any matters which may be inquired into under Rule 26.02, and the answers may be used to the extent permitted by the rules of evidence.

(2) An interrogatory otherwise proper is not necessarily objectionable merely because an answer to the interrogatory involves an opinion or contention that relates to fact or the application of law to fact, but the court may order that such an interrogatory need not be answered until after designated discovery has been completed or until a pre-trial conference or other later time.

HISTORY: Amended eff. 10–1–71; adopted eff. 7–1–53

CR 33.03   Option to produce business records

Where the answer to an interrogatory may be derived or ascertained from the business records of the party upon whom the interrogatory has been served or from an examination, audit or inspection of such business records, or from a compilation, abstract or summary based thereon, and the burden of deriving or ascertaining the answer is substantially the same for the party serving the interrogatory as for the party served, it is a sufficient answer to such interrogatory to specify the records from which the answer may be derived or ascertained and to afford to the party serving the interrogatory reasonable opportunity to examine, audit or inspect such records and to make copies, compilations, abstracts or summaries.

HISTORY: Adopted eff. 10–1–71

CR 34   Production of documents and things and entry upon land for inspection and other purposes

CR 34.01   Scope

Any party may serve on any other party a request (a) to produce and permit the party making the request, or someone acting on his behalf, to inspect and copy any designated documents (including writings, drawings, graphs, charts, photographs, phono-records, and other data compilations from which information can be obtained, translated, if necessary, by the respondent through detection devices into reasonably usable form), or to inspect and copy, test, or sample any tangible things which constitute or contain matters within the scope of Rule 26.02 and which are in the possession, custody or control of the party upon whom the request is served; or (b) to permit entry upon designated land or other property in the possession or control of the party upon whom the request is served for the purpose of inspection and measuring, surveying, photographing, testing, or sampling the property or any designated object or operation thereon, within the scope of Rule 26.02.

HISTORY: Amended eff. 10–1–71; adopted eff. 7–1–53

CR 34.02 Procedure

(1) The request may, without leave of court, be served upon the plaintiff after commencement of the action and upon any other party with or after service of the summons upon that party. The request shall set forth the items to be inspected either by individual item or by category, and describe each item and category with reasonable particularity. The request shall specify a reasonable time, place, and manner of making the inspection and performing the related acts.

(2) The party upon whom the request is served shall serve a written response within 30 days after the service of the request, except that a defendant may serve a response within 45 days after service of the summons upon that defendant. The court may allow a shorter or longer time. The response shall state, with respect to each item or category, that inspection and related activities will be permitted as requested, unless the request is objected to, in which event the reasons for objection shall be stated. If objection is made to part of an item or category, the part shall be specified. The party submitting the request may move for an order under Rule 37.01 with respect to any objection to or other failure to respond to the request or any part thereof, or any failure to permit inspection as requested.

HISTORY: Adopted eff. 10–1–71

CR 34.03 Persons not parties

Rule 34 does not preclude an independent action against a person not a party for production of documents and things and permission to enter upon land.

HISTORY: Adopted eff. 10–1–71

CR 35 Physical and mental examination of persons

CR 35.01 Order for examination

When the mental or physical condition (including the blood group) of a party, or of a person in the custody or under the legal control of a party, is in controversy, the court in which the action is pending may order the party to submit to a physical or mental examination by a physician, dentist or appropriate health care expert, or to produce for examination the person in his custody or legal control. The order may be made only on motion for good cause shown and upon notice to the person to be examined and to all parties and shall specify the time, place, manner, conditions, and scope of the examination and the person or persons by whom it is to be made.

HISTORY: Amended by Order 91–2, eff. 11–15–91; prior amendment eff. 10–1–71; adopted eff. 7–1–53

CR 35.02 Report of examining physician or health care expert

(1) If requested by the party against whom an order is made under Rule 35.01 or the person examined, the party causing the examination to be made shall deliver to that person or party a copy of a detailed written report of the examining health care expert setting out all findings, including results of all tests made, diagnoses and conclusions, together with like reports of all earlier examinations of the same condition. After delivery, the party causing the examination shall be entitled upon request to receive from the party against whom the order is made a like report of any examination, previously or thereafter made, of the same condition, unless, in the case of a report of examination of a person not a party, the party shows an inability to obtain it. The court on motion may make an order against a party requiring delivery of a report on such terms as are just, and if a physician or examining health care expert fails or refuses to make a report the court may exclude such testimony if offered at the trial.

(2) This rule applies to examinations made by agreement of the parties, unless the agreement expressly provides otherwise. This rule does not preclude discovery of a report of an examining physician or health care expert or the taking of a deposition of the physician or health care expert in accordance with the provisions of any other rule.

HISTORY: Amended by Order 91–2, eff. 11–15–91; prior amendment eff. 10–1–71; adopted eff. 7–1–53

CR 36 Requests for admission

CR 36.01 Request for admission

(1) A party may serve upon any other party a written request for the admission, for purposes of the pending action only, of the truth of any matters within the scope of Rule 26.02 set forth in the request that relate to statements or opinions of fact or of the application of law to fact, including the genuineness of any documents described in the request. Copies of documents shall be served with the request unless they have been or are otherwise furnished or made available for inspection and copying. The request may, without leave of court, be served upon the plaintiff after commencement of the action and upon any other party with or after service of the summons upon that party.

(2) Each matter of which an admission is requested shall be separately set forth. The matter is admitted unless, within 30 days after service of the request, or within such shorter or longer time as the court may allow, the party to whom the request is directed serves upon the party requesting the admission a written answer or objection addressed to the matter, signed by the party or by his attorney, but, unless the court shortens the time, a defendant shall not be required to serve answers or objections before the expiration of 45 days after service of the summons upon him. If objection is made, the reasons therefor shall be stated. The answer shall specifically deny the matter or set forth in detail the reasons why the answering party cannot truthfully admit or deny the matter. A denial shall fairly meet the substance of the requested admission, and when good faith requires that a party qualify his answer or deny only a part of the matter of which an admission is requested, he shall specify so much of it as is true and qualify or deny the remainder. An answering party may not give lack of information or knowledge as a reason for failure to admit or deny unless he states that he has made reasonable inquiry and that the information known or readily obtainable by him is insufficient to enable him to admit or deny. A party who considers that a matter of which an admission has been requested presents a genuine issue for trial may not, on that ground alone, object to the request; he may, subject to the provisions of Rule 37.03, deny the matter or set forth reasons why he cannot admit or deny it.

(3) The party who has requested the admissions may move to determine the sufficiency of the answers or objections. Unless the court determines that an objection is justified, it shall order that an answer be served. If the court determines that an answer does not comply with the requirements of this Rule, it may order either that the matter is admitted or that an amended answer be served. The court may, in lieu of these orders, determine that final disposition of the request be made at a pretrial conference or at a designated time prior to trial. The provisions of Rule 37.01(4)[1] apply to the award of expenses incurred in relation to the motion.

HISTORY: Amended eff. 10–1–71; adopted eff. 7–1–53

[1] So in original.

CR 36.02   Effect of admission

Any matter admitted under Rule 36 is conclusively established unless the court on motion permits withdrawal or amendment of the admission. Subject to the provisions of Rule 16 governing amendment of a pretrial order, the court may permit withdrawal or amendment when the presentation of the merits of the action will be subserved thereby and the party who obtained the admission fails to satisfy the court that withdrawal or amendment will prejudice him in maintaining his action or defense on the merits. An admission made by a party under Rule 36 is for the purpose of the pending action only and is not an admission by him for any other purpose nor may it be used against him in any other proceeding.

HISTORY: Amended eff. 10–1–71; adopted eff. 7–1–53

CR 37   Failure to make discovery; sanctions

CR 37.01   Motion for order compelling discovery

A party, upon reasonable notice to other parties and all persons affected thereby, may apply for an order compelling discovery as follows:

(a) Appropriate court.

An application for an order to a party may be made to the court in which the action is pending, or, on matters relating to a deposition, to the court of equivalent jurisdiction in the county where the deposition is being taken.

(b) Motion.

(i) If a deponent fails to answer a question propounded or submitted under Rule 30 or 31, or a corporation or other entity fails to make a designation under Rule 30.02(6) or 31.01(2), or a party fails to answer an interrogatory submitted under Rule 33, or if a party, in response to a request for inspection submitted under Rule 34, fails to respond that inspection will be permitted as requested or fails to permit inspection as requested, the discovering party may move for an order compelling an answer, or a designation, or an order compelling inspection in accordance with the request. When taking a deposition on oral examination, the proponent of the question may complete or adjourn the examination before he applies for an order.

(ii) If the court denies the motion in whole or in part, it may make such protective order as it would have been empowered to make on a motion made pursuant to Rule 26.03.

(c) Evasive or incomplete answer.

For the purposes of this rule an evasive or incomplete answer is to be treated as a failure to answer.

(d) Award of expenses of motion.

(i) If the motion is granted the court shall, after opportunity for hearing, require the party or deponent whose conduct necessitated the motion or the party or attorney advising such conduct or both of them to pay to the moving party the reasonable expenses incurred in obtaining the order, including attorney's fees, unless the court finds that the opposition to the motion was substantially justified or that other circumstances make an award of expenses unjust.

(ii) If the motion is denied, the court shall, after opportunity for hearing, require the moving party or the attorney advising the motion or both of them to pay to the party or deponent who opposed the motion the reasonable expenses incurred in opposing the motion, including attorney's fees, unless the court finds that the making of the motion was substantially justified or that other circumstances make an award of expenses unjust.

(iii) If the motion is granted in part and denied in part, the court may apportion the reasonable expenses incurred in relation to the motion among the parties and persons in a just manner.

HISTORY: Amended eff. 1–1–78; prior amendments eff. 7–1–76, 10–1–71; adopted eff. 7–1–53

CR 37.02   Failure to comply with order

(1) Sanctions by court in judicial district where deposition is taken.

If a deponent fails to be sworn or to answer a question after being directed to do so by the court in the judicial district in which the deposition is being taken, the failure may be considered a contempt of that court.

(2) Sanctions by court in which action is pending.

If a party or an officer, director, or managing agent of a party or a person designated under Rule 30.02(6) or 31.01(2) to testify on behalf of a party fails to obey an order to provide or permit discovery, including an order made under Rule 37.01 or Rule 35, the court in which the action is pending may make such orders in regard to the failure as are just, and among others the following:

(a) An order that the matters regarding which the order was made or any other designated facts shall be taken to be established for the purposes of the action in accordance with the claim of the party obtaining the order;

(b) An order refusing to allow the disobedient party to support or oppose designated claims or defenses, or prohibiting him from introducing designated matters in evidence;

(c) An order striking out pleadings or parts thereof, or staying further proceedings until the order is obeyed, or dismissing the action or proceeding or any part thereof, or rendering a judgment by default against the disobedient party;

(d) In lieu of any of the foregoing orders or in addition thereto, an order treating as a contempt of court the failure to obey any orders except an order to submit to a physical or mental examination;

(e) Where a party has failed to comply with an order under Rule 35.01 requiring him to produce another for examination, such orders as are listed in subparagraphs (a), (b) and (c) of this paragraph (2), unless the party failing to comply shows that he is unable to produce such person for examination.

(3) Expenses on failure to obey order.

In lieu of any of the foregoing orders or in addition thereto, the court shall require the party failing to obey the order or the attorney advising him or both to pay the reasonable expenses, including attorney's fees,

caused by the failure, unless the court finds that the failure was substantially justified or that other circumstances make an award of expenses unjust.

HISTORY: Amended eff. 1–1–78; prior amendment eff. 10–1–71; adopted eff. 7–1–53

CR 37.03   Expenses on failure to admit

If a party fails to admit the genuineness of any document or the truth of any matter as requested under Rule 36, and if the party requesting the admissions thereafter proves the genuineness of the document or the truth of the matter, he may apply to the court for an order requiring the other party to pay him the reasonable expenses incurred in making that proof, including reasonable attorney's fees. The court shall make the order unless it finds that (a) the request was held objectionable pursuant to Rule 36.01, or (b) the admission sought was of no substantial importance, or (c) the party failing to admit had reasonable ground to believe that he might prevail on the matter, or (d) there was other good reason for the failure to admit.

HISTORY: Amended eff. 10–1–71; adopted eff. 7–1–53

CR 37.04   Failure of party to attend at own deposition or serve answers to interrogatories or respond to request for inspection

(1) If a party or an officer, director, or managing agent of a party or a person designated under Rule 30.02(6) or 31.01(2) to testify on behalf of a party fails (a) to appear before the officer who is to take his deposition, after being served with a proper notice, or (b) to serve answers or objections to interrogatories submitted under Rule 33, after proper service of the interrogatories, or (c) to serve a written response to a request for inspection submitted under Rule 34, after proper service of the request, the court in which the action is pending on motion may make such orders in regard to the failure as are just, and among others it may take any action authorized under subparagraphs (a), (b) and (c) of Rule 37.02(2). In lieu of any order or in addition thereto, the court shall require the party failing to act or the attorney advising him or both to pay the reasonable expenses, including attorney's fees, caused by the failure, unless the court finds that the failure was substantially justified or that other circumstances make an award of expenses unjust.

(2) The failure to act described in this rule may not be excused on the ground that the discovery sought is objectionable unless the party failing to act has applied for a protective order as provided by Rule 26.03.

HISTORY: Amended eff. 1–1–78; prior amendment eff. 10–1–71; adopted eff. 7–1–53

CR 37.05   Expenses against the Commonwealth

Expenses and attorney's fees are not to be imposed upon the Commonwealth under Rule 37.

HISTORY: Amended eff. 10–1–71

CR 37.06   Expenses against the Commonwealth— Renumbered

HISTORY: Renumbered eff. 10–1–71

VI   TRIALS

CR 38   Jury trials of right

CR 38.01   Right preserved

The right of trial by jury as declared by the Constitution of Kentucky or as given by a statute of Kentucky shall be preserved to the parties inviolate.

HISTORY: Adopted eff. 7–1–53

CR 38.02   Demand

Any party may demand a trial by jury of any issue triable of right by a jury by serving upon the other parties a demand therefor in writing at any time after the commencement of the action and not later than 10 days after the service of the last pleading directed to such issue. Such demand may be indorsed upon a pleading of the party, and if indorsed on the complaint, the filing of the complaint shall constitute service of the demand.

HISTORY: Adopted eff. 7–1–53

CR 38.03   Same; specification of issues

In his demand a party may specify the issues which he wishes so tried; otherwise he shall be deemed to have demanded trial by jury for all the issues so triable. If he has demanded trial by jury for only some of the issues, any other party within 10 days after service of the demand, or within the time for answering if the demand is indorsed upon the complaint, or within such lesser time as the court may order, may serve a demand for trial by jury of any other or all of the issues of fact in the action.

HISTORY: Adopted eff. 7–1–53

CR 38.04   Waiver

The failure of a party to serve a demand as required by this rule and to file it as required by Rule 5.05 constitutes a waiver by him of trial by jury. A demand for trial by jury made as herein provided may not be withdrawn without the consent of the parties.

HISTORY: Adopted eff. 7–1–53

CR 39   Trial by jury or by the court

CR 39.01   By jury

When trial by jury has been demanded as provided in Rule 38, the action shall be designated upon the docket as a jury action. The trial of all issues so demanded shall be by jury, unless (a) the parties or their attorneys of record, by written stipulation filed with the court or by an oral stipulation made in open court and entered in the record, consent to trial by the court sitting without a jury, or (b) the court upon motion or of its own initiative finds that a right of trial by jury of some or all of the issues does not exist under the Constitution or Statutes of Kentucky.

HISTORY: Amended by Order 96–1, eff. 1–1–97; prior amendment eff. 1–1–78; adopted eff. 7–1–53

CR 39.02   By the court

Issues not demanded for trial by jury as provided in Rule 38 shall be tried by the court; but, notwithstanding the failure of a party to demand a jury in an action in which such a demand might have been made out of right, the court in its discretion upon motion may order a trial by jury of any or all issues.

HISTORY: Adopted eff. 7–1–53

CR 39.03   Advisory jury and trial by consent

In all actions not triable of right by a jury the court upon motion or of its own initiative may try any issue with an advisory jury; or the court, with the consent of all parties noted of record, may order a trial with a jury whose verdict has the same effect as if trial by jury had been a matter of right.

HISTORY: Amended eff. 7–1–69; adopted eff. 7–1–53

CR 40   Assignment of cases for trial

No case shall be assigned for trial without giving reasonable notice to all parties not in default of the day on which a trial date will be fixed.

HISTORY: Amended eff. 6–1–60; adopted eff. 7–1–53

CR 41   Dismissal of actions

CR 41.01   Voluntary dismissal; effect thereof
(1) By plaintiff; by stipulation.

Subject to the provisions of Rule 23.05, of Rule 66, and of any statute, an action, or any claim therein, may be dismissed by the plaintiff without order of court, by filing a notice of dismissal at any time before service by the adverse party of an answer or of a motion for summary judgment, whichever first occurs, or by filing a stipulation of dismissal signed by all parties who have appeared in the action. Unless otherwise stated in the notice of dismissal or stipulation, the dismissal is without prejudice, except that a notice of dismissal operates as an adjudication upon the merits when filed by a plaintiff who has once dismissed in any court of this state, of the United

States or of any state an action based on or including the same claim.

(2) By order of court.

Except as provided in paragraph (1) of this rule, an action, or any claim therein, shall not be dismissed at the plaintiff's instance save upon order of the court and upon such terms and conditions as the court deems proper. If a counterclaim has been pleaded by a defendant prior to the service upon him of the plaintiff's motion to dismiss, the action shall not be dismissed against the defendant's objection unless the counterclaim can remain pending for independent adjudication by the court. Unless otherwise specified in the order, a dismissal under this section is without prejudice.

HISTORY: Amended by Order 2000–1, eff. 2–1–01; prior amendment eff. 1–1–78; adopted eff. 7–1–53

CR 41.02　Involuntary dismissal; effect thereof

(1) For failure of the plaintiff to prosecute or to comply with these rules or any order of the court, a defendant may move for dismissal of an action or of any claim against him.

(2) In an action tried by the court without a jury, after the plaintiff has completed the presentation of his evidence, the defendant, without waiving his right to offer evidence in the event the motion is not granted, may move for a dismissal on the ground that upon the facts and the law the plaintiff has shown no right to relief. The court as trier of the facts may then determine them and render judgment against the plaintiff or may decline to render any judgment until the close of all the evidence. If the court renders judgment on the merits against the plaintiff, the court shall make findings as provided in Rule 52.01.

(3) Unless the court in its order for dismissal otherwise specifies, a dismissal under this Rule, and any dismissal not provided for in Rule 41, other than a dismissal for lack of jurisdiction, for improper venue, for want of prosecution under Rule 77.02(2), or for failure to join a party under Rule 19, operates as an adjudication upon the merits.

HISTORY: Amended by Order 89–1, eff. 8–28–89; prior amendment eff. 7–1–69; adopted eff. 7–1–53

CR 41.03　Dismissal of counterclaim, cross-claim, or third-party claim

The provisions of Rule 41 apply to the dismissal of any counterclaim, cross-claim, or third-party claim. A voluntary dismissal by the claimant alone pursuant to paragraph (1) of Rule 41.01 shall be made before a responsive pleading is served or, if there is none, before the introduction of evidence at the trial or hearing.

HISTORY: Amended eff. 1–1–78; prior amendment eff. 4–1–63; adopted eff. 7–1–53

CR 41.04　Costs of previously dismissed action

If a plaintiff who has once dismissed an action in any court commences an action based upon or including the same claim against the same defendant, the court may make such order for the payment of costs of the action previously dismissed as it may deem proper and may stay the proceedings in the action until the plaintiff has complied with the order.

HISTORY: Adopted eff. 7–1–53

CR 42　Consolidation; separate trials

CR 42.01　Consolidation

When actions involving a common question of law or fact are pending before the court, it may order a joint hearing or trial of any or all the matters in issue in the actions; it may order all the actions consolidated; and it may make such orders concerning proceedings therein as may tend to avoid unnecessary costs or delay.

HISTORY: Adopted eff. 7–1–53

CR 42.02　Separate trials

If the court determines that separate trials will be in furtherance of convenience or will avoid prejudice, or will be conducive to expedition and economy, it shall order a separate trial of any claim, cross-claim, counterclaim, or third-party claim, or of any separate issue or of any number of claims, cross-claims, counterclaims, third-party claims or issues.

HISTORY: Amended eff. 7–1–69; adopted eff. 7–1–53

CR 43　Trial procedure and the introduction of evidence

CR 43.01　Burden of proof

(1) The party holding the affirmative of an issue must produce the evidence to prove it.

(2) The burden of proof in the whole action lies on the party who would be defeated if no evidence were given on either side.

HISTORY: Adopted eff. 7–1–53

CR 43.02　Order of proceeding in trial

When the jury has been sworn, the trial shall proceed in the following order, unless the court, for special reasons otherwise directs:

(a) The plaintiff must briefly state his claim and the evidence by which he expects to sustain it.

(b) The defendant must then briefly state his defense and the evidence he expects to offer in support of it.

(c) The party on whom rests the burden of proof in the whole action must first produce his evidence; the adverse party will then produce his evidence. The party who begins the case must ordinarily exhaust his evidence before the other begins. But the order of proof shall be regulated by the court so as to expedite the trial and enable the tribunal to obtain a clear view of the whole evidence.

(d) The parties will then be confined to rebutting evidence, unless the court, for good reasons in furtherance of justice, permits them to offer evidence in chief.

(e) The parties may submit or argue the case to the jury. In the argument, the party having the burden of proof shall have the conclusion and the adverse party the opening. If there be more than one speech on either side, or if several defendants having separate defenses appear by different counsel, the court shall arrange the relative order of argument.

HISTORY: Amended eff. 1–1–78; adopted eff. 7–1–53

CR 43.03   Postponement of trial; motion and affidavit

A motion to postpone a trial on account of the absence of evidence may be made only upon affidavit showing the materiality of the evidence expected to be obtained, and that due diligence has been used to obtain it. If the motion is based on the absence of a witness, the affidavit must show what facts the affiant believes the witness will prove, and not merely the effect of such facts in evidence, and that the affiant believes them to be true. If the adverse party will consent that, on the trial, the affidavit may be read as the deposition of the absent witness, the trial shall not be postponed on account of his absence.

HISTORY: Adopted eff. 7–1–53

CR 43.04   Form of evidence; trial by deposition
(1) Form of evidence.

In all trials concerning alimony or divorce; the enforcement of a lien or the satisfaction of a judgment; judicial sale; surcharge or accounting; settlement of estates; the division of land; or the allotment of dower, the testimony shall be taken by deposition, unless the court by order or by local rule directs the testimony to be heard under oath and orally in open court. In all other trials the testimony of witnesses shall be heard under oath and orally in open court, unless otherwise provided by these rules or by statute, except that the court may upon motion or upon its own initiative, and with due regard to the importance of presenting the testimony of witnesses orally in open court, order the testimony to be taken by deposition upon any issue which is to be tried by the court without a jury.

(2) Time of taking depositions.

In all cases where proof is to be taken by deposition without an order of court the plaintiff shall complete his evidence by deposition 30 days after the service of the last pleading directed to the issue. In cases where evidence is ordered taken by deposition the plaintiff shall complete his evidence by deposition 30 days after service of the order directing proof to be so heard. The court may in either case order a shorter or longer period for good cause. The defendant shall complete his proof by deposition 30 days after the termination of the period allowed the plaintiff by this rule or by the court, unless the court for good cause orders a shorter or longer period. The parties shall each have 10 days in which to take rebuttal depositions, unless a longer period is allowed by the court.

(3) Procedure.

The provisions of Rule 26, 28, 29, 30, 31, 32 and 37 shall apply to depositions to be used under this rule, except that the party taking a deposition shall give prompt notice of its filing to all other parties; and no objection to the competency, relevancy or materiality of testimony shall be regarded unless made at the taking of the deposition or subsequently made in writing, specifying the grounds of objection, and served and filed prior to the submission of the case.

HISTORY: Adopted eff. 7–1–53

CR 43.05   Scope of examination and cross-examination; leading questions—Deleted

HISTORY: Deleted by Order 2004–5, eff. 1–1–05; prior amendment eff. 1–1–78; adopted eff. 7–1–53

CR 43.06   Same; examination of adverse party—Deleted

HISTORY: Deleted by Order 2004–5, eff. 1–1–05; adopted eff. 7–1–53

CR 43.07   Impeachment of witnesses—Deleted

HISTORY: Deleted by Order 2004–5, eff. 1–1–05; adopted eff. 7–1–53

CR 43.08   Same; prior contradictory statements—Deleted

HISTORY: Deleted by Order 2004–5, eff. 1–1–05; adopted eff. 7–1–53

CR 43.09   Separation of witnesses—Deleted

HISTORY: Deleted by Order 2004–5, eff. 1–1–05; adopted eff. 7–1–53

CR 43.10   Avowals—Deleted

HISTORY: Deleted by Order 2004–5, eff. 1–1–05; adopted eff. 7–1–53

CR 43.11   Affirmation in lieu of oath—Deleted

HISTORY: Deleted by Order 2004–5, eff. 1–1–05; adopted eff. 7–1–53

CR 43.12   Evidence on motions

When a motion is based on facts not appearing of record the court may hear the matter on affidavits presented by the respective parties, but the court may direct that the matter be heard wholly or partly on oral testimony or depositions.

HISTORY: Adopted eff. 7–1–53

CR 43.13   Affidavits; definition and content

(1) Affidavits authorized or permitted under these rules, or in any statutory proceeding, shall be a written statement or declaration sworn to or affirmed before an officer authorized to take depositions by Rule 28. If a party is absent from the county, or mentally incapable of taking an oath, or physically unable to attend before an officer, his agent or attorney may make such affidavit, unless otherwise provided by these rules or any statute. Such an affidavit shall state the absence or incapacity of the party and the capacity of the affiant.

(2) Every affidavit shall be subscribed by the affiant; and the certificate of the officer or person before whom it is made shall be written separately, following the signature of the affiant, and shall be proof of the time and manner of the affidavit being made.

HISTORY: Adopted eff. 7–1–53

CR 44   Proof of official record

CR 44.01   Authentication of copy

An official record or an entry therein, when admissible for any purpose, may be evidenced by an official publication thereof or by a copy attested by the officer having the legal custody of the record, or by his deputy if the record is in the custody of an officer of this state, and if the record is in the custody of an officer outside this state such attested copy shall be accompanied with a certificate that such officer has the custody. If the office in which the record is kept is within the United States or within a territory or insular possession subject to the dominion of the United States, the certificate may be made by a judge of a court of record of the district or political subdivision in which the record is kept, authenticated by the seal of the court, or may be made by any public officer having a seal of office and having official duties in the district or political subdivision in which the record is kept, authenticated by the seal of his office. If the

office in which the record is kept is in a foreign state or country, the certificate may be made by a secretary of embassy or legation, consul general, consul, vice consul, or consular agent or by any officer in the foreign service of the United States stationed in the foreign state or country in which the record is kept, and authenticated by the seal of his office.

HISTORY: Amended eff. 4–1–63; adopted eff. 7–1–53

CR 44.02   Proof of lack of record—Deleted

HISTORY: Deleted by Order 2004–5, eff. 1–1–05; adopted eff. 7–1–53

CR 44.03   Other proof

Rule 44 does not prevent the proof of official records or of entry or lack of entry therein by any other method authorized by law.

HISTORY: Amended eff. 7–1–69; adopted eff. 7–1–53

CR 45   Subpoena

CR 45.01   Form; issuance

(1) Every subpoena shall state the court from which it is issued, the title of the action, the court in which the action is pending, and its civil action number; and the name, address, telephone number and e-mail address of the attorney or pro-se party causing the subpoena to be issued. Every subpoena shall command each person to whom it is directed to attend and give testimony and/or to produce designated documents or tangible things in that person's possession, custody, or control, or to permit inspection of premises, at the time and place therein specified.

(2) The clerk or other authorized deputy shall issue a subpoena signed but otherwise in blank, to a party requesting it, who shall fill it in before service. An attorney licensed to practice law in this state may also issue and sign a subpoena on behalf of the court. A command to produce documents or tangible things or to permit the inspection of premises may be included in a subpoena commanding attendance at a deposition, hearing, or trial, or may be set out in a separate subpoena.

AOC-025 Doc. Code: RS		Case No. _____
Page 1 of 1	[ ] SUBPOENA	Court _____
Commonwealth of Kentucky		County _____
Court of Justice www.courts.ky.gov		Date _____
CR 45; RCr 7.02	[ ] SUBPOENA DUCES TECUM	

PLAINTIFF

VS

DEFENDANT

The Commonwealth of Kentucky to:

Name _____

Address _____

_____

You are commanded to appear before: *(select one of three choices)*

[ ] _____ Court   [ ] The Grand Jury of _____ County

[ ] Other _____

You are to appear at: _____

on the _____ day of _____, 20____ at _____ [ ] a.m. OR [ ] p.m. [ ] Eastern [ ] Central Time

    [ ] To testify in behalf of _____

    [ ] To produce _____

_____

    [ ] To give depositions

You are commanded to produce and permit inspection and copying of the following documents or objects (or to permit inspection of premises): _____

_____

on the _____ day of _____, 20____ at _____ [ ] a.m. OR [ ] p.m. [ ] Eastern [ ] Central Time
at the following address: _____

_____

| Issuing Officer/Attorney Licensed in Kentucky | Name of Requesting Attorney |
| By: _____ | Phone # _____ |

PROOF OF SERVICE

This subpoena was served by delivery of a true copy to: _____

_____

This _____ day of _____, 20_____ By: _____

_____ Title

HISTORY: Amended by Order 2012–10, eff. 1–1–13, prior amendments eff. 4–1–09 (Order 2009–01), 11–15–91 (Order 91–1); adopted eff. 7–1–53

CR 45.02   For production of documentary evidence

The court, upon motion made promptly and in any event at or before the time specified in the subpoena for compliance therewith, may (a) quash or modify the subpoena if it is unreasonable and oppressive or (b) condition denial of the motion upon the advancement by the person in whose behalf the subpoena is issued of the reasonable cost of producing the books, papers, documents, or tangible things.

HISTORY: Amended by Order 2009–01, eff. 4–1–09; prior amendment eff. 1–1–78; adopted eff. 7–1–53

CR 45.03   Service; notice

(1) A subpoena may be served in any manner that a summons might be served. It may also be served by any person over eighteen years of age, and the affidavit endorsed thereon by such person shall be proof of service or the witnesses may acknowledge service in writing on the subpoena. Service of the subpoena shall be made by delivering or offering to deliver a copy thereof to the person to whom it is directed. A subpoena may be served at any place within this state. Proof of service shall be made by filing with the issuing court a statement showing the date and manner of service and the names of the persons served. The statement must be certified by the server.

(2) Copies of all documents received in response to the subpoena shall be forthwith furnished to all other parties to the action, except on motion and for good cause shown. Any other tangible evidence received in response to the subpoena shall be forthwith made available for inspection by all other parties to the action.

(3) Before any subpoena is served, notice of that subpoena, except those issued for trial, shall be served on each party and any person or entity whose information is being requested.

HISTORY: Amended by Order 2012–10, eff. 1–1–13; prior amendments eff. 4–1–09 (Order 2009–01), eff. 11–15–91 (Order 91–2); adopted eff. 7–1–53

CR 45.04   Protection of a person subject to a subpoena

(1) A subpoena that commands the person to whom it is directed to produce designated documents or tangible things or to permit inspection of premises may relate only to matters within the scope of discovery permitted by Rule 26.02. Every subpoena will be subject to the provisions of Rule 26.03.

(2) The person to whom a subpoena is directed may, within ten (10) days after the service thereof or on or before the time specified in the subpoena for compliance if such time is less than ten (10) days after service, serve upon the attorney or pro se party designated in the subpoena written objection to inspection or copying of any or all of the designated materials. If objection is made, the party serving the subpoena shall not be entitled to inspect and copy the materials except pursuant to an order of the court from which the subpoena was issued. The party serving discovery may, upon notice, move for an appropriate order.

(3) A resident of the state may be required to attend an examination only in the county wherein he resides or is employed or transacts his business in person, or at such other convenient place as is fixed by an order of the court. A person commanded to produce documents or tangible things, or to permit the inspection of premises, need not appear in person at the place of production or inspection unless also commanded to appear for a deposition, hearing, or trial.

HISTORY: Amended by Order 2009–01, eff. 4–1–09; prior amendment eff. 10–1–71; adopted eff. 7–1–53

CR 45.05   Subpoena for a hearing or trial; personal attendance

(1) Subject to the provisions of paragraph (2) of this rule a witness whose deposition might be used under Rule 32.01(c) shall not be compelled to appear in court for oral examination, unless he/she failed, when duly subpoenaed, to give his/her deposition.

(2) Upon the affidavit of a party or his/her attorney that the testimony of a witness is important, and that the just and proper effect of that testimony can not in a reasonable degree be obtain without oral examination in court, the court may, in its discretion, order the personal attendance of the witness, although such witness may otherwise be exempt from personal attendance.

HISTORY: Amended by Order 2009–01, eff. 4–1–09; prior amendments eff. 1–1–78, 10–1–71, 4–1–63; adopted eff. 7–1–53

CR 45.06   Contempt

Disobedience of a subpoena or a refusal to be sworn or to answer as a witness may be punished as a contempt of the court in which the action is pending.

HISTORY: Adopted eff. 7–1–53

CR 46   Exceptions unnecessary

Formal exceptions to rulings or orders of the court are unnecessary; but for all purposes for which an exception has heretofore been necessary it is sufficient that a party, at the time the ruling or order of the court is made or sought, makes known to the court the action which he desires the court to take or his objection to the action of the court, and on request of the court, his grounds therefor; and, if a party has no opportunity to object to a ruling or order at the time it is made, the absence of an objection does not thereafter prejudice him.

HISTORY: Adopted eff. 7–1–53

CR 47   Jurors

CR 47.01   Examination of jurors

The court may permit the parties or their attorneys to conduct the examination of prospective jurors or may itself conduct the examination. In the latter event, the court shall permit the parties or their attorneys to supplement the examination by such further inquiry as it deems proper or shall itself submit to the prospective jurors such additional questions of the parties or their attorneys as it deems proper.

HISTORY: Adopted eff. 7–1–53

CR 47.02   Alternate jurors

At any time before either side has exercised a peremptory challenge or challenges, but not thereafter, the court may direct the clerk to draw from the jury box, in addition to the number of jurors required by law to comprise the jury, one (1) or two (2) cards bearing numbers identifying prospective jurors. All jurors so drawn shall be empaneled and shall hear the case. Should it become necessary for any reason to excuse a juror, the trial shall continue unless the number of jurors be reduced below the number required by law. If the membership of the jury exceeds the number required by law, immediately before the jury retires to consider its verdict the clerk, in open court, shall place in a box the cards bearing numbers identifying the jurors empaneled to hear the case and, after thoroughly mixing them, withdraw from the box at random a sufficient number of cards (one or two, as the case may be) to reduce the jury to the number required by law, whereupon the jurors so selected for elimination shall be excused.

HISTORY: Amended eff. 1–1–80; prior amendment eff. 10–1–71; adopted eff. 7–1–53

CR 47.03   Peremptory challenges

(1) In civil cases each opposing side shall have three peremptory challenges, but co-parties having antagonistic interests shall have three peremptory challenges each.

(2) If one or two additional jurors are called, the number of peremptory challenges for each side and antagonistic co-party shall be increased by one.

(3) After the parties have been given the opportunity of challenging jurors for cause, each side or party having the right to exercise peremptory challenges shall be handed a list of qualified jurors drawn from the box equal to the number of jurors to be seated plus the number of allowable peremptory challenges for all parties. Peremptory challenges shall be exercised simultaneously by striking names from the list and returning it to the trial judge. If the number of prospective jurors remaining on the list exceeds the number of jurors to be seated, the cards bearing numbers identifying the prospective jurors shall be placed in a box and thoroughly mixed, following which the clerk shall draw at random the number of cards necessary to comprise the jury or, if so directed by the court, a sufficient number of cards to reduce the jury to the number required by law, in which latter

event the prospective jurors whose identifying cards remain in the box shall be empaneled as the jury.

HISTORY: Adopted eff. 1–1–80

CR 48   Juries of less than twelve; majority verdict

The parties may stipulate that the jury shall consist of any number less than provided by law or that a verdict or a finding of a stated majority of the jurors shall be taken as the verdict or finding of the jury.

HISTORY: Adopted eff. 7–1–53

CR 49   Special verdicts and interrogatories

CR 49.01   Special verdicts

The court may require a jury to return only a special verdict in the form of a special written finding upon each issue of fact. In that event the court may submit to the jury written questions susceptible of categorical or other brief answers or may submit written forms of the several special findings which might properly be made under the pleadings and evidence; or it may use such other method of submitting the issues and requiring the written findings thereon as it deems most appropriate. The court shall give to the jury such written instructions concerning the matter thus submitted as may be necessary to enable the jury to make its findings upon each issue. If in so doing the court omits any issue of fact raised by the pleadings or by the evidence, each party waives his right to a trial by jury of the issue so omitted unless before the jury retires he demands its submission to the jury. As to an issue omitted without such demand the court may make a finding; or, if it fails to do so, it shall be deemed to have made a finding in accord with the judgment on the special verdict.

HISTORY: Adopted eff. 7–1–53

CR 49.02   General verdict accompanied by answer to interrogatories

The court may submit to the jury, together with appropriate forms for a general verdict, written interrogatories upon one or more issues of fact the decision of which is necessary to a verdict. The court shall give such written instructions as may be necessary to enable the jury both to make answers to the interrogatories and to render a general verdict, and the court shall direct the jury both to make written answers and to render a general verdict. When the general verdict and the answers are harmonious, the court shall direct the entry of the appropriate judgment upon the verdict and answers. When the answers are consistent with each other but one or more is inconsistent with the general verdict, the court may direct the entry of judgment in accordance with the answers, notwithstanding the general verdict, or may return the jury for further consideration of its answers and verdict or may order a new trial. When the answers are inconsistent with each other and one or more is likewise inconsistent with the general verdict, the court shall not direct the entry of judgment but may return the jury for further consideration of its answers and verdict or may order a new trial.

HISTORY: Adopted eff. 7–1–53

CR 50   Motion for a directed verdict and for judgment notwithstanding the verdict

CR 50.01   Motion for directed verdict

A party who moves for a directed verdict at the close of the evidence offered by an opponent may offer evidence in the event that the motion is not granted, without having reserved the right so to do and to the same extent as if the motion had not been made. A motion for a directed verdict which is not granted is not a waiver of trial by jury even though all parties to the action have moved for directed verdicts. A motion for a directed verdict shall state the specific grounds therefor. The order of the court granting a motion for a directed verdict is effective without any assent of the jury.

HISTORY: Amended eff. 7–1–69; adopted eff. 7–1–53

CR 50.02   Motion for judgment notwithstanding the verdict; alternative motion for new trial

Not later than 10 days after entry of judgment, a party who has moved for a directed verdict at the close of all the evidence may move to have the verdict and any judgment entered thereon set aside and to have judgment entered in accordance with his motion for a directed verdict; or if a verdict was not returned, such party within 10 days after the jury has been discharged may move for judgment in accordance with his motion for a directed verdict. A motion for a new trial may be joined with this motion, or a new trial may be prayed for in the alternative. If a verdict was returned the court may allow the judgment to stand or may reopen the judgment and either order a new trial or direct the entry of judgment as if the requested verdict had been directed. If no verdict was returned the court may direct the entry of judgment as if the requested verdict had been directed or may order a new trial.

HISTORY: Amended eff. 7–1–69; prior amendment eff. 4–1–63; adopted eff. 7–1–53

CR 50.03   Conditional rulings on grant or denial of motion for judgment notwithstanding the verdict

(1) If the motion for judgment notwithstanding the verdict, provided for in Rule 50.02, is granted, the court shall also rule on the motion for a new trial, if any, by determining whether it should be granted if the judgment is thereafter vacated or reversed, and

shall specify the grounds for granting or denying the motion for the new trial. If the motion for a new trial is thus conditionally granted, the order thereon does not affect the finality of the judgment. In case the motion for a new trial has been conditionally granted and the judgment is reversed on appeal, the new trial shall proceed unless the appellate court has otherwise ordered. In case the motion for a new trial has been conditionally denied, the appellee on appeal may assert error in that denial; and if the judgment is reversed on appeal, subsequent proceedings shall be in accordance with the order of the appellate court.

(2) The party whose verdict has been set aside on motion for judgment notwithstanding the verdict may serve a motion for a new trial pursuant to Rule 59 not later than 10 days after entry of the judgment notwithstanding the verdict.

(3) If the motion for judgment notwithstanding the verdict is denied, the party who prevailed on that motion may, as appellee, assert grounds entitling him to a new trial in the event the appellate court concludes that the trial court erred in denying the motion for judgment notwithstanding the verdict. If the appellate court reverses the judgment, nothing in Rule 50 precludes it from determining that the appellee is entitled to a new trial, or from directing the trial court to determine whether a new trial shall be granted.

HISTORY: Amended eff. 7–1–69; adopted eff. 7–1–53

CR 50.04   Judgment notwithstanding verdict; assessment of damages

Where the trial court orders, or an appellate court directs, judgment notwithstanding a verdict, in favor of a party entitled to recover damages, the trial court shall, unless a jury is waived, submit to a jury solely the question of assessing damages.

HISTORY: Amended eff. 7–1–76; adopted eff. 7–1–53

CR 51   Instructions to jury; objections

(1) At any time before or during the trial, the court may direct the parties to tender written instructions. At the close of the evidence any party may move the court to instruct the jury on any matter appropriate to the issues in the action.

(2) After considering any tendered instructions and motions to instruct and before the commencement of the argument, the court shall show the parties the written instructions it will give the jury, allowing them an opportunity to make objections out of the hearing of the jury. Thereafter, and before argument to the jury, the written instructions shall be given.

(3) No party may assign as error the giving or the failure to give an instruction unless he has fairly and adequately presented his position by an offered instruction or by motion, or unless he makes objection before the court instructs the jury, stating specifically

the matter to which he objects and the ground or grounds of his objection.

HISTORY: Amended eff. 7–1–69; adopted eff. 7–1–53

CR 52   Findings of the court

CR 52.01   When required; effect

In all actions tried upon the facts without a jury or with an advisory jury, the court shall find the facts specifically and state separately its conclusions of law thereon and render an appropriate judgment; and in granting or refusing temporary injunctions or permanent injunctions the court shall similarly set forth the findings of fact and conclusions of law which constitute the grounds of its action. Requests for findings are not necessary for purposes of review except as provided in Rule 52.04. Findings of fact, shall not be set aside unless clearly erroneous, and due regard shall be given to the opportunity of the trial court to judge the credibility of the witnesses. The findings of a commissioner, to the extent that the court adopts them, shall be considered as the findings of the court. If an opinion or memorandum of decision is filed, it will be sufficient if the findings of fact and conclusions of law appear therein. Findings of fact and conclusions of law are unnecessary on decisions of motions under Rules 12 or 56 or any other motion except as provided in Rule 41.02.

HISTORY: Amended by Order 2012–10, eff. 1–1–13; prior amendments eff. 3–1–74, eff. 4–1–63; adopted eff. 7–1–53

CR 52.02   Amendment

Not later than 10 days after entry of judgment the court of its own initiative, or on the motion of a party made not later than 10 days after entry of judgment, may amend its findings or make additional findings and may amend the judgment accordingly. The motion may be made with a motion for a new trial pursuant to Rule 59.

HISTORY: Amended eff. 4–1–63; adopted eff. 7–1–53

CR 52.03   Sufficiency of evidence to support findings

When findings of fact are made in actions tried by the court without a jury, the question of the sufficiency of the evidence to support the findings may thereafter be raised whether or not the party raising the question has made in the trial court an objection to such findings or has made a motion to amend them or a motion for judgment or a motion for a new trial.

HISTORY: Adopted eff. 4–1–63

CR 52.04   Failure to make finding on essential issue of fact; necessity for request

A final judgment shall not be reversed or remanded because of the failure of the trial court to make a finding of fact on an issue essential to the judgment unless such failure is brought to the attention of the trial court by a written request for a finding on that issue or by a motion pursuant to Rule 52.02.

HISTORY: Adopted eff. 3–1–74

CR 53   Master Commissioners of Circuit Courts

CR 53.01   Appointments; deputies

Each circuit court may appoint a master commissioner and a receiver as authorized by statute. Other master commissioners, deputy master commissioners, receivers, and their assistants may be appointed only upon express authority of the Chief Justice. A master commissioner or deputy master commissioner shall hold no other public office of the Court of Justice except a master commissioner or deputy master commissioner may also serve as a trial commissioner for the district court pursuant to SCR 5.010, or a domestic relations commissioner as approved by the Chief Justice. Master commissioners and deputy master commissioners shall be qualified as attorneys.

HISTORY: Amended by Order 2010–09, eff. 1–1–11; prior amendments eff. 9–15–90 (Order 90–1), 1–1–89, 1–1–80; adopted eff. 1–1–78

CR 53.02   Judicial sales; settlements; receiverships; qualifications of commissioner

(1) Judicial sales under order or judgment of the circuit court may be executed and accounts of estates may be settled by a master commissioner under such terms and conditions as are specified by the circuit court either in its order or judgment or by rule. A master commissioner may act as a receiver under terms and conditions likewise specified by the circuit court. A master commissioner may draft and execute such instruments as are necessary to complete any responsibility. A master commissioner performing any of these functions and appointed after December 31, 1977, shall be qualified as an attorney or experienced as a fiduciary. The master commissioner shall serve notice of the date, time and place of the judicial sale upon every party who is not in default for failure to appear.

(2) Civil matters pertaining to bills of discovery of assets of judgment debtors and claim and delivery may be referred to a master commissioner who shall be qualified as an attorney.

(3) All other references to master commissioners shall be warranted only in special cases. Cases may be regarded as special due to complexity of issues, damages which are difficult to calculate, a multiplicity of claims the priority of which must be established, matters of account involving complex or numerous transactions, or similar exceptional circumstances. A

master commissioner performing this function shall be qualified as an attorney.

HISTORY: Amended by Order 2010–09, eff. 1–1–11; prior amendments eff. 8–28–89 (Order 89–1), 1–1–89; adopted eff. 1–1–78

CR 53.03   Powers

An order of reference to a master commissioner or local rules of court may specify or limit his or her powers and may direct him or her to report only upon particular issues or to do or perform particular acts or to receive and report evidence only and may fix the time and place for beginning and closing the hearings and for the filing of the master commissioner's report. Subject to the specifications and limitations stated in the order or local rules of court, the master commissioner has and shall exercise the power to regulate all proceedings in every hearing before him or her and to do all acts and take all measures necessary or proper for the efficient performance of his or her duties under the order or local rules of court. He or she may require the production before him of evidence upon all matters embraced in the reference, including the production of all books, papers, vouchers, documents, and writings applicable thereto. He or she may rule upon the admissibility of evidence unless otherwise directed by the order of reference and has the authority to put witnesses on oath and may himself or herself examine them and may call the parties to the action and examine them upon oath. When a party so requests, the master commissioner shall make a record of the evidence offered and excluded in the same manner and subject to the same limitations as provided in Rule 43.10 for a court sitting without a jury.

HISTORY: Amended and renumbered by Order 2010–09, eff. 1–1–11; prior amendment eff. 1–1–89 (Order 88–7); adopted eff. 1–1–78

CR 53.04   Proceedings

(1) **Meetings.** When a reference is made other than automatic references provided by local rules of court, the clerk shall forthwith furnish the master commissioner with a copy of the order of reference. Upon receipt thereof unless he or she otherwise provides, the master commissioner shall forthwith set a time and place for the first meeting of the parties or their attorneys to be held within 20 days after the date of the order of reference and shall notify the parties or their attorneys. It is the duty of the master commissioner to proceed with all reasonable diligence. Either party, on notice to the parties and master commissioner, may apply to the court for an order requiring the commissioner to speed the proceedings and to make his report. If a party fails to appear at the time and place appointed, the master commissioner may proceed ex parte or, in his discretion, adjourn the proceedings to a future day, giving notice to the absent party of the adjournment.

(2) **Witnesses.** The parties may procure the attendance of witnesses before the master commissioner by the issuance and service of subpoenas as provided in Rule 45. If without adequate excuse a witness fails to appear or give evidence, he may be punished as for a contempt and be subjected to the consequences, penalties, and remedies provided in Rules 37 and 45.

(3) **Statement of accounts.** When matters of accounting are in issue before the master commissioner, he or she may prescribe the form in which the accounts shall be submitted and in any proper case may require or receive in evidence a statement by a certified public accountant who is called as a witness. Upon objection of a party to any of the items thus submitted or upon a showing that the form of statement is insufficient, the master commissioner may require a different form of statement to be furnished, or the accounts or specific items thereof to be proved by oral examination of the accounting parties or upon written interrogatories or in such other manner as he or she directs.

HISTORY: Amended and renumbered by Order 2010–09, eff. 1–1–11; prior amendment eff. 1–1–89 (Order 88–7); adopted eff. 1–1–78

CR 53.05   Report

(1) **Contents and filing.** The master commissioner shall prepare a report of recommendations to the court upon the matters submitted by the order of reference or local rules of court and, if required to make findings of fact and conclusions of law, the master commissioner shall set them forth in the report and shall file the report and sufficient copies for all parties with the clerk of the court. The clerk shall forthwith serve the report and notice of the filing upon all parties who have appeared in the action. A transcript of reported proceedings may be ordered by any party at that party's expense. In the case of proceedings recorded on video the untranscribed recording shall constitute the official record.

(2) **Action on report.** Within 10 days after being served with notice of the filing of the report any party may serve written objections thereto upon the other parties. Application to the court for action upon the report and upon objections thereto shall be by motion and upon notice as prescribed in CR 6.04. The court after hearing may adopt the report, or may modify it, or may reject it in whole or in part, or may receive further evidence, or may recommit it with instructions.

(3) **Stipulation as to findings.** The effect of a master commissioner's report is the same whether or not the parties have consented to the reference, but, when the parties stipulate that a master commissioner's findings of fact shall be final, only questions of law arising upon the report shall thereafter be considered.

(4) **Draft report.** Before filing his report a master commissioner may submit a draft thereof to counsel

for all parties for the purpose of receiving their suggestions.

(5) Report as security. The master commissioner shall not retain his report as security for his compensation; but when the party ordered to pay the compensation allowed by the court does not pay it after notice and within the time prescribed by the court, the master commissioner is entitled to a writ of execution against the delinquent party.

(6) The report shall be promptly acted upon by the court.

HISTORY: Amended and renumbered by Order 2010–09, eff. 1–1–11; prior amendments eff. 1–1–07 (Order 2006–09), 1–1–03 (Order 2002–1), 2–1–01 (Order 2000–1), 11–1–95 (Order 95–1), 1–1–89; adopted eff. 1–1–78

CR 53.06 Compensation

The compensation of master commissioners shall be by fee charged upon such of the parties or paid out of any fund or subject matter of the action which is in the custody or control of the circuit court. Deputies and other assistants of master commissioners shall be compensated and office expenses shall be paid from the fees of the office. Rates of compensation shall be in accordance with a schedule or schedules established by the Supreme Court.

HISTORY: Amended and renumbered by Order 2010–09, eff. 1–1–11; prior amendment eff. 1–1–89 (Order 88–7); adopted eff. 1–1–78

CR 53.07 Limit on compensation

All master commissioners shall be limited in their total personal compensation derived from fees to not more than $48,000 per annum, unless approved by the Chief Justice. Fees in excess of the personal compensation of the commissioner and office expenses and

salaries shall be remitted as provided in Rule 53.09, however, anticipated three (3) months expenses may be retained.

HISTORY: Amended and renumbered by Order 2010–09, eff. 1–1–11; prior amendments eff. 2–1–01 (Order 2000–2), 2–1–01 (Order 2000–1), 1–1–89 (Order 88–7); adopted eff. 1–1–78

CR 53.08 Accounting

(1) Each master commissioner shall account to the circuit judge under whose direction he or she is acting, for all amounts received and distributed, for all proceeds of sales disbursed, and for all fees collected. These accounts shall be in the manner directed by the circuit judge who shall approve the accounts by his or her signature. The master commissioner shall file the approved accounts with the circuit clerk who shall include them with the applicable case file. Each master commissioner shall maintain a current record, kept in the office of the circuit clerk, or in the office of the master commissioner if the Chief Circuit Judge so directs, of each case in which a fee has been received.

(2) Each master commissioner shall annually provide to the Administrative Office of the Courts a complete accounting for all amounts received and distributed and for all fees collected in accordance with the Rules of Administrative Procedure of the Court of Justice, Part IV. Excess fees referred to in Rule 53.07 shall be remitted with the report and may be added to the existing surplus. A copy of this report shall at the same time be provided to the finance and administration cabinet.

HISTORY: Amended and renumbered by Order 2010–09, eff. 1–1–11; prior amendments eff. 2–1–01 (Order 2000–1), 1–1–89 (Order 88–7); adopted eff. 1–1–78

VII JUDGMENT

CR 54 Judgments; costs

CR 54.01 Definition and construction

A judgment is a written order of a court adjudicating a claim or claims in an action or proceeding. A final or appealable judgment is a final order adjudicating all the rights of all the parties in an action or proceeding, or a judgment made final under Rule 54.02. Where the context requires, the term "judgment" as used in these rules shall be construed "final judgment" or "final order".

HISTORY: Amended eff. 4–1–63; adopted eff. 7–1–53

CR 54.02 Judgment upon multiple claims or involving multiple parties

(1) When more than one claim for relief is presented in an action, whether as a claim, counterclaim, cross-claim, or third-party claim, or when multiple parties are involved, the court may grant a final

judgment upon one or more but less than all of the claims or parties only upon a determination that there is no just reason for delay. The judgment shall recite such determination and shall recite that the judgment is final. In the absence of such recital, any order or other form of decision, however designated, which adjudicates less than all the claims or the rights and liabilities of less than all the parties shall not terminate the action as to any of the claims or parties, and the order or other form of decision is interlocutory and subject to revision at any time before the entry of judgment adjudicating all the claims and the rights and liabilities of all the parties.

(2) When the remaining claim or claims in a multiple claim action are disposed of by judgment, that judgment shall be deemed to readjudicate finally as of that date and in the same terms all prior interlocutory orders and judgments determining claims which are not specifically disposed of in such final judgment.

(3) For the purposes of this rule demands in an action for both injunctive relief and damages may be treated as separate claims.

HISTORY: Amended by Order 91–2, eff. 11–15–91; prior amendments eff. 7–1–69, 4–1–63, 6–1–60; adopted eff. 7–1–53

CR 54.03   Demand for judgment

(1) Judgment by default for want of appearance shall not be different in kind from or exceed in amount that prayed for in the demand for judgment. If the demand for judgment is for an unliquidated sum, and therefore unspecified as required by CR 8.02(2), then the amount of the default judgment shall not exceed the amount proved.

(2) Except as to a party against whom a judgment is entered by default for want of appearance, every final judgment shall grant the relief to which the party in whose favor it is rendered is entitled, even if the party has not demanded such relief in his pleadings.

HISTORY: Amended by Order 89–1, eff. 8–28–89; prior amendment eff. 1–1–88; adopted eff. 7–1–53

CR 54.04   Costs

(1) Costs shall be allowed as of course to the prevailing party unless the court otherwise directs; but costs against the Commonwealth, its officers and agencies shall be imposed only to the extent permitted by law. In the event of a partial judgment or a judgment in which neither party prevails entirely against the other, costs shall be borne as directed by the trial court.

(2) A party entitled to recover costs shall prepare and serve upon the party liable therefor a bill itemizing the costs incurred by him in the action, including filing fees, fees incident to service of process and summoning of witnesses, jury fees, warning order attorney, and guardian ad litem fees, costs of the originals of any depositions (whether taken stenographically or by other than stenographic means), fees for extraordinary services ordered to be paid by the court, and such other costs as are ordinarily recoverable by the successful party. If within five days after such service no exceptions to the bill are served on the prevailing party, the clerk shall endorse on the face of the judgment the total amount of costs recoverable as a part of the judgment. Exceptions shall be heard and resolved by the trial court in the form of a supplemental judgment.

HISTORY: Amended by Order 87–1, eff. 1–1–88; prior amendments eff. 3–1–78, 1–1–78, 4–1–63; adopted eff. 7–1–53

CR 55   Default

CR 55.01   Judgment

When a party against whom a judgment for affirmative relief is sought has failed to plead or otherwise defend as provided by these rules, the party entitled to a judgment by default shall apply to the court therefor. If the party against whom judgment by default is sought has appeared in the action, he, or if appearing by representative, his representative shall be served with written notice of the application for judgment at least three days prior to the hearing on such application. The motion for judgment against a party in default for failure to appear shall be accompanied by a certificate of the attorney that no papers have been served on him by the party in default. If, in order to enable the court to enter judgment or to carry it into effect, it is necessary to take an account or to determine the amount of damages or to establish the truth of any averment by evidence or to make an investigation of any other matter, the court, without a jury, shall conduct such hearings or order such references as it deems necessary and proper, unless a jury is demanded by a party entitled thereto or is mandatory by statute or by the Constitution. A party in default for failure to appear shall be deemed to have waived his right of trial by jury.

HISTORY: Amended eff. 3–1–55; adopted eff. 7–1–53

CR 55.02   Setting aside default

For good cause shown the court may set aside a judgment by default in accordance with Rule 60.02.

HISTORY: Adopted eff. 7–1–53

CR 55.03   Plaintiffs, counterclaimants, cross-claimants

The provisions of this rule apply whether the party entitled to the judgment by default is a plaintiff, a third-party plaintiff, or a party who has pleaded a cross-claim or counterclaim. In all cases a judgment by default is subject to the limitations of Rule 54.03.

HISTORY: Adopted eff. 7–1–53

CR 55.04   Judgment against the Commonwealth or the United States

No judgment by default shall be entered against the Commonwealth or an officer or agency thereof or against the United States of America or an officer or agency thereof unless the claimant establishes his claim or right to relief by evidence satisfactory to the Court.

HISTORY: Amended by Order 84–2, eff. 1–1–85; prior amendment eff. 1–1–78; adopted eff. 7–1–53

CR 56   Summary judgment

CR 56.01   For claimant

A party seeking to recover upon a claim, counterclaim, or cross-claim or to obtain a declaratory judgment may, at any time after the expiration of 20 days from the commencement of the action or after service of a motion for summary judgment by the adverse party, move with or without supporting affidavits for a summary judgment in his favor upon all or any part thereof.

HISTORY: Adopted eff. 7–1–53

CR 56.02   For defending party

A party against whom a claim, counterclaim, or cross-claim is asserted or a declaratory judgment is sought may, at any time, move with or without supporting affidavits for a summary judgment in his favor as to all or any part thereof.

HISTORY: Adopted eff. 7–1–53

CR 56.03   Motion and proceedings thereon

The motion shall be served at least 10 days before the time fixed for the hearing. The adverse party prior to the day of hearing may serve opposing affidavits. The judgment sought shall be rendered forthwith if the pleadings, depositions, answers to interrogatories, stipulations, and admissions on file, together with the affidavits, if any, show that there is no genuine issue as to any material fact and that the moving party is entitled to a judgment as a matter of law. A summary judgment, interlocutory in character, may be rendered on the issue of liability alone although there is a genuine issue as to the amount of damages.

HISTORY: Amended eff. 4–1–63; adopted eff. 7–1–53

CR 56.04   Case not fully adjudicated on motion

If on motion under this rule judgment is not rendered upon the whole case or for all the relief asked and a trial is necessary, the court at the hearing of the motion, by examining the pleadings and the evidence before it and by interrogating counsel, shall if practicable ascertain what material facts exist without substantial controversy and what material facts are actually and in good faith controverted. It shall thereupon make an order specifying the facts that appear without substantial controversy, including the extent to which the amount of damages or other relief is not in controversy, and directing such further proceedings in the action as are just. Upon the trial of the action the facts so specified shall be deemed established, and the trial shall be conducted accordingly.

HISTORY: Adopted eff. 7–1–53

CR 56.05   Form of affidavits; further testimony

Supporting and opposing affidavits shall be made on personal knowledge, shall set forth such facts as would be admissible in evidence, and shall show affirmatively that the affiant is competent to testify to the matters stated therein. Sworn or certified copies of all papers or parts thereof referred to in an affidavit shall be attached thereto or served therewith. The court may permit affidavits to be supplemented or opposed by depositions or by further affidavits.

HISTORY: Adopted eff. 7–1–53

CR 56.06   When affidavits are unavailable

Should it appear from the affidavits of a party opposing the motion that he cannot for reasons stated present by affidavit facts essential to justify his opposition, the court may refuse the application for judgment or may order a continuance to permit affidavits to be obtained or depositions to be taken or discovery to be had or may make such other order as is just.

HISTORY: Adopted eff. 7–1–53

CR 56.07   Affidavits made in bad faith

Should it appear to the satisfaction of the court at any time that any of the affidavits presented pursuant to this rule are presented in bad faith or solely for the purpose of delay, the court shall forthwith order the party employing them to pay to the other party the amount of the reasonable expenses which the filing of the affidavits caused him to incur, including reasonable attorney's fees, and any offending party or attorney may be adjudged guilty of contempt.

HISTORY: Adopted eff. 7–1–53

CR 57   Declaratory judgments

The procedure for obtaining a declaratory judgment pursuant to statute shall be in accordance with these rules, and the right to trial by jury may be demanded under the circumstances and in the manner provided in Rules 38 and 39. The existence of another adequate remedy does not preclude a judgment for declaratory relief in cases where it is appropriate. The court may order a speedy hearing of an action for a declaratory judgment and may advance it on the calendar.

HISTORY: Adopted eff. 7–1–53

CR 58   Signing and entry of judgments and orders in trial courts

(1) Before a judgment or order may be entered in a trial court it shall be signed by the judge. The clerk, forthwith upon receipt of the signed judgment or order, shall note it in the civil docket as provided by CR 79.01. The notation shall constitute the entry of the judgment or order, which shall become effective at the time of such notation; however, an authorized order for pre-trial adult or juvenile release or detention, or a signed emergency protective order, shall be effective when issued and does not require prior entry in the clerk's office to become effective. The additional notation required by CR 77.04(2) or by RCr 12.06(2) shall govern the running of time for appeal under CR 73.02.

(2) In the district court, if more than one judgment is entered on a single page, one signature by the judge following the last judgment on the page will be sufficient compliance with paragraph (1) of this Rule 58. For purposes of Rule 79.05, either the original or a photocopy or comparable duplicate of the signed page on which the judgment appears shall constitute the judgment.

HISTORY: Amended by Order 95–1, eff. 11–1–95; prior amendments eff. 1–1–78, 7–1–76, 4–1–63; adopted eff. 7–1–53

CR 59   New trials;   amendment of judgments

CR 59.01   Grounds

A new trial may be granted to all or any of the parties and on all or part of the issues for any of the following causes:

(a) Irregularity in the proceedings of the court, jury or prevailing party, or an order of the court, or abuse of discretion, by which the party was prevented from having a fair trial.

(b) Misconduct of the jury, of the prevailing party, or of his attorney.

(c) Accident or surprise which ordinary prudence could not have guarded against.

(d) Excessive or inadequate damages, appearing to have been given under the influence of passion or prejudice or in disregard of the evidence or the instructions of the court.

(e) Error in the assessment of the amount of recovery whether too large or too small.

(f) That the verdict is not sustained by sufficient evidence, or is contrary to law.

(g) Newly discovered evidence, material for the party applying, which he could not, with reasonable diligence, have discovered and produced at the trial.

(h) Errors of law occurring at the trial and objected to by the party under the provisions of these rules.

HISTORY: Amended eff. 1–1–78; adopted eff. 7–1–53

CR 59.02   Time for motion

A motion for a new trial shall be served not later than 10 days after the entry of the judgment.

HISTORY: Adopted eff. 7–1–53

CR 59.03   Time for serving affidavits

When a motion for a new trial is supported by affidavits the opposing party has 10 days after the service within which to serve opposing affidavits, which period may be extended for an additional period not exceeding 20 days either by the court for good cause shown or by the parties by written stipulation. The court may permit reply affidavits.

HISTORY: Adopted eff. 7–1–53

CR 59.04   On initiative of court

Not later than 10 days after entry of judgment the court of its own initiative may order a new trial for any reason for which it might have granted a new trial on motion of a party. After giving the parties notice and an opportunity to be heard on the matter, the court may grant a motion for a new trial, timely served, for a reason not stated in the motion. In either case, the court shall specify in the order the grounds therefor.

HISTORY: Amended eff. 7–1–69; adopted eff. 7–1–53

CR 59.05   Motion to alter, amend or vacate a judgment

A motion to alter or amend a judgment, or to vacate a judgment and enter a new one, shall be served not later than 10 days after entry of the final judgment.

HISTORY: Amended eff. 4–1–63; prior amendment eff. 6–1–60; adopted eff. 7–1–53

CR 59.06   Preservation of error

Allegations of error, otherwise properly preserved, in respect to rulings, orders or instructions of the court need not be presented in a motion for a new trial in order to be preserved for appellate review.

HISTORY: Adopted eff. 7–1–53

CR 59.07   Proceedings in lieu of new trial

On motion for a new trial in an action tried without a jury, the court may grant a new trial or it may open the judgment if one has been entered, take additional testimony, amend findings of fact and conclusions of law or make new findings and conclusions, and enter a new judgment.

HISTORY: Adopted eff. 7–1–53

CR 60   Relief from judgment or order

CR 60.01   Clerical mistakes

Clerical mistakes in judgments, orders or other parts of the record and errors therein arising from oversight or omission may be corrected by the court at any time of its own initiative or on the motion of any party and after such notice, if any, as the court orders. During the pendency of an appeal, such mistakes may be so corrected before the appeal is docketed in the appellate court, and thereafter while the appeal is pending may be so corrected with leave of the appellate court.

HISTORY: Adopted eff. 7–1–53

CR 60.02   Mistake; inadvertence; excusable neglect; newly discovered evidence; fraud, etc.

On motion a court may, upon such terms as are just, relieve a party or his legal representative from its final judgment, order, or proceeding upon the following grounds: (a) mistake, inadvertence, surprise or excusable neglect; (b) newly discovered evidence which by due diligence could not have been discovered in time to move for a new trial under Rule 59.02; (c) perjury or falsified evidence; (d) fraud affecting the proceedings, other than perjury or falsified evidence; (e) the judgment is void, or has been satisfied, released, or discharged, or a prior judgment upon which it is based has been reversed or otherwise vacated, or it is no longer equitable that the judgment should have prospective application; or (f) any other reason of an extraordinary nature justifying relief. The motion shall be made within a reasonable time, and on grounds (a), (b), and (c) not more than one year after the judgment, order, or proceeding was entered or taken. A motion under this rule does not affect the finality of a judgment or suspend its operation.

HISTORY: Amended eff. 1–1–78; prior amendment eff. 6–1–60; adopted eff. 7–1–53

CR 60.03   Independent actions

Rule 60.02 shall not limit the power of any court to entertain an independent action to relieve a person from a judgment, order or proceeding on appropriate equitable grounds. Relief shall not be granted in an independent action if the ground of relief sought has been denied in a proceeding by motion under Rule 60.02, or would be barred because not brought in time under the provisions of that rule.

HISTORY: Adopted eff. 6–1–60

CR 60.04   When appeal pending

If a proceeding by motion or independent action is commenced under Rule 60.02 or 60.03 while an appeal is pending from the original judgment and prior to the time an opinion is rendered by the appellate court, the party commencing such proceeding shall promptly move the appellate court to abate the appeal until a final order is entered therein. When the trial court has entered such final order, the party who moved for abatement shall promptly file with the clerk of the appellate court a certified copy thereof.

HISTORY: Amended eff. 7–1–76; adopted eff. 6–1–60

CR 60.05   Writs abolished

Writs of coram nobis, coram vobis, audita querela, and bills of review and bills in the nature of a bill of review, are abolished, and the procedure for obtaining any relief from a judgment shall be as provided in Rule 60.02 or 60.03.

HISTORY: Adopted eff. 6–1–60

CR 61   Errors; harmless; substantial

CR 61.01   Harmless error

No error in either the admission or the exclusion of evidence and no error or defect in any ruling or order

or in anything done or omitted by the court or by any of the parties is ground for granting a new trial or for setting aside a verdict or for vacating, modifying, or otherwise disturbing a judgment or order, unless refusal to take such action appears to the court inconsistent with substantial justice. The court at every stage of the proceeding must disregard any error or defect in the proceeding which does not affect the substantial rights of the parties.

HISTORY: Adopted eff. 7–1–53

CR 61.02   Substantial error

A palpable error which affects the substantial rights of a party may be considered by the court on motion for a new trial or by an appellate court on appeal, even though insufficiently raised or preserved for review, and appropriate relief may be granted upon a determination that manifest injustice has resulted from the error.

HISTORY: Amended eff. 7–1–76; adopted eff. 7–1–53

CR 62   Stay of proceedings to enforce a judgment

CR 62.01   Motions after verdict or judgment

A motion for a new trial or to alter, amend or vacate a judgment made pursuant to Rule 59, or a motion for judgment in accordance with a motion for a directed verdict made pursuant to Rule 50, or a motion for amendment to the findings or for additional findings made pursuant to Rule 52.02 shall operate to stay the execution of or any proceedings to enforce a judgment pending the disposition of any such motion or motions, provided that such motion is filed with the court within the time prescribed for the making of or service of such motion. In its discretion and on such conditions for the security of the adverse party as are proper, the court may stay the execution of or any proceedings to enforce a judgment pending the disposition of a motion for relief from a judgment or order made pursuant to Rule 60. Unless otherwise ordered by the court, a final judgment in an action for an injunction shall not be stayed during the period after its entry and until an appeal is taken.

HISTORY: Amended eff. 4–1–63; adopted eff. 7–1–53

CR 62.02   Pending appeal of injunction judgments

When an appeal is taken from any final judgment granting or denying injunctive relief, the judgment may be stayed as provided in Rule 65.08.

HISTORY: Amended eff. 4–1–63; prior amendment eff. 6–1–60; adopted eff. 7–1–53

CR 62.03   Pending appeal of judgment other than injunction judgment

(1) When an appeal is taken the appellant may stay enforcement of the judgment by giving a supersedeas

bond as provided in Rule 73.04. The bond may be given at or after the time of filing the notice of appeal. The stay is effective when the supersedeas bond is approved by the court or the clerk, and the clerk shall give prompt notice of such approval to the party or parties in whose favor the judgment was rendered.

(2) If the appellant is a governmental unit exempted from the execution of a bond under the provisions of Rule 81A, the filing of a notice of appeal by such party shall stay enforcement of the judgment as to it in all cases where the giving of a supersedeas bond would effect such a stay.

HISTORY: Amended eff. 4–1–63; adopted eff. 7–1–53

CR 62.04   Stay of judgment upon multiple claims

When a court has granted a final judgment on some but not all of the claims presented in the action under the conditions stated in Rule 54.02, the court may stay enforcement of that judgment until the entering of a subsequent judgment or judgments and may prescribe such conditions as are necessary to secure the benefit thereof to the party in whose favor the judgment is entered.

HISTORY: Adopted eff. 7–1–53

CR 63   Disability of a judge

CR 63   Disability of a judge

If by reason of death, sickness, or other disability, a judge before whom an action has been tried is unable to perform the duties to be performed by the court under these rules after a verdict is returned or finding of fact and conclusions of law are filed, then any successor or special judge sitting in or assigned to the court in which the action was tried may perform those duties; but if such other judge is satisfied that he cannot perform those duties because he did not preside at the trial or for any other reason, he may in his discretion grant a new trial.

HISTORY: Adopted eff. 7–1–53

VIII   PROVISIONAL AND FINAL REMEDIES AND SPECIAL PROCEEDINGS

CR 64   Seizure of person or property

CR 64   Seizure of person or property

At the commencement of and during the course of an action, all remedies providing for seizure of person or property for the purpose of securing satisfaction of the judgment ultimately to be entered in the action are available under the circumstances and in the manner provided by law.

HISTORY: Adopted eff. 7–1–53

CR 65   Injunctions

CR 65.01   Injunctive relief

A party may obtain injunctive relief in the circuit court by (a) restraining order, (b) temporary injunction, or (c) permanent injunction in a final judgment. A restraining order shall only restrict the doing of an act. An injunction may restrict or mandatorily direct the doing of an act. Injunctive relief shall not be granted in any action in the district court except as specifically authorized by statute.

HISTORY: Amended eff. 3–1–78; prior amendments eff. 1–1–78, 6–1–60; adopted eff. 7–1–53

CR 65.02   Requisites of restraining order or injunction; parties bound

(1) Every restraining order or injunction shall be specific in terms and shall describe in reasonable detail, and not by reference to the complaint or other document, the act restrained or enjoined.

(2) Every restraining order or injunction shall be binding upon the parties to the action, their officers, agents, and attorneys; and upon other persons in active concert or participation with them who receive actual notice of the restraining order or injunction by personal service or otherwise.

HISTORY: Amended eff. 6–1–60; adopted eff. 7–1–53

CR 65.03   Restraining order
(1) When authorized.

A restraining order may be granted at the commencement of an action, or during the pendency thereof, without written or oral notice to the adverse party or his attorney only if (a) it clearly appears from specific facts shown by verified complaint or affidavit that the applicant's rights are being or will be violated by the adverse party and the applicant will suffer immediate and irreparable injury, loss or damage before the adverse party or his attorney can be heard in opposition, and (b) the applicant's attorney certifies to the court in writing the efforts, if any, which have been made to give notice and the reasons supporting his claims that notice should not be required.

(2) Officers who may grant or dissolve.

A restraining order may be granted (a) by a judge of the circuit court in which the action is pending, (b) by a district judge of that judicial district if no judge of that circuit court is present in the county, (c) by a district trial commissioner of that county if he is an attorney *and* if neither a judge of the circuit court in which the action is pending nor a district judge of that judicial district is present in the county, or (d) by any circuit judge if no judge of the circuit court in which the action is pending is present in his judicial circuit. A restraining order may be dissolved on motion by the judge of the circuit court in which the action is pending or, if no judge of that court is present in his judicial circuit, by any circuit judge. For the purposes of this paragraph a disqualification or disability preventing a judge from acting shall be considered as tantamount to an absence from his judicial circuit. Before a restraining order may be granted or dissolved by one other than a judge of the circuit court in which the action is pending, the party applying for such relief shall show by his affidavit the absence, disqualification, or disability of the circuit judge or judges and the fact that no judge has refused such relief.

(3) Issuance, signing and filing.

Every restraining order shall be endorsed with the date and hour of issuance, shall be signed by the officer granting it, and shall forthwith be filed in the clerk's office. Every restraining order granted without notice shall, in addition to the other requirements of this subparagraph, define the injury and state why it is irreparable and why the order was granted without notice.

(4) Service.

A copy of the restraining order for each party to be restrained shall be delivered to a person authorized to serve a summons. Such person shall forthwith serve the order as provided by Rule 4.04, and forthwith make return thereof on the order. If a restraining order is issued at the commencement of an action, a copy shall be served with the summons.

(5) Binding effect and duration.

A restraining order becomes effective and binding on the party to be restrained at the time of service or when he is informed of the order, whichever is earlier. Unless it provides an earlier termination date, a restraining order shall remain in force until, and not after, (a) the time set for a hearing on a motion to dissolve the restraining order unless there is then pending a motion for a temporary injunction, or (b) the entry of an order on a motion for a temporary injunction, or (c) the entry of a final judgment, whichever is earlier.

HISTORY: Amended by Order 85–2, eff. 1–1–86; prior amendments eff. 1–1–78, 6–1–60; adopted eff. 7–1–53

CR 65.04   Temporary injunction

(1) When authorized.

A temporary injunction may be granted during the pendency of an action on motion if it is clearly shown by verified complaint, affidavit, or other evidence that the movant's rights are being or will be violated by an adverse party and the movant will suffer immediate and irreparable injury, loss, or damage pending a final judgment in the action, or the acts of the adverse

party will tend to render such final judgment ineffectual.

(2) Officers who may grant, modify or dissolve.

A temporary injunction may be granted, modified or dissolved on motion by the judge of the court in which the action is pending, or if he is disqualified or absent from his judicial district, by any circuit judge.

(3) Issuance, filing and entry.

Every temporary injunction shall be indorsed with the date and hour of issuance, and shall forthwith be filed in the clerk's office and entered.

(4) Binding effect and duration.

A temporary injunction becomes effective and binding on the party enjoined when the order is entered. It shall remain in force until modified or dissolved on motions or until a permanent injunction is granted or denied.

(5) Findings of fact and conclusions of law.

In granting, denying, or modifying a temporary injunction, the court shall set forth findings of fact and conclusions of law which constitute the grounds of its action, as required by Rule 52.01.

HISTORY: Amended eff. 6–1–60; adopted eff. 7–1–53

CR 65.05   Restraining order and injunction bond

(1) No restraining order or temporary injunction shall be granted except upon the giving of a bond by the applicant, with surety, in such sum as the court or the officer to whom application is made deems proper, for the payment of such costs and damages as may be incurred or suffered by any person who is found to have been wrongfully restrained or enjoined. The address of the surety shall be shown on the bond.

(2) A surety upon a bond under this rule submits himself to the jurisdiction of the court. His liability may be enforced on motion without the necessity of an independent action. The motion shall be served on the surety as provided by Rule 5 at least 20 days prior to the date of the hearing thereon.

(3) A party restrained or enjoined may move the court for additional security; and if it appear on such motion that the surety is insufficient, or the amount of the bond is insufficient, the court may vacate the restraining order or temporary injunction, unless in a reasonable time sufficient security is given.

HISTORY: Amended by Order 85–2, eff. 1–1–86; prior amendments eff. 4–1–63, 6–1–60; adopted eff. 7–1–53

CR 65.06   Enforcement of restraining orders and injunctions

Compliance with a restraining order or an injunction, other than an injunction granted under Rule 65.08, may be compelled or its disobedience punished as a contempt by the judge of the court in which the action is pending, or if he is disqualified or absent from his judicial district, by any circuit judge. Upon a showing by affidavit or other evidence of the breach of a restraining order or injunction, the circuit judge may proceed by rule and attachment against the person committing the breach. If an appellate court grants an injunction pending appeal under Rule 65.08, compliance therewith shall be compelled or disobedience punished by the appellate court.

HISTORY: Amended eff. 7–1–76; prior amendment eff. 6–1–60; adopted eff. 7–1–53

CR 65.07   Interlocutory relief in Court of Appeals prior to final judgment

(1) When a circuit court by interlocutory order has granted, denied, modified, or dissolved a temporary injunction, a party adversely affected may within 20 days after the entry thereof move the Court of Appeals for relief from such order. If the order dissolves a temporary injunction theretofore granted, the circuit court may in its discretion suspend the operation of the order for a period not exceeding 20 days to permit such party to proceed under this rule.

(2) The original and four copies of the motion shall be filed in the office of the appellate court clerk, and the movant shall pay the filing fee required by CR 76.42(2)(a)(viii). The format of the motion shall be the same as for other motions filed in the appellate court under CR 76.34. The motion shall state clearly the procedural history of the case, the factual history of the dispute, and the grounds on which movant's claim for relief is based.

(3) There shall be filed with the motion the original or a certified copy or photocopy of such portion of the record or proceedings as may be necessary to a proper consideration and disposition of the motion.

(4) Any respondent may file a response within ten days of the date on which the motion is served.

(5)(a) The motion and any responses shall be submitted to a panel for decision. Oral argument will not be held unless ordered by the Court sua sponte or on the motion of a party.

(b) The basis of affirmative relief shall be the grounds specified in Rule 65.04(1), and if such relief is granted, a bond may be required to be executed in the circuit court as provided by Rule 65.05.

(6) If a movant will suffer irreparable injury before the motion will be considered by a panel, the movant may request emergency relief from a member of the Court which may be granted ex parte if necessary. If such relief is sought ex parte the motion shall state why it is impractical to notify opposing counsel so that they may appear, in person or by phone, before the judge to whom the request for emergency relief is presented.

(7) A signed copy of the order entered on the motion shall be sent forthwith to the clerk of the circuit court where the action is pending, and when filed in the clerk's office shall have the same effect as an order entered by such circuit court.

(8) A ruling granting or denying interlocutory relief under Rule 65.07 will not be reconsidered.

HISTORY: Amended by Order 91–2, eff. 11–15–91; prior amendments eff. 12–31–80, 9–1–80, 6–1–60; adopted eff. 7–1–53

CR 65.08   Interlocutory relief pending appeal from final judgment

(1) After an appeal is taken from a final judgment granting or denying an injunction any party may move the circuit court to grant, suspend or modify injunctive relief during the pendency of the appeal. The circuit court, in its discretion, may provide in the order ruling on the motion that the status existing immediately before the entry of the final judgment shall be maintained for a specified limited time to protect a party wishing to proceed promptly under paragraph (2) of this rule.

(2) A party adversely affected by a ruling by the circuit court under paragraph (1) of this rule, may move the Court of Appeals for relief.

(3) Relief shall be sought in the Court of Appeals by filing the original and four copies of a motion complying in all respects with other motions filed in the appellate court under CR 76.34. If no request was made to the trial court under paragraph (1) of this rule, the motion shall state why such request was impractical.

(4) There shall be filed with a motion made in the Court of Appeals under this rule the original, a photocopy or a certified copy of such portion of the record or proceedings as may be necessary to a proper consideration and disposition of the motion.

(5) Any party may file a response to the motion within ten days of the date on which the motion was served.

(6) The motion and any responses shall be submitted to a panel of the Court for decision. No oral argument will be heard unless ordered by the Court on its own motion or on motion of a party.

(7) If a movant will suffer irreparable injury before the Court of Appeals may hear the motion, the movant may request emergency relief from a member of the Court which may be granted ex parte if necessary. If such relief is sought ex parte the motion shall state why it is impractical to notify opposing counsel so that they may appear, in person or by phone, before the judge to whom the request for emergency relief is presented.

(8) Any order entered under this rule may fix such terms as are proper to secure the rights of the parties, including the execution of an injunction bond subject to the provisions of Rule 65.05.

(9) A ruling granting or denying interlocutory relief under Rule 65.08 will not be reconsidered.

HISTORY: Amended by Order 91–2, eff. 11–15–91; prior amendments eff. 12–31–80, 9–1–80, 1–1–78, 4–1–63, 6–1–60; adopted eff. 7–1–53

CR 65.09   Interlocutory relief in Supreme Court

(1) Any party adversely affected by an order of the Court of Appeals in a proceeding under Rule 65.07 or Rule 65.08 may within five (5) days after the date on which such order was entered, move the Supreme Court to vacate or modify it. The decision whether to review such order shall be discretionary with the Supreme Court. Such a motion will be entertained only for extraordinary cause shown in the motion. Ten copies of the motion and the response, if any, shall be filed.

(2) There shall be filed with the motion the original or certified copies or photocopies of the order or orders of the Court of Appeals and all other papers, exhibits and briefs filed in that court.

(3) If a Court of Appeals judge has granted or denied emergency relief under CR 65.07(6) or CR 65.08(7), any party adversely affected by that order may move the Supreme Court for relief in the same manner as provided in subsection (1) of this rule.

(a) If the Supreme Court declines to exercise its discretion to immediately review the ruling, the motion for relief in the Court of Appeals will be assigned to a panel of that Court for decision.

(b) If the Supreme Court decides to exercise its discretion to immediately review the ruling, the Supreme Court review shall encompass both the emergency motion and the motion for relief under CR 65.07 or CR 65.08.

(c) Failure of a party to seek Supreme Court emergency review under this paragraph (3) shall not affect the party's right to seek review under paragraph (1) of a decision of a Court of Appeals panel disposing of the motion for relief under CR 65.07 or 65.08.

HISTORY: Amended by Order 91–2, eff. 11–15–91; prior amendments eff. 9–15–90, 1–1–88, 9–1–80, 1–1–78; adopted eff. 7–1–76

CR 66   Receivers

CR 66   Receivers

An action wherein a receiver has been appointed shall not be dismissed except by order of the court. The practice in the administration of estates by receivers or by other similar officers appointed by the court shall be in accordance with the Kentucky Revised Statutes and with the practice heretofore followed in the courts of this state. In all other respects, the action in which the appointment of a receiver is sought or which is brought by or against a receiver is governed by these rules.

HISTORY: Adopted eff. 7–1–53

CR 67   Deposit in court

CR 67.01   In an action

In an action in which any part of the relief sought is a judgment for a sum of money or the disposition of a sum of money or the disposition of any other thing capable of delivery, a party, upon notice to every other party, and by leave of court, may deposit with the court all or any part of such sum or thing. Money paid into court under this rule shall be deposited in an interest-bearing account or invested in an interest-bearing instrument approved by the court. At the conclusion of the action, the interest accruing on any such account or instrument shall be paid to the person to whom the principal amount of the account is paid.

HISTORY: Amended by Order 90–1, eff. 9–15–90; prior amendment eff. 1–1–87; adopted eff. 7–1–53

CR 67.02   Court may order deposit or seizure of property

When it is admitted by the pleading or examination of a party that he has in his possession or control any money or other thing capable of delivery which being the subject of the litigation, is held by him as trustee for another party, or which belongs or is due to another party, the court may order the same to be deposited in court or delivered to such other party, with or without security, subject to further direction. If such order is disobeyed, the court may punish the disobedience as a contempt, and may also require the sheriff or other proper officer to take the money or property and deposit or deliver it in accordance with the direction given. Money paid into court under this rule shall be deposited in an interest-bearing account or invested in an interest-bearing instrument approved by the court. At the conclusion of the action, the interest accruing on any such account or instrument shall be paid to the person to whom the principal amount of the account is paid.

HISTORY: Amended by Order 90–1, eff. 9–15–90; prior amendment eff. 1–1–87; adopted eff. 7–1–53

CR 67.03   Money paid into court

Where the money is paid into court to abide the result of any legal proceeding, the judge may order it deposited in one or more designated federally insured state or national banks or savings banks, to the credit of the court in the action or proceeding in which the money was paid. The money, including earned interest, so deposited shall be paid only upon the check of the clerk of the court, annexed to its certified order for the payment, and in favor of the person to whom the order directs the payment to be made. Any interest which may have accrued shall also be paid to that same person.

HISTORY: Amended by Order 90–1, eff. 9–15–90; prior amendment eff. 1–1–87; adopted eff. 7–1–53

CR 68   Offer of judgment

CR 68   Offer of judgment

(1) At any time more than 10 days before the trial begins, a party defending against a claim may serve upon the adverse party an offer to allow judgment to be taken against him for the money or property, or to the effect specified in his offer, with costs then accrued. The offer may be conditioned upon the party's failure in his defense. If within 10 days after service of the offer the adverse party serves written notice that the offer is accepted, either party may then file the offer and notice of acceptance, together with the proof of service thereof, and thereupon judgment shall be rendered accordingly, except when the offer is one conditioned upon failure in defense, in which case the judgment shall be rendered when the defense has failed.

(2) When the liability of one party to another has been determined by verdict or order or judgment, but the amount or extent of the liability remains to be determined by further proceedings, the party adjudged liable may make an offer of judgment, which shall have the same effect as an offer made before the trial if it is served within a reasonable time not less than 10 days prior to the commencement of hearings to determine the amount or extent of liability.

(3) An offer not accepted shall be deemed withdrawn and evidence thereof is not admissible except in a proceeding to determine costs. If the judgment finally obtained by the offeree is not more favorable than the offer, the offeree must pay the costs incurred after the making of the offer. The fact that an offer is made but not accepted does not preclude a subsequent offer.

HISTORY: Amended eff. 7–1–69; prior amendment eff. 4–1–63; adopted eff. 7–1–53

CR 69   Provisional remedies and enforcement of judgments

CR 69.01   Service upon defendants in respect to proceedings for attachment or writ of possession

Service of summons, notice and other required papers upon defendants in respect to proceedings for attachment or writ of possession shall be made as prescribed in Rule 4, or may be served by any person authorized to serve a subpoena pursuant to Rule 45.03, or may be directed by the plaintiff to the defendant at his last known place of residence by certified mail, return receipt requested. Expenses shall be recoverable as costs.

HISTORY: Adopted eff. 6–1–78

CR 69.02   Post-judgment garnishment; service; answer; disposition of funds

(1) Service of post-judgment orders of attachment or garnishment upon third-party garnishees, such as employers and financial institutions, shall be served as prescribed in Rule 4 or, at the option of the plaintiff, may be directed by the plaintiff to the garnishee by regular first class or certified mail, or may be personally served by any person authorized to serve a subpoena pursuant to Rule 45.03. Expenses shall be recoverable as costs.

(2) Upon receiving a post-judgment order of garnishment, the garnishee shall answer within the time required by Rule 12.01, and unless otherwise ordered by the court shall make payments directly to the attorney for the party in whose behalf the order of garnishment was issued. If such party has no attorney of record, as, for example, in the instance of a "small claim," payments by the garnishee shall be made to the clerk of the court.

Except for child support arrearages, where wages are garnisheed, the attorney for the party in whose behalf the order of wage garnishment was issued, or the clerk of the court if such party has no attorney of record, shall safely hold the garnisheed funds in escrow for a period of fifteen (15) days from the issuance date of the employer's garnishment check. If the debtor files an objection within that period, the funds shall continue to be held until the court rules upon the objection. If an exemption is asserted and a hearing held, the attorney or clerk of the court shall disburse the garnisheed funds as ordered by the court. If no exemption is asserted the attorney or clerk of the court shall after the fifteen (15) day period disburse the funds to the party in whose behalf the order of garnishment was issued.

HISTORY: Amended by Order 88–4, eff. 1–1–89; adopted eff. 6–1–78

CR 69.03   Execution

Process to enforce a judgment for the payment of money shall be a writ of execution, unless the court directs otherwise. The procedure on execution, in proceedings supplementary to and in aid of a judgment, and in proceedings on and in aid of execution shall be in accordance with the Kentucky Revised Statutes. In aid of the judgment or execution, the judgment creditor, or his successor in interest when that interest appears of record, may obtain discovery from any person, including the judgment debtor, in the manner provided in these Rules.

HISTORY: Adopted eff. 6–1–78

CR 70   Judgment for specific acts

CR 70   Judgment for specific acts

If a judgment directs a party to execute a conveyance of land or to deliver deeds or other documents or to perform any other specific act and the party fails to comply within the time specified, the court may direct the act to be done at the cost of the disobedient party by some other person appointed by the court and the act when so done has like effect as if done by the party. On application of the party entitled to performance, the clerk shall issue a writ of attachment against the property of the disobedient party to compel obedience to the judgment. The court may also in proper cases adjudge the party in contempt. When any order or judgment is for money, land, or for the delivery of possession, the party in whose favor it is entered is entitled to a writ of execution upon application to the clerk.

HISTORY: Adopted eff. 7–1–53

CR 71   Process in behalf of and against persons not parties

CR 71   Process in behalf of and against persons not parties

When an order is made in favor of a person who is not a party to the action, he may enforce obedience to the order by the same process as if he were a party; and, when obedience to an order may be lawfully enforced against a person who is not a party, he is liable to the same process for enforcing obedience to the order as if he were a party.

HISTORY: Adopted eff. 7–1–53

IX   APPEALS

CR 72   Appeals from district courts

CR 72.01   Scope of rule

Rule 72 applies only to appeals from the district court to the circuit court.

HISTORY: Adopted eff. 1–1–78

CR 72.02   When and how taken

(1) Appeals from the district court to the circuit court in civil cases shall be taken by filing a notice of appeal in the district court and paying the required filing fee.

(2) Two or more persons entitled to appeal may file a joint notice of appeal, or may later join in appeal, if practicable, after filing separate notices of appeal and they shall thereafter proceed as a single appellant.

(3) Rules 73.02, 73.03 and 74 are applicable to appeals from the district court to the circuit court except when otherwise provided in statutes creating special remedies, including but not limited to:

Remedy		Time to File Notice of Appeal
Small Claims Statute	KRS 24A.340	10 days;
Paternity Statute	KRS 406.051	60 days;
Forcible Entry and Detainer Statute	KRS 383.255	7 days.

HISTORY: Amended by Order 2004–5, eff. 1–1–05; prior amendment eff. 11–15–91 (Order 91–2); adopted eff. 1–1–78

CR 72.04   Record on appeal from district court

The record on appeal to the circuit court shall consist of the entire original record of proceedings in the district court, including untranscribed electronic recordings made under the supervision and remaining in the custody of the district court or clerk. It need not be certified unless and until the Court of Appeals grants a motion for review of the final action of the circuit court disposing of the appeal.

HISTORY: Amended by Order 2006–09, eff. 1–1–07; adopted eff. 1–1–78

CR 72.06   Perfecting appeals and cross-appeals from district court

(1) To perfect an appeal from the district court the appellant shall file with the clerk of the circuit court the statement of appeal required by Rule 72.10.

(2) To perfect a cross-appeal from the district court the party taking it shall file with the clerk of the circuit court the counterstatement required by Rule 72.12.

HISTORY: Amended by Order 81–4, eff. 7–1–81; adopted eff. 1–1–78

CR 72.08   Time in which appeal from district court must be perfected

An appeal from the district court must be perfected within 30 days after the date of filing the first notice of appeal.

HISTORY: Adopted eff. 1–1–78

CR 72.10   Statement of appeal from district court

(1) A party or parties appealing from the judgment or a final order of the district court shall file with the clerk of the circuit court and serve on the appellee or appellees a statement of appeal signed by counsel for the appellant and setting forth:

(a) The style of the case and the district court docket number;

(b) The name, mailing address, and telephone number of each attorney whose appearance is entered in the case, together with the name of the party represented by the attorney;

(c) The name of the district judge who presided over the matter being appealed;

(d) The date on which the notice of appeal was filed and the date on which any notice of cross-appeal was filed;

(e) A statement as to whether the matter has been before the circuit court on any previous occasion and whether reference to the record of the prior appeal is necessary;

(f) The type of litigation;

(g) A statement as to whether the appellant wants an oral argument;

(h) A fair and accurate summary of the evidence heard by the district court, or a statement that the appeal does not require consideration of the evidence;

(i) A concise statement of the legal questions and propositions on which the appellant relies for a reversal of the judgment, with citations of pertinent authority;

(j) A concise statement of the relief to which the appellant contends he/she is entitled.

(2) In a criminal case appealed from district court to circuit court, a statement of appeal shall be served upon both the county attorney and the Commonwealth's attorney.

HISTORY: Amended by Order 98–2, eff. 1–1–99; prior amendments eff. 11–1–95 (Order 95–1), 9–1–93, 1–1–85; adopted eff. 1–1–78

CR 72.12   Appellee's counterstatement

Within 30 days after the date on which the appellant's statement of appeal from the district court was filed the appellee shall file and serve a counterstatement, not exceeding 10 pages, signed by counsel for the appellee and setting forth:

(a) The same information required for cross-appeals from the circuit court;

(b) A statement of whether the appellee or cross-appellant wants an oral argument;

(c) A statement of whether the appellant's summary of the evidence is accepted and, if not, a fair and accurate counterstatement of the evidence in question; and

(d) A response to the appellant's statement of legal points and propositions.

HISTORY: Amended by Order 95–1, eff. 11–1–95; prior amendments eff. 9–1–93, 7–1–81; adopted eff. 1–1–78

CR 72.13   Costs

Upon final disposition of an appeal in the circuit court the clerk shall send the parties a statement of what portion, if any, of the filing fee or fees mentioned in Rule 73.02(1)(c) shall be reimbursed by one party to the other, to the end that such costs shall be borne by the unsuccessful party or parties, except, however, that in criminal cases no reimbursement shall be required of the Commonwealth or a municipality. Liability for reimbursement of costs may be enforced on motion without the necessity of an independent action.

HISTORY: Amended by Order 82–2, eff. 10–1–82; adopted eff. 1–1–78

CR 73   All appeals

CR 73.01   General provisions

(1) Rules 73, 74, 75 and 76 apply to all appeals in civil actions except as otherwise provided in Rule 72, Rule 98 or in statutes creating special remedies.

(2) All appeals shall be taken to the next higher court by filing a notice of appeal in the court from which the appeal is taken. Appeals from family courts that are established pursuant to Ky. Const. § 110 (5) (b) or Ky. Const. § 112 (6) shall be taken to the Court of Appeals. After such filing, if the appeal is from a circuit court, any party may file a motion for transfer of the case to the Supreme Court as provided in CR 74.02. A motion for discretionary review by the Supreme Court of a decision of the Court of Appeals, or by the Court of Appeals of an appellate decision of the circuit court, shall be made as provided in Rule 76.20.

(3) Two or more persons entitled to appeal may file a joint notice of appeal, or may later join in appeal, if practicable, after filing separate notices of appeal, and they shall thereafter proceed as a single appellant.

(4) The taking of an appeal from a final order or judgment in any action in which the trial court has denied a defense asserted under Rule 12.02 based upon (a) lack of jurisdiction over the person, or (b) improper venue, or (c) insufficiency of process, or (d) insufficiency of service of process, shall not constitute an entry of appearance in said action in any court by the appellant.

HISTORY: Amended by Order 2006–09, eff. 1–1–07; prior amendments eff. 1–1–97 (Order 96–1), 11–15–91, 10–1–82, 1–1–78, 7–1–76, 7–1–69, 4–1–63; adopted eff. 7–1–53

CR 73.02   When and how taken

(1) (a) The notice of appeal shall be filed within 30 days after the date of notation of service of the judgment or order under Rule 77.04(2).

(b) If an appeal or cross-appeal is from an order or judgment of the circuit court, the filing fee required by Rule 76.42(2)(a)(i) or (ii) shall be paid to the clerk of the circuit court at the time the notice of appeal or cross-appeal is tendered, and the notice shall not be docketed or noted as filed until such payment is made. Motions to proceed in forma pauperis on such an appeal or cross-appeal must be addressed to the circuit court. If timely tendered and accompanied by a motion to proceed in forma pauperis supported by an affidavit, a notice of appeal or cross-appeal shall be considered timely but shall not be filed until the motion to proceed in forma pauperis is granted or, if denied, the filing fee is paid. If the motion to proceed in forma pauperis is denied, the party shall have 30 days within which to pay the filing fee or to appeal the denial to the appropriate appellate court. Time for further steps in the appeal or cross-appeal shall run from the date that the notice of appeal is filed upon payment of the filing fee or the granting of the motion to proceed in forma pauperis.

(c) If an appeal or cross-appeal is from an order or judgment of the district court, the filing fee required by KRS 23A.210 or 23A.205(1) shall be paid to the clerk of the district court at the time the notice of appeal or cross-appeal is filed, and the notice shall not be docketed or noted as filed until such payment is made.

(d) Upon a showing of excusable neglect based on a failure of a party to learn of the entry of the judgment or an order which affects the running of the time for taking an appeal, the trial court may extend the time for appeal, not exceeding 10 days from the expiration of the original time.

(e) The running of the time for appeal is terminated by a timely motion pursuant to any of the Rules hereinafter enumerated, and the full time for appeal fixed in this Rule commences to run upon entry and service under Rule 77.04(2) of an order granting or denying a motion under Rules 50.02, 52.02 or 59, except when a new trial is granted under Rule 59.

(i) If a party files a notice of appeal after the date of the docket notation of service of the judgment required by CR 77.04(2), but before disposition of any of the motions listed in this rule, the notice of appeal becomes effective when an order disposing of the last such remaining motion is entered.

(ii) A party intending to challenge a post-judgment order listed in this rule, or a judgment altered or amended upon such motion, must file a notice of appeal, or an amended notice of appeal, within the time prescribed by this rule measured by the date of the CR 77.04(2) docket notation regarding service of the order disposing of the last such remaining motion.

(iii) No additional fee is required to file an amended notice.

(2) The failure of a party to file timely a notice of appeal, cross-appeal, or motion for discretionary review shall result in a dismissal or denial. Failure to comply with other rules relating to appeals or motions for discretionary review does not affect the validity of the appeal or motion, but is ground for such action as the appellate court deems appropriate, which may include:

(a) A dismissal of the appeal or denial of the motion for discretionary review,

(b) Striking of pleadings, briefs, record or portions thereof,

(c) Imposition of fines on counsel for failing to comply with these rules of not more than $500, and

(d) Such further remedies as are specified in any applicable Rule.

(3) When the right of appeal in special civil cases is granted by statute, such appeals shall be prosecuted as provided in KRS 446.190.

(4) If an appellate court determines that an appeal or motion is frivolous, it may award just damages and single or double costs to the appellee or respondent. An appeal or motion is frivolous if the court finds that it is so totally lacking in merit that it appears to have been taken in bad faith.

HISTORY: Amended by Order 2010–09, eff. 1–1–11; prior amendments eff. 4–1–09 (Order 2009–01), 2–1–01 (Order 2000–1), 1–1–99 (Order 98–2), 11–15–91 (Order 91–2), 8–28–89, 1–1–87, 7–5–85, 1–1–85, 7–1–81, 1–1–78, 7–1–76, 7–1–69, 4–1–63, 6–1–60; adopted eff. 7–1–53

Legislative Research Commission Note: The appeal from the Small Claims Division of District Court is governed by KRS 24A.340, which provides that an appeal may be taken within 10 days of the judgment to the appropriate Circuit Court.

CR 73.03   Notice of appeal

(1) The notice of appeal shall specify by name all appellants and all appellees ("et al." and "etc." are not proper designation of parties) and shall identify the judgment, order or part thereof appealed from. It shall contain a certificate that a copy of the notice has been served upon all opposing counsel, or parties, if unrepresented, at their last known address.

(2) When the notice of appeal is filed, the clerk shall serve notice of its filing by mailing a copy showing the date filed and a copy of the official docket sheet to the clerk of the appellate court and to the attorney of record of each party or to the party, if unrepresented. The clerk shall note in the civil docket the names of the parties mailed the copies, with the date of mailing. Failure of the clerk to comply with this rule does not affect the validity of the appeal.

HISTORY: Amended by Order 2002–1, eff. 1–1–03; prior amendments eff. 11–15–91 (Order 91–2), 1–1–85, 1–1–78, 7–1–76, 7–1–69; adopted eff. 7–1–53

CR 73.04   Supersedeas bond

(1) Whenever an appellant entitled thereto desires a stay on appeal, as provided in Rule 62.03, he may present to the clerk or the court for approval an executed supersedeas bond with good and sufficient surety. The address of the surety shall be shown on the bond. The bond shall be in a fixed amount and conditioned for the satisfaction of the judgment in full together with costs, interest and damages for delay, if the appeal is dismissed or if the judgment is affirmed, and to satisfy in full such modification of the judgment

and such costs, including costs on the appeal and interest as the appellate court may adjudge.

(2) When the judgment is for the recovery of money not otherwise secured, the amount of the bond shall be fixed at such sum as will cover the whole amount of the judgment remaining unsatisfied, costs on the appeal, interest, and damages for delay, unless the trial court after notice and hearing and for good cause shown fixes a different amount or orders security other than the bond.

(3) When the judgment determines the disposition of the property in controversy as in real actions or replevin, or when such property is in the custody of the sheriff, or when the proceeds of such property or a bond for its value is in the custody or control of the court, the amount of the supersedeas bond shall be fixed at such sum only as will secure the amount recovered for the use and detention of the property, the costs of the action, costs on appeal, interest, and damages for delay. A supersedeas bond may be given to stay proceedings on a part of a judgment, and in such case the bond need only secure the part superseded.

HISTORY: Amended by Order 91–2, eff. 11–15–91; prior amendments eff. 7–1–76, 4–1–63, 6–1–60; adopted eff. 7–1–53

CR 73.05   Bond on appeal—Repealed
HISTORY: Repealed eff. 1–1–78; prior amendment eff. 7–1–76; adopted eff. 7–1–53

CR 73.06   Failure to file or insufficiency of supersedeas bond

(1) The sufficiency of the bond or the surety may be determined by the trial court upon motion and hearing.

(2) During an appeal, the trial court shall retain original jurisdiction to determine all matters relating to the right to file a supersedeas bond, the amount and sufficiency thereof and the surety thereon.

HISTORY: Amended by Order 91–2, eff. 11–15–91; prior amendments eff. 8–28–89, 1–1–86, 1–1–78, 7–1–76, 7–1–69; adopted eff. 7–1–53

CR 73.07   Judgment against surety

By entering into a supersedeas bond, the surety submits to the jurisdiction of the court with which the bond is filed and liability may be enforced on motion without the necessity of an independent action. The motion shall be served on the surety as provided by Rule 5 at least 20 days prior to the date of the hearing.

HISTORY: Amended by Order 91–2, eff. 11–15–91; prior amendments eff. 1–1–78, 6–1–60; adopted eff. 7–1–53

CR 73.08   Certification of record on appeal

The record on appeal as constituted under Rule 75 or Rule 76 shall be prepared and certified by the clerk

of the court from which the appeal is taken within 10 days after the filing of the transcript of evidence by the court reporter. If the proceedings were taken exclusively by video recording, if there are no proceedings to transcribe, or if the appeal is from a Circuit Court order determining paternity, dependency, abuse, neglect, domestic violence, or juvenile status offense, then the record on appeal shall be certified by the clerk within 30 days after the date of filing the first notice of appeal. In Forma Pauperis cases, the time for certifying the record on appeal in cases taken exclusively by video recording or where there are no proceedings to transcribe shall run from the date the Motion to Proceed In Forma Pauperis is granted. If CR 76.03 applies to the appeal, the time for certifying the record shall begin to run as provided in CR 76.03. The appellate court, in its discretion, may extend the time for certification of the record upon motion and a showing of good cause.

HISTORY: Amended by Order 2006–09, eff. 1–1–07; prior amendments eff. 11–15–91 (Order 91–2), 8–28–89, 7–14–88, 1–1–85, 1–1–78, 7–1–76, 6–1–60; adopted eff. 7–1–53

CR 74   Cross-appeals—Deleted
HISTORY: Deleted by Order 91–2, eff. 11–15–91; prior amendments eff. 7–1–76, 7–1–69, 3–1–55; adopted eff. 7–1–53

CR 74.01   Cross-appeals

(1) Any party properly named as an appellee or cross-appellee may take a cross-appeal from a judgment of the trial court. A cross-appeal shall be denominated as such and shall be prosecuted like a regular appeal and governed by the Rules applicable thereto, except that the notice of cross-appeal shall be filed not later than 10 days after the last day allowed for the filing of a notice of appeal. The failure of a party taking an appeal to prosecute the appeal, or that party's dismissal of it shall not prevent any party taking a cross-appeal from prosecuting the cross-appeal.

(2) A cross-appellant may name as cross-appellee any party to the circuit court action against whom relief is sought on the cross-appeal.

(3) Any cross-appellee, who has not previously filed a notice of appeal or cross-appeal from the judgment to be reviewed, may file an additional cross-appeal within ten (10) days of the filing of the notice of cross-appeal which first names that cross-appellee as a party to the appellate action seeking review of this particular judgment.

HISTORY: Amended by Order 93–1, eff. 9–1–93; adopted eff. 11–15–91

CR 74.02   Transfer of appeal from Court of Appeals to Supreme Court
(1) General.

Within 10 days after the date on which a notice of appeal to the Court of Appeals has been filed any party may serve and file a motion in the Supreme Court for transfer of the case to that Court. A copy of the notice of appeal shall accompany a motion for transfer filed in the Supreme Court. The requirements of Rule 76.20, excepting paragraphs (1), (2), (9)(a), and (9)(b), shall apply to such motions.

(2) Considerations governing transfer.

Such transfer is within the discretion of the Supreme Court and will be granted only upon a showing that the case is of great and immediate public importance, except that if separate appeals in a criminal case to the Supreme Court and to the Court of Appeals arise from the same trial, the Supreme Court in its discretion, on motion of the appellant whose appeal lies to the Court of Appeals, may transfer the latter appeal to the Supreme Court. The filing of a notice of appeal in a case in which a death penalty has been imposed will automatically serve to transfer the appeal to the Supreme Court.

(3) Running of time.

Filing of the motion shall suspend the running of time for further steps in the appeal, and the full time for such steps shall be computed from the date of the order granting or denying the transfer.

(4) Granting of motion.

If the motion is granted, the appeal shall be perfected and prosecuted as in the instance of appeals taken as a matter of right unless otherwise directed by the Supreme Court.

(5) Recommendation by Court of Appeals.

The Supreme Court may at any time, upon recommendation of the Court of Appeals, transfer to the Supreme Court any case pending before the Court of Appeals that falls within the criteria set forth in paragraph (2) of CR 74.02. The entry of a recommendation for transfer by the Court of Appeals shall suspend the running of time for any further steps in the appeal, and the full time for such steps shall be computed from the date of the order of the Supreme Court granting or denying the transfer.

(6) Costs.

Payment of the filing fee specified in Rule 76.42(2)(a) shall be required with the motion.

HISTORY: Amended by Order 2002–1, eff. 1–1–03; adopted by Order 91–2, eff. 11–15–91.

CR 75   Record on appeal

CR 75.01   Procedures for designation of evidence or proceedings reported by a court reporter

(1) Unless an agreed statement of the case is certified as provided in Rule 75.15, the proceedings were taken exclusively by video recording as governed by Rule 98, or there are no proceedings to transcribe, the appellant shall file a designation of untranscribed material. The designation shall be filed with the clerk of

the trial court and shall be served on the appellee, the court reporter, and the clerk of the appellate court. The designation shall be filed with the clerk of the trial court within 10 days of the filing of the notice of appeal unless Rule 76.03 applies to the appeal, in which case, the designation shall be filed within 10 days of the order ending the prehearing procedure under Rule 76.03(3). The designation shall: (1) list such untranscribed portions of the proceedings stenographically or electronically recorded as appellant wishes to be included in the record on appeal and (2) list any depositions or portions thereof as have been filed with the clerk but were not read into evidence and are thus required by Rule 75.07(1) to be excluded from the record on appeal. Within 10 days after the service and filing of such designation, or within 10 days after the time for filing of such designation has expired, any other party to the appeal may file a designation of additional portions of the untranscribed proceedings stenographically or electronically recorded as that party wishes to be included. If an appellee files the original designation, the parties shall proceed under Rule 75.01 in the same manner as if the original designation had been filed by the appellant. If no designation is required, a statement identifying such depositions, if any, or any portions thereof, as have been filed with the clerk but were not read into evidence and are thus required by Rule 75.07(1) to be excluded from the record on appeal, shall be filed with the clerk of the trial court and served upon the appellee and the clerk of the appellate court within the time periods set forth in this rule.

(2) If any part of the proceedings are to be transcribed by a court reporter there shall be attached to the designation a certificate signed by the designating counsel and by the court reporter stating:

(a) Date on which transcript was requested;

(b) Estimated number of pages;

(c) Estimated completion date; and

(d) That satisfactory financial arrangements have been made between counsel and reporter for the transcription.

(3) Except in cases in which the death penalty was sought at trial, the court reporter shall prepare the transcript of evidence within 50 days from the date of service of the designation of record. If the transcript of evidence cannot be completed within 50 days, it shall be the duty of the court reporter to make a written request to the appellant's attorney who shall file in the appropriate appellate court for an extension of time. If the transcript cannot be completed within 110 days of the service of the designation of the record, the reporter is required to make another written request to the appellant's attorney for an extension and must reduce the transcript preparation fee by 10% for every 30 days over the 110 days.

(4) In cases in which the death penalty had been sought at trial, the court reporter shall prepare the

transcript of evidence within 170 days from the date of the service of the designation of record. If the transcript cannot be completed within 170 days, it shall be the duty of the court reporter to make a written request to the appellant's attorney who shall file in the Supreme Court of Kentucky for an extension of time. If the transcript cannot be completed within 230 days of the service of the designation of record, the reporter is required to make another written request to the appellant's attorney for an extension and must reduce the transcript preparation fee by 10% for every 30 days over the 230 days.

(5) All written requests for extensions by the court reporter to the appellant's attorney must be made at least ten (10) days before the expiration of the period as originally prescribed or as extended by a previous order.

(6) The court reporter shall immediately notify all counsel of record of the completion and filing of the transcript of evidence and one (1) copy with the clerk of the circuit court.

HISTORY: Amended by Order 2006–09, eff. 1–1–07; prior amendments eff. 1–1–03 (Order 2002–1), 1–1–99 (Order 98–2), 1–1–97 (Order 96–1), 9–1–93, 11–15–91, 8–28–89, 1–1–89, 7–1–81, 7–1–79, 1–1–78, 7–1–76, 7–1–69; adopted eff. 7–1–53

CR 75.02   Transcript of evidence and proceedings

(1) If there be designated for inclusion any proceedings that were not electronically recorded but were stenographically recorded, the court reporter shall file promptly in the trial court the original and one copy of the transcript of the portion or portions thereof included in the designation. If the designation includes only a portion or portions of the reporter's transcript, the court reporter at the request of the appellant shall file such additional portions as the appellee would reasonably require to enable him or her to complete the record on appeal and if the appellant fails to do so the trial court on motion may require the additional material needed to be so furnished. Initially the cost of a transcript will be borne by the party designating it.

(2) Except in cases in which the death penalty was sought at trial, unless otherwise directed by the court, the transcript of proceedings shall include only those portions of the voir dire or opening statements and closing arguments by counsel which were properly objected to in the proceedings in the trial court and which are designated by one of the parties to be a part of the record on appeal.

(3) In the event any of the proceedings designated for inclusion have been electronically recorded, it shall not be necessary that they be transcribed, and in lieu of a transcript the original tapes or recordings shall be transmitted by the clerk pursuant to Rule 75.07.

HISTORY: Amended by Order 2006–09, eff. 1–1–07; prior amendments eff. 1–1–99 (Order 98–2), 11–15–91 (Order 91–2), 1–1–88, 1–1–84, 7–1–81, 1–1–78, 7–1–76, 6–1–60; adopted eff. 7–1–53

CR 75.03   Form of testimony

Testimony of witnesses designated for inclusion may be either in question and answer form or in narrative form. A party may prepare and file with his designation a condensed statement in narrative form of all or part of the testimony, and any other party to the appeal, if dissatisfied with the narrative statement may require testimony in question and answer form to be substituted for all or part thereof.

HISTORY: Adopted eff. 7–1–53

CR 75.04   Statement of points—Repealed

HISTORY: Repealed eff. 1–1–78; prior amendment eff. 7–1–76; adopted eff. 7–1–53

CR 75.05   Record to be abbreviated

No party shall designate any matter not essential to the decision of the questions presented by the appeal. For any infraction of this rule or for the unnecessary substitution by one party of evidence in question and answer form for a fair narrative statement proposed by another, the appellate court may withhold or impose costs as the circumstances of the case and discouragement of like conduct in the future may require; and costs may be imposed upon offending attorneys or parties. On motion the trial court may require a party filing a counterdesignation under Rule 75.01 to advance all or part of the costs of the additional record if it does not appear reasonably necessary to the disposition of the appeal.

HISTORY: Amended eff. 7–1–76; prior amendment eff. 7–1–69; adopted eff. 7–1–53

CR 75.06   Stipulation as to record

Instead of serving designations as provided in Rule 75.01, the parties by stipulation filed with the clerk of the trial court may designate the parts of the proceedings and evidence to be included in the record on appeal.

HISTORY: Amended eff. 1–1–78; prior amendment eff. 7–1–76; adopted eff. 7–1–53

CR 75.07   Record to be prepared and transmitted by clerk

(1) The clerk of the trial court shall prepare and certify the entire original record on file in his or her office, in accordance with the requirements of paragraphs (10) and (11) of this Rule 75.07, including the designations or stipulations of the parties with respect to proceedings stenographically or electronically recorded and a certified copy (rather than the original) of the docket assigned to the action, but excluding depositions not read into evidence.

(2) The transcript of proceedings stenographically recorded (or tapes or recordings of proceedings electronically recorded), or such lesser portions thereof as have been designated or agreed upon by stipulation,

shall when filed with the clerk be certified as a part of the record on appeal.

(3) Except for (a) documents, (b) maps and charts, and (c) other papers reasonably capable of being enclosed in envelopes, exhibits shall be retained by the clerk and shall not be transmitted to the appellate court unless specifically directed by the appellate court on motion of a party or upon its own motion.

(4) The written record on appeal shall include the juror strike sheets made pursuant to RCr 9.36.

(5) The matter certified under subsections (1), (2), (3), and (4) of this Rule and Rule 98 shall constitute the record on appeal. It is the responsibility of the appellant or counsel for the appellant, if any, to see that the record is prepared and certified by the clerk within the time prescribed by Rule 73.08.

(6) If the appeal is to the Court of Appeals or Supreme Court, the clerk of the circuit court or of the Court of Appeals in workers' compensation cases, or original proceedings pursuant to CR 76.36(7) shall immediately notify the clerk of the appellate court when the record has been completed and certified as required by this Rule, and shall simultaneously serve copies of such notification upon all parties to the appeal. Such notification shall indicate the name or names of counsel for the appellant. The clerk shall enter the fact and date of such notification in the docket of the case, and the date of such docket entry shall govern the time for perfecting the appeal.

(7) The record on appeal shall be retained under the responsibility and control of the clerk of the trial court until it is transmitted to the clerk of the appellate court. It will be made available first to counsel for the appellant and then to counsel for the appellee. If it is removed from the clerk's office, counsel for the appellant shall return it before submitting his or her brief to the appellate court in order that it may be available to counsel for the appellee. Counsel for the appellee shall return it before submitting his or her brief to the appellate court. If it is withdrawn by counsel for the appellant for the purpose of preparing a reply brief it shall be returned before such brief is submitted to the appellate court. In no event shall the original of an electronic recording be removed from the clerk's office, nor shall a record on appeal be retained by counsel beyond the filing date on which his or her appellate brief is due.

(8) Whenever the clerk permits a record on appeal to be withdrawn by counsel, the original of the reporter's transcript, including evidentiary exhibits, shall be retained in the clerk's office until it is transmitted to the appellate court.

(9) Withdrawals and returns of the record on appeal shall be noted by the clerk on the docket kept for that action (which, in the instance of appeals from the district court, shall be the circuit court's appellate docket).

(10) All parts of the written record on appeal shall be arranged in the order in which they were filed or entered. If the record comprises more than 150 pages, it shall be divided into two or more volumes not exceeding 150 pages each. Each volume shall be securely bound at the left side.

(11) There shall be a general index at the beginning of the record and an index to each volume in the front thereof which shall show, in the order in which they appear, the pages on which all pleadings, orders, judgments, instructions, and papers may be found, together with the name of each witness and the pages on which his or her examination and cross-examination appear. All exhibits filed with the record shall be sufficiently identified and the index shall direct where they may be found.

(12) If the appeal is to the Court of Appeals or Supreme Court, the clerk of the trial court shall transmit the record on appeal to the appellate court when so requested by the clerk of that court.

HISTORY: Amended by Order 2010–09, eff. 1–1–11; prior amendments eff. 1–1–07 (Order 2006–09), 1–1–03 (Order 2002–1), 1–1–99 (Order 98–2), 10–1–94 (Order 94–1), 7–1–81, 9–1–80, 7–1–78, 1–1–78, 7–1–76, 7–1–69, 4–1–63, 6–1–60; adopted eff. 7–1–53

CR 75.08   Power of court to correct or modify record

It is not necessary for the record on appeal to be approved by the trial court or judge thereof except as provided in Rule 75.12, Rule 75.13, and Rule 76, but if any difference arises as to whether the record truly discloses what occurred in the trial court, the difference shall be submitted to and settled by that court and the record made to conform to the truth. If anything material to either party is omitted from the record on appeal by error or accident or is misstated therein, the parties by stipulation, or the trial court, either before or after the record is transmitted to the appellate court, or the appellate court, on a proper suggestion or of its own initiative, may direct that the omission or misstatement shall be corrected, and if necessary that a supplemental record shall be certified and transmitted by the clerk of the trial court. All other questions as to the content and form of the record shall be presented to the appellate court.

HISTORY: Amended eff. 7–1–76; adopted eff. 7–1–53

CR 75.09   Orders as to original papers—Repealed
HISTORY: Repealed eff. 7–1–76; adopted eff. 7–1–53

CR 75.10   Record for preliminary hearing in an appellate court

If at any time before the record on appeal to the Court of Appeals or Supreme Court has been transmitted to the appellate court a party desires to move that court for a dismissal, for a stay pending appeal, or for any other intermediate order, the clerk of the trial court at his request shall prepare for transmission to the appellate court a photocopy of the judgment or order from which the appeal is taken, the notice of appeal and such other portions of the record as the parties may request or as may be necessary including a copy of the certificate as to transcript under Rule 75.01(2), if applicable.

HISTORY: Amended by Order 89–1, eff. 8–28–89; prior amendments eff. 12–31–80, 1–1–78, 7–1–76, 7–1–69; adopted eff. 7–1–53

CR 75.11   Several appeals

When more than one appeal is taken to an appellate court from the same judgment, a single record on appeal shall be prepared containing all the matter designated or agreed upon by the parties, without duplication. If there are separate appeals to the Supreme Court and Court of Appeals in a criminal case, a copy of the original record shall be made up and certified as the record on appeal to the Court of Appeals.

HISTORY: Amended eff. 10–1–78; prior amendment eff. 7–1–76; adopted eff. 7–1–53

CR 75.12   Appeals in forma pauperis—Deleted

HISTORY: Deleted by Order 91–2, eff. 11–15–91; prior amendments eff. 2–13–81, 7–1–76; adopted eff. 7–1–53

CR 75.13   Narrative statement

(1) In the event no stenographic or electronic record of the evidence or proceedings at a hearing or trial was made or, if so, cannot be transcribed or are not clearly understandable from the tape or recording, the appellant may prepare a narrative statement thereof from the best available means, including his/her recollection, for use instead of a transcript or for use as a supplement to or in lieu of an insufficient electronic recording. This statement shall be served on the appellee, who may serve objections or proposed amendments thereto within 10 days after service upon him/her. Thereupon the statement, with the objections or proposed amendments, shall be submitted to the trial court for settlement and approval, and as settled and approved shall be included in the record on appeal.

(2) By agreement of the parties a narrative statement of all or any part of the evidence or other proceedings at a hearing or trial may be substituted for or used in lieu of a stenographic transcript or an electronic recording.

HISTORY: Amended by Order 2006–09, eff. 1–1–07; prior amendments eff. 1–1–99 (Order 98–2), 7–1–81 (Order 81–4), 7–1–79, 7–1–76; adopted eff. 7–1–53

CR 75.14   Bystanders bill

In the event that the trial judge refuses or is unable for any reason to approve a record of the proceedings and evidence when submitted to him for settlement; or in the event he approves such a record or enters a correction thereon over a party's objection, an aggrieved party may, within five days after the trial judge's action, serve an exception as written by him, if its truth is attested by the affidavits of two bystanders, but its truth may be controverted and maintained by other affidavits so served, not exceeding five on either side. Affidavits controverting must be filed within five days after the serving of the correction and those maintaining within 10 days after the serving of the correction.

HISTORY: Adopted eff. 7–1–53

CR 75.15   Record on appeal; agreed statement

When the questions presented by an appeal can be determined without an examination of all the proceedings and evidence in the trial court, the parties may prepare and sign a statement of the case showing how the questions arose and were decided in the trial court and setting forth only so many of the facts averred and proved or sought to be proved as are essential to a decision of the questions by the appellate court. The statement shall include a copy of the judgment appealed from, a copy of the notice of appeal with its filing date, and a concise statement of the points to be relied on by the appellant. If the statement conforms to the proceedings and evidence it shall, with such additions as the trial court may consider necessary fully to present the questions raised by the appeal, be approved by the trial court and shall then be certified to the appellate court as the record on appeal in lieu of the record specified in Rule 75.07.

HISTORY: Adopted eff. 1–1–78

CR 76   Practice and procedure in Court of Appeals and Supreme Court

CR 76.01   Scope of rule

(1) Rule 76 applies only to practice and procedure in the Court of Appeals and Supreme Court. Wherever "court" or "appellate court" is used it means the court to which an appeal is or may be taken or in which it is pending, "judge" means either a judge or justice of that court, and "clerk" means the clerk of that court, unless the context indicates otherwise. Wherever the appellate court is called by its title the rule shall apply to that court alone.

(2) Appeals to the Supreme Court from judgments and final orders in proceedings originating in the Court of Appeals shall be governed by Rule 76.36(7), and the provisions of Rules 76.02 and 76.04 with respect to perfecting appeals and submission of briefs shall not apply.

HISTORY: Amended by Order 89–1, eff. 8–28–89; prior amendment eff. 12–31–80; adopted eff. 1–1–78

CR 76.02   Perfecting appeals and cross-appeals

(1) To perfect an appeal from the circuit court the appellant shall: (a)(i) cause the clerk's notice required by CR 75.07(6) to be transmitted to the clerk of the appellate court or (ii) if the appeal is taken of a case recorded pursuant to CR 98(1), cause the clerk's notice required by paragraph CR 98(3)(c) to be transmitted to the clerk of the appellate court; and (b) file with the clerk of the appellate court the brief required by Rule 76.12.

(2) When an appeal has been perfected and so noted on the docket the clerk shall forthwith mail notice of the date of such entry to the attorneys for the parties as shown on the notice of appeal.

(3) To perfect a cross-appeal the party taking it shall file with the clerk of the appellate court the brief required by Rule 76.12.

HISTORY: Amended by Order 2010–09, eff. 1–1–11; prior amendments eff. 1–1–07 (Order 2006–09), 1–1–97 (Order 96–1), 9–1–93, 11–15–91, 7–1–81; adopted eff. 1–1–78

CR 76.03   Prehearing conference

(1) This Rule, 76.03, applies to all civil actions appealed to the Court of Appeals, except prisoner applications seeking relief relating to confinement or conditions of confinement and appeals from Circuit Court orders determining paternity, dependency, abuse, neglect, domestic violence, or juvenile status offense.

(2) Upon the filing of a notice of appeal to the Court of Appeals in a civil case to which this rule applies, the clerk of the circuit court shall forthwith transmit a copy of the notice of appeal to the Clerk of the Court of Appeals, together with copies of (a) the docket sheet of the court from which the appeal is taken; (b) the judgment or order sought to be reviewed; and (c) any opinion or findings of the circuit court or administrative agency.

(3) In any appeal to which this Rule, 76.03, applies, following the filing of the notice of appeal, the running of time for further steps shall not run until so ordered by the Court of Appeals except for the following: (a) the filing of a notice of cross-appeal under Rule 74.01; (b) the filing of a motion to transfer under Rule 74.02; or the filing of a prehearing statement under this Rule, 76.03. Unless otherwise ordered by the Court of Appeals, the full time for such further steps shall be computed from the date of entry of the order stating that no prehearing conference shall be held pursuant to this rule, or from the date of entry of the order reciting the actions taken and the agreements reached by the parties during a prehearing conference held pursuant to this rule.

(4) Within twenty days after filing the notice of appeal or notice of cross-appeal in the circuit court, each appellant and cross-appellant shall file with the Clerk of the Court of Appeals, with service on all other parties, a prehearing statement, on a form to be supplied by the clerk of the circuit court at the time the notice of appeal is filed, setting forth the following information:

(a) The style of the case and circuit court docket number;

(b) The name, mailing address, and telephone number of each attorney whose appearance is entered in the case, together with the name of the party represented by the attorney;

(c) The name of the judge who presided over the matter being appealed;

(d) The date on which the notice of appeal and the date on which any notice of cross-appeal was filed;

(e) A statement as to whether the matter has been before the Court of Appeals, on a previous occasion, in which case the clerk shall, if necessary, obtain the old record from the clerk of the trial court, and shall place the old record with the new one;

(f) The type of litigation;

(g) A brief description of the claims, defenses, and issues litigated;

(h) A brief statement of the facts and issues proposed to be raised on appeal, including jurisdictional challenges;

(i) A statement, based on counsel's present knowledge, as to whether the appeal involves a question of first impression;

(j) A statement as to whether the determination of the appeal will turn on the interpretation or application of a particular case or statute and, if so, the name of the case or the number of the statute;

(k) A statement, based upon counsel's present knowledge, as to whether there is pending before the Court of Appeals or the Supreme Court another case arising from substantially the same case or controversy or involving an issue which is substantially the same, similar or related to an issue in this appeal.

(5) In any civil case to which this rule applies in which the constitutionality of a statute is challenged by any party as an issue in the appeal, a copy of the prehearing statement shall be served upon the Attorney General. The Attorney General may file within 10 days of the filing of the prehearing statement an entry of appearance. If no entry of appearance is filed in such a case by the Attorney General, then no further filings or briefs shall be served on the Attorney General.

(6) Within ten days after the filing of appellant's or cross-appellant's prehearing statement each appellee or cross-appellee may file with the Clerk of the Court of Appeals, with service on all other parties, a supplemental statement containing any other information needed to clarify the issues on appeal and on cross-appeal, and a statement as to whether in the opinion of counsel, the appeal should be designated a special appeal pursuant to CR 76.05.

(7) All civil cases shall be reviewed to determine if a prehearing conference would be of assistance to the Court or the parties; and any party may move for a prehearing conference at the time of filing the pre-hearing statement or supplemental statement. Such a conference may be conducted by a judge of the Court of Appeals or a staff attorney of the Court known as a conference attorney.

(8) A party shall be limited on appeal to issues in the prehearing statement except that when good cause is shown the appellate court may permit additional issues to be submitted upon timely motion.

(9) A judge of the Court of Appeals designated by the Chief Judge of the Court of Appeals or a conference attorney designated by the Chief Judge of the Court of Appeals may direct the attorneys for all parties to attend a prehearing conference, in person or by telephone, to be held as soon as practicable after the filing of the prehearing statement.

(10) The purpose of the conference shall be to consider the possibility of settlement, the simplification of issues, the contents of the record, the time for filing the record and briefs, and any other matters which the judge or conference attorney determines may aid in the handling or disposition of the proceedings.

(11) At the conclusion of the prehearing conference, the judge or conference attorney shall enter an order reciting the actions taken and the agreements reached by the parties and that order shall govern the subsequent course of the proceedings.

(12) The comments made during the prehearing conference are confidential, except to the extent disclosed by the prehearing order entered pursuant to CR 76.03(10), and shall not be disclosed by the conference judge or conference attorney nor by counsel in briefs or argument.

(13) In the event of default by any party in any action required by a prehearing conference order, the Clerk of the Court of Appeals shall issue a notice to the party in default providing a 10–day period within which to file an affidavit showing good cause for the default and including when the required action will be taken.

(14) Upon failure of a party or attorney to comply with the provisions of this rule or the provisions of the prehearing conference order, the Court of Appeals may assess reasonable expenses caused by the failure, including attorney's fees; assess all or a portion of the appellate costs; or dismiss the appeal.

(15) A judge who participates in a prehearing conference or becomes involved in settlement discussions pursuant to this rule shall not sit as a member of the panel assigned to hear the appeal.

HISTORY: Amended by Order 2006–09, eff. 1–1–07; prior amendments eff. 2–1–01 (Order 2000–1), 1–1–99 (Order 98–2), 1–1–97 (Order 96–1), 8–1–92; adopted eff. 11–15–91

CR 76.04   Time in which appeals and cross-appeals must be perfected—Deleted
HISTORY: Deleted by Order 2004–5, eff. 1–1–05; prior amendment eff. 7–1–78; adopted eff. 1–1–78

CR 76.05   Special Appeals of the Court of Appeals—Deleted
HISTORY: Deleted by Order 2000–1, eff. 2–1–01; adopted by Order 91–2, eff. 11–15–91

CR 76.06   Statement of appeal—Deleted
HISTORY: Deleted by Order 91–2, eff. 11–15–91; prior amendment eff. 7–1–79; adopted eff. 1–1–78

CR 76.08   Statement of cross-appeal—Deleted
HISTORY: Deleted by Order 91–2, eff. 11–15–91; adopted eff. 1–1–78

CR 76.10   Record of previous appeal—Deleted
HISTORY: Deleted by Order 91–2, eff. 11–15–91; adopted eff. 1–1–78

CR 76.12   Briefs
(1) When required.

Unless otherwise directed by the appellate court, before any appeal is taken under submission for final disposition on the merits briefs shall be filed by the respective parties. An appellant or cross-appellant may file a reply brief. No further briefs will be considered without leave of the court. The combining of arguments on an appeal and cross-appeal into one brief is both permitted and encouraged. Should the appellant or appellants fail to file a brief, no brief shall be required of the appellees unless so ordered by the court.

(2) Time for filing.

(a) Civil cases. In civil cases, including workers' compensation appeals, except appeals from Circuit Court orders determining paternity, dependency, abuse, neglect, domestic violence or juvenile status offense, the appellant's brief shall be filed with the clerk of the appellate court within 60 days after the date of the notation on the docket of the notification required by Rule 75.07(6). The appellee's brief (or combined briefs, if the appellee is also a cross–appellant) shall be so filed within 60 days after the date on which the appellant's brief was filed. The appellant's reply brief shall be filed within 15 days after the date on which the last appellee's brief was filed or due to be filed. If the appellant is also a cross-appellee, a combined brief may be filed within 60 days after the date on which the last appellee's brief is filed or due to be filed. When a motion for discretionary review has been granted by the Supreme Court, the time in which the movant's brief must be filed shall be computed from the date of entry of the order granting review.

(i) Civil appeals from Circuit Court orders determining paternity, dependency, abuse, neglect, domestic violence or juvenile status offense. Appeals in these cases shall be expedited. The appellant's brief shall be filed with the clerk of the appellate court within 30 days after the date of the notation on the docket of the notification required by Rule 75.07(6). The appellee's brief shall be filed within 30 days after the date of filing of the appellant's brief. The appellant's reply brief shall be filed within 10 days after the date of filing of the appellee's brief. Motions for extension of time will not be considered except under extraordinary circumstances.

(b) Criminal cases. The times in which briefs are required to be filed in criminal cases shall be the same as in civil cases, except as follows:

(i) If counsel for the appellant is the Public Advocate of the Commonwealth or the Attorney General of the Commonwealth, or designee, the appellant's brief shall be filed within 60 days after the date on which the record on appeal was received by the clerk of the appellate court (notice of which shall be sent); and

(ii) If counsel for the appellant is someone other than the Public Advocate of the Commonwealth or the Attorney General of the Commonwealth, or designee, the appellee's brief shall be filed within 60 days after the date on which the appellant's brief was filed or within 60 days after the date on which the record on appeal was received by the clerk of the appellate court, whichever is the later.

(3) Number of copies.

(a) Briefs in the Court of Appeals shall be filed in quintuplicate. In the Supreme Court ten copies shall be filed.

(b) Filing of Electronic Briefs on Diskette or CD–ROM. Any party filing a brief on the merits with the Clerk of the Supreme Court or the Court of Appeals may, and is encouraged to, file with the required copies of the paper brief an electronic brief thereof on a floppy disk or CD–ROM (preferred). The appellate court clerk shall receive and file the floppy disk or CD–ROM with the papers of that case.

(i) All electronic briefs shall be on a 3.5 floppy disk or CD–ROM that can be read via Microsoft Windows and shall contain in a single file all information contained in the paper brief, including the cover, the table of contents, and the certifications, in the same order as the paper brief. The electronic briefs may also contain hypertext links or bookmarks to cases, statutes and other reference materials available on the Internet or appended to the brief.

(ii) An electronic brief must be formatted in Microsoft Word, WordPerfect, or in a .pdf document (preferred).

(iii) An electronic brief shall contain a label indicating:

(a) The style and docket number of the case,

(b) The name of the document contained on the diskette or CD–ROM, and

(c) The language format of the document.

(4) Form and content.

(a) Printed or typewritten brief. In the Supreme Court and the Court of Appeals, all briefs may be printed or typewritten. "Printed briefs" are those which have been typeset. A brief produced on a computer printer is considered to be typewritten.

(i) If *printed*, briefs shall be in black ink on unglazed opaque white paper 6 1/8 by 9 1/4 inches in dimension, in type no smaller than 11–point, and enclosed in covers colored as specified in this rule.

(ii) If *typewritten*, briefs shall be on unglazed white paper 8 1/2 by 11 inches in dimension in black type no smaller than 12 point set at standard width. Typing shall be double spaced and clearly readable. The brief shall have a 1 1/2 inch margin on the left side and a 1 inch margin on all other edges. Briefs shall be enclosed (front and back) in covers colored as specified in this rule. Typewritten briefs shall be securely bound at the left side.

(iii) *Covers.* All briefs shall be enclosed (front and back) in covers colored as follows: Appellants—red; Appellees—blue; Appellants reply brief—yellow; Amicus curiae—brown; Petitions for Rehearing—green; Response—gray; Other—white. Brief covers shall show the file number(s) of the appeal(s), the file number(s) of the circuit court action(s), a caption containing at least the lead appellants and appellees, the name of the party on whose behalf the brief is submitted, and the certificate required by subsection (6) of this rule. See official forms 24 and 25.

(b) Length.

(i) In the Court of Appeals, unless otherwise ordered by that court, the appellant's brief and the appellee's brief in response shall be limited to 25 pages each, excluding the introduction, statement of points and authorities, exhibits and appendices. Reply briefs shall be limited to five pages each, except that when an appellant is called upon to respond to more than one appellee brief the appellant is permitted up to five additional pages for each additional appellee brief. A brief combining arguments as an appellee and cross-appellant shall be limited to 40 pages. A brief combining an appellant's reply and a cross-appellee brief shall be limited to 30 pages.

(ii) In the Supreme Court, unless otherwise permitted by order of that Court the appellant's brief and the appellee's brief in response shall be limited to 50 pages each, excluding the introduction, statement of points and authorities, exhibits and appendices, and reply briefs shall be limited to 10 pages each. A brief combining arguments on an appeal and cross-appeal to the Supreme Court shall not exceed 65 pages. A brief combining a reply and a response to a cross-appeal shall not exceed 25 pages in length. If the appellant is called upon to respond to more than one appellee's brief, the appellant shall be permitted up to five additional pages for each additional appellee's brief.

(iii) In cases where the death penalty has been imposed, upon motion made at least 20 days prior to the filing deadline, and upon good cause shown, the appellant's brief and the appellee's brief may be extended to no more than 150 pages, excluding the introduction, statement of points and authorities, exhibits and appendices. Upon similar motion, for good cause shown, made at least 5 days prior to the filing deadline, a reply brief may be extended to no more than 25 pages.

(c) Organization and contents–Appellant's brief. The organization and contents of the appellant's brief shall be as follows:

(i) A brief "INTRODUCTION" indicating the nature of the case, and not exceeding two simple sentences, such as, "This is a murder case in which the defendant appeals from a judgment convicting him of 1st -degree manslaughter and sentencing him to 20 years in prison," or "This is a case in which an insurance company appeals from a judgment construing its policy as applicable, and a co-defendant's policy as not applicable, to the plaintiff's accident claim. Plaintiff also appeals against the co-defendant."

(ii) A "STATEMENT CONCERNING ORAL ARGUMENT" indicating whether the appellant desires oral argument and why appellant believes that oral argument would or would not be helpful to the Court in deciding the issues presented. This Statement should be no longer than one brief paragraph. The appellant's statement is not binding on the Court and does not preclude a party's right to file a motion to reconsider the Court's ruling that oral argument will be dispensed with. Failure to include a statement concerning oral argument will be treated as indicating that appellant does not desire oral argument in the appeal.

(iii) A "STATEMENT OF POINTS AND AUTHORITIES," which shall set forth, succinctly and in the order in which they are discussed in the body of the argument, the appellant's contentions with respect to each issue of law relied upon for a reversal, listing under each the authorities cited on that point and the respective pages of the brief on which the argument appears and on which the authorities are cited.

(iv) A "STATEMENT OF THE CASE" consisting of a chronological summary of the facts and procedural events necessary to an understanding of the issues presented by the appeal, with ample references to the specific pages of the record, or tape and digital counter number in the case of untranscribed videotape or audiotape recordings, or date and time in the case of all other untranscribed electronic recordings, supporting each of the statements narrated in the summary.

(v) An "ARGUMENT" conforming to the statement of Points and Authorities, with ample supportive references to the record and citations of authority pertinent to each issue of law and which shall contain at the beginning of the argument a statement with reference to the record showing whether the issue was properly preserved for review and, if so, in what manner.

(vi) A "CONCLUSION" setting forth the specific relief sought from the appellate court.

(vii) An "APPENDIX" with appropriate extruding tabs containing copies of the findings of fact, conclusions of law, and judgment of the trial court, any written opinions filed by the trial court in support of the judgment, the opinion or opinions of the court from which the appeal is taken, and any pleadings or exhibits to which ready reference may be considered by the appellant as helpful to the appellate court. The first item of the appendix shall be a listing or index of all documents included in the appendix. The index shall set forth where the documents may be found in the record. The appellant shall place the judgment, opinion, or order under review immediately after the appendix list so that it is most readily available to the court. Except for matters of which the appellate court may take judicial notice, materials and documents not included in the record shall not be introduced or used as exhibits in support of briefs. In workers' compensation cases the appendix shall include the opinions of the Administrative Law Judge, the Workers' Compensation Board and the Court of Appeals.

(viii) Any "INDEX" the appellant may wish to provide.

(d) Organization and contents–Appellee's brief. The organization and contents of the appellee's brief shall be as follows:

(i) A "STATEMENT CONCERNING ORAL ARGUMENT" responsive to appellant's statement indicating why appellee believes that oral argument would or would not assist the Court in deciding the issues presented.

(ii) A "COUNTERSTATEMENT OF POINTS AND AUTHORITIES" similar to the statement required of the appellant by paragraph (4)(c)(iii) of this Rule.

(iii) A "COUNTERSTATEMENT OF THE CASE" stating whether the appellee accepts the appellant's Statement of the Case and, if not, setting forth the matters the appellee considers essential to a fair and adequate statement of the case in accordance with the requirements of paragraph (4)(c)(iv) of this Rule.

(iv) An "ARGUMENT" conforming to the appellee's Statement of Points and Authorities and to the requirements of paragraph (4)(c)(v) of this Rule with reference to record-references and citations of authority.

(v) An "APPENDIX" with appropriate extruding tabs containing copies of any papers or exhibits, not included in the appellant's brief to which ready reference may be considered by the appellee as helpful to the appellate court. The first item of the appendix shall be a listing or index of all documents included in the appendix. The index shall set forth where the documents may be found in the record.

(vi) Any "INDEX" the appellee may wish to provide.

(e) Organization and contents—other briefs. Other briefs permitted by these Rules shall have a "STATEMENT OF POINTS AND AUTHORITIES" conforming to paragraph (4)(c)(iii) of this Rule, shall state the purpose of the brief and the particular issues to which it is directed and shall contain an ARGUMENT consistent with the requirements of paragraph (4)(c)(v) of this Rule. The brief shall conclude with a statement of the relief sought, if pertinent, and may include an appendix or an index as in the instance of the briefs mentioned in paragraphs (4)(c) and (4)(d) of this Rule. Reply briefs shall be confined to points raised in the briefs to which they are addressed, and shall not reiterate arguments already presented.

(f) Organization and contents—Briefs of five pages or less. The requirements of this Rule with respect to a "STATEMENT OF POINTS AND AUTHORITIES" shall not apply to any brief of five pages or less.

(g) Form of citations. All citations of Kentucky Statutes shall be made from the official edition of the Kentucky Revised Statutes and may be abbreviated "KRS." The citation of Kentucky cases reported after January 1, 1951, shall be in the following form for decisions of the Supreme Court and its predecessor court: Doe v. Roe, ___ S.W.2d ___ or ___ S.W.3d ___ (Ky. [date]), or for reported decisions of the present Court of Appeals, Doe v. Roe, ___ S.W.2d ___ or ___ S.W.3d ___ (Ky. App. [date]). Case names may be italicized or underlined.

(5) Service of briefs on adverse parties and courts from which appeals have been taken.

Before filing any brief in the appellate court a party shall serve, in the manner provided by CR 5.02, a copy of it on each adverse party to the appeal and on the judge whose decision is under review. In criminal cases both the defendant and the attorney general also shall serve copies of their briefs on the Commonwealth's attorney of the district in which the case was tried.

(6) Certificate required.

Every brief shall bear on the front cover a signed statement, in accordance with Rule 5.03, by the attorney or party that service has been made as required by this Rule, which statement shall identify by name the persons so served. Except for briefs on appeals from the Court of Appeals to the Supreme Court, the statement shall further certify that the record on appeal has been returned to the clerk of the trial court or that it was not withdrawn by the party filing the

brief. The name or names of the attorneys submitting a brief and responsible for its contents shall appear following its "Conclusion."

(7) Amicus curiae briefs.

A brief for an amicus curiae shall not be filed except on order of the appellate court pursuant to a motion specifying with particularity the nature of the movant's interest, the points to be presented, and their relevance to the disposition of the case. Payment of the filing fee specified in Rule 76.42(2)(a) shall be required with a motion for leave to file an amicus curiae brief and said motion shall be filed within fifteen (15) days of the filing of appellant's brief. An amicus curiae brief shall not exceed fifteen (15) pages, shall not contain appendices and shall be tendered with the motion.

(8) Penalties.

(a) A brief may be stricken for failure to comply with any substantial requirement of this Rule 76.12.

(b) If the appellant's brief has not been filed within the time allowed, the appeal may be dismissed.

(c) If the appellee's brief has not been filed within the time allowed, the court may: (i) accept the appellant's statement of the facts and issues as correct; (ii) reverse the judgment if appellant's brief reasonably appears to sustain such action; or (iii) regard the appellee's failure as a confession of error and reverse the judgment without considering the merits of the case.

HISTORY: Amended by Order 2010–09, eff. 1–1–11; prior amendments eff. 1–1–07 (Order 2006–09), 1–1–05 (Order 2004–5), 1–1–03 (Order 2002–1), 2–1–01 (Order 2000–2, 2000–1), 1–1–99 (Order 98–2), 1–1–97 (Order 96–1), 11–1–95, 10–1–94, 11–15–91, 1–1–89, 1–1–86, 1–1–85, 4–15–83, 7–1–81, 12–31–80, 5–1–80, 7–1–79, 7–1–78, 6–1–78; adopted eff. 1–1–78

CR 76.14   Prehearing conference—Deleted

HISTORY: Deleted by Order 91–2, eff. 11–15–91; prior amendments eff. 1–1–88, 1–1–87, 7–5–85, 7–1–85, 4–17–85, 1–1–85; adopted eff. 1–1–78

CR 76.15   Special appeals of the Court of Appeals—Deleted

HISTORY: Deleted by Order 91–2, eff. 11–15–91; adopted eff. 1–1–88

CR 76.16   Oral arguments

(1) Oral arguments on the merits will be heard in all cases appealed from the circuit court unless the appellate court directs otherwise on its own motion or on motion of one or more of the parties to the appeal. CR 76.12(4) provides for the parties to include in their brief statements concerning the need for oral argument in the appeal. In any case where the court orders on its own motion that oral argument shall be dispensed with, any party shall have ten (10) days from the date of the order in which to object and ask

for reconsideration. No opinion shall be rendered until the time has expired for making such objection and motion for reconsideration, or if such objection and motion is made, until it can be decided.

(2) In an oral argument the party upon whom the burden rests shall have the right to open and close. Unless otherwise directed each side will be allowed 15 minutes. Visual aids based on the record may be used at oral argument with leave of the court.

(3) Counsel representing an amicus curiae shall not participate in the oral argument without specific permission by the appellate court granted on motion.

(4) A person who is not an attorney at law will be permitted to make an oral argument only with special leave of the court.

(5)(a) In death penalty cases in which the appellant has been granted permission to file a brief exceeding fifty (50) pages, appellant shall file and serve upon appellee not later than fourteen (14) days before oral argument a notice of issues that appellant intends to argue orally, with specific reference to the argument number and page numbers of each issue in appellant's brief. If appellant fails to do so, without good cause, appellant's oral argument shall be limited to answering questions from the Court.

In death penalty cases, appellant shall file any motion for leave to cite supplemental authority for oral argument not later than fourteen (14) days before oral argument, unless good cause is shown for a later filing. In death penalty cases, appellee shall file any motion for leave to cite supplemental authority for oral argument not later than ten (10) days before oral argument or ten (10) days after service of appellant's designation of issues for oral argument, whichever is earlier, unless good cause is shown for a later filing.

(b) In all cases before the Supreme Court to which paragraph (5)(a) of this Rule does not apply, appellant or cross-appellant shall file and serve upon each appellee or cross-appellee not later than ten (10) days before oral argument a notice of issues in the order to be argued that the appellant or cross-appellant intends to argue orally, with specific reference to the argument number and page numbers of each issue in the appellant's or cross-appellant's brief. If the appellant or cross-appellant fails to do so, without good cause, the appellant's oral argument or the portion of the cross-appellant's oral argument devoted to issues raised in the cross-appeal shall be limited to answering questions from the court.

HISTORY: Amended by Order 2004–5, eff. 1–1–05; prior amendments eff. 2–1–01 (Order 2000–1), 1–1–99 (Order 98–2), 11–1–95 (Order 95–1), 9–15–90, 1–1–89, 10–1–82; adopted eff. 1–1–78

CR 76.18 Transfer of appeal from Court of Appeals to Supreme Court—Deleted

HISTORY: Deleted by Order 91–2, eff. 11–15–91; prior amendments eff. 1–1–89, 1–1–87, 9–1–80, 1–1–80, 10–1–78; adopted eff. 1–1–78

CR 76.20 Motion for discretionary review

(1) General.

A motion for discretionary review by the Supreme Court of a decision of the Court of Appeals, and a motion for such review by the Court of Appeals of a judgment of the circuit court in a case appealed to it from the district court, shall be prosecuted as provided by this Rule 76.20 and in accordance with the Rules generally applicable to other motions. Such review is a matter of judicial discretion and will be granted only when there are special reasons for it.

(2) Time for Motion.

(a) A motion for discretionary review by the Court of Appeals of a circuit court judgment in a case appealed from the district court shall be filed within 30 days after the date on which the judgment of the circuit court was entered, subject to the provisions of Rule 77.04(2) and Criminal Rule 12.06(2).

(b) A motion for discretionary review by the Supreme Court of a Court of Appeals decision shall be filed within 30 days after the date of the order or opinion sought to be reviewed unless (i) a timely petition under Rule 76.32 or (ii) a timely motion for reconsideration under Rule 76.38(2) has been filed or an extension of time has been granted for that purpose, in which event a motion for discretionary review shall be filed within 30 days after the date of the order denying the petition or motion for reconsideration or, if it was granted, within 30 days after the date of the opinion or order finally disposing of the case in the Court of Appeals.

(c) The failure of a party to file a Motion for Discretionary Review within the time specified in this Rule, or as extended by a previous order, shall result in a dismissal of the Motion for Discretionary Review.

(3) The Motion.

The motion shall designate the parties as Movant(s) and Respondent(s), shall not exceed fifteen (15) pages in length, unless otherwise authorized by the Court, and shall contain the following:

(a) The name of each movant and each respondent and the names and addresses of their counsel,

(b) The date of entry of the judgment sought to be reviewed, or the date of final disposition by the Court of Appeals, as the case may be,

(c) A statement of whether a supersedeas bond, or bail on appeal, has been executed,

(d) A clear and concise statement of (i) the material facts, (ii) the questions of law involved, and (iii) the specific reason or reasons why the judgment should be reviewed; and

(e) If the motion is addressed to the Supreme Court, a statement that the movant does not have a petition for rehearing or motion for reconsideration pending in the Court of Appeals,

(f) A statement showing whether any other party to the proceeding has a petition for rehearing or motion for reconsideration pending in the Court of Appeals.

(4) Record on Motion.

There shall be filed with each motion photocopies of the final order or judgment, any findings of fact, conclusions of law and opinion of the trial court, and any opinion or final order of the appellate court, including any decision on any petition for rehearing or motion for reconsideration. In administrative agency cases, copies of the findings of fact, conclusions of law and award or order of the administrative agency shall be filed. No other record on the motion shall be required unless the court to which the motion is addressed so orders.

(5) Response to Motion.

Each respondent may file a response to the motion within 30 days after the motion is filed. Said response shall not exceed fifteen (15) pages in length, unless otherwise authorized by the Court. No reply to a response shall be filed unless requested by the Court.

(6) Form, Signing, and Number of Copies Required.

The motion and the response shall be either printed or reproduced by an acceptable duplicating process, and shall be signed by each party or his counsel in his individual name, which signature shall constitute a certification that the statements of fact therein are true. Ten copies shall be filed for a motion in the Supreme Court, and five in the Court of Appeals.

(7) Service of Motion and Response.

Before filing, the motion and the response shall be served on the other parties and on the clerk of the court whose decision is sought to be reviewed, and such service shall be shown as provided in Rules 5.02 and 5.03.

(8) Submission.

The motion shall be submitted to the court for consideration when the response is filed or when the time for filing such response has expired, whichever is sooner.

(9) Disposition of Motion.

(a) If the motion is denied the decision shall stand affirmed, and if a supersedeas bond has been executed, damages for delay shall be recoverable pursuant to KRS Chapter 26A. The denial of a motion for discretionary review does not indicate approval of the opinion or order sought to be reviewed and shall not be cited as connoting such approval.

(b) If the motion is in the Supreme Court and is granted, the times prescribed in Rule 76.12(2) for the filing of briefs shall be computed from the date of the entry of the order granting the motion, the movant being regarded as the appellant and the respondent as the appellee.

(c) If the motion is in the Court of Appeals and is granted, the appeal shall be perfected in the same time and manner as if it were an appeal as a matter of right, unless otherwise directed by the court. Evidence designated under Rule 75.01 must be transcribed. The time prescribed by Rule 73.08 for preparation and certification of the record, and by Rule 75.01 for designation of the evidence or other proceedings requiring transcription, shall be computed from the date of the order granting the motion.

(d) A motion for discretionary review in the Supreme Court will not be ruled upon during the pendency of a petition for rehearing or motion for reconsideration in the Court of Appeals. If a party files a timely petition for rehearing or motion for reconsideration in the Court of Appeals after another party has filed a motion for discretionary review in the Supreme Court, the clerk shall withhold submission of the latter pending final disposition of the case in the Court of Appeals.

(e) A ruling by the Court of Appeals granting or denying a motion for discretionary review will not be reconsidered by the Court of Appeals. A ruling by the Supreme Court granting or denying a motion for discretionary review will not be reconsidered by the Supreme Court. A motion for reconsideration, however styled, shall not be accepted for filing by the clerk of the Supreme Court or Court of Appeals.

(f) Copies of the order shall be sent forthwith by the clerk of the appellate court to counsel for each party and to the clerk of the court whose decision is sought to be reviewed.

(10) Costs.

Payment of the filing fee specified in Rule 76.42(2)(a) shall be required with the motion.

HISTORY: Amended by Order 2000–2, eff. 2–1–01; prior amendments eff. 2–1–01 (Order 2000–1), 1–1–99 (Order 98–2), 9–1–93 (Order 93–1), 8–1–92, 8–28–89, 1–1–89, 1–1–85, 1–1–84, 7–1–81, 5–1–80, 7–1–79, 3–1–78; adopted eff. 1–1–78

CR 76.21   Cross motion for discretionary review

(1) If a motion for discretionary review is granted, the respondent shall then be permitted ten days thereafter in which to file a cross motion for discretionary review designating issues raised in the original appeal which are not included in the motion for discretionary review but which should be considered in reviewing the appeal in order to properly dispose of the case.

(2) This cross motion for discretionary review will be practiced in conformity with Rule 76.34, motion practice in appellate courts. Each cross respondent may file a response to the cross motion within 10 days after the cross motion is filed. No reply to a cross response shall be filed unless requested by the court. Ten copies of any cross motion or cross response shall be filed in the Supreme Court, and five in the Court of Appeals.

(3) The filing of a cross motion for discretionary review shall suspend the running of time for briefing discretionary review as heretofore granted, and the full time for briefing shall be computed from the date of the order granting or denying the cross motion for discretionary review.

(4) If the cross motion for discretionary review is granted, the moving party shall brief the new issues thus raised in this brief responding to the brief on behalf of the original movant, and the original movant shall then be permitted to reply to these further issues in the reply brief permitted by Rule 76.12.

HISTORY: Amended by Order 86–3, eff. 1–1–87; adopted eff. 1–1–86

CR 76.22 Advancement

Appeals may be advanced for good cause shown.

HISTORY: Amended by Order 2004–5, eff. 1–1–05; adopted eff. 1–1–78

CR 76.24 Substitution of parties

(a) Death of a Party. If a party dies after a notice of appeal is filed or while a proceeding is otherwise pending in the appellate court, the personal representative of the deceased party may be substituted as a party on motion filed by the representative or by any party with the clerk of the appellate court. The motion of a party shall be served upon the representative in accordance with the provisions of Rule 25. If the deceased party has no representative, any party may suggest the death on the record and proceedings shall then be had as the appellate court may direct. If a party against whom an appeal may be taken dies after entry of a judgment or order in the trial court but before a notice of appeal is filed, an appellant may proceed as if death had not occurred. After the notice of appeal is filed substitution shall be effected in the appellate court in accordance with this subdivision. If a party entitled to appeal shall die before filing a notice of appeal, the notice of appeal may be filed by his personal representative, or, if he has no personal representative, by his attorney of record within the time prescribed by these rules. After the notice of appeal is filed substitution shall be effected in the appellate court in accordance with this substitution.

(b) Substitution for Other Causes. If substitution of a party in the appellate court is necessary for any reason other than death, substitution shall be effected in accordance with the procedure prescribed in subdivision (a).

(c) Public Officers; Death or Separation from Office.

(1) When a public officer is a party to an appeal or other proceeding in the appellate court in his official capacity and during its pendency dies, resigns or otherwise ceases to hold office, the action does not abate and his successor is automatically substituted as a party. Proceedings following the substitution shall be in the name of the substituted party, but any misnomer not affecting the substantial rights of the parties shall be disregarded. An order of substitution may be entered at any time, but the failure to enter such an order shall not affect the substitution.

(2) When a public officer is a party to an appeal or other proceeding in his official capacity he may be described as a party by his official title rather than by name; but the court may require his name to be added.

HISTORY: Amended by Order 90–1, eff. 9–15–90; adopted eff. 1–1–78

CR 76.25 Review of Workers' Compensation Board decisions

(1) General.

Pursuant to Section 111(2) of the Kentucky Constitution and SCR 1.030(3), decisions of the Workers' Compensation Board shall be subject to direct review by the Court of Appeals in accordance with the procedures set out in this Rule.

(2) Time for Petition.

Within 30 days of the date upon which the Board enters its final decision pursuant to KRS 342.285(3) any party aggrieved by that decision may file a petition for review by the Court of Appeals and pay the filing fee required by CR 76.42(2)(a)(xi). Failure to file the petition within the time allowed shall require dismissal of the petition.

(3) Number of Copies.

An original and four (4) copies of the petition shall be filed with the Clerk of the Court of Appeals. The petition shall conform in all respects to CR 7.02(4) and be secured on the left side. Petitions shall be covered in red. Responses shall be covered in blue.

(4) Petition.

The petition shall designate the parties as appellant(s) and appellee(s) and shall contain the following:

(a) The name of each appellant and each appellee and the names and addresses of their respective counsel. The appellant shall specifically designate as appellees all adverse parties and the Workers' Compensation Board.

(b) The petition shall state the date of the entry of the decision by the administrative law judge and the date of entry of the final decision of the Workers' Compensation Board.

(c) Each petition shall begin with a table of points and authorities stating the issues to be raised. The petition shall contain a clear and concise statement of (i) the material facts, (ii) the questions of law involved, and (iii) the specific reason(s) why relief from the Board's decision should be granted by the Court of Appeals. The petition shall be prepared with the expectation that it will be the only pleading filed by the appellant in the appeal.

(d) Copies of the following documents shall be attached to the original and each copy of the petition filed in the Court of Appeals: (i) the decision of the administrative law judge, (ii) the final decision of the Workers' Compensation Board, and (iii) a set of the briefs filed with the Board by the appellant and each appellee. If review is sought of a decision on a motion to reopen, copies of the motion to reopen, any responses thereto, and decisions on that motion by the administrative law judge and the Board shall be attached.

(e) The petition shall clearly state whether there is or is not any other action concerning the injury pending before any other state or federal court or administrative body.

(5) Record.

Upon receipt of the petition, the clerk of the Court of Appeals will request that the original record of the Workers' Compensation Board be prepared by the board in conformity with CR 75.07(9) and (10), certified within a maximum of sixty (60) days, and transported forthwith to the office of the Clerk of the Court of Appeals.

(6) Response to Petition.

Each appellee may file an original and four copies of a response to the petition within 20 days of the date on which the petition was filed with the Court of Appeals. No reply to the response shall be filed without leave of Court.

(7) Certification.

The petition and the response shall be signed by each party or his counsel and that signature shall constitute a certification that the statements therein are true and made in good faith.

(8) Service of Petition and Response.

Before filing, a copy of the petition and any response shall be served on counsel of record, or on any party not represented by counsel, and on the Workers' Compensation Board. Such service shall be shown by certificate on the petition or response when filed in the Court of Appeals pursuant to CR 5.02 and CR 5.03. In any case in which the constitutionality of a statute is questioned, a copy of the petition and response shall be served on the Attorney General of the Commonwealth by the party challenging the validity of the statute. The Attorney General may file an entry of appearance within ten (10) days of the date of such service. If no entry of appearance is filed, no further pleadings need be served on the Attorney General.

(9) Cross-Petition; Response.

(a) Any party designated as an appellee may file a cross-petition within twenty (20) days following filing of the petition. The cross-petition shall state the name of each cross-appellant and each cross-appellee and the names and addresses of their respective counsel. The cross-petition shall contain a clear and con-

cise statement of the issues which the cross-appellant seeks to raise and any material facts relevant to those issues not presented in the petition.

(b) Any cross-appellee may file a response to the cross-petition within twenty (20) days of the filing of the cross-petition.

(c) The original and four copies of the cross-petition and response shall be filed with the Clerk of the Court of Appeals.

(d) Cross-petitions and responses shall be signed in accordance with paragraph (7) of this Rule, and shall be served in accordance with paragraph (8) of this Rule, with colored covers and binding in accordance with paragraph (3) of this Rule.

(10) Submission.

The petition, any responses, cross-petitions, and the record shall be submitted to the Court of Appeals for review, and the matter shall proceed further as directed by order of the Court of Appeals. The court may order the filing of briefs under CR 76.12 or direct that the appeal be submitted for decision based only upon the petition and response.

(11) Disposition.

After the Court of Appeals issues a decision, the Clerk of the Court of Appeals shall send a copy of the decision of the Court of Appeals to counsel for each party and to the Workers' Compensation Board.

(12) Procedure for Further Review.

Further review may be sought in the Supreme Court of a final decision or final order of the Court of Appeals in a Workers' Compensation matter, and shall be prosecuted in accordance with the rules generally applicable to other appeals pursuant to CR 76.12 and CR 76.36.

HISTORY: Amended by Order 2001–2, eff. 1–1–02; prior amendments eff. 1–1–99 (Order 98–2), 10–1–94 (Order 94–1), 9–1–93, 11–15–91, 8–28–89, 5–4–88; adopted eff. 1–15–88

CR 76.26　Submission of appeals

Appeals will be submitted for consideration on the merits by the appellate court when all briefs have been filed or when the time for such filing has expired, whichever is sooner. No paper filed or tendered after submission will be considered unless filed with leave of court.

HISTORY: Adopted eff. 1–1–78

CR 76.28　Opinions
(1) Written Opinions.

(a) Appellate court opinions and orders may be announced orally but shall be reduced to writing and, except for unanimous actions of the Supreme Court, shall list the names of the members concurring or dissenting and indicate the name of any member who did not participate in the decision.

(b) Opinions and orders finally deciding a case on the merits shall include an explanation of the legal reasoning underlying the decision.

(2) Time of Announcement.

Unless otherwise determined by the Supreme Court, opinions of the Supreme Court will be released for publication on Thursdays. Opinions of the Court of Appeals shall be released on Fridays. However, if a Friday is a state holiday, the Court of Appeals, at the discretion of the Chief Judge may render opinions on the last working day before the holiday. The time of publication shall be 10:00 A.M. prevailing Frankfort time.

(3) Distribution of Copies.

Promptly after an opinion is handed down the clerk shall send a copy to the trial judge, to any intermediate court which made a decision in the case, and to each attorney in the case. Copies shall be furnished to other persons as directed by the court.

(4) Publication.

(a) When a motion for discretionary review under Rule 76.20 is filed with the Supreme Court, the opinion of the Court of Appeals in the case under review shall not be published until the Supreme Court rules on the motion for discretionary review or until the Court permits the motion to be withdrawn. Unless otherwise ordered by the Supreme Court, upon entry of an order denying the motion for discretionary review or granting withdrawal of the motion, the opinion of the Court of Appeals shall be published if the opinion was designated "To Be Published" by the Court of Appeals. Upon entry of an order of the Supreme Court granting a motion for discretionary review the opinion of the Court of Appeals shall not be published, unless otherwise ordered by the Supreme Court. All other opinions of the appellate courts will be published as directed by the court issuing the opinion. Every opinion shall show on its face whether it is "To Be Published" or "Not To Be Published."

(b) The court rendering an opinion that is to be published shall provide a copy of it forthwith to the reporter for West Publishing Company. Except for those that are not to be published, opinions of an appellate court shall be released for publication by its clerk.

(c) Opinions that are not to be published shall not be cited or used as binding precedent in any other case in any court of this state; however, unpublished Kentucky appellate decisions, rendered after January 1, 2003, may be cited for consideration by the court if there is no published opinion that would adequately address the issue before the court. Opinions cited for consideration by the court shall be set out as an unpublished decision in the filed document and a copy of the entire decision shall be tendered along with the document to the court and all parties to the action.

(5) Withdrawal of Opinions.

Parties to an appeal may not by agreement dismiss an appeal and have an opinion withdrawn after it has been issued.

HISTORY: Amended by Order 2009–01, eff. 4–1–09; prior amendments eff. 1–1–07 (Order 2006–09), 1–1–99 (Order 98–2), 8–1–92 (Order 92–1), 8–28–89, 1–1–88, 1–1–86, 1–1–85, 1–1–84, 10–1–82, 7–1–81, 5–1–80, 1–1–80; adopted eff. 1–1–78

CR 76.30   Effective date of opinions

(1) Scope of Rule.

This Rule 76.30 applies to any final decision of an appellate court styled an "Opinion." A decision styled an "Opinion and Order" is an order, and is governed by Rule 76.38.

(2) Finality.

(a) An opinion of the Supreme Court becomes final on the 21st day after the date of its rendition unless a petition under Rule 76.32 has been timely filed or an extension of time has been granted for that purpose. An opinion of the Court of Appeals becomes final on the 31st day after the date of its rendition unless a petition under Rule 76.32 or a motion for review under Rule 76.20 has been timely filed or an extension of time has been granted for one of those purposes.

(b) In the event of a timely motion for review under Rule 76.20, the opinion becomes final immediately upon denial of the motion.

(c) In the event of a timely petition under Rule 76.32, (i) if it is in the Supreme Court and is denied, the opinion becomes final immediately upon such denial, but if the petition is granted and a new or revised opinion is rendered, the new or revised opinion becomes final on the 21st day after the date of its rendition unless otherwise ordered, or unless a further petition under Rule 76.32 has been timely filed or an extension of time has been granted for that purpose; (ii) if it is in the Court of Appeals and is denied, the opinion becomes final on the 31st day after the date the petition was denied unless a motion for review under Rule 76.20 has been timely filed; (iii) if it is in the Court of Appeals and is granted, and a new or revised opinion rendered, the new or revised opinion becomes final on the 31st day after the date of its rendition unless otherwise ordered, or unless a further petition under Rule 76.32 or a motion for review under Rule 76.20 has been timely filed or an extension of time has been granted for one of those purposes.

(d) Unless otherwise ordered, (i) in no event shall an opinion become final pending final disposition of a timely petition under Rule 76.32 or a timely motion for review under Rule 76.20; and (ii) in every case it shall become final when no such motion or petition has been filed within the time allowed for that purpose.

(e) When an opinion has become final, the clerk of the appellate court that rendered it shall forthwith send to the clerk of the trial court and, if the opinion results from a review of the decision of another appellate court, to the clerk of that court also, a copy of the opinion with an endorsement stamped thereon showing the date upon which it became final, whereupon the clerk of the trial court shall forthwith file the opinion as enclosed in the original record and note the filing on the proper docket. In the event a final opinion directs that an administrative agency, board, or commission conduct further proceedings with respect to such action, the clerk of the trial court shall forthwith remand the action to the administrative agency, board, or commission before which said action originated without further order of the trial court.

(f) No mandate shall be required to effectuate the final decision of an appellate court, whether entered by order or by opinion.

HISTORY: Amended by Order 98–2, eff. 1–1–99; prior amendments eff. 1–1–88 (Order 87–1), 7–1–81; adopted eff. 1–1–78

CR 76.32 Petitions for rehearing
(1) When authorized.

(a) A party adversely affected by an opinion of the Supreme Court or Court of Appeals in an appealed case may petition the Court for (i) a rehearing or (ii) a modification or extension of the opinion, or both, and the opposing party may file a response. When final disposition of an appeal is made by an order, or an "opinion and order," the party adversely affected may move for a reconsideration as provided by Rule 76.38(2), but a petition for rehearing is not authorized.

(b) Except in extraordinary cases when justice demands it, a petition for rehearing shall be limited to a consideration of the issues argued on the appeal and will be granted only when it appears that the court has overlooked a material fact in the record, or a controlling statute or decision, or has misconceived the issues presented on the appeal or the law applicable thereto.

(c) When it is desired to point out and have corrected any inaccuracies in statements of law or fact contained in an opinion of the court, or to extend the opinion to cover matters in issue not discussed therein, and the result reached in the opinion is not questioned, a party may request a modification or extension.

(d) In the event a petition for rehearing is granted, a party adversely affected by the new opinion may petition for a rehearing, modification or extension under the same rules governing the original petition for rehearing, modification or extension, but unless the court directs otherwise there shall be no response to the second or any further petition for rehearing.

(e) A party who has moved for a discretionary review by the Supreme Court under Rule 76.20 shall not be authorized to file a petition for rehearing of the same case in the Court of Appeals unless the order or opinion sought to be reviewed is revised or set aside pursuant to a petition for rehearing filed by another party, in which event the pending motion for discretionary review shall be dismissed without prejudice to a subsequent motion for discretionary review of the order or opinion finally disposing of the case in the Court of Appeals. The filing of a subsequent motion for discretionary review following a dismissal without prejudice under this paragraph (e) shall not require payment of another filing fee under Rule 76.42(2)(a)(iv).

(2) Time for filing.

A petition for rehearing, modification or extension shall be filed within 20 days after the date on which the opinion was issued, and any response thereto shall be filed within 20 days after the date on which the petition was filed. The failure of a party to timely file the petition shall result in the appeal becoming final.

(3) Form.

(a) All petitions and responses shall be in the form prescribed by Rule 76.12(4), but with covers colored as follows: Petition—Green; Response—Gray.

(b) Every petition shall bear the style of the court's opinion, shall indicate in the caption whether it is presented by the appellant or appellee, and shall include a copy of the opinion of which complaint is made.

(c) Petitions for rehearing and responses shall be limited to 10 pages each, exclusive of copies of the opinion.

(4) Number of copies.

Petitions and responses in the Court of Appeals shall be filed in quintuplicate. In the Supreme Court ten copies shall be filed.

(5) Service and certification.

Every petition and response shall be served as required by Rule 76.12(5) for briefs and shall bear on the front cover a signed statement, in accordance with Rule 5.03, by the attorney or party that service has been made as required by this rule, which statement shall identify by name the persons so served. The name or names of the attorneys submitting a petition for rehearing, extension or modification or response thereto, and responsible for its contents, shall appear at its conclusion.

(6) Disposition.

(a) *In the Supreme Court.*

A petition for rehearing will be assigned to a justice other than the one who prepared the opinion.

(b) *In the Court of Appeals.*

A petition for rehearing will be assigned to a member of the panel that decided the case, other than the member who prepared the opinion.

(7) Costs.

Payment of the filing fee specified in Rule 76.42(2)(a) shall be required with a petition for rehearing or modification or extension of an opinion.

HISTORY: Amended by Order 93–1, eff. 9–1–93; prior amendments eff. 11–15–91, 7–1–81, 5–1–80, 7–1–79; adopted eff. 1–1–78

CR 76.33 Intermediate relief in appellate court

(1) When Authorized.

At any time after a notice of appeal or a motion for discretionary review pursuant to Rule 76.20 has been filed, a party to the appeal or motion may move the appellate court for intermediate relief upon a satisfactory showing that otherwise he will suffer immediate and irreparable injury before a hearing may be had on the motion.

(2) Record Required.

Unless the record on appeal has been transmitted to the appellate court, a motion pursuant to this rule shall be accompanied by a partial record pursuant to CR 75.10.

(3) Costs.

Payment of the filing fee specified in Rule 76.42(2)(a) shall be required with the motion.

HISTORY: Amended by Order 91–2, eff. 11–15–91; prior amendments eff. 8–28–89, 1–1–87, 1–1–86, 7–1–81; adopted eff. 1–1–78

CR 76.34 Motions

(1) Applicability of Other Rules.

Rules 5.01, 5.02, 5.03, 5.05, 6.04, 6.05 and 7.02 shall apply to all motions other than motions for transfer to the Supreme Court and motions for discretionary review, except that the movant shall not specify a time for hearing in the motion or notice unless the time has been set as provided by paragraph (4) of this Rule 76.34.

(2) Response.

The opposing party may file a response, accompanied by a certificate of service, within 10 days after the date the motion was served or within the time otherwise designated by the court.

(3) Number of Copies.

Five (5) copies of motions and responses in the Court of Appeals shall be filed. Except as otherwise required by Rule 65.09(1), Rule 74.02(1), Rule 76.20(6) and Rule 76.37(11), five (5) copies of motions and responses in the Supreme Court shall be filed, unless the Court directs otherwise.

(4) Hearing and Disposition.

(a) Except for motions that call for final disposition of an appeal or original action in the appellate court, any member of the court designated by the Chief Justice or Chief Judge may hear and dispose of any motion; and

(b) Any intermediate order of a procedural nature pending final disposition of a proceeding pending in an appellate court may be issued on the signature of any judge of that court.

(5) Oral Arguments.

No motion will be heard on oral argument except by prearrangement with an authorized representative of the appellate court or with the judge to whom the motion is addressed or has been assigned.

(6) Motion to Dismiss Appeal or Cross–Appeal.

(a) In addition to any other relief provided by these Rules, an adversary party may move to dismiss an appeal or cross-appeal because it is not within the jurisdiction of the appellate court or because it has not been prosecuted in conformity with the Rules; and

(b) Timely filing of a motion to dismiss shall suspend the running of time for procedural steps otherwise required with regard to the appeal and any cross-appeal in the same proceeding, and the time will continue to run as provided by Rule 76.12(2) after the date an order is entered denying the motion or passing it to the merits.

HISTORY: Amended by Order 93–1, eff. 9–1–93; prior amendments eff. 8–28–89, 1–1–85, 7–1–79; adopted eff. 1–1–78

CR 76.36 Original proceedings in appellate court

(1) Petition for relief.

Original proceedings in an appellate court may be prosecuted only against a judge or agency whose decisions may be reviewed as a matter of right by that appellate court. All other actions must be prosecuted in accordance with applicable law. Original proceedings in an appellate court may be prosecuted upon the payment of the filing fee required by CR 76.42(2)(a) and the filing of a petition setting forth:

(a) The name of each respondent against whom relief is sought;

(b) The style and file number of the underlying action before the respondent(s);

(c) The facts upon which petitioner claims entitlement to relief;

(d) The relief sought;

(e) A memorandum of authorities in support of the petition.

A copy of the petition shall be served on each respondent and each real party in interest as defined in this Rule, Section (8), and shall bear proof of service as required by Rule 5.03. Immediately upon the filing of the petition, the clerk shall mail to each respondent and real party in interest notice of the date the petition was filed.

(2) Response.

The party against whom relief is sought and real party in interest as defined in this Rule, section (8), may within 20 days after the date of filing of the petition file a response, bearing proof of service as required by Rule 5.03, accompanied by a memorandum of authorities in support of his defense.

(3) Number of copies.

Petitions and responses shall be filed in quintuplicate.

(4) Intermediate relief.

If the petitioner requires any relief prior to the expiration of 20 days after the date of filing the petition he/she may move the court on notice for a temporary order on the ground that he/she will suffer immediate and irreparable injury before a hearing may be had on the petition.

(5) Evidence.

Evidence in support of or against the petition, other than that which may be attached to the petition and response in the form of exhibits, affidavits, and counter-affidavits, will be permitted only by order of the court, and it shall be in the form of affidavits or depositions taken in accordance with the Rules applicable to proceedings in trial courts. Oral testimony will not be heard in the appellate court.

(6) Submission and disposition.

Original actions will be submitted for decision when the response is filed or the time for filing it has expired, whichever is sooner, unless otherwise ordered by the court.

(7) Appeals to the Supreme Court.

(a) An appeal may be taken to the Supreme Court as a matter of right from a judgment or final order in any proceeding originating in the Court of Appeals.

(b) The notice of appeal and the filing fee required by CR 76.42(2)(a)(i) shall be filed with the Clerk of the Court of Appeals within 30 days after the date the judgment or order appealed from was entered and shall conform to the requirements of Rule 73.03. A cross-appeal may be taken in the time and manner specified by Rule 74.01 except that the notice of cross-appeal and filing fee shall be timely filed by the Clerk of the Court of Appeals.

(c) To perfect the appeal the appellant shall, within thirty (30) days after filing a notice of appeal, file with the Clerk of the Supreme Court a brief setting forth argument for reversal or modification of the judgment or order from which the appeal is taken. In workers' compensation cases, briefing shall proceed according to CR 76.12.

(d) When the appeal has been perfected and entered in the docket book the clerk of the Supreme Court shall forthwith mail notice of the date of such entry to the attorneys for the parties.

(e) To perfect a cross-appeal, within 30 days after the mailing of the clerk's notice mentioned in the preceding subparagraph (d) of this Rule 76.36(7), or within 30 days after expiration of the time allowed for the appellant to perfect the appeal, whichever is the

sooner, the party taking the cross-appeal shall file with the clerk of the Supreme Court a brief setting forth the arguments for reversal or modification of the judgment or order from which the cross-appeal is taken and against the relief sought by the appellant.

(f) Briefs in response to an appeal or cross-appeal shall be required. Such briefs shall be filed in accord with the provisions of CR 76.12(2)(a) and (b).

Where an appeal is taken against a judge in the Court of Justice and concerns performance of an official act, the party appealing shall serve notice on the real party in interest as defined in this Rule, section (8), who shall then be required to file a brief on behalf of the judge against whom the appeal or cross-appeal is taken; provided, however, no attorney shall be required or permitted to file such a brief where to do so would conflict with the interest of his or her client.

(g) Ten (10) copies of the briefs shall be filed. Briefs need not be printed.

(h) The clerk of the Court of Appeals shall transmit all or any portion of the original record of the proceedings to the Supreme Court when so requested by the clerk of that court.

(8) Real party in interest.

For the purpose of this rule only, the term "real party in interest" is any party in the circuit court action from which the original action arises who may be adversely affected by the relief sought pursuant to this Rule.

HISTORY: Amended by Order 2010–09, eff. 1–1–11; prior amendments eff. 4–1–09 (Order 2009–01), 1–1–07 (Order 2006–09), 2–1–01 (Order 2000–1), 10–1–94 (Order 94–1), 9–1–93, 11–15–91, 9–15–90, 1–1–85, 7–1–79; adopted eff. 1–1–78

CR 76.37   Certification of question of law

(1) Power to answer.

If there are involved in any proceeding before the Supreme Court of the United States, any Court of Appeals of the United States, any District Court of the United States, the highest appellate court of any other state, or the District of Columbia, questions of law of this state which may be determinative of the cause then pending before the originating court and as to which it appears to the party or the originating court that there is no controlling precedent in the decisions of the Supreme Court and the Court of Appeals of this state, the Kentucky Supreme Court may answer those questions of law when certified to it by the originating court, or after judgment in the District Court upon petition of any party to the proceeding.

(2) Method of invoking.

This Rule may be invoked by an order of any of the courts referred to in paragraph (1) of this Rule upon the court's own motion or upon the motion of any party to the cause.

(3) Contents of certification order.

A certification order shall set forth

(a) the questions of law to be answered;

(b) a statement of all facts relevant to the questions certified and showing fully the nature of the controversy in which the questions arose;

(c) the names of each appellant and appellee; and

(d) the names and addresses of counsel for each appellant and appellee.

(4) Preparation of certification order.

The certification order shall be prepared by the certifying court, signed by the judge presiding at the hearing, and forwarded to the Supreme Court by the clerk of the certifying court under its official seal. The Supreme Court may require the original or copies of all or such portion of the record before the certifying court as it deems necessary to a determination of the questions certified to it.

(5) Costs of certification.

Fees and costs shall be the same as in civil appeals docketed before the Supreme Court and shall be equally divided between the parties unless otherwise ordered by the certifying court in its order of certification and each party shall pay its share of the filing fee within the 30–day period allowed by paragraph (6) of this Rule for filing of briefs.

(6) Briefs and argument.

Each of the parties desiring to be heard shall within 30 days after the date of the order of the Kentucky Supreme Court accepting certification file with the clerk of the Supreme Court 10 copies of a brief setting forth his arguments. Oral arguments will not be required or permitted unless so ordered by the Supreme Court.

(7) Opinion.

The written opinion of the Supreme Court stating the law governing the questions certified shall be sent by the clerk under the seal of the Supreme Court to the certifying court and to the parties.

(8) Power to certify.

The Supreme Court on its own motion or the motion of any party may order certification of questions of law to the highest court of any state or the District of Columbia when it appears to the certifying court that there are involved in any proceeding before the court questions of law of the receiving state or district which may be determinative of the cause then pending in the certifying court and it appears to the certifying court that there are no controlling precedents in the decisions of the highest court or intermediate appellate courts of the receiving state.

(9) Procedure on certifying.

The procedures for certification from this state to the receiving state shall be those provided in the laws of the receiving state or district.

(10) Certification of law by the Commonwealth.

A request by the Commonwealth of Kentucky pursuant to Section 115 of the Constitution of Kentucky for a certification of law shall be initiated in the Supreme Court. The request shall be initiated within thirty (30) days of a final order adverse to the Commonwealth. The Commonwealth shall initiate the certification procedure by motion requesting the Supreme Court to accept the question(s) for review. The motion shall contain the same elements as provided in this Rule, section (3), for a certification order. The motion shall be served and response permitted in conformity with the rules applicable to motion practice in the Supreme Court. If the motion is sustained, thereafter the case shall proceed in the same manner as any other appeal.

(11) Ten (10) copies of the certification order from another court or the request for certification by the Commonwealth, and the response, if any, shall be filed with the Clerk of the Supreme Court.

HISTORY: Amended by Order 93–1, eff. 9–1–93; prior amendments eff. 8–28–89, 1–1–86, 1–1–85, 1–1–84, 10–1–82; adopted eff. 9–1–78

CR 76.38 Effective date and reconsideration of orders

(1) Effective date.

Unless otherwise directed, all orders of an appellate court, including those in original proceedings under Rule 76.36, are effective upon entry and filing with the clerk. A decision or ruling styled an "Opinion and Order" is an order.

(2) Reconsideration.

Unless otherwise provided by these Rules or ordered by the court, a party adversely affected by a decision rendered by order may within 10 days after the date of its entry move the court to reconsider it. On ex parte motion the court may suspend the effectiveness of such order pending disposition of the motion to reconsider. The timely filing of a motion to reconsider an order granting or denying a motion to dismiss shall suspend the running of time to the same extent as provided by Rule 76.34(6)(b) with respect to the filing of a motion to dismiss.

(3) Paragraph (2) of this Rule 76.38 shall not apply to orders granting or denying interlocutory relief under Rule 65.07 or Rule 65.08, to orders granting or denying transfer under Rule 74.02, to orders granting or denying discretionary review under Rule 76.20, or to orders granting or denying a petition for rehearing under Rule 76.32, which orders will not be reconsidered.

(4) Orders granting or denying reconsideration under this Rule will not be reconsidered.

HISTORY: Amended by Order 2009–01, eff. 4–1–09; prior amendments eff. 1–1–97 (Order 96–1), 9–1–93, 8–28–89, 7–1–81, 12–31–80, 7–1–79; adopted eff. 1–1–78

CR 76.40   Time

(1) Computation and extension.

The computation of any period of time under these rules shall be governed by Rule 6.01. Extensions of time, unless restricted by the applicable rule, may be obtained as provided by Rule 6.02. Parties may not by agreement extend time without leave of court.

(2) Timely filing.

To be timely filed, a document must be received by the Clerk of the Supreme Court or the Clerk of the Court of Appeals within the time specified for filing, except that any document shall be deemed timely filed if it has been transmitted by United States registered (not certified) or express mail, or by other recognized mail carriers, with the date the transmitting agency received said document from the sender noted by the transmitting agency on the outside of the container used for transmitting, within the time allowed for filing.

HISTORY: Amended by Order 93–1, eff. 9–1–93; prior amendments eff. 1–1–85, 1–1–84, 10–1–82; adopted eff. 1–1–78

CR 76.42   Costs

(1) Costs taxable.

Except for a filing fee, no costs shall be taxed in proceedings in the Supreme Court and Court of Appeals unless depositions are taken in an original action as authorized by Rule 76.36(5), in which event the reporter's fees for taking and transcribing the depositions shall be charged to the unsuccessful party.

(2) Filing fees.

(a) Filing fees for docketing the following in the Court of Appeals or in the Supreme Court shall be:

(i)	Appeal, cross appeal or certification of law	$150.00
(ii)	Appeals or cross appeals from Circuit Court, Family Division, to the Court of Appeals, from orders determining:	$ 75.00
	(a) Paternity	
	(b) Dependency, neglect or abuse	
	(c) Domestic violence	
	(d) Juvenile status offense	
(iii)	Motion for transfer	$150.00
(iv)	Motion or cross-motion for discretionary review	$150.00
(v)	Petition for rehearing, modification or extension of opinion	$150.00
(vi)	Motion for leave to file amicus curiae brief	$150.00
(vii)	Motion for extension of time for certification of record, for intermediate relief, or for dismissal of an adversary party's appeal, if the filing fee has not been paid theretofore	$150.00
(viii)	Motion for relief under Rules 65.07 or 65.09	$150.00
(ix)	Original proceeding	$150.00
(x)	Motion for reconsideration of a final order or "Opinion and Order" under Rule 76.38	$150.00
(xi)	Petition or cross-petition for review of a decision by the Workers' Compensation Board	$150.00

(b) If prior to its perfection an appeal has been docketed for purposes of a motion for extension of time for certification of the record on appeal, for intermediate relief, or for dismissal of an adversary party's appeal, no further filing fee shall be required in order to perfect or make any other motion pertaining to that appeal during its pendency. No filing fee shall be payable in a criminal proceeding in which the appellant or appellants are represented by the Public Defender. No filing fee shall be payable by the Commonwealth, but in civil actions it shall be liable for reimbursement of costs as provided by paragraph (3) of this Rule to the same extent as any other unsuccessful party. Judicial officers of the Court of Justice who are litigants in their official capacities shall not be liable for reimbursement or for the payment of filing fees except as may be required by the Supreme Court in actions arising under Rule 4 (Judicial Retirement and Removal Commission).

(3) Collection.

Forthwith upon the final disposition of any action in an appellate court, the clerk shall send the parties a statement of what portion, if any, of the filing fee or fees mentioned in paragraph (2) of this Rule 76.42 shall be reimbursed by one party to the other, to the end that the costs of each appeal or original action shall be borne by the unsuccessful party or parties. Liability for reimbursement of costs may be enforced on motion without necessity of an independent proceeding.

HISTORY: Amended by Order 2008–01, eff. 7–1–08; prior amendments eff. 1–1–07 (Order 2006–09), 1–1–97 (Order 96–1), 9–1–93, 1–1–90, 5–4–88, 1–15–88, 1–1–88, 10–1–82, 7–1–81, 12–31–80, 3–1–78; adopted eff. 1–1–78

CR 76.43   Number of documents required for docketing

Required number of documents for docketing in the Court of Appeals and/or Supreme Court shall be:

	Supreme Court	Court of Appeals	Rule References
(a) Motion Interlocutory Relief		5	67.07 and 65.08
(b) Motion Interlocutory Relief	10		65.09
(c) Briefs	10	5	76.12
(d) Petition for Rehearing & Responses thereto	10	5	76.32
(e) Prehearing Conference Statement	N/A	1	76.03
(f) Position Statement (Special Appeals)	N/A	5	76.05
(g) Motion to Transfer & Responses thereto	10	N/A	74.02
(h) Motion for Discretionary Review & Responses thereto (including Cross Motion)	10	5	76.20

	Supreme Court	Court of Appeals	Rule References
(i) Petition for Review Workers' Compensation Proceedings	N/A	5	76.25
(j) Motions/Responses (unless the court directs otherwise), except: Motion to Transfer, Motion for Discretionary Review, Certification of Law and CR 65.09	5	5	76.34 (including 76.38 Reconsideration)
(k) Original Proceedings (Mandamus/Prohibition) and Responses thereto	10	5	76.36
(*l*) Certification of Law	10	N/A	76.37

For other requirements, refer to appropriate Rule.

HISTORY: Amended by Order 94–1, eff. 10–1–94; prior amendment eff. 8–1–92; adopted eff. 8–28–89

CR 76.44 Stay pending review by United States Supreme Court

The taking of an appeal to the Supreme Court of the United States or the filing in that court of a petition for review on a writ of certiorari does not affect the finality of an opinion or final order. An order staying execution or enforcement of an opinion or final order may be entered upon motion under the following conditions and circumstances and for the periods designated:

(a) When an appeal is taken to the Supreme Court of the United States by the filing of a notice of appeal with the clerk of an appellate court as required by Rule 10 of the Rules of the Supreme Court of the United States and otherwise in accordance with Part IV of the Rules of that court, a stay during the pendency of the appeal may be granted on motion by any judge of the appellate court from which the appeal is taken, and shall be granted in appeals involving a sentence of death. The stay may be conditioned upon the giving of security to be fixed and approved by the judge that the appeal will be duly perfected and prosecuted as required by the Rules of the Supreme

Court of the United States, and if the stay is to act as a supersedeas, a supersedeas bond shall be required in accordance with Rule 18 of the Rules of the Supreme Court of the United States. (Supreme Court Rules may be found in 28 U.S.C.A. Rules, Supreme Court); and

(b) When a party desires to make application for a writ of certiorari, a stay may be granted by any judge of the appellate court for such specified number of days not exceeding 90, as may reasonably be required to enable the writ to be obtained, and may be conditioned upon the giving of adequate security as specified in Title 28, Section 2101(f), U.S. Code.

HISTORY: Amended by Order 84–2, eff. 1–1–85; prior amendment eff. 7–1–81; adopted eff. 1–1–78

CR 76.46 Preservation and disposition of records

(1) Withdrawal from custody of clerk.

Records or parts thereof shall be taken from the custody of the clerk of the appellate court only under extraordinary circumstances and upon order of the court, except that unless otherwise directed by the Supreme Court the attorney general and public defender may be permitted by the clerk of an appellate court to have temporary custody of records in criminal and quasi-criminal cases for the purpose of preparing briefs.

(2) Transmittal from Court of Appeals to Supreme Court.

Upon the granting of a motion for review by the Supreme Court the clerk of the Court of Appeals shall forward the record on appeal to the clerk of the Supreme Court, together with the briefs and all other relevant papers on file in his office.

(3) Return to trial court.

Upon final disposition of an appeal the clerk shall return the original record to the clerk of the trial court. All other records shall be retained or microfilmed. Clearly legible microfilms may be retained in lieu of hard copies. Physical exhibits may be disposed of at any time as the court directs.

HISTORY: Amended by Order 81–4, eff. 7–1–81; adopted eff. 1–1–78

X COURTS AND CLERKS

CR 77 Courts and clerks

CR 77.01 Courts always open

The courts of this Commonwealth shall be deemed always open for the purpose of filing any pleading or other proper paper, of issuing and returning mesne and final process, and of making and directing all interlocutory motions, orders and rules.

HISTORY: Adopted eff. 7–1–53

CR 77.02 Trials and hearings; orders in chambers; review of trial dockets

(1) All trials upon the merits, except as provided in Rule 43.04, shall be conducted in open court and, so far as convenient, in a regular court room. All other acts or proceedings, except jury trials, may be done or conducted by a judge in chambers without the attendance of the clerk or other court officials, and at any place either within or without the judicial district; but no hearing, other than one ex parte, shall be conduct-

ed outside the judicial district without the consent of all parties affected thereby.

(2) At least once each year trial courts shall review all pending actions on their dockets. Notice shall be given to each attorney of record of every case in which no pretrial step has been taken within the last year, that the case will be dismissed in thirty days for want of prosecution except for good cause shown. The court shall enter an order dismissing without prejudice each case in which no answer or an insufficient answer to the notice is made.

HISTORY: Amended by Order 89–1, eff. 8–28–89; prior amendment eff. 1–1–78; adopted eff. 7–1–53

CR 77.03   Clerk's office and orders by clerk

The office of the clerk with the clerk or deputy in attendance shall be open during business hours on all days except Sundays and legal holidays. All motions and applications in the clerk's office for issuing mesne process, for issuing final process to enforce and execute judgments, and for other proceedings which do not require allowance or order of the court are grantable of course by the clerk; but his action may be suspended or altered or rescinded by the court upon cause shown.

HISTORY: Adopted eff. 7–1–53

CR 77.04   Notice of entry of judgments and orders

(1) Immediately upon the entry in the trial court of a judgment, a final order, an order which affects the running of time for taking an appeal, or an order which by its terms is required to be served, the clerk shall serve a notice of the entry by mail in the manner provided in Rule 5 upon every party who is not in default for failure to appear. Service of notice of entry of any judgment or order under this rule may be waived by the filing of a writing signed by the party or his attorney of record.

(2) The clerk shall make a note in the case docket of the service required in paragraph (1) of this rule and the notation shall show the date of service. The date of the notation on the docket of the service of notice of entry, or the date of filing a waiver if prior thereto, shall be the date of entry for the purpose of fixing the running of the time for appeal under Rule 73.02(1).

(3) The trial court shall require in the order, service of notice of entry of all orders made under Rules 6.03(2), 12.01, 12.05, 43.04, 50.02, 52.02, 54.02, 59, 62.01, 62.04, and 65.08(1), and all orders heard ex parte, or any other order it deems advisable.

(4) Failure of the trial court to require service of notice of entry of any judgment or order under this rule or the failure of the clerk to serve such notice, or the failure of a party to receive notice, shall not affect the validity of the judgment or order, and does not affect the time to appeal or relieve or authorize the court to relieve a party for failure to appeal within the time allowed, except as permitted in Rule 73.02(1).

(5) The provisions of this Rule 77.04 do not apply to trial courts other than circuit or district courts.

HISTORY: Amended eff. 1–1–78; prior amendments eff. 7–1–76, 4–1–63, 6–1–60; adopted eff. 7–1–53

CR 78   Motion days; submission of motions

CR 78   Motion days; submission of motions

(1) Each circuit and district court shall establish by rule regular motion days as required by statute, and a copy of the rules shall be certified to the Supreme Court as provided in SCR 1.040(3)(a).

(2) To expedite its business, the court may make provision by rule or order for the submission and determination of motions without oral hearing upon brief written statements of reasons in support and opposition.

HISTORY: Amended by Order 2000–1, eff. 2–1–01; prior amendment eff. 7–1–76; adopted eff. 7–1–53

CR 79   Books and records to be kept by clerks of courts

CR 79.01   Dockets

(1) The clerk of each trial court shall keep a docket for each original action filed in that court. Actions shall be assigned consecutive file numbers as prescribed in the Circuit Clerks Manual published by the Administrative Office of the Courts. The file number of each action shall be inscribed on the heading of the page of the docket on which the first entry of the action is made. All papers filed with the clerk, process issued and returns made, appearances, orders, verdicts, and judgments shall be marked with the file number and shall be noted chronologically in the docket on the page or pages of the docket assigned to the action. These notations shall be brief but shall show the nature of each paper filed or issued and the substance of each order or judgment of the court and of the returns showing execution of process. The notation of an order or judgment shall show the date the notation is made. When a trial by jury has been properly demanded or ordered the clerk shall enter the word "jury" on the heading of the page of the docket on which the first entry of the action is made.

(2) The circuit court clerk shall keep for each action appealed to that court a separate appellate docket. Such actions shall be assigned consecutive file numbers as prescribed in the Circuit Clerks Manual published by the Administrative Office of the Courts. The provisions of paragraph (1) of this Rule 79.01 relating to entries on the docket shall apply also to the appellate docket.

HISTORY: Amended eff. 1–1–78; prior amendments eff. 7–1–76, 4–1–63; adopted eff. 7–1–53

CR 79.02   Entry of satisfaction of judgment

When a judgment has been satisfied such satisfaction may be certified upon the records of the Circuit Court as follows:

(1) Upon the return of an execution showing that a judgment has been satisfied the clerk shall thus enter satisfaction on the judgment: "Satisfaction by execution." A party or his attorney receiving satisfaction of a judgment otherwise than by execution may make, date and sign this entry on the margin of the judgment: "Satisfaction in full." The court may upon motion compel an entry of satisfaction to be made.

(2) The satisfaction of the judgment may be shown by the entry of a document styled satisfaction of judgment indicating that it has been satisfied in full. The aforesaid Satisfaction of Judgment should be executed by the party or his attorney having received said satisfaction. The court may upon motion compel an entry of satisfaction to be made.

HISTORY: Amended by Order 89–1, eff. 8–28–89; prior amendments eff. 1–1–78, 7–1–76, 4–1–63; adopted eff. 7–1–53

CR 79.03   Indices and calendars

Suitable indices of the dockets required by Rule 79.01 and Criminal Rule 13.01 shall be kept by the clerk of each trial court in the form and manner prescribed in the Circuit Clerks Manual published by the Administrative Office of the Courts. The clerk shall prepare, under the direction of the trial court, calendars of all actions assigned for trial which shall distinguish "jury actions" from "court actions."

HISTORY: Amended eff. 1–1–78; prior amendment eff. 7–1–76; adopted eff. 7–1–53

CR 79.04   Other records

The clerk of each trial court shall keep such other records as may be required by the Circuit Clerks Manual published by the Administrative Office of the Courts.

HISTORY: Amended eff. 1–1–78; prior amendment eff. 7–1–76; adopted eff. 7–1–53

CR 79.05   Original record; removal and transfer

(1) General.

The clerk of each trial court shall maintain separately all papers filed, entered, issued or returned in each action, which with the docket required by Rule 79.01 or by Criminal Rule 13.01 shall constitute the original record. Except when transmitted to an appellate court or withdrawn by counsel pursuant to Rule 75.07, no original record shall be removed from the office of the clerk unless by a court order. However, when necessary in the hearing of a motion or in the taking of some step in an action or proceeding that is to be conducted by the court out of the county in which the record is kept, an attorney of record in the action, or if a party is not represented by an attorney, the party himself, may make a written and signed request to the clerk that the original record be transferred to the circuit clerk of the county wherein the hearing is to be conducted. Upon receipt of such request the clerk shall forthwith transmit the record as requested. The record shall be returned promptly after completion of the event necessitating the transfer.

(2) Recording of wills.

When a will is admitted to probate the clerk shall lodge the original will and a certified copy of the order admitting it with the county clerk for recording. It shall be the responsibility of the proponent of the will to see that the will and certified copy of the order are duly recorded and to pay the county clerk's recording fee. The original order admitting the will to probate and a certified copy of the will shall be retained in the record of the probate action.

(3) Exhibits.

The clerk may dispose of exhibits six (6) months after the action becomes final, unless sooner withdrawn by the parties.

HISTORY: Amended by Order 89–1, eff. 8–28–89; prior amendments eff. 3–1–78, 1–1–78, 7–1–76; adopted eff. 7–1–53

CR 79.06   Clerks of the Court of Appeals and Supreme Court

(1) Scope of rule.

Rule 79.06 applies only to the clerks of the Court of Appeals and Supreme Court.

(2) General docket.

The clerk of each appellate court shall keep a general docket in which shall be recorded all appeals and original proceedings in that court. It shall show the number and style of each case and the dates it is docketed, submitted, or sent to the court, and decided. In appealed cases it shall show also the county from which appealed, whether it is civil or criminal, and if advanced; the dates briefs are filed; the dates a petition for rehearing, modification or extension is filed and ruled on and the nature of the ruling; and the date the order or opinion became final.

(3) Docketing of appeals.

No action in or appeal to the Court of Appeals or Supreme Court will be docketed until the filing fee required by Rule 76.42(2) is paid. Subject to that requirement, an appeal shall be docketed when the appellate court clerk receives copies of the notice of appeal, judgment, and receipt for the filing fee from the appropriate court clerk. A motion for relief under Rule 65.07 or 65.09 shall also be treated as an appeal and shall be docketed when it is filed and the filing fee is paid. A motion for relief under CR 65.08 shall be treated as an interlocutory motion in the pending appeal from the final judgment and shall not receive a separate docketing number in the Court of Appeals.

(4) Docket sheets.

The clerk shall attach to each case record a docket sheet which shall bear the style and file number of the case, a brief indication of the subject-matter, the names and addresses of the attorneys, and in appealed cases the county and appellate district from which appealed and the name and address of the trial judge. Every step taken in the case shall when taken be entered by the clerk on the docket sheet.

(5) Docket of motions for transfer and review.

The clerk of the Supreme Court shall keep a special docket of motions for transfer of cases from the Court of Appeals and a special docket of motions for review of cases from the Court of Appeals. They shall show the style of each case, the county from which it comes, the dates of filing, responding, submission and ruling, and the nature of the ruling. After the motion is granted, the appeal shall be transferred to the general docket at the time specified in paragraph (3) of this Rule 79.06.

(6) Filing of papers.

Nothing lodged with the clerk in connection with an original proceeding or an appealed case, or on which action of any kind by the court is sought, shall be docketed or noted as a step in a proceeding unless (a) it is tendered within the time allowed for its filing and otherwise conforms to these rules and (b) the filing fee mentioned in paragraph (3) of this Rule 79.06 has been paid. A late, unauthorized, or otherwise nonconforming paper will be considered only by leave of the court.

(7) Request for transmittal of record on appeal.

(a) Transmittal of the record on appeal from the clerk of the trial court shall be requested by the clerk of the appellate court when the appellant's reply brief is filed or at the expiration of the time allowed for its filing, whichever is the sooner, with the following exceptions in criminal cases (including proceedings under RCr 11.42):

(i) If the notification required by Rule 75.07(5) indicates that counsel for the appellant is the Public Advocate of the Commonwealth or the Attorney General of the Commonwealth, the clerk of the appellate court shall request transmittal of the record forthwith; or

(ii) If the notification required by CR 75.07(5) indicates that counsel for the appellant is someone other than the Public Advocate of the Commonwealth or the Attorney General of the Commonwealth or that the appellant is acting pro-se, the clerk of the appellate court shall request transmittal of the record when the appellant's brief is filed. Should the appellant fail to file a brief, the clerk need not request the record unless so directed by the court.

(b) The record on appeal in a civil case shall not be requested by the clerk until the appellant has complied with the applicable provisions of Rule 76.02.

HISTORY: Amended by Order 98–2, eff. 1–1–99; prior amendments eff. 11–1–95 (Order 95–1), 7–1–81, 7–1–79; adopted eff. 1–1–78

CR 80 Stenographic report or transcript as evidence

CR 80 Stenographic report or transcript as evidence

Whenever the testimony of a witness at a trial or hearing which was stenographically reported is admissible in evidence at a later trial, it may be proved by the transcript thereof duly certified by the person who reported the testimony.

HISTORY: Adopted eff. 7–1–53

XI GENERAL APPLICATION OF THESE RULES

CR 81 Relief heretofore available by common law writs

CR 81 Relief heretofore available by common law writs

Relief heretofore available by the remedies of mandamus, prohibition, scire facias, quo warranto, or of an information in the nature of a quo warranto, may be obtained by original action in the appropriate court.

HISTORY: Amended eff. 1–1–78; adopted eff. 7–1–53

CR 81A Exemption of governmental units from giving bond

CR 81A Exemption of governmental units from giving bond

Whenever a bond is or may be required by these rules in order to take any proceeding, to indemnify any party, or to stay proceedings under or the enforcement of a judgment, such requirement shall not apply to the United States, the Commonwealth or any of its municipal corporations or political subdivisions, or any of their agencies or officers acting for or on their behalf. Unless otherwise exempted by law such governmental unit shall be obligated to the same extent as if it had given the bond required.

HISTORY: Adopted eff. 4–1–63

CR 82 Jurisdiction and venue unaffected

CR 82 Jurisdiction and venue unaffected

These rules shall not be construed to extend or limit the jurisdiction of any court of this Commonwealth or the venue of actions therein.

HISTORY: Adopted eff. 7–1–53

CR 83   Local rules—Abolished

CR 83   Local rules—Abolished

HISTORY: Abolished by Order 82–3, eff. 10–1–82; prior amendment eff. 7–1–76; adopted eff. 7–1–53

CR 84   Forms—Deleted

CR 84   Forms—Deleted

HISTORY: Deleted by Order of Supreme Court, eff. 1–1–13; adopted eff. 7–1–53

CR 85   Title

CR 85   Title—Repealed

HISTORY: Repealed eff. 1–1–78; adopted eff. 7–1–53

CR 86   Effective date

CR 86   Effective date

(1) The rules adopted by orders of the Court of Appeals dated December 19, 1952 and February 6, 1953 shall take effect on July 1, 1953. Amendments to these rules shall become effective when so designated by the Supreme Court.

(2) The original rules and any amendments thereto govern all proceedings in actions brought after they take effect and also further proceedings in actions then pending, except to the extent that in the opinion of the proper court, expressed by its order, their application in a particular action pending when the original rules or amendments thereto take effect would not be feasible, or would work injustice, in which event the procedure existing at the time the action was brought applies.

HISTORY: Amended eff. 7–1–76; prior amendment eff. 4–1–63; adopted eff. 7–1–53

CR 87   Amendment of rules

CR 87   Amendment of rules

(1) Suggestions for amendment of these rules may be submitted directly to the Supreme Court for its consideration.

(2) Unless otherwise ordered by the court by reason of exigent circumstances, all substantial amendments will be published in an official publication of the Kentucky Bar Association or mailed to the members of the Kentucky Bar Association at least 60 days before they become effective.

HISTORY: Amended eff. 5–1–76; adopted eff. 7–1–75

XII   SPECIAL RULES OF THE CIRCUIT COURT FOR THE ECONOMICAL LITIGATION DOCKET

CR 88   Scope of rules relating to the economical litigation docket

CR 88   Scope of rules relating to the economical litigation docket

Rules 89 through 97 shall apply only in those circuits or divisions thereof specified by order of the Supreme Court.

HISTORY: Adopted by Order 82–3, eff. 10–1–82

CR 89   Economical litigation docket

CR 89   Economical litigation docket

(1) The economical litigation docket shall consist of all cases falling substantially within the following categories:

(a) contracts;

(b) personal injury;

(c) property damages;

(d) property rights;

(e) termination of parental rights.

(2) Practice and procedure for cases on the economical litigation docket shall be governed by Rules 1 through 87 and the local rules of the trial court except as modified by Rules 89 through 97 relating to the economical litigation docket.

HISTORY: Adopted by Order 82–3, eff. 10–1–82

CR 90   Discovery and status conference

CR 90   Discovery and status conference

(1) A discovery and status conference shall be held in each case for the purpose of scheduling each event in the case and determining the period of time necessary to complete discovery. The conference shall be set within fifteen (15) days after service of the last responsive pleading or the last day a responsive pleading could have been served. A date for a pretrial conference shall be set for a date not more than sixty (60) days following the discovery and status conference and a trial date shall be set not more than thirty (30) days after the pretrial conference. However, in the discretion of the trial judge these times may be extended or reduced to meet the needs of the individual case.

(2) Motions for exceptions to the rules of the economical litigation docket relating to discovery must be made at the discovery and status conference.

(3) All parties shall be represented at the discovery and status conference and shall be prepared to have firm dates set for the pretrial conference and the trial.

HISTORY: Adopted by Order 82–3, eff. 10–1–82

CR 91   Telephone conferences

CR 91   Telephone conferences

At the discretion of the trial judge, any motion may be heard and any conference may be held by a telephone conference call among the trial judge and counsel for the respective parties.

HISTORY: Adopted by Order 82–3, eff. 10–1–82

CR 92   Motions; enlargement of time; summary judgment

CR 92   Motions; enlargement of time; summary judgment

(1) Except as provided in Rule 91, motions respecting cases on the economical litigation docket shall be heard at the court's regular motion hour.

(2) Motions for enlargement of time or continuances shall state the reasons therefor and will be granted only for good cause. Agreed orders pertaining to such matters will not be accepted.

(3) Motions for summary judgment must be made ten (10) days prior to the pretrial conference.

HISTORY: Adopted by Order 82–3, eff. 10–1–82

CR 93   Discovery

CR 93.01   Depositions

Depositions are permitted as a matter of right of parties only. The plaintiff shall be required to give his deposition before any other discovery takes place unless the defendant elects not to examine the plaintiff or the court otherwise directs. Except as otherwise ordered by the court, a deposition of a witness shall be permitted only if it will be introduced at trial according to the provisions of Rule 32.01.

HISTORY: Adopted by Order 82–3, eff. 10–1–82

CR 93.02   Interrogatories

The scope and manner of discovery by means of interrogatories shall be governed by Rule 33, except that the interrogatories to any party shall not exceed twenty (20) in number, each of which shall be limited to a single question.

HISTORY: Adopted by Order 82–3, eff. 10–1–82

CR 93.03   Production of documents and things and entry upon land for inspection and other purposes

Procedures respecting the production of documents and things and entry upon land for inspection and other purposes shall be as provided in Rule 34, except that notwithstanding the provisions of Rule 34.02(2), the party upon whom the request is served shall permit the inspection or copying of documents or other things or allow the entry upon land as the case might be within fifteen (15) days after service unless an objection is filed within that period. If objection is made to a part of an item or category, the part shall be specified. The party submitting the request may move for an order under Rule 37.01 with respect to any objection to or other failure to respond to the request or any part thereof or any failure to permit inspection as requested.

HISTORY: Adopted by Order 82–3, eff. 10–1–82

CR 93.04   Exchange of information

(1) Not later than ten (10) days prior to the pretrial conference each party shall disclose the following material to all other parties with a copy to the court:

(a) Name, address and telephone number of any witness whom the party may call at trial together with a copy of any statement of such person or if there is not such statement, a summary of the testimony the person is expected to give. However, no party shall be required to furnish any statement (written or taped) protected by the attorney-client privilege or work product rule.

(b) A description, drawing or photograph of any physical evidence which is to be presented at trial.

(c) A copy of any document or writing which is to be presented at trial.

(d) A brief summary of the qualifications of any expert witness the party may call at trial together with a report or statement of any such expert witness which sets forth the subject matter of the expert witnesses' anticipated testimony; the substance of the facts and opinions to which the expert is expected to testify, and a summary of the grounds for each opinion.

(e) A statement summarizing each contention in support of every claim or defense which the party will present at trial and a brief statement of the facts upon which the contentions are based.

(f) Offers of stipulation.

(g) A concise statement of each issue of law and each issue of fact recognized by the party.

(2) Each party is under a continuing duty promptly to supplement all prior discovery or pretrial disclosures rendered pursuant to this Rule 93.04 with any pertinent after-acquired information.

(3) Parties are required to refine issues that are to be tried in the case. If an order of stipulation is rejected and the matter is subsequently proved at trial, the rejecting party shall be subject to sanctions according to Rule 96.

HISTORY: Amended by Order 88–4, eff. 1–1–89; adopted eff. 10–1–82

CR 94   Certificate of compliance

CR 94   Certificate of compliance

A certificate of compliance with Rule 93 shall be filed by each party upon the completion of discovery.

HISTORY: Adopted by Order 82–3, eff. 10–1–82

CR 95   Pretrial conference

CR 95   Pretrial conference

A pretrial conference shall be scheduled in all cases at the discovery and status conference. The pretrial conference shall be for the purpose of:

(a) Simplifying the issues and agreeing upon the issues of law and upon the issues of fact to be tried.

(b) Exploring the possibility of settlement.

(c) Disposing of all remaining motions.

(d) Considering amendments to pleadings.

(e) Exploring possible admissions of fact and documents that will avoid unnecessary proof.

(f) Limiting the number of expert witnesses.

(g) Any other matter that will aid in disposition of the case.

HISTORY: Adopted by Order 82–3, eff. 10–1–82

CR 96   Sanctions

CR 96   Sanctions

If a party fails to comply with Rules 88 through 97, the trial judge may impose as appropriate any of the sanctions specified in Rule 37.02, in the same manner as if an order of the court had been violated.

HISTORY: Adopted by Order 82–3, eff. 10–1–82

CR 97   Presence of counsel

CR 97   Presence of counsel

Trial counsel of record must be present in order to make binding stipulations and set firm hearing dates at all hearings. Alternate counsel may be designated only if that counsel is empowered to stipulate on matters and has counsel of record's office calendar information so that he may firmly bind counsel of record in event-setting and other decisions.

HISTORY: Adopted by Order 82–3, eff. 10–1–82

CR 98   Procedures for video recorded court proceedings and appeals

CR 98   Procedures for video recorded court proceedings and appeals

(1) Scope of Rule.

The provisions of this Rule shall apply to any court proceeding presided over by, or to any appeal from a judgment entered by, a trial judge upon his/her activation and use of video recording equipment to record the court proceeding.

(2) Record of Trial Court Proceedings.

In addition to those provisions of the Kentucky Rules of Court relating to video recorded court proceedings the following procedures shall apply:

(a) Video Recordings. The official record of these court proceedings shall be constituted as follows:

1. two (2) videotape recordings, recorded simultaneously, of court proceedings utilizing video cassette equipment; or,

2. two (2) copies of the digital video recording when court proceedings are otherwise electronically recorded.

Upon the filing of a notice of appeal, one of the two video recordings, or a court-certified copy of that portion thereof recording the court proceeding being appealed shall be filed with the clerk and certified by the clerk as part of the record on appeal. The second video recording, or a court-certified copy of that portion thereof recording the court proceeding being appealed, also shall be retained by the clerk.

(i) Method of identification. For identification purposes, the clerk shall designate on each of the two video recordings, on one line, the judicial circuit or district number, the court division number (if any), the last two digits of the current year, the letters "VR", the number of the video recording (counting all video records used since the start of the current calendar year), either the letter "A", if the video recording is retained by the clerk, or the letter "B", if the video recording is filed with the clerk, the number of the video recording used in the proceeding being identified, and the case file number of the proceeding being identified (for example: 22–3–06–VR–015–A–1, 06–CR–123). On the second line, the clerk shall designate the caption of the proceeding recorded on the video (for example: Smith v. Jones) or refer to the video recording log for the captions of the proceedings when multiple proceedings are recorded thereon. On the third line, the clerk shall designate the date on with which the video record was made (for example: 10/27/06).

(ii) Duplicate copies. The clerk shall arrange for the recording of duplicate copies of video recordings for use by counsel in preparing an appeal. The clerk shall charge the person requesting a duplicate video recording a reasonable fee, which shall be set by the Administrative Office of the Courts, for each duplicate video tape, disk or other media requested.

(b) Exhibit List: Trial Log. The trial judge or his/her designee shall make a written exhibit list, a written trial log, and a written log listing the date and time of where each witness' testimony begins and ends on the video recording. The trial judge shall keep one copy of each log and list as part of the record, and shall place a second copy of each log and list with the video recording, or portion thereof.

(c) Exhibits. By pretrial order, the trial judge may require that at the time an exhibit is introduced into evidence, a photograph or photographs of the exhibit be submitted and included as part of the record, in lieu of the exhibit itself being retained by the clerk as part of the record. The photograph(s) shall serve as part of the official record, and the exhibit itself may be returned for safekeeping to the custody of the party introducing the exhibit. The clerk shall not be required to certify the exhibit itself as part of the record on appeal, unless so ordered by the appellate court.

(d) Depositions. In a court proceeding in which video recording equipment is being used to record the proceeding, the official record of a deposition admitted into evidence may be, in the trial judge's discretion, either the transcript of the deposition or the video recording of the deposition.

(e) Court Reporters in Mechanically Recorded Proceedings. Any party to the case may have a stenographic reporter present as part of the public or at counsel table and the court shall, to the extent it can do so without unduly disrupting its proceeding, accommodate the reporter inside the bar.

(3) Record on Appeal.

Unless otherwise ordered by the court, no transcript of court proceedings shall be made a part of the record on appeal except as provided in Paragraph 4 of this rule. The official video recordings, together with the clerk's written record, shall constitute the entire original record on appeal. To facilitate the timely preparation and certification of the record as set out in this rule, appellant or counsel for appellant, if any, shall provide the clerk with a list setting out the dates on which video recordings were made for all pre-trial and post-trial proceedings necessary for inclusion in the record on appeal. Designation of the video recordings shall be filed within the ten (10) day time limitation and in the manner described in Rule 75.01(1). Supplemental designation by other parties shall likewise conform with the requirements of Rule 75.01(1).

(a) Preparation and Certification by Clerk. The circuit court clerk shall prepare and certify the entire original record on file in his/her office. All parts of the written record on appeal shall be arranged in the order in which they were filed or entered. If the record comprises more than 150 pages, it shall be divided into two or more volumes not exceeding 150 pages each. Each volume shall be securely bound at the left side. There shall be a general index at the beginning of the record and an index to each volume in the front thereof which shall show, in the order in which they appear, the pages on which all pleadings, orders, judgments, instructions, and papers may be found. Except for documents, maps and charts, and other papers reasonably capable of being enclosed in envelopes, exhibits, unless otherwise ordered by the trial court pursuant to paragraph (2)(c) of this rule, shall be retained by the clerk and shall not be transmitted to the appellate court unless specifically directed by the appellate court on motion of a party or upon its own motion. All exhibits filed with the record shall be sufficiently identified and the index shall direct where they may be found.

(b) Time for Certification. The record on appeal shall be prepared and certified by the circuit court clerk as soon after the filing of the notice of appeal as possible, but in any event within thirty (30) days after the date of filing the notice of appeal. Extension of time for certification shall be by motion for cause filed with the court to which the appeal is taken.

The matter certified under this section shall constitute the record on appeal. It is the responsibility of the appellant to see that the record is prepared and certified by the clerk within the time prescribed by this rule.

(c) Notice of Certification. The circuit court clerk shall immediately give written notice to the clerk of the appellate court when the record has been completed and certified as required herein, and shall simultaneously serve copies of such notice upon all parties to the appeal. The clerk shall enter the fact and date of such notice in the docket of the case.

(d) Withdrawal and Transmission of Record on Appeal. The circuit court clerk shall transmit the record on appeal to the appellate court when so requested by the clerk of the appellate court. Until the record on appeal is so requested, the record on appeal shall be retained under the responsibility and control of the clerk of the circuit court. Except for the official video recording of the proceedings which shall be retained by the clerk until transmitted to the appellate court, the record on appeal will be made available first to counsel for the appellant and then to the counsel for the appellee. If the record on appeal is removed from the clerk's office, counsel for the appellant shall return it before submitting his/her brief to the appellate court in order that it may be available to counsel for the appellee. If it is withdrawn by counsel for the appellant for the purpose of preparing a reply brief it shall be returned before such brief is submitted to the appellate court. A record on appeal shall not be retained by counsel beyond the filing date on which his/her brief is due. Withdrawals and returns of the record on appeal shall be noted by the clerk on the docket kept for that action.

(e) Perfection of Appeal. An appeal shall be perfected within sixty (60) days after the date of the notation on the docket of the service of notice required by paragraph (3)(c) of this rule. To perfect an appeal, the appellant shall: (1) cause the clerk's notice required by paragraph (3)(c) of this rule to be transmitted to the clerk of the appellate court; and (2) file with the clerk of the appellate court the brief required by CR 76.12.

(4) Briefs.

The provisions of CR 76.12 pertaining to briefs shall apply to appeals taken pursuant to this rule, as well as the following provisions:

(a) Video Recording Reference. Each reference in a brief to a segment of the video recordings shall set forth in parentheses the letters "VR", the number of the video recording, and the month, day, year, hour, minute, and second at which the reference begins as recorded on the video recording. For example: (VR No. 1: 10/27/06; 14:24:05).

(b) Evidentiary Appendix. An appendix of the evidence (hereinafter, evidentiary appendix) that consists of a transcription of the evidence or other court proceeding may be attached to a brief on appeal. The filing of an evidentiary appendix and index attached to a brief shall not exceed fifty (50) pages if filed in the Supreme Court, nor twenty-five (25) pages if filed in the Court of Appeals, except that an evidentiary appendix and index attached to a reply brief shall not exceed fifteen (15) pages. An evidentiary appendix shall contain transcriptions of only those parts of the video recording that support the specific issues or contentions raised in a brief on appeal, or that relate to the question of whether an alleged error was properly preserved for appellate review.

(i) Organization of Appendix. At the top of each page of an evidentiary appendix, there shall be a video recording reference which corresponds to the transcription on each page of the appendix. Each evidentiary appendix shall include an index setting forth: (a) a list of video recording references cross-indexed to pages of the appendix; (b) an alphabetical list of witnesses whose testimony is transcribed in the appendix, listing the video recording references with the pages of the appendix where each witness' testimony begins; (c) the name of each witness at the place in the appendix where the testimony of that witness begins.

(ii) Purpose of Appendix: Sanctions. The purpose of this evidentiary appendix is to facilitate the efforts of each appellate judge in studying the briefs in a meaningful way. Inclusion of transcript unnecessary to the disposition of the case imposes a burden on both the parties and the court and may subject counsel to sanctions set forth below:

(a) The appellate court may deny costs to, or assess costs against, a party who has been responsible for the insertion of unnecessary material into an evidentiary appendix. Moreover, any counsel who so multiplies an appendix in any brief as to increase delay or costs may be required by the court to satisfy personally such excess costs, and may be subject to the imposition of fines as set forth in CR 73.02(2)(c).

(b) The appellate court may strike any part or all of an evidentiary appendix, or brief to which it is attached, which has been determined by the appellate court to contain unnecessary material.

(5) Further Provisions.

(a) Transcription for Appellate Court. The appellate court may request the Administrative Office of the Courts to transcribe any portion of the video recordings it determines is necessary for a decision in the case. The costs of transcriptions under this paragraph shall be certified by the Director of the Administrative Office of the Courts, or his or her designee, and shall be paid by the parties to the appeal in such proportions as directed by the appellate court requesting the transcription.

(b) Effect of Rule on Practice in Court of Appeals. Nothing in this rule shall be construed to supersede the provisions of CR 76.03.

HISTORY: Amended by Order 2006–09, eff. 1–1–07; prior amendments eff. 1–1–03 (Order 2002–1), 2–1–01 (Order 2000–2, 2000–1), 1–1–99 (Order 98–2), 10–1–94 (Order 94–1), 8–1–92, 9–15–90; adopted eff. 8–28–89

APPENDIX OF OFFICIAL FORMS

Research Note

No attempt is made to furnish a manual of forms. The following forms are, under Rule 84, sufficient to withstand attack under the rules, and the practitioner using them may rely on them to that extent. In addition, they serve as examples of the simplicity and brevity of pleading required by the rules. Each form assumes the action to be brought in the Franklin Circuit Court. If the court in which an action is brought has branches or divisions, the branch or division should be indicated in the caption.

Except when otherwise indicated each pleading, motion, and other paper should have a caption similar to that of Form 2, with the designation of the particular paper substituted for the word "Complaint." In the caption of the Complaint all parties must be named, but in other pleadings and papers, it is sufficient to state the name of the first party on either side, with an appropriate indication of other parties. See Rules 4.02, 7.02(2) and 10.01.

Each pleading, motion, and other paper is to be signed in his individual name by at least one attorney of record (Rule 11). The attorney's name is to be followed by his address. If a party is not represented by an attorney, the signature and address of the party are required in place of those of the attorney.

APPENDIX OF OFFICIAL FORMS

Form
1 Summons—Deleted
2 Complaint on a promissory note—Deleted
3 Complaint on an account—Deleted
4 Complaint for goods sold and delivered—Deleted
5 Complaint for money lent—Deleted
6 Complaint for money paid by mistake—Deleted
7 Complaint for money had and received—Deleted
8 Complaint for negligence—Deleted
9 Complaint for negligence where plaintiff is unable to determine definitely whether the person responsible is A.B. or C.D. or whether both are responsible and where his evidence may justify a finding of wilfulness or of negligence—Deleted
10 Complaint for conversion—Deleted
11 Complaint for specific performance of contract to convey land—Deleted
12 Complaint on claim for debt and to set aside fraudulent conveyance under Rule 18.02—Deleted
13 Complaint for interpleader and declaratory relief—Deleted
14 Motion to dismiss, presenting defenses of failure to state a claim, of lack of service of process, and of lack of jurisdiction under Rule 12.02—Deleted
15 Answer presenting defenses under Rule 12.02—Deleted
16 Answer to complaint set forth in Form 7 with counterclaim for interpleader—Deleted
17 Motion to bring in third-party defendant—Deleted
18 Motion to intervene as a defendant under Rule 24—Deleted
19 Request for production of documents, etc., under Rule 34—Deleted
20 Request for admission under Rule 36—Deleted
21 Allegation of reason for omitting party—Deleted
22 Notice of appeal under Rule 73.03—Deleted
23 Certificate as to transcript under Rule 75.01(2)—Deleted
24 Cover of brief to be filed in the Court of Appeals—Deleted
25 Cover of brief to be filed in the Supreme Court of Kentucky—matter of right appeal—Deleted

Form 1   Summons—Deleted

HISTORY: Deleted by Order of Supreme Court, eff. 1–1–13; prior amendments eff. 7–1–75; 6–1–60; adopted eff. 7–1–53

Form 2   Complaint on a promissory note—Deleted

HISTORY: Deleted by Order of Supreme Court, eff. 1–1–13; adopted eff. 7–1–53

Form 3   Complaint on an account—Deleted

HISTORY: Deleted by Order of Supreme Court, eff. 1–1–13; prior amendment eff. 1970; adopted eff. 7–1–53

Form 4   Complaint for goods sold and delivered— Deleted

HISTORY: Deleted by Order of Supreme Court, eff. 1–1–13; adopted eff. 7–1–53

Form 5   Complaint for money lent—Deleted

HISTORY: Deleted by Order of Supreme Court, eff. 1–1–13; adopted eff. 7–1–53

Form 6   Complaint for money paid by mistake— Deleted

HISTORY: Deleted by Order of Supreme Court, eff. 1–1–13; adopted eff. 7–1–53

Form 7   Complaint for money had and received— Deleted

HISTORY: Deleted by Order of Supreme Court, eff. 1–1–13; adopted eff. 7–1–53

Form 8   Complaint for negligence—Deleted

HISTORY: Deleted by Order of Supreme Court, eff. 1–1–13; prior amendment eff. 6–1–60; adopted eff. 7–1–53

Form 9   Complaint for negligence where plaintiff is unable to determine definitely whether the person responsible is A.B. or C.D. or whether

both are responsible and where his evidence may justify a finding of wilfulness or of negligence—Deleted

HISTORY: Deleted by Order of Supreme Court, eff. 1–1–13; prior amendment eff. 6–1–60; adopted eff. 7–1–53

Form 10 Complaint for conversion—Deleted

HISTORY: Deleted by Order of Supreme Court, eff. 1–1–13; adopted eff. 7–1–53

Form 11 Complaint for specific performance of contract to convey land—Deleted

HISTORY: Deleted by Order of Supreme Court, eff. 1–1–13; adopted eff. 7–1–53

Form 12 Complaint on claim for debt and to set aside fraudulent conveyance under Rule 18.02—Deleted

HISTORY: Deleted by Order of Supreme Court, eff. 1–1–13; prior amendment eff. 1970; adopted eff. 7–1–53

Form 13 Complaint for interpleader and declaratory relief—Deleted

HISTORY: Deleted by Order of Supreme Court, eff. 1–1–13; adopted eff. 7–1–53

Form 14 Motion to dismiss, presenting defenses of failure to state a claim, of lack of service of process, and of lack of jurisdiction under Rule 12.02—Deleted

HISTORY: Deleted by Order of Supreme Court, eff. 1–1–13; adopted eff. 7–1–53

Form 15 Answer presenting defenses under Rule 12.02—Deleted

HISTORY: Deleted by Order of Supreme Court, eff. 1–1–13; adopted eff. 7–1–53

Form 16 Answer to complaint set forth in Form 7 with counterclaim for interpleader—Deleted

HISTORY: Deleted by Order of Supreme Court, eff. 1–1–13; adopted eff. 7–1–53

Form 17 Motion to bring in third-party defendant—Deleted

HISTORY: Deleted by Order of Supreme Court, eff. 1–1–13; prior amendment eff. 1970; adopted eff. 7–1–53

Form 18 Motion to intervene as a defendant under Rule 24—Deleted

HISTORY: Deleted by Order of Supreme Court, eff. 1–1–13; adopted eff. 7–1–53

Form 19 Request for production of documents, etc., under Rule 34—Deleted

HISTORY: Deleted by Order of Supreme Court, eff. 1–1–13; prior amendment eff. 10–1–71; adopted eff. 7–1–53

Form 20 Request for admission under Rule 36—Deleted

HISTORY: Deleted by Order of Supreme Court, eff. 1–1–13; adopted eff. 7–1–53

Form 21 Allegation of reason for omitting party—Deleted

HISTORY: Deleted by Order of Supreme Court, eff. 1–1–13; adopted eff. 7–1–53

Form 22 Notice of appeal under Rule 73.03—Deleted

HISTORY: Deleted by Order of Supreme Court, eff. 1–1–13; prior amendments eff. 1–1–78; 7–1–76; 1970; adopted eff. 7–1–53

Form 23 Certificate as to transcript under Rule 75.01(2)—Deleted

HISTORY: Deleted by Order of Supreme Court, eff. 1–1–13; adopted eff. 7–1–81 (Order 81–4)

Form 24 Cover of brief to be filed in the Court of Appeals—Deleted

HISTORY: Deleted by Order of Supreme Court, eff. 1–1–13; adopted eff. 2–1–01 (Order 2000–1)

Form 25 Cover of brief to be filed in the Supreme Court of Kentucky—matter of right appeal—Deleted

HISTORY: Deleted by Order of Supreme Court, eff. 1–1–13; prior amendment eff. 2–1–01 (Order 2000–2); adopted eff. 2–1–01 (Order 2000–1)

FAMILY COURT RULES OF PROCEDURE AND PRACTICE

Effective January 1, 2011

I. TITLE AND SCOPE OF RULES

FCRPP 1   Title and Scope

(1) Pursuant to KRS 403.130, these rules constitute a separate section of the civil rules and shall be known as the Kentucky Family Court Rules of Procedure and Practice. They may be cited as such, or by the abbreviation "FCRPP."

(2) These Rules shall be applicable to the procedure and practice in all actions pertaining to dissolution of marriage; custody and child support; visitation and timesharing; property division; maintenance; domestic violence; paternity; dependency; neglect or abuse; termination of parental rights; adoption; and status offenses, or any other matter exclusively within family law jurisdiction, except for any special statutory proceedings, which shall prevail over any inconsistent procedures set forth in these Rules.

(3) Self represented litigants shall be held to knowledge of these rules the same as parties represented by counsel.

(4) The Rules of Civil and Criminal Procedure shall apply to family law matters to the extent they are not inconsistent with these Rules.

HISTORY: Amended by Order 2012–10, eff. 1–1–13; adopted eff. 1–1–11

II. DISSOLUTIONS AND PROPERTY DIVISION

FCRPP 2 Preliminary Matters

(1) **Original Pleadings.** All original pleadings, including forms, in a dissolution action shall be signed by the preparer, filed with the clerk of the court, and if applicable, shall include, unless otherwise ordered by the court, the following:

(a) A verified petition;

(b) Proof of service;

(c) A verified response, or a verified entry of appearance in lieu of a response;

(d) Unless waived by the court pursuant to KRS 403.180(4)(b), a verified separation agreement;

(e) The Final Verified Disclosure Statement;

(f) A verified waiver of notice of final hearing;

(g) A verified deposition or interrogatories for proof of the allegations of the petition if done without a hearing;

(h) A divorce education certificate; and

(i) A child support work sheet.

(2) **Multiple Actions.** When actions concerning the same subject matter are filed in different circuits, the first action filed shall be the controlling action, subject to transfer by the court of that circuit on a motion for forum non conveniens or other appropriate legal grounds. A motion for transfer shall be filed prior to or with the response. On notice to the parties, the courts in both circuits may confer concerning the proper venue.

(3) **Preliminary Mandatory Disclosure.** The AOC–238, Preliminary Verified Disclosure Statement, shall be exchanged between the parties within 45 days of service of the petition on the respondent, and objections thereto shall be exchanged 20 days thereafter but the disclosures shall not be filed in the record unless ordered by the court or required by local rule.

(4) **Exchange of Information and Documents.** The parties shall sign and return specific releases for relevant information and documents unless objected to in writing. Such releases shall contain a provision directing that any information and/or documents provided in writing to the requesting counsel or pro se party shall simultaneously be transmitted to the other counsel or pro se party, at requesting party's expense. Upon objection, the requesting party may file a motion to compel.

(5) **Status Quo Orders.** Without limiting a party's relief under CR 65, upon notice and opportunity to be heard, a court may enter a status quo order regarding disposition of the marital estate. Any such order may be entered on the AOC–237. A status quo order may include but not be limited to the following:

(a) Neither party shall, except as necessary to pay reasonable living expenses, incur unreasonable debt, sell, encumber, gift, bequeath or in any manner transfer, convey or dissipate any property, cash, stocks or other assets currently in their possession or in the control of another person, company, legal entity or family member without permission of the court or an agreed order signed by both parties or their attorneys.

(b) Neither party shall allow the cancellation or lapse of any health, life, automobile, casualty or disability insurance currently covering themselves or a family member or change the named beneficiaries on such policies prior to receiving permission of the court or filing an agreed order signed by both parties or their attorneys.

(6) **Case Management.**

(a) Mediation.

(1) The parties may agree to mediate at any time. After notice and opportunity to be heard and unless prohibited by KRS 403.036 (domestic violence), the parties may be ordered to mediate any issues before further proceedings.

(2) Within 10 days of a final mediation, if the parties have been unable to resolve all issues, the petitioner shall file a motion for a case management conference or final hearing date, unless previously scheduled by the court.

(b) Case Management Conference.

(1) Unless notice is given to the court that a case is being mediated, within 60 days of service of the petition upon the respondent, the petitioner shall file a motion for a case management conference.

(2) Both parties and their counsel shall attend the conference, unless otherwise ordered by the court.

(3) Each party shall file the following documents at least 7 days prior to the conference:

(i) Any related motions; and

(ii) Any stipulations or agreements reached.

(4) In the event of failure of a party or parties to appear at the conference, the court may, in accordance with its order, conduct a hearing in which proof may be taken or the case dismissed, as the court may determine appropriate.

(7) **Trial.** The trial shall not be continued except as otherwise ordered for good cause shown on the record.

(8) **Temporary Motions.**

(a) Any ex parte motion shall be accompanied by a supporting affidavit sufficient to state grounds for injunctive relief, and if granted, shall be set for hearing with all parties at the earliest available date.

(b) Any pendente lite motions shall be served on the opposing party and set for a hearing before the court unless otherwise agreed to by the parties.

HISTORY: Amended by Order 2012–10, eff. 1–1–13; adopted eff. 1–1–11

FCRPP 3 Obtaining a Decree of Dissolution

(1) Matters Not Requiring a Trial.

(a) If the parties reach an agreement on all issues, a decree of dissolution may be obtained without a trial by filing a motion or agreed order to submit for decree of dissolution of marriage, and the parties shall further comply with any local rule requiring additional filings.

(b) A decree shall not be final until the original is signed by the court and entered by the clerk.

(c) If the parties reach an agreement on individual issues short of settling the entire case, the agreement, signed by both parties, may be submitted to the court for approval and entry.

(2) Default Cases.

In all cases of default, the motion to submit for decree shall state the following:

(a) That no answer or pleadings have been received by the moving party or counsel;

(b) That the respondent was personally served and 20 days have elapsed since service, or that a warning order attorney was appointed, has filed a report and affidavit and that 50 days have elapsed since appointment of the warning order attorney; and,

(c) Shall include certification that the motion and notice of trial or submission has been served on the opposing party at the party's last known address; and if the party is on active military duty, that the provisions of the Servicemembers' Civil Relief Act have been followed.

(3) Matters Requiring a Trial.

(a) If the parties do not reach an agreement on any or all issues, a trial shall be held, on motion, as set by the court.

(b) No later than 5 days prior to the trial, the parties shall file an AOC–239, Final Verified Disclosure Statement, in the record if property matters are in dispute at that trial; or the parties may file an affidavit that there are no changes in circumstance since the completion of the AOC–238, Preliminary Verified Disclosure Statement, if filed.

(c) A copy of AOC–239, Final Verified Disclosure Statement, or the affidavit in (b) above, together with any supporting documentation, shall be provided to the opposing party 15 days prior to trial unless otherwise ordered by the court.

(4) Evidence and Exhibits.

(a) A court-appointed expert's report shall be in lieu of live testimony, unless either party subpoenas the expert to testify or unless the court orders otherwise. The party who subpoenas the expert shall be responsible for paying the expert's fee for appearance at trial, unless otherwise ordered by the court.

(b) In the trial order, the court shall order parties to exchange the list of exhibits to be submitted at trial. Absent good cause shown, failure to provide an exhibit list may result in the exclusion of such exhibit at trial.

(c) Originals of depositions, interrogatories or requests for admissions, shall not be filed in the court record unless offered as proof. The attorney who noticed the taking of a deposition, or propounded the interrogatories or requests for admissions, shall be the custodian of the record for the originals, and shall present them when directed by the court or at the request of any party.

(5) Post–Decree Litigation.

A fee of $50.00 shall be paid by the movant in domestic relations cases reopened after 6 months from the entry of the decree for the purpose of modifying the decree. This does not include motions in 42 U.S.C. Title IV–D cases for child support enforcement. The clerk shall collect any fee upon the filing of the motion, unless the movant files a motion to proceed in forma pauperis.

(a) Reopening for purposes of this rule means any motion for modification of an order filed more than 6 months after entry of the order. A case is considered reopened until all matters in the motion are resolved.

(b) Once a case is reopened and the fee is paid, another fee will not be required unless 6 months or more have elapsed since entry of the order on the motion that re-opened the case.

(c) This fee shall not be required for motions to enforce an order and which are so titled.

HISTORY: Amended by Order 2012–10, eff. 1–1–13; adopted eff. 1–1–11

FCRPP 4 Procedures Before the Domestic Relations Commissioner

(1) In jurisdictions having no family court, the circuit judge may appoint a domestic relations commissioner, who shall serve at the pleasure of the court. The court may refer domestic relations matters under KRS Chapter 403 to the domestic relations commissioner, except for domestic violence proceedings, contempt proceedings and injunctive relief proceedings. Any local rules relating to domestic relations commissioners shall be approved by the Chief Justice and be uniform in all divisions of circuit court within each county of each circuit.

(2) Each domestic relations commissioner shall have been licensed to practice law for at least eight years at the time of appointment, unless otherwise authorized by the Chief Justice, and shall satisfy the annual continuing legal education minimum require-

ment with domestic relations law education. Additionally, each domestic relations commissioner shall attend a training program, at least once every two years, which focuses on the dynamics and effects of domestic violence including the availability of community resources, victims' services and reporting requirements. Domestic relations commissioners shall not otherwise engage in the practice of domestic relations law.

(3) The domestic relations commissioner shall hear all matters and file a report promptly pursuant to KRS 454.350(2). Testimony may be heard orally before the commissioner or by deposition or interrogatory. All actions involving indigents shall be heard by the commissioner without fee. Proceedings before the commissioner shall be recorded by audio or video and a recording log shall be kept. The domestic relations commissioner shall file the recorded hearings and the recording log in the record with the clerk of the court. Transcriptions shall not be required for any purpose within this Rule.

(4) The domestic relations commissioner shall have the authority to make recommendations to the judge regarding motions for temporary orders of custody, support and maintenance. All temporary and final decrees and orders shall be entered by the court upon review of the recommendations of the domestic relations commissioner as set forth below:

(a) Within 10 days after being served with a copy of the commissioner's recommendations, any party may file written objections thereto with the court. After hearing the court may adopt the recommendations, modify them, or reject them in whole or in part, or may receive further evidence or may recommit them for further hearing.

(b) The circuit court shall sign any recommended temporary or post-decree order within 10 days after the time for filing exceptions has run unless a motion for a hearing on the exceptions has been filed. All temporary recommendations of the domestic relations commissioner which become orders of the court shall be without prejudice and subject to the court's de novo review on final hearing.

(c) If the parties stipulate that the commissioner's findings of fact shall be final, only questions of law arising upon the recommendations shall thereafter be considered.

(d) All final decrees shall be entered by the court within 20 days of submission if no exceptions have been filed. If exceptions have been filed, entry of the final decree shall occur within 10 days of disposition of the exceptions.

(5) For any case assigned, the domestic relations commissioner shall receive a fee of $60 per hour, assessed at a rate of $15.00 for each quarter hour or part thereof. Such fees shall be paid through the office of circuit court clerk to the commissioner and shall be due on the fifth working day following the

conclusion of the hearing. No more than $600 shall be assessed in any case regardless of the number and length of hearings unless recommended by the circuit judge and approved by the Chief Justice for extraordinary circumstances shown. If a case is reopened additional fees totaling not more than $200 may be assessed. No more than $15 shall be assessed in any uncontested divorce.

(6) The compensation of domestic relations commissioners shall be by fee charged upon the parties, or paid out of any fund or subject matter of the action which is in the custody or control of the circuit court. This compensation shall be paid to the circuit court clerk, who shall issue payment to the commissioner.

(7) All domestic relations commissioners shall be limited in their total personal compensation derived from fees to not more than $48,000 per annum unless approved by the Chief Justice. Fees in excess of the personal compensation of the commissioner shall be remitted to the Administrative Office of the Courts with the annual accounting for all amounts received.

(8) The Administrative Office of the Courts shall establish audit and accounting standards, prescribe bookkeeping and accounting practices and procedures, and otherwise perform audits and oversee the financial accounts of domestic relations commissioners. A copy of any audit shall be submitted by the Administrative Office of the Courts to the chief judge of the circuit. In the event that the audit reveals an accounting or other irregularity, a copy shall also be submitted to the Chief Justice.

(9) The commissioner shall not retain his or her recommendations as security for his or her compensation. When the party ordered to pay the compensation allowed by the court does not pay it after notice and within the time prescribed by the court, that party may be subject to civil contempt.

HISTORY: Amended by Order 2012–10, eff. 1–1–13; adopted eff. 1–1–11

FCRPP 5   Maintenance

(1) A motion for temporary maintenance shall be accompanied by copies of the movant's last three pay stubs or, if movant is self-employed, proof of the movant's current income, and by an affidavit setting forth movant's monthly expenses and income and the monthly income of the party from whom maintenance is sought.

(2) The notice of hearing accompanying a motion for temporary maintenance shall contain the following statement: "You must file with the Court, at least 24 hours prior to the time of the hearing, a responsive affidavit setting forth your net monthly income and expenses and attach copies of your last three pay stubs or, if self-employed, proof of your current income."

(3) Motions to Establish or Modify Permanent Maintenance

(a) All motions to establish or modify permanent maintenance shall be accompanied by the following:

(i) A statement from movant setting forth the amount of maintenance requested.

(ii) Copies of the movant's last three pay stubs or, if movant is self-employed, proof of the movant's current income.

(iii) An affidavit setting forth movant's monthly expenses and income and the monthly income of the party against whom the motion is brought, if known.

(iv) The most recently filed federal and state income tax return.

(b) The respondent shall file the above financial information with the court and serve it on the opposing party 5 days prior to the hearing.

(c) The notice of hearing accompanying a motion to establish or modify permanent maintenance shall contain the following statement: "You must file with the court, at least 24 hours prior to the time of the hearing, copies of your last three pay stubs, or if self-employed, proof of your current income and by an affidavit setting forth your monthly expenses and income, and the most current federal and state tax returns."

(4) All post-decree matters regarding the maintenance issues shall be submitted with a statement of monthly living expenses, supporting documentation of all year to date gross income from all sources, and the most recently filed federal and state income tax returns. The responding party is to similarly file this financial information. All parties shall exchange said information 10 days prior to the hearing. In addition, counsel shall certify, prior to any hearing being held, that reasonable efforts were made to resolve the issues in dispute.

HISTORY: Amended by Order 2012–10, eff. 1–1–13; adopted eff. 1–1–11

III. CUSTODY, SHARED PARENTING, VISITATION AND SUPPORT

FCRPP 6   General Provisions

(1) The provisions of this section shall apply to all actions in which there are disputes regarding custody, shared parenting, visitation or support.

(2) A parent or custodian may move for, or the court may order, one or more of the following, which may be apportioned at the expense of the parents or custodians:

(a) A custody evaluation;

(b) Psychological evaluation(s) of a parent or parents or custodians, or child(ren);

(c) Family counseling;

(d) Mediation;

(e) Appointment of a guardian *ad litem*;

(f) Appointment of such other professional(s) for opinions or advice which the court deems appropriate; or,

(g) Such other action deemed appropriate by the court.

(3) The court or domestic relations commissioner shall conduct a hearing on any motion for temporary custody, time sharing, visitation or child support, within 60 days of the filing of the motion except for good cause stated on the record. Nothing herein prevents the parties from entering into an agreement on these issues.

(4) In all proceedings for the dissolution of marriage in which children of the marriage are minors, or in any custody proceedings, the court may order the parents or custodians and children to participate in counseling or divorce education on a case-by-case basis, which shall be at the expense of the parties.

HISTORY: Amended by Order 2012–10, eff. 1–1–13; adopted eff. 1–1–11

FCRPP 7   Custody

(1) Unless otherwise ordered by the court, in any action in which the permanent custody or time-sharing of the child(ren) is in issue, each party shall, not less than 14 days prior to the day set for hearing, provide the other party(ies) with a list of the names and addresses of every person and a short statement of the subject of their testimony, other than a parent or the child(ren) of the parents, expected to be called as a witness, as well as a list of exhibits to be entered.

(2) **Relocation.**

(a) Before a joint custodian seeks to relocate, written notice shall be filed with the court and notice shall be served on the non-relocating joint custodian. Either party may file a motion for change of custody or time-sharing within 20 days of service of the notice if the custodians are not in agreement; or, the parties shall file an agreed order if the time sharing arrangement is modified by agreement. See Pennington v. Marcum, 266 S.W.3d 759 (Ky. 2008) and Wilson v. Messinger, 840 S.W.2d 203 (Ky.1992).

(b) Before a sole custodian seeks to relocate, written notice shall be filed with the court and notice shall be served on the non-custodial parent. If the court ordered visitation is affected by the relocation, the non-custodial parent may file a motion contesting the change in visitation within 20 days of service of the notice.

HISTORY: Amended by Order 2012–10, eff. 1–1–13; adopted eff. 1–1–11

Supreme Court Standing Committee on the FCRPP (2012) Commentary

Pursuant to KRS 403.770, if the relocating custodian has an active Emergency Protective Order or Domestic Violence Order against the other parent or custodian, the relocating custodian must not be required to disclose to the other party the relocation destination. The court and clerks will strictly comply with the statutory mandates set forth in KRS 403.770. If the domestic violence action is not pending in the same circuit, the court may require the relocating custodian to disclose the relocation destination provided only if the location is filed under seal, with strict confidentiality maintained by the court and clerk, and the location is not disclosed to the opposing party.

FCRPP 8　Time-Sharing/Visitation

(1) A parent shall be entitled to time-sharing/visitation as ordered by the court, which may be in accordance with the Model Time–Sharing/Visitation Guidelines, unless otherwise agreed to by the parties or ordered by the court.

(2) Model Time–Sharing/Visitation Guidelines are set forth in Appendix A to these Rules or other guidelines may be applied and set forth in local rules.

HISTORY: Amended by Order 2012–10, eff. 1–1–13; adopted eff. 1–1–11

FCRPP 9　Support

(1) Once support has been set by the court, it shall continue in full force and effect unless modified by the court, or ended by operation of law.

(2) An order directing the payment of child support shall be entered utilizing the AOC–152, Uniform Child Support Order and/or Wage/Income Withholding Order which is the form prescribed by the Administrative Office of the Courts pursuant to KRS 205.713 and KRS 205.802. This form shall be located on the Court of Justice website and shall include the following:

(a) The amount and frequency of the support payments;

(b) That the payment shall be paid

(i) By wage/income withholding, to begin immediately; or,

(ii) If wage/income withholding is not ordered to begin immediately for good cause shown, as ordered by the court and as directed in KRS 403.215; or,

(iii) According to a written agreement reached between both parties which provides for an alternative arrangement to wage/income withholding.

(c) In non–IV–D cases the federal Income Withholding[1] for Support (IWO) form OMB 0970–0154, and in IV–D cases the state CS–89, shall be utilized to notify the employer/income withholder of any wage/income withholding ordered by the court.

(d) The party responsible for medical and other ordered expenses of the child(ren); and,

(e) The social security numbers of the parties and child(ren), CR 7.03 notwithstanding.

(3) Notice of any wage/income withholding shall be served upon the employer and the employee as follows:

(a) In non–IV–D cases, the OMB 0970–0154 shall be accompanied by the underlying AOC–152.

(b) In IV–D cases, the CS–89 shall be utilized.

(4) Motions to Establish or Modify Child Support.

(a) A motion to establish or modify child support shall be accompanied by the following:

(1) A completed child support guidelines worksheet.

(2) Copies of the movant's last three pay stubs or, if movant is self-employed, proof of the movant's current income.

(3) The most recently filed federal and state income tax returns.

(4) Verification of the cost of health insurance for the child(ren) only.

(5) A notice of hearing accompanying a motion for child support which shall contain the following statement: "You must file with the Court, at least 24 hours prior to the time of the hearing, a completed child support guidelines worksheet and copies of your last three pay stubs or, if self-employed, proof of your current income and the most current federal and state tax returns."

(b) The responding party is to similarly file this financial information at least 24 hours prior to the hearing.

(c) All parties shall exchange said information 10 days prior to the hearing.

(d) In addition, counsel shall certify, prior to the hearing being held, that reasonable efforts were made to resolve all the issues in dispute.

(5) Motions to Modify Support.

(a) All motions to modify support shall set forth the current child support and shall be accompanied by a completed child support guidelines worksheet and by copies of the movant's last three pay stubs or, if movant is self-employed, proof of the movant's current income.

(b) The notice of hearing accompanying a motion to modify child support shall contain the following statement: "You must file with the court, at least 24 hours prior to the time of the hearing, a completed child support guidelines worksheet and copies of your last three pay stubs or, if self-employed, proof of your current income."

(6) All post-decree matters regarding modification of child support shall be submitted with a child support worksheet, documentation of all year to date gross income from all sources, the most recently filed federal and state income tax returns, verification of the cost of health insurance for the child(ren) only, and verification of child care expenses. The responding party is to similarly file financial information. All parties shall exchange said information 10 days prior to the hearing. In addition counsel shall certify, prior

to any hearing being held, that reasonable efforts were made to resolve the issues in dispute.

HISTORY: Amended by Order 2012–10, eff. 1–1–13; adopted eff. 1–1–11

[1]So in original.

IV. DOMESTIC VIOLENCE

FCRPP 10 Issuance of Summons

(1) If an emergency protective order is not issued due to an insufficient relationship as identified in KRS 403.720(2) or (4), or for failure to state an act or threat of domestic violence between the parties, the finding of the insufficient relationship or failure to state an act or threat of domestic violence shall be noted on the petition by the judge, and no summons shall be issued.

(2) If the relationship is one recognized under KRS 403.720(2) or (4) and there is a finding of domestic violence and abuse and a finding of immediate and present danger, an emergency protective order shall be issued.

(3) If there is no finding of an immediate and present danger of domestic violence and abuse, when the relationship is one recognized under KRS 403.720(2) or (4), but the court determines that domestic violence and abuse exists, a summons shall be issued and a hearing shall be held to determine if a domestic violence order should be issued. Any finding at the hearing shall constitute an appealable order.

HISTORY: Adopted by Order 2010–09, eff. 1–1–11

FCRPP 11 Contempt Proceedings

(1) No petitioner shall be held in contempt for failure to appear at a domestic violence hearing or for failing to prosecute a civil or criminal contempt violation of a protective order except for good cause shown on the record. Failure to appear may result in denial of the petition.

(2) When the court conducts contempt proceedings in domestic violence actions, the party subject to contempt shall be represented by counsel, unless waived, and an attorney shall be appointed by the court if the party qualifies as an indigent.

HISTORY: Adopted by Order 2010–09, eff. 1–1–11

FCRPP 12 Reissuance of Emergency Protective Order Upon Transfer to Another Circuit

When the local domestic violence protocol requires that a case be transferred to another circuit due to a pending dissolution case, an emergency protective order shall continue and the summons shall be re-issued by the initiating court, pursuant to KRS 403.740(4), for a period not to exceed 14 days if service has not been made on the adverse party by the date of transfer, or as the court determines is necessary for the protection of the petitioner. Thereafter, reissuance of the summons shall occur as needed in the court of transfer.

HISTORY: Adopted by Order 2010–09, eff. 1–1–11

FCRPP 13 Domestic Violence Protocols

(1) Domestic violence cases shall be conducted according to the local domestic violence protocol.

(2) The court shall not limit or restrict a victim's access to seek a protective order for domestic violence.

(3) The court shall provide 24–hour access to protection from domestic violence.

(4) Domestic violence cases shall retain the domestic violence case file number even if heard with another matter.

(5) The court shall establish schedules for domestic violence hearings and shall provide them to anyone authorized to verify domestic violence petitions.

(6) The court shall inform the respondent regarding the purchase of a firearm, and the surrender of same, in compliance with 18 U.S.C. Section 922(g)(8), during the pendency of an emergency protective order or domestic violence order, and shall inform the respondent regarding the confiscation, retention and return of firearms.

HISTORY: Adopted by Order 2010–09, eff. 1–1–11

V. PATERNITY ACTIONS

FCRPP 14 Paternity Reopenings

(1) A fee of $50.00 shall be paid by the movant in paternity cases reopened after 6 months from the entry of the paternity judgment for the purpose of modifying any support, custody or visitation ordered. This does not include motions in 42 U.S.C. Title IV–D cases for child support enforcement. The clerk shall collect any fee upon the filing of the motion, unless the movant files a motion to proceed in forma pauperis.

(a) Reopening for purposes of this rule means any motion for modification of an order filed more than 6 months after entry of the order. A case is considered reopened until all matters in the motion are resolved.

(b) Once a case is reopened and the fee is paid, another fee will not be required unless 6 months or more have elapsed since entry of the order on the motion that reopened the case.

(c) This fee shall not be required for motions to enforce an order and which are so titled.

(2) Nothing in this Rule shall preclude the district court from declining jurisdiction on custody and visitation and referring the action to the circuit court pursuant to KRS 406.051(2); nor shall this Rule preclude an action for custody, visitation or support from being filed in the circuit court by a party after the entry of a judgment of paternity in district court. In either event the appropriate filing fee shall be paid by the moving party, unless the movant/petitioner files a motion to proceed in forma pauperis.

(3) In family court jurisdictions nothing in this Rule shall preclude the family court judge from ordering the custody, visitation and support matters in a paternity action be initiated in a circuit action. In such instance, a new circuit civil petition shall be filed by the movant/petitioner and the appropriate filing fee shall be paid unless in forma pauperis status is granted by the court.

HISTORY: Amended by Order 2012–10, eff. 1–1–13; adopted eff. 1–1–11

FCRPP 15   Genetic Testing

When paternity is an issue in any action, the court may order the mother, child and the putative father to submit to genetic tests as follows:

(1) In a case in which paternity is denied or in which the parties request genetic testing, on motion made by any party, a pretrial order shall be entered by the court forthwith which requires both parties and the child to submit to genetic tests in accordance with KRS 406.081 or 406.091 unless an agreed order is entered.

(2) Within 30 days of receipt of the genetic report, the petitioner shall file the original report with the court in support of a motion to dismiss, a motion for trial or a motion for summary judgment. This does not preclude prehearing conferencing in the interim which may extend the 30 days by agreement or resolve the issues.

(3) In those cases in which the genetic test report excludes the defendant from the paternity of the child, the court, after the expiration of 30 days from the date of the filing of the exclusionary report, shall enter an order of dismissal in favor of the defendant unless a motion for additional testing pursuant to KRS 406.091 is filed prior to the expiration of the 30 days.

HISTORY: Amended by Order 2012–10, eff. 1–1–13; adopted eff. 1–1–11

VI. DEPENDENCY, NEGLECT OR ABUSE

FCRPP 16 Orders in Dependency, Neglect or Abuse Actions

To the extent not otherwise specified, any order entered in a dependency or neglect or abuse action shall be on the appropriate Administrative Office of the Courts forms.

HISTORY: Adopted by Order 2010–09, eff. 1–1–11

FCRPP 17 Notice in Dependency, Neglect or Abuse Actions

(1) Judicial Notice. In making any determinations with regard to a child in a dependency or neglect or abuse action, the court may consider the findings of fact and court orders from any other court proceeding in any other court file involving the child or the child's parents or the person exercising custodial control or supervision, if the court is aware of such proceedings. To the extent that the court relies on such, the court shall include a copy of that material in the record.

(2) Notice and Opportunity to be Heard. Prior to any review or permanency hearing, the state child welfare agency shall inform the court of the name and address of the foster parents, pre-adoptive parents and any relatives who are providing care for the child. The clerk shall provide notice of any review or permanency hearing to all parties and to the child's foster parents, pre-adoptive parents, and any relatives who are providing care for the child. The foster parents, pre-adoptive parents or any relative who is providing

care for the child shall have an opportunity to be heard and may be subject to cross examination but shall not be designated as a party to such a proceeding solely on the basis of such notice and right to be heard.

HISTORY: Amended by Order 2012–10, eff. 1–1–13; adopted eff. 1–1–11

FCRPP 18 Service

(1) A copy of the petition and summons, and an emergency custody order, if any, shall be served upon parents or persons exercising custodial control or supervision or who have been awarded legal custody by a court or claims a right to legal custody under the law of this state. It may be served by any person authorized to serve process except the state child protective service agency.

(2) A notice and statement of the rights and a blank affidavit of indigency, utilizing AOC–DNA–2.2, Notice of Emergency Removal, and AOC–DNA–11, Financial Statement, Affidavit of Indigence, Request for Counsel and Order, shall be served with the emergency custody order.

HISTORY: Amended by Order 2012–10, eff. 1–1–13; adopted eff. 1–1–11

Supreme Court Standing Committee on the FCRPP (2012) Commentary

If a permanent custody motion is filed within a Dependency, Neglect and Abuse (DNA) action pursuant to KRS 620.027, the movant shall ensure that personal service of the permanent custody motion has been perfected upon both parents and any other legal custodian, except as otherwise directed by the Uniform Child Custody Jurisdiction and Enforcement Act (UCCJEA). Personal service shall be perfected in accordance with the Kentucky Rules of Civil Procedure, CR 4, et. seq. If said service has not been properly perfected in the DNA action, the court should deny the motion and require the movant to file a proper petition for child custody pursuant to KRS Chapter 403.

FCRPP 19 Emergency Custody Orders in Dependency, Neglect or Abuse Actions

(1) Any request for an emergency custody order in a dependency, neglect or abuse case shall be in writing and shall be accompanied by an AOC–DNA–2.1, Affidavit for Emergency Custody Order, alleging dependency, or neglect or abuse, and shall be presented to the judge with any other documentation presented at the time of the filing of the request.

(2) The person seeking the emergency custody order shall indicate on the affidavit whether there are other proceedings pending, or any orders of custody, related to the child in the Commonwealth or any other state.

(3) The emergency custody order shall be on AOC–DNA–2, Emergency Custody Order. In no event shall a child be removed pursuant to KRS 620.060 only on a verbal order.

(a) Upon issuance of an emergency custody order by the judge, the person seeking the emergency custody order shall file the emergency custody order and the affidavit with the clerk no later than the close of the next work day and the clerk shall assign a case number.

(b) If not filed with the emergency custody order, a petition shall be filed with the clerk within 72 hours of taking the child into custody in the same case file as the emergency custody order and affidavit.

(c) The court may, after issuing an emergency custody order, transfer the case for forum non conveniens to the county where the dependency, abuse or neglect is alleged to have occurred and shall notify the court to which the case is being transferred, upon issuance of the transfer order.

HISTORY: Adopted by Order 2010–09, eff. 1–1–11

FCRPP 20 Petition

(1) A petition pursuant to KRS Chapter 620 shall be filed on AOC–DNA–1, Dependency Neglect or Abuse Petition. In proceedings involving siblings, separate petitions shall be filed for each child and individual case numbers shall be assigned by the clerk of the court, but all siblings' files shall be assigned to the same judge.

(2) When a petition is filed a copy shall be mailed or provided by the clerk to the parents or other person exercising custodial control or supervision, the state child protective service agency, the county attorney, any guardian *ad litem*, and any counsel of record,

no later than the business day following the filing of the petition.

HISTORY: Adopted by Order 2010–09, eff. 1–1–11

FCRPP 21 Notice of Temporary Removal Hearing

(1) The clerk shall provide notification of the temporary removal hearing to the parents or other person exercising custodial control or supervision, county attorney, the state child protective service agency, any guardian *ad litem* and any counsel of record.

(2) The order entered at the hearing shall be on AOC–DNA–3, Order–Temporary Removal Hearing.

HISTORY: Adopted by Order 2010–09, eff. 1–1–11

FCRPP 22 Orders from Hearings

(1) Adjudication Hearing. The order entered at the hearing shall be on AOC–DNA–4, Order–Adjudication Hearing.

(2) Disposition Hearing. The order entered at the hearing shall be on AOC–DNA–5, Order–Disposition Hearing

(3) Permanency Hearing. The order entered at the hearing shall be on AOC–DNA–6, Order–Disposition Hearing.

(4) Permanent Custody Order. Any order of permanent custody entered pursuant to KRS 620.027 shall be on AOC–DNA–9, Order–Permanent Custody.

(5) Verbal Approval or Stamped Signatures. No order in a dependency, neglect and abuse action may be entered on verbal approval or stamped signature.

HISTORY: Amended by Order 2012–10, eff. 1–1–13; adopted eff. 1–1–11

Supreme Court Standing Committee on the FCRPP (2012) Commentary

Faxed or scanned original signatures and encrypted or otherwise secure digital signatures authorized by the Supreme Court have been deemed to be acceptable methods of signature for purposes of these Rules.

FCRPP 23 Continuances

(1) If the court grants an extension of time or a continuance for any hearing other than the annual permanency hearing, it shall make written or oral findings on the record that the continuance is necessary in the best interest of the child, for discovery or presentation of evidence or witnesses, to protect the rights of a party, or for other good cause shown.

(2) The annual permanency review hearing shall be conducted at least annually and shall not be continued beyond 12 months from the placement of the child in foster care for any reason, including good cause.

HISTORY: Amended by Order 2012–10, eff. 1–1–13; adopted eff. 1–1–11

Supreme Court Standing Committee on the FCRPP (2012) Commentary

Pursuant to 45 C.F.R. 1356.21(b)(2)(i), the state child welfare agency must obtain a judicial determination that it has made reasonable efforts to finalize the permanency plan that is in effect (whether the plan is reunification, adoption, legal guardianship, placement with a fit and willing relative, or placement in another planned permanent living arrangement) within 12 months of the date the child is considered to have entered foster care and at least every 12 months thereafter while the child is in foster care. Under 45 C.F.R. 1356.21(b)(2)(ii), if such a judicial determination is not made, the child becomes ineligible under title IV–E at the end of the month in which the judicial determination was required to have been made, and remains ineligible until such a determination is made.

FCRPP 24   Dismissal

Once filed, a petition shall be dismissed only upon court order.

HISTORY: Adopted by Order 2010–09, eff. 1–1–11

FCRPP 25   Transfer

Cases shall not be transferred from one county to another prior to adjudication except on a specific finding of improper venue or forum nonconveniens.

HISTORY: Adopted by Order 2010–09, eff. 1–1–11

FCRPP 26   Appearances

Any attorney appearing on behalf of a party in a dependency, neglect or abuse action shall file a written entry of appearance unless an order appointing the attorney as guardian *ad litem* or court-appointed counsel has been entered. An attorney shall not withdraw from representation except upon motion to withdraw granted by the court.

HISTORY: Amended by Order 2012–10, eff. 1–1–13; adopted eff. 1–1–11

FCRPP 27   Records and Transcripts

(1) An electronic or stenographic record of interviews with children, including a recording of any in-camera proceedings, shall be filed under seal with the clerk and may be made available to the parties or their counsel on motion and written order of the court.

(2) In courts that have more than one county in their jurisdiction any recordings made in a county other than where the action is filed shall be delivered to the clerk of the county where the action is filed by the court ordering the hearing.

HISTORY: Amended by Order 2012–10, eff. 1–1–13; adopted eff. 1–1–11

FCRPP 28   Reports

Any dispositional report shall be filed three days prior to a dispositional hearing on AOC–DNA–12, Dependency, Neglect or Abuse Dispositional Report.

HISTORY: Adopted by Order 2010–09, eff. 1–1–11

FCRPP 29   Case Plan and Case Progress Reports

The court shall require the following to be filed in the court record and provided to all parties:

(1) The out of home case plan;

(2) Any visitation agreement for the case plan or the case permanency plan; and,

(3) Any prevention plan or safety plan developed by the child protective service agency.

(4) The state child welfare agency shall provide the names and addresses of the child's foster parents, pre-adoptive parents or relatives providing care to the child, court appointed special advocate, and foster care review board member assigned to the case with the case permanency plan or case progress report filed with the court on a form prescribed by the Administrative Office of the Courts.

HISTORY: Amended by Order 2012–10, eff. 1–1–13; adopted eff. 1–1–11

FCRPP 30   Reviews

(1) **Permanent Placement Review.** In addition to the annual permanency hearing mandated by KRS 610.125, the court shall conduct a permanency progress review no later than 6 months after a child is placed in foster care, in the home of a non-custodial parent, or other person or agency, when that child was sixteen years of age or younger at the time of the filing of a dependency, neglect or abuse petition.

(2) **Independent Living Review.** In addition to the permanent placement review and the annual permanency hearing, and when the child remains in foster care or committed to the state child welfare agency, the court shall conduct an independent living review at least 6 months prior to the child turning 18 years of age to ensure that training on independent living and other appropriate services have been included in the case plan and are being provided to the child.

HISTORY: Amended by Order 2012–10, eff. 1–1–13; adopted eff. 1–1–11

Supreme Court Standing Committee on the FCRPP (2012) Commentary

With respect to FCRPP 30(1), if a permanent custody motion is filed within a Dependency, Neglect or Abuse (DNA) action pursuant to KRS 620.027, the movant shall ensure that personal service (of the DNA action) has been perfected upon both parents and any other legal custodian, except as otherwise directed by the Uniform Child Custody Jurisdiction and Enforcement Act (UCCJEA). Personal service shall be perfected in accordance with the Kentucky Rules of Civil Procedure, CR 4, et. seq. If said service has not been properly perfected in the DNA action, the court should deny the motion and require the movant to file a proper petition for child custody pursuant to KRS Chapter 403.

FCRPP 31   New Action

Any new allegation or request for removal after a child has achieved permanency shall be filed as a new action.

HISTORY: Adopted by Order 2010–09, eff. 1–1–11

VII. ADOPTION AND TERMINATION OF PARENTAL RIGHTS

FCRPP 32   Venue and Petition

(1) **Venue**. When filed in the same county in which a KRS Chapter 620 proceeding has been held, a proceeding under KRS Chapter 625 shall be assigned to the same family court division that heard the KRS Chapter 620 action. Otherwise, venue shall proceed according to KRS 625.050(4).

(2) **Petition.**

(a) A separate petition shall be filed for each child and individual case numbers shall be assigned by the clerk of the court in proceedings filed pursuant to KRS Chapters 199 and 625, and in the case of siblings, shall be heard by the same judge.

(b) Every petition in an adoption or termination of parental rights action shall include the case number of any underlying juvenile case, specifically dependency, neglect or abuse or termination of parental rights cases, and shall include the name of any guardian *ad litem* previously appointed.

HISTORY: Amended by Order 2012–10, eff. 1–1–13; adopted eff. 1–1–11

FCRPP 33   Adoption

(1) No request for final hearing shall be made prior to the filing of the state child protective service agency report pursuant to KRS 199.510, and the guardian *ad litem* report, if any, pursuant to KRS 199.515.

(2) In the event of an uncontested adoption, a hearing shall be held within 60 days of the filing of a request for a final hearing.

(3) A continuance of any final hearing date shall not be granted except upon good cause shown. Annual permanency review hearings shall continue to be held in any dependency, neglect and abuse action as required by FCRPP 23 until finalization of the adoption.

HISTORY: Amended by Order 2012–10, eff. 1–1–13; adopted eff. 1–1–11

FCRPP 34   Involuntary Termination

(1) Immediately upon the filing of any petition for involuntary termination of parental rights, the petitioner shall obtain a pretrial date. In the event the parents are not served prior to the pretrial date, the pretrial date shall be used as a case status review to expedite the proceeding.

(2) A continuance of any final hearing date shall not be granted except upon good cause shown. The annual permanency review hearings shall continue to be held in any dependency, neglect and abuse action as required by FCRPP 23 until permanency is achieved.

HISTORY: Amended by Order 2012–10, eff. 1–1–13; adopted eff. 1–1–11

FCRPP 35   Orders Terminating Parental Rights

The clerk of the court shall send two certified copies of the order terminating parental rights to the state child protective agency. The prospective adoptive parent or his or her attorney, if any, may obtain a certified copy of the order terminating parental rights from the state child protective agency to attach to the adoption petition.

HISTORY: Adopted by Order 2010–09, eff. 1–1–11

FCRPP 36   Post-Termination of Parental Rights Review

If an order terminating parental rights is entered, a copy of the order shall also be certified to the record in the underlying dependency, neglect and abuse case which shall be identified in the order. The clerk of the court in the underlying dependency, neglect and abuse case shall docket the matter for a review hearing within 90 days from the date of the entry of the order of termination of parental rights and shall docket the matter as directed by the court at least annually thereafter until permanency is achieved.

HISTORY: Amended by Order 2012–10, eff. 1–1–13; adopted eff. 1–1–11

VIII. STATUS OFFENDERS

FCRPP 37   Review

At any time during a status offense action, the court on its own motion, or on motion of any interested person, may determine that a status matter is more appropriate as a KRS Chapter 620 proceeding and direct the state child welfare agency to investigate and/or provide services to the child and/or family; amend the petition pursuant to KRS 610.010(13) and order it served; or, require a new petition to be filed. See also KRS 605.130(3).

HISTORY: Amended by Order 2012–10, eff. 1–1–13; adopted eff. 1–1–11

FCRPP 38   Interstate Compact on Placement of Children

Pursuant to KRS Chapter 615, the child shall be presented forthwith to the court without formal petition. The court shall utilize the forms provided pursuant to the Interstate Compact.

HISTORY: Adopted by Order 2010–09, eff. 1–1–11

FCRPP 39   Diversion

Prior to the court issuing an order for a formal hearing or the county attorney requesting a formal hearing, the case shall be processed by the court designated worker pursuant to KRS 610.030.

HISTORY: Amended by Order 2012–10, eff. 1–1–13; adopted eff. 1–1–11

FCRPP 40   Petition

(1) Every petition shall be accompanied by the AOC–JW–40, Preliminary Inquiry Formal/Informal Processing Criteria and Recommendations; and where diversion has been attempted pursuant to KRS 630.050, shall also include an AOC–40.1, Unsuccessful Diversion Agreement, which includes preliminary intake inquiry findings.

(2) A habitual truancy petition shall be accompanied by AOC–JV–41, Affidavit and Truancy Evaluation Form in compliance with KRS 159.140.

(3) A beyond control of school petition shall be accompanied by AOC–JV–38.1, Affidavit and Beyond Control of School Evaluation Form.

(4) A beyond control of parent petition shall be accompanied by AOC–JV–38, Affidavit and Beyond Control of Parent Evaluation Form.

(5) A habitual runaway petition shall be accompanied by the AOC–JW–39, Pre–Adjudicative Detention Criteria, with attachments.

HISTORY: Adopted by Order 2010–09, eff. 1–1–11

FCRPP 41   Summons

Upon the filing of the petition, the clerk shall issue a summons to the parent(s) or other person exercising custodial control or supervision of the child, setting a date for initial appearance as directed by the presiding judge.

HISTORY: Adopted by Order 2010–09, eff. 1–1–11

FCRPP 42   Proceedings

(1) Pursuant to KRS 610.060, the judge shall explain to the child on the record his or her rights and the charge, and shall utilize AOC–JV–49, Notice of Juvenile Rights and Consequences for Status Offenders.

(2) A public advocate shall be appointed for the child unless otherwise waived on the record by obtaining private counsel. The court may place the child on terms which address the child's alleged behavior(s), and may order participation in a service, program or local resource to assist the child.

(3) A pretrial conference may be held in the court's discretion.

(4) For disposition, the court shall utilize, AOC–JV–36, Juvenile Status Offender Order, to order terms, services, programs and/or resources to address the needs of the child and family pursuant to KRS 630.120(5). These orders may not require an involuntary drug screen of the parent(s) or other person exercising custodial control or supervision in the status offense case. The court may also adopt recommendations in the dispositional report. For a child who is committed to the state child protective service agency, the court shall also utilize the AOC–JV–31, Juvenile Status or Delinquency Disposition.

HISTORY: Adopted by Order 2010–09, eff. 1–1–11

FCRPP 43   Informal Adjustments

(1) For any status offender petition resolved by an informal adjustment as defined by KRS 600.020(31), unless explicitly stated otherwise, the terms of the informal adjustment shall remain in effect for a period not to exceed one year or until the child's eighteenth birthday, whichever comes first.

(2) On notice of a violation of the terms of an informal adjustment to the county attorney, and motion filed with the court and noticed to the interested parties, the court shall re-docket the case, set aside the informal adjustment, and reinstate the original petition upon a showing that the violation could not be remedied without court intervention.

(3) In the event that the alleged violation of the terms of the informal adjustment would constitute grounds for an original petition the county attorney may move to file an amended petition or file a new petition after consulting with the case worker and the family involved.

HISTORY: Adopted by Order 2010–09, eff. 1–1–11

FCRPP 44   Detention of Status Offenders

(1) Pursuant to KRS 630.100, no status offender shall be placed in secure detention unless:

(a) The offender is alleged to be an habitual runaway; or,

(b) The offender is alleged to be in contempt of a valid court order entered on AOC–JV–36, Juvenile Status Offender Order; or a finding of contempt of court has been entered in a formal court proceeding and a valid court order has been entered on AOC–JV–36, Juvenile Status Offender Order.

(2) Any status offender appearing before the court shall be provided a public advocate or shall be provided the opportunity to retain private counsel.

(3) Release of a child in detention to non-secure alternatives may be to:

(a) The child's parents or legal guardians; or

(b) The state child protective service agency if the child is committed to that agency; or

(c) The state juvenile justice agency for alternative detention services, if the child qualifies for such a placement; or

(d) A non-secure crisis or other mental health unit/facility.

(4) If the parents or legal guardians are unavailable or unwilling to accept the child and there is no other alternative under Section (3) above:

(a) Another responsible adult relative or other interested adult with an established relationship with the child, including the person who may have been exercising custodial control or supervision but does not have actual legal custody, shall be contacted as directed by the presiding judge and the child released to his/her care; or

(b) The child shall be placed in an alternative placement, with possible referral to the state child protective service agency.

(5) No child shall be detained for more than twenty-four (24) hours in secure detention without a hearing before the court within that twenty-four (24) hour period of the detainment, exclusive of weekends and holidays. Each court shall establish a local protocol to assure that the hearing is scheduled within twenty-four (24) hours, exclusive of weekends and holidays.

(6) A judge shall conduct a due process hearing prior to detaining a child in a secure detention facility for contempt and shall consider any alternatives to a secure detention placement, and other alternatives identified in agency reports submitted within 48 hours pursuant to KRS 610.265(3)(d)(3). If the court has determined by findings on the record that no less restrictive alternatives are available or appropriate, then the child may be securely detained. Any such court order shall indicate the length of detainment.

HISTORY: Adopted by Order 2010–09, eff. 1–1–11

IX. APPENDIX A

Appendix A Model Time-Sharing Visitation Guidelines

Model Time–Sharing/Visitation Guidelines

The following schedules are suggested as **guidelines** for the parents and the court in establishing time-sharing/visitation schedules. Each case will present unique facts or circumstances which shall be considered by the court in establishing a time-sharing/visitation schedule and **the final schedule established by the court or agreed to by the parents may or may not be what these guidelines suggest.**

1. The time-sharing/visitation schedule set by the court for holidays, school breaks and summer break should control over regularly scheduled time-sharing/visitation time, even if this allows successive time-sharing/visitation periods.

2. The parent exercising time–sharing/visitation should be responsible for timely picking up the child(ren) at the beginning of the time-sharing/visitation period and returning the child(ren) in a timely manner at the end of the time-sharing/visitation period.

3. Times in a time-sharing/visitation schedule should be set in the time zone where the child primarily resides.

4. For time-sharing/visitation times pertaining to school holidays, whether in a formal school or home-schooled, the school holidays where the child(ren) primarily resides should apply.

5. Each parent should provide to the other parent contact numbers and addresses (unless a domestic violence order is in effect) where the child(ren) can be located during their scheduled time-sharing/visitation time.

6. The parent exercising time-sharing/visitation should be given a minimum of every other weekend as time-sharing/visitation time with the child(ren) and one midweek overnight time-sharing/visitation. The parent having such time-sharing/visitation should be responsible for delivering the child(ren) to school, child care, or the other parent's home as specifically ordered by the court or agreed to by the parents.

7. Holidays.

a. If a holiday is celebrated on a Monday following a parent's regularly scheduled time-sharing/visitation, then that parent should be permitted to extend parenting time until 6:00 p.m. on the holiday, unless the parents agree otherwise.

b. Other holidays.

(i) Parent exercising time-sharing/visitation.

1) During the first full year after divorce/custody proceedings have been filed, the non-residential parent should have time-sharing/visitation scheduled as follows:

a) New Year's Day and July 4th from 8:00 a.m. until 6:00 p.m.

b) Thanksgiving, beginning at 6:00 p.m. the day school ends until 3:00 p. m. Thanksgiving Day.

c) Christmas/Winter Break, beginning at 6:00 p.m. the day school ends until noon on December 25.

d) Holidays not listed that are of special interest to the family should be assigned to the non-residential parent in time amounts similar to those in a), b) and c) above.

2) Holiday time not scheduled above to the parent exercising time-sharing/visitation should be with the other parent.

3) Mother's Day and Father's Day, regardless of any conflict with the above proposed schedule, should be spent with the appropriate parent from 8:00 a.m. until 6:00 p.m.

4) Fall Break or Spring Break, as allowed by the child(ren)'s school calendar, should be scheduled for the parent with whom the child(ren)

primarily resides in the first full year after the divorce/custody proceedings are filed from 6:00 p.m. the day school ends until 6:00 p.m. the following Friday. If school breaks are longer than one week due to the school schedule, the parent with whom the child(ren) primarily resides should be scheduled for the first half of the break and the other parent should be scheduled for the last half.

5) Summer Break should be scheduled to allow the parent exercising time-sharing/visitation a minimum of two periods of two consecutive weeks during the Summer Break. Each parent should provide the time periods he or she desires to the other parent before the end of the school year, or at least 60 days in advance of the requested time. If a child(ren) must attend summer school in order to pass to the next grade, summer time-sharing/visitation should not prevent school time.

6) Birthdays: Unless the birthday falls on a regularly scheduled time-sharing/visitation day, the parent exercising time-sharing/visitation should be scheduled for birthday time from 5:00 p.m. until 8:00 p.m. If it is a regular day of the parent exercising time-sharing/visitation where the child(ren) does not primarily reside, the other parent should have birthday time from 5:00 p.m. until 8:00 p.m.

(ii) Alternating years: For each year thereafter, the time-sharing/visitation set out above should alternate between the parent with whom the child(ren) primarily resides and the parent exercising time-sharing/visitation.

8. Waiting/Tardiness/Cancellations.

a. In the event either parent will be more than 30 minutes late, due to reasonable unforeseen circumstances, to pick up the child(ren), he or she should provide direct notice to the other parent or a designated third party and make suitable arrangements for exchange of the child(ren).

b. If time-sharing/visitation is missed through no fault of the parent, and reasonable notice has been given, that time should be made up, if reasonable to do so.

c. If the child(ren) is ill, the parent who has the child should give 24–hour notice, if possible, to allow for appropriate plans to be made.

9. Transportation: The parents should transport the child(ren) in a safe manner, which includes utilizing the appropriate child restraint systems and not driving under the influence of intoxicants.

HISTORY: Adopted by Order 2010–09, eff. 1–1–11

RULES OF CRIMINAL PROCEDURE

Including Amendments Received Through January 1, 2013

I   GENERAL PROVISIONS

RCr 1.02   Title and scope of rules

(1) The title of these rules is Kentucky Rules of Criminal Procedure. They may be cited as such, or as the Criminal Rules, or by the abbreviation "RCr."

(2) These rules govern procedure and practice in all criminal proceedings in the Court of Justice. To the extent that they are not inconsistent with these rules, the regulations, administrative procedures, and manuals published by the Administrative Office of the Courts upon authorization of the Supreme Court relating to internal policy and administration within the Court of Justice shall have the same effect as if incorporated in the rules.

HISTORY: Amended by Order 81–5, eff. 9–1–81; prior amendment eff. 1–1–78; adopted eff. 1–1–63

RCr 1.04   Purpose and construction

The Rules of Criminal Procedure are intended to provide for a just determination of every criminal proceeding. They shall be construed to secure simplicity in procedure, fairness in administration and the elimination of unjustifiable expense and delay.

HISTORY: Adopted eff. 1–1–63

RCr 1.06   Definitions

As used in these rules, unless the context indicates otherwise:

(a) "Judge" means any judge or justice of the Court of Justice or a trial commissioner of the district court acting under the authority of SCR 5.030.

(b) "Attorney for the Commonwealth" means the attorney general, the Commonwealth's attorney, county attorney, or special prosecutor, exercising functions assigned to them by law, and an authorized assistant of any of them.

(c) "Court" means both the circuit and district court. Wherever a court is named by its title the rule shall apply to that court alone.

HISTORY: Amended by Order 81–5, eff. 9–1–81; prior amendments eff. 1–1–78, 1–1–64; adopted eff. 1–1–63

RCr 1.08   Papers; form, filing, service

(1) All pleadings and papers, other than exhibits and printed briefs, filed in the courts shall be typewritten in black ink on unglazed white paper 8 1/2 by 11 inches in dimension, leaving at least a double space between lines, and shall be clearly readable. This requirement shall not apply to computer print-outs or similar reproductions prescribed by the Administrative Office of the Courts for use in the district court, nor shall it apply to those papers filed by a party pro se.

(2) Whenever these Rules do not specify the manner of filing and service of papers the following shall apply:

(a) Every order required by its terms to be served, every paper relating to discovery required to be served upon a party unless the court otherwise orders, every written motion other than one that may be heard ex parte, and every written notice, appearance, demand, designation of record on appeal, and similar papers shall be served upon each party.

(b) Whenever under these Rules service is required or permitted to be made upon a party represented by an attorney, the service shall be made upon the attorney unless service upon the party himself or herself is ordered by the court. Service upon the attorney or upon a party shall be made by delivering a copy to him or her or by mailing it to him or her at his or her last known address or, if no address is known, by leaving it with the clerk of the court. Delivery of a copy within this rule means handing it to the attorney or to the party; or leaving it at his or her office with the person in charge thereof; or, if there is no one in charge, leaving it in a conspicuous place therein; or, if the office is closed or the person to be served has no office, leaving it at his or her dwelling house or usual place of abode with some person of suitable age and discretion then residing therein. Service by mail is complete upon mailing.

(c) Whenever any pleading or other paper is served under subparagraphs (a) and (b), proof of the time and manner of such service shall be filed before action is to be taken thereon by the court or the parties. Proof may be by certificate of a member of the bar of the court or by affidavit of the person who served the papers, or by any other proof satisfactory to the court.

(d)(i) All papers required to be served upon a party shall be filed with the court either before service or within a reasonable time thereafter.

(ii) The filing of papers with the court as required by these Rules shall be made by filing them with the clerk of the court, except that the judge may permit the papers to be filed with him or her, in which event the judge shall note thereon the filing date and forthwith transmit them to the office of the clerk.

(iii) The clerk shall endorse upon every paper filed in an action the date of its filing. Such endorsement shall constitute the filing of the pleading or other paper, and no order of court shall be required.

HISTORY: Amended by Order 98–3, eff. 3–1–99; prior amendments eff. 9–1–81 (Order 81–5), 1–1–78; adopted eff. 1–1–63

RCr 1.10 Time

Whenever these Rules do not provide otherwise with respect to time, the following shall apply:

(a) In computing any period of time prescribed or allowed by these Rules, by order of court or by any applicable statute, the day of the act, event or default after which the designated period of time begins to run is not to be included. The last day of the period so computed is to be included unless it is a Saturday, a Sunday or a legal holiday. When the period of time prescribed or allowed is less than seven (7) days, intermediate Saturdays, Sundays and legal holidays shall be excluded in the computation.

(b) Whenever by statute, by these Rules or by a notice given thereunder, or by order of court an act is required or allowed to be done at or within a specified time, the court for cause shown may, at any time in its discretion, (i) with or without motion or notice order the period enlarged if request therefor is made before the expiration of the period originally prescribed or as extended by a previous order, or (ii) upon motion made after the expiration of the specified period, permit the act to be done if the failure to act was the result of excusable neglect.

(c)(i) A written motion, other than one which may be heard ex parte, and notice of the hearing thereof shall be served a reasonable time before the time specified for the hearing unless a specific period is fixed by these Rules or by order of the court. Such an order may for cause shown be made on ex parte application.

(ii) When a motion is supported by affidavit, the affidavit shall be served with the motion; and, except as otherwise provided in Rule 10.08, opposing affidavits may be served not later than one (1) day before the hearing unless the court permits them to be served at some other time.

(d) Whenever a party has the right or is required to do some act or take some proceedings within a prescribed period after the service of a notice or other paper upon that party and the notice or paper is served by mail, three (3) days shall be added to the prescribed period.

(e) The time for a motion for a new trial or for taking an appeal or cross-appeal shall not be extended. The time for certification of the record on appeal shall not be extended except as provided in Civil Rule 73.08.

HISTORY: Amended by Order 98–3, eff. 3–1–99; prior amendments eff. 9–1–81 (Order 81–5), 1–1–78; adopted eff. 1–1–63

II ARREST

RCr 2.02 Complaint

The complaint is a written statement of the essential facts constituting the offense charged. It shall be made under oath and signed by the complaining party before a judge or a person who (a) is legally empowered to administer oaths and (b) has been authorized to administer such oaths to a complaining party by written order of a judge for the county having venue of the offense charged.

HISTORY: Amended by Order 81–5, eff. 9–1–81; prior amendment eff. 6–1–78; adopted eff. 1–1–63

RCr 2.04 Warrant or summons; issuance

(1) If from an examination of the complaint it appears to the judge (or clerk authorized to issue warrants pursuant to KRS 15.725(5)) that there is probable cause to believe that an offense has been committed and that the defendant committed it, the judge (or clerk) shall issue a warrant for the arrest of the defendant except in the case of offenses for which a summons is mandatory pursuant to KRS 431.410, and except that a summons may issue instead of a warrant if there are reasonable grounds to believe that the defendant will appear in response, or if the defendant is a corporation.

(2) If there are reasonable grounds to believe that a defendant duly summoned will fail to appear, a warrant of arrest shall issue without the necessity of an additional supporting affidavit or complaint.

(3) More than one warrant or summons may issue on the same complaint.

HISTORY: Amended by Order 2000–1, eff. 2–1–01; prior amendments eff. 3–1–99 (Order 98–3), 9–1–81 (Order 81–5), 1–1–78; adopted eff. 1–1–63

RCr 2.05 Bench warrants

Whenever a witness or defendant fails to appear in court as duly required, the presiding judge may issue a warrant for his or her arrest without the necessity of a supporting affidavit or complaint.

HISTORY: Amended by Order 98–3, eff. 3–1–99; adopted by Order 81–5, eff. 9–1–81

RCr 2.06   Warrant or summons; requisites

(1) A warrant of arrest shall be in writing and in the name of the Commonwealth, shall be signed by the issuing officer with the title of the office and shall state the date when issued and the court to which it is returnable. It shall name or describe the offenses charged to have been committed and the county in which they are alleged to have occurred, specify the name of the defendant, or, if the defendant's name is unknown, any name or description by which the defendant can be identified with reasonable certainty, and the name of the complaining party or parties. The warrant shall be directed to all peace officers in the Commonwealth and shall direct that the defendant be arrested and brought before the court to which it is returnable.

(2) A summons shall be in the same form as a warrant except that it shall summon the defendant to appear at a stated time and place before the court to which it is returnable.

(3) If the offense charged is bailable, the judge issuing a warrant of arrest shall fix the amount of bail and type of security, if any, and endorse it on the warrant.

(4) A copy of the warrant and of the complaint pursuant to which it is issued shall be served on the arrested party at the time of the arrest or as soon thereafter as practicable.

HISTORY: Amended by Order 98–3, eff. 3–1–99; prior amendments eff. 9–1–81 (Order 81–5), 1–1–78, 1–1–64; adopted eff. 1–1–63

RCr 2.08   Defective warrant, summons or citation

No person arrested under a warrant or appearing in response to a summons or citation shall be discharged from custody or dismissed because of any defect of form in the warrant, summons, or citation, but the warrant, summons, or citation may be amended to remedy any such defect.

HISTORY: Amended by Order 81–5, eff. 9–1–81; adopted eff. 1–1–63

RCr 2.10   Warrant and summons; execution and service

(1) A warrant of arrest may be executed by any peace officer. The officer need not have the warrant in his or her possession at the time of arrest. In any event, the officer shall inform the defendant of the offense charged and the fact that a warrant has been issued.

(2) (a) A summons may be served by any peace officer. It shall be served upon a defendant by delivering a copy to the defendant personally, or by leaving it at the defendant's dwelling house or usual place of abode with some person of suitable age and discretion then residing therein.

(b) Upon the direction of the judge or the attorney for the Commonwealth a summons may be served as provided in Civil Rule 4.01(1)(a).

(c) Any peace officer who does not have the summons in his or her possession may serve it by delivering to the defendant a citation containing the information contained in the summons.

(3) A summons to a corporation shall be served by delivering a copy to an officer or managing or general agent or to any other agent authorized by appointment or by law to receive process, or by mail addressed to any of such officers or agents and mailed in accordance with paragraph (2)(b) of this Rule.

HISTORY: Amended by Order 98–3, eff. 3–1–99; prior amendments eff. 9–1–81 (Order 81–5), 1–1–78; adopted eff. 1–1–63

RCr 2.12   Warrant or summons; return

(1) The officer executing a warrant shall make return thereof to the court to which it was made returnable within a reasonable time of its execution. The executing officer shall deliver the warrant with the return endorsed thereon, together with a copy of the complaint pursuant to which the warrant was issued, to the court to which the warrant was made returnable.

(2) The officer serving a summons shall make return thereof to the court to which it was made returnable on or before the day named therein for the appearance of the defendant. The return may be made by mail. If the summons was not served on the defendant personally, the return shall show the name of the person to whom the summons was delivered, the date and hour of service, and the address at which the summons was left.

HISTORY: Amended by Order 98–3, eff. 3–1–99; prior amendments eff. 9–1–81 (Order 81–5), 1–1–78; adopted eff. 1–1–63

RCr 2.14   Right to contact attorney

(1) A person in custody shall have the right to make communications as soon as practicable for the purpose of securing the services of an attorney.

(2) Any attorney at law entitled to practice in the courts of this Commonwealth shall be permitted, at the request of the person in custody or of some one acting in that person's behalf, to visit the person in custody.

HISTORY: Amended by Order 98–3, eff. 3–1–99; prior amendment eff. 9–1–81 (Order 81–5); adopted eff. 1–1–63

III INITIAL APPEARANCE AND PRELIMINARY HEARING BEFORE DISTRICT COURT

RCr 3.02 Initial appearance before the judge

(1) An officer making an arrest under a warrant issued upon a complaint shall take the arrested person without unnecessary delay before a judge as commanded in the warrant. If the arrest is made in a county other than that in which the warrant was issued and the arrested person is not taken as commanded in the warrant, the arrested person shall be taken before a judge of the county in which the arrest is made, who shall consider the defendant for release on personal recognizance and so release the arrested person or admit the arrested person to bail for his or her appearance before the proper judge to whom the bail bond and other papers may be transmitted by mail. If the offense is nonbailable, or if the person arrested is unable to give bail, the judge shall commit that person to jail and he or she shall be taken as commanded in the warrant within a reasonable time by an officer of the county in which it was issued.

(2) Any person making an arrest without a warrant shall take the arrested person without unnecessary delay before a judge and shall file with the court a post-arrest complaint specifying the offense for which the arrest was made and the essential facts constituting probable cause on which the complaint is based. Such complaint need not be verified but shall be signed by the person making the arrest. If the judge before whom the arrested person is taken is in a county other than the county in which the offense was committed, the judge shall proceed as directed in paragraph (1) of this Rule 3.02 as on an arrest under warrant in a county other than that in which the warrant was issued.

(3) If no judge is available in the county in which the arrest was made the defendant shall be taken to jail, and any documents relating to the arrest shall be given to the jailer. If the defendant is ineligible to post bail under Rule 4.20 or cannot make the bail endorsed on the arrest warrant, the jailer shall take the defendant before the judge without unnecessary delay.

(4) Any documents relating to the arrest that are in the possession of the jailer shall be delivered to the clerk on or before the next business day.

HISTORY: Amended by Order 98–3, eff. 3–1–99; prior amendments eff. 9–1–81 (Order 81–5), 6–19–76; adopted eff. 1–1–63

RCr 3.04 Trial or preliminary hearing—Abolished

HISTORY: Abolished by Order 81–5, eff. 9–1–81; prior amendment eff. 6–19–76; adopted eff. 1–1–63

RCr 3.05 Cautioning of accused; appointment of counsel

(1) At the time of the defendant's appearance the judge shall inform the defendant of the charge against him or her and of his or her right to a preliminary hearing or a trial, and shall advise the defendant of his or her right to have counsel. The defendant shall be informed also that he or she is not required to make a statement and that any statement made by him or her may be used against him or her. The judge shall notify the attorney for the Commonwealth, allow the defendant reasonable time and opportunity to consult counsel, and release the defendant on personal recognizance or admit the defendant to bail if the offense is bailable.

(2) If the crime of which the defendant is charged is punishable by confinement and the defendant is financially unable to employ counsel, the judge shall appoint counsel to represent the defendant unless he or she elects to proceed without counsel. The defendant has the burden of first establishing his or her indigency before counsel may be appointed. If the defendant demonstrates that he or she is a needy person as defined in KRS 31.120 and the court so concludes, then the appointment shall continue for all future stages of the criminal proceeding, including appeal. Such appointment may be terminated by the court in which the proceeding is pending at any time upon a showing that defendant is able to employ counsel.

HISTORY: Amended by Order 98–3, eff. 3–1–99; adopted by Order 81–5, eff. 9–1–81

RCr 3.06 Bail for good behavior—Abolished

HISTORY: Abolished by Order 81–5, eff. 9–1–81; prior amendment eff. 6–19–76; adopted eff. 1–1–63

RCr 3.07 Trial or preliminary hearing

When a person is brought or appears before a judge having authority to try the offense charged, the judge shall proceed in accordance with Chapters VI—XIII of these Rules. If the judge does not have authority to try the offense charged but does have venue to hold a preliminary hearing, the judge shall proceed in accordance with the remainder of Chapter III. A defendant who has not been indicted is entitled to a preliminary hearing, unless waived, when charged with an offense requiring an indictment pursuant to Section 12 of the Kentucky Constitution. If the judge does not have authority to try the case or venue to hold the preliminary hearing, the judge shall order the defendant to be taken before the proper court for further proceedings and may release the defendant on personal recognizance or admit the defendant to bail for his or her appearance before that court, if the offense is bailable, or commit the defendant to jail to await trial or preliminary hearing.

HISTORY: Amended by Order 98–3, eff. 3–1–99; adopted by Order 81–5, eff. 9–1–81

RCr 3.08 Cautioning of accused; appointment of counsel—Abolished

HISTORY: Abolished by Order 81–5, eff. 9–1–81; prior amendments eff. 6–19–76, 8–24–72, 1–1–66; adopted eff. 1–1–63

RCr 3.10 Preliminary hearing; waiver

(1) The defendant may waive a preliminary hearing.

(2) If the defendant does not waive the preliminary hearing, such hearing shall be held within a reasonable time but no later than 10 days following the initial appearance if the defendant is in custody and no later than 20 days if the defendant is not in custody, provided, however, that the preliminary hearing shall not be held if the defendant is indicted before the date set for the hearing. In the event the preliminary hearing is not held within the above time period, the defendant shall be discharged from custody, and he or she shall thereafter be proceeded against on that charge by indictment only. Unless the defendant consents to an extension, time limits may be extended by the court only upon a showing that extraordinary circumstances exist and that delay is indispensable to the interests of justice.

(3) Notwithstanding waiver of the preliminary hearing, at any time before the defendant has been indicted the attorney for the Commonwealth shall, upon demand, be entitled to a preliminary hearing for the purpose of examining witnesses. The defendant may cross-examine the witnesses offered by the Commonwealth.

HISTORY: Amended by Order 98–3, eff. 3–1–99; prior amendments eff. 9–1–81 (Order 81–5), 1–1–78; adopted eff. 1–1–63

RCr 3.12 Transfer of defendant to another county

If it appears from either the complaint or evidence introduced at the hearing that the offense was committed in a county other than that in which the hearing is being held, the judge may release the defendant on personal recognizance or admit the defendant to bail for his or her appearance before the proper judge of the county in which the offense was committed on a day named in the bond, if the offense is bailable, or shall commit the defendant to jail to await transfer within a reasonable time to the latter county by a peace officer of that county. The bond and other papers shall be transmitted to the clerk of the court before which the defendant is bound to appear. Cash deposits shall also be transmitted to the court having authority over the defendant's case.

HISTORY: Amended by Order 98–3, eff. 3–1–99; prior amendments eff. 9–1–81 (Order 81–5), 6–19–76; adopted eff. 1–1–63

RCr 3.13 Defective complaint

If before or during the preliminary hearing of any person arrested pursuant to a warrant, or appearing in response to a summons or citation, it appears that the complaint does not properly name or describe the defendant, or the offense with which the defendant is charged, or that although not guilty of the offense specified in the complaint, there is probable cause to believe that the defendant is guilty of some other offense, the judge shall not discharge or dismiss the defendant but shall permit the attorney for the Commonwealth to amend the complaint if substantial rights of the defendant are not prejudiced.

HISTORY: Amended by Order 98–3, eff. 3–1–99; adopted by Order 81–5, eff. 9–1–81

RCr 3.14 Probable cause finding

(1) If the defendant waives the preliminary hearing or if from the evidence it appears to the judge that there is probable cause to believe that an offense required to be prosecuted by indictment pursuant to Section 12 of the Kentucky Constitution has been committed and that the defendant committed it, the judge shall hold the defendant to answer in the circuit court and commit the defendant to jail, release the defendant on personal recognizance or admit the defendant to bail if the offense is bailable; otherwise the defendant shall be discharged.

(2) The finding of probable cause may be based upon hearsay evidence in whole or in part. The defendant may cross-examine witnesses against him or her and may introduce evidence in his or her own behalf.

(3) Objections to evidence on the ground that it was acquired by unlawful means are not properly made at the preliminary hearing. Motions to suppress must be made to the trial court as provided in Rule 9.78.

HISTORY: Amended by Order 98–3, eff. 3–1–99; prior amendments eff. 9–1–81 (Order 81–5), 6–19–76; adopted eff. 1–1–63

RCr 3.16 Record of testimony

The preliminary hearing shall be recorded unless waived by all parties. Either party may obtain a copy of the tape or recording upon request and payment therefor.

HISTORY: Amended by Order 81–5, eff. 9–1–81; adopted eff. 1–1–63

RCr 3.18 Order of commitment; bail

Whenever a person is committed to jail the judge shall direct the clerk to issue a written order of commitment, which shall be delivered to the jailer by the peace officer who executes it. If the offense is bailable, the judge must fix the sum for which bail is to be given and direct the clerk to enter it on the order of commitment. Thereafter, the bail shall be taken by the clerk of the court in which the defendant is held to appear.

HISTORY: Amended by Order 81–5, eff. 9–1–81; adopted eff. 1–1–63

RCr 3.20   Recognizance of witnesses

When the defendant has been held to answer the charge the judge shall cause each of the material witnesses on behalf of the Commonwealth and, at the defendant's request, each of such witnesses for the defendant as the defendant may suggest, to enter into a recognizance before the judge to the effect that the witness will attend and testify in the court to which the defendant has been held to answer, or forfeit a sum not less than one hundred dollars ($100) to the Commonwealth of Kentucky. If witnesses for the defendant are recognized, it shall be so stated in the recognizance.

HISTORY: Amended by Order 98–3, eff. 3–1–99; prior amendment eff. 9–1–81 (Order 81–5); adopted eff. 1–1–63

RCr 3.22   Transmission of papers

If at the conclusion of the preliminary hearing the defendant is held to answer, the clerk shall transmit all papers in the proceedings to the clerk of the court to which the defendant has been held.

HISTORY: Amended by Order 81–5, eff. 9–1–81; prior amendment eff. 6–19–76; adopted eff. 1–1–63

IV   BAIL

RCr 4.00   Recognizance and bail; definitions of terms

As used in these rules the following terms mean:

(a) "Bail bond" means a written undertaking, executed by the defendant or one or more sureties, that the defendant designated in such instrument will, while at liberty as a result of an order fixing bail and of the execution of a bail bond in satisfaction thereof, appear in a designated criminal action or proceeding when the defendant's attendance is required and otherwise render himself or herself amenable to the orders and processes of the court, and that in the event the defendant fails to do so, the signers of the bond will pay to the court the amount of money specified in the order fixing bail.

(b) "Cash bail bond" means a sum of money, in the amount designated in an order fixing bail, posted by a defendant or by another person on the defendant's behalf with a court or other authorized public officer upon condition that such money will be forfeited if the defendant does not comply with the directions of a court requiring the defendant's attendance at the criminal action or proceeding involved and does not otherwise render himself or herself amenable to the orders and processes of the court.

(c) "Conditions of release" may include financial as well as nonfinancial requirements upon which the defendant's release is dependent. All methods of pretrial release include the conditions of release requiring the defendant to appear before court when required and to submit himself or herself to the orders and processes of the court.

(d) "Pre-trial release" is release of a defendant from custody before his or her trial date. It may be secured by any authorized method of pre-trial release including but not limited to release on personal recognizance, on nonfinancial conditions or upon execution of a bail bond. It does not include the procedure for issuance of citation as provided in KRS 431.015.

(e) "Pre-trial services agency" means the agency established or authorized by Supreme Court order to provide pre-trial release investigation and services for trial courts having jurisdiction of criminal causes.

(f) "Release on personal recognizance" means release of a defendant on personal recognizance when, having acquired control over the defendant's person, the court permits the defendant to be at liberty during the pendency of the criminal action or proceeding upon the defendant's written promise to appear whenever his or her attendance before court may be required and to render himself or herself amenable to the orders and processes of the court.

(g) "Surety" means a person other than the defendant who executes a bail bond and assumes the obligations therein.

(h) "Unsecured bail bond" means a bail bond for which the defendant is fully liable upon failure to appear in court when ordered to do so or upon breach of a material condition of release, but which is not secured by any deposit of or lien upon property.

HISTORY: Amended by Order 98–3, eff. 3–1–99; prior amendment eff. 1–1–78; adopted eff. 6–19–76

RCr 4.02   Bailable offenses; eligibility for pretrial release

(1) All persons shall be bailable before conviction, except when death is a possible punishment for the offense or offenses charged and the proof is evident or the presumption is great that the defendant is guilty.

(2) All defendants charged with bailable offenses shall be considered for pretrial release without making formal application except when a capital offense is charged. A person charged with a capital offense must make an application for pretrial release.

(3) On the hearing of an application for admission to pretrial release made before or after indictment for a capital offense, the burden of showing that the proof is evident or the presumption is great that the defendant is guilty is on the Commonwealth.

HISTORY: Amended eff. 6–19–76; adopted eff. 1–1–63

RCr 4.04   Authorized methods of pretrial release

(1) The only authorized methods of pretrial release are on the following or any combination thereof as the court determines:

(a) personal recognizance

(b) unsecured bail bond

(c) nonfinancial conditions

(d) executed bail bond

  (i) with sufficient personal surety acceptable to the court; or

  (ii) with a deposit with the court of a sum of money equal to at least ten percent of the bond; or

  (iii) with a deposit with the court of cash equal to the amount of the bond; or

  (iv) with stocks or bonds which are not exempt from execution and which over and above all liabilities and encumbrances have a value equal to the total amount of the bond; or

  (v) with real property having a value over and above all liabilities and encumbrances, equal to twice the value of the bond; or

  (vi) in cases of motor vehicle traffic violations, with a guaranteed arrest bond certificate as provided in KRS 431.020[1].

(2) Nonfinancial conditions may be imposed upon any bail bond in the manner provided in RCr 4.14.

(3) The court shall determine the method of pretrial release and the manner in which a bail bond is executed.

HISTORY: Amended by Order 86–3, eff. 1–1–87; prior amendments eff. 9–1–81, 6–19–76; adopted eff. 1–1–63

  [1] So in original.

RCr 4.06   Duties of pretrial services agency

The duties of a pretrial services agency authorized by the Administrative Office of the Courts to serve the trial court shall include interviewing defendants eligible for pretrial release, verifying information obtained from defendants, making recommendations to the court as to whether defendants interviewed should be released on personal recognizance, identifying veterans, and any other duties ordered by the Supreme Court. When a defendant requests appointment of counsel, the Pretrial Release Officer shall, where practical, interview the defendant, assist in preparing the affidavit of indigency set out in KRS 31.120, and provide the affidavit to the court and the defendant.

HISTORY: Amended by Order 2012–10, eff. 1–1–13; prior amendments eff. 1–1–03; (Order 2002–1), 6–19–76, adopted eff. 1–1–63

RCr 4.07   Officers authorized to take bail; responsibility—Abolished

Publisher's Note: RCr 4.07 was not included in the 1976 amendment to Part IV of these Rules.

RCr 4.08   Confidentiality of pre-trial services agency records

Information supplied by a defendant to a representative of the pre-trial services agency during the defendant's initial interview or subsequent contacts, or information obtained by the pre-trial services agency as a result of the interview or subsequent contacts, shall be deemed confidential and shall not be subject to subpoena or to disclosure without the written consent of the defendant except in the following circumstances:

(a) information relevant to the imposition of conditions of release shall be presented to the court on a standardized form when the court is considering what conditions of release to impose;

(b) information furnished by the defendant to the pre-trial services agency and recorded on a completed interview form shall be furnished to law enforcement officials upon request if the defendant fails to appear in court when required;

(c) information concerning compliance with any conditions of release imposed by the court shall be furnished to the court upon its request for consideration of modification of conditions of release or of sentencing or of probation;

(d) information relevant to sentencing or probation shall be furnished to the court upon its request for consideration in imposing sentence or probation;

(e) at its discretion, the court may permit the probation officer, for the purpose of preparing the presentence investigation report, and the defense attorney to inspect the completed interview form;

(f) any person conducting an evaluation of the pretrial release program may have access to all completed interview forms upon order of the Supreme Court.

(g) all information obtained from the defendant and all information provided to the court shall be provided to the defendant's attorney.

(h) information relating to a defendant's status as a military veteran may be shared with the Department of Veterans Affairs in order to facilitate the provision of services available to the defendant.

At the beginning of the initial interview with a representative of the pretrial services agency, the defendant shall be advised of the above uses of information supplied by the defendant or obtained as a result of information supplied by the defendant.

HISTORY: Amended by Order 2012–10, eff. 1–1–13; prior amendments eff. 1–1–03 (Order 2002–1), eff. 3–1–99 (Order 98–3), 1–1–85 (Order 84–2), 11–1–78, 1–1–78, 6–19–76; adopted eff. 1–1–63

RCr 4.10   Release on personal recognizance; unsecured bail bond

A defendant shall be released on personal recognizance or upon an unsecured bail bond unless the court determines, in the exercise of its discretion, that such release will not reasonably assure the appearance of the defendant as required. In the exercise of such discretion the court shall give due consideration to recommendations of the local pretrial services agency when made as authorized by order of the Supreme Court.

HISTORY: Amended eff. 6–19–76; prior amendment eff. 5–31–68; adopted eff. 1–1–63

RCr 4.12   Release on nonfinancial conditions

If a defendant's promise to appear or his or her execution of an unsecured bail bond alone is not deemed sufficient to insure his or her appearance when required, the court shall impose the least onerous conditions reasonably likely to insure the defendant's appearance as required. Such conditions of release may include but are not limited to placing the defendant in the custody of a designated person or organization agreeing to supervise the defendant or to placing restrictions on the defendant's travel, association or place of abode during the period of release.

Commensurate with the risk of nonappearance the court may impose any other condition including a condition requiring the defendant to return to custody after specified hours.

HISTORY: Amended by Order 98–3, eff. 3–1–99; prior amendment eff. 6–19–76; adopted eff. 1–1–63

RCr 4.13   Motor vehicle traffic violations; guaranteed arrest bond certificate—Abolished

Publisher's Note: RCr 4.13 was not included in the 1976 amendment to Part IV of these Rules.

RCr 4.14   Nonfinancial conditions on release

The court shall cause the issuance of an order containing a statement of any conditions imposed upon the defendant for his or her release. The defendant shall sign the statement of conditions and receive a copy thereof. The order shall inform the defendant of penalties applicable to violation of conditions and advise that a warrant for the defendant's arrest will be issued if conditions are violated. The court shall also inform the local pre-trial services agency of the conditions of release.

HISTORY: Amended by Order 98–3, eff. 3–1–99; prior amendment eff. 6–19–76; adopted eff. 1–1–63

RCr 4.16   Amount of bail

(1) The amount of bail shall be sufficient to insure compliance with the conditions of release set by the court. It shall not be oppressive and shall be commensurate with the gravity of the offense charged. In determining such amount the court shall consider the defendant's past criminal acts, if any, the defendant's reasonably anticipated conduct if released and the defendant's financial ability to give bail.

(2) If a defendant is charged with an offense punishable by fine only, the amount of bail shall not exceed the amount of the maximum penalty and costs.

(3) Amount of bail may also be set in accordance with the uniform schedule of bail prescribed for designated misdemeanors and violations in Appendix A—Uniform Schedule of Bail, of these rules.

HISTORY: Amended by Order 98–3, eff. 3–1–99; prior amendment eff. 6–19–76; adopted eff. 1–1–63

RCr 4.18   Motor vehicle traffic violations; guaranteed arrest bond certificate

(1) Notwithstanding any other provisions of these rules, a guaranteed arrest bond certificate presented by the person whose signature appears thereon shall be accepted in lieu of cash bail in an amount not to exceed five hundred dollars ($500) as a bail bond to guarantee the appearance of such person in any court of this Commonwealth, at the time required by such court, when such person is arrested for violation of any law of this Commonwealth or traffic ordinance of any municipality therein relating to the operation of a motor vehicle. A guaranteed arrest bond certificate so presented as a bail bond is subject to the same forfeiture and enforcement provisions as a bail bond or cash bail. However:

(a) The violation must have been committed prior to the expiration date shown on the guaranteed arrest bond certificate, and

(b) A guaranteed arrest bond certificate may not be accepted when a person is arrested for violation of KRS Chapter 281 or subsection (2) of KRS 189.520.

(2) As used in this Rule 4.18, "guaranteed arrest bond certificate" means a printed card or other certificate issued by the association to any of its members, which is signed by the member and contains a printed statement that such association and a surety company licensed to do business in this Commonwealth;

(a) Guarantee the appearance of the person whose signature appears on the card or certificate, and

(b) Will, in the event of the failure of such person to appear in court at the time set for appearance, pay any fine or forfeiture imposed upon such person in an amount not to exceed five hundred dollars ($500).

HISTORY: Amended by Order 98–3, eff. 3–1–99; prior amendments eff. 1–1–84 (Order 83–4), 1–1–78, 6–19–76; adopted eff. 1–1–63

RCr 4.20   Use of uniform schedule of bail

(1) The defendant may execute a bail bond in accordance with the uniform schedule of bail (Appendix A) for designated misdemeanors and violations without appearing before a judge. If a defendant chooses to execute a bail bond in accordance with the schedule without appearing before a judge and proceeds to do so, that defendant waives his or her statutory right to be considered for other authorized methods of pre-trial release. Before said waiver is effective, the defendant must be informed of his or her right to appear before a judge without unnecessary delay, and to be considered for release on personal recognizance.

(2) In the exercise of its reasonable discretion the court may refuse to set bail in the amount prescribed by Appendix A, but must record written reasons for the deviation.

(3) Each court may by local rule establish a uniform schedule of bail for violations of ordinances of cities and counties over which it has jurisdiction; provided, however, that when the ordinance is punishable by a fine only, the amount of the bond set shall not exceed the amount of the maximum penalty and costs.

HISTORY: Amended by Emergency Order 2012–12, eff. 10–21–12; prior amendments eff. 1–1–13 (Order 2012–10), eff. 3–1–99 (Order 98–3), eff. 9–1–81 (Order 81–5), 11–1–78, 6–19–76; adopted eff. 1–1–63

RCr 4.22 Ten percent deposit

(1) If a ten percent cash deposit to the court is accepted, in no event shall it be less than ten dollars.

(2) A ten percent deposit will not be accepted to secure bail in the amount designated on the uniform schedule for bail for traffic, boating, fish and wildlife offenses listed therein.

HISTORY: Amended eff. 6–19–76; adopted eff. 1–1–63

RCr 4.24 Officers authorized to take bail

When the amount of bail has been fixed either by the court or by the uniform schedule of bail, it may be taken by the clerk of the court in which the defendant is held to appear. Another bonded public officer shall be authorized by the chief judge of the circuit court to take bail. The authorized bonded public officer shall take bail when the clerk of the court is unavailable. The individual with whom deposits are made shall ascertain that the amount deposited is no less than the amount fixed by the court.

HISTORY: Amended by Order 2000–1, eff. 2–1–01; prior amendments eff. 9–1–81 (Order 81–5), 6–19–76; adopted eff. 1–1–63

RCr 4.26 Receipt for and record of cash deposit and bond

(1) When an authorized officer receives a cash deposit the officer shall give a receipt to the person from whom the officer receives the money on a uniform receipt form provided by the Administrative Office of the Courts.

(2) The person who takes the bail bond shall see that the bond form is completed. That person shall give one copy to the defendant and one to the clerk of the court in which the defendant is held to appear. The clerk shall file the copy in the case file.

HISTORY: Amended by Order 98–3, eff. 3–1–99; prior amendments eff. 9–1–81 (Order 81–5), 6–19–76; adopted eff. 1–1–63

RCr 4.28 Custody of cash deposits and bond

The court copy of the bond and the cash deposited with an individual authorized to take bail in the absence of the clerk shall be delivered to the clerk by the next business day. The clerk shall forthwith deposit the money in an escrow account for all cash deposits and bail, which account may include other funds held by the court.

HISTORY: Amended by Order 81–5, eff. 9–1–81; prior amendments eff. 1–1–78, 6–19–76; adopted eff. 1–1–63

RCr 4.30 Qualification of sureties

(1) Each surety, except a corporate surety that is approved as provided by law, shall be a resident or owner of real estate within the Commonwealth and shall file an affidavit in which the surety shall describe the property by which the surety proposes to secure the bond. The provisions of this paragraph (1) shall not apply to a surety who posts a full cash bond.

(2) No attorney at law, sheriff, deputy sheriff, judge, clerk, deputy clerk, trial commissioner, master commissioner or pretrial release officer shall be taken as surety on any bail bond, including bail on appeal under Rule 12.78.

(3) No bond shall be approved unless the surety thereon appears to be qualified.

HISTORY: Amended by Order 98–3, eff. 3–1–99; prior amendments eff. 9–1–81 (Order 81–5), 6–19–76; adopted eff. 1–1–63

RCr 4.32 Sufficiency of sureties

If there is only one (1) surety, that surety shall be worth the amount specified in the bond exclusive of the amount of any other undertaking on which the surety may be principal or surety, and exclusive of property exempt from execution and over and above liabilities. If there are several sureties they shall in the aggregate be worth that amount exclusive of the amount of other undertakings, and of the exemptions and liabilities mentioned above. Any person authorized to take bail shall refuse any surety offered in a bail bond to be taken by that person who is, in that person's opinion, insufficient.

HISTORY: Amended by Order 98–3, eff. 3–1–99; prior amendment eff. 9–1–81 (Order 81–5); adopted eff. 6–19–76

RCr 4.34 Justification of security

(1) If the bail bond is secured by real estate, the defendant or surety must file with the bond a sworn schedule and a statement of value from the property valuation administrator of the county in which the real estate is located. The sworn schedule shall contain:

(a) legal description of the real estate;

(b) description of any and all encumbrances on the real estate including the amount of each and the holder thereof; and

(c) market value of the unencumbered equity owned by the affiant or affiants.

(2) If the bail bond is secured by stocks and bonds, the defendant or surety must file with the bond a sworn schedule which shall contain:

(a) descriptions sufficient for identification of the stocks and bonds deposited;

(b) present market value of each stock and bond; and

(c) total market value of stocks and bonds listed.

(3) In either case, unless the defendant or the defendant's relative is using his or her own property as security, a statement must be filed stating that the property has not been used or accepted as security on a bail bond in the Commonwealth during the twelve months preceding the date of the bond.

(4) The sworn schedule in either case must further include a statement that affiant or affiants are the sole owners of the unencumbered equity; that the property is not exempt from execution; and that the property is security for the appearance of the defendant in accordance with the conditions of release imposed by the court.

(5) If a bail bond is to be secured by real estate, the unencumbered equity of the real estate must have a fair market value at least double the amount of the bail bond.

HISTORY: Amended by Order 98–3, eff. 3–1–99; prior amendments eff. 9–1–81 (Order 81–5), 11–1–78; adopted eff. 6–19–76

RCr 4.36   Recording of a real property bond

A certified copy of the bail bond and a schedule of real estate accompanied by necessary recording fee which shall be paid by the defendant or sureties, must be filed by the clerk of court requiring bail bond in the office of the county clerk of each county in which the real estate is situated.

The county court clerk must record copies of the bail bond and schedule and the Commonwealth then has lien upon the real estate. Such records shall be kept in the miscellaneous encumbrance book provided by county court clerk.

HISTORY: Amended by Order 98–3, eff. 3–1–99; adopted eff. 6–19–76

RCr 4.38   Mandatory review after twenty-four hours

If a defendant continues to be detained 24 hours from the time of the imposition of conditions of release because of inability to meet such conditions, the court that imposed the conditions must review them on defendant's written application or may do so on its own motion. If the court declines to modify them, the judge shall record in writing the reasons for that decision. It shall be the duty of the pretrial release officer to inform the court of those defendants in custody who are not released from jail after 24 hours.

HISTORY: Amended by Order 98–3, eff. 3–1–99; prior amendment eff. 9–1–81 (Order 81–5); adopted eff. 6–19–76

RCr 4.40   Review of conditions of release

(1) The defendant or the Commonwealth may by written motion apply for a change of conditions of release at any time before the defendant's trial. The motion shall state the grounds on which the change is sought. The moving party may request an adversary hearing on the motion, and is entitled to such hearing the first time the moving party requests it. Requests for adversary hearings made in subsequent motions for review of conditions of release shall lie within the discretion of the court.

(2) Whenever the court denies the specific relief requested, the judge shall record in writing the reasons for so doing.

(3) Motion for change of conditions of release must be in good faith. Where the defendant has appeared when required at previous proceedings in the case, the Commonwealth must demonstrate by clear and convincing evidence the need to modify existing conditions of release.

HISTORY: Amended by Order 98–3, eff. 3–1–99; prior amendment eff. 9–1–81 (Order 81–5); adopted eff. 6–19–76

RCr 4.42   Change of conditions of release; bond forfeiture

(1) If at any time following the release of the defendant and before the defendant is required to appear for trial the court is advised of a material change in the defendant's circumstances or that the defendant has not complied with all conditions imposed upon his or her release, the court having jurisdiction may order the defendant's arrest and require the defendant or the defendant's surety or sureties to appear and show cause why the bail bond should not be forfeited or the conditions of release be changed, or both.

(2) A copy of said order shall be served on the defendant and the defendant's surety or sureties. The court shall order the arrest of the defendant only when it has good cause to believe the defendant will not appear voluntarily upon notice to appear.

(3) Where the court is acting on advice that the defendant has not complied with all conditions imposed upon his or her release, the court shall not change the conditions of release or order forfeiture of the bail bond unless it finds by clear and convincing evidence that the defendant has wilfully violated one of the conditions of his or her release or that there is a substantial risk of nonappearance.

(4) Where the court is acting on advice of a material change in the defendant's circumstances, it shall not change the conditions of release or order forfeiture of

the bail bonds unless it finds by clear and convincing evidence that a material change in circumstances exists and that there is a substantial risk of nonappearance.

(5) Before the court may make the findings required for change of conditions or forfeiture of bail under this rule, the defendant and the defendant's surety or sureties shall be granted an adversary hearing comporting with the requirements of due process. Whenever the court changes conditions of release (except upon motion of the defendant) or orders forfeiture of bail, it must furnish the defendant and the defendant's surety or sureties with written reasons for so doing.

HISTORY: Amended by Order 98–3, eff. 3–1–99; prior amendments eff. 11–1–95 (Order 95–1), 7–8–83, 9–1–81 (Order 81–5); adopted eff. 6–19–76

RCr 4.43   Appellate review of bail; habeas corpus

(1) Any defendant aggrieved by a decision of the circuit court on a motion to change the conditions of bail may appeal that decision to the Court of Appeals pursuant to the following procedures:

(a) The notice of appeal from the order of the trial court shall be filed in the manner and within the time fixed by Rule 12.04.

(b) Upon the filing of the notice of appeal the clerk of the circuit court shall prepare and certify the original or a copy of such portion of the record as relates to the question of bail and is needed for the purpose of deciding the issue on appeal. The abbreviated record shall be filed with the clerk of the appellate court within 30 days after filing of the notice of appeal.

(c) The appellant shall within 15 days after filing of the record file the statement of appeal and brief required by Civil Rules 76.06 and 76.12. The brief shall be abbreviated and shall not exceed five (5) double-spaced typewritten pages. It shall be served on the local Commonwealth's attorney and on the attorney general. No brief shall be required of the Commonwealth, but the Commonwealth may file a brief within 10 days after the date the appellant's statement of appeal and brief were filed, such brief not to exceed five (5) double-spaced typewritten pages. No other briefs shall be filed unless requested by the appellate court.

(d) The appeal shall stand submitted for final disposition 10 days after the date on which the appeal was perfected by the appellant. The court shall proceed immediately to a hearing thereof and complete the same as soon as practicable.

(e) Neither the filing of the notice of appeal nor the pendency of the appeal shall stay further proceedings in the prosecution.

(2) The writ of habeas corpus remains the proper method for seeking circuit court review of the action of a district court respecting bail.

(3) This Rule 4.43 shall apply only to appellate review of bail conditions prior to entry of a judgment of conviction. After entry of a judgment of conviction, appellate review of bail on appeal shall be by intermediate motion filed pursuant to RCr 12.82 in the appeal of the conviction.

HISTORY: Amended by Order 89–1, eff. 8–28–89; adopted eff. 9–1–81

RCr 4.44   Record of discharge

(1) When the court orders a discharge upon the defendant's compliance with conditions of release, the clerk of the court that required a bail bond or released on personal recognizance shall make a record of the discharge and the date of discharge.

(2) Upon discharge of the defendant's and surety's obligations under the bail bond, the court shall return all stocks and bonds and cash deposited with the court except when a 10% deposit was made. In such cases the clerk of court shall retain 10% of the 10% deposit, in no event less than five dollars.

(3) If the defendant was released on a property bond, the clerk of the court requiring the bond shall notify in writing the county court clerk of each county where the real estate is situated. The lien on real estate must be discharged and the release recorded on the margin by that county court clerk.

HISTORY: Amended eff. 8–1–76; adopted eff. 6–19–76

RCr 4.46   Application of deposit to fine or costs

(1) Upon a final rendition of judgment against the defendant for a fine and costs, or either, in the prosecution of a cause in which money has been deposited as bail by the defendant himself or herself, if the money still remains on deposit and unforfeited, and such fine and costs, or either, have not been paid, such money, or so much thereof as may be necessary, shall be applied to the payment of such fine and costs, or either.

(2) Upon motion by the defendant, the court may order the amount repayable to the defendant to be paid to the defendant's attorney.

HISTORY: Amended by Order 98–3, eff. 3–1–99; adopted eff. 6–19–76

RCr 4.48   Forfeiture of bail

(1) If the court has ordered forfeiture of bail following a show-cause hearing as described in Rule 4.42(5), or following the willful failure of the defendant to appear in court when required, the court shall serve a copy of the forfeiture order on the defendant and the defendant's surety or sureties at their last-known addresses. If the defendant or the defendant's surety or sureties do not appear within 20 days after service of the order or return of not found and satisfy the court that appearance or compliance by the defendant was impossible and without his or her fault, the court

may order judgment against the defendant and the defendant's surety for the amount of the bail or any part thereof and the costs of the proceedings.

(2) If the declaration of forfeiture is made by a trial court other than the circuit court and the amount of bail is beyond its jurisdiction, or a lien on real estate is involved, the bond shall be filed with the clerk of the circuit court of the county where the amount of forfeiture may be determined and collection proceedings may be so instituted.

(3) A forfeiture may be set aside upon such conditions as the forfeiting court may impose if it appears that justice does not require its enforcement.

(4) When bail is forfeited, the clerk of the court shall enter a record of the forfeiture and date of forfeiture. When real estate is affected, the clerk shall forthwith send notice of the forfeiture and date thereof to the county clerk of each county where the real estate is situated. The county clerk of the latter county shall make an appropriate entry at the end or on the margin of the record of the Commonwealth's lien on the real estate.

HISTORY: Amended by Order 2009–01, eff. 4–1–09; prior amendment eff. 3–1–99 (Order 98–3); adopted eff. 6–19–76

RCr 4.50   Surrender of defendant; exoneration

(1) At any time before forfeiture, any surety may procure a certified copy of the bail bond which shall authorize any peace officer to whom it is presented to arrest the defendant in any county within the Commonwealth and to deliver the defendant and the certified copy of the bail bond to the jailer in the county in which the prosecution is pending. The jailer shall acknowledge the surrender in writing.

(2) Upon presentation of the writing executed by the jailer, the court before which the defendant has been held to answer shall, after five (5) days' notice to the county attorney, order that the surety or sureties be exonerated from liability on the bond or recognizance and that any money or bonds that have been deposited as bail be returned to the person making the deposit.

HISTORY: Amended by Order 98–3, eff. 3–1–99; prior amendment eff. 1–1–78; adopted eff. 6–19–76

RCr 4.52   Judgment against surety

(1) By entering into a bail bond (including bail on appeal under Rules 12.78 to 12.82, inclusive) the surety submits himself or herself to the jurisdiction of the court or courts in which the charge is or may thereafter be pending. The surety's liability may be enforced on motion without an independent action. The motion shall be served on the surety at the surety's address which shall be shown on the bond, or at the surety's last known address, at least 20 days prior to the date of hearing thereon. In the event of bail pending appeal, for purposes of this Rule 4.52 the court from

which the appeal is or may be taken shall be considered to be the court in which the charge is pending.

(2) After entry of judgment the court for sufficient cause may remit wholly or in part the sum specified in the bail bond.

(3) Unless there are reasonable grounds to believe that the principal has caused himself or herself to be incarcerated elsewhere, or elects to remain under such detention though able to secure his or her release through bail or otherwise, for the purpose of delaying or avoiding appearance, the court shall not declare a forfeiture of bail (or, having declared a forfeiture, shall remit the amount thereof) if it is proved that the defendant's appearance is prevented by detention in a jail or penitentiary outside the Commonwealth or in custody of the United States. An affidavit of the jailer, warden or other responsible officer of such jail or penitentiary or appropriate federal officer, shall be adequate evidence of such detention, and other affidavits may be considered as evidence.

HISTORY: Amended by Order 98–3, eff. 3–1–99; prior amendment eff. 1–1–78; adopted eff. 6–19–76

RCr 4.54   Continuation of bail

(1) Except as provided in Rule 5.22 and Rule 12.78, bail taken at any stage of the proceedings shall continue in effect to insure the appearance of the defendant for any and all purposes at all stages of the proceedings, including appeal. In the event a defendant waives the charges to the Grand Jury, or following a preliminary hearing is ordered bound over to the circuit court, control over bail, including any conditions thereof, shall remain with the district court until indictment is returned, at which time control shall pass to the circuit court. Upon the conviction of a defendant, bail may be increased, decreased, revoked, or modified by the trial court without being subject to the hearing requirements of Rule 4.42, and control over bail shall remain with the trial court throughout any appeal.

(2) Subject to RCr 5.22, bail shall terminate (a) when the principal is acquitted or the prosecution is dismissed; (b) when the principal, following conviction, fails to file a notice of appeal within the time limit under Rule 12.04; (c) when the appeal taken by the defendant is dismissed; or (d) on the effective date of an appellate decision affirming the conviction.

(3) In the event of a reversal of a conviction by an appellate court granting the defendant a new trial, the defendant shall be entitled to the rights of pre-trial release under Rule 4.04 as if upon an initial appearance.

(4) The efficacy of a bail bond shall not be affected by the fact that the defendant is prosecuted for an alleged offense or offenses different from but arising

out of the same occurrence as the charge named in the bail bond.

HISTORY: Amended by Order 2009–01, eff. 4–1–09; prior amendments eff. 3–1–99 (Order 98–3), 9–1–81 (Order 81–5), 1–1–78; adopted eff. 6–19–76

RCr 4.56 Defects in bond or recognizance

(1) Neither a bail bond nor a recognizance shall be invalid because of any defects of form, omission, recital, or condition, or because of any other irregularity, provided the official before whom it was entered into was legally authorized to take it, the amount of bail is stated, and it can be ascertained therefrom before which magistrate or court the principal is bound to appear.

(2) If no day is fixed for the appearance of the defendant, or an impossible day, or a day in vacation, the bond or recognizance shall bind the defendant to appear in court within twenty (20) days from the time the bond is issued to have a date set for his or her appearance at any preliminary proceeding or trial.

HISTORY: Amended by Order 98–3, eff. 3–1–99; prior amendment eff. 9–15–90 (Order 90–1); adopted eff. 6–19–76

RCr 4.58 Credit for incarceration

Any person incarcerated on a bailable offense who does not supply bail or is not otherwise released and against whom a fine is levied on conviction of such offense should be allowed a credit of $5.00 for each day so incarcerated prior to conviction except that in no case shall the amount so allowed or credited exceed the amount of the fine.

HISTORY: Adopted eff. 6–19–76

V GRAND JURY

RCr 5.02 Charge to grand jury

The court shall swear the grand jurors and charge them to inquire into every offense for which any person has been held to answer and for which an indictment or information has not been filed, or other offenses which come to their attention or of which any of them has knowledge. The court shall further instruct the grand jurors concerning (a) their right to exclude the attorney for the Commonwealth while questioning witnesses, (b) their rights and duties to juvenile cases as provided in KRS 640.010, and (c) any other matter affecting their rights and duties as grand jurors which the court believes will assist them in the conduct of their business.

HISTORY: Amended by Order 93–1, eff. 9–1–93; prior amendment eff. 9–1–81; adopted eff. 1–1–63

RCr 5.04 Foreperson; oath to witnesses

The grand jury shall elect one of its members to be foreperson, who shall administer an oath, prescribed by the Supreme Court, to each witness who testifies before the grand jury.

HISTORY: Amended by Order 98–3, eff. 3–1–99; prior amendments eff. 9–1–80 (Order 80–2), 1–1–78; adopted eff. 1–1–63

RCr 5.06 Attendance of witnesses before the Grand Jury

The Clerk, upon request of the foreperson of the Grand Jury or of the attorney for the Commonwealth, shall issue subpoenas for witnesses. The attendance of witnesses may be coerced as in other judicial proceedings, unless, and until, excused, or modified, by the requesting party. RCr 7.02 shall apply to Grand Jury subpoenas except that a subpoena issued pursuant to this rule may command the person to whom it is directed to produce the books, papers, documents or other objects designated therein to the foreperson of the Grand Jury or the Commonwealth's Attorney or his/her agent, without requiring the personal appearance of the witness before the Grand Jury.

HISTORY: Amended by Order 2005–4, eff. 6–21–05; prior amendments eff. 1–1–05 (Order 2004–5), 3–1–99 (Order 98–3), 9–1–81 (Order 81–5); adopted eff. 1–1–63

RCr 5.08 Evidence for defendant

If the defendant notifies the attorney for the Commonwealth in writing of his or her desire to present evidence before the grand jury, the attorney for the Commonwealth shall so inform the grand jury. The grand jurors may hear evidence for the defendant but are not required to do so.

HISTORY: Amended by Order 98–3, eff. 3–1–99; prior amendment eff. 9–1–81 (Order 81–5); adopted eff. 1–1–63

RCr 5.10 Evidence supporting indictment

The grand jurors shall find an indictment where they have received what they believe to be sufficient evidence to support it, but no indictment shall be quashed or judgment of conviction reversed on the ground that there was not sufficient evidence before the grand jury to support the indictment.

HISTORY: Amended by Order 81–5, eff. 9–1–81; adopted eff. 1–1–63

RCr 5.12 Compelling testimony

When a witness before the grand jury refuses to testify or to answer a question put to him or her, the foreperson shall state the refusal to the court in the presence of the witness. After hearing the witness, if the court decides that the witness is bound to testify or answer and the witness persists in his or her refusal, the court shall proceed against the witness as in cases of similar refusal in open court.

HISTORY: Amended by Order 98–3, eff. 3–1–99; adopted eff. 1–1–63

RCr 5.14 Duties of prosecuting attorney

(1) The attorney for the Commonwealth, or an assistant, designated by the attorney for the Commonwealth, shall attend the grand jurors when requested by them, and he or she may do so on his or her own initiative, for the purpose of examining witnesses in their presence, or of giving the grand jurors legal advice regarding any matter cognizable by them. The attorney for the Commonwealth or designated assistant shall also, when requested by them, draft indictments.

(2) At the time of the return of the indictment of a defendant the attorney for the Commonwealth shall inform the court of the defendant's status with respect to bail.

HISTORY: Amended by Order 98–3, eff. 3–1–99; prior amendment eff. 9–1–81 (Order 81–5); adopted eff. 1–1–63

RCr 5.16 Transcript of testimony

(1) The attorney for the Commonwealth shall cause all of the testimony before a grand jury to be recorded. For this purpose the attorney for the Commonwealth may appoint a stenographer to take in shorthand the testimony of witnesses or may cause the testimony to be taken by a recording device, but the record so made shall include the testimony of all witnesses. The shorthand notes or the recordings and transcript of the same, if any, shall be delivered to and retained by the attorney for the Commonwealth.

(2) Failure to have a record made, if required by paragraph (1) of this Rule 5.16, shall be ground for dismissal of the indictment unless the Commonwealth can show good cause for the failure. Mechanical failure of the recording device shall constitute good cause.

(3) The stenographer or operator of the recording device and any typist who transcribes the stenographer's notes or recordings shall be sworn by the court not to disclose any testimony or the names of any witnesses except to the attorney for the Commonwealth or when testifying in court, and except that any person indicted by the grand jury shall have a right to procure a transcript of any stenographic report or a duplicate of any mechanical recording relating to his or her indictment or any part thereof upon payment of its reasonable cost.

HISTORY: Amended by Order 98–3, eff. 3–1–99; prior amendment eff. 9–1–81 (Order 81–5); adopted eff. 1–1–63

RCr 5.18 Presence of other persons with grand jury

No person except the attorney or attorneys for the Commonwealth, a stenographer or operator of a recording device appointed by the attorney for the Commonwealth, the witness under examination, an interpreter, if needed, a parent, guardian or custodian of a minor witness or other person under disability, and the grand jurors shall be present while the grand jury is in session. No person other than the grand jurors shall be present while the grand jury is deliberating or voting. Any person violating this rule may be held in contempt of court.

HISTORY: Amended by Order 81–5, eff. 9–1–81; prior amendment eff. 1–1–65; adopted eff. 1–1–63

RCr 5.20 Return of indictment

All indictments shall be returned to the circuit judge by the foreperson in the presence of the grand jury in open court, and thereupon shall be filed with the clerk of the court and retained in the clerk's office as public records. An indictment for a misdemeanor not joined with a felony charged in the same indictment shall be docketed in the district court.

HISTORY: Amended by Order 98–3, eff. 3–1–99; prior amendments eff. 9–1–81 (Order 81–5), 5–1–80; adopted eff. 1–1–63

RCr 5.22 Procedure upon failure to indict

(1) If the defendant has been held to answer and the votes of the grand jurors are insufficient in number to find an indictment, the foreperson shall so report forthwith to the circuit court in writing. The circuit court shall order a discharge of the defendant from custody, and exoneration of the bail or a refund of any money or bonds deposited as bail, as the case may be.

(2) Final adjournment of a grand jury without its having indicted a defendant who has been held to answer, pursuant to RCr 3.14(1), shall effect the defendant's discharge from custody or, if the defendant is free on bail that has not been forfeited, shall exonerate the bail and any conditions thereon unless the grand jury refers the matter to the next grand jury, which referral must be in writing to the circuit court. Money or bonds deposited in lieu of bail shall be refunded upon such discharge. In any event, a defendant who has been held to answer, pursuant to RCr 3.14(1), for longer than sixty (60) days without having been indicted shall be entitled to a discharge from custody.

(3) Failure of the grand jury to return an indictment does not prevent the charge from being submitted to another grand jury.

HISTORY: Amended by Order 2012–10, eff. 1–1–13, prior amendments eff. 1–1–11 (Order 2010–09), eff. 1–1–03 (Order 2002–1), 3–1–99 (Order 98–3), 9–1–81 (Order 81–5), 1–1–65; adopted eff. 1–1–63

RCr 5.24 Secrecy of proceedings; disclosure

(1) Subject to the right of a person indicted to procure a transcript or recording as provided by Rule

5.16(3), and subject to the authority of the court at any time to direct otherwise, all persons present during any part of the proceedings of a grand jury shall keep its proceedings and the testimony given before it secret, except that counsel may divulge such information as may be necessary in preparing the case for trial or other disposition.

(2) The court may direct that an indictment be kept secret until the defendant is in custody or has given bail, in which event the clerk shall seal the indictment and no person shall disclose the finding of the indictment except when necessary for the issuance and execution of a warrant or summons.

(3) A violation of this Rule 5.24 shall be punishable as a contempt of court.

HISTORY: Amended by Order 81–5, eff. 9–1–81; prior amendments eff. 1–1–78, 1–1–65; adopted eff. 1–1–63

VI   INDICTMENT AND INFORMATION

RCr 6.02   Use of indictment and information

(1) All offenses required to be prosecuted by indictment pursuant to Section 12 of the Kentucky Constitution shall be prosecuted by indictment unless the defendant waives indictment by notice in writing to the circuit court, in which event the offense may be prosecuted forthwith by information.

(2) All other offenses shall be prosecuted by indictment, information, complaint, post-arrest complaint, or, in the case of traffic offenses or fish and wildlife offenses, may be prosecuted by uniform citation.

HISTORY: Amended by Order 81–5, eff. 9–1–81; adopted eff. 1–1–63

RCr 6.04   Information

The attorney for the Commonwealth may file an information charging the commission of an offense either upon such attorney's own knowledge, information, and belief, or in his or her discretion upon the basis of a verified complaint submitted to such attorney.

HISTORY: Amended by Order 98–3, eff. 3–1–99; adopted eff. 1–1–63

RCr 6.06   Signatures

All indictments shall be signed by the foreperson of the grand jury. All informations shall be signed by an attorney for the Commonwealth. No objection to an indictment or information on the ground that it was not signed as herein required may be made after a plea to the merits has been filed or entered.

HISTORY: Amended by Order 98–3, eff. 3–1–99; adopted eff. 1–1–63

RCr 6.08   Names of witnesses

The names of all the witnesses who were examined shall be endorsed on the indictment. The names of all persons upon whose statements the information is based shall be endorsed thereon. Failure to endorse the names shall not affect the validity or sufficiency of the indictment or information, but the court, on motion of the defendant, shall direct the names to be endorsed, and may grant such continuance of the case as it deems necessary in the interest of justice.

HISTORY: Adopted eff. 1–1–63

RCr 6.10   Requisites of indictment or information

(1) The indictment or information shall contain a caption setting forth the name of the court and the names of the parties, and the caption shall be a part of the indictment or information.

(2) The indictment or information shall contain, and shall be sufficient if it contains, a plain, concise and definite statement of the essential facts constituting the specific offense with which the defendant is charged. It need not contain any other matter not necessary to such statement, nor need it negative any exception, excuse or proviso contained in any statute creating or defining the offense charged.

(3) Allegations made in one count may be incorporated by a reference in another count. It may be alleged in any count that the means by which the defendant committed the offense are unknown or that the defendant committed it by one or more specified means. The indictment or information shall state for each count the official or customary citation of any applicable statute, rule, regulation or other provision of law which the defendant is alleged therein to have violated; but error in the citation or its omission shall not be ground for dismissal of the indictment or information or for reversal of a conviction if the error or omission did not mislead the defendant to his or her prejudice.

(4) The date on which it was returned in open court shall be endorsed on the indictment by the clerk.

HISTORY: Amended by Order 98–3, eff. 3–1–99; prior amendments eff. 9–1–81 (Order 81–5), 7–1–79, 1–1–78; adopted eff. 1–1–63

RCr 6.12   Effect of defects

An indictment, information, complaint or citation shall not be deemed invalid, nor shall the trial, judgment or other proceedings thereon be stayed, arrested or in any manner affected by reason of a defect or imperfection that does not tend to prejudice the substantial rights of the defendant on the merits.

HISTORY: Amended by Order 81–5, eff. 9–1–81; adopted eff. 1–1–63

RCr 6.14   Surplusage

Unnecessary allegations may be disregarded as surplusage, and on motion of the defendant may be stricken from the indictment, information, complaint or citation.

HISTORY: Amended by Order 81–5, eff. 9–1–81; adopted eff. 1–1–63

RCr 6.16   Amendment

The court may permit an indictment, information, complaint or citation to be amended any time before verdict or finding if no additional or different offense is charged and if substantial rights of the defendant are not prejudiced. If justice requires, however, the court shall grant the defendant a continuance when such an amendment is permitted.

HISTORY: Amended by Order 81–5, eff. 9–1–81; adopted eff. 1–1–63

RCr 6.18   Joinder of offenses

Two (2) or more offenses may be charged in the same complaint or two (2) or more offenses whether felonies or misdemeanors, or both, may be charged in the same indictment or information in a separate count for each offense, if the offenses are of the same or similar character or are based on the same acts or transactions connected together or constituting parts of a common scheme or plan.

HISTORY: Amended by Order 81–5, eff. 9–1–81; adopted eff. 1–1–63

RCr 6.20   Joinder of defendants

Two (2) or more defendants may be charged in the same indictment, information or complaint if they are alleged to have participated in the same act or transaction or in the same series of acts or transactions constituting an offense or offenses. Such defendants may be charged in one or more counts together or separately, and all of the defendants need not be charged in each count.

HISTORY: Amended by Order 81–5, eff. 9–1–81; adopted eff. 1–1–63

RCr 6.22   Bill of particulars

The court for cause shall direct the filing of a bill of particulars. A motion for such bill may be made at any time prior to arraignment, or thereafter in the discretion of the court. A bill of particulars may be amended at any time subject to such conditions as justice requires.

HISTORY: Adopted eff. 1–1–63

RCr 6.24   Prior judicial approval for grand jury subpoena of an attorney or attorney's agent to obtain evidence concerning attorney's client

A prosecutor shall not subpoena an attorney to a grand jury without prior judicial approval in circumstances where the prosecutor seeks to compel the attorney/witness to provide evidence concerning a person who is represented by the attorney/witness. A prosecutor shall not in comparable circumstances subpoena an agent of the attorney, such as an investigator or a paralegal, without prior judicial approval.

HISTORY: Amended by Order 98–3, eff. 3–1–99; adopted by Order 91–2, eff. 11–15–91

RCr 6.52   Warrant or summons upon indictment or information; issuance

Upon the return of an indictment or the issuance of an information, the clerk shall issue a summons for each defendant named instead of a warrant unless a warrant is requested by the attorney for the Commonwealth or directed by the court. Upon request of the attorney for the Commonwealth, the clerk shall issue more than one warrant or summons for the same defendant. The clerk shall deliver the warrant or summons to a peace officer for execution or service. If a defendant fails to appear in response to the summons, a warrant shall issue.

HISTORY: Amended by Order 2012–10, eff. 1–1–13, prior amendments eff. 3–1–99 (Order 98–3), eff. 1–1–78; adopted eff. 1–1–63

RCr 6.54   Warrant or summons; requisites

(1) The requisites of a warrant on an indictment or information shall be the same as for a warrant issued on a complaint except that it shall be signed by the clerk, it shall name or describe the offense charged in the indictment or information, and it shall command that the defendant be arrested and brought before the court. If the offense is bailable the court shall fix the amount of bail and endorse it on the warrant.

(2) The summons shall be in the same form as the warrant except that it shall summon the defendant to appear before the court at a stated time and place.

HISTORY: Amended eff. 1–1–78; prior amendment eff. 1–1–64; adopted eff. 1–1–63

RCr 6.56   Warrant or summons; execution or service and return

(1) The warrant shall be executed or the summons served as provided for the execution of warrants or the service of summons issued upon complaints pursuant to Rule 2.10.

(2) The return of the warrant or summons shall be made as provided in Rule 2.12.

HISTORY: Amended by Order 81–5, eff. 9–1–81; prior amendment eff. 1–1–78; adopted eff. 1–1–63

VII PRODUCTION OF EVIDENCE

RCr 7.02 Subpoenas

(1) A subpoena shall be issued by the clerk. It shall state the name of the court and title, if any, of the proceeding, and shall command each person to whom it is directed to attend and give testimony at the time and place specified therein. The clerk shall issue a subpoena, signed but otherwise in blank, to a party requesting it, who shall fill in the blanks before it is served.

(2) A subpoena for an unmarried infant shall be served upon the infant's resident guardian if there is one known to the party requesting it or, if none, by serving either the infant's father or mother within this state or, if none, by serving the person within this state having control of the infant, and shall command each person to whom it is directed to attend with the infant for the purpose of the infant giving testimony at a time and place for the party therein specified.

(3) A subpoena may also command the person to whom it is directed to produce the books, papers, documents or other objects designated therein. The court on motion made promptly may quash or modify the subpoena if compliance would be unreasonable or oppressive. The court may direct that books, papers, documents or objects designated in the subpoena be produced before the court at a time prior to the trial or prior to the time when they are to be offered in evidence and may upon their production permit the books, papers, documents or objects or portions thereof to be inspected by the parties and their attorneys.

(4) A subpoena may be served by any officer by whom a summons might be served. It may also be served by any person eighteen years of age or over, and that person's affidavit endorsed thereon shall be proof of service or the witness may acknowledge service in writing on the subpoena. Service of the subpoena shall be made by delivering or offering to deliver a copy thereof to the person to whom it is directed.

(5) A subpoena requiring the attendance of a witness at a hearing or trial may be served at any place within the Commonwealth. Failure to tender to the witnesses any compensation for expenses shall not be a sufficient ground for failure to respond to the subpoena.

(6) (a) An order to take a deposition authorizes the clerk of the court in which the deposition is to be taken to issue subpoenas for the persons named or described therein.

(b) The witness whose deposition is to be taken may be required by subpoena to attend at any place designated by the trial court, taking into account the convenience of the witness and the parties.

(7) Failure by any person without adequate excuse to obey a subpoena served upon that person shall be punishable as a contempt of court, provided the appearance of an unmarried infant as specified in the subpoena shall be deemed compliance by the person served on behalf of the infant. Immediate attendance of the witness for the purpose for which the witness was subpoenaed may be compelled by bench warrant issued pursuant to Rule 2.05. A show-cause order may also issue for the purpose of determining whether the witness should be held in contempt.

HISTORY: Amended by Order 98–3, eff. 3–1–99; prior amendments eff. 1–1–85 (Order 84–2), 9–1–81 (Order 81–5); adopted eff. 1–1–63

RCr 7.04 Attendance of witnesses—Abolished
HISTORY: Abolished by Order 81–5, eff. 9–1–81; adopted eff. 1–1–63

RCr 7.06 Indispensable witness

(1) If it appears by affidavit in any criminal proceeding that the testimony of a person is indispensable and that there are reasonable grounds to believe that it will be impracticable to secure that person's attendance by subpoena, the court may issue an order to any peace officer to bring the witness before the court. A hearing shall then be held without unnecessary delay at which the witness shall be present and represented by counsel unless waived, and the court may require the witness to give bail for his or her appearance as a witness. The applicable provisions governing bail shall apply to bail for indispensable witnesses. If the witness fails to give bail, the court may commit him or her to custody pending a final disposition of the proceeding in which the testimony is needed. The court may order the witness's release if he or she has been detained for an unreasonable length of time and may modify at any time the requirement as to bail.

(2) If such witness is committed for failure to give bail, the court on written motion of the witness and upon notice to the parties may direct that the witness's deposition be taken. After the deposition has been taken the court shall discharge the witness.

HISTORY: Amended by Order 98–3, eff. 3–1–99; prior amendments eff. 1–1–85 (Order 84–2), 9–1–81 (Order 81–5); adopted eff. 1–1–63

RCr 7.08 Documentary evidence—Abolished
HISTORY: Abolished by Order 81–5, eff. 9–1–81; adopted eff. 1–1–63

RCr 7.10 Grounds for taking depositions

(1) If it appears that a prospective witness may be unable to attend or is or may be prevented from attending a trial or hearing or is or may become a nonresident of the Commonwealth, that the witness's testimony is material and that it is necessary to take

the witness's deposition in order to prevent a failure of justice, in any pending proceeding the court may upon motion and notice to the parties order that the witness's testimony be taken by deposition and that any designated books, papers, documents or tangible objects, not privileged, be produced at the same time and place.

(2) If a witness is committed for failure to give bail pursuant to Rule 7.06, the court on written motion of the witness and upon notice to the parties may direct that the witness's deposition be taken. After the deposition has been taken the court shall discharge the witness.

(3) Nothing in this Rule 7.10 precludes the taking of a deposition, orally or upon written questions, or the use of a deposition, by agreement of the parties.

HISTORY: Amended by Order 98–3, eff. 3–1–99; prior amendment eff. 9–1–81 (Order 81–5); adopted eff. 1–1–63

RCr 7.12   Taking depositions

(1) The order authorizing the taking of a deposition shall contain such specifications as will fully protect the rights of personal confrontation and cross-examination of the witness by the defendant. Whenever it is practicable to do so, the court shall direct that the deposition be taken in the county where the criminal case is pending, and the attendance of witnesses may be compelled by subpoena in the same manner as at trial.

(2) If a deposition is taken at the instance of the Commonwealth, the Commonwealth shall pay in advance the reasonable expenses of travel and subsistence of the defendant and the defendant's attorney in attending such examination.

(3) If a defendant is in custody, he or she shall be produced at the examination by the officer having the defendant in custody and kept in the presence of the witness during the examination.

HISTORY: Amended by Order 98–3, eff. 3–1–99; prior amendments eff. 9–1–81 (Order 81–5), 1–1–78; adopted eff. 1–1–63

RCr 7.14   Notice of taking depositions

(1) In the absence of agreement the party at whose insistence the deposition is to be taken shall give to every party reasonable written notice of the time and place for taking the deposition. In the absence of good cause shown, notice of less than 72 hours shall not be deemed reasonable for the purposes of this rule.

(2) The notice shall state the name and address of each person to be examined. On motion of a party upon whom the notice is served, the court for cause shown may change the time or place of taking.

HISTORY: Amended by Order 84–2, eff. 1–1–85; prior amendment eff. 9–1–81; adopted eff. 1–1–63

RCr 7.16   Defendant's counsel

Upon the application for taking depositions if a defendant is without counsel, the court shall advise the defendant of his or her right thereto and assign counsel to represent the defendant unless the defendant elects to proceed without counsel or is able to obtain counsel.

HISTORY: Amended by Order 98–3, eff. 3–1–99; adopted eff. 1–1–63

RCr 7.18   Manner of taking depositions

A deposition shall be taken in the manner provided in the Civil Rules. The court at the request of a defendant may direct that a deposition be taken on written interrogatories in the manner provided in the Civil Rules.

HISTORY: Adopted eff. 1–1–63

RCr 7.20   Use of depositions; objections

(1) At the trial or upon any hearing, a part or all of a deposition, so far as otherwise admissible under the rules of evidence, may be used if it appears: that the witness is dead; or that the witness is out of the Commonwealth of Kentucky, unless it appears that the absence of the witness was procured by the party offering the deposition; or that the witness is unable to attend or testify because of sickness or infirmity; or that the party offering the deposition had been unable to procure the attendance of the witness by subpoena. Any deposition may also be used by any party for the purpose of contradicting or impeaching the testimony of the deponent as a witness. If only a part of a deposition is offered in evidence by a party, any other party may require the offering party to introduce at that time all of it which is relevant to the part introduced or may later introduce any other parts so relevant.

(2) Objections may be made at the trial or hearing to receiving in evidence any deposition or part thereof for any reason that would require exclusion of the evidence if the witness were then present and testifying; provided, however, that:

(a) objections to the competency of a witness or to the competency, relevancy or materiality of testimony are not waived by failure to make them before or during the taking of the deposition unless the ground of the objection is one that might have been obviated or removed if presented at that time;

(b) errors and irregularities occurring at the oral examination in the manner of taking the deposition, in the form of the questions or answers, in the oath or affirmation or in the conduct of parties, and errors of any kind that might be obviated, removed, or cured if promptly presented, are waived unless seasonable objection is made at the taking of the deposition; and

(c) objections to the form of written questions are waived unless served in writing on the party propounding them within the time allowed for serving the succeeding cross or other questions and within three (3) days after service of the last questions authorized.

HISTORY: Amended by Order 98–3, eff. 3–1–99; prior amendments eff. 9–1–81 (Order 81–5), 1–1–78; adopted eff. 1–1–63

RCr 7.22 Transcript of previous testimony

For purposes of Rule 7.20 a duly authenticated transcript of testimony given by a witness in a previous trial of the same offense in any district or circuit court on the same charge shall be the equivalent of a deposition.

HISTORY: Amended by Order 81–5, eff. 9–1–81; prior amendments eff. 1–1–78; adopted eff. 1–1–65

RCr 7.24 Discovery and inspection

(1) Upon written request by the defense, the attorney for the Commonwealth shall disclose the substance, including time, date, and place, of any oral incriminating statement known by the attorney for the Commonwealth to have been made by a defendant to any witness, and to permit the defendant to inspect and copy or photograph any relevant (a) written or recorded statements or confessions made by the defendant, or copies thereof, that are known by the attorney for the Commonwealth to be in the possession, custody, or control of the Commonwealth, and (b) results or reports of physical or mental examinations, and of scientific tests or experiments made in connection with the particular case, or copies thereof, that are known by the attorney for the Commonwealth to be in the possession, custody or control of the Commonwealth, and (c) upon written request by the defense, the attorney for the Commonwealth shall furnish to the defendant a written summary of any expert testimony that the Commonwealth intends to introduce at trial. This summary must identify the witness and describe the witness's opinions, the bases and reasons for those opinions, and the witness's qualifications.

(2) On motion of a defendant the court may order the attorney for the Commonwealth to permit the defendant to inspect and copy or photograph books, papers, documents or tangible objects, or copies or portions thereof, that are in the possession, custody or control of the Commonwealth, upon a showing that the items sought may be material to the preparation of the defense and that the request is reasonable. This provision authorizes pretrial discovery and inspection of official police reports, but not of memoranda, or other documents made by police officers and agents of the Commonwealth in connection with the investigation or prosecution of the case, or of statements made to them by witnesses or by prospective witnesses (other than the defendant).

(3)(a) If the defendant requests disclosure under RCr 7.24(1)(b), upon compliance to such request by

the Commonwealth, and upon written request of the Commonwealth, the defendant, subject to objection for cause, shall permit the Commonwealth to inspect, copy, or photograph any results or reports of physical or mental examinations and of scientific tests or experiments made in connection with the particular case, or copies thereof, within the possession, custody, or control of the defendant, which the defendant intends to introduce as evidence or which were prepared by a witness whom the defendant intends to call at trial when the results or reports relate to the witness's testimony. If the defendant requests disclosure of the Commonwealth's experts under RCr 7.24(1)(c), then upon written request by the attorney for the Commonwealth, the defense shall furnish to the attorney for the Commonwealth a written summary of any expert testimony that the defense intends to introduce at trial. This summary must identify the witness and describe that witness's opinions, the bases and reasons for those opinions, and the witness's qualifications.

(b) If the defendant requests disclosure under Rule 7.24(2), upon compliance with such request by the Commonwealth, and upon motion of the Commonwealth, the court may order that the defendant permit the Commonwealth to inspect, copy, or photograph books, papers, documents or tangible objects which the defendant intends to introduce into evidence and which are in the defendant's possession, custody, or control.

(B)(i) If a defendant intends to introduce expert testimony relating to a mental disease or defect or any other mental condition of the defendant bearing upon the issue of his or her guilt or punishment, the defendant shall, at least 20 days prior to trial, or at such other time as the court may direct upon reasonable notice to the parties, notify the attorney for the Commonwealth in writing of such intention and file a copy of such notice with the clerk. The court may for cause shown allow late filing of the notice or grant additional time to the parties to prepare for trial or make such other order as may be appropriate.

(ii) When a defendant has filed the notice required by paragraph (B)(i) of this rule, the court may, upon motion of the attorney for the Commonwealth, order the defendant to submit to a mental examination. No statement made by the defendant in the course of any examination provided for by this rule, whether the examination be with or without the consent of the defendant, shall be admissible into evidence against the defendant in any criminal proceeding. No testimony by the expert based upon such statement, and no fruits of the statement shall be admissible into evidence against the defendant in any criminal proceeding except upon an issue regarding mental condition on which the defendant has introduced testimony. If the examination ordered under this rule pertains to the issue of punishment (excluding a pretrial hearing under KRS 532.135), the court shall enter an order prohibiting disclosure to the attorneys for either party of any self-incriminating information divulged by the defendant until the defendant is found guilty of a felony offense, unless the parties otherwise enter into an agreement regulating disclosure.

(C) If there is a failure to give notice when required by this rule or to submit to an examination ordered by the court under this rule, the court may exclude such evidence or the testimony of any expert witness offered by the defendant on the issue of his or her mental condition.

(D) Evidence of an intention as to which notice was given pursuant to this rule, but later withdrawn, shall not be admissible, in any civil or criminal proceeding, against the person who gave said notice.

(4) If the case has been set for trial, a request for relief under this rule shall be made a reasonable time in advance of the trial date, and the granting of a continuance by reason of such request shall lie within the sound discretion of the court.

(5) An order granting relief under this rule shall specify the time, place and manner of making the discovery and inspection permitted and may prescribe such terms and conditions as are just.

(6) On a sufficient showing the court may at any time order that the discovery or inspection be denied, restricted or deferred, or make such other order as is appropriate. On motion the court may permit the Commonwealth to make such showing, in whole or part, in the form of a written statement to be inspected by the court privately; and if the court thereupon grants relief following such private inspection the entire text of the Commonwealth's statement shall be sealed and preserved in the records of the court to be made available to the appellate court in the event of an appeal by the defendant.

(7) One (1) motion shall exhaust the relief available to the movant under this rule, except that a subsequent motion may be sustained on a showing of just cause.

(8) If subsequent to compliance with an order issued pursuant to this rule, and prior to or during trial, a party discovers additional material previously requested which is subject to discovery or inspection under the rule, that party shall promptly notify the other party or the other party's attorney, or the court, of the existence thereof.

(9) If at any time during the course of the proceedings it is brought to the attention of the court that a party has failed to comply with this rule or an order issued pursuant thereto, the court may direct such party to permit the discovery or inspection of materials not previously disclosed, grant a continuance, or prohibit the party from introducing in evidence the material not disclosed, or it may enter such other order as may be just under the circumstances.

HISTORY: Amended by Order 2012–10, eff. 1–1–13, prior amendments eff. 1–1–11 (Order 2010–09), eff. 1–1–05 (Order 2004–5), 1–1–03 (Order 2002–1), 3–1–99 (Order 98–3), 1–1–99 (Order 98–2), 10–1–94 (Order 94–1), 9–1–93, 1–1–88, 1–1–87, 1–1–86; adopted eff. 1–1–65

RCr 7.26 Demands for production of statement and reports

(1) Except for good cause shown, not later than forty-eight (48) hours prior to trial, the attorney for the Commonwealth shall produce all statements of any witness in the form of a document or recording in its possession which relates to the subject matter of the witness's testimony and which (a) has been signed or initialed by the witness or (b) is or purports to be a substantially verbatim statement made by the witness. Such statement shall be made available for examination and use by the defendant.

(2) If the Commonwealth claims that a statement to be produced under this Rule 7.26 does not relate to the subject matter of the witness's testimony, the court shall examine the statement privately and, before making it available for examination and use by the defendant, excise the portions that do not so relate. The entire text of the statement shall be sealed and preserved in the records of the court to be made available to the appellate court in the event of an appeal by the defendant.

HISTORY: Amended by Order 96–1, eff. 1–1–97; prior amendments eff. 1–1–86, 9–1–81; adopted eff. 1–1–65

VIII ARRAIGNMENT AND PLEADINGS

RCr 8.01 Initial appearance after indictment or information

Within a reasonable time after service of the warrant or summons on the indictment or information, the judge shall proceed as provided in Rule 3.05 and shall also proceed with or set a time for arraignment.

HISTORY: Amended by Order 2000–1, eff. 2–1–01; adopted by Order 81–5, eff. 9–1–81

RCr 8.02 Arraignment

Arraignment shall be conducted in open court and shall consist of reading or stating to the defendant the substance of the charge and calling upon the defendant to plead in response to it. Defendants who are jointly charged may be arraigned separately or together, in the discretion of the court.

HISTORY: Amended by Order 98–3, eff. 3–1–99; prior amendments eff. 9–1–81 (Order 81–5), 1–1–67; adopted eff. 1–1–63

RCr 8.03 Pretrial procedure

At any time after the filing of the indictment or information the court on motion of any party or on its own motion may order counsel for all parties to appear before it for one or more conferences to consider such matters as will promote a fair and expeditious trial. At the conclusion of a conference the court shall prepare and file an order noting the matters agreed upon. This rule shall not be invoked in the case of a defendant who is not represented by counsel.

HISTORY: Amended by Order 81–5, eff. 9–1–81; adopted eff. 1–1–65

RCr 8.04 Pretrial diversion

(1) Generally. The attorney for the Commonwealth and the defendant may agree, subject to the approval of the trial court, that the prosecution will be suspended for a specified period after which it will be dismissed on the condition that the defendant not commit a crime during that period, or other conditions agreed upon by the parties. The agreement (or any mutually agreed upon subsequent modifications to the agreement) must be in writing and signed by the parties.

(2) Limitations on agreements. The agreement may not specify a period longer than could be imposed upon probation after conviction of the crime charged. The agreement may include conditions that could be imposed upon probation.

(3) Filing of agreement; release. Promptly after the agreement is made, the Attorney for the Commonwealth shall file the agreement together with a statement that pursuant to the agreement the prosecution is suspended for a period specified in the statement. Upon this filing and approval by the trial court, the defendant must be released from custody on the charges for which diversion is granted.

(4) Termination of agreement; resumption of prosecution.

(a) The defendant may unilaterally terminate this agreement by filing a written notice of termination. Upon filing of the notice of termination, the prosecution may resume as if there had been no agreement.

(b) The court may order the agreement terminated and the prosecution resumed if, prior to completion of the agreement by the defendant, the court finds at a hearing the existence of one of the following:

(i) Either party misrepresented material facts affecting the agreement;

(ii) The defendant has committed a material violation of the agreement or has failed to complete the terms of the agreement.

(5) Termination of the agreement; automatic dismissal. Upon the expiration of the period of suspension of prosecution and upon the completion of the agreement and where there is no motion by the Attorney for the Commonwealth to terminate the agreement upon any grounds permitted under this Rule, the indictment, complaint or charges which are the subject matter of the agreement shall be dismissed with prejudice. In the event that there may be a pending motion by the Commonwealth to termi-

nate the agreement, if the Court shall rule that the motion be denied, then upon entry of said order the indictment, complaint or charges shall be dismissed with prejudice.

HISTORY: Adopted by Order 98–2, eff. 1–1–99

RCr 8.06 Incapacity to stand trial

If upon arraignment or during the proceedings there are reasonable grounds to believe that the defendant lacks the capacity to appreciate the nature and consequences of the proceedings against him or her, or to participate rationally in his or her defense, all proceedings shall be postponed until the issue of incapacity is determined as provided by KRS 504.100.

HISTORY: Amended by Order 98–3, eff. 3–1–99; prior amendments eff. 1–1–87 (Order 86–3), 9–1–81 (Order 81–5); adopted eff. 1–1–63

RCr 8.07 Mental issues

(1) Insanity Defense; Notice; Mental Examination.

(A) Notice by Defendant. A defendant who intends to assert a defense of insanity at the time of the alleged offense shall, not less than ninety (90) days before the date set for commencement of trial of the alleged offense, file a notice in writing of this intention with the clerk and serve a copy of the notice upon the attorney for the Commonwealth and all other parties. The court shall, for good cause, allow the defendant to file the notice late, grant a continuance of the trial or of any other proceedings, modify scheduling orders, or make other appropriate orders.

(B) Motion by Commonwealth for Examination of Defendant. If the defendant files a notice under Rule 8.07(1)(A), the attorney for the Commonwealth may, within ten (10) days of the filing of that notice, file a motion with the clerk for the court to order the defendant to be examined under KRS 504.070 and serve a copy of the motion upon counsel for the defendant. The court shall, for good cause, allow the attorney for the Commonwealth to file the motion late, grant a continuance of the trial or of any other proceedings, modify scheduling orders, or make other appropriate orders.

(C) Mental Examination; Authority to Order Examination; Procedures. If the defendant files a notice under Rule 8.07(1)(A), the court shall, upon the Commonwealth's motion under Rule 8.07(1)(B), order the defendant to be examined under KRS 504.070(3).

(D) Reports of Psychiatric or Psychological Examination. A report of a psychiatric or psychological examination ordered pursuant to Rule 8.07(1)(C) shall be prepared by the examiner designated to conduct the psychiatric or psychological examination. The report shall include—

(i) the defendant's history;

(ii) a description of the psychiatric, psychological, and medical tests that were employed and their results; and

(iii) the examiner's findings opinions and diagnosis as to whether the defendant was insane at the time of the offense charged.

(E) Filing and Disclosing Results and Reports of Psychiatric or Psychological Examination. The examiner designated to conduct the psychiatric or psychological examination under Rule 8.07(1)(C) shall, immediately upon completion of the report, deliver it as directed in the referring order of the court. The court shall order the report to be filed under seal and notice of the filing be given to all parties.

(2) Mental Disease, Mental Defect or Other Mental Condition Bearing on Issue of Guilt or Issue of Punishment; Notice; Mental Examination.

(A) Notice by Defendant. A defendant who intends to introduce expert evidence relating to a mental disease or defect or any other mental condition of the defendant bearing on—

(i) the issue of guilt;

(ii) the issue of punishment; or

(iii) the issue of guilt and the issue of punishment;

shall, not less than ninety (90) days before the date set for commencement of trial of the alleged offense, file a notice in writing of this intention with the clerk and serve a copy of the notice upon the attorney for the Commonwealth and all other parties. The notice shall specify whether the defendant intends to introduce expert evidence bearing on the issue of guilt, the issue of punishment or both such issues. The court shall, for good cause, allow the defendant to file the notice late, grant a continuance of the trial or of any other proceedings, modify scheduling orders, or make other appropriate orders.

(B) Motion by Commonwealth for Examination of Defendant. If the defendant files a notice under Rule 8.07(2)(A), the attorney for the Commonwealth may, within ten (10) days of the filing of that notice, file a motion with the clerk for the court to order the defendant to be examined and serve a copy of the motion upon counsel for the defendant and all other parties. The court shall, for good cause, allow the attorney for the Commonwealth to file the motion late, grant a continuance of the trial or of any other proceedings, modify scheduling orders, or make other appropriate orders.

(C) Mental Examination; Authority to Order Examination; Procedures. If the defendant files a notice under Rule 8.07(2)(A), the court may, upon the Commonwealth's motion under Rule 8.07(2)(B), order the defendant to be examined under procedures ordered by the court. The order shall specify that the examination relates to a claim that defendant suffers, or has suffered, from a mental disease or defect or

any other mental condition of the defendant that bears on—

(i) the issue of guilt;

(ii) the issue of punishment; or

(iii) the issue of guilt and the issue of punishment.

(D) Reports of Psychiatric or Psychological Examination. A report of a psychiatric or psychological examination ordered pursuant to Rule 8.07(2)(C) shall be prepared by the examiner designated to conduct the psychiatric or psychological examination. The report shall include—

(i) the defendant's history;

(ii) a description of the psychiatric, psychological, and medical tests that were employed and their results; and

(iii) the examiner's findings, opinions and diagnosis as to whether:

(a) if the examination is ordered under Rule 8.07(2)(C)(i), whether the defendant is, or was at the time of the offense charged, suffering from a mental disease, mental defect or other mental condition bearing on the issue of guilt;

(b) if the examination is ordered under Rule 8.07(2)(C)(ii), whether the defendant is, or was at the time of the offense charged, suffering from a mental disease, mental defect or other mental condition bearing on the issue of punishment; or

(c) if the examination is ordered under Rule 8.07(2)(C)(iii), whether the defendant is, or was at the time of the offense charged, suffering from a mental disease, mental defect or other mental condition bearing on the issue of guilt and the issue of punishment.

(E) Filing and Disclosing Results and Reports of Psychiatric or Psychological Examination. The examiner designated to conduct the psychiatric or psychological examination under Rule 8.07(2)(C)(i) shall, upon completion of the report, immediately deliver it as directed in the referring order of the court. The court shall order the report to be filed under seal and notice of the filing be given to all parties.

(3) Inadmissibility of a Defendant's Statements Made In Course of Examination Under Rules 8.06, 8.07(1) and 8.07(2).

No statement made by a defendant in the course of any examination conducted under Rules 8.06, 8.07(1) or 8.07(2) (whether conducted with or without the defendant's consent), no testimony by an expert based on any such statement, and no other fruits of any such statement may be admitted into evidence against the defendant in any criminal proceeding except on an issue regarding mental condition on which the defendant:

(A) has introduced evidence of incompetency or incapacity to stand trial under Rule 8.06;

(B) has introduced evidence requiring notice under Rule 8.07(1)(A); or

(C) has introduced evidence requiring notice under Rule 8.07(2)(A).

(4) Failure to Comply with Rules 8.07(1) and 8.07(2).

(A) Defendant's Failure to Give Notice or to Submit to Examination. The court may exclude any expert evidence from the defendant on the issue of the defendant's—

(i) sanity or insanity, if the defendant fails to give notice under Rule 8.07(1)(A) or to submit to an examination when ordered under Rule 8.07(1)(C); or

(ii) mental disease, mental defect, or any other mental condition bearing on the defendant's guilt or the issue of punishment, if the defendant fails to give notice under 8.07(2)(A) or to submit to an examination when ordered under Rule 8.07(2)(C).

(B) Commonwealth's Failure to Move for Examination. The court may decline to order the defendant to be examined if the attorney for the Commonwealth fails to file a motion under Rule 8.07(1)(B) or Rule 8.07(2)(B) for the defendant to be examined.

(5) Inadmissibility of Withdrawn Intention As to Which Notice Was Given Under Rules 8.07(1)(A) and 8.07(2)(A).

Evidence of an intention as to which notice was given under Rule 8.07(1)(A) or 8.07(2)(A), later withdrawn, is not, in any civil, or criminal, administrative or other proceeding, admissible against the person who gave notice of the intention.

HISTORY: Adopted by Order 2012–10, eff. 1–1–13.

RCr 8.08   Pleas

A defendant may plead not guilty, guilty or guilty but mentally ill. The court may refuse to accept a plea of guilty or guilty but mentally ill, and shall not accept the plea without first determining that the plea is made voluntarily with understanding of the nature of the charge. If a defendant refuses to plead or if the court refuses to accept a plea of guilty or guilty but mentally ill or if a defendant corporation fails to appear, the court shall enter a plea of not guilty.

HISTORY: Amended by Order 84–2, eff. 1–1–85; adopted eff. 1–1–63

RCr 8.09   Conditional plea

With the approval of the court a defendant may enter a conditional plea of guilty, reserving in writing the right, on appeal from the judgment, to review of the adverse determination of any specified trial or pretrial motion. A defendant shall be allowed to withdraw such plea upon prevailing on appeal.

HISTORY: Amended by Order 91–2, eff. 11–15–91; adopted eff. 1–1–87

RCr 8.10   Withdrawal of plea

At any time before judgment the court may permit the plea of guilty or guilty but mentally ill, to be withdrawn and a plea of not guilty substituted.

If the court rejects the plea agreement, the court shall, on the record, inform the parties of this fact, advise the defendant personally in open court or, on a showing of good cause, in camera, that the court is not bound by the plea agreement, afford the defendant the opportunity to then withdraw the plea, and advise the defendant that if the defendant persists in that guilty plea the disposition of the case may be less favorable to the defendant than that contemplated by the plea agreement.

The court can defer accepting or rejecting the plea agreement until there has been an opportunity to consider the presentence report.

HISTORY: Amended by Order 98–3, eff. 3–1–99; prior amendments eff. 8–28–89 (Order 89–1), 1–1–85; adopted eff. 1–1–63

RCr 8.12   Pleadings

Pleadings in criminal proceedings shall be the indictment, information, complaint or uniform citation, and the plea of guilty, guilty but mentally ill, or not guilty. No other plea, demurrer, or motion to quash shall be used, and defense or objections that before the effective date of these rules could have been raised by one or more of them shall be raised only by motion to dismiss or to grant appropriate relief.

HISTORY: Amended by Order 84–2, eff. 1–1–85; prior amendment eff. 9–1–81; adopted eff. 1–1–63

RCr 8.14   Motions

An application to the court for an order shall be by motion which shall be in writing unless made during a hearing or trial, shall state with particularity the grounds therefor, and shall set forth the relief or order sought.

HISTORY: Adopted eff. 1–1–63

RCr 8.16   Motions that may be made before trial

A party may raise by pretrial motion any defense, objection, or request that the court can determine without a trial of the general issue.

HISTORY: Amended by Order 2012–10, eff. 1–1–13. Adopted eff. 1–1–63

RCr 8.18   Defenses which must be raised by motion

Defenses and objections based on defects in the institution of the prosecution or in the indictment or information other than that it fails to show jurisdiction in the court or to charge an offense may be raised only by motion before trial. The motion shall include all such defenses and objections then available to the defendant. Failure to present any such defense or objection as herein provided constitutes a waiver thereof, but the court for cause shown may grant relief from the waiver. Lack of jurisdiction or the failure of the indictment or information to charge an offense shall be noticed by the court at any time during the proceedings.

HISTORY: Adopted eff. 1–1–63

RCr 8.20   Motion deadline; ruling on motion

(1) Motion Deadline. The court may, at the arraignment or as soon afterward as practicable, set a deadline for the parties to make pretrial motions and may also schedule a motion hearing.

(2) Ruling on a Motion. The court shall decide every pretrial motion within a reasonable time before the date of trial unless it finds good cause to defer a ruling. When factual issues are involved in deciding a motion, the court shall state its essential findings on the record.

HISTORY: Amended by Order 2012–10, eff. 1–1–13. Adopted eff. 1–1–63

RCr 8.22   Hearing on motion

A pretrial motion raising defenses or objections shall be determined before trial unless the court orders that it be deferred for determination at the trial of the general issue, but no such determination shall be deferred if a party's right to appeal is adversely affected. An issue of fact shall be tried by a jury if a jury trial is required by law. All other issues of fact shall be determined by the court with or without a jury or on affidavits or in such other manner as the court may direct. A verbatim record shall be made of all proceedings at the hearing, including such findings of fact and conclusions of law as are made orally.

HISTORY: Amended by Order 81–5, eff. 9–1–81; adopted eff. 1–1–63

RCr 8.24   Effect of determination

(1) If a motion is determined adversely to the defendant the defendant shall be permitted to plead if the defendant has not previously done so. A plea previously entered shall not be affected by the adverse determination of a motion.

(2) If the court grants a motion based on a defect in the institution of the prosecution or in the indictment, information or complaint, it may also order that the defendant be held in custody or that the defendant's bail be continued for a period of time not to exceed the date of discharge of the grand jury next assembled or 60 days, whichever is sooner, pending the filing of a new indictment, information or complaint.

HISTORY: Amended by Order 98–3, eff. 3–1–99; prior amendment eff. 9–1–81 (Order 81–5); adopted eff. 1–1–63

RCr 8.26   Improper venue; transfer

If it appears from either the indictment, information or evidence that the offense was committed in a county other than that in which the trial is being held, the defendant may move for a transfer of the prosecution to the proper venue. If the motion is sustained, the court shall order a transfer of the original papers including the bail bond, if any, or certified copies thereof, and any cash deposits on the bond made by the defendant to the clerk of the court of the county to which the transfer of the prosecution is made. The court also may order that the bail be continued for the defendant's appearance or that the defendant be held in custody to await his or her transfer to the county to which the prosecution is transferred by a peace officer of that county. The defendant shall be deemed to be held to answer in the court of the county in which the offense was committed from the date of the sustaining of the motion.

HISTORY: Amended by Order 98–3, eff. 3–1–99; prior amendments eff. 1–1–78, 6–19–76; adopted eff. 1–1–63

RCr 8.28   Presence of defendant

(1) The defendant shall be present at the arraignment, at every critical stage of the trial including the empaneling of the jury and the return of the verdict, and at the imposition of the sentence. The defendant's voluntary absence after the trial has been commenced in his or her presence shall not prevent proceeding with the trial up to and including the verdict. The defendant may be permitted to remain on bail during the trial. Upon a hearing and finding by the trial court, that a defendant in custody on any charge, including a felony, intentionally refuses to appear for any proceeding, including trial, short of physical force, such refusal shall be deemed a waiver of the defendant's right to appear at that proceeding.

(2) A defendant who persists in engaging in disruptive conduct after being warned by the court that such conduct will cause him or her to be removed may be excluded from the courtroom.

(3) A corporation may appear by counsel for all purposes.

(4) In prosecutions for misdemeanors or violations the court may permit arraignment, plea, trial and imposition of sentence in the defendant's absence. However, no plea of guilty to a violation of KRS 189A or KRS 218A may be entered in the defendant's absence, unless the defendant first executes a written waiver of his or her right to be present.

(5) During his or her appearance in court before a jury the defendant shall not be required to wear the distinctive clothing of a prisoner. Except for good cause shown the judge shall not permit the defendant to be seen by the jury in shackles or other devices for physical restraint.

HISTORY: Amended by Order 2009–01, eff. 4–1–09; prior amendments eff. 3–1–99 (Order 98–3), 10–1–94 (Order 94–1), 9–1–81 (Order 81–5); adopted eff. 1–1–63

RCr 8.30 Separate counsel for defendants; when required

(1) If the crime of which the defendant is charged is punishable by a fine of more than $500, or by confinement, no attorney shall be permitted at any stage of the proceedings to act as counsel for the defendant while at the same time engaged as counsel for another person or persons accused of the same offense or of offenses arising out of the same incident or series of related incidents unless (a) the judge of the court in which the proceeding is being held explains to the defendant or defendants the possibility of a conflict of interests on the part of the attorney in that what may be or seem to be in the best interests of one client may not be in the best interests of another, and (b) each defendant in the proceeding executes and causes to be entered in the record a statement that the possibility of a conflict of interests on the part of the attorney has been explained to the defendant by the court and that the defendant nevertheless desires to be represented by the same attorney.

(2) The procedure set forth in paragraph (1) of this Rule 8.30 shall be followed in each court in which the defendant requires the assistance of counsel, excepting the Court of Appeals and Supreme Court.

(3) Upon receipt of any information reasonably suggesting that what is best for one client may not be best for another, counsel shall explain its significance to the defendant and disclose it to the court, and shall withdraw as counsel for one client or the other unless (a) each such client who is a defendant in the proceeding executes a written waiver setting forth the circumstances and reiterating the client's desire for continued representation by the same counsel and (b) such waiver is entered in the record of the proceeding.

HISTORY: Amended by Order 98–3, eff. 3–1–99; prior amendment eff. 1–1–78; adopted eff. 1–1–78

[SPECIMEN FORM]

FRANKLIN CIRCUIT COURT No. _____

COMMONWEALTH OF KENTUCKY
      PLAINTIFF

vs.

TOM THOMS AND DAN DRUMMER
      DEFENDANTS

WAIVER OF DUAL
OR MULTIPLE
REPRESENTATION
[RCr 8.30(1)]

The undersigned, Tom Thoms, a defendant before this court charged with the offense of theft (KRS 514.030), acknowledges that the court has explained to him and that he understands the possibility of a conflict of interests on the part of his attorney, Hon. Uriah Micawber, in that what may be or seem to be to the best interests of this defendant may not be to the best interests of his codefendant, Dan Drummer, or of Wilkins Primrose, who is not a defendant in this proceeding but is known to be under police investigation as a possible receiver of stolen goods from this defendant, both Drummer and Primrose being also represented by Mr. Micawber. With that understanding, the undersigned nevertheless desires that Mr. Micawber represent him in this proceeding and has no objection to his continu-

ing to act as counsel for the other persons mentioned in this waiver as being involved in a possible conflict of interests.

Signed in open court this ___ day of _____, 1978.

_____
Tom Thoms

Adopted eff. 1–1–78.

RCr 8.32 Transfer from the circuit or district for plea and sentence

(1) A defendant arrested, held, or present in a county of a circuit or district other than that in which an indictment or information is pending against that defendant may state in writing that he or she wishes to plead guilty, to waive trial in the county of the circuit or district in which the indictment or information is pending, and to consent to disposition of the case in the county of the circuit or district in which the defendant was arrested, held, or present, subject to the approval of the Commonwealth's attorney for each county when the matter is in circuit court or the county attorney for each county when the matter is in district court. Upon receipt of the defendant's statement and of the written approval of the Commonwealth's attorney or county attorney for each county, the clerk of the court in which the indictment or information is pending shall transmit the papers in the proceeding or certified copies thereof to the clerk of the court for the county in the circuit or district in which the defendant is arrested, held, or present, and the prosecution shall continue in that county of the circuit or district.

(2) A defendant arrested, held, or present in a county of a circuit or district other than the county of the circuit or district in which a complaint is pending against that defendant may state in writing that he or she wishes to plead guilty, to waive trial in the county of the circuit or district in which the warrant or summons was issued, and to consent to disposition of the case in the county of the circuit or district in which the defendant was arrested, held, or present subject to the approval of the Commonwealth's attorney for each county when the matter is in circuit court or the county attorney for each county when the matter is in district court. Upon receipt of the defendant's statement and of the written approval of the Commonwealth's attorney or county attorney for each county and upon filing of an information or the return of an indictment, the clerk of the court for the county of the circuit or district in which the warrant or summons was issued shall transmit the papers in the proceeding or certified copies thereof to the clerk of the court for the county of the circuit or district in which the defendant was arrested, held, or present, and the prosecution shall continue in that county of the circuit or district.

(3) If after the proceeding has been transferred pursuant to paragraphs (1) or (2) of this Rule the defendant pleads not guilty, the clerk shall return the

papers to the court in which the prosecution was commenced and the proceeding shall be restored to the docket of that court. The defendant's statement that he or she wishes to plead not guilty shall not be used against the defendant.

HISTORY: Amended by Order 98–3, eff. 3–1–99; adopted by Order 84–2, eff. 1–1–85

IX TRIAL

A. GENERAL

RCr 9.02 Time of hearing or trial

All prosecutions shall proceed when the defendant appears or is brought before the court unless postponed for cause. The trials of all persons in custody under arrest shall be held as promptly as reasonably possible.

HISTORY: Amended eff. 1–1–67; adopted eff. 1–1–63

RCr 9.04 Postponement of hearing or trial; motion and affidavit

The court, upon motion and sufficient cause shown by either party, may grant a postponement of the hearing or trial. A motion by the defendant for a postponement on account of the absence of evidence may be made only upon affidavit showing the materiality of the evidence expected to be obtained, and that due diligence has been used to obtain it. If the motion is based on the absence of a witness, the affidavit must show what facts the affiant believes the witness will prove, and not merely the effect of such facts in evidence, and that the affiant believes them to be true. If the attorney for the Commonwealth consents to the reading of the affidavit on the hearing or trial as the deposition of the absent witness, the hearing or trial shall not be postponed on account of the witness's absence. If the Commonwealth does not consent to the reading of the affidavit, the granting of a continuance is in the sound discretion of the trial judge.

HISTORY: Amended by Order 98–3, eff. 3–1–99; prior amendments eff. 8–28–89 (Order 89–1), 1–1–78; adopted eff. 1–1–63

RCr 9.08 Pretrial procedure—Renumbered

HISTORY: Renumbered by Order 81–5, eff. 9–1–81; adopted eff. 1–1–65

RCr 9.12 Consolidation of offenses for trial

The court may order two (2) or more indictments, informations, complaints or uniform citations to be tried together if the offenses, and the defendants, if more than one (1), could have been joined in a single indictment, information, complaint or uniform citation. The procedure shall be the same as if the prosecution were under a single indictment, information, complaint or uniform citation.

HISTORY: Amended by Order 81–5, eff. 9–1–81; adopted eff. 1–1–63

RCr 9.14 Misjoinder of offenses

If two (2) or more offenses are charged in the same indictment, information, complaint or uniform citation and they cannot be properly joined, the Commonwealth may be required to elect which offense it will prosecute.

HISTORY: Amended by Order 81–5, eff. 9–1–81; adopted eff. 1–1–63

RCr 9.16 Separate trials

If it appears that a defendant or the Commonwealth is or will be prejudiced by a joinder of offenses or of defendants in an indictment, information, complaint or uniform citation or by joinder for trial, the court shall order separate trials of counts, grant separate trials of defendants or provide whatever other relief justice requires. A motion for such relief must be made before the jury is sworn or, if there is no jury, before any evidence is received. No reference to the motion shall be made during the trial. In ruling on a motion by a defendant for severance the court may order the attorney for the Commonwealth to deliver to the court for inspection in camera any statements or confessions made by the defendants that the Commonwealth intends to introduce in evidence at the trial.

HISTORY: Amended by Order 81–5, eff. 9–1–81; prior amendment eff. 1–1–67; adopted eff. 1–1–63

RCr 9.22 Objections, exceptions unnecessary

Formal exceptions to rulings or orders of the court are unnecessary; but for all purposes for which an exception has heretofore been necessary it is sufficient that a party, at the time the ruling or order of the court is made or sought, makes known to the court the action which that party desires the court to take or any objection to the action of the court, and on request of the court, the grounds therefor; and, if a party has no opportunity to object to a ruling or order at the time it is made, the absence of an objection does not thereafter prejudice that party.

HISTORY: Amended by Order 98–3, eff. 3–1–99; adopted eff. 1–1–63

RCr 9.24 Harmless error

No error in either the admission or the exclusion of evidence and no error or defect in any ruling or order, or in anything done or omitted by the court or by any of the parties, is ground for granting a new trial or for setting aside a verdict or for vacating, modifying or otherwise disturbing a judgment or order unless it appears to the court that the denial of such relief would be inconsistent with substantial justice. The court at every stage of the proceeding must disregard any error or defect in the proceeding that does not affect the substantial rights of the parties.

HISTORY: Amended by Order 81–5, eff. 9–1–81; adopted eff. 1–1–63

RCr 9.26   Trial by jury or by the court

(1) Cases required to be tried by jury shall be so tried unless the defendant waives a jury trial in writing with the approval of the court and the consent of the Commonwealth.

(2) In a case tried without a jury the court shall make a general finding and shall in addition, on request made before the general finding, find the facts specially. Such findings may be oral. If an opinion or memorandum of decision is filed, it will be sufficient if the findings of fact appear in it.

HISTORY: Adopted by Order 81–5, eff. 9–1–81

B. JURY

RCr 9.30   Selection of jury

(1) (a) In a jury trial in circuit court the clerk, in open court, shall draw from the jury box sufficient names of the persons selected and summoned for jury service to compose a jury as required by law. If one or more of them is challenged, the clerk shall draw from the box as many more as are necessary to complete the jury.

(b) If there is an irregularity in drawing from the jury box, the names of the jurors so drawn shall be returned to the box.

(c) When it appears that the names in the jury box are about to become exhausted, the judge may obtain additional jurors by drawing from the drum, or, with the consent of the parties, by ordering the sheriff or a bailiff appointed by the court to summon any number of qualified persons.

(2) The jury-selection process shall be conducted in accordance with Part Two (2) of the Administrative Procedures of the Court of Justice.

HISTORY: Amended by Order 81–5, eff. 9–1–81; prior amendment eff. 7–1–76; adopted eff. 1–1–63

RCr 9.32   Alternate Jurors

(1) In General. The court may impanel alternate jurors to hear a case. Should it become necessary to excuse a juror, the trial shall proceed unless the number of jurors is reduced below the number required by law. If the membership of the jury exceeds the number required by law, the alternate juror or jurors may be designated by agreement of the parties and the Court; otherwise, immediately before the jury retires to consider its verdict, the clerk, in open court,

shall by random selection reduce the jury to the number required by law.

(2) Recalling Alternate Jurors. The court may require alternate jurors to remain sworn and subject to recall after the jury retires to deliberate provided they have been properly admonished. If recalled, the court must ensure that an alternate has complied with the admonition. If an alternate is recalled after deliberations have begun, the court must instruct the jury to begin its deliberations anew. Alternate jurors shall be recalled in the same sequence in which they were excused.

HISTORY: Adopted by Order 2010–09, eff. 1–1–11

RCr 9.33   Jurors from adjoining counties

If the judge of the court is satisfied after having made a fair effort, in good faith, for that purpose, that, from any cause, it will be impracticable to obtain a jury free of bias in the county wherein the prosecution is pending, the judge shall be authorized to order the sheriff to summon a sufficient number of qualified jurors from some adjoining county in which the judge shall believe there is the greatest probability of obtaining impartial jurors. When so ordered the sheriff shall go to the circuit judge of such adjoining county, if such judge is in the county at the time, and request the judge to draw from the jury drum a list of names sufficient in number to equal the number ordered summoned; and to record the names upon paper, certify and sign it. Whereupon the said sheriff shall summon the number ordered to be summoned from such list. If the circuit judge is not in the county at the time, then the sheriff shall select such jurors from the panels which served, and whose names appeared of record, as jurors at the previous regular term of court in such adjoining county. If the jurors who served at the preceding term are not sufficient in number to meet the number ordered summoned then the sheriff shall select the remainder from the list which served at the next to the last preceding term. From the persons so summoned the jury may be formed.

HISTORY: Amended by Order 98–3, eff. 3–1–99; adopted eff. 1–1–63

RCr 9.34   Challenge to panel

A motion raising an irregularity in the selection or summons of the jurors or formation of the jury must precede the examination of the jurors.

HISTORY: Adopted eff. 1–1–63

RCr 9.36   Challenges to individual jurors

(1) Challenges for cause shall be made first by the Commonwealth and then by the defense. No peremptory challenge shall be permitted before the voir dire has been completed for all parties. When there is reasonable ground to believe that a prospective juror

cannot render a fair and impartial verdict on the evidence, that juror shall be excused as not qualified.

(2) After the parties have been given the opportunity of challenging jurors for cause, each side or party having the right to exercise peremptory challenges shall be handed a list of qualified jurors drawn from the box equal to the number of jurors to be seated plus the number of allowable peremptory challenges for all parties. Peremptory challenges shall be exercised simultaneously by striking names from the list and returning it to the trial judge. If the number of prospective jurors remaining on the list exceeds the number of jurors to be seated, the cards bearing numbers identifying the prospective jurors shall be placed in a box and thoroughly mixed, following which the clerk shall draw at random the number of cards necessary to comprise the jury or, if so directed by the court, a sufficient number of cards to reduce the jury to the number required by law, in which latter event the prospective jurors whose identifying cards remain in the box shall be empaneled as the jury.

(3) All challenges must be made before the jury is sworn. No prospective juror may be challenged after being accepted unless the court for good cause permits it.

(4) If trial counsel so moves, the written record on appeal shall include the juror strike sheets.

HISTORY: Amended by Order 98–3, eff. 3–1–99; prior amendments eff. 9–1–93 (Order 93–1), 9–1–81 (Order 81–5), 1–1–80, 1–1–78, 1–1–67; adopted eff. 1–1–63

RCr 9.38 Examination of jurors

The court may permit the attorney for the Commonwealth and the defendant or the defendant's attorney to conduct the examination of prospective jurors or may itself conduct the examination. In the latter event the court shall permit the attorney for the Commonwealth and the defendant or the defendant's attorney to supplement the examination by such further inquiry as it deems proper. The court may itself submit to the prospective jurors such additional questions submitted by the parties or their attorneys as it deems proper. When the Commonwealth seeks the death penalty, individual voir dire out of the presence of other prospective jurors is required if questions regarding capital punishment, race or pretrial publicity are propounded. Further, upon request, the Court shall permit the attorney for the defendant and the Commonwealth to conduct the examination on these issues.

HISTORY: Amended by Order 96–1, eff. 1–1–97; prior amendment eff. 1–1–89; adopted eff. 1–1–63

RCr 9.40 Peremptory challenges

(1) If the offense charged is a felony, the Commonwealth is entitled to eight (8) peremptory challenges and the defendant or defendants jointly to eight (8) peremptory challenges. If the offense charged is a misdemeanor, the Commonwealth is entitled to three (3) peremptory challenges and the defendant or defendants jointly to three (3) peremptory challenges.

(2) If one (1) or two (2) additional jurors are called, the number of peremptory challenges allowed each side and each defendant shall be increased by one (1).

(3) If more than one defendant is being tried, each defendant shall be entitled to at least one additional peremptory challenge to be exercised independently of any other defendant.

HISTORY: Amended by Order 94–1, eff. 10–1–94; prior amendments eff. 9–15–90, 1–1–78, 1–1–64; adopted eff. 1–1–63

C. PROCEEDINGS

RCr 9.42 Order of proceeding

The jury shall be sworn to try the issue after which the trial shall proceed in the following order, unless the court for special reasons otherwise directs:

(a) The attorney for the Commonwealth shall state to the jury the nature of the charge and the evidence upon which the Commonwealth relies to support it;

(b) The defendant or the defendant's attorney may state the defense and the evidence upon which the defendant relies to support it or the defendant may reserve opening statement until the conclusion of the evidence for the Commonwealth;

(c) The attorney for the Commonwealth must offer the evidence in support of the charge;

(d) The defendant or the defendant's attorney may make opening statement, if reserved, and offer evidence in support of the defense;

(e) The parties respectively may offer rebutting evidence, unless the court, for good reason in furtherance of justice, permits them to offer evidence-in-chief;

(f) The parties may submit or argue the case to the jury. In the argument, the attorney for the Commonwealth shall have the conclusion and the defendant or the defendant's attorney the opening. If more than one (1) counsel is to take part in the closing argument on either side, or if several defendants have separate defenses and appear by different counsel, the court shall arrange the order of argument, always giving the attorney for the Commonwealth the closing argument.

HISTORY: Amended by Order 98–3, eff. 3–1–99; prior amendment eff. 1–1–78; adopted eff. 1–1–63

RCr 9.44 Proof of official record

(1) An official record or an entry therein, when admissible for any purpose, may be evidenced by an official publication thereof or by a copy attested by the officer having the legal custody of the record, or by the officer's deputy if the record is in the custody of an officer of this state, and if the record is in the

custody of an officer outside this state such attested copy shall be accompanied by a certificate that such officer has the custody. If the office in which the record is kept is within the United States or within a territory or insular possession subject to the dominion of the United States, the certificate may be made by a judge of a court of record of the district or political subdivision in which the record is kept, authenticated by the seal of the court, or may be made by any public officer having a seal of office and having official duties in the district or political subdivision in which the record is kept, authenticated by the seal of his or her office. If the office in which the record is kept is in a foreign state or country, the certificate may be made by a secretary of embassy or legation, consul-general, consul, vice consul, or consular agent or by any officer in the foreign service of the United States stationed in the foreign state or country in which the record is kept, and authenticated by the seal of his or her office.

(2) A written statement signed by an officer having the custody of an official record or by the officer's deputy that after diligent search no record or entry of a specified tenor is found to exist in the records of his or her office, accompanied by a certificate as provided above in paragraph (1), is admissible as evidence that the records of his or her office contain no such record or entry.

(3) This Rule 9.44 does not prevent the proof of official records or of entry or lack of entry therein by any other method authorized by law.

HISTORY: Amended by Order 98–3, eff. 3–1–99; prior amendment eff. 9–1–81 (Order 81–5); adopted eff. 1–1–63

RCr 9.46   Expert witnesses—Deleted

HISTORY: Deleted by Order 2004–5, eff. 1–1–05; prior amendment eff. 3–1–99 (Order 98–3); adopted eff. 1–1–63

RCr 9.48   Separation of witnesses—Deleted

HISTORY: Deleted by Order 2004–5, eff. 1–1–05; prior amendment eff. 3–1–99 (Order 98–3); adopted eff. 1–1–63

RCr 9.50   Exclusion of infants from courtroom

In any criminal proceeding in which there will be evidence or testimony presented of a violent or sexual nature, the judge may exclude from the courtroom, and from the hearing of the testimony and arguments, any or all children under the age of sixteen years.

HISTORY: Amended by Order 2010-09, eff. 1–1–11; adopted eff. 1–1–63.

RCr 9.52   Avowals—Deleted

HISTORY: Deleted by Order 2004–5, eff. 1–1–05; prior amendments eff. 3–1–99 (Order 98–3), 9–1–81 (Order 81–5); adopted eff. 1–1–63

RCr 9.54   Instructions

(1) It shall be the duty of the court to instruct the jury in writing on the law of the case, which instruc-

tions shall be read to the jury prior to the closing summations of counsel. These requirements may not be waived except by agreement of both the defense and the prosecution.

(2) No party may assign as error the giving or the failure to give an instruction unless the party's position has been fairly and adequately presented to the trial judge by an offered instruction or by motion, or unless the party makes objection before the court instructs the jury, stating specifically the matter to which the party objects and the ground or grounds of the objection.

(3) The instructions shall not make any reference to a defendant's failure to testify unless so requested by the defendant, in which event the court shall give an instruction to the effect that a defendant is not compelled to testify and that the jury shall not draw any inference of guilt from the defendant's election not to testify and shall not allow it to prejudice the defendant in any way.

HISTORY: Amended by Order 98–3, eff. 3–1–99; prior amendments eff. 9–1–93 (Order 93–1), 1–1–85, 9–1–81 (Order 81–5), 3–1–74, 10–1–68; adopted eff. 1–1–63

RCr 9.55   Jury instruction on the disposition of a defendant when the jury is instructed on the absence of criminal responsibility

On request of either party in a trial by jury of the issue of absence of criminal responsibility for criminal conduct, the court shall instruct the jury at the guilt/innocence phase as to the dispositional provisions applicable to the defendant if the jury returns a verdict of not criminally responsible by reason of mental illness or retardation, or guilty but mentally ill.

HISTORY: Amended by Order 94–1, eff. 10–1–94; adopted eff. 11–15–91

RCr 9.56   Reasonable doubt

(1) In every case the jury shall be instructed substantially as follows: "The law presumes the defendant to be innocent of a crime, and the indictment shall not be considered as evidence or as having any weight against him or her. You shall find the defendant not guilty unless you are satisfied from the evidence alone, and beyond a reasonable doubt, that he or she is guilty. If upon the whole case you have a reasonable doubt that he or she is guilty, you shall find him or her not guilty."

(2) The instructions should not attempt to define the term "reasonable doubt."

HISTORY: Amended by Order 98–3, eff. 3–1–99; prior amendments eff. 7–1–78, 7–1–76; adopted eff. 1–1–63

RCr 9.57   Deadlocked jury; instruction; polling

(1) If a jury reports to a court that it is unable to reach a verdict and the court determines further deliberations may be useful, the court shall not give any instruction regarding the desirability of reaching

a verdict other than one which contains only the following elements:

(a) in order to return a verdict, each juror must agree to that verdict;

(b) jurors have a duty to consult with one another and to deliberate with a view to reaching an agreement, if it can be done without violence to individual judgment;

(c) each juror must decide the case, but only after an impartial consideration of the evidence with the other jurors;

(d) in the course of deliberations, a juror should not hesitate to reexamine his or her own views and change his or her opinion if convinced it is erroneous; and

(e) no juror should surrender his or her honest conviction as to the weight or effect of the evidence solely because of the opinion of other jurors, or for the mere purpose of returning a verdict.

(2) The Court shall not poll the jury before a verdict is returned.

HISTORY: Amended by Order 98–3, eff. 3–1–99; prior amendment eff. 1–1–99 (Order 98–2); adopted by Order 92–1, eff. 8–1–92

RCr 9.58   Questions of law

All questions of law arising during the trial or proceedings shall be decided by the court, and the jury shall be bound to take the decisions of the court on points of law as the law of the case.

HISTORY: Adopted eff. 1–1–63

RCr 9.60   Corroboration of confession

A confession of a defendant, unless made in open court, will not warrant a conviction unless accompanied by other proof that such an offense was committed.

HISTORY: Amended by Order 80–2, eff. 9–1–80; adopted eff. 1–1–63

RCr 9.62   Testimony of accomplice—Abolished

HISTORY: Abolished by Order 80–2, eff. 9–1–80; adopted eff. 1–1–63

RCr 9.64   Dismissal of indictment

The attorney for the Commonwealth, with the permission of the court, may dismiss the indictment, information, complaint or uniform citation prior to the swearing of the jury or, in a non-jury case, prior to the swearing of the first witness.

HISTORY: Amended by Order 81–5, eff. 9–1–81; adopted eff. 1–1–63

RCr 9.66   Sequestration of jurors

Whether the jurors in any case shall be sequestered shall be within the discretion of the court, except that in the trial of a felony charge, after the case is submitted for their verdict, they shall be sequestered unless otherwise agreed by the parties with approval of the court.

HISTORY: Amended eff. 7–1–75; adopted eff. 1–1–63

RCr 9.68   Oath of officers in charge of jury

When the jury is kept together in charge of officers, the officers must be sworn to keep the jurors together, and to suffer no person to speak to, or communicate with, them on any subject connected with the trial, and not to do so themselves.

HISTORY: Adopted eff. 1–1–63

RCr 9.70   Admonition to jury

The jurors, whether permitted to separate or kept in charge of officers, must be admonished by the court that it is their duty not to permit anyone to speak to, or communicate with, them on any subject connected with the trial, and that all attempts to do so should be immediately reported by them to the court, and that they should not converse among themselves on any subject connected with the trial, nor form, nor express any opinion thereon, until the cause be finally submitted to them. This admonition must be given or referred to by the court at each adjournment.

HISTORY: Adopted eff. 1–1–63

RCr 9.72   Jury to take exhibits

Upon retiring for deliberation the jury may take all papers and other things received as evidence in the case. The jurors shall be permitted to take into the jury room during their deliberations any notes they may have made during the course of the trial, but upon request of either party the jury shall be admonished that the notes made by jurors shall not be given any more weight in deliberation than the memory of other jurors.

HISTORY: Amended by Order 81–5, eff. 9–1–81; adopted eff. 1–1–63

RCr 9.74   Information after case submitted

No information requested by the jury or any juror after the jury has retired for deliberation shall be given except in open court in the presence of the defendant (unless the defendant is being tried in absentia) and the entire jury, and in the presence of or after reasonable notice to counsel for the parties.

HISTORY: Amended by Order 98–3, eff. 3–1–99; adopted eff. 1–1–63

RCr 9.76   Court open while jury deliberating

While the jurors are deliberating on their verdict the court shall be deemed open for every purpose connected with the case submitted to the jury until the verdict is returned or the jury is discharged.

HISTORY: Amended by Order 81–5, eff. 9–1–81; adopted eff. 1–1–63

RCr 9.78   Confessions, searches, and witness identification; suppression of evidence

If at any time before trial a defendant moves to suppress, or during trial makes timely objection to the admission of evidence consisting of (a) a confession or other incriminating statements alleged to have been made by the defendant to police authorities, (b) the fruits of a search, or (c) witness identification, the trial court shall conduct an evidentiary hearing outside the presence of the jury and at the conclusion thereof shall enter into the record findings resolving the essential issues of fact raised by the motion or objection and necessary to support the ruling. If supported by substantial evidence the factual findings of the trial court shall be conclusive.

HISTORY: Amended by Order 2004–5, eff. 1–1–05; prior amendment eff. 3–1–99 (Order 98–3); adopted eff. 1–1–78

D.   VERDICT

RCr 9.82   Verdict

(1) The verdict shall be unanimous. It shall be returned by the jury in open court.

(2) If there are two or more defendants, the jury at any time during its deliberation may return a verdict or verdicts with respect to a defendant or defendants as to whom it has agreed; if the jury cannot agree with respect to all, the defendant or defendants as to whom it does not agree may be tried again.

HISTORY: Adopted eff. 1–1–63

RCr 9.84   Penalty

(1) When the jury returns a verdict of guilty it shall fix the degree of the offense and the penalty except that the court may fix the penalty (a) in cases where the penalty is fixed by law and (b) in cases where the court is otherwise authorized by law to fix the penalty.

(2) When the defendant enters a plea of guilty the court may fix the penalty, except that in cases involving offenses punishable by death the defendant may demand that his or her punishment be fixed by the jury.

HISTORY: Amended by Order 98–3, eff. 3–1–99; prior amendment eff. 1–1–89 (Order 88–4); adopted eff. 1–1–63

RCr 9.86   Limitations on conviction

The defendant may be found guilty of an offense included in the offense charged or of an attempt to commit either the offense charged or an offense included therein if the attempt is an offense.

HISTORY: Adopted eff. 1–1–63

RCr 9.88   Poll of jury

When the verdict is announced, either party may require the jury to be polled, which is done by the clerk's or court's asking each juror if it is his or her verdict. If upon the poll, there is not unanimous concurrence, the verdict cannot be received.

HISTORY: Amended by Order 98–3, eff. 3–1–99; adopted eff. 1–1–63

RCr 9.90   Insanity

(1) If the defense of insanity is made by the defendant, the jury must be instructed to state the finding of insanity in their verdict if they acquit the defendant on that ground.

(2) When such a verdict is returned the court may on motion of the prosecuting attorney or on its own initiative dispose of the defendant in accordance with KRS 504.030.

HISTORY: Amended by Order 98–3, eff. 3–1–99; prior amendment eff. 9–1–81 (Order 81–5); adopted eff. 1–1–63

X   NEW TRIAL

RCr 10.02   Motion for new trial

(1) Upon motion of a defendant, the court may grant a new trial for any cause which prevented the defendant from having a fair trial, or if required in the interest of justice. If trial was by the court without a jury, the court may vacate the judgment, take additional testimony and direct the entry of a new judgment.

(2) Not later than ten (10) days after return of the verdict, the court on its own initiative may order a new trial for any reason for which it might have granted a new trial on motion of a defendant, and in the order shall specify the grounds therefor.

HISTORY: Adopted eff. 1–1–63

RCr 10.04   Examination of jurors after verdict

A juror cannot be examined to establish a ground for a new trial, except to establish that the verdict was made by lot.

HISTORY: Adopted eff. 1–1–63

RCr 10.06   Time for motion

(1) The motion for a new trial shall be served not later than five (5) days after return of the verdict. A motion for a new trial based upon the ground of newly discovered evidence shall be made within one (1) year after the entry of the judgment or at a later time if the court for good cause so permits.

(2) After a motion for a new trial is filed and if there is an appeal pending, either party may move the appellate court for a stay of the proceedings in the appellate court, whereupon the clerk of the appellate

court shall notify the clerk of the trial court that the motion has been filed. The clerk of the trial court shall notify the clerk of the appellate court of the trial court's ruling on the motion for a new trial.

HISTORY: Amended by Order 81–5, eff. 9–1–81; adopted eff. 1–1–63

RCr 10.08 Time for serving affidavits

When a motion for a new trial is supported by affidavits, the Commonwealth has ten (10) days after service of the motion within which to serve opposing affidavits, which period may be extended for an additional period not exceeding twenty (20) days either by the court for good cause shown or by the parties by written stipulation. The court may permit reply affidavits.

HISTORY: Amended by Order 98–3, eff. 3–1–99; adopted eff. 1–1–63

RCr 10.10 Clerical mistakes

Clerical mistakes in judgments, orders or other parts of the record and errors therein arising from oversight or omission may be corrected by the court at any time on its own initiative or on the motion of any party and after such notice, if any, as the court orders. During the pendency of an appeal, such mistakes may be so corrected before the appeal is perfected in the appellate court, and thereafter while the appeal is pending may be so corrected with leave of the appellate court.

HISTORY: Amended by Order 81–5, eff. 9–1–81; adopted eff. 1–1–63

RCr 10.12 Preservation of error

Allegations of error, properly preserved by objections as provided in these rules, in respect to rulings, orders or instructions of the court need not be pre-sented in a motion for a new trial in order to be preserved for appellate review.

HISTORY: Adopted eff. 1–1–63

RCr 10.22 Arrest of judgment—Abolished

HISTORY: Abolished by Order 81–5, eff. 9–1–81; adopted eff. 1–1–63

RCr 10.24 Motion for judgment of acquittal

Not later than five (5) days after the return of a verdict finding a defendant guilty of one or more offenses, or after the discharge of the jury following their having not returned a verdict, a defendant who has moved for a directed verdict of acquittal at the close of all the evidence may move to have the verdict set aside and a judgment of acquittal entered, or for a judgment of acquittal. Likewise, if a defendant has been found guilty under any instruction to which at the close of all the evidence such defendant objected upon the ground that the evidence was not sufficient to support a verdict of guilty under that instruction, that defendant may move that to that extent the verdict be set aside and a judgment of acquittal entered. A motion for a new trial may be joined with this motion.

HISTORY: Amended by Order 98–2, eff. 1–1–99; adopted eff. 7–1–79

RCr 10.26 Substantial error

A palpable error which affects the substantial rights of a party may be considered by the court on motion for a new trial or by an appellate court on appeal, even though insufficiently raised or preserved for review, and appropriate relief may be granted upon a determination that manifest injustice has resulted from the error.

HISTORY: Adopted by Order 81–5, eff. 9–1–81

XI JUDGMENT; EXECUTION

RCr 11.02 Sentence

(1) Sentence shall be imposed without unreasonable delay. Pending sentence the court may commit the defendant or continue or alter the bail. Before imposing sentence the court shall, if the defendant is guilty of a felony, cause a presentence investigation to be conducted, examine and consider the report, and furnish a copy of the report to the attorney for the Commonwealth and the attorney for the defendant no later than two (2) business days prior to final sentencing. The defendant may waive the presentence investigation report pursuant to KRS 532.050. The court shall consider the possibility of probation or conditional discharge and shall afford the defendant and the defendant's counsel an opportunity to make a state-ment or statements in the defendant's behalf and to present any information in mitigation of punishment.

(2) After imposing sentence in a case tried on a plea of not guilty, the court shall advise the defendant of his or her right to appeal and of the right of a person who is unable to pay the cost of an appeal, or unable to employ counsel, to apply for leave to appeal in forma pauperis and to have the continued assistance of counsel to perfect and prosecute the appeal. If the defendant is proceeding without counsel and so requests, the clerk of the court shall prepare a notice of appeal for the defendant's signature and shall file the notice forthwith.

HISTORY: Amended by Order 2009–01, eff. 4–1–09; prior amendments eff. 3–1–99 (Order 98–3), 9–1–81 (Order 81–5), 1–1–67; adopted eff. 1–1–63

RCr 11.04 Contents and entry of judgment

(1) A judgment of conviction shall set forth the plea, the verdict or findings, the adjudication and sentence, a statement as to whether the defendant is entitled to bail, the amount of bail and the day of the execution of a death sentence, which shall be at least thirty (30) days after the entry of the judgment. If two (2) or more sentences are imposed, the judgment shall state whether they are to be served concurrently or consecutively.

(2) If the defendant is found "not guilty" or for any other reason is entitled to be discharged, judgment shall be entered accordingly.

(3) The judgment shall be signed by the judge and entered by the clerk.

(4) In the district court, if more than one judgment is entered on a single page, one signature by the judge following the last judgment on the page will be sufficient compliance with paragraph (3) of this rule. For purposes of Civil Rule 79.05 either the original or a photocopy or comparable duplicate of the signed page on which the judgment appears shall constitute the judgment.

HISTORY: Amended by Order 81–5, eff. 9–1–81; adopted eff. 1–1–63

RCr 11.22 Execution of judgment

(1) If the judgment imposes a sentence of death or confinement in the penitentiary, two (2) certified copies thereof shall be furnished forthwith to the sheriff, who shall execute the same by delivering the defendant and a certified copy of the judgment to the person in charge of the institution of confinement and filing a written return thereof in the office of the clerk of the court within ten (10) days thereafter.

(2) If the judgment imposes a sentence of confinement for a misdemeanor, the clerk shall issue a commitment on which shall be stated the period of confinement as established by the judgment. Two (2) certified copies of this order shall be furnished to the sheriff for execution as provided above in paragraph (1).

(3) All court orders, opinions, or judgments relating to the custody of a convicted felon shall be served upon the Warden of the Assessment Center, Department of Corrections by the Clerk of the Court in which said document is entered. Failure of the clerk to perform the duty imposed herein shall not affect the validity of said order, opinion, or judgment.

HISTORY: Amended by Order 95–1, eff. 11–1–95; prior amendment eff. 9–1–81; adopted eff. 1–1–63

RCr 11.32 Disability of judge

If by reason of death, sickness, or other disability, a judge before whom the defendant has been tried is unable to perform the duties to be performed by the court after a verdict or finding of guilty, any successor or special judge sitting in or assigned to the court in which the case was tried may perform those duties; but if such other judge is satisfied that he or she cannot perform those duties because he or she did not preside at the trial or for any other reason, such judge may in his or her discretion grant a new trial.

HISTORY: Amended by Order 98–3, eff. 3–1–99; adopted eff. 1–1–63

RCr 11.42 Motion to vacate, set aside or correct sentence

(1) A prisoner in custody under sentence or a defendant on probation, parole or conditional discharge who claims a right to be released on the ground that the sentence is subject to collateral attack may at any time proceed directly by motion in the court that imposed the sentence to vacate, set aside or correct it.

(2) The motion shall be signed and verified by the movant and shall state specifically the grounds on which the sentence is being challenged and the facts on which the movant relies in support of such grounds. Failure to comply with this section shall warrant a summary dismissal of the motion.

(3) The motion shall state all grounds for holding the sentence invalid of which the movant has knowledge. Final disposition of the motion shall conclude all issues that could reasonably have been presented in the same proceeding.

(4) The clerk of the court shall notify the attorney general and the Commonwealth's attorney in writing that such motion (whether it be styled a motion, petition or otherwise) has been filed, and the Commonwealth's attorney shall have 20 days after the date of mailing of notice by the clerk to the Commonwealth's attorney in which to serve an answer on the movant.

(5) Affirmative allegations contained in the answer shall be treated as controverted or avoided of record. If the answer raises a material issue of fact that cannot be determined on the face of the record the court shall grant a prompt hearing and, if the movant is without counsel of record and if financially unable to employ counsel, shall upon specific written request by the movant appoint counsel to represent the movant in the proceeding, including appeal.

(6) At the conclusion of the hearing or hearings, the court shall make findings determinative of the material issues of fact and enter a final order accordingly. If it appears that the movant is entitled to relief, the court shall vacate the judgment and discharge, resentence, or grant him or her a new trial, or correct the sentence as may be appropriate. A final order shall not be reversed or remanded because of the failure of the court to make a finding of fact on an issue essential to the order unless such failure is brought to the attention of the court by a written request for a finding on that issue or by a motion pursuant to Civil Rule 52.02.

(7) Either the movant or the Commonwealth may appeal from the final order or judgment of the trial court on a motion brought under this rule. If the trial court finds the movant received ineffective assistance of appellate counsel and the Commonwealth fails to pursue a timely appeal, the movant may appeal the trial court's order by filing a notice of appeal within sixty (60) days after the date of notation of service of the judgment or order under Criminal Rule 12.06(2). If neither party has filed a notice of appeal within this sixty (60) day period, the trial court shall issue to the movant an order to show cause within ten (10) days why the judgment vacated on his behalf should not be reinstated. If the movant fails to respond within ten (10) days or fails to show cause, the trial court shall reinstate the vacated judgment. If upon the movant's showing the trial court is satisfied that the movant's failure to appeal should not be deemed a waiver of his right to do so, it shall grant the movant an additional thirty (30) days in which to file notice of his appeal.

(8) The final order of the trial court on the motion shall not be effective until expiration of time for notice of appeal under RCr 12.04 and shall remain suspended until final disposition of an appeal duly taken and perfected.

(9) Original applications for relief of the nature described in this Rule 11.42 that are addressed directly to a court other than the one in which the sentence was imposed shall be transmitted to the court in which the sentence was imposed for further disposition in the manner above set forth.

(10) Any motion under this rule shall be filed within three years after the judgment becomes final, unless the motion alleges and the movant proves either:

(a) that the facts upon which the claim is predicated were unknown to the movant and could not have been ascertained by the exercise of due diligence; or

(b) that the fundamental constitutional right asserted was not established within the period provided for herein and has been held to apply retroactively.

If the judgment becomes final before the effective date of this rule, the time for filing the motion shall commence upon the effective date of this rule. If the motion qualifies under one of the foregoing exceptions to the three year time limit, the motion shall be filed within three years after the event establishing the exception occurred. Nothing in this section shall preclude the Commonwealth from relying upon the defense of laches to bar a motion upon the ground of unreasonable delay in filing when the delay has prejudiced the Commonwealth's opportunity to present relevant evidence to contradict or impeach the movant's evidence.

HISTORY: Amended by Order 2012–09, eff. 9–12–12; prior amendments eff. 3–1–99 (Order 98–3), 10–1–94 (Order 94–1), 1–1–86, 1–1–85, 9–1–81 (Order 81–5), 11–1–78, 1–1–78, 7–1–76, 9–1–70, 1–1–70, 1–1–65; adopted eff. 1–1–63

XII APPEALS

RCr 12.02 Applicability of Civil Rules

Civil Rules 72, 73.01(2), 73.02(1)(e), 73.02(2)(c), 73.02(4), 73.08, 75.01, 75.06 to 75.15 inclusive, and 76 shall apply also in criminal actions, except that an appeal from a judgment imposing a sentence of death, life imprisonment, or imprisonment for 20 years or more shall be taken directly to the Supreme Court. Payment of the filing fee prescribed by Civil Rule 73.02(1)(b) and (c) is required.

HISTORY: Amended by Order 2006–09, eff. 1–1–07; prior amendments eff. 7–5–85 (Order 85–2), 9–1–81; adopted eff. 1–1–78

RCr 12.04 When and how taken

(1) An appeal is taken by filing a notice of appeal in the trial court.

(2) The notice of appeal shall name all of the appellants and appellees and designate the judgment from which the appeal is being taken. The clerk shall serve notice of the filing of the notice of appeal by mailing a copy thereof to the clerk of the appellate court and to the attorney for each appellee, shall note on each copy thus served the date on which the notice of appeal was filed, and shall note in the docket the names of the parties served and date or dates on which the copies were mailed.

(3) The time within which an appeal may be taken shall be thirty (30) days after the date of entry of the judgment or order from which it is taken, subject to Rule 12.06, but if a timely motion has been made for a new trial an appeal from a judgment of conviction may be taken within thirty (30) days after the date of entry of the order denying the motion; provided, however, that in the case of a motion for new trial made later than five (5) days after return of the verdict, the appeal must be from the order overruling or denying the motion, and the review on appeal shall be limited to the grounds timely raised by the motion as provided by Rule 10.06. If a motion to proceed in forma pauperis is denied, the party shall have thirty (30) days within which to pay the filing fee or to appeal the denial to the appropriate appellate court.

(4) The timely filing of a notice of appeal from a judgment of the district court shall stay proceedings on the judgment as long as the case remains on appeal, except for the requirement of bail. Stays in juvenile dispositions shall be discretionary with the court.

(5) If an inmate files a notice of appeal in a criminal case, the notice shall be considered filed if its envelope is officially marked as having been deposited in the institution's internal mail system on or before the last

day for filing with sufficient First Class postage prepaid.

HISTORY: Amended by Order 2010–09, eff. 1–1–11; prior amendments eff. 4–1–09 (Order 2009–01), 1–1–99 (Order 98–2), 9–1–81 (Order 81–5), 10–1–78; adopted eff. 1–1–78

RCr 12.05 Petition for rehearing and discretionary review motion not required for exhaustion

In all appeals from criminal convictions or post-conviction relief matters a litigant shall not be required to petition for rehearing or to file a motion for discretionary review to either the Kentucky Court of Appeals or Kentucky Supreme Court following an adverse decision of either the circuit court or Court of Appeals in order to be deemed to have exhausted all available state remedies respecting a claim of error. Rather, when the claim has been presented to the appellate court, and relief has been denied, the litigant shall be deemed to have exhausted all available state remedies available for that claim. If rehearing or discretionary review is sought on less than all of the claims of error presented on appeal, the litigant, nevertheless, shall be deemed to have exhausted all available state remedies respecting the claim(s) of error for which rehearing or discretionary review is not sought. Finality of the opinion for all claims of error is governed by CR 76.30(2).

HISTORY: Adopted by Order 2004–5, eff. 1–1–05

RCr 12.06 Notice of entry of judgments and orders

(1) Immediately upon the entry in the trial court of a judgment, a final order, or an order that affects the running of time for taking an appeal, the clerk shall serve a written notice of the entry, either by mail or by personal delivery, upon counsel of record for each defendant, affected by the judgment or order, or upon the defendant personally if the defendant is without counsel of record. Service of notice under this Rule may be waived in writing by either the defendant or the defendant's counsel of record.

(2) The clerk shall make a note in the criminal docket of the service required by paragraph (1) of this Rule, which notation shall show the date and manner of service. Unless notice has been waived, the date of such notation shall be the date of entry for purposes of Rule 12.04(3) or, in a bond forfeiture proceeding, for purposes of Civil Rule 73.02(1)(a).

(3) This Rule 12.06 shall apply only in felony cases, and it shall not apply to a judgment entered pursuant to a plea of guilty.

HISTORY: Amended by Order 98–3, eff. 3–1–99; prior amendment eff. 6–1–78; adopted eff. 1–1–78

RCr 12.08 Expiration date of Rule 12—Repealed

HISTORY: Repealed eff. 1–1–78; adopted eff. 7–1–76

RCr 12.52 Manner of taking; notice—Repealed

HISTORY: Repealed eff. 1–1–78; amended eff. 7–1–76, 1–1–65; adopted eff. 1–1–63

RCr 12.54 Time for taking—Repealed

HISTORY: Repealed eff. 1–1–78; amended eff. 7–1–76, 9–1–71, 1–1–67; adopted eff. 1–1–63

RCr 12.55 Notice of entry of judgments and orders—Repealed

HISTORY: Repealed eff. 1–1–78; amended eff. 11–10–76; adopted eff. 7–1–75

RCr 12.56 Record on appeal—Repealed

HISTORY: Repealed eff. 1–1–78; amended eff. 7–1–76; adopted eff. 1–1–63

RCr 12.58 Filing record on appeal—Repealed

HISTORY: Repealed eff. 1–1–78; amended eff. 7–1–76; adopted eff. 1–1–63

RCr 12.60 Correction or modification of record—Repealed

HISTORY: Repealed eff. 1–1–78; amended eff. 7–1–76; adopted eff. 1–1–63

RCr 12.61 Order as to original papers—Repealed

HISTORY: Repealed eff. 7–1–76

RCr 12.62 Record for preliminary hearing in an appellate court—Repealed

HISTORY: Repealed eff. 1–1–78; amended eff. 7–1–76; adopted eff. 1–1–63

RCr 12.63 Appeals in forma pauperis—Repealed

HISTORY: Repealed eff. 1–1–78; amended eff. 7–1–76; adopted eff. 1–1–63

RCr 12.64 Transcript of evidence and proceedings—Repealed

HISTORY: Repealed eff. 1–1–78; amended eff. 7–1–76; adopted eff. 1–1–63

RCr 12.66 Several appeals—Repealed

HISTORY: Repealed eff. 1–1–78; amended eff. 7–1–76; adopted eff. 1–1–63

RCr 12.68 Appeals when no stenographic report is available—Repealed

HISTORY: Repealed eff. 1–1–78; amended eff. 7–1–76; adopted eff. 1–1–63

RCr 12.70 Bystanders bill—Repealed

HISTORY: Repealed eff. 1–1–78; adopted eff. 1–1–63

RCr 12.72   Agreed statement—Repealed

HISTORY: Repealed eff. 1–1–78; amended eff. 7–1–76; adopted eff. 1–1–63

RCr 12.74   Preference—Abolished

HISTORY: Abolished by Order 81–5, eff. 9–1–81; adopted eff. 1–1–63

RCr 12.76   Stay of execution

(1) (Death.)

A sentence of death shall be stayed pending review by an appellate court, but the defendant may be transferred to the penitentiary.

(2) (Imprisonment.)

The execution of a sentence of imprisonment shall be stayed if an appeal is taken and the defendant is admitted to bail.

(3) (Fine.)

A sentence to pay a fine or a fine and costs, if an appeal is taken, may be stayed by the trial court upon such terms as the court deems proper.

(4) (Probation.)

A sentence of probation may be stayed if an appeal from the conviction or sentence is taken. If the sentence is stayed, the court shall fix the terms of the stay.

HISTORY: Amended by Order 2009–01, eff. 4–1–09; prior amendments eff. 2–1–01 (Order 2000–1), 1–1–89 (Order 88–4), 7–1–76; adopted eff. 1–1–63

RCr 12.78   Bail on appeal

(1) Bail may be allowed by the trial judge pending appeal notwithstanding that service of the sentence has commenced, except when the defendant has been sentenced to death or life imprisonment.

(2) When a person has been convicted of an offense and only a fine has been imposed the amount of bail shall not exceed the amount of the fine and costs.

(3) The applicable provisions governing bail shall apply to bail on appeal.

(4) The court allowing bail may at any time revoke the order admitting the defendant to bail.

HISTORY: Amended by Order 91–2, eff. 11–15–91; prior amendments eff. 9–1–81, 6–19–76; adopted eff. 1–1–63

RCr 12.80   Execution and approval of bond

The bond for bail pending appeal may be given at or after the time of filing the notice of appeal. The stay is effective when the bond is accepted by the court or the clerk, and the clerk shall give prompt notice of such acceptance to the attorney for the Commonwealth.

HISTORY: Amended by Order 81–5, eff. 9–1–81; prior amendment eff. 1–1–78; adopted eff. 1–1–63

RCr 12.82   Application for relief pending review

If an application is made to the appropriate appellate court for bail pending appeal, for an extension of time for filing the record on appeal, or for any other relief, the application shall be upon notice and shall show that application to the trial court is not practicable or that application has been made and denied, with reasons given for the denial, or that the action on the application did not afford the relief to which the applicant considers himself or herself to be entitled. The decision of the trial court regarding bail will not be disturbed by an appellate court unless it is demonstrated that the trial judge failed to exercise sound discretion.

HISTORY: Amended by Order 98–3, eff. 3–1–99; prior amendments eff. 8–28–89 (Order 89–1), 9–1–81 (Order 81–5); adopted eff. 1–1–63

XIII   MISCELLANEOUS

RCr 13.01   Records

Civil Rules 79.01, 79.02(1), 79.03, 79.04, 79.05(1), and 79.06 shall apply also to criminal actions. The general docket of criminal cases in the trial court shall be kept separately from the general dockets of civil and appellate cases. The general docket for criminal cases in the trial court shall include only those cases originating in that court. Appeals from the district court in criminal cases shall be included in the general docket of appellate cases in the circuit court. All cases in which an indictment is returned or an information filed in the circuit court shall be docketed as original actions in that court.

HISTORY: Adopted eff. 1–1–78

RCr 13.02   Local rules

Each court may make and amend rules governing its practice not inconsistent with these rules. A copy of the rules and amendments so made shall, upon their adoption, be certified to the Chief Justice of the Supreme Court for approval. They shall become effective upon such approval. In all cases not provided for by rule, the courts may regulate their practice in any manner not inconsistent with these rules.

HISTORY: Amended by Order 81–5, eff. 9–1–81; prior amendment eff. 1–1–78; adopted eff. 1–1–63

RCr 13.03   Review of trial dockets

At least once each year trial courts shall review all pending criminal actions on their dockets. Notice shall be given to each attorney of record of every case in which no pretrial step has been taken within the last year, that the case will be dismissed in thirty days for want of prosecution except for good cause shown. The court shall enter an order dismissing without prejudice each case in which no answer or an insufficient answer to the notice is made. This rule shall not apply to cases where the trial court has issued an arrest warrant based on the defendant's failure to appear in the case.

HISTORY: Adopted by Order 2004–5, eff. 1–1–05

RCr 13.04 Application of Civil Rules to criminal procedure

The Rules of Civil Procedure shall be applicable in criminal proceedings to the extent not superseded by or inconsistent with these Rules of Criminal Procedure.

HISTORY: Amended by Order 81–5, eff. 9–1–81; prior amendment eff. 7–1–75; adopted eff. 1–1–63

RCr 13.06 Forms

The forms contained in the Appendix of Forms are sufficient under these rules and illustrate the simplicity of statement contemplated.

HISTORY: Adopted eff. 1–1–63

RCr 13.08 Amendment of rules

(1) Suggestions for amendment of these rules may be submitted directly to the Supreme Court for its consideration.

(2) Unless otherwise directed by the Supreme Court all substantial amendments will be published in an official publication of the Kentucky Bar Association or mailed to the members of the Kentucky Bar Association at least 60 days before they become effective.

HISTORY: Amended by Order 81–5, eff. 9–1–81; prior amendments eff. 1–1–78, 5–1–76, 1–1–65; adopted eff. 1–1–63

RCr 13.10 Search warrant; who may issue

(1) Upon affidavit sufficient under Section 10 of the Kentucky Constitution and sworn to before an officer authorized to administer oaths as provided in Rule 2.02 for the swearing of complaints, a search warrant may be issued by a judge or other officer authorized by statute to issue search warrants.

(2) A copy of the search warrant and supporting affidavit shall be retained by the issuing officer and filed by such officer with the clerk of the court to which the warrant is returnable.

(3) The officer executing a search warrant shall make return thereof to the appropriate court within a reasonable time of its execution. The return shall show the date and hour of service.

HISTORY: Amended by Order 98–3, eff. 3–1–99; prior amendments eff. 9–1–81 (Order 81–5); adopted eff. 1–1–63

APPENDIX A—UNIFORM
SCHEDULE OF BAIL

(1) (a) Except as indicated in (1)(b), bail for any violation of KRS Chapter 150 shall be $45.

   (b) Bail for violations of the following statutes shall be as indicated:

150.235 (3)	$70
150.390	$120
150.460	$120

(2) Bail for any violation of KRS Chapter 186 shall be $35 except that, bail for a person charged with a violation of KRS 186.620(2) shall be $200, and bail for a person charged with being a habitual violator under KRS 186.641 to 186.649 and bail for a person charged with theft of a motor vehicle registration plate under KRS 186.990(6) shall be set by the court.

(3) (a) Except as indicated in (3)(b) and (c), bail for any violation of KRS Chapter 189 shall be set at the minimum fine and court cost for the offense.

   (b) Bail for violations of the following statutes shall be as indicated:

189.370 (1)	$100
189.393	100
189.505	50
189.530	100
189.565	50
189.580 (1)	200
189.860	100
189.920	100
189.930	100
189.940	100
189.950	100
Abandoning Vehicle	50

   (c) Bail for the following offenses shall be as indicated:

   Overweight or overdimension (KRS 189.221 – 189.223)
   The bond shall not exceed the maximum fine that can be levied for the offense and in no event more than $500.

   DWI (KRS 189.520)
   The bond shall be set by the court.

(4) Bail for the following violations of KRS Chapter 218A shall be as indicated:

218A.990 (6)	$2000 with 10% deposit
218A.990 (7)	1000 with 10% deposit
218A.990 (10)	1000 with 10% deposit
218A.140 (6)	1000 with 10% deposit

(5) Bail for any violation of KRS Chapter 235 shall be $35.

(6) Bail for violations of KRS Chapter 244 shall be $1000 with a 10% deposit except that, bail for a person charged with a violation of KRS 244.020 shall be $300 with a 10% deposit, and bail for a person charged with a violation of KRS 244.170 shall be set by the court.

(7) Bail for violations of KRS Chapter 257 shall be $50.

OFFENSE, PENALTY AND BAIL SCHEDULE
(Misdemeanors)
Kentucky Penal Code

Publisher's Note: Asterisks indicate misdemeanors added or changes made by Publisher's Editorial Staff, based upon legislative amendment of KRS sections referred to herein, pending amendment of this Schedule by Supreme Court Order. Bracketed material added by the Publisher's Editorial Staff is for clarification and not due to legislative amendments. KRS 431.540 was amended by 2008 c 186, § 1, eff. 7–15–08, and added nonviolent Class D felonies as additional crimes of which the Supreme Court may prescribe a uniform schedule of amounts of bail per order or rule. [Amended eff. 8–1–79; prior amendment eff. 8–1–76; adopted eff. 6–19–76.]

SECTION		FINE		JAIL			BAIL Percentum	
		Min.	Max.	Min.	Max.	Other	Deposit	Bail Bond
506.010.	Criminal Attempt [when crime attempted is Class C or D felony].		$500		12 Mos.	Section (4)(d)*	$200	$2000
	[when crime attempted is misdemeanor]		$250		90 Days	Section (4)(e)*	$100	$1000
506.030.	Criminal Solicitation [when crime committed is Class C or D felony].		$500		12 Mos.	Section (2)(d)*	$200	$2000
	[when crime committed is misdemeanor]		$250		90 Days	Section (2)(c)*	$100	$1000
506.040.	Criminal Conspiracy [when object of conspiratorial agreement is Class C or D felony].		$500		12 Mos.	Section (2)(d)*	$200	$2000
	[when object of conspiratorial agreement is misdemeanor]		$250		90 Days	Section (2)(e)*	$100	$1000
506.050.	Conspiracy — General Provisions.	X	X	X	X	X		
506.060.	Criminal Solicitation or Conspiracy — Defense of Renunciation	X	X	X	X	X		
506.080.	Criminal Facilitation [when crime facilitated is Class C or D felony].		$500		12 Mos.	Section (2)(b)	$200	$2000
	[when crime facilitated is misdemeanor]		$250		90 Days	Section (2)(c)	$100	$1000
506.140.	Criminal Gang Recruitment.*		$500		12 Mos.	Section (3)*	$200	$2000
508.030.	Assault in the fourth degree.*		$500		12 Mos.		$200	$2000

*Misdemeanor added or change made by Publisher's Editorial Staff, based upon legislative change, pending amendment by Supreme Court Order.

†Changed to a Class D felony, eff. 7-13-84.
†*Changed to a Class D felony, eff. 7-14-92.
†*†Changed to a Class D felony, eff. 7-15-02.

SECTION		FINE		JAIL			BAIL	
		Min.	Max.	Min.	Max.	Other	Percentum Deposit	Bail Bond
508.040.	Assault under extreme emotional disturbance.		$250		90 Days	Section (2)(b)	S 100	$1000
508.050.	Menacing.		$250		90 Days		S 100	$1000
508.070.	Wanton endangerment in the second degree.		$500		12 Mos.		S 200	$2000
508.080.	Terroristic threatening in the third degree.*		$500		12 Mos.		S 200	$2000
508.120.*	Criminal abuse in the third degree.		$500		12 Mos.		S 200	$2000
508.150.*	Stalking in the second degree.		$500		12 Mos.		S 200	$2000
509.030.*	Unlawful imprisonment in the second degree.		$500		12 Mos.		S 200	$2000
509.070.	Custodial Interference.†							
509.080.*	Criminal coercion.		$500		12 Mos.		S 200	$2000
510.100.*	Sodomy in the fourth degree.		$500		12 Mos.		S 200	$2000
510.120.	Sexual abuse in the second degree.		$500		12 Mos.		S 200	$2000
510.130.	Sexual abuse in the third degree.		$250		90 Days		S 100	$1000
510.140.	Sexual misconduct.		$500		12 Mos.		S 200	$2000
510.150.	Indecent Exposure.		$250		90 Days		S 100	$1000
511.050.	Possession of burglar's tools.		$500		12 Mos.		S 200	$2000
511.060.	Criminal trespass in the first degree.		$500		12 Mos.		S 200	$2000
511.070.	Criminal trespass in the second degree.		$250		90 Days		S 100	$1000
511.080.	Criminal trespass in the third degree.		$250				None pay full cash bond.	$ 50
512.030.	Criminal mischief in the second degree.		$500		12 Mos.		S 200	$2000
512.040.	Criminal mischief in the third degree [violation].		$250		90 Days		S 100	$1000
512.050.	Criminal use of noxious substance.		$250		90 Days		S 100	$1000

*Misdemeanor added or change made by Publisher's Editorial Staff, based upon legislative change, pending amendment by Supreme Court Order.

†Changed to a Class D felony, eff. 7-13-84.

††Changed to a Class D felony, eff. 7-14-92.

†††Changed to a Class D felony, eff. 7-15-02.

| SECTION | | FINE | | JAIL | | | Percentum | BAIL |
		Min.	Max.	Min.	Max.	Other	Deposit	Bail Bond
512.060.	Criminal possession of noxious substance.		$250		90 Days		$100	$1000
512.070.	Criminal littering.		$500*		12 Mos.*		$200*	$2000*
512.080.	Unlawfully posting advertisements [violation].		$250				$50	$500
514.030.	Theft by unlawful taking or disposition [under $300, unless firearm or anhydrous ammonia taken].*		$500		12 Mos.	Section (2)	$50	$500
514.040.	Theft by deception [under $300].		$500		12 Mos.	Section (8)*	$100	$1000
514.050.	Theft of property [under $300].		$500		12 Mos.	Section (2)	$100	$1000
514.060.	Theft of services [under $300].		$500		12 Mos.	Section (4)*	$100	$1000
514.065.*	Possession, use or transfer of device for theft of telecommunications services [first offense].		$500		12 Mos.	Section (4)	$100	$1000
514.070.	Theft by failure to make required disposition of property [under $300].		$500		12 Mos.	Section (4)	$100	$1000
514.080.	Theft by extortion [under $300].		$500		12 Mos.	Section (3)	$100	$1000
514.090.	Theft of labor [under $300].		$500		12 Mos.	Section (3)	$100	$1000
514.100.	Unauthorized use of vehicle [first offense].		$500		12 Mos.	Section (2)*	$200	$2000

*Misdemeanor added or change made by Publisher's Editorial Staff, based upon legislative change, pending amendment by Supreme Court Order.

†Changed to a Class D felony, eff. 7-13-84.

††Changed to a Class D felony, eff. 7-14-92.

†††Changed to a Class D felony, eff. 7-15-02.

SECTION		FINE		JAIL			BAIL	
		Min.	Max.	Min.	Max.	Other	Percentum Deposit	Bail Bond
514.110.	Receiving stolen property [under $300, unless firearm taken].		$500		12 Mos.	Section (3)	$200	$2000
514.120.	Obscuring identity of machine [under $300].		$500		12 Mos.	Section (4)*	$200	$2000
516.040.	Forgery in the third degree.		$500		12 Mos.		$200	$2000
516.070.	Criminal possession of forged instrument in the third degree.		$500		12 Mos.		$200	$2000
516.110.	Criminal simulation.		$500		12 Mos.		$200	$2000
516.130.	Using slugs in the second degree.		$250		90 Days		$100	$1000
517.020.	Deceptive business practices.		$500		12 Mos.		$200	$2000
517.030.	False advertising.		$500		12 Mos.		$200	$2000
517.040.	Bait advertising.		$500		12 Mos.		$200	$2000
517.050.	Falsifying business records.		$500		12 Mos.		$200	$2000
517.060.	Defrauding secured creditors [under $100].		$500		12 Mos.	Section (2)*	$200	$2000
517.070.	Defrauding judgment creditors.		$500		12 Mos.		$200	$2000
517.080.	Fraud in insolvency.		$500		12 Mos.		$200	$2000
517.090.	Issuing false financial statement.		$500		12 Mos.		$200	$2000
517.110.	Misapplication of entrusted property.		$500		12 Mos.		$200	$2000
518.020.	Commercial bribery.		$500		12 Mos.		$200	$2000
518.030.	Receiving commercial bribe.		$500		12 Mos.		$200	$2000
518.060.	Tampering with or rigging sports contest.		$500		12 Mos.		$200	$2000
518.070.	Ticket scalping [violation].		$250				None pay full cash bond.	$ 50

*Misdemeanor added or change made by Publisher's Editorial Staff, based upon legislative change, pending amendment by Supreme Court Order.

†Changed to a Class D felony, eff. 7-13-84.

††Changed to a Class D felony, eff. 7-14-92.

†††Changed to a Class D felony, eff. 7-15-02.

SECTION		FINE		JAIL			BAIL Percentum	
		Min.	Max.	Min.	Max.	Other	Deposit	Bail Bond
518.090.	Assault of sports official.*		$500		12 Mos.	Sections (3) and (4)*	$200	$2000
519.020.	Obstructing governmental operations.		$500		12 Mos.		$200	$2000
519.030.	Compounding a crime.		$500		12 Mos.		$200	$2000
519.040.	Falsely reporting an incident.		$500		12 Mos.		$200	$2000
519.050.	Impersonating a public servant.		$500		12 Mos.		$200	$2000
519.060.	Tampering with public records.††							
520.040.	Escape in the third degree.		$250		90 Days		$100	$1000
520.060.	Promoting contraband in the second degree.		$500		12 Mos.		$200	$2000
520.080.	Bail jumping in the second degree.		$500		12 Mos.		$200	$2000
520.090.	Resisting arrest.		$500		12 Mos.		$200	$2000
520.100.	Fleeing or evading police in the second degree.		$500		12 Mos.		$200	$2000
520.130.	Hindering prosecution or apprehension in the second degree.		$500		12 Mos.		$200	$2000
521.030.	Soliciting unlawful compensation.		$250		90 Days		$100	$1000
521.040.	Receiving unlawful compensation.		$500		12 Mos.		$200	$2000
522.020.	Official misconduct in the first degree.		$500		12 Mos.		$200	$2000
522.030.	Official misconduct in the second degree.		$250		90 Days		$100	$1000
523.030.	Perjury in the second degree.		$500		12 Mos.		$200	$2000
523.040.	False swearing.		$250		90 Days		$100	$1000
523.100.	Unsworn falsification to authorities.		$250		90 Days		$100	$1000
523.110.*	Giving Peace officer false name or address.		$250		90 Days		$100	$1000

*Misdemeanor added or change made by Publisher's Editorial Staff, based upon legislative change, pending amendment by Supreme Court Order.

†Changed to a Class D felony, eff. 7-13-84.
††Changed to a Class D felony, eff. 7-14-92.
†††Changed to a Class D felony, eff. 7-15-02.

| SECTION | | FINE | | JAIL | | | BAIL | |
		Min.	Max.	Min.	Max.	Other	Percentum Deposit	Bail Bond
524.050.	Tampering with a witness.†††							
524.090.	Jury tampering.†††							
524.110.	Simulating legal process.		$250		90 Days		$100	$1000
524.130.	Unauthorized practice of law.*		$250		90 Days		$100	$1000
525.030.	Riot in the second degree.		$500		12 Mos.		$200	$2000
525.040.	Inciting to riot.		$500		12 Mos.		$200	$2000
525.050.	Unlawful assembly.		$250		90 Days		$100	$1000
525.060.	Disorderly conduct.		$250		90 Days		$100	$1000
525.070.	Harassment [violation].*		$250				$ 30	$ 30
			$250		90 Days	Section (2)(b)*	$100	$1000
525.080.	Harassing communications.		$250		90 Days		$100	$1000
525.090.	Loitering [violation].		$250				None pay full cash bond.	$ 50
525.100.	Public intoxication.		$250		90 Days		$ 30	$ 300
525.110.	Desecration of venerated objects in the second degree.*		$500		12 Mos.		$200	$2000
525.115.*	Violating graves [first offense].		$500		12 Mos.	Section (3)	$200	$2000
525.120.	Abuse of corpse.		$500		12 Mos.	Section (2)*	$200	$2000
525.130.	Cruelty to animals in the second degree.*		$500		12 Mos.		$200	$2000
525.140.	Obstructing a highway or other public passage		$250		90 Days		$100	$1000
525.150.	Disrupting meetings or processions.		$250		90 Days		$100	$1000
525.160.*	Failure to disperse.		$250		90 Days		$100	$1000
525.205.	Assault on service animal in the second degree.*		$250		90 Days		$100	$1000
526.040.	Possession of eavesdropping device.		$500		12 Mos.		$200	$2000

*Misdemeanor added or change made by Publisher's Editorial Staff, based upon legislative change, pending amendment by Supreme Court Order.

†Changed to a Class D felony, eff. 7-13-84.

††Changed to a Class D felony, eff. 7-14-92.

†††Changed to a Class D felony, eff. 7-15-02.

SECTION		FINE		JAIL			BAIL	
		Min.	Max.	Min.	Max.	Other	Percentum Deposit	Bail Bond
526.050.	Tampering with private communications.		$500		12 Mos.		$200	$2000
526.060.	Divulging illegally obtained information.		$500		12 Mos.		$200	$2000
527.020.	Carrying concealed deadly weapon.*		$500		12 Mos.	Section (5)*	$200	$2000
527.030.	Defacing a firearm.		$500		12 Mos.		$200	$2000
527.050.	Possession of defaced firearm.		$500		12 Mos.		$200	$2000
527.100*	Possession of handgun by minor [first offense].		$500		12 Mos.	Section (3)	$200	$2000
528.030.	Promoting gambling in the second degree.		$500		12 Mos.		$200	$2000
528.060.	Possession of gambling records in the second degree.		$500		12 Mos.		$200	$2000
528.070.	Permitting gambling.		$250		90 Days		$100	$1000
528.080.	Possession of gambling device.		$500		12 Mos.		$200	$2000
528.110	Messenger betting.*		$500		12 Mos.		$200	$2000
528.120.*	Off-track acceptance of money for pari-mutuel wagering.		$500		12 Mos.		$200	$2000
529.020.	Prostitution.		$250		90 Days		$100	$1000
529.050.	Promoting prostitution in the third degree.		$500		12 Mos.		$200	$2000
529.070.	Permitting prostitution.		$250		90 Days		$100	$1000
529.080.*	Loitering for prostitution purposes [second offense].		$250		90 Days	Section (2)(b)*	$100	$1000
529.090.*	Committing prostitution knowing one tested positive for sexually transmitted disease.		$500		12 Mos.		$200	$2000
530.030.	Concealing birth of infant.		$500		12 Mos.		$200	$2000

*Misdemeanor added or change made by Publisher's Editorial Staff, based upon legislative change, pending amendment by Supreme Court Order.

†Changed to a Class D felony, eff. 7-13-84.

††Changed to a Class D felony, eff. 7-14-92.

†††Changed to a Class D felony, eff. 7-15-02.

SECTION		FINE		JAIL			BAIL Percentum	
		Min.	Max.	Min.	Max.	Other	Deposit	Bail Bond
530.050.	Non-support and flagrant nonsupport.*		$500		12 Mos.	Sections (5) and (6)*	$100	$1000
530.060.	Endangering welfare of minor.		$500		12 Mos.		$100	$1000
530.070.	Unlawful transaction with minor in the third degree.*		$500		12 Mos.		$100	$1000
530.080.*	Endangering welfare of incompetent person		$500		12 Mos.		$200	$2000
531.020.	Distribution of obscene matter [when defendant possesses more than one unit of material].		$500		12 Mos.	Section (2)	$200	$2000
	[distribution a Class B misdemeanor]		$250		90 Days		$100	$1000
531.030.	Distribution of obscene matter to minors.		$500		12 Mos.	Section (2)	$200	$2000
531.040.	Using minors to distribute obscene material.		$500		12 Mos.	Section (2)	$200	$2000
531.050.	Advertising obscene material.		$250		90 Days		$100	$1000

*Misdemeanor added or change made by Publisher's Editorial Staff, based upon legislative change, pending amendment by Supreme Court Order.

†Changed to a Class D felony, eff. 7-13-84.

††Changed to a Class D felony, eff. 7-14-92.

†††Changed to a Class D felony, eff. 7-15-02.

SECTION		FINE		JAIL			BAIL	
		Min.	Max.	Min.	Max.	Other	Percentum Deposit	Bail Bond
531.060.	Promoting sale of obscenity [second offense].		$500		12 Mos.	Section (2)	$200	$2000
	[first offense]		$250		90 Days		$100	$1000
531.335.*	Possession of matter portraying a sexual performance by a minor [first offense].		$500		12 Mos.	Section (2)	$200	$2000
531.340.*	Distribution of matter portraying sexual performance by minor.††							
531.350.*	Promoting sale of material portraying sexual performance by minor [first offense].		$500		12 Mos.	Section (2)	$200	$2000
531.360.*	Advertising material portraying sexual performance by minor.		$500		12 Mos.		$200	$2000

NOTE: SPECIAL SCHEDULE FOR KRS
517.020, .030, .040.

Residents $100

Nonresidents $500

[Amended eff. 8-1-79; prior amendment eff. 8-1-76; adopted eff. 6-19-76]

*Misdemeanor added or change made by Publisher's Editorial Staff, based upon legislative change, pending amendment by Supreme Court Order.

†Changed to a Class D felony, eff. 7-13-84.

††Changed to a Class D felony, eff. 7-14-92.

†††Changed to a Class D felony, eff. 7-15-02.

KENTUCKY RULES OF EVIDENCE

Effective July 1, 1992

Including Amendments Received Through January 1, 2013

Rule
KRE 1104   Use of official commentary

ARTICLE I
GENERAL PROVISIONS

KRE 101   Scope

These rules govern proceedings in the courts of the Commonwealth of Kentucky, to the extent and with the exceptions stated in KRE 1101. The rules should be cited as "KRE," followed by the rule number to which the citation relates.

HISTORY: 1992 c 324, § 34, eff. 7–1–92; 1990 c 88, § 1

KRE 102   Purpose and construction

These rules shall be construed to secure fairness in administration, elimination of unjustifiable expense and delay, and promotion of growth and development of the law of evidence to the end that the truth may be ascertained and proceedings justly determined.

HISTORY: 1992 c 324, § 34, eff. 7–1–92; 1990 c 88, § 2

KRE 103   Rulings on evidence

(a) Effect of erroneous ruling.   Error may not be predicated upon a ruling which admits or excludes evidence unless a substantial right of the party is affected; and

   (1) Objection.   If the ruling is one admitting evidence, a timely objection or motion to strike appears of record, stating the specific ground of objection, if the specific ground was not apparent from the context; or

   (2) Offer of proof.   If the ruling is one excluding evidence, the substance of the evidence was made known to the court by offer or was apparent from the context within which questions were asked.

(b) Record of offer and ruling.   The court may add any other or further statement which shows the character of the evidence, the form in which it was offered, the objection made, and the ruling thereon. It may direct the making of an offer in question and answer form.

(c) Hearing of jury.   In jury cases, proceedings shall be conducted, to the extent practicable, so as to prevent inadmissible evidence from being suggested to the jury by any means, such as making statements or offers of proof or asking questions in the hearing of the jury.

(d) Motions in limine.   A party may move the court for a ruling in advance of trial on the admission or exclusion of evidence. The court may rule on such a motion in advance of trial or may defer a decision on admissibility until the evidence is offered at trial. A motion in limine resolved by order of record is sufficient to preserve error for appellate review. Nothing in this rule precludes the court from reconsidering at trial any ruling made on a motion in limine.

(e) Palpable error.   A palpable error in applying the Kentucky Rules of Evidence which affects the substantial rights of a party may be considered by a trial court on motion for a new trial or by an appellate court on appeal, even though insufficiently raised or preserved for review, and appropriate relief may be granted upon a determination that manifest injustice has resulted from the error.

Evidence Rules Review Commission Notes (2007)

The 2007 amendment to this provision of the Rules makes two changes in the original (1992) rules on preserving errors for review. Both of the changes are in the first subsection of the provision (KRE 103(a)). None of the other subsections are affected by the 2007 amendment.

The first of the changes involves the requirement that a party make "specific" rather than "general" objections when the party desires exclusion of offered evidence. Under the 1992 version of this rule, a party was required to give grounds for objection only when requested to do so by the trial court; under the 2007 amendment, a party is required to state grounds for an objection in order to preserve error for review (and not just when requested to do so by the court) unless the ground for the objection was apparent from the context. The reasons for making this change include all of the following:

(1) One of the reasons for requiring specific objections is to impose on lawyers an obligation to assist the trial judge with difficult issues of evidence law so that the judge may rule intelligently and quickly on those issues. This policy is sufficiently sound to require a statement of grounds in all instances and not merely upon request by the court.

(2) The amendment brings KRE 103(a)(1) into alignment with FRE 103(a)(1). Uniformity with the Federal Rules has been consistently pursued by drafters of the Kentucky Rules and would be advanced by this amendment.

(3) The amendment would bring Kentucky law into alignment with the prevailing if not universal rule of other states and would bring the law into alignment with a proposal made by the drafters of the 1992 version of the Kentucky Rules. See Study Committee, Kentucky Rules of Evidence, Final Draft, pp. 2–4 (Nov. 1989).

The second of the changes involves the requirement that a party made a "proper offer" of proof in order to preserve error when offered evidence is excluded by the trial judge. Under the 1992 version of this rule, lawyers were required to use witnesses when making a record of evidence ruled inadmissible by the judge; the rule left no room for what is known widely as a "proffer" of evidence (i.e., where the lawyer states for the record what the witness would have said if allowed to testify). Under the 2007 amendment, lawyers are required to make the substance of excluded testimony "known to the court by offer" but are not required to do so through testimony of witnesses (thereby opening the door to the use of "proffers" of evidence). The reasons for this change include all of the following:

(1) It is more efficient and less burdensome to allow the lawyers to state for the record what a witness would say in testimony if permitted (using the "proffer") and should in some instances enhance the fluidity of the production of evidence, all without imposing any

burden on the opposing party or on the affected courts (trial and appeal).

(2) The amendment brings KRE 103(a)(2) into alignment with FRE 103(a)(2), brings Kentucky's law into alignment with the law of most if not all other states, and adopts a position first advanced by the original drafters of Kentucky's Rules of Evidence. See Study Committee, Kentucky Rules of Evidence, Final Draft, pp. 2–3 (Nov. 1989).

(3) The amendment also serves to eliminate an ambiguity in KRE 103 because of the inconsistency of saying on the one hand that an offer of excluded evidence must come from the witness (as in the original version of KRE 103(a)(2)) but then saying on the other hand that the trial judge "may direct the making of an offer in question and answer form" (as has always been stated in KRE 103(b)).

HISTORY: Amended by Supreme Court Order 2007–02, eff. 5–1–07; 1992 c 324, § 1, 34, eff. 7–1–92; 1990 c 88, § 3

KRE 104   Preliminary questions

(a) Questions of admissibility generally. Preliminary questions concerning the qualification of a person to be a witness, the existence of a privilege, or the admissibility of evidence shall be determined by the court, subject to the provisions of subdivision (b) of this rule. In making its determination it is not bound by the rules of evidence except those with respect to privileges.

(b) Relevancy conditioned on fact. When the relevancy of evidence depends upon the fulfillment of a condition of fact, the court shall admit it upon, or subject to, the introduction of evidence sufficient to support a finding of the fulfillment of the condition.

(c) Hearing of jury. Hearings on the admissibility of confessions or the fruits of searches conducted under color of law shall in all cases be conducted out of the hearing of the jury. Hearings on other preliminary matters shall be so conducted when the interests of justice require, or when an accused is a witness and so requests.

(d) Testimony by accused. The accused does not, by testifying upon a preliminary matter, become subject to cross-examination as to other issues in the case.

(e) Weight and credibility. This rule does not limit the right of a party to introduce before the jury evidence relevant to weight or credibility, including evidence of bias, interest, or prejudice.

HISTORY: 1992 c 324, § 2, 34, eff. 7–1–92; 1990 c 88, § 4

KRE 105   Limited admissibility

(a) When evidence which is admissible as to one (1) party or for one (1) purpose but not admissible as to another party or for another purpose is admitted, the court, upon request, shall restrict the evidence to its proper scope and admonish the jury accordingly. In the absence of such a request, the admission of the evidence by the trial judge without limitation shall not be a ground for complaint on appeal, except under the palpable error rule.

(b) When evidence described in subdivision (a) above is excluded, such exclusion shall not be a ground for complaint on appeal, except under the palpable error rule, unless the proponent expressly offers the evidence for its proper purpose or limits the offer of proof to the party against whom the evidence is properly admissible.

HISTORY: 1992 c 324, § 34, eff. 7–1–92; 1990 c 88, § 5

KRE 106   Remainder of or related writings or recorded statements

When a writing or recorded statement or part thereof is introduced by a party, an adverse party may require the introduction at that time of any other part or any other writing or recorded statement which ought in fairness to be considered contemporaneously with it.

HISTORY: 1992 c 324, § 34, eff. 7–1–92; 1990 c 88, § 6

KRE 107   Miscellaneous provisions

(a) Parol evidence. The provisions of the Kentucky Rules of Evidence shall not operate to repeal, modify, or affect the parol evidence rule.

(b) Effective date. The Kentucky Rules of Evidence shall take effect on the first day of July, 1992. They shall apply to all civil and criminal actions and proceedings originally brought on for trial upon or after that date and to pretrial motions or matters originally presented to the trial court for decision upon or after that date if a determination of such motions or matters requires an application of evidence principles; provided, however, that no evidence shall be admitted against a criminal defendant in proof of a crime committed prior to July 1, 1992, unless that evidence would have been admissible under evidence principles in existence prior to the adoption of these rules.

HISTORY: 1992 c 324, § 34, eff. 7–1–92; 1990 c 88, § 7

ARTICLE II
JUDICIAL NOTICE

KRE 201   Judicial notice of adjudicative facts

(a) Scope of rule. This rule governs only judicial notice of adjudicative facts.

(b) Kinds of facts. A judicially noticed fact must be one not subject to reasonable dispute in that it is either:

(1) Generally known within the county from which the jurors are drawn, or, in a nonjury matter,

the county in which the venue of the action is fixed; or

(2) Capable of accurate and ready determination by resort to sources whose accuracy cannot reasonably be questioned.

(c) When discretionary. A court may take judicial notice, whether requested or not.

(d) When mandatory. A court shall take judicial notice if requested by a party and supplied with the necessary information.

(e) Opportunity to be heard. A party is entitled upon timely request to an opportunity to be heard as to the propriety of taking judicial notice and the tenor of the matter noticed. In the absence of prior notification, the request may be made after judicial notice has been taken.

(f) Time of taking notice. Judicial notice may be taken at any stage of the proceeding.

(g) Instructing the jury. The court shall instruct the jury to accept as conclusive any fact judicially noticed.

HISTORY: 1992 c 324, § 34, eff. 7–1–92; 1990 c 88, § 8

ARTICLE III
PRESUMPTIONS IN CIVIL ACTIONS AND PROCEEDINGS

KRE 301 Presumptions in general in civil actions and proceedings

In all civil actions and proceedings when not otherwise provided for by statute or by these rules, a presumption imposes on the party against whom it is directed the burden of going forward with evidence to rebut or meet the presumption, but does not shift to such party the burden of proof in the sense of the risk of nonpersuasion, which remains throughout the trial upon the party on whom it was originally cast.

HISTORY: 1992 c 324, § 34, eff. 7–1–92; 1990 c 88, § 9

KRE 302 Applicability of federal law or the law of other states in civil actions and proceedings

In civil actions and proceedings, the effect of a presumption respecting a fact which is an element of a claim or defense as to which the federal law or the law of another state supplies the rule of decision is determined in accordance with federal law or the law of the other state.

HISTORY: 1992 c 324, § 34, eff. 7–1–92; 1990 c 88, § 10

ARTICLE IV
RELEVANCY AND RELATED SUBJECTS

KRE 401 Definition of "relevant evidence"

"Relevant evidence" means evidence having any tendency to make the existence of any fact that is of consequence to the determination of the action more probable or less probable than it would be without the evidence.

HISTORY: 1992 c 324, § 34, eff. 7–1–92; 1990 c 88, § 11

KRE 402 General rule of relevancy

All relevant evidence is admissible, except as otherwise provided by the Constitutions of the United States and the Commonwealth of Kentucky, by Acts of the General Assembly of the Commonwealth of Kentucky, by these rules, or by other rules adopted by the Supreme Court of Kentucky. Evidence which is not relevant is not admissible.

HISTORY: 1992 c 324, § 34, eff. 7–1–92; 1990 c 88, § 12

KRE 403 Exclusion of relevant evidence on grounds of prejudice, confusion, or waste of time

Although relevant, evidence may be excluded if its probative value is substantially outweighed by the danger of undue prejudice, confusion of the issues, or misleading the jury, or by considerations of undue delay, or needless presentation of cumulative evidence.

HISTORY: 1992 c 324, § 3, 34, eff. 7–1–92; 1990 c 88, § 13

KRE 404 Character evidence and evidence of other crimes

(a) Character evidence generally. Evidence of a person's character or a trait of character is not admissible for the purpose of proving action in conformity therewith on a particular occasion, except:

(1) Character of accused. Evidence of a pertinent trait of character or of general moral character offered by an accused, or by the prosecution to rebut the same, or if evidence of a trait of character of the alleged victim of the crime is offered by an accused and admitted under Rule 404(a)(2), evidence of the same trait of character of the accused offered by the prosecution;

(2) Character of victim generally. Evidence of a pertinent trait of character of the victim of the crime offered by an accused, other than in a prosecution for criminal sexual conduct, or by the prosecution to rebut the same, or evidence of a character trait of peacefulness of the victim

offered by the prosecution in a homicide case to rebut evidence that the victim was the first aggressor;

(3) Character of witnesses. Evidence of the character of witnesses, as provided in KRE 607, KRE 608, and KRE 609.

(b) Other crimes, wrongs, or acts. Evidence of other crimes, wrongs, or acts is not admissible to prove the character of a person in order to show action in conformity therewith. It may, however, be admissible:

(1) If offered for some other purpose, such as proof of motive, opportunity, intent, preparation, plan, knowledge, identity, or absence of mistake or accident; or

(2) If so inextricably intertwined with other evidence essential to the case that separation of the two (2) could not be accomplished without serious adverse effect on the offering party.

(c) Notice requirement. In a criminal case, if the prosecution intends to introduce evidence pursuant to subdivision (b) of this rule as a part of its case in chief, it shall give reasonable pretrial notice to the defendant of its intention to offer such evidence. Upon failure of the prosecution to give such notice the court may exclude the evidence offered under subdivision (b) or for good cause shown may excuse the failure to give such notice and grant the defendant a continuance or such other remedy as is necessary to avoid unfair prejudice caused by such failure.

Evidence Rules Review Commission Notes (2007)

The 2007 amendment to this rule makes a change with respect to the admissibility of evidence of the character of an accused (as provided in subsection (a)(1) of the provision) and leaves all of the other provisions of the rule unchanged.

The change expands the circumstances under which the prosecution is permitted to prove a defendant's character to show the commission of a criminal act. Under the 1992 version of this rule, the prosecution could not introduce evidence of a defendant's character except in rebuttal of character evidence first offered by the defendant (i.e., the defendant's character was not in issue until he had put it in issue). The change opens the door for the prosecution to prove the bad character of a defendant after the defense has attacked the character of the victim (although keeping his own character out of the issues of the case).

The drafters of the Federal Rules made this same change in year 2000 and offered the following explanation for doing so:

"The amendment makes clear that the accused cannot attack the alleged victim's character and yet remain shielded from the disclosure of equally relevant evidence concerning the same character trait of the accused. For example, in a murder case with a claim of self-defense, the accused, to bolster this defense, might offer evidence of the alleged victim's violent disposition. If the government has evidence that the accused has a violent disposition, but is not allowed to offer this evidence as part of its rebuttal, the jury has only part of the information it needs for an informed assessment of the probabilities as to who was the initial aggressor ... Thus, the amendment is designed to permit a more balanced presentation of character evidence when an accused chooses to attack the character of the alleged victim." See Fed.R.Evid. 404, Advisory Committee Notes, 2000 Amendment.

Needless to say, the 2007 amendment to the Kentucky Rules serves to bring KRE 404(a)(1) into full alignment with its counterpart in the Federal Rules.

It needs to be noted, as stated in the commentary to the Federal Rules that "the amendment does not permit proof of the accused's character when the accused attacks the alleged victim's character as a witness under Rule 608 or 609." See Fed.R.Evid. 404, Advisory Committee Notes, 2000 Amendment.

HISTORY: Amended by Supreme Court Order 2007–02, eff. 5–1–07; 1992 c 324, § 4, 34, eff. 7–1–92; 1990 c 88, § 14

KRE 405   Methods of proving character

(a) Reputation or opinion. In all cases in which evidence of character or a trait of character of a person is admissible, proof may be made by testimony as to general reputation in the community or by testimony in the form of opinion.

(b) Inquiry on cross-examination. On cross-examination of a character witness, it is proper to inquire if the witness has heard of or knows about relevant specific instances of conduct. However, no specific instance of conduct may be the subject of inquiry under this provision unless the cross-examiner has a factual basis for the subject matter of the inquiry.

(c) Specific instances of conduct. In cases in which character or a trait of character of a person is an essential element of a charge, claim, or defense, proof may also be made of specific instances of that person's conduct.

HISTORY: 1992 c 324, § 5, 34, eff. 7–1–92; 1990 c 88, § 15

KRE 406   Habit; routine practice

Evidence of the habit of a person or of the routine practice of an organization, whether corroborated or not and regardless of the presence of eyewitnesses, is relevant to prove that the conduct of the person or organization on a particular occasion was in conformity with the habit or routine practice.

COMMENT

Most jurisdictions (perhaps all but Kentucky and one other) recognize the propriety of proving that a person acted in a particular way on a given occasion by showing that he had a "habit" of so acting. At the same time, most if not all jurisdictions refuse to allow litigants to prove that a person acted in a particular way on a given occasion by showing that he had a particular trait of character (except in criminal cases pursuant to KRE 404). Evidence that a person habitually stops at a railroad crossing before moving across, offered to show that he stopped on a given occasion, is a classic illustration of the former; evidence that a person has a general disposition toward carefulness, offered to prove that he stopped at a crossing on a given occasion, is an illustration of the latter.

Rule 406 authorizes the introduction of evidence of a person's habit (and the routine practice of an organization) without opening the gates to the introduction of evidence of character or generalized disposition. The provision contains no definition of "habit" or "routine practice" but the following definition from the Advisory Committee Notes on Federal Rule 406 is both helpful and typical:

"Character and habit are close akin. Character is a generalized description of one's disposition, or of one's disposition in respect to a general trait, such as honesty, temperance, or peacefulness. 'Habit,' in modern usage, both lay and psychological, is more specific. It describes one's regular response to a repeated specific situation. If we speak of character for care, we think of the person's tendency to act prudently in all the varying situations of life, in business, family life, in handling automobiles and in walking across the street. A habit, on the other hand, is the person's regular practice of meeting a particular kind of situation with a specific type of conduct, such as the habit of going down a particular stairway two stairs at a time, or of giving the hand-signal for a left turn, or of alighting from railway cars while they are moving. The doing of the habitual acts may become semi-automatic." Fed.R.Evid. 406, Advisory Committee's Note.

It is contemplated that testimony about a driver's specific behavior (such as activating turn signals) would be admissible under the provision but that testimony about a driver's general behavior (such as always driving carefully) would be inadmissible.

The provision does not attempt to address the following questions: (1) How many times does a response to a specific stimulus have to occur in order to constitute a habit for purposes of the rule? (2) How much behavioral uniformity is required for multiple repetitive responses to qualify as habitual under the rule? With respect to these questions, drafters of the Federal Rules made the following points:

". . . The extent to which instances must be multiplied and consistency of behavior maintained in order to rise to the status of habit inevitably gives rise to differences of opinion . . . While adequacy of sampling and uniformity of response are key factors, precise standards for measuring their sufficiency for evidence purposes cannot be formulated." Fed.R.Evid. 406, Advisory Committee's Note.

Evidence authorities believe that the lack of certainty on these points is insufficient reason for an exclusion of all habit evidence and that these are matters that can be resolved by the trial judge (as he/she resolves other matters of relevance) on a case-by-case basis. The same is true with respect to matters involving the methods by which habit can be proved (a single witness who has seen 50 responses or 50 witnesses who have seen 1 response). With respect to all such matters, the trial judge is well-suited to resolve issues bearing on admissibility and, of course, the trial judge has the discretion under Rule 403 to exclude such evidence when its probative value is substantially outweighed by such undesirable effects as undue delay, waste of time, confusion of the jury, and others.

Rule 406 is borrowed from the Federal Rules without modification.

Rule 406 changes Kentucky law. The Supreme Court ruled repeatedly during the last century that evidence of habit could not be used to prove conduct in conformity with habit. *See e.g., Lexington R. Co. v. Herring*, 96 S.W. 558 (Ky. 1906); *Cincinnati, N.O. & T.P. Ry. Co. v. Hare's Adm'x*, 178 S.W.2d 835 (Ky. 1944). Recently, however, a majority of the Court expressed the view that habit evidence should be admissible to prove conduct in conformity with habit, although a majority held that such evidence could not be admitted without explicit authorization for such in the Rules of Evidence. See *Burchett v. Commonwealth*, 98 S.W.3d 492 (Ky. 2003). Rule 406 adopts the view of the Court's majority and brings Kentucky law into line with that of nearly all other states and the Federal Rules.

HISTORY: Adopted by Supreme Court Order 2006–06, eff. 7-1-06

KRE 407   Subsequent remedial measures

When, after an event, measures are taken which, if taken previously, would have made an injury or harm allegedly caused by the event less likely to occur, evidence of the subsequent measures is not admissible to prove negligence, culpable conduct, a defect in a product, a defect in a product's design, or a need for a warning or instruction. This rule does not require the exclusion of evidence of subsequent measures when offered for another purpose, such as proving ownership, control, or feasibility of precautionary measures, if controverted, or impeachment.

Evidence Rules Review Commission Notes (2006)

The objective of the amendment is to modify the existing law to prohibit the introduction of evidence of subsequent remedial measures in products liability litigation (what some think of as strict liability litigation). The original federal rule was silent with respect to whether evidence of subsequent remedial measures was admissible or inadmissible in strict liability litigation and federal courts split over the issue, with a strong majority holding the prohibition applicable in such cases. In 1997, the federal counterpart to Rule 407 was amended to make this majority holding a part of the rule. The amendment of Kentucky's Rule 407 brings the Kentucky law into conformity with the federal law.

The following statement from a federal case decided before amendment of the federal provision describes well the rationale for the amendment:

"The rationale behind Rule 407 is that people in general would be less likely to take subsequent remedial measures if these repairs or improvements would be used against them in a lawsuit arising out of a prior accident. By excluding this evidence defendants are encouraged to make such improvements. It is difficult to understand why this policy should apply any differently where the complaint is based on strict liability as well as negligence. From a defendant's point of view it is the fact that the evidence may be used against him which will inhibit subsequent repairs or improvements. It makes no difference to the defendant on what theory the evidence is admitted; his inclination to make subsequent improvements will be similarly repressed. The reasoning behind the asserted distinction we believe to be hypertechnical, for the suit is against the manufacturer, not against the product." Werner v. Upjohn Co., Inc., 628 F.2d 848, 857 (4th Cir. 1980).

The argument against this position is that a mass producer of goods will not be deterred from taking subsequent remedial measures by the thought that its actions might be used against it in litigation, thereby leaving the prohibition without a rationale and having the effect of excluding relevant evidence. The difficulty of confirming or denying this claim and the very high probability of prejudice from the introduction of this kind of evidence tilts the scales in favor of exclusion of the evidence without regard to whether the case is based on a theory of negligence or a theory of strict liability.

HISTORY: Amended by Supreme Court Order 2006–06, eff. 7-1-06; 1992 c 324, § 6, 34, eff. 7-1-92; 1990 c 88, § 17

KRE 408   Compromise and offers to compromise

Evidence of:

(1)   Furnishing or offering or promising to furnish; or

(2)   Accepting or offering or promising to accept a valuable consideration in compromising or attempting to compromise a claim which was disputed as to either validity or amount, is not admissible to prove liability for or invalidity of the claim or its amount. Evidence of conduct or statements made in compromise negotiations is likewise not admissible. This rule does not require the exclusion of any evidence otherwise discoverable merely because it is presented in the course of compromise negotiations. This rule also does not require exclusion when the evidence is offered for another purpose, such as proving bias or prejudice of a witness, negativing a contention of undue delay, or proving an effort to obstruct a criminal investigation or prosecution.

HISTORY: 1992 c 324, § 34, eff. 7-1-92; 1990 c 88, § 18

KRE 409 Payment of medical and similar expenses

Evidence of furnishing or offering or promising to pay medical, hospital, or similar expenses occasioned by an injury is not admissible to prove liability for the injury.

HISTORY: 1992 c 324, § 34, eff. 7–1–92; 1990 c 88, § 19

KRE 410 Inadmissibility of pleas, plea discussions, and related statements

Except as otherwise provided in this rule, evidence of the following is not, in any civil or criminal proceeding, admissible against the defendant who made the plea or was a participant in the plea discussions:

(1)   A plea of guilty which was later withdrawn;

(2)   A plea of nolo contendere in a jurisdiction accepting such pleas;

(3)   Any statement made in the course of formal plea proceedings, under either state procedures or Rule 11 of the Federal Rules of Criminal Procedure, regarding either of the foregoing pleas; or

(4)   Any statement made in the course of plea discussions with an attorney for the prosecuting authority which do not result in a plea of guilty or which result in a plea of guilty later withdrawn.

However, such a plea or statement is admissible (i) in any proceeding wherein another statement made in the course of the same plea or plea discussions has been introduced and the statement ought in fairness be considered contemporaneously with it, or (ii) in a criminal proceeding for perjury or false statement if the statement was made by the defendant under oath, on the record and in the presence of counsel.

Evidence Rules Review Commission Notes (2007)

The overall purpose of KRE 410 is to bar the use of certain pleas and plea discussions when later offered into evidence in a civil or criminal trial. The 2007 amendment to this provision of the Rules makes two changes. The first change is minor but substantive and the second is solely for the purpose of correcting an error made in the original enactment of the Rules.

The first change is to eliminate some language that was unwisely added to the rule during the course of its original enactment, specifically the language prohibiting the use of "a plea under Alford v. North Carolina, 394 U.S. 956 (1969)." (A so-called "Alford plea" is a guilty plea by a criminal defendant who refuses to acknowledge guilt but waives trial and accepts all the consequences of a conviction.) This added language created a question as to whether prior convictions based on "Alford pleas" might be introduced as evidence (for impeachment purposes or to prove persistent felony offender status), which the Supreme Court has resolved in favor of admissibility. See Pettiway v. Commonwealth, 860 S.W.2d 766 (Ky. 1993). The proposed change eliminates language from the rule that serves no useful purpose and simultaneously brings the Kentucky provision into alignment with its federal counterpart.

The second change is designed to correct an error that was made upon the original enactment of the Rules. By mistake, the last sentence of the provision (beginning with the words "However, such a statement is admissible:" and ending with the words "in the presence of counsel.") has been published as an exception applicable only to

subsection (4) of the rule when it was intended by drafters, the Supreme Court, and the General Assembly to be an exception applicable to all of the subsections of the rule. See Study Committee, Kentucky Rules of Evidence, Final Draft, p. 33 (Nov. 1989). The proposed change modifies the rule as needed to accomplish its original objective, while simultaneously achieving uniformity between the Kentucky and Federal Rules on this point.

HISTORY: Amended by Supreme Court Order 2007–02, eff. 5–1–07; 1992 c 324, § 7, 34, eff. 7–1–92; 1990 c 88, § 20

KRE 411 Liability insurance

Evidence that a person was or was not insured against liability is not admissible upon the issue whether the person acted negligently or otherwise wrongfully. This rule does not require the exclusion of evidence of insurance against liability when offered for another purpose, such as proof of agency, ownership, or control, or bias or prejudice of a witness.

HISTORY: 1992 c 324, § 34, eff. 7–1–92; 1990 c 88, § 21

KRE 412 Rape and similar cases; admissibility of victim's character and behavior

(a) Evidence generally inadmissible. The following evidence is not admissible in any civil or criminal proceeding involving alleged sexual misconduct except as provided in subdivisions (b) and (c):

(1) Evidence offered to prove that any alleged victim engaged in other sexual behavior.

(2) Evidence offered to prove any alleged victim's sexual predisposition.

(b) Exceptions:

(1) In a criminal case, the following evidence is admissible, if otherwise admissible under these rules:

(A) evidence of specific instances of sexual behavior by the alleged victim offered to prove that a person other than the accused was the source of semen, injury, or other physical evidence;

(B) evidence of specific instances of sexual behavior by the alleged victim with respect to the person accused of the sexual misconduct offered by the accused to prove consent or by the prosecution; and

(C) any other evidence directly pertaining to the offense charged.

(2) In a civil case, evidence offered to prove the sexual behavior or sexual predisposition of any alleged victim is admissible if it is otherwise admissible under these rules and its probative value substantially outweighs the danger of harm to any victim and of unfair prejudice to any party. Evidence of an alleged victim's reputation is admissible only if it has been placed in controversy by the alleged victim.

(c) Procedure to determine admissibility.

(1) A party intending to offer evidence under subdivision (b) must:

(A) file a written motion at least fourteen (14) days before trial specifically describing the evidence and stating the purpose for which it is offered unless the court, for good cause requires a different time for filing or permits filing during trial; and

(B) serve the motion on all parties and notify the alleged victim or, when appropriate, the alleged victim's guardian or representative.

(2) Before admitting evidence under this rule the court must conduct a hearing in camera and afford the victim and parties a right to attend and be heard. The motion, related papers, and the record of the hearing must be sealed and remain under seal unless the court orders otherwise.

HISTORY: Amended by Supreme Court Order 2003-3, eff. 7-1-03; 1992 c 324, § 29, 34, eff. 7-1-92; 1990 c 88, § 22

ARTICLE V
PRIVILEGES

KRE 501　General rule

Except as otherwise provided by Constitution or statute or by these or other rules promulgated by the Supreme Court of Kentucky, no person has a privilege to:

(1)　Refuse to be a witness;

(2)　Refuse to disclose any matter;

(3)　Refuse to produce any object or writing; or

(4)　Prevent another from being a witness or disclosing any matter or producing any object or writing.

HISTORY: 1992 c 324, § 34, eff. 7-1-92; 1990 c 88, § 23

KRE 502　[Number not yet utilized]

KRE 503　Lawyer-client privilege

(a) Definitions.　As used in this rule:

(1) "Client" means a person, including a public officer, corporation, association, or other organization or entity, either public or private, who is rendered professional legal services by a lawyer, or who consults a lawyer with a view to obtaining professional legal services from the lawyer.

(2) "Representative of the client" means:

(A) A person having authority to obtain professional legal services, or to act on advice thereby rendered on behalf of the client; or

(B) Any employee or representative of the client who makes or receives a confidential communication:

(i) In the course and scope of his or her employment;

(ii) Concerning the subject matter of his or her employment; and

(iii) To effectuate legal representation for the client.

(3) "Lawyer" means a person authorized, or reasonably believed by the client to be authorized to engage in the practice of law in any state or nation.

(4) "Representative of the lawyer" means a person employed by the lawyer to assist the lawyer in rendering professional legal services.

(5) A communication is "confidential" if not intended to be disclosed to third persons other than those to whom disclosure is made in furtherance of the rendition of professional legal services to the client or those reasonably necessary for the transmission of the communication.

(b) General rule of privilege.　A client has a privilege to refuse to disclose and to prevent any other person from disclosing a confidential communication made for the purpose of facilitating the rendition of professional legal services to the client:

(1) Between the client or a representative of the client and the client's lawyer or a representative of the lawyer;

(2) Between the lawyer and a representative of the lawyer;

(3) By the client or a representative of the client or the client's lawyer or a representative of the lawyer to a lawyer or a representative of a lawyer representing another party in a pending action and concerning a matter of common interest therein;

(4) Between representatives of the client or between the client and a representative of the client; or

(5) Among lawyers and their representatives representing the same client.

(c) Who may claim the privilege.　The privilege may be claimed by the client, the client's guardian or conservator, the personal representative of a deceased client, or the successor, trustee, or similar representative of a corporation, association, or other organization, whether or not in existence. The person who was the lawyer or the lawyer's representative at the time of the communication is presumed to have authority to claim the privilege but only on behalf of the client.

(d) Exceptions.　There is no privilege under this rule:

(1) Furtherance of crime or fraud. If the services of the lawyer were sought or obtained to enable

or aid anyone to commit or plan to commit what the client knew or reasonably should have known to be a crime or fraud;

(2) *Claimants through same deceased client.* As to a communication relevant to an issue between parties who claim through the same deceased client, regardless of whether the claims are by testate or intestate succession or by transaction inter vivos;

(3) *Breach of duty by a lawyer or client.* As to a communication relevant to an issue of breach of duty by a lawyer to the client or by a client to the lawyer;

(4) *Document attested by a lawyer.* As to a communication relevant to an issue concerning an attested document to which the lawyer is an attesting witness; and

(5) *Joint clients.* As to a communication relevant to a matter of common interest between or among two (2) or more clients if the communication was made by any of them to a lawyer retained or consulted in common, when offered in an action between or among any of the clients.

HISTORY: 1992 c 324, § 8, 34, eff. 7–1–92; 1990 c 88, § 25

Legislative Research Commission Note (6–8–11): When this rule was enacted in 1990, it was intended to mirror Section 502 of the Uniform Rules of Evidence Act which was recommended for enactment in all the states by the National Conference of Commissioners on Uniform State Laws. Section 502, subsection (b)(3) contained the words "to a lawyer or a representative of a lawyer" preceding the word "representing." However, that phrase was omitted during the drafting of 1990 HB 214, Section 25 (1990 Ky. Acts ch. 88) because the drafter apparently erroneously considered it to be duplicative of prior text and an error in the language of the Uniform Rule. It is clear to the Reviser of Statutes that it is not duplicative since it is describing to whom a privileged communication may be made. The Reviser of Statutes has reinserted that phrase into subsection (b)(3) to correct that manifest clerical or typographical error under the authority of KRS 7.136.

KRE 504   Husband-wife privilege

(a) *Spousal testimony.* The spouse of a party has a privilege to refuse to testify against the party as to events occurring after the date of their marriage. A party has a privilege to prevent his or her spouse from testifying against the party as to events occurring after the date of their marriage.

(b) *Marital communications.* An individual has a privilege to refuse to testify and to prevent another from testifying to any confidential communication made by the individual to his or her spouse during their marriage. The privilege may be asserted only by the individual holding the privilege or by the holder's guardian, conservator, or personal representative. A communication is confidential if it is made privately by an individual to his or her

spouse and is not intended for disclosure to any other person.

(c) *Exceptions.* There is no privilege under this rule:

(1) In any criminal proceeding in which the court determines that the spouses conspired or acted jointly in the commission of the crime charged;

(2) In any proceeding in which one (1) spouse is charged with wrongful conduct against the person or property of:

  (A) The other;

  (B) A minor child of either;

  (C) An individual residing in the household of either; or

  (D) A third person if the wrongful conduct is committed in the course of wrongful conduct against any of the individuals previously named in this sentence; or

(3) In any proceeding in which the spouses are adverse parties.

(d) *Minor child.* The court may refuse to allow the privilege in any proceeding if the interests of a minor child of either spouse may be adversely affected.

Evidence Rules Review Commission Notes (2006)

The 2006 amendment to this provision of the Rules makes two modifications in the 1992 provision on husband-wife privilege. The first is substantive; the second merely clarifies part of the original provision in order to eliminate ambiguity concerning one of the exceptions to the privilege.

KRE 504(c)(1) denies claims of spousal privileges in criminal proceedings when it is established that the spouses were jointly involved in the commission of crimes. (It should be noted that this exception is similar to the crime/fraud exception to the lawyer-client privilege.) The original provision of this rule provided for loss of the privilege when there was "evidence sufficient to support a finding" of joint criminal activity by the spouses. This yardstick is normally used in the evidence rules for deciding preliminary questions involving what is called "conditional relevance" (in KRE 104(b)). A greater proof requirement (preponderance of the evidence) is used for determining all other preliminary questions upon which admissibility of evidence depends (in KRE 104(a)). The preliminary question upon which loss of the spousal privilege depends under KRE 504(c)(1) is not a conditional relevance question but is instead a so-called "competency" question that needs to be resolved by the standard set forth in KRE 104(a). The proposed amendment would make this change with respect to the "joint crime" exception to spousal privileges. It should be noted that the Supreme Court adopted this same position with respect to the crime/fraud exception to the lawyer-client privilege in Stidham v. Clark, 74 S.W.3d 719 (Ky. 2002).

KRE 504(c)(2), as originally adopted, was ambiguous, as indicated in the following statement: "The last sentence of KRE 504(c)(2)(D) is ambiguous (perhaps partly because it seems to be out of place in the provision) but seems to create an entirely separate exception to spousal privileges that would require a trial judge to deny any and all spousal privilege claims determined to be adverse 'to the interests of a minor child of either spouse.'" Lawson, The Kentucky Evidence Law Handbook 376 (4th ed. 2003). The drafters of the original provision clearly indicated in their Commentary that the intent was to create a separate exception when spousal testimony was needed for determination of matters involving "the best interests of a minor child":

"The final sentence of the rule [KRE 504(c)(2)] provides that a judge may refuse to recognize the privilege in any kind of action if convinced that spousal testimony is needed to decide what is in the best interests of a minor child of either spouse." Evidence Rules Study Committee, Kentucky Rules of Evidence—Final Draft, p. 45 (November 1989).

The proposed amendment eliminates this ambiguity in the original provision by separating the last sentence of KRE 504(c)(2) from that provision and moving it to a new subsection of the rule, thereby clearly indicating that there is a separate exception to spousal privileges for testimony needed to determine matters involving "the best interests of a minor child." The new separate exception is now numbered KRE 504(d).

HISTORY: Amended by Supreme Court Order 2006–06, eff. 7-1-06; 1992 c 324, § 9, 34, eff. 7-1-92; 1990 c 88, § 26

KRE 505   Religious privilege

(a) Definitions. As used in this rule:

(1) A "clergyman" is a minister, priest, rabbi, accredited Christian Science practitioner, or other similar functionary of a religious organization, or an individual reasonably believed so to be by the person consulting him.

(2) A communication is "confidential" if made privately and not intended for further disclosure except to other persons present in furtherance of the purpose of the communication.

(b) General rule of privilege. A person has a privilege to refuse to disclose and to prevent another from disclosing a confidential communication between the person and a clergyman in his professional character as spiritual adviser.

(c) Who may claim the privilege. The privilege may be claimed by the person, by his guardian or conservator, or by his personal representative if he is deceased. The person who was the clergyman at the time of the communication is presumed to have authority to claim the privilege but only on behalf of the communicant.

HISTORY: 1992 c 324, § 10, 34, eff. 7-1-92; 1990 c 88, § 27

KRE 506   Counselor-client privilege

(a) Definitions. As used in this rule:

(1) A "counselor" includes:

(A) A certified school counselor who meets the requirements of the Kentucky Board of Education and who is duly appointed and regularly employed for the purpose of counseling in a public or private school of this state;

(B) A sexual assault counselor, who is a person engaged in a rape crisis center, as defined in KRS Chapter 421, who has undergone forty (40) hours of training and is under the control of a direct services supervisor of a rape crisis center, whose primary purpose is the rendering of advice, counseling, or assistance to victims of sexual assault;

(C) A certified professional art therapist who is engaged to conduct art therapy under KRS 309.130 to 309.1399;

(D) A licensed marriage and family therapist as defined in KRS 335.300 who is engaged to conduct marriage and family therapy pursuant to KRS 335.300 to 335.399;

(E) A licensed professional clinical counselor or a licensed professional counselor associate as defined in KRS 335.500;

(F) An individual who provides crisis response services as a member of the community crisis response team or local community crisis response team under KRS 36.250 to 36.270;

(G) A victim advocate as defined in KRS 421.570 except a victim advocate who is employed by a Commonwealth's attorney under KRS 15.760 or a county attorney pursuant to KRS 69.350; and

(H) A certified fee-based pastoral counselor as defined in KRS 335.600 who is engaged to conduct fee-based pastoral counseling under KRS 335.600 to 335.699.

(2) A "client" is a person who consults or is interviewed or assisted by a counselor for the purpose of obtaining professional or crisis response services from the counselor.

(3) A communication is "confidential" if it is not intended to be disclosed to third persons, except persons present to further the interest of the client in the consultation or interview, persons reasonably necessary for the transmission of the communication, or persons present during the communication at the direction of the counselor, including members of the client's family.

(b) General rule of privilege. A client has a privilege to refuse to disclose and to prevent any other person from disclosing confidential communications made for the purpose of counseling the client, between himself, his counselor, and persons present at the direction of the counselor, including members of the client's family.

(c) Who may claim the privilege. The privilege may be claimed by the client, his guardian or conservator, or the personal representative of a deceased client. The person who was the counselor (or that person's employer) may claim the privilege in the absence of the client, but only on behalf of the client.

(d) Exceptions. There is no privilege under this rule for any relevant communication:

(1) If the client is asserting his physical, mental, or emotional condition as an element of a claim or defense; or, after the client's death, in any proceeding in which any party relies upon the condition as an element of a claim or defense.

(2) If the judge finds:

(A) That the substance of the communication is relevant to an essential issue in the case;

(B) That there are no available alternate means to obtain the substantial equivalent of the communication; and

(C) That the need for the information outweighs the interest protected by the privilege. The court may receive evidence in camera to make findings under this rule.

HISTORY: 2002 c 99, § 7, eff. 3–28–02; 2002 c 79, § 11, eff. 7–15–02; 1998 c 525, § 13, c 86, § 6, eff. 7–15–98; 1996 c 364, § 13, c 189, § 3, c 316, § 6, eff. 7–15–96; 1994 c 352, § 13, c 337, § 11, eff. 7–15–94; 1992 c 324, § 11, 34, eff. 7–1–92; 1990 c 88, § 28

Legislative Research Commission Note (7–15–02): This section was amended by 2002 Ky. Acts chs. 79 and 99, which do not appear to be in conflict and have been codified together.

Legislative Research Commission Note (10–31–96): The original codification of the changes to this statute from the 1996 Regular Session inadvertently omitted from subdivision (a)(2) the words "or assisted by" after the word "interviewed" and the words "or crisis response" after the word "professional."

KRE 507 Psychotherapist-patient privilege

(a) Definitions. As used in this rule:

(1) A "patient" is a person who, for the purpose of securing diagnosis or treatment of his or her mental condition, consults a psychotherapist.

(2) A "psychotherapist" is:

(A) A person licensed by the state of Kentucky, or by the laws of another state, to practice medicine, or reasonably believed by the patient to be licensed to practice medicine, while engaged in the diagnosis or treatment of a mental condition;

(B) A person licensed or certified by the state of Kentucky, or by the laws of another state, as a psychologist, or a person reasonably believed by the patient to be a licensed or certified psychologist;

(C) A licensed clinical social worker, licensed by the Kentucky Board of Social Work; or

(D) A person licensed as a registered nurse or advanced registered nurse practitioner by the board of nursing and who practices psychiatric or mental health nursing.

(3) A communication is "confidential" if not intended to be disclosed to third persons other than those present to further the interest of the patient in the consultation, examination, or interview, or persons reasonably necessary for the transmission of the communication, or persons who are present during the communication at the direction of the psychotherapist, including members of the patient's family.

(4) "Authorized representative" means a person empowered by the patient to assert the privilege granted by this rule and, until given permission by the patient to make disclosure, any person whose communications are made privileged by this rule.

(b) General rule of privilege. A patient, or the patient's authorized representative, has a privilege to refuse to disclose and to prevent any other person from disclosing confidential communications, made for the purpose of diagnosis or treatment of the patient's mental condition, between the patient, the patient's psychotherapist, or persons who are participating in the diagnosis or treatment under the direction of the psychotherapist, including members of the patient's family.

(c) Exceptions. There is no privilege under this rule for any relevant communications under this rule:

(1) In proceedings to hospitalize the patient for mental illness, if the psychotherapist in the course of diagnosis or treatment has determined that the patient is in need of hospitalization;

(2) If a judge finds that a patient, after having been informed that the communications would not be privileged, has made communications to a psychotherapist in the course of an examination ordered by the court, provided that such communications shall be admissible only on issues involving the patient's mental condition; or

(3) If the patient is asserting that patient's mental condition as an element of a claim or defense, or, after the patient's death, in any proceeding in which any party relies upon the condition as an element of a claim or defense.

HISTORY: 1996 c 369, § 18, eff. 7–15–96; 1994 c 367, § 13, eff. 7–15–94; 1992 c 324, § 12, 34, eff. 7–1–92; 1990 c 88, § 29

KRE 508 Identity of informer

(a) General rule of privilege. The Commonwealth of Kentucky and its sister states and the United States have a privilege to refuse to disclose the identity of a person who has furnished information relating to or assisting in an investigation of a possible violation of a law to a law enforcement officer or member of a legislative committee or its staff conducting an investigation.

(b) Who may claim. The privilege may be claimed by an appropriate representative of the public entity to which the information was furnished.

(c) Exceptions:

(1) Voluntary disclosure; informer as a witness. No privilege exists under this rule if the identity of the informer or his interest in the subject matter of his communication has been disclosed by the holder of the privilege or by the informer's own action, or if the informer appears as a witness for the state. Disclosure within a law

enforcement agency or legislative committee for a proper purpose does not waive the privilege.

(2) Testimony on relevant issue. If it appears that an informer may be able to give relevant testimony and the public entity invokes the privilege, the court shall give the public entity an opportunity to make an in camera showing in support of the claim of privilege. The showing will ordinarily be in the form of affidavits, but the court may direct that testimony be taken if it finds that the matter cannot be resolved satisfactorily upon affidavits. If the court finds that there is a reasonable probability that the informer can give relevant testimony, and the public entity elects not to disclose this identity, in criminal cases the court on motion of the defendant or on its own motion shall grant appropriate relief, which may include one (1) or more of the following:

(A) Requiring the prosecuting attorney to comply;

(B) Granting the defendant additional time or a continuance;

(C) Relieving the defendant from making disclosures otherwise required of him;

(D) Prohibiting the prosecuting attorney from introducing specified evidence; and

(E) Dismissing charges.

(d) In civil cases, the court may make any order the interests of justice require if the informer has pertinent information. Evidence presented to the court shall be sealed and preserved to be made available to the appellate court in the event of an appeal, and the contents shall not otherwise be revealed without consent of the informed public entity.

HISTORY: 1992 c 324, § 13, 34, eff. 7–1–92; 1990 c 88, § 30

KRE 509   Waiver of privilege by voluntary disclosure

A person upon whom these rules confer a privilege against disclosure waives the privilege if he or his predecessor while holder of the privilege voluntarily discloses or consents to disclosure of any significant part of the privilege matter. This rule does not apply if the disclosure itself is privileged. Disclosure of communications for the purpose of receiving third-party payment for professional services does not waive any privilege with respect to such communications.

HISTORY: 1992 c 324, § 34, eff. 7–1–92; 1990 c 88, § 31

KRE 510   Privileged matter disclosed under compulsion or without opportunity to claim privilege

A claim of privilege is not defeated by a disclosure which was:

(1)   Compelled erroneously; or

(2)   Made without opportunity to claim the privilege.

HISTORY: 1992 c 324, § 34, eff. 7–1–92; 1990 c 88, § 32

KRE 511   Comment upon or inference from claim of privilege; instruction

(a) Comment or inference not permitted. The claim of a privilege, whether in the present proceeding or upon a prior occasion, is not a proper subject of comment by judge or counsel. No inference may be drawn therefrom.

(b) Claiming privilege without knowledge of jury. In jury cases, proceedings shall be conducted, to the extent practicable, so as to facilitate the assertion of claims of privilege without the knowledge of the jury.

(c) Jury instruction. Upon request, any party against whom the jury might draw an adverse inference from a claim of privilege is entitled to an instruction that no inference may be drawn therefrom.

HISTORY: 1992 c 324, § 34, eff. 7–1–92; 1990 c 88, § 33

ARTICLE VI
WITNESSES

KRE 601   Competency

(a) General. Every person is competent to be a witness except as otherwise provided in these rules or by statute.

(b) Minimal qualifications. A person is disqualified to testify as a witness if the trial court determines that he:

(1) Lacked the capacity to perceive accurately the matters about which he proposes to testify;

(2) Lacks the capacity to recollect facts;

(3) Lacks the capacity to express himself so as to be understood, either directly or through an interpreter; or

(4) Lacks the capacity to understand the obligation of a witness to tell the truth.

HISTORY: 1992 c 324, § 34, eff. 7–1–92; 1990 c 88, § 34

KRE 602   Lack of personal knowledge

A witness may not testify to a matter unless evidence is introduced sufficient to support a finding that the witness has personal knowledge of the matter. Evidence to prove personal knowledge may, but need not, consist of the witness' own testimony. This rule is subject to the provisions of KRE 703, relating to opinion testimony by expert witnesses.

HISTORY: 1992 c 324, § 34, eff. 7–1–92; 1990 c 88, § 35

KRE 603   Oath or affirmation

Before testifying, every witness shall be required to declare that the witness will testify truthfully, by oath or affirmation administered in a form calculated to awaken the witness' conscience and impress the witness' mind with the duty to do so.

HISTORY: 1992 c 324, § 34, eff. 7–1–92; 1990 c 88, § 36

KRE 604   Interpreters

An interpreter is subject to the provisions of these rules relating to qualifications of an expert and the administration of an oath or affirmation to make a true translation.

HISTORY: 1992 c 324, § 34, eff. 7–1–92; 1990 c 88, § 37

KRE 605   Competency of judge as witness

The judge presiding at the trial may not testify in that trial as a witness. No objection need be made in order to preserve the point.

HISTORY: 1992 c 324, § 34, eff. 7–1–92; 1990 c 88, § 38

KRE 606   Competency of juror as witness

A member of the jury may not testify as a witness before that jury in the trial of the case in which the juror is sitting. No objection need be made in order to preserve the point.

HISTORY: 1992 c 324, § 34, eff. 7–1–92; 1990 c 88, § 39

KRE 607   Who may impeach

The credibility of a witness may be attacked by any party, including the party calling the witness.

HISTORY: 1992 c 324, § 34, eff. 7–1–92; 1990 c 88, § 40

KRE 608   Evidence of character and conduct of witness

(a) Opinion and reputation evidence of character. The credibility of a witness may be attacked or supported by evidence in the form of opinion or reputation, but subject to these limitations: (1) the evidence may refer only to character for truthfulness or untruthfulness, and (2) evidence of truthful character is admissible only after the character of the witness for truthfulness has been attacked by opinion or reputation evidence or otherwise.

(b) Specific instances of conduct. Specific instances of the conduct of a witness, for the purpose of attacking or supporting the witness' credibility, other than conviction of crime as provided in Rule 609, may not be proved by extrinsic evidence. They may, however, in the discretion of the court, if probative of truthfulness or untruthfulness, be inquired into on cross–examination of the witness: (1) concerning the witness' character for truthfulness or untruthfulness, or (2) concerning the character for truthfulness or untruthfulness of another witness as to which character the witness being

cross–examined has testified. No specific instance of conduct of a witness may be the subject of inquiry under this provision unless the cross–examiner has a factual basis for the subject matter of his inquiry.

The giving of testimony, whether by an accused or by any other witness, does not operate as a waiver of the accused's or the witness' privilege against self–incrimination when examined with respect to matters which relate only to credibility.

HISTORY: Amended by Supreme Court Order 2003–3, eff. 7–1–03; 1992 c 324, § 14, 34, eff. 7–1–92; 1990 c 88, § 41

KRE 609   Impeachment by evidence of conviction of crime

(a) General rule. For the purpose of reflecting upon the credibility of a witness, evidence that the witness has been convicted of a crime shall be admitted if elicited from the witness or established by public record if denied by the witness, but only if the crime was punishable by death or imprisonment for one (1) year or more under the law under which the witness was convicted. The identity of the crime upon which conviction was based may not be disclosed upon cross-examination unless the witness has denied the existence of the conviction. However, a witness against whom a conviction is admitted under this provision may choose to disclose the identity of the crime upon which the conviction is based.

(b) Time limit. Evidence of a conviction under this rule is not admissible if a period of more than ten (10) years has elapsed since the date of the conviction unless the court determines that the probative value of the conviction substantially outweighs its prejudicial effect.

(c) Effect of pardon, annulment, or certificate of rehabilitation. Evidence of a conviction is not admissible under this rule if the conviction has been the subject of a pardon, annulment, or other equivalent procedure based on a finding of innocence.

HISTORY: 1992 c 324, § 15, 34, eff. 7–1–92; 1990 c 88, § 42

KRE 610   Religious beliefs or opinions

Evidence of the beliefs or opinions of a witness on matters of religion is not admissible for the purpose of showing that by reason of their nature the witness' credibility is impaired or enhanced.

HISTORY: 1992 c 324, § 34, eff. 7–1–92; 1990 c 88, § 43

KRE 611   Mode and order of interrogation and presentation

(a) Control by court. The court shall exercise reasonable control over the mode and order of interrogating witnesses and presenting evidence so as to:

  (1) Make the interrogation and presentation effective for the ascertainment of the truth;

(2) Avoid needless consumption of time; and

(3) Protect witnesses from harassment or undue embarrassment.

(b) Scope of cross-examination. A witness may be cross-examined on any matter relevant to any issue in the case, including credibility. In the interests of justice, the trial court may limit cross-examination with respect to matters not testified to on direct examination.

(c) Leading questions. Leading questions should not be used on the direct examination of a witness except as may be necessary to develop the witness' testimony. Ordinarily leading questions should be permitted on cross-examination, but only upon the subject matter of the direct examination. When a party calls a hostile witness, an adverse party, or a witness identified with an adverse party, interrogation may be by leading questions.

HISTORY: 1992 c 324, § 34, eff. 7–1–92; 1990 c 88, § 44

KRE 612   Writing used to refresh memory

Except as otherwise provided in the Kentucky Rules of Criminal Procedure, if a witness uses a writing during the course of testimony for the purpose of refreshing memory, an adverse party is entitled to have the writing produced at the trial or hearing or at the taking of a deposition, to inspect it, to cross-examine the witness thereon, and to introduce in evidence those portions which relate to the testimony of the witness. If it is claimed that the writing contains matters not related to the subject matter of the testimony, the court shall examine the writing in camera, excise any portions not so related, and order delivery of the remainder to the party entitled thereto. Any portion withheld over objections shall be preserved and made available to the appellate court in the event of an appeal.

HISTORY: 1992 c 324, § 34, eff. 7–1–92; 1990 c 88, § 45

KRE 613   Prior statements of witnesses

(a) Examining witness concerning prior statement. Before other evidence can be offered of the witness having made at another time a different statement, he must be inquired of concerning it, with the circumstances of time, place, and persons present, as correctly as the examining party can present them; and, if it be in writing, it must be shown to the witness, with opportunity to explain

it. The court may allow such evidence to be introduced when it is impossible to comply with this rule because of the absence at the trial or hearing of the witness sought to be contradicted, and when the court finds that the impeaching party has acted in good faith.

(b) This provision does not apply to admissions of a party-opponent as defined in KRE 801A.

HISTORY: 1992 c 324, § 16, 34, eff. 7–1–92; 1990 c 88, § 46

KRE 614   Calling and interrogation of witnesses by court

(a) Calling by court. The court may, on its own motion or at the suggestion of a party, call witnesses, and all parties are entitled to cross-examine witnesses thus called.

(b) Interrogation by court. The court may interrogate witnesses, whether called by itself or by a party.

(c) Interrogation by juror. A juror may be permitted to address questions to a witness by submitting them in writing to the judge who will decide at his discretion whether or not to submit the questions to the witness for answer.

(d) Objections. Objections to the calling of witnesses by the court, to interrogation by the court, or to interrogation by a juror may be made out of the hearing of the jury at the earliest available opportunity.

HISTORY: 1992 c 324, § 17, 34, eff. 7–1–92; 1990 c 88, § 47

KRE 615   Exclusion of witnesses

At the request of a party the court shall order witnesses excluded so that they cannot hear the testimony of other witnesses and it may make the order on its own motion. This rule does not authorize exclusion of:

(1) A party who is a natural person;

(2) An officer or employee of a party which is not a natural person designated as its representative by its attorney; or

(3) A person whose presence is shown by a party to be essential to the presentation of the party's cause.

HISTORY: 1992 c 324, § 34, eff. 7–1–92; 1990 c 88, § 48

ARTICLE VII
OPINIONS AND EXPERT TESTIMONY

KRE 701   Opinion testimony by lay witnesses

If the witness is not testifying as an expert, the witness' testimony in the form of opinions or inferences is limited to those opinions or inferences which are:

(a) Rationally based on the perception of the witness;

(b) Helpful to a clear understanding of the witness' testimony or the determination of a fact in issue; and

(c) Not based on scientific, technical, or other specialized knowledge within the scope of Rule 702.

Evidence Rules Review Commission Notes (2007)

With the adoption by the Kentucky Supreme Court of the analysis
required by the decision in Daubert v. Merrell Dow Pharmaceuticals,
509 U.S. 579 (1993), there was a risk that courts could be asked to
avoid the reliability standards set out in that case by the simple
process of offering "scientific, technical, or other specialized knowledge" evidence through a witness that an attorney sought to identify
as a "lay witness." The Federal Rules of Evidence, Rule 701, avoided
this error, by specifically adding language that excludes such evidence
from the operation of Rule 701. The addition of subsection © to
Kentucky Rule of Evidence, Rule 702, follows the exact language of
the Federal Rule amendment. This subsection requires that an
attempt to introduce testimony that is a part of "scientific, technical,
or other specialized knowledge," must be tested for reliability under
Rule 702.

The amendments to Rules 701 and 702 must be read together. The
introduction and reliability of the evidence is determined not by
asking whether the *witness* is lay or expert, but, instead, by asking
whether the *testimony* to be offered is lay or "scientific, technical, or
other specialized knowledge." If it is of the former, then Rule 701 is
applicable. If it is of the latter, then Rule 702 must be used.

HISTORY: Amended by Supreme Court Order 2007–02, eff.
5–1–07; 1992 c 324, § 34, eff. 7–1–92; 1990 c 88, § 49

KRE 702   Testimony by experts

If scientific, technical, or other specialized knowledge
will assist the trier of fact to understand the evidence
or to determine a fact in issue, a witness qualified as
an expert by knowledge, skill, experience, training, or
education, may testify thereto in the form of an opinion or otherwise, if:

(1) The testimony is based upon sufficient facts or
data;

(2) The testimony is the product of reliable principles
and methods; and

(3) The witness has applied the principles and methods reliably to the facts of the case.

Evidence Rules Review Commission Notes (2007)

When the Kentucky Rules of Evidence were adopted in 1992, Ky.
Rule 702 used the same language as Federal Rule of Evidence 702.
In addition, the Kentucky Rule was interpreted to follow the tradi-
tional rule of Frye v. United States, 293 F. 1013 (D.C. Cir. 1923).
The "Frye Test" would allow admission of scientific evidence if it was
generally accepted in the scientific community.

The United States Supreme Court in Daubert v. Merrell Dow
Pharmaceuticals, 509 U.S. 579 (1993) overruled the "Frye Test" and
interpreted Federal Rule of Evidence 702 to require an analysis of
factors by the trial judge in order to determine whether the scientific
evidence was admissible. In order to admit such evidence the trial
court was to act as a "gatekeeper" and make a preliminary determination that the underlying science was, in fact, "valid." In Kumho Tire
Co., Ltd. v. Carmichael, 526 U.S. 137 (1999), the "Daubert Test" was
extended to cover not only "scientific" evidence, but also any evidence
of "scientific, technical, or other specialized knowledge."

In 2000, Rule 702 of the Federal Rules of Evidence was amended in
order to codify the approach taken in Daubert. The items listed as
numbers (1), (2), and (3) are not intended to specifically state the
factors found in Daubert and Kumho Tire. They are, instead, intended to indicate that the court is to determine the reliability of such
evidence based upon the flexible factors suggested by such cases.
Although there is no attempt to codify the specific factors from that
case, the purpose of the amendment is clearly stated by the Federal
Advisory Committee Notes to that amendment.

No attempt has been made to "codify" these specific factors.
Daubert itself emphasized that the factors were neither exclusive nor
dispositive. Other cases have recognized that not all of the specific
Daubert factors can apply to every type of expert testimony . . . The
standards set forth in the amendment are broad enough to require
consideration of any or all of the specific Daubert factors where
appropriate.

In 1995, the Kentucky Supreme Court followed the lead of the
United States Supreme Court and adopted the rationale of the
Daubert decision as the appropriate interpretation of the language of
Rule 702. Mitchell v. Commonwealth, 908 S.W.2d 100 (Ky. 1995). In
2004, the Kentucky Supreme Court restated the flexible standard
originally espoused in Daubert in Toyota Motor Corp. v. Gregory, 136
S.W.3d 35 (Ky. 2004).

The 2007 amendment to Kentucky Rule of Evidence, Rule 702 is
designed to follow the development and adopts exact language set by
the Federal Rules. The amendment will codify the approach taken in
the Daubert case, followed in the Toyota Motor Corp. case and allow
the trial court to act as gatekeeper to the introduction of "scientific,
technical, or other specialized knowledge." The amendment does not
specifically require the use of all or any one of the factors suggested
by the court. It allows the trial court to use those factors that are
appropriate to the case at trial.

HISTORY: Amended by Supreme Court Order 2007–02, eff.
5–1–07; 1992 c 324, § 34, eff. 7–1–92; 1990 c 88, § 50

KRE 703   Bases of opinion testimony by experts

(a) The facts or data in the particular case upon which
an expert bases an opinion or inference may be
those perceived by or made known to the expert at
or before the hearing. If of a type reasonably
relied upon by experts in the particular field in
forming opinions or inferences upon the subject,
the facts or data need not be admissible in evidence.

(b) If determined to be trustworthy, necessary to
illuminate testimony, and unprivileged, facts or
data relied upon by an expert pursuant to subdivision (a) may at the discretion of the court be
disclosed to the jury even though such facts or
data are not admissible in evidence. Upon request the court shall admonish the jury to use
such facts or data only for the purpose of evaluating the validity and probative value of the expert's
opinion or inference.

(c) Nothing in this rule is intended to limit the right
of an opposing party to cross-examine an expert
witness or to test the basis of an expert's opinion
or inference.

HISTORY: 1992 c 324, § 34, eff. 7–1–92; 1990 c 88, § 51

KRE 704   [Number not yet utilized]

KRE 705   Disclosure of facts or data underlying expert opinion

The expert may testify in terms of opinion or inference and give reasons therefor without prior disclosure of the underlying facts or data, unless the court
requires otherwise. The expert may in any event be
required to disclose the underlying facts or data on
cross-examination.

HISTORY: 1992 c 324, § 18, 34, eff. 7–1–92; 1990 c 88, § 53

KRE 706   Court-appointed experts

(a) Appointment. The court may on its own motion or on the motion of any party enter an order to show cause why expert witnesses should not be appointed, and may require the parties to submit nominations. The court may appoint any expert witnesses agreed upon by the parties, and may appoint expert witnesses of its own selection. An expert witness shall not be appointed by the court unless the witness consents to act. A witness so appointed shall be informed of the witness' duties by the court in writing, a copy of which shall be filed with the clerk, or at a conference in which the parties shall have opportunity to participate. A witness so appointed shall advise the parties of the witness' findings, if any; the witness' deposition may be taken by any party; and the witness may be called to testify by the court or any party. The witness shall be subject to cross-examination by each party, including a party calling the witness.

(b) Compensation. Expert witnesses so appointed are entitled to reasonable compensation in whatever sum the court may allow. Except as otherwise provided by law, the compensation shall be paid by the parties in such proportions and at such time as the court directs, and thereafter charged in like manner as other costs.

HISTORY: 1992 c 324, § 19, 34, eff. 7-1-92; 1990 c 88, § 54

ARTICLE VIII
HEARSAY

KRE 801   Definitions

(a) Statement. A "statement" is:

(1) An oral or written assertion; or

(2) Nonverbal conduct of a person, if it is intended by the person as an assertion.

(b) Declarant. A "declarant" is a person who makes a statement.

(c) Hearsay. "Hearsay" is a statement, other than one made by the declarant while testifying at the trial or hearing, offered in evidence to prove the truth of the matter asserted.

HISTORY: 1992 c 324, § 34, eff. 7-1-92; 1990 c 88, § 55

KRE 801A   Prior statements of witnesses and admissions

(a) Prior statements of witnesses. A statement is not excluded by the hearsay rule, even though the declarant is available as a witness, if the declarant testifies at the trial or hearing and is examined concerning the statement, with a foundation laid as required by KRE 613, and the statement is:

(1) Inconsistent with the declarant's testimony;

(2) Consistent with the declarant's testimony and is offered to rebut an express or implied charge against the declarant of recent fabrication or improper influence or motive; or

(3) One of identification of a person made after perceiving the person.

(b) Admissions of parties. A statement is not excluded by the hearsay rule, even though the declarant is available as a witness, if the statement is offered against a party and is:

(1) The party's own statement, in either an individual or a representative capacity;

(2) A statement of which the party has manifested an adoption or belief in its truth;

(3) A statement by a person authorized by the party to make a statement concerning the subject;

(4) A statement by the party's agent or servant concerning a matter within the scope of the agency or employment, made during the existence of the relationship; or

(5) A statement by a coconspirator of a party during the course and in furtherance of the conspiracy.

(c) Admission by privity:

(1) Wrongful death. A statement by the deceased is not excluded by the hearsay rule when offered as evidence against the plaintiff in an action for wrongful death of the deceased.

(2) Predecessors in interest. Even though the declarant is available as a witness, when a right, title, or interest in any property or claim asserted by a party to a civil action requires a determination that a right, title, or interest existed in the declarant, evidence of a statement made by the declarant during the time the party now claims the declarant was the holder of the right, title, or interest is not excluded by the hearsay rule when offered against the party if the evidence would be admissible if offered against the declarant in an action involving that right, title, or interest.

(3) Predecessors in litigation. Even though the declarant is available as a witness, when the liability, obligation, or duty of a party to a civil action is based in whole or in part upon the liability, obligation, or duty of the declarant, or when the claim or right asserted by a party to a civil action is barred or diminished by a breach of duty by the declarant, evidence of a statement made by the declarant is not excluded by the hearsay rule when offered against the party if the evidence would be admissible against the

declarant in an action involving that liability, obligation, duty, or breach of duty.

HISTORY: 1992 c 324, § 20, 34, eff. 7-1-92; 1990 c 88, § 56

KRE 802   Hearsay rule

Hearsay is not admissible except as provided by these rules or by rules of the Supreme Court of Kentucky.

HISTORY: 1992 c 324, § 21, 34, eff. 7-1-92; 1990 c 88, § 57

KRE 803   Hearsay exceptions: availability of declarant immaterial

The following are not excluded by the hearsay rules, even though the declarant is available as a witness:

(1) Present sense impression. A statement describing or explaining an event or condition made while the declarant was perceiving the event or condition, or immediately thereafter.

(2) Excited utterance. A statement relating to a startling event or condition made while the declarant was under the stress of excitement caused by the event or condition.

(3) Then existing mental, emotional, or physical condition. A statement of the declarant's then existing state of mind, emotion, sensation, or physical condition (such as intent, plan, motive, design, mental feeling, pain, and bodily health), but not including a statement of memory or belief to prove the fact remembered or believed unless it relates to the execution, revocation, identification, or terms of declarant's will.

(4) Statements for purposes of medical treatment or diagnosis. Statements made for purposes of medical treatment or diagnosis and describing medical history, or past or present symptoms, pain, or sensations, or the inception or general character of the cause or external source thereof insofar as reasonably pertinent to treatment or diagnosis.

(5) Recorded recollection. A memorandum or record concerning a matter about which a witness once had knowledge but now has insufficient recollection to enable the witness to testify fully and accurately, shown to have been made or adopted by the witness when the matter was fresh in the witness' memory and to reflect that knowledge correctly. If admitted, the memorandum or record may be read into evidence but may not be received as an exhibit unless offered by an adverse party.

(6) Records of regularly conducted activity. A memorandum, report, record, or data compilation, in any form, of acts, events, conditions, opinions, or diagnoses, made at or near the time by, or from information transmitted by, a person with knowledge, if kept in the course of a regularly conducted business activity, and if it was the regular practice of that business activity

to make the memorandum, report, record, or data compilation, all as shown by the testimony of the custodian or other qualified witness, unless the source of information or the method or circumstances of preparation indicate lack of trustworthiness. The term "business" as used in this paragraph includes business, institution, association, profession, occupation, and calling of every kind, whether or not conducted for profit.

(A) Foundation exemptions. A custodian or other qualified witness, as required above, is unnecessary when the evidence offered under this provision consists of medical charts or records of a hospital that has elected to proceed under the provisions of KRS 422.300 to 422.330, business records which satisfy the requirements of KRE 902(11), or some other record which is subject to a statutory exemption from normal foundation requirements.

(B) Opinion. No evidence in the form of an opinion is admissible under this paragraph unless such opinion would be admissible under Article VII of these rules if the person whose opinion is recorded were to testify to the opinion directly.

(7) Absence of entry in records kept in accordance with the provisions of paragraph (6). Evidence that a matter is not included in the memoranda, reports, records, or data compilations, in any form, kept in accordance with the provisions of paragraph (6), to prove the nonoccurrence or nonexistence of the matter, if the matter was of a kind of which a memorandum, report, record, or other data compilation was regularly made and preserved, unless the sources of information or other circumstances indicate lack of trustworthiness.

(8) Public records and reports. Unless the sources of information or other circumstances indicate lack of trustworthiness, records, reports, statements, or other data compilations in any form of a public office or agency setting forth its regularly conducted and regularly recorded activities, or matters observed pursuant to duty imposed by law and as to which there was a duty to report, or factual findings resulting from an investigation made pursuant to authority granted by law. The following are not within this exception to the hearsay rule:

(A) Investigative reports by police and other law enforcement personnel;

(B) Investigative reports prepared by or for a government, a public office, or an agency when offered by it in a case in which it is a party; and

(C) Factual findings offered by the government in criminal cases.

(9) Records of vital statistics. Records or data compilations, in any form, of births, fetal deaths,

deaths, or marriages, if the report thereof was made to a public office pursuant to requirements or law.

(10) Absence of public record or entry. To prove the absence of a record, report, statement, or data compilation, in any form, or the nonoccurrence or nonexistence of a matter of which a record, report, statement, or data compilation, in any form, was regularly made and preserved by a public office or agency, evidence in the form of a certification in accordance with KRE 902, or testimony, that diligent search failed to disclose the record, report, statement, or data compilation, or entry.

(11) Records of religious organizations. Statements of births, marriages, divorces, deaths, legitimacy, ancestry, relationships by blood or marriage, or other similar facts of personal or family history, contained in a regularly kept record of a religious organization.

(12) Marriage, baptismal, and similar certificates. Statements of fact contained in a certificate that the maker performed a marriage or other ceremony or administered a sacrament, made by a clergyman, public official, or other person authorized by the rules or practices of a religious organization or by law to perform the act certified, and purporting to have been issued at the time of the act or within a reasonable time thereafter.

(13) Family records. Statements of births, marriages, divorces, deaths, legitimacy, ancestry, relationship by blood or marriage, or other similar facts of personal or family history contained in family Bibles, genealogies, charts, engravings on rings, inscriptions on family portraits, engravings on urns, crypts, or tombstones, or the like.

(14) Records of documents affecting an interest in property. The record of a document purporting to establish or affect an interest in property, as proof of the content of the original recorded document and its execution and delivery by each person by whom it purports to have been executed, if the record is a record of a public office and an applicable statute authorizes the recording of documents of that kind in that office.

(15) Statements in documents affecting an interest in property. A statement contained in a document purporting to establish or affect an interest in property if the matter stated was relevant to the purpose of the document, unless dealings with the property since the document was made have been inconsistent with the truth of the statement or the purport of the document.

(16) Statements in ancient documents. Statements in a document in existence twenty (20) years or more the authenticity of which is established.

(17) Market reports, commercial publications. Market quotations, tabulations, lists, directories, or other published compilations, generally used and relied upon by the public or by persons in particular occupations.

(18) Learned treatises. To the extent called to the attention of an expert witness upon cross-examination or relied upon by the expert witness in direct examination, statements contained in published treatises, periodicals, or pamphlets on a subject of history, medicine, or other science or art, established as a reliable authority by the testimony or admission of the witness or by other expert testimony or by judicial notice. If admitted, the statements may be read into evidence but may not be received as exhibits.

(19) Reputation concerning personal or family history. Reputation among members of a person's family by blood, adoption, or marriage, or among a person's associates, or in the community, concerning a person's birth, adoption, marriage, divorce, death, legitimacy, relationship by blood, adoption, or marriage, ancestry, or other similar fact of his personal or family history.

(20) Reputation concerning boundaries or general history. Reputation in a community, arising before the controversy, as to boundaries of or customs affecting lands in the community, and reputation as to events of general history important to the community or state or nation in which located.

(21) Reputation as to character. Reputation of a person's character among associates or in the community.

(22) Judgment of previous conviction. Evidence of a final judgment, entered after a trial or upon a plea of guilty (but not upon a plea of nolo contendere), adjudging a person guilty of a crime punishable by death or imprisonment under the law defining the crime, to prove any fact essential to sustain the judgment, but not including, when offered by the prosecution in a criminal case for purposes other than impeachment, judgments against persons other than the accused.

(23) Judgment as to personal, family, or general history, or boundaries. Judgments as proof of matters of personal, family, or general history, or boundaries, essential to the judgment, if the same would be provable by evidence of reputation.

HISTORY: 1994 c 279, § 5, eff. 7–15–94

Legislative Research Commission Note (12–12–94): Although subsection (12) of this statute was enacted with the phrase "authorized by the rules or practices or a religious organization," see 1990 Ky. Acts ch. 88, sec. 58, it is clear from context and from Fed. R. Evid. 803(12) that this should read "authorized by the rules or practices of a religious organization." This phrase has been corrected pursuant to KRS 7.136(1)(h).

KRE 804 Hearsay exceptions: declarant unavailable

(a) Definition of unavailability. "Unavailability as a witness" includes situations in which the declarant:

(1) Is exempted by ruling of the court on the ground of privilege from testifying concerning the subject matter of the declarant's statement;

(2) Persists in refusing to testify concerning the subject matter of the declarant's statement despite an order of the court to do so;

(3) Testifies to a lack of memory of the subject matter of the declarant's statement;

(4) Is unable to be present or to testify at the hearing because of death or then existing physical or mental illness or infirmity; or

(5) Is absent from the hearing and the proponent of the statement has been unable to procure the declarant's attendance by process or other reasonable means.

A declarant is not unavailable as a witness if his exemption, refusal, claim of lack of memory, inability, or absence is due to the procurement or wrongdoing of the proponent of a statement for the purpose of preventing the witness from attending or testifying.

(b) Hearsay exceptions. The following are not excluded by the hearsay rule if the declarant is unavailable as a witness:

(1) Former testimony. Testimony given as a witness at another hearing of the same or a different proceeding, or in a deposition taken in compliance with law in the course of the same or another proceeding, if the party against whom the testimony is now offered, or, in a civil action or proceeding, a predecessor in interest, had an opportunity and similar motive to develop the testimony by direct, cross, or redirect examination.

(2) Statement under belief of impending death. In a criminal prosecution or in a civil action or proceeding, a statement made by a declarant while believing that the declarant's death was imminent, concerning the cause or circumstances of what the declarant believed to be his impending death.

(3) Statement against interest. A statement which was at the time of its making so far contrary to the declarant's pecuniary or proprietary interest, or so far tended to subject the declarant to civil or criminal liability, or to render invalid a claim by the declarant against another, that a reasonable person in the declarant's position would not have made the statement unless believing it to be true. A statement tending to expose the declarant to criminal liability is not admissible unless corroborating circumstances clearly indicate the trustworthiness of the statement.

(4) Statements of personal or family history.

(A) A statement concerning the declarant's own birth, adoption, marriage, divorce, legitimacy, relationship by blood, adoption, or marriage, ancestry, or other similar fact of personal or family history, even though declarant had no means of acquiring personal knowledge of the matter stated; or

(B) A statement concerning the foregoing matters, and death also, of another person, if the declarant was related to the other by blood, adoption, or marriage or was so intimately associated with the other's family as to be likely to have accurate information concerning the matter declared.

(5) Forfeiture by wrongdoing. A statement offered against a party that has engaged or acquiesced in wrongdoing that was intended to, and did, procure the unavailability of the declarant as a witness.

HISTORY: Amended by Supreme Court Order 2004-1, eff. 7–1–04; 1992 c 324, § 23, 34, eff. 7–1–92; 1990 c 88, § 59

KRE 805 Hearsay within hearsay

Hearsay included within hearsay is not excluded under the hearsay rule if each part of the combined statements conforms with an exception to the hearsay rule provided in these rules.

HISTORY: 1992 c 324, § 34, eff. 7–1–92; 1990 c 88, § 60

KRE 806 Attacking and supporting credibility of declarant

When a hearsay statement has been admitted in evidence, the credibility of the declarant may be attacked, and if attacked may be supported, by any evidence which would be admissible for those purposes if declarant had testified as a witness. Evidence of a statement or conduct by the declarant at any time, inconsistent with the declarant's hearsay statement, is not subject to any requirement that the declarant may have been afforded an opportunity to deny or explain. If the party against whom a hearsay statement has been admitted calls the declarant as a witness, the party is entitled to examine the declarant on the statement as if under cross-examination.

HISTORY: 1992 c 324, § 34, eff. 7–1–92; 1990 c 88, § 61

ARTICLE IX
AUTHENTICATION AND IDENTIFICATION

KRE 901   Requirement of authentication or identification

(a) *General provision.* The requirement of authentication or identification as a condition precedent to admissibility is satisfied by evidence sufficient to support a finding that the matter in question is what its proponent claims.

(b) *Illustrations.* By way of illustration only, and not by way of limitation, the following are examples of authentication or identification conforming with the requirements of this rule:

(1) *Testimony of witness with knowledge.* Testimony that a matter is what it is claimed to be.

(2) *Nonexpert testimony on handwriting.* Nonexpert opinion as to the genuineness of handwriting, based upon familiarity not acquired for the purposes of litigation.

(3) *Comparison by trier or expert witness.* Comparison by the trier of fact or by expert witnesses with specimens which have been authenticated.

(4) *Distinctive characteristics and the like.* Appearance, contents, substance, internal patterns, or other distinctive characteristics, taken in conjunction with circumstances.

(5) *Voice identification.* Identification of a voice, whether heard firsthand or through mechanical or electronic transmission or recording, by opinion based upon hearing the voice at any time under circumstances connecting it with the alleged speaker.

(6) *Telephone conversations.* Telephone conversations, by evidence that a call was made to the number assigned at the time by the telephone company to a particular place or business if:

(A) In the case of a person, circumstances, including self-identification, show the person answering to be the one called; or

(B) In the case of a business, the call was made to a place of business and the conversation related to business reasonably transacted over the phone.

(7) *Public records or reports.* Evidence that a writing authorized by law to be recorded or filed and in fact recorded or filed in a public office, or a purported public record, report, statement, or data compilation, in any form, is from the public office where items of this nature are kept.

(8) *Ancient documents or data compilation.* Evidence that a document or data compilation, in any form:

(A) Is in such condition as to create no suspicion concerning its authenticity;

(B) Was in a place where it, if authentic, would likely be; and

(C) Has been in existence twenty (20) years or more at the time it is offered.

(9) *Process or system.* Evidence describing a process or system used to produce a result and showing that the process or system produces an accurate result.

(10) *Methods provided by statute or rule.* Any method of authentication or identification provided by act of the General Assembly or by rule prescribed by the Supreme Court of Kentucky.

HISTORY: 1992 c 324, § 34, eff. 7–1–92; 1990 c 88, § 62

KRE 902   Self-authentication

Extrinsic evidence of authenticity as a condition precedent to admissibility is not required with respect to the following:

(1) *Domestic public documents under seal.* A document bearing a seal purporting to be that of the United States, or of any state, district, Commonwealth, territory, or insular possession thereof, or the Panama Canal Zone, or the Trust Territory of the Pacific Islands, or of a political subdivision, department, officer, or agency thereof, and a signature purporting to be an attestation or execution.

(2) *Domestic public documents not under seal.* A document purporting to bear the signature in the official capacity of an officer or employee of any entity included in paragraph (1) of this rule, having no seal, if a public officer having a seal and having official duties in the district or political subdivision of the officer or employee certifies under seal that the signer has the official capacity and that the signature is genuine.

(3) *Foreign public documents.* A document purporting to be executed, or attested in an official capacity by a person authorized by the laws of a foreign country to make the execution or attestation, and accompanied by a final certification as to the genuineness of the signature of official position:

(A) Of the executing or attesting person; or

(B) Of any foreign official whose certificate of genuineness of signature and official position relates to the execution or attestation.

A final certification may be made by a secretary of embassy or legation, consul general, consul, vice consul, or consular agent of the United

States, or a diplomatic or consular official of the foreign country assigned or accredited to the United States. If reasonable opportunity has been given to all parties to investigate the authenticity and accuracy of official documents, the court may, for good cause shown, order that they be treated as presumptively authentic without final certification or permit them to be evidenced by an attested summary with or without final certification.

(4) *Official records.* An official record or an entry therein, when admissible for any purpose, may be evidenced by an official publication thereof or by a copy attested by an official having the legal custody of the record. If the office in which the record is kept is outside the Commonwealth of Kentucky, the attested copy shall be accompanied by a certificate that the official attesting to the accuracy of the copy has the authority to do so. The certificate accompanying domestic records (those from offices within the territorial jurisdiction of the United States) may be made by a judge of a court of record of the district or political subdivision in which the record is kept, authenticated by the seal of the court, or may be made by any public officer having a seal of office and having official duties in the district or political subdivision in which the record is kept, authenticated by the seal of office. The certificate accompanying foreign records (those from offices outside the territorial jurisdiction of the United States) may be made by a secretary of embassy or legation, consul general, consul, vice consul, or consular agent or by any officer in the foreign service of the United States stationed in the foreign state or country in which the record is kept, and authenticated by the seal of office. A written statement prepared by an official having the custody of a record that after diligent search no record or entry of a specified tenor is found to exist in the records of the office, complying with the requirements set out above, is admissible as evidence that the records of the office contain no such record of entry.

(5) *Official publications.* Books, pamphlets, or other publications purporting to be issued by public authority.

(6) *Books, newspapers, and periodicals.* Printed materials purporting to be books, newspapers, or periodicals.

(7) *Trade inscriptions and the like.* Inscriptions, signs, tags, or labels purporting to have been affixed in the course of business and indicating ownership, control, or origin.

(8) *Acknowledged documents.* Documents accompanied by a certificate of acknowledgement executed in the manner provided by law before a notary public or other officer authorized by law to take acknowledgements.

(9) *Commercial paper and related documents.* Commercial paper, signatures thereon, and documents relating thereto to the extent provided by the general commercial law.

(10) *Documents which self-authenticate by the provisions of statutes or other rules of evidence.* Any signature, document, or other matter which is declared to be presumptively genuine by Act of Congress or the General Assembly of Kentucky or by rule of the Supreme Court of Kentucky.

(11) *Business records.*

(A) Unless the sources of information or other circumstances indicate lack of trustworthiness, the original or a duplicate of a record of regularly conducted activity within the scope of KRE 803(6) or KRE 803(7), which the custodian thereof certifies:

(i) Was made, at or near the time of the occurrence of the matters set forth, by (or from information transmitted by) a person with knowledge of those matters;

(ii) Is kept in the course of the regularly conducted activity; and

(iii) Was made by the regularly conducted activity as a regular practice.

(B) A record so certified is not self-authenticating under this paragraph unless the proponent makes an intention to offer it known to the adverse party and makes it available for inspection sufficiently in advance of its offer in evidence to provide the adverse party with a fair opportunity to challenge it.

(C) As used in this paragraph, "certifies" means, with respect to a domestic record, a written declaration under oath subject to the penalty of perjury, and, with respect to a foreign record, a written declaration which, if falsely made, would subject the maker to criminal penalty under the laws of that country. The certificate relating to a foreign record must be accompanied by a final certification as to the genuineness of the signature and official position:

(i) Of the individual executing the certificate; or

(ii) Of any foreign official who certifies the genuineness of signature and official position of the executing individual or is the last in a chain of certificates that collectively certify the genuineness of signature and official position of the executing individual.

A final certification must be made by a secretary of embassy or legation, consul general, consul, vice consul, or consular agent or by an officer in the foreign service of the United States stationed in the foreign state or country in which the record is kept, and authenticated by the seal of office.

HISTORY: 1992 c 324, § 24, 34, eff. 7–1–92; 1990 c 88, § 63

KRE 903   Subscribing witness' testimony unnecessary

The testimony of a subscribing witness is not necessary to authenticate a writing unless required by the laws of the jurisdiction whose laws govern the validity of the writing.

HISTORY: 1992 c 324, § 34, eff. 7–1–92; 1990 c 88, § 64

ARTICLE X
CONTENTS OF WRITINGS, RECORDINGS, AND PHOTOGRAPHS

KRE 1001   Definitions

For purposes of this article the following definitions are applicable:

(1)   Writings and recordings. "Writings" and "recordings" consist of letters, words, or numbers, or their equivalent, set down by handwriting, typewriting, printing, photostating, photographing, magnetic impulse, mechanical or electronic recording, or other form of data compilation.

(2)   Photographs. "Photographs" include still photographs, X-ray films, video tapes, and motion pictures.

(3)   Original. An "original" of a writing or recording is the writing or recording itself or any counterpart intended to have the same effect by a person executing or issuing it. An "original" of a photograph includes the negative or any print therefrom. If data are stored in a computer or similar device, any printout or other output readable by sight, shown to reflect the data accurately, is an "original."

(4)   Duplicate. A "duplicate" is a counterpart produced by the same impression as the original, or from the same matrix, or by means of photography, including enlargements and miniatures, or by mechanical or electronic rerecording, or by chemical reproduction, or by other equivalent technique which accurately reproduces the original.

HISTORY: 1992 c 324, § 34, eff. 7–1–92; 1990 c 88, § 65

KRE 1002   Requirement of original

To prove the content of a writing, recording, or photograph, the original writing, recording, or photograph is required, except as otherwise provided in these rules, in other rules adopted by the Kentucky Supreme Court, or by statute.

HISTORY: 1992 c 324, § 34, eff. 7–1–92; 1990 c 88, § 66

KRE 1003   Admissibility of duplicates

A duplicate is admissible to the same extent as an original unless:

(1)   A genuine question is raised as to the authenticity of the original; or

(2)   In the circumstances it would be unfair to admit the duplicate in lieu of the original.

HISTORY: 1992 c 324, § 34, eff. 7–1–92; 1990 c 88, § 67

KRE 1004   Admissibility of other evidence of contents

The original is not required, and other evidence of the contents of a writing, recording, or photograph is admissible if:

(1)   Originals lost or destroyed. All originals are lost or have been destroyed, unless the proponent lost or destroyed them in bad faith;

(2)   Original not obtainable. No original can be obtained by any available judicial process or procedure; or

(3)   Original in possession of opponent. At a time when an original was under the control of the party against whom offered, that party was put on notice, by the pleadings or otherwise, that the contents would be a subject of proof at the hearing, and that party does not produce the original at the hearing.

HISTORY: 1992 c 324, § 25, 34, eff. 7–1–92; 1990 c 88, § 68

KRE 1005   Public records

The contents of an official record, or of a document authorized to be recorded or filed and actually recorded or filed with a governmental agency, either federal, state, county, or municipal, in a place where official records or documents are ordinarily filed, including data compilations in any form, if otherwise admissible, may be proved by copy, certified as correct in accordance with KRE 902 or testified to be correct by a witness who has compared it with the original. If a copy which complies with the foregoing cannot be obtained by the exercise of reasonable diligence, then other evidence of the contents may be given.

HISTORY: 1992 c 324, § 34, eff. 7–1–92; 1990 c 88, § 69

KRE 1006   Summaries

The contents of voluminous writings, recordings, or photographs which cannot conveniently be examined in court may be presented in the form of a chart, summary, or calculation. A party intending to use such a summary must give timely written notice of his intention to use the summary, proof of which shall be filed with the court. The originals, or duplicates, shall be made available for examination or copying, or both, by other parties at reasonable time and place. The court may order that they be produced in court.

HISTORY: 1992 c 324, § 34, eff. 7–1–92; 1990 c 88, § 70

KRE 1007   Testimony or written admission of party

Contents of writings, recordings, or photographs may be proved by the testimony or deposition of the party against whom offered or by that party's written admission, without accounting for the nonproduction of the original.

HISTORY: 1992 c 324, § 34, eff. 7–1–92; 1990 c 88, § 71

KRE 1008   Functions of court and jury

When the admissibility of other evidence of contents of writings, recordings, or photographs under these rules depends upon the fulfillment of a condition of fact, the question whether the condition has been fulfilled is ordinarily for the court to determine in accordance with the provisions of KRE 104. However, when an issue is raised:

(a) Whether the asserted writing ever existed;

(b) Whether another writing, recording, or photograph produced at the trial is the original;

(c) Whether other evidence of contents correctly reflects the contents,

the issue is for the trier of fact to determine as in the case of other issues of fact.

HISTORY: 1992 c 324, § 34, eff. 7–1–92; 1990 c 88, § 72

ARTICLE XI
MISCELLANEOUS RULES

KRE 1101   Applicability of rules

(a) Courts. These rules apply to all the courts of this Commonwealth in the actions, cases, and proceedings and to the extent hereinafter set forth.

(b) Proceedings generally. These rules apply generally to civil actions and proceedings and to criminal cases and proceedings, except as provided in subdivision (d) of this rule.

(c) Rules on privileges. The rules with respect to privileges apply at all stages of all actions, cases, and proceedings.

(d) Rules inapplicable. The rules (other than with respect to privileges) do not apply in the following situations:

(1) Preliminary questions of fact. The determination of questions of fact preliminary to admissibility of evidence when the issue is to be determined by the court under KRE 104.

(2) Grand jury. Proceedings before grand juries.

(3) Small claims. Proceedings before the small claims division of the District Courts.

(4) Summary contempt proceedings. Contempt proceedings in which the judge is authorized to act summarily.

(5) Miscellaneous proceedings. Proceedings for extradition or rendition; preliminary hearings in criminal cases; sentencing by a judge; granting or revoking probation; issuance of warrants for arrest, criminal summonses, and search warrants; and proceedings with respect to release on bail or otherwise.

HISTORY: 1992 c 324, § 34, eff. 7–1–92; 1990 c 88, § 73

KRE 1102   Amendments

(a) Supreme Court. The Supreme Court of Kentucky shall have the power to prescribe amendments or additions to the Kentucky Rules of Evidence. Amendments or additions shall not take effect until they have been reported to the Kentucky General Assembly by the Chief Justice of the Supreme Court at or after the beginning of a regular session of the General Assembly but not later than the first day of March, and until the adjournment of that regular session of the General Assembly; but if the General Assembly within that time shall by resolution disapprove any amendment or addition so reported it shall not take effect. The effective date of any amendment or addition so reported may be deferred by the General Assembly to a later date or until approved by the General Assembly. However, the General Assembly may not disapprove any amendment or addition or defer the effective date of any amendment or addition that constitutes rules of practice and procedure under Section 116 of the Kentucky Constitution.

(b) General Assembly. The General Assembly may amend any proposal reported by the Supreme Court pursuant to subdivision (a) of this rule and may adopt amendments or additions to the Kentucky Rules of Evidence not reported to the General Assembly by the Supreme Court. However, the General Assembly may not amend any proposals reported by the Supreme Court and may not adopt amendments or additions to the Kentucky Rules of Evidence that constitute rules of practice and procedure under Section 116 of the Constitution of Kentucky.

(c) Review of proposals for change. Neither the Supreme Court nor the General Assembly should undertake to amend or add to the Kentucky Rules of Evidence without first obtaining a review of proposed amendments or additions from the Evidence Rules Review Commission described in KRE 1103.

HISTORY: 1992 c 324, § 26, 34, eff. 7–1–92; 1990 c 88, § 74

KRE 1103   Evidence Rules Review Commission

(a) The Chief Justice of the Supreme Court or a designated justice shall serve as chairman of a permanent Evidence Rules Review Commission which shall consist of the Chief Justice or a designated justice, one (1) additional member of the judiciary appointed by the Chief Justice, the chairman of the Senate Judiciary Committee, the chairman of the House Judiciary Committee, a member of the Board of Governors of the Kentucky Bar Association appointed by the President of the Kentucky Bar Association, and five (5) additional members of the Kentucky bar appointed to four (4) year terms by the Chief Justice.

(b) The Evidence Rules Review Commission shall meet at the call of the Chief Justice or a designated justice for the purpose of reviewing proposals for amendment or addition to the Kentucky Rules of Evidence, as requested by the Supreme Court or General Assembly pursuant to KRE 1102. The Commission shall act promptly to assist the Supreme Court or General Assembly and shall perform its review function in furtherance of the ideals and objectives described in KRE 102.

HISTORY: Amended by Supreme Court Order 2007–02, eff. 5–1–07; 1992 c 324, § 27, 34, eff. 7–1–92; 1990 c 88, § 75

KRE 1104   Use of official commentary

The commentary accompanying the Kentucky Rules of Evidence may be used as an aid in construing the provisions of the Rules, but shall not be binding upon the Court of Justice.

HISTORY: 1992 c 324, § 28, 34, eff. 7–1–92; 1990 c 88, § 76

RULES OF THE SUPREME COURT

Including Amendments Received Through January 1, 2013

I   POLICY AND ADMINISTRATION

SCR 1.000   Title and scope

These rules shall be called the Rules of the Supreme Court and may be cited by their full title or by the abbreviation SCR. Rule 1 covers matters of policy and administration within the Court of Justice.

HISTORY: Adopted eff. 1–1–78

SCR 1.010   Authority

The policy-making and administrative authority of the Court of Justice is vested in the Supreme Court and the Chief Justice. All fiscal management, personnel actions and policies, development and distribution of statistical information, and pretrial release services come within that authority.

HISTORY: Adopted eff. 1–1–78

SCR 1.020   The Supreme Court

(1) Conduct of business.

(a) *Final decisions and matters of policy.*

The final disposition of all appeals and original actions in the Supreme Court and matters of policy or administration shall be decided by a concurrence of at least four of its members, except that in appealed cases if one member is disqualified or does not sit and the court is equally divided, the order or judgment appealed from shall stand affirmed.

(b) *The Chief Justice.*

The Chief Justice shall be the presiding officer of the court. Orders of the court shall be signed by the Chief Justice or one of its members acting on his behalf, unless otherwise provided by these rules. Whenever the Chief Justice is absent or otherwise unable to act, the remaining six members shall act for and in his behalf in the order of their seniority on the court unless otherwise directed by the Chief Justice. Members whose terms of service are equal shall have precedence according to seniority in age.

(2) Terms.

(a) There shall be one annual term of the Supreme Court, coinciding with the calendar year.

(b) The provisions of CR 6.03(1) and CR 77.01 apply to the transaction of business in the Supreme Court.

(3) Sessions.

The Supreme Court will sit in open session for scheduled oral arguments and on such other occasions as it may determine.

(4) Court personnel.

Officers and employees of the Supreme Court shall not engage in the practice of law.

HISTORY: Amended by Order 83–4, eff. 7–8–83; prior amendments eff. 10–1–82, 5–1–80; adopted eff. 1–1–78

SCR 1.030   The Court of Appeals

(1) Headquarters.

The headquarters of the Court of Appeals shall be in Frankfort. Each judge shall maintain an office in his district.

(2) Continuous session.

The Court of Appeals shall be a court of continuous session.

(3) Powers of the Court.

The Court of Appeals may administer oaths, punish contempts, and issue necessary orders to give control over lower courts. Proceedings in the nature of mandamus or prohibition against a circuit judge shall originate in the Court of Appeals. Final decisions of the Workers' Compensation Board are subject to review by the Court of Appeals in accordance with procedures set out in the Rules of Civil Procedure.

(4) Style of process.

All process from the Court of Appeals shall be issued in the name of the court and signed by the clerk, and shall be styled "The Commonwealth of Kentucky, Court of Appeals."

(5) Court personnel.

The Court of Appeals may appoint law clerks and secretaries for each judge and may appoint staff attorneys for the court. Other court service personnel shall be employed by the Administrative Office of the Courts. Officers and employees of the Court of Appeals shall not practice law.

(6) Chief judge.

(a) Selection.

The judges of the Court of Appeals shall elect one of their number to serve as chief judge for a term of four years. The chief judge shall appoint a chief judge pro tem to serve at his pleasure. The chief judge pro tem shall perform the functions of the chief judge when the latter is absent or unable to act.

(b) Duties.

In addition to the powers and duties imposed by these rules, the chief judge shall have such other powers and duties as the Supreme Court by rule or special order shall direct.

(7) Panels.

(a) Division.

The Court of Appeals shall be divided from time to time into panels of three judges each to conduct hearings at the times and in the places necessary to discharge the business before the court. The assignment of judges to panels, the times and places for holding hearings, and the assignment of cases shall be determined by the chief judge in conformity with the administrative policies set forth in subsection (b) of this rule. Judges may be assigned to more than one panel at the same time.

(b) Assignment of judges.

The assignment of judges to panels shall be rotated in such manner that over the course of each year (i) each judge sits with each of the other members of the court, other than the chief judge, with substantially the same frequency and (ii) each judge other than the chief judge sits in each appellate district with substantially the same frequency as each of the other judges.

(c) Presiding judge.

The chief judge shall preside over any panel of which he is a member, and shall designate the presiding judge of other panels. The presiding judge of each panel shall preside at the hearings and perform such other functions as the Court of Appeals or Supreme Court by rule or order shall direct.

(d) Finality of decisions.

The decision of a majority of the judges of a panel shall constitute the decision of the Court of Appeals. If prior to the time the decision of a panel is announced it appears that the proposed decision is in conflict with the decision of another panel on the same question, the chief judge may reassign the case to the entire court. If a panel is unable to reach a decision on a case under consideration by it, the chief judge may reassign the case to a larger or different panel or to the entire court.

(8) Authority of Supreme Court opinions; denial of discretionary review.

(a) Precedents.

The Court of Appeals is bound by and shall follow applicable precedents established in the opinions of the Supreme Court and its predecessor court.

(b) Denial of discretionary review.

The denial of a motion for discretionary review by the Supreme Court or by the Court of Appeals shall not be taken as indicating its approval of the opinion or order sought to be reviewed, and shall not be cited as connoting such approval.

HISTORY: Amended by Order 88–1, eff. 1–15–88; prior amendments eff. 7–8–83, 5–1–80, 1–1–80; adopted eff. 1–1–78

SCR 1.040   The circuit and district courts

(1) Territorial assignment.

All judicial proceedings at the trial level shall be regularly conducted by the circuit and district judges elected or appointed from the respective circuits or districts in which such proceedings have been filed or are pending. No judge shall conduct any judicial proceeding, other than the issuance of warrants, outside his own circuit or district unless designated by the chief justice or by the chief judge of an administrative region. When so designated, a judge conducting proceedings in another circuit or district shall be styled a "special judge."

(2) Selection of chief judge.

Except as may be provided otherwise in the Regional Administration Charter in each circuit or district in which there are two or more judges a chief judge shall be selected biennially by the judges of that circuit or district on the basis of his administrative qualifications, and not by rotation or seniority. If the judges of the circuit or district fail to do so within a reasonable time, the chief justice shall designate the chief judge.

(3) Duties of chief judge.

The chief judge shall:

(a) Prepare with the assistance of appropriate committees such proposed local rules as are consistent with the Rules of Civil Procedure, Rules of Criminal Procedure, and Rules of the Supreme Court, and as are required to expedite and facilitate the business of the court, including the establishment of times for conducting regular sessions of the court within the circuit or district; submit such proposed rules for consideration by the judges of the circuit or district and, upon tentative approval by a majority of such judges, have the proposed rules published and submitted to the local bar and circuit court clerk(s) for consideration and recommendations; and after a majority of the judges have finally recommended the rules, submit copies to the Chief Justice for review and final approval. No local rules shall be of binding effect unless in writing, approved by the Chief Justice, and filed with the Supreme Court Clerk who shall compile such rules and make them available for general distribution.

(b) Designate one of the judges as acting chief judge to act in his absence or inability to act;

(c) Assign the business of the circuit or district among the several judges as equally as possible and have published for general distribution copies of a current court calendar setting forth the assignments of the judges, the times and places assigned for hearing the various types of court business, and any special calendaring requirements adopted by the court for such hearings;

(d) Reassign cases from one judge to another as necessary or convenient;

(e) Call such meetings of the judges as may be necessary;

(f) Appoint such standing and special committees of judges as may be advisable to assist in the proper performance of the duties and functions of the court;

(g) Supervise the administrative business of the court and have general direction and supervision of the nonjudicial personnel assigned to that court;

(h) Provide for proper liaison between the court and other governmental and civic agencies;

(i) When appropriate, meet with or designate a judge or judges to meet with any committee of the bench, bar and news media to review problems and to promote understanding of the principles of fair trial and free press; and

(j) Provide for an appropriate orientation program for new judges as soon as is feasible after appointment or election.

(k) The chief judge of the circuit court shall also develop and coordinate with the circuit court clerk and the chief district court judge a local plan for jury management and shall chair the advisory board for the pretrial services agency and, as appropriate, submit to the Administrative Office of the Courts recommendations for improvement of the agency.

(4) Distribution of business.

Except as otherwise provided by law, the business of the court in each county shall be distributed by the chief judge according to the following:

(a) The chief judge or his designee shall regulate the assignment of cases to the judges on a random basis.

(b) A district judge may be assigned exclusively to juvenile cases for a period not to exceed two years, at the end of which he shall be assigned to other cases. Cases arising in all other jurisdictional categories shall be equally apportioned among the district judges.

(c) In the absence of good cause to the contrary, all matters connected with a pending or supplemental proceeding shall be heard by the judge to whom the proceeding was originally assigned.

(5) Conformity with precedents.

On all questions of law the circuit and district courts are bound by and shall follow applicable precedents established in the opinions of the Supreme Court and its predecessor court and, when there are no such precedents, those established in the opinions of the Court of Appeals.

(6) Mandamus and prohibition.

Proceedings for relief in the nature of mandamus or prohibition against a district judge shall originate in the circuit court.

(7) Extended absences from the circuit or district.

Circuit and district judges of single-judge circuits and districts shall, before leaving the circuit or district for an extended period, make arrangements through the Regional Administration Program or the Administrative Office of the Courts for a special judge to be designated to dispose of urgent matters.

HISTORY: Amended by Order 95–1, eff. 11–1–95; prior amendments eff. 1–1–89, 11–1–83, 10–1–82, 2–1–81, 1–1–80; adopted eff. 1–1–78

SCR 1.050 The Administrative Office of the Courts

(1) The Administrative Office of the Courts shall act as the administrative and fiscal agency of the Court of Justice. Policies and procedures developed by the Administrative Office of the Courts and issued by it with the approval of the Supreme Court shall have the same effect as if issued by the Supreme Court.

(2) All personnel actions shall conform to the requirements of the judicial personnel system approved by the Supreme Court.

(3) No funds, excepting in-state travel, shall be expended or otherwise obligated without prior review and approval of the Administrative Office of the Courts.

(4) All courts, clerks and court reporters within the Court of Justice shall keep such records and report such statistics as may be required by the Administrative Office of the Courts with the approval of the Supreme Court.

(5) The internal management of juries shall be in accordance with the Rules of Civil and Criminal Procedure as implemented by the procedures issued by the Administrative Office of the Courts with the approval of the Supreme Court.

(6) Requests for branch court sites shall first be presented to the Administrative Office of the Courts for review and recommendation to the Supreme Court.

(7) Requests for certification of necessity for trial commissioners or new judicial positions shall be submitted to the chief justice with a copy to the Administrative Office of the Courts.

(8) All attorneys shall notify the Administrative Office of the Courts forthwith, in writing and with a copy to the judge, when any action stands submitted for final adjudication. When the decision has been rendered, the circuit clerk shall notify the Administrative Office of the Courts.

The Administrative Office of the Courts shall keep records of all cases under submission and report monthly to the chief justice on the status of cases under submission.

The chief justice shall report to the judicial retirement and removal commission regarding any case under submission for longer than ninety (90) days in which the district or circuit judge has not reported the reason for the delay to the chief justice as required by KRS 454.350.

(9) The Administrative Office of the Courts shall make available, at least once every two years, a training program designed for Circuit and Deputy Circuit Clerks which focuses on the dynamics and effects of domestic violence including the availability of community resources, victims services and reporting requirements.

HISTORY: Amended by Order 96–1, eff. 1–1–97; prior amendment eff. 1–1–84; adopted eff. 1–1–78

SCR 1.060 Circuit court clerks

(1) Pursuant to Section 100 of the Constitution of Kentucky no person shall be eligible to seek the office of circuit clerk unless he shall have procured from a judge of the Court of Appeals, or a judge of the circuit court, a certificate that he has been examined by the clerk of his court under his supervision, and that he is qualified for the office for which he is a candidate.

(2) No such certificate shall be issued to any person unless that person has received a passing grade of 70% or more on a standard examination to be prepared and administered by the Administrative Office of the Courts. The examination shall include questions pertaining to the materials included in the Circuit Clerk's Manual, Circuit Clerk's Accounting Manual, and the Personnel Policies of the Court of Justice.

(3) The examination shall be given once not less than 30 days nor more than 60 days before the deadline for filing for election in the year in which circuit clerks are elected. No person shall be eligible to appear on any election ballot for the office for circuit clerk who has not successfully completed an examination and been so certified, except no incumbent circuit clerk shall be required to be re-certified.

(4) In the event of a vacancy in the office of circuit clerk, a special examination shall be prepared by the Administrative Office of the Courts to be administered to such person or persons designated by the chief circuit judge responsible for filling the vacancy by appointment, and to be administered to prospective candidates for election to fill the unexpired term.

HISTORY: Amended by Order 2001–2, eff. 1–1–02; adopted by Order 85–2, eff. 1–1–87

II ADMISSION OF PERSONS TO PRACTICE LAW

SCR 2.000 Office of Bar Admissions

There is hereby created an Office of Bar Admissions which shall be comprised of the Kentucky Board of Bar Examiners, as defined in SCR 2.020 and the

Character and Fitness Committee, as defined in SCR 2.040.

Subject to the approval of the Supreme Court, the Board and Committee shall have the power to adopt and amend rules and regulations governing the manner in which each carries out its duties.

HISTORY: Amended by Order 2001–2, eff. 1–1–02; prior amendments eff. 2–1–00 (Order 99–1), 8–1–92 (Order 92–1), 10–29–91, 7–1–84, 7–1–81; adopted eff. 1–1–78

SCR 2.002   Fiscal provisions

(1) The fees collected by the Kentucky Office of Bar Admissions shall constitute a fund to provide for the ordinary and necessary expenses of the administration of the bar examination and the operation of both the Board of Bar Examiners and the Character and Fitness Committee.

(2) An annual budget including all income and expenditures shall be prepared by the Board and the Committee and submitted to the Supreme Court not less than four (4) months prior to the commencement of the next fiscal year. The budget shall distinctly set forth expected revenues according to source, together with carryover funds from the previous year, and shall list budgeted amounts for each category of expenditure in sufficient detail to identify clearly the nature of the respective expenditures.

(3) Upon approval by the court, the budget shall govern the fiscal operation of the Board and the Committee. Each expenditure category may be increased or decreased by not more than ten (10) percent. Further departure from the budget allotments may be made only upon approval of the court.

(4) All fees collected by the Kentucky Office of Bar Admissions for the Board and the Committee shall be recorded and deposited promptly in a joint account of the Board of Bar Examiners and Character and Fitness Committee. Each repository of funds and each bank account shall be designated by the Board and the Committee and approved by the Court.

(5) All disbursements shall be in accordance with the budget and recorded. Checks shall bear such signatures and countersignatures as the Board and the Committee shall direct.

(6) At least once each quarter a financial report shall be prepared at the direction of the Board and the Committee and transmitted to the Court.

(7) Each member of the Board and the Committee and each employee given responsibility by the Board and the Committee for the receipt or disbursement of funds shall be bonded in an amount specified by the Board and the Committee.

(8) There shall be an annual audit of the Board and the Committee by the Administrative Office of the Courts or, at the election of the Board and the Committee, a private accounting firm approved by the Court. The report of the audit shall be submitted to the Court. Each annual audit shall be paid for by the Board and the Committee.

(9) The Board and the Committee may employ such personnel as the Court authorizes. Their compensation shall be fixed by the Board and the Committee subject to approval by the Court. The compensation of members of the Board and Committee shall be fixed by the Court.

(10) Printing and purchasing shall be regulated by procedures established through the Administrative Office of the Courts except that the duplicating of bar examinations shall be accomplished in such manner as the Board designates in order to preserve the security thereof.

HISTORY: Amended by Order 2009–12, eff. 1–1–10; prior amendments eff. 8–1–92 (Order 92–1); adopted eff. 2–1–81

SCR 2.005   Travel

(1) In the conduct of business for the Board and Committee, its members and employees shall be reimbursed for lodging, meals and travel expenses in accordance with the travel regulations of the Administrative Office of the Courts.

(2) Whenever it appears to the Board or Committee that the above limitations will result in unfair hardship because actual and necessary expenses exceed the limits fixed, the Board or Committee may allow additional reimbursements.

HISTORY: Amended by Order 99–1, eff. 2–1–00; adopted by Order 81–2, eff. 2–1–81

SCR 2.007   Qualification, compensation, expenses, and assistants of board of bar examiners and committee on character and fitness

Each member of the Board of Bar Examiners and each member of the Character and Fitness Committee shall have the qualifications of a circuit judge, and shall be engaged in the active practice of law, including active practice before the Supreme Court. Except for compensated expenses and allowances for services rendered as members of the Board and of the Committee as authorized by the Supreme Court to be paid out of special funds for such purposes, no member of the Board of Bar Examiners and no member of the Character and Fitness Committee shall knowingly receive, or agree to receive, directly or indirectly, compensation for any services rendered or to be rendered, either by himself/herself or another, in any matter which is before the Kentucky Supreme Court relating to the admission of a person to practice law in this state. As appointees of the Supreme Court, neither the members of the Board of Bar Examiners nor the members of the Character and Fitness Committee constitute officers or employees of any agency within the meaning of KRS 45A.335, 45A.340 and 61.990. Subject to the approval of the Supreme Court, the Board of Bar Examiners and the Character and Fitness Committee each may employ such personnel as it deems appropriate, compensation therefore to be paid out of special funds for such purposes.

HISTORY: Amended by Order 2009–12, eff. 1–1–10; adopted by Order 2001–2, eff. 1–1–02

SCR 2.008 Confidentiality

The Office of Bar Admissions shall not disclose to anyone other than an applicant any information with respect to the character and fitness or the examination results of any applicant except:

(a) upon written authority of such applicant and upon payment of any fees required by the Board for copies of such reports;

(b) in response to a valid subpoena from a Court of competent jurisdiction;

(c) to the Director, Kentucky Bar Association.

HISTORY: Adopted by Order 2001–2, eff. 1–1–02

SCR 2.009 Immunity

Any person who communicates information to a member of the Board, Committee or its affiliates concerning an applicant for admission to the Kentucky Bar shall be granted immunity from all civil liability which might result from said communications.

HISTORY: Adopted by Order 2001–2, eff. 1–1–02

SCR 2.010 Requirements for admission to the Kentucky bar

All applicants for admission to the bar of this state must meet certain basic requirements regardless of whether admission is sought by examination (SCR 2.022), without examination (SCR 2.110), for a limited certificate (SCR 2.111) or as an attorney participant in a defender or legal services program (SCR 2.112). Those requirements are set forth in the following sections SCR 2.011 through SCR 2.015.

HISTORY: Amended by Order 2001–2, eff. 1–1–02; prior amendments eff. 1–1–88 (Order 87–2), 2–24–86, 7–5–85, 2–1–84, 10–1–82, 11–1–78, 1–1–78, 3–10–73

SCR 2.011 Moral character and fitness

All applicants for admission to the bar of this state must be of good moral character and general fitness requisite for an attorney.

(1) Every applicant shall be of good moral character. The applicant shall have the burden of proving that he or she is possessed of good moral character. The term "good moral character" includes qualities of honesty, fairness, responsibility, knowledge of the laws of the state and the nation and respect for the rights of others and for the judicial process. Good moral character is a functional assessment of character and fitness of a prospective lawyer. The purpose of requiring an applicant to possess present good moral character is to exclude from the practice of law those persons possessing character traits that are likely to result in injury to future clients, in the obstruction of the administration of justice, or in a violation of the Code of Professional Responsibility.

(2) Fitness is the assessment of mental and emotional health as it affects the competence of a prospective lawyer. The purpose of requiring an applicant to possess this fitness is to exclude from the practice of law any person having a mental or emotional illness or condition which would be likely to prevent the person from carrying out duties to clients, Courts or the profession. A person may be of good moral character, but may be incapacitated from proper discharge of his duties as a lawyer by such illness or condition. The fitness required is a present fitness, and prior mental or emotional illness or conditions are relevant only so far as they indicate the existence of a present lack of fitness.

(3) If the Committee's initial review and investigation into the character and fitness of an applicant reveals any of the following conduct, further detailed investigation shall be undertaken, as determined to be warranted, prior to the Committee's determination regarding whether the applicant possesses the requisite character and fitness to practice law in Kentucky:

A. Unlawful conduct

B. Academic misconduct

C. Making a false statement, including omissions of material information

D. Misconduct in employment

E. Acts involving dishonesty, fraud, deceit or misrepresentation

F. Abuse of legal process

G. Neglect of financial responsibilities

H. Neglect or disregard of ethical or professional obligations

I. Violation of an order of court

J. Conduct indicating mental or emotional instability impairing the ability of an applicant to perform the functions of an attorney

K. Conduct indicating substance abuse impairing the ability of an applicant to perform the functions of an attorney

L. Denial of admission to the bar in another jurisdiction on character and fitness grounds

M. Disciplinary complaints or disciplinary action by an attorney disciplinary agency or a professional disciplinary agency of any jurisdiction.

(4) Each applicant for admission to the Kentucky Bar shall pay all investigative fees, reporting fees or other expenses required and assessed by the Character and Fitness Committee as deemed necessary in determining the character and fitness of the applicant.

HISTORY: Amended by Order 2007–007, eff. 2–1–08; adopted by Order 2001–2, eff. 1–1–02

SCR 2.012   Oath of allegiance

No person who advocates the overthrow of the government of the United States or of this State by any unconstitutional means, shall be certified to the Supreme Court for admission and a license to practice law. Therefore every applicant shall be required to take the oath to support the Constitutions of the United States and Kentucky.

HISTORY: Amended by Order 2001–2, eff. 1–1–02; adopted by Order 91–2, eff. 11–15–91

SCR 2.013   Intent to practice law in Commonwealth

Every applicant must intend to engage in the practice of law in Kentucky and agree to abide by the rules, duties and standards imposed upon attorneys of this state. No person shall seek admission to the Bar of Kentucky for the primary purpose of using such admission as a basis for obtaining admission to the Bar of some sister state or the District of Columbia or to circumvent the admission requirements of such sister state or District. The giving of erroneous information as to intention to practice law in the State of Kentucky shall be grounds for denying the applicant's application or for disbarment.

HISTORY: Adopted by Order 2001–2, eff. 1–1–02

SCR 2.014   Legal education

(1) Every applicant for admission to the Kentucky Bar must have completed degree requirements for a J.D. or equivalent professional degree from a law school approved by the American Bar Association or by the Association of American Law Schools.

(2) An attorney who received a legal education in the United States but is not eligible for admission by virtue of not having attended a law school approved by the American Bar Association or the Association of American Law Schools may nevertheless be considered for admission by examination provided the attorney satisfies the following requirements:

(a) The attorney holds a J.D. Degree, which is not based on study by correspondence, from a law school accredited in the jurisdiction where it exists and which requires the equivalent of a three-year course of study that is the substantial equivalent of the legal education provided by approved law schools located in Kentucky. The applicant shall bear the cost of the evaluation of his/her legal education, as determined by the Board, and the application shall not be processed until the applicant's legal education is approved by the Board of Bar Examiners; and

(b) The attorney has been actively and substantially engaged in lawful practice of law as his or her principal business or occupation for at least three of the last five years immediately preceding the filing of the application; and

(c) In evaluating the education received the Board of Bar Examiners shall consider, but not be limited to, such factors as the admission of the applicant to the bar of another state or the District of Columbia, the similarity of the curriculum taken to that offered in law schools approved by the American Bar Association or by the Association of American Law Schools, and that the school at which the applicant's legal education was received has been examined and approved by other state bar associations examining the legal qualifications of non-ABA law school graduates.

(d) The attorney meets all other requirements contained in the Rules of the Supreme Court of Kentucky pertaining to Admission of Persons to Practice Law.

(3) An attorney who received a legal education in a foreign country and is not eligible for admission by virtue of not having attended a law school approved by the American Bar Association or the Association of American Law Schools may nevertheless be considered for admission by examination provided the attorney satisfies the following requirements:

(a) The foreign attorney's legal education is the substantial equivalent of the legal education provided by approved law schools located in Kentucky. The applicant shall bear the cost of the evaluation of their legal education, as determined by the Board, and the application shall not be processed until the applicant's legal education is approved by the Board of Bar Examiners.

(b) In evaluating the education received the Board of Bar Examiners shall consider, but not be limited to, such factors as the admission of the applicant to the bar of another state or the District of Columbia, the similarity of the curriculum taken to that offered in law schools approved by the American Bar Association or by the Association of American Law Schools, that the school at which the applicant's legal education was received has been examined and approved by other state bar associations examining the legal qualifications of foreign law school graduates, and the applicant's proficiency in written and spoken English.

(c) The applicant shall, in order to qualify to sit for the Bar examination, also submit a certified copy of the record or license of the court or agency which admitted the applicant to practice law in such country, and satisfy the requirement that the applicant has been actively and substantially engaged in the lawful practice of law as his or her principal business or occupation for at least three of the last five years immediately preceding the filing of the application, in addition to any other requirements authorized by these rules.

(4) For purposes of (2)(b) and (3)(c), the active engagement in the teaching of the law shall be considered active engagement in the practice of law.

HISTORY: Amended by Order 2012–01, eff. 3–1–12; prior amendments eff. 1–1–02 (Order 2001–2), 2–1–00 (Order 99–1); adopted by Order 92–1, eff. 8–1–92

SCR 2.015 Professional responsibility examinations

(1) No person shall be eligible for admission to the Kentucky Bar until that person has first passed the Multi–State Professional Responsibility Examination administered by the National Conference of Bar Examiners by attaining a scaled score thereon of at least 75.

(2) No person shall sit for the Bar Examinations administered under SCR 2.080, 3.500 or 3.510 unless he or she has first passed the Multi–State Professional Responsibility Examination administered by the National Conference of Bar Examiners by attaining a scaled score thereon of at least 75.

HISTORY: Amended by Order 2003–4, eff. 1–1–04; prior amendments eff. 1–1–02 (Order 2001–2), 2–24–86 (Order 86-2), 3–10–73

SCR 2.016 Application for early registration as a law student—Deleted

HISTORY: Deleted by Order 99–1, eff. 2–1–00; prior amendment eff. 1–1–97 (Order 96–1); adopted eff. 8–1–92

SCR 2.018 Application packets

(1) All applications for admission to the Kentucky Bar shall be on forms approved by the Board and Committee. Application packets will be available upon written request to the Kentucky Office of Bar Admissions and accompanied by a fee of $10.00 made payable to the Kentucky Office of Bar Admissions.

(2) The applicant must give full and complete response to all inquiries on the application as well as furnish any additional documents requested in relation to the application.

(3) Any application received that is incomplete shall be returned to the applicant and a fee of $20.00 shall be submitted along with the complete application prior to said application being acted upon. If an applicant fails to return the requested information within 30 days, the application will be held in abeyance and no further action will be taken and no fees shall be refundable. If the requested information is submitted after the 30 days, the Committee will determine whether or not the applicant is permitted to take the forthcoming examination.

(4) The application is to be signed by the applicant and notarized. All answers on the application form must be completely candid. Lack of candor could result in possible denial of character and fitness certification. An applicant is required to submit in writing any circumstance or occurrence that may reflect on their character or fitness.

HISTORY: Amended by Order 2009–12, eff. 1–1–10; adopted by Order 2001–2, eff. 1–1–02

SCR 2.020 Board of Bar Examiners

(1) There is hereby created a Board of Bar Examiners known and designated as Kentucky Board of Bar Examiners, hereinafter referred to as "Board".

(2) The Board shall be composed of seven (7) attorneys appointed by the Supreme Court of Kentucky for terms of three years, the members to serve until the expirations of their terms and until their successors are appointed. The Supreme Court of Kentucky shall appoint the Chair of the Board, and the Board shall select from its membership a secretary.

(3) The Board is charged with the responsibility of administering the bar examination to qualified applicants for admission to the bar of the Commonwealth.

HISTORY: Amended by Order 2001–2, eff. 1–1–02; prior amendments eff. 2–1–00 (Order 99–1), 1–1–97 (Order 96–1), 9–1–93, 8–1–92, 1–15–88, 1–1–88, 7–1–87, 4–15–86, 2–24–86, 7–5–85, 7–1–81, 1–1–78, 9–24–75, 3–6–74, 3–10–73

SCR 2.021 Late filing of application for admission by examination—Deleted

HISTORY: Deleted by Order 2001–2, eff. 1–1–02; prior amendment eff. 2–1–00 (Order 99–1); adopted by Order 92–1, eff. 8–1–92

SCR 2.022 Application for admission by examination

The application for Admission by Examination shall be on a verified form approved by the Board. Applications may not be filed more than 90 days before the filing deadline outlined below.

(1) An applicant must file a complete Application for Admission by Examination form accompanied by a fee of $625.00 (cashier's or certified check or money order) at the time of filing. The filing deadline is October 1 for the February Bar examination and February 1 for the July Bar examination.

(2) **ATTORNEY APPLICANT:** An attorney applicant who is admitted in another jurisdiction must file a complete Application for Admission By Examination form along with a fee of $675.00 (cashier's or certified check or money order). The filing deadline is October 1 for the February Bar examination and February 1 for the July Bar examination.

(3) Every person who intends to apply for admission to the Kentucky Bar by examination shall file with the Kentucky Office of Bar Admissions, a verified application on a form provided by the Kentucky Office of Bar Admissions. The applicant shall provide such information as requested on the form. An application must be complete at the time of filing including a properly executed Authorization & Release form.

(4) The Dean of each law school shall certify to the Committee as to the character and fitness of each applicant. Each applicant shall pay all additional investigation expenses that exceed the $200.00 fee required by the Committee in conducting the background investigation necessary for certification of eli-

gibility. These costs are incurred when circumstances require a more intensive background investigation. The cost of any record, document or inquiry concerning an application or transcript of record as a result of a hearing shall be paid by the applicant. Any additional expenses incurred must be paid prior to the release of any examination results for the applicant.

(5) Any applicant whose application to the Bar of another state has been refused for any reason is ineligible to take the Bar examination in this state unless the refusal was based upon a failure to pass the Bar examination in that state.

(6) Any applicant who is a member of the bar in another jurisdiction must produce a certificate of good standing with the application. The applicant must also produce a statement from the disciplinary board of that jurisdiction indicating whether any complaints have been filed against the applicant and their disposition. Any applicant who has a complaint(s) pending, is under disciplinary action, suspended, or any other action that would prohibit the practice of law as a member of the bar in another jurisdiction is not eligible for admission in Kentucky. Any applicant who is disbarred in another jurisdiction is not eligible for admission in Kentucky.

(7) An applicant who wishes to withdraw from the Bar examination must notify the Kentucky Office of Bar Admissions, in writing, not later than five (5) days prior to the examination date or have a verified excuse, otherwise, the Bar examination fee shall be forfeited.

(8) No part of any fees or expenses as stated in the paragraphs above shall be refundable.

HISTORY: Amended by Order 2009–12, eff. 1–1–10; prior amendments eff. 1–1–02 (Order 2001–2), 2–1–00 (Order 99–1); adopted by Order 92–1, eff. 8–1–92

SCR 2.023   Late filing of application for admission by examination

(1) An applicant who has failed to timely file an Application for Admission by Examination under SCR 2.022 may file a late application for Admission by Examination form from October 2 to November 10, prior to the February Bar examination and from February 2, to March 10, for the July Bar examination, accompanied by a late fee of $200 along with the application fee (cashier's or certified check or money order).

(2) An applicant who has failed to file an Application for Admission by Examination form by the late deadlines prescribed in paragraph (1) of this rule, may file under the extended late deadlines of November 11 to December 10 for the February Bar examination and March 11 to May 10 for the July Bar examination accompanied by an extended late fee of $400 along with the application fee.

(3) When an Application for Admission by Examination form is filed later than the prescribed deadlines of SCR 2.022, the Committee will determine whether or not the applicant is permitted to take the forthcoming examination.

(4) Under no circumstances will an application to sit for the Bar examination be accepted after the above stated extended late filing deadline.

HISTORY: Adopted by Order 2001–2, eff. 1–1–02

SCR 2.024   Re-application for admission by examination

An applicant who withdraws from or fails the bar examination shall be permitted to re-apply for the next scheduled bar examination on a form approved by the Board along with a fee of $75.00. The $175.00 examination fee is also required of applicants who failed the bar examination. The re-application form must be filed by November 10 prior to the February examination and May 10 prior to the July examination.

HISTORY: Amended by Order 2006–09, eff. 1–1–07; adopted by Order 2001–2, eff. 1–1–02

SCR 2.025   Re-certification of character and fitness—Deleted

HISTORY: Deleted by Order 2001–2, eff. 1–1–02; prior amendments eff. 2–1–00 (Order 99–1), 1–1–97 (Order 96–1); adopted eff. 8–1–92

SCR 2.030   Disposition of application and fee—Abolished

HISTORY: Abolished by Order 81–2, eff. 2–1–81; prior amendments eff. 1–1–78, 3–10–73

SCR 2.040   Character and Fitness Committee; nominations

(1) There is hereby created a Committee on Character and Fitness, hereinafter referred to as the Committee, to be composed of five attorneys, appointed by the Supreme Court for terms of three years, the members to serve until the expiration of their terms and until their successors are appointed. The Supreme Court of Kentucky shall appoint the Chair of the Committee.

(2) Subject to the approval of the Supreme Court, the committee shall have the power to adopt and amend rules and regulations governing the manner in which it carries out its duties. The Character and Fitness Committee may appoint from the bar of the state associate members of the Character and Fitness Committee.

(3) The Committee on Character and Fitness is charged with the responsibility of determining the age, character and fitness, education and general qualifications of those applicants for admission to the bar of the Commonwealth whose applications are referred to it by the Clerk of the Supreme Court. The Character and Fitness Committee is further charged with the duty of certifying to the Supreme Court persons who

appear qualified to perform legal services as interns under Rule 2.540.

(4) The Character and Fitness Committee, in determining the character and fitness of an applicant for admission to the bar of the Commonwealth, and in determining the character and fitness of a person seeking to perform legal services as an intern under Rule 2.540, may have such persons investigated by associate members of the Character and Fitness Committee, members of the bar of the state, the National Conference of Bar Examiners or any other reputable investigative agency. Subject to the approval of the Supreme Court the Character and Fitness Committee may compensate any person or agency making such investigation out of funds held for that purpose.

(5) The Character and Fitness Committee shall submit to the Board of Bar Examiners the names and addresses of all applicants to take the examination who will be eligible upon approval from the standpoint of character and fitness and upon submission of the required recommendations of their law school deans. Said list shall be submitted no later than 30 days after the extended late deadline. At least ten days prior to each Bar examination the Character and Fitness Committee shall certify to the Secretary of the Board of Bar Examiners the names and addresses of all applicants who are qualified to take that Bar examination.

(6) From time to time, the Character and Fitness Committee shall recommend to the Supreme Court admission to the bar without examination of applicants for such admission who qualify therefor under the provisions of Rule 2.110.

(7) The Character and Fitness Committee shall have the power to issue subpoenas and to assess costs as it shall determine necessary.

HISTORY: Amended by Order 2009–12, eff. 1–1–10; prior amendments eff. 2–1–00 (Order 99–1), 1–1–97 (Order 96–1), 8–1–92, 2–24–86, 1–1–78, 3–10–73

SCR 2.041   Immunity—Deleted

HISTORY: Deleted by Order 2001–2, eff. 1–1–02; adopted by Order 96–1, eff. 1–1–97

SCR 2.042   Conditional admission, restoration and reinstatement

(1) As a part of its certification process for all applicants, including applicants for restoration or reinstatement under SCR 3.500 or 3.510, the Character and Fitness Committee may require that an applicant enter into an agreement as a condition of his/her admission to the Bar. The conditions of admission, as determined by the Character and Fitness Committee, shall be set forth in a written agreement with specific terms and conditions. These terms and conditions shall be monitored by the Committee or its agents or designees.

(2) Upon failure to comply with the terms and conditions of the agreement, the Committee may:

(a) extend the term and impose additional condition(s).

(b) recommend to the Court revocation of the license to practice law.

(3) Additionally, in the event of failure to comply with the conditions of the agreement, or other conditions imposed by the Court upon admission, restoration or reinstatement, the Office of Bar Counsel may:

(a) request that the Court extend the term and impose additional condition(s).

(b) recommend to the Court revocation of the license to practice law.

(4) All information relating to conditional admission of an applicant or an attorney shall remain confidential in accordance with SCR 2.008.

(5) Any member whose license is revoked by the Court for failure to comply with the terms of a conditional admission agreement shall be deemed to have been subject to a disciplinary action and restoration or reinstatement shall be subject to the rules set forth in SCR 3.510.

HISTORY: Amended by Order 2006–09, eff. 1–1–07; prior amendments eff. 1–1–04 (Order 2003-4), 1–1–02 (Order 2001-2), 2–1–00 (Order 99–1); adopted by Order 96–1, eff. 1–1–97

SCR 2.050   Formal and informal hearings

In the event an area of concern appears, whether on the application or is discovered during the investigation process, the applicant may be requested to appear before one or more Committee member(s) for an informal hearing. Notice will be served on the applicant not less than fourteen days prior to said hearing.

At the discretion of the member(s) present at the informal hearing, a formal hearing before the full Committee may be required of the applicant. The applicant shall be given written notice of the date, time and place of said hearing not less than fourteen days prior to the hearing. The hearing shall be of record and the applicant may have counsel present and present testimony. The costs involved in this hearing shall be included with costs outlined in SCR 2.011.

At the time a formal hearing is requested, the applicant will be notified in writing that he/she may not sit for the bar examination unless a final decision is submitted by the Committee prior to the examination.

A written recommendation will be submitted by the Committee to the Court either recommending the applicant be certified from a character and fitness standpoint to sit for the bar examination or that the applicant be denied certification of character and fitness. The applicant shall be supplied a copy of the recommendation. If said recommendation results in denial of the applicant's certification to sit for the bar examination, the applicant has the right to appeal such decision, as noted in SCR 2.060.

HISTORY: Amended by Order 2001–2, eff. 1–1–02; adopted by Order 91–2, eff. 11–15–91

SCR 2.060   Committee's decision as to eligibility

The decision of the Character and Fitness Committee as to the eligibility of an applicant for admission to the Bar of this state shall be final unless, on motion by the applicant filed within 30 days after notice of an adverse decision has been mailed to applicant's last known address, the Supreme Court upon review of the record overrules such decision.

HISTORY: Amended by Order 99–1, eff. 2–1–00; prior amendments eff. 1–1–78, 3–10–73

SCR 2.062   Re-certification of character and fitness

Certification of character and fitness eligibility of the applicant shall be valid for a period of three years. An applicant whose certification of eligibility is granted three years or more from the date of the examination for which they are applying must apply for re-certification of character and fitness on a form provided by the Committee along with a fee of $200.00.

HISTORY: Adopted by Order 2001–2, eff. 1–1–02

SCR 2.070   Legal education—Deleted

HISTORY: Deleted by Order 2001–2, eff. 1–1–02; prior amendments eff. 2–1–00 (Order 99–1), 11–1–95 (Order 95–1), 11–15–91, 7–1–87, 7–5–85, 11–1–81, 1–1–78, 3–10–73

SCR 2.080   Bar examinations

(1) The Board of Bar Examiners shall examine such applicants as are certified to it as provided in Rule 2.040. The examination shall cover a period of two days and may cover the following subjects:

(a) Administrative Law and Administrative Procedure

(b) Conflict of Laws

(c) Contracts

(d) Constitutional Law

(e) Business Entities (corporations, partnerships and/or others)

(f) Criminal Law and Procedure

(g) Civil Procedure

(h) Domestic Relations

(i) Property (real and/or personal)

(j) Federal Taxation

(k) Torts

(l) Uniform Commercial Code (sales, secured transactions and/or negotiable instruments)

(m) Estates (wills and/or trusts)

(n) Evidence

(o) Such other subjects as the Board may select from among questions proposed by the National Conference of Bar Examiners.

Prior to or at the time of the examination, each applicant shall certify that he or she has successfully completed a course of study in law school in the subject of ethics, and that if admitted to practice, the applicant will adhere to the Code of Ethics prescribed by the Supreme Court. The Character and Fitness Committee of the Kentucky Office of Bar Admissions may, in exceptional cases, waive the requirement that an applicant have successfully completed a course of study in law school in the subject of ethics.

(2) The Board may cover the subject matter in any manner that it sees fit, including or not including the multi-state essay examinations, multi-state performance examinations and/or multi-state Bar examinations.

(3) The Board of Bar Examiners shall, thirty (30) days before each examination, report to the Supreme Court the method by which the examination shall be administered.

(4) An applicant must pass both the essay and Multistate (MBE) portions of the examination. A general average of 75% or higher on the essay portion of the examination shall be deemed a passing score on the essay portion of the examination. A scaled score of 132 or higher on the Multistate (MBE) portion of the examination shall be deemed a passing score on the Multistate portion of the examination. After failing to pass five (5) Kentucky Bar Examinations, an applicant shall not be permitted to sit for the Kentucky Bar Examination. An applicant who has failed only one portion of the exam must only reapply to sit for the failed portion; however, a passing score on one portion of the exam may only be used for a period of three years to exempt the applicant from taking that portion of the examination. An applicant who has taken the Multistate (MBE) examination in another jurisdiction within three years of the date of the Kentucky examination may transfer a score of 132 or higher and need only sit for the essay portion of the examination. In situations where the applicant has first passed the Kentucky essay portion of the examination, subsequently has taken the Multistate (MBE) examination in another jurisdiction, and wishes to be admitted by transferring in a score of 132 or higher that applicant must first file an update form for a character and fitness re-certification as prescribed in SCR 2.062.

(5) The Board of Bar Examiners at the beginning of the first session shall give each applicant a numbered envelope. The applicant shall write his/her name upon a slip of paper, seal the name in the envelope and return the envelope to the Secretary of the Board. All papers will then be signed by the applicant only with the number upon his/her envelope. When the applicant has completed answering the questions on any given subject, he/she shall deposit

his/her written answers thereto with the Secretary of the Board.

(6) The papers containing the questions and written answers given by applicants will be preserved by the Secretary of the Board for a period of one year from the time that the application for admission has passed upon by the Supreme Court, and longer if so ordered by the Court.

(7) Upon recommendation of the Board of Bar Examiners, the Supreme Court may appoint qualified members of the bar, to be known as Bar Examination Graders, to assist the Examiners in the grading of examination papers. Persons so appointed shall hold those positions for terms of one year and until the appointment of their successors.

HISTORY: Amended by Order 2009–12, eff. 1–1–10; prior amendment eff. 1–1–02 (Order 2001–2); adopted by Order 88–2, eff. 1–1–89

SCR 2.082   Non standard test accommodations

(1) The bar examination shall be administered by the Bar Examining authority to all eligible applicants in a manner that is fair and equitable.

(2) An applicant with a disability, who is eligible to take the bar examination, may file an application for reasonable non standard test accommodations. For the purpose of this rule disability shall be defined as a physical or mental impairment that; (a) substantially limits one or more major life activities, (b) substantially limits the ability of an applicant to demonstrate, under standard test conditions, the skills, abilities and knowledge tested on the Kentucky bar examination, (c) this applicant has a record of having, or (d) this applicant is regarded as having.

(3) An Application for Non Standard Test Accommodations shall be submitted on a form approved by the Board. The application forms may be obtained from the Kentucky Office of Bar Admissions.

(4) Individuals requesting non standard test accommodations shall submit a complete Application for Non Standard Test Accommodations, including all required supporting documentation by the filing deadlines prescribed in SCR 2.022(1).

(5) The Bar Examining authority shall make reasonable modification in the manner in which the examination is administered to an applicant with a disability whose application for non standard test accommodations has been approved by the Board, while maintaining the security and integrity of the examination.

(6) An emergency request for non standard accommodations may be filed after the prescribed deadlines stated above if the applicant did not have the disability at the time of filing the application to take the bar examination. Due to processing complexities, an emergency request may not be granted if; a) time constraints preclude the applicant from being able to provide necessary justification for the accommodations sought, or b) there is insufficient time for the bar examining authority to properly evaluate the applicant's request or make the necessary arrangements for the non-standard test accommodations.

HISTORY: Adopted by Order 2001–2, eff. 1–1–02

SCR 2.085   Approval of certificate of admission to practice law

(1) When an applicant has passed an examination as provided by Rule 2.080, the Board of Bar Examiners shall certify that fact to the Supreme Court together with a recommendation that the applicant be admitted to practice law. The Court may approve or disapprove the recommendations and, if approved, shall authorize the Clerk of the Court to issue a certificate of admission.

(2) When the Character and Fitness Committee determines that an applicant is eligible for admission to the Kentucky Bar without examination, the Committee's recommendation as provided for in Rule 2.040(6) shall be certified to the Supreme Court, and the recommendation for admission to the practice of law shall be considered as set forth in paragraph (1) of this rule.

(3) When the Supreme Court has granted approval for the issuance of a certificate of admission based upon the recommendation submitted under paragraph (1) or (2), the applicant must be admitted to the Kentucky Bar within two years of said date. If an applicant fails to be admitted within the two-year period, the applicant must make new application for admission.

HISTORY: Adopted by Order 2001–2, eff. 1–1–02

SCR 2.090   Bar examinations—Deleted

HISTORY: Deleted by Order 2001–2, eff. 1–1–02; prior amendments eff. 2–1–00 (Order 99–1), 11–15–91 (Order 91–2), 1–1–89, 1–1–88, 2–24–86, 7–5–85, 7–1–84, 11–1–81, 2–1–81, 5–1–80, 1–1–78, 3–6–74, 3–10–73, 3–26–71

SCR 2.091   Special testing accommodations—Deleted

HISTORY: Deleted by Order 2001–2, eff. 1–1–02; adopted by Order 96–1, eff. 1–1–97

SCR 2.095   Approval of certificate of admission to practice law—Deleted

HISTORY: Deleted by Order 2001–2, eff. 1–1–02; prior amendments eff. 3–1–98 (Order 97–3), 2–24–86 (Order 86–2), 7–5–85, 11–1–81, 7–1–79, 1–1–78, 3–10–73

SCR 2.100   Requirement of admission to practice law; prerequisites—Deleted

HISTORY: Deleted by Order 2001–2, eff. 1–1–02; prior amendments eff. 2–1–00 (Order 99–1), 8–1–92 (Order 92–1), 1–1–89, 2–24–86, 11–1–81; adopted eff. 7–1–79

SCR 2.110　Admission without examination

(1) Any person who has been admitted to the highest Court of the District of Columbia or some sister state and who has been engaged in the active practice of law, in a state or jurisdiction which has reciprocity or comity with Kentucky, for five of the seven years next preceding the filing of an application may be admitted to the bar of this state without examination provided the applicant meets all requirements for admission to the bar under these Rules. Active engagement in the teaching of the law shall be considered active engagement in the practice of law.

(2) An attorney applying for admission under this Rule shall file with the Kentucky Office of Bar Admissions, on the form provided for application for admission, such information as shall be requested thereon accompanied by a fee of twelve hundred dollars ($1200), no part of which shall be refunded. An applicant shall file with the Character and Fitness Committee such other affidavits, certificates, documents and materials as shall be required to satisfy the Committee of the applicant's good moral character and fitness to be a member of the bar of this state. With respect to character and fitness, the Character and Fitness Committee shall process such applications pursuant to Rule 2.040.

(3) Admission under this Rule shall be conditioned on the applicant establishing that the district or state from which the applicant applies and in which the applicant performs the major portion of his or her professional activities has rules or other provisions providing for admission without examination and by reciprocity or comity which are no more restrictive than the rules of this Commonwealth.

(4) Notwithstanding the requirements stated above, if the applicant has practiced five of the last seven years in a jurisdiction that permits the admission without examination of attorneys from Kentucky, the Character & Fitness Committee may approve admission without examination under the same provisions that allow admission of Kentucky attorneys.

HISTORY: Amended by Order 2012–01, eff. 3–1–12; prior amendments eff. 1–1–10 (Order 2009–12), 1–1–04 (Order 2003–4), 1–1–02 (Order 2001–2), 2–1–00 (Order 99–1), 8–1–92 (Order 92–1), 11–15–91, 1–1–88, 2–24–86, 7–1–81, 1–1–78, 9–24–75, 3–6–74, 3–10–73.

SCR 2.111　Limited certificate of admission to practice law

(1) Every attorney not a member of the Bar of this Commonwealth who performs legal services in this Commonwealth solely for his/her employer, its parent, subsidiary, or affiliated entities, shall file with the Kentucky Office of Bar Admissions on a form provided, an application for limited certificate of admission to practice law in this Commonwealth. Such application shall be reviewed by the Character and Fitness Committee. If approved, a limited certificate of admission to practice law shall be granted, and shall be effective as of the date such application is approved, provided that the following prerequisites are satisfied.

(a) The applicant must be admitted to practice in the highest court of another state or the District of Columbia, and be a member in good standing at the Bar of such court, or in such state, at the time of filing such application.

(b) The attorney applying for limited certificate of admission to practice law shall sign a sworn statement certifying to the Court that:

(i) He/she has completed the study of law in an accredited law school;

(ii) He/she has been admitted to practice in the highest Court of another state or the District of Columbia;

(iii) He/she is presently in good standing at the Bar of such Court, or such state;

(iv) He/she will perform legal services in this Commonwealth solely for his employer, its parent, subsidiary, or affiliated entities.

(c) A statement signed by a representative of such applicant's employer stating that such applicant is an employee for such employer, and performs legal services in this Commonwealth for such employer, its parent, subsidiary, or affiliated entities, shall be filed with the application.

(2) Such applicant shall pay to the Kentucky Office of Bar Admissions, at the time of submission of such application a fee of one thousand dollars ($1,000) and shall make payment of the current annual dues or fees to the Kentucky Bar Association, as authorized under SCR 3.040.

(3) Upon granting of such limited certificate of admission to practice law, and issuance of said limited certificate by the Clerk of the Supreme Court of Kentucky, such applicant shall be and shall remain, during the period the limited certificate of admission to practice law remains in effect, an active member of the Kentucky Bar Association, subject to all duties and obligations of members admitted under SCR 2.110, SCR 2.120, and SCR 3.661.

(4) The only restrictions and limitations applicable to such membership in the Kentucky Bar Association and to such attorney's right to practice in this Commonwealth shall be:

(a) Such attorney shall perform legal services in this Commonwealth solely for his employer, its parent, subsidiary, or affiliated entities, and shall not provide legal services in this Commonwealth, to any other individual or entity.

(b) Such attorney shall not appear as attorney of record for his employer, its parent, subsidiary or affiliated entities, in any case or matter pending before the Courts of this Commonwealth, without first engaging a member of the Association, admitted under SCR 2.120 or SCR 2.110, as co-counsel, whose presence shall be necessary, when required by the

Court, at all trials or other times specified by the Court. Nothing herein shall prevent such attorney from appearing on his/her own behalf or representing himself/herself in any case or matter to which he/she is a party, or appearing in the Small Claims Division of the District Court as otherwise provided in Rule 3.020.

(5) The performance of legal services in this Commonwealth solely for such attorney's employer, its parent, subsidiary, or affiliated entities, following admission to the Kentucky Bar on a limited certificate shall be considered to be the active engagement in the practice of law for all purposes.

(6) The limited certificate of admission to practice law in this Commonwealth shall expire if such attorney is granted a certificate of admission to practice, or is admitted to the Bar of this Commonwealth under any other rule of this Court, or if such attorney ceases to be an employee for the employer or its parent, subsidiary, or affiliated entities, listed on such attorney's application, whichever shall first occur; *provided, however,* that if such attorney, within thirty (30) days of ceasing to be an employee for the employer or its parent, subsidiary, or affiliated entities listed on such attorney's application, becomes employed by another employer for which such attorney shall solely perform legal services, such attorney may maintain his admission under this Rule by promptly filing with the Clerk of the Supreme Court a statement to such effect, stating the date on which his prior employment ceased and his new employment commenced, identifying his new employer and reaffirming that he shall not provide legal services, in this Commonwealth, to any other individual or entity. In the event that the employment of an attorney admitted under this rule shall cease with no subsequent employment by a successor employer within thirty (30) days, such attorney shall promptly file with the Clerk of the Supreme Court a statement to such effect, stating the date that such employment ceased.

(7) Except as specifically limited herein, the rules, rights and privileges governing the practice of law shall be applicable to an attorney admitted under this Rule.

HISTORY: Amended by Order 2009–12, eff. 1–1–10; prior amendments eff. 1–1–04 (Order 2003–4), 1–1–02 (Order 2001–2), 2–1–00 (Order 99–1), 8–1–92 (Order 92–1), 1–13–86; adopted eff. 7–5–85

SCR 2.112 Attorney participants in defender or legal services programs

(a) **Scope.** This rule applies to an attorney who is not a member of the Bar of this Commonwealth but who, after having completed the study of law in a law school approved by the American Bar Association or by the Association of American Law Schools and having been admitted to practice in the highest Court of another state, wishes to become an employee of an organized public defender program or an organized legal services program in this Commonwealth providing legal assistance to indigent persons.

(b) **General Rule.** An attorney to whom this rule applies shall be admitted to practice before the Courts of this Commonwealth in all matters in which the attorney is associated with an organized public defender program or an organized legal services program which program is sponsored, approved or recognized by the Kentucky Bar Association. Admission to practice under this rule shall be limited to the matters specified in the preceding sentence. An application for admission to practice under this rule shall include or be accompanied by:

(1) A certificate of the highest Court or agency of any other state having jurisdiction over admission to the bar and the practice of law stating that the applicant is in good standing at the bar of such Court or in such state.

(2) A statement signed by a representative of an organized public defender program showing compliance with paragraph (a) of this rule. Any such statement shall also contain an undertaking by the program to notify the Clerk of the Supreme Court immediately whenever the attorney ceases to be an employee of such program.

(3) Such other affidavits or materials as shall be deemed necessary by the Character and Fitness Committee in order to satisfy the Committee of the applicant's moral character and fitness to practice before the Courts of this Commonwealth.

(4) Payment of a fee of one hundred dollars ($100.00) made payable to the Kentucky Office of Bar Admissions (cashier's or certified check or money order).

(c) **Subscription and Action.** The application for admission shall be subscribed to by a member of the bar of this Commonwealth in good standing. If the application and related documents are in proper order and if the Character and Fitness Committee finds that the applicant has the moral character and fitness to practice before the Courts of this Commonwealth, the Clerk of the Supreme Court shall enter the name of the applicant upon the docket of persons specially admitted to the bar of this Commonwealth subject to the restrictions of this rule and shall issue an appropriate certificate in evidence thereof.

(d) **Expiration of Admission.** When an attorney admitted under this rule ceases to be associated in a program as set forth in the motion previously filed, a written statement to that effect shall be filed with the Clerk of the Supreme Court by a representative of the public defender program or legal services program. Admission to practice under this rule shall expire after eighteen months, or when the attorney ceases to be an employee of the program, whichever shall first occur.

(e) **Rules Governing the Practice of Law.** Except for Rules 2.110 and 3.030(2), the Rules governing the practice of law shall be applicable to an attorney admitted under this rule.

HISTORY: Amended by Order 2009–12, eff. 1–1–10; prior amendments eff. 1–1–02 (Order 2001–2), 2–1–00 (Order 99–1), 3–1–98 (Order 97–3), 10–1–94 (Order 94–1), 2–24–86; adopted eff. 6–1–79

SCR 2.115 Qualification, compensation, expenses, and assistants of board of bar examiners and committee on character and fitness—Deleted

HISTORY: Deleted by Order 2001–2, eff. 1–1–02; prior amendments eff. 1–1–78, 3–10–73

SCR 2.120 Administration of oath and issuance of certificate of admission to practice law

An applicant approved for admission under SCR 2.085, 2.110, 2.111 or 2.112 must apply for and be granted a certificate of admission prior to engaging in the practice of law in this state. As prerequisites for the issuance of such a certificate an applicant shall pay the current annual dues or fees of the Kentucky Bar Association authorized under SCR 3.040, pay a fee of fifty dollars ($50.00) to the Kentucky Office of Bar Admissions, and shall be administered the Constitutional Oath of Office either by a Justice of the Supreme Court or by the Clerk of the Supreme Court. Upon completion of the prerequisites, the Clerk shall deliver to the applicant a Certificate of Admission on a form approved by the Court, and the issuance of the certificate shall be duly recorded by the Clerk.

HISTORY: Amended by Order 2012–01, eff. 3–1–12; prior amendment eff. 1–1–10 (Order 2009–12), 1–1–02 (Order 2001–2); adopted by Order 86–2, eff. 2–24–86

SCR 2.300 Reinstatement of persons to practice law scope and purpose of reinstatement guidelines

Scope and Purpose of Reinstatement Guidelines.

The guidelines set forth in SCR 2.300 apply to applications for reinstatement filed by any person who has been suspended from the practice of law, who seeks reinstatement under the provisions of SCR 3.510, and whose application is referred by the Kentucky Bar Association to the Office of Bar Admissions, Character and Fitness Committee.

These guidelines have been formulated to govern the manner in which Reinstatement Applications are processed so that all parties, including the public at large, are insured that a systematic and thorough character and fitness investigation is conducted and applicants are assured that their applications are addressed in a timely and procedurally consistent manner.

(1) Initial Reinstatement Application Process:

(a) The initial forms necessary to apply for reinstatement may be obtained from the Kentucky Bar Association. Completed applications for reinstatement, along with the necessary fees, must be delivered or mailed to the Kentucky Bar Association in accordance with SCR 3.500 and SCR 3.510.

(b) Any applicant for reinstatement who is a member of the bar in any other jurisdiction must provide, along with the application, a statement from the disciplinary authority of each jurisdiction listing any complaint or charge that has been filed against the applicant and its disposition. Reciprocal discipline, based on a Kentucky disciplinary order, shall also be disclosed.

(c) Any applicant who is permanently disbarred in another jurisdiction is not eligible to apply for reinstatement in Kentucky.

(d) Upon receipt of a complete application for reinstatement and payment of necessary fees by an applicant who has been suspended more than one hundred eighty (180) days (and in some cases where the suspension has been less than one hundred eighty (180) days) the Kentucky Bar Association will refer the application to the Kentucky Office of Bar Admissions, Character and Fitness Committee for investigation, for a hearing, if necessary, and for a formal recommendation regarding the disposition of the application in accordance with SCR 3.500, SCR 3.505, and SCR 3.510.

(e) Upon receipt of a Reinstatement Application from the Kentucky Bar Association, the Kentucky Office of Bar Admissions, Character and Fitness Committee will immediately send the applicant an Application for Admission to the Bar. The applicant must complete that form and return it to the Character and Fitness Committee with documentation specified in instructions accompanying the application.

(f) The submission of an incomplete application or the failure of an applicant to submit necessary documentation and/or fees will delay the Character and Fitness Committee's ability to render a timely recommendation. Failure of an applicant to submit the application for admission to the Bar within thirty (30) days or failure of an applicant to perfect an application within thirty (30) days of the date a notice of deficiency is sent to the applicant by the Committee may result in an unfavorable recommendation.

(2) Investigative Process:

Upon receipt of a fully complete application the Character and Fitness Committee will immediately begin the necessary investigatory process, which may or may not involve the use of independent investigators. During this initial investigative period the applicant will be notified that he/she has sixty (60) days to obtain and submit any additional evidence he/she wants considered. The initial sixty (60) day period may be extended upon proper justification being submitted to the Committee in a written request by the applicant.

(3) Informal Hearings:

At the conclusion of the investigative period a member of the Character and Fitness Committee, or a designee appointed by the Committee, may elect to conduct an informal hearing in an effort to clarify or narrow issues. The informal hearing proceeding shall not be stenographically reported and sworn testimony shall not be taken.

The applicant shall be given written notice of the date, time and place of any informal hearing. Notice shall be given no less than fourteen days before the hearing. Failure of the Applicant to fully cooperate with and participate in the informal hearing process shall be a basis for an unfavorable recommendation regarding the application for readmission.

(4) Formal Hearings:

(a) At the conclusion of the investigative period, and following the informal hearing, if one is held, the applicant and Kentucky Bar Association Counsel will be given a right to request a formal hearing before the Committee pursuant to SCR 3.505(3). If a formal hearing is not requested, the Committee may elect to hold a hearing or act upon the evidence of record and issue a decision within sixty (60) days of the day the parties decline a formal hearing.

(b) If the applicant or Bar Counsel requests a formal hearing then such a hearing will be held within sixty (60) days of the request. Notice of the hearing date will be served on the parties not less than fourteen days before said hearing. The hearing shall be of record and the applicant may have counsel present and present testimony. The costs involved in this hearing shall be included with costs outlined in SCR 2.040(7) and will be paid by the applicant.

(c) The Character and Fitness Committee shall, at the hearing, inquire fully into all matters at issue, and shall not be bound by common law or statutory rules of evidence, or by technical or formal rules of procedure. The Committee shall receive into evidence the testimony of the witnesses and parties, the evidence of record, and such additional evidence as may be submitted. However, the Committee may entertain the objections of any party to the evidence submitted under this section.

(d) The conduct of the hearings and the order in which allegations and evidence shall be presented shall be within the discretion of the Character and Fitness Committee.

(5) Formal Recommendation:

Following the Formal Hearing if there are material factual disputes, the Character and Fitness Committee must resolve them by making findings of fact. Such findings of fact must be supported by the existence or absence of clear and convincing evidence. Such findings will be set forth in a formal recommendation. A formal recommendation will be issued within thirty (30) days of the date of receipt of the hearing transcript.

(6) Burden of Proof:

While the burden of proof in a disciplinary proceeding rests with the KBA, in reinstatement cases the applicant has the burden of proving by clear and convincing evidence that he/she possesses the requisite character, fitness and moral qualification for readmission to the practice of law. (SCR 3.330) Issues that will be considered include, but are not limited to, the following:

(a) Whether the applicant has presented clear and convincing evidence that he/she has complied with every term of the order of suspension or disbarment.

(b) Whether the applicant has presented clear and convincing evidence that his/her conduct while under suspension shows that he/she is worthy of the trust and confidence of the public.

(c) Whether the applicant has presented clear and convincing evidence that he/she possesses sufficient professional capabilities to serve the public as a lawyer.

(d) Whether the applicant has presented clear and convincing evidence that he/she presently exhibits good moral character.

(e) Whether the applicant has presented clear and convincing evidence that he/she appreciates the wrongfulness of his/her prior misconduct, that he/she has manifest contrition for his/her prior professional misconduct, and has rehabilitated himself/herself from past derelictions.

Failure to meet any of these criteria may constitute a sufficient basis for denial of a petitioner's application.

(7) Presumptions and Weight of Evidence:

A petitioner for reinstatement will be held to a substantially more rigorous standard than a first time applicant for an initial admission to the Bar. The prior determination that he/she engaged in professional misconduct continues to be evidence against him or her and the proof presented must be sufficient to overcome that prior adverse judgment.

Among the considerations to be weighed are:

The nature of the misconduct for which the applicant was suspended or disbarred.

The applicant's conception of the serious nature of his or her act.

The applicant's sense of wrongdoing.

The applicant's previous and subsequent conduct and attitude toward the courts and the practice, including the element of time elapsed since disbarment.

The applicant's candor in dealing with the Character and Fitness Committee.

The relevant knowledge of witnesses called by the applicant.

HISTORY: Amended by Order 2012–01, eff. 3–1–12; prior amendment eff. 1–1–10 (Order 2009–12); adopted by Order 99–1, eff. 2–1–00

SCR 2.540   Limited student practice

Any student who has successfully completed two-thirds of the academic hour requirement for the first degree in law at an approved law school and is participating in a law school sponsored clinic, intern, extern, or public service program may provide legal services to, and may appear in any proceeding in any court of this state on behalf of any person financially unable to employ counsel, or, on behalf of the Commonwealth or the United States' Attorney; and any student who has successfully completed two-thirds of the academic hour requirements for the first degree in law may provide legal advice, counseling and negotiation services to a college or university student, regardless of that student's financial status, pursuant to an approved law school clinical program provided:

(a) Such student is providing such services to, or appearing in such proceeding on behalf of, a person assigned to the student through a clinic, intern, extern, or public service program operated by an approved law school under the direction of a full or part time law school director.

(b) The Chief Justice of the Supreme Court of Kentucky, the dean of the student's law school, and the director of the law school program in which such student is participating, have filed written approval of such student with the clerk of the Supreme Court, the clerk of the courts before which the student is to appear, and the clerk of the circuit court in the county wherein the student's law school is located.

(c) A member in good standing of the bar of this state personally supervises all activities of the student in each case, with the exception that the student may consult with the client or potential clients, but may not advise, negotiate or appear alone in administrative proceedings or in the courts of this state in civil or criminal matters without personal appearance and supervision by a member in good standing of the bar of this state, and as otherwise provided in this Rule.

In all criminal cases involving crime for which the defendant may be punished by a fine of more than $500.00 or by confinement for more than twelve months, personal supervision of the activities of the student requires that a member in good standing of the bar of this state be present for all proceedings which take place before a judge.

In the defense of any criminal case which involves a crime for which the defendant may be punished by a fine of more than $500.00 or by confinement for more than twelve months, and which is to be prosecuted in a county not having a formal public defender program, the attorney who is to supervise the student must be appointed by the judge of the court before whom the cause is pending.

No student authorized to perform legal services under this Rule shall ask for or receive any compensation or remuneration of any kind for the services. This Rule does not prevent a law school from awarding scholarships or fellowships to a law student authorized to perform legal services under this Rule.

Unless earlier revoked, approval to perform legal services under this Rule shall be effective until the Monday following the distribution of results of the first bar examination for which an approved law graduate could be admitted to practice under the Rules of the Court.

Any student authorized to perform legal services under this Rule must subscribe to the following oath.

OATH OF LEGAL INTERN UNDER STUDENT PRACTICE RULE

I, _____, do solemnly swear that I will, as a Legal Intern, support and defend the Constitution of the United States and the Constitution of the State of Kentucky; that cognizant of the trust placed in me and the responsibility it carries, I will conduct myself in all matters to the extent given me as an officer of the court with the utmost fidelity toward the court and all persons whose affairs are in any way entrusted to me; that I will neither take part in deception of the court, nor allow deception to take place, and should any be practiced will inform the court; that I will accept no remuneration for services performed as a Legal Intern except those specifically provided by the Rules of the Supreme Court; that I subscribe to and will abide by the Rules of Professional Conduct as adopted by the Supreme Court of Kentucky; and that I will so exercise these privileges given me that it may be alike useful in the service of justice and in my preparation to assume full responsibility later as a member of the bar.

The above and foregoing Oath was subscribed to by the above named Legal Intern and administered to him/her by me, on this _____ day of _____, 19___.

Notary Public

HISTORY: Amended by Order 99–1, eff. 2–1–00; prior amendments eff. 3–1–98 (Order 97–4), 3–1–98 (Order 97–3), 10–1–94 (Order 94–1), 7–1–78, 1–1–78

SCR 2.550   Repeal of previous rules—Deleted

HISTORY: Deleted by Order of Supreme Court, eff. 1–1–78

III PRACTICE OF LAW

SCR 3.010 General definitions

As used throughout this Rule 3, the following definitions shall apply unless the context clearly requires a different meaning:

"Association" is the Kentucky Bar Association.

"Attorney" is a person licensed or authorized to practice law.

"Board" is the Board of Governors of the Association.

"Bylaws" means the bylaws of the Association.

"Charge" means the pleading by which the Association charges an attorney with unprofessional conduct.

"Circuit clerk" is the clerk of the court of respondent's present or last known residence.

"Clerk" is the Clerk of the Supreme Court of Kentucky.

"Committee" means the Committee on Character and Fitness as defined in Rule 2.040.

"Complainant" means the party who causes to be initiated an investigation of an attorney, or who causes to be initiated a proceeding under Rule 3.160. The complainant may be a person or entity.

"Court" is the Supreme Court of Kentucky.

"Director" is the Director of the Association.

"District" means a prescribed geographical and political area of the state.

"Governor" is an elected member of the board.

"Law student" means any person enrolled in an approved law school who has successfully completed the first year therein.

"Member" means an attorney in good standing as required by the rules of the court.

"Officer" means a member elected or appointed pursuant to the rules.

"President" is the President of the Association.

"President–Elect" is the President–Elect of the Association.

"Registrar" is the Registrar of the Association.

"Respondent" is an attorney against whom a charge is filed.

"Rules" are the rules of the Court.

"Section" means a body of members actively interested in and promoting improvements in a particular branch of law.

"Time" is computed as under the Rules of Civil Procedure.

"Treasurer" is the Treasurer of the Association.

"Trial commissioner" means the commissioner appointed pursuant to the provisions of Rule 3.230 and other rules governing disciplinary procedures.

"Vice–President" is the Vice–President of the Association.

HISTORY: Amended by Order 2005–10, eff. 1–1–06; prior amendments eff. 1–1–04 (Order 2003–4), 11–15–91 (Order 91–2), 9–15–90, 4–1–82, 7–1–78, 1–1–78, 7–2–71

SCR 3.020 Practice of law defined

The practice of law is any service rendered involving legal knowledge or legal advice, whether of representation, counsel or advocacy in or out of court, rendered in respect to the rights, duties, obligations, liabilities, or business relations of one requiring the services. But nothing herein shall prevent any natural person not holding himself out as a practicing attorney from drawing any instrument to which he is a party without consideration unto himself therefor. An appearance in the small claims division of the district court by a person who is an officer of or who is regularly employed in a managerial capacity by a corporation or partnership which is a party to the litigation in which the appearance is made shall not be considered as unauthorized practice of law.

HISTORY: Amended eff. 11–1–78; prior amendment eff. 7–2–71

SCR 3.022 Forms of practice of law

Lawyers may engage in the practice of law in Kentucky in the following forms:

a. As sole practitioners;

b. As employees of a private corporation, a United States government agency or department, or a state, county or municipal government agency, a legal aid society, or a corporation organized to provide public defender services (but if for a private corporation, may render professional services in that employment only for the employing corporation and its subsidiaries and not the general public; except pro bono or legal aid);

c. As instructors or professors of law in a law school located in Kentucky;

d. As a judge of the Court of Justice, a federal court or as an administrative law judge in federal or state government;

e. As employees or general partners of a Kentucky general partnership organized for the practice of law;

f. As employees of or partners, shareholders, members or co-owners of a registered limited liability partnership, professional service corporation, or limited liability company or any other limited liability entity organized pursuant to applicable statutes.

Subject to judicial or prosecutorial immunity which may be recognized by law, each lawyer practicing law in Kentucky shall be personally liable and accountable to his or her clients for (i) all of his or her acts, errors, and omissions in the practice of law; and (ii) the acts, errors, and omissions of other lawyers under such lawyer's direct supervision.

HISTORY: Adopted by Order 99–1, eff. 2–1–00

SCR 3.024   Requirements of practicing law in limited liability entities

Lawyers may engage in the practice of law as a partner, shareholder, member, manager, co-owner or employee of a registered limited liability partnership, professional service corporation, limited liability company or any other limited liability entity recognized by the Commonwealth so long as such entity maintains at all times adequate professional liability insurance in force and effect or has established and maintains at all times other acceptable forms of adequate financial coverage for the acts, errors and omissions of its partners, shareholders, members, managers, co-owners and employees arising out of the performance of legal services.

For purposes of the preceding sentence, "adequate insurance" shall mean one or more policies of lawyers professional liability insurance which shall insure the limited liability entity and its individual owners and employees. The insurance shall be in an amount of at least $50,000 per claim, multiplied by the number of attorneys of the limited liability entity, with an aggregate maximum limit of liability per policy year for all claims in the amount of at least $100,000, multiplied by the number of attorneys of the limited liability entity, provided that i) the minimum insurance coverage that a limited liability entity shall be required to carry is $250,000 per claim and $500,000 for all claims during the policy year and ii) no limited liability entity shall be required to carry insurance in excess of $5,000,000 per claim and $10,000,000 for all claims during the policy year. Each co-owner of a limited liability entity shall remain jointly and severally liable for acts, errors and omissions excluded from coverage by such insurance policies, but in no event shall that joint and several liability exceed, for each claim and for all claims during the policy year, an amount (net of the payment of any insurance claims in such year) equal to the minimum amount of coverage per claim and for all claims during the policy year described in the second sentence of this paragraph.

For purposes of this Rule, a limited liability entity has established "other acceptable forms of adequate financial coverage" if the limited liability entity provides funds (in amounts no less than as described in the next sentence) specifically designated and segregated for the satisfaction of judgments against the limited liability entity and/or the co-owners by:

1. deposit in trust, or in bank escrow of cash, bank certificates of deposit, or United States Treasury obligations; or

2. a bank letter of credit, or

3. a surety bond to be payable to any person presenting a valid final judgment of any court of competent jurisdiction in the Commonwealth of Kentucky, or a foreign judgment registered in a Kentucky federal court, or a settlement or mediation award for acts, errors and omissions arising out of the performance of professional legal services by the limited liability entity. The funds required to be so designated and segregated shall be no less than $50,000 multiplied by the number of attorneys employed by the limited liability entity, with the minimum amounts of funding for the year to be no less than $250,000 and the maximum limit of funding for the year shall not be required to exceed $5,000,000.

Nothing in this Rule shall relieve a co-owner of a limited liability entity from personal liability for the acts, errors and omissions committed by such individual or any person under his or her direct supervision and control arising out of the performance of professional legal services.

HISTORY: Adopted by Order 99–1, eff. 2–1–00

SCR 3.025   Kentucky Bar Association

The mission and purpose of the association is to maintain a proper discipline of the members of the bar in accordance with these rules and with the principles of the legal profession as a public calling, to initiate and supervise, with the approval of the court, appropriate means to insure a continuing high standard of professional competence on the part of the members of the bar, and to bear a substantial and continuing responsibility for promoting the efficiency and improvement of the judicial system.

HISTORY: Adopted by Order 80–3, eff. 12–31–80

SCR 3.026   Local divisions of the Kentucky Bar Association

(1) Members of the Association who reside in any judicial circuit may elect to form a local Bar Association which shall, upon approval by the Board as provided herein, become a division of the Association.

(2) A local Bar Association which elects to become a division of the Association may be organized as an unincorporated association.

(3) In order for a local Bar Association to become a division of the Association, the local Bar Association, in conjunction with the chief judge of the judicial circuit, must submit for approval by the Board a copy of by-laws adopted by majority vote of the members of the proposed local Bar Association. Such by-laws may contain any provisions not inconsistent with SCR 3 and must contain the following:

(a) a definition of the geographic area encompassed by the local Bar Association;

(b) a provision that any member of the Association who desires to join the local Bar Association may do so;

(c) a statement of the purposes for which the local Bar Association is organized;

(d) provisions defining the officers and governing body of the local Bar Association and their respective duties and providing for the election of such officers and members of such governing body at least bi-annually;

(e) provisions establishing the place and time of meetings of the local Bar Association and the manner of notifying members of the local Bar Association of such meetings;

(f) a statement that, notwithstanding any other provision of the by-laws, the activities of the local Bar Association shall, at all times, conform to the standards established by SCR 3;

(g) provisions establishing the manner of assessing and collecting dues for membership in the local Bar Association and setting forth the purposes for which the dues may be used;

(h) provisions for the manner of amendment of the by-laws.

(4) Upon approval of the by-laws of any proposed local Bar Association, the Board shall issue a charter upon which the local Bar Association is chartered as a division of the Association.

HISTORY: Adopted by Order 88–4, eff. 1–1–89

SCR 3.030   Membership, practice by nonmembers and classes of membership

(1) All persons admitted to the practice of law in this state shall be, and they are, members of the association upon the completion of the prerequisites under Rule 2.100.

(2) A person admitted to practice in another state, but not in this state, shall be permitted to practice a case in this state only if that attorney subjects himself or herself to the jurisdiction and rules of the Supreme Court of Kentucky, pays a one time per case fee of two hundred seventy dollars ($270.00) to the Kentucky Bar Association and engages a member of the association as co-counsel, whose presence shall be necessary at all trials and at other times when required by the court. No motion for permission to practice in any state court in this jurisdiction shall be granted without submission to the admitting court of a certification from the Kentucky Bar Association of receipt of this fee.

(3) The association, by its bylaws, may create honorary memberships. All other attorneys shall be active members.

(4) A new class of membership is established to be known as "Senior Retired Inactive Member." Any member who reaches the age of 70 years and no longer is actively practicing law and who has met the necessary CLE requirements for inactive status pursuant to SCR 3.666(2), shall upon notification to the

Executive Director be classified as Senior Retired Inactive and shall not be required to pay annual dues.

HISTORY: Amended by Order 2012–01, eff. 3–1–12; prior amendments eff. 1–1–05 (Order 2004–5), 1–1–02 (Order 2001–2), 4–1–82 (Order 82–1), 1–1–78, 7–2–71

SCR 3.040   Dues: date of payment and amount

(1) On or before July 1 of each year every member of the Association, including every justice or judge of the Kentucky Court of Justice and United States judge in or who is appointed from or maintains a residence in Kentucky, except board-designated honorary members, shall be assessed dues for the ensuing twelve months. Dues shall be fixed by the Supreme Court on recommendation of the Board. Dues shall be paid to the treasurer on or before September 1 of each year.

(2) Any member of the association shall be relieved of the payment of dues for any fiscal year in which the member serves actively for a period of not less than six months in the armed services of the United States of America, other than as a career member of the armed forces.

(3) The class of membership designated Senior Retired Inactive Member, established by the Supreme Court in SCR 3.030, shall not be required to pay annual dues.

(4) Any member of the bar may apply in writing to the Kentucky Bar Association to be relieved of the payment of dues by reason of undue hardship arising from disability, sickness or financial condition. The application shall be copied to the Governors from the district in which the attorney lives, who may or may not recommend in writing to the President that such relief be granted, giving the reasons therefor. Thereupon the President shall have the authority to rule on the application and to notify the Treasurer by written order that the attorney is relieved of the payment of dues. The President shall file the order with the registrar along with the recommendation(s) of the Governor(s).

HISTORY: Amended by Order 2012–01, eff. 3–1–12; prior amendments eff. 1–1–02 (Order 2001–2), 4–1–82 (Order 82–1), 2–1–81, 2–1–78, 1–1–78, 10–14–74, 7–2–71

SCR 3.050   Collection of dues; suspension for non-payment

If dues are not paid on or before September 1, then an additional late payment fee of fifty dollars ($50.00) shall be assessed. On or before September 15 of each year, the Treasurer shall notify a member in writing of his or her delinquency and late fee. On or before October 15 of each year, the Treasurer shall in writing certify to the Board the names of all members who remain delinquent. The Board shall cause to be sent to the member a notice of delinquency by certified mail, return receipt requested, at the member's bar roster address. Such notice shall require the member to show cause within thirty (30) days from the date of the mailing why the member's law license should not be suspended for failure to pay dues and the late fee. In addition, such notice shall inform the member that if such dues and late fee, as well as costs in the amount of fifty ($50.00), are not paid within thirty (30) days, or unless good cause is shown within thirty (30) days that a suspension should not occur, the lawyer will be stricken from the membership roster as an active member of the KBA and suspended from the practice of law. At the conclusion of the thirty (30) days, unless the dues, late fees and additional costs payment have been received, or unless good cause has been shown as to why the member should not be suspended, the Board of Governors will vote to suspend any such member from the practice of law. A copy of the suspension notice shall be sent by the Director to the member, the Clerk of the Supreme Court of Kentucky, the Director of Membership, and the Circuit Clerk of the member's roster address district for recording and indexing. The suspended member may apply for restoration to membership under the provisions of SCR 3.500. A member may appeal to the Supreme Court of Kentucky from such suspension within thirty (30) days of the date the suspension notice is recorded in the membership records. Such appeal shall include an affidavit showing good cause why the suspension should be revoked.

HISTORY: Amended by Order 2012–01, eff. 3–1–12; prior amendments eff. 1–1–04 (Order 2003–4), 2–1–00 (Order 99–1), 9–15–90 (Order 90–1), 1–1–78, 10–14–74, 7–2–71

SCR 3.060   Records to show status of members

(1) The records of the association shall show the status as to membership and standing of each member and former member of the association. Specifically, those records shall show at least the following data:

(a) As to each present member of the association concerning whom the information is known, and as to each new member hereafter admitted, the date of his admission to the bar and where the court's order granting such admission may be found.

(b) When known, the year of each member's death.

(c) The fact and date of each honorary membership, the reason therefor, and, when the honorary membership terminates, the fact and date of such termination and the reason therefor.

(d) The final disposition of each motion to resign, and where the court's order finally disposing of each such motion may be found, and, where the motion to resign is sustained, the effective date of the resignation.

(e) The effective date of each disbarment, suspension and reinstatement and where the court's judgment or order of disbarment, suspension or reinstatement may be found, and in the case of suspension, the length of time for which the respondent has been suspended.

(f) In the case of any disciplinary action other than disbarment or suspension (as, for instance, public reprimand), the date when such disciplinary action was ordered, where the court's judgment or order directing such disciplinary action may be found, and the date when and manner in which such judgment or order was carried out.

(g) The final disposition of each contemplated proceeding brought against a former member of the association under the provisions of Rule 3.460, and where the court's judgment or final order in such proceeding may be found, and the date and manner in which the punishment, if any, adjudged therein was inflicted.

(h) Disciplinary complaints filed with the director pursuant to Rule 3.160(1) against attorneys that have been dismissed by the inquiry tribunal shall be maintained by the director for a period of one (1) year after final disposition of the complaint.

(i) Those records which are disciplinary complaints against attorneys that have resulted in discipline of attorneys shall be maintained by the director until five (5) years after the death of the attorneys.

(j) At the end of the period stated in paragraphs (h) and (i) of this rule, the director shall destroy the described complaints and/or records.

HISTORY: Amended by Order 82–1, eff. 4–1–82; prior amendments eff. 1–1–78, 1–1–74, 7–2–71

SCR 3.070   The board; functions and membership

The Board is the governing body of the Association and the agent of the Court for the purpose of administering and enforcing the Rules. It shall consist of the President, the President–Elect, the Vice–President, the immediate Past President, the Chair of the Young Lawyer's Section, and two attorneys elected from the membership of the Association in each appellate district of the state as presently existing or hereafter created.

HISTORY: Amended by Order 2005–10, eff. 1–1–06; prior amendments eff. 9–15–90 (Order 90–1), 1–1–78, 7–2–71

SCR 3.080   Selection and tenure of board of governors; filling vacancies on the board

The elected members of the board for each appellate district shall be nominated and elected, in the manner prescribed in the bylaws, by the members of the association residing in the appellate district. Each governor shall hold office for two years and/or until his successor is elected and qualified. No governor who has served three consecutive full terms, after July 1, 1971, shall be eligible to again serve without at least one term of said office intervening. The terms of the two governors from each appellate district shall expire in alternate years. Bylaws shall provide for an annual election, to be held simultaneously in all appellate districts in which more than one person has been nominated as governor, for the purpose of electing successors to those governors whose terms of office shall expire. Any vacancy on the board may be filled for the remainder of the term in such manner as the bylaws may prescribe. The KENTUCKY BENCH & BAR shall in the April and July issues prior to the expiration of the term of governor carry a notice to the membership of the expiration.

HISTORY: Amended eff. 1–1–78; prior amendment eff. 7–2–71

SCR 3.090   Duties and powers of the board

It shall be the board's duty to perform the functions prescribed in Rule 3.070, and it shall have power to do everything necessary or appropriate to enable it to perform those functions. The board shall adopt by-laws, subject to the approval of the court and not in conflict with these rules, relating to the performance of its functions and providing for the conduct of its business. The board's power to perform its function as the governing body of the association expressly includes the power to engage in any program designed to educate and inform the bar and the public.

HISTORY: Amended eff. 1–1–78; prior amendment eff. 7–2–71

SCR 3.100   Officers of the board and association

The officers of the board shall be a president, a president-elect, a vice-president, a director, a treasurer, a registrar and such other officers as the bylaws may provide for. The registrar shall be appointed by and hold office during the pleasure of the Chief Justice of the court. The registrar shall perform the duties required of him by the rules, keep the records required by Rule 3.060, keep an indexed file of advisory opinions rendered pursuant to Rule 3.530, and perform such other duties as the court may from time to time prescribe for him. He shall maintain an office in Frankfort, Kentucky. The offices of director, registrar and treasurer may, but need not, be held by the same person. The manner of selection, tenure and duties of other officers shall be prescribed in bylaws.

HISTORY: Amended eff. 1–1–78; prior amendment eff. 7–2–71

SCR 3.110   The house; functions, membership, terms and vacancies—Deleted

HISTORY: Deleted by Order 2005–10, eff. 1–1–06; prior amendments eff. 1–1–02 (Order 2001–2), 7–1–84 (Order 84–2), 1–1–78, 7–2–71

SCR 3.115   Bar center headquarters

(1) A board of trustees of the association's bar center headquarters is created. It shall consist of the president, ex officio, a non-voting executive director appointed by the trustees, and six members of the association, three appointed by the court and three by the board of governors. Both the court and the board of governors shall appoint persons for staggered

terms of three years each, commencing December 1 of the year of appointment.

(2) The powers and duties of the trustees shall include the right to act for and in the name of the association with respect to all matters incident to the ownership, management and control of the bar center headquarters to be located in Frankfort, and for the purpose of carrying out such purposes, the right:

(a) To hold the legal title to all real estate acquired in the future for the bar center headquarters building, and to acquire and hold, by lease, purchase, gift, bequest or devise, such additional real estate as may reasonably be required for additions to or incident to the reasonable use of the bar center headquarters building.

(b) To construct, purchase, lease or otherwise acquire such additions to a bar center headquarters building as may reasonably be required, to incur such indebtedness as may be required in the opinion of the trustees in order to finance the acquisition of additional land for and additions to the bar center headquarters building, and to secure the payment of such indebtedness by mortgage or pledge of the property, real and personal, of the trust.

(c) To control, manage, and maintain the bar center headquarters building and all real and personal property incident thereto.

(d) To receive and accept any gifts, devises and bequests of real and personal property, and to hold, sell, mortgage, expend, invest, reinvest and otherwise control and use the same or the proceeds thereof for any purposes incident to the bar center headquarters building.

(e) To accept and hold in trust real and personal property given, devised and bequeathed for any use and purpose germane to the acquisition, maintenance and expansion of the bar center headquarters building, and to administer such trust in accordance with the terms thereof.

(f) To institute, intervene in, or defend any action or proceeding at law or in equity in any state or federal court wherein any issue involving the trustees, the real or personal property within their charge, or the trust is or may be presented.

(g) The trustees shall, annually on or before September 15 of each year, render to this court and to the board of governors of the association, or more often if either shall so direct, a complete account of their administration and transactions.

HISTORY: Amended by Order 82–1, eff. 4–1–82; adopted eff. 1–1–78

SCR 3.120   Fiscal provisions

(1) The dues and bar registration fees prescribed in Rule 3.040 shall constitute a general fund to provide for the ordinary and necessary expenses of the operation of the Kentucky Bar Association, including, as

appropriate, compensation of employees; expenses of the Board and officers; publications; maintenance of the client's security fund and the bar center fund and the discharge of the disciplinary, educational and other functions specified by these rules. Other fees, subscriptions, and contributions authorized by these Rules or approved by the court shall constitute a special fund or funds to provide for the specific purpose or purposes of each such collection including the annual and midyear conventions and other undertakings for which specific collections are authorized. Excesses in the special fund may be transferred to the general fund on order of the Board. Voluntary section funds or contributions may be retained by the sections annually with the approval of the Board.

(2) An annual budget including all income and expenditures shall be prepared by a budget and finance committee composed of the President-Elect and two members of the Board appointed by him/her; the Vice-President; two members at large appointed by the President-Elect; a member of the Inquiry Commission; a member of the Continuing Legal Education Commission; a member of the IOLTA Trustees; a member of the Clients' Security Fund Trustees; and the Director. The President-Elect shall act as chair.

(3) Not less than four (4) months prior to the commencement of the next fiscal year, the budget shall be submitted by the Board to the court for its approval. The Board shall include in its budget proposal the budget of the continuing legal education commission. The budget shall distinctly set forth expected revenues according to source, together with carry-over funds from the previous year, and shall list budgeted amounts for each category of expenditure in sufficient detail to identify clearly the nature of the respective expenditures.

(4) Upon approval by the court, the budget shall govern the fiscal operations of the Association. Each expenditure category may be increased or decreased by not more than ten (10) percent. Further departures from the budget allotments may be made only upon approval of the court.

(5) All receipts of the Association shall be recorded in a cash receipts journal and deposited promptly. Each repository of funds and bank account shall be designated by the Board and approved by the court.

(6) All disbursements shall be in accordance with the budget, made by the treasurer and recorded in a cash disbursements journal. Each check shall bear such countersignatures as the Board may direct.

(7) The director, treasurer and such other employees as the Board designates shall be bonded for the accounting of all funds collected. The bonds shall be in the amount or amounts specified by the Board.

(8) There shall be an annual audit of the Association by the Administrative Office of the Courts or, at the election of the court, a private accounting firm approved by the court. The report of the audit shall be submitted to the court. Each annual audit shall be paid for by the Association.

(9) The compensation of employees of the Association shall be fixed by the Board.

(10) Printing and purchasing shall be regulated by procedures established through the Administrative Office of the Courts.

HISTORY: Amended by Order 2005–10, eff. 1–1–06; prior amendments eff. 9–1–93 (Order 93–1), 2–1–81, 7–1–78, 1–1–78, 10–14–74, 4–9–74, 7–2–71

SCR 3.125   Travel—Abolished

HISTORY: Abolished by Order 97–3, eff. 3–1–98; adopted by Order 81–2, eff. 2–1–81

KENTUCKY RULES OF PROFESSIONAL CONDUCT

SCR 3.130   Kentucky Rules of Professional Conduct

Preamble: A Lawyer's Responsibilities

I. The Preamble and this note on Scope provide general orientation. The Comment accompanying each Rule explains and illustrates the meaning and purpose of the Rule. The Comments are intended as guides to interpretation, but the text of each Rule is authoritative.

II. A lawyer, as a member of the legal profession, is a representative of clients, an officer of the legal system and a public citizen having special responsibility for the quality of justice.

III. As a representative of clients, a lawyer performs various functions. As advisor, a lawyer provides a client with an informed understanding of the client's legal rights and obligations and explains their practical implications. As advocate, a lawyer zealously asserts the client's position under the rules of the adversary system. As negotiator, a lawyer seeks a result advantageous to the client but consistent with requirements of honest dealings with others. As an evaluator, a lawyer acts by examining a client's legal affairs and reporting about them to the client or to others.

IV. In addition to these representational functions, a lawyer may serve as a third-party neutral, a nonrepresentational role helping the parties to resolve a dispute or other matter. Some of these Rules apply directly to lawyers who are or have served as third-party neutrals. See, e.g., Rules 1.12 and 2.4. In addition, there are Rules that apply to lawyers who are not active in the practice of law or to practicing lawyers even when they are acting in a nonprofessional capacity. For example, a lawyer who commits fraud in the conduct of a business is subject to discipline for engaging in conduct involving dishonesty, fraud, deceit or misrepresentation. See Rule 8.4.

V. In all professional functions a lawyer shall be competent, prompt and diligent. A lawyer shall maintain communication with a client concerning the representation. A lawyer shall keep in confidence information relating to representation of a client except so far as disclosure is required or permitted by the Rules of Professional Conduct or other law.

VI. A lawyer's conduct shall conform to the requirements of the law, both in professional service to clients and in the lawyer's business and personal affairs. A lawyer shall use the law's procedures only for legitimate purposes and not to harass or intimidate others. A lawyer shall demonstrate respect for the legal system and for those who serve it, including judges, other lawyers and public officials. While it is a lawyer's duty, when necessary, to challenge the rectitude of official action, it is also a lawyer's duty to uphold legal process.

VII. As a public citizen, a lawyer should seek improvement of the law, access to the legal system, the administration of justice and the quality of service rendered by the legal profession. As a member of a learned profession, a lawyer should cultivate knowledge of the law beyond its use for clients, employ that knowledge in reform of the law and work to strengthen legal education. In addition, a lawyer should further the public's understanding of and confidence in the rule of law and the justice system because legal institutions in a constitutional democracy depend on popular participation and support to maintain their authority. A lawyer should be mindful of deficiencies in the administration of justice and of the fact that the poor, and sometimes persons who are not poor, cannot afford adequate legal assistance. Therefore, all lawyers should devote professional time and resources and use civic influence to ensure equal access to our system of justice for all those who because of economic or social barriers cannot afford or secure adequate legal counsel. A lawyer should aid the legal profession in pursuing these objectives and should help the bar regulate itself in the public interest.

VIII. Many of a lawyer's professional responsibilities are prescribed in the Rules of Professional Conduct, as well as substantive and procedural law. However, a lawyer is also guided by personal conscience and the approbation of professional peers. A lawyer should strive to attain the highest level of skill, to improve the law and the legal profession and to exemplify the legal profession's ideals of public service.

IX. A lawyer's responsibilities as a representative of clients, an officer of the legal system and a public citizen are usually harmonious. Thus, when an opposing party is well represented, a lawyer can be a zealous advocate on behalf of a client and at the same time assume that justice is being done. So also, a lawyer can be sure that preserving client confidences ordinarily serves the public interest because people are more likely to seek legal advice, and thereby heed their legal obligations, when they know their communications will be private.

X. In the nature of law practice, however, conflicting responsibilities are encountered. Virtually all difficult ethical problems arise from conflict between a lawyer's responsibilities to clients, to the legal system and to the lawyer's own interest in remaining an ethical person while earning a satisfactory living. The Rules of Professional Conduct often prescribe terms for resolving such conflicts. Within the framework of these Rules, however, many difficult issues of professional discretion can arise. Such issues must be resolved through the exercise of sensitive professional and moral judgment guided by the basic principles underlying the Rules. These principles include the lawyer's obligation zealously to protect and pursue a client's legitimate interests, within the bounds of the law, while maintaining a professional, courteous and civil attitude toward all persons involved in the legal system.

XI. The legal profession is largely self-governing. Although other professions also have been granted powers of self-government, the legal profession is unique in this respect because of the close relationship between the profession and the processes of government and law enforcement. This connection is manifested in the fact that ultimate authority over the legal profession is vested largely in the courts.

XII. To the extent that lawyers meet the obligations of their professional calling, the occasion for government regulation is obviated. Self-regulation also helps maintain the legal profession's independence from government domination. An independent legal profession is an important force in preserving government under law, for abuse of legal authority is more readily challenged by a profession whose members are not dependent on government for the right to practice.

XIII. The legal profession's relative autonomy carries with it special responsibilities of self-government. The profession has a responsibility to assure that its regulations are conceived in the public interest and not in furtherance of parochial or self-interested concerns of the bar. Every lawyer is responsible for observance of the Rules of Professional Conduct. A lawyer should also aid in securing their observance by other lawyers. Neglect of these responsibilities compromises the independence of the profession and the public interest which it serves.

XIV. Lawyers play a vital role in the preservation of society. The fulfillment of this role requires an understanding by lawyers of their relationship to our legal system. The Rules of Professional Conduct, when properly applied, serve to define that relationship.

Scope

XV. The Rules of Professional Conduct are rules of reason. They should be interpreted with reference to the purposes of legal representation and of the law itself. Some of the Rules are imperatives, cast in the terms "shall" or "shall not." These define proper conduct for purposes of professional discipline. Others, generally cast in the term "may," are permissive and define areas under the Rules in which the lawyer has discretion to exercise professional judgment. No disciplinary action should be taken when the lawyer chooses not to act or acts within the bounds of such discretion. Other Rules define the nature of relationships between the lawyer and others. The Rules are thus partly obligatory and disciplinary and partly constitutive and descriptive in that they define a lawyer's professional role. Many of the Comments use the term "should." Comments do not add obligations to the Rules but provide guidance for practicing in compliance with the Rules.

XVI. The Rules presuppose a larger legal context shaping the lawyer's role. That context includes court rules and statutes relating to matters of licensure, laws defining specific obligations of lawyers and substantive and procedural law in general. The Comments are sometimes used to alert lawyers to their responsibilities under such other law.

XVII. Compliance with the Rules, as with all law in an open society, depends primarily upon understanding and voluntary compliance, secondarily upon reinforcement by peer and public opinion and finally, when necessary, upon enforcement through disciplinary proceedings. The Rules do not, however, exhaust the moral and ethical considerations that should inform a lawyer, for no worthwhile human activity can be completely defined by legal rules. The Rules simply provide a framework for the ethical practice of law.

XVIII. Furthermore, for purposes of determining the lawyer's authority and responsibility, principles of substantive law external to these Rules determine whether a client-lawyer relationship exists. Most of the duties flowing from the client-lawyer relationship attach only after the client has requested the lawyer to render legal services and the lawyer has agreed to do so. But there are some duties, such as that of confidentiality under Rule 1.6, that attach when the lawyer agrees to consider whether a client-lawyer relationship shall be established. See Rule 1.18. Whether a client-lawyer relationship exists for any specific purpose can depend on the circumstances and may be a question of fact.

XIX. Under various legal provisions, including constitutional, statutory and common law, the responsibilities of government lawyers may include authority concerning legal matters that ordinarily reposes in the client in private client-lawyer relationships. For example, a lawyer for a government agency may have authority on behalf of the government to decide upon settlement or whether to appeal from an adverse judgment. Such authority in various respects is generally vested in the attorney general and the state's attorney in state government, and their federal counterparts, and the same may be true of other government law officers. Also, lawyers under the supervision of these officers may be authorized to represent several government agencies in intragovernmental legal controversies in circumstances where a private lawyer could not represent multiple private clients. These Rules do not abrogate any such authority.

XX. Failure to comply with an obligation or prohibition imposed by a Rule is a basis for invoking the disciplinary process. The Rules presuppose that disciplinary assessment of a lawyer's conduct will be made on the basis of the facts and circumstances as they existed at the time of the conduct in question and in recognition of the fact that a lawyer often has to act upon uncertain or incomplete evidence of the situation. Moreover, the Rules presuppose that whether or not discipline should be imposed for a violation, and the severity of a sanction, depend on all the circumstances, such as the willfulness and seriousness of the violation, extenuating factors and whether there have been previous violations.

XXI. Violation of a Rule should not itself give rise to a cause of action against a lawyer nor should it create any presumption in such a case that a legal duty has been breached. In addition, violation of a Rule does not necessarily warrant any other nondisciplinary remedy, such as disqualification of a lawyer in pending litigation. The Rules are designed to provide guidance to lawyers and to provide a structure for regulating conduct through disciplinary agencies. They are not designed to be a basis for civil liability. Furthermore, the purpose of the Rules can be subverted when they are invoked by opposing parties as procedural weapons. The fact that a Rule is a just basis for a lawyer's self-assessment, or for sanctioning a lawyer under the administration of a disciplinary authority, does not imply that an antagonist in a collateral proceeding or transaction has standing to seek enforcement of the Rule. Nevertheless, since the Rules do establish standards of conduct by lawyers, a lawyer's violation of a Rule may be evidence of breach of the applicable standard of conduct.

XXII. The Comment accompanying each Rule explains and illustrates the meaning and purpose of the Rule. The Preamble and this note on Scope provide general orientation. The Comments are intended as guides to interpretation, but the text of each Rule is authoritative.

HISTORY: Amended by Order 2009–05, eff. 7–15–09; adopted by Order 89–1, eff. 1–1–90

SCR 3.130(1.0) Terminology

(a) "Belief" or "believes" denotes that the person involved actually supposed the fact in question to be true. A person's belief may be inferred from circumstances.

(b) "Confirmed in writing," when used in reference to the informed consent of a person, denotes informed consent that is given in writing by the person or a writing that a lawyer promptly transmits to the person confirming an oral informed consent. See paragraph (e) for the definition of an informed consent. If it is not feasible to obtain or transmit the writing at the time the person gives informed consent, then the lawyer must obtain or transmit it within a reasonable time thereafter.

(c) "Firm" or "law firm" denotes a lawyer or lawyers in a, law partnership, professional corporation, sole proprietorship or other association authorized to practice law; or lawyers employed in a legal services organization or the legal department of a corporation or other organization.

(d) "Fraud" or "fraudulent" denotes conduct that is fraudulent under the substantive or procedural law of the applicable jurisdiction and has a purpose to deceive.

(e) "Informed consent" denotes the agreement by a person to a proposed course of conduct after the lawyer has communicated adequate information and explanation about the material risks of and reasonably available alternatives to the proposed course of conduct.

(f) "Knowingly," "known," or "knows" denotes actual knowledge of the fact in question. A person's knowledge may be inferred from circumstances.

(g) "Partner" denotes a member of a partnership, a shareholder in a law firm organized as a professional corporation, or a member of an association authorized to practice law.

(h) "Reasonable" or "reasonably" when used in relation to conduct by a lawyer denotes the conduct of a reasonably prudent and competent lawyer.

(i) "Reasonable belief" or "reasonably believes" when used in reference to a lawyer denotes that the lawyer believes the matter in question and that the circumstances are such that the belief is reasonable.

(j) "Reasonably should know" when used in reference to a lawyer denotes that a lawyer of reasonable prudence and competence would ascertain the matter in question.

(k) "Screened" denotes the isolation of a lawyer from any participation in a matter through the timely imposition of procedures within a firm that are reasonably adequate under the circumstances to protect information that the isolated lawyer is obligated to protect under these Rules or other law.

(l) "Substantial" when used in reference to degree or extent denotes a material matter of clear and weighty importance.

(m) "Tribunal" denotes a court, an arbitrator in a binding arbitration proceeding or a legislative body, administrative agency, disciplinary or admissions entity created by the Supreme Court, or other body acting in an adjudicative capacity. A legislative body, administrative agency or other body acts in an adjudicative capacity when a neutral official, after the presentation of evidence or legal argument by a party or parties, will render a binding legal judgment directly affecting a party's interests in a particular matter.

(n) "Writing" or "written" denotes a tangible or electronic record of a communication or representation, including handwriting, typewriting, printing, photostating, photography, audio or videorecording and e-mail. A "signed" writing includes an electronic sound, symbol or process attached to or logically associated with a writing and executed or adopted by a person with the intent to sign the writing.

HISTORY: Adopted by Order 2009–05, eff. 7–15–09

Supreme Court Commentary

2009:

Confirmed in Writing

(1) If it is not feasible to obtain or transmit a written confirmation at the time the client gives informed consent, then the lawyer must obtain or transmit it within a reasonable time thereafter. If a lawyer has obtained a client's informed consent, the lawyer may act in reliance on that consent so long as it is confirmed in writing within a reasonable time thereafter.

Firm

(2) Whether two or more lawyers constitute a firm within paragraph (c) can depend on the specific facts. For example, two practitioners who share office space and occasionally consult or assist each other ordinarily would not be regarded as constituting a firm. However, if they present themselves to the public in a way that suggests that they are a firm or conduct themselves as a firm, they should be regarded as a firm for purposes of the Rules. The terms of any formal agreement between associated lawyers are relevant in determining whether they are a firm, as is the fact that they have mutual access to information concerning the clients they serve. Furthermore, it is relevant in doubtful cases to consider the underlying purpose of the Rule that is involved. A group of lawyers could be regarded as a firm for purposes of the Rule that the same lawyer should not represent opposing parties in litigation, while it might not be so regarded for purposes of the Rule that information acquired by one lawyer is attributed to another.

(3) With respect to the law department of an organization, including the government, there is ordinarily no question that the members of the department constitute a firm within the meaning of the Rules of Professional Conduct. There can be uncertainty, however, as to the identity of the client. For example, it may not be clear whether the law department of a corporation represents a subsidiary or an affiliated corporation, as well as the corporation by which the members of the department are directly employed. A similar question can arise concerning an unincorporated association and its local affiliates.

(4) Similar questions can also arise with respect to lawyers in legal aid and legal services organizations. Depending upon the structure of the organization, the entire organization or different components of it may constitute a firm or firms for purposes of these Rules.

Fraud

(5) When used in these Rules, the terms "fraud" or "fraudulent" refer to conduct that is characterized as such under the substantive or procedural law of the applicable jurisdiction and has a purpose to deceive. This does not include merely negligent misrepresentation or negligent failure to apprise another of relevant information. For purposes of these Rules, it is not necessary that anyone has suffered damages or relied on the misrepresentation or failure to inform.

Informed Consent

(6) Many of the Rules of Professional Conduct require the lawyer to obtain the informed consent of a client or other person (e.g., a former client or, under certain circumstances, a prospective client) before accepting or continuing representation or pursuing a course of conduct. See, e.g., Rules 1.2(c), 1.6(a) and 1.7(b). The communication necessary to obtain such consent will vary according to the Rule involved and the circumstances giving rise to the need to obtain informed consent. The lawyer must make reasonable efforts to ensure that the client or other person possesses information reasonably adequate to make an informed decision. Ordinarily, this will require communication that includes a disclosure of the facts and circumstances giving rise to the situation, any explanation reasonably necessary to inform the client or other person of the material advantages and disadvantages of the proposed course of conduct and a discussion of the client's or other person's options and alternatives. In some circumstances it may be appropriate for a lawyer to advise a client or other person to seek the advice of other counsel. A lawyer need not inform a client or other person of facts or implications already known to the client or other person; nevertheless, a lawyer who does not personally inform the client or other person assumes the risk that the client or other person is inadequately informed and the consent is invalid. In determining whether the information and explanation provided are reasonably adequate, relevant factors include whether the client or other person is experienced in legal matters generally and in making decisions of the type involved, and whether the client or other person is independently represented by other counsel in giving the consent. Normally, such persons need less information and explanation than others, and generally a client or other person who is independently represented by other counsel in giving the consent should be assumed to have given informed consent.

(7) Obtaining informed consent will usually require an affirmative response by the client or other person. In general, a lawyer may not assume consent from a client's or other person's silence. Consent may be inferred, however, from the conduct of a client or other person who has reasonably adequate information about the matter. A number of Rules require that a person's consent be confirmed in writing. See Rules 1.7(b) and 1.9(a). For a definition of "writing" and "confirmed in writing," see paragraphs (n) and (b). Other Rules require that a client's consent be obtained in a writing signed by the client. See, e.g., Rules 1.8(a) and (g). For a definition of "signed," see paragraph (n).

Screened

(8) This definition applies to situations when screening of a personally disqualified lawyer is permitted to remove imputation of a conflict of interest under Rules 1.10, 1.11, 1.12 or 1.18.

(9) The purpose of screening is to assure the affected parties that confidential information known by the personally disqualified lawyer remains protected. The personally disqualified lawyer should acknowledge the obligation not to communicate with any of the other lawyers in the firm with respect to the matter. Similarly, other lawyers in the firm who are working on the matter should be informed that the screening is in place and that they may not communicate with the personally disqualified lawyer with respect to the matter. Additional screening measures that are appropriate for the particular matter will depend on the circumstances. To implement, reinforce and remind all affected lawyers of the presence of the screening, it may be appropriate for the firm to undertake such procedures as a written undertaking by the screened lawyer to avoid any communication with other firm personnel and any contact with any firm files or other materials relating to the matter, written notice and instructions to all other firm personnel forbidding any communication with the screened lawyer relating to the matter, denial of access by the screened lawyer to firm files or other materials relating to the matter and periodic reminders of the screen to the screened lawyer and all other firm personnel.

(10) In order to be effective, screening measures must be implemented as soon as practical after a lawyer or law firm knows or reasonably should know that there is a need for screening.

SCR 3.130(1.1)　Competence

A lawyer shall provide competent representation to a client. Competent representation requires the legal knowledge, skill, thoroughness and preparation reasonably necessary for the representation.

HISTORY: Amended by Order 2009–05, eff. 7–15–09; adopted by Order 89–1, eff. 1–1–90

Supreme Court Commentary

2009:

Legal Knowledge and Skill

(1) In determining whether a lawyer employs the requisite knowledge and skill in a particular matter, relevant factors include the relative complexity and specialized nature of the matter, the lawyer's general experience, the lawyer's training and experience in the field in question, the preparation and study the lawyer is able to give the matter and whether it is feasible to refer the matter to, or associate or consult with, a lawyer of established competence in the field in question. In many instances, the required proficiency is that of a general practitioner. Expertise in a particular field of law may be required in some circumstances.

(2) A lawyer need not necessarily have special training or prior experience to handle legal problems of a type with which the lawyer is unfamiliar. A newly admitted lawyer can be as competent as a practitioner with long experience. Some important legal skills, such as the analysis of precedent, the evaluation of evidence and legal drafting, are required in all legal problems. Perhaps the most fundamental legal skill consists of determining what kind of legal problems a situation may involve, a skill that necessarily transcends any particular specialized knowledge. A lawyer can provide adequate representation in a wholly novel field through necessary study. Competent representation can also be provided through the association of a lawyer of established competence in the field in question.

(3) In an emergency a lawyer may give advice or assistance in a matter in which the lawyer does not have the skill ordinarily required where referral to or consultation or association with another lawyer would be impractical. Even in an emergency, however, assistance should be limited to that reasonably necessary in the circumstances, for ill-considered action under emergency conditions can jeopardize the client's interest.

(4) A lawyer may accept representation where the requisite level of competence can be achieved by reasonable preparation. This applies as well to a lawyer who is appointed as counsel for an unrepresented person. See also Rule 6.2.

Thoroughness and Preparation

(5) Competent handling of a particular matter includes inquiry into and analysis of the factual and legal elements of the problem, and use of methods and procedures meeting the standards of competent practitioners. It also includes adequate preparation. The required attention and preparation are determined in part by what is at stake; major litigation and complex transactions ordinarily require more extensive treatment than matters of lesser complexity and consequence. An agreement between the lawyer and the client regarding the scope of the representation may limit the matters for which the lawyer is responsible. See Rule 1.2(c).

Maintaining Competence

(6) To maintain the requisite knowledge and skill, a lawyer should keep abreast of changes in the law and its practice, engage in continuing study and education and comply with all continuing legal education requirements to which the lawyer is subject.

SCR 3.130(1.2)　Scope of representation and allocation of authority between client and lawyer

(a) Subject to paragraphs (c) and (d), a lawyer shall abide by a client's decisions concerning the objectives of representation and, as required by Rule 1.4, shall consult with the client as to the means by which they are to be pursued. A lawyer may take such action on behalf of the client as is impliedly authorized to carry out the representation. A lawyer shall abide by a client's decision whether to settle a matter. In a criminal case, the lawyer shall abide by the client's decision, after consultation with the lawyer, as to a plea to be entered, whether to waive jury trial and whether the client will testify.

(b) A lawyer's representation of a client, including representation by appointment, does not constitute an endorsement of the client's political, economic, social or moral views or activities.

(c) A lawyer may limit the scope of the representation if the limitation is reasonable under the circumstances and the client gives informed consent.

(d) A lawyer shall not counsel a client to engage, or assist a client, in conduct that the lawyer knows is criminal or fraudulent, but a lawyer may discuss the legal consequences of any proposed course of conduct with a client and may counsel or assist a client to make a good faith effort to determine the validity, scope, meaning or application of the law.

HISTORY: Amended by Order 2009–05, eff. 7–15–09; adopted by Order 89–1, eff. 1–1–90

Supreme Court Commentary

2009:

Allocation of Authority between Client and Lawyer

(1) Paragraph (a) confers upon the client the ultimate authority to determine the purposes to be served by legal representation, within the limits imposed by law and the lawyer's professional obligations. The decisions specified in paragraph (a), such as whether to settle a civil matter, must also be made by the client. See Rule 1.4(a)(1) for the lawyer's duty to communicate with the client about such decisions. With respect to the means by which the client's objectives are to be pursued, the lawyer shall consult with the client as required by Rule 1.4(a)(2) and may take such action as is impliedly authorized to carry out the representation.

(2) On occasion, however, a lawyer and a client may disagree about the means to be used to accomplish the client's objectives. Clients normally defer to the special knowledge and skill of their lawyer with respect to the means to be used to accomplish their objectives, particularly with respect to technical, legal and tactical matters. Conversely, lawyers usually defer to the client regarding such questions as the expense to be incurred and concern for third persons who might be adversely affected. Because of the varied nature of the matters about which a lawyer and client might disagree and because the actions in question may implicate the interests of a tribunal or other persons, this Rule does not prescribe how such disagreements are to be resolved. Other law, however, may be applicable and should be consulted by the lawyer. The lawyer should also consult with the client and seek a mutually acceptable resolution of the disagreement. If such efforts are unavailing and the lawyer has a fundamental disagreement with the client, the lawyer may withdraw from the representation. See Rule 1.16(b)(4). Conversely, the client may resolve the disagreement by discharging the lawyer. See Rule 1.16(a)(3).

(3) At the outset of a representation, the client may authorize the lawyer to take specific action on the client's behalf without further consultation. Absent a material change in circumstances and subject to Rule 1.4, a lawyer may rely on such an advance authorization. The client may, however, revoke such authority at any time.

(4) In a case in which the client appears to be suffering diminished capacity, the lawyers duty to abide by the clients decisions is to be guided by reference to Rule 1.14.

Independence from Client's Views or Activities

(5) Legal representation should not be denied to people who are unable to afford legal services, or whose cause is controversial or the subject of popular disapproval. By the same token, representing a client does not constitute approval of the client's views or activities.

Agreements Limiting Scope of Representation

(6) The scope of services to be provided by a lawyer may be limited by agreement with the client or by the terms under which the lawyer's services are made available to the client. When a lawyer has been retained by an insurer to represent an insured, for example, the representation may be limited to matters related to the insurance coverage. A limited representation may be appropriate because the client has limited objectives for the representation. In addition, the terms upon which representation is undertaken may exclude specific means that might otherwise be used to accomplish the client's objectives. Such limitations may exclude actions that the client thinks are too costly or that the lawyer regards as repugnant or imprudent.

(7) Although this Rule affords the lawyer and client substantial latitude to limit the representation, the limitation must be reasonable under the circumstances. If, for example, a client's objective is limited to securing general information about the law the client needs in order to handle a common and typically uncomplicated legal problem, the lawyer and client may agree that the lawyer's services will be limited to a brief telephone consultation. Such a limitation, however, would not be reasonable if the time allotted was not sufficient to yield advice upon which the client could rely. Although an agreement for a limited representation does not exempt a lawyer from the duty to provide competent representation, the limitation is a factor to be considered when determining the legal knowledge, skill, thoroughness and preparation reasonably necessary for the representation. See Rule 1.1.

(8) All agreements concerning a lawyer's representation of a client must accord with the Rules of Professional Conduct and other law. See, e.g., Rules 1.1, 1.8 and 5.6.

Criminal, Fraudulent and Prohibited Transactions

(9) Paragraph (d) prohibits a lawyer from knowingly counseling or assisting a client to commit a crime or fraud. This prohibition, however, does not preclude the lawyer from giving an honest opinion about the actual consequences that appear likely to result from a client's conduct. Nor does the fact that a client uses advice in a course of action that is criminal or fraudulent of itself make a lawyer a party to the course of action. There is a critical distinction between presenting an analysis of legal aspects of questionable conduct and recommending the means by which a crime or fraud might be committed with impunity.

(10) When the client's course of action has already begun and is continuing, the lawyer's responsibility is especially delicate. The lawyer is required to avoid assisting the client, for example, by drafting or delivering documents that the lawyer knows are fraudulent or by suggesting how the wrongdoing might be concealed. A lawyer may not continue assisting a client in conduct that the lawyer originally supposed was legally proper but then discovers is criminal or fraudulent. The lawyer must, therefore, withdraw from the representation, of the client in the matter. See Rule 1.16(a). In some cases, withdrawal alone might be insufficient. It may be necessary for the lawyer to give notice of the fact of withdrawal and to disaffirm any opinion, document, affirmation or the like. See Rule 4.1.

(11) Where the client is a fiduciary, the lawyer may be charged with special obligations in dealings with a beneficiary.

(12) Paragraph (d) applies whether or not the defrauded party is a party to the transaction. Hence, a lawyer must not participate in a transaction to effectuate criminal or fraudulent avoidance of tax liability. Paragraph (d) does not preclude undertaking a criminal defense incident to a general retainer for legal services to a lawful enterprise. The last clause of paragraph (d) recognizes that determining the validity or interpretation of a statute or regulation may require a course of action involving disobedience of the statute or regulation or of the interpretation placed upon it by governmental authorities.

(13) If a lawyer comes to know or reasonably should know that a client expects assistance not permitted by the Rules of Professional Conduct or other law or if the lawyer intends to act contrary to the client's instructions, the lawyer must consult with the client regarding the limitations on the lawyer's conduct. See Rule 1.4(a)(5).

SCR 3.130(1.3)　Diligence

A lawyer shall act with reasonable diligence and promptness in representing a client.

HISTORY: Amended by Order 2009–05, eff. 7–15–09; adopted by Order 89–1, eff. 1–1–90.

Supreme Court Commentary

2009:

(1) A lawyer should pursue a matter on behalf of a client despite opposition, obstruction or personal inconvenience to the lawyer, and take whatever lawful and ethical measures are required to vindicate a client's cause or endeavor. A lawyer must also act with commitment and dedication to the interests of the client and with zeal in advocacy upon the client's behalf. A lawyer is not bound, however, to press for every advantage that might be realized for a client. For example, a lawyer may have authority to exercise professional discretion in determining the means by which a matter should be pursued. See Rule 1.2. The lawyer's duty to act with reasonable diligence does not require the use of offensive tactics or preclude the treating of all persons involved in the legal process with courtesy and respect.

(2) A lawyer's work load must be controlled so that each matter can be handled competently.

(3) Perhaps no professional shortcoming is more widely resented than procrastination. A client's interests often can be adversely affected by the passage of time or the change of conditions; in extreme instances, as when a lawyer overlooks a statute of limitations, the client's legal position may be destroyed. Even when the client's interests are not affected in substance, however, unreasonable delay can cause a client needless anxiety and undermine confidence in the lawyer's trustworthiness. A lawyer's duty to act with reasonable promptness, however, does not preclude the lawyer from agreeing to a reasonable request for a postponement that will not prejudice the lawyer's client.

(4) Unless the relationship is terminated as provided in Rule 1.16, a lawyer should carry through to conclusion all matters undertaken for a client. If a lawyer's employment is limited to a specific matter, the relationship terminates when the matter has been resolved. If a lawyer has served a client over a substantial period in a variety of matters, the client sometimes may assume that the lawyer will continue to serve on a continuing basis unless the lawyer gives notice of withdrawal. Doubt about whether a client-lawyer relationship still exists should be clarified by the lawyer, preferably in writing, so that the client will not mistakenly suppose the lawyer is looking after the client's affairs when the lawyer has ceased to do so. For example, if a lawyer has handled a judicial or administrative proceeding that produced a result adverse to the client and the lawyer and the client have not agreed that the lawyer will handle the matter on appeal, the lawyer must consult with the client about the possibility of appeal before relinquishing responsibility for the matter. See Rule 1.4(a)(2). Whether the lawyer is obligated to prosecute the appeal for the client depends on the scope of the representation the lawyer has agreed to provide to the client. See Rule 1.2.

SCR 3.130(1.4)　Communication

(a) A lawyer shall:

(1) promptly inform the client of any decision or circumstance with respect to which the client's informed consent, as defined in Rule 1.0(e), is required by these Rules;

(2) reasonably consult with the client about the means by which the client's objectives are to be accomplished;

(3) keep the client reasonably informed about the status of the matter;

(4) promptly comply with reasonable requests for information; and

(5) consult with the client about any relevant limitation on the lawyer's conduct when the lawyer knows that the client expects assistance not permitted by the Rules of Professional Conduct or other law.

(b) A lawyer shall explain a matter to the extent reasonably necessary to permit the client to make informed decisions regarding the representation.

HISTORY: Amended by Order 2009–05, eff. 7–15–09; adopted by Order 89–1, eff. 1–1–90.

Supreme Court Commentary

2009:

(1) Reasonable communication between the lawyer and the client is necessary for the client effectively to participate in the representation.

Communicating with Client

(2) If these Rules require that a particular decision about the representation be made by the client, paragraph (a)(1) requires that the lawyer promptly consult with and secure the client's consent prior to taking action unless prior discussions with the client have resolved what action the client wants the lawyer to take. For example, a lawyer who receives from opposing counsel an offer of settlement in a civil controversy or a proffered plea bargain in a criminal case must promptly inform the client of its substance unless the client has previously communicated to the lawyer that the proposal will be acceptable or unacceptable or has authorized the lawyer to accept or to reject the offer. See Rule 1.2(a).

(3) Paragraph (a)(2) requires the lawyer to reasonably consult with the client about the means to be used to accomplish the client's objectives. In some situations—depending on both the importance of the action under consideration and the feasibility of consulting with the client—this duty will require consultation prior to taking action. In other circumstances, such as during a trial when an immediate decision must be made, the exigency of the situation may require the lawyer to act without prior consultation. In such cases the lawyer must nonetheless act reasonably to inform the client of actions the lawyer has taken on the client's behalf. Additionally, paragraph (a)(3) requires that the lawyer keep the client reasonably informed about the status of the matter, such as significant developments affecting the timing or the substance of the representation.

(4) A lawyer's regular communication with clients will minimize the occasions on which a client will need to request information concerning the representation. When a client makes a reasonable request for information, however, paragraph (a)(4) requires prompt compliance with the request, or if a prompt response is not feasible, that the lawyer, or a member of the lawyer's staff, acknowledge receipt of the request and advise the client when a response may be expected. Client telephone calls should be promptly returned or acknowledged.

Explaining Matters

(5) The client should have sufficient information to participate intelligently in decisions concerning the objectives of the representation and the means by which they are to be pursued, to the extent the client is willing and able to do so. Adequacy of communication depends in part on the kind of advice or assistance that is involved. For example, when there is time to explain a proposal made in a negotiation, the lawyer should review all important provisions with the client before proceeding to an agreement. In litigation a lawyer should explain the general strategy and prospects of success and ordinarily should consult the client on tactics that are likely to result in significant expense or to injure or coerce others. On the other hand, a lawyer ordinarily will not be expected to describe trial or negotiation strategy in detail. The guiding principle is that the lawyer should fulfill reasonable client expectations for information consistent with the duty to act in the client's best interests, and the client's overall requirements as to the character of representation. In certain circumstances, such as when a lawyer asks a client to consent to a representation affected by a conflict of interest, the client must give informed consent, as defined in Rule 1.0(e).

(6) Ordinarily, the information to be provided is that appropriate for a client who is a comprehending and responsible adult. However,

fully informing the client according to this standard may be impracticable, for example, where the client is a child or suffers from diminished capacity. See Rule 1.14. When the client is an organization or group, it is often impossible or inappropriate to inform every one of its members about its legal affairs; ordinarily, the lawyer should address communications to the appropriate officials of the organization. See Rule 1.13. Where many routine matters are involved, a system of limited or occasional reporting may be arranged with the client.

Withholding Information

(7) In some very unusual circumstances, a lawyer may be justified in delaying transmission of information when the client would be likely to react imprudently to an immediate communication. Thus, a lawyer might withhold a psychiatric diagnosis of a client when the examining psychiatrist indicates that disclosure would harm the client. A lawyer may not withhold information to serve the lawyer's own interest or convenience or the interests or convenience of another person. Rules or court orders governing litigation may provide that information supplied to a lawyer may not be disclosed to the client. Rule 3.4(c) directs compliance with such rules or orders.

SCR 3.130(1.5)   Fees

(a) A lawyer shall not make an agreement for, charge, or collect an unreasonable fee or an unreasonable amount for expenses. The factors to be considered in determining the reasonableness of a fee include the following:

(1) the time and labor required, the novelty and difficulty of the questions involved, and the skill requisite to perform the legal service properly;

(2) the likelihood that the acceptance of the particular employment will preclude other employment by the lawyer;

(3) the fee customarily charged in the locality for similar legal services;

(4) the amount involved and the results obtained;

(5) the time limitations imposed by the client or by the circumstances;

(6) the nature and length of the professional relationship with the client;

(7) the experience, reputation, and ability of the lawyer or lawyers performing the services; and

(8) whether the fee is fixed or contingent.

(b) The scope of the representation and the basis or rate of the fee and expenses for which the client will be responsible shall be communicated to the client, preferably in writing, before or within a reasonable time after commencing the representation, except when the lawyer will charge a regularly represented client on the same basis or rate. Any changes in the basis or rate of the fee or expenses shall also be communicated to the client.

(c) A fee may be contingent on the outcome of the matter for which the service is rendered, except in a matter in which a contingent fee is prohibited by paragraph (d) or other law. Such a fee must meet the requirements of Rule 1.5(a). A contingent fee agreement shall be in a writing signed by the client and shall state the method by which the fee is to be determined, including the percentage or percentages

that shall accrue to the lawyer in the event of settlement, trial or appeal; litigation and other expenses to be deducted from the recovery; and whether such expenses are to be deducted before or after the contingent fee is calculated. The agreement must clearly notify the client of any expenses for which the client will be liable whether or not the client is the prevailing party. Upon conclusion of a contingent fee matter, the lawyer shall provide the client with a written statement stating the outcome of the matter and, if there is a recovery, showing the remittance to the client and the method of its determination.

(d) A lawyer shall not enter into an arrangement for, charge, or collect:

(1) any fee in a domestic relations matter, the payment or amount of which is contingent upon the securing of a divorce or upon the amount of alimony, maintenance, support, or property settlement in lieu thereof, provided this does not apply to liquidated sums in arrearage; or

(2) a contingent fee for representing a defendant in a criminal case.

(e) A division of a fee between lawyers who are not in the same firm may be made only if:

(1) the division is in proportion to the services performed by each lawyer, or, each lawyer assumes joint responsibility for the representation;

(2) the client agrees to the arrangement and the agreement is confirmed in writing; and

(3) the total fee is reasonable.

(f) A fee may be designated as a non-refundable retainer. A non-refundable retainer fee agreement shall be in a writing signed by the client evidencing the client's informed consent, and shall state the dollar amount of the retainer, its application to the scope of the representation and the time frame in which the agreement will exist.

HISTORY: Amended by Order 2009–05, eff. 7–15–09; adopted by Order 89–1, eff. 1–1–90

Supreme Court Commentary

2009:

Reasonableness of Fee and Expenses

(1) Paragraph (a) requires that lawyers charge fees that are reasonable under the circumstances. The factors specified in (1) through (8) are not exclusive. Nor will each factor be relevant in each instance. Paragraph (a) also requires that expenses for which the client will be charged must be reasonable. A lawyer may seek reimbursement for the cost of services performed in-house, such as copying, or for other expenses incurred in-house, such as telephone charges, either by charging a reasonable amount to which the client has agreed in advance or by charging an amount that reasonably reflects the cost incurred by the lawyer.

Basis or Rate of Fee

(2) When the lawyer has regularly represented a client, they ordinarily will have evolved an understanding concerning the basis or rate of the fee and the expenses for which the client will be responsible. In a new client-lawyer relationship, however, an understanding as to fees and expenses must be promptly established. Generally, it is desirable to furnish the client with at least a simple memorandum or copy of the lawyer's customary fee arrangements that states the

general nature of the legal services to be provided, the basis, rate or total amount of the fee and whether and to what extent the client will be responsible for any costs, expenses or disbursements in the course of the representation. A written statement concerning the terms of the engagement reduces the possibility of misunderstanding.

(3) Contingent fees, like any other fees, are subject to the reasonableness standard of paragraph (a) of this Rule. In determining whether a particular contingent fee is reasonable, or whether it is reasonable to charge any form of contingent fee, a lawyer must consider the factors that are relevant under the circumstances. Applicable law may impose limitations on contingent fees, such as a ceiling on the percentage allowable, or may require a lawyer to offer clients an alternative basis for the fee. Applicable law also may apply to situations other than a contingent fee, for example, government regulations regarding fees in certain tax matters.

Terms of Payment

(4) A lawyer may require advance payment of a fee, but is obliged to return any unearned portion. See Rule 1.16(d). A lawyer may accept property in payment for services, such as an ownership interest in an enterprise, providing this does not involve acquisition of a proprietary interest in the cause of action or subject matter of the litigation contrary to Rule 1.8(i). However, a fee paid in property instead of money may be subject to the requirements of Rule 1.8(a) because such fees often have the essential qualities of a business transaction with the client.

(5) An agreement may not be made whose terms might induce the lawyer improperly to curtail services for the client or perform them in a way contrary to the client's interest. For example, a lawyer should not enter into an agreement whereby services are to be provided only up to a stated amount when it is foreseeable that more extensive services probably will be required, unless the situation is adequately explained to the client. Otherwise, the client might have to bargain for further assistance in the midst of a proceeding or transaction. However, it is proper to define the extent of services in light of the client's ability to pay. A lawyer should not exploit a fee arrangement based primarily on hourly charges by using wasteful procedures.

Prohibited Contingent Fees

(6) Paragraph (d) prohibits a lawyer from charging a contingent fee in a domestic relations matter when payment is contingent upon the securing of a divorce or upon the amount of alimony or support or property settlement to be obtained. This provision does not preclude a contract for a contingent fee for legal representation in connection with the recovery of post-judgment balances due under support, alimony or other financial orders because such contracts do not implicate the same policy concerns.

Division of Fee

(7) A division of fee is a single billing to a client covering the fee of two or more lawyers who are not in the same firm. A division of fee facilitates association of more than one lawyer in a matter in which neither alone could serve the client as well, and most often is used when the fee is contingent and the division is between a referring lawyer and a trial specialist. Paragraph (e) permits the lawyers to divide a fee either on the basis of the proportion of services they render or if each lawyer assumes responsibility for the representation as a whole. In addition, the client must agree to the arrangement and the agreement must be confirmed in writing. Contingent fee agreements must be in a writing signed by the client and must otherwise comply with paragraph (c) of this Rule. Joint responsibility for the representation entails financial and ethical responsibility for the representation as if the lawyers were associated in a partnership. A lawyer should only refer a matter to a lawyer whom the referring lawyer reasonably believes is competent to handle the matter. See Rule 1.1.

(8) Paragraph (e) does not prohibit or regulate division of fees to be received in the future for work done when lawyers were previously associated in a law firm.

Disputes over Fees

(9) If a procedure has been established for resolution of fee disputes, such as an arbitration or mediation procedure established by the bar, the lawyer must comply with the procedure when it is mandatory, and, even when it is voluntary, the lawyer should conscientiously consider submitting to it. Law may prescribe a procedure for determining a lawyer's fee, for example, in representation of an executor or administrator, a class or a person entitled to a reasonable fee as part of the measure of damages. The lawyer entitled to such a fee and a lawyer representing another party concerned with the fee should comply with the prescribed procedure.

Advance Fee Arrangements

(10) If a lawyer collects an advance deposit on a fee or for expenses, or a flat fee for services to be performed, the lawyer must deposit the funds in the lawyer's trust account until the fee is earned or the expense incurred, at which time the funds shall be promptly distributed. In the event the full amount that is held is not ultimately earned, or due to other factors, such as termination of the attorney-client relationship, is not reasonable, the funds must be returned to the client as provided in Rule 1.16(d).

Non-refundable Retainers

(11) A lawyer may designate a fee arrangement as a non-refundable retainer and upon receipt deposit such funds in the lawyer's operating account. The amount of a non-refundable retainer fee must be reasonable in amount and comply with Rule 1.5.

SCR 3.130(1.6) Confidentiality of information

(a) A lawyer shall not reveal information relating to the representation of a client unless the client gives informed consent, the disclosure is impliedly authorized in order to carry out the representation or the disclosure is permitted by paragraph (b).

(b) A lawyer may reveal information relating to the representation of a client to the extent the lawyer reasonably believes necessary:

(1) to prevent reasonably certain death or substantial bodily harm;

(2) to secure legal advice about the lawyer's compliance with these Rules;

(3) to establish a claim or defense on behalf of the lawyer in a controversy between the lawyer and the client, to establish a defense to a criminal charge or civil claim against the lawyer based upon conduct in which the client was involved, or to respond to allegations in any proceeding, including a disciplinary proceeding, concerning the lawyer's representation of the client; or

(4) to comply with other law or a court order.

HISTORY: Amended by Order 2009–05, eff. 7–15–09; adopted by Order 89–1, eff. 1–1–90

Supreme Court Commentary

2009:

(1) This Rule governs the disclosure by a lawyer of information relating to the representation of a client during the lawyer's representation of the client. See Rule 1.18 for the lawyer's duties with respect to information provided to the lawyer by a prospective client, Rule 1.9(c)(2) for the lawyer's duty not to reveal information relating to the lawyer's prior representation of a former client and Rules 1.8(b) and 1.9(c)(1) for the lawyer's duties with respect to the use of such information to the disadvantage of clients and former clients.

(2) A fundamental principle in the client-lawyer relationship is that, in the absence of the client's informed consent, the lawyer must not reveal information relating to the representation. See Rule 1.0(e) for the definition of informed consent. This contributes to the trust that is the hallmark of the client-lawyer relationship. The client is thereby encouraged to seek legal assistance and to communicate fully and frankly with the lawyer even as to embarrassing or legally damaging subject matter. The lawyer needs this information to represent the client effectively and, if necessary, to advise the client to refrain from wrongful conduct. Almost without exception, clients come to lawyers

in order to determine their rights and what is, in the complex of laws and regulations, deemed to be legal and correct. Based upon experience, lawyers know that almost all clients follow the advice given, and the law is upheld.

(3) The principle of client-lawyer confidentiality is given effect by related bodies of law: the attorney-client privilege, the work product doctrine and the rule of confidentiality established in professional ethics. The attorney-client privilege and work-product doctrine apply in judicial and other proceedings in which a lawyer may be called as a witness or otherwise required to produce evidence concerning a client. The rule of client-lawyer confidentiality applies in situations other than those where evidence is sought from the lawyer through compulsion of law. The confidentiality rule, for example, applies not only to matters communicated in confidence by the client but also to all information relating to the representation, whatever its source. A lawyer may not disclose such information except as authorized or required by the Rules of Professional Conduct or other law. See also Scope.

(4) Paragraph (a) prohibits a lawyer from revealing information relating to the representation of a client. This prohibition also applies to disclosures by a lawyer that do not in themselves reveal protected information but could reasonably lead to the discovery of such information by a third person. A lawyer's use of a hypothetical to discuss issues relating to the representation is permissible so long as there is no reasonable likelihood that the listener will be able to ascertain the identity of the client or the situation involved.

Authorized Disclosure

(5) Except to the extent that the client's instructions or special circumstances limit that authority, a lawyer is impliedly authorized to make disclosures about a client when appropriate in carrying out the representation. In some situations, for example, a lawyer may be impliedly authorized to admit a fact that cannot properly be disputed or, to make a disclosure that facilitates a satisfactory conclusion to a matter. Lawyers in a firm may, in the course of the firm's practice, disclose to each other information relating to a client of the firm, unless the client has instructed that particular information be confined to specified lawyers.

Disclosure Adverse to Client

(6) Although the public interest is usually best served by a strict rule requiring lawyers to preserve the confidentiality of information relating to the representation of their clients, the confidentiality rule is subject to limited exceptions. Paragraph (b)(1), recognizes the overriding value of life and physical integrity and permits disclosure reasonably necessary to prevent reasonably certain death or substantial bodily harm. Such harm is reasonably certain to occur if it will be suffered imminently or if there is a present and substantial threat that a person will suffer such harm at a later date if the lawyer fails to take action necessary to eliminate the threat. Thus, a lawyer who knows that a client has accidentally discharged toxic waste into a town's water supply may reveal this information to the authorities if there is a present and substantial risk that a person who drinks the water will contract a life-threatening or debilitating disease and the lawyer's disclosure is necessary to eliminate the threat or reduce the number of victims.

(7) A lawyer's confidentiality obligations do not preclude a lawyer from securing confidential legal advice about the lawyer's personal responsibility to comply with these Rules. In most situations, disclosing information to secure such advice will be impliedly authorized for the lawyer to carry out the representation. Even when the disclosure is not impliedly authorized, paragraph (b)(4) permits such disclosure because of the importance of a lawyer's compliance with the Rules of Professional Conduct. SCR 3.530, Advisory opinion—informal and formal, authorizes a lawyer to request an advisory opinion from the requester's Supreme Court District Committee member regarding ethics and unauthorized practice of law questions. The question may be submitted in writing or by telephone using the KBA Ethics Hotline. Communications between the requester and any District Committee member or Ethics Committee member are granted confidentiality by SCR 3.530 and are permitted disclosure by paragraph (b)(4).

(8) Where a legal claim or disciplinary charge alleges complicity of the lawyer in a client's conduct or other misconduct of the lawyer involving representation of the client, the lawyer may respond to the extent the lawyer reasonably believes necessary to establish a de-

fense. The same is true with respect to a claim involving the conduct or representation of a former client. Such a charge can arise in a civil, criminal, disciplinary or other proceeding and can be based on a wrong allegedly committed by the lawyer against the client or on a wrong alleged by a third person, for example, a person claiming to have been defrauded by the lawyer and client acting together. The lawyer's right to respond arises when an assertion of such complicity has been made. Paragraph (b)(5) does not require the lawyer to await the commencement of an action or proceeding that charges such complicity, so that the defense may be established by responding directly to a third party who has made such an assertion. Lawyers may also report incidents of potential malpractice that have not ripened into a client claim to a lawyer's liability insurer for legal advice and to comply with policy reporting requirements provided the report is made on a confidential basis and protected by the attorney-client privilege. The right to defend also applies, of course, where a proceeding has been commenced.

(9) A lawyer entitled to a fee is permitted by paragraph (b)(5) to prove the services rendered in an action to collect it. This aspect of the Rule expresses the principle that the beneficiary of a fiduciary relationship may not exploit it to the detriment of the fiduciary.

(10) Other law may require that a lawyer disclose information about a client. Whether such a law supersedes Rule 1.6 is a question of law beyond the scope of these Rules. When disclosure of information relating to the representation appears to be required by other law, the lawyer must discuss the matter with the client to the extent required by Rule 1.4. If, however, the other law supersedes this Rule and requires disclosure, paragraph (b)(6) permits the lawyer to make such disclosures as are necessary to comply with the law.

(11) A lawyer may be ordered to reveal information relating to the representation of a client by a court or by another tribunal or governmental entity claiming authority pursuant to other law to compel the disclosure. Absent informed consent of the client to do otherwise, the lawyer should assert on behalf of the client all nonfrivolous claims that the order is not authorized by other law or that the information sought is protected against disclosure by the attorney-client privilege or other applicable law. In the event of an adverse ruling, the lawyer must consult with the client about the possibility of appeal to the extent required by Rule 1.4. Unless review is sought, however, paragraph (b)(6) permits the lawyer to comply with the court's order.

(12) Paragraph (b) permits disclosure only to the extent the lawyer reasonably believes the disclosure is necessary to accomplish one of the purposes specified. Where practicable, the lawyer should first seek to persuade the client to take suitable action to obviate the need for disclosure. In any case, a disclosure adverse to the client's interest should be no greater than the lawyer reasonably believes necessary to accomplish the purpose. If the disclosure will be made in connection with a judicial proceeding, the disclosure should be made in a manner that limits access to the information to the tribunal or other persons having a need to know it and appropriate protective orders or other arrangements should be sought by the lawyer to the fullest extent practicable.

(13) Paragraph (b) permits but does not require the disclosure of information relating to a client's representation to accomplish the purposes specified in paragraphs (b)(1) through (b)(6). In exercising the discretion conferred by this Rule, the lawyer may consider such factors as the nature of the lawyer's relationship with the client and with those who might be injured by the client, the lawyer's own involvement in the transaction and factors that may extenuate the conduct in question. A lawyer's decision not to disclose as permitted by paragraph (b) does not violate this Rule. Disclosure may be required, however, by other Rules. Some Rules require disclosure only if such disclosure would be permitted by paragraph (b). See Rules 1.2(d), 4.1(b), 8.1 and 8.3. Rule 3.3, on the other hand, requires disclosure in some circumstances regardless of whether such disclosure is permitted by this Rule. See Rule 3.3(c).

Acting Competently to Preserve Confidentiality

(14) A lawyer must act competently to safeguard information relating to the representation of a client against inadvertent or unauthorized disclosure by the lawyer or other persons who are participating in the representation of the client or who are subject to the lawyer's supervision. See Rules 1.1, 5.1 and 5.3.

(15) When transmitting a communication that includes information relating to the representation of a client, the lawyer must take reasonable precautions to prevent the information from coming into the hands of unintended recipients. This duty, however, does not require that the lawyer use special security measures if the method of communication affords a reasonable expectation of privacy. Special circumstances, however, may warrant special precautions. Factors to be considered in determining the reasonableness of the lawyer's expectation of confidentiality include the sensitivity of the information and the extent to which the privacy of the communication is protected by law or by a confidentiality agreement. A client may require the lawyer to implement special security measures not required by this Rule or may give informed consent to the use of a means of communication that would otherwise be prohibited by this Rule.

Former Client

(16) The duty of confidentiality continues after the client-lawyer relationship has terminated. See Rule 1.9(c)(2). See Rule 1.9(c)(1) for the prohibition against using such information to the disadvantage of the former client.

SCR 3.130(1.7) Conflict of interest: current clients

(a) Except as provided in paragraph (b), a lawyer shall not represent a client if the representation involves a concurrent conflict of interest. A concurrent conflict of interest exists if:

(1) the representation of one client will be directly adverse to another client; or

(2) there is a significant risk that the representation of one or more clients will be materially limited by the lawyer's responsibilities to another client, a former client or a third person or by a personal interest of the lawyer.

(b) Notwithstanding paragraph (a), a lawyer may represent a client if:

(1) the lawyer reasonably believes that the lawyer will be able to provide competent and diligent representation to each affected client;

(2) the representation is not prohibited by law;

(3) the representation does not involve the assertion of a claim by one client against another client represented by the lawyer in the same litigation or other proceeding before a tribunal; and

(4) each affected client gives informed consent, confirmed in writing. The consultation shall include an explanation of the implications of the common representation and the advantages and risks involved.

HISTORY: Amended by Order 2009–05, eff. 7–15–09; adopted by Order 89–1, eff. 1–1–90

Supreme Court Commentary

2009:

General Principles

(1) Loyalty and independent judgment are essential elements in the lawyer's relationship to a client. Concurrent conflicts of interest can arise from the lawyer's responsibilities to another client, a former client or a third person or from the lawyer's own interests. For specific Rules regarding certain concurrent conflicts of interest, see Rule 1.8. For former client conflicts of interest, see Rule 1.9. For conflicts of interest involving prospective clients, see Rule 1.18. For definitions of "informed consent" and "confirmed in writing," see Rule 1.0(e) and (b).

(2) Resolution of a conflict of interest problem under this Rule requires the lawyer to: 1) clearly identify the client or clients; 2) determine whether a conflict of interest exists; 3) decide whether the representation may be undertaken despite the existence of a conflict, i.e., whether the conflict is consentable; and 4) if so, consult with the clients affected under paragraph (a) and obtain their informed consent, confirmed in writing. The clients affected under paragraph (a) include both of the clients referred to in paragraph (a)(1) and the one or more clients whose representation might be materially limited under paragraph (a)(2).

(3) A conflict of interest may exist before representation is undertaken, in which event the representation must be declined, unless the lawyer obtains the informed consent of each client under the conditions of paragraph (b). To determine whether a conflict of interest exists, a lawyer should adopt reasonable procedures, appropriate for the size and type of firm and practice, to determine in both litigation and non-litigation matters the persons and issues involved. See also Comment to Rule 5.1. Ignorance caused by a failure to institute such procedures will not excuse a lawyer's violation of this Rule. As to whether a client-lawyer relationship exists or, having once been established, is continuing, see Comment to Rule 1.3 and Scope.

(4) If a conflict arises after representation has been undertaken, the lawyer ordinarily must withdraw from the representation, unless the lawyer has obtained the informed consent of the client under the conditions of paragraph (b). See Rule 1.16. Where more than one client is involved, whether the lawyer may continue to represent any of the clients is determined both by the lawyer's ability to comply with duties owed to the former client and by the lawyer's ability to represent adequately the remaining client or clients, given the lawyer's duties to the former client. See Rule 1.9. See also Comments (5) and (29).

(5) Unforeseeable developments, such as changes in corporate and other organizational affiliations or the addition or realignment of parties in litigation, might create conflicts in the midst of a representation, as when a company sued by the lawyer on behalf of one client is bought by another client represented by the lawyer in an unrelated matter. Depending on the circumstances, the lawyer may have the option to withdraw from one of the representations in order to avoid the conflict. The lawyer must seek court approval where necessary and take steps to minimize harm to the clients. See Rule 1.16. The lawyer must continue to protect the confidences of the client from whose representation the lawyer has withdrawn. See Rule 1.9(c).

Identifying Conflicts of Interest: Directly Adverse

(6) Loyalty to a current client prohibits undertaking representation directly adverse to that client without that client's informed consent. Thus, absent consent, a lawyer may not act as an advocate in one matter against a person the lawyer represents in some other matter, even when the matters are wholly unrelated. The client as to whom the representation is directly adverse is likely to feel betrayed, and the resulting damage to the client-lawyer relationship is likely to impair the lawyer's ability to represent the client effectively. In addition, the client on whose behalf the adverse representation is undertaken reasonably may fear that the lawyer will pursue that client's case less effectively out of deference to the other client, i.e., that the representation may be materially limited by the lawyer's interest in retaining the current client. Similarly, a directly adverse conflict may arise when a lawyer is required to cross-examine a client who appears as a witness in a lawsuit involving another client, as when the testimony will be damaging to the client who is represented in the lawsuit. On the other hand, simultaneous representation in unrelated matters of clients whose interests are only economically adverse, such as representation of competing economic enterprises in unrelated litigation, does not ordinarily constitute a conflict of interest and thus may not require consent of the respective clients.

(7) Directly adverse conflicts can also arise in transactional matters. For example, if a lawyer is asked to represent the seller of a business in negotiations with a buyer represented by the lawyer, not in the same transaction but in another, unrelated matter, the lawyer could not undertake the representation without the informed consent of each client.

Identifying Conflicts of Interest: Material Limitation

(8) Even where there is no direct adverseness, a conflict of interest exists if there is a significant risk that a lawyer's ability to consider, recommend or carry out an appropriate course of action for the client

will be materially limited as a result of the lawyer's other responsibilities or interests. For example, a lawyer asked to represent several individuals seeking to form a joint venture is likely to be materially limited in the lawyer's ability to recommend or advocate all possible positions that each might take because of the lawyer's duty of loyalty to the others. The conflict in effect forecloses alternatives that would otherwise be available to the client. The mere possibility of subsequent harm does not itself require disclosure and consent. The critical questions are the likelihood that a difference in interests will eventuate and, if it does, whether it will materially interfere with the lawyer's independent professional judgment in considering alternatives or foreclose courses of action that reasonably should be pursued on behalf of the client.

Lawyer's Responsibilities to Former Clients and Other Third Persons

(9) In addition to conflicts with other current clients, a lawyer's duties of loyalty and independence may be materially limited by responsibilities to former clients under Rule 1.9 or by the lawyer's responsibilities to other persons, such as fiduciary duties arising from a lawyer's service as a trustee, executor or corporate director.

Personal Interest Conflicts

(10) The lawyer's own interests should not be permitted to have an adverse effect on representation of a client. For example, if the probity of a lawyer's own conduct in a transaction is in serious question, it may be difficult or impossible for the lawyer to give a client detached advice. Similarly, when a lawyer has discussions concerning possible employment with an opponent of the lawyer's client, or with a law firm representing the opponent, such discussions could materially limit the lawyer's representation of the client. In addition, a lawyer may not allow related business interests to affect representation, for example, by referring clients to an enterprise in which the lawyer has an undisclosed financial interest. See Rule 1.8 for specific Rules pertaining to a number of personal interest conflicts, including business transactions with clients. See also Rule 1.10 (personal interest conflicts under Rule 1.7 ordinarily are not imputed to other lawyers in a law firm).

(11) When lawyers representing different clients in the same matter or in substantially related matters are closely related by blood or marriage, there may be a significant risk that client confidences will be revealed and that the lawyer's family relationship will interfere with both loyalty and independent professional judgment. As a result, each client is entitled to know of the existence and implications of the relationship between the lawyers before the lawyer agrees to undertake the representation. Thus, a lawyer related to another lawyer, e.g., as parent, child, sibling or spouse, ordinarily may not represent a client in a matter where that lawyer is representing another party, unless each client gives informed consent. The disqualification arising from a close family relationship is personal and ordinarily is not imputed to members of firms with whom the lawyers are associated. See Rule 1.10.

(12) A lawyer is prohibited from engaging in sexual relationships with a client unless the sexual relationship predates the formation of the client-lawyer relationship. See Rule 1.8(j).

Interest of Person Paying for a Lawyer's Service

(13) A lawyer may be paid from a source other than the client, including a co-client, if the client is informed of that fact and consents and the arrangement does not compromise the lawyer's duty of loyalty or independent judgment to the client. See Rule 1.8(f). If acceptance of the payment from any other source presents a significant risk that the lawyer's representation of the client will be materially limited by the lawyer's own interest in accommodating the person paying the lawyer's fee or by the lawyer's responsibilities to a payer who is also a co-client, then the lawyer must comply with the requirements of paragraph (b) before accepting the representation, including determining whether the conflict is consentable and, if so, that the client has adequate information about the material risks of the representation.

Prohibited Representations

(14) Ordinarily, clients may consent to representation notwithstanding a conflict. However, as indicated in paragraph (b), some conflicts are nonconsentable, meaning that the lawyer involved cannot properly ask for such agreement or provide representation on the basis of the client's consent. When the lawyer is representing more than one client, the question of consentability must be resolved as to each client.

(15) Consentability is typically determined by considering whether the interests of the clients will be adequately protected if the clients are permitted to give their informed consent to representation burdened by a conflict of interest. Thus, under paragraph (b)(1), representation is prohibited if in the circumstances the lawyer cannot reasonably conclude that the lawyer will be able to provide competent and diligent representation. See Rule 1.1 (competence) and Rule 1.3 (diligence).

(16) Paragraph (b)(2) describes conflicts that are nonconsentable because the representation is prohibited by applicable law. For example, in some states substantive law provides that the same lawyer may not represent more than one defendant in a capital case, even with the consent of the clients, and under federal criminal statutes certain representations by a former government lawyer are prohibited, despite the informed consent of the former client. In addition, decisional law in some states limits the ability of a governmental client, such as a municipality, to consent to a conflict of interest.

(17) Paragraph (b)(3) describes conflicts that are nonconsentable because of the institutional interest in vigorous development of each client's position when the clients are aligned directly against each other in the same litigation or other proceeding before a tribunal. Whether clients are aligned directly against each other within the meaning of this paragraph requires examination of the context of the proceeding. Although this paragraph does not preclude a lawyer's multiple representation of adverse parties to a mediation (because mediation is not a proceeding before a "tribunal" under Rule 1.0(m)), such representation may be precluded by paragraph (b)(1).

Informed Consent

(18) Informed consent requires that each affected client be aware of the relevant circumstances and of the material and reasonably foreseeable ways that the conflict could have adverse effects on the interests of that client. See Rule 1.0(e) (informed consent). The information required depends on the nature of the conflict and the nature of the risks involved. When representation of multiple clients in a single matter is undertaken, the information must include the implications of the common representation, including possible effects on loyalty, confidentiality and the attorney-client privilege and the advantages and risks involved. See Comments [30] and [31] (effect of common representation on confidentiality).

(19) Under some circumstances it may be impossible to make the disclosure necessary to obtain consent. For example, when the lawyer represents different clients in related matters and one of the clients refuses to consent to the disclosure necessary to permit the other client to make an informed decision, the lawyer cannot properly ask the latter to consent. In some cases the alternative to common representation can be that each party may have to obtain separate representation with the possibility of incurring additional costs. These costs, along with the benefits of securing separate representation, are factors that may be considered by the affected client in determining whether common representation is in the client's interests.

Consent Confirmed in Writing

(20) Paragraph (b) requires the lawyer to obtain the informed consent of the client, confirmed in writing. Such a writing may consist of a document executed by the client or one that the lawyer promptly records and transmits to the client following an oral consent. See Rule 1.0(b). See also Rule 1.0(n) (writing includes electronic transmission). If it is not feasible to obtain or transmit the writing at the time the client gives informed consent, then the lawyer must obtain or transmit it within a reasonable time thereafter. See Rule 1.0(b). The requirement of a writing does not supplant the need in most cases for the lawyer to talk with the client, to explain the risks and advantages, if any, of representation burdened with a conflict of interest, as well as reasonably available alternatives, and to afford the client a reasonable opportunity to consider the risks and alternatives and to raise questions and concerns. Rather, the writing is required in order to impress upon clients the seriousness of the decision the client is being asked to make and to avoid disputes or ambiguities that might later occur in the absence of a writing.

Revoking Consent

(21) A client who has given consent to a conflict may revoke the consent and, like any other client, may terminate the lawyer's representation at any time. Whether revoking consent to the client's own representation precludes the lawyer from continuing to represent other clients depends on the circumstances, including the nature of the conflict, whether the client revoked consent because of a material change in circumstances, the reasonable expectations of the other clients and whether material detriment to the other clients or the lawyer would result.

Consent to Future Conflict

(22) Whether a lawyer may properly request a client to waive conflicts that might arise in the future is subject to the test of paragraph (b). The effectiveness of such waivers is generally determined by the extent to which the client reasonably understands the material risks that the waiver entails. The more comprehensive the explanation of the types of future representations that might arise and the actual and reasonably foreseeable adverse consequences of those representations, the greater the likelihood that the client will have the requisite understanding. Thus, if the client agrees to consent to a particular type of conflict with which the client is already familiar, then the consent ordinarily will be effective with regard to that type of conflict. If the consent is general and open-ended, then the consent ordinarily will be ineffective, because it is not reasonably likely that the client will have understood the material risks involved. On the other hand, if the client is an experienced user of the legal services involved and is reasonably informed regarding the risk that a conflict may arise, such consent is more likely to be effective, particularly if, e.g., the client is independently represented by other counsel in giving consent and the consent is limited to future conflicts unrelated to the subject of the representation. In any case, advance consent cannot be effective if the circumstances that materialize in the future are such as would make the conflict nonconsentable under paragraph (b).

Conflicts in Litigation

(23) Paragraph (b)(3) prohibits representation of opposing parties in the same litigation, regardless of the clients' consent. On the other hand, simultaneous representation of parties whose interests in litigation may conflict, such as coplaintiffs or codefendants, is governed by paragraph (a)(2). A conflict may exist by reason of substantial discrepancy in the parties' testimony, incompatibility in positions in relation to an opposing party or the fact that there are substantially different possibilities of settlement of the claims or liabilities in question. Such conflicts can arise in criminal cases as well as civil. The potential for conflict of interest in representing multiple defendants in a criminal case is so grave that ordinarily a lawyer should decline to represent more than one codefendant. On the other hand, common representation of persons having similar interests in civil litigation is proper if the requirements of paragraph (b) are met.

(24) Ordinarily a lawyer may take inconsistent legal positions in different tribunals at different times on behalf of different clients. The mere fact that advocating a legal position on behalf of one client might create precedent adverse to the interests of a client represented by the lawyer in an unrelated matter does not create a conflict of interest. A conflict of interest exists, however, if there is a significant risk that a lawyer's action on behalf of one client will materially limit the lawyer's effectiveness in representing another client in a different case; for example, when a decision favoring one client will create a precedent likely to seriously weaken the position taken on behalf of the other client. Factors relevant in determining whether the clients need to be advised of the risk include: where the cases are pending, whether the issue is substantive or procedural, the temporal relationship between the matters, the significance of the issue to the immediate and long-term interests of the clients involved and the clients' reasonable expectations in retaining the lawyer. If there is significant risk of material limitation, then absent informed consent of the affected clients, the lawyer must refuse one of the representations or withdraw from one or both matters.

(25) When a lawyer represents or seeks to represent a class of plaintiffs or defendants in a class-action lawsuit, unnamed members of the class are ordinarily not considered to be clients of the lawyer for purposes of applying paragraph (a)(1) of this Rule. Thus, the lawyer does not typically need to get the consent of such a person before representing a client suing the person in an unrelated matter. Simi-

larly, a lawyer seeking to represent an opponent in a class action does not typically need the consent of an unnamed member of the class whom the lawyer represents in an unrelated matter.

Nonlitigation Conflicts

(26) Conflicts of interest under paragraphs (a)(1) and (a)(2) arise in contexts other than litigation. For a discussion of directly adverse conflicts in transactional matters, see Comment (7). Relevant factors in determining whether there is significant potential for material limitation include the duration and intimacy of the lawyer's relationship with the client or clients involved, the functions being performed by the lawyer, the likelihood that disagreements will arise and the likely prejudice to the client from the conflict. The question is often one of proximity and degree. See Comment (8).

(27) For example, conflict questions may arise in estate planning and estate administration. A lawyer may be called upon to prepare wills for several family members, such as husband and wife, and, depending upon the circumstances, a conflict of interest may be present. In estate administration the identity of the client may be unclear under the law of a particular jurisdiction. Under one view, the client is the fiduciary; under another view the client is the estate or trust, including its beneficiaries. In order to comply with conflict of interest Rules, the lawyer should make clear the lawyer's relationship to the parties involved.

(28) Whether a conflict is consentable depends on the circumstances. For example, a lawyer may not represent multiple parties to a negotiation whose interests are fundamentally antagonistic to each other, but common representation is permissible where the clients are generally aligned in interest even though there is some difference in interest among them. Thus, a lawyer may seek to establish or adjust a relationship between clients on an amicable and mutually advantageous basis; for example, in helping to organize a business in which two or more clients are entrepreneurs, working out the financial reorganization of an enterprise in which two or more clients have an interest or arranging a property distribution in settlement of an estate. The lawyer seeks to resolve potentially adverse interests by developing the parties' mutual interests. Otherwise, each party might have to obtain separate representation, with the possibility of incurring additional cost, complication or even litigation. Given these and other relevant factors, the clients may prefer that the lawyer act for all of them.

Special Considerations in Common Representation

(29) In considering whether to represent multiple clients in the same matter, a lawyer should be mindful that if the common representation fails because the potentially adverse interests cannot be reconciled, the result can be additional cost, embarrassment and recrimination. Ordinarily, the lawyer will be forced to withdraw from representing all of the clients if the common representation fails. In some situations, the risk of failure is so great that multiple representation is plainly impossible. For example, a lawyer cannot undertake common representation of clients where contentious litigation or negotiations between them are imminent or contemplated. Moreover, because the lawyer is required to be impartial between commonly represented clients, representation of multiple clients is improper when it is unlikely that impartiality can be maintained. Generally, if the relationship between the parties has already assumed antagonism, the possibility that the clients' interests can be adequately served by common representation is not very good. Other relevant factors are whether the lawyer subsequently will represent both parties on a continuing basis and whether the situation involves creating or terminating a relationship between the parties.

(30) A particularly important factor in determining the appropriateness of common representation is the effect on client-lawyer confidentiality and the attorney-client privilege. With regard to the attorney-client privilege, the prevailing Rule is that, as between commonly represented clients, the privilege does not attach. Hence, it must be assumed that if litigation eventuates between the clients, the privilege will not protect any such communications, and the clients should be so advised.

(31) As to the duty of confidentiality, continued common representation will almost certainly be inadequate if one client asks the lawyer not to disclose to the other client information relevant to the common representation. This is, so because the lawyer has an equal duty of loyalty to each client, and each client has the right to be informed of anything bearing on the representation that might affect that client's

interests and the right to expect that the lawyer will use that information to that client's benefit. See Rule 1.4. The lawyer should, at the outset of the common representation and as part of the process of obtaining each client's informed consent, advise each client that information will be shared and that the lawyer will have to withdraw if one client decides that some matter material to the representation should be kept from the other. In limited circumstances, it may be appropriate for the lawyer to proceed with the representation when the clients have agreed, after being properly informed, that the lawyer will keep certain information confidential. For example, the lawyer may reasonably conclude that failure to disclose one client's trade secrets to another client will not adversely affect representation involving a joint venture between the clients and agree to keep that information confidential with the informed consent of both clients.

(32) When seeking to establish or adjust a relationship between clients, the lawyer should make clear that the lawyer's role is not that of partisanship normally expected in other circumstances and, thus, that the clients may be required to assume greater responsibility for decisions than when each client is separately represented. Any limitations on the scope of the representation made necessary as a result of the common representation should be fully explained to the clients at the outset of the representation. See Rule 1.2(c).

(33) Subject to the above limitations, each client in the common representation has the right to loyal and diligent representation and the protection of Rule 1.9 concerning the obligations to a former client. The client also has the right to discharge the lawyer as stated in Rule 1.16.

Organizational Clients

(34) A lawyer who represents a corporation or other organization does not, by virtue of that representation, necessarily represent any constituent or affiliated organization, such as a parent or subsidiary. See Rule 1.13(a). Thus, the lawyer for an organization is not barred from accepting representation adverse to an affiliate in an unrelated matter, unless the circumstances are such that the affiliate should also be considered a client of the lawyer, there is an understanding between the lawyer and the organizational client that the lawyer will avoid representation adverse to the client's affiliates, or the lawyer's obligations to either the organizational client or the new client are likely to limit materially the lawyer's representation of the other client.

(35) A lawyer for a corporation or other organization who is also a member of its board of directors should determine whether the responsibilities of the two roles may conflict. The lawyer may be called on to advise the corporation in matters involving actions of the directors. Consideration should be given to the frequency with which such situations may arise, the potential intensity of the conflict, the effect of the lawyer's resignation from the board and the possibility of the corporation's obtaining legal advice from another lawyer in such situations. If there is material risk that the dual role will compromise the lawyer's independence of professional judgment, the lawyer should not serve as a director or should cease to act as the corporation's lawyer when conflicts of interest arise. The lawyer should advise the other members of the board that in some circumstances matters discussed at board meetings while the lawyer is present in the capacity of director might not be protected by the attorney-client privilege and that conflict of interest considerations might require the lawyer's recusal as a director or might require the lawyer and the lawyer's firm to decline representation of the corporation in a matter.

SCR 3.130(1.8) Conflict of interest: current clients; specific rules

(a) A lawyer shall not enter into a business transaction with a client or knowingly acquire an ownership, possessory, security or other pecuniary interest adverse to a client unless:

(1) the transaction and terms on which the lawyer acquires the interest are fair and reasonable to the client and are fully disclosed and transmitted in writing in a manner that can be reasonably understood by the client;

(2) the client is advised in writing of the desirability of seeking and is given a reasonable opportunity to seek the advice of independent legal counsel on the transaction; and

(3) the client gives informed consent, in a writing signed by the client, to the essential terms of the transaction and the lawyer's role in the transaction, including whether the lawyer is representing the client in the transaction.

(b) A lawyer shall not use information relating to representation of a client to the disadvantage of the client unless the client gives informed consent, except as permitted or required by these Rules.

(c) A lawyer shall not solicit any substantial gift from a client, including a testamentary gift, or prepare on behalf of a client an instrument giving the lawyer or a person related to the lawyer any substantial gift unless the lawyer or other recipient of the gift is related to the client. For purposes of this paragraph, related persons include a spouse, child, grandchild, parent, grandparent or other relative or individual with whom the lawyer or the client maintains a close, familial relationship.

(d) Prior to the conclusion of representation of a client, a lawyer shall not make or negotiate an agreement giving the lawyer literary or media rights to a portrayal or account based in substantial part on information relating to the representation.

(e) A lawyer shall not provide financial assistance to a client in connection with pending or contemplated litigation, except that:

(1) a lawyer may advance court costs and expenses of litigation, the repayment of which may be contingent on the outcome of the matter; and

(2) a lawyer representing an indigent client may pay court costs and expenses of litigation on behalf of the client.

(f) A lawyer shall not accept compensation for representing a client from one other than the client unless:

(1) the client gives informed consent;

(2) there is no interference with the lawyer's independence of professional judgment or with the client-lawyer relationship; and

(3) information relating to representation of a client is protected as required by Rule 1.6.

(g) A lawyer who represents two or more clients shall not participate in making an aggregate settlement of the claims of or against the clients, or in a criminal case an aggregated agreement as to guilty or nolo contendere pleas, unless each client gives informed consent, in a writing signed by the client. The lawyer's disclosure shall include the existence and nature of all the claims or pleas involved and of the participation of each person in the settlement.

(h) A lawyer shall not:

(1) make an agreement prospectively limiting the lawyer's liability to a client for malpractice unless the client is independently represented in making the agreement; or

(2) settle a claim or potential claim for such liability with an unrepresented client or former client unless that person is advised in writing of the desirability of seeking and is given a reasonable opportunity to seek the advice of independent legal counsel in connection therewith.

(i) A lawyer shall not acquire a proprietary interest in the cause of action or subject matter of litigation the lawyer is conducting for a client, except that the lawyer may:

(1) acquire a lien authorized by law to secure the lawyer's fee or expenses; and

(2) contract with a client for a reasonable contingent fee in a civil case.

(j) A lawyer shall not have sexual relations with a client unless a consensual sexual relationship existed between them before the client-lawyer relationship commenced.

(k) While lawyers are associated in a firm, a prohibition in the foregoing paragraphs (a) through (i) that applies to any one of them shall apply to all of them.

HISTORY: Amended by Order 2012–01, eff. 3–1–12; prior amendment eff. 7–15–09 (Order 2009–05); adopted by Order 89–1, eff. 1–1–90.

Supreme Court Commentary

2009:

Business Transactions Between Client and Lawyer

(1) A lawyer's legal skill and training, together with the relationship of trust and confidence between lawyer and client, create the possibility of overreaching when the lawyer participates in a business, property or financial transaction with a client, for example, a loan or sales transaction or a lawyer investment on behalf of a client. The requirements of paragraph (a) must be met even when the transaction is not closely related to the subject matter of the representation, as when a lawyer drafting a will for a client learns that the client needs money for unrelated expenses and offers to make a loan to the client. It also applies to lawyers purchasing property from estates they represent. It does not apply to ordinary fee arrangements between client and lawyer, which are governed by Rule 1.5, although its requirements must be met when the lawyer accepts an interest in the client's business or other nonmonetary property as payment of all or part of a fee. In addition, the Rule does not apply to standard commercial transactions between the lawyer and the client for products or services that the client generally markets to others, for example, banking or brokerage services, medical services, products manufactured or distributed by the client, and utilities' services. In such transactions, the lawyer has no advantage in dealing with the client, and the restrictions in paragraph (a) are unnecessary and impracticable.

(2) Paragraph (a)(1) requires that the transaction itself be fair to the client and that its essential terms be communicated to the client, in writing, in a manner that can be reasonably understood. Paragraph (a)(2) requires that the client also be advised, in writing, of the desirability of seeking the advice of independent legal counsel. It also requires that the client be given a reasonable opportunity to obtain such advice. Paragraph (a)(3) requires that the lawyer obtain the client's informed consent, in a writing signed by the client, both to the essential terms of the transaction and to the lawyer's role. When necessary, the lawyer should discuss both the material risks of the proposed transaction, including any risk presented by the lawyer's

involvement, and the existence of reasonably available alternatives and should explain why the advice of independent legal counsel is desirable. See Rule 1.0(e) (definition of informed consent).

(3) The risk to a client is greatest when the client expects the lawyer to represent the client in the transaction itself or when the lawyer's financial interest otherwise poses a significant risk that the lawyer's representation of the client will be materially limited by the lawyer's financial interest in the transaction. Here the lawyer's role requires that the lawyer must comply, not only with the requirements of paragraph (a), but also with the requirements of Rule 1.7. Under that Rule, the lawyer must disclose the risks associated with the lawyer's dual role as both legal adviser and participant in the transaction, such as the risk that the lawyer will structure the transaction or give legal advice in a way that favors the lawyer's interests at the expense of the client. Moreover, the lawyer must obtain the client's informed consent. In some cases, the lawyer's interest may be such that Rule 1.7 will preclude the lawyer from seeking the client's consent to the transaction.

(4) If the client is independently represented in the transaction, paragraph (a)(2) of this Rule is inapplicable, and the paragraph (a)(1) requirement for full disclosure is satisfied either by a written disclosure by the lawyer involved in the transaction or by the client's independent counsel. The fact that the client was independently represented in the transaction is relevant in determining whether the agreement was fair and reasonable to the client as paragraph (a)(1) further requires.

Use of Information Related to Representation

(5) Use of information relating to the representation to the disadvantage of the client violates the lawyer's duty of loyalty. Paragraph (b) applies when the information is used to benefit either the lawyer or a third person, such as another client or business associate of the lawyer. For example, if a lawyer learns that a client intends to purchase and develop several parcels of land, the lawyer may not use that information to purchase one of the parcels in competition with the client or to recommend that another client make such a purchase. The Rule does not prohibit uses that do not disadvantage the client. For example, a lawyer who learns a government agency's interpretation of trade legislation during the representation of one client may properly use that information to benefit other clients. Paragraph (b) prohibits disadvantageous use of client information unless the client gives informed consent, except as permitted or required by these Rules. See Rules 1.2(d), 1.6, 1.9(c), 3.3, 4.1(b), 8.1 and 8.3.

Gifts to Lawyers

(6) A lawyer may accept a gift from a client, if the transaction meets general standards of fairness. For example, a simple gift such as a present given at a holiday or as a token of appreciation is permitted. If a client offers the lawyer a more substantial gift, paragraph (c) does not prohibit the lawyer from accepting it, although such a gift may be voidable by the client under the doctrine of undue influence, which treats client gifts as presumptively fraudulent. In any event, due to concerns about overreaching and imposition on clients, a lawyer may not suggest that a substantial gift be made to the lawyer or for the lawyer's benefit, except where the lawyer is related to the client as set forth in paragraph (c).

(7) If effectuation of a substantial gift requires preparing a legal instrument such as a will or conveyance, the client should have the detached advice that another lawyer can provide. The sole exception to this Rule is where the client is a relative of the donee.

(8) This Rule does not prohibit a lawyer from seeking to have the lawyer or a partner or associate of the lawyer named as executor of the client's estate or to another potentially lucrative fiduciary position. Nevertheless, such appointments will be subject to the general conflict of interest provision in Rule 1.7 when there is a significant risk that the lawyer's interest in obtaining the appointment will materially limit the lawyer's independent professional judgment in advising the client concerning the choice of an executor or other fiduciary. In obtaining the client's informed consent to the conflict, the lawyer should advise the client concerning the nature and extent of the lawyer's financial interest in the appointment, as well as the availability of alternative candidates for the position.

Literary Rights

(9) An agreement by which a lawyer acquires literary or media rights concerning the conduct of the representation creates a conflict

between the interests of the client and the personal interests of the lawyer. Measures suitable in the representation of the client may detract from the publication value of an account of the representation. Paragraph (d) does not prohibit a lawyer representing a client in a transaction concerning literary property from agreeing that the lawyer's fee shall consist of a share in ownership in the property, if the arrangement conforms to Rule 1.5 and paragraphs (a) and (i).

Financial Assistance

(10) Lawyers may not subsidize lawsuits or administrative proceedings brought on behalf of their clients, including making or guaranteeing loans to their clients for living expenses, because to do so would encourage clients to pursue lawsuits that might not otherwise be brought and because such assistance gives lawyers too great a financial stake in the litigation. These dangers do not warrant a prohibition on a lawyer lending a client court costs and litigation expenses, including the expenses of medical examination and the costs of obtaining and presenting evidence, because these advances are virtually indistinguishable from contingent fees and help ensure access to the courts. Similarly, an exception allowing lawyers representing indigent clients to pay court costs and litigation expenses regardless of whether these funds will be repaid is warranted.

Person Paying for a Lawyer's Services

(11) Lawyers are frequently asked to represent a client under circumstances in which a third person will compensate the lawyer, in whole or in part. The third person might be a relative or friend, an indemnitor (such as a liability insurance company) or a co-client (such as a corporation sued along with one or more of its employees). Because third-party payers frequently have interests that differ from those of the client, including interests in minimizing the amount spent on the representation and in learning how the representation is progressing, lawyers are prohibited from accepting or continuing such representations unless the lawyer determines that there will be no interference with the lawyer's independent professional judgment and there is informed consent from the client. See also Rule 5.4(c) (prohibiting interference with a lawyer's professional judgment by one who recommends, employs or pays the lawyer to render legal services for another).

(12) Sometimes, it will be sufficient for the lawyer to obtain the client's informed consent regarding the fact of the payment and the identity of the third-party payer. If, however, the fee arrangement creates a conflict of interest for the lawyer, then the lawyer must comply with Rule 1.7. The lawyer must also conform to the requirements of Rule 1.6 concerning confidentiality. Under Rule 13(a), a conflict of interest exists if there is significant risk that the lawyer's representation of the client will be materially limited by the lawyer's own interest in the fee arrangement or by the lawyer's responsibilities to the third-party payer (for example, when the third-party payer is a co-client). Under Rule 13(b), the lawyer may accept or continue the representation with the informed consent of each affected client, unless the conflict is nonconsentable under that paragraph. Under Rule 1.7(b), the informed consent must be confirmed in writing.

Aggregate Settlements

(13) Differences in willingness to make or accept an offer of settlement are among the risks of common representation of multiple clients by a single lawyer. Under Rule 1.7, this is one of the risks that should be discussed before undertaking the representation, as part of the process of obtaining the clients' informed consent. In addition, Rule 1.2(a) protects each client's right to have the final say in deciding whether to accept or reject an offer of settlement and in deciding whether to enter a guilty or nolo contendere plea in a criminal case. The Rule stated in this paragraph is a corollary of both these Rules and provides that, before any settlement offer or plea bargain is made or accepted on behalf of multiple clients, the lawyer must inform each of them about all the material terms of the settlement, as described herein.

A non-certified, non-class aggregate settlement is a settlement of the claims of two or more individual claimants in which the resolution of the claims is interdependent. The resolution of claims in a non-class aggregate settlement is interdependent if the defendant's acceptance of the settlement is contingent upon the acceptance by a specified number or percentage of the claimants or specified dollar amount of claims; or the value of each claim is not based solely on individual case-by-case facts and negotiations. In such situations

potential conflicts of interest stemming from interdependency exist, thus posing a risk of unfairness to individual claimants.

When the terms of an aggregate settlement do not determine individual amounts to be distributed to each client, detailed disclosures are required. For example, if a lump sum is offered in an aggregate settlement and the claimants' attorney is involved in dividing the settlement sum, that attorney must disclose to each client the number of his or her clients participating, specifics of each client's claim relevant to the settlement, and the method of dividing the lump sum. In addition, the attorney must disclose the total attorney fees and costs to be paid, payments to be made other than to clients, to their attorneys and for costs, the method by which the costs are to be apportioned among the clients and ultimately the amount each client receives.

By contrast, if the terms of the aggregate settlement establish the method of calculating and distributing payments to each claimant, based upon the individual claim for liability and/or damages, the disclosures to each client represented by the same attorney do not need to be as detailed. In that instance, each client should be generally informed of the terms of the aggregate settlement offer, how such terms apply specifically to such client, the fact that the attorney represents multiple clients in the settlement and, if applicable, any contingency in the settlement requiring a percentage of claimants to accept the settlement. The claimants' attorney must also disclose fees and costs to each client (including how costs are apportioned among the joint clients) but attorney fees may be stated as a percentage of the total recovery as opposed to a specific dollar amount.

Limiting Liability and Settling Malpractice Claims

(14) Agreements prospectively limiting a lawyer's liability for malpractice are prohibited unless the client is independently represented in making the agreement because they are likely to undermine competent and diligent representation. Also, many clients are unable to evaluate the desirability of making such an agreement before a dispute has arisen, particularly if they are then represented by the lawyer seeking the agreement. This paragraph does not, however, prohibit a lawyer from entering into an agreement with the client to arbitrate legal malpractice claims, provided such agreements are enforceable and the client is fully informed of the scope and effect of the agreement. Nor does this paragraph limit the ability of lawyers to practice in the form of a limited-liability entity, where permitted by law, provided that each lawyer remains personally liable to the client for his or her own conduct and the firm complies with any conditions required by law, such as provisions requiring client notification or maintenance of adequate liability insurance. Nor does it prohibit an agreement in accordance with Rule 1.2 that defines the scope of the representation, although a definition of scope that makes the obligations of representation illusory will amount to an attempt to limit liability.

(15) Agreements settling a claim or a potential claim for malpractice are not prohibited by this Rule. Nevertheless, in view of the danger that a lawyer will take unfair advantage of an unrepresented client or former client, the lawyer must first advise such a person in writing of the appropriateness of independent representation in connection with such a settlement. In addition, the lawyer must give the client or former client a reasonable opportunity to find and consult independent counsel.

Acquiring Proprietary Interest in Litigation

(16) Paragraph (i) states the traditional general rule that lawyers are prohibited from acquiring a proprietary interest in litigation. Like paragraph (e), the general rule has its basis in common law champerty and maintenance and is designed to avoid giving the lawyer too great an interest in the representation. In addition, when the lawyer acquires an ownership interest in the subject of the representation, it will be more difficult for a client to discharge the lawyer if the client so desires. The Rule is subject to specific exceptions developed in decisional law and continued in these Rules. The exception for certain advances of the costs of litigation is set forth in paragraph (e). In addition, paragraph (i) sets forth exceptions for liens authorized by law to secure the lawyer's fees or expenses and contracts for reasonable contingent fees. The law of each jurisdiction determines which liens are authorized by law. These may include liens granted by statute, liens originating in common law and liens acquired by contract with the client. When a

lawyer acquires by contract a security interest in property other than that recovered through the lawyer's efforts in the litigation, such an acquisition is a business or financial transaction with a client and is governed by the requirements of paragraph (a). Contracts for contingent fees in civil cases are governed by Rule 1.5.

Client–Lawyer Sexual Relationships

(17) The relationship between lawyer and client is a fiduciary one in which the lawyer occupies the highest position of trust and confidence. The relationship is almost always unequal; thus, a sexual relationship between lawyer and client can involve unfair exploitation of the lawyer's fiduciary role, in violation of the lawyer's basic ethical obligation not to use the trust of the client to the client's disadvantage. In addition, such a relationship presents a significant danger that, because of the lawyer's emotional involvement, the lawyer will be unable to represent the client without impairment of the exercise of independent professional judgment. Moreover, a blurred line between the professional and personal relationships may make it difficult to predict to what extent client confidences will be protected by the attorney-client evidentiary privilege, since client confidences are protected by privilege only when they are imparted in the context of the client-lawyer relationship. Because of the significant danger of harm to client interests and because the client's own emotional involvement renders it unlikely that the client could give adequate informed consent, this Rule prohibits the lawyer from having sexual relations with a client regardless of whether the relationship is consensual and regardless of the absence of prejudice to the client.

(18) Sexual relationships that predate the client-lawyer relationship are not prohibited. Issues relating to the exploitation of the fiduciary relationship and client dependency are diminished when the sexual relationship existed prior to the commencement of the client-lawyer relationship. However, before proceeding with the representation in these circumstances, the lawyer should consider whether the lawyer's ability to represent the client will be materially limited by the relationship. See Rule 11(a)(2).

(19) When the client is an organization, paragraph (j) of this Rule prohibits a lawyer for the organization (whether inside counsel or outside counsel) from having a sexual relationship with a constituent of the organization who supervises, directs or regularly consults with that lawyer concerning the organization's legal matters.

Imputation of Prohibitions

(20) Under paragraph (k), a prohibition on conduct by an individual lawyer in paragraphs (a) through (i) also applies to all lawyers associated in a firm with the personally prohibited lawyer. For example, one lawyer in a firm may not enter into a business transaction with a client of another member of the firm without complying with paragraph (a), even if the first lawyer is not personally involved in the representation of the client. The prohibition set forth in paragraph (j) is personal and is not applied to associated lawyers.

SCR 3.130(1.9)   Duties to former clients

(a) A lawyer who has formerly represented a client in a matter shall not thereafter represent another person in the same or a substantially related matter in which that person's interests are materially adverse to the interests of the former client unless the former client gives informed consent, confirmed in writing.

(b) A lawyer shall not knowingly represent a person in the same or a substantially related matter in which a firm with which the lawyer formerly was associated had previously represented a client

(1) whose interests are materially adverse to that person; and

(2) about whom the lawyer had acquired information protected by Rules 1.6 and 1.9(c) that is material to the matter; unless the former client gives informed consent, confirmed in writing.

(c) A lawyer who has formerly represented a client in a matter or whose present or former firm has formerly represented a client in a matter shall not thereafter:

(1) use information relating to the representation to the disadvantage of the former client except as these Rules would permit or require with respect to a client, or when the information has become generally known; or

(2) reveal information relating to the representation except as these Rules would permit or require with respect to a client.

HISTORY: Amended by Order 2009–05, eff. 7-15-09; prior amendment eff. 2-1-00 (Order 99-1); adopted by Order 89-1, eff. 1-1-90

Supreme Court Commentary

2009:

(1) After termination of a client-lawyer relationship, a lawyer has certain continuing duties with respect to confidentiality and conflicts of interest and thus may not represent another client except in conformity with this Rule. Under this Rule, for example, a lawyer could not properly seek to rescind on behalf of a new client a contract drafted on behalf of the former client. So also a lawyer who has prosecuted an accused person could not properly represent the accused in a subsequent civil action against the government concerning the same transaction. Nor could a lawyer who has represented multiple clients in a matter represent one of the clients against the others in the same or a substantially related matter after a dispute arose among the clients in that matter, unless all affected clients give informed consent. See Comment [9]. Current and former government lawyers must comply with this Rule to the extent required by Rule 1.11.

(2) The scope of a "matter" for purposes of this Rule depends on the facts of a particular situation or transaction. The lawyer's involvement in a matter can also be a question of degree. When a lawyer has been directly involved in a specific transaction, subsequent representation of other clients with materially adverse interests in that transaction clearly is prohibited. On the other hand, a lawyer who recurrently handled a type of problem for a former client is not precluded from later representing another client in a factually distinct problem of that type even though the subsequent representation involves a position adverse to the prior client. Similar considerations can apply to the reassignment of military lawyers between defense and prosecution functions within the same military jurisdictions. The underlying question is whether the lawyer was so involved in the matter that the subsequent representation can be justly regarded as a changing of sides in the matter in question.

(3) Matters are "substantially related" for purposes of this Rule if they involve the same transaction or legal dispute or if there otherwise is a substantial risk that confidential factual information as would normally have been obtained in the prior representation would materially advance the client's position in the subsequent matter. For example, a lawyer who has represented a business person and learned extensive private financial information about that person may not then represent that person's spouse in seeking a divorce. Similarly, a lawyer who has previously represented a client in securing environmental permits to build a shopping center would be precluded from representing neighbors seeking to oppose rezoning of the property on the basis of environmental considerations; however, the lawyer would not be precluded, on the grounds of substantial relationship, from defending a tenant of the completed shopping center in resisting eviction for nonpayment of rent. Information that has been disclosed to the public or to other parties adverse to the former client ordinarily will not be disqualifying. Information acquired in a prior representation may have been rendered obsolete by the passage of time, a circumstance that may be relevant in determining whether two representations are substantially related. In the case of an organizational client, general knowledge of the client's policies and practices ordinarily will not preclude a subsequent representation; on the other

hand, knowledge of specific facts gained in a prior representation that are relevant to the matter in question ordinarily will preclude such a representation. A former client is not required to reveal the confidential information learned by the lawyer in order to establish a substantial risk that the lawyer has confidential information to use in the subsequent matter. A conclusion about the possession of such information may be based on the nature of the services the lawyer provided the former client and information that would in ordinary practice be learned by a lawyer providing such services.

Lawyers Moving Between Firms

(4) When lawyers have been associated within a firm but then end their association, the question of whether a lawyer should undertake representation is more complicated. There are several competing considerations. First, the client previously represented by the former firm must be reasonably assured that the principle of loyalty to the client is not compromised. Second, the rule should not be so broadly cast as to preclude other persons from having reasonable choice of legal counsel. Third, the rule should not unreasonably hamper lawyers from forming new associations and taking on new clients after having left a previous association. In this connection, it should be recognized that today many lawyers practice in firms, that many lawyers to some degree limit their practice to one field or another, and that many move from one association to another several times in their careers. If the concept of imputation were applied with unqualified rigor, the result would be radical curtailment of the opportunity of lawyers to move from one practice setting to another and of the opportunity of clients to change counsel.

(5) Historically, another rubric used for dealing with disqualification has been the appearance of impropriety proscribed in Canon 9 of the ABA Model Code of Professional Responsibility. This rubric has a two-fold problem. First, the appearance of impropriety can be taken to include any new client-lawyer relationship that might make a former client feel anxious. If that meaning were adopted, disqualification would become little more than a question of subjective judgment by the former client. Second, since "impropriety" is undefined, the term "appearance of impropriety" is question-begging. It therefore has to be recognized that the problem of disqualification cannot be properly resolved either by simple analogy to a lawyer practicing alone or by the very general concept of appearance of impropriety. Notwithstanding the deletion of this standard from the Rules of Professional Conduct, the Kentucky Supreme Court, in *Lowell v. Winchester, Ky.*, 941 S.W.2d 466 (1997), opined that "Although the appearance of impropriety formula is vague and leads to uncertain results, it nonetheless serves the useful function of stressing that disqualification properly may be imposed to protect the reasonable expectations of former and present clients. The impropriety standard also promotes the public's confidence in the integrity of the legal profession. For these reasons, courts still retain the appearance of impropriety standard as an independent basis of assessment."

(6) Paragraph (b) operates to disqualify the lawyer only when the lawyer involved has actual knowledge of information protected by Rules 1.6 and 1.9(c). Thus, if a lawyer while with one firm acquired no knowledge or information relating to a particular client of the firm, and that lawyer later joined another firm, neither the lawyer individually nor the second firm is disqualified from representing another client in the same or a related matter even though the interests of the two clients conflict. See Rule 1.10(b) for the restrictions on a firm once a lawyer has terminated association with the firm.

(7) Application of paragraph (b) depends on a situation's particular facts, aided by inferences, deductions or working presumptions that reasonably may be made about the way in which lawyers work together. A lawyer may have general access to files of all clients of a law firm and may regularly participate in discussions of their affairs; it should be inferred that such a lawyer in fact is privy to all information about all the firm's clients. In contrast, another lawyer may have access to the files of only a limited number of clients and participate in discussions of the affairs of no other clients; in the absence of information to the contrary, it should be inferred that such a lawyer in fact is privy to information about the clients actually served but not those of other clients. In such an inquiry, the burden of proof should rest upon the firm whose disqualification is sought.

(8) Independent of the question of disqualification of a firm, a lawyer changing professional association has a continuing duty to preserve confidentiality of information about a client formerly represented. See Rules 1.6 and 1.9(c).

(9) Paragraph (c) provides that information acquired by the lawyer in the course of representing a client may not subsequently be used or revealed by the lawyer to the disadvantage of the client. However, the fact that a lawyer has once served a client does not preclude the lawyer from using generally known information about that client when later representing another client.

(10) The provisions of this Rule are for the protection of former clients and can be waived if the client gives informed consent, which consent must be confirmed in writing under paragraphs (a) and (b). See Rule 1.0(e). With regard to the effectiveness of an advance waiver, see Comment (22) to Rule 1.7. With regard to disqualification of a firm with which a lawyer is or was formerly associated, see Rule 1.10.

SCR 3.130(1.10) Imputation of conflicts of interest: general rule

(a) While lawyers are associated in a firm, none of them shall knowingly represent a client when any one of them practicing alone would be prohibited from doing so by Rules 1.7 or 1.9, unless the prohibition is based on a personal interest of the prohibited lawyer and does not present a significant risk of materially limiting the representation of the client by the remaining lawyers in the firm.

(b) When a lawyer has terminated an association with a firm, the firm is not prohibited from thereafter representing a person with interests materially adverse to those of a client represented by the formerly associated lawyer and not currently represented by the firm, unless:

(1) the matter is the same or substantially related to that in which the formerly associated lawyer represented the client; and

(2) any lawyer remaining in the firm has information protected by Rules 1. 6 and 1.9(c) that is material to the matter.

(c) A disqualification prescribed by this rule may be waived by the affected client under the conditions stated in Rule 1.7.

(d) A firm is not disqualified from representation of a client if the only basis for disqualification is representation of a former client by a lawyer presently associated with the firm, sufficient to cause that lawyer to be disqualified pursuant to Rule 1.9 and:

(1) the disqualified lawyer is screened from any participation in the matter and is apportioned no specific part of the fee therefrom; and

(2) written notice is given to the former client.

(e) The disqualification of lawyers associated in a firm with former or current government lawyers is governed by Rule 1.11.

HISTORY: Amended by Order 2009–05, eff. 7–15–09; prior amendment eff. 2–1–00 (Order 99–1); adopted by Order 89–1, eff. 1–1–90

Supreme Court Commentary

2009:

Definition of "Firm"

(1) For purposes of the Rules of Professional Conduct, the term "firm" denotes lawyers in a law partnership, professional corporation, sole proprietorship or other association authorized to practice law; or lawyers employed in a legal services organization or the legal department of a corporation or other organization. See Rule 1.0(c). Whether two or more lawyers constitute a firm within this definition can depend on the specific facts. See Rule 1.0, Comments [2]–[4].

Principles of Imputed Disqualification

(2) The rule of imputed disqualification stated in paragraph (a) gives effect to the principle of loyalty to the client as it applies to lawyers who practice in a law firm. Such situations can be considered from the premise that a firm of lawyers is essentially one lawyer for purposes of the rules governing loyalty to the client, or from the premise that each lawyer is vicariously bound by the obligation of loyalty owed by each lawyer with whom the lawyer is associated. Paragraph (a) operates only among the lawyers currently associated in a firm. When a lawyer moves from one firm to another, the situation is governed by Rules 1.9(b) and 1.10(b).

(3) The rule in paragraph (a) does not prohibit representation where neither questions of client loyalty nor protection of confidential information are presented. Where one lawyer in a firm could not effectively represent a given client because of strong political beliefs, for example, but that lawyer will do no work on the case and the personal beliefs of the lawyer will not materially limit the representation by others in the firm, the firm should not be disqualified. On the other hand, if an opposing party in a case were owned by a lawyer in the law firm, and others in the firm would be materially limited in pursuing the matter because of loyalty to that lawyer, the personal disqualification of the lawyer would be imputed to all others in the firm.

(4) The rule in paragraph (a) also does not prohibit representation by others in the law firm where the person prohibited from involvement in a matter is a nonlawyer, such as a paralegal or legal secretary. Nor does paragraph (a) prohibit representation if the lawyer is prohibited from acting because of events before the person became a lawyer, for example, work that the person did while a law student. Such persons, however, ordinarily must be screened from any personal participation in the matter to avoid communication to others in the firm of confidential information that both the nonlawyers and the firm have a legal duty to protect. See Rules 1.0(k) and 5.3.

(5) Rule 1.10(b) operates to permit a law firm, under certain circumstances, to represent a person with interests directly adverse to those of a client represented by a lawyer who formerly was associated with the firm. The Rule applies regardless of when the formerly associated lawyer represented the client. However, the law firm may not represent a person with interests adverse to those of a present client of the firm, which would violate Rule 1.7. Moreover, the firm may not represent the person where the matter is the same or substantially related to that in which the formerly associated lawyer represented the client and any other lawyer currently in the firm has material information protected by Rules 1.6 and 1.9.

(6) Rule 1.10(c) removes imputation with the informed consent of the affected client or former client under the conditions stated in Rule 1.7. The conditions stated in Rule 1.7 require the lawyer to determine that the representation is not prohibited by Rule 1.7(b) and that each affected client or former client has given informed consent to the representation, confirmed in writing. In some cases, the risk may be so severe that the conflict may not be cured by client consent. For a discussion of the effectiveness of client waivers of conflicts that might arise in the future, see Rule 1.7, Comment [22]. For a definition of informed consent, see Rule 1.0(e).

(7) Rule 1.10(d) removes the imputation in some cases when the disqualified lawyer is screened. See Rule 1.0(k) and Comments [8]–[10] for minimum requirements of screening.

(8) When a lawyer has joined a private firm after having represented the government, imputation is governed by Rule 1.11(b) and (c), not this Rule. Under Rule 1.11(d), when a lawyer represents the government after having served clients in private practice, nongovernmental employment or in another government agency, former client conflicts are not imputed to government lawyers associated with the individually disqualified lawyer.

(9) Where a lawyer is prohibited from engaging in certain transactions under Rule 1.8, paragraph (k) of that Rule, and not this Rule,

determines whether that prohibition also applies to other lawyers associated in a firm with the personally prohibited lawyer.

SCR 3.130(1.11) Special conflicts of interest for former and current government officers and employees

(a) Except as law may otherwise expressly permit, a lawyer who has formerly served as a public officer or employee of the government:

(1) is subject to Rule 1.9(c); and

(2) shall not otherwise represent a client in connection with a matter in which the lawyer participated personally and substantially as a public officer or employee, unless the appropriate government agency gives its informed consent, confirmed in writing, to the representation.

(b) When a lawyer is disqualified from representation under paragraph (a), no lawyer in a firm with which that lawyer is associated may knowingly undertake or continue representation in such a matter unless:

(1) the disqualified lawyer is timely screened from any participation in the matter and is apportioned no part of the fee therefrom; and

(2) written notice is promptly given to the appropriate private public body or government agency to enable it to ascertain compliance with the provisions of this Rule.

(c) Except as law may otherwise expressly permit, a lawyer having information that the lawyer knows is confidential government information about a person acquired when the lawyer was a public officer or employee, may not represent a private client whose interests are adverse to that person in a matter in which the information could be used to the material disadvantage of that person. As used in this Rule, the term "confidential government information" means information that has been obtained under governmental authority and which, at the time this Rule is applied, the government is prohibited by law from disclosing to the public or has a legal privilege not to disclose and which is not otherwise available to the public. A firm with which that lawyer is associated may undertake or continue representation in the matter only if the disqualified lawyer is timely screened from any participation in the matter and is apportioned no part of the fee therefrom.

(d) Except as law may otherwise expressly permit, a lawyer currently serving as a public officer or employee:

(1) is subject to Rules 1.7 and 1.9; and

(2) shall not:

(i) participate in a matter in which the lawyer participated personally and substantially while in private practice or nongovernmental employment, unless the appropriate government agency gives its informed consent, confirmed in writing; or

(ii) negotiate for private employment with any person who is involved as a party or as attorney for a party in a matter in which the lawyer is participating personally and substantially, except that a lawyer serving as a law clerk to a judge, other adjudicative officer or arbitrator may negotiate for private employment as permitted by Rule 1.12(b) and subject to the conditions stated in Rule 1.12(b).

(e) As used in this Rule, the term "matter" includes:

(1) any judicial or other proceeding, application, request for a ruling or other determination, contract, claim, controversy, investigation, charge, accusation, arrest or other particular matter involving a specific party or parties, and

(2) any other matter covered by the conflict of interest rules of the appropriate government agency.

HISTORY: Amended by Order 2009–05, eff. 7–15–09; adopted by Order 89–1, eff. 1–1–90.

Supreme Court Commentary

2009:

(1) A lawyer who has served or is currently serving as a public officer or employee is personally subject to the Rules of Professional Conduct, including the prohibition against concurrent conflicts of interest stated in Rule 1.7. In addition, such a lawyer may be subject to statutes and government regulations regarding conflict of interest. Such statutes and regulations may circumscribe the extent to which the government agency may give consent under this Rule. See Rule 1.0(e) for the definition of informed consent.

(2) Paragraphs (a)(1), (a)(2) and (d)(1) restate the obligations of an individual lawyer who has served or is currently serving as an officer or employee of the government toward a former government or private client. Rule 1.10 is not applicable to the conflicts of interest addressed by this Rule. Rather, paragraph (b) sets forth a special imputation Rule for former government lawyers that provides for screening and notice. Because of the special problems raised by imputation within a government agency, paragraph (d) does not impute the conflicts of a lawyer currently serving as an officer or employee of the government to other associated government officers or employees, although ordinarily it will be prudent to screen such lawyers.

(3) Paragraphs (a)(2) and (d)(2) apply regardless of whether a lawyer is adverse to a former client and are thus designed not only to protect the former client, but also to prevent a lawyer from exploiting public office for the advantage of another client. For example, a lawyer who has pursued a claim on behalf of the government may not pursue the same claim on behalf of a later private client after the lawyer has left government service, except when authorized to do so by the government agency under paragraph (a). Similarly, a lawyer who has pursued a claim on behalf of a private client may not pursue the claim on behalf of the government, except when authorized to do so by paragraph (d). As with paragraphs (a)(1) and (d)(1), Rule 1.10 is not applicable to the conflicts of interest addressed by these paragraphs.

(4) This Rule represents a balancing of interests. On the one hand, where the successive clients are a government agency and another client, public or private, the risk exists that power or discretion vested in that agency might be used for the special benefit of the other client. A lawyer should not be in a position where benefit to the other client might affect performance of the lawyer's professional functions on behalf of the government. Also, unfair advantage could accrue to the other client by reason of access to confidential government information about the client's adversary obtainable only through the lawyer's government service. On the other hand, the rules governing lawyers presently or formerly employed by a government agency should not be so restrictive as to inhibit transfer of employment to and from the government. The government has a legitimate

need to attract qualified lawyers as well as to maintain high ethical standards. Thus a former government lawyer is disqualified only from particular matters in which the lawyer participated personally and substantially. The provisions for screening and waiver in paragraph (b) are necessary to prevent the disqualification rule from imposing too severe a deterrent against entering public service. The limitation of disqualification in paragraphs (a)(2) and (d)(2) to matters involving a specific party or parties, rather than extending disqualification to all substantive issues on which the lawyer worked, serves a similar function.

(5) When a lawyer has been employed by one government agency and then moves to a second government agency, it may be appropriate to treat that second agency as another client for purposes of this Rule, as when a lawyer is employed by a city and subsequently is employed by a federal agency. However, because the conflict of interest is governed by paragraph (d), the latter agency is not required to screen the lawyer as paragraph (b) requires a law firm to do. The question of whether two government agencies should be regarded as the same or different clients for conflict of interest purposes is beyond the scope of these Rules. See Rule 1.13 Comment [9].

(6) Paragraphs (b) and (c) contemplate a screening arrangement. See Rule 1.0(k) (requirements for screening procedures). These paragraphs do not prohibit a lawyer from receiving a salary or partnership share established by prior independent agreement, but that lawyer may not receive compensation directly relating the attorney's compensation to the fee in the matter in which the lawyer is disqualified.

(7) Notice, including a description of the screened lawyer's prior representation and of the screening procedures employed, generally should be given as soon as practicable after the need for screening becomes apparent.

(8) Paragraph (c) operates only when the lawyer in question has knowledge of the information, which means actual knowledge; it does not operate with respect to information that merely could be imputed to the lawyer.

(9) Paragraphs (a) and (d) do not prohibit a lawyer from jointly representing a private party and a government agency when doing so is permitted by Rule 1.7 and is not otherwise prohibited by law.

(10) For purposes of paragraph (e) of this Rule, a "matter" may continue in another form. In determining whether two particular matters are the same, the lawyer should consider the extent to which the matters involve the same basic facts, the same or related parties, and the time elapsed.

SCR 3.130(1.12) Judge, arbitrator, mediator or other third-party neutral

(a) Except as stated in paragraph (d), a lawyer shall not represent anyone in connection with a matter in which the lawyer participated personally and substantially as a judge or other adjudicative officer or law clerk to such a person or as an arbitrator, mediator or other third-party neutral, unless all parties to the proceeding give informed consent, confirmed in writing.

(b) A lawyer shall not negotiate for employment with any person who is involved as a party or as attorney for a party in a matter in which the lawyer is participating personally and substantially as a judge or other adjudicative officer, or as an arbitrator, mediator or other third-party neutral. This rule does not prohibit an arbitrator, mediator, or third-part neutral from negotiating future cases. A lawyer serving as a law clerk to a judge or other adjudicative officer may negotiate for employment with a party or lawyer involved in a matter in which the clerk is participating personally and substantially, but only after the lawyer has notified the judge or other adjudicative officer.

(c) If a lawyer is disqualified by paragraph (a), no lawyer in a firm with which that lawyer is associated may knowingly undertake or continue representation in the matter unless:

(1) the disqualified lawyer is timely screened from any participation in the matter and is apportioned no part of the fee therefrom; and

(2) written notice is promptly given to the parties and any appropriate tribunal to enable them to ascertain compliance with the provisions of this Rule.

(d) An arbitrator selected as a partisan of a party in a multimember arbitration panel is not prohibited from subsequently representing that party.

HISTORY: Amended by Order 2009–05, eff. 7–15–09; adopted by Order 89–1, eff. 1–1–90.

Supreme Court Commentary

2009:

(1) This Rule generally parallels Rule 1.11. The term "personally and substantially" signifies that a judge who was a member of a multimember court, and thereafter left judicial office to practice law, is not prohibited from representing a client in a matter pending in the court, but in which the former judge did not participate. So also the fact that a former judge exercised administrative responsibility in a court does not prevent the former judge from acting as a lawyer in a matter where the judge had previously exercised remote or incidental administrative responsibility that did not affect the merits. Compare the Comment to Rule 1.11. The term "adjudicative officer" includes such officials as judges pro tempore, referees, special masters, hearing officers and other parajudicial officers, and also lawyers who serve as part-time judges. Compliance Canons A(2), B(2) and C of the Model Code of Judicial Conduct provide that a part-time judge, judge pro tempore or retired judge recalled to active service, may not "act as a lawyer in any proceeding in which he served as a judge or in any other proceeding related thereto." Although phrased differently from this Rule, those rules correspond in meaning.

(2) Like former judges, lawyers who have served as arbitrators, mediators or other third-party neutrals may be asked to represent a client in a matter in which the lawyer participated personally and substantially. This Rule forbids such representation unless all of the parties to the proceedings give their informed consent, confirmed in writing. See Rule 1.0(e) and (b). Other law or codes of ethics governing third-party neutrals may impose more stringent standards of personal or imputed disqualification. See Rule 2.4.

(3) Although lawyers who serve as third-party neutrals do not have information concerning the parties that is protected under Rule 1.6, they typically owe the parties an obligation of confidentiality under law or codes of ethics governing third-party neutrals. Thus, paragraph (c) provides that conflicts of the personally disqualified lawyer will be imputed to other lawyers in a law firm unless the conditions of this paragraph are met.

(4) Requirements for screening procedures are stated in Rule 1.0(k). Paragraph (c)(1) does not prohibit the screened lawyer from receiving a salary or partnership share established by prior independent agreement, but that lawyer may not receive compensation directly related to the matter in which the lawyer is disqualified.

(5) Notice, including a description of the screened lawyer's prior representation and of the screening procedures employed, generally should be given as soon as practicable after the need for screening becomes apparent.

SCR 3.130(1.13)   Organization as client

(a) A lawyer employed or retained by an organization represents the organization acting through its duly authorized constituents.

(b) If a lawyer for an organization knows that an officer, employee or other person associated with the organization is engaged in action, intends to act or refuses to act in a matter related to the representation that is a violation of a legal obligation to the organization, or a violation of law that reasonably might be imputed to the organization, and that is likely to result in substantial injury to the organization, then the lawyer shall proceed as is reasonably necessary in the best interest of the organization. Unless the lawyer reasonably believes that it is not necessary in the best interest of the organization to do so, the lawyer shall refer the matter to higher authority in the organization, including, if warranted by the circumstances, to the highest authority that can act in behalf of the organization as determined by applicable law.

(c) Except as provided in paragraph (d), if,

(1) despite the lawyer's efforts in accordance with paragraph (b), the highest authority that can act on behalf of the organization insists upon or fails to address in a timely and appropriate manner an action, or a refusal to act, that is clearly a violation of law, and

(2) the lawyer reasonably believes that the violation is reasonably certain to result in substantial injury to the organization, then the lawyer may reveal information relating to the representation whether or not Rule 1.6 permits such disclosure, but only if and to the extent the lawyer reasonably believes necessary to prevent substantial injury to the organization.

(d) Paragraph (c) shall not apply with respect to information relating to a lawyer's representation of an organization to investigate an alleged violation of law, or to defend the organization or an officer, employee or other constituent associated with the organization against a claim arising out of an alleged violation of law.

(e) A lawyer who reasonably believes that he or she has been discharged because of the lawyer's actions taken pursuant to paragraphs (b) or (c), or who withdraws under circumstances that require or permit the lawyer to take action under either of those paragraphs, shall proceed as the lawyer reasonably believes necessary to assure that the organization's highest authority is informed of the lawyer's discharge or withdrawal.

(f) In dealing with an organization's directors, officers, employees, members, shareholders or other constituents, a lawyer shall explain the identity of the client when the lawyer knows or reasonably should know that the organization's interests are adverse to those of the constituents with whom the lawyer is dealing.

(g) A lawyer representing an organization may also represent any of its directors, officers, employees, members, shareholders or other constituents, subject to the provisions of Rule 1.7. If the organization's consent to the dual representation is required by Rule

1.7, the consent shall be given by an appropriate official of the organization other than the individual who is to be represented, or by the shareholders.

HISTORY: Amended by Order 2009–05, eff. 7–15–09; adopted by Order 89–1, eff. 1–1–90.

Supreme Court Commentary

2009:

The Entity as the Client

(1) An organizational client is a legal entity, but it cannot act except through its officers, directors, employees, shareholders and other constituents. Officers, directors, employees and shareholders are the constituents of the corporate organizational client. The duties defined in this Comment apply equally to unincorporated associations. "Other constituents" as used in this Comment means the positions equivalent to officers, directors, employees and shareholders held by persons acting for organizational clients that are not corporations.

(2) When one of the constituents of an organizational client communicates with the organization's lawyer in that person's organizational capacity, the communication is protected by Rule 1.6. Thus, by way of example, if an organizational client requests its lawyer to investigate allegations of wrongdoing, interviews made in the course of that investigation between the lawyer and the client's employees or other constituents are covered by Rule 1.6. This does not mean, however, that constituents of an organizational client are the clients of the lawyer. The lawyer may not disclose to such constituents information relating to the representation except for disclosures explicitly or impliedly authorized by the organizational client in order to carry out the representation or as otherwise permitted by Rule 1.6.

(3) When constituents of the organization make decisions for it, the decisions ordinarily must be accepted by the lawyer even if their utility or prudence is doubtful. Decisions concerning policy and operations, including ones entailing serious risk, are not as such in the lawyer's province. Paragraph (b) makes clear, however, that when the lawyer knows that the organization is likely to be substantially injured by action of an officer or other constituent that violates a legal obligation to the organization or is in violation of law that might be imputed to the organization, the lawyer must proceed as is reasonably necessary in the best interest of the organization. As defined in Rule 1.0(f), knowledge can be inferred from circumstances, and a lawyer cannot ignore the obvious.

(4) In determining how to proceed under paragraph (b), the lawyer should give due consideration to the seriousness of the violation and its consequences, the responsibility in the organization and the apparent motivation of the person involved, the policies of the organization concerning such matters, and any other relevant considerations. Ordinarily, referral to a higher authority would be necessary. In some circumstances, however, it may be appropriate for the lawyer to ask the constituent to reconsider the matter; for example, if the circumstances involve a constituent's innocent misunderstanding of law and subsequent acceptance of the lawyer's advice, the lawyer may reasonably conclude that the best interest of the organization does not require that the matter be referred to higher authority. If a constituent persists in conduct contrary to the lawyer's advice, it will be necessary for the lawyer to take steps to have the matter reviewed by a higher authority in the organization. If the matter is of sufficient seriousness and importance or urgency to the organization, referral to higher authority in the organization may be necessary even if the lawyer has not communicated with the constituent. Any measures taken should, to the extent practicable, minimize the risk of revealing information relating to the representation to persons outside the organization. Even in circumstances where a lawyer is not obligated by Rule 1.13 to proceed, a lawyer may bring to the attention of an organizational client, including its highest authority, matters that the lawyer reasonably believes to be of sufficient importance to warrant doing so in the best interest of the organization.

(5) Paragraph (b) also makes clear that when it is reasonably necessary to enable the organization to address the matter in a timely and appropriate manner, the lawyer must refer the matter to higher authority, including, if warranted by the circumstances, the highest authority that can act on behalf of the organization under applicable law. The organization's highest authority to whom a matter may be referred ordinarily will be the board of directors or similar governing body. However, applicable law may prescribe that under certain conditions the highest authority reposes elsewhere, for example, in the independent directors of a corporation.

Relation to Other Rules

(6) The authority and responsibility provided in this Rule are concurrent with the authority and responsibility provided in other Rules. In particular, this Rule does not limit or expand the lawyer's responsibility under Rule 1.8, 1.16, 3.3 or 4.1. Paragraph (c) of this Rule supplements Rule 1.6(b) by providing an additional basis upon which the lawyer may reveal information relating to the representation, but does not modify, restrict, or limit the provisions of Rule 1.6(b)(1)–(4). Under paragraph (c) the lawyer may reveal such information only when the organization's highest authority insists upon or fails to address threatened or ongoing action that is clearly a violation of law, and then only to the extent the lawyer reasonably believes necessary to prevent reasonably certain substantial injury to the organization. It is not necessary that the lawyer's services be used in furtherance of the violation, but it is required that the matter be related to the lawyer's representation of the organization. If the lawyer's services are being used by an organization to further a crime or fraud by the organization, Rule 1.6 may permit the lawyer to disclose confidential information. In such circumstances Rule 1.2(d) may also be applicable, in which event, withdrawal from the representation under Rule 1.16(a)(1) may be required.

(7) Paragraph (d) makes clear that the authority of a lawyer to disclose information relating to a representation in circumstances described in paragraph (c) does not apply with respect to information relating to a lawyer's engagement by an organization to investigate an alleged violation of law or to defend the organization or an officer, employee or other person associated with the organization against a claim arising out of an alleged violation of law. This is necessary in order to enable organizational clients to enjoy the full benefits of legal counsel in conducting an investigation or defending against a claim.

(8) A lawyer who reasonably believes that he or she has been discharged because of the lawyer's actions taken pursuant to paragraph (b) or (c), or who withdraws in circumstances that require or permit the lawyer to take action under either of these paragraphs, must proceed as the lawyer reasonably believes necessary to assure that the organization's highest authority is informed of the lawyer's discharge or withdrawal.

Government Agency

(9) The duty defined in this Rule applies to governmental organizations. Defining precisely the identity of the client and prescribing the resulting obligations of such lawyers may be more difficult in the government context and is a matter beyond the scope of these Rules. See Scope [XIX]. Although in some circumstances the client may be a specific agency, it may also be a branch of government, such as the executive branch, or the government as a whole. For example, if the action or failure to act involves the head of a bureau, either the department of which the bureau is a part or the relevant branch of government may be the client for purposes of this Rule. Moreover, in a matter involving the conduct of government officials, a government lawyer may have authority under applicable law to question such conduct more extensively than that of a lawyer for a private organization in similar circumstances. Thus, when the client is a governmental organization, a different balance may be appropriate between maintaining confidentiality and assuring that the wrongful act is prevented or rectified, for public business is involved. In addition, duties of lawyers employed by the government or lawyers in military service may be defined by statutes and regulation. This Rule does not limit that authority. See Scope.

Clarifying the Lawyer's Role

(10) There are times when the organization's interest may be or become adverse to those of one or more of its constituents. In such circumstances the lawyer should advise any constituent, whose interest the lawyer finds adverse to that of the organization of the conflict or potential conflict of interest, that the lawyer cannot represent such constituent, and that such person may wish to obtain independent representation. Care must be taken to assure that the individual understands that, when there is such adversity of interest, the lawyer for the organization cannot provide legal representation for that

constituent individual, and that discussions between the lawyer for the organization and the individual may not be privileged.

(11) Whether such a warning should be given by the lawyer for the organization to any constituent individual may turn on the facts of each case.

Dual Representation

(12) Paragraph (g) recognizes that a lawyer for an organization may also represent a principal officer or major shareholder. If the organization is closely held it is possible that the owners of the organization will have an expectation that the lawyer represents the organization and the organization's owners. In this situation, when the lawyer reasonably should know that the owners have an expectation of dual representation, the lawyer should advise the owners and the representatives of the organization, preferably in writing, the identify of the lawyer's client and the ramifications of a client conflict.

Derivative Actions

(13) Under generally prevailing law, the shareholders or members of a corporation may bring suit to compel the directors to perform their legal obligations in the supervision of the organization. Members of unincorporated associations have essentially the same right. Such an action may be brought nominally by the organization, but usually is, in fact, a legal controversy over management of the organization.

(14) The question can arise whether counsel for the organization may defend such an action. The proposition that the organization is the lawyer's client does not alone resolve the issue. Most derivative actions are a normal incident of an organization's affairs, to be defended by the organization's lawyer like any other suit. However, if the claim involves serious charges of wrongdoing by those in control of the organization, a conflict may arise between the lawyer's duty to the organization and the lawyers relationship with the board. In those circumstances, Rule 1.7 governs who should represent the directors and the organization.

SCR 3.130(1.14)   Client with diminished capacity

(a) When a client's capacity to make adequately considered decisions in connection with a representation is diminished, whether because of minority, age, mental impairment or for some other reason, the lawyer shall, as far as reasonably possible, maintain a normal client-lawyer relationship with the client.

(b) When the lawyer reasonably believes that the client has diminished capacity, is at risk of substantial physical, financial or other harm unless action is taken and cannot adequately act in the client's own interest, the lawyer may take reasonably necessary protective action, including consulting with individuals or entities that have the ability to take action to protect the client and, in appropriate cases, seeking the appointment of a guardian ad litem, conservator or guardian.

(c) Information relating to the representation of a client with diminished capacity is protected by Rule 1.6. When taking protective action pursuant to paragraph (b), the lawyer is impliedly authorized under Rule 1.6(a) to reveal information about the client, but only to the extent reasonably necessary to protect the client's interests.

HISTORY: Amended by Order 2009–05, eff. 7–15–09; adopted by Order 89–1, eff. 1–1–90

Supreme Court Commentary

2009:

(1) The normal client-lawyer relationship is based on the assumption that the client, when properly advised and assisted, is capable of making decisions about important matters. When the client is a minor or suffers from a diminished mental capacity, however, maintaining the ordinary client-lawyer relationship may not be possible in all respects. In particular, a severely incapacitated person may have no power to make legally binding decisions. Nevertheless, a client with diminished capacity often has the ability to understand, deliberate upon, and reach conclusions about matters affecting the client's own well-being. For example, children as young as five or six years of age, and certainly those of ten or twelve, are regarded as having opinions that are entitled to weight in legal proceedings concerning their custody. So also, it is recognized that some persons of advanced age can be quite capable of handling routine financial matters while needing special legal protection concerning major transactions.

(2) The fact that a client suffers a disability does not diminish the lawyer's obligation to treat the client with attention and respect. Even if the person has a legal representative, the lawyer should as far as possible accord the represented person the status of client, particularly in maintaining communication.

(3) The client may wish to have family members or other persons participate in discussions with the lawyer. When necessary to assist in the representation, the presence of such persons generally does not affect the applicability of the attorney-client evidentiary privilege. Nevertheless, the lawyer must keep the client's interests foremost and, except for protective action authorized under paragraph (b), must to look to the client, and not family members, to make decisions on the client's behalf.

(4) If a legal representative has already been appointed for the client, the lawyer should ordinarily look to the representative for decisions on behalf of the client. In matters involving a minor, whether the lawyer should look to the parents as natural guardians may depend on the type of proceeding or matter in which the lawyer is representing the minor. If the lawyer represents the guardian as distinct from the ward, and is aware that the guardian is acting adversely to the ward's interest, the lawyer may have an obligation to prevent or rectify the guardian's misconduct. See Rule 1.2(d).

Taking Protective Action

(5) If a lawyer reasonably believes that a client is at risk of substantial physical, financial or other harm unless action is taken, and that a normal client-lawyer relationship cannot be maintained as provided in paragraph (a) because the client lacks sufficient capacity to communicate or to make adequately considered decisions in connection with the representation, then paragraph (b) permits the lawyer to take protective measures deemed necessary. Such measures could include: consulting with family members, using a reconsideration period to permit clarification or improvement of circumstances, using voluntary surrogate decisionmaking tools such as durable powers of attorney or consulting with support groups, professional services, adult-protective agencies or other individuals or entities that have the ability to protect the client. In taking any protective action, the lawyer should be guided by such factors as the wishes and values of the client to the extent known, the client's best interests and the goals of intruding into the client's decisionmaking autonomy to the least extent feasible, maximizing client capacities and respecting the client's family and social connections.

(6) In determining the extent of the client's diminished capacity, the lawyer should consider and balance such factors as: the client's ability to articulate reasoning leading to a decision, variability of state of mind and ability to appreciate consequences of a decision; the substantive fairness of a decision; and the consistency of a decision with the known long-term commitments and values of the client. In appropriate circumstances, the lawyer may seek guidance from an appropriate diagnostician.

(7) If a legal representative has not been appointed, the lawyer should consider whether appointment of a guardian ad litem, conservator or guardian is necessary to protect the client's interests. Thus, if a client with diminished capacity has substantial property that should be sold for the client's benefit, effective completion of the transaction may require appointment of a legal representative. In addition, rules of procedure in litigation sometimes provide that minors or persons with diminished capacity must be represented by a guardian or next friend if they do not have a general guardian. In many circumstances, however, appointment of a legal representative may be more expensive or traumatic for the client than circumstances in fact require. Evaluation of such circumstances is a matter entrusted to the professional judgment of the lawyer. In considering

alternatives, however, the lawyer should be aware of any law that requires the lawyer to advocate the least restrictive action on behalf of the client.

Disclosure of the Client's Condition

(8) Disclosure of the client's diminished capacity could adversely affect the client's interests. For example, raising the question of diminished capacity could, in some circumstances, lead to proceedings for involuntary commitment. Information relating to the representation is protected by Rule 1.6. Therefore, unless authorized to do so, the lawyer may not disclose such information. When taking protective action pursuant to paragraph (b), the lawyer is impliedly authorized to make the necessary disclosures, even when the client directs the lawyer to the contrary. Nevertheless, given the risks of disclosure, paragraph (c) limits what the lawyer may disclose in consulting with other individuals or entities or seeking the appointment of a legal representative. At the very least, the lawyer should determine whether it is likely that the person or entity consulted with will act adversely to the client's interests before discussing matters related to the client. The lawyer's position in such cases is an unavoidably difficult one.

Emergency Legal Assistance

(9) In an emergency where the health, safety or a financial interest of a person with seriously diminished capacity is threatened with imminent and irreparable harm, a lawyer may take legal action on behalf of such a person even though the person is unable to establish a client-lawyer relationship or to make or express considered judgments about the matter, when the person or another acting in good faith on that person's behalf has consulted with the lawyer. Even in such an emergency, however, the lawyer should not act unless the lawyer reasonably believes that the person has no other lawyer, agent or other representative available. The lawyer should take legal action on behalf of the person only to the extent reasonably necessary to maintain the status quo or otherwise avoid imminent and irreparable harm. A lawyer who undertakes to represent a person in such an exigent situation has the same duties under these Rules as the lawyer would with respect to a client.

(10) A lawyer who acts on behalf of a person with seriously diminished capacity in an emergency should keep the confidences of the person as if dealing with a client, disclosing them only to the extent necessary to accomplish the intended protective action. The lawyer should disclose to any tribunal involved and to any other counsel involved the nature of his or her relationship with the person. The lawyer should take steps to regularize the relationship or implement other protective solutions as soon as possible. Normally, a lawyer would not seek compensation for such emergency actions taken.

SCR 3.130(1.15) Safekeeping property

(a) A lawyer shall hold property of clients or third persons that is in a lawyer's possession in connection with a representation separate from the lawyer's own property. Funds shall be kept in a separate account maintained in the state where the lawyer's office is situated, or elsewhere with the consent of the client, third person, or both in the event of a claim by each to the property. The separate account referred to in the preceding sentence shall be maintained in a bank which has agreed to notify the Kentucky Bar Association in the event that any overdraft occurs in the account. Other property shall be identified as such and appropriately safeguarded. Complete records of such account funds and other property shall be kept by the lawyer and shall be preserved for a period of five years after termination of the representation.

(b) Upon receiving funds or other property in which a client or third person has an interest, a lawyer shall promptly notify the client, third person, or both in the event of claims by each to the property. Except as stated in this Rule or otherwise permitted by law or by agreement with the client, third person, or both in the event of a claim by each to the property, a lawyer shall promptly deliver to the client or third person any funds or other property that the client or third person is entitled to receive and, upon request by the client or third person, shall promptly render a full accounting regarding such property.

(c) When in the course of representation a lawyer is in possession of property in which two or more persons (one of whom may be the lawyer) claim interests, the property shall be kept separate by the lawyer until the dispute is resolved. The lawyer shall promptly distribute all portions of the property as to which the interests are not in dispute.

(d) A lawyer may deposit the lawyer's own funds in a client trust account for the sole purpose of paying bank service charges on that account, but only in an amount necessary for that purpose.

(e) Except for non refundable fees as provided in 1.5(f), a lawyer shall deposit into a client trust account legal fees and expenses that have been paid in advance, to be withdrawn by the lawyer only as fees are earned or expenses incurred.

HISTORY: Amended by Order 2009–05, eff. 7–15–09; prior amendment eff. 10–1–98 (Order 98–1); adopted by Order 89–1, eff. 1–1–90

Supreme Court Commentary

2009:

(1) A lawyer should hold property of others with the care required of a professional fiduciary. Securities should be kept in a safe deposit box, except when some other form of safekeeping is warranted by special circumstances. All property which is the property of clients or third persons, including prospective clients, must be kept separate from the lawyer's business and personal property and, if monies, in one or more trust accounts. Separate trust accounts may be warranted when administering estate monies or acting in similar fiduciary capacities. A lawyer should maintain on a current basis books and records in accordance with generally accepted accounting practice and comply with any recordkeeping rules established by law or court order. See, e.g., ABA Model Financial Recordkeeping Rule.

(2) Lawyers often receive funds from which the lawyer's fee will be paid. The lawyer is not required to remit to the client funds that the lawyer reasonably believes represent fees owed. However, a lawyer may not hold funds to coerce a client into accepting the lawyer's contention. The disputed portion of the funds must be kept in a trust account and the lawyer should suggest means for prompt resolution of the dispute, such as arbitration. The undisputed portion of the funds shall be promptly distributed.

(3) Paragraph (c) describes the handling of disputes, including those between the lawyer and the client, the lawyer and third persons (or entities), and the client and third parties. Paragraph (c) recognizes that third parties may have lawful claims against specific funds or other property in a lawyer's custody, such as a client's creditor who has a lien on funds recovered in a personal injury action. A lawyer may have a duty under applicable law to protect such third-party claims against wrongful interference by the client. In such cases, when the third-party claim is not frivolous under applicable law, the lawyer must refuse to surrender the property until the claims are resolved. Generally, if the claim is based on a contract obligation, writing signed by the client, statutory lien, court order, legal obligation to ensure payment to a third party employed by the attorney to provide services in furtherance of the client's claim, or other law, the lawyer may not disburse the funds until the dispute is resolved. In these circumstances the client should also be advised of the risks of

not paying a valid claim. A lawyer should not unilaterally assume to arbitrate a dispute between the client and the third party, but, when there are substantial grounds for dispute as to the person entitled to the funds, the lawyer may file an action to have a court resolve the dispute.

(4) While normally it is impermissible to commingle the lawyer's own funds with client funds, paragraph (d) provides that it is permissible when necessary to pay bank service charges on that account. Accurate records must be kept regarding which part of the funds are the lawyer's. A lawyer may deposit funds in a trust account to provide funds for restitution of the defalcation caused by others, if necessary under any legal obligation to a banking institution, client or third party whose funds have been converted.

(5) Paragraph (e) requires that when a lawyer has collected an advance deposit on a fee or for expenses or a flat fee for services not yet completed, the funds must be deposited in the trust account until earned, at which time they should be promptly distributed to the lawyer. The foregoing shall not apply to non refundable fees. At the termination of the client-lawyer relationship the lawyer must return any amount held that was not earned or was an unreasonable fee, as provided by Rules 1.5 and 1.16(d).

(6) The obligations of a lawyer under this Rule are independent of those arising from activity other than rendering legal services. For example, a lawyer who serves only as an escrow agent is governed by the applicable law relating to fiduciaries even though the lawyer does not render legal services in the transaction and is not governed by this Rule.

SCR 3.130(1.16) Declining or terminating representation

(a) Except as stated in paragraph (c), a lawyer shall not represent a client or, where representation has commenced, shall withdraw from the representation of a client if:

(1) the representation will result in violation of the Rules of Professional Conduct or other law; or

(2) the lawyer's physical or mental condition materially impairs the lawyer's ability to represent the client; or

(3) the lawyer is discharged.

(b) Except as stated in paragraph (c), a lawyer may withdraw from representing a client if:

(1) withdrawal can be accomplished without material adverse effect on the interests of the client; or

(2) the client persists in a course of action involving the lawyer's services that the lawyer reasonably believes is criminal or fraudulent; or

(3) the client has used the lawyer's services to perpetrate a crime or fraud; or

(4) the client insists upon taking action that the lawyer considers repugnant or with which the lawyer has a fundamental disagreement; or

(5) the client fails substantially to fulfill an obligation to the lawyer regarding the lawyer's services and has been given reasonable warning that the lawyer will withdraw unless the obligation is fulfilled; or

(6) the representation will result in an unreasonable financial burden on the lawyer or has been rendered unreasonably difficult by the client; or

(7) other good cause for withdrawal exists.

(c) A lawyer must comply with applicable law requiring notice to or permission of a tribunal when terminating a representation. When ordered to do so by a tribunal, a lawyer shall continue representation notwithstanding good cause for terminating the representation.

(d) Upon termination of representation, a lawyer shall take steps to the extent reasonably practicable to protect a client's interests, such as giving reasonable notice to the client, allowing time for employment of other counsel, surrendering papers and property to which the client is entitled and refunding any advance payment of fee or expense that has not been earned or incurred. The lawyer may retain papers relating to the client to the extent permitted by other law.

HISTORY: Amended by Order 2009–05, eff. 7–15–09; adopted by Order 89–1, eff. 1–1–90

Supreme Court Commentary

2009:

(1) A lawyer should not accept representation in a matter unless it can be performed competently, promptly, without improper conflict of interest and to completion. Ordinarily, a representation in a matter is completed when the agreed-upon assistance has been concluded. See Rules 1.2(c) and 6.5. See also Rule 1.3, Comment (4).

Mandatory Withdrawal

(2) A lawyer ordinarily must decline or withdraw from representation if the client demands that the lawyer engage in conduct that is illegal or violates the Rules of Professional Conduct or other law. The lawyer is not obliged to decline or withdraw simply because the client suggests such a course of conduct; a client may make such a suggestion in the hope that a lawyer will not be constrained by a professional obligation.

(3) When a lawyer has been appointed to represent a client, withdrawal ordinarily requires approval of the appointing authority. See also Rule 6.2. Similarly, court approval or notice to the court is often required by applicable law before a lawyer withdraws from pending litigation. Difficulty may be encountered if withdrawal is based on the client's demand that the lawyer engage in unprofessional conduct. The court may request an explanation for the withdrawal, while the lawyer may be bound to keep confidential the facts that would constitute such an explanation. The lawyer's statement that professional considerations require termination of the representation ordinarily should be accepted as sufficient. Lawyers should be mindful of their obligations to both clients and the court under Rules 1.6 and 3.3.

Discharge

(4) A client has a right to discharge a lawyer at any time, with or without cause, subject to liability for payment for the lawyer's services. Where future dispute about the withdrawal may be anticipated, it may be advisable to prepare a written statement reciting the circumstances.

(5) Whether a client can discharge appointed counsel may depend on applicable law. A client seeking to do so should be given a full explanation of the consequences. These consequences may include a decision by the appointing authority that appointment of successor counsel is unjustified, thus requiring self-representation by the client.

(6) If the client has severely diminished capacity, the client may lack the legal capacity to discharge the lawyer, and in any event the discharge may be seriously adverse to the client's interests. The lawyer should make special effort to help the client consider the consequences and may take reasonably necessary protective action as provided in Rule 1.14.

Optional Withdrawal

(7) A lawyer may withdraw from representation in some circumstances. The lawyer has the option to withdraw if it can be accomplished without material adverse effect on the client's interests. Withdrawal is also justified if the client persists in a course of action

that the lawyer reasonably believes is criminal or fraudulent, for a lawyer is not required to be associated with such conduct even if the lawyer does not further it. Withdrawal is also permitted if the lawyer's services were misused in the past even if that would materially prejudice the client. The lawyer also may withdraw where the client insists on taking action that the lawyer considers repugnant or with which the lawyer has a fundamental disagreement.

(8) A lawyer may withdraw if the client refuses to abide by the terms of an agreement relating to the representation, such as an agreement concerning fees or court costs or an agreement limiting the objectives of the representation.

Assisting the Client upon Withdrawal

(9) Even if the lawyer has been unfairly discharged by the client, a lawyer must take all reasonable steps to mitigate the consequences to the client. A lawyer must return the client's file, papers, and property after termination if the client requests the file. The lawyer may retain a copy of the file. A lawyer may charge a reasonable copying charge, but may not condition return of a client's files, papers, and property upon payment of the copying charge, unless the lawyer has previously provided a copy, either during the representation or after cessation of the representation. A lawyer must make one copy of the file and materials available to the client even without payment if the client's interests will be substantially prejudiced without the documents.

(10) The lawyer may not condition return of the client's file, papers, and property upon payment of a fee. KRS 376.460 gives a lawyer the right to have payment of fees secured by a judgment the client recovers as a result of the lawyer's efforts. However, a lawyer may withhold uncompensated work product from the client's returned files (*e.g.*, draft of pleadings, agreements and the like), unless the client's interests will be substantially prejudiced without the uncompensated work product. Documents or other relevant evidence, the original or its equivalent that may be required for trial preparation or as evidence for trial or in other legal proceedings, must be surrendered in their original form. See Rule 1.15 for guidance on resolving disputed claims for client funds.

SCR 3.130(1.17)   Sale of law practice

A lawyer or a law firm may sell or purchase a law practice, or a field of practice, including good will, if the following conditions are satisfied:

(a) The seller ceases to engage in:

(1) the private practice of law; or

(2) the field(s) of practice sold; or

(3) the practice of law in the geographic area in which the practice has been conducted, all as the seller and purchaser may agree, all as the seller and purchaser may agree;

(b) The entire practice, or the entire field of practice is sold to one or more lawyers or law firms;

(c) The seller gives written notice to each of the seller's clients regarding:

(1) the proposed sale;

(2) the client's right to retain other counsel or to take possession of the file; and

(3) the fact that the client's consent to the transfer of the client's files will be presumed if the client does not take any action or does not otherwise object within ninety (90) days of the date the notice was sent.

(d) The fees charged clients shall not be increased by reason of the sale.

(e) If a client with active matters cannot be given notice, the file(s) of that client may be transferred to the purchaser only upon entry of an order by the circuit court in the county of the principal place of business of the seller. The seller may disclose to the court in camera information relating to the representation only to the extent necessary to obtain an order authorizing the transfer of the file. Notification of the entry of the order shall be sent to the Kentucky Bar Association.

(f) In the event the sale includes files that are closed matters, and the attorney has mailed notice to the client's last known address, the client's consent to the transfer of the client's files will be presumed if the client does not take any action or does not otherwise object within ninety (90) days of the date the notice was sent.

HISTORY: Adopted by Order 2009–05, eff. 7–15–09

Supreme Court Commentary

2009:

(1) The practice of law is a profession, not merely a business. Clients are not commodities that can be purchased and sold at will. Pursuant to this Rule, when a lawyer or an entire firm ceases to practice, or ceases to practice in a field of law, and other lawyers or firms take over the representation, the selling lawyer or firm may obtain compensation for the reasonable value of the practice as may withdrawing partners of law firms. See Rules 5.4 and 5.6.

Termination of Practice by the Seller

(2) The requirement that all of the private practice, or all of a field of practice, or the practice of law in a particular geographic area be sold is satisfied if the seller in good faith makes the entire practice, or the field of practice, or the practice of law in a particular geographic area available for sale to the purchasers. The fact that a number of the seller's clients decide not to be represented by the purchasers but take their matters elsewhere, therefore, does not result in a violation. Return to private practice as a result of an unanticipated change in circumstances does not necessarily result in a violation. For example, a lawyer who has sold the practice to accept an appointment to judicial office does not violate the requirement that the sale be attendant to cessation of practice if the lawyer later resumes private practice upon being defeated in a contested or a retention election for the office or resigns from a judiciary position.

(3) The requirement that the seller cease to engage in the private practice of law does not prohibit employment as a lawyer on the staff of a public agency or a legal services entity that provides legal services to the poor, or as in-house counsel to a business.

(4) The Rule permits a sale of an entire practice attendant upon retirement from the private practice of law within the geographical area. Its provisions, therefore, accommodate the lawyer who sells the practice upon the occasion of moving to another geographical area in the state.

(5) This Rule also permits a lawyer or law firm to sell a field of practice. If a field of practice is sold and the lawyer remains in the active practice of law, the lawyer must cease accepting any matters in the field of practice that has been sold, either as counsel or co-counsel or by assuming joint responsibility for a matter in connection with the division of a fee with another lawyer as would otherwise be permitted by Rule 1.5(e). For example, a lawyer with a substantial number of estate planning matters and a substantial number of probate administration cases may sell the estate planning portion of the practice but remain in the practice of law by concentrating on probate administration; however, that practitioner may not thereafter accept any estate planning matters. Although a lawyer who leaves a jurisdiction or geographical area typically would sell the entire practice, this Rule permits the lawyer to limit the sale to one or more fields of the practice, thereby preserving the lawyer's right to continue practice in the fields of the practice that were not sold.

Sale of Entire Practice or Entire Field of Practice

(6) The Rule requires that the seller's entire practice, or field(s) of practice or the practice of law in a particular geographic area, be sold. The prohibition against sale of less than an entire field of practice protects those clients whose matters are less lucrative and who might find it difficult to secure other counsel if a sale could be limited to substantial fee-generating matters. The purchasers are required to undertake all client matters in the practice, the field of practice, or in the geographic area in which the practice has been conducted, subject to client consent. This requirement is satisfied, however, even if a purchaser is unable to undertake a particular client matter because of a conflict of interest.

Client Confidences, Consent and Notice

(7) Negotiations between seller and prospective purchaser prior to disclosure of information relating to a specific representation of an identifiable client no more violate the confidentiality provisions of Model Rule 1.6 than do preliminary discussions concerning the possible association of another lawyer or mergers between firms, with respect to which client consent is not required. Providing the purchaser access to client-specific information relating to the representation and to the file, however, requires client consent. The Rule provides that, before such information can be disclosed by the seller to the purchaser, the client must be given actual written notice of the contemplated sale, including the identity of the purchaser, and must be told that the decision to consent or make other arrangements must be made within 90 days. If nothing is heard from the client within that time, consent to the sale is presumed.

(8) A lawyer or law firm ceasing to practice cannot be required to remain in practice because some clients cannot be given actual notice of the proposed purchase. Since these clients cannot themselves consent to the purchase or direct any other disposition of their files, the Rule requires an order by the circuit court in the county of the principal place of business of the seller authorizing their transfer or other disposition. The Court can be expected to determine whether reasonable efforts to locate the client have been exhausted, and whether the absent client's legitimate interests will be served by authorizing the transfer of the file so that the purchaser may continue the representation. Preservation of client confidences requires that the petition for a court order be considered in camera. See paragraph (f) for guidance on transferring files of former clients that cannot be given actual notice.

(9) All the elements of client autonomy, including the client's absolute right to discharge a lawyer and transfer the representation to another, survive the sale of the practice or field of practice.

Fee Arrangements Between Client and Purchaser

(10) The sale may not be financed by increases in fees charged the clients of the practice. Existing agreements between the seller and the client as to fees and the scope of the work must be honored by the purchaser.

Other Applicable Ethical Standards

(11) Lawyers participating in the sale of a law practice or a practice field are subject to the ethical standards applicable to involving another lawyer in the representation of a client. These include, for example, the seller's obligation to exercise competence in identifying a purchaser qualified to assume the practice and the purchaser's obligation to undertake the representation competently (see Rule 1.1); the obligation to avoid disqualifying conflicts, and to secure the client's informed consent for those conflicts that can be agreed to (see Rule 1.7 regarding conflicts and Rule 1.0(e) for the definition of informed consent); and the obligation to protect information relating to the representation (see Rules 1.6 and 1.9).

(12) If approval of the substitution of the purchasing lawyer for the selling lawyer is required by the Rules of any tribunal in which a matter is pending, such approval must be obtained before the matter can be included in the sale (see Rule 1.16).

Applicability of the Rule

(13) This Rule applies to the sale of a law practice by representatives of a deceased, disabled or disappeared lawyer. Thus, the seller may be represented by a non-lawyer representative not subject to these Rules. Since, however, no lawyer may participate in a sale of a law practice which does not conform to the requirements of this Rule, the representatives of the seller as well as the purchasing lawyer can be expected to see to it that they are met.

(14) Admission to or retirement from a law partnership or professional association, retirement plans and similar arrangements, and a sale of tangible assets of a law practice, do not constitute a sale or purchase governed by this Rule.

(15) This Rule does not apply to the transfers of legal representation between lawyers when such transfers are unrelated to the sale of a practice or a field of practice.

SCR 3.130(1.18)   Duties to prospective client

(a) A person who discusses with a lawyer the possibility of forming a client-lawyer relationship with respect to a matter is a prospective client.

(b) Even when no client-lawyer relationship ensues, a lawyer who has had discussions with a prospective client shall not use or reveal information learned in the consultation, except as Rule 1.9 would permit with respect to information of a former client.

(c) A lawyer subject to paragraph (b) shall not represent a client with interests materially adverse to those of a prospective client in the same or a substantially related matter if the lawyer received information from the prospective client that could be significantly harmful to that person in the matter, except as provided in paragraph (d). If a lawyer is disqualified from representation under this paragraph, no lawyer in a firm with which that lawyer is associated may knowingly undertake or continue representation in such a matter, except as provided in paragraph (d).

(d) When the lawyer has received disqualifying information as defined in paragraph (c), representation is permissible if:

(1) both the affected client and the prospective client have given informed consent, confirmed in writing, or;

(2) the lawyer who received the information took reasonable measures to avoid exposure to more disqualifying information than was reasonably necessary to determine whether to represent the prospective client; and

(i) the disqualified lawyer is timely screened from any participation in the matter and is apportioned no part of the fee therefrom; and

(ii) written notice is promptly given to the prospective client.

HISTORY: Adopted by Order 2009–05, eff. 7–15–09

Supreme Court Commentary

2009:

(1) Prospective clients, like clients, may disclose information to a lawyer, place documents or other property in the lawyer's custody, or rely on the lawyer's advice. A lawyer's discussions with a prospective client usually are limited in time and depth and leave both the prospective client and the lawyer free (and sometimes required) to proceed no further. Hence, prospective clients should receive some but not all of the protection afforded clients.

(2) Not all persons who communicate information to a lawyer are entitled to protection under this Rule. A person who communicates information unilaterally to a lawyer, without any reasonable expectation that the lawyer is willing to discuss the possibility of forming a client-lawyer relationship, is not a "prospective client" within the meaning of paragraph (a).

(3) It is often necessary for a prospective client to reveal information to the lawyer during an initial consultation prior to the decision about formation of a client-lawyer relationship. The lawyer often must learn such information to determine whether there is a conflict of interest with an existing client and whether the matter is one that the lawyer is willing to undertake. Paragraph (b) prohibits the lawyer from using or revealing that information, except as permitted by Rule 1.9, even if the client or lawyer decides not to proceed with the representation. The duty exists regardless of how brief the initial conference may be.

(4) In order to avoid acquiring disqualifying information from a prospective client, a lawyer considering whether or not to undertake a new matter should limit the initial interview to only such information as reasonably appears necessary for that purpose. Where the information indicates that a conflict of interest or other reason for non-representation exists, the lawyer should so inform the prospective client or decline the representation. If the prospective client wishes to retain the lawyer, and if consent is possible under Rule 1.7, then consent from all affected present or former clients must be obtained before accepting the representation.

(5) A lawyer may condition conversations with a prospective client on the person's informed consent that no information disclosed during the consultation will prohibit the lawyer from representing a different client in the matter. See Rule 1.0(e) for the definition of informed consent. If the agreement expressly so provides, the prospective client may also consent to the lawyer's subsequent use of information received from the prospective client.

(6) Even in the absence of an agreement, under paragraph (c), the lawyer is not prohibited from representing a client with interests adverse to those of the prospective client in the same or a substantially related matter unless the lawyer has received from the prospective client information that could be significantly harmful if used in the matter.

(7) Under paragraph (c), the prohibition in this Rule is imputed to other lawyers as provided in Rule 1.10, but, under paragraph (d)(1), imputation may be avoided if the lawyer obtains the informed consent, confirmed in writing, of both the prospective and affected clients. In the alternative, imputation may be avoided if the conditions of paragraph (d)(2) are met and all disqualified lawyers are timely screened and written notice is promptly given to the prospective client. See Rule 1.0(k) (requirements for screening procedures). Paragraph (d)(2)(i) does not prohibit the screened lawyer from receiving a salary or partnership share established by prior independent agreement, but that lawyer may not receive compensation directly related to the matter in which the lawyer is disqualified.

(8) Notice, including a general description of the subject matter about which the lawyer was consulted, and of the screening procedures employed, generally should be given as soon as practicable after the need for screening becomes apparent.

(9) For the duty of competence of a lawyer who gives assistance on the merits of a matter to a prospective client, see Rule 1.1. For a lawyer's duties when a prospective client entrusts valuables or papers to the lawyer's care, see Rule 1.15.

SCR 3.130(1.19) Dissolution of law firm

Upon dissolution of a law firm or of any legal professional corporation, the partners shall make reasonable arrangements for the maintenance of client trust account.

HISTORY: Adopted by Order 2012–01, eff. 3–1–12

SCR 3.130(1.20) Sale of law practice

Upon the sale of a law practice, the seller shall make reasonable arrangements for the maintenance of client trust account records.

HISTORY: Adopted by Order 2012–01, eff. 3–1–12

COUNSELOR

SCR 3.130(2.1) Advisor

In representing a client, a lawyer shall exercise independent professional judgment and render candid advice. In rendering advice, a lawyer may refer not only to law but to other considerations such as moral, economic, social and political factors, that may be relevant to the client's situation.

HISTORY: Amended by Order 2009–05, eff. 7–15–09; adopted by Order 89–1, eff. 1–1–90

Supreme Court Commentary

2009:

Scope of Advice

(1) A client is entitled to straightforward advice expressing the lawyer's honest assessment. Legal advice often involves unpleasant facts and alternatives that a client may be disinclined to confront. In presenting advice, a lawyer endeavors to sustain the client's morale and may put advice in as acceptable a form as honesty permits. However, a lawyer should not be deterred from giving candid advice by the prospect that the advice will be unpalatable to the client.

(2) Advice couched in narrow legal terms may be of little value to a client, especially where practical considerations, such as cost or effects on other people, are predominant. Purely technical legal advice, therefore, can sometimes be inadequate. It is proper for a lawyer to refer to relevant moral and ethical considerations in giving advice. Although a lawyer is not a moral advisor as such, moral and ethical considerations impinge upon most legal questions and may decisively influence how the law will be applied.

(3) A client may expressly or impliedly ask the lawyer for purely technical advice. When such a request is made by a client experienced in legal matters, the lawyer may accept it at face value. When such a request is made by a client inexperienced in legal matters, however, the lawyer's responsibility as advisor may include indicating that more may be involved than strictly legal considerations.

(4) Matters that go beyond strictly legal questions may also be in the domain of another profession. Family matters can involve problems within the professional competence of psychiatry, clinical psychology or social work; business matters can involve problems within the competence of the accounting profession or of financial specialists. Where consultation with a professional in another field is itself something a competent lawyer would recommend, the lawyer should make such a recommendation. At the same time, a lawyer's advice at its best often consists of recommending a course of action in the face of conflicting recommendations of experts.

Offering Advice

(5) In general, a lawyer is not expected to give advice until asked by the client. However, when a lawyer knows that a client proposes a course of action that is likely to result in substantial adverse legal consequences to the client, the lawyer's duty to the client under Rule 1.4 may require that the lawyer offer advice if the client's course of action is related to the representation. A lawyer ordinarily has no duty to initiate investigation of a client's affairs or to give advice that the client has indicated is unwanted, but a lawyer may initiate advice to a client when doing so appears to be in the client's interest.

SCR 3.130(2.2) Intermediary—Deleted

HISTORY: Deleted by Order 2009–05, eff. 7–15–09; adopted by Order 89–1, eff. 1–1–90

SCR 3.130(2.3) Evaluation for use by third persons

(a) A lawyer may provide an evaluation of a matter affecting a client for the use of someone other than the client if the lawyer reasonably believes that making the evaluation is compatible with other aspects of the lawyer's relationship with the client.

(b) When the lawyer knows or reasonably should know that the evaluation is likely to affect the client's interests materially and adversely, the lawyer shall not provide the evaluation unless the client gives informed consent.

(c) Except as disclosure is authorized in connection with a report of an evaluation, information relating to the evaluation is otherwise protected by Rule 1.6.

HISTORY: Amended by Order 2009–05, eff. 7–15–09; adopted by Order 89–1, eff. 1–1–90

Supreme Court Commentary

2009:

Definition

(1) An evaluation may be performed at the client's direction or when impliedly authorized in order to carry out the representation. See Rule 1.2. Such an evaluation may be for the primary purpose of establishing information for the benefit of third parties; for example, an opinion concerning the title of property rendered at the behest of a vendor for the information of a prospective purchaser, or at the behest of a borrower for the information of a prospective lender. In some situations, the evaluation may be required by a government agency; for example, an opinion concerning the legality of the securities registered for sale under the securities laws. In other instances, the evaluation may be required by a third person, such as a purchaser of a business.

(2) A legal evaluation should be distinguished from an investigation of a person with whom the lawyer does not have a client-lawyer relationship. For example, a lawyer retained by a purchaser to analyze a vendor's title to property does not have a client-lawyer relationship with the vendor. So also, an investigation into a person's affairs by a government lawyer, or by special counsel employed by the government, is not an evaluation as that term is used in this Rule. The question is whether the lawyer is retained by the person whose affairs are being examined. When the lawyer is retained by that person, the general rules concerning loyalty to client and preservation of confidences apply, which is not the case if the lawyer is retained by someone else. For this reason, it is essential to identify the person by whom the lawyer is retained. This should be made clear not only to the person under examination, but also to others to whom the results are to be made available.

Duties Owed to Third Person and Client

(3) When the evaluation is intended for the information or use of a third person, a legal duty to that person may or may not arise. That legal question is beyond the scope of this Rule. However, since such an evaluation involves a departure from the normal client-lawyer relationship, careful analysis of the situation is required. The lawyer must be satisfied as a matter of professional judgment that making the evaluation is compatible with other functions undertaken in behalf of the client. For example, if the lawyer is acting as advocate in defending the client against charges of fraud, it would normally be incompatible with that responsibility for the lawyer to perform an evaluation for others concerning the same or a related transaction. Assuming no such impediment is apparent, however, the lawyer should advise the client of the implications of the evaluation, particularly the lawyer's responsibilities to third persons and the duty to disseminate the findings.

Access to and Disclosure of Information

(4) The quality of an evaluation depends on the freedom and extent of the investigation upon which it is based. Ordinarily a lawyer should have whatever latitude of investigation seems necessary as a matter of professional judgment. Under some circumstances, however, the terms of the evaluation may be limited. For example, certain issues or sources may be categorically excluded, or the scope of search may be limited by time constraints or the noncooperation of persons having relevant information. Any such limitations which are material to the evaluation should be described in the report. If after

a lawyer has commenced an evaluation, the client refuses to comply with the terms upon which it was understood the evaluation was to have been made, the lawyer's obligations are determined by law, having reference to the terms of the client's agreement and the surrounding circumstances. In no circumstances is the lawyer permitted to knowingly make a false statement of material fact or law in providing an evaluation under this Rule. See Rule 4.1.

Obtaining Client's Informed Consent

(5) Information relating to an evaluation is protected by Rule 1.6. In many situations, providing an evaluation to a third party poses no significant risk to the client; thus, the lawyer may be impliedly authorized to disclose information to carry out the representation. See Rule 1.6(a). Where, however, it is reasonably likely that providing the evaluation will affect the client's interests materially and adversely, the lawyer must first obtain the client's consent after the client has been adequately informed concerning the important possible effects on the client's interests. See Rules 1.6(a) and 1.0(e).

Financial Auditors' Requests for Information

(6) When a question concerning the legal situation of a client arises at the instance of the client's financial auditor and the question is referred to the lawyer, the lawyer's response may be made in accordance with procedures recognized in the legal profession. Such a procedure is set forth in the American Bar Association Statement of Policy Regarding Lawyers' Responses to Auditors' Requests for Information, adopted in 1975.

SCR 3.130(2.4)   Lawyer serving as third-party neutral

(a) A lawyer serves as a third-party neutral when the lawyer assists two or more persons who are not clients of the lawyer to reach a resolution of a dispute or other matter that has arisen between them. Service as a third-party neutral may include service as an arbitrator, a mediator or in such other capacity as will enable the lawyer to assist the parties to resolve the matter.

(b) A lawyer serving as a third-party neutral shall inform unrepresented parties that the lawyer is not representing them. When the lawyer knows or reasonably should know that a party does not understand the lawyer's role in the matter, the lawyer shall explain the difference between the lawyer's role as a third-party neutral and a lawyer's role as one who represents a client.

HISTORY: Adopted by Order 2009–05, eff. 7–15–09

Supreme Court Commentary

2009:

(1) Alternative dispute resolution has become a substantial part of the civil justice system. Aside from representing clients in dispute-resolution processes, lawyers often serve as third-party neutrals. A third-party neutral is a person, such as a mediator, arbitrator, conciliator or evaluator, who assists the parties, represented or unrepresented, in the resolution of a dispute or in the arrangement of a transaction. Whether a third-party neutral serves primarily as a facilitator, evaluator or decisionmaker depends on the particular process that is either selected by the parties or mandated by a court.

(2) The role of a third-party neutral is not unique to lawyers, although, in some court-connected contexts, only lawyers are allowed to serve in this role or to handle certain types of cases. In performing this role, the lawyer may be subject to court Rules or other law that apply either to third-party neutrals generally or to lawyers serving as third-party neutrals. Lawyer-neutrals may also be subject to various codes of ethics, such as the Code of Ethics for Arbitration in Commercial Disputes prepared by a joint committee of the American Bar Association and the American Arbitration Association or the Model Standards of Conduct for Mediators jointly prepared by the

American Bar Association, the American Arbitration Association and the Society of Professionals in Dispute Resolution.

(3) A lawyer serving as a third-party neutral may experience unique problems as a result of differences between the role of a third-party neutral and a lawyer's service as a client representative. The potential for confusion is significant when the parties are unrepresented in the process. Thus, paragraph (b) requires a lawyer-neutral to inform unrepresented parties that the lawyer is not representing them. For some parties, particularly parties who frequently use dispute-resolution processes, this information will be sufficient. For others, particularly those who are using the process for the first time, more information will be required. Where appropriate, the lawyer should inform unrepresented parties of the important differences between the lawyer's role as third-party neutral and a lawyer's role as a client representative, including the inapplicability of client confidentiality and the attorney-client privilege. The extent of disclosure required under this paragraph will depend on the particular parties involved and the subject matter of the proceeding, as well as the particular features of the dispute-resolution process selected.

(4) A lawyer who serves as a third-party neutral subsequently may be asked to serve as a lawyer representing a client in the same matter. The conflicts of interest that arise for both the individual lawyer and the lawyer's law firm are addressed in Rule 1.12.

(5) Lawyers who represent clients in alternative dispute-resolution processes are governed by the Rules of Professional Conduct. When the dispute-resolution process takes place before a tribunal, as in binding arbitration (see Rule 1.0(m)), the lawyer's duty of candor is governed by Rule 3.3. Otherwise, the lawyer's duty of candor toward both the third-party neutral and other parties is governed by Rule 4.1.

ADVOCATE

SCR 3.130(3.1) Meritorious claims and contentions

A lawyer shall not knowingly bring or defend a proceeding, or assert or controvert an issue therein, unless there is a basis in law and fact for doing so that is not frivolous, which includes a good faith argument for an extension, modification or reversal of existing law. A lawyer for the defendant in a criminal proceeding, or the respondent in a proceeding that could result in incarceration, may nevertheless so defend the proceeding as to require that every element of the case be established.

HISTORY: Amended by Order 2009–05, eff. 7–15–09; adopted by Order 89–1, eff. 1–1–90

Supreme Court Commentary

2009:

(1) The advocate has a duty to use legal procedure for the fullest benefit of the client's cause, but also a duty not to abuse legal procedure. The law, both procedural and substantive, establishes the limits within which an advocate may proceed. However, the law is not always clear and never is static. Accordingly, in determining the proper scope of advocacy, account must be taken of the law's ambiguities and potential for change.

(2) The filing of an action or defense or similar action taken for a client is not frivolous merely because the facts have not first been fully substantiated or because the lawyer expects to develop vital evidence only by discovery. What is required of lawyers, however, is that they inform themselves sufficiently about the facts of their clients' cases and the applicable law and determine that they can make good faith arguments in support of their clients' positions. Such action is not frivolous even though the lawyer believes that the client's position ultimately will not prevail. The action is frivolous, however, if the lawyer is unable either to make a good faith argument on the merits of the action taken or to support the action taken by a

good faith argument for an extension, modification or reversal of existing law.

(3) The lawyer's obligations under this Rule are subordinate to federal or state constitutional law that entitles a defendant in a criminal matter to the assistance of counsel in presenting a claim or contention that otherwise would be prohibited by this Rule.

SCR 3.130(3.2) Expediting litigation

A lawyer shall make reasonable efforts to expedite litigation consistent with the interests of the client.

HISTORY: Amended by Order 2009–05, eff. 7–15–09; adopted by Order 89–1, eff. 1–1–90

Supreme Court Commentary

2009:

Dilatory practices bring the administration of justice into disrepute. Although there will be occasions when a lawyer may properly seek a postponement for personal reasons, it is not proper for a lawyer to routinely fail to expedite litigation solely for the convenience of the advocates. Nor will a failure to expedite be reasonable if done for the purpose of frustrating an opposing party's attempt to obtain rightful redress or repose. It is not a justification that similar conduct is often tolerated by the bench and bar. The question is whether a competent lawyer acting in good faith would regard the course of action as having some substantial purpose other than delay. Realizing financial or other benefit from otherwise improper delay in litigation is not a legitimate interest of the client.

SCR 3.130(3.3) Candor toward the tribunal

(a) A lawyer shall not knowingly:

(1) make a false statement of fact or law to a tribunal or fail to correct a false statement of material fact or law previously made to the tribunal by the lawyer;

(2) fail to disclose to the tribunal published legal authority in the controlling jurisdiction known to the lawyer to be directly adverse to the position of the client and not disclosed by opposing counsel; or

(3) offer evidence that the lawyer knows to be false. If a lawyer, the lawyer's client, or a witness called by the lawyer, has offered material evidence and the lawyer comes to know of its falsity, the lawyer shall take reasonable remedial measures, including, if necessary, disclosure to the tribunal. A lawyer may refuse to offer evidence, other than the testimony of a defendant in a criminal matter, that the lawyer reasonably believes is false.

(b) A lawyer who represents a client in an adjudicative proceeding and who knows that a person intends to engage, is engaging or has engaged in criminal or fraudulent conduct related to the proceeding shall take reasonable remedial measures, including, if necessary, disclosure to the tribunal.

(c) The duties stated in paragraphs (a) and (b) continue to the conclusion of the proceeding, and apply even if compliance requires disclosure of information otherwise protected by Rule 1.6.

(d) In an ex parte proceeding, a lawyer shall inform the tribunal of all material facts known to the lawyer which will enable the tribunal to make an informed decision, whether or not the facts are adverse.

HISTORY: Amended by Order 2009–05, eff. 7–15–09; adopted by Order 89–1, eff. 1–1–90

Supreme Court Commentary

2009:

(1) This Rule governs the conduct of a lawyer who is representing a client in the proceedings of a tribunal. See Rule 1.0(m) for the definition of "tribunal." It also applies when the lawyer is representing a client in an ancillary proceeding conducted pursuant to the tribunal's adjudicative authority, such as a deposition. Thus, for example, paragraph (a)(3) requires a lawyer to take reasonable remedial measures if the lawyer comes to know that a client who is testifying in a deposition has offered evidence that is false.

(2) This Rule sets forth the special duties of lawyers as officers of the court to avoid conduct that undermines the integrity of the adjudicative process. A lawyer acting as an advocate in an adjudicative proceeding has an obligation to present the client's case with persuasive force. Performance of that duty while maintaining confidences of the client, however, is qualified by the advocate's duty of candor to the tribunal. Consequently, although a lawyer in an adversary proceeding is not required to present an impartial exposition of the law or to vouch for the evidence submitted in a cause, the lawyer must not allow the tribunal to be misled by false statements of law or fact or evidence that the lawyer knows to be false.

Representations by a Lawyer

(3) An advocate is responsible for pleadings and other documents prepared for litigation, but is usually not required to have personal knowledge of matters asserted therein, for litigation documents ordinarily present assertions by the client, or by someone on the client's behalf, and not assertions by the lawyer. Compare Rule 3.1. However, an assertion purporting to be on the lawyer's own knowledge, as in an affidavit by the lawyer or in a statement in open court, may properly be made only when the lawyer knows the assertion is true or believes it to be true on the basis of a reasonably diligent inquiry. There are circumstances where failure to make a disclosure is the equivalent of an affirmative misrepresentation. The obligation prescribed in Rule 1.2(d) not to counsel a client to commit or assist the client in committing a fraud applies in litigation. Regarding compliance with Rule 1.2(d), see the Comment to that Rule. See also the Comment to Rule 8.4(b).

Legal Argument

(4) Legal argument based on a knowingly false representation of law constitutes dishonesty toward the tribunal. A lawyer is not required to make a disinterested exposition of the law, but must recognize the existence of pertinent legal authorities. Furthermore, as stated in paragraph (a)(2), an advocate has a duty to disclose directly adverse published authority in the controlling jurisdiction that has not been disclosed by the opposing party. The underlying concept is that legal argument is a discussion seeking to determine the legal premises properly applicable to the case.

Offering Evidence

(5) Paragraph (a)(3) requires that the lawyer refuse to offer evidence that the lawyer knows to be false, regardless of the client's wishes. This duty is premised on the lawyer's obligation as an officer of the court to prevent the trier of fact from being misled by false evidence. A lawyer does not violate this Rule if the lawyer offers the evidence for the purpose of establishing its falsity.

(6) If a lawyer knows that the client intends to testify falsely or wants the lawyer to introduce false evidence, the lawyer should seek to persuade the client that the evidence should not be offered. If the persuasion is ineffective and the lawyer continues to represent the client, the lawyer must refuse to offer the false evidence. If only a portion of a witness's testimony will be false, the lawyer may call the witness to testify but may not elicit or otherwise permit the witness to present the testimony that the lawyer knows is false.

(7) The duties stated in paragraphs (a) and (b) apply to all lawyers, including defense counsel in criminal cases. In some jurisdictions, however, courts have required counsel to present the accused as a witness or to give a narrative statement if the accused so desires,

even if counsel knows that the testimony or statement will be false. The obligation of the advocate under the Rules of Professional Conduct is subordinate to such requirements. See also Comment (9).

(8) The prohibition against offering false evidence only applies if the lawyer knows that the evidence is false. A lawyer's reasonable belief that evidence is false does not preclude its presentation to the trier of fact. A lawyer's knowledge that evidence is false, however, can be inferred from the circumstances. See Rule 1.0(f). Thus, although a lawyer should resolve doubts about the veracity of testimony or other evidence in favor of the client, the lawyer cannot ignore an obvious falsehood.

(9) Although paragraph (a)(3) only prohibits a lawyer from offering evidence the lawyer knows to be false, it permits the lawyer to refuse to offer testimony or other proof that the lawyer reasonably believes is false. Offering such proof may reflect adversely on the lawyer's ability to discriminate in the quality of evidence and thus impair the lawyer's effectiveness as an advocate. Because of the special protections historically provided criminal defendants, however, this Rule does not permit a lawyer to refuse to offer the testimony of such a client where the lawyer reasonably believes but does not know that the testimony will be false. Unless the lawyer knows the testimony will be false, the lawyer must honor the client's decision to testify. See also Comment (7).

Remedial Measures

(10) Having offered material evidence in the belief that it was true, a lawyer may subsequently come to know that the evidence is false. Or, a lawyer may be surprised when the lawyer's client, or another witness called by the lawyer, offers testimony the lawyer knows to be false, either during the lawyer's direct examination or in response to cross-examination by the opposing lawyer. In such situations or if the lawyer knows of the falsity of testimony elicited from the client during a deposition, the lawyer must take reasonable remedial measures. In such situations, the advocate's proper course is to remonstrate with the client confidentially, advise the client of the-lawyer's duty of candor to the tribunal and seek the client's cooperation with respect to the withdrawal or correction of the false statements or evidence. If that fails, the advocate must take further remedial action. If withdrawal from the representation is not permitted or will not undo the effect of the false evidence, the advocate must make such disclosure to the tribunal as is reasonably necessary to remedy the situation, even if doing so requires the lawyer to reveal information that otherwise would be protected by Rule 1.6. It is for the tribunal then to determine what should be done—making a statement about the matter to the trier of fact, ordering a mistrial or perhaps nothing.

(11) The disclosure of a client's false testimony can result in grave consequences to the client, including not only a sense of betrayal but also loss of the case and perhaps a prosecution for perjury. But the alternative is that the lawyer cooperate in deceiving the court, thereby subverting the truth-finding process which the adversary system is designed to implement. See Rule 1.2(d). Furthermore, unless it is clearly understood that the lawyer will act upon the duty to disclose the existence of false evidence, the client can simply reject the lawyer's advice to reveal the false evidence and insist that the lawyer keep silent. Thus the client could in effect coerce the lawyer into being a party to fraud on the court.

Preserving Integrity of Adjudicative Process

(12) Lawyers have a special obligation to protect a tribunal against criminal or fraudulent conduct that undermines the integrity of the adjudicative process, such as bribing, intimidating or otherwise unlawfully communicating with a witness, juror, court official or other participant in the proceeding, unlawfully destroying or concealing documents or other evidence or failing to disclose information to the tribunal when required by law to do so. Thus, paragraph (b) requires a lawyer to take reasonable remedial measures, including disclosure if necessary, whenever the lawyer knows that a person, including the lawyer's client, intends to engage, is engaging or has engaged in criminal or fraudulent conduct related to the proceeding.

Duration of Obligation

(13) A practical time limit on the obligation to rectify false evidence or false statements of law and fact has to be established. The conclusion of the proceeding is a reasonably definite point for the termination of the obligation. A proceeding has concluded within the

meaning of this Rule when a final judgment in the proceeding has been affirmed on appeal or the time for review has passed.

Ex Parte Proceedings

(14) Ordinarily, an advocate has the limited responsibility of presenting one side of the matters that a tribunal should consider in reaching a decision; the conflicting position is expected to be presented by the opposing party. However, in any ex parte proceeding, such as an application for a temporary restraining order, there is no balance of presentation by opposing advocates. The object of an ex parte proceeding is nevertheless to yield a substantially just result. The judge has an affirmative responsibility to accord the absent party just consideration. The lawyer for the represented party has the correlative duty to make disclosures of material facts known to the lawyer and that the lawyer reasonably believes are necessary to an informed decision.

Withdrawal

(15) Normally, a lawyer's compliance with the duty of candor imposed by this Rule does not require that the lawyer withdraw from the representation of a client whose interests will be or have been adversely affected by the lawyer's disclosure. The lawyer may, however, be required by Rule 1.16(a) to seek permission of the tribunal to withdraw if the lawyer's compliance with this Rule's duty of candor results in such an extreme deterioration of the client-lawyer relationship that the lawyer can no longer competently represent the client. Also see Rule 1.16(b) for the circumstances in which a lawyer will be permitted to seek a tribunal's permission to withdraw. In connection with a request for permission to withdraw that is premised on a client's misconduct, a lawyer may reveal information relating to the representation only to the extent reasonably necessary to comply with this Rule or as otherwise permitted by Rule 1.6.

SCR 3.130(3.4) Fairness to opposing party and counsel

A lawyer shall not:

(a) unlawfully obstruct another party's access to evidence or unlawfully alter, destroy or conceal a document or other material having potential evidentiary value. A lawyer shall not counsel or assist another person to do any such act;

(b) knowingly falsify evidence, counsel or assist a witness to testify falsely, or offer an inducement to a witness that is prohibited by law;

(c) knowingly disobey an obligation under the rules of a tribunal except for an open refusal based on an assertion that no valid obligation exists;

(d) in pretrial procedure, make a frivolous discovery request or deliberately fail to make reasonably diligent effort to comply with a legally proper discovery request by an opposing party;

(e) in trial, allude to any matter that the lawyer does not reasonably believe is relevant or that will not be supported by admissible evidence, assert personal knowledge of facts in issue except when testifying as a witness, or state a personal opinion as to the justness of a cause, the credibility of a witness, the culpability of a civil litigant or the guilt or innocence of an accused; or

(f) present, participate in presenting, or threaten to present criminal or disciplinary charges solely to obtain an advantage in any civil or criminal matter; or

(g) request a person other than a client to refrain from voluntarily giving relevant information to another party unless:

(1) the person is a relative or agent who supervises, directs or regularly consults with the client concerning the matter or has authority to obligate the client with respect to the matter;

(2) the lawyer reasonably believes that the person's interests will not be adversely affected by refraining from giving such information.

HISTORY: Amended by Order 2009–05, eff. 7–15–09; adopted by Order 89–1, eff. 1–1–90

Supreme Court Commentary

2009:

(1) The procedure of the adversary system contemplates that the evidence in a case is to be marshalled competitively by the contending parties. Fair competition in the adversary system is secured by prohibitions against destruction or concealment of evidence, improperly influencing witnesses, obstructive tactics in discovery procedure, and the like.

(2) Documents and other items of evidence are often essential to establish a claim or defense. Subject to evidentiary privileges, the right of an opposing party, including the government, to obtain evidence through discovery or subpoena is an important procedural right. The exercise of that right can be frustrated if relevant material is altered, concealed or destroyed. Applicable law in many jurisdictions makes it an offense to destroy material for the purpose of impairing its availability in a pending proceeding or one whose commencement can be foreseen. Falsifying evidence is also generally a criminal offense. Paragraph (a) applies to evidentiary material generally, including computerized information. Applicable law may permit a lawyer to take temporary possession of physical evidence of client crimes for the purpose of conducting a limited examination that will not alter or destroy material characteristics of the evidence. In such a case, applicable law may require the lawyer to turn the evidence over to the police or other prosecuting authority, depending on the circumstances.

(3) With regard to paragraph (b), it is not improper to pay a witness's expenses or to compensate an expert witness on terms permitted by law. The common law rule in most jurisdictions is that it is improper to pay an occurrence witness any fee for testifying and that it is improper to pay an expert witness a contingent fee.

(4) Paragraph (g) permits a lawyer to request relatives or employees or other agents of a client to refrain from giving information to another party. Such persons may identify their interests with those of the client. Caveat Rules 1.13(f), 4.2, and 4.3. The lawyer must reasonably believe that the person's interests will not be adversely affected by compliance with the request. The Rule does not require that the lawyer know or ascertain the person's interest, but any such knowledge, communication, or other information available to the lawyer may suggest that such a belief is not reasonable. See Rule 1.0 (a), (f), (h), (i), and (j). A request that a person refrain from giving information to prosecutors or law enforcement and regulatory officials will almost never be proper, because that person could violate the law or otherwise be adversely affected by a lack of cooperation with such persons, and such a request might involve the lawyer's violations of other provisions of these Rules and other law. A request in a civil matter may or may not be proper under the Rule, depending upon the person's interests in the matter, if any, and upon what a lawyer would reasonably believe in the circumstances.

SCR 3.130(3.5) Impartiality and decorum of the tribunal

A lawyer shall not:

(a) seek to influence a judge, juror, prospective juror or other official by means prohibited by law;

(b) communicate ex parte with such a person as to the merits of the cause except as permitted by law or court order;

(c) communicate with a juror or prospective juror after discharge of the jury if:

(1) the communication is prohibited by law, local rule, or court order;

(2) the juror has made known to the lawyer a desire not to communicate; or

(3) the communication involves misrepresentation, coercion, duress or harassment; or

(d) engage in conduct intended to disrupt a tribunal.

HISTORY: Amended by Order 2009–05, eff. 7–15–09; adopted by Order 89–1, eff. 1–1–90.

Supreme Court Commentary

2009:

(1) Many forms of improper influence upon a tribunal are proscribed by criminal law. Others are specified in the ABA Model Code of Judicial Conduct, with which an advocate should be familiar. A lawyer is required to avoid contributing to a violation of such provisions.

(2) During the proceeding a lawyer may not communicate ex parte as to the merits of the cause with persons serving in an official capacity in the proceeding, such as judges, commissioners or jurors, unless authorized to do so by law or court order.

(3) A lawyer may on occasion want to communicate with a juror or prospective juror after the jury has been discharged. The lawyer may do so unless the communication is prohibited by law or a court order but must respect the desire of the juror not to talk with the lawyer. The lawyer may not engage in improper conduct during the communication.

(4) The advocate's function is to present evidence and argument so that the cause may be decided according to law. Refraining from abusive or obstreperous conduct is a corollary of the advocate's right to speak on behalf of litigants. A lawyer may stand firm against abuse by a judge but should avoid reciprocation; the judge's default is no justification for similar dereliction by an advocate. An advocate can present the cause, protect the record for subsequent review and preserve professional integrity by patient firmness no less effectively than by belligerence or theatrics.

(5) The duty to refrain from disruptive conduct applies to any proceeding of a tribunal, including a deposition. See Rule 1.0(m).

SCR 3.130(3.6) Trial publicity

(a) A lawyer who is participating or has participated in the investigation or litigation of a matter shall not make an extrajudicial statement that the lawyer knows or reasonably should know will be disseminated by means of public communication it and will have a substantial likelihood of materially prejudicing an adjudicative proceeding in the matter.

(b) Notwithstanding paragraph (a), a lawyer may state:

(1) the claim, offense or defense involved and, except when prohibited by law, the identity of the persons involved;

(2) information contained in a public record;

(3) that an investigation of the matter is in progress;

(4) the scheduling or result of any step in litigation;

(5) a request for assistance in obtaining evidence and information necessary thereto;

(6) a warning of danger concerning the behavior of a person involved, when there is reason to believe that there exists the likelihood of substantial harm to an individual or to the public interest; and

(7) in a criminal case, in addition to subparagraphs (1) through (6):

(i) the identity, residence, occupation and family status of the accused;

(ii) if the accused has not been apprehended, information necessary to aid in apprehension of that person;

(iii) the fact, time and place of arrest; and

(iv) the identity of investigating and arresting officers or agencies and the length of the investigation.

(c) Notwithstanding paragraph (a), a lawyer may make a statement that a reasonable lawyer would believe is required to protect a client from the substantial undue prejudicial effect of recent publicity not initiated by the lawyer or the lawyer's client. A statement made pursuant to this paragraph shall be limited to such information as is necessary to mitigate the recent adverse publicity.

(d) No lawyer associated in a firm or government agency with a lawyer subject to paragraph (a) shall make a statement prohibited by paragraph (a).

HISTORY: Amended by Order 2009–05, eff. 7–15–09; adopted by Order 89–1, eff. 1–1–90.

Supreme Court Commentary

2009:

(1) It is difficult to strike a balance between protecting the right to a fair trial and safeguarding the right of free expression. Preserving the right to a fair trial necessarily entails some curtailment of the information that may be disseminated about a party prior to trial, particularly where trial by jury is involved. If there were no such limits, the result would be the practical nullification of the protective effect of the rules of forensic decorum and the exclusionary rules of evidence. On the other hand, there are vital social interests served by the free dissemination of information about events having legal consequences and about legal proceedings themselves. The public has a right to know about threats to its safety and measures aimed at assuring its security. It also has a legitimate interest in the conduct of judicial proceedings, particularly in matters of general public concern. Furthermore, the subject matter of legal proceedings is often of direct significance in debate and deliberation over questions of public policy.

(2) Special rules of confidentiality may validly govern proceedings in juvenile, domestic relations and mental disability proceedings, and perhaps other types of litigation. Rule 3.4(c) requires compliance with such Rules.

(3) The Rule sets forth a basic general prohibition against a lawyer making statements that the lawyer knows or should know will have a substantial likelihood of materially prejudicing an adjudicative proceeding. Recognizing that the public value of informed commentary is great and the likelihood of prejudice to a proceeding by the commentary of a lawyer who is not involved in the proceeding is small, the Rule applies only to lawyers who are, or who have been involved in the investigation or litigation of a case, and their associates.

(4) Paragraph (b) identifies specific matters about which a lawyer's statements would not ordinarily be considered to present a substantial likelihood of material prejudice, and should not in any event be considered prohibited by the general prohibition of paragraph (a). Paragraph (b) is not intended to be an exhaustive listing of the

subjects upon which a lawyer may make a statement, but statements on other matters may be subject to paragraph (a).

(5) There are, on the other hand, certain subjects that are more likely than not to have a material prejudicial effect on a proceeding, particularly when they refer to a civil matter triable to a jury, a criminal matter, or any other proceeding that could result in incarceration. These subjects relate to:

(1) the character, credibility, reputation or criminal record of a party, suspect in a criminal investigation or witness, or the identity of a witness, or the expected testimony of a party or witness;

(2) in a criminal case or proceeding that could result in incarceration, the possibility of a plea of guilty to the offense or the existence or contents of any confession, admission, or statement given by a defendant or suspect or that person's refusal or failure to make a statement;

(3) the performance or results of any examination or test or the refusal or failure of a person to submit to an examination or test, or the identity or nature of physical evidence expected to be presented;

(4) any opinion as to the guilt or innocence of a defendant or suspect in a criminal case or proceeding that could result in incarceration;

(5) information that the lawyer knows or reasonably should know is likely to be inadmissible as evidence in a trial and that would, if disclosed, create a substantial risk of prejudicing an impartial trial; or

(6) the fact that a defendant has been charged with a crime, unless there is included therein a statement explaining that the charge is merely an accusation and that the defendant is presumed innocent until and unless proven guilty.

(6) Another relevant factor in determining prejudice is the nature of the proceeding involved. Criminal jury trials will be most sensitive to extrajudicial speech. Civil trials may be less sensitive. Non-jury hearings and arbitration proceedings may be even less affected. The Rule will still place limitations on prejudicial comments in these cases, but the likelihood of prejudice may be different depending on the type of proceeding.

(7) Finally, extrajudicial statements that might otherwise raise a question under this Rule may be permissible when they are made in response to statements made publicly by another party, another party's lawyer, or third persons, where a reasonable lawyer would believe a public response is required in order to avoid prejudice to the lawyer's client. When prejudicial statements have been publicly made by others, responsive statements may have the salutary effect of lessening any resulting adverse impact on the adjudicative proceeding. Such responsive statements should be limited to contain only such information as is necessary to mitigate undue prejudice created by the statements made by others.

(8) See Rule 3.8(e) for additional duties of prosecutors in connection with extrajudicial statements about criminal proceedings.

SCR 3.130(3.7)   Lawyer as witness

(a) A lawyer shall not act as advocate at a trial in which the lawyer is likely to be a necessary witness unless:

(1) the testimony relates to an uncontested issue;

(2) the testimony relates to the nature and value of legal services rendered in the case; or

(3) disqualification of the lawyer would work substantial hardship on the client.

(b) A lawyer may act as advocate in a trial in which another lawyer in the lawyer's firm is likely to be called as a witness unless precluded from doing so by Rule 1.7 or Rule 1.9.

HISTORY: Amended by Order 2009–05, eff. 7–15–09; adopted by Order 89–1, eff. 1–1–90

Supreme Court Commentary

2009:

(1) Combining the roles of advocate and witness can prejudice the tribunal and the opposing party and can also involve a conflict of interest between the lawyer and client.

Advocate–Witness Rule

(2) The tribunal has proper objection when the trier of fact may be confused or misled by a lawyer serving as both advocate and witness. The opposing party has proper objection where the combination of roles may prejudice that party's rights in the litigation. A witness is required to testify on the basis of personal knowledge, while an advocate is expected to explain and comment on evidence given by others. It may not be clear whether a statement by an advocate-witness should be taken as proof or as an analysis of the proof.

(3) To protect the tribunal, paragraph (a) prohibits a lawyer from simultaneously serving as advocate and necessary witness except in those circumstances specified in paragraphs (a)(1) through (a)(3). Paragraph (a)(1) recognizes that if the testimony will be uncontested, the ambiguities in the dual role are purely theoretical. Paragraph (a)(2) recognizes that where the testimony concerns the extent and value of legal services rendered in the action in which the testimony is offered, permitting the lawyers to testify avoids the need for a second trial with new counsel to resolve that issue. Moreover, in such a situation the judge has firsthand knowledge of the matter in issue; hence, there is less dependence on the adversary process to test the credibility of the testimony.

(4) Apart from these two exceptions, paragraph (a)(3) recognizes that a balancing is required between the interests of the client and those of the tribunal and the opposing party. Whether the tribunal is likely to be misled or the opposing party is likely to suffer prejudice depends on the nature of the case, the importance and probable tenor of the lawyer's testimony, and the probability that the lawyer's testimony will conflict with that of other witnesses. Even if there is risk of such prejudice, in determining whether the lawyer should be disqualified, due regard must be given to the effect of disqualification on the lawyer's client. It is relevant that one or both parties could reasonably foresee that the lawyer would probably be a witness. The conflict of interest principles stated in Rules 1.7, 1.9 and 1.10 have no application to this aspect of the problem.

(5) Because the tribunal is not likely to be misled when a lawyer acts as advocate in a trial in which another lawyer in the lawyer's firm will testify as a necessary witness, paragraph (b) permits the lawyer to do so except in situations involving a conflict of interest.

Conflict of Interest

(6) In determining if it is permissible to act as advocate in a trial in which the lawyer will be a necessary witness, the lawyer must also consider that the dual role may give rise to a conflict of interest that will require compliance with Rules 1.7 or 1.9. For example, if there is likely to be substantial conflict between the testimony of the client and that of the lawyer, the representation involves a conflict of interest that requires compliance with Rule 1.7. This would be true even though the lawyer might not be prohibited by paragraph (a) from simultaneously serving as advocate and witness because the lawyer's disqualification would work a substantial hardship on the client. Similarly, a lawyer who might be permitted to simultaneously serve as an advocate and a witness by paragraph (a)(3) might be precluded from doing so by Rule 1.9. The problem can arise whether the lawyer is called as a witness on behalf of the client or is called by the opposing party. Determining whether or not such a conflict exists is primarily the responsibility of the lawyer involved. If there is a conflict of interest, the lawyer must secure the client's informed consent, confirmed in writing. In some cases, the lawyer will be precluded from seeking the client's consent. See Rule 1.7. See Rule 1.0(b) for the definition of "confirmed in writing" and Rule 1.0(e) for the definition of "informed consent."

(7) Paragraph (b) provides that a lawyer is not disqualified from serving as an advocate because a lawyer with whom the lawyer is associated in a firm is precluded from doing so by paragraph (a). If, however, the testifying lawyer would also be disqualified by Rule 1.7 or Rule 1.9 from representing the client in the matter, other lawyers in the firm will be precluded from representing the client by Rule 1.10 unless the client gives informed consent under the conditions stated in Rule 1.7.

SCR 3.130(3.8) Special responsibilities of a prosecutor

The prosecutor in a criminal case shall:

(a) refrain from prosecuting a charge that the prosecutor knows is not supported by probable cause;

(b) make reasonable efforts to assure that the accused has been advised of the right to, and the procedure for obtaining, counsel and has been given reasonable opportunity to obtain counsel;

(c) make timely disclosure to the defense of all evidence or information known to the prosecutor that tends to negate the guilt of the accused or mitigates the offense, and, in connection with sentencing, disclose to the defense and to the tribunal all unprivileged mitigating information known to the prosecutor, except when the prosecutor is relieved of this responsibility by a protective order of the tribunal;

(d) not subpoena a lawyer in a grand jury or other criminal proceeding to present evidence about a past or present client unless the prosecutor reasonably believes:

(1) the information sought is not protected from disclosure by any applicable privilege;

(2) the evidence sought is essential to the successful completion of an ongoing investigation or prosecution; and

(3) there is no other feasible alternative to obtain the information;

(e) refrain, except for statements that are necessary to inform the public of the nature and extent of the prosecutor's action and that serve a legitimate law enforcement purpose, from making extrajudicial comments that have a substantial likelihood of heightening public condemnation of the accused and exercise reasonable care to prevent investigators, law enforcement personnel, employees or other persons under the supervision of the prosecutor in a criminal case from making an extrajudicial statement that the prosecutor would be prohibited from making under Rule 3.6 or this Rule.

HISTORY: Amended by Order 2009–05, eff. 7–15–09; adopted by Order 89–1, eff. 1–1–90

Supreme Court Commentary

2009:

(1) A prosecutor has the responsibility of a minister of justice and not simply that of an advocate. This responsibility carries with it specific obligations to see that the defendant is accorded procedural justice and that guilt is decided upon the basis of sufficient evidence. Precisely how far the prosecutor is required to go in this direction is a matter of debate and varies in different jurisdictions. Many jurisdictions have adopted the ABA Standards of Criminal Justice Relating to the Prosecution Function, which in turn are the product of prolonged and careful deliberation by lawyers experienced in both criminal prosecution and defense. Applicable law may require other measures by the prosecutor and knowing disregard of those obligations or a systematic abuse of prosecutorial discretion could constitute a violation of Rule 8.4.

(2) The exception in paragraph (c) recognizes that a prosecutor may seek an appropriate protective order from the tribunal if disclo-

sure of information to the defense could result in substantial harm to an individual or to the public interest.

(3) Paragraph (d) is intended to limit the issuance of lawyer subpoenas in grand jury and other criminal proceedings to those situations in which there is a genuine need to intrude into the client-lawyer relationship.

(4) Paragraph (e) supplements Rule 3.6, which prohibits extrajudicial statements that have a substantial likelihood of prejudicing an adjudicatory proceeding. In the context of a criminal prosecution, a prosecutor's extrajudicial statement can create the additional problem of increasing public condemnation of the accused. Although the announcement of an indictment, for example, will necessarily have severe consequences for the accused, a prosecutor can, and should, avoid comments which have no legitimate law enforcement purpose and have a substantial likelihood of increasing public opprobrium of the accused. Nothing in this Comment is intended to restrict the statements which a prosecutor may make which comply with Rule 3.6(b) or 3.6(c).

(5) Like other lawyers, prosecutors are subject to Rules 5.1 and 5.3, which relate to responsibilities regarding lawyers and nonlawyers who work for or are associated with the lawyer's office. Paragraph (e) reminds the prosecutor of the importance of these obligations in connection with the unique dangers of improper extrajudicial statements in a criminal case. In addition, paragraph (e) requires a prosecutor to exercise reasonable care to prevent persons under the supervision of the prosecutor from making improper extrajudicial statements. Ordinarily, the reasonable care standard will be satisfied if the prosecutor issues the appropriate cautions to law-enforcement personnel and other relevant individuals.

SCR 3.130(3.9) Advocate in nonadjudicative proceedings

A lawyer representing a client before a legislative body or administrative agency in a nonadjudicative proceeding shall disclose that the appearance is in a representative capacity and shall conform to the provisions of Rules 3.3(a) through (c), 3.4(a) through (c), and 3.5.

HISTORY: Amended by Order 2009–05, eff. 7–15–09; adopted by Order 89–1, eff. 1–1–90

Supreme Court Commentary

2009:

(1) In representation before bodies such as legislatures, municipal councils, and executive and administrative agencies acting in a rule-making or policy-making capacity, lawyers present facts, formulate issues and advance argument in the matters under consideration. The decision-making body, like a court, should be able to rely on the integrity of the submissions made to it. A lawyer appearing before such a body must deal with it honestly and in conformity with applicable rules of procedure. See Rules 3.3(a) through (c), 3.4(a) through (c) and 3.5.

(2) Lawyers have no exclusive right to appear before nonadjudicative bodies, as they do before a court. The requirements of this Rule therefore may subject lawyers to regulations inapplicable to advocates who are not lawyers. However, legislatures and administrative agencies have a right to expect lawyers to deal with them as they deal with courts.

(3) This Rule only applies when a lawyer represents a client in connection with an official hearing or meeting of a governmental agency or a legislative body to which the lawyer or the lawyer's client is presenting evidence or argument. It does not apply to representation of a client in a negotiation or other bilateral transaction with a governmental agency or in connection with an application for a license or other privilege or the client's compliance with generally applicable reporting requirements, such as the filing of income-tax returns. Nor does it apply to the representation of a client in connection with an investigation or examination of the client's affairs conducted by government investigators or examiners. Representation in such matters is governed by Rules 4.1 through 4.4.

TRANSACTIONS WITH PERSONS OTHER THAN CLIENTS

SCR 3.130(4.1) Truthfulness in statements to others

In the course of representing a client a lawyer:

(a) shall not knowingly make a false statement of material fact or law to a third person; and

(b) if a false statement of material fact or law has been made, shall take reasonable remedial measures to avoid assisting a fraudulent or criminal act by a client including, if necessary, disclosure of a material fact, unless prohibited by Rule 1.6.

HISTORY: Amended by Order 2009–05, eff. 7–15–09; adopted by Order 89–1, eff. 1–1–90

Supreme Court Commentary

2009:

Misrepresentation

(1) A lawyer is required to be truthful when dealing with others on a client's behalf, but generally has no affirmative duty to inform an opposing party of relevant facts. A misrepresentation can occur if the lawyer incorporates or affirms a statement of another person that the lawyer knows is false. Misrepresentations can also occur by partially true but misleading statements or omissions that are the equivalent of affirmative false statements. For dishonest conduct that does not amount to a false statement or for misrepresentations by a lawyer other than in the course of representing a client, see Rule 8.4.

Statements of Fact

(2) This Rule refers to statements of fact. Whether a particular statement should be regarded as one of fact can depend on the circumstances. Under generally accepted conventions in negotiation, certain types of statements ordinarily are not taken as statements of material fact. Estimates of price or value placed on the subject of a transaction and a party's intentions as to an acceptable settlement of a claim are ordinarily in this category, and so is the existence of an undisclosed principal except where nondisclosure of the principal would constitute fraud. Lawyers should be mindful of their obligations under applicable law to avoid criminal and tortious misrepresentation.

Crime or Fraud by Client

(3) Under Rule 1.2(d), a lawyer is prohibited from counseling or assisting a client in conduct that the lawyer knows is criminal or fraudulent. Paragraph (b) states a specific application of the principle set forth in Rule 1.2(d) and addresses the situation where a client's crime or fraud takes the form of a lie or misrepresentation. Ordinarily a lawyer can avoid assisting in a client's crime or fraud by withdrawing from the representation. Nonetheless, sometimes a lawyer is required to take more overt measures such as giving notice of the fact of withdrawal, disaffirming an opinion, document, affirmation or the like, to prevent the lawyer's services' being used to further the client's crime or fraud. In extreme cases, substantive law may require a lawyer to disclose information relating to the representation to avoid being deemed to have assisted in the client's crime or fraud. If the lawyer can avoid assisting a client's crime or fraud only by disclosing this information, then under paragraph (b) the lawyer is required to do so, unless the disclosure is prohibited by Rule 1.6. [See also, Rules 1.6(b), 1.13 (c) and 8.4(c).]

SCR 3.130(4.2) Communication with person represented by counsel

In representing a client, a lawyer shall not communicate about the subject of the representation with a person the lawyer knows to be represented by another lawyer in the matter, unless the lawyer has the consent of the other lawyer or is authorized to do so by law or a court order.

HISTORY: Amended by Order 2009–05, eff. 7–15–09; adopted by Order 89–1, eff. 1–1–90

Supreme Court Commentary

2009:

(1) This Rule contributes to the proper functioning of the legal system by protecting a person who has chosen to be represented by a lawyer in a matter against possible overreaching by other lawyers who are participating in the matter, interference by those lawyers with the client-lawyer relationship and the uncounseled disclosure of information relating to the representation.

(2) This Rule applies to communications with any person, who is represented by counsel concerning the matter to which the communication relates.

(3) The Rule applies even though the represented person initiates or consents to the communication. A lawyer must immediately terminate communication with a person if, after commencing communication, the lawyer learns that the person is one with whom communication is not permitted by this Rule.

(4) This Rule does not prohibit communication with a represented person, or an employee or agent of such a person, concerning matters outside the representation. For example, the existence of a controversy between a government agency and a private party, or between two organizations, does not prohibit a lawyer for either from communicating with nonlawyer representatives of the other regarding a separate matter. Nor does this Rule preclude communication with a represented person who is seeking advice from a lawyer who is not otherwise representing a client in the matter. A lawyer may not make a communication prohibited by this Rule through the acts of another. See Rule 8.4(a). Parties to a matter may communicate directly with each other, and a lawyer is not prohibited from advising a client concerning a communication that the client is legally entitled to make. Also, a lawyer having independent justification or legal authorization for communicating with a represented person is permitted to do so.

(5) Communications authorized by law may include communications by a lawyer on behalf of a client who is exercising a constitutional or other legal right to communicate with the government. Communications authorized by law may also include investigative activities of lawyers representing governmental entities, directly or through investigative agents, prior to the commencement of criminal or civil enforcement proceedings. When communicating with the accused in a criminal matter, a government lawyer must comply with this Rule in addition to honoring the constitutional rights of the accused.

(6) A lawyer who is uncertain whether a communication with a represented person is permissible may seek a court order. A lawyer may also seek a court order in exceptional circumstances to authorize a communication that would otherwise be prohibited by this Rule, for example, where communication with a person represented by counsel is necessary to avoid reasonably certain injury.

(7) In the case of a represented organization, this Rule prohibits communications to a constituent of the organization who supervises, directs or regularly consults with the organization's lawyer concerning the matter or has authority to obligate the organization with respect to the matter or whose act or omission in connection with the matter may be imputed to the organization for purposes of civil or criminal liability. Consent of the organization's lawyer is not required for communication with a former constituent. If a constituent of the organization is represented in the matter by his or her own counsel, the consent by that counsel to a communication will be sufficient for purposes of this Rule. Compare Rule 3.4(g). In communicating with a current or former constituent of an organization, a lawyer must not use methods of obtaining evidence that violate the legal rights of the organization. See Rule 4.4.

(8) The prohibition on communications with a represented person only applies in circumstances where the lawyer knows that the person is in fact represented in the matter to be discussed. This means that the lawyer has actual knowledge of the fact of the representation; but such actual knowledge may be inferred from the circumstances. See

Rule 1.0(f). Thus, the lawyer cannot evade the requirement of obtaining the consent of counsel by closing eyes to the obvious.

(9) In the event the person with whom the lawyer communicates is not known to be represented by counsel in the matter, the lawyer's communications are subject to Rule 4.3.

SCR 3.130(4.3)   Dealing with unrepresented person

In dealing on behalf of a client with a person who is not represented by counsel, a lawyer shall not state or imply that the lawyer is disinterested. When the lawyer knows or reasonably should know that the unrepresented person misunderstands the lawyer's role in the matter, the lawyer shall make reasonable efforts to correct the misunderstanding. The lawyer shall not give legal advice to an unrepresented person. The lawyer may suggest that the unrepresented person secure counsel.

HISTORY: Amended by Order 2009–05, eff. 7–15–09; adopted by Order 89–1, eff. 1–1–90

Supreme Court Commentary

2009:

(1) An unrepresented person, particularly one not experienced in dealing with legal matters, might assume that a lawyer is disinterested in loyalties or is a disinterested authority on the law even when the lawyer represents a client. In order to avoid a misunderstanding, a lawyer will typically need to identify the lawyer's client and, where necessary, explain that the client has interests opposed to those of the unrepresented person. For misunderstandings that sometimes arise when a lawyer for an organization deals with an unrepresented constituent, see Rule 1.13(f). Unlike Rule 4.3 of the ABA Model Rules of Professional Conduct (2003), this Rule provides that under no circumstances shall a lawyer give legal advice to an unrepresented person.

(2) The Rule distinguishes between situations involving unrepresented persons whose interests may be adverse to those of the lawyer's client and those in which the person's interests are not in conflict with the client's. In the former situation, the possibility that the lawyer will compromise the unrepresented person's interests is so great that the Rule prohibits the giving of any advice, apart from the suggestion to obtain counsel. Whether the discussion of the client's position impermissibly assumes the character of rendering legal advice may depend on the experience and sophistication of the unrepresented person, as well as the setting in which the behavior and Comments occur. This Rule does not prohibit a lawyer from negotiating the terms of a transaction or settling a dispute with an unrepresented person. So long as the lawyer has explained that the lawyer represents an adverse party and is not representing the person, the lawyer may inform the person of the terms on which the lawyer's client will enter into an agreement or settle a matter, prepare documents that require the person's signature and explain the client's position as to the meaning of the document or explain the lawyer's view of the underlying legal obligations.

SCR 3.130(4.4)   Respect for rights of third persons

(a) In representing a client, a lawyer shall not use means that have no substantial purpose other than to embarrass, delay, or burden a third person, or use methods of obtaining evidence that violate the legal rights of such a person.

(b) A lawyer who receives a document relating to the representation of the lawyer's client and knows or reasonably should know that the document was inadvertently sent shall:

(1) refrain from reading the document,

(2) promptly notify the sender, and

(3) abide by the instructions of the sender regarding its disposition.

HISTORY: Amended by Order 2009–05, eff. 7–15–09; adopted by Order 89–1, eff. 1–1–90

Supreme Court Commentary

2009:

(1) Responsibility to a client requires a lawyer to subordinate the interests of others to those of the client, but that responsibility does not imply that a lawyer may disregard the rights of third persons. It is impractical to catalogue all such rights, but they include legal restrictions on methods of obtaining evidence from third persons and unwarranted intrusions into privileged relationships. such as the client-lawyer relationship.

(2) Paragraph (b) recognizes that lawyers sometimes receive documents or other communications that were mistakenly sent or produced by opposing parties or their lawyers. If it is clear from the circumstances that the document was not intended for the receiving lawyer, that lawyer must avoid reading the substance of the communication, notify the sender of the mistake, and comply with any reasonable request of the sender, allowing for protective measures (e.g. returning to sender, deleting or otherwise destroying the communication). The question whether the privileged status of such a document has been waived is a matter of law beyond the scope of these Rules Similarly, this Rule does not address the legal duties of a lawyer who received a document that the lawyer knows or reasonably should know may have been wrongfully obtained by the sending person. For purposes of this Rule, "document" includes e-mail or other electronic modes of transmission subject to being read or put into readable form.

LAW FIRMS AND ASSOCIATIONS

SCR 3.130(5.1)   Responsibilities of partners, managers and supervisory lawyers

(a) A partner in a law firm, and a lawyer who individually or together with other lawyers possesses comparable managerial authority in a law firm, shall make reasonable efforts to ensure that the firm has in effect measures giving reasonable assurance that all lawyers in the firm conform to the Rules of Professional Conduct.

(b) A lawyer having direct supervisory authority over another lawyer shall make reasonable efforts to ensure that the other lawyer conforms to the Rules of Professional Conduct.

(c) A lawyer shall be responsible for another lawyers violation of the Rules of Professional Conduct if:

(1) the lawyer orders or, with knowledge of the specific conduct, ratifies the conduct involved; or

(2) the lawyer is a partner or has comparable managerial authority in the law firm in which the other lawyer practices, or has direct supervisory authority over the other lawyer, and knows of the conduct at a time when its consequences can be avoided or mitigated but fails to take reasonable remedial action.

HISTORY: Amended by Order 2009–05, eff. 7–15–09; adopted by Order 89–1, eff. 1–1–90

Supreme Court Commentary

2009:

(1) Paragraph (a) applies to lawyers who have managerial authority over the professional work of a firm. See Rule 1.0(c). This includes members of a partnership, the shareholders in a law firm organized as a professional corporation, and members of other associations authorized to practice law; lawyers having comparable managerial authority in a legal services organization or a law department of an enterprise or government agency; and lawyers who have intermediate managerial responsibilities in a firm. Paragraph (b) applies to lawyers who have supervisory authority over the work of other lawyers in a firm.

(2) Paragraph (a) requires lawyers with managerial authority within a firm to make reasonable efforts to establish internal policies and procedures designed to provide reasonable assurance that all lawyers in the firm will conform to the Rules of Professional Conduct. Such policies and procedures include those designed to detect and resolve conflicts of interest, identify dates by which actions must be taken in pending matters, account for client funds and property and ensure that inexperienced lawyers are properly supervised.

(3) Other measures that may be required to fulfill the responsibility prescribed in paragraph (a) can depend on the firm's structure and the nature of its practice. In a small firm of experienced lawyers, informal supervision and periodic review of compliance with the required systems ordinarily will suffice. In a large firm, or in practice situations in which difficult ethical problems frequently arise, more elaborate measures may be necessary. Some firms, for example, have a procedure whereby junior lawyers can make confidential referral of ethical problems directly to a designated senior partner or special committee. See Rule 5.2. Firms, whether large or small, may also rely on continuing legal education in professional ethics. In any event, the ethical atmosphere of a firm can influence the conduct of all its members and the partners may not assume that all lawyers associated with the firm will inevitably conform to the Rules.

(4) Paragraph (c) expresses a general principle of personal responsibility for acts of another. See also Rule 8.4(a).

(5) Paragraph (c)(2) defines the duty of a partner or other lawyer having comparable managerial authority in a law firm, as well as a lawyer who has direct supervisory authority over performance of specific legal work by another lawyer. Whether a lawyer has supervisory authority in particular circumstances is a question of fact. Partners and lawyers with comparable authority have at least indirect responsibility for all work being done by the firm, while a partner or manager in charge of a particular matter ordinarily also has supervisory responsibility for the work of other firm lawyers engaged in the matter. Appropriate remedial action by a partner or managing lawyer would depend on the immediacy of that lawyer's involvement and the seriousness of the misconduct. A supervisor is required to intervene to prevent avoidable consequences of misconduct if the supervisor knows that the misconduct occurred. Thus, if a supervising lawyer knows that a subordinate misrepresented a matter to an opposing party in negotiation, the supervisor as well as the subordinate has a duty to correct the resulting misapprehension.

(6) Professional misconduct by a lawyer under supervision could reveal a violation of paragraph (b) on the part of the supervisory lawyer even though it does not entail a violation of paragraph (c) because there was no direction, ratification or knowledge of the violation.

(7) Apart from this Rule and Rule 8.4(a), a lawyer does not have disciplinary liability for the conduct of a partner, associate or subordinate. Whether a lawyer may be liable civilly or criminally for another lawyer's conduct is a question of law beyond the scope of these Rules.

(8) The duties imposed by this Rule on managing and supervising lawyers do not alter the personal duty of each lawyer in a firm to abide by the Rules of Professional Conduct. See Rule 5.2(a).

SCR 3.130(5.2) Responsibilities of a subordinate lawyer

(a) A lawyer is bound by the Rules of Professional Conduct notwithstanding that the lawyer acted at the direction of another person.

(b) A subordinate lawyer does not violate the Rules of Professional Conduct if that lawyer acts in accor-

dance with a supervisory lawyer's reasonable resolution of an arguable question of professional duty.

HISTORY: Adopted by Order 89-1, eff. 1-1-90

Supreme Court Commentary

1989:

[1] Although a lawyer is not relieved of responsibility for a violation by the fact that the lawyer acted at the direction of a supervisor, that fact may be relevant in determining whether a lawyer had the knowledge required to render conduct a violation of the Rules. For example, if a subordinate filed a frivolous pleading at the direction of a supervisor, the subordinate would not be guilty of a professional violation unless the subordinate knew of the document's frivolous character.

[2] When lawyers in a supervisor-subordinate relationship encounter a matter involving professional judgment as to ethical duty, the supervisor may assume responsibility for making the judgment. Otherwise a consistent course of action or position could not be taken. If the question can reasonably be answered only one way, the duty of both lawyers is clear and they are equally responsible for fulfilling it. However, if the question is reasonably arguable, someone has to decide upon the course of action. That authority ordinarily reposes in the supervisor, and a subordinate may be guided accordingly. For example, if a question arises whether the interests of two clients conflict under Rule 1.7, the supervisor's reasonable resolution of the question should protect the subordinate professionally if the resolution is subsequently challenged.

SCR 3.130(5.3) Responsibilities regarding nonlawyer assistants

With respect to a nonlawyer employed or retained by or associated with a lawyer:

(a) a partner, and a lawyer who individually or together with other lawyers possesses comparable managerial authority in a law firm shall make reasonable efforts to ensure that the firm has in effect measures giving reasonable assurance that the person's conduct is compatible with the professional obligations of the lawyer;

(b) a lawyer having direct supervisory authority over the nonlawyer shall make reasonable efforts to ensure that the person's conduct is compatible with the professional obligations of the lawyer; and

(c) a lawyer shall be responsible for conduct of such a person that would be a violation of the Rules of Professional Conduct if engaged in by a lawyer only if:

(1) the lawyer orders or, with the knowledge of the specific conduct, ratifies the conduct involved; or

(2) the lawyer is a partner or has comparable managerial authority in the law firm in which the person is employed, or has direct supervisory authority over the person, and knows of the conduct at a time when its consequences can be avoided or mitigated but fails to take reasonable remedial action.

HISTORY: Amended by Order 2009–05, eff. 7–15–09; adopted by Order 89–1, eff. 1–1–90

Supreme Court Commentary

2009:

(1) Lawyers generally employ assistants in their practice, including secretaries, investigators, law student interns, and paraprofessionals. Such assistants, whether employees or independent contractors, act for the lawyer in rendition of the lawyer's professional services. A

lawyer must give such assistants appropriate instruction and supervision concerning the ethical aspects of their employment, particularly regarding the obligation not to disclose information relating to representation of the client, and should be responsible for their work product. The measures employed in supervising nonlawyers should take account of the fact that they do not have legal training and are not subject to professional discipline.

(2) Paragraph (a) requires lawyers with managerial authority within a law firm to make reasonable efforts to establish internal policies and procedures designed to provide reasonable assurance that nonlawyers in the firm will act in a way compatible with the Rules of Professional Conduct. See Comment [1] to Rule 5.1. Paragraph (b) applies to lawyers who have supervisory authority over the work of a nonlawyer. Paragraph (c) specifies the circumstances in which a lawyer is responsible for conduct of a nonlawyer that would be a violation of the Rules of Professional Conduct if engaged in by a lawyer.

SCR 3.130(5.4) Professional independence of a lawyer

(a) A lawyer or law firm shall not share legal fees with a nonlawyer, except that:

(1) an agreement by a lawyer with the lawyer's firm, partner, or associate may provide for the payment of money, over a reasonable period of time after the lawyer's death, to the lawyer's estate or to one or more specified persons;

(2) a lawyer who purchases the practice of a deceased, disabled, or disappeared lawyer may, pursuant to the provisions of Rule 1.17, pay to the estate or other representative of that lawyer the agreed-upon purchase price;

(3) a lawyer or law firm may include nonlawyer employees in a compensation or retirement plan, even though the plan is based in whole or in part on a profit-sharing arrangement; and

(b) A lawyer shall not form a partnership with a nonlawyer if any of the activities of the partnership consist of the practice of law.

(c) A lawyer shall not permit a person who recommends, employs, or pays the lawyer to render legal services for another to direct or regulate the lawyer's professional judgment in rendering such legal services.

(d) A lawyer shall not practice with or in the form of a professional corporation or association authorized to practice law for a profit, if:

(1) a nonlawyer owns any interest therein, except that a fiduciary representative of the estate of a lawyer may hold the stock or interest of the lawyer for a reasonable time during administration;

(2) a nonlawyer is a corporate director or officer thereof or occupies the position of similar responsibility in any form of association other than a corporation; or

(3) a nonlawyer has the right to direct or control the professional judgment of a lawyer.

HISTORY: Amended by Order 2009–05, eff. 7–15–09; adopted by Order 89–1, eff. 1–1–90

Supreme Court Commentary

2009:

(1) The provisions of this Rule express traditional limitations on sharing fees. These limitations are to protect the lawyer's professional independence of judgment. Where someone other than the client pays the lawyer's fee or salary, or recommends employment of the lawyer, that arrangement does not modify the lawyer's obligation to the client. As stated in paragraph (c), such arrangements should not interfere with the lawyer's professional judgment.

(2) This Rule also expresses traditional limitations on permitting a third party to direct or regulate the lawyer's professional judgment in rendering legal services to another. See also Rule 1.8(f) (lawyer may accept compensation from a third party as long as there is no interference with the lawyer's independent professional judgment and the client gives informed consent).

SCR 3.130(5.5) Unauthorized practice of law; multijurisdictional practice of law

(a) A lawyer shall not practice law in a jurisdiction in violation of the regulation of the legal profession in that jurisdiction, or assist another in doing so.

(b) A lawyer who is not admitted to practice in this jurisdiction shall not:

(1) except as authorized by these Rules or other law, establish or maintain an office or other presence in this jurisdiction for the practice of law; or

(2) hold out to the public or otherwise represent that the lawyer is admitted to practice law in this jurisdiction.

(c) A lawyer admitted in another United States jurisdiction, and not disbarred or suspended from practice in any jurisdiction, may provide legal services on a temporary basis in this jurisdiction if such services:

(1) comply with SCR 3.030(2), or they do not require compliance with SCR 3.030(2) due to federal statute, rule or regulation; or

(2) are in, or reasonably related to, a pending or potential proceeding before a tribunal or alternative dispute resolution proceeding in another jurisdiction for a client, or prospective client pursuant to Rule 1.18, if the services arise out of, or are reasonably related to, the lawyer's practice in a jurisdiction in which the lawyer is admitted to practice and are not services for which the forum requires pro hac vice admission pursuant to SCR 3.030(2); or

(3) are not within paragraph (c) (2) and arise out of, or are reasonably related to, the representation of the lawyer's client in the jurisdiction in which the lawyer is admitted.

(d) A lawyer admitted in another United States jurisdiction, and not disbarred or suspended from practice in any jurisdiction, may provide legal services in this jurisdiction that:

(1) comply with SCR 2.111 regarding a Limited Certificate of Admission to Practice Law in this jurisdiction; or

(2) are services that the lawyer is authorized to provide by federal law or other law of this jurisdiction.

(e) A lawyer authorized to provide legal services under this Rule shall be subject to the Kentucky Rules of Professional Conduct and shall comply with SCR 3.030(2) or, if such legal services do not require compliance with that Rule, the lawyer must actively participate in, and assume responsibility for, the representation of the client.

HISTORY: Amended by Order 2012–01, eff. 3–1–12; prior amendment eff. 7–15–09 (Order 2009–05); adopted by Order 89–1, eff. 1–1–90

Supreme Court Commentary

2009:

(1) A lawyer may practice law only in a jurisdiction in which the lawyer is authorized to practice. A lawyer may be admitted to practice law in a jurisdiction on a regular basis or may be authorized by court rule or order or by law to practice for a limited purpose or on a restricted basis. Paragraph (a) applies to unauthorized practice of law by a lawyer, whether through the lawyer's direct action or by the lawyer assisting another person.

(2) The definition of the practice of law is established by law and varies from one jurisdiction to another. The practice of law in Kentucky is defined in SCR 3.020. Whatever the definition, limiting the practice of law to members of the bar protects the public against rendition of legal services by unqualified persons. This Rule does not prohibit a lawyer from employing the services of paraprofessionals and delegating functions to them, so long as the lawyer supervises the delegated work and retains responsibility for their work. See Rule 5.3.

(3) A lawyer may provide professional advice and instruction to nonlawyers whose employment requires knowledge of the law; for example, claims adjusters, employees of financial or commercial institutions, social workers, accountants and persons employed in government agencies. Lawyers also may assist independent nonlawyers, such as paraprofessionals, who are authorized by the law of a jurisdiction to provide particular law-related services. In addition, a lawyer may counsel nonlawyers who wish to proceed pro se.

(4) Other than as authorized by law or this Rule, a lawyer who is not admitted to practice generally in this jurisdiction violates paragraph (b) if the lawyer establishes or maintains an office in this jurisdiction for the practice of law. A lawyer may violate paragraph (b) by establishing or maintaining an office even if the lawyer is not physically present here. Such a lawyer must not hold out to the public or otherwise represent that the lawyer is admitted to practice law in this jurisdiction. See Rules 7.15 and 7.50. For example, advertising in media specifically targeted to Kentucky residents or initiating contact with Kentucky residents for solicitation purposes could be viewed as conduct in Kentucky in violation of paragraph (b). See also Comment [20].

(5) There are occasions in which a lawyer admitted to practice in another United States jurisdiction, and not disbarred or suspended from practice in any jurisdiction, may provide legal services on a temporary basis in this jurisdiction under circumstances that do not create an unreasonable risk to the interests of their clients, the public or the courts. Paragraph (c) identifies three such circumstances. The fact that conduct is not so identified does not imply that the conduct is or is not authorized. With the exception of paragraphs (d)(1) and (d)(2), this Rule does not authorize a lawyer to establish or maintain an office in this jurisdiction without being admitted to practice generally here.

(6) There is no single test to determine whether a lawyer's services are provided on a "temporary basis" in this jurisdiction, and may therefore be permissible under paragraph (c). Services may be "temporary" even though the lawyer provides services in this jurisdiction on a recurring basis, or for an extended period of time, as when the lawyer is representing a client in a single lengthy negotiation or litigation.

(7) Paragraphs (c) and (d) apply to lawyers who are admitted to practice law in any United States jurisdiction, which includes the District of Columbia and any state, territory or commonwealth of the United States. The word "admitted" contemplates that the lawyer is authorized to practice in the jurisdiction in which the lawyer is admitted and excludes a lawyer who, while technically admitted, is not authorized to practice, because, for example, the lawyer is on inactive status.

(8) Paragraph (c)(1) recognizes that the interests of clients and the public are protected if a lawyer admitted only in another jurisdiction associates with a lawyer licensed to practice in this jurisdiction. For this paragraph to apply, however, the lawyer admitted to practice in this jurisdiction must comply with SCR 3.030(2) or, if such legal services do not require compliance with that Rule, the lawyer must actively participate in, and show responsibility for, the representation of the client.

(9) Lawyers not admitted to practice generally in a jurisdiction may be authorized by law or order of a court or federal administrative agency to appear before the court or agency. This authority may be granted pursuant to formal rules governing admission pro hac vice or pursuant to rules of the federal administrative agency. Under paragraph (c)(1) and (2), a lawyer does not violate this Rule when the lawyer appears before a court or agency pursuant to such authority. To the extent that a court rule or other law of this jurisdiction requires a lawyer who is not admitted to practice in this jurisdiction to obtain admission pro hac vice before appearing before a court or agency, this Rule requires the lawyer to obtain that authority.

(10) Paragraph (c)(2) provides that a lawyer rendering services in this jurisdiction on a temporary basis does not violate this Rule when the lawyer engages in conduct in anticipation of a proceeding or hearing in a jurisdiction in which the lawyer is authorized to practice law. Examples of such conduct include meetings with the client, interviews of potential witnesses, and the review of documents. Similarly, a lawyer admitted only in another jurisdiction may engage in conduct temporarily in this jurisdiction in connection with pending litigation in another jurisdiction in which the lawyer is or reasonably expects to be authorized to appear, including taking depositions in this jurisdiction. Paragraph (c)(2) also permits conduct by lawyers who are associated with that lawyer in the matter, but who do not expect to appear before the court or administrative agency. For example, subordinate lawyers may conduct research, review documents, and attend meetings with witnesses in support of the lawyer responsible for the litigation.

(11) Paragraph (c)(2) also permits a lawyer admitted to practice law in another jurisdiction to perform services on a temporary basis in this jurisdiction if those services are in or reasonably related to a pending or potential arbitration, mediation, or other alternative dispute resolution proceeding in another jurisdiction, if the services arise out of or are reasonably related to the lawyer's practice in a jurisdiction in which the lawyer is admitted to practice. The lawyer, however, must obtain admission pro hac vice in the case of a court-annexed arbitration or mediation or otherwise if court rules or law so require.

(12) Paragraph (c)(3) permits a lawyer admitted in another jurisdiction to provide certain legal services on a temporary basis in this jurisdiction that arise out of or are reasonably related to the lawyer's representation of a client in a jurisdiction in which the lawyer is admitted but are not within paragraph (c)(2). These services include both legal services and services that nonlawyers may perform but that are considered the practice of law when performed by lawyers.

(13) Paragraphs (c)(2) and (c)(3) require that the services arise out of or be reasonably related to the lawyer's practice in a jurisdiction in which the lawyer is admitted. A variety of factors evidence such a relationship. The lawyer's client may have been previously represented by the lawyer, or may be resident in or have substantial contacts with the jurisdiction in which the lawyer is admitted. The matter, although involving other jurisdictions, may have a significant connection with that jurisdiction. In other cases, significant aspects of the lawyer's work might be conducted in that jurisdiction or a significant aspect of the matter may involve the law of that jurisdiction. The necessary relationship might arise when the client's activities or the legal issues involve multiple jurisdictions, such as when the officers of a multinational corporation survey potential business sites and seek the services of their lawyer in assessing the relative merits of each. In addition, the services may draw on the lawyer's recognized expertise developed through the regular practice of law on behalf of clients in matters involving a particular body of federal, nationally-uniform, foreign, or international law.

(14) Paragraph (d) identifies two circumstances in which a lawyer who is admitted to practice in another United States jurisdiction, and is not disbarred or suspended from practice in any jurisdiction, may establish or maintain an office in this jurisdiction for the practice of law as well as provide legal services on a temporary basis. Except as provided in paragraphs (d)(1) and (d)(2), a lawyer who is admitted to practice law in another jurisdiction and who establishes or maintains an office in this jurisdiction must become admitted to practice law generally in this jurisdiction.

(15) Paragraph (d)(1) applies to a lawyer who is employed by a client to provide legal services to the client or its organizational affiliates, i.e., entities that control, are controlled by, or are under common control with the employer. This paragraph does not authorize the provision of personal legal services to the employer's officers or employees. The paragraph applies to in-house corporate lawyers and others who are employed to render legal services to the employer. The lawyer's ability to represent the employer outside the jurisdiction in which the lawyer is licensed generally serves the interests of the employer and does not create an unreasonable risk to the client and others because the employer is well situated to assess the lawyer's qualifications and the quality of the lawyer's work.

(16) If an employed lawyer under paragraph (d)(1) performs legal services in this jurisdiction, the lawyer is subject to the rules, rights and privileges governing the practice of law under SCR 2.111.

(17) Paragraph (d)(2) recognizes that a lawyer may provide legal services in a jurisdiction in which the lawyer is not licensed when authorized to do so by federal law or other law of this jurisdiction.

(18) A lawyer who practices law in this jurisdiction pursuant to paragraphs (c) or (d) or otherwise is subject to the disciplinary authority of this jurisdiction. See Rule 8.5(a).

(19) In some circumstances, a lawyer who practices law in this jurisdiction pursuant to paragraphs (c) or (d) may have to inform the client that the lawyer is not licensed to practice law in this jurisdiction. For example, that may be required when the representation occurs primarily in this jurisdiction and requires knowledge of the law of this jurisdiction. See Rule 1.4(b).

(20) Paragraphs (c) and (d) do not authorize communications advertising legal services to prospective clients in this jurisdiction by lawyers who are admitted to practice in other jurisdictions. Whether and how lawyers may communicate the availability of their services to prospective clients in this jurisdiction is governed by Rules 7.01 to 7.50.

SCR 3.130(5.6) Restrictions on right to practice

A lawyer shall not participate in offering or making:

(a) a partnership or, shareholders, operating, employment, or other similar type of agreement that restricts the right of a lawyer to practice after termination of the relationship, except an agreement concerning benefits upon retirement; or

(b) an agreement in which a restriction on the lawyer's right to practice is part of the settlement of a client controversy.

HISTORY: Amended by Order 2009–05, eff. 7–15–09; adopted by Order 89–1, eff. 1–1–90

Supreme Court Commentary

2009:

(1) An agreement restricting the right of lawyers to practice after leaving a firm not only limits their professional autonomy but also limits the freedom of clients to choose a lawyer. Paragraph (a) prohibits such agreements except for restrictions incident to provisions concerning retirement benefits for service with the firm.

(2) Paragraph (b) prohibits a lawyer from agreeing not to represent other persons in connection with settling any controversy on behalf of a client.

(3) This Rule does not apply to prohibit restrictions that may be included in the terms of the sale of a law practice pursuant to Rule 1.17.

PUBLIC SERVICE

SCR 3.130(6.1) Donated legal services

A lawyer is encouraged to voluntarily render public interest legal service. A lawyer is encouraged to accept and fulfill this responsibility to the public by rendering a minimum of fifty (50) hours of service per calendar year by providing professional services at no fee or a reduced fee to persons of limited means, and/or by financial support for organizations that provide legal service to persons of limited means. Donated legal services may be reported on the annual dues statement furnished by the Kentucky Bar Association. Lawyers rendering a minimum of fifty (50) hours of donated legal services shall receive a recognition award for such service from the Kentucky Bar Association.

HISTORY: Amended by Order 94–1, eff. 10–1–94; prior amendment eff. 8–1–92; adopted eff. 1–1–90

Supreme Court Commentary

1989:

[1] The ABA House of Delegates has formally acknowledged "the basic responsibility of each lawyer engaged in the practice of law to provide public interest legal services" without fee, or at a substantially reduced fee, in one or more of the following areas: poverty law, civil rights law, public rights law, charitable organization representation and the administration of justice. This Rule expresses that policy but is not intended to be enforced through disciplinary process.

[2] The rights and responsibilities of individuals and organizations in the United States are increasingly defined in legal terms. As a consequence, legal assistance in coping with the web of statutes, rules and regulations is imperative for persons of modest and limited means, as well as for the relatively well-to-do.

[3] The basic responsibility for providing legal services for those unable to pay ultimately rests upon the individual lawyer, and personal involvement in the problems of the disadvantaged can be one of the most rewarding experiences in the life of a lawyer. Every lawyer, regardless of professional prominence or professional workload, should find time to participate in or otherwise support the provision of legal services to the disadvantaged. The provision of free legal services to those unable to pay reasonable fees continues to be an obligation of each lawyer as well as the profession generally, but the efforts of individual lawyers are often not enough to meet the need. Thus, it has been necessary for the profession and government to institute additional programs to provide legal services. Accordingly, legal aid offices, lawyer referral services and other related programs have been developed, and others will be developed by the profession and government. Every lawyer should support all proper efforts to meet this need for legal services.

SCR 3.130(6.2) Accepting appointments

A lawyer should not seek to avoid appointment by a tribunal to represent a person except for good cause, such as:

(a) Representing the client is likely to result in violation of the Rules of Professional Conduct or other law;

(b) Representing the client is likely to result in an unreasonable financial burden on the lawyer; or

(c) The client or the cause is so repugnant to the lawyer as to be likely to impair the client-lawyer relationship or the lawyer's ability to represent the client.

HISTORY: Adopted by Order 89–1, eff. 1–1–90

Supreme Court Commentary

1989:

[1] A lawyer ordinarily is not obliged to accept a client whose character or cause the lawyer regards as repugnant. The lawyer's freedom to select clients is, however, qualified. All lawyers have a responsibility to assist in providing pro bono publico service. See Rule 6.1. An individual lawyer fulfills this responsibility by accepting a fair share of unpopular matters or indigent or unpopular clients. A lawyer may also be subject to appointment by a court to serve unpopular clients or persons unable to afford legal services.

Appointed Counsel

[2] For good cause a lawyer may seek to decline an appointment to represent a person who cannot afford to retain counsel or whose cause is unpopular. Good cause exists if the lawyer could not handle the matter competently, see Rule 1.1, or if undertaking the representation would result in an improper conflict of interest, for example, when the client or the cause is so repugnant to the lawyer as to be likely to impair the client-lawyer relationship or the lawyer's ability to represent the client. A lawyer may also seek to decline an appointment if acceptance would be unreasonably burdensome, for example, when it would impose a financial sacrifice so great as to be unjust.

[3] An appointed lawyer has the same obligations to the client as retained counsel, including the obligations of loyalty and confidentiality, and is subject to the same limitations on the client-lawyer relationship, such as the obligation to refrain from assisting the client in violation of the Rules.

SCR 3.130(6.3) Membership in legal services organization

A lawyer may serve as a director, officer or member of a legal services organization, apart from the law firm in which the lawyer practices, notwithstanding that the organization serves persons having interests adverse to a client of the lawyer. The lawyer shall not knowingly participate in a decision or action of the organization:

(a) If participating in the decision would be incompatible with the lawyer's obligations to a client under Rule 1.7; or

(b) Where the decision could have a material adverse effect on the representation of a client who will be served by lawyers provided by the organization whose interests are adverse to a client of the lawyer.

HISTORY: Adopted by Order 89–1, eff. 1–1–90

Supreme Court Commentary

1989:

[1] Lawyers should be encouraged to support and participate in legal service organizations. A lawyer who is an officer or a member of such an organization does not thereby have a client-lawyer relationship with persons served by the organization. However, there is potential conflict between the interests of such persons and the interests of the lawyer's clients. If the possibility of such conflict disqualified a lawyer from serving on the board of a legal services organization, the profession's involvement in such organizations would be severely curtailed.

[2] It may be necessary in appropriate cases to reassure a client of the organization that the representation will not be affected by conflicting loyalties of a member of the board. Established, written policies in this respect can enhance the credibility of such assurances.

SCR 3.130(6.4) Law reform activities affecting client interests

A lawyer may serve as a director, officer or member of an organization involved in reform of the law or its administration notwithstanding that the reform may affect the interests of a client of the lawyer. When the lawyer knows that the interests of a client may be materially affected by a decision in which the lawyer participates, the lawyer shall disclose that fact but need not identify the client.

HISTORY: Amended by Order 2009–05, eff. 7–15–09; adopted by Order 89–1, eff. 1–1–90

Supreme Court Commentary

2009:

Lawyers involved in organizations seeking law reform generally do not have a client-lawyer relationship with the organization. Otherwise, it might follow that a lawyer could not be involved in a bar association law reform program that might indirectly affect a client. See also Rule 1.2(b). For example, a lawyer specializing in antitrust litigation might be regarded as disqualified from participating in drafting revisions of rules governing that subject. In determining the nature and scope of participation in such activities, a lawyer should be mindful of obligations to clients under other Rules, particularly Rule 1.7. A lawyer is professionally obligated to protect the integrity of the program by making an appropriate disclosure within the organization when the lawyer knows a private client might be materially affected.

SCR 3.130(6.5) Nonprofit and court-annexed limited legal services programs

(a) A lawyer who, under the auspices of a program sponsored by a nonprofit organization or court, provides short-term limited legal services to a client without expectation by either the lawyer or the client that the lawyer will provide continuing representation in the matter:

(1) is subject to Rules 1.7 and 1.9(a) only if the lawyer knows that the representation of the client involves a conflict of interest; and

(2) is subject to Rule 1.10 only if the lawyer knows that another lawyer associated with the lawyer in a law firm is disqualified by Rule 1.7 or 1.9(a) with respect to the matter.

(b) Except as provided in paragraph (a)(2), Rule 1.10 is inapplicable to a representation governed by this Rule.

HISTORY: Adopted by Order 2009–05, eff. 7–15–09

Supreme Court Commentary

2009:

(1) Legal services organizations, courts and various nonprofit organizations have established programs through which lawyers provide short-term limited legal services, such as advice or the completion of legal forms, that will assist persons to address their legal problems without further representation by a lawyer. In these programs, such as legal-advice hotlines, advice-only clinics or pro se counseling programs, a client-lawyer relationship is established, but there is no expectation that the lawyer's representation of the client will continue beyond the limited consultation. Such programs are normally operated under circumstances in which it is not feasible for a lawyer to systematically screen for conflicts of interest as is generally required

before undertaking a representation. See, e.g., Rules 1.7, 1.9 and 1.10.

(2) A lawyer who provides short-term limited legal services pursuant to this Rule must secure the client's informed consent to the limited scope of the representation. See Rule 1.2(c). If a short-term limited representation would not be reasonable under the circumstances, the lawyer may offer advice to the client but must also advise the client of the need for further assistance of counsel. Except as provided in this Rule, the Rules of Professional Conduct, including Rules 1.6 and 1.9(c), are applicable to the limited representation.

(3) Because a lawyer who is representing a client in the circumstances addressed by this Rule ordinarily is not able to check systematically for conflicts of interest, paragraph (a) requires compliance with Rules 1.7 or 1.9(a) only if the lawyer knows that the representation presents a conflict of interest for the lawyer, and with Rule 1.10 only if the lawyer knows that another lawyer in the lawyer's firm is disqualified by Rules 1.7 or 1.9(a) in the matter.

(4) Because the limited nature of the services significantly reduces the risk of conflicts of interest with other matters being handled by the lawyer's firm, paragraph (b) provides that Rule 1.10 is inapplicable to a representation governed by this Rule except as provided by paragraph (a)(2). Paragraph (a)(2) requires the participating lawyer to comply with Rule 1.10 when the lawyer knows that the lawyer's firm is disqualified by Rules 1.7 or 1.9(a). By virtue of paragraph (b), however, a lawyer's participation in a short-term limited legal services program will not preclude the lawyer's firm from undertaking or continuing the representation of a client with interests adverse to a client being represented under the program's auspices. Nor will the personal disqualification of a lawyer participating in the program be imputed to other lawyers participating in the program.

(5) If, after commencing a short-term limited representation in accordance with this Rule, a lawyer undertakes to represent the client in the matter on an ongoing basis, Rules 1.7, 1.9(a) and 1.10 become applicable.

INFORMATION ABOUT LEGAL SERVICES

SCR 3.130(7.01) Applicability

Rule 7 shall apply to advertisements of legal services directed to residents of the Commonwealth of Kentucky or which originate in the Commonwealth of Kentucky.

HISTORY: Amended by Order 2001–2, eff. 1–1–02; adopted by Order 92–1, eff. 8–1–92

SCR 3.130(7.02) Definitions

For the purposes of Rule 7, the following definitions shall apply:

(1) "Advertise" means to furnish any information or communication containing a lawyer's name or other identifying information, and an "advertisement" is any information containing a lawyer's name or other identifying information, except the following:

(a) A professional card of a lawyer identifying the lawyer by name and giving the lawyer's address(es), telephone number(s), fax number(s), e-mail address(es), but no other information. A professional card of a law firm may also give the names of members and associates, and jurisdictions in which the lawyers are licensed to practice.

(b) A public service broadcast announcement identifying the sponsor as a lawyer or law firm, by name, address(es), telephone number(s), but no other information.

(c) A professional announcement stating new or changed associations or addresses or change of firm name. It shall not state biographical data except to the extent necessary to identify the lawyer or to explain the change in his or her association, but it may state the immediate past position of the lawyer and jurisdictions in which the lawyer is licensed to practice. It may give the names and dates of predecessor firms in a continuing line of succession.

(d) A regularly published professional directory. Each separate office maintained by a lawyer may have a separate listing.

(e) A sign on or near the law office and in the building directory identifying the law office and containing only the information specified in subsection (a) of this section.

(f) A letterhead of a lawyer containing addresses, telephone numbers, fax numbers, email addresses, the name of the law firm, associates, and the jurisdictions in which the lawyer is licensed to practice. A letterhead of a law firm may also give the names of members and associates, and names and dates relating to deceased and retired members. A lawyer may be designated "Of Counsel" on a letterhead if there is a continuing relationship with a lawyer or law firm, other than as a partner or associate. A lawyer or law firm may be designated "General Counsel" or by similar professional reference on stationery of a client if the lawyer or the firm devotes a substantial amount of professional time in the representation of that client. The letterhead of a law firm may give the names and dates of predecessor firms in a continuing line of succession.

(g) Any communication by a lawyer to third parties that is further distributed by a third party who is not in any way controlled by the lawyer, and for which distribution the lawyer pays no consideration, shall be exempt from all the provisions of these Rules except Rule 7.10, 7.15 and 8.4.

(h) Communication to prospective clients as defined in SCR 3.130(1.18) and communication to, for, or on behalf of an existing client shall not be included within the definition herein. It is not the intention of the Rules to designate such communications performed in the regular course of representation of an existing client as advertising.

(i) A communication otherwise exempt under these Rules is not disqualified by the inclusion of any truthful information pertaining to national certification by an organization that the attorney demonstrates is qualified to grant such certification, to attorneys who meet objective and consistently applied standards relevant to practice in a particular area of the law.

(j) Information and communication by a lawyer to members of the public in public speaking forums, radio, television broadcasts or postings on the internet that permit real time communication and exchanges on topics of general interest in legal issues, provided there is no reference to an offer by the lawyer to render legal services. This exception includes any republication or rebroadcasts of such communications.

(2) "Legal Services" means the practice of law as defined in SCR 3.020.

(3) "Commission" when used in SCR 3.130(7) means Attorneys' Advertising Commission.

HISTORY: Amended by Order 2012–16, eff. 12–11–12; prior amendments eff. 7–15–09 (Order 2009–05), eff. 1–1–06 (Order 2005–10), eff. 1–1–02 (Order 2001–2), 9–1–93 (Order 93–1), adopted eff. 8–1–92

Supreme Court Commentary

2009:

SCR 3.130(7.02)(i) adopts standards set forth and discussed in *Peel v. Attorney Registration and Disciplinary Commission of Illinois,* 496 U.S. 91, 110 S.Ct. 2281 (1990).

SCR 3.130(7.03) Attorneys' advertising commission

(1) There shall be created an Attorneys' Advertising Commission which shall perform such functions in regulating lawyer advertising as prescribed in these Rules.

(2) The Commission shall consist of nine (9) persons appointed by the President and approved by the Board. Each Commission member shall be appointed for a term of three years, with terms so established that the terms of the Commission members shall be staggered. Vacancies for unexpired terms shall be filled in the same manner as original appointees, but the appointees shall hold office only to the end of the unexpired term. No member may serve more than two (2) terms in succession, and may be removed at any time by a majority vote of the Board.

(3) Each Commission member shall be a citizen of the United States and licensed to practice law in the Courts of the Commonwealth.

(4) The Board shall appoint a Chair from among the Commission members. The term shall be one (1) year; however, the Chair may serve more than one (1) term.

(5) The Commission shall be provided with sufficient administrative assistance from the Director as from time to time may be required.

(6) The Commission shall prepare a budget for the succeeding year and shall submit same to the Board of Governors for inclusion with the budget of the Association.

(a) Issue and promulgate regulations and such forms as may be necessary, subject to prior approval by the Board. Each member of the Association shall be given at least sixty (60) days advance notice of any proposed regulations and an opportunity to comment thereon. Notice may be given by publication in the journal of the Kentucky Bar Association.

(b) Report to the Board at its last meeting preceding the Annual Convention of the Association, and otherwise as required, on the status of advertising with such recommendations or forms as advisable.

(c) Delegate to an employee of the KBA designated by the Director of the Kentucky Bar Association the authority to review advertisements on its behalf.

(d) Review advertisements, issue advisory opinions concerning the compliance of an advertisement with the Advertising Rules and Advertising Regulations, conduct such proceedings or investigations as it deems necessary, or delegate this authority to a Commission member or a hearing officer who shall proceed in the name of the Commission.

(e) Seek out violations of the Advertising Rules and the Advertising Regulations, resolve the violations under Rule 7.06(4), or refer violations to the Inquiry Commission. Referral to the Inquiry Commission may be by any panel or by a majority of a quorum of the entire Commission.

(7) The Commission shall prepare a budget for the succeeding year and shall submit same to the Board of Governors for inclusion with the budget of the Association.

(8) The Commission shall act upon advertisements, or issue advisory opinions in panels of three (3) persons. A quorum to act upon an advertisement shall consist of not fewer than two (2) members of a panel. A quorum to do business in meetings of the entire Commission shall consist of not fewer than five of its members in attendance.

(9) Nothing in these rules shall be construed as creating any cause of action for any party or right of suit against any member of the Commission. The Kentucky Bar Association, the Board of Governors, the Attorneys' Advertising Commission, the Executive Director of the Association, the Office of Bar Counsel, all of their officers, members, employees or agents shall be immune from civil liability for all acts in the course of their official duties in regulating lawyer advertising.

HISTORY: Amended by Order 2012–01, eff. 3–1–12; prior amendments eff. 1–1–06 (Order 2005–10), 1–17–03 (Order 2003–1), 1–1–02 (Order 2001–2), 1–1–97 (Order 96–1); adopted eff. 8–1–92

SCR 3.130(7.04) Advertising of fees

(1) A lawyer who advertises a fee for routine services and accepts the employment must perform such services for the amount advertised. In addition, a detailed description of what services are included in the "routine services" must be supplied to the Commission with each advertisement and to each prospective client who requests such a description.

(2) If an advertisement mentions a fee for legal services, including reference to a contingent fee, disclosure shall be made as to the responsibility for court costs and case expenses. If the client is required to

pay court costs and/or case expenses in addition to the attorney's fee, the advertisement shall state in all capital letters, "COURT COSTS AND CASE EXPENSES WILL BE THE RESPONSIBILITY OF THE CLIENT."

HISTORY: Amended by Order 2009–05, eff. 7–15–09; prior amendments eff. 1–1–06 (Order 2005–10), 1–1–02 (Order 2001–2); adopted by Order 92–1, eff. 8–1–92

SCR 3.130(7.05)   Filing of advertisements

No lawyer may advertise unless the lawyer complies with SCR 3.130 (7.02)–(7.50).

(1)(a) A lawyer may employ the following in an advertisement:

1. Name, including name of law firm and names of professional associates, addresses, telephone numbers, fax numbers and e-mail addresses;

2. One or more fields of law in which the lawyer or law firm practices, or a statement that practice is limited to one or more fields of law, to the extent authorized under Rule 7.40;

3. Date and place of birth;

4. Date and place of admission to the bar of state and federal courts;

5. Schools attended, with dates of graduation, degrees and other scholastic distinctions;

6. Public or quasi-public offices;

7. Military services;

8. Authorships;

9. Teaching positions;

10. Memberships, offices and committee assignments, in bar associations;

11. Membership and offices in legal fraternities and legal societies;

12. Technical and professional licenses;

13. Memberships in scientific, technical and professional associations and societies;

14. Foreign language ability;

15. Names and addresses of bank references;

16. With their written consent, names of clients regularly represented;

17. Prepaid or group legal services programs in which the lawyer participates;

18. Whether credit cards or other credit arrangements are accepted;

19. Office and telephone answering service hours;

20. Fee for an initial consultation;

21. Availability upon request of a written schedule of fees and/or an estimate of the fee to be charged for specific services;

22. Contingent fee rates provided that the statement discloses whether percentages are computed before or after deduction of court costs and case expenses;

23. Range of fees for services, provided that the statement discloses that the specific fee within the range which will be charged will vary depending upon the particular matter to be handled for each client and the client is entitled to without obligation to an estimate of the fee within the range likely to be charged, in print size equivalent to the largest print used in setting forth the fee information;

24. Hourly rate, provided that the statement discloses that the total fee charged will depend upon the number of hours which must be devoted to the particular matter to be handled for each client and the client is entitled to without obligation an estimate of the fee likely to be charged, in print size at least equivalent to the largest print used in setting forth the fee information;

25. Fixed fees for specific legal services to the extent authorized under these Rules; or

26. Any other information specified in any regulation adopted by the Commission. Any lawyer may petition the Commission for the adoption of such a regulation in which case the petition shall be published as provided in these Rules.

(b) If the advertisement contains only those items listed in SCR 3.130(7.05)(1)(a), or in AAC Regulation 2, the lawyer shall mail or deliver to the Commission, c/o the Director of the Kentucky Bar Association, three (3) copies of the advertisement, or electronically transmit the advertisement via facsimile or email in PDF (Portable Document Format) to the Attorneys' Advertising Commission address attorney advertising@kybar.org. If the advertisement is to be published by broadcast media, including radio or television, a fair and accurate representation of the advertisement plus three (3) copies of a typed transcript of the words spoken shall be submitted. Any such advertisement is exempt from a fee for submission. Submission under this subsection shall occur no later than the publication of the advertisement.

(2) If the advertisement does not qualify under SCR 3.130(7.05)(1) for submission without a fee, the lawyer shall mail or deliver to the Commission, c/o the Director of the Kentucky Bar Association, three (3) copies of the advertisement. If the advertisement is to be published by broadcast media, including radio or television, a fair and accurate representation of the advertisement plus three (3) copies of a typed transcript of the words spoken shall be submitted. Website advertisements that do not qualify for submission without a fee must be submitted in electronic format on a data disc in PDF (Portable Document Format), or other such data storage media as the Commission may designate by regulation. Three (3) copies of the data disc should be mailed or delivered to the Commission, c/o the Director of the Kentucky Bar Association. A filing fee of seventy five-dollars ($75.00) for

each advertisement filed under this subsection shall accompany each submission. Submission under this subsection shall occur no later than the publication of the advertisement. An additional administrative fee of one hundred dollars ($100.00) may be imposed for late submissions. Additionally, advertisements of more than 100 pages, or longer than 10 minutes of video or audio, will require a supplemental fee of one hundred dollars ($100.00). The same fees are required if an advisory opinion has been sought under SCR 3.130(7.06)(1).

(3) The fair and accurate representation of a broadcast media advertisement required in SCR 3.130 (7.05)(1) and (2) shall include three (3) copies of a video cassette (VHS), digital video disc (DVD), or audio cassette plus three (3) copies of a typed transcript of the advertisement.

(4) The lawyer shall retain a copy or recording of all advertisements utilized by the lawyer, as well as a record of when and where it was used, for two (2) years after its last dissemination. Electronic retention is permitted if in PDF format, or such other formats as the Commission may designate by regulation. In the event of the pendency of any disciplinary action before the Inquiry Commission, Board of Governors or Court, the lawyer shall continue to retain a copy until the termination of that proceeding.

HISTORY: Amended by Order 2012–01, eff. 3–1–12; prior amendments eff. 7–15–09 (Order 2009–05), 1–1–06 (Order 2005–10), 8–19–04 (Order 2004–4), 1–1–02 (Order 2001–2), 3–1–98 (Order 97–3), 11–1–95 (Order 95–1); adopted eff. 8–1–92

SCR 3.130(7.06)   Advisory opinions

(1) For any advertisement submitted as required by SCR 3.130(7.05)(2), a lawyer may request an advisory opinion by the Commission before the advertisement is published. Such request shall be in writing made at least 30 days before the advertisement is published. The request shall be accompanied by the filing fee, and any required administrative fees as set forth in SCR 3.130(7.05)(2). Within 30 days after such request is received, the Commission shall issue its advisory opinion as to the compliance of the advertisement with the Advertising Rules and Advertising Regulations.

(2) If a lawyer has received an advisory opinion that an advertisement complies with the Advertising Rules and Advertising Regulations, that lawyer shall not be disciplined for any use of that advertisement, except as otherwise provided in SCR 3.130 (7.06)(6).

(3) If a lawyer has requested an advisory opinion and the Commission finds that the advertisement does not comply with the requirements of the Advertising Rules or the Advertising Regulations, the Commission, or its designee, shall issue an advisory letter setting forth the factual and legal basis for the opinion. The lawyer may submit a corrected advertisement under SCR 3.130(7.05)(2) that conforms to the

advice in the advisory letter with no additional fee required.

(4) if an advertisement is discovered to be false, misleading or deceptive, or information provided to the Commission in connection with the submission is discovered to be false, misleading or deceptive after the Commission has issued its advisory opinion, it, or its designee, may notify the Advertising lawyer that all prior advisory opinions concerning such advertisement are withdrawn and the advisory opinion shall not constitute a defense to the subsequent use of the advertisement.

HISTORY: Amended by Order 2009–05, eff. 7–15–09; prior amendments eff. 1–1–06 (Order 2005–10), 1–1–02 (Order 2001–2); adopted by Order 92–1, eff. 8–1–92

SCR 3.130(7.07)   Review of filings

(1) For any advertisement on which an advisory opinion has not been sought, the Commission, or its designee, may review such filings for compliance with the Advertising Rules and Advertising Regulations. If the Commission, or its designee, determines a violation of the Advertising Rules or Advertising Regulations has occurred, it may notify the advertising attorney that a violation has occurred, and it may refer the matter to the Inquiry Commission.

(2) If the Commission determines that the Advertising Rules or Advertising Regulations have been violated by a lawyer, it shall determine whether the violation can be dealt with administratively, or can be presumed to be intentional. The Commission may address administrative violations. Intentional violations include but are not limited to: (1) publishing the advertisement after receiving notice that the advertisement is in violation of the Advertising Rules or the Advertising Regulations; (2) a manifest indifference to the Advertising Rules or Advertising Regulations; or (3) a pattern of repeated disregard for these Advertising Rules or Advertising Regulations. Intentional violations may be referred to the Inquiry Commission.

(3) If the Commission has notified the lawyer that the advertisement violated the Advertising Rules or Advertising Regulations, and has further determined that the publication of the advertisement may be contrary to the public interest, the Commission or its designee shall notify the lawyer whose advertisement is under consideration and the Director of the Association. The Director may, upon receiving such notification, bring an action in compliance with this Rule.

HISTORY: Amended by Order 2009–05, eff. 7–15–09; prior amendments eff. 1–1–06 (Order 2005–10), 1–1–02 (Order 2001–2), 11–1–95 (Order 95–1); adopted eff. 8–1–92

Supreme Court Commentary

2009:

Any advisory opinion under SCR 3.130(7.06) or any letters of notification under SCR 3.130(7.07) that an advertisement does not comply with the Advertising Rules or any Advertising Regulations of the Commission does not prohibit the lawyer from using any such advertisement. However, the lawyer, as with all other Rules of

Professional Conduct, is obligated to comply with the Advertising Rules and Advertising Regulations and may face disciplinary sanctions if the advertisement used is found to be in violation of the Advertising Rules or Advertising Regulations.

SCR 3.130(7.08) Records of the commission

All advertisements and the records of all actions taken by the Commission on submitted advertisements shall be available for inspection and copying at the offices of the Bar Association at reasonable times and upon reasonable notice. Any expense incurred shall be borne by the requesting party.

HISTORY: Amended by Order 2009–05, eff. 7–15–09; prior amendment eff. 1–1–02 (Order 2001–2); adopted by Order 92–1, eff. 8–1–92

SCR 3.130(7.09) Direct contact with potential clients

(1) No lawyer shall directly or through another person, by in person, live telephone, or real-time electronic means, initiate contact or solicit professional employment from a potential client unless:

(a) the lawyer has an immediate family relationship with the potential client;

(b) the lawyer has a current attorney-client relationship with the potential client; or

(c) the lawyer is advocating a public interest issue and is not significantly motivated by the lawyer's pecuniary gain.

This Rule shall not prohibit response to inquiries initiated by persons who may become potential clients at the time of any other incidental contact not designed or intended by the lawyer to solicit employment.

(2) A lawyer shall not solicit professional employment from a potential client even when not otherwise prohibited by paragraph (1) if:

(a) The potential client has made known to the lawyer a desire not to be solicited by the lawyer; or

(b) the solicitation involves coercion, duress or harassment.

(3) Every written, recorded or electronic communication from a lawyer soliciting professional employment from a potential client known or reasonably believed to be in need of legal services in a particular matter, must contain the words "THIS IS AN ADVERTISEMENT" in all capital letters prominently displayed in type at least as large as the type in the body of the communication unless:

(a) the lawyer has an immediate family relationship with the potential client; or

(b) the lawyer has a current attorney-client relationship with the potential client.

Further, in each such written or recorded or electronic communication the envelope, document, or container, by which such communication is transmitted shall contain the word "ADVERTISEMENT" in all capital

letters, and in type large enough to be conspicuous and placed in a conspicuous location on the same side of the envelope, document, or container upon which the lawyer's name and/or address appears. If an electronic communication is sent by or on behalf of the lawyer to a potential client in a container or on a disc or other format on which words may appear, the outside of the container, or disc, or other format shall be marked as provided in this rule. If a recorded telephone, electronic, video, or digital communication is sent under this rule, a speaker must first recite the language "THE FOLLOWING IS AN ADVERTISEMENT" and shall further state at the end of the communication the language "THIS MESSAGE HAS BEEN AN ADVERTISEMENT".

(4) No communication pursuant to SCR 3.130(7.09)(3) shall be sent to those potential clients who have been involved in a disaster as defined in SCR 3.130(7.60) until thirty (30) days have elapsed from the occurrence of the disaster.

(5) Notwithstanding the prohibitions in SCR 3.130(7.09)(1), a lawyer may participate with a prepaid or group legal service plan operated by an organization not owned or directed by the lawyer that uses in-person or telephone contact to solicit memberships or subscriptions for the plan from persons who are not known to need legal services in a particular manner covered by the plan.

HISTORY: Amended 2012–01, eff. 3–1–12; prior amendments eff. 7–15–09 (Order 2009–05), 1–1–02 (Order 2001–2); adopted by Order 92–1, eff. 8–1–92

Supreme Court Commentary

2009:

(1) Communications to prior clients are not prohibited if the lawyer is required by the circumstances of the representation to communicate with a prior client to advise the client of changes in the law that would result in additional legal work.

(2) SCR 3.130(7.04)(5) permits a lawyer to participate with an organization that uses personal contact to solicit members for its group or prepaid legal service plan, provided that personal contact is not undertaken by any lawyer who would be a provider of legal services through the plan. The organization must not be owned by or directed (whether as manager or otherwise) by any lawyer or law firm that participates in the plan. For example, paragraph (5) would not permit a lawyer to create an organization controlled directly or indirectly by the lawyer and use the organization for the in-person or telephone solicitation of legal employment of the lawyer through memberships in the plan or otherwise. The communication permitted by these organizations also must not be directed to a person known to need legal services in a particular matter, but should be designed to inform potential plan members generally of another means of affordable legal services. Lawyers who participate in a legal service plan must make reasonable efforts to determine that the plan sponsors are in compliance with the Rules.

(3) Neither this rule nor SCR 3.130(7.20) prohibits communications authorized by law, such as notice to members of a class in class action litigation.

SCR 3.130(7.10) Waiver and forfeiture of fees for prohibited solicitation

If a lawyer illegally or unethically solicited a client for which compensation is paid or payable, all fees arising from such transaction shall be deemed waived and forfeited and shall be returned to the client. A civil action for recovery of such fees may be brought in a court of competent jurisdiction.

HISTORY: Amended by Order 2001–2, eff. 1–1–02; adopted by Order 92–1, eff. 8–1–92

SCR 3.130(7.15) Communications concerning a lawyer's service

A lawyer shall not make a false, deceptive or misleading communication about the lawyer or the lawyer's service. A communication is false, deceptive or misleading if it:

(a) Contains a material misrepresentation of fact or law, or omits a fact necessary to make the statement considered as a whole not materially misleading; or

(b) Is likely to create an unjustified expectation about results the lawyer can achieve, or states or implies that the lawyer can achieve results by means that violate the rules of professional conduct or other law; or

(c) Compares the lawyer's services with other lawyers' services, unless the comparison can be factually substantiated.

HISTORY: Amended by Order 2009–05, eff. 7–15–09; prior amendment eff. 1–1–06 (Order 2005–10); adopted by Order 2001–2, eff. 1–1–02

Supreme Court Commentary

2009:

(1) This Rule governs all communications about a lawyer's services, including advertising permitted by SCR 3.130(7.20). Whatever means are used to make known a lawyer's services; statements about them must be truthful. Truthful statements that are misleading are also prohibited by this Rule. A truthful statement is misleading if it omits a fact necessary to make the lawyer's communication considered as a whole not materially misleading. A truthful statement is also misleading if there is a substantial likelihood that it will lead a reasonable person to formulate a specific conclusion about the lawyer or the lawyer's services for which there is no reasonable factual foundation.

(2) The prohibition in SCR 3.130(7.15)(b) of statements that may create "unjustified expectations" may preclude advertisements about results obtained on behalf of a client, such as the amount of a damage award or the lawyer's record in obtaining favorable verdicts, and advertisements containing client endorsements. An advertisement that truthfully reports a lawyer's achievements on behalf of clients or former clients may be misleading if presented in a manner that may lead a reasonable person to form an unjustified expectation that the same results could be obtained for other clients in similar matters without reference to the specific factual and legal circumstances of each client's case.

(3) Similarly, an unsubstantiated comparison of the lawyer's services or fees with the services or fees of other lawyers may be misleading.

SCR 3.130(7.20) Advertising

(1) A lawyer may advertise legal services through communications in compliance with these Rules.

(2) A lawyer shall not give anything of value to a non-lawyer for recommending the lawyer's services, except that a lawyer may:

(a) pay the reasonable cost of advertising or communication permitted by this Rule; and,

(b) pay the usual charges of a legal service plan, not to include a division of fees, operated by an organization not owned or directed by the lawyer, or,

(c) pay the usual charges of a not-for-profit or qualified lawyer referral service that has been approved by the highest court in the jurisdiction where the service operates an agency designated by that court or by the Kentucky Bar Association.

(3) Any communication made pursuant to these Rules shall include the name of at least one lawyer licensed in Kentucky, or law firm any of whose members are licensed in Kentucky, responsible for its contents.

(4) Communication by a lawyer with a person or entity with whom that lawyer has an immediate family or current attorney-client relationship, or a communication in response to an inquiry from any person or entity seeking information, shall be exempt from the provisions of the Advertising Rules and the Advertising Regulations, with the exception of SCR 3.130(7.15).

(5) If a lawyer or a law firm advertises legal services and a lawyer's name or image is used to present the advertisement, the lawyer must be the lawyer who will actually perform the service advertised unless the advertisement prominently discloses that the service may be performed by other lawyers. If the advertising lawyer or firm is advertising for clients for the purpose of referring the client to another lawyer or firm, that fact must be disclosed prominently in the advertisement.

HISTORY: Amended by Order 2009–05, eff. 7–15–09; prior amendment eff. 1–1–02 (Order 2001–2); adopted by Order 92–1, eff. 8–1–92

Supreme Court Commentary

2009:

(1) Neither this Rule nor SCR 3.130 (7.3) prohibits communications authorized by law, such as notice to members of a class in class action litigation.

(2) A lawyer is allowed to pay for advertising permitted by this Rule, but otherwise is not permitted to pay another person for channeling professional work. This restriction does not prevent an organization or person other than the lawyer from advertising or recommending the lawyer's services. Thus, a legal aid agency or prepaid legal services plan may pay to advertise legal services provided under its auspices. Likewise, a lawyer may participate in not-for-profit lawyer referral programs and pay the usual fees charged by such programs. Paragraph (b) does not prohibit paying regular compensation to an assistant, such as a secretary, to prepare communications permitted by this Rule.

(3) A lawyer may pay the usual charges of a legal service plan or a not-for-profit qualified lawyer referral service. A legal service plan is a prepaid or group legal service plan or a similar delivery system that assists potential clients to secure legal representation. This Rule only permits a lawyer to pay the usual charges of a not-for-profit qualified lawyer referral service. A not-for-profit qualified lawyer referral service is one that is approved by the highest court of the jurisdiction where the service operates or by an agency designated by the highest court in that jurisdiction to handle such approvals, or in Kentucky by the Kentucky Bar Association.

(4) A lawyer who accepts assignments or referrals from a legal service plan or referrals from a lawyer referral service must make reasonable efforts to determine that the activities of the plan or

service are compatible with the lawyer's professional obligations. Legal service plans and lawyer referral services may communicate with potential clients, but such communication must conform with the Advertising Rules and Advertising Regulations. For example, the plan may not engage in advertising that is false or misleading, as would be the case if the communications of a group advertising program or a group legal services plan mislead potential clients to believe that the plan was a lawyer referral service sponsored by a state agency or bar association. Similarly, the lawyer may not allow in-person, telephonic, or real-time contacts by the plan that would violate SCR 3.130(1.5)(e).

(5) This Rule does not address the circumstances under which a lawyer may be permitted to share or split a fee with other lawyers. For ethical requirements applicable to fee sharing arrangements see SCR 3.130(1.5)(e).

SCR 3.130(7.25)   Identification of advertisements

All advertisements must include the words "THIS IS AN ADVERTISEMENT", unless excepted by SCR 3.130(7.09). In recorded telephone, electronic, video, or digital communications, other than television, the speaker must first state "THE FOLLOWING IS AN ADVERTISEMENT" and must further state at the end of the communication "THIS MESSAGE HAS BEEN AN ADVERTISEMENT". All television communication, video recording or digital recording must prominently display the words "THIS IS AN ADVERTISEMENT" on the screen for as long as the lawyer's or firm's name appears on the screen. If a television communication video recording, or digital recording is longer than 60 seconds, the words "THIS IS AN ADVERTISEMENT" must be displayed throughout the entire communication. The words "THIS IS AN ADVERTISEMENT" must be prominently displayed on every page of any advertisement in writing, and displayed without scrolling on the first screen of every page of a website.

HISTORY: Amended by Order 2009–05, eff. 7–15–09; prior amendment eff. 1–1–02 (Order 2001–2); adopted by Order 92–1, eff. 8–1–92

SCR 3.130(7.30)   Direct contact with prospective client—Deleted

HISTORY: Deleted by Order 2001–2, eff. 1–1–02; adopted by Order 92–1, eff. 8–1–92

SCR 3.130(7.40)   Communication of fields of practice

A lawyer may communicate the fact that the lawyer does or does not practice in particular fields of law. A lawyer who concentrates in, limits his or her practice to, or wishes to announce a willingness to accept cases in a particular field may advertise or publicly state that information in any manner otherwise permitted by these Rules. Any such advertisement or statement shall be strictly factual and shall not contain any form of the words "certified", "specialist", "expert", or "authority", except as follows:

(1) A lawyer admitted to engage in patent practice before the United States Patent and Trademark Office may use the designation "Patent Lawyer" or a substantially similar designation.

(2) A lawyer certified by an appropriate governmental agency in admiralty practice may use the designation "Admiralty", "Proctor in Admiralty", or a substantially similar designation.

(3) A lawyer may state or imply that he or she is "certified", a "specialist", an "expert" or "authority" in a particular field of law only if:

(a) the lawyer has been certified as a specialist by an organization that has been approved by an appropriate state authority or by a national organization that the attorney demonstrates is qualified to grant such certification to attorneys who meet objective and consistently applied standards relevant to practice in a particular area of the law; and

(b) the name of the certifying organization is clearly identified in the communication; and

(c) if the lawyer is licensed to practice law in Kentucky, the communication must state that Kentucky does not certify specialties in legal fields. The communication may occur only for as long as the lawyer remains so certified and in good standing.

HISTORY: Amended by Order 2009–05, eff. 7–15–09; prior amendment eff. 1–1–02 (Order 2001–2); adopted by Order 92–1, eff. 8–1–92

Supreme Court Commentary

2009:

(1) This Rule permits a lawyer to indicate areas of practice in communications about the lawyer's services. If a lawyer practices only in certain fields, or will not accept matters except in such fields, the lawyer is permitted to so indicate.

(2) Recognition of specialization in patent matters is a matter of long-established policy of the Patent and Trademark Office. Designation of admiralty practice has a long historical tradition associated with maritime commerce and the federal courts.

(3) Certificates discussed in SCR 3.130(7.40)(3) must meet the criteria set forth in *Peel v. Attorney Registration and Disciplinary Commission of Illinois*, 496 U.S. 91, 110 S.Ct. 2281 (1990). Stating or implying that the lawyer is certified as a "specialist", an "expert" or "authority" is not permitted except as provided in this rule. The lawyer may state or imply that he or she is certified as a specialist, expert or authority only if the certification is granted by an organization approved by an appropriate state authority, such as a state bar association, or by an organization that qualifies under *Peel v. Attorney Registration and Disciplinary Commission of Illinois*, 496 U.S. 91, 110 S.Ct. 2281 (1990). Certifying organizations are expected to apply standards of experience, knowledge and proficiency to insure that a lawyer's recognition as a specialist is meaningful and reliable. To insure that consumers can obtain access to useful information about an organization granting certification, the name of the certifying organization must be included in any communication about certification, and the communication must state that Kentucky does not certify specialties in legal fields. If the Commission is not satisfied that the certifying organization's standards and procedures are sufficiently meaningful and rigorous to make the communication truthful, it may disapprove the communication under SCR 3.130(7.15).

(4) Refer to SCR 3.130(702)(1)(i) for other applications of *Peel v. Attorney Registration and Disciplinary Commission of Illinois*, 496 U.S. 91, 110 S.Ct. 2281 (1990).

SCR 3.130(7.50)   Firm names and letterheads

(1) A lawyer shall not use a firm name, letterhead or other professional designation that violates Rule 7.15.

(2) A law firm with offices in more than one jurisdiction may use the same name in each jurisdiction, but identification of the lawyers in an office of the firm shall indicate the jurisdictional limitations on those not licensed to practice in the jurisdiction where the office is located.

(3) The name of a lawyer holding a public office shall not be used in the name of a law firm, or in communications on its behalf, during any period in which the lawyer is not actively and regularly practicing with the firm.

(4) Lawyers may state or imply that they practice in a legal entity only if that is the fact.

(5) The name of a lawyer who is suspended by the Supreme Court from the practice of law may not be used by the law firm in any manner until the lawyer is reinstated. A lawyer who has been permanently disbarred shall not be included in a firm name, letterhead, or any other professional designation or advertisement.

HISTORY: Amended by Order 2009–05, eff. 7–15–09; prior amendment eff. 1–1–02 (Order 2001–2); adopted by Order 92–1, eff. 8–1–92

Supreme Court Commentary

2009:

With regard to paragraph (4), lawyers sharing office facilities, but who are not in fact partners, may not denominate themselves as, for example, "Smith and Jones," for that title suggests partnership in the practice of law.

SCR 3.130(7.60) Kentucky Bar Association disaster response plan

(a) It is the purpose of the Kentucky Disaster Response Plan to:

(1) address the problems that occur when lawyers and non-lawyers, who are not subject to the disciplinary jurisdiction of the Association and the Kentucky Supreme Court, engage in the provision of legal services, legal advice, and outright solicitation of persons and their families affected by a Disaster;

(2) provide information to the public regarding the availability of legal services, as well as information regarding the legal rights available to persons affected by disasters.

(3) monitor the conduct of all attorneys, both members and non-members of the Association, and thereby deter violations of the rules of ethical conduct and the rules of the Association.

(4) inform the public of the levels of conduct required of members of the Association and notify the public that it is improper for attorneys to solicit employment either in person or through runners, agents, solicitors, or others in such a manner as to create direct contact between the attorney seeking such employment and the potential claimant.

(b) It is the policy of the Association to encourage and promote the highest ethical standards among attorneys practicing within its borders. Realizing the emotional distress and grief that are inevitable immediately following a Disaster, the Kentucky Bar Association Disaster Response Plan (hereafter Plan) is established to facilitate the handling of these situations in a manner that best protects the interests of the persons involved as well as the legal community.

(c) For purposes of the Plan, a "Disaster" shall mean the type of emergency or disaster that draws persons to solicit clients. This includes, but is not limited to, air crash, major fire, explosion, sea disaster, hazardous material contamination, flood, landslide, major rail or traffic accident, earthquake, or other circumstances resulting in substantial loss of life, substantial personal injury, or substantial property damage.

(d) It shall be the responsibility of the Immediate Past President of the Association (hereafter Past President) or if the Past President is absent from the state or physically or mentally unable to act, the Director of the Association, or their designee, to identify a Disaster.

(e) The Kentucky Mass Disaster Task Force, (hereafter "Task Force") is hereby created from the Association membership in a sufficient number of "units" at the discretion of the Board to provide Disaster services. A unit of the Task Force shall consist of at least one member of the Board; one member of the Court of Justice; and one or more additional designees to each unit as appointed by the Past President.

(f) The Task Force shall meet promptly upon learning of an identified Disaster and shall establish a "legal service information center."

(g) The Task Force shall be provided with printed literature identifying the purpose of the Task Force, a press release identifying the unit of the Task Force, and any additional materials and equipment that the Past President, the Director, or the unit members themselves believe necessary to accomplish their purpose.

(h) The units of the Task Force shall be prepared to inform affected persons that:

(1) decisions regarding most legal matters and legal claims (other than those requiring immediate attention for the preservation of life or health of a person) are generally decisions that are better made after reasonable and thoughtful consideration and after consultation with the appropriate professionals, including attorneys;

(2) legal services are available to persons affected by Disasters;

(3) persons and entities who sustain damage by reason of the wrongful conduct of another may be entitled to recover damages;

(4) "Statutes of Limitations" exist which apply to various causes of action within the Commonwealth of

Kentucky and, in certain circumstances, to Federal causes of action;

(5) any person or entity believing he or she has been damaged by the wrongful acts of another should seek legal advice to determine the applicable statute of limitations;

(6) only those persons who have been admitted to practice law in the Commonwealth of Kentucky and those persons who are lawfully associated with them in practice may appear and present claims within the Courts of the Commonwealth of Kentucky;

(7) no person affected by a Disaster is obligated by law to furnish information regarding the occurrence to any representative of the media, or to investigators, insurance agents and adjusters (other than as required by the persons own insurers), attorneys, or other members of the public, except that a person who has observed conduct that may be identified as "criminal activity" is obligated to furnish information pertaining to criminal activity to lawfully constituted legal authorities;

(8) the affected persons should make a diligent effort to observe all conditions pertaining to the Disaster, and to make such appropriate records or notations as necessary in the circumstances to memorialize their recollections of the Disaster;

(9) if there are witnesses to the Disaster, it may be important to obtain the names, addresses, and telephone numbers of those witnesses, and to retain them for future reference;

(10) that Kentucky law does not certify specialties and that the members of the unit and their partners, associates, members of their firms, and other lawyers associated with them are not permitted to accept employment for the provision of legal services regarding the Disaster;

(11) the services provided by the unit are for informational purposes only; and

(12) each person or entity interested in legal services should seek the advice of private counsel selected by that person or entity.

(i) The Task Force shall investigate to determine if runners, attorneys, or others have been soliciting or attempting to solicit victims, relatives of victims, or others as clients for matters related to the Disaster. The Task Force shall designate from its members a person to receive any complaints or inquiries concerning suspected improper solicitation. As soon as is reasonably practicable, such designee shall furnish such information to the Director Association or his designee.

(j) The Task Force shall be subject to the following restrictions:

(1) no member of the Task Force shall offer specific legal advice to anyone regarding the Disaster, nor shall he refer a person to a particular lawyer or law firm. Upon inquiry and to the extent necessary to respond, a member of the Task Force may refer a person to other agencies or groups for information or assistance.

(2) no member of the unit assigned to a particular Disaster, nor any of his partners, members of his firm, associates, or other lawyers associated with the member shall be permitted to accept any employment relating to any matter arising out of that Disaster.

(3) the Task Force shall not issue any news releases or make any public statements on behalf of the Association without the specific prior approval of the Director.

(k) The reasonable expenses incurred by each unit member of the Task Force in training and providing services as contemplated herein, as well as the cost of the equipment and supplies necessary to provide the service shall be paid from the General Fund of the Association unless the same expenses shall be provided from IOLTA funds of the Association, funds obtained from private sources, grants or donations; or from funds otherwise appropriated by the Kentucky General Assembly, including discretionary funds of the Governor of Kentucky or other elected officials. Each unit of the Task Force shall be authorized to obtain when necessary such secretarial and clerical assistance as appropriate in the circumstances of the particular Disaster.

HISTORY: Amended by Order 2009–05, eff. 7–15–09; prior amendment eff. 1–1–06 (Order 2005–10); adopted by Order 92–1, eff. 8–1–92

SCR 3.130(7.1)　Communications concerning a lawyer's services—Deleted

HISTORY: Deleted by Order 92–1, eff. 8–1–92; adopted eff. 1–1–90

SCR 3.130(7.2)　Advertising—Deleted

HISTORY: Deleted by Order 92–1, eff. 8–1–92; adopted eff. 1–1–90

SCR 3.130(7.3)　Direct contact with prospective clients—Deleted

HISTORY: Deleted by Order 92–1, eff. 8–1–92; prior amendment eff. 11–1–90; adopted eff. 1–1–90

SCR 3.130(7.4)　Communication of fields of practice—Deleted

HISTORY: Deleted by Order 92–1, eff. 8–1–92; adopted eff. 1–1–90

SCR 3.130(7.5)　Firm names and letterheads—Deleted

HISTORY: Deleted by Order 92–1, eff. 8–1–92; adopted eff. 1–1–90

MAINTAINING THE INTEGRITY OF THE PROFESSION

SCR 3.130(8.1) Bar admission and disciplinary matters

An applicant for admission to the bar, or a lawyer in connection with a bar admission application or in connection with a disciplinary matter, shall not:

(a) knowingly make a false statement of material fact; or

(b) fail to disclose a fact necessary to correct a misapprehension known by the person to have arisen in the matter, or knowingly fail to respond to a lawful demand for information from an admissions or disciplinary authority, except that this Rule does not require disclosure of information otherwise protected by Rule 1.6.

HISTORY: Amended by Order 2009–05, eff. 7–15–09; adopted by Order 89–1, eff. 1–1–90

Supreme Court Commentary

2009:

(1) The duty imposed by this Rule extends to persons seeking admission to the bar as well as to lawyers. Hence, if a person makes a material false statement in connection with an application for admission, it may be the basis for subsequent disciplinary action if the person is admitted, and in any event may be relevant in a subsequent admission application. The duty imposed by this Rule applies to a lawyer's own admission or discipline as well as that of others. Thus, it is a separate professional offense for a lawyer to knowingly make a misrepresentation or omission in connection with a disciplinary investigation of the lawyer's own conduct. Paragraph (b) of this Rule also requires correction of any prior misstatement in the matter that the applicant or lawyer may have made and affirmative clarification of any misunderstanding on the part of the admissions or disciplinary authority of which the person involved becomes aware.

(2) This Rule is subject to the provisions of the fifth amendment of the United States Constitution and corresponding provisions of state constitutions. A person relying on such a provision in response to a question, however, should do so openly and not use the right of nondisclosure as a justification for failure to comply with this Rule.

(3) A lawyer representing an applicant for admission to the bar, or representing a lawyer who is the subject of a disciplinary inquiry or proceeding, is governed by the rules applicable to the client-lawyer relationship, including Rule 1.6 and, in some cases, Rule 3.3.

SCR 3.130(8.2) Judicial and legal officials

(a) A lawyer shall not make a statement that the lawyer knows to be false or with reckless disregard as to its truth or falsity concerning the qualifications or integrity of a judge, adjudicatory officer or public legal officer, or of a candidate for election or appointment to judicial or legal office.

(b) A lawyer who is a candidate for judicial office shall comply with the applicable provisions of the Code of Judicial Conduct.

HISTORY: Adopted by Order 89–1, eff. 1–1–90

Supreme Court Commentary

1989:

[1] Assessments by lawyers are relied on in evaluating the professional or personal fitness of persons being considered for election or appointment to judicial office and to public legal offices, such as attorney general, prosecuting attorney and public defender. Expressing honest and candid opinions on such matters contributes to improving the administration of justice. Conversely, false statements by a lawyer can unfairly undermine public confidence in the administration of justice.

[2] When a lawyer seeks judicial office, the lawyer should be bound by applicable limitations on political activity.

[3] To maintain the fair and independent administration of justice, lawyers are encouraged to continue traditional efforts to defend judges and courts unjustly criticized.

SCR 3.130(8.3) Reporting professional misconduct

(a) A lawyer who knows that another lawyer has committed a violation of the Rules of Professional Conduct that raises a substantial question as to the lawyer's honesty, trustworthiness or fitness as a lawyer in other respects, shall inform the Association's Bar Counsel.

(b) A lawyer who knows that a judge has committed a violation of applicable rules of judicial conduct that raises a substantial question as to the judge's fitness for office shall report such violation to the Judicial Conduct Commission.

(c) A lawyer is not required to report information that is protected by Rule 1.6 or by other law. Further, a lawyer or a judge does not have a duty to report or disclose information that is received in the course of participating in the Kentucky Lawyer Assistance Program or Ethics Hotline.

(d) A lawyer acting in good faith in the discharge of the lawyer's professional responsibilities required by paragraphs (a) and (b) or when making a voluntary report of other misconduct shall be immune from any action, civil or criminal, and any disciplinary proceeding before the Bar as a result of said report, except for conduct prohibited by Rule 3.4(f).

(e) As provided in SCR 3.435, a lawyer who is disciplined as a result of a lawyer disciplinary action brought before any authority other than the Association shall report that fact to Bar Counsel.

(f) As provided in SCR 3.166(2), a lawyer prosecuting a case against any member of the Association to a plea of guilty, conviction by judge or jury or entry of judgment, should immediately notify Bar Counsel of such event.

HISTORY: Amended by Order 2012–01, eff. 3–1–12; prior amendment eff. 7–15–09 (Order 2009–05); adopted by Order 89–1, eff. 1–1–90

Supreme Court Commentary

2009:

(1) Self-regulation of the legal profession requires that members of the profession initiate a disciplinary investigation when they know that another lawyer has violated certain minimum standards of behavior as described in the Rule. Lawyers have a similar obligation with respect to judicial misconduct. An apparently isolated violation may indicate a pattern of misconduct that only a disciplinary investigation can uncover. Reporting a violation is especially important where the victim is unlikely to discover the offense.

(2) If a lawyer were obliged to report every violation of the Rules, the failure to report any violation would itself be a professional offense. Such a requirement exists in many jurisdictions but has

proved unenforceable. The Rule limits the reporting obligation to those violations that a self-regulating profession must vigorously endeavor to prevent. A measure of judgment is, therefore, required in complying with the provisions of this Rule. The term "substantial" refers to the seriousness of the possible offense and not the quantum of evidence of which the lawyer is aware. A report should be made to the bar disciplinary agency unless some other agency, such as a peer review agency is more appropriate in the circumstances. Similar considerations apply to the reporting of judicial conduct. Lawyers requiring assistance in determining the need to report a violation may confer with their Supreme Court District Committee member. Pursuant to SCR 3.530(7) a lawyer's communications with a District Committee member are confidential.

(3) A lawyer who knows that a judge has committed a violation of the Code of Judicial Conduct that raises a substantial question as to the judge's fitness shall, at a minimum, file a report with the Judicial Conduct Commission. The term "substantial" refers to the seriousness of the possible offense.

(4) The duty to report professional misconduct does not apply to a lawyer retained to represent a lawyer whose professional conduct is in question. Such a situation is governed by the rules applicable to the client-lawyer relationship.

(5) The duty to report misconduct is an important aspect of self-regulation, and is intended to advance societal goals. In order to protect a lawyer who makes a report in compliance with the Rule and to encourage a lawyer to make a voluntary report of other acts of misconduct, the Rule provides qualified immunity to the reporting lawyer thereby removing the fear of retaliation by the reported lawyer or judge. The Rule's immunity provision is founded upon a similar rule of immunity provided by SCR 4.300, Canon 3D(3) of the Kentucky Code of Judicial Conduct.

SCR 3.130(8.4)   Misconduct

It is professional misconduct for a lawyer to:

(a) violate or attempt to violate the Rules of Professional Conduct, knowingly assist or induce another to do so, or do so through the acts of another;

(b) commit a criminal act that reflects adversely on the lawyer's honesty, trustworthiness or fitness as a lawyer in other respects;

(c) engage in conduct involving dishonesty, fraud, deceit or misrepresentation;

(d) state or imply an ability to influence improperly a government agency or official or to achieve results by means that violate the Rules of Professional Conduct or other law; or

(e) knowingly assist a judge or judicial officer in conduct that is a violation of applicable Rules of Judicial Conduct or other law.

HISTORY: Amended by Order 2009–05, eff. 7–15–09; adopted by Order 89–1, eff. 1–1–90.

Supreme Court Commentary
2009:

(1) Lawyers are subject to discipline when they violate or attempt to violate the Rules of Professional Conduct, knowingly assist or induce another to do so or do so through the acts of another, as when they request or instruct an agent to do so on the lawyer's behalf. Paragraph (a), however, does not prohibit a lawyer from advising a client concerning action the client is legally entitled to take.

(2) Many kinds of illegal conduct reflect adversely on fitness to practice law, such as offenses involving fraud and the offense of willful failure to file an income tax return. However, some kinds of offenses carry no such implication. Traditionally, the distinction was drawn in terms of offenses involving "moral turpitude." That concept can be construed to include offenses concerning some matters of personal

morality, such as adultery and comparable offenses, that have no specific connection to fitness for the practice of law. Although a lawyer is personally answerable to the entire criminal law, a lawyer should be professionally answerable only for offenses that indicate lack of those characteristics relevant to law practice. Offenses involving violence, dishonesty, breach of trust, or serious interference with the administration of justice are in that category. A pattern of repeated offenses, even ones of minor significance when considered separately, can indicate indifference to legal obligation.

(3) A lawyer may refuse to comply with an obligation imposed by law upon a good faith belief that no valid obligation exists. The provisions of Rule 1.2(d) concerning a good faith challenge to the validity, scope, meaning or application of the law apply to challenges of legal regulation of the practice of law.

SCR 3.130(8.5)   Disciplinary authority; choice of law

(a) Disciplinary Authority. A lawyer admitted to practice in this jurisdiction is subject to the disciplinary authority of this jurisdiction, regardless of where the lawyer's conduct occurs. A lawyer not admitted in this jurisdiction is also subject to the disciplinary authority of this jurisdiction if the lawyer provides or offers to provide any legal services in this jurisdiction. A lawyer may be subject to the disciplinary authority of both this jurisdiction and another jurisdiction for the same conduct.

(b) Choice of Law. In any exercise of the disciplinary authority of this jurisdiction, the Rules of Professional Conduct to be applied shall be as follows:

(1) for conduct in connection with a matter pending before a tribunal, the rules of the jurisdiction in which the tribunal sits, unless the rules of the tribunal provide otherwise; and

(2) for any other conduct, the rules of the jurisdiction in which the lawyer's conduct occurred, or, if the predominant effect of the conduct is in a different jurisdiction, the rules of that jurisdiction shall be applied to the conduct. A lawyer shall not be subject to discipline if the lawyer's conduct conforms to the rules of a jurisdiction in which the lawyer reasonably believes the predominant effect of the lawyer's conduct will occur.

HISTORY: Adopted by Order 2009–05, eff. 7–15–09

Supreme Court Commentary
2009:

Disciplinary Authority

(1) It is longstanding law that the conduct of a lawyer admitted to practice in this jurisdiction is subject to the disciplinary authority of this jurisdiction. Extension of the disciplinary authority of this jurisdiction to other lawyers who provide or offer to provide legal services in this jurisdiction is for the protection of the citizens of this jurisdiction. Reciprocal enforcement of a jurisdiction's disciplinary findings and sanctions will further advance the purposes of this Rule. *See*, Rules 6 and 22, ABA *Model Rules for Lawyer Disciplinary Enforcement.* A lawyer who is subject to the disciplinary authority of this jurisdiction under Rule 8.5(a) appoints an official to be designated by this Court to receive service of process in this jurisdiction. The fact that the lawyer is subject to the disciplinary authority of this jurisdiction may be a factor in determining whether personal jurisdiction may be asserted over the lawyer for civil matters.

Choice of Law

(2) A lawyer may be potentially subject to more than one set of rules of professional conduct which impose different obligations. The lawyer may be licensed to practice in more than one jurisdiction with differing rules, or may be admitted to practice before a particular court with rules that differ from those of the jurisdiction or jurisdictions in which the lawyer is licensed to practice. Additionally, the lawyer's conduct may involve significant contacts with more than one jurisdiction.

(3) Paragraph (b) seeks to resolve such potential conflicts. Its premise is that minimizing conflicts between rules, as well as uncertainty about which rules are applicable, is in the best interest of both clients and the profession (as well as the bodies having authority to regulate the profession). Accordingly, it takes the approach of (i) providing that any particular conduct of a lawyer shall be subject to only one set of rules of professional conduct, (ii) making the determination of which set of rules applies to particular conduct as straightforward as possible, consistent with recognition of appropriate regulatory interests of relevant jurisdictions, and (iii) providing protection from discipline for lawyers who act reasonably in the face of uncertainty.

(4) Paragraph (b)(1) provides that as to a lawyer's conduct relating to a proceeding pending before a tribunal, the lawyer shall be subject only to the rules of the jurisdiction in which the tribunal sits unless the rules of the tribunal, including its choice of law rule, provide otherwise. As to all other conduct, including conduct in anticipation of a proceeding not yet pending before a tribunal, paragraph (b)(2) provides that a lawyer shall be subject to the rules of the jurisdiction in which the lawyer's conduct occurred, or, if the predominant effect of the conduct is in another jurisdiction, the rules of that jurisdiction shall be applied to the conduct. In the case of conduct in anticipation of a proceeding that is likely to be before a tribunal, the predominant effect of such conduct could be where the conduct occurred, where the tribunal sits or in another jurisdiction.

(5) When a lawyer's conduct involves significant contacts with more than one jurisdiction, it may not be clear whether the predominant effect of the lawyer's conduct will occur in a jurisdiction other than the one in which the conduct occurred. So long as the lawyer's conduct conforms to the rules of a jurisdiction in which the lawyer reasonably believes the predominant effect will occur, the lawyer shall not be subject to discipline under this Rule.

(6) If two admitting jurisdictions were to proceed against a lawyer for the same conduct, they should, applying this Rule, identify the same governing ethics rules. They should take all appropriate steps to see that they do apply the same rule to the same conduct, and in all events should avoid proceeding against a lawyer on the basis of two inconsistent rules.

(7) The choice of law provision applies to lawyers engaged in transnational practice, unless international law, treaties or other agreements between competent regulatory authorities in the affected jurisdictions provide otherwise.

SCR 3.135   Advertisement of legal services—Deleted

HISTORY: Deleted by Order 92–1, eff. 8–1–92; prior amendments eff. 11–1–90, 1–1–88, 1–1–87, 7–8–83, 10–1–82, 7–1–79; adopted eff. 6–1–78

SCR 3.140   Appointment of inquiry commission

(1) The Chief Justice, with the consent of the Court, shall appoint an Inquiry Commission consisting of nine persons, six of whom shall be lawyers possessing the qualifications of a Circuit Judge and three of whom shall be citizens of the Commonwealth of at least thirty (30) years of age who are not lawyers. One lawyer member shall be designated by the Chief Justice as Chair of the Commission and of each panel. No lawyer members shall serve more than two (2) consecutive terms of three (3) years. No non-lawyer member shall serve more than three (3) consecutive terms of two (2) years.

(2) The Commission shall meet and act in panels of three (3) persons comprised of two (2) lawyers and one (1) non-lawyer to promptly dispose of all complaints and matters referred to it pursuant to SCR 3.170. When the Commission meets in a panel of three (3), any two (2) members must be present in order that a quorum exist. At least one (1) panel of the Commission shall meet each month if there is unresolved business to conduct.

(3) The terms of the lawyer and non-lawyer members of the Inquiry Commission shall be appointed by the Chief Justice, with the consent of the Court, in such a manner that their terms shall be staggered.

(4) The Inquiry Commission may adopt administrative regulations for the discharge of its responsibility subject to approval of the Court during its regular term. The Commission shall meet as a whole for administrative purposes, at which six (6) persons shall constitute a quorum. The Commission, through its administrative regulations, will provide for the rotation of its members among the different panels.

HISTORY: Amended by Order 98–1, eff. 10–1–98; prior amendments eff. 9–15–90 (Order 90–1), 4–1–82, 1–1–78, 7–2–71

SCR 3.150   Access to disciplinary information

(1) **Confidentiality.** In a discipline matter, prior to a rendition of a finding of a violation of these Rules by the Trial Commissioner or the Board and the recommendation of the imposition of a public sanction, the proceeding is confidential.

(2)(a) Notwithstanding subsection (1), the pendency, subject matter and status may be disclosed by Bar Counsel if:

    i.   The Respondent has waived confidentiality;

    ii.   The proceeding involves public reciprocal discipline;

    iii.   The disclosure of any information is made for the purpose of conducting an investigation by the Inquiry Commission or the Office of Bar Counsel, or;

    iv.   A Motion for Temporary Suspension is pending.

(b) After considering the protection of the public, the interests of the Bar, and the interest of the Respondent in maintaining the confidentiality of the proceeding prior to a finding of a violation of the Rules, the pendency, subject matter and status may also be disclosed by Bar Counsel at the discretion of the Chair of the Inquiry Commission, or of the Chair's lawyer member designee, if:

    i.   The proceeding is based upon an allegation that the Respondent has been charged with a crime arising from the same nexus of facts; or

ii. The proceeding is based upon a finding by a court in a civil matter that an attorney has committed conduct that may constitute a violation of the Rules of Professional Conduct.

(3) Duty of Participants. All Participants in a proceeding under these Rules shall conduct themselves so as to maintain the confidentiality requirement of this Rule. Nothing in the rule shall prohibit the Respondent from discussing the disciplinary matter with any potential witness or entity in order to respond in a disciplinary proceeding, or to disclose to any tribunal, or to disclose any information for the purpose of conducting a defense. This provision shall not apply to the Complainant or the Respondent after the Inquiry Commission or its Chair has taken action on a Complaint including the issuance of a charge, the issuance of a private admonition, or a dismissal, including those pursuant to SCR 3.160(3).

(4)(a) Request for Non-Public Information. A request for non-public information to the Office of Bar Counsel may be considered by the Inquiry Commission and may be granted if the request relates to an investigation by the requestor and is made by:

  i. The Character and Fitness Committee;

  ii. A Lawyer Disciplinary Enforcement Agency;

  iii. A Judicial Disciplinary Enforcement Agency;

(b) A request for non-public information to the Office of Bar Counsel may be considered by the Court if the request is made by a Law Enforcement Agency, or other official authorized by federal or any state's law to investigate or prosecute misdemeanors or felonies, or the equivalent thereof, in any jurisdiction, provided that the agency or official certifies under oath with specificity that the information is necessary to a pending investigation. In this event the Respondent shall receive notice unless the Court determines that disclosure of the request would seriously prejudice the investigation.

(c) In the absence of a third party request, the Court may permit the disclosure of any non-public information to any of the entities listed in (4)(a) or (b) upon application to it by the Office of Bar Counsel.

(d) In the event of a request under (4)(a) or (c) no notice to the Respondent is required, although either the Inquiry Commission or Court may require notice upon review of the application.

(5) Public Proceedings. Upon a finding by the Trial Commissioner or the Board that an attorney has committed a violation of these rules meriting public discipline, or upon the filing of a petition for reinstatement, the record of the Disciplinary Clerk, and any further proceedings before the Board or Court, shall be public except for:

(a) deliberations of the Inquiry Commission, Board of Governors, or the Court; or

(b) information with respect to which a protective order has been issued.

(6) Protective Orders. The Inquiry Commission, the Trial Commissioner, the Board, or the Court, which at the time the order is sought has the case pending before it, may, upon application of any person or entity, and for good cause shown, issue a protective order. Such an order may protect the interests of a Complainant, witness, third party, Respondent, or Bar Counsel. The order may prohibit the disclosure of specific information otherwise privileged or confidential and direct that the proceedings be conducted so as to implement the order, including requiring that the hearing be conducted in such a way as to preserve the confidentiality of the information that is the subject of the application.

(7) Notice to National Discipline Data Bank. The Disciplinary Clerk shall transmit notice of all public discipline imposed against a lawyer and reinstatements to the National Discipline Data Bank maintained by the American Bar Association.

HISTORY: Amended by Order 2007–007, eff. 2–1–08; prior amendments eff. 1–1–99 (Order 98–2), 10–1–98 (Order 98–1), 1–1–87 (Order 86–3), 1–1–86, 10–1–82, 4–1–82, 1–1–80, 7–2–71

SCR 3.155 Appointment and duties of Bar Counsel

(1) The Board shall appoint a Bar Counsel and such Deputy Bar Counsel as may from time to time be appropriate. Bar Counsel shall be responsible for investigating and prosecuting all disciplinary cases and such other duties as the Board may designate.

(2) Bar Counsel, and such Deputies as may be appointed, shall serve at the pleasure of the Board.

(3) Bar Counsel and all Deputies shall be attorneys licensed to practice law in the Commonwealth.

(4) The Board may employ such Bar Counsel staff as may be appropriate.

(5) Annually, on or before November 1, the Inquiry Commission shall submit to the Board a recommended budget for the succeeding fiscal year along with any recommended changes in annual membership dues to cover costs of administering the duties of the Inquiry Commission and the office of Bar Counsel.

HISTORY: Adopted by Order 98–1, eff. 10–1–98

SCR 3.157 Appointment and duties of Disciplinary Clerk

The Board shall appoint a Disciplinary Clerk and such Deputy Clerks as may from time to time become appropriate. The Disciplinary Clerk shall have such qualifications as the Board deems appropriate, and shall be responsible for accepting the filing of charges issued by the Inquiry Commission, pleadings or other paper, issuing process, and the preparation and maintenance of the records of each disciplinary proceeding, other than the files of the Office of Bar Counsel, and other duties as are assigned by the Board.

HISTORY: Amended by Order 2007–007, eff. 2–1–08; adopted by Order 98–1, eff. 10–1–98

SCR 3.160   Initiation of disciplinary cases

(1) After review by Bar Counsel pursuant to sub-paragraph (3) of this Rule, any sworn written statement of complaint against an attorney for unprofessional conduct shall be filed with the Disciplinary Clerk who shall promptly notify the attorney by certified mail, sent to the address maintained by the Director pursuant to SCR 3.175, or other means consistent with the Supreme Court Rules and Civil Rules, of the complaint, and that he/she has twenty (20) days to respond to the complaint. Upon completion of the investigation by the Office of Bar Counsel the matter shall be assigned to an Inquiry Commission panel by rotation.

(2) Notwithstanding the provisions of paragraph (1), when it comes to the attention of the Inquiry Commission from any source that an attorney may have engaged in unprofessional conduct, the Inquiry Commission, or a three-person panel thereof, may initiate and conduct an investigation, and if it believes from its investigation that there is sufficient evidence to justify its filing a complaint against the attorney it may file such a complaint.

(3)(A) Upon receipt of a verbal, or written allegation of a violation of the Rules of Professional Conduct, or sworn complaint, the Office of Bar Counsel will initially determine, under the direction of the Chair and Inquiry Commission, whether the matter is appropriate for alternative disposition. Alternative disposition may include, but is not limited to:

i.   Informal resolution

ii. Referral to Fee Arbitration under SCR 3.810

iii. Legal negligence arbitration under SCR 3.800

iv. Legal or management education programs

v.   Remedial ethics education programs

vi. Referral to KYLAP under SCR 3.970(1)(c)

vii. Issuance of a warning letter.

(B) A complaint is not suitable for alternative disposition if it alleges serious misconduct in which the sanction would more than likely result in a suspension. Additionally, some ethical violations warranting a private or public reprimand may not, under all circumstances, be eligible for alternative disposition.

(C) After review and such preliminary investigation as may reasonably be necessary, the Office of Bar Counsel may attempt informal resolution and subsequently close the Complaint. If the acts or course of conduct complained of merit referral under 3(A)(ii)–(vii), and do not warrant a greater degree of discipline, the Office of Bar Counsel may issue a warning letter, which will be maintained in the investigative file of the Office of Bar Counsel but not be considered as discipline, or it may recommend remedial ethics, related legal or management education programs, fee arbitration, or KYLAP, completion of which would result in the complaint being dismissed.

(D) If Bar Counsel deems a written and sworn complaint to state an ethical violation, such that alternative disposition is not appropriate or the Respondent will not consent to or complete the alternative disposition program, the matter shall proceed under subsection (1) above.

(E) If Bar Counsel deems any written and sworn complaint against a member not to state an ethical violation and it is not suitable for alternative disposition, it may decline, without investigation, to entertain it.

(4) Neither the Association, the Board, the Director, the Inquiry Commission, the Trial Commission, the Office of Bar Counsel, nor their officers, employees, agents, delegates or members shall be liable, to any person or entity initiating a complaint or investigation, or to any member of the bar or any other person or entity being charged or investigated by, or at the direction of, the Inquiry Commission, for any damages incident to such investigation or any complaint, charge, prosecution, proceeding or trial.

HISTORY: Amended by Order 2007–007, eff. 2–1–08; prior amendments eff. 4–1–07 (Order 2007–01), 1–1–06 (Order 2005–10), 10–1–98 (Order 98–1), 1–13–86 (Order 86–1), 7–1–79, 1–1–78, 7–2–71

SCR 3.165   Temporary suspension by the Supreme Court

(1) On petition of the Inquiry Commission, authorized by its Chair, or the Chair's lawyer member designee, and supported by an affidavit, an attorney may be temporarily suspended from the practice of law by order of the Court provided:

(a) It appears that probable cause exists to believe that an attorney is or has been misappropriating funds the attorney holds for others to his/her own use or has been otherwise improperly dealing with said funds; or

(b) It appears that probable cause exists to believe that an attorney's conduct poses a substantial threat of harm to his clients or to the public; or

(c) An attorney has been convicted of a crime as set out in SCR 3.320 and it appears from the record of such conviction that the attorney has so acted as to put in grave issue whether he/she has the moral fitness to continue to practice law; or,

(d) It appears that probable cause exists to believe that an attorney is mentally disabled or is addicted to intoxicants or drugs and probable cause exists to believe he/she does not have the physical or mental fitness to continue to practice law. If the attorney denies that he/she is mentally disabled or denies that he/she is addicted to intoxicants or drugs, the Court may order the attorney to submit to a physical or mental examination by a physician or other health care professional appointed by the Court. The examining health care professional shall file with the Clerk of the Court a detailed written report setting out the findings of the health care professional, including results of all tests made, diagnosis and conclusions, together with like reports of all earlier examinations by any health care professional of the same condition. The Clerk of the Court shall furnish a copy of the examining health care professional's entire report to the attorney and to Bar Counsel. The Court may order the attorney to produce to the Court and Bar Counsel any relevant medical, psychiatric, psychological or other health care or treatment records, including alcohol or drug abuse patient records, evidencing prior or ongoing treatment for mental disability or addiction to drugs or to execute appropriate releases which would comply with applicable federal and state law in order to permit the treating health care professional to release those records to the Court and Bar Counsel. Any such order and the resulting records regarding the treatment shall be confidential and sealed in the record.

(2) Any such order of temporary suspension may restrict the attorney in dealing with client funds and shall, when served on any bank maintaining any account upon which said attorney may make withdrawals, serve as an injunction to prevent said bank from making further payment from such account or accounts on any obligation except in accordance with restrictions imposed by the Court, and shall direct such bank not to disclose (except to those entitled to withdraw from the account or accounts or to receive payment of such obligation, or upon the express written permission of at least one of such persons as to each such account or obligations) that such order has been received or the contents thereof. Any fees tendered to such attorney thereafter shall be deposited in a trust fund from which withdrawals may be made only in accordance with restrictions imposed by the Court. The Court may appoint a trustee to receive, transfer, or disburse any funds that are in the possession of or are under the control of the attorney if the funds came into the attorney's possession from the attorney's clients or from third parties during or as a result of the practice of law prior to suspension. The Court may require the trustee to render an accounting of said funds to the Court and to furnish a copy of the accounting to the Director.

(3) The petition of temporary suspension authorized by this rule shall be filed with the Clerk of the Court. The Chair of the Commission, or the Chair's designee, or the Commission's counsel, shall certify that a copy of the petition has been served on the Respondent or Respondent's attorney at his/her bar roster address. The Respondent shall file a response to the petition within twenty (20) days of the date the petition was filed with the Clerk. The Court may schedule an oral argument or a show cause hearing after the filing of the response or after the expiration of the time for a response to be filed.

(4) The Respondent may for good cause request dissolution or amendment of any such temporary order by petition filed with the Court, a copy of which will be served on the Director and on Bar Counsel, who shall respond on behalf of the Association. The Court may refer such petition for dissolution to a person who possesses the qualifications of a Trial Commissioner under Rule 3.230 sitting as a Special Commissioner for immediate hearing. The Special Commissioner shall hear evidence and argument upon such petition forthwith and submit his/her report and recommendations to the Court within thirty (30) days. Upon receipt of the foregoing report, the Court may refer the matter to the Character and Fitness Committee for recommendation and/or may modify its order if deemed appropriate until final disposition of all pending disciplinary charges against said attorney.

(5) Within twenty (20) days from the date of the entry of the order of temporary suspension, the attorney shall notify all clients in writing of his/her inability to continue to represent them and shall furnish copies of all such letters of notice to the Director.

(6) Upon the issuance of an order of temporary suspension, the attorney affected shall immediately, to the extent reasonably possible, cancel and cease any advertising activities in which the attorney is engaged, and remove the attorney's name from any firm with which the attorney is associated.

(7) Failure to comply with this rule shall subject the Respondent to a charge of contempt of court.

HISTORY: Amended by Order 2007–007, eff. 2–1–08; prior amendments eff. 10–1–98 (Order 98–1), 10–1–94 (Order 94–1), 11–15–91, 5–1–80; adopted eff. 1–1–78

SCR 3.166 Automatic suspension after conviction of a felony

(1) Any member of the Kentucky Bar Association who pleads guilty to a felony, including a no contest plea or a plea in which the member allows conviction but does not admit the commission of a crime, or is convicted by a judge or jury of a felony, in this State or in any other jurisdiction, shall be automatically suspended from the practice of law in this Commonwealth. "Felony" means an offense for which a sentence to a term of imprisonment of at least one (1) year is authorized by law. The imposition of probation, parole, diversion or any other type of discharge prior to the service of sentence, if one is imposed, shall not affect the automatic suspension. The suspension shall take effect automatically beginning on the day following the plea of guilty or finding of guilt by a judge or jury or upon the entry of judgment whichever occurs first. The suspension under this rule shall remain in effect until dissolved or superseded by order of the Court. Within thirty (30) days of the plea of guilty, or the finding of guilt by a judge or

jury, or entry of judgment, whichever occurs first, the suspended attorney may file a motion with the Clerk of the Supreme Court of Kentucky setting forth any grounds which the attorney believes justify dissolution or modification of the suspension.

(2) The attorney prosecuting the case to a plea of guilty, conviction by judge or jury or entry of judgment, whichever occurs first, shall immediately notify Bar Counsel and the Clerk of the Supreme Court that such plea, finding or entry of judgment has been made.

(3) The suspended attorney shall serve a copy of any motion filed under paragraph (1) above on Bar Counsel by mailing a copy to 514 West Main Street, Frankfort, Kentucky 40601. Bar Counsel shall file a response to the suspended attorney's motion within twenty (20) days of receipt of the motion.

(4) Any attorney suspended under this rule shall notify all clients in writing of the attorney's inability to continue to represent them and shall furnish copies of all such letters to the Director. These letters shall be mailed to the client within ten (10) days after the plea of guilty, conviction by judge or jury, or entry of judgment has been made. The attorney shall make arrangements to return all active files to the client or new counsel and shall return all unearned attorney fees and client property to the client and shall advise the Director of such arrangements within the same ten (10) day period.

(5) Any attorney suspended under this rule shall immediately, to the extent possible, cancel and cease any advertising activities in which the attorney is engaged, and remove the attorney's name from any firm with which the attorney is associated.

(6) Disciplinary proceedings against such attorney shall be initiated by the Inquiry Commission pursuant to SCR 3.160, unless already begun or unless the suspended attorney resigns under terms of disbarment.

HISTORY: Amended by Order 2012–01, eff. 3–1–12; prior amendments eff. 2–1–08 (Order 2007–007), 1–1–06 (Order 2005–10), 1–1–04 (Order 2003–4), 10–1–98 (Order 98–1); adopted by Order 94–1, eff. 10–1–94

SCR 3.170 Processing disciplinary cases

Upon the expiration of sixty (60) days after service upon Respondent by certified mail or other means, or receipt of a response to a complaint, whichever is later, the Office of Bar Counsel shall refer the matter, together with such investigative evidence as may have been obtained, to the Inquiry Commission to determine whether the complaint should be dismissed or a charge should be filed. Upon motion by Bar Counsel, and with good cause shown, the Inquiry Commission may direct that the complaint be returned to Bar Counsel for further investigation.

HISTORY: Amended by Order 2005–10, eff. 1–1–06; prior amendments eff. 10–1–98 (Order 98–1), 7–2–71

SCR 3.175 Efficient enforcement; notice of attorney's address

(1) In order to facilitate the efficient enforcement of the Kentucky Rules of Professional Conduct, the rules of the Continuing Legal Education Commission, the dues obligations of attorneys, and such other communications of importance to the profession as the Supreme Court may consider appropriate, each attorney licensed by the Supreme Court to practice law in this Commonwealth shall:

(a) maintain with the Director a current address at which he or she may be communicated with by mail, the said address to be known as the member's Bar Roster address, and shall upon a change of that address notify the Director within thirty (30) days of the new address; and

(b) include his or her five (5) digit member identification number in all communications to the Association including, but not limited to, any and all communications relating to his or her membership status, membership record, dues obligations, compliance with continuing legal education requirements or disciplinary proceedings in which he or she is a respondent.

(c) If the member provides a Post Office address, he or she must also provide a current address for service of process.

(d) Failure to maintain a current address which allows for physical service of process with the Director may be prosecuted in the same manner as a violation of the Rules of Professional Conduct.

(2) After July 1, 2004, every member of the Association shall be deemed to have appointed the Director as that member's agent for service of any document that is required to be served upon that member by any provision of Supreme Court Rule 2 or 3, provided that service of a document upon the Director shall constitute constructive service of that document upon the member only upon proof that all of the following requirements have been satisfied:

(a) Reasonable efforts have been made to achieve actual service of the document upon the member;

(b) Two (2) true copies of the document have been provided to the Director, accompanied by a written request that the Director serve the document upon the member at the member's current Bar Roster address;

(c) Within seven (7) days after receipt of such request, the Director mailed one (1) copy of the document to the member at the aforesaid address, posted by certified mail, return receipt requested, restricted delivery—addressee only, in an envelope bearing the return address of the Director and marked on the outside as "OFFICIAL COMMUNICATION—IMMEDIATE ATTENTION REQUIRED"; and

(d) No less than thirty (30) days after mailing the document pursuant to subparagraph (c), the Director shall enter a Return of Service which attests:

(i) that the Director mailed one of the copies of the document mentioned in subparagraph (b) to the member's Bar Roster address in accordance with the requirements of subparagraph (c);

(ii) that the Director has attached to the Return of Service all communications received in response to the service or attempted service of the document, including any certified mail receipt or other postal notice or return receipt relating to the delivery or attempted delivery of the document and any communication from the member of the Association or other person acting on behalf of such member; and

(iii) that the Director has provided a true copy of the Return of Service, with copies of all attachments, to the person or entity who requested service of the document upon the member of the Association.

(3) After July 1, 2004, the Association may reject any communication to the Association which fails to comply with paragraph (1)(b) of this Rule 3.175, provided that a member's failure to include his or her member identification number in a document shall not result in a default in any disciplinary proceeding.

HISTORY: Amended by Order 2005–10, eff. 1–1–06; prior amendment eff. 1–1–04 (Order 2003–4); adopted by Order 98–1, eff. 10–1–98

SCR 3.180   Investigations and trials to be prompt; subpoena power

(1) All investigations and the trial of all disciplinary cases shall be begun, prosecuted, and completed as promptly as the ends of justice will permit. Neither the unwillingness of the complainant to prosecute, nor an offer of settlement, compromise or restitution shall delay the investigation, trial or report to the Board.

(2) Proceedings may be deferred by the Inquiry Commission if there is pending civil or criminal litigation directly involving the Respondent or proposed Respondent involving substantially similar material allegations to that or those in the disciplinary proceedings, provided, however, that the Respondent-attorney proceeds with reasonable dispatch to insure the prompt disposition of the pending litigation. Proceedings deferred pursuant to this subsection shall be reviewed quarterly by the Inquiry Commission.

(3) Upon application of Bar Counsel to the Inquiry Commission and after a hearing of which Respondent is given at least five (5) days' notice, for good cause shown the inquiry Commission may authorize the Director or the Disciplinary Clerk to issue a subpoena to a Respondent, or any other person or legal entity, to produce to Bar Counsel any evidence deemed by the Inquiry Commission to be material to the investigation of a complaint and to testify regarding such production. Such an application may be made in connection with complaints against more than one Respondent if the complaints are based on the same or a related set of facts. The person or entity so

subpoenaed will not divulge, except to his/her own attorney, that such a subpoena has been served nor what evidence is sought or obtained. The Respondent may be present at the time the evidence or material is examined or obtained by Bar Counsel and will be furnished copies of all documents obtained, unless obtained from the Respondent.

(4) If any witness refuses to testify concerning any matter for which he or she may lawfully be interrogated, upon application of the Inquiry Commission to the Circuit Court of the county in which the witness resides, the Circuit Court may compel obedience by proceedings for contempt as in the case of disobedience of a subpoenas issued from the Circuit Court.

HISTORY: Amended by Order 2012–01, eff. 3–1–12; prior amendments eff. 10–1–98 (Order 98–1), 4–1–82 (Order 82–1), 1–1–78, 7–2–71

SCR 3.181   Assistance to other lawyer disciplinary jurisdictions

(1) Upon receipt by the Director of a subpoena certified to be duly issued under the rules or laws of another lawyer disciplinary jurisdiction, or by a clients' security fund of any jurisdiction, the Inquiry Commission may authorize the Director or Disciplinary Clerk to issue a subpoena directing a person domiciled or found within the Commonwealth of Kentucky to give testimony and/or produce documents or other things for use in the other lawyer disciplinary or clients' security fund proceedings as directed in the subpoena of the other jurisdiction.

(2) The testimony or production shall be only in the county wherein the person resides or is employed, or as otherwise fixed by the Inquiry Commission for good cause shown, and shall be taken as provided in CR 28.01.

(3) Any attack on the validity of a subpoena issued by another jurisdiction may be heard and determined by the disciplinary authority of the other state in accordance with the law of the issuing jurisdiction.

(4) In addition to the relief available under the law of the requesting disciplinary jurisdiction or clients' security fund, upon motion made by a party or by the person from whom appearance or production is sought, and for good cause shown, the Inquiry Commission may make any order which justice requires to protect a party or person from annoyance, embarrassment, oppression, or undue burden or expense, including one or more of the following: (a) that the testimony or production not be had; (b) that it may be had only on specified terms and conditions, including a designation of the time or place; (c) that it may be had only by a method other than that selected by the party seeking testimony or production; (d) that certain matters not be inquired into, or that the scope of the subpoena be limited to certain matters; (e) that the testimony be taken with no one present except persons designated by the Inquiry Commission; (f)

that testimony may be sealed to be opened only by order of the original issuing jurisdiction; (g) that a trade secret or other confidential research, development, or commercial information not be disclosed or be disclosed only in a designated way; (h) that the parties simultaneously file specified documents or information enclosed in sealed envelopes to be opened as directed by the original issuing jurisdiction.

HISTORY: Adopted by Order 2012–01, eff. 3–1–12

SCR 3.185 Informal admonition procedure

After a complaint against an attorney for unprofessional conduct is investigated and a response filed, the Inquiry Commission may direct a private admonition, with or without conditions, to the attorney if the acts or course of conduct complained of are shown not to warrant a greater degree of discipline. The attorney so admonished may, within twenty (20) days from the date of the admonition, reject such admonition and request that a charge be issued and filed as is provided by Rule 3.190; whereupon, the issues shall be processed under the applicable rules. The Inquiry Commission may also issue a warning or a conditional dismissal letter including, but not limited to, conditions such as referral to KYLAP, or attendance at a remedial ethics program or related classes as directed by the Office of Bar Counsel.

HISTORY: Amended by Order 2012–01, eff. 3–1–12; prior amendments eff. 2–1–08 (Order 2007–007), 4–1–07 (Order 2007–01), 10–1–98 (Order 98–1), 1–1–78; adopted eff. 6–14–72

SCR 3.190 Charges; form; by whom and where filed

If a panel of or the entire Inquiry Commission determines, by a majority vote, that probable cause exists for a charge to be filed, it shall cause to be prepared such charge stating the name and bar roster address of the attorney and facts alleged to constitute unprofessional conduct. The charge shall be signed by a member of the panel which considers the case. It shall then be filed with the Disciplinary Clerk within twenty (20) days. Upon notice to the respondent, the Inquiry Commission may amend the charge upon its own motion, or that of the Office of Bar Counsel, or the Respondent, at any time before hearing or submission by default.

HISTORY: Amended by Order 2007–007, eff. 2–1–08; prior amendments eff. 1–1–06 (Order 2005–10), 10–1–98 (Order 98–1), 7–2–71

SCR 3.200 Notice of filing charges; time to answer

Upon the filing of a charge, the Disciplinary Clerk shall furnish the Respondent with a copy, by certified mail return receipt requested to the Respondent's bar roster address, or by service on the Director as set forth in SCR 3.175, and notify the Respondent that within twenty (20) days after receipt of the notice,

he/she must file an answer and three (3) copies with the Disciplinary Clerk for transmittal to the Inquiry Commission. The Inquiry Commission may rule on motions to file late answers for good cause shown as set forth in CR 6.02.

HISTORY: Amended by Order 2007–007, eff. 2–1–08; prior amendments eff. 1–1–06 (Order 2005–10), 10–1–98 (Order 98–1), 1–1–78, 7–2–71

SCR 3.210 Processing cases of default, admissions of violations or answers raising only issues of law

(1) If no answer is filed after a Respondent is notified, the Inquiry Commission shall order the record, together with such investigative evidence as may have been obtained, to be submitted to the Board.

(2) If the parties agree that the answer raises only issues of law, or the Respondent admits the violation, the case shall be submitted directly to the Board. Bar Counsel may file a brief within twenty (20) days, and the Respondent may file a brief within twenty (20) days, thereafter. After briefs are filed, or the time within which briefs may be filed has expired, the record and briefs shall be forwarded to the President for assignment to a member of the Board for a report.

(3) The Board, by a vote of a majority of the Board present and voting, may return the entire record to the Disciplinary Clerk for appointment of a Trial Commissioner pursuant to SCR 3.230 to conduct an evidentiary hearing, which proceeding will be confidential pursuant to 3.150.

HISTORY: Amended by Order 98–1, eff. 10–1–98; prior amendments eff. 1–1–78, 7–2–71

SCR 3.220 When charge shall not be taken as confessed—Deleted

HISTORY: Deleted by Order 98–1, eff. 10–1–98; prior amendments eff. 1–1–78, 7–2–71

SCR 3.225 Appointment of trial commission

The Chief Justice shall appoint, subject to the approval of the Supreme Court, from among the membership of the Bar Association, a Trial Commission and shall designate a chair from the Commission. Members of the Trial Commission shall be lawyers licensed in the Commonwealth who possess the qualifications of a Circuit Judge. To the extent practicable, the Chief Justice shall, with the consent of the Court, appoint Trial Commissioners from each appellate district. Such Trial Commissioners shall be authorized to serve terms of two (2) years.

HISTORY: Amended by Order 2012–01, eff. 3–1–12; prior amendments eff. 1–1–06 (Order 2005–10), 11–8–04 (Order 2004–6); adopted by Order 98–1, eff. 10–1–98

SCR 3.230 Procedure when answer raises issues of fact

After an answer is filed raising issues of fact, the Disciplinary Clerk shall appoint the next available member of the Trial Commission to serve as a commissioner upon approval by the Chief Justice. The Trial Commissioner shall reside in a different Supreme Court district from that of the Respondent. The Disciplinary Clerk shall immediately notify the Trial Commissioner of his/her appointment and provide the Trial Commissioner a copy of the pleadings.

HISTORY: Amended by Order 2007–007, eff. 2–1–08; prior amendments eff. 10–1–98 (Order 98–1), 1–1–87 (Order 86–3), 1–1–78, 7–2–71.

SCR 3.240 Notice of appointment of Trial Commissioner and hearing

(1) Upon the appointment of a Trial Commissioner, the Disciplinary Clerk shall notify the parties of his/her name and address. The Trial Commissioner shall fix the time and place of the hearing and the Disciplinary Clerk shall give notice thereof to the parties. Such hearing shall be held not less than thirty (30) days, nor more than sixty (60) days, after the date of the notice, but for good cause shown, or by agreement, said time may be extended by the Trial Commissioner.

(2) Any time, not later than ten (10) days after the appointment of a Trial Commissioner or at such point in the proceeding that facts become known sufficient for such challenge, the Respondent may, by motion, challenge for cause the Trial Commissioner. If the challenge is such as might disqualify a Circuit Judge, the Chief Justice shall relieve the challenged member and direct the Disciplinary Clerk to immediately fill the vacancy.

(3) The Trial Commissioner may convene a pretrial conference. The Trial Commissioner shall have the authority to demand the appearance of counsel representing the respective parties at the pretrial conference or such other conferences as he/she may convene in person or by telephone for the purpose of disposing of pretrial matters or motions.

HISTORY: Amended by Order 2005–10, eff. 1–1–06; prior amendments eff. 10–1–98 (Order 98–1), 1–1–78, 7–2–71.

SCR 3.250 Challenge to qualifications of trial commissioner—Deleted

HISTORY: Deleted by Order 98–1, eff. 10–1–98; prior amendments eff. 1–1–78, 7–2–71.

SCR 3.260 Joinder and consolidation

(1) Any number of acts or omissions, and any number of separate and distinct transactions, alleged to constitute unprofessional conduct on the part of any attorney may be alleged in a single charge in separate counts. Separate charges may, by order of the Inquiry Commission, be consolidated and tried as a single disciplinary case.

(2) A charge may be filed against two or more attorneys if based on the same or related state of facts, and separate charges against two or more attorneys based upon the same or related state of facts may, by order of the Inquiry Commission, be consolidated and tried as a single disciplinary proceeding. Where two or more attorneys are proceeded against in the same proceeding, the Trial Commissioner shall report to the Board as to each.

(3) Charges against two or more attorneys may be consolidated by order of the Inquiry Commission for limited purposes including, but not limited to, preservation of testimony, out of state depositions, or document production pursuant to subpoena.

(4) Any party may file a motion with the Inquiry Commission to sever separate charges against any attorney as provided in subsection (1), or to sever charges against two or more attorneys as provided in subsection (2) or (3). However, the filing of such motions shall not delay the evidentiary hearing or the Board's consideration of the case.

HISTORY: Amended by Order 2012–01, eff. 3–1–12; prior amendments eff. 2–1–08 (Order 2007–007), 10–1–98 (Order 98–1), 1–1–78, 7–2–71.

SCR 3.270 Absent respondents; appointment of attorney—Deleted

HISTORY: Deleted by Order 98–1, eff. 10–1–98; prior amendments eff. 1–1–78, 7–2–71.

SCR 3.280 Pleadings and preliminary motions—Deleted

HISTORY: Deleted by Order 98–1, eff. 10–1–98; prior amendments eff. 1–1–78, 7–2–71.

SCR 3.285 Motion to reconsider or dismiss a charge

(1) Either party may file a motion with the Inquiry Commission to reconsider or dismiss a charge prior to the case being submitted to the Trial Commissioner for determination of factual issues, or to the Board if it presents only a legal issue. However, the filing of such motion shall not delay the evidentiary hearing or the Board's consideration of the case.

(2) The motion shall be verified unless filed by the Office of Bar Counsel, and shall state specifically the reasons why the matter should be reconsidered or dismissed and may be accompanied by supporting affidavits and exhibits. The motion shall be filed in the office of the Disciplinary Clerk within ten (10) days of service of the charge. Any response shall be filed within twenty (20) days of service of the motion. No other motion to reconsider or dismiss shall be permitted in regard to the reconsideration of a charge by the Inquiry Commission, unless good cause is

shown. The Commission shall rule on the motion at the next meeting of the issuing panel.

(3) Upon such reconsideration, the Inquiry Commission may dismiss a charge, issue a private admonition under SCR 3.185, or deny the motion and direct the Trial Commissioner to proceed with the hearing or refer the matter to the Board for action.

HISTORY: Amended by Order 2005–10, eff. 1–1–06; prior amendment eff. 10–1–98 (Order 98–1); adopted by Order 87–1, eff. 1–1–88

SCR 3.290 Filing and processing of pleadings and other papers

(1) Promptly after a charge is filed all further pleadings, notices, motions, orders, and briefs shall be sent to the Disciplinary Clerk. The Disciplinary Clerk shall file the original and forward one copy each: to the Inquiry Commission, through the Office of Bar Counsel, or to the Trial Commissioner, if after appointment, to Respondent or Respondent's counsel of record and to the Office of Bar Counsel. However, a motion to reconsider, dismiss, or amend a charge shall be sent only to the Inquiry Commission and to counsel of record. All other reports, inquiries, letters and letters of transmittal, and other communications shall be sent to and processed by the Clerk; however, any communication between the parties concerning negotiations for an agreed sanction shall not be transmitted to the Disciplinary Clerk or Trial Commissioner nor filed of record unless the sanction proposal is approved by the Court. No such paper or copy thereof shall be sent by, or on behalf of, any party to the Court, the Board, the Trial Commissioner, Inquiry Commission, or any member thereof.

(2) All pleadings, notices, motions, orders, and briefs shall be filed with sufficient copies to allow service by the Disciplinary Clerk on all persons listed above.

HISTORY: Amended by Order 2005–10, eff. 1–1–06; prior amendments eff. 2–1–00 (Order 99–1), 10–1–98 (Order 98–1), 1–1–78, 7–2–71

SCR 3.300 Rights of respondent against whom a charge has been filed

The Respondent against whom a charge has been filed shall have the right to be represented by counsel. The Respondent shall have all the rights secured to a party by the Rules of Civil Procedure and Kentucky Rules of Evidence with respect to the introduction of evidence. The Respondent shall have the right to compel the attendance of witnesses and the production of books, papers and documents or other writings, except those contained in the investigative file of Bar Counsel, to the hearing or to such depositions as are permitted under SCR 3.340. The Respondent shall have the right to an oral argument or to file a brief before the Trial Commissioner. The Respondent shall be afforded a full opportunity to defend himself/herself by the introduction of evidence, and to cross-examine witnesses. If the facts in the charge would give rise to a criminal proceeding, respondent shall not be compelled to give evidence against himself or herself. If the Respondent is unable to employ counsel, the Chair, or Chair's lawyer member designee, upon written request accompanied by an *in forma pauperis* affidavit, made within twenty (20) days after service of the charge, shall appoint counsel for the Respondent.

HISTORY: Amended by Order 2007–007, eff. 2–1–08; prior amendments eff. 10–1–98 (Order 98–1), 4–1–82 (Order 82–1), 1–1–78, 7–2–71

SCR 3.310 Mental disability after misconduct charged—Deleted

HISTORY: Deleted by Order of Supreme Court, eff. 1–1–78

Supreme Court Commentary

1977:

This rule has been superseded by Rule 3.165.

SCR 3.320 Procedure where an attorney has been convicted of a misdemeanor or a felony

When any member of the Association has been convicted of a felony or class "A" misdemeanor, a copy of the judgment shall be filed by the Respondent and the attorney prosecuting the case to a plea of guilty, or conviction by judge or jury, with Bar Counsel for action under SCR 3.160. Bar Counsel shall submit copies of the judgment to the Inquiry Commission which may take action under SCR 3.165.

HISTORY: Amended by Order 2005–10, eff. 1–1–06; prior amendments eff. 10–1–98 (Order 98–1), 1–1–78, 7–2–71

SCR 3.330 Order of proceedings and burden of proof

The Trial Commissioner shall determine and regulate the order of proceedings at the hearing. Upon the application of a party or upon direction of the Trial Commissioner, the Disciplinary Clerk shall issue subpoenas for the attendance of witnesses or the production of evidence at the hearing. Prehearing discovery shall proceed in accordance with this rule as directed by the Trial Commissioner rather than by the Kentucky Rules of Civil Procedure. If reasonably necessary to prepare the case for hearing, the Trial Commissioner may allow the taking of depositions and require the production of documents. The burden of proof shall rest upon the Association in a disciplinary proceeding, and the facts must be proven by a preponderance of the evidence. In reinstatement hearings the burden shall rest upon the Applicant, and he/she must demonstrate by clear and convincing evidence his/her suitability for reinstatement. Before submission the Trial Commissioner may direct such oral argument as he/she deems appropriate and receive briefs from all parties on such terms as he/she may impose.

HISTORY: Amended by Order 2007–007, eff. 2–1–08; prior amendments eff. 10–1–98 (Order 98–1), 4–1–82 (Order 82–1), 1–1–78, 7–2–71

SCR 3.340 Introduction and admissibility of evidence, evidence taken in other proceedings

The testimony at all hearings shall be in person, except that the parties may use depositions under the same standards as those prescribed by the Kentucky Rules of Civil Procedure. The rules of evidence applicable in civil actions shall apply, and the Trial Commissioner will rule on all evidentiary issues.

Where, in any proceeding, evidence has been taken under oath upon due notice to the Respondent, and at the taking of which Respondent has appeared, either in person or by counsel, or as attorney for any party, a duly certified transcript, videotape or digital recording made by a court reporter or official of a court, of all, or the essential portions, of such proceedings may be used as evidence in any hearing or in any investigation antecedent to or in connection with any disciplinary case involving the same charge, or any charge growing out of the matters connected therewith. Such transcript, tapes, or digital recordings of the record, or parts thereof, may be made a part of the record on any hearing or investigation.

HISTORY: Amended by Order 2007–007, eff. 2–1–08; prior amendments eff. 10–1–98 (Order 98–1), 7–2–71

SCR 3.350 Transcript of evidence

The proceedings before the Trial Commissioner shall be reported by videotape, where possible, or if not possible, by a reporter appointed by the Trial Commissioner. If a transcript must be prepared, it shall be completed within sixty (60) days of the hearing.

HISTORY: Amended by Order 98–1, eff. 10–1–98; prior amendments eff. 1–1–78, 7–2–71

SCR 3.360 Trial commissioner to file report with disciplinary clerk

(1) When a disciplinary proceeding has been finally submitted, the Trial Commissioner shall promptly file with the Disciplinary Clerk a written report setting forth his/her findings of fact and conclusions of law as to whether a violation of the rules has occurred. The Trial Commissioner's Report shall contain a concise statement of:

(a) the charge(s) made and the defense(s) offered by the Respondent;

(b) the proceedings had;

(c) the facts which the Commissioner deems proved by a preponderance of the evidence, and;

(d) the sanction, if any, recommended.

(2) The Trial Commissioner's report shall constitute a part of the record in the case. The report shall be advisory.

The Trial Commissioner shall file the report with the Disciplinary Clerk within thirty (30) days after the transcript of evidence or videotape has been filed with the Disciplinary Clerk. Said deadline may be extended by agreement of the parties or by the President upon verified motion by the Trial Commissioner. If an extension is sought by the Trial Commissioner, a verified motion stating with particularity the grounds for the extension of time shall be filed with the Disciplinary Clerk, with service on the parties. The President may grant up to a sixty (60) day extension of time for the Trial Commissioner to file the report. If the Trial Commissioner fails to timely file the report or a verified motion for extension of time, the Board shall request the Supreme Court to issue a show cause order to the Trial Commissioner.

(3) Within ten (10) days after the filing of the report with the Disciplinary Clerk, either party may move to amend the findings or for additional findings of fact or conclusions of law by the Trial Commissioner. Such motion shall be ruled upon within thirty (30) days.

(4) Within thirty (30) days after the filing with the Disciplinary Clerk of: (a) the report, (b) an order ruling on a motion under SCR 3.360(3), or (c) an amended report, whichever is later, either party may file a notice of appeal with the Disciplinary Clerk. If no notice of appeal is timely filed, the entire record shall be forwarded to the Court for entry of a final order pursuant to SCR 3.370(10).

(5) Upon finality of the report, the Trial Commissioner shall return to the Disciplinary Clerk the entire transcript of the proceeding, the transcript of testimony and such papers as may have been filed and are in the possession of the Trial Commissioner.

(6) Upon the finality of the report of the Trial Commissioner, the Disciplinary Clerk shall certify the record of the proceedings and send notice of certification to the parties.

HISTORY: Amended by Order 2012–01, eff. 3–1–12; prior amendments eff. 1–1–06 (Order 2005–10), 10–1–98 (Order 98–1), 8–28–89 (Order 89–1), 1–1–87, 1–1–78, 7–2–71

SCR 3.365 Notice of appeal

(1) A notice of appeal, if any, shall be filed within thirty (30) days of the final report of the Trial Commissioner.

(2) The notice of appeal shall specify by name the appellant and the report appealed from.

(3) The notice of appeal shall be filed with the Disciplinary Clerk pursuant to SCR 3.290.

HISTORY: Amended by Order 2012–01, eff. 3–1–12; adopted by Order 98–1, eff. 10–1–98

SCR 3.370 Procedure before the Board and the Court

(1) Thirty (30) days after the filing of the notice of appeal, the Appellant shall file a brief supporting his/her position on the merits of the case. Fifteen (15) days thereafter, the Appellee shall file his/her brief. No reply brief shall be permitted.

(2) Upon motion by the parties or upon the Board's own motion, oral arguments may be scheduled before the Board.

(3) Within sixty (60) days of completion of briefing by the parties, the Board shall consider and act upon the entire record. Only the President, the President–Elect, the Vice–President, the fourteen (14) duly-elected members of the Board from their respective Supreme Court Districts, and four (4) adult citizens of the Commonwealth who are not lawyers appointed by the Chief Justice as hereinafter described, shall be eligible to be present, participate in and vote on any disciplinary case. Any member, including a non-lawyer member, who has participated in any phase of a disciplinary case submitted to the Board under this rule, or who has been challenged on grounds sufficient to disqualify a Circuit Judge shall be disqualified. If disqualification or absence results in lack of a quorum the Chief Justice shall appoint a member or members (or, if applicable, non-lawyer participants) sufficient to provide a quorum to consider and act on the cases. Any challenge to a member's qualifications shall be determined by the Chief Justice in accordance with KRS 26A.015, et seq.

(4) Eleven (11) of those qualified to sit in a disciplinary matter must be present to constitute a quorum for consideration of such matters.

(5)(a) The Board, after deliberation, and consideration of oral argument, if any, shall decide, by a roll call vote:

(i.) To accept the Trial Commissioner's Report as to the guilt, innocence, and the discipline imposed, by concluding that the Trial Commissioner's report is supported by substantial evidence and is not clearly erroneous as a matter of law, or,

(ii.) To conduct a *de novo* review, in its discretion. In that event it shall make findings as to the guilt or innocence on each Count, and the appropriate discipline to be imposed, if any, and take separate votes as to each. If the Board votes to take de novo review of the case, said review shall be confined to the evidence presented and the record of the case. The Board may consider the admissibility of evidence as well as the appropriate weight of it. The Board shall state, in its written report required by subsection (8), the difference between its findings and recommendations and the report of the Trial Commissioner.

(b) In the event of a case submitted under SCR 3.210, the Board shall decide, by a roll call vote, guilt or innocence on each Count and the appropriate discipline to be imposed, if any. It shall make findings of fact in the event of a disputed fact, and make conclusions of law. Failure to answer may be deemed an admission of the facts stated in the charge.

(c) Each roll call vote under (5)(a)(b) shall be agreed upon by eleven (11) or three-fourths (3/4) of the members of the Board present and voting on the proceedings, whichever is less.

(d) At any time during deliberations the Board by a vote of a majority of the Board present and voting, may remand the case to the Inquiry Commission for reconsideration of the form of the charge or remand the case to the Trial Commissioner for clarification of the Trial Commissioner's report or for an evidentiary hearing on points specified in the order of remand. The Board may order the parties to file additional briefs on specific issues.

(6) The Board shall issue a written decision within forty five (45) days of voting on the cases. The Disciplinary Clerk shall mail copies of such report to the Respondent, counsel of record, and to each member of the Inquiry Commission. The Disciplinary Clerk shall place ten (10) copies of the report in the record and file the entire record of the case with the Court, unless the Board has taken actions under subsection (5)(d), in which case the matter will proceed in accordance with the Board's direction.

(7) Within thirty (30) days after the Board's decision is filed with the Disciplinary Clerk, Bar Counsel or the Respondent may file with the Court a Notice for the Court to review the Board's decision stating reasons for review, accompanied by a brief, not to exceed thirty (30) pages in length, supporting his/her position on the merits of the case. The opposing party may file a brief, not to exceed thirty (30) pages in length, within thirty (30) days thereafter. No reply brief shall be filed unless by order of the Court.

(8) If no notice of review is filed by either party, the Court may notify Bar Counsel and Respondent that it will review the decision. If the Court so acts, Bar Counsel and Respondent may each file briefs, not to exceed thirty (30) pages in length, within thirty (30) days, with no right to file reply briefs unless by order of the Court, whereupon the case shall stand submitted. Thereafter, the Court shall enter such orders or opinion as it deems appropriate on the entire record.

(9) If no notice of review is filed by either of the parties, or the Court under paragraph eight (8) of this rule, the Court shall enter an order adopting the decision of the Board or the Trial Commissioner, whichever the case may be, relating to all matters.

(10) When the Respondent is proceeded against by warning order, the notice in paragraph two (2) and paragraph eight (8) of this rule shall be deemed to have been served thirty (30) days after the date of the making of the warning order.

(11) In each case to be presented to the Trial Commissioner, there shall be supplied with the Disci-

plinary Clerk's file a sealed envelope containing a statement of the Respondent's years of membership in the Association, all orders of unprofessional conduct, and all withdrawals from the association and reasons therefor. The envelope will be opened only if the Trial Commissioner makes a finding of a violation and may be considered in deciding what discipline to impose. Such statement will become part of the record of the case and be transmitted with the rest of the file to the Disciplinary Clerk, Board and/or Supreme Court. Before submission of a case to the Trial Commissioner or the Board a copy of said statement shall be sent to the Respondent, who may review documents relative to it at the Bar Center, and may comment to the Trial Commissioner or the Board upon the statement and point out errors contained in it.

HISTORY: Amended by Order 2011–11, eff. 11–15–11; prior amendments eff. 1–1–07 (Order 2006–09), 1–1–06 (Order 2005–10), 1–1–04 (Order 2003–4), 10–1–98 (Order 98–1), 9–15–90 (Order 90–1), 8–28–89, 1–1–87, 4–1–82, 7–1–79, 1–1–78, 7–2–71.

SCR 3.375 Appointment of non-lawyer members to Board

The Chief Justice, with the approval of the Court, shall appoint four (4) adult citizens of the Commonwealth who are not lawyers to serve as members of the Board in disciplinary cases. Persons so appointed shall be entitled to participate and vote in any disciplinary case. The terms of such non-lawyer members shall be appointed in such a manner that the terms shall be staggered. No such member shall serve more than three (3) consecutive terms of two (2) years.

HISTORY: Adopted by Order 98–1, eff. 10–1–98

SCR 3.380 Degrees of discipline

Upon findings of a violation of these rules, discipline may be administered by way of private reprimand, public reprimand, suspension from practice for a definite time, all of which may be with or without such conditions as the Court may impose, or permanent disbarment.

HISTORY: Amended by Order 2005–10, eff. 1–1–06; prior amendments eff. 10–1–98 (Order 98–1), 4–1–82 (Order 82–1), 1–1–78, 7–2–71.

SCR 3.390 Notice to client of suspension or disbarment

(a) Any order suspending a lawyer from the practice of law, other than an order of suspension under SCR 3.165 or 3.166, shall take effect on the tenth (10th) day following its entry unless otherwise provided within the order. The suspended lawyer shall promptly take all reasonable steps to protect the interests of the lawyer's clients. A lawyer suspended from the practice of law shall not during the term of suspension accept new clients or collect unearned fees, and shall comply with the provisions of SCR 3.130–7.50(5).

(b) Within ten (10) days after the issuance of an order of disbarment, or suspension under SCR 3.050 or SCR 3.669(4), or upon issuance of an order of suspension from the practice of law for more than sixty (60) days, the disbarred or suspended lawyer shall notify, by letter duly placed with the United States Postal Service, all courts or other tribunals in which that lawyer has matters pending, and all clients of the lawyer's inability to represent them and of the necessity and urgency of promptly retaining new counsel. The lawyer shall simultaneously provide a copy of all such letters of notification to the Office of Bar Counsel. Upon issuance of an order of disbarment or suspension, the affected lawyer shall immediately cancel any pending advertisements, to the extent possible, and shall terminate any advertising activity for the duration of the term of suspension or disbarment.

HISTORY: Amended by Order 2012–01, eff. 3–1–12; prior amendments eff. 10–1–98 (Order 98–1), 1–1–87 (Order 86–3), 4–1–82, 1–1–78, 7–2–71.

SCR 3.395 Appointment of special commissioner to protect clients' interests

(1) When it comes to the attention of the Director that: (a) an attorney has been temporarily suspended pursuant to SCR 3.165 and has failed to notify his/her clients of the suspension as required by Court order; or (b) an attorney has been suspended or disbarred pursuant to SCR 3.370 and has failed to notify his/her clients of his/her suspension or disbarment pursuant to SCR 3.390; or (c) an attorney has resigned pursuant to SCR 3.480 and has failed to notify his/her clients of his/her resignation as required by Court order; or (d) an attorney dies; or (e) an attorney abandons his/her law practice or his/her whereabouts are unknown, and no law partner, personal representative of the deceased attorney's estate, or other responsible person capable of conducting the attorney's business affairs is known to exist, the Director may petition the Court, and the Court for good cause may order the appointment of one or more members of the Association to serve as Special Commissioners of the Court.

The Director shall give notice to the attorney by mailing a copy of the petition to the attorney's last known address, except where the attorney is deceased. Within twenty (20) days after the date on which the Director files the petition with the Court, the attorney may file a response to the petition with the Court. The Clerk of the Court shall mail a copy of the Court's order ruling on the petition to the attorney's last known address, to the Director and to the Special Commissioner. The Director in his/her petition may suggest to the Court the names of one or more members of the Association to serve as a Special Commissioner.

(2) A Special Commissioner appointed under this rule may be authorized by the Court to take possession of the files and records of an attorney described in subsection (1) above, to make an inventory of the files, to give notice to the attorney's clients of the unavailability or inability of the attorney to continue to represent the clients, to deliver to the clients all papers and other property to which the clients are entitled, to take any other action which the clients are entitled and to take any other action which the Court deems necessary to protect the interests of the clients.

(3) The Special Commissioner shall not disclose any information contained in any files which are the subject of an inventory without the consent of the client to whom such files relate, except as reasonably necessary to carry out the orders of the Court.

(4) The Special Commissioner shall file a written report with the Court containing a summary and explanation of the actions taken by the Special Commissioner to fulfill the duties assigned to the Special Commissioner by the Court. The Special Commissioner shall mail a copy of the report to the Director and to the attorney's last known address.

(5) If the Special Commissioner takes possession of files of an attorney and the Special Commissioner is unable after a diligent effort to deliver the files to the clients or to new attorneys representing the clients, the Special Commissioner may request the Court to enter an order providing for the storage and safekeeping of such files.

(6) The Special Commissioner shall be entitled to reasonable compensation with the amount to be determined by the Court and to also be reimbursed for necessary expenses actually incurred. In order to receive such compensation or reimbursement of expenses, the Special Commissioner shall file with the Court a motion containing an itemized list of the time spent on the case, the work performed, and receipts for the expenses incurred. The Special Commissioner's compensation and expenses which are approved by the Court shall be paid by the Association, but any amounts disbursed by the Association to the Special Commissioner may be assessed as costs against the attorney pursuant to SCR 3.450 if the appointment of the Special Commissioner arose out of a disciplinary proceeding.

HISTORY: Amended by Order 98–1, eff. 10–1–98; adopted by Order 84–2, eff. 7–1–84

SCR 3.400   Rehearing by Trial Commissioner

Rehearing shall not be permitted except for newly discovered evidence so material to the rights of either party as to affect the finding and recommendation which could not have been discovered by the exercise of reasonable diligence and then only if such evidence is first presented in affidavit form, together with the affidavit of counsel that such evidence could not have been discovered sooner by the exercise of reasonable

diligence. After the Trial Commissioner has made his/her report to the Board, no rehearing shall be permitted by the Trial Commissioner. After the Board has conducted its review, no rehearing shall be permitted by the Board. After the Board has filed its order under Rule 3.370, the Court may remand the case to the Board for such action as the Court may direct.

HISTORY: Amended by Order 98–1, eff. 10–1–98; prior amendments eff. 1–1–78, 7–2–71

SCR 3.410   Procedure in the court—Deleted

HISTORY: Deleted by Order of the Supreme Court, eff. 1–1–78

Supreme Court Commentary

1977:
This rule has been superseded by Rule 3.370.

SCR 3.420   Attorney general may represent the board—Deleted

HISTORY: Deleted by Order 98–1, eff. 10–1–98; amended eff. 7–2–71

SCR 3.430   Duty to file brief—Deleted

HISTORY: Deleted by Order 98–1, eff. 10–1–98; amended eff. 7–2–71

SCR 3.435   Reciprocal discipline

(1) Any attorney subject to the provisions of this Rule shall, upon being subjected to professional disciplinary action in another jurisdiction, promptly inform the Bar Counsel of such action. Upon being informed that an attorney subject to the provisions of these Rules has been subjected to discipline in another jurisdiction, the Bar Counsel shall obtain a certified copy of such disciplinary order and shall file the same with this Court.

(2) Upon receipt of a certified copy of an order demonstrating that an attorney admitted to practice in this State has been disciplined in another jurisdiction, this Court shall forthwith issue a notice directed to the attorney containing:

(a) a copy of said order from the other jurisdiction; and

(b) an order directing that the attorney inform the Court, within twenty (20) days from the service of the notice, of any claim by the attorney predicated upon the grounds set forth in paragraph (4) hereof that the imposition of the identical discipline in this State would be unwarranted and the reasons therefor.

(3) In the event the discipline imposed in the other jurisdiction has been stayed there, any reciprocal discipline imposed in this State shall be deferred until such stay expires.

(4) Upon the expiration of thirty (30) days from the service of the notice issued pursuant to the provisions of (2) above, this Court shall impose the identical

discipline unless Respondent proves by substantial evidence:

(a) a lack of jurisdiction or fraud in the out-of-state disciplinary proceeding, or

(b) that misconduct established warrants substantially different discipline in this State.

(c) In all other respects, a final adjudication in another jurisdiction that an attorney has been guilty of misconduct shall establish conclusively the misconduct for purposes of a disciplinary proceeding in this State.

HISTORY: Amended by Order 98–1, eff. 10–1–98; adopted eff. 1–1–78

SCR 3.440 Disposition of case

The provisions of the Rules regarding petition for rehearing shall apply. The Clerk shall promptly furnish a copy of the order of disposition to all parties, Bar Counsel, and the Director. Every final order or opinion shall be published as are other opinions of the Court.

HISTORY: Amended by Order 98–1, eff. 10–1–98; prior amendments eff. 4–1–82 (Order 82–1), 1–1–78, 7–2–71

SCR 3.450 Recovery of appropriate costs

In any case to be submitted to the Court, the Disciplinary Clerk shall file with the Court the entire record of the proceedings together with a certified bill of costs, which shall include the expenses incurred by the Kentucky Bar Association in connection with the investigation and prosecution of the matter, including the expenses associated with the trial commissioner's hearing.

Every final order of the Board or the Court which adjudges the Respondent guilty of unprofessional conduct shall provide for the recovery of appropriate costs. Immediately upon the effective date of the order, the Clerk shall furnish a bill for said costs to the Respondent. If the bill is not satisfied within ten (10) days thereafter, the Clerk shall notify the Director of the Association.

HISTORY: Amended by Order 2012–01, eff. 3–1–12; prior amendments eff. 10–1–98 (Order 98–1), 4–1–82 (Order 82–1), 1–1–78, 7–2–71

SCR 3.455 Subpoena power

Upon application by the Office of Bar Counsel or a claimant, or upon the initiation of the Trustees of the Client's Security Fund, the Director may issue a subpoena to any person or legal entity to appear before it and to produce to the Trustees any evidence deemed by the Trustees to be material to the investigation of a claim for compensation being considered under the Client's Security Fund Plan of the Association. The Director shall mail a copy of the application to the person or legal entity to be subpoenaed, to the claimant, the Office of Bar Counsel, and to the attorney against whom the claim is made, each of whom shall have twenty (20) days from the date of the application to file an objection. If no objection is made, or a timely objection is overruled by the Chair of the Trustees the Director shall issue the subpoena. The subpoenaed party shall appear or produce the documents, whichever is directed by the subpoena. Any such documents will be produced to the Clients' Security Fund Trustees by delivery to the Office of Bar Counsel, which shall provide copies to the claimant and the attorney against whom the claim is made.

HISTORY: Amended by Order 2005–10, eff. 1–1–06; prior amendment eff. 10–1–98 (Order 98–1); adopted by Order 84–2, eff. 7–1–84

SCR 3.460 Unauthorized practices proceeding

(1) When it comes to the attention of the Director that any person or entity not having the right to practice law is directly or indirectly practicing law, the Director shall have the authority to cause such investigation to be made concerning the matter as he deems appropriate. Bar Counsel may participate in such investigation. The Director shall have the authority to subpoena any person or entity to produce any evidence relevant to the investigation including testimony by deposition pursuant to the Rules of Civil Procedure. Any motion to quash a subpoena shall be filed in and ruled on by the Supreme Court. If the Director determines that any person or entity has been engaged in the unauthorized practice of law, the Director shall send a letter or warning by certified mail, return receipt requested, to the person's or entity's last known address, requesting that the unauthorized practice of law be discontinued. If future violations occur and in the opinion of the Board action should be taken, it shall direct that a motion in the name of the Association for a show cause rule be filed with the Clerk. The Clerk shall docket the motion and issue a rule against the alleged offender to show cause why he/she should not be held in contempt for unauthorized practice of law. The rule shall be returnable on the 15th day following service. When procedure is by warning order, service shall be deemed to have been made thirty (30) days after the date of making the warning order.

(2) If the Respondent fails to file due response on the rule's return day or files a response admitting the offense, the rule shall forthwith be made absolute, and the Court shall enter such orders as it deems appropriate to deter and punish, which may include injunctive relief.

(3) If the Respondent timely files response denying the offense, the Court shall within twenty (20) days refer the case to a Trial Commissioner appointed under Rule 3.230 sitting as a Special Commissioner, who shall thereupon hold a hearing within sixty (60) days at such time and place as he/she may fix, at which hearing the Association shall be represented by counsel designated by the Board for that purpose.

The parties may obtain compulsory attendance of witnesses and the production of documents as provided in the Civil Rules. The Special Commissioner, at the conclusion of the hearing, may permit the filing of briefs by the parties, with each brief being filed within thirty (30) days, and shall make and submit to the Court written findings of fact and recommendations within thirty (30) days thereafter.

(4) Upon filing of the Special Commissioner's report, the Court may permit the filing of briefs by the parties or may summarily dispose of the matter and shall enter such order as may be appropriate. The Clerk shall furnish counsel and the Director copies of every order entered under this rule and every such order shall be reported and published as are other opinions of the Court.

(5) If the Respondent is adjudged guilty, he/she shall be liable for all Court costs, and the provisions of Civil Rule 73.07 shall apply.

HISTORY: Amended by Order 98–1, eff. 10–1–98; prior amendments eff. 1–1–86 (Order 85–2), 1–1–78, 10–14–74, 7–2–71

SCR 3.470   Attorney aiding unauthorized practice

Any attorney who knowingly aids, assists or abets in any way, form, or manner any person or entity in the unauthorized practice of law shall be guilty of unprofessional conduct.

HISTORY: Amended by Order 98–1, eff. 10–1–98; prior amendment eff. 7–2–71

SCR 3.475   Furnishing legal services pursuant to a pre-paid legal services plan

As used in this Rule, a pre-paid legal services plan means a plan, program, or insurance policy under which a member of the Association is paid (in whole or in part) legal fees or a member of the plan is reimbursed for legal fees for services rendered to a member of the plan.

A member of the Association may furnish legal services to a member of a pre-paid legal services plan, as heretofore defined, provided that the plan provides that no agent, servant or employee of the plan or the plan itself shall interfere with or control the performance of the duties of the attorney.

HISTORY: Amended by Order 98–1, eff. 10–1–98; adopted by Order 88–4, eff. 1–1–89

SCR 3.476   Furnishing legal services pursuant to a prepaid legal services plan—Abolished

HISTORY: Abolished by Order 88–4, eff. 1–1–89; prior amendments eff. 7–1–84, 1–1–78; adopted eff. 5–16–72

SCR 3.477   Member's financial interest in plan or group

Any member of the Association who is actively engaged in the practice of law as defined in Rule 3.020 shall not have any financial interest whatsoever in any group or plan contemplated within Rule 3.475.

HISTORY: Amended by Order 98–1, eff. 10–1–98; prior amendment eff. 1–1–78; adopted eff. 5–16–72

SCR 3.480   Withdrawal from the association; negotiated sanctions

(1) Any member who desires to withdraw from membership and is not under investigation pursuant to Rule 3.160(2), and does not have a complaint or charge pending against him/her in any jurisdiction, shall file a written motion to that effect with the Court and serve a copy on the Registrar and the Inquiry Commission. The motion shall be docketed by the Clerk. The Registrar shall, after consultation with the Inquiry Commission, within ten (10) days after the filing of the motion, certify in writing to the Court whether the movant is an active member in good standing of the Association and whether movant is under a disciplinary investigation by the Inquiry Commission or has a complaint or charge pending against him/her in this or any jurisdiction. Said motion may be granted if movant is an active member in good standing and has no pending disciplinary investigation, complaints, or charges.

(2) The Court may consider negotiated sanctions of disciplinary investigations, complaints or charges if the parties agree. Any member who is under investigation pursuant to SCR 3.160(2) or who has a complaint or charge pending in this jurisdiction, and who desires to terminate such investigation or disciplinary proceedings at any stage of it may request Bar Counsel to consider a negotiated sanction. If the member and Bar Counsel agree upon the specifics of the facts, the rules violated, and the appropriate sanction, the member shall file a motion with the Court which states such agreement, and serve a copy upon Bar Counsel, who shall, within ten (10) days of the Clerk's notice that the motion has been docketed, respond to its merits and confirm its agreement. The Disciplinary Clerk shall submit to the Court within the ten (10) day period the active disciplinary files to which the motion applies. The Court may approve the sanction agreed to by the parties, or may remand the case for hearing or other proceedings specified in the order of remand.

(3) Any member who has been engaged in unethical or unprofessional conduct and desires to withdraw his membership under terms of permanent disbarment shall file a verified motion with the Court stating as follows:

(a) He/she has violated the Rules of Professional Conduct, or his/her conduct fails to comply with those rules, the specifics of which shall be detailed in the motion.

(b) He/she will not seek reinstatement and understands the provisions of SCR 3.510 and SCR 3.520 do not apply.

(c) He/she will not practice law in the Commonwealth of Kentucky subsequent to the permanent disbarment order.

The motion shall be served on Bar Counsel and docketed by the Clerk. Bar Counsel may file a response within 10 days after the filing of the motion to resign under terms of permanent disbarment. Simultaneously with service of the motion on Bar Counsel, the member will immediately cancel all advertising for which the member has contracted and shall direct the publisher of such advertising to immediately cease publication of such advertising insofar as the medium of that advertising makes such action practicable and whether or not the member has paid for the advertising in advance. The Disciplinary Clerk shall, within ten (10) days after the filing of such a motion, submit to the Court any active disciplinary files maintained by the Inquiry Commission relating to movant. The Court will then enter an appropriate order, stating the conditions, if any, under which the motion is granted, or deny the motion and direct the completion of disciplinary proceedings under these rules.

(4) Any member suspended or disbarred by order of this Court shall:

(a) Take all steps necessary and practicable to cease all forms of advertisement of the member's practice immediately upon entry of an order of suspension or disbarment and shall report the fact and effect of those steps to the Director in writing within twenty (20) days after the order of suspension or disbarment is entered.

(b) Pay all costs of the disciplinary investigation and proceedings in accordance with Rule 3.450, and

(c) Comply with the provisions of Rule 3.390 regarding notice to clients of suspension or disbarment.
HISTORY: Amended by Order 2009–12, eff. 1–1–10; prior amendments eff. 2–1–00 (Order 99–1), 10–1–98 (Order 98–1), 4–1–82 (Order 82–1), 7–2–71

SCR 3.490 Mental disability in absence of misconduct—Deleted
HISTORY: Deleted by Order of Supreme Court, eff. 1–1–78

Supreme Court Commentary
1977:
This rule is superseded by Rule 3.165.

SCR 3.500 Restoration to membership
(1) A former member who has withdrawn from membership pursuant to SCR 3.480(1), or who was suspended for failure to pay dues as provided by SCR 3.050, or for failure to comply with the continuing legal education requirements of SCR 3.661 may be restored to membership upon compliance with the conditions set forth in this rule. No application for restoration shall be effective until entry of an order of restoration by the Board of Governors or the Court, as provided herein. Until the entry of such an order,

the suspension or withdrawal from membership remains in force.

(2) A former member whose withdrawal or suspension from membership has prevailed for less than five (5) years may apply for restoration by:

(a) Submitting an application for restoration using the forms provided by the Director, with a fee of three hundred fifty dollars ($350.00) and all applicable unpaid Bar Association dues; and

(b) Submitting with the application a certificate from the Office of Bar Counsel that the former member has no pending disciplinary matters; and

(c) Submitting with the application a certificate from the Director of Continuing Legal Education pursuant to SCR 3.675.

(d) Upon the filing of the foregoing items, the Office of Bar Counsel shall present the matter to the Board at its next meeting. Within thirty (30) days of its review of the complete application materials, the Board may restore the applicant to membership or refer the matter to the Character and Fitness Committee of the Kentucky Office of Bar Admissions for proceedings pursuant to SCR 2.040 and SCR 2.011, and subsequent review by the Supreme Court. If the matter is referred to the Character and Fitness Committee, the applicant shall pay a fee of two hundred fifty dollars ($250.00) to the Kentucky Office of Bar Admissions. Upon completion of its review, the Character and Fitness Committee shall submit its recommendation to the Board for its action and recommendation to the Court.

(3) A former member whose withdrawal or suspension from membership has prevailed for five (5) years or longer may apply for restoration by:

(a) Submitting an application for restoration using the forms provided by the Director, with a fee of seven hundred fifty dollars ($750.00) and all applicable unpaid Bar Association dues; and

(b) Submitting with the application a certificate from the Office of Bar Counsel that the former member has no pending disciplinary matters; and

(c) Submitting with the application a certificate from the Director of Continuing Legal Education pursuant to SCR 3.675.

(d) Upon the filing of the foregoing items, the Director shall refer the application to the Character and Fitness Committee of the Kentucky Office of Bar Admissions for proceedings pursuant to SCR 2.040 and SCR 2.011. An additional fee of five hundred dollars ($500.00) shall be paid to the Kentucky Office of Bar Admissions. Upon completion of its review, the Character and Fitness Committee shall submit its recommendation to the Board of Governors for its action and recommendation to the Court.

(e) If the Character and Fitness Committee recommends approval of the application and the Board concurs, the application shall be referred to the Board of Bar Examiners of the Kentucky Office of Bar Admissions, for the administration of a written examination which includes the subject of professional ethics and five (5) of the subjects listed in SCR 2.080(1). A general average score of 75% or higher shall be deemed a passing score. Fees required by SCR 2.022, and SCR 2.023 shall be paid prior to taking the examination. As an alternative and upon referral from the Board of Governors, if the Applicant has practiced in a reciprocal jurisdiction after withdrawal pursuant to SCR 3.480 and meets all requirements of SCR 2.110, the Applicant may elect to have the Character and Fitness Committee consider an application for admission without examination under SCR 2.110. All fees required by that rule shall be paid prior to the processing of the application.

If the Applicant passes the examination or is approved for admission without examination, such fact shall be certified to the Court and to the Director, together with a recommendation for the Applicant's restoration to membership. Upon this certification, the Disciplinary Clerk shall transmit the record to the Court for its consideration of the application for restoration. If the applicant fails the examination, the Board of Bar Examiners shall certify the fact of the failure to the Court and the Director. Upon that certification, the Disciplinary Clerk shall transmit the record to the Court for entry of an order denying restoration.

The provisions of SCR 2.015, SCR 2.080, and SCR 2.110 shall apply where not inconsistent with these provisions.

(f) If the Character and Fitness Committee recommends disapproval of the application, the matter shall be referred to the Board of Governors for its review. The Applicant and the KBA may file briefs and an oral argument may be held upon the request of either party. If, after its consideration, the Board concurs in the disapproval of the application, its findings and recommendation shall be filed with the Disciplinary Clerk, and the record shall be sent to the Clerk of the Supreme Court. Upon receipt of the record, the Clerk of the Supreme Court shall send notice of the filing by certified mail, return receipt requested, to the Applicant's bar roster address. Within twenty (20) days, the Applicant may petition the Court for review of the action of the Board. If the Court reverses the Board's disapproval of the application, it shall refer the matter to the Board of Bar Examiners for the procedure set forth above in paragraph 3(e).

(4) All costs incurred in excess of the filing fee shall be paid by the Applicant. Upon referral to the Character and Fitness Committee, a cash or corporate surety bond in the amount of two thousand five hundred dollars ($2500.00) to secure the costs to be incurred shall be paid to the Office of Bar Admissions by the Applicant.

(5) The burden of proof for establishing the Applicant's present qualifications to practice law in Kentucky is on the Applicant.

(6) If the Character and Fitness Committee or the Board of Governors recommends restoration of membership on conditions as provided in SCR 2.042, such conditions may be imposed by the Board, for application processed by it under subsection (2)(d) of this rule, or by the Court in any order of restoration.

HISTORY: Amended by Order 2012–01, eff. 3–1–12; prior amendments eff. 1–1–10 (Order 2009–12), 1–1–07 (Order 2006–09), 1–1–04 (Order 2003–4), 2–1–00 (Order 99–1), 10–1–98 (Order 98–1), 3–1–98 (Order 97–3), 9–15–90 (Order 90–1), 1–1–89, 1–1–88, 1–1–86, 7–1–84, 4–1–82, 1–1–78, 7–2–71

SCR 3.505 Character and Fitness Committee; reinstatements

(1) The Character and Fitness Committee created by SCR 2.040 shall, in addition to the powers and duties conferred in that rule, consider all applications for reinstatement to the practice of law by persons who:

(a) have been suspended for more than one hundred eighty (180) days;

(b) have been suspended for one hundred eighty (180) days or less, but whose reinstatement has been opposed by Bar Counsel.

(2) The Character and Fitness Committee may act upon the application and such investigative material as it may gather or Bar Counsel may tender to it, all of which information not submitted by the Applicant shall be made available to the Applicant.

(3) The Applicant or Bar Counsel shall have the right to a hearing before the Character and Fitness Committee prior to the issuance of its decision. The hearing shall be held within sixty (60) days from the request. The report of the Committee shall be filed within sixty (60) days of receipt of the transcript of hearing.

(4) If either party requests a hearing before the Character and Fitness Committee, the Applicant shall have the rights accorded a Respondent in a disciplinary proceeding pursuant to SCR 3.300, except that the Character and Fitness Committee shall hold the hearing rather than a Trial Commissioner. The burden of proof of one's good character and fitness to practice law shall be on the Applicant.

HISTORY: Amended by Order 2003–4, eff. 1–1–04; adopted by Order 98–1, eff. 10–1–98

SCR 3.510 Reinstatement in case of disciplinary suspension

(1) No former member of the Association who has been suspended for a disciplinary case for more than one hundred eighty (180) days shall resume practice until he/she is reinstated by order of the Court. Application for reinstatement shall be on forms provided

by the Director and Continuing Legal Education Commission, filed with the Director, and shall be accompanied by a filing fee of $250.00 which shall be made payable to the Kentucky Bar Association. An additional filing fee of $1250.00 shall be made payable to the Kentucky Office of Bar Admissions. The Director shall not accept an application for filing unless alt costs incurred in the suspension proceeding have been paid by the former member, the Office of Bar Counsel has certified to the Applicant that there is no pending disciplinary file, and the costs in the reinstatement proceeding (whether costs of the Association or of the Character and Fitness Committee or of the Kentucky Office of Bar Admissions) have been secured by the posting of a cash or corporate surety bond of $2500.00. Any additional costs will be paid by Applicant. The Director shall refer the application to the Continuing Legal Education Commission within ten (10) days of receipt for certification under Rule 3.675. The Continuing Legal Education Commission shall make its certification within twenty (20) days of the referral which shall be added to the record in the reinstatement proceedings.

(2) If the period of suspension has prevailed for one hundred eighty (180) days or less, the suspension shall expire by its own terms upon the filing with the Clerk and Bar Counsel of an affidavit of compliance with the terms of the suspension, which must include a certification from the CLE Commission that the Applicant has complied with SCR 3.675. The Registrar of the Association will make an appropriate entry in the records of the Association reflecting that the member has been reinstated; provided, however, that such suspension shall not expire by its own terms if, not later than ten (10) days preceding the time the suspension would expire, Bar Counsel files with the Inquiry Commission an opposition to the termination of suspension wherein Bar Counsel details such information as may exist to indicate that the member does not, at that time, possess sufficient professional capabilities and qualifications properly to serve the public as an active practitioner or is not of good moral character. A copy of such objection shall be provided to the Character and Fitness Committee, to the member concerned, and to the Registrar. If such an objection has been filed by Bar Counsel, and is not withdrawn within thirty (30) days, the Character and Fitness Committee shall conduct proceedings under SCR 2.300. In cases where a suspension has prevailed for one hundred eighty (180) days or less and the reinstatement application is referred to the Character and Fitness Committee, a fee of $1250.00 shall be made payable to the Kentucky Office of Bar Admissions.

(3) If the period of suspension has prevailed for more than one hundred eighty (180) days, the matter shall be referred to the Character and Fitness Committee for proceedings under SCR 2.300. The Character and Fitness Committee will determine whether the application of a member who has been suspended one hundred eighty (180) days or less but whose termination of suspension has been objected to, or a member who has been suspended for more than one hundred eighty (180) days, should be approved. The Character and Fitness Committee shall file with the Director and the Clerk the entire record, including a written report and recommendation by the Character and Fitness Committee. The Board shall review the record and report and recommend approval or disapproval of the application to the Court. The Court may enter an order reinstating the Applicant to the practice of law or deny the application.

(4) If the period of suspension has prevailed for more than five (5) years, the Director shall refer the application to the Character and Fitness Committee for proceedings under SCR 2.300. The Committee shall file a written report and recommendation with the Director and the Clerk. The Board shall review the record and report and recommend approval or disapproval of the application to the Court. If the Committee and the Board recommend approval of the application, the Committee shall refer the application to the Board of Bar Examiners for processing in accordance with Rule 3.500(3) and shall file the entire record with the Clerk, including the written report and recommendation of the Committee. The Board of Bar Examiners shall certify the results of the examination to the Director and the Court. If the Applicant successfully completes the examination, the Court may, at its discretion, enter an order reinstating the suspended member to the practice of law. However, if the Applicant fails to pass the examination, the Court shall enter an order denying the application.

(5) A suspended member of the Association who desires to resume practice as quickly as possible following a period of suspension may file an application to do so at any time during the last ninety (90) days of the period of suspension.

(6) If the Committee and Board recommend approval of reinstatement on conditions, as provided in SCR 2.042, or approval with such additional conditions as the Board may recommend, the Court may include such conditions in any order of reinstatement.

HISTORY: Amended by Order 2009–12, eff. 1–1–10; prior amendments eff. 1–1–07 (Order 2006–09), 1–1–04 (Order 2003–4), 2–1–00 (Order 99–1), 10–1–98 (Order 98–1), 9–15–90 (Order 90–1), 1–1–88, 2–24–86, 7–1–84, 4–1–82, 1–1–78, 7–2–71

SCR 3.520   Reinstatement in case of disbarment—Deleted

HISTORY: Deleted by Order 98–1, eff. 10–1–98; prior amendments eff. 9–15–90 (Order 90–1), 2–24–86, 1–1–86, 7–1–84, 4–1–82, 1–1–78, 7–2–71

SCR 3.530   Ethics Committee and Unauthorized Practice Committee—advisory opinions—informal and formal

(1) The Ethics Committee and the Unauthorized Practice Committee are authorized to issue informal

opinions, and to submit to the Board for its action formal opinions, on questions of ethics or unauthorized practice, as applicable.

(2) Any attorney licensed in Kentucky or admitted under SCR 3.030(2), who is in doubt as to the ethical propriety of any professional act contemplated by that attorney may request an informal opinion. The President shall designate members of the Ethics Committee to respond to such requests. Ordinarily, the request shall be directed to a member of the requestor's Supreme Court district. Such request shall be in writing or by telephone followed by a request in writing. The committee member to whom the request is directed shall attempt to furnish the requesting attorney with a prompt telephonic answer and written informal letter opinion as to the ethical propriety of the act or course of conduct in question. A copy of any such informal opinion shall be provided to the Director for safekeeping and statistical purposes, and to the Chair of the Ethics Committee, to determine whether the informal opinion has broader application.

(3) Communications between the requesting attorney and the Ethics Committee member shall be confidential. However, the requesting and giving of advice under this Rule does not create an attorney-client relationship. In order to promote uniformity of advice, redacted copies of informal opinions may be circulated among members of the Ethics Committee, as applicable, provided that such confidentiality is preserved.

(4) If the Ethics Committee determines an ethical issue to be of sufficient importance, the Committee may issue and furnish to the Board of Governors a proposed opinion authorized by such Committee for approval as a formal opinion. Such approval shall require a vote of three-fourths of the voting members present at the meeting of the Board. If the Board is unable to approve of the opinion as written, then the Board may return the matter to the Committee for further review and consideration, or may modify the opinion and approve the opinion as modified by the three-fourths vote, or may direct the Committee to furnish the requesting attorney, if any, with an informal opinion in the form of a Chair's letter opinion, with a copy to the Director.

(5) Both informal and formal opinions shall be advisory only; however, no attorney shall be disciplined for any professional act performed by that attorney in compliance with an informal opinion furnished by the Ethics Committee member pursuant to such attorney's written request, provided that the written request clearly, fairly, accurately and completely states such attorney's contemplated professional act.

(6) Any attorney licensed in Kentucky who is in doubt as to the propriety of any course of conduct or act of any person or entity which may constitute the unauthorized practice of law may make a request in writing, or in emergencies, by telephone, to the Chair of the Unauthorized Practice Committee, or such oth-

er members of the Unauthorized Practice Committee as are designated by the Chair, for an advisory opinion thereon. Local bar associations may also request advisory opinions. The Committee member to whom the request is directed shall bring this matter to the attention of the Committee at its next meeting. The Committee may attempt to furnish the requesting attorney with a prompt telephonic answer and written informal letter opinion as to whether the conduct constitutes the unauthorized practice of law. A copy of such informal opinion shall be provided to the Director and the Chair of the Unauthorized Practice Committee.

(7) Any attorney licensed in Kentucky or admitted under SCR 3.030(2) who is in doubt as to the ethical propriety of any professional act contemplated by that attorney with respect to the unauthorized practice of law shall be referred to the Ethics Committee district member for an informal opinion as set forth in (2) and (3). Communications about such an inquiry between the requesting attorney and the unauthorized practice committee member, and between the committee members of the two committees, shall be confidential.

(8) The requesting and giving of advice by the Unauthorized Practice Committee under this Rule does not create an attorney/client relationship.

(9) If the Unauthorized Practice Committee determines an issue regarding the unauthorized practice of law to be of sufficient importance, the Committee may issue and furnish to the Board of Governors a proposed opinion authorized by such Committee for approval as a formal opinion. Such approval shall require a vote of three-fourths of the voting members present at the meeting of the Board. If the Board is unable to approve the opinion as written, then the Board may return the matter to the Committee for further review and consideration, or may modify the opinion and approve the opinion as modified by the three-fourths vote, or may direct the Committee to furnish the requesting attorney, if any, with an informal opinion in the form of a Chair's letter opinion, with a copy to the Director.

(10) Ethics Committee and Unauthorized Practice Committee members shall be immune from suit for advice given in the performance of duties under this Rule.

(11) All formal opinions of the Board arising from either Committee shall be published in full or in synopsis form, as determined by the Director, in the edition of the KENTUCKY BENCH & BAR next issued after the adoption of the opinion.

(12) Any person or entity aggrieved or affected by a formal opinion of the Board may file with the clerk within thirty (30) days after the end of the month of publication of the KENTUCKY BENCH & BAR in which the full opinion or a synopsis thereof is published, a copy of the opinion, and, upon motion and reasonable notice in writing to the Director, obtain a

review of the Board's opinion by the Court. The Court's action thereon shall be final and the Clerk shall furnish copies of the formal order to the original petitioner, if any, the movant and the Director. The movant shall file a brief in support of the review, and the Director may file a response brief thirty days thereafter.

(13) The filing fee for docketing a motion under paragraph (7) of this Rule 3.530 shall be as provided by Civil Rule 76.42(1) for original actions in the Supreme Court.

HISTORY: Amended by Order 2006–09, eff. 1–1–07; prior amendments eff. 1–1–97 (Order 96–1), 11–1–95, 11–15–91, 12–31–80, 1–1–78, 12–4–74, 7–2–71

SCR 3.540   Legal internship—Renumbered

HISTORY: Renumbered eff. 3–10–73

SCR 3.550   Amendments—Deleted

HISTORY: Deleted by Order of Supreme Court, eff. 1–1–78

SCR 3.600   Continuing legal education definitions

As used in SCR 3.610–3.690, the following definitions shall apply unless the context clearly requires a different meaning:

"Approved activity" is a continuing legal education activity that has been approved for credit by the CLE Commission.

"Attorney Identification Number" is the five (5) digit number assigned to each member of the Association upon admission.

"Award" is the Continuing Legal Education Award.

"Commission" is the Continuing Legal Education Commission.

"Continuing legal education," or "CLE," is any legal educational activity or program which is designed to maintain or improve the professional competency of the practicing attorneys and is accredited by the Commission.

"Credit" is a unit for measuring continuing legal education activity.

"Educational year" is the reporting period for mandatory continuing legal education and runs from July 1st each year through June 30th of the successive year.

"Ethics, professional responsibility and professionalism" is the category by which "ethics credits" shall be earned and includes, but is not limited to programs or seminars or designated portions thereof with instruction focusing on the Rules of Professional Conduct independently or as they relate to law firm management, malpractice avoidance, attorneys fees, legal ethics, and the duties of attorneys to the judicial system, the public, clients and other attorneys.

"In-house activity" is an activity sponsored by a single law firm, single corporate law department, or single governmental office for lawyers who are members or employees of the firm, department or office.

"Legal writing" is a publication which contributes to the legal competency of the applicant, other attorneys or judges and is approved by the Commission. Writing for which the author is paid shall not be approved.

"Non-compliance" means not meeting continuing legal education requirements set forth in Rule 3.661 and Rule 3.652 and includes both lack of certification and lack of completion of activities prior to established time requirements.

"Technological transmission" is a CLE activity delivery method other than live seminars and includes video tape, DVD, audio tape, CD–ROM, computer online services, or other appropriate technology as approved by the Commission.

HISTORY: Amended by Order 2012–01, eff. 3–1–12; adopted by Order 2003–4, eff. 1–1–04

SCR 3.610   The commission; functions and membership

The Continuing Legal Education Commission shall consist of seven attorneys, one of whom shall be from each appellate district of the state as presently existing or hereafter created. Under the policy direction of the Court and the Board, the Commission shall be responsible for the administration and regulation of all continuing legal education programs and activities for the members of the Association.

HISTORY: Amended by Order 90–1, eff. 9–15–90; adopted eff. 7–1–78

SCR 3.620   Selection and tenure of the commission, filling vacancies on the commission

The Court shall appoint all members of the Commission from a list consisting of three times the number to be appointed submitted to the Court by the Board. A chairman shall be designated by the Court for such time as the Court may direct. Of the members first appointed, three shall be appointed for one year, two for two years and two for three years. Thereafter, appointments shall be made for a three-year term. Members may be reappointed but no member shall serve more than two successive three-year terms. Each member shall serve until a successor is appointed and qualified. Vacancies occurring through death, disability, inability or disqualification to serve or by resignation shall be filled for the vacant term in the same manner as initial appointments are made by the Court. Members of the Commission shall serve without compensation but shall be paid their reasonable and necessary expenses incurred in the performance of their duties. The Association shall have the responsibility of funding the Commission and any necessary staff who shall be employees of the Association.

HISTORY: Amended by Order 2012–01, eff. 3–1–12; adopted eff. 7–1–78

SCR 3.630   Commission member's qualifications

Each Commission member must be a citizen of the United States, licensed to practice law in the courts of this Commonwealth and have been a resident in the appellate district from which nominated for two years immediately preceding the appointment.

HISTORY: Amended by Order 2012–01, eff. 3–1–12; adopted eff. 7–1–78

SCR 3.635   Commission quorum

A quorum consisting of at least four (4) Commission members is required for conducting the business of the Commission.

HISTORY: Amended by Order 2012–01, eff. 3–1–12; adopted by Order 91–2, eff. 11–15–91

SCR 3.640   Commission staff

The Commission shall be provided with a Director for Continuing Legal Education and sufficient administrative and secretarial assistants as are from time to time required. Selection and qualifications of the Director for Continuing Legal Education shall be determined by the Board except that the person selected shall be an attorney licensed to practice law in the courts of this Commonwealth. The Director for Continuing Legal Education shall be responsible to the Commission for the proper administration of the rules applying to the Commission and any regulations issued by the Commission.

HISTORY: Amended by Order 2012–01, eff. 3–1–12; prior amendment eff. 9–15–90 (Order 90–1); adopted eff. 7–1–78

SCR 3.650   Commission duties

The Commission shall be responsible for the administration of these continuing legal education rules, subject to policy approval and other direction by the Board and the Court. In discharging this responsibility, the Commission shall:

(1) Encourage and promote the offering of high quality continuing legal education.

(2) Conduct, sponsor, or otherwise provide high quality continuing legal education, specifically including, but not limited to, one (1) twelve and one-half (12.5) credit seminar in each Supreme Court District each year.

(3) Encourage and promote quality legal writing.

(4) Approve or deny promptly all applications provided for by these rules.

(5) Establish standards, procedures, and forms to evaluate applications made pursuant to these rules.

(6) Promulgate rules and regulations for the administration of the mandatory continuing legal education program subject to approval of the Board and the Court.

(7) Report annually, on or before September 15, and as otherwise required, to the Board and the Court on the status of continuing legal education in the Commonwealth. Such report shall include recommended changes to these rules and regulations and their implementation.

(8) Submit to the Board annually, on or before November 1, a recommended budget for the succeeding year with any recommended changes in annual membership dues to cover costs of administering these rules.

(9) Perform such other acts and duties, not inconsistent with these rules, as are necessary and proper to improve the continuing legal education programs within the Commonwealth.

When in the course of undertaking the duties set forth above, the Commission receives information which may raise questions regarding a member's competence to represent clients or to otherwise practice law as defined at SCR 3.020, or which may raise any of the issues covered at SCR 3.165(b), the Commission has an affirmative duty to report such information to the Office of Bar Counsel for review by the Inquiry Commission.

HISTORY: Amended by Order 2012–01, eff. 3–1–12; prior amendments eff. 2–1–01 (Order 2000–1), 7–1–95 (Order 95–1), 9–15–90, 1–1–88, 7–1–84, 2–1–81; adopted eff. 7–1–78

SCR 3.651   Kentucky law update seminars in each appellate district

(1) Each educational year, the Commission shall conduct a twelve and one-half (12.5) credit continuing legal education seminar in each Supreme Court District. Subjects taught at each seminar shall include the latest Kentucky Supreme Court and Court of Appeals decisions, procedural rule changes, Federal Court decisions, legal ethics, professional responsibility and professionalism, Kentucky statutory changes and other subjects relating to improvements in basic legal skills. Each program shall include a minimum of two (2.0) credits for subjects specifically addressing legal ethics, professional responsibility and professionalism.

(2) Registration for the Kentucky Law Update seminars shall be free to all members in good standing of the Association.

(3) Members may attend Kentucky Law Update seminars in any location. The maximum credit that may be earned for attending any one (1) Kentucky Law Update seminar is twelve (12.5) credits. However, if different tracks of programs are attended at different locations, additional credit may be approved by the Commission. Pursuant to Rule 3.664 (1) duplicate credits shall not be earned by attending the same program at a different location.

HISTORY: Amended by Order 2012–01, eff. 3–1–12; prior amendment eff. 7–1–95 (Order 95–1); adopted eff. 9–15–90

SCR 3.652   New lawyer program

(1) At least twice each educational year, the Commission shall provide or cause to be provided a New Lawyer Program of not less than twelve and one-half (12.5) credits. The Commission may in its discretion, accredit a New Lawyer Program proposed by other CLE providers.

(2) Continuing legal education credits for the New Lawyer Program shall be awarded in a number consistent with the award of credits for other continuing legal education programs.

(3) The New Lawyer Program shall include at least two (2) hours of ethics, a course on law practice management and other subjects determined appropriate by the Commission.

(4) The Commission or other provider accredited under SCR 3.652(1) may charge a reasonable registration fee approved by the Court for the New Lawyer Program.

(5) Within twelve (12) months following the date of admission as set forth on the certificate of admission, each person admitted to membership to the Association shall complete the New Lawyer Program.

(6) Each individual attending the New Lawyer Program shall certify to the Director the completion of the Program on the attendance certificate provided for that purpose. Such certification shall be submitted to the Director upon completion of the program and in no case shall the certification be submitted later than thirty (30) days after completion of the program. Continuing legal education credits awarded for the program shall be applied to the educational year in which the program is attended, and if applied to a year in which the individual so attending is otherwise exempt from CLE requirements under SCR 3.666(1)(b), then said credits shall carry forward in accordance with SCR 3.661(5) and (6).

(7) Members required to complete the New Lawyer Program pursuant to paragraph (5) of this Rule may, upon application to and approval by the Commission, be exempted from the requirement if the member is admitted to practice in another jurisdiction for a minimum of five (5) years, and will certify such prior admission to the Commission, or if the member has attended a mandatory new lawyer training program of at least twelve and one-half (12.5) credits, including two (2) ethics credits, offered by the state bar association of another jurisdiction and approved by the Director.

(8) The time for completion and certification set forth in paragraphs (5) and (6) of this Rule may, upon written application to and approval by the Commission or its designee, be extended. Written applications for an extension under this paragraph must be received by the Commission no later than thirty (30) days after the member's deadline to complete the Program as set forth in paragraph (5) of this Rule. All applications must be signed by the member. The Commission may approve extensions for completing the Program under the following circumstances:

(a) Where the member demonstrates hardship or other good cause clearly warranting relief. Requests for relief under this subsection must set forth all circumstances upon which the request is based, including supporting documentation. In these circumstances, the member shall complete the requirement set forth in paragraphs (5) and (6) as soon as reasonably practicable as determined by the Commission or its designee; or

(b) Where the member fails to demonstrate hardship or other good cause clearly warranting relief, the member must pay a fee of two hundred fifty dollars ($250.00) and complete the requirement set forth in paragraphs (5) and (6) at the next regularly scheduled New Lawyer Program.

(9) Failure to complete and certify attendance for the New Lawyer Program pursuant to paragraphs (5), (6), or (8) of this Rule shall be grounds for suspension from the practice of law in the Commonwealth or other sanctions as deemed appropriate by the Court. Ninety (90) days prior to the end of the twelve (12) month period all individuals not certifying completion of the New Lawyer Program pursuant to paragraphs (5), (6) or (8) shall be notified in writing that the program must be completed before the end of the twelve (12) month period, indicating the date. Names of all individuals not submitting certification of completion of the New Lawyer Program within the twelve (12) month period or not being granted an extension of time, pursuant to paragraph (8) of this Rule, shall be submitted to the Court by the Director, certifying the member's failure to comply with the New Lawyer Program requirement. The Clerk shall docket the matter and the Court shall issue each such member a rule returnable within twenty (20) days thereafter to show cause why the member should not be suspended from the practice of law or otherwise sanctioned as deemed appropriate by the Court. The Commission shall be permitted to file a reply within ten (10) days following the filing of a response by a member. Unless good cause is shown by the return date of the rule, or within such additional time as may be allowed by the Court, an Order shall be entered suspending respondent from the practice of law or imposing such other sanctions as may be deemed appropriate by the Court. An attested copy of the Order shall forthwith be delivered by the Clerk to the member, the Director, and in the case of suspension, to the Circuit Clerk of the district wherein the member resides for recording and indexing as required by Rule 3.480.

HISTORY: Amended by Order 2012–01, eff. 3–1–12; prior amendments eff. 2–1–08 (Order 2007–007), 1–1–04 (Order 2003–4), 1–1–97 (Order 96–1), 7–1–95; adopted eff. 9–1–93

SCR 3.660   Commission quorum—Deleted

HISTORY: Deleted by Order 91–2, eff. 11–15–91; adopted eff. 7–1–78

SCR 3.661 Continuing legal education requirements: compliance and certification

(1) Each educational year, every person licensed to practice law in this Commonwealth, not specifically exempted pursuant to the provisions of Rule 3.666, shall complete and certify a minimum of twelve and one-half (12.5) credit hours in continuing legal education activities approved by the Commission, including a minimum of two (2) credit hours devoted to continuing legal education specifically addressing the topics of legal ethics, professional responsibility or professionalism. All continuing legal education activities must be completed not later than June 30 of each educational year.

(2) Certification of completion of approved CLE activities must be received by the Director no later than August 10th immediately following the educational year in which the activity is completed. Certification shall be submitted to the Director by the sponsor of the accredited activity or by individual attorneys. Sponsors submitting certifications to the Director shall comply with all requirements set forth in SCR 3.665(6).

(3) Programs or seminars or designated portions thereof devoted to legal ethics, professional responsibility or professionalism include but are not limited to programs or seminars, or designated portions thereof, with instruction focusing on the Rules of Professional Conduct independently or as they relate to law firm management, malpractice avoidance, attorneys fees, legal ethics, and the duties of attorneys to the judicial system, the public, clients and other attorneys.

(4) Integration of legal ethics, professional responsibility or professionalism issues into substantive law topics is encouraged, but shall not count toward the two (2) credit minimum annual requirement.

(5) A member who accumulates an excess over the twelve and one-half (12.5) credit requirement may carry forward the excess credits into the two successive educational years for the purpose of satisfying the minimum requirement for those years. Carry-forward credits are limited to a total of twenty-five (25) credits. All excess credits above a total of twenty-five (25) credits will remain on the member's records but may not be carried forward.

(6) Carry-forward credits shall be allowed to satisfy the two (2) credit annual requirement for continuing legal education addressing the topics of legal ethics, professional responsibility and professionalism, and may be carried forward into the two years immediately succeeding the year in which the hours were earned. Carry-forward credits for ethics, professional responsibility and professionalism are limited to a total of four (4) credits.

(7) Certification may be submitted by sponsors or by individuals on approved Association forms, uniform certificates, or any other format adopted by the Commission.

(8) Compliance and certification requirements concerning the New Lawyer Program are set forth at SCR 3.652(5) and (6).

HISTORY: Amended by Order 2012–01, eff. 3–1–12; prior amendments eff. 1–1–04 (Order 2003–4), 1–1–97 (Order 96–1), 7–1–95, 9–1–93, 8–1–92; adopted eff. 9–15–90

SCR 3.662 Qualifying continuing legal education activity standards and credit limits

(1) A continuing legal education activity qualifies for accreditation if the Commission determines that the activity conforms to the following standards:

(a) The activity is an organized program of learning (including a course of study, workshop, symposium or lecture) which contributes directly to the legal competence of an attorney.

(b) The activity deals primarily with substantive legal issues directly related to the practice of law, or practice management and includes consideration of any related issues of ethics, professional responsibility, or professionalism.

(c) The activity has significant intellectual or practical content which is timely.

(d) The activity has as its primary objective to increase the participant's professional competence as an attorney.

(e) The activity must be offered by a sponsor having substantial, recent experience in offering continuing legal education. Demonstrated ability arises partly from the extent to which individuals with legal training or educational experience are involved in the planning, instruction and supervision of the activity.

(f) The activity itself must be taught and conducted by an individual or group qualified by practical or academic experience. The activity, including the named advertised participants, must be conducted substantially as planned, subject to emergency alterations.

(g) Thorough, high-quality, readable, timely, useful and carefully prepared written materials must be made available to all participants at or before the time the activity is presented, unless the absence of such materials is recognized as reasonable and approved by the Commission. A brief outline without citations or explanatory notations will not be sufficient.

(h) At the conclusion of the activity, each participating attorney must be given the opportunity to complete an evaluation questionnaire addressing the quality of the particular activity.

(i) The cost of the activity itself to participating attorneys must be reasonable considering the subject matter and instructional level.

(j) The activity may be presented live or by technological transmission as defined in Rule 3.600. If presented by technological transmission, the transmission must be produced from an activity submitted and approved by the Commission pursuant to SCR 3.665.

Activities including audio components must have high quality audio reproductions so that listeners may easily hear the content of the activity. Activities including video components must have high quality video reproductions so that observers may easily view the content of the activity. If activities are presented by technological transmission and an attorney facilitator is available for purposes of answering questions and leading discussions, that activity is considered a live seminar.

(k) In cases of in-house activity, as defined in SCR 3.600, such activities may be approved if all standards set forth herein for accreditation are met. A maximum of six (6.0) credits per educational year earned at in-house activities may be applied to meet the annual twelve and one-half (12.5) credit requirement. The following additional requirements must also be met for accreditation of in-house activities:

(i) At least half the instruction hours must be provided by qualified persons having no continuing relationship or employment with the sponsoring firm, department or agency. For technologically transmitted activities, the activities must meet all standards for qualifying continuing legal education activities as set forth in SCR 3.662 and must be included as part of the application as set forth at SCR 3.662(1)(k).

(ii) Members of the Court, the Commission or a Commission designee may attend or participate in any such program to observe compliance without payment of registration or other fees.

(*l*) In cases of law school classes attended by members, the member may receive continuing legal education credit provided the following requirements are met:

(i) The member registers for the class with the law school.

(ii) The member completes the course as required by the terms of registration, for credit or by audit.

(iii) Credit is calculated pursuant to Rule 3.663.

(2) The following categories of activities shall not qualify as a continuing legal education activity.

(a) Activities designed primarily for non-lawyers.

(b) In-house activities for which less than half the instruction is provided by qualified persons outside the firm, department or agency, and for which members of the Court, the Commission or Commission designee are prohibited from observing for compliance without charge of fees.

(c) Seminars or meetings sponsored by law firms or other organizations which are determined by the Commission to be in the nature of client development.

(d) Technological transmissions as set forth at SCR 3.662(1)(j) which do not meet the standards set forth in SCR 3.662 and which have not been submitted and accredited pursuant to SCR 3.665, or which are of such poor audio and video quality that participants cannot see or hear the content under reasonable circumstances.

(e) Home study or self-study which does not meet the standards set forth in SCR 3.662 and which has not been submitted and accredited pursuant to SCR 3.665.

(f) Bar review courses taken in preparation for bar examinations for admission to the highest court in a state or jurisdiction.

(g) Correspondence classes.

(h) Any activity completed prior to admission to practice in Kentucky except the program required pursuant to SCR 3.661(8) and 3.652(5).

(i) Undergraduate law or law-related classes.

(j) Programs taken in preparation for licensure exams for non-lawyer professionals.

(k) Business meetings or committee meetings of legal and law-related associations.

(3) Continuing legal education credit may be earned as set forth in Rule 3.663 for the following additional activities.

(a) Teaching or participating as a panel member or seminar leader in an approved activity. No credit may be earned for teaching or participating as a panel member or seminar leader for activities that do not meet standards set forth in Rule 3.662. A maximum of twelve and one-half (12.5) credits earned under this Rule per educational year may be applied to meet the annual minimum requirement.

(b) Researching, writing or editing material to be presented at an approved activity. No credit may be earned for researching, writing, or editing materials for activities that do not meet the standards set forth in Rule 3.662. A maximum of twelve and one-half (12.5) credits earned under this Rule per educational year may be applied to meet the annual minimum requirement.

(c) Publication of legal writing. A legal writing is a publication which contributes to the legal competency of the applicant, other attorneys or judges and is approved by the Commission. Writing for which the author is paid shall not be approved. A maximum of six (6.0) credits earned under this Rule per educational year may be applied to meet the annual minimum requirement.

(d) Public speaking. Upon application, by teaching or participating as a panel member, mock trial coach or seminar leader for law-related public service speeches to civic organizations or school groups. A maximum of two (2.0) credits earned under this Rule per educational year may be applied to meet the annual minimum requirement. Speaking for which the member is paid shall not be approved. Written copies of presentations must accompany such applications; provided, however, that, where appropriate, a narrative summary of the material presented may be sufficient.

(e) Seminars designed for non-lawyer professionals which in, case-by-case situations, will benefit the lawyer by allowing clients improved services in unique areas of practice. Credits earned for this category of seminar or activity shall not count toward the twelve and one-half (12.5) credit annual minimum requirement but may count toward continuing legal education award credits as determined by the Commission.

(4) Accreditation of activities may be withdrawn by the Commission in cases where there is evidence that any of the above standards and criteria have not been met or that circumstances surrounding the actual content or transmission of the activity are not as originally represented to the Commission during the application process such that withdrawal of accreditation is warranted.

HISTORY: Amended by Order 2012–01, eff. 3–1–12; prior amendments eff. 1–1–04 (Order 2003–4), 2–1–00 (Order 99–1), 3–1–98 (Order 97–3), 9–1–93 (Order 93–1), 8–1–92; adopted eff. 9–15–90

SCR 3.663 Calculation and reporting of continuing legal education credits: formulas and limits

Credits granted for continuing legal education activities vary depending on the nature of the activity. Credit will be granted, or is calculated, and in some instances limited, as set forth below.

(1) Members completing or participating in the course of study of an approved activity will be granted one (1) credit for each sixty (60) minutes of actual instructional time. Instructional time shall not include introductory remarks, breaks, or business meetings held in conjunction with a continuing legal education activity. For activities involving technologically transmitted programming, actual instructional time may be deemed inappropriate for assigning credit hours. In such circumstances credits claimed will be limited by the total assigned by the Commission. The Commission's assignment of credit hours for such activities will include consideration of the sponsor's estimates of average completion time, volume of material, opportunities for interaction, duration of program and other factors as deemed appropriate. No additional credit is given for completing or participating in duplicate activities at different times or locations. Duplicate completion of or participation in any course of study of any accredited activity shall not result in duplicate continuing legal education credits awarded. Continuing legal education credit shall be claimed on forms provided by the Association, or any uniform certificate adopted by the Association, and shall be forwarded to the Director.

(2) Members teaching or participating as panel members or seminar leaders in an approved activity will be granted one credit for each sixty (60) minutes of actual instructional time. Credit shall be claimed on forms provided by the Association, or any uniform certificate adopted by the Association, and shall be forwarded to the Director.

(3) Members may be granted preparation credit as follows:

(a) One (1) credit for each two (2) hours spent in preparation for teaching or participating as a panel member or seminar leader in an approved activity, up to a maximum of twelve and one-half (12.5) credits per educational year.

(b) One (1) credit for each two (2) hours spent researching, writing or editing material presented by another member at an approved continuing legal education activity, up to a maximum of twelve and one-half (12.5) credits per educational year.

(4) Credit for attending a law school class as set forth in Rule 3.662 shall equal twice the number of semester or credit hours awarded by the law school for successful completion of the course for credit or by audit. Actual instruction time shall not be used to determine continuing legal education credit for attending law school classes. Continuing legal education credit shall be claimed on forms provided by the Association, or any uniform certificate adopted by the Association, and shall be forwarded to the Director.

(5) Members may earn credits for publication of legal writing up to a maximum of six (6.0) credits per year. One (1) credit is granted for each two (2) hours of actual preparation time including research, writing, and editing. Any excess credits will be applied toward the award established in Rule 3.680. The Commission may grant up to twenty (20) credit hours for published legal writing toward the award, but may only grant up to six (6.0) credits to meet the annual minimum requirement. Applications for continuing legal education credit for a published legal writing shall be made on forms provided by the Association and shall be accompanied by a copy of the published legal writing for which credit is sought. Said application shall be forwarded to the Director.

(6) Members completing or participating in an accredited in-house activity will be granted credit as set forth in Rule 3.663(1). A maximum of six (6.0) credits may be applied to meet the minimum requirement set forth in Rule 3.661.

(7) Members completing or participating in an accredited technologically transmitted activity, as set forth in SCR 3.662(1)(j) will be granted credit as set forth in Rule 3.663(1). A maximum of six (6.0) credits may be applied to meet the minimum requirement set forth in Rule 3.661.

(8) The Commission shall grant a maximum of six (6.0) credits to meet the annual minimum requirement for any combination of credits earned pursuant to SCR 3.663(6) and (7).

(9) The Commission shall grant a maximum of two (2.0) credits to meet the annual minimum requirement

for public speaking credit earned pursuant to SCR 3.662(3)(d).

HISTORY: Amended by Order 2012–01, eff. 3–1–12; prior amendments eff. 2–1–00 (Order 99–1), 3–1–98 (Order 97–3), 7–1–95 (Order 95–1), 8–1–92, 11–15–91; adopted eff. 9–15–90

SCR 3.664 Procedure for accreditation of sponsors and obligations of accredited sponsors— Deleted

HISTORY: Deleted by Order 96–1, eff. 1–1–97; prior amendments eff. 9–1–93, 8–1–92; adopted eff. 9–15–90

SCR 3.665 Procedure for accreditation of continuing legal education activities and obligations of sponsors

(1) Educational activities may be approved for credit upon application to the Commission. Application for accreditation may be made by a member or former member without involving the sponsor, or application for accreditation may be made by an activity sponsor. Application for accreditation shall be made to the Director not less than thirty (30) days in advance of the scheduled date of the activity. Sponsors failing to submit the application for accreditation as set forth in this rule shall result in an application fee double the amount set forth in Rule 3.665(2)(a)–(c). It is the obligation of the attorney seeking credit to ensure the activity has been approved. Completion of a non-accredited activity shall be at the risk of the attorney.

(2) Application for accreditation of continuing legal education activities shall be made by members, former members or activity sponsors using forms provided by the Association or using uniform applications adopted by the Association. Applications must provide all information required by the form in order to be reviewed. All applications shall be accompanied by the appropriate application fee as follows:

(a) Applications submitted by sponsors for activities greater than two hours in length–$50.00 per activity. Activities repeated on different dates or at different locations are separate activities and require separate applications and separate fees.

(b) Applications submitted by sponsors for activities two hours or less in length–$20.00 per activity. Activities repeated on different dates or at different locations are separate activities and require separate applications and separate fees.

(c) Applications submitted by members or former members, regardless of length of activity–$20.00. Each separate activity submitted for accreditation is a separate application requiring a separate fee.

(3) To receive accreditation the application must include evidence that the activity for which accreditation is sought will meet the standards set forth in Rule 3.662.

(4) Activity sponsors which apply for accreditation and receive approval prior to the activity may announce in advertising materials, "This activity has been approved by the Kentucky Bar Association Continuing Legal Education Commission for a maximum of XX.XX credits, including XX.XX ethics credits." Sponsors who have made application for accreditation of activities that have not yet been approved may announce in advertising materials, "Application for approval of this activity for a maximum of XX.XX credits, including XX.XX ethics credits, is PENDING before the Kentucky Bar Association Continuing Legal Education Commission." Sponsors may not advertise accreditation if accreditation has not been granted by the Commission and notice of such accreditation received by the sponsor.

(5) Technologically transmitted activities produced from live programs or studio productions must be accredited separately from the live or studio activity from which they are produced and applications for accreditation must include a copy of the tape or other instructions for prior access to the activity by the Commission for evaluation purposes in addition to other information as required by the application provided by the Association.

(6) Sponsors of accredited activities shall comply with the obligations and requirements set forth below.

(a) Ensure that all education activities comply with Rule 3.662.

(b) Permit Commission members and staff or one designee to monitor without payment of registration or other fees, any approved activity.

(c) Utilize the activity code provided by the Kentucky Bar Association in its notification of accreditation in identifying the activity in all correspondence regarding the activity and provide the activity code to members for use in reporting their credits.

(d) Provide to each Kentucky attorney completing an approved activity an Association approved credit reporting form and activity code. Credit reporting forms and activity numbers shall be made available to sponsors upon request from the Association for use at approved activities.

(e) Collect credit reporting forms from Kentucky attorneys and submit to the Commission all forms received within thirty (30) days of completion of the program. Failure to submit completed credit reporting forms within thirty (30) days of the activity shall be accompanied by a late filing fee from the sponsor of ten dollars ($10.00) per form or certificate. Submit all attendance forms or certificates for activities held during the month of June no later than July 10th, immediately following the end of the educational year on June 30th. For programs held during June this provision of the rule supersedes the thirty (30) day submission provided above. Failure to submit forms or certificates pursuant to this schedule will result in the sponsor's obligation to pay a late filing fee of ten dollars ($10.00) perform or certificate.

(f) Sponsors may submit member activity certifications to the Director as required by SCR 3.661(2), via electronic means so long as the sponsor maintains the member's original certification, or copy thereof, of the completion of the activity on file for two (2) subsequent educational years following the year in which the activity was completed.

HISTORY: Amended by Order 2012–01, eff. 3–1–12; prior amendments eff. 1–1–06 (Order 2005–10), 1–1–04 (Order 2003–4), 2–1–00 (Order 99–1), 3–1–98 (Order 97–3), 1–1–97 (Order 96–1), 9–1–93, 8–1–92, 11–15–91; adopted eff. 9–15–90

SCR 3.666 Exemptions and removal of exemptions

(1) With respect to each educational year, the following members of the Association shall be exempt from the requirements of Rule 3.661:

(a) Members who, during any portion of that educational year, are serving as Justices or Judges of the Kentucky Court of Justice or Justices, Judges, or Magistrates of the Court of the United States, or full-time administrative law judges for an agency of the United States or Commonwealth of Kentucky executive branch, and because of such positions are prohibited from practicing law and have significant continuing education requirements by statute or rule of court as a result of the position they hold.

(b) New lawyers who have been admitted less than one full educational year as of the June 30th deadline. Such members shall be subject to the provisions of SCR 3.652.

(c) Members who are at least 75 years of age or at least 50 year members, including members who will become 75 years of age and those who become 50 year members within the educational year.

(2) Upon application to the Commission, the following members may be exempted from the requirements of Rule 3.661:

(a) Members who do not practice law, as defined in Rule 3.020, within the Commonwealth and agree to refrain from such practice until the Commission approves an application for removal of the exemption.

(b) Members who practice law within the Commonwealth, but demonstrate that meeting the requirements of Rule 3.661 would work an undue hardship by reason of disability, sickness, or other clearly mitigating circumstances.

(c) Members required to complete the New Lawyer Program following procedures set forth in SCR 3.652(7).

(d) Any member who, for any portion of an educational year, was on active duty in the United States armed forces.

(3) Every member seeking an exemption from the mandatory continuing legal education requirement of Rule 3.661 pursuant to Rule 3.666(2) shall submit an application on forms provided by the Association or shall make other such written request providing information necessary for determination by the Commission of circumstances warranting exemption.

(4) Exemptions granted pursuant to Rule 3.666(2)(a) shall not be effective retroactively unless the applicant certifies that he or she has not practiced law, as defined in Rule 3.020, within the Commonwealth, for all time periods covered by such exemption. Members shall not practice law as defined in Rule 3.020 while said exemption is in effect. Practice of law as defined in Rule 3.020, within the Commonwealth, during the effective period of an exemption pursuant to Rule 3.666(2)(a) shall constitute unauthorized practice. Information known by the Commission regarding the practice of law during any period for which a member has certified non-practice status pursuant to SCR 3.666(2)(a) and SCR 3.666(3) is not confidential as provided at SCR 3.690 and shall be provided along with the member's continuing legal education transcript by the Director to the Office of Bar Counsel and the Inquiry Commission in writing.

(5) Exemptions granted pursuant to Rule 3.666(2)(b) and SCR 3.666(2)(d) based on hardship including military service are considered temporary in nature unless specifically designated otherwise. In order to maintain an exemption based on a temporary hardship, including an exemption based on military service, annual application is necessary. Failure to so certify will result in loss of the exempt status.

(6) A member seeking removal of a non-practice exemption granted pursuant to Rule 3.666(2)(a) shall be required to file a written application with the Commission, addressed to the Director, for the removal of said exemption. Required as attachment to the application for removal of said exemption shall be certification of completion of sufficient continuing legal education credits to meet the minimum annual continuing legal education requirement for each educational year during which he or she was exempt, excluding the current educational year. The member shall be notified in writing, via certified mail, of the Commission's action on the application for the removal of the exemption. In no case shall a member be required to certify completion of more than twenty-five (25) credits, including applicable ethics credits, as a condition of removal of the exemption. Timely certification shall include only continuing legal education credits earned during the current educational year and two prior educational years. This Rule in no way affects the member's responsibility to complete the current year minimum annual education requirement by June 30th. The current year minimum educational requirement must be completed as set forth at SCR 3.661.

(7) Application for removal of an exemption as provided in SCR 3.666(6) shall be made by completion of forms provided by the Association. The application shall include certification of completion of such continuing legal education activities as required by these rules, including SCR 3.661(3), SCR 3.662, SCR 3.663, SCR 3.665, or as otherwise specified by the Commission.

(8) The Commission shall approve the application for removal of a non-practice exemption if it appears that the member has satisfied the requirements of this Rule.

(9) Application for removal of an exemption granted pursuant to SCR 3.666(2)(a) may not be made within thirty (30) days of the granting of the exemption.

HISTORY: Amended by Order 2012–01, eff. 3–1–12; prior amendments eff. 1–1–07 (Order 2006–09), 1–1–06 (Order 2005–10), 3–1–98 (Order 97–3), 7–1–95 (Order 95–1), 9–1–93, 8–1–92, 11–15–91, 9–15–90, 1–1–89, 1–1–88, 10–29–85, 6–25–85; adopted eff. 7–1–84

SCR 3.667   Extension of time requirements

(1) The time requirements associated with completion of continuing legal education and certification thereof, as set forth in Rule 3.661(1) and (8), may be extended by the Commission in case of hardship or other good cause clearly warranting relief. Requests for time extensions for completion of activities or certification thereof shall be made to the Commission in writing. All requests for time extension must be received by the Commission no later than the September 10th following the end of the educational year for which the time extension is sought. Requests must set forth all circumstances upon which the request is based, including supporting documentation. Applications for time extensions for completion of the New Lawyer Program may be submitted pursuant to SCR 3.652(8).

(2) A member who fails to complete the requirements of Rule 3.661 for any educational year, and who cannot show hardship or other good cause clearly warranting relief, may submit a plan for making up his or her delinquency, provided that the Commission has not approved such a plan for the member for either of the two preceding educational years. The plan must be received by the Commission no later than the September 10th immediately following the end of the educational year for which the time extension is sought. The plan will be approved only if the member pays a filing fee of two hundred fifty dollars ($250.00) and the plan lists activities which would provide, by the September 10th immediately following the end of the educational year, the credit hours needed to make up the deficiency. Such plan shall be deemed accepted by the Commission unless within fifteen (15) days after receipt of the compliance plan and filing fee, the Commission notifies the applicant to the contrary.

(3) Failure to comply with extended time requirements granted by the Commission pursuant to Rule 3.667(1) or (2), including both completion of continuing legal education activities and certification thereof, shall subject the member to the sanctions of Rule 3.669: Suspension for Non–Compliance.

HISTORY: Amended by Order 2012–01, eff. 3–1–12; prior amendments eff. 9–1–93 (Order 93–1), 8–1–92, 11–15–91; adopted eff. 9–15–90

SCR 3.668   Non-compliance, definition

(1) Delinquency of Certification. Any certification of continuing legal education activity for an educational year (July 1–June 30) which is submitted after the August 10th immediately following the close of that educational year, shall be deemed past due and in non-compliance. All past due reports shall be accompanied by a late filing fee of fifty dollars ($50.00) per certificate or report to cover the administrative costs of recording credits to the prior year. All past due reports for completion of an activity in the immediately preceding educational year must be received by the Commission with the late fee of fifty dollars ($50.00) per certificate or report no later than the close of the current educational year (June 30). Past due reports shall be accepted only until the end of the educational year (June 30) immediately following the year during which the activity is completed. This deadline (June 30) will not apply in instances where the member or former member is in the process of removing an exemption per SCR 3.666(6) or attempting certification per SCR 3.675, but the late fee of fifty dollars ($50.00) per certificate or report shall be applied if the report is received after the August 10th reporting deadline described above.

(2) Delinquency of Credits. Failure to acquire a minimum of twelve and one-half (12.5) credits to meet the minimum continuing legal education requirements of Rule 3.661 and associated certification requirements shall be grounds for suspension by the Court from the practice of law.

HISTORY: Amended by Order 2012–01, eff. 3–1–12; prior amendments eff. 1–1–07 (Order 2006–09), 1–1–97 (Order 96–1), 9–15–90, 1–1–88, 6–25–85; adopted eff. 7–1–84

SCR 3.669   Non-compliance: procedure and sanctions

(1) As soon as practicable after August 20th of each year, the Commission shall notify a member in writing of existing delinquencies of record. The writing may consist of a computer generated form setting forth said delinquency. If any statement incorrectly reflects the continuing legal education status of the member it shall be the duty of the member to promptly notify the Commission of any claimed discrepancy in the education statement.

(2) If, by the first day of November immediately following, a member has neither certified completion by the June 30th immediately prior, of the minimum continuing legal education requirements set forth in Rule 3.661, nor applied for and satisfied the conditions of an extension under Rule 3.667 or exemption under Rule 3.666, the Commission shall certify the name of that member to the Board.

(3) The Board shall cause to be sent to the member a notice of delinquency by certified mail, return receipt requested, at the member's bar roster address. Such notice shall require the attorney to show cause

within thirty (30) days from the date of the mailing why the attorney's license should not be suspended for failure to meet the mandatory minimum CLE requirements of SCR 3.661. Such response shall be in writing, sent to the attention of the Director for CLE, and shall be accompanied by costs in the amount of fifty dollars ($50.00) payable to the Kentucky Bar Association.

(4) Unless good cause is shown by the return date of the rule, or within such additional time as may be allowed by the Board, the lawyer will be stricken from the membership roster as an active member of the KBA and will be suspended from the practice of law or will be otherwise sanctioned as deemed appropriate by the Board. A copy of the suspension notice shall be delivered by the Director to the member, the Clerk of the Kentucky Supreme Court, the Director of Membership, and to the Circuit Clerk of the district wherein the member resides for recording and indexing as required by Rule 3.480.

(5) A member suspended under this Rule may apply for restoration to membership under the provisions of Rule 3.500.

(6) A member may appeal to the Kentucky Supreme Court from such suspension order within thirty (30) days of the effective date of the suspension. Such appeal shall include an affidavit showing good cause why the suspension should be set aside.

HISTORY: Amended by Order 2012–01, eff. 3–1–12; prior amendments eff. 2–1–00 (Order 99–1), 1–1–97 (Order 96–1), 9–1–93, 8–1–92, 9–15–90, 1–1–88, 1–1–86; adopted eff. 7–1–84

SCR 3.670   Appeal of commission actions

(1) The Commission shall state the reason or reasons for any adverse Commission decision and shall notify the person or organization affected.

(2) Any person or organization may request in writing reconsideration of an adverse decision within fifteen (15) days of the notice of the decision. The Commission shall consider any pertinent material submitted and shall permit the aggrieved party the opportunity to appear at a meeting of the Commission for oral presentation of information to be considered.

(3) Any person or organization may appeal to the Board from an adverse decision of the Commission by filing a written notice in the Office of the Director within thirty (30) days of the notice of the decision or of a refusal to reconsider a decision. The review of the Board shall be limited to the record considered by the Commission. The entire record, including a transcript of Commission proceedings, shall be submitted to the Board, with costs born by the unsuccessful party.

(4) Any person or organization may appeal to the Supreme Court of Kentucky from an adverse decision of the Board by filing a written petition, together with ten (10) copies, in the office of the Clerk of the Court, accompanied by a certificate of service on the Director

and a filing fee of $100.00, within thirty (30) days of the notice of the decision. The review of the Court shall be limited to the record considered by the Commission and the Board.

(5) Commission certification of non-compliance filed with the Supreme Court pursuant to SCR 3.652 (9) or SCR 3.669 may not be appealed under Sections (3) and (4) of this Rule.

HISTORY: Amended by Order 2012–01, eff. 3–1–12; prior amendment eff. 8–1–92 (Order 92–1); adopted eff. 9–15–90

SCR 3.675   Continuing legal education requirements for restoration or reinstatement to membership: procedures

(1) Every former member, applying for or otherwise seeking restoration or reinstatement to membership pursuant to Rules 3.500 or 3.510, shall be required to have completed the minimum annual continuing legal education requirement for each year during which he or she was not a member in good standing, including any year prior to disbarment, suspension or withdrawal under threat of disbarment or suspension, during which the minimum annual continuing legal education requirement was not fulfilled. Completion of such credits shall be certified to the Commission as a condition precedent to reinstatement or restoration. In no case shall a member be required to attend more than sixty-two and one-half (62.5) continuing legal education credits, including applicable ethics credits, as a condition precedent of restoration or reinstatement to membership.

(2) The application or affidavit of compliance submitted for restoration or reinstatement shall include certification from the Director for CLE of completion of continuing legal education activities as required by these Rules, or otherwise specified by the Commission or Court. Applicants or affiants shall request said certification from the Director for CLE in writing and shall submit with said written request a fee of fifty dollars ($50.00) to cover the expense of the record search and certification. Applications or affidavits of compliance submitted for restoration or reinstatement which do not include the required certification of continuing legal education credits, including verification of fee payment for the certification, shall be considered incomplete and shall not be processed.

(3) The requirements for completion of continuing legal education as a condition to restoration or reinstatement as set forth above may only be satisfied with credits earned in the current educational year during which the application is submitted and the preceding two educational years. Credits so earned shall be applicable to requirements imposed by the Commission upon application or other actions undertaken in pursuit of restoration or reinstatement.

(4) The Commission shall approve such applications if it appears that the former member has satisfied the requirements of this Rule.

(5) Approval of the application or provision of a certification for an affidavit of compliance shall satisfy the requirement of the applicant under Rule 3.661 for the current educational year.

(6) In the event that a new educational year begins after approval of the application or certification for an affidavit of compliance by the Commission, but prior to Supreme Court entry of an Order of Reinstatement or Restoration, or Registrar's certification of member's name to the active roster of membership the new year minimum continuing legal education requirement must be completed and the application updated before the reinstatement or restoration can proceed to the Board of Governors or to the Court, unless a maximum of sixty-two and one-half (62.5) credits has been completed.

HISTORY: Amended by Order 2012–01, eff. 3–1–12; prior amendments eff. 1–1–06 (Order 2005–10), 1–1–04 (Order 2003–4), 1–1–02 (Order 2001–2), 7–1–95 (Order 95–1), 8–1–92, 11–15–91; adopted eff. 9–15–90

SCR 3.680   Continuing legal education award

(1) Any member who completes a minimum of sixty-two and one-half (62.5) credit hours approved by the Commission within a period of three or fewer educational years, is eligible for a Continuing Legal Education Award which shall consist of a dignified certificate issued by the Association attesting to the educational accomplishment.

(2) The Commission shall notify the member and issue the award.

(3) Approved awards are valid for one year, beginning on the first day of July of the year of application award notification.

(4) The validity of an award may be renewed for an additional year following the initial awards date, in which the member who holds the award completes a minimum of twenty (20) approved credit.

(5) Failure to earn twenty (20) credits in any educational year following the initial award date shall disqualify the member from further renewals of that award. The member may only become eligible for another award by earning sixty-two and one-half (62.5) approved credit hours in a period separate and distinct from the period for which a prior award was issued.

(6) Each member who holds a valid, unexpired award shall receive a 25% discount from the normal registration fee for the Kentucky Bar Association Annual Convention.

(7) Application for renewal of a Continuing Legal Education Award shall be made by members following the same procedure required for initial award application pursuant to this Rule.

(8) Each member who holds a valid, unexpired award shall receive a 25% discount from the normal registration fee for the Kentucky Bar Association Annual Convention.

HISTORY: Amended by Order 2012–01, eff. 3–1–12; prior amendment eff. 7–1–95 (Order 95–1); adopted eff. 9–15–90

SCR 3.685   Annual publication of educational achievement

The Association may publish annually in leading daily newspapers of general circulation throughout the Commonwealth an announcement of the members who during the preceding educational year have earned the Continuing Legal Education Award. The announcement shall describe the basis of the award and shall set forth in alphabetical order the name and geographical location of each recipient. A similar annual announcement may be included in the Kentucky *Bench and Bar*.

HISTORY: Adopted by Order 90–1, eff. 9–15–90

SCR 3.690   Commission records confidential

The files and records of the Commission shall be deemed confidential and shall not be disclosed except in furtherance of the duties of the Commission, as set forth at SCR 3.650, or of the Board, or upon request of the member affected, or as directed by the Supreme Court of Kentucky. This rule specifically excludes from confidentiality information provided by a member to the Commission as a part of a member's application for relief from the requirements of these rules.

HISTORY: Amended by Order 2000–1, eff. 2–1–01; prior amendment eff. 11–15–91 (Order 91–2); adopted eff. 9–15–90

SCR 3.695   Continuing legal education appeals— Withdrawn

HISTORY: Withdrawn by Order 90–1, eff. 9–15–90; adopted eff. 1–1–88

SCR 3.700   Provisions relating to paralegals

PRELIMINARY STATEMENT: The availability of legal services to the public at a price it can afford is a goal to which the Bar is committed, and one which finds support in Canons 2 and 8 of the Code of Professional Responsibility. The employment of paralegals furnishes a means by which lawyers may expand the public's opportunity for utilization of their services at a reduced cost.

For purposes of this rule, a paralegal is a person under the supervision and direction of a licensed lawyer, who may apply knowledge of law and legal procedures in rendering direct assistance to lawyers engaged in legal research; design, develop or plan modifications or new procedures, techniques, services, processes or applications; prepare or interpret legal documents and write detailed procedures for practicing in certain fields of law; select, compile and use technical information from such references as digests, encyclopedias or practice manuals; and analyze and follow procedural problems that involve independent decisions.

PURPOSE: Rapid growth in the employment of paralegals increases the desirability and necessity of establishing guidelines for the utilization of paralegals by the legal community. This rule is not intended to stifle the proper development and expansion of paralegal services, but to provide guidance and ensure growth in accordance with the Code of Professional Responsibility, statutes, court rules and decisions, rules and regulations of administrative agencies, and opinions rendered by committees on professional ethics and unauthorized practice of law.

While the responsibility for compliance with standards of professional conduct rests with members of the Bar, a paralegal should understand those standards. It is, therefore, incumbent upon the lawyer employing a paralegal to inform him of the restraints and responsibilities incident to the job and supervise the manner in which the work is completed. However, the paralegal does have an independent obligation to refrain from illegal conduct. Additionally, and notwithstanding the fact that the Code of Professional Responsibility is not binding upon lay persons, the very nature of a paralegal's employment imposes an obligation to refrain from conduct which would involve the lawyer in a violation of the Code.

SUB–RULE 1

A lawyer shall ensure that a paralegal in his employment does not engage in the unauthorized practice of law.

SUB–RULE 2

For purposes of this rule, the unauthorized practice of law shall not include any service rendered involving legal knowledge or legal advice, whether representation, counsel or advocacy, in or out of court, rendered in respect to the acts, duties, obligations, liabilities or business relations of the one requiring services where:

A. The client understands that the paralegal is not a lawyer;

B. The lawyer supervises the paralegal in the performance of his duties; and

C. The lawyer remains fully responsible for such representation, including all actions taken or not taken in connection therewith by the paralegal to the same extent as if such representation had been furnished entirely by the lawyer and all such actions had been taken or not taken directly by the lawyer.

D. The services rendered under this Rule shall not include appearing formally in any court or administrative tribunal except under Sub-rule 3 below, nor shall it include questioning of witnesses, parties or other persons appearing in any legal or administrative action including but not limited to depositions, trials, and hearings.

SUB–RULE 3

For purposes of this Rule 3.700, the unauthorized practice of law shall not include representation before any administrative tribunal or court where such service or representation is rendered pursuant to a court rule or decision which authorizes such practice by nonlawyers.

SUB–RULE 4

A lawyer shall instruct a paralegal employee to preserve the confidences and secrets of a client and shall exercise care that the paralegal does so.

SUB–RULE 5

A lawyer shall not form a partnership with a paralegal if any part of the partnership's activities consists of the practice of law, nor shall a lawyer share on a proportionate basis, legal fees with a paralegal.

SUB–RULE 6

The letterhead of a lawyer may include the name of a paralegal where the paralegal's status is clearly indicated: A lawyer may permit his name to be included in a paralegal's business card, provided that the paralegal's status is clearly indicated.

SUB–RULE 7

A lawyer shall require a paralegal, when dealing with a client, to disclose at the outset that he is not a lawyer. A lawyer shall also require such a disclosure when the paralegal is dealing with a court, administrative agency, attorney or the public, if there is any reason for their believing that the paralegal is a lawyer or is associated with a lawyer.

HISTORY: Amended by Order 89–1, eff. 8–28–89; prior amendment eff. 1–8–81; adopted eff. 1–1–80

Supreme Court Commentary

1979:

Sub-rule 1

The Kentucky Constitution, Section 109, creates one Court of Justice for the Commonwealth. Section 116 empowers the Kentucky Supreme Court to promulgate rules of practice and procedure for the Court of Justice. In addition, the Supreme Court has statutory authority to govern the conduct and activity of members of the Bar. KRS 21A.160.

Pursuant to constitutional and statutory authority, the Kentucky Supreme Court has adopted rules which govern the unauthorized practice of law. SCR 3.020 defines the practice of law in general and descriptive terms. SCR 3.470 provides that any attorney who aids another in the unauthorized practice of law shall be guilty of unprofessional conduct. SCR 3.460 delineates the procedure to be followed when a person or entity "not having the right to practice law" engages in the practice of law.

As of January 1, 1978, the American Bar Association Code of Professional Responsibility was accepted as a sound statement of professional conduct for members of the Kentucky Bar Association, with the exception of provisions which conflict with *Bates v. State Bar of Arizona.* SCR 3.130.

Canon 3 of the Code of Professional Responsibility provides that "A lawyer should assist in preventing the unauthorized practice of law." Further, "A lawyer shall not aid a non-lawyer in the unauthorized practice of law." DR 3–101(A). The rationale of this sub-rule may be found in EC 3–1 through EC 3–6 of the Code of Professional Responsibility.

The foregoing authorities demonstrate that paralegals cannot, any more than any other person or entity, engage in the unauthorized practice of law. Members of the Bar who employ paralegals incur a professional responsibility to ensure that their paralegal employees do not transgress the rules governing the practice of law contained in these authorities and thereby involve their employers in violations of their own professional responsibilities. A lawyer may, however, allow a paralegal to perform services involving the practice of law, provided that such services comply with the requirements of Sub-rule 2 and Sub-rule 3.

Sub-rule 2

The Code of Professional Responsibility, in particular EC 3–6, recognizes the value of utilizing the services of paralegals under certain conditions:

"A lawyer often delegates tasks to clerks, secretaries, and other lay persons. Such delegation is proper if the lawyer maintains a direct relationship with his client, supervises the delegated work, and has complete professional responsibility for the work product. This delegation enables a lawyer to render legal services more economically and efficiently."

Maintaining a "direct relationship" with the client does not preclude a paralegal from meeting with the client nor does it mandate regular and frequent meetings between the lawyer and client. However, when it appears that consultation between the lawyer and the client is necessary, the lawyer should talk directly to the client.

Sub-rule 3

Notwithstanding the restrictions imposed upon nonlawyers with respect to engaging in the practice of law, exceptions exist by virtue of statute, administrative rule or regulation, or court rule or decision. Under certain circumstances, lay representation of parties does not constitute the unauthorized practice of law. For example, the Federal Administrative Procedure Act, Title 5, U.S.C. Section 555(b) authorizes federal administrative agencies to permit nonlawyers to represent parties in proceedings before the agencies. Such lay representation is also provided for in statutes and regulations governing administrative proceedings involving the Public Assistance (AFDC), Medicaid, and Food Stamp Programs. See, 42 U.S.C. Section 601, Section 602 (1977); 42 U.S.C. Section 1396 (1977); 7 U.S.C. Section 2019 (1977); and the implementing regulations, 45 C.F.R. Section 205.10(a), and 7 C.F.R. Section 271.1(a)(1) (1977).

The Kentucky Department for Human Resources has implemented these federal regulations. Lay representation is specifically provided for in regulations governing hearings and appeals in certain programs. 904 KAR 2:055, Section 1–12.

The United States Supreme Court has held that federal law controls the administration of federal grant-in-aid programs. See, King v. Smith, 392 U.S. 309, 332–333 (1968); Rosado v. Wyman, U.S. 397, 421–422 (1970). Additionally, the court has held that in federally regulated areas, federal statutes and regulations prevail over a state's power to define and regulate the practice of law. See, Sperry v. Florida, 373 U.S. 379, 385 (1963); and Keller v. State Bar of Wisconsin, 374 U.S. 102 (1963), citing Sperry.

Sub-rule 4

This sub-rule reiterates the Code of Professional Responsibility. Canon 4, DR 4–101(D) provides in part that:

"(D) A lawyer shall exercise reasonable care to prevent his employees, associates, and others whose services are utilized by him from disclosing or using confidences or secrets of a client...."

This obligation is emphasized in EC 4–2 under Canon 4:

"... It is a matter of common knowledge that the normal operation of a law office exposes confidential professional information to non-lawyer employees of the office, particularly secretaries and those having access to the files; and this obligates a lawyer to exercise care in selecting and training his employees so that the sanctity of all confidences and secrets of his clients may be preserved."

Sub-rule 5

This sub-rule is based on the express provisions of DR 3–102(A) and DR 3–103(A) of the Code of Professional Responsibility. In accordance with these provisions, the compensation of a paralegal

may not include a percentage of the fees received by his employer, or any remuneration, directly or indirectly, for referring matters of a legal nature to the employer.

DR 3–103(A) provides that: "A lawyer shall not form a partnership with a non-lawyer if any of the activities of the partnership consist of the practice of law." The rationale is found in EC 3–8: "Since a lawyer should not aid or encourage a layman to practice law, he should not practice law in association with a layman...." However, "A lawyer or law firm may include non-lawyer employees in a retirement plan, even though the plan is based in whole or in part on a profit-sharing arrangement." DR 3–102(A)(3).

This Disciplinary Rule also reflects the rationale of EC 3–8:

"Since a lawyer should not aid or encourage a layman to practice law, he should not... share legal fees with a layman."

"Profit-sharing retirement plans of a lawyer or law firm which include non-lawyer office employees are not improper. These limited exceptions to the rule against sharing legal fees with laymen are permissible since they do not aid or encourage laymen to practice law."

Sub-rule 6

The Code of Professional Responsibility, in particular DR 2–102(A)(4), provides direction concerning the information which may be provided on a lawyer's letterhead. In keeping with the spirit of DR 2–102(A)(4), paralegals may be listed on the letterhead if there is a clear indication of their status, i.e., they are not lawyers. These names should properly be listed under the separate heading of "Paralegals."

A paralegal may have a business card with the lawyer's name or law firm's name on it, provided the status of the paralegal is clearly indicated. It is not necessary that any lawyer's name appear on such business card. The card is designed to identify the paralegal and to state by whom the paralegal is employed. The business card of a paralegal shall be approved, in form and substance, by the lawyer-employer.

Sub-rule 7

A lawyer should instruct a paralegal employee to disclose at the beginning of any dealings with a client that he is not an attorney. Whenever any person dealing with a paralegal has reason to believe that the paralegal is a lawyer or associated with a lawyer, the paralegal shall make clear that he is not a lawyer. Even if a paralegal appears before an administrative agency or court in which a lay person is entitled to represent a party, the paralegal should nevertheless disclose his status to the tribunal. Routine early disclosure of nonlawyer status is necessary to ensure that there will be no misunderstanding as to the responsibilities and role of the paralegal. Disclosure may be made in any way that avoids confusion. Common sense suggests a routine disclosure at the outset of communication.

If a paralegal is designated as the individual in the office of a lawyer or law firm who should be contacted, disclosure of his or her nonlawyer status should be made at the time of such designation.

SCR 3.800   Legal negligence arbitration

(1) Purpose.

The purpose of this Rule 3.800 is to establish a procedure whereby claims of legal negligence in the amount of fifty thousand dollars ($50,000.00) or less arising from attorney and client relationships may be resolved by submission to binding arbitration.

(2) Definitions.

(A) "Attorney" means an attorney-at-law who is a member in good standing of the Association, or an attorney admitted to practice pursuant to SCR 3.030 when the dispute arises from that representation.

(B) "Association" means the Kentucky Bar Association.

(C) "Director" means the Director of the Kentucky Bar Association.

(D) "Dispute" shall mean any claim of legal negligence in the amount of fifty thousand dollars ($50,000.00) or less. This includes a matter that is the subject of a diversion pursuant to SCR 3.160(3), or a matter referred for negligence arbitration by the Court.

(E) "Amount in Controversy" means the amount of direct loss claimed as a result of the claimed negligence of an attorney.

(F) "Panel" means the arbitrator or arbitrators appointed to arbitrate a claim of legal negligence.

(3) Scope of Authority.

(A) The Rules and Procedures herein shall be available to resolve any dispute as herein defined only when the amount in controversy exceeds the jurisdictional maximum specified in KRS 24A.230 and all parties to the dispute agree in writing to submit the claim of negligence to the arbitration procedures herein and further, agree in writing that they shall be fully bound by the decision and award of the Panel.

(B) These Rules shall not be used unless the parties to the dispute certify in writing that a good faith effort has been made by them to resolve the dispute.

(C) These Rules shall not be used if the dispute is the subject matter of a pending lawsuit, unless the parties follow the procedures of KRS 417.060(4).

(D) Except as otherwise provided herein, the substantive law of the Commonwealth of Kentucky will apply to any dispute arbitrated under this plan.

(4) Institution of Proceedings.

(A) Proceedings hereunder shall be begun by the filing of a petition with the Association. The signed petition shall state the origin and details of the dispute, the acts or omissions deemed to be negligent, and the amount claimed due as a result of the negligence alleged. The petitioner shall also sign an arbitration agreement. The petition and arbitration agreement shall be on forms provided by the Association.

(B) Upon the filing of the petition, the Director shall determine whether it presents a dispute under these Rules. The decision of the Director on that matter shall be final. The Director shall have full power to require additional information from the petitioner as is deemed necessary.

(C) If the Director determines that the Association shall not accept jurisdiction, the petition shall be returned to the petitioner indicating why the Association has not accepted jurisdiction and will not arbitrate the matter.

(D) If the Director determines that the Association shall accept jurisdiction, a copy of the petition and the arbitration agreement signed by the petitioner shall be forwarded to the other party to the dispute to sign and return to the Director with the answer to the petition. Twenty (20) days shall be allowed in which to answer unless additional time is requested. Upon receipt of the answer, the Director shall forward to the petitioner a signed copy of the arbitration agreement and the answer submitted by the other party to the dispute.

(E) If the other party to the dispute refuses to submit to arbitration, or fails to sign and return the arbitration agreement and answer within the time allowed, the Director shall so notify the petitioner, and the file of the Association shall be closed.

(F) If the dispute is referred to arbitration as referenced in 2(D) above, then sections 4(B) and (C) of this rule are not applicable. The attorney involved in the dispute shall be deemed the petitioner and shall file a petition with the Director.

(G) Upon the filing of a petition with the Association, any applicable statute of limitations is tolled until dismissal or final award is entered.

(5) Arbitration Panel.

(A) Composition.

(i) Where the amount in controversy is ten thousand dollars ($10,000.00) or less, the Panel shall consist of one (1) practicing attorney.

(ii) Where the amount in controversy exceeds ten thousand dollars ($10,000.00), but is not in excess of fifty thousand dollars ($50,000.00), the Panel shall consist of three (3) practicing attorneys.

(iii) The practicing attorneys referred to in paragraph (5)(A)(i) and (5)(A)(ii) above shall each:

(a) be a member in good standing of the Association;

(b) be appointed for a particular dispute by the Director;

(c) if engaged in the private practice of law, maintain an office and carry on such practice within a reasonable proximity to the county in which the petitioner resides.

(iv) Any attorney appointed by the Director may refuse to serve. Such refusal shall be by written notice to the Director within ten (10) days of the appointment.

(v) The Director, in cases of a three-member Panel, shall designate one member of the Panel as Chair of the Panel.

(B) Objections.

Either party to the dispute may object for cause to any of the Panel members. Such objection shall be in writing and shall be made within twenty (20) days of written notification of the composition of the Panel. Failure to object within twenty (20) days shall constitute a waiver of any objection to the composition of the Panel.

Objections to Panel members shall be made to the Director and shall be determined in accordance with KRS 26A.015 et seq. The decision of the Director shall be final.

(C) Compensation.

The Panel shall not be compensated for its services. Reasonable transportation costs may be reimbursed.

(D) Vacancies.

If any arbitrator should be unable to act, the Director shall declare the office vacant and, if the matter has already been heard by the Panel, it shall not be reheard if the remaining members concur in the Award. If the sole member of the Panel is unable to act or the remaining members of the Panel do not concur in the Award, a new member shall be selected and the matter will be reheard. If the Panel has not yet heard the matter a new arbitration Panel member shall be selected in accordance with these Rules.

(E) Communication Between the Parties and Panel Members.

There shall be no ex parte communication between the parties and the Panel upon the subject matter of the arbitration other than at arbitration proceedings, or in documents filed with the Association as part of the proceedings. This limitation does not apply to administrative communications between the Panel and the parties regarding the scheduling of the hearing.

(6) Hearings.

(A) Location.

Hearings shall be held in a county that reasonably limits the travel required by the parties to attend the hearing.

(B) Notice.

The Chair of the Panel shall fix the time and cause written notice of time and place to be served upon all parties to the dispute by Certified Mail not fewer than ten (10) days prior to the time set for the hearing. Such notice of hearing shall also inform the parties of their right to be represented by an attorney and their right to present evidence in support of their respective positions.

(C) Stenographic Record.

(i) Any party may have a hearing before a Panel reported by a Certified Shorthand Reporter at the expense of the requesting party by written notice presented to the Panel Chair at least seven (7) days prior to the date of the hearing. Any other party to the arbitration shall be entitled to acquire, at their own expense, a copy of the reporter's transcript of the testimony by arrangements made directly with the reporter.

(ii) In the event the Panel determines it appropriate or necessary to record the hearing, it may be recorded by digital or video means with costs being assessed as the Panel deems just. A party to the dispute, at its own expense, may request a copy of the record so recorded.

(D) Production of Records and Subpoenas.

(i) The parties to a dispute have the obligation to provide all documents needed for the Panel to resolve the questions presented for resolution. The discovery provisions of the Kentucky Rules of Civil Procedure are not strictly applicable. When a party fails to provide documents determined necessary by the Panel, the Panel may accept the negative factual inferences created by the failure to provide the requested documents.

(ii) When the Panel determines the provisions of KRS 417.110 should be utilized, it may request permission in writing from the Director for the authority to issue a subpoena for the documents specified in its request.

(E) Oath of Panel Members.

The Panel shall take a written oath to be filed with the Director to decide the dispute submitted to them according to the law and evidence and the equity of the case to the best of their judgment without favor, affection or prejudice.

(F) Conduct of Hearings.

(i) The testimony of all witnesses shall be given under oath. The Panel Chair shall administer oaths to witnesses.

(ii) The Panel Chair shall preside at the hearing and shall be the judge of the relevancy and materiality of the evidence offered, shall rule on questions of procedure, and shall exercise all powers relating to the conduct of the hearing. Strict compliance with the rules of evidence shall not be required.

(iii) In cases involving a three (3) member Panel, if at the time set for any hearing all three members of the Panel are not available to participate, the hearing shall be postponed, or, with consent of the parties shall proceed with the hearing with one (1) member of the Panel chosen by the parties as the sole arbitrator.

(iv) If any party to an arbitration who has been duly notified fails to appear at a scheduled hearing, the Panel may proceed with the hearing and determine the dispute upon the evidence produced.

(v) The Panel Chair may adjourn the hearing from time to time as necessary. Upon request of a party to the arbitration for good cause, the Panel Chair may postpone the hearing from time to time.

(vi) No briefs or legal memorandum shall be submitted by the parties unless specifically requested by the Panel or a majority thereof.

(7) The Award.

(A) Rendition and Form.

(i) The Panel shall render its award within thirty (30) days after the close of the hearing. The Award shall be made by a majority of the Panel.

(ii) The original Award shall be in writing and shall be signed by the member(s) of the Panel concurring therein. The Award shall include a determination of all questions submitted to the Panel, the decision of which shall be necessary to resolve the dispute. Copies of the Award shall have the same legal force and effect as the original.

(iii) While it is not required that the Award be in any particular form, it should, in general, consist of a preliminary statement reciting the jurisdictional facts, i.e., that a hearing was held upon notice pursuant to a written agreement to arbitrate, the parties were given an opportunity to testify and cross-examine, etc., a brief statement of the dispute, findings, conclusions, and the amount, if any, to be paid or reimbursed. The Panel shall avoid reciting information in the text of the Award that is privileged unless the parties specifically waive any privilege.

(iv) An Award may also be entered by consent of all parties to the dispute.

(v) The Award signed by the member(s) of the Panel shall be provided to the Director, who shall cause it to be mailed to the parties by Certified Mail.

(B) Correction of Errors.

If, upon receiving the Award, a party determines it contains significant factual or accounting errors or omissions, the party may bring this information to the attention of the Director within fifteen (15) days from the receipt of the Award. The Director will present the information to the other party and to the Panel for consideration along with the comments from the other party to the dispute. If the Panel determines that modification of the Award is appropriate, the Panel will issue a modified Award reflecting any changes made and will provide the modified Award to the Director for service on the parties as indicated above. This procedure is not intended to provide a party the opportunity to submit new evidence or to reargue the merits of the dispute.

(C) Effect and Enforcement.

The provisions of KRS 417.180 and of the arbitration agreement of the parties shall govern and determine the effect and enforcement of the Award. The law of the Commonwealth of Kentucky will govern the award of interest of any judgment.

(8) Records.

With the exception of the Award itself all records, documents, files, proceedings and hearings pertaining to arbitration of any dispute under these Rules shall not be open to the public or to any person not involved in the dispute with the exception of disputes referred to arbitration as stated in section 2(D) above. In that circumstance, a copy of the Award may be provided to the referring activity or agency.

(9) Death or Incompetence of a Party.

In the event of the death or incompetence of a party to the arbitration proceedings before the hearing has been concluded, the proceedings shall be abated without prejudice to either party to seek such relief as may be proper. In the event of death or incom-

petence of a party after the close of the hearing, but prior to issuance of the Award, the decision rendered shall be binding upon the heirs, administrators, or executors of the deceased and on the estate or guardian of the incompetent.

(10) No Charge for Arbitration Services.

No charge or fee shall be required of any party requesting or making use of the arbitration services provided by these Rules.

(11) Indemnity Provision.

By agreeing to the procedures authorized herein, the parties further agree to indemnify and hold harmless the Association, its employees and the Panel concerning any action arising out of the procedures set forth by this rule and for any and all conduct of the Panel in the exercise of the procedures herein.

HISTORY: Amended by Order 2007–007, eff. 2–1–08; prior amendments eff. 1–1–06 (Order 2005–10), 1–1–97 (Order 96–1), 1–1–89, 1–1–86; adopted eff. 7–1–84

SCR 3.810   Legal fee arbitration

(1) Purpose.

The purpose of this Rule 3.810 is to establish a procedure whereby fee disputes arising from attorney and client relationships may be resolved by submission to binding arbitration.

(2) Definitions.

(A) "Attorney" means an attorney-at-law who is a member in good standing of the Kentucky Bar Association, or an attorney admitted to practice pursuant to SCR 3.030 when the dispute arises from that representation.

(B) "Association" means the Kentucky Bar Association.

(C) "Director" means the Director of the Kentucky Bar Association.

(D) "Dispute" means a disagreement between an attorney and a client relative to the fee due the attorney for particular legal services rendered, or a disagreement between attorneys concerning the amount of the fees due each attorney for particular legal services rendered. This includes a matter that is the subject of a diversion pursuant to SCR 3.160(3), or a matter referred for fee arbitration by the Court.

(E) "Amount in controversy" means the difference between the sum of money an attorney proposes to charge for legal services and the sum of money the client offers to pay for such services, or the total amount of the fee to be divided between attorneys.

(F) "Panel" means the arbitrator or arbitrators appointed to arbitrate the dispute.

(3) Scope of Authority.

(A) The Rules and Procedures herein set forth shall be available to resolve any dispute when the amount in controversy exceeds the jurisdictional maximum specified in KRS 24A.230 and all parties to the dispute agree in writing to submit the dispute to these Rules and further agree in writing that they shall be fully bound by the decision and Award of the Panel.

(B) These Rules shall not be used unless the parties to the dispute certify in writing that a good faith effort has been made by them to resolve the dispute.

(C) These Rules shall not be used if the dispute is the subject matter of a pending lawsuit, unless the parties follow the procedures of KRS 417.060(4).

(4) Institution of Proceedings.

(A) Proceedings hereunder shall be begun by the filing of a petition with the Association. The signed petition shall state the origin and details of the dispute, the nature and degree of legal services rendered, and the amount claimed due as a result of the dispute alleged. The petitioner shall also sign an arbitration agreement. The petition and arbitration agreement shall be on forms provided by the Association.

(B) Upon the filing of the petition, the Director shall determine whether it presents a dispute under these Rules. The decision of the Director on that matter shall be final. The Director shall have full power to require additional information from the petitioner as is deemed necessary to determine whether the Association shall accept jurisdiction of the dispute under these Rules.

(C) If the Director determines that the Association shall not accept jurisdiction of a fee dispute, the petition shall be returned to the petitioner indicating why the Association has not accepted jurisdiction of the matter.

(D) If the Director determines that the Association shall accept jurisdiction, a copy of the petition and the arbitration agreement signed by the petitioner shall be forwarded to the other party to the dispute to sign and return to the Director with the answer to the petition. Twenty (20) days shall be allowed in which to answer, unless additional time is requested. Upon receipt of the answer, the Director shall forward to the petitioner a signed copy of the arbitration agreement and of the answer submitted by the other party to the dispute.

(E) If the other party to the dispute refuses to submit the fee dispute to arbitration, or fails to sign and return the arbitration agreement and answer within the time allowed, the Director shall so notify the petitioner and the file of the Association shall be closed.

(F) If the dispute is referred to arbitration as referenced in 2(D) above, then sections 4(B) and (C) of this rule are not applicable. The attorney involved in the dispute shall be deemed the petitioner and shall file a petition with the Director.

(G) Upon the filing of a petition with the Association, any applicable statute of limitations is tolled until dismissal or a final award is entered.

(5) Arbitration Panel.

(A) Composition.

(i) Where the amount in controversy is ten thousand dollars ($10,000.00) or less, the Panel shall consist of one (1) person who shall be a practicing Attorney.

(ii) Where the amount in controversy exceeds ten thousand dollars ($10,000.00), the Panel shall consist of three (3) persons, two (2) of whom shall be practicing Attorneys and the third (3rd) member shall be a non-lawyer.

(iii) The practicing Attorney(s) referred to in paragraph (5)(A)(i) and (5)(A)(ii) above, shall each:

(a) be a member in good standing of the Association;

(b) be appointed for a particular dispute by the Director; and

(c) if engaged in the private practice of law shall maintain an office and carry on such practice within a reasonable proximity to the county in which the petitioner in the dispute resides.

(iv) Any attorney appointed by the Director may refuse to serve. Such refusal shall be by written notice to the Director within ten (10) days of the appointment.

(v) The non-lawyer referred to in paragraph (5)(A)(ii) shall be selected by the senior presiding judge or Chief Circuit Judge of the county where the attorney involved in the fee dispute maintains a principal office for the practice of law. If the dispute is between two attorneys, the selection of the non-lawyer member of the Panel shall be made by the senior presiding judge or Chief Circuit Judge of the county where the attorney petitioning for arbitration maintains a principal office for the practice of law.

(vi) In cases of a three-member Panel, the Director shall designate one member of the Panel as Chair of the Panel.

(B) Objections.

Either party to a fee dispute may object for cause to any of the Panel members. Such objection shall be in writing and shall be made within twenty (20) days of written notification of the composition of the Panel. Failure to object within twenty (20) days shall constitute a waiver of any objection to the composition of the Panel.

Objections to Panel members shall be made to the Director and shall be determined in accordance with KRS 26A.015 et seq. The decision of the Director shall be final.

(C) Compensation.

The Panel shall not be compensated for its services. Reasonable transportation expenses may be reimbursed.

(D) Vacancies.

If any arbitrator should be unable to act, the Director shall declare the office vacant and, if the matter has already been heard by the Panel, it shall not be reheard if the remaining members concur in the Award. If the sole member of the Panel is unable to act or the remaining members of the Panel do not concur in the Award, a new member shall be selected and the matter will be reheard. If the Panel has not yet heard the matter a new arbitration Panel member shall be selected in accordance with these Rules.

(E) Communication Between the Parties and Panel Members.

There shall be no ex parte communication between the parties and the Panel upon the subject matter of the arbitration other than at arbitration proceedings, or in documents filed with the Association as part of the proceedings. This limitation does not apply to administrative communications between the Panel and the parties regarding the scheduling of the hearing.

(6) Hearings.

(A) Location.

Hearings shall be held in a county that reasonably limits the travel required by the parties to attend the hearing.

(B) Notice.

The Chair of the Panel shall fix the time and place for the hearing and shall cause written notice of time and place to be served upon all parties to the dispute by Certified Mail not fewer than ten (10) days prior to the time set for the hearing. Such notice of hearing shall also inform the parties of their right to be represented by an attorney and their right to present evidence in support of their respective positions.

(C) Stenographic Record.

(i) Any party may have a hearing before a Panel reported by a Certified Shorthand Reporter at the expense of the requesting party by written notice presented to the Panel Chair at least seven (7) days prior to the date of the hearing. Any other party to the arbitration shall be entitled to acquire at their own expense, a copy of the reporter's transcript of the testimony by arrangements made directly with the reporter.

(ii) In the event the Panel determines it appropriate or necessary to record the hearing, it may be recorded by digital or video means with costs being assessed as the Panel deems just. A party to the dispute, at its own expense, may request a copy of the record so recorded.

(D) Production of Records and Subpoenas.

(i) The parties to a dispute have the obligation to provide all documents needed for the Panel to resolve the questions presented for resolution. The discovery provisions of the Kentucky Rules of Civil Procedure are not strictly applicable. When a party fails to provide documents determined necessary by the Panel, the Panel may accept the negative factual inferences created by the failure to provide the requested documents.

(ii) When the Panel determines the provisions of KRS 417.110 should be utilized, it may request permission in writing from the Director for the authority to issue a subpoena for the documents specified in its request.

(E) Oath of Panel Members.

The Panel shall take a written oath to be filed with the Director to decide the dispute submitted to them according to the law and evidence and the equity of the case to the best of their judgment without favor, affection or prejudice.

(F) Conduct of Hearings.

(i) The testimony of all witnesses shall be given under oath. The Panel Chair shall administer oaths to witnesses.

(ii) The Panel Chair shall preside at the hearing and shall be the judge of the relevancy and materiality of the evidence offered, shall rule on questions of procedure, and shall exercise all powers relating to the conduct of the hearing. Strict compliance with the rules of evidence shall not be required.

(iii) In cases involving a three (3) member Panel, if at the time set for any hearing all three members of the panel are not available to participate, the hearing shall be postponed, or, with consent of the parties shall proceed with the hearing with one (1) member of the panel chosen by the parties as the sole arbitrator.

(iv) If any party to an arbitration who has been duly notified fails to appear at a scheduled hearing, the Panel may proceed with the hearing and determine the dispute upon the evidence produced.

(v) The Panel Chair may adjourn the hearing from time to time as necessary. Upon request of a party to the arbitration for good cause, the Panel Chair may postpone the hearing from time to time.

(vi) No briefs or legal memorandum shall be submitted by the parties unless specifically requested by the Panel or a majority thereof.

(7) The Award.

(A) Rendition and Form.

(i) The Panel shall render its Award within thirty (30) days after the close of the hearing. The Award of the Panel shall be made by a majority of the Panel.

(ii) The original Award shall be in writing and shall be signed by the member(s) of the Panel concurring therein. The Award shall include a determination of all questions submitted to the Panel, the decision of which shall be necessary to resolve the controversy. Copies of the Award shall have the same legal force and effect as the original.

(iii) While it is not required that the Award be in any particular form, it should, in general, consist of a preliminary statement reciting the jurisdictional facts, i.e., that a hearing was held upon notice pursuant to a written agreement to arbitrate, the parties were given an opportunity to testify and cross-examine, etc., a brief statement of the dispute, findings, conclusions, and the amount to be paid or reimbursed. The Panel shall avoid reciting information in the text of the Award that is privileged unless the parties specifically waive any privilege.

(iv) An Award may also be entered by consent of all parties to the dispute.

(v) The award signed by the member(s) of the Panel shall be provided to the Director, who shall cause it to be mailed to the parties by Certified Mail.

(B) Correction of Errors.

If, upon receiving the Award, a party determines it contains significant factual or accounting errors or omissions, the party may bring this information to the attention of the Director within fifteen (15) days from the receipt of the Award. The Director will present the information to the other party and to the Panel for consideration along with any comments by the other party to the dispute. If the Panel determines that modification of the Award is appropriate, the Panel will issue a modified Award reflecting any changes made and will provide the modified Award to the Director for service on the parties as indicated above. This procedure is not intended to provide a party the opportunity to submit new evidence or to reargue the merits of the dispute.

(C) Effect and Enforcement.

The provisions of KRS 417.180 and of the arbitration agreement of the parties shall govern and determine the effect and enforcement of the Award. The law of the Commonwealth of Kentucky will govern the Award of interest on any judgment.

(8) Records.

With the exception of the Award itself all records, documents, files, proceedings and hearings pertaining to arbitration of any fee dispute under these Rules shall not be open to the public or to any person not involved in the dispute with the exception of disputes referred to arbitration as stated in section 2(D) above. In that circumstance, a copy of the Award may be provided to the referring activity or agency.

(9) Death or Incompetence of a Party.

In the event of the death or incompetence of a party to the arbitration proceedings before the hearing has been concluded, the proceedings shall be abated without prejudice to either party to seek such relief as may be proper. In the event of death or incompetence of a party after the close of the hearing but prior to issuance of the Award, the decision rendered shall be binding upon the heirs, administrators, or executors of the deceased and on the estate or guardian of the incompetent.

(10) Arbitration of Fee Disputes Between and Among Attorneys.

(A) The Association may accept jurisdiction of any fee dispute between or among attorneys when such a dispute has been submitted to the Association in accordance with these Rules.

(B) These Rules shall be applied by the Association in the resolution of fee disputes between and among attorneys except that in rendering its Award the Panel shall determine whether the fee in dispute should be divided and if so, in what proportions it should be divided between or among the parties to the arbitration.

(C) Service of a copy of such Award on the attorneys shall conclusively limit all claim and interest of the participating attorneys in the disputed fee in accordance with the division of the fee, if any, set forth in the Award.

(11) No Charge for Arbitration Service.

No charge or fee shall be required of any party requesting or making use of the fee arbitration services provided by these Rules.

(12) Indemnity Provision.

By agreeing to the procedures authorized herein, the parties further agree to indemnify and hold harmless the Association, its employees and the Panel concerning any action arising out of the procedures set forth by this rule and for any and all conduct of the Panel in the exercise of the procedures herein.

HISTORY: Amended by Order 2007–007, eff. 2–1–08; prior amendments eff. 1–1–06 (Order 2005–10), 1–1–97 (Order 96–1), 1–1–89, 1–1–88, 1–1–86; adopted eff. 7–1–84

SCR 3.815 Mediation and arbitration

(1) Purpose.

The purpose of this Rule 3.815 is to establish a procedure whereby disputes arising among attorneys from their professional and economic relationships may be resolved by submission to mediation, binding arbitration, or non-binding arbitration.

(2) Definitions.

(A) "Attorney" means an attorney-at-law who is a member in good standing of the Association.

(B) "Association" means the Kentucky Bar Association.

(C) "Director" means the Director of the Kentucky Bar Association.

(D) "Vice-President" means Vice-President of the Kentucky Bar Association.

(E) "Controversy" means a dispute or disagreement between attorneys relative to questions of representation of clients, questions arising when law firms or other legal associations between attorneys are dissolved or otherwise terminated, or other economic disputes between attorneys.

(F) "Panel" means the arbitrator or arbitrators appointed or designated to assist in resolving the controversy as hereinafter provided.

(3) Scope of Authority.

(A) The Rules and Procedures herein set forth shall be available to settle or resolve any controversy as herein defined only when all parties to the controversy agree and bind themselves in writing to submit such controversy to the arbitration or mediation procedures herein set forth and further, agree in writing that they shall be fully bound by the decision and award of the arbitrator(s).

(B) The provisions of these Rules shall not be used unless the parties to the dispute certify in writing that a good faith effort has been made by them to resolve the dispute and has failed.

(C) The provisions of these Rules shall not be used if the dispute proposed to be submitted is the subject matter of a pending lawsuit, unless the parties follow the procedures of KRS 417.060.

(4) Institution of Proceedings.

(A) Proceedings hereunder shall be begun by completing three copies of a petition. The petition must be signed by one of the parties to the dispute. The petition shall state the origin and details of the dispute, acts or omissions deemed to be in controversy, and the relief desired from the mediation or arbitration. Upon the filing of the petition, the petitioner shall also sign three copies of an arbitration or mediation agreement, as applicable. The petition and agreement shall be on forms provided by the Association and when completed shall be filed in the office of the Association.

(B) Upon the filing of the petition, the Director of the Association shall forward a copy of the petition to the Vice-President. The Vice-President, upon receipt of the petition, shall determine whether the plan and this rule apply, and the Vice-President's decision on that matter shall be final. The Vice-President shall have full power to require additional information from the petition in all disputes wherein additional information is deemed desirable or necessary.

(C) If the Vice-President determines that the Association shall not accept jurisdiction of a controversy, the petition shall be returned to the Director, or other designated employee of the Association with a brief explanation as to why jurisdiction has been refused. The Director shall then notify the petitioner that the Association has not accepted jurisdiction and will not arbitrate or mediate the controversy and shall advise the petitioner why the Association has not accepted jurisdiction of the matter.

(D) If the Vice-President determines that the Association shall accept jurisdiction, the Vice-President shall notify the Director and shall return the petition to the Director or other designated employee of the Association. The Director shall then forward to respondent a copy of the petition and three copies of the agreement signed by the petitioner, and he or she shall require the respondent to sign and return to the Director two copies of the agreement and three copies of the respondent's answer to the petition. The letter to the respondent shall state that respondent has twenty days in which to answer and return the two signed agreements, and that if respondent's answer is not received within twenty days, the Association will construe such failure to answer as constituting a refusal to submit to arbitration or mediation. Upon receipt of the respondent's answer, the Director shall forthwith forward to the petitioner one signed copy of the agreement and one copy of the respondent's answer.

(E) If the respondent's refusal to submit the controversy to arbitration or mediation, or failure within twenty days following receipt of the documents described in (4)(D) to sign and return the agreement, the Director shall so notify the petitioner and the file of the Association shall be closed.

(5) Arbitration panel.

(A) Composition.

(i) Where the matter is to be mediated, the mediator shall consist of one person who shall be a practicing Attorney.MP21(ii) Where the matter is to be arbitrated, the arbitration panel shall consist of one practicing Attorney, if the amount in controversy is $2,500.00 or less, or if it exceeds $2,500.00, the panel shall consist of three persons, all of whom shall be practicing Attorneys.

(iii) The practicing Attorney(s) referred to in paragraph (5)(A)(i) and (5)(A)(ii) above, shall each:

(a) be a member in good standing of the Association;

(b) be appointed or designated for a particular controversy by the Vice–President;

(c) if a panel member or sole arbitrator is engaged in the private practice of law shall maintain or carry on a private law practice in an office more than fifty (50) miles from the county seat of the county where the attorneys who are parties to the controversy maintain their principal offices for the practice of law.

(iv) Any attorney appointed or designated by the Vice–President may refuse to serve. Such refusal shall be by written notice to the Director within ten (10) days of the appointment.

(v) The Vice–President, in cases of a three-member panel, shall designate one member of the panel as Chairperson of the panel.

(B) Objections.

(i) Either party to a controversy may object for cause to any of the panel members. Such objection shall be in writing and shall be made within twenty (20) days of written notification of the names of the panel members. Failure to object within twenty

(20) days shall constitute a waiver of any objection to the composition of the panel. The following shall constitute grounds for objection for cause to a proposed panel member serving:

(a) If the member is associated in any business or profession with or related in any way to any of the parties or their attorneys;

(b) If the member has a personal or financial interest or any bias or prejudice regarding any of the parties or the nature of the controversy;

(c) If the member has pending any business transactions or controversy as a party with any party to the controversy or their attorney or has then pending any business transactions or controversies as an attorney with any party to the controversy or any attorney for a party, and there is such a conflict that it would render the arbitrator incapable of fairly exercising independent judgment.

(ii) Objections to panel members shall be made to the Chair of the panel and shall be ruled upon by the Chair of the panel whose decision shall be final. Each side may have one peremptory strike.

(C) Compensation.

Members of the panel shall not be paid or compensated for their services.

(D) Vacancies.

If any arbitrator or mediator should resign, die, withdraw, refuse to act or be disqualified or unable to act, the Vice–President shall declare the office vacant and, if the matter has already been heard, shall be reheard, unless the parties otherwise agree. In the absence of such agreement, a new arbitration panel shall be selected in accordance with these Rules.

(E) Communication Between the Parties and Panel Members.

There shall be no communication between the parties and the members of the arbitration or mediation panel upon the subject matter of the arbitration or mediation other than at arbitration or mediation proceedings. Copies of any written communication between members of the panel and any party, or any attorney for any parties or between parties or their attorneys and the panel shall be furnished contemporaneously to each participant in the proceeding and filed with the Director.

(6) Hearings.

(A) The mediation shall be held in the county where the attorneys involved in the controversy maintain their principal offices for the practice of law, or in the event the dispute is between two or more attorneys, the hearings shall be held in the county where the attorney petitioning for arbitration maintains that attorney's principal office for the practice of law.

(B) Arbitration hearings shall be held and conducted as follows:

(i) Notice: The Chair of the panel shall fix the time and place for the hearing and shall cause written notice of time and place to be served upon all parties to the dispute by Certified Mail not less than ten (10) days prior to the time set for the hearing. Such notice of hearing shall also inform the parties of their right to be represented by an attorney and their right to present evidence in support of their respective positions.

(ii) Stenographic Record: Any party may have a hearing before a panel reported by a Certified Shorthand Reporter at their expense by written request presented to the Director at least four (4) days prior to the date of the hearing. In such event, any other party to the arbitration or mediation shall be entitled to acquire, at their own expense, a copy of the reporter's transcript of the testimony by arrangements made directly with the reporter. When no party to the arbitration or mediation requests that the hearing be reported, and the panel or sole arbitrator deems it necessary to have the hearing reported, the panel or sole arbitrator may record the proceedings or employ a Certified Shorthand Reporter for such purpose if authorized to do so by the Director. Costs of making a record will be assessed by the panel or sole arbitrator as a part of the award. Prior to assessment of such costs, the Association will pay same upon notice to the Director.

(iii) Subpoenas: The provisions of KRS 417.110 shall apply to proceedings under these Rules.

(iv) Oath of Panel Members: Panel members shall take a written oath to be filed with the Director to decide the controversies submitted to them according to the law and evidence and the equity of the case to the best of their judgment without favor, affection or prejudice.

(v) Conduct of Hearings:

(a) The testimony of all witnesses shall be given under oath. When so requested, the member of the panel presiding at the hearing may administer oaths to witnesses.

(b) The panel Chair, or sole arbitrator, shall preside at the hearing. The member of the panel who is presiding shall be the judge of the relevancy and materiality of the evidence offered and shall rule on questions of procedure and shall exercise all powers relating to the conduct of the hearing. However, strict conformity to rules of evidence shall not be required.

(c) In cases involving a three (3) member panel, if at the time set for any hearing all three members of the panel are not present, the hearing shall be postponed, or, with consent of the parties to proceed with the hearing with one (1) member of the panel chosen by the parties as the sole arbitrator. In no event shall a hearing be conducted by or proceed with two (2) members of the panel acting as arbitrators.

(d) If any party to an arbitration or mediation who has been duly notified fails to appear at a scheduled hearing, the panel may proceed with the hearing and determine the controversy upon the evidence produced, notwithstanding such failure to appear.

(e) The panel Chair, or if the hearing is conducted by a sole arbitrator, then the latter, may adjourn the hearing from time to time as necessary. Upon request of a party to the arbitration for good cause, or upon their own determination, the panel Chair or sole arbitrator may postpone the hearing from time to time.

(f) No briefs or legal memorandum shall be submitted by the parties unless specifically requested by the panel or a majority thereof.

(7) The Award.

(A) If the mediator is able to mediate the controversy successfully and the parties are able to reach agreement, that agreement shall be reduced to a written agreement and executed by the parties. The agreement shall consist of a preliminary statement reciting the jurisdictional facts, the nature of the controversy, and the specific agreement reached. The agreement will be thereafter enforceable and have the same force and effect as a judgment in a court of law in the Commonwealth of Kentucky.

(B) *Arbitration Award Rendition and Form.*

(i) The panel shall render its award within fifteen (15) days after the close of the hearing or final hearing if more than one has been held. The award of the panel shall be made by a majority of the panel when heard by three (3) members, or by the sole arbitrator.

(ii) The original and four (4) copies of the award shall be in writing and shall be signed by the members of the panel concurring therein unless the hearing shall have been conducted by a sole arbitrator, in which event the original and copies of the award shall be signed only by the sole arbitrator. The award shall include a determination of all questions submitted to the panel, the decision of which shall be necessary to resolve the controversy.

(iii) While it is not required that the award be in any particular form, it should, in general, consist of a preliminary statement reciting the jurisdictional facts, i.e., that a hearing was held upon notice pursuant to a written agreement to arbitrate, the parties were given an opportunity to testify and cross-examine, etc., a brief statement of the dispute, findings, conclusions, and the amount to be paid or reimbursed. The panel shall avoid reciting information in the text of the award that is privileged unless the client specifically waives any privilege.

(iv) An award may also be entered by consent of all parties to the dispute.

(C) *Effect and Enforcement.*

The provisions of KRS 417.180 and of the arbitration agreement of the parties shall govern and determine the effect and enforcement of the award. The law of the Commonwealth of Kentucky will govern the award of interest on any judgment.

(D) If the parties selected non-binding arbitration, they may agree to have the award be binding and enterable as a judgment.

(8) Confidentiality.

By agreeing to participate in the proceedings authorized by this rule, the parties agree to hold in confidence the award, all records, documents, files, proceedings and other matters pertaining to the procedures authorized herein, and such records shall not be opened to the public or to any person not involved in the dispute.

(9) Death or Incompetence of a Party.

In the event of the death or incompetence of a party to the arbitration proceedings, during the course of arbitration but prior to the rendering of a decision, the proceedings shall be abated without prejudice to either party to proceed in a court of proper jurisdiction to seek such relief as may be proper. In the event of death or incompetence of a party after the close of the proceedings but prior to a decision, the decision rendered shall be binding upon the heirs, administrators, or executors of the deceased and on the estate or guardian of the incompetent.

(10) Indemnity Provision.

By agreeing to the procedures authorized herein, the parties further agree to indemnify and hold harmless the hearing officer, arbitrator, mediator or presiding officer or panel concerning any action arising out of the procedures set forth by this rule and for any and all conduct of the hearing officer, arbitrator, mediator or presiding officer or panel presiding over the procedures herein.

(11) Costs.

(A) Costs shall be allowed to the prevailing party unless otherwise directed by the mediator/sole arbitrator/panel. In the event of a partial award in favor of a party, or of an award in which neither party prevails entirely against the other, costs of the proceeding may be apportioned and shall be borne as directed by the mediator/sole arbitrator/panel.

(B) A party to a mediation/arbitration procedure entitled to recover costs shall prepare and serve promptly upon the party liable for costs a bill itemizing the costs incurred in the mediation/arbitration proceeding, including fees incident to summoning witnesses, transmittal of documents to the parties and the mediator/sole arbitrator/panel, the cost of depositions used in lieu of live testimony at any hearing, if permitted by the mediator/sole arbitrator/panel, the costs associated with the location of the hearing, if any, except that no costs for the location will be assessed for any hearing conducted on the premises of the Kentucky Bar Center, travel, lodging and meal expenses of the mediator/sole arbitrator/panel, and fees for extraordinary services, if specifically awarded by the mediator/sole arbitrator/panel. If a stenographic record of the hearing has been ordered by the mediator/sole arbitrator/panel pursuant to paragraph (6)(B)(ii), and the costs billed to or paid by the Association, the mediator/sole arbitrator/panel shall assess the costs in accordance with this rule. Any party to the mediation/arbitration who requests a stenographic or other record pursuant to paragraph (6)(B)(ii) shall bear the cost of that record.

(C) Prohibited recovery: Notwithstanding the provisions of paragraph (B) above, no award of costs shall be made to any party for attorney's fees incurred in the mediation/arbitration, nor shall any recovery be allowed to any party or witness for lost wages or other expenses incurred as a result of attendance at the hearing.

HISTORY: Amended by Order 2005–10, eff. 1–1–06; prior amendments eff. 3–1–98 (Order 97–3), 1–1–97 (Order 96–1); adopted eff. 9–1–93

SCR 3.820   Client's Security Fund

There shall be maintained a special fund for the purpose of providing indemnification to clients who may suffer pecuniary loss by reason of fraudulent or dishonest acts on the part of a member of the Kentucky Bar Association. The fund shall be named, held, administered and disbursed in accordance with the provisions hereinafter set forth.

(1)   Purpose and Scope

(a) The purpose of the Clients' Security Fund is to promote public confidence in the administration of justice and the integrity of the legal profession by reimbursing losses caused by the dishonest conduct of lawyers admitted and licensed to practice law in the courts of this State occurring in the course or arising out of a lawyer-client relationship between the lawyer and the claimant.

(b) Every lawyer has an obligation to the public to participate in the collective effort of the bar to reimburse persons who have lost money or property as a result of the dishonest conduct of another lawyer. Contribution to the Clients' Security Fund is an acceptable method of meeting this obligation.

(2)   Establishment

(a) There is established the Clients' Security Fund to reimburse claimants for losses caused by dishonest conduct committed in this state by lawyers admitted to practice in this State.

(b) There is established, under the supervision of the Supreme Court of Kentucky, the Clients' Security Fund Board of Trustees, which shall receive, hold, manage and disburse from the Fund such monies as may from time to time be allocated to the Fund.

(c) These rules shall be effective for claims filed with the Trustees after October 20, 1971 and the Trustees shall not pay claims for losses incurred as a result of dishonest conduct committed prior thereto.

(3)   Funding

(a) The Court shall provide for funding by the lawyers of the State in amounts adequate for the proper payment of claims and the costs of administering the Fund.

(b) A lawyer's failure to pay any fee assessed shall be a cause for suspension from practice until payment has been made.

(c) A lawyer whose dishonest conduct has resulted in reimbursement to a claimant shall make restitution to the Fund including interest and the expense incurred by the Fund in processing the claim. A lawyer's failure to make satisfactory arrangements for restitution shall be cause for suspension, disbarment, or denial of an application for reinstatement.

(4)   Funds

All monies or other assets of the Fund shall constitute a trust and shall be held in the name of the Fund, subject to the direction of the Trustees.

(5)   Composition and Officers of the Board

(a) The Trustees shall consist of three lawyers and two nonlawyers appointed by the Board of Governors for initial terms as follows:

(1) One lawyer for one year;

(2) One nonlawyer for two years;

(3) One lawyer for two years;

(4) One nonlawyer for three years; and

(5) One lawyer for three years.

Subsequent appointments shall be for a term of three years. The Board of Governors may limit the number of successive terms that Trustees may serve.

(b) Trustees shall serve without compensation but shall be reimbursed for their actual and necessary expenses incurred in the discharge of their duties.

(c) Vacancies shall be filled by appointment by the Board for any unexpired terms.

(d) The Trustees shall select a chairperson and such other officers as they deem appropriate.

(6)   Board Meetings

(a) The Trustees shall meet as frequently as necessary to conduct the business of the Fund and to timely process claims.

(b) The Chairperson shall call a meeting at any reasonable time or upon the request of at least two Trustees.

(c) A quorum for any meeting of the Board shall be three Trustees.

(d) A record of meetings shall be taken and maintained.

(7)   Duties and Responsibilities of the Trustees

The Trustees shall have the following duties and responsibilities:

(a) to receive, evaluate, determine and pay claims;

(b) to promulgate rules of procedure not inconsistent with these Rules, subject to approval by the Board of Governors;

(c) to prudently invest such portions of the funds as may not be needed currently to pay losses;

(d) to provide a full report at least annually to the Court and to make other reports as necessary;

(e) to publicize its activities to the public and the bar;

(f) to retain and compensate consultants, auditors, actuaries, agents, legal counsel, special commissioners appointed under SCR 3.395, and other persons as necessary;

(g) to prosecute for restitution to which the Fund is entitled;

(h) to engage in studies and programs for client protection and prevention of dishonest conduct by lawyers; and

(i) to perform all other acts necessary or proper for the fulfillment of the purposes and effective administration of the Fund.

(8) Conflict of Interest

(a) A Trustee who has or has had a lawyer-client relationship or a financial relationship with a claimant or lawyer who is the subject of a claim shall not participate in the investigation or adjudication of a claim involving that claimant or lawyer.

(b) A Trustee with a past or present relationship, other than as provided in section (a), with a claimant or the lawyer whose alleged conduct is the subject of the claim, shall disclose such relationship to the panel and, if the panel deems appropriate, that Trustee shall not participate in any proceeding relating to such claim.

(9) Immunity

The Trustees, employees and agents of the panel shall be absolutely immune from civil liability for all acts in the course of their official duties. Absolute immunity shall also extend to claimants and lawyers who assist claimants for all communications to the Fund.

(10) Eligible Claims

(a) The loss must be caused by the dishonest conduct of the lawyer and shall have arisen out of or in the course of a lawyer-client relationship between the lawyer and the claimant.

(b) The claim shall have been filed no later than two years after the claimant knew or should have known of the dishonest conduct of the lawyer.

(c) As used in these Rules, "dishonest conduct" means:

(1) Wrongful acts committed by a lawyer in the nature of theft or embezzlement of money or the wrongful taking or conversion of money, property or other things of value, or

(2) Refusal to refund unearned fees received in advance where the lawyer performed no services or such an insignificant portion of the services that the refusal to refund the unearned fees constitutes a wrongful taking or conversion of money.

(d) Except as provided by section (e) of this Rule, the following losses shall not be reimbursable:

(1) Losses incurred as a result of any negligent act of malpractice,

(2) Losses incurred by spouses, children, parents, grandparents, siblings, partners, associates and employees of lawyer(s) causing the losses;

(3) Losses covered by any bond, surety agreement, or insurance contract to the extent covered thereby, including any loss to which any bonding agent, surety or insurer is subrogated, to the extent of that subrogated interest;

(4) Losses incurred by any financial institution which are recoverable under a "banker's blanket bond" or similar commonly available insurance or surety contract;

(5) Losses incurred by any business entity controlled by the lawyer, any person or entity described in section (d)(1), (2), or (3) hereof;

(6) Losses incurred by any governmental entity or agency.

(e) In cases of extreme hardship or special and unusual circumstances, the panel of Trustees may, in its discretion, recognize a claim which would otherwise be excluded under these Rules.

(f) In cases where it appears that there would be unjust enrichment, or the claimant unreasonably or knowingly contributed to the loss, the panel of Trustees may in its discretion, deny the claim.

(11) Procedures and Responsibilities for Claimants

(a) The Trustees shall prepare and approve a form for claiming reimbursement.

(b) The form shall include at least the following information provided by the claimant under penalty of perjury:

(1) the name and address of claimant, home and business telephone, occupation and employer, social security number;

(2) the name, address and telephone number of the lawyer alleged to have dishonestly taken the claimant's money or property, and any family or business relationship of the claimant to the lawyer;

(3) the legal or other fiduciary services the lawyer was to perform for the claimant;

(4) the amount paid to the lawyer;

(5) the copy of any written agreement pertaining to the claim;

(6) the form of the claimant's loss involved (e.g. money, securities or other property);

(7) the amount of loss and the date when the loss occurred;

(8) the date when the claimant discovered the loss, and how the claimant discovered the loss;

(9) the lawyer's dishonest conduct and the names and addresses of any persons who have knowledge of the loss;

(10) the name of the person, if any, to whom the loss has been reported (e.g. prosecuting attorney, police, disciplinary agency, or other person or entity) and a copy of any complaint and description of any action that was taken;

(11) the source, if any, from which the loss can be reimbursed including any insurance, fidelity or surety agreement;

(12) the description of any steps taken to recover the loss directly from the lawyer, or any other source.

(13) the circumstances under which the claimant has been or will be, reimbursed for any part of the claim (including the amount received, or to be received, and the source); along with a statement that the claimant agrees to notify the Board of any reimbursements the claimant receives during the pendency of the claim;

(14) the existence of facts believed to be important to the Fund's consideration of the claim;

(15) the manner in which the claimant learned about the Fund;

(16) the name, address and telephone number of the claimant's present lawyer;

(17) the claimant's agreement to cooperate with the Board in reference to the claim or as required by SCR 3.820 (16), in reference to civil actions which may be brought in the name of the Board pursuant to a subrogation and assignment clause which shall also be contained within the claim.

(18) the name and address of any other State Fund to which the claimant has applied or intends to apply for reimbursement, together with a copy of the application.

(19) a statement that the client agrees to the publication of appropriate information about the nature of the claim and the amount of reimbursement if reimbursement is made.

(c) The claimant shall have the responsibility to complete the claim form and provide satisfactory evidence of a reimbursable loss.

(d) The claim shall be filed with the Trustees in the manner and place designated in the rules governing claims with the Fund.

(12) Processing Claims

(a) Whenever it appears that a claim is not eligible for reimbursement pursuant to SCR 3.820 (10), the claimant shall be advised of the reasons why the claim may not be eligible for reimbursement, and that unless additional facts to support eligibility are submitted to the Fund, the claim file shall be closed.

(b) A copy of an order disciplining a lawyer for the same dishonest act or conduct alleged in a claim, or a final judgment imposing civil or criminal liability therefor, may be considered by the Trustees as evidence that the lawyer committed such dishonest act or conduct.

(c) The lawyer disciplinary agency shall be promptly notified of the claim and requested to furnish a report of its investigation on the matter to the Trustees. The lawyer disciplinary agency shall allow the Fund's representative access to its records during an investigation of a claim. The Trustees shall evaluate whether the investigation is complete and determine whether the Trustees should conduct additional investigation or await the pendency of any disciplinary investigation or proceeding involving the same act or conduct that is alleged in the claim.

(d) The Trustees may conduct their own investigation when deemed appropriate.

(e) A copy of the claim shall be served upon the lawyer, or the lawyer's representative. The lawyer or representative shall have 20 days in which to respond.

(f) The Trustees may request that testimony be presented to complete the record. Upon request, the claimant or lawyer, or their representative, will be given an opportunity to be heard.

(g) A determination by the Trustees of dishonest conduct for purposes of adjudicating a claim shall not constitute a finding of dishonest conduct for purposes of professional discipline.

(h) When the record is complete, the claim shall be determined on the basis of all available evidence, and notice shall be given to the claimant and the lawyer of the Board's determination and the reasons therefor. The approval or denial of a claim shall require the affirmative votes of at least three trustees.

(i) Any proceeding upon a claim need not be conducted according to technical rules relating to evidence, procedure and witnesses. Any relevant evidence shall be admitted if it is the sort of evidence on which responsible persons are accustomed to rely in the conduct of serious affairs, regardless of the existence of any common law or statutory rule which might make improper the admission of such evidence over objection in court proceedings. The claimant shall have the duty to supply relevant evidence to support the claim.

(j) The Trustees shall determine the order and manner of payment and pay all approved claims, but unless the Trustees direct otherwise, no claim should be approved during the pendency of a disciplinary proceeding involving the same act or conduct that is alleged in the claim.

(k) Both the claimant and the lawyer shall be advised of the status of the Trustees' consideration of the claim and shall be informed of the final determination.

(*l*) The claimant or respondent lawyer may request reconsideration within 30 days of the denial or determination of the amount of a claim. The request shall plainly state the reasons for such reconsideration. The Trustees shall grant or deny this request within 30 days after the request is filed with the KBA administrator. If the claimant fails to make a request or the request is denied, the decision of the Board is final.

(13) Payment of Reimbursement

(a) The Board of Governors, with the approval of the Supreme Court, may from time to time fix a maximum amount on reimbursement that is payable by the Fund.

(b) Claimants shall be reimbursed for losses in amounts to be determined by the Trustees. No claim shall be paid for consequential damages flowing from the wrongful act of a practicing attorney. Claims shall be limited to actual pecuniary amounts retained, embezzled, stolen, or otherwise taken from or withheld from the claimant by the practicing attorney.

(c) Payment of reimbursement shall be made in such amounts and at such times as the Trustees deem appropriate and may be paid in lump sum or installment amounts.

(d) If a claimant is a minor or an incompetent, the reimbursement may be paid to any person or entity for the benefit of the claimant.

(14) Reimbursement from Fund is a Matter of Grace

No person shall have the legal right to reimbursement from the Fund whether as claimant, third-party beneficiary, or otherwise.

(15) Restitution and Subrogation

(a) A lawyer whose dishonest conduct results in reimbursement to a claimant shall be liable to the Fund for restitution; and the Trustees may bring such action as it deems advisable to enforce such obligation.

(b) As a condition of reimbursement, a claimant shall be required to provide the Fund with a *pro tanto* transfer of the claimant's rights against the lawyer, the lawyer's legal representative, estate or assigns; and of the claimant's rights against any third party or entity who may be liable for the claimant's loss.

(c) Upon commencement of an action by the Clients' Security Fund as subrogee or assignee of a claim, it shall advise the claimant, who may then join in such action to recover the claimant's unreimbursed losses.

(d) In the event that the claimant commences an action to recover unreimbursed losses against the lawyer or another entity who may be liable for the claimant's loss, the claimant shall be required to notify the Trustees of such action.

(e) The claimant shall be required to agree to cooperate in all efforts that the Trustees undertake to achieve restitution for the Fund.

(16) Judicial Relief

(a) The Trustees may make application to the appropriate court for relief to protect the interests of claimants or the Fund where:

(1) the assets of client appear to be in danger of misappropriation or loss, or to secure the claimant's or Fund's rights to restitution or subrogation; or

(2) the disciplinary agency has failed to exercise jurisdiction.

(b) A court's jurisdiction in such proceedings shall include the authority to appoint and compensate custodial receivers to conserve the assets and practices of missing, incapacitated and deceased lawyers.

(17) Confidentiality

(a) Claims, proceedings and reports involving claims for reimbursement are confidential until the Trustees authorize reimbursement to the claimant, except as provided below. After payment of the reimbursement, the Trustees may publicize the nature of the claim, the amount of reimbursement, and the name of the lawyer. The name and the address of the claimant shall not be publicized by the Trustees unless specific permission has been granted by the claimant.

(b) This Rule shall not be construed to deny access to relevant information by professional discipline agencies or other law enforcement authorities as the Trustees shall authorize, or the release of statistical information which does not disclose the identity of the lawyer or the parties.

(18) Compensation for Representing Claimants

No lawyer shall accept any payment for prosecuting a claim on behalf of a claimant.

HISTORY: Amended by Order 2007–007, eff. 2–1–08; prior amendments eff. 11–1–95 (Order 95–1), 8–1–92, 1–1–89, 1–1–88; adopted eff. 7–1–84

SCR 3.830   Kentucky IOLTA Fund

The Kentucky Bar Foundation, Inc., a nonprofit corporation, shall maintain a special fund for the purpose of depositing interest from Kentucky Bar Association members' trust accounts, as hereinafter provided, and the name of the fund shall be the Kentucky IOLTA Fund ("IOLTA").

Except as set forth in paragraph (14) of this rule, a lawyer or law firm shall create and maintain in a participating financial institution, as defined in paragraph (4) below, an interest-bearing trust account for clients' funds which are nominal in amount or to be held for a short period of time so that they could not earn interest income for the client in excess of the costs incurred to secure such income (hereinafter sometimes referred to as an "IOLTA account") in compliance with the following provisions:

(1) No funds may be deposited in any IOLTA account when either the amount or the period of time that the funds are held would earn for the client interest above the costs that would otherwise be incurred to generate such interest.

(2) No earnings from an IOLTA account shall be made available to a lawyer or law firm.

(3) An IOLTA account shall be established with a participating financial institution (i) authorized by federal or state law to do business in Kentucky, and (ii) insured by the Federal Deposit Insurance Corporation or its equivalent. Funds in each IOLTA account shall be subject to withdrawal upon request and without delay and without risk to principal by reason of said withdrawal.

(4) Participating financial institutions that maintain IOLTA accounts shall pay on the accounts the highest interest rate or dividend generally available from the institution to its non-IOLTA account customers when IOLTA accounts meet or exceed the same minimum balance or other account eligibility qualifications. In determining the highest interest rate or dividend generally available from the institution, participating financial institutions may consider factors, in addition to the IOLTA account balance, that are customarily considered by the institution when setting interest rates or dividends for its non-IOLTA customers. Such factors should not discriminate between IOLTA accounts and accounts of non-IOLTA customers. All interest earned net of fees or charges shall be remitted to IOLTA, which is designated in paragraph (16) of this rule to organize and administer the IOLTA program, and the depository participating institution shall submit reports thereon as set forth below.

(5) A participating financial institution may satisfy the comparability requirements set forth in paragraph (4) above by electing one of the following options: (i) Pay an amount on funds that would otherwise qualify for the investment options equal to 70% of the federal funds targeted rate as of the first business day of the month or other IOLTA remitting period, which is deemed to be already net of allowable reasonable service charges or fees. The foregoing option of paying 70% of the federal funds targeted rate shall only apply when such rate is established in the range of 1.0% to 4.0% unless otherwise agreed to by IOLTA and the participating financial institution. (ii) Pay a yield rate specified by IOLTA, if IOLTA so chooses, which is agreed to by the participating financial institution. The rate would be deemed to be already net of allowable reasonable fees and would be in effect for and remain unchanged during a period of no more than twelve months from the inception of the agreement between the financial institution and IOLTA.

(6) IOLTA accounts may be established as: (i) An interest-bearing checking account such as a negotiable order of withdrawal account; (ii) a checking account with an automated investment feature, such as an overnight and investment in repurchase agreements or money market funds invested solely in or fully collateralized by U.S. Government Securities, including U. S. Treasury obligations and obligations issued or guaranteed as to principal and interest by the United States or any agency or instrument thereof; (iii) a checking account paying preferred interest rates, such as money market or indexed rates; (iv) any other suitable interest-bearing deposit account offered by the institution to its non-IOLTA customers.

(7) A daily financial institution repurchase agreement shall be fully collateralized by United States Government Securities and may be established only with an eligible institution that is "well capitalized" or "adequately capitalized" as those terms are defined by applicable federal statutes and regulations. An open-end money market fund shall be invested solely in United States Government Securities or repurchase agreements fully collateralized by United States Government Securities, shall hold itself out as a "money market fund" as that term is defined by federal statutes and regulations under the Investment Company Act of 1940 and, at the time of the investment, the money market fund shall have total assets of at least two hundred fifty million dollars ($250,000,000).

(A) Nothing in this rule shall preclude a participating financial institution from paying a higher interest or dividend than described above or electing to waive any service charges or fees on IOLTA accounts.

(B) Interest and dividends shall be calculated in accordance with the participating financial institution's standard practice for non-IOLTA customers.

(C) Allowable reasonable service charges or fees may be deducted from interest or dividends on an IOLTA account only at the rates and in accordance with the customary practices of the eligible institution for non-IOLTA customers. No fees or service charges other than allowable reasonable fees may be assessed against the accrued interest or dividends on an IOLTA account.

(D) Any IOLTA account which has or may have the net effect of costing IOLTA more in fees than earned in interest over a period of any time, may, at the discretion of IOLTA, be exempted from and removed from the IOLTA program. Exemption of an IOLTA account from the IOLTA program revokes the permission to use IOLTA's tax identification number for that account. Exemption of such account from the IOLTA program shall not relieve the lawyer and/or law firm from the obligation to maintain the property of client funds separately, as required above, in a trust account and also will not relieve the lawyer of the annual IOLTA certification.

(8) Lawyers or law firms depositing client funds in an IOLTA account established pursuant to this rule shall, on forms approved by IOLTA, direct the depository institution:

(A) to remit all interest or dividends, net of reasonable service charges or fees, if any, on the average monthly balance in the account, or as otherwise computed in accordance with the institution's standard accounting practice, at least quarterly, solely to IOLTA. The depository institution may remit the interest or dividends on all of its IOLTA accounts in a lump sum; however, the depository institution must provide, for each individual IOLTA account, the information to the lawyer or law firm and to IOLTA required by subparagraphs (8)(B) and (8)(C) of this rule;

(B) to transmit with each remittance to IOLTA a statement showing the name of the lawyer or law firm for whom the remittance is sent, the rate of interest applied, average daily balance, service charges, if any, and such other information as is reasonably required by IOLTA;

(C) to transmit to the depositing lawyer or law firm a periodic account statement for the IOLTA account reflecting the amount of interest paid to IOLTA, the rate of interest applied, the average account balance for the period for which the interest was earned, and such other information as is reasonably required by IOLTA; and

(D) to waive any reasonable service charge that exceeds the interest earned on any IOLTA account during a reporting period ("excess charge").

(9) The IOLTA program will issue refunds when interest has been remitted in error, whether the error is the bank's or the lawyer's. Requests for refunds must be submitted in writing by the bank, the lawyer, or the law firm on a timely basis, accompanied by documentation that confirms the amount of interest paid to the IOLTA program. As needed for auditing purposes, the IOLTA program may request additional documentation to support the request. The refund will be remitted to the appropriate financial institution for transmittal at the lawyer's direction after appropriate accounting and reporting. In no event will the refund exceed the amount of interest actually received by the IOLTA program.

(10) All interest transmitted to IOLTA shall be held, invested and distributed periodically in accordance with a plan of distribution which shall be prepared by IOLTA and approved at least annually by the Supreme Court of Kentucky, for the following purposes:

(A) to pay or provide for all costs, expenses and fees associated with the administration of the IOLTA program;

(B) to establish appropriate reserves;

(C) to assist or help establish approved legal services and pro bono programs;

(D) for such other law-related programs for the benefit of the public as are specifically approved by the Supreme Court from time to time.

(11) The information contained in the statements forwarded to IOLTA under paragraph (8)(B) of this rule shall remain confidential, and the provisions of any other Supreme Court Rules providing for confidentiality are not hereby abrogated; therefore, IOLTA shall not release any information contained in any such statement other than as a compilation of data from such statements, except as directed in writing by the Supreme Court.

(12) IOLTA shall have full authority to and shall, from time to time, prepare and submit to the Supreme Court for approval, forms, procedures, instructions and guidelines necessary and appropriate to implement the provisions set forth in this rule and, after approval thereof by the Court, shall promulgate same.

(13) On or before September 1 of each year, every lawyer admitted to practice in Kentucky shall certify to IOLTA, in such form as IOLTA shall provide ("IOLTA Certification Form"), that the member is in compliance with, or is exempt from, the provisions of this rule. The IOLTA Certification Form shall include the participating financial institution, account numbers, name of law firm or lawyer accounts and such other information as IOLTA shall require. If the lawyer is exempt from the IOLTA program, the lawyer must still submit an IOLTA Certification Form annually to certify to IOLTA that the lawyer is exempt from the provisions in this rule. Each lawyer shall keep and maintain records supporting the information submitted in the IOLTA Certification Form. The lawyer shall maintain these records for a period of three years from the end of the period for which the IOLTA Certification Form is filed, and these records shall be submitted to IOLTA upon written request.

(14) The lawyer is exempt from this rule if:

(A) not engaged in the private practice of law;

(B) does not have a trust account in a financial institution within the Commonwealth of Kentucky;

(C) serving full time as a judge, attorney general, public defender, U.S. attorney, commonwealth attorney, county attorney, on duty with the armed services or employed by a local, state or federal government, and is not otherwise engaged in the private practice of law;

(D) is a corporate counsel or teacher of law and is not otherwise engaged in the private practice of law;

(E) has been exempted by an order of general or special application of this Court which is cited in the certification;

(F) compliance with Rule 3.830 would work an undue hardship on the lawyer or would be extremely impractical, based on the geographic distance between the lawyer's principal office and the closest participating financial institution, or on other compelling and necessary factors; or

(G) does not manage or handle client trust funds.

(15) The determination of whether a client's funds are nominal or short-term so that they could not earn income in excess of costs shall rest in the sound judgment of the lawyer or law firm. No lawyer shall be charged with an ethical impropriety or other breach of professional conduct based on the good faith exercise of such judgment.

(16) IOLTA is hereby designated as the entity to organize and administer the program established by this rule in accordance with the following provisions:

(A) The determination of whether or not a financial institution is a participating institution as defined in paragraph (4) above, and whether it is meeting the requirements of this rule shall be made by IOLTA. IOLTA shall maintain a list of participating financial institutions, and shall provide a copy of the list to any Kentucky lawyer upon request.

(B) Lawyers may only maintain IOLTA accounts in participating financial institutions. Participating financial institutions are those that voluntarily offer IOLTA accounts and comply with the requirements of this rule. If a financial institution becomes non-participatory, the lawyer or law firm must move its IOLTA account to a participating financial institution as described in paragraph (4) above, upon ninety (90) days written notice by IOLTA, and recertify to IOLTA the transfer.

(17) If the IOLTA Certification Form is timely filed, indicating compliance, there will be no acknowledgment. Should an IOLTA Certification Form not be filed by a lawyer or if filed, fail to evidence compliance, IOLTA shall contact the lawyer and attempt to resolve the non-compliance administratively.

(18) Lawyers licensed in Kentucky must notify IOLTA in writing within thirty (30) days of any change in IOLTA status, including the opening or closing of any IOLTA accounts, except as provided in paragraph (16)(B) above.

(19) For the purpose of administering the funds deposited in the Kentucky IOLTA Fund, the Kentucky Bar Foundation is authorized to create a separate Board of Trustees to administer this fund, which shall consist of ten (10) members of the Association. One (1) member will be from each of the seven (7) Supreme Court Districts of the Commonwealth. The remaining three (3) members will be the Chief Justice of the Supreme Court of Kentucky, the President of the Kentucky Bar Association and the Chair of the Kentucky Bar Foundation, or a member of the Association appointed by each of such persons. These three (3) persons will serve year to year at the pleasure of the appointing person.

(A) Members of the Board of Trustees from the Supreme Court Districts shall be appointed by the Board of Governors of the Kentucky Bar Association and approved by the Supreme Court. Appointments shall be made for a three-year term. Members may be reappointed, but no member shall serve more than two (2) successive three-year terms. Each member shall serve until a successor is appointed and qualified. Vacancies occurring through death, disability, inability, or disqualification to serve, or by resignation, shall be filled for the remainder of the vacant term in the same manner as the initial appointments are made by the Court. The members of the Board of Trustees of the Kentucky IOLTA Fund shall serve without compensation, but shall be paid their reasonable and necessary expenses incurred in the performance of their duties. The staff support for the Board of Trustees shall be paid by IOLTA.

(B) The IOLTA Board of Trustees (the "Trustees") shall have general supervisory authority over the administration of the IOLTA program, subject to the continuing jurisdiction of the Supreme Court.

(C) The Trustees shall receive the net earnings from IOLTA accounts established in accordance with this rule and shall make appropriate temporary investments of IOLTA program funds pending disbursement of such funds.

(D) The Trustees shall, by grants, appropriations and other appropriate measures, make disbursements from the IOLTA program funds, including current and accumulated net earnings, in accordance with the plan of distribution approved by the Supreme Court on at least an annual basis.

(E) The Trustees shall maintain proper records of all IOLTA program receipts and disbursements, which records shall be audited or reviewed annually by a certified public accountant approved by the Supreme Court.

(F) The Trustees shall be indemnified by IOLTA against any liability or expense arising directly or indirectly out of the good faith performance of their duties.

(G) The Trustees shall present an annual administrative budget request to the Board of Governors for their approval, after which the budget shall be forwarded to the Supreme Court for approval. Staff for the operation of IOLTA shall be under the supervision and responsible to the Executive Director of the Bar Association.

(H) The Trustees shall monitor attorney compliance with the provisions of this rule and will report to the Supreme Court those attorneys not in compliance.

(I) In the event the IOLTA program or its administration by IOLTA is terminated, all assets of the IOLTA program, including any program funds then on hand, shall be transferred in accordance with the Order of the Supreme Court terminating the IOLTA program or its administration by IOLTA; provided, such transfer shall be to an entity which will not violate the requirements IOLTA must observe regarding transfer of its assets in order to retain its tax-exempt status under the Internal Revenue Code of 1986, as amended, or similar future provisions of law.

HISTORY: Amended by Order 2009–12, eff. 1–1–10; prior amendments eff. 11–15–91 (Order 91–2), 8–28–89, 7–1–86; adopted eff. 7–1–86

SCR 3.900   Definitions

As used in SCR 3.900 through SCR 3.980:

(1) "Impairment" means and includes any mental, psychological or emotional condition that impairs or may foreseeably impair a person's ability to practice law or serve on the bench. Impairment may result from addiction to intoxicants or drugs, chemical dependency, substance abuse, mental disease, mental disorder or defect, or psychological or emotional illness.

(2) "The Kentucky legal community" means and includes (a) all members of the Kentucky Bar Association, including judges; (b) all applicants for admission to the practice of law in Kentucky; (c) all students enrolled at law schools in the Commonwealth; and (d) all members of the Association who have been suspended from the practice of law pursuant to the Rules of the Supreme Court.

HISTORY: Adopted by Order 2003–4, eff. 1–1–04; temporary amendment adopted eff. 3–17–03 (Order 2003–2)

SCR 3.910   Kentucky lawyer assistance program (KYLAP)

(1) There is hereby established a state-wide program to be called the Kentucky Lawyer Assistance Program (or "KYLAP"), which shall be operated by the Association in accordance with these Rules. It shall be the mission and purpose of KYLAP to address impairment issues within the Kentucky legal community in a manner that serves and promotes the general mission and purpose of the Association as set forth in SCR 3.025.

(2) KYLAP shall offer certain types of assistance as described in this Rule to members of the Kentucky legal community who suffer from actual or potential impairment, and may proceed to provide such assistance to any member of the said community as requested or authorized. The types of assistance offered and provided by KYLAP in a particular case may include lay counseling and encouragement; assisting, planning and execution of interventions; providing information about treatment alternatives; monitoring progress of recovery from impairment, which may include assistance in arranging, scheduling and tracking attendance at recovery programs, appointments with counselors, therapists and medical care providers and compliance with alcohol or drug screens; monitoring compliance with voluntary or involuntary treatment or recovery programs, which may

include documentation and reports concerning compliance or non-compliance; obtaining authorizations in conformity with federal and state law; and other related tasks that may assist a member of the said community in addressing an actual or potential impairment; provided, however, that KYLAP shall perform the aforesaid types of assistance in such a manner that KYLAP's staff does not render legal or medical advice and does not engage in any activity which constitutes the practice of law or medicine.

(3) KYLAP shall develop and present educational programs for the Kentucky legal community regarding issues of impairment and shall pursue other appropriate opportunities to increase awareness and understanding of such matters and cultivate an environment in which issues of impairment are properly addressed.

(4) KYLAP shall serve as a resource within the Association with respect to matters of impairment, so that all functions and activities of the Association may benefit from KYLAP's information and expertise in matters of impairment.

(5) KYLAP may engage in other activities consistent with these Rules and as authorized by the operating policies and procedures adopted by the KYLAP Commission.

(6) KYLAP shall perform all of the aforementioned duties in a manner consistent with the confidentiality provisions of Rule 3.990.

(7) KYLAP shall be funded from the annual dues collected by the Association pursuant to these Rules. KYLAP may also charge reasonable and appropriate fees for services rendered and accept monetary gifts in support of its activities, to the extent authorized by the KYLAP Commission and approved by the Board.

(8) KYLAP may, with the approval of the Board, establish such non-profit tax exempt Foundations as are necessary for the purpose of carrying out its mission. This may include establishment of a Foundation to obtain donations in order to furnish financial assistance, in the form of loans, to enable members of the legal community to obtain treatment for their impairment. The Board will appoint the Directors of any such Foundation.

HISTORY: Amended by Order 2012–01, eff. 3–1–12; adopted by Order 2003–4, eff. 1–1–04; temporary amendment adopted eff. 3–17–03 (Order 2003–2)

SCR 3.920   Kentucky Lawyer Assistance Program Commission (KYLAP Commission)

(1) The Board of Governors shall appoint a Commission to be called the Kentucky Lawyer Assistance Program Commission or "KYLAP Commission", which shall have general responsibility for the administration of KYLAP in accordance with these Rules.

(2) The Commission shall consist of fifteen (15) persons, as follows: (a) two members of the Board of Governors; (b) an active member of the Association

(either a lawyer or judge) from each of the seven Supreme Court Districts; (c) two other active members of the Association (either lawyers or judges); and (d) four (4) citizens of the Commonwealth who are not members of the Kentucky legal community. The Board shall appoint persons who have a demonstrated interest in issues of impairment and shall also endeavor to make appointments which create a diversity of knowledge and life experience within the Commission's membership.

(3) Each member of the Commission shall be appointed for a period of four (4) years. However, in order to achieve staggered terms, the initial members of the Commission shall be appointed as follows:

(a) Five of the Commission members who are lawyers or judges shall be appointed for two-year terms;

(b) Four of the Commission members who are lawyers or judges shall be appointed for three-year terms;

(c) Two of the Commission members who are lawyers or judges shall be appointed for four-year terms;

(d) Two of the Commission members who are not members of the Kentucky legal community shall be appointed for three-year terms; and

(e) Two of the Commission members who are not members of the Kentucky legal community shall be appointed for four-year terms.

Thereafter, when any vacancy occurs in the membership of the Commission, that vacancy shall be filled by appointment by the Board of Governors. When a vacancy occurs prior to the expiration of a member's term, the new member shall be appointed for the remainder of the unexpired term. When a vacancy occurs because of the expiration of a term, the new member shall be appointed for a four-year term.

(4) The Commission shall have a Chair and a Vice–Chair. The Chair shall be appointed annually by the Board of Governors with input from the Commission and the KYLAP Director. The Vice–Chair shall be elected annually by the members of the Commission.

(5) The Commission shall meet quarterly or upon call of the Chair or upon the request of five (5) or more members. A member's failure to attend three (3) consecutive meetings will automatically result in the vacancy of that member's position on the Commission.

(6) The Commission shall have general responsibility for the administration of KYLAP in accordance with these Rules. In discharging its responsibility KYLAP shall have the authority to:

(a) Adopt operating policies and procedures as necessary and appropriate to implement these Rules and administer KYLAP, provided that, before such policies and procedures are implemented, they shall receive approval of the Board; and

(b) Make reports to the Board and Court annually or as otherwise required, provided that such reports shall be of a statistical and summary nature and shall not compromise the confidentiality of any referral under SCR 3.950 or any assignment under SCR 3.960.

HISTORY: Adopted by Order 2003–4, eff. 1–1–04; temporary amendment adopted eff. 3–17–03 (Order 2003–2)

SCR 3.930   KYLAP Program Director and Staff

The Board of Governors, through the Executive Director of the Association, shall appoint a KYLAP Program Director and sufficient staff to provide administrative support for the KYLAP Commission and the KYLAP program. The Program Director shall be responsible for the administration of KYLAP.

HISTORY: Adopted by Order 2003–4, eff. 1–1–04; temporary amendment adopted eff. 3–17–03 (Order 2003–2)

SCR 3.940   KYLAP Volunteer Counselors

KYLAP may enlist volunteer counselors to assist KYLAP in discharging KYLAP's duties under these Rules. Such volunteer counselors shall be subject to all provisions of these Rules including the provisions of SCR 3.910(2) limiting the types of assistance provided by KYLAP and the confidentiality requirements of SCR 3.990.

HISTORY: Adopted by Order 2003–4, eff. 1–1–04; temporary amendment adopted eff. 3–17–03 (Order 2003–2)

SCR 3.950   Self–Referrals

Any member of the Kentucky legal community may contact KYLAP to obtain information about KYLAP's services or to request assistance from KYLAP regarding an actual or potential impairment. Any such communication with KYLAP shall be confidential in nature and shall be held in strict confidence by KYLAP's staff and by all other persons involved in the implementation and delivery of KYLAP's services. Upon receiving any such inquiry, KYLAP may offer assistance of the nature described in Rule 3.910(2) as appropriate to the person's situation and circumstances, and may proceed to provide such assistance as authorized by that person.

HISTORY: Adopted by Order 2003–4, eff. 1–1–04; temporary amendment adopted eff. 3–17–03 (Order 2003–2)

SCR 3.960   Third Party Referrals

(1) Any person may contact KYLAP and request or suggest that KYLAP offer assistance to a member of the Kentucky legal community who is suffering or may be suffering from an actual or potential impairment.

(2) When a person contacts KYLAP pursuant to this Rule, his or her communication with KYLAP shall be confidential in nature and shall be held in strict confidence by KYLAP's staff and by all other persons involved in the implementation and delivery of KY-

LAP's services. Further, if KYLAP proceeds to communicate with the member of the Kentucky legal community who is the subject matter of the contact, KYLAP shall not disclose any information about its communications with the person who made the third-party referral, except as authorized by that person.

(3) Any person who contacts KYLAP pursuant to this Rule shall be immune from any liability to the person who is the subject matter of the contact, or to any other person, by reason of contacting KYLAP.

HISTORY: Adopted by Order 2003–4, eff. 1–1–04; temporary amendment adopted eff. 3–17–03 (Order 2003–2)

SCR 3.970   Agency Referrals

(1) A member of the Kentucky legal community who is the subject of a pending admission, disciplinary or continuing legal education proceeding before an agency of the Supreme Court of Kentucky may authorize that agency to make a confidential request for assistance from KYLAP in evaluating or addressing any actual or potential impairment that may be relevant to the issues which the agency is charged with considering in the proceeding. In particular:

(a) A member of the Kentucky legal community who is the subject of an application for admission, restoration or reinstatement to the practice of law in the Commonwealth may authorize the Office of Bar Admissions to communicate in confidence with KYLAP for the purpose of requesting assistance from KYLAP in evaluating and addressing any actual or potential impairment that may be relevant to the OBA's consideration or disposition of the application for admission, restoration or reinstatement.

(b) A member or former member of the Association who is the subject of a disciplinary complaint or investigation pending before the Inquiry Commission may authorize that Commission to communicate in confidence with KYLAP for the purpose of requesting assistance from KYLAP in evaluating and addressing any actual or potential impairment that may be relevant to that Commission's consideration or disposition of that complaint or investigation.

(c) A member or former member of the Association who is the subject of an investigation or prosecution by the Office of Bar Counsel may authorize OBC to communicate in confidence with KYLAP for the purpose of requesting assistance from KYLAP in evaluating and addressing any actual or potential impairment that may be relevant to OBC's recommended disposition of that investigation or prosecution.

(d) A member or former member of the Association who is the subject of a continuing legal education proceeding pursuant to Rule 3.669 by the Continuing Legal Education Commission may authorize the Director for Continuing Legal Education

to communicate in confidence with KYLAP for the purpose of requesting assistance from KYLAP in evaluating and addressing any actual or potential impairment that may be relevant to the CLE Commission's recommended disposition of that proceeding.

(2) Before an agency of the Court makes any contact with KYLAP pursuant to paragraph (1) of this Rule, it shall obtain a written authorization from the person who is the subject of the proposed assistance clearly evidencing the fact that such person has authorized the agency to communicate with KYLAP for one or more purposes set forth in paragraph (1).

(3) Upon receiving any request for assistance from an agency of the Court pursuant to paragraph (1) of this Rule, KYLAP shall satisfy itself: (a) that the person who is the subject of the proposed assistance has authorized the agency to communicate with KYLAP, in accordance with paragraphs (1) and (2) of this Rule; and (b) that the requested assistance falls within the scope of KYLAP's mission and services as set forth in Rule 3.910. KYLAP shall not take any other steps in response to the request until it has satisfied itself of these two threshold matters.

(4) After satisfying itself of the threshold matters set forth in paragraph (3), KYLAP shall determine whether it is able to provide any assistance to the requesting agency and respond appropriately to that agency. KYLAP is not obligated by these Rules to accept any request for assistance or become involved in any proceeding before any agency of the Court, and shall do so only when it determines that it is able to provide assistance in accordance with these Rules.

(5) Before providing any assistance pursuant to a request from an agency of the Court, KYLAP shall obtain a written authorization, waiver and release from the person who is the subject of the proposed assistance, in which that person authorizes KYLAP to:

(a) provide appropriate status reports to the requesting agency, and to any other appropriate agencies of the Court, regarding any aspect of the assistance provided by KYLAP after the date KYLAP has accepted the request for assistance, including, without limitation, (i) any assessment or diagnosis of the person's condition rendered after the date KYLAP has accepted the request for assistance, (ii) the person's progress in addressing the actual or potential impairment after the date KYLAP has accepted the request for assistance, and (iii) the person's compliance or non-compliance with any terms or conditions imposed by the Court, any agency of the Court, or KYLAP, after the date KYLAP has accepted the request for assistance;

(b) disclose to the requesting agency, and to any other appropriate agencies of the Court, any information gathered or received by KYLAP after the date KYLAP has accepted the request for assistance, for use as evidence in any admission, disciplinary, restoration or reinstatement proceeding, subject to the rules of evidence and procedure in that proceeding; and

(c) provide testimony in any admission, disciplinary, restoration or reinstatement proceeding regarding assistance provided by KYLAP after the date KYLAP has accepted the request for assistance, subject to the rules of evidence and procedure in that proceeding.

HISTORY: Amended by Order 2005–10, eff. 1–1–06; adopted by Order 2003–4, eff. 1–1–04; temporary amendment adopted eff. 3–17–03 (Order 2003–2)

SCR 3.980 Supreme Court Assignments to KYLAP

(1) The Supreme Court may assign appropriate tasks and responsibilities to KYLAP relating to the evaluation of an impairment or the monitoring of a person's progress toward recovery from impairment as part of the Court's final disposition of any application for admission to the bar, petition for temporary suspension, charge of professional misconduct or application for restoration or reinstatement, where an issue of impairment has been raised in the proceeding, provided that in no event shall KYLAP become involved in any proceeding prior to the final disposition of that proceeding without the consent of the lawyer.

(2) The Board of Governors may recommend that the Court assign appropriate tasks and responsibilities to KYLAP as described in paragraph (1) of this Rule as part of the Board's recommendation to the Court in any disciplinary, restoration or reinstatement proceeding, where an issue of impairment has been raised in the proceeding.

(3) When KYLAP receives a matter by assignment from the Court pursuant to paragraph (1) of this Rule:

(a) KYLAP shall proceed to provide assistance of the nature described in Rule 3.910(2) in accordance with the terms of the Court's order, and may impose additional requirements on the person who is the subject of the assignment as necessary to perform the assignment;

(b) KYLAP may provide reports to the Court, and to one or more agencies of the Court, as authorized or required by the terms of the Court's order;

(c) Any information gathered or received by KYLAP after the date of the Court's order and in the course of discharging the tasks and responsibilities assigned by the Court as part of a final disposition under paragraph (1) of this Rule may be used as evidence in any admission, disciplinary, continuing legal education, restoration or reinstatement proceeding regarding the person who is the subject of the assignment, subject to the rules of evidence and procedure in that proceeding; and

(d) One or more representatives of KYLAP may be called as witnesses in any admission, disciplinary,

continuing legal education, restoration or reinstatement proceeding for the purpose of testifying about information gathered or received by KYLAP after the date of the Court's order and in the course of discharging the tasks and responsibilities assigned by the Court as part of a final disposition under paragraph (1) of this Rule, subject to the rules of evidence and procedure in that proceeding.

HISTORY: Amended by Order 2005–10, eff. 1–1–06; adopted by Order 2003–4, eff. 1–1–04; temporary amendment adopted eff. 3–17–03 (Order 2003–2)

SCR 3.990 Confidentiality

(1) All communications to KYLAP and all information gathered, records maintained and actions taken by KYLAP shall be confidential, shall be kept in strict confidence by KYLAP's staff and volunteers, shall not be disclosed by KYLAP to any person or entity, including any agency of the Court and any department of the Association, and shall be excluded as evidence in any proceeding before the Board of Governors or the Office of Bar Admissions, except that:

(a) if the person who is the subject of KYLAP's assistance has provided a written release authorizing disclosure of communications to KYLAP or information gathered, records maintained or actions taken by KYLAP, KYLAP may disclose such information in strict accordance with the terms and conditions of that written release;

(b) if the matter was assigned to KYLAP by the Court pursuant to paragraph SCR 3.980, KYLAP may issue reports, disclose information and provide testimony as set forth in paragraph (3) of that Rule, and this Rule 3.990 shall not be construed as a basis for excluding otherwise admissible evidence from any admission, disciplinary, restoration or reinstatement proceeding; and

(c) if KYLAP provided assistance pursuant to an agency referral under SCR 3.970, KYLAP may issue reports, disclose information and provide testimony as set forth in paragraph (5) of that Rule, and this Rule 3.990 shall not be construed as a basis for excluding otherwise admissible evidence from any admission, disciplinary, restoration or reinstatement proceeding.

(2) The foregoing requirement of confidentiality shall apply to all members of the KYLAP Commission, all KYLAP staff members and volunteers, all employees of the Association, all volunteer counselors, all persons who provide information or other assistance to KYLAP in connection with any referral or assignment, and all other persons who participate in the performance or delivery of KYLAP's services.

HISTORY: Adopted by Order 2003–4, eff. 1–1–04; temporary amendment adopted eff. 3–17–03 (Order 2003–2)

SCR 3.995 Immunity

The duties imposed by these Rules are duties owed to the Supreme Court, not to any other person or entity. Nothing in these Rules shall be construed as creating any cause of action or right of suit against any person or entity.

HISTORY: Adopted by Order 2003–4, eff. 1–1–04; temporary amendment adopted eff. 3–17–03 (Order 2003–2)

IV JUDICIAL CONDUCT COMMISSION

SCR 4.000 Scope

This Part IV of these rules applies to all proceedings before the Judicial Conduct Commission involving the discipline, retirement or removal of justices of the Supreme Court and judges of the Court of Appeals, circuit court and district court, pursuant to section 121 of the Constitution of Kentucky, as well as the disciplining of lawyers seeking judicial office who during their candidacy shall be deemed subject to the jurisdiction and discipline of the Commission.

HISTORY: Amended by Order 98–2, eff. 1–1–99; prior amendment eff. 3–8–83 (Order 83–2); adopted eff. 10–1–76

SCR 4.010 Definitions

In Part IV of these rules, unless the context or subject-matter otherwise requires:

(a) "Commission" means the Kentucky Judicial Conduct Commission.

(b) "Court of Justice" means the Supreme Court, Court of Appeals, circuit court and district court.

(c) "Judge" means any judge or justice of the Court of Justice or other officer of the Court of Justice performing judicial functions. In addition, where context so requires, the term judge shall include lawyer or layperson subject to the jurisdiction of the Commission.

(d) "Chair" includes the acting chair or vice-chair.

(e) "Counsel" means the lawyer designated by the Commission to gather and present evidence before the Commission with respect to the charges against a judge.

(f) "Mail" includes but is not limited to registered and certified mail.

HISTORY: Amended by Order 98–2, eff. 1–1–99; prior amendment eff. 1–1–78; adopted eff. 10–1–76

SCR 4.020 Jurisdiction

(1) Commission shall have authority:

(a) To order a temporary or permanent retirement of any judge whom it finds to be suffering from a mental or physical disability that seriously interferes with the performance of his duties, and to suspend temporarily from the performance of his duties, without affecting his pay status, any judge (i) against whom there is pending in any court of the United States an indictment or information charging him with a crime punishable as a felony, or (ii) after notice and an opportunity to be heard, and upon a finding that it will be in the best interest of justice that he be suspended from acting in his official capacity as a judge until final adjudication of the complaint, any judge against whom formal proceedings have been initiated under Rule 4.180.

(b) To impose the sanctions, separately or collectively of (1) admonition, private reprimand, public reprimand or censure; (2) suspension without pay or removal or retirement from judicial office, upon any judge of the Court of Justice or lawyer while a candidate for judicial office, who after notice and hearing the Commission finds guilty of any one or more of the following:

(i) Misconduct in office.

(ii) Persistent failure to perform his duties.

(iii) Incompetence.

(iv) Habitual intemperance.

(v) Violation of The Code of Judicial Conduct, Rule 4.300.

(vi) Any willful refusal or persistent failure to conform to official policies and directives adopted by the Supreme Court and issued by the Chief Justice in his constitutional capacity as Chief Executive Officer of the Court of Justice.

(vii) Conviction of a crime punishable as a felony.

(c) After notice and hearing, to remove a judge whom it finds to lack the constitutional and statutory qualifications for the judgeship in question.

(d) To refer any judge of the Court of Justice or lawyer while a candidate for judicial office, after notice and hearing found by the Commission to be guilty of misconduct, to the Kentucky Bar Association for possible suspension or disbarment from the practice of law.

(2) Any erroneous decision made in good faith shall not be subject to the jurisdiction of the Commission.

HISTORY: Amended by Order 89–1, eff. 8–28–89; prior amendments eff. 3–8–83, 9–1–80, 1–1–78; adopted eff. 10–1–76

SCR 4.025 Authority of commission in certain situations

(1) The Commission shall have the authority set out in SCR 4.020 without regard to separation of a judge from office or defeat of a candidate in an election, except as specifically limited in SCR 4.000 to SCR 4.300.

(2) For any violation related to campaign conduct in a primary or general election, the authority of the

Commission to take action shall be barred unless notice of preliminary investigation pursuant to SCR 4.170 has been issued by the Commission within 180 days of the date of the general election following the campaign as to which the conduct relates.

(3) For any violation other than a campaign violation, the authority of the Commission to take action against a judge who has left office shall be barred unless notice of preliminary investigation pursuant to SCR 4.170 has been issued within 180 days after the date the judge leaves office.

(4) Nothing in SCR 4.000 to 4.300 shall bar proceedings against sitting judges who have left judicial office after a prior term of office concerning conduct not previously adjudicated by the Commission.

HISTORY: Amended by Order 98–2, eff. 1–1–99; adopted eff. 1–1–80

SCR 4.030   Powers of commission

As provided in KRS 34.330, the commission may administer oaths, take testimony under oath, compel the attendance of witnesses, and compel the production of records and other evidence. It may also order the judge to undergo a physical or mental examination in appropriate cases.

HISTORY: Adopted eff. 10–1–76

SCR 4.040   Court of Appeals member

The Court of Appeals shall elect one of its judges as its representative on the commission in accordance with procedures to be established by the chief judge.

HISTORY: Adopted eff. 10–1–76

SCR 4.050   Circuit court member

(1) Nominating ballot.

The administrative director of the courts shall send to each circuit judge a nominating ballot on which shall be listed in alphabetical order the names of all circuit judges together with instructions to vote for one nominee and to return the ballot by a certain named date. Subject to the provisions of paragraph (3) of this rule regarding a tie vote, the two persons receiving the highest number of votes shall be nominees.

(2) Second ballot.

The names of the nominees shall be placed in alphabetical order on a second ballot which shall be sent by the administrative director of the courts to all judges, with the same instructions as provided on the nominating ballot. Subject to paragraph (3) of this rule, the person receiving the highest number of votes shall be the circuit court representative on the commission.

(3) Tie vote.

If the winners of the nominating ballot or the second ballot cannot be determined because of a tie

vote among the candidates, the election shall be determined by lot in such manner as the administrative director of the courts directs, in the presence of not less than three other persons.

HISTORY: Amended eff. 1–1–78; adopted eff. 10–1–76

SCR 4.060   District court member

The district court representative on the commission shall be elected by the judges of the district court in the same manner as the circuit court member.

HISTORY: Adopted eff. 10–1–76

SCR 4.070   Bar association member

The board of governors of the Kentucky Bar Association shall appoint a member of the bar as the bar representative on the commission in the same manner in which it makes other appointments.

HISTORY: Adopted eff. 10–1–76

SCR 4.075   Alternate members

At the time and in the same manner as the Court of Appeals, circuit court and district court members are elected, an alternate member for each shall be elected. At the time and in the same manner as the bar association member is appointed an alternate member shall be appointed. The alternate member shall serve on the commission during such time as the member disqualifies or is otherwise unable to serve or a vacancy exists.

HISTORY: Adopted eff. 1–1–78

SCR 4.080   Vacancies

When a judge ceases to be a judge of the class of court from which he was elected, or whenever any member of the commission becomes ineligible for membership thereon, his membership shall terminate. Elections to fill uncompleted terms shall be conducted in the same manner as provided herein for regular elections.

HISTORY: Adopted eff. 10–1–76

SCR 4.090   Disqualification

(1) Grounds. A member or alternate member shall disqualify from participation as a member in all matters in which the member has an interest, relationship or bias that would disqualify a judge in a judicial proceeding.

(2) Procedure.

(a) A party seeking disqualification of a member or alternate member shall file a verified motion with the executive secretary who shall forthwith transmit the motion to the challenged member.

(b) The challenged member shall promptly file with the Executive Secretary a written response stating whether the member recuses. The response may include explanation of the member's position.

(c) If a member refuses to recuse, the recusal issue shall be decided by majority vote of the other members of the Commission by written findings not later than the meeting next following the filing of the member's response to the motion to recuse.

(d) Upon disqualification of a member, the disqualified member's alternate shall serve. If there be no alternate for the disqualified member, the matter shall be determined by the remaining members of the Commission.

HISTORY: Amended by Order 99–1, eff. 2–1–00; prior amendment eff. 1–1–99 (Order 98–2); adopted eff. 10–1–76

SCR 4.095   Term of office: transitional provisions

(1) The 4-year terms of office of all members and alternate members of the commission shall be deemed as having commenced on the first Monday in January of 1976 except for the district court member and alternate member, whose terms shall commence on the first Monday in January of 1978. Selection or appointment of the initial member shall be for the unexpired portions of the respective terms of office.

(2) Except for the district court member the commission shall be fully constituted by election or appointment of its members as soon as practicable after initial appointment of the members of the Court of Appeals. The initial district court member and alternate member and the initial Court of Appeals, circuit court and bar association alternate members shall be selected as soon as practicable after the first Monday in January of 1978.

(3) Pending selection of the initial district court member the commission shall exercise the powers and authorities conferred upon it by section 121 of the Constitution and by these rules, except that beginning on the first Monday in January of 1978 the district court membership, though temporarily vacant, shall be counted in determining what is a majority vote of the commission under KRS 34.340 and Rule 4.120.

HISTORY: Amended eff. 1–1–78; adopted eff. 10–1–76

SCR 4.100   Officers

The members of the commission shall elect one of their number as chairman and one as vice-chairman, provided however that a judge member of the commission shall not be eligible to serve as chairman or vice-chairman. The commission shall employ an executive secretary and such other employees as the Chief Justice approves, subject to budgetary exigencies. The executive secretary shall have custody of its records.

HISTORY: Amended eff. 1–1–78; adopted eff. 10–1–76

SCR 4.110   Counsel

The commission may request the attorney general to gather and present evidence before the commission and before the Supreme Court upon judicial review;

or it may designate or employ any member of the Kentucky bar for that purpose.

HISTORY: Adopted eff. 10–1–76

SCR 4.120   Quorum

A quorum shall be four members. The commission may act by majority vote of members present except in the suspension, retirement, censure or removal of a judge for good cause, when it must act by a majority of the full commission. Absence of a member or a vacancy upon the commission shall not invalidate its action.

HISTORY: Amended eff. 1–1–78; adopted eff. 10–1–76

SCR 4.130   Confidentiality

All papers and information obtained by or on behalf of the Commission shall be confidential except as provided in this rule or by order of the Supreme Court.

(1) Following the procedure set forth in SCR 4.170, upon filing of an answer to a notice of formal proceedings, or expiration of time for filing an answer, the notice and all subsequent pleadings filed with the Commission shall not be confidential, except that the Commission's internal papers such as investigative reports and staff memoranda, and similar matters, shall remain confidential and shall not be a part of the formal file.

(a) Following the procedure set forth in SCR 4.170, upon filing of an answer to a notice of formal proceedings, or expiration of time for filing an answer, the notice and all subsequent pleadings filed with the Commission shall not be confidential, except that the Commission's internal papers such as investigative reports and staff memoranda, and similar matters, shall remain confidential and shall not be a part of the formal file.

(b) The Commission may reveal information to appropriate law enforcement authorities or to the judge under investigation that it believes is reasonable necessary in order to protect the public or the administration of justice.

(2) Hearings in formal proceedings shall be public, except that the Commission shall deliberate in executive session in reaching any decision involved in such hearings.

(3) The Commission may on its own initiative, and shall upon request of the director or Board of Governors of the Kentucky Bar Association, make available to the Kentucky Bar Association any of the Commission's records pertinent to a disciplinary matter or inquiry under investigation by the Commission or by the Association.

(4) Breach of confidentiality may be deemed contempt of court and grounds for removal of a member

of the Commission and for discharge of any of its agents or employees.

HISTORY: Amended by Order 2012–01, eff. 3–1–12; prior amendments eff. 1–1–99 (Order 98–2), 1–1–80, 1–1–78; adopted eff. 10–1–76

SCR 4.140   Privilege

The filing of papers with or the giving of testimony before the commission shall be privileged in any action for defamation. No other publication of such papers or proceedings shall be so privileged, except that the record filed by the commission in the Supreme Court shall continue to be privileged.

HISTORY: Adopted eff. 10–1–76

SCR 4.150   Service of papers

Service of notices and other papers may be by personal service or by mail. Papers served on the judge shall be marked "Personal and Confidential."

HISTORY: Adopted eff. 10–1–76

SCR 4.160   Civil rules apply

To the extent applicable and not inconsistent with these rules, the Rules of Civil Procedure shall apply to proceedings before the commission, except that the proof shall be by clear and convincing evidence.

HISTORY: Amended eff. 1–1–78; adopted eff. 10–1–76

SCR 4.170   Complaint; preliminary investigation

(1) Upon its own motion or upon receiving a written complaint alleging facts indicating that there is probable cause for action concerning a judge, the Commission shall make a preliminary investigation to determine whether formal proceedings should be initiated.

(2) Notice of the investigation shall be given to the judge, and he shall be given an opportunity to appear informally before the commission. The name of the complainant shall not be included in the notice.

(3) If the commission concludes after its preliminary investigation that formal proceedings should not be initiated, it shall so inform the judge.

(4) After the preliminary investigation is completed and before formal proceedings are initiated under Rule 4.180, the Commission shall afford the judge under investigation an opportunity to examine all factual information, including the name of the complainant if relevant, and shall afford the judge an opportunity to furnish to the Commission any information the judge may desire bearing on the investigation.

(5) The Commission shall decide whether to initiate formal proceedings under SCR 4.180 within 180 days of commencement of preliminary investigation, unless within such period or extension thereof the Commission for good cause shown and with the agreement of the judge extends such period for a period or periods

not exceeding an additional 180 days. The judge shall be informed of such extensions.

HISTORY: Amended by Order 98–2, eff. 1–1–99; prior amendment eff. 1–1–78; adopted eff. 10–1–76

SCR 4.180   Formal proceedings

If the commission concludes that formal proceedings should be initiated, it shall notify the judge. He may file an answer within 15 days after service of the notice. Upon the filing of his answer, or the expiration of time for so filing, the commission shall set a time and place for the hearing and shall give reasonable notice thereof to the judge.

HISTORY: Adopted eff. 10–1–76

SCR 4.190   Amendments to notice or answer

The notice or answer may be amended to conform to proof or to set forth additional facts, whether occurring before or after the commencement of the hearing. In case such an amendment is made, the judge shall be given reasonable time both to answer the amendment and to prepare and present his defense against the matters charged thereby.

HISTORY: Adopted eff. 10–1–76

SCR 4.200   Extension of time

The chairman of the commission may extend the time for filing an answer and for the commencement of a hearing before the commission.

HISTORY: Adopted eff. 10–1–76

SCR 4.210   Procedural rights of judge

(1) In proceedings involving his censure, retirement or removal, a judge shall have the right and reasonable opportunity to defend against the charges by the introduction of evidence, to be represented by counsel, and to examine and cross-examine witnesses. He shall also have the right to the issuance of subpoenas for attendance of witnesses to testify or produce books, papers, and other evidentiary matter.

(2) When a transcript of the testimony has been prepared at the expense of the commission, a copy thereof shall, upon request, be available for use by the judge and his counsel in connection with the proceedings. The judge shall have the right, without any order or approval, to have all or any portion of the testimony in the proceedings transcribed at the expense of the commission.

(3) Except as herein otherwise provided, whenever these rules provide for giving notice or sending any matter to the judge, such notice or matter shall be sent to the judge at his residence unless he requests otherwise, and a copy thereof shall be mailed to his counsel of record.

(4) If the judge is adjudged insane or incompetent, or if it appears to the commission at any time during the proceedings that he is not competent to act for

himself, it shall appoint a guardian ad litem unless the judge has a committee who will represent him. In the appointment of such guardian ad litem, preference shall be given, whenever possible, to members of the judge's immediate family. The committee or guardian ad litem may claim and exercise any right and privilege and make any defense for the judge with the same force and effect as if claimed, exercised, or made by the judge, if competent, and whenever these rules provide for serving or giving notice or sending any matter to the judge, such notice or matter shall be served, given, or sent to the committee or guardian ad litem.

HISTORY: Amended eff. 1–1–78; adopted eff. 10–1–76

SCR 4.220   Hearing

(1) At the time and place set for hearing, the commission shall proceed with the hearing whether or not the judge has filed an answer or appears at the hearing. Counsel shall present the case in support of the charges.

(2) The failure of the judge to answer or to appear at the hearing shall not, standing alone, be taken as evidence of the truth of the facts alleged to constitute grounds for censure, suspension, retirement or removal. The failure of the judge to testify in his own behalf or to submit to a medical examination requested by the commission may be considered, unless it appears that such failure was occasioned by circumstances beyond his control.

(3) In a hearing before the commission not less than five members shall be present when the evidence is produced.

HISTORY: Amended eff. 1–1–78; adopted eff. 10–1–76

SCR 4.230   Reporter; transcript

The proceedings shall be reported by a qualified court reporter or by mechanical means, but shall not be transcribed unless so directed by the commission or requested by the judge as provided in Rule 4.210(2).

HISTORY: Amended eff. 1–1–78; adopted eff. 10–1–76

SCR 4.240   Evidence

At a hearing before the commission legal evidence only shall be received, and oral evidence shall be taken only on oath or affirmation.

HISTORY: Adopted eff. 10–1–76

SCR 4.250   Hearing additional evidence

The commission may order a hearing for the taking of additional evidence at any time while the matter is pending before it. The order shall set the time and place of hearing and shall indicate the matters on which the evidence is to be taken. A copy of such order shall be sent by mail to the judge at least 10 days prior to the date of hearing.

HISTORY: Adopted eff. 10–1–76

SCR 4.260   Commission findings; order

(1) The commission shall make written findings of fact and conclusions of law which shall be filed with the record in the case.

(2) A certified copy of the commission's findings of fact, conclusions of law and final order shall be served on the judge immediately after entry.

(3) The Commission shall make final disposition in formal proceedings as provided in this section within 180 days of notice of such proceedings, except that within such period or extension thereof the Commission may for good cause extend such period for a period or periods not exceeding an additional 180 days. The judge shall be informed of such extensions.

HISTORY: Amended by Order 98–2, eff. 1–1–99; prior amendment eff. 1–1–78; adopted eff. 10–1–76

SCR 4.270   Commission orders

Commission orders shall become effective ten days after service on the judge unless he appeals therefrom within that time. Upon its effective date, a certified copy of an order of public censure, suspension, removal or retirement shall be given to appropriate persons such as the Chief Justice, the executive department for finance and administration and the judicial retirement board. Notice of a private reprimand shall not be given to any person other than the judge.

A judge who is retired for a permanent disability shall thereupon become eligible for retirement benefits under KRS 21.345 to KRS 21.455.

A judge who is placed on temporary retirement shall continue to draw full compensation the same as if he were on active duty, and for retirement purposes shall be considered as continuing in active service.

HISTORY: Adopted eff. 10–1–76

SCR 4.280   Certification of commission order

Upon making a determination ordering the censure, suspension, retirement or removal of a judge, the commission shall promptly file a copy of the order certified by the chairman or secretary of the commission, together with the findings and conclusions and the record of the proceedings, in a permanent file.

HISTORY: Adopted eff. 10–1–76

SCR 4.290   Judicial review

(1) To the extent applicable and not inconsistent with SCR 4, the Rules of Civil Procedure (CR) applicable to other types of proceedings shall apply to the judicial review of commission orders by the Supreme Court.

(2) A notice of appeal of the commission's final order shall be filed with the clerk of the Supreme Court within ten days after service of notice of the order upon the judge. A copy of the notice of appeal shall be served on the commission.

(3) The commission shall thereupon promptly transmit to the court the entire original record upon which the order is based, unless by stipulation of the commission and the judge an abbreviated or substitute record is agreed upon. A transcript of testimony shall not be included in the record unless designated by the commission or the judge, but may be ordered by the Supreme Court at any time.

(4) The judge shall file his brief within 20 days after the record is filed and the commission shall file its brief within 20 days thereafter. The time for filing of briefs may be extended by the court upon motion of either party.

(5) The court shall have power to affirm, modify or set aside in whole or in part the order of the commission, or to remand the action to the commission for further proceedings.

HISTORY: Amended eff. 1–1–78; adopted eff. 10–1–76

SCR 4.300   Kentucky Code of Judicial Conduct

APPLICATION OF THE CODE OF JUDICIAL CONDUCT

PREAMBLE

Our legal system is based on the principle that an independent, fair and competent judiciary will interpret and apply the laws that govern us. The role of the judiciary is central to American and Kentucky concepts of justice and the rule of law. Intrinsic to all sections of this Code are the precepts that judges, individually and collectively, must respect and honor the judicial office as a public trust and strive to enhance and maintain confidence in our legal system. The judge is an arbiter of facts and law for the resolution of disputes and a highly visible symbol of government under the rule of law.

The Code of Judicial Conduct is intended to establish standards for ethical conduct of judges. It consists of broad statements called Canons, specific rules set forth in Sections under each Canon, a Terminology Section, An Application Section and Commentary. The text of the Canons and the Sections, including the Terminology and Application Sections, is authoritative. The Commentary, by explanation and example, provides guidance with respect to the purpose and meaning of the Canons and Sections. The Commentary is not intended as a statement of additional rules. When the text uses "shall" or "shall not," it is intended to impose binding obligations the violation of which can result in disciplinary action. When "should" or "should not" is used, the text is intended as hortatory and as a statement of what is or is not appropriate conduct but not as a binding rule under which a judge may be disciplined. When "may" is used, it denotes permissible discretion or, depending on the context, it refers to action that is not covered by specific proscriptions.

The Canons and Sections are rules of reason. They should be applied consistent with constitutional requirements, statutes, other court rules and decisional law and in the context of all relevant circumstances, including the varying degrees of responsibility and administrative functions of different levels of courts. The Code is to be construed so as not to impinge on the essential discretion of judges in making judicial decisions.

The Code is designed to provide guidance to judges and candidates for judicial office and to provide a structure for regulating conduct through disciplinary agencies. It is not designed or intended as a basis for civil liability or criminal prosecution. Furthermore, the purpose of the Code would be subverted if the Code were invoked by lawyers for mere tactical advantage in a proceeding.

The text of the Canons and Sections is intended to govern conduct of judges and to be binding upon them. It is not intended, however, that every transgression will result in disciplinary action. Whether disciplinary action is appropriate, and the degree of discipline to be imposed, should be determined through a reasonable and reasoned application of the text and should depend on such factors as the seriousness of the transgression, whether there is a pattern of improper activity and the effect of the improper activity on others or on the judicial system.

The Code of Judicial Conduct is not intended as an exhaustive guide for the conduct of judges. They should also be governed in their judicial and personal conduct by general ethical standards. The Code is intended, however, to state basic standards which should govern the conduct of all judges and to provide guidance to assist judges in establishing and maintaining high standards of judicial and personal conduct.

TERMINOLOGY

"Appropriate authority" denotes the authority with responsibility for initiation of disciplinary process with respect to the violation to be reported.

"Candidate." A candidate is a person seeking selection for or retention in judicial office by election or appointment. A person becomes a candidate for judicial office as soon as he or she makes a public announcement of candidacy, declares or files as a candidate with the election or appointment authority, or authorizes solicitation or acceptance of contributions or support. The term "candidate" has the same meaning when applied to a judge seeking election or appointment to non-judicial office.

"Court personnel" does not include the lawyers in a proceeding before a judge.

"De minimis" denotes an insignificant interest that could not raise reasonable question as to a judge's impartiality.

"Economic interest" denotes ownership of a more than de minimis legal or equitable interest, or a relationship as officer, director, advisor or other active participant in the affairs of a party, except that:

(i) ownership of an interest in a mutual or common investment fund that holds securities is not an economic interest in such securities unless the judge participates in the management of the fund or a proceeding pending or impending before the judge could substantially affect the value of the interest;

(ii) service by a judge as an officer, director, advisor or other active participant in an educational, religious, charitable, fraternal or civic organization, or service by a judge's spouse, parent or child as an officer, director, advisor or other active participant in any organization does not create an economic interest in securities held by that organization;

(iii) a deposit in a financial institution, the proprietary interest of a policy holder in a mutual insurance company, of a depositor in a mutual savings association or of a member in a credit union, or a similar proprietary interest, is not an economic interest in the organization unless a proceeding pending or impending before the judge could substantially affect the value of the interest;

(iv) ownership of government securities is not an economic interest in the issuer unless a proceeding pending or impending before the judge could substantially affect the value of the securities.

"Fiduciary" includes such relationships as executor, administrator, trustee, and guardian.

"Knowingly," "knowledge," "known" or "knows" denotes actual knowledge of the fact in question. A person's knowledge may be inferred from circumstances.

"Law" denotes court rules as well as statutes, constitutional provisions and decisional law.

"Member of the candidate's family" denotes a spouse, child, grandchild, parent, grandparent or other relative or person with whom the candidate maintains a close familial relationship.

"Member of the judge's family" denotes a spouse, child, grandchild, parent, grandparent, or other relative or person with whom the judge maintains a close familial relationship.

"Member of the judge's family residing in the judge's household" denotes any relative of a judge by blood or marriage, or a person treated by a judge as a member of the judge's family, who resides in the judge's household.

"Nonpublic information" denotes information that, by law, is not available to the public. Nonpublic information may include but is not limited to: information that is sealed by statute or court order, impounded or communicated in camera; and information offered in grand jury proceedings, presentencing reports, dependency cases or psychiatric reports.

"Political organization" denotes a political party or other group, the principal purpose of which is to further the election or appointment of candidates to political office.

"Public election." This term includes primary and general elections; it includes partisan elections, nonpartisan elections and retention elections.

"Require." The rules prescribing that a judge "require" certain conduct of others are, like all of the rules in this Code, rules of reason. The use of the term "require" in that context means a judge is to exercise reasonable direction and control over the conduct of those persons subject to the judge's direction and control.

"Third degree of relationship." The following persons are relatives within the third degree of relationship: great–grandparent, grandparent, parent, uncle, aunt, brother, sister, child, grandchild, great-grandchild, nephew or niece.

CANON 1
CANON 1: A JUDGE SHALL UPHOLD THE INTEGRITY AND INDEPENDENCE OF THE JUDICIARY

An independent and honorable judiciary is indispensable to justice in our society. A judge should actively participate in establishing, maintaining and enforcing high standards of conduct, and shall personally observe those standards so that the integrity and independence of the judiciary will be preserved. The provisions of this Code are to be construed and applied to further that objective.

Commentary

Deference to the judgments and rulings of courts depends upon public confidence in the integrity and independence of judges. The integrity and independence of judges depends in turn upon their acting without fear or favor. Although judges should be independent, they must comply with the law, including the provisions of this Code. Public confidence in the impartiality of the judiciary is maintained by the adherence of each judge to this responsibility. Conversely, violation of this Code diminishes public confidence in the judiciary and thereby does injury to the system of government under law. This Code is intended to apply to every aspect of judicial behavior except purely legal decisions made in good faith in the performance of judicial duties. Such decisions are subject to judicial review. Reference is made to SCR 4.020(2).

CANON 2

CANON 2: A JUDGE SHALL AVOID IMPROPRIETY AND THE APPEARANCE OF IMPROPRIETY IN ALL OF THE JUDGE'S ACTIVITIES

A. A judge shall respect and comply with the law and shall act at all times in a manner that promotes public confidence in the integrity and impartiality of the judiciary.

Commentary

Public confidence in the judiciary is eroded by irresponsible or improper conduct by judges. A judge must avoid all impropriety and appearance of impropriety. A judge must expect to be the subject of constant public scrutiny. A judge must therefore accept restrictions on the judge's conduct that might be viewed as burdensome by the ordinary citizen and should do so freely and willingly.

The prohibition against behaving with impropriety or the appearance of impropriety applies to both the professional and personal conduct of a judge. Because it is not practicable to list all prohibited acts, the proscription is necessarily cast in general terms that extend to conduct by judges that is harmful although not specifically mentioned in the Code. Actual improprieties under this standard include violations of law, court rules or other specific provisions of this Code. The test for appearance of impropriety is whether the conduct would create in reasonable minds a perception that the judge's ability to carry out judicial responsibilities with integrity, impartiality and competence is impaired. See also Commentary under Section 2E.

B. A judge may properly lend the prestige of the judge's office to advance the public interest in the administration of justice.

C. A judge may actively support public agencies or interests or testify voluntarily on public matters concerning the law, the legal system, the provision of legal services, and the administration of justice.

D. A judge shall not allow family, social, political or other relationships to impair the judge's objectivity. A judge shall not lend the prestige of judicial office to advance the private interests of the judge or others; nor shall a judge convey or permit others to convey the impression that they are in a special position to

influence the judge. A judge shall not testify voluntarily as a character witness.

Commentary

Maintaining the prestige of judicial office is essential to a system of government in which the judiciary functions independently of the executive and legislative branches. Respect for the judicial office facilitates the orderly conduct of legitimate judicial functions. Judges should distinguish between proper and improper use of the prestige of office in all of their activities. For example, it would be improper for a judge to allude to his or her judgeship to gain a personal advantage such as deferential treatment when stopped by a police officer for a traffic offense. Similarly, judicial letterhead must not be used for conducting a judge's personal business.

A judge must avoid lending the prestige of judicial office for the advancement of the private interests of others. For example, a judge must not use the judge's judicial position to gain advantage in a civil suit involving a member of the judge's family. In contracts for publication of a judge's writings, a judge should retain control over the advertising to avoid exploitation of the judge's office. As to the acceptance of awards, see Section 4D(5)(a) and Commentary. A judge should be careful in the use of the judge's letterhead.

Although a judge should be sensitive to possible abuse of the prestige of office, a judge may, based on the judge's personal knowledge, serve as a reference or provide a letter of recommendation. However, a judge must not initiate the communication of information to a sentencing judge or a probation or corrections officer but may provide to such persons information for the record in response to a formal request.

Judges may participate in the process of judicial selection by cooperating with appointing authorities and screening committees seeking names for consideration, and by responding to official inquiries concerning a person being considered for a judgeship. See also Canon 5 regarding use of a judge's name in political activities.

A judge must not testify voluntarily as a character witness because to do so may lend the prestige of the judicial office in support of the party for whom the judge testifies. Moreover, when a judge testifies as a witness, a lawyer who regularly appears before the judge may be placed in the awkward position of cross-examining the judge. A judge may, however, testify when properly summoned. Except in unusual circumstances where the demands of justice require, a judge should discourage a party from requiring the judge to testify as a character witness.

E. A judge shall not hold membership in any organization that practices invidious discrimination on the basis of race, sex, religion or national origin. Invidious discrimination includes any action by an organization that appears to regard some immutable individual trait, such as a person's race, gender, religion or national origin, as odious or inferior, which is used to justify arbitrary exclusion of persons possessing those traits from membership or participation in the organization. On the other hand, organizations dedicated to the preservation of religious, fraternal, sororal, spiritual, charitable, civic, or cultural values, which do not stigmatize any excluded persons as inferior and therefore unworthy of membership, are not considered to discriminate invidiously.

Commentary

Membership of a judge in an organization that practices invidious discrimination gives rise to perceptions that the judge's impartiality is impaired. Section 2E refers to the current practices of the organization. Whether an organization practices invidious discrimination is often a complex question to which judges should be sensitive. The answer cannot be determined from a mere examination of an organization's current membership rolls but rather depends on how the organization selects members and other relevant factors, such as that the organization is dedicated to the preservation of religious, ethnic or cultural values of legitimate common interest to its members, or that it is in fact and effect an intimate, purely private organization whose membership limitations could not be constitutionally prohibited.

An organization is generally said to discriminate invidiously if it arbitrarily excludes from membership on the basis of race, religion, sex or national origin persons who would otherwise be admitted to membership. *See New York State Club Ass'n., Inc. v. City of New York*, 108 S. Ct. 2225, 101 L. Ed. 2d 1 (1988); *Board of Directors of Rotary International v. Rotary Club of Duarte*, 481 U.S. 537, 107 S. Ct. 1940, [(1987)] 95 L. Ed. 2d 474 *(1987)*; *Roberts v. United States Jaycees*, 468 U.S. 609, 104 S. Ct. 3244, 82 L. Ed. 2d 462 (1984).

Although Section 2E relates only to membership in organizations that invidiously discriminate on the basis of race, sex, religion or national origin, a judge's membership in an organization that engages in any discriminatory membership practices prohibited by the law of the jurisdiction also violates Canon 2 and Section 2A and gives the appearance of impropriety. In addition, it would be a violation of Canon 2 and Section 2A for a judge to arrange a meeting at a club that the judge knows practices invidious discrimination on the basis of race, sex, religion or national origin in its membership or other policies, or for the judge to regularly use such a club. Moreover, public manifestation by a judge of the judge's knowing approval of invidious discrimination on any basis gives the appearance of impropriety under Canon 2 and diminishes public confidence in the integrity and impartiality of the judiciary, in violation of Section 2A.

When a person who is a judge on the date this Code becomes effective learns that an organization to which the judge belongs engages in invidious discrimination that would preclude membership under Section 2E or under Canon 2 and Section 2A, the judge is permitted, in lieu of resigning, to make immediate efforts to have the organization discontinue its invidiously discriminatory practices, but is required to suspend participation in any other activities of the organization. If the organization fails to discontinue its invidiously discriminatory practices as promptly as possible (and in all events within a year of the judge's first learning of the practices), the judge is required to resign immediately from the organization.

CANON 3

CANON 3: A JUDGE SHALL PERFORM THE DUTIES OF JUDICIAL OFFICE IMPARTIALLY AND DILIGENTLY

A. Judicial Duties in General. The judicial duties of a judge take precedence over all the judge's other activities. The judge's judicial duties include all the duties of the judge's office prescribed by law. In the performance of these duties, the following standards apply.

B. Adjudicative Responsibilities.

(1) A judge shall hear and decide matters assigned to the judge except those in which disqualification is required.

(2) A judge shall be faithful to the law and maintain professional competence in it. A judge shall not be swayed by partisan interests, public clamor or fear of criticism.

(3) A judge shall require order and decorum in proceedings before the judge.

(4) A judge shall be patient, dignified and courteous to litigants, jurors, witnesses, lawyers and others with whom the judge deals in an official capacity, and shall require similar conduct of lawyers, and of staff, court officials and others subject to the judge's direction and control.

Commentary
The duty to hear all proceedings fairly and with patience is not inconsistent with the duty to dispose promptly of the business of the court. Judges can be efficient and businesslike while being patient and deliberate.

(5) A judge shall perform judicial duties without bias or prejudice. A judge shall not, in the performance of judicial duties, by words or conduct manifest bias or prejudice, including but not limited to bias or prejudice based upon race, sex, religion, national origin, disability, age, sexual orientation or socioeconomic status, and in proceedings before the judge, shall not permit staff, court officials and others subject to the judge's direction and control to do so.

Commentary
A judge must refrain from speech, gestures or other conduct that could reasonably be perceived as sexual harassment and must require the same standard of conduct of others subject to the judge's direction and control.

A judge must perform judicial duties impartially and fairly. A judge who manifests bias on any basis in a proceeding impairs the fairness of the proceeding and brings the judiciary into disrepute. Facial expression and body language, in addition to oral communication, can give to parties or lawyers in the proceeding, jurors, the media and others an appearance of judicial bias. A judge must be alert to avoid behavior that may be perceived as prejudicial.

(6) A judge shall require lawyers in proceedings before the judge to refrain from manifesting by words or conduct bias or prejudice based upon race, sex, religion, national origin, disability, age, sexual orientation or socioeconomic status, against parties, witnesses, counsel or others. This Section 3B(6) does not preclude legitimate advocacy when race, sex, religion, national origin, disability, age, sexual orientation or socioeconomic status, or other similar factors, are issues in the proceeding.

(7) A judge shall accord to every person who has a legal interest in a proceeding, or that person's lawyer, the right to be heard according to law. With regard to a pending or impending proceeding, a judge shall not initiate, permit, or consider ex parte communications with attorneys and shall not initiate, encourage or consider ex parte communications with parties, except that:

(a) Where circumstances require, ex parte communications for scheduling, initial fixing of bail, administrative purposes or emergencies that do not deal with substantive matters or issues on the merits are authorized; provided:

(i) the judge reasonably believes that no party will gain a procedural or tactical advantage as a result of the ex parte communication, and

(ii) the judge makes provision promptly to notify all other parties of the substance of the ex parte communication and allows an opportunity to respond.

(b) As a part of legal research, a judge may obtain the advice of a disinterested expert on the law applicable to a proceeding before the judge.

(c) A judge may consult with court personnel whose function is to aid the judge in carrying out the judge's adjudicative responsibilities or with other judges.

(d) A judge may, with the consent of the parties, confer separately with the parties and their lawyers in an effort to mediate or settle matters pending before the judge.

(e) A judge may initiate or consider any ex parte communications when expressly authorized by law to do so.

Commentary

The proscription against communications concerning a proceeding includes communications from lawyers, and other persons who are not participants in the proceeding, except to the limited extent permitted.

To the extent reasonably possible, all parties or their lawyers shall be included in communications with a judge.

Whenever presence of a party or notice to a party is required by Section 3B(7), it is the party's lawyer, or if the party is unrepresented the party, who is to be present or to whom notice is to be given.

An appropriate and often desirable procedure for a court to obtain the advice of a disinterested expert on legal issues is to invite the expert to file a brief amicus curiae.

Certain ex parte communication is approved by Section 3B(7) to facilitate scheduling and other administrative purposes and to accommodate emergencies. In general, however, a judge must discourage ex parte communication and allow it only if all the criteria stated in Section 3B(7) are clearly met. A judge must disclose to all parties all ex parte communications described in Sections 3B(7)(a) regarding a proceeding pending or impending before the judge.

A judge must not independently investigate facts in a case and must consider only the evidence presented.

A judge may request a party to submit proposed findings of fact and conclusions of law, so long as the other parties are apprised of the request and are given an opportunity to respond to the proposed findings and conclusions.

A judge must make reasonable efforts, including the provision of appropriate supervision, to ensure that Section 3B(7) is not violated through law clerks or other personnel on the judge's staff.

If communication between the trial judge and the appellate court with respect to a proceeding is permitted, a copy of any written communication or the substance of any oral communication should be provided to all parties.

(8) A judge shall dispose of all judicial matters promptly, efficiently and fairly.

Commentary

In disposing of matters promptly, efficiently and fairly, a judge must demonstrate due regard for the rights of the parties to be heard and to have issues resolved without unnecessary cost or delay. Containing costs while preserving fundamental rights of parties also protects the interests of witnesses and the general public. A judge should monitor and supervise cases so as to reduce or eliminate dilatory practices, avoidable delays and unnecessary costs. A judge should encourage and seek to facilitate settlement, but parties should not feel coerced into surrendering the right to have their controversy resolved by the courts.

Prompt disposition of the court's business requires a judge to devote adequate time to judicial duties, to be punctual in attending court and expeditious in determining matters under submission, and to insist that court officials, litigants and their lawyers cooperate with the judge to that end.

(9) A judge shall not, while a proceeding is pending or impending in any court, make any public comment that might reasonably be expected to affect its outcome or impair its fairness or make any nonpublic comment that might substantially interfere with a fair trial or hearing. The judge shall require similar abstention on the part of court personnel subject to the judge's direction and control. This Section does not prohibit judges from making public statements in the course of their official duties or from explaining for public information the procedures of the court. This Section does not apply to proceedings in which the judge is a litigant in a personal capacity.

Commentary

The requirement that judges abstain from public comment regarding a pending or impending proceeding continues during any appellate process and until final disposition. This Section does not prohibit a judge from commenting on proceedings in which the judge is a litigant in a personal capacity, but in cases such as a writ of mandamus where the judge is a litigant in an official capacity, the judge must not comment publicly. The conduct of lawyers relating to trial publicity is governed by SCR 3.130(3.6).

(10) A judge shall not commend or criticize jurors for their verdict other than in a court order or opinion in a proceeding, but may express appreciation to jurors for their service to the judicial system and the community.

Commentary

Commending or criticizing jurors for their verdict may imply a judicial expectation in future cases and may impair a juror's ability to be fair and impartial in a subsequent case.

(11) A judge shall not disclose or use, for any purpose unrelated to judicial duties, nonpublic information acquired in a judicial capacity.

C.   Administrative Responsibilities.

(1) A judge shall diligently discharge the judge's administrative responsibilities without bias or prejudice and maintain professional competence in judicial administration, and should cooperate with other judges and court officials in the administration of court business.

(2) A judge shall require a judge's staff and those subject to the judge's direction and control and should encourage other court officials to observe the standards of fidelity and diligence that apply to the judge and to refrain from manifesting bias or prejudice in the performance of their official duties.

(3) A judge with supervisory authority for the judicial performance of other judges shall take reasonable measures to assure the prompt disposition of matters before them and the proper performance of their other judicial responsibilities.

(4) A judge shall not make unnecessary appointments. A judge shall exercise the power of appointment impartially and on the basis of merit. A judge shall avoid nepotism and favoritism. A judge shall not approve compensation of appointees beyond the fair value of services rendered.

Commentary

Appointees of a judge include assigned counsel, officials such as referees, commissioners, special masters, receivers and guardians and personnel such as clerks, secretaries and bailiffs. Consent by the parties to an appointment or an award of compensation does not relieve the judge of the obligation prescribed by Section 3C(4).

D. Disciplinary Responsibilities.

(1) A judge who receives information indicating a substantial likelihood that another judge has committed a violation of this Code should take appropriate action. A judge having knowledge that another judge has committed a violation of this Code that raises a substantial question as to the other judge's fitness for office should inform the appropriate authority.

(2) A judge who receives information indicating a substantial likelihood that a lawyer has committed a violation of the Kentucky Rules of Professional Conduct should take appropriate action. A judge having knowledge that a lawyer has committed a violation of the Kentucky Rules of Professional Conduct that raises a substantial question as to the lawyer's honesty, trustworthiness or fitness as a lawyer in other respects should inform the appropriate authority.

(3) A judge acting in good faith in the discharge of disciplinary responsibilities required or permitted by Sections 3D(1) and 3D(2) shall be immune from any action, civil or criminal.

Commentary

Appropriate action may include direct communication with the judge or lawyer who has committed the violation, other direct action if available, and reporting the violation to the appropriate authority or other agency or body. A judge should comply with KRS 26A.080.

E. Disqualification.

(1) A judge shall disqualify himself or herself in a proceeding in which the judge's impartiality might reasonably be questioned, including but not limited to instances where:

Commentary

Under this rule, a judge is disqualified whenever the judge's impartiality might reasonably be questioned, regardless whether any of the specific rules in Section 3E(1) apply. For example, if a judge were in the process of negotiating for employment with a law firm, the judge would be disqualified from any matters in which that law firm appeared, unless the disqualification was waived by the parties after disclosure by the judge.

A judge should disclose on the record information that the judge believes the parties or their lawyers might consider relevant to the question of disqualification, even if the judge believes there is no real basis for disqualification.

By decisional law, the rule of necessity may override the rule of disqualification. For example, a judge might be required to participate in judicial review of a judicial salary statute, or might be the only judge available in a matter requiring immediate judicial action, such as a hearing on probable cause or a temporary restraining order. In the latter case, the judge must disclose on the record the basis for possible disqualification and use reasonable efforts to transfer the matter to another judge as soon as practicable.

(a) the judge has a personal bias or prejudice concerning a party or a party's lawyer, or personal knowledge of disputed evidentiary facts concerning the proceeding;

Commentary

Dislike of a party or a party's lawyer does not, by itself, constitute a personal bias or prejudice.

(b) the judge served as a lawyer in the matter in controversy, or a lawyer with whom the judge previously practiced law served during such association as a lawyer concerning the matter, or the judge has been a material witness concerning it;

Commentary

A lawyer in a government agency does not ordinarily have an association with other lawyers employed by that agency within the meaning of Section 3E(1)(b); a judge formerly employed by a government agency, however, should disqualify himself or herself in a proceeding if the judge's impartiality might reasonably be questioned because of such association.

(c) the judge knows that he or she, individually or as a fiduciary, or the judge's spouse, parent or minor child residing in the judge's household, has any interest, more than a de minimis interest, in the subject matter in controversy or in a party to the proceeding that could be substantially affected by the proceeding;

(d) the judge or the judge's spouse, or a person within the third degree of relationship to either of them, or the spouse of such a person:

(i) is a party to the proceeding, or an officer, director or trustee of a party;

(ii) is acting as a lawyer in the proceeding;

(iii) is known by the judge to have a more than de minimis interest that could be substantially affected by the proceeding;

(iv) is to the judge's knowledge likely to be a material witness in the proceeding.

Commentary

The fact that a lawyer in a proceeding is affiliated with a law firm with which a relative of the judge is affiliated does not of itself disqualify the judge. Under appropriate circumstances, the fact that "the judge's impartiality might reasonably be questioned" under Section 3E(1), or that the relative is known by the judge to have an interest in the law firm that could be "substantially affected by the outcome of the proceeding" under Section 3E(1)(d)(iii) may require the judge's disqualification.

(2) A judge shall keep informed about the judge's personal and fiduciary economic interests, and make a reasonable effort to keep informed about the personal economic interests of the judge's spouse and minor children residing in the judge's household.

F. Remittal of Disqualification.
A judge disqualified by the terms of Section 3E may disclose on the record the basis of the judge's disqualification and may ask the parties and their lawyers to consider, out of the presence of the judge, whether to waive disqualification. If following disclosure of any basis for disqualification other than personal bias or prejudice concerning a party, the parties and lawyers, without participation by the judge, all agree that the judge should not be disqualified, and the judge is then willing to participate, the judge may participate in the proceeding. The agreement, signed by all parties and

lawyers, shall be incorporated in the record of the proceeding.

Commentary

A remittal procedure provides the parties an opportunity to proceed without delay if they wish to waive the disqualification. To assure that consideration of the question of remittal is made independently of the judge, a judge must not solicit, seek or hear comment on possible remittal or waiver of the disqualification unless the lawyers jointly propose remittal after consultation as provided in the rule. A party may act through counsel if counsel represents on the record that the party has been consulted and consents.

CANON 4

CANON 4: A JUDGE SHALL SO CONDUCT THE JUDGE'S EXTRA–JUDICIAL ACTIVITIES AS TO MINIMIZE THE RISK OF CONFLICT WITH JUDICIAL OBLIGATIONS

A. Extra–judicial Activities in General. A judge shall conduct all of the judge's extra-judicial activities so that they do not:

(1) cast reasonable doubt on the judge's capacity to act impartially as a judge;

(2) demean the judicial office; or

(3) interfere with the proper performance of judicial duties.

Commentary

Complete separation of a judge from extra-judicial activities is neither possible nor wise; a judge should not become isolated from the community in which the judge lives.

Expressions of bias or prejudice by a judge, even outside the judge's judicial activities, may cast reasonable doubt on the judge's capacity to act impartially as a judge. Expressions which may do so include jokes or other remarks demeaning individuals on the basis of their race, sex, religion, national origin, disability, age, sexual orientation or socioeconomic status. See Section 2E and accompanying Commentary.

B. Avocational Activities. A judge may speak, write, lecture, teach and participate in other extra-judicial activities concerning the law, the legal system, the administration of justice and non-legal subjects, subject to the requirements of this Code.

Commentary

As a judicial officer and person specially learned in the law, a judge is in a unique position to contribute to the improvement of the law, the legal system, and the administration of justice, including revision of substantive and procedural law and improvement of criminal and juvenile justice. To the extent that time permits, a judge is encouraged to do so, either independently or through a bar association, judicial conference or other organization dedicated to the improvement of the law. Judges may participate in efforts to promote the fair administration of justice, the independence of the judiciary and the integrity of the legal profession and may express opposition to the persecution of lawyers and judges in other countries because of their professional activities.

In this and other Sections of Canon 4, the phrase "subject to the requirements of this Code" is used, notably in connection with a judge's governmental, civic or charitable activities. This phrase is included to remind judges that the use of permissive language in various Sections of the Code does not relieve a judge from the other requirements of the Code that apply to the specific conduct.

C. Governmental, Civic or Charitable Activities.

(1) A judge shall not appear at a public hearing before, or otherwise consult with, an executive or legislative body or official except on matters concerning the law, the legal system or the administration of justice or except when acting pro se in a matter involving the judge or the judge's interests.

Commentary

See Section 2D regarding the obligation to avoid improper influence.

(2) A judge shall not accept appointment to a governmental committee or commission or other governmental position that is concerned with issues of fact or policy on matters other than the improvement of the law, the legal system or the administration of justice. A judge may accept appointment to a governmental committee or commission where a judicial appointment is authorized or required by law. A judge may represent a country, state or locality on ceremonial occasions or in connection with historical, educational or cultural activities.

Commentary

Section 4C(2) prohibits a judge from accepting any governmental position except one relating to the law, legal system or administration of justice as authorized by Section 4(C)(3). The appropriateness of accepting extra-judicial assignments must be assessed in light of the demands on judicial resources created by crowded dockets and the need to protect the courts from involvement in extra-judicial matters that may prove to be controversial. Judges should not accept governmental appointments that are likely to interfere with the effectiveness and independence of the judiciary.

Section 4C(2) does not govern a judge's service in a nongovernmental position. See Section 4C(3) permitting service by a judge with organizations devoted to the improvement of the law, the legal system or the administration of justice and with educational, religious, charitable, fraternal or civic organizations not conducted for profit.

(3) A judge may serve as an officer, director, trustee or non-legal advisor of an organization or governmental agency devoted to the improvement of the law, the legal system or the administration of justice or of an educational, religious, charitable, fraternal or civic organization not conducted for profit, subject to the following limitations and the other requirements of this Code.

Commentary

Section 4C(3) does not apply to a judge's service in a governmental position unconnected with the improvement of the law, the legal system or the administration of justice; see Section 4C(2).

See Commentary to Section 4B regarding use of the phrase "subject to the following limitations and the other requirements of this Code." As an example of the meaning of the phrase, a judge permitted by Section 4C(3) to serve on the board of a fraternal institution may be prohibited from such service by Sections 2C or 4A if the institution practices invidious discrimination or if service on the board otherwise casts reasonable doubt on the judge's capacity to act impartially as a judge.

Service by a judge on behalf of a civic or charitable organization may be governed by other provisions of Canon 4 in addition to Section 4C. For example, a judge is prohibited by Section 4G from serving as a legal advisor to a civic or charitable organization.

(a) A judge shall not serve as an officer, director, trustee or non-legal advisor if it is likely that the organization

(i) will be engaged in proceedings that would ordinarily come before the judge, or

(ii) will be engaged frequently in adversary proceedings in the court of which the judge is a member or in any court subject to the appellate jurisdiction of the court of which the judge is a member.

(iii) by reason of its purpose, will have a substantial interest in other proceedings in the Court in which the judge is a member or in any court subject to the appellate jurisdiction of the court of which the judge is a member.

Commentary

The changing nature of some organizations and of their relationship to the law makes it necessary for a judge regularly to reexamine the activities of each organization with which the judge is affiliated to determine if it is proper for the judge to continue the affiliation. For example, in many jurisdictions charitable hospitals are now more frequently in court than in the past. Similarly, the boards of some legal aid organizations now make policy decisions that may have political significance or imply commitment to causes that may come before the courts for adjudication. Some educational, religious, charitable, fraternal or civic organizations are so large, or have such an impact on the public, that they are either frequently before the courts or are substantially interested in other similar organizations who are frequently before the courts.

(b) A judge as an officer, director, trustee or non-legal advisor, or as a member or otherwise:

(i) may assist such an organization in planning fund-raising and may participate in the management and investment of the organization's funds, but shall not personally participate in the solicitation of funds or other fund-raising activities;

(ii) may make recommendations to public and private fund-granting organizations on projects and programs concerning the law, the legal system or the administration of justice;

(iii) shall not personally participate in membership solicitation if the solicitation might reasonably be perceived as coercive or if the membership solicitation is essentially a fund-raising mechanism;

(iv) shall not use or permit the use of the prestige of judicial office for fund-raising or membership solicitation.

Commentary

A judge may solicit membership or endorse or encourage membership efforts for an organization devoted to the improvement of the law, the legal system or the administration of justice or a nonprofit educational, religious, charitable, fraternal or civic organization as long as the solicitation cannot reasonably be perceived as coercive and is not essentially a fund-raising mechanism. Solicitation of funds for an organization and solicitation of memberships similarly involve the danger that the person solicited will feel obligated to respond favorably to the solicitor if the solicitor is in a position of influence or control. A judge must not engage in direct, individual solicitation of funds or memberships in person, in writing or by telephone except in the following cases: 1) a judge may solicit for memberships other judges over whom the judge does not exercise supervisory or appellate authority, 2) a judge may solicit other persons for membership in the organizations described above if neither those persons nor persons with whom they are affiliated are likely ever to appear before the court on which the judge serves and 3) a judge who is an officer of

such an organization may send a general membership solicitation mailing over the judge's signature.

Use of an organization letterhead for fund-raising or membership solicitation does not violate Section 4C(3)(b) provided the letterhead lists only the judge's name and office or other position in the organization, and, if comparable designations are listed for other persons, the judge's judicial designation. In addition, a judge must also make reasonable efforts to ensure that the judge's staff, court officials and others subject to the judge's direction and control do not solicit funds on the judge's behalf for any purpose, charitable or otherwise.

A judge must not be a speaker or guest of honor at an organization's fund-raising event, but mere attendance at such an event is permissible if otherwise consistent with this Code.

D. Financial Activities.

(1) A judge shall not engage in financial and business dealings that:

(a) may reasonably be perceived to exploit the judge's judicial position, or

(b) involve the judge in frequent transactions or continuing business relationships with those lawyers or other persons likely to come before the court on which the judge serves.

Commentary

The Time for Compliance provision of this Code (Application, Section F) postpones the time for compliance with certain provisions of this Section in some cases.

When a judge acquires in a judicial capacity information, such as material contained in filings with the court, that is not yet generally known, the judge must not use the information for private gain. See Section 2B; see also Section 3B(11).

A judge must avoid financial and business dealings that involve the judge in frequent transactions or continuing business relationships with persons likely to come either before the judge personally or before other judges on the judge's court. In addition, a judge should discourage members of the judge's family from engaging in dealings that would reasonably appear to exploit the judge's judicial position. This rule is necessary to avoid creating an appearance of exploitation of office or favoritism and to minimize the potential for disqualification. With respect to affiliation of relatives of judges with law firms appearing before the judge, see Commentary to Section 3E(1) relating to disqualification.

Participation by a judge in financial and business dealings is subject to the general prohibitions in Section 4A against activities that tend to reflect adversely on impartiality, demean the judicial office, or interfere with the proper performance of judicial duties. Such participation is also subject to the general prohibition in Canon 2 against activities involving impropriety or the appearance of impropriety and the prohibition in Section 2B against the misuse of the prestige of judicial office. In addition, a judge must maintain high standards of conduct in all of the judge's activities, as set forth in Canon 1. See Commentary for Section 4B regarding use of the phrase "subject to the requirements of this Code."

(2) A judge may, subject to the requirements of this Code, hold and manage investments of the judge and members of the judge's family, including real estate, and engage in other remunerative activity.

Commentary

This Section provides that, subject to the requirements of this Code, a judge may hold and manage investments owned solely by the judge, investments owned solely by a member or members of the judge's family, and investments owned jointly by the judge and members of the judge's family.

(3) A judge may serve as an officer, director, manager, general partner, advisor or employee of any

business entity subject to the following limitations and the other requirements of this Code:

(a) A judge shall not be involved with any business entity

(i) generally held in disrepute in the community, or

(ii) likely to be engaged in proceedings that would ordinarily come before the judge, or

(iii) likely to be engaged frequently in adversary proceedings in the court of which the judge is a member or in any court subject to the appellate jurisdiction of the court of which the judge is a member.

(b) A judge involved with any business entity may assist such a business entity in planning fund-raising and may participate in the management and investment of the entity's funds, but shall not personally participate in the solicitation of funds, the raising of capital or the selling of stock in such a manner as to use or permit the use of the prestige of judicial office for promotion of the business entity.

Commentary

Subject to the requirements of this Code, a judge may participate in a business. Although participation by a judge in a business might otherwise be permitted by Section 4D(3), a judge may be prohibited from participation by other provisions of this Code when, for example, the business entity frequently appears before the judge's court or the participation requires significant time away from judicial duties. Similarly, a judge must avoid participating in a business if the judge's participation would involve misuse of the prestige of judicial office.

(4) A judge shall manage the judge's investments and other financial interests to minimize the number of cases in which the judge is disqualified. As soon as the judge can do so without serious financial detriment, the judge shall divest himself or herself of investments and other financial interests that might require frequent disqualification.

(5) A judge shall not accept, and shall urge members of the judge's family residing in the judge's household, not to accept, a gift, bequest, favor or loan from anyone except for:

Commentary

Section 4D(5) does not apply to contributions to a judge's campaign for judicial office, a matter governed by Canon 5.

Because a gift, bequest, favor or loan to a member of the judge's family residing in the judge's household might be viewed as intended to influence the judge, a judge must inform those family members of the relevant ethical constraints upon the judge in this regard and discourage those family members from violating them. A judge cannot, however, reasonably be expected to know or control all of the financial or business activities of all family members residing in the judge's household.

(a) a gift incident to a public testimonial, books, tapes and other resource materials supplied by publishers on a complimentary basis for official use, or an invitation to the judge and the judge's spouse or guest to attend a bar-related function or an activity devoted to the improvement of the law, the legal system or the administration of justice;

Commentary

Acceptance of an invitation to a law-related function is governed by Section 4D(5)(a); acceptance of an invitation paid for by an individual lawyer or group of lawyers is governed by Section 4D(5)(h).

A judge may accept a public testimonial or a gift incident thereto only if the donor organization is not an organization whose members comprise or frequently represent the same side in litigation, and the testimonial and gift are otherwise in compliance with other provisions of this Code. See Sections 4A(1) and 2D.

(b) a gift, award or benefit incident to the business, profession or other separate activity of a spouse or other family member of a judge residing in the judge's household, including gifts, awards and benefits for the use of both the spouse or other family member and the judge (as spouse or family member), provided the gift, award or benefit could not reasonably be perceived as intended to influence the judge in the performance of judicial duties;

(c) ordinary social hospitality or customary expressions of sympathy;

(d) a gift from a relative or friend, for a special occasion, such as a wedding, anniversary or birthday, if the gift is fairly commensurate with the occasion and the relationship;

Commentary

A gift to a judge, or to a member of the judge's family living in the judge's household, that is excessive in value raises questions about the judge's impartiality and the integrity of the judicial office and might require disqualification of the judge where disqualification would not otherwise be required. See, however, Section 4D(5)(e).

(e) a gift, bequest, favor or loan from a relative or close personal friend whose appearance or interest in a case would in any event require disqualification under Section 3E;

(f) a loan from a lending institution in its regular course of business on the same terms generally available to persons who are not judges;

(g) a scholarship or fellowship awarded on the same terms and based on the same criteria applied to other applicants; or

(h) any other gift, bequest, favor or loan, only if: the donor is not a party or other person who has come or is likely to come or whose interests have come or are likely to come before the judge.

Commentary

Section 4D(5)(h) prohibits judges from accepting gifts, favors, bequests or loans from lawyers or their firms if they have come or are likely to come before the judge; it also prohibits gifts, favors, bequests or loans from clients of lawyers or their firms when the clients' interests have come or are likely to come before the judge.

E. Fiduciary Activities.

(1) A judge shall not serve as executor, administrator or other personal representative, trustee, guardian, attorney in fact or other fiduciary, except for the estate, trust or person of a member of the judge's family, and then only if such service will not interfere with the proper performance of judicial duties.

(2) A judge shall not serve as a fiduciary if it is likely that the judge as a fiduciary will be engaged in proceedings that would ordinarily come before the judge, or if the estate, trust or ward becomes involved in adversary proceedings in the court on which the judge serves or one under its appellate jurisdiction.

(3) The same restrictions on financial activities that apply to a judge personally also apply to the judge while acting in a fiduciary capacity.

Commentary

The Time for Compliance provision of this Code (Application, Section F) postpones the time for compliance with certain provisions of this Section in some cases.

The restrictions imposed by this Canon may conflict with the judge's obligation as a fiduciary. For example, a judge should resign as trustee if detriment to the trust would result from divestiture of holdings the retention of which would place the judge in violation of Section 4D(4).

F. **Service as Arbitrator or Mediator.** A judge shall not act as an arbitrator or mediator or otherwise perform judicial functions in a private capacity unless expressly authorized by law.

Commentary

Section 4F does not prohibit a judge from participating in arbitration, mediation or settlement conferences performed as part of judicial duties.

G. **Practice of Law.** A judge shall not practice law. Notwithstanding this prohibition, a judge may act pro se and may, without compensation, give legal advice to and draft or review documents for a member of the judge's family.

Commentary

This prohibition refers to the practice of law in a representative capacity and not in a pro se capacity. A judge may act for himself or herself in all legal matters, including matters involving litigation and matters involving appearances before or other dealings with legislative and other governmental bodies. However, in so doing, a judge must not abuse the prestige of office to advance the interests of the judge or the judge's family. See Section 2D.

The Code allows a judge to give legal advice to and draft legal documents for members of the judge's family, so long as the judge receives no compensation. A judge must not, however, act as an advocate or negotiator for a member of the judge's family in a legal matter.

H. **Compensation, Reimbursement and Reporting.**

(1) **Compensation and Reimbursement.** A judge may receive compensation and reimbursement of expenses for the extra-judicial activities permitted by this Code, if the source of such payments does not give the appearance of influencing the judge's performance of judicial duties or otherwise give the appearance of impropriety.

(a) Compensation shall not exceed a reasonable amount nor shall it exceed what a person who is not a judge would receive for the same activity.

(b) Expense reimbursement shall be limited to the actual cost of travel, food and lodging reasonably incurred by the judge and, where appropriate to the occasion, by the judge's spouse or guest.

Any payment in excess of such an amount is compensation.

(2) All candidates for judicial office and judges shall comply with KRS 61.710, et seq.

Commentary

See Section 4D(5) regarding gifts, bequests and loans.

The Code does not prohibit a judge from accepting honoraria or speaking fees provided that the compensation is reasonable and commensurate with the task performed. A judge should ensure, however, that no conflicts are created by the arrangement. A judge must not appear to trade on the judicial position for personal advantage. Nor should a judge spend significant time away from court duties to meet speaking or writing commitments for compensation. In addition, the source of the payment must not raise any question of undue influence or the judge's ability or willingness to be impartial.

I. Disclosure of a judge's income, debts, investments or other assets is required only to the extent provided in this Canon and in Sections 3E and 3F, or as otherwise required by law.

Commentary

Section 3E requires a judge to disqualify himself or herself in any proceeding in which the judge has an economic interest. See "economic interest" as explained in the Terminology Section. A judge has the rights of any other citizen, including the right to privacy of the judge's financial affairs, except to the extent that limitations established by law are required to safeguard the proper performance of the judge's duties.

CANON 5

CANON 5: A JUDGE OR JUDICIAL CANDIDATE SHALL REFRAIN FROM INAPPROPRIATE POLITICAL ACTIVITY

A. **Political Conduct in General.**

(1) A judge or a candidate for election to judicial office shall not:

(a) act as a leader or hold any office in a political organization;

(b) make speeches for or against a political organization or candidate or publicly endorse or oppose a candidate for public office;

(c) solicit funds for or pay an assessment or make a contribution to a political organization or candidate, except as authorized in subsection A(2);

Commentary

A judge or a candidate for election to judicial office retains the right to participate in the political process as a voter.

Where false information concerning a judicial candidate is made public, a judge or candidate having knowledge of the facts is not prohibited by Section 5A(1) from making the facts public.

Section 5A(1) does not prohibit a judge or candidate from privately expressing his or her views on judicial candidates or other candidates for public office.

(2) A judge or a candidate for election to judicial office may purchase tickets to political gatherings for the judge or candidate and one guest, may attend political gatherings and may speak to such gatherings on the judge's or candidate's own behalf. A judge or candidate shall not identify himself or herself as a member of a political party in any form of advertising,

or when speaking to a gathering. If not initiated by the judge or candidate for such office, and only in answer to a direct question, the judge or candidate may identify himself or herself as a member of a particular political party.

Commentary

A judge or candidate, in purchasing tickets to political gatherings, should be careful that he or she doesn't create the impression that the purchase is not for the advancement of the judge or candidate but is solely a contribution to another candidate or political organization, which is prohibited.

(3) A judge shall resign office when the judge becomes a candidate either in a party primary or in a general election for a non-judicial office, except that the judge may continue to hold judicial office while being a candidate for election to or serving as a delegate in a state constitutional convention, if otherwise permitted by law.

(4) A judge shall not engage in any other political activity except on behalf of measures to improve the law, the legal system, or the administration of justice, as provided in Canon 2B and C.

Commentary

A judge or candidate for judicial office shall encourage members of his or her family to adhere to the same standards of political conduct in support of the candidate that apply to the candidate. Family members are free to participate in other political activity.

B. Campaign Conduct.

(1) A judge or candidate for election to judicial office:

(a) shall maintain the dignity appropriate to judicial office, and shall encourage members of the candidate's family to adhere to the same standards of political conduct;

(b) shall prohibit public officials or employees subject to the candidate's direction and control from doing for the candidate what the candidate is prohibited from doing under this Canon; and except to the extent authorized under subsection B(2), the candidate should not allow any other person to do for the candidate what the candidate is prohibited from doing under this Canon;

(c) shall not, in connection with cases, controversies, or issues that are likely to come before the court, make pledges, promises or commitments that are inconsistent with the impartial performance of the adjudicative duties of judicial office.

Commentary

The making of a pledge, promise or commitment is not dependent upon, or limited to, the use of any specific words or phrases; instead, the totality of the statement must be examined to determine if a reasonable person would believe that the candidate for judicial office has specifically undertaken to reach a particular result. Pledges, promises, or commitments must be contrasted with statements or announcements of personal views on legal, political, or other issues, which are not prohibited. When making such statements, a judge should acknowledge the overarching judicial obligation to apply and uphold the law, without regard to his or her personal views.

A judicial candidate may make campaign promises related to judicial organization, administration, and court management, such as a promise to dispose of a backlog of cases, start court sessions on time, or avoid favoritism in appointments and hiring. A candidate may also pledge to take action outside the courtroom, such as working toward an improved jury selection system, or advocating for more funds to improve the physical plant and amenities of the courthouse.

Judicial candidates may receive questionnaires or requests for interviews from the media and from issue advocacy or other community organizations that seek to learn their views on disputed or controversial legal or political issues. Section 5B(1)(c) does not specifically address judicial responses to such inquiries. Depending upon the wording and format of such questionnaires, candidates' responses might be viewed as pledges, promises or commitments to perform the adjudicative duties of office other than in an impartial way. To avoid violating Section 5B(1)(c), therefore, candidates who respond to media and other inquiries should also give assurances that they will keep an open mind and will carry out their adjudicative duties faithfully and impartially if elected. Candidates who do not respond may state their reasons for not responding, such as the danger that answering might be perceived by a reasonable person as undermining a successful candidate's independence or impartiality, or that it might lead to frequent disqualifications.

(d) shall file the report referred to in Canon 4H(2).

(2) A judge or a candidate for judicial office shall not solicit campaign funds, but may establish committees of responsible persons to secure and manage the expenditure of funds for the campaign and to obtain public statements of support for the candidacy. A candidate's committees may solicit funds for the campaign no earlier than 180 days before a primary election. A candidate's committees may not solicit funds after a general election (See KRS 121.150). A candidate shall not use or permit the use of campaign contributions for the private benefit of the candidate or a member of the candidate's family.

Commentary

Section 5B(2) permits a candidate to establish campaign committees to solicit and accept political support and reasonable financial contributions. At the start of the campaign, the candidate should instruct his or her campaign committees to solicit or accept only contributions that are reasonable under the circumstances. The candidate should instruct his or her campaign committees as to the requirements of Canon 5 of this Code. The candidate is responsible for the actions of his or her campaign committees.

APPLICATION OF THE CODE OF JUDICIAL CONDUCT

Anyone, whether or not a lawyer, who is an officer of a judicial system performing judicial functions, including an officer such as a court commissioner, is a judge for the purpose of this Code. All judges should comply with this Code except as provided below.

A. Part-Time Judge or Special Judge. A part-time judge is a judge who serves on a continuing or periodic basis, but is permitted by law to devote time to some other profession or occupation and whose compensation for that reason is less than that of a full-time judge.

(1) is not required to comply with Canon 4D(3), E, F, and G;

(2) should not practice law in the court on which the judge serves or in any court subject to the appellate

jurisdiction of the court on which the judge serves, or act as a lawyer in a proceeding in which the judge has served as a judge or in any other proceeding related thereto. This provision shall not, however, prevent a trial commissioner of the District Court or a commissioner of the Circuit Court from practicing in the court of which that person is a commissioner so long as that person has not taken and does not take any action as such commissioner with respect to the matter or matters in which that person practices as an attorney.

B. Judge Pro Tempore. A judge pro tempore is a person who is appointed to act temporarily as a judge.

(1) While acting as such, a judge pro tempore is not required to comply with Canon 4D(3), (4), E, F, and G.

(2) A person who has been a judge pro tempore should not act as lawyer in a proceeding in which that person has served as a judge or in any other proceeding related thereto.

HISTORY: Amended by Order 2010–11, eff. 12–15–10; prior amendments eff. 2–16–06 (Order 2006–03); 9–15–05 (Order 2005–9), 1–1–05 (Order 2004–5), 2–1–00 (Order 99–1), 1–1–99 (Order 98–2), 11–1–95 (Order 95–1), 4–4–91, 1–1–87, 10–1–82, 7–1–81, 1–1–80, 7–1–79, 1–29–79, 6–1–78, 3–1–78, 2–22–78, 1–1–78; adopted eff. 1–1–78

SCR 4.310 Judicial ethics committee and opinions

(1) There shall be an ethics committee of the Kentucky judiciary consisting of one judge each of the Court of Appeals, the circuit court and the district court and two members of the Kentucky Bar Association appointed by the board of governors, none of whom shall be members of the judicial retirement and removal commission. The judicial members shall be selected by the members of their courts in the manner which each court selects. Each member shall serve for a term of four years from the date of his appointment. A chairman shall be elected by the ethics committee.

(2) Opinions as to the propriety of any act or conduct and the construction or application of any canon shall be provided by the committee upon request from any justice, judge, trial commissioner or by any judicial candidate. Communications between the questioner and the Judicial Ethics Committee and its members shall be confidential. If the committee finds the question of limited significance, it shall provide an informal opinion to the questioner. If, however, it finds the question of sufficient general interest and importance, it shall render a formal opinion, in which event it shall cause the opinion to be published in complete or synopsis form, without specific identification of the questioner. Likewise, the committee may issue formal opinions on its own motion under such circumstances as it finds appropriate.

(3) Both formal and informal opinions shall be advisory only; however, the commission and the Supreme Court shall consider reliance by a justice, judge, trial commissioner or by any judicial candidate upon the ethics committee opinion.

(4) Any person affected by a formal opinion of the ethics committee may obtain a review thereof by the Supreme Court by filing with the clerk of that court within thirty (30) days after the end of the month in which it was published a motion for review stating the grounds upon which the movant is dissatisfied with the opinion. The motion shall be accompanied by a copy of the opinion or synopsis as published and shall be served upon the ethics committee and, if the movant is someone other than the party who initiated the request for the opinion, upon the initiating justice, judge or commissioner. The filing fee for docketing such motion shall be as provided by Civil Rule 76.42(1) for original actions in the Supreme Court. The ethics committee may file a response to the motion for review within thirty (30) days after its receipt of the motion. Notwithstanding the provisions of this subsection of the rule, the Supreme Court on its own initiative may review a judicial ethics opinion at any time.

HISTORY: Amended by Order 2012–01, eff. 3–1–12; prior amendment eff. 1–1–04 (Order 2003–4); adopted eff. 7–1–79

V TRIAL COMMISSIONERS OF THE DISTRICT COURT

SCR 5.000 Scope

Rule 5 applies to all trial commissioners of the district court.

HISTORY: Adopted eff. 1–1–78

SCR 5.010 Appointment

In each county in which no district judge resides, the chief judge of the district shall appoint a trial commissioner subject to the approval of the Chief Justice. Any trial commissioner may be removed by order of the Supreme Court. Every other trial commissioner shall be appointed by the chief judge of the district upon certification of the necessity therefor by the Supreme Court, which certification shall be initiated by a request from the chief judge of the district stating the circumstances requiring the appointment.

HISTORY: Amended by Order 2005–10, eff. 1–1–06; prior amendment eff. 11–1–95 (Order 95–1); adopted eff. 1–1–78

SCR 5.020 Qualifications and terms of office

Each trial commissioner shall be a resident of the county for which he or she is appointed, shall be an attorney if one is qualified and available at the time of such appointment, and shall serve at the pleasure of the chief judge of the district during the remainder of the judge's current term of office. Prior to the appointment of a non-lawyer to serve as trial commissioner, the Chief District Judge shall certify to the Chief Justice in writing that no attorney is qualified and available to serve.

Each trial commissioner, in addition to maintaining applicable continuing education requirements, shall, at least once every two years, attend a training program which focuses on the dynamics and effects of domestic violence including the availability of community resources, victims services and reporting requirements.

HISTORY: Amended by Order 96–1, eff. 1–1–97; prior amendment eff. 11–1–95; adopted eff. 1–1–78

SCR 5.030 Powers

Subject to review by the chief district judge or by another judge of the district designated for that purpose by the chief judge, in the county for which he is appointed a trial commissioner shall have, unless otherwise specified in the certificate of necessity authorizing his appointment, the authority of a district judge with respect to the following:

(a) In criminal cases,

(i) To issue search warrants and warrants of arrest;

(ii) To examine any charge and commit the defendant to jail or hold him to bail or other form of pretrial release; and

(iii) To accept a plea of guilty, at the time the charge is examined, and impose sentence for any offense punishable only by fine of $500 or less;

(b) In juvenile cases,

(i) To hear and determine if children in custody should be held in detention;

(ii) To conduct preliminary inquiries, informally adjust juvenile cases, and cause juvenile petitions to be brought;

(iii) To order physical and mental examinations of children before the juvenile court; and

(iv) To issue orders for the temporary custody of children whose welfare is threatened under emergency conditions;

(c) In probate matters,

(i) To admit to record or reject any will offered for probate;

(ii) To appoint executors and administrators of wills and estates, and to fix and approve bond as required;

(d) In civil proceedings,

(i) To authorize orders of attachment and garnishment and writs of possession;

(ii) To conduct judicial sales if so authorized by the chief judge of the district; and

(iii) To issue emergency protective orders in domestic violence and abuse cases.

(iv) To issue forthwith orders of arrest in domestic violence and abuse cases.

(e) To issue writs of forcible entry and detainer and warrants of restitution;

(f) In mental health cases, to conduct all preliminary proceedings relating to involuntary commitments, and, specifically:

(i) to issue a warrant or summons for the respondent if he is not already detained;

(ii) to release persons for whom no warrant has been taken pursuant to KRS 202A.041;

(iii) to order immediate mental examinations pursuant to KRS 202A.041 and 202A.051;

(iv) to appoint counsel for respondent;

(v) to set and conduct preliminary hearings in involuntary commitment cases pursuant to KRS 202A.041, 202A.051 and 202A.071; and

(vi) to order the detention of the respondent pending the preliminary and final hearings.

(g) To compel the attendance of witnesses and the production of evidence with respect to any proceeding before him.

HISTORY: Amended by Order 86–3, eff. 7–1–86; prior amendments eff. 7–1–84, 9–10–82, 3–1–78; adopted eff. 1–1–78

SCR 5.040 Temporary assignment in another county

A trial commissioner may be temporarily assigned by the chief judge of the district to serve in any county within the district and shall, while so serving, have the same authority as in the county of his residence.

HISTORY: Adopted eff. 1–1–78

SCR 5.050 Disqualification

A trial commissioner shall disqualify himself in all matters in which he has an interest, relationship or bias that would disqualify a judge.

HISTORY: Adopted eff. 1–1–78

SCR 5.060 Service as attorney

A trial commissioner shall not personally engage in the practice of criminal law in the district court of the district in which he serves as commissioner and shall not act as an attorney in any other matter in which he has taken any action as a trial commissioner. If a trial commissioner anticipates employment as an attorney in a matter coming before him, he may decline to act in the matter.

HISTORY: Amended eff. 1–1–80; adopted eff. 1–1–78

SCR 5.070 Retirement and removal

All trial commissioners shall be subject to the provisions of section 121 of the Constitution and to the rules of the Supreme Court relating to the retirement and removal of judges.

HISTORY: Amended eff. 1–1–78; adopted eff. 1–1–78

VI JUDICIAL NOMINATING COMMISSION

SCR 6.000 Activating the judicial nominating commission

(1) Whenever a vacancy occurs in the office of justice of the Supreme Court, judge of the Court of Appeals, judge of the circuit court, or judge of the district court, the chief justice or his designee shall notify each member of the appropriate judicial nominating commission that such vacancy exists and that the commission will convene to consider its nominations.

(2) If the governor has not yet made the appointments to the commission as provided in section 118(2) of the Kentucky Constitution, the chief justice or his designee shall ask the governor to do so.

(3) If a justice or judge submits a letter of resignation which is to become effective on a date subsequent or if a judicial position is created by act of the general assembly, or a justice or judge is elected to another judicial office; the commission shall proceed as if a vacancy exists as of the date the resignation is submitted, the election occurs or the date on which the act is signed by the governor or becomes law without his signature, and the commission may convene to make its nominations so that the governor may prepare to make his appointment at the time the vacancy becomes effective.

HISTORY: Amended by Order 83–5, eff. 11–1–83; adopted eff. 1–1–79

SCR 6.010 Call for nominations

The chief justice or his designee shall cause notice to be given in the appropriate district in a manner likely to alert the general public to the fact that a judicial vacancy exists. The notice shall contain a declaration that the public is invited to submit the names of qualified individuals to the commission. The notice shall also contain the constitutional qualifications for the office, the latest date by which names should be submitted and the address of the commission.

HISTORY: Adopted eff. 1–1–79

SCR 6.020 Questionnaires

(1) Each person whose name is submitted shall be sent a questionnaire in a form approved by the Supreme Court. It shall be designed to elicit information about the potential nominee concerning his qualifications, experience and interests bearing upon his fitness for the judicial office, and a statement to the effect that by submitting the questionnaire the applicant agrees to accept the appointment of the governor should he be so selected. The questionnaire shall be subscribed and dated by the applicant and returned to the commission.

(2) If a name is submitted by someone other than the applicant himself, a letter from the chief justice or his designee shall be included with the questionnaire, stating that the applicant's name has been submitted and that he should complete and return the enclosed questionnaire if he is willing to be considered.

(3) As questionnaires are returned, they shall be photocopied and distributed to each member of the commission. The names of applicants to whom questionnaires have been directed but not yet returned shall be made available to the members of the commission upon request, or may be distributed to the members at any time by the chief justice or his designee.

HISTORY: Adopted eff. 1–1–79

SCR 6.030 Time constraints

The chief justice or his designee may in the interest of good order establish the latest date by which names should be submitted and questionnaires returned. However, the date shall be merely directory, and no name or questionnaire shall be withheld from the commission for failure to meet such date.

HISTORY: Adopted eff. 1–1–79

SCR 6.040 Commission meeting; procedures

(1) The chief justice shall call the meeting of the commission. When assembled, it shall proceed to consider its nominations in whatever manner it selects. The commission shall not be limited in its deliberations to those who have applied but may nominate any qualified individual.

(2) The chief justice shall submit the names of the three nominees to the governor by letter. The names shall be presented in alphabetical order with no expression of preference among them.

HISTORY: Adopted eff. 1–1–79

SCR 6.050 Confidential records and proceedings

The records and proceedings of the commission shall be confidential and the meetings of the commission shall be closed to the public. However, the members of the commission are not prohibited from revealing the identity of the applicants when seeking information about their qualifications, and the names of the nominees may be made public at any time after they have been transmitted to the governor.

HISTORY: Adopted eff. 1–1–79

SCR 6.060   Records of the commission

The permanent records of the commission shall consist of a dated copy of the call for nominations, the minutes of the commission's meetings and a copy of the letter of submittal from the chief justice to the governor. All other records generated in connection with the commission's work shall be destroyed one year after the meeting.

HISTORY: Adopted eff. 1–1–79

VII   ELECTION OF BAR REPRESENTATIVES TO JUDICIAL NOMINATING COMMISSIONS

SCR 7.000   Definitions

Except for the definition of "Court," the definitions set forth in Rule 3.010 shall apply also to Part VII of these rules.

HISTORY: Adopted eff. 3–12–76

SCR 7.010   Terms of office

The terms of office of bar representatives on the judicial nominating commissions described in section 118 of the Constitution shall be deemed to have commenced on January 1, 1976. The initial elections in 1976 shall be special elections for the purpose of filling the unexpired terms. Regular elections shall be held on the first Tuesday following the first Monday in November of 1980 and every fourth year thereafter.

HISTORY: Adopted eff. 3–12–76

SCR 7.020   Qualifications

Candidates for election as bar representatives on the commissions shall be members of the association who reside in this state and do not hold any other public office or any office in a political party or organization.

HISTORY: Adopted eff. 3–12–76

SCR 7.030   Nomination and election—regular elections

(1) Candidates for election as bar representatives on the commission shall be nominated by the board or by written petition as herein provided.

(2) On or before June 1 of the years in which regular elections are to be held under this rule the board shall by majority vote nominate candidates for election to the various commissions as specified in paragraph (c) of this rule. The board shall immediately certify the names of its nominees to the director. On or before July 1 the director shall publish by appropriate means to the members specified in paragraph (c) of this rule a list or lists of the candidates so nominated.

(3)(a) For the commission for the Supreme Court and the Court of Appeals the board shall nominate one (1) qualified member from each appellate district.

The director shall publish by appropriate means a list of the candidates so nominated to each member residing in the Commonwealth of Kentucky.

(b) For the commissions for each judicial circuit the board shall nominate two (2) qualified members. To the extent practicable, in multi-county circuits the board shall nominate candidates from different counties in the circuit. The director shall publish by appropriate means a list of the candidates so nominated to each member residing in the circuit.

(c) Lists of the board's nominees for election to the various commissions may be combined as one list and may be included in one publication of names.

(4) Any other qualified member may file a written petition for candidacy for the commission for the Supreme Court and the Court of Appeals, signed by himself and not less than ten (10) other members residing in the Commonwealth of Kentucky, or may file a written petition for candidacy for the commission for a judicial circuit, signed by himself and not less than two (2) other members residing in the circuit. In his petition the member shall state that he does not hold any other public office or any office in a political party or organization. All such petitions shall be filed with the director on or before August 15 of the year in which the regular election for members of the commissions is to be held. The director shall acknowledge receipt of each candidate's petition by return mail. All petitions shall be considered public records and shall be available for inspection at reasonable hours. On or before September 1 the director shall publish by appropriate means to the members specified in paragraph (c) of this rule a list or lists of the candidates, including those nominated by the board and those nominated by petition.

(5) The eligibility of a candidate in a regular election may be challenged by any member entitled to vote in the election of the commission for which the challenged party is a candidate. Such challenge shall be in writing signed by the challenger, certifying that a copy has been served upon the challenged party or parties, and filed with the director on or before September 15 of the year in which the election is to be held. It shall be summarily heard by a hearing committee consisting of three (3) disinterested mem-

bers appointed by the president. The parties shall be entitled to appear in person or by or with counsel. The hearing shall be held and a final decision rendered in writing on or before the following September 25. The party or parties aggrieved by such decision may appeal to the Supreme Court by a petition for review filed with the clerk of that court on or before the following October 1 and certifying that a copy has been served on the adversary party or parties. The matter shall be summarily heard and determined as ordered by the court.

(6) Ballots shall be prepared by the director. The various commissions shall be on separate ballots but may be included in one mailing. The ballot for each commission shall include the names of the candidates, listed in alphabetical order, and the addresses at which they reside. There shall be printed on each ballot in boldface type the words "This ballot must be received by the director on or before the first Tuesday following the first Monday in November" and the words, "You must vote for two and two only or your ballot will not be counted."

(7) On or before October 10 of the year in which the election is to be held the ballots shall be mailed, with return envelopes, to the following members: A ballot for the commission for the Supreme Court and the Court of Appeals shall be sent to each member residing in the Commonwealth of Kentucky; a ballot for the commission for each judicial circuit shall be sent to each member residing in the circuit.

(8) The completed ballot shall be sealed in an unmarked inner envelope which shall be sealed in an outer return envelope. The outer envelope shall be addressed to the director and shall contain the words "Official Ballot—Not to be opened until the day of the regular election" and lines for the signature and county of residence of the attorney casting the ballot. Failure to sign or to indicate the proper county of residence shall invalidate the ballot.

(9) All ballots must be received by the director on or before the day of the regular election. On or before the following December 1 a canvassing board consisting of five (5) members appointed by the president shall meet in the office of the director and tabulate the votes. Each candidate or a representative designated by him in writing may be present at the meeting of the canvassing board.

(10) The two (2) candidates for each commission receiving the highest number of votes shall be elected. If two (2) or more candidates are found to have received an equal number of votes, the election shall be fairly determined by lot under the supervision of and in the presence of the canvassing board.

(11) The canvassing board shall immediately make and forward to the Chief Justice and the director a written certification of the election. The director shall promptly notify each candidate of the results of the

election and shall publish the results in the next official association publication.

(12) On or before December 10 following the election any defeated candidate may contest the election of his successful opponent or opponents. Such contest shall be by written petition to the Supreme Court stating the grounds of contest and certifying that a copy has been served on the adversary party or parties. The matter shall be summarily heard and determined in such manner, and relief granted or denied upon such grounds, as the court shall deem fair and equitable.

(13) As soon as practicable after the election the director shall certify to the Supreme Court for its approval an itemization of all costs incurred in the election of members to the commissions. Upon its approval of such costs the court shall order payment to the association out of the state treasury.

(14) Within sixty (60) days after the election the director shall transmit all petitions, ballots and other applicable records to the administrative director of the courts.

HISTORY: Amended by Order 2012–01, eff. 3–1–12; prior amendment eff. 1–1–78; adopted eff. 3–12–76

SCR 7.040 Nomination and election—special elections

(1) On or before ten (10) days after receipt of the notice to the director (hereinafter referred to as "Director's notice") of the need for a special election, to fill an unexpired term resulting from a vacancy in the bar representation on any commission, the board shall nominate the bar representative for each vacancy in the same manner as provided in Rule 7.030(2) and (3).

(2) On or before twenty (20) days after the director's notice, the director shall cause to be published by appropriate means to each member residing in the circuit or jurisdiction concerned a list of candidates nominated by the board.

(3) Between 20 and 30 days after the director's notice, other nominating petitions conforming to the requirements of Rule 7.030(4) may be filed with the director.

(4) On or before 40 days after the director's notice, the director shall cause the appropriate ballots to be prepared and mailed in the manner provided by Rule 7.030(6) and (7). He shall use first-class postal service.

(5) All ballots to be counted must be received by the director on or before 50 days after the director's notice.

(6) On or before 54 days after the director's notice, a canvassing board constituted in the manner as set forth in Rule 7.030(9) shall meet and tabulate the ballots, and upon completion thereof shall certify the results in the manner provided by Rule 7.030(11).

(7) On or before 65 days of the director's notice, the director shall certify the costs of the election in the manner provided by Rule 7.030(13).

HISTORY: Amended by Order 2012–01, eff. 3–1–12; adopted eff. 1–1–78

SCR 7.050   Vacancies—Deleted

HISTORY: Deleted by Order of Supreme Court, eff. 1–1–78

VIII   MANDATORY CONTINUING JUDICIAL EDUCATION FOR THE KENTUCKY JUDICIARY

SCR 8.000   Purpose

Only by continuing their legal education can members of the judiciary fulfill their obligation to competently serve the Commonwealth. These rules establish minimum requirements for such continuing judicial education and the means by which the requirements shall be enforced.

HISTORY: Adopted by Order 83–4, eff. 7–8–83

SCR 8.010   The Commission; functions and membership

The Mandatory Continuing Judicial Education Commission shall consist of fourteen (14) members. The Commission shall be responsible for regulating the mandatory continuing judicial education for the judges of Kentucky.

HISTORY: Amended by Order 89–1, eff. 8–28–89; adopted eff. 7–8–83

SCR 8.020   Selection and tenure of the Commission

(1) The Chief Justice of the Kentucky Supreme Court or his designee shall serve as chair of the Commission;

(2) One (1) member of the Court of Appeals to be appointed by the Chief Judge of the Court of Appeals;

(3) The Chair of the Circuit Judges' Education Committee and two (2) circuit judges to be appointed by the President of the Circuit Judges' Association;

(4) The Chair of the District Judges' Education Committee and two (2) district judges to be appointed by the President of the District Judges' Association;

(5) One (1) representative of the University of Kentucky College of Law to be appointed by the Dean of the College; one (1) representative of the University of Louisville School of Law to be appointed by the Dean of the School; one (1) representative of the Northern Kentucky University Chase College of Law to be appointed by the Dean of the College.

(6) Chair, or the chair's designee, of the House Judiciary Committee for a term concurrent with the term as chair.

(7) Chair, or the chair's designee, of the Senate Judiciary Committee for a term concurrent with the term as chair.

(8) All appointments shall be for a term of three (3) years or so long as they remain chair of their respective judicial or legislative committees. Vacancies occurring through death, disability, inability or disqualification to serve or by resignation shall be filled for the remainder of the term in the same manner as initial appointments.

HISTORY: Amended by Order 99–1, eff. 2–1–00; prior amendment eff. 8–28–89 (Order 89–1); adopted eff. 7–8–83

SCR 8.030   Staff for Commission

The Manager of the Division of Education Services of the Administrative Office of the Courts shall serve as Executive Secretary to the Commission.

HISTORY: Amended by Order 99–1, eff. 2–1–00; adopted by Order 83–4, eff. 7–8–83

SCR 8.040   Expenses of Commission members

Members of the Commission shall not be compensated but shall be reimbursed for actual expenses incurred by them in attending the Commission meetings in accordance with the current travel regulations of the Court of Justice.

HISTORY: Amended by Order 99–1, eff. 2–1–00; adopted by Order 83–4, eff. 7–8–83

SCR 8.050   Duties of Commission

The Commission shall perform the following duties:

(a) Exercise general supervisory authority over the administration of this rule, subject to the approval of the Supreme Court;

(b) Accredit sponsors of courses, programs and other educational activities which will satisfy the educational requirements of this rule;

(c) Submit to the Supreme Court proposed regulations not inconsistent with this rule to govern the operations and activities of the Commission;

(d) Report within six (6) months after the close of each biennium to the Supreme Court concerning its activities and, from time to time, make recommendations to the Supreme Court concerning this rule and the enforcement thereof.

HISTORY: Adopted by Order 83–4, eff. 7–8–83

SCR 8.060   Commission meetings and quorum

The Commission will meet at least once an educational biennium before the end of the fiscal year and at such other times as called by the Chair. A quorum to do business in meetings of the Commission shall require the attendance of not less than seven members of the Commission. Commission actions relating to the accreditation of sponsors of courses, programs and other educational activities which will satisfy the educational requirements of this rule may be taken by mail, e-mail, telephone conference or other electronic means where not less than seven members of the Commission by such means vote on said actions.

HISTORY: Amended by Order 2001–2, eff. 1–1–02; prior amendments eff. 2–1–00 (Order 99–1), 8–28–89 (Order 89–1), 1–1–88; adopted eff. 7–8–83

SCR 8.070   Continuing judicial education requirements

Every appellate judge and justice and every trial judge, not exempted, shall attend a minimum of twenty-five (25) hours in continuing judicial education courses approved by the Judicial Education Commission each educational biennium. At least once every two years, a portion of the required continuing judicial education shall consist of programs which focus on the dynamics and effects of domestic violence including the availability of community resources, victims services and reporting requirements. An educational biennium shall begin on July 1 and end two years later on June 30 of each even-numbered year. To satisfy the minimum attendance requirement for any educational biennium a judge is authorized to carry forward any excess attendance over twenty-five (25) hours earned in the immediately preceding biennium.

HISTORY: Amended by Order 99–1, eff. 2–1–00; prior amendments eff. 1–1–97 (Order 96–1), 11–1–95; adopted eff. 7–8–83

SCR 8.080   Exemptions

The Mandatory Judicial Education Commission shall have the authority to relieve any judge of the requirement to meet the minimum attendance in any biennium if attendance would impose an undue hardship by reason of disability or for good cause found by the Commission. A judge shall file for an exemption as soon as practicable after the need for the exemption is known, but no later than July 1 of each even-numbered year.

HISTORY: Adopted by Order 83–4, eff. 7–8–83

SCR 8.090   Appeals

Any decision of the Commission denying an exemption requested under this rule may be appealed to the Supreme Court. Regulations of the Commission shall provide a procedure for timely appeals by the judges who desire to avail themselves of this right of appeal.

HISTORY: Adopted by Order 83–4, eff. 7–8–83

SCR 8.100   Reporting

Every judge, not exempted, shall certify in writing on forms provided by the Administrative Office of the Courts, no later than July 31 following the close of the educational biennium, that the minimum continuing judicial education requirements have been met. Certification shall be made to the Commission in the manner and form prescribed by regulations of the Commission.

The truth and accuracy of the certification shall be the individual responsibility of the certifying judge. Intentional filing of a false report shall be a basis for disciplinary action as prescribed in Rule 8.110.

Each June 1 of even-numbered years, the Executive Secretary will notify each judge of the filing deadline.

HISTORY: Adopted by Order 83–4, eff. 7–8–83

SCR 8.110   Sanctions

As soon as practicable after July 31st of the educational biennium, the Commission shall request the Executive Secretary to notify a judge in writing of their delinquency unless prior to July 1st the judge has requested an exemption which has not been ruled on by the Commission. If such judge remains delinquent on the 30th day of August, the Executive Secretary shall forthwith, in writing, certify the judge's name to the Judicial Retirement and Removal Commission.

HISTORY: Amended by Order 89–1, eff. 8–28–89; adopted eff. 7–8–83

SCR 8.120   Expenses

Judges attending judicial education programs sponsored by the Administrative Office of the Courts shall be reimbursed for their expenses in accordance with Court of Justice Travel Regulations. Expenses for attendance at any other education program shall be borne by the judge unless prior approval is obtained from the Manager of the Education Services Unit of the Administrative Office of the Courts.

HISTORY: Amended by Order 99–1, eff. 2–1–00; adopted by Order 83–4, eff. 7–8–83

IX MONITORING OF DISTRICT COURT PROBATIONERS BY PRIVATE AGENCY

SCR 9.000 Monitoring of District Court probationers by private agency

KRS 533.010(12) permits a court to order a defendant to submit to probation monitoring by a private agency when it is in the best interest of the defendant and the public to do so. (Effective July 15, 1998). The following rules shall apply when a district court orders a private agency to supervise a defendant who has been convicted of a misdemeanor or traffic offense and placed on probation as an alternative sentence to imprisonment.

HISTORY: Adopted by Order 99–1, eff. 2–1–00

SCR 9.010 When referral to a private agency is permitted

A district court may refer a defendant convicted of a misdemeanor or a traffic offense to a private agency for monitoring in accordance with KRS 533.010(12) only when probation monitoring services are not being and cannot be performed by a governmental agency, a not-for-profit agency or volunteers.

HISTORY: Adopted by Order 99–1, eff. 2–1–00

SCR 9.020 Requirements of private agency

To receive referrals from the district court, the private agency must:

A. be an independent contractor and not an agent, servant, or employee of the court;

B. have no individual or fiduciary financial relationship with a judge of the district in which the agency has been approved to provide services, nor with the judge's spouse, nor with a minor child of the judge residing within the judge's household;

C. not have as a principal officer, director or trustee, or the spouse of said officer, director or trustee, anyone related by blood or marriage within the third degree of relationship to any judge or the spouse of any judge in the district for which the agency has been approved to provide services;

D. maintain and provide upon request liability insurance in an amount equal to a minimum of $1 million dollars;

E. agree in writing to accept pro bono referrals from the district court on a proportional basis with all other private probation companies providing approved services to a district court;

F. must provide the district court a written schedule of fees to be charged, including a sliding scale fee schedule for indigent defendants based upon the individual's ability to pay; and,

G. agree in writing to assess fees in strict conformity with the fee schedule submitted to and approved by the district court.

HISTORY: Adopted by Order 99–1, eff. 2–1–00

SCR 9.030 Requirements of district court in referring a convicted offender to a private agency

When utilizing a private agency for probation monitoring, the district court must:

A. assure the private agency has no discretion as to the terms or conditions of probation, including, but not limited to the condition of or the amount of restitution;

B. assure the private agency shall not collect any fines, fees and court costs for the district court;

C. approve all fees to be charged by the private agency, and assure all fees actually charged comply with the approved schedule of fees submitted to the district court;

D. assure no employee of the private agency is seated inside the bar within the courtroom;

E. assure the terms of probation or conditional discharge are clearly stated on the court's docket or other forms provided by the Administrative Office of the Courts and not on forms provided by the private agency;

F. assign pro bono cases proportionately to all private agencies approved by the district court to provide services to the court;

G. require all private agencies to report to the district court on a monthly basis all pro bono cases referred to such agency by the court and whether such agency accepted or rejected the pro bono referral and, if rejected, the reasons for such rejection.

HISTORY: Adopted by Order 99–1, eff. 2–1–00

SCR 9.040 Disqualification

Non-compliance with the rule by any private agency shall constitute grounds for the district court to deny or rescind approval for the private agency to provide services to the district court.

HISTORY: Adopted by Order 99–1, eff. 2–1–00

STANDARDS OF CONDUCT AND TECHNOLOGY GOVERNING ELECTRONIC MEDIA AND STILL PHOTOGRAPHY COVERAGE OF JUDICIAL PROCEEDINGS

Effective July 1, 1981

---

1. Equipment and personnel

(a) Not more than one portable television camera [film camera—16mm sound on film (self blimped) or video tape electronic camera], operated by not more than one camera person, shall be permitted in any trial court proceeding. Not more than two television cameras, operated by not more than one camera person each, shall be permitted in any appellate court proceeding.

(b) Not more than one still photographer, utilizing not more than two still cameras with not more than two lenses for each camera and related equipment for print purposes shall be permitted in any proceeding in a trial or appellate court.

(c) Not more than one audio system for radio broadcast purposes shall be permitted in any proceeding in a trial or appellate court. Audio pickup for all media purposes shall be accomplished from existing audio systems present in the court facility. If no technically suitable audio system exists in the court facility, microphones and related wiring essential for media purposes shall be unobtrusive and shall be located in places designated in advance of any proceeding by the presiding judge.

(d) Requests for coverage, which need not be in any particular form, shall be made to the presiding judge. Subject to the provisions of 1(e), approval of such requests shall be regarded as approval of coverage for the print (photographs) and/or broadcast (radio and television) media generally.

(e) Any "pooling" arrangements among the media required by these limitations on equipment and personnel shall be the sole responsibility of the media without calling upon the presiding judge to mediate any dispute as to the appropriate media representative or equipment authorized to cover a particular proceeding. In the absence of advance media agreement on disputed equipment or personnel issues, the presiding judge shall exclude all contesting media personnel from a proceeding.

2. Sound and light criteria

(a) Only television photographic and audio equipment which does not produce distracting sound or light shall be employed to cover judicial proceedings. Specifically, such photographic and audio equipment shall produce no greater sound or light than the equipment designated in Schedule A annexed hereto, when such equipment is in good working order. No artificial lighting device of any kind shall be employed in connection with the television camera.

(b) Only still camera equipment which does not produce distracting sound or light shall be employed to cover judicial proceedings. Specifically, such still camera equipment shall produce no greater sound or light than a 35mm Leica "M" Series Rangefinder camera, including blimped still reflex cameras, e.g., Nikon F2 or F3, which meet this sound and light criteria. No artificial lighting device of any kind shall be employed in connection with a still camera.

(c) It shall be the affirmative duty of media personnel to demonstrate to the presiding judge adequately in advance of any proceeding that the equipment sought to be utilized meets the sound and light criteria enunciated herein. A failure to obtain advance judicial approval for equipment shall preclude its use in any proceeding.

3. Location of equipment personnel

(a) Television camera equipment shall be positioned in such location in the courtroom as shall be designated by the presiding judge. The area designated shall provide reasonable access to coverage. If and when areas remote from the courtroom which permit reasonable access to coverage are provided, all television camera and audio equipment shall be positioned only in such area. Video tape recording equipment which is not a component part of a television camera shall be located in an area remote from the courtroom.

(b) A still camera photographer shall position himself in such location in the courtroom as shall be designated by the presiding judge. The area designated shall provide reasonable access to coverage. Still camera photographers shall assume a fixed position within the designated area and, once a photographer has established himself in a shooting position, he shall act so as not to call attention to himself through further movement. Still camera photographers shall not be permitted to move about in order to obtain photographs of court proceedings.

(c) Broadcast media representatives shall not move about the court facility while proceedings are in session, and microphones or taping equipment once positioned as required by 1.(c) above shall not be moved during the proceeding.

4. Movement during proceedings

News media photographic or audio equipment shall not be placed in or removed from the courtroom except prior to commencement or after adjournment of proceedings each day, or during a recess. Neither television film magazines nor still camera film or lenses shall be changed in the courtroom except during a recess in the proceeding.

5. Courtroom light sources

With the concurrence of the presiding judge, modifications and additions may be made in light sources existing in the facility, provided such modifications or additions are installed and maintained without public expense.

6. Conferences of counsel

To protect the attorney-client privilege and the effective right to counsel, there shall be no audio pickup or broadcast of conferences which occur in the courtroom between attorneys and their clients, between co-counsel of a client, or between counsel and the presiding judge held at the bench.

7. Impermissible use of media material

None of the film, video tape, still photographs or audio reproductions developed during or by virtue of coverage of a judicial proceeding shall be admissible as evidence in the proceeding out of which it arose, any proceeding subsequent or collateral thereto, or upon any retrial or appeal of such proceedings.

(Schedule A)

No.	Maker	Models
1.	Ikegami	HL–74A, HL–53, HL–77, HL–33, HL–34, HL–35, HL–51, HL–79, HL–78A, HL–79A, HL–79D, ITC–350, ITC–240
2.	RCA	TK76, TK78
3.	Sony	DXC–1600 TRINICON, BVP–200, BVP–3000, DXC–1640
3a.	ASACA	ACC–2006
4.	Hitachi	SK80, SK90
5.	Hitachi	FP–3030, FP–3060A, FP–205, FP–405, GP7
6.	Philips	LDK–25
7.	Sony BVP–200	ENG Camera
8.	Fernseh	Video Camera
9.	JVC–8800u	ENG Camera
10.	AKAI	CVC–150, VTS–150
11.	Panasonic	WV–3085, NV–3085, AK–750, WV–3800
12.	JVC	GC–4800u, KY–2000

HISTORY: Adopted by Order 81–4, eff. 7–1–81

SPECIAL RULES FOR SELF-CONSENT
ABORTION BY A MINOR

Adopted November 13, 1986
Amended September 2, 1988

The purpose of these rules is to provide an expedited and confidential procedure for minors seeking to apply for self-consent for an abortion, pursuant to KRS 311.732, and for appeals therefrom. Confidentiality shall be enforced in the same manner as subsection (1) of the Adoptions Records Statute, KRS 199.570(1).

Insofar as there exists a conflict between the Kentucky Rules of Civil Procedure and these Special Rules for Self–Consent Abortion by a Minor, the Rules of Civil Procedure shall be suspended.

The adoption of these special rules does not, either expressly or impliedly reflect on the ultimate constitutionality of the statute involved.

A. In order to protect the anonymity of persons making a petition for self-consent for an abortion pursuant to KRS 311.732, the following provisions shall apply:

(1) Petitions shall be styled "In re self-consent for an abortion by a minor."

(2) The petition and all information relating thereto shall be confidential, shall not be a public record, and shall not be released to the public. For the purpose of record keeping, petitions shall contain the initials of the petitioner, a name, address, and telephone number where the petitioner can be reached, and where necessary, an alternate address and telephone number for the petitioner.

(3) For the purpose of court public record keeping, petitions shall contain the initials of the petitioner, the date the petition is filed and the disposition of the petition.

(4) Hearings on petitions shall be held before the judge, and shall be confidential. The hearings may be conducted in an informal manner. Only the parties before the court may be admitted to the hearing. Witnesses shall be admitted only for the duration of their testimony.

B. In order to assure expeditious hearings on petitions filed pursuant to KRS 311.732, the following provisions shall apply:

(1) The Administrative Office of the Courts shall design a suitable form to be utilized as a petition for matters covered by KRS 311.732.

(2) The circuit or district clerk shall assist, where necessary, petitioners in the preparation of petitions under KRS 311.732.

(3) Upon the filing of a petition pursuant to KRS 311.732, the appropriate circuit or district judge in whose court the petition was filed shall set the time, date, and place of the hearing thereon. The clerk shall then promptly notify the petitioner thereof.

(4) The judge shall, within seventy-two (72) hours, weekends or holidays included, convene a hearing and decide the matter in question and the judge shall advise the petitioner of her right to an immediate appeal to the Court of Appeals in the event of the judge's failure to render a decision within the seventy-two (72) hour time limit.

(5) Unless additional time is required for review of reports, the judge shall render his decision immediately following the hearing and shall give the petitioner a written order containing the decision.

(6) If additional time is required for review of reports, the judge shall give the reasons therefor, make them part of the record, and shall render a decision within seventy-two (72) hours of the time of the filing of the petition, unless the petitioner requests an extension of time.

(7) If the decision is not rendered immediately following the hearing then the petitioner shall be responsible for contacting the clerk of the court for notification of the decision.

(8) If the judge does not render a decision within the seventy-two (72) hour time limit, the petitioner may immediately submit the matter to the Court of Appeals.

C. In order to assure expeditious appeals on petitions filed pursuant to KRS 311.732, the following provisions shall apply:

(1) All appeals shall be directly to the Court of Appeals.

(2) The circuit or district clerk shall assist, where necessary, petitioners in the preparation of appeals on petitions filed under KRS 311.732.

(3) At the conclusion of the hearing in the district or circuit court, the judge shall notify the petitioner of

the right to appeal, with whom the appeal must be filed and the procedures relating thereto.

(4) The clerk of the circuit court shall expedite completion and certification of the record on appeal so that in no case shall a period of more than five calendar days elapse between the filing of a notice of appeal in the trial court and the filing of the appeal in the Court of Appeals.

(5) Upon the filing of an appeal with the Clerk of the Court of Appeals, the Clerk shall forthwith notify the Chief Judge of the Court of Appeals or his deputy or designated substitute of the filing of the appeal, and the Chief Judge or his designee shall assign the matter to a member of the Court of Appeals who shall immediately consider the appeal. The judge designated to consider the matter shall convene a panel of the court without delay. Final disposition shall be by a panel.

(6) The Court of Appeals shall within seventy-two (72) hours of the filing consider the appeal in a confidential manner.

(7) Printed and bound materials on appeal shall not be required. Simple, precise and direct statements of appeal are to be encouraged.

(8) The Court of Appeals shall render its decision following the hearing if at all possible, but in no event shall the time for the rendering of the decision exceed seventy-two (72) hours from the time of the filing thereof unless an extension is requested by the petitioner. A written decision is required.

(9) If the decision on the appeal is not rendered immediately following the hearing then the petitioner shall be responsible for contacting the clerk of the court for notification of the decision. All notification pursuant to this procedure shall be confidential.

HISTORY: Amended eff. 9–2–88; adopted eff. 11–13–86

AOC–260   Abortion Petition

AOC-260 Doc. Code: PAB Rev. 4-01 01/11/2011 02:31 pm Page 1 of 2 Ver. 1.01 Commonwealth of Kentucky Court of Justice KRS 311.732	**ABORTION PETITION**	Case No. _____ Court _____ County _____

IN RE: SELF-CONSENT FOR AN ABORTION BY A MINOR

NOTICE TO PETITIONER: *The Clerk will assist you in preparing and filing this Petition if necessary. Anonymity of the Petitioner is required by KRS 311.732.*

Comes the Petitioner, _____, a minor under the age of 18, *(check one)*
(initials)

☐ by herself;

☐ by counsel; or

☐ by her next friend _____.
                                          (Name)

and in support of this Petition for an order of self-consent for an abortion by a minor states that the minor is pregnant and *(check all that apply)*

☐ The minor is mature and well-informed enough to make the abortion decision on her own;

☐ Performance of the abortion is in the minor's best interest.

WHEREFORE, Petitioner prays for the Court to set a hearing within 72 hours of the filing of this Petition, inclusive of weekends and holidays; appoint a guardian *ad litem*, and

☐ appoint counsel; OR

☐ proceed without payment of fees because the minor has insufficient funds to pursue this procedure.

Initials of Petitioner _____

(address where
Petitioner can be reached)   _____
                                          _____
                                          _____

(telephone number for Petitioner)   _____

(2nd address where
Petitioner can be reached)   _____
                                          _____
                                          _____

(2nd telephone number for Petitioner)   _____

Signature of Petitioner's Next Friend: _____

Signature of Petitioner's Counsel: _____

Date Petition Filed: _____, 2_____

Print	Page 1 of 2	Reset Form

AOC-260
Rev. 4-01
Page 2 of 2

Pursuant to special rules of the Kentucky Supreme Court, this Petition and all information relating thereto shall be confidential; shall not be a public record; and shall not be released to the public.

To be completed by clerk:

NOTICE TO PETITIONER:

A **hearing** on this matter **has been set** for _____, 2_____, at _____ ☐ a.m. / ☐ p.m. which is within 72 hours (inclusive of weekends and holidays) from the filing of the Petition. **You must attend**. It will occur at:

_____
_____

_____ has been appointed as your **guardian *ad litem***.

_____ has been appointed as your **counsel** (if requested).

Should this Court fail to render a decision within 72 hours (inclusive of weekends and holidays) from the filing of this Petition, you may take an immediate appeal to the Kentucky Court of Appeals. **Should this Court fail to render a decision immediately following the hearing, you are responsible for contacting the clerk of the trial court** for notification of the Judge's decision. The 72-hour time period may be extended by you.

Distribution:
    Petitioner
    Guardian *ad litem*
    Counsel

Print	Page 2 of 2	Reset Form

JUDICIAL GUIDELINES FOR PRETRIAL RELEASE AND MONITORED CONDITIONAL RELEASE

Current with Amendments Received Through January 1, 2013

Section 1 Purpose

KRS 27A.096 states:

(a) The Supreme Court shall establish recommended guidelines for judges to use when ordering pretrial release and monitored conditional release for defendants whose pretrial risk assessments indicate that they are moderate or high risk and would otherwise be ordered to a local correctional facility while waiting for trial.

(b) The Supreme Court shall establish recommended guidelines for judges to use to determine whether defendants whose pretrial risk assessments indicate that they are moderate to high risk and are eligible for pretrial supervision.

(c) Judges shall consider the guidelines established by the Supreme Court pursuant to this section when setting terms of pretrial supervision.

HISTORY: Adopted by Order 2011–12, eff. 12–15–11

Section 2 Definitions

As used in these sections, unless the context otherwise requires:

(a) "Conditions of release" has the same meaning as that set forth in RCr 4.00(c).

(b) "High risk defendant" means a defendant who has been determined through the pretrial risk assessment to pose a high risk of flight and anticipated criminal conduct. Under KRS 431.066 and these guidelines, level of risk also includes a determination by the court as to the defendant's likelihood of appearing for trial and risk of danger to others.

(c) "Individual risk and needs" means behaviors and conditions identified by scientific evidence to contribute to an individual defendant's risk of flight and anticipated criminal conduct, as determined by the pretrial interview, investigation and risk assessment.

(d) "Low risk defendant" means a defendant who has been determined through the pretrial risk assessment to pose a low risk of flight and anticipated criminal conduct. Under KRS 431.066 and these guidelines, level of risk also includes a determination by the court as to the defendant's likelihood of appealing for trial and risk of danger to others.

(e) "Moderate risk defendant" means a defendant who has been determined through the pretrial risk assessment to pose a moderate risk of flight and anticipated criminal conduct. Under KRS 431.066 and these guidelines, level of risk also includes a determination by the court as to the defendant's likelihood of appearing for trial and risk of danger to others.

(f) "Pretrial risk assessment" means an objective, research based, validated assessment tool that measures a defendant's risk of flight and risk of anticipated criminal conduct while on pretrial release pending adjudication.

(g) "Risk level" means (1) the assessed predictability of a defendant's risk of flight and anticipated criminal conduct based upon the validated Kentucky pretrial risk assessment and (2) the assessed risk of a defendant appearing for trial and posing a danger to others based upon the court's determination.

(h) "Risk reduction plan" means the conditions of release, as recommended to the court by a pretrial officer. The risk reduction plan will be based on the individual risk and needs of a defendant in order to mitigate risk of reoffending or failing to appear.

(i) "Supervision strategy" means conditions, strategies and supervision levels that pretrial officers employ given both the risk level of the defendant and the ability of the defendant to manage his or her own behavior in the community. Because strategies may change during the course of pretrial supervision, periodic modifications to the supervision risk reduction plan may be necessary.

HISTORY: Adopted by Order 2011–12, eff. 12–15–11

Section 3   Pretrial interview, investigation and risk assessment

(a) Pretrial Services will assemble reliable and objective information relevant to the court's determination concerning pretrial release and supervision, drawing upon information obtained through the interview of the defendant, its investigation and the risk assessment. Pretrial Services will present to the court an assessment of risks posed by the defendant and will recommend ways of responding to the risks through use of appropriate conditions of release.

(b) The interview, investigation and assessment may include, but are not limited to, information such as:

(1) the defendant's age, physical and mental condition, family ties, employment status and history, financial resources, length of residence in the community, community ties, past conduct, history relating to drug or alcohol abuse, criminal history, and record concerning appearance at court proceedings;

(2) whether, at the time of the current offense or arrest, the defendant was on probation, parole, or other release pending trial, sentencing, appeal, or completion of sentence for an offense;

(3) the availability of persons who could verify information and who agree to assist the defendant in attending court at the proper time;

(4) other information relevant to successful supervision in the community;

(5) facts justifying a concern that the defendant will violate the law if released without restrictions; and

(6) whether there are specific factors that may make the defendant an appropriate subject for conditional release and supervision options, including participation in available drug, mental health or other treatment.

(c) The presentation of the Pretrial Service's information and the recommendations made to the court will link assessments of the risk of flight and of public safety to appropriate release options designed to respond to the specific risk and supervision needs identified. Suggested release options or conditions will be objectively and consistently applied and will constitute the least restrictive conditions necessary to assure the defendant's appearance for scheduled court events and protect the safety of the community and individual persons.

HISTORY: Adopted by Order 2011–12, eff. 12–15–11

Section 4   Initial presentation and re-examination of the release decision

(a) Information obtained by Pretrial Services through the interview of the defendant, its investigation and the risk assessment will be presented to the court within 12 hours of the defendant's incarceration. Failure by Pretrial Services to present this information to the court within 12 hours will not result in the automatic release of a defendant.

(b) Pretrial Services must inform the court of those defendants in custody who are not released from jail 24 hours alter the initial presentation by the pretrial officer. If a defendant continues to be detained 24 hours from the time of the imposition of conditions of release because of the inability to meet such conditions, the court that imposed the conditions must review the conditions on the defendant's written application or may do so on its own motion. If the court declines to modify the conditions, the judge will record in writing the reasons for that decision.

(c) Pretrial Services will inform the court of those defendants in custody who have not appeared before the court and who are not released from jail after 48 hours. In addition to the information obtained through the interview, investigation and risk assessment, the pretrial officer will provide the court with the current charge and information from the arrest document for a probable cause determination.

(d) Pretrial Services will provide the court with a weekly report that lists the name of the defendants, the status of the bail and the current charge for defendants who remain in custody pending adjudication.

HISTORY: Adopted by Order 2011–12, eff. 12–15–11

Section 5   Factors to consider

(a) Utilizing the pretrial interview, investigation and risk assessment, the pretrial officer will determine whether a defendant poses a low, moderate or high risk of flight or anticipated criminal conduct and will recommend an appropriate risk reduction plan to the court.

(b) In determining whether there is a substantial risk of nonappearance or threat to the community, any person, or the integrity of the judicial process if the defendant is released, the court should consider the pretrial risk assessment and the pretrial recommendation regarding appropriate conditions of release.

(c) Factors utilized in the pretrial risk assessment and in making the pretrial recommendation include, but are not limited to, the factors set forth in Section 3.

HISTORY: Adopted by Order 2011–12, eff. 12–15–11

Section 6   Low-risk defendants

Pursuant to KRS 431.066(2), if, based upon the pretrial risk assessment, the court determines that a defendant poses a low risk of flight and of anticipated criminal conduct, and the court determines that the defendant is likely to appear for trial and is not likely to be a danger to others, the court shall order the defendant released on unsecured bond or on the defendant's own recognizance subject to such other conditions as the court may order.

If the court in its discretion determines that the nature and circumstances of the offense necessitate conditions to ensure public safety and future court appearances, the court should consider, and may place on low-risk defendants, the least restrictive conditions of release.

HISTORY: Adopted by Order 2011–12, eff. 12–15–11

Section 7   Moderate risk defendants

Pursuant to KRS 431.066(3), if, based upon the pretrial risk assessment, the court determines that a defendant poses a moderate risk of flight and of anticipated criminal conduct, and the court determines that the defendant has a moderate risk of not appearing for trial and poses a moderate risk of danger to others, the court shall release the defendant on unsecured bond or on the defendant's own recognizance, but the court shall consider global positioning system (GPS) monitoring, controlled substance testing, increased supervision, or such other conditions as the court may order.

For a moderate risk defendant, the court may place conditions of release that are related to the defendant's individual risk factors. Through the pretrial interview, investigation and risk assessment, the pretrial officer will identify the defendant's individual risk factors and will recommend to the court an appropriate risk reduction plan and supervision strategy.

HISTORY: Adopted by Order 2011–12, eff. 12–15–11

Section 8   High risk defendants

If, based upon the pretrial risk assessment, a defendant is determined to pose a high risk of flight or a high risk of anticipated criminal conduct, or the court determines that the defendant has a high risk of not appearing for trial or poses a high risk of danger to others, the pretrial officer will develop and recommend to the court a risk reduction plan and a supervision strategy. The risk reduction plan will take into consideration the defendant's individual risk factors and the conditions of release set forth in Section 9.

HISTORY: Adopted by Order 2011–12, eff. 12–15–11

Section 9   Conditions of release

(a) If the court sets conditions of release, the court shall consider imposing the least restrictive release conditions reasonably necessary to ensure the defendant's appearance in court, to protect the safety of the community or any person, to prevent intimidation of witnesses or interference with the orderly administration of justice and to safeguard the integrity of the judicial process. In addition, the court should, in every case, (1) require that the defendant attend all court proceedings as ordered and (2) prohibit the commission of any criminal offense.

(b) The court will have (1) a wide array of programs or options available to promote pretrial release on conditions that ensure appearance and protect the safety of the community, victims and witnesses pending trial and (2) the capacity to develop release options appropriate to the risks and special needs posed by defendants released to the community. When no conditions of release are sufficient to accomplish the aims of pretrial release, defendants must be detained.

(c) In setting conditions of release, the court should consider the pretrial officer's recommended risk reduction plan. The conditions of release should be reasonably related to the defendant's risks of nonappearance and danger to public safety that have been identified by the court.

(d) When conditions of release are imposed, the court may direct the pretrial officer to (1) monitor the defendant's compliance with the nonfinancial conditions and (2) make reports to the court concerning the defendant's compliance with the conditions.

(e) If a court determines, in the exercise of its discretion, that release on personal recognizance or the execution of an unsecured bail bond will not reasonably assure the appearance of the defendant, KRS 431.520 requires the court to impose any of the conditions of release listed in KRS 431.520(1) through (5) or any other condition deemed reasonably necessary to assure the defendant's appearance as required by the court. Conditions of release may include, but are not limited to:

(1) reporting to the pretrial officer;

(2) prohibition against consuming alcohol or illegal drugs;

(3) prohibition against possession of weapons;

(4) prohibition against driving;

(5) alcohol/drug abuse assessment/evaluation;

(6) alcohol/drug treatment;

(7) random drug testing;

(8) electronic and global positioning system monitoring;

(9) restriction of association;

(10) restricting place of abode;

(11) restricting travel by structuring inclusion and exclusion zones that prohibit travel to specific locations;

(12) no contact orders;

(13) telephone or other curfews;

(14) home incarceration or GPS monitoring;

(15) educational and/or employment requirements; and

(16) payment of court-ordered obligations.

(f) The defendant shall be notified of upcoming court dates.

(g) Pretrial officers shall inform the court if a defendant fails to appear in court or is charged with a new crime while on pretrial release.

HISTORY: Adopted by Order 2011–12, eff. 12–15–11

Section 10   Release decision order provisions

In the release decision order, the court should

(a) include all the conditions to which the release is subject, in a manner sufficiently clear and specific to serve as a guide for the defendant's conduct.

(b) advise the defendant of:

(1) the consequences of violating a condition of release, including the immediate issuance of a warrant for the defendant's arrest and possible criminal penalties;

(2) the prohibitions against threats, force, or intimidation of witnesses, jurors and officers of the court, obstruction of criminal investigations and retaliation against a witness, victim or informant; and

(3) the prohibition against any criminal conduct during pretrial release.

(d) document the reasons for:

(1) setting a bail amount that exceeds the maximum amount set forth in KRS 431.525(2) through (5) because the defendant presents a flight risk or is a danger to others;

(2) denying a defendant release via bail credit under KRS 431.066 because:

(A) the defendant is convicted of, pleading guilty to, or entering an Afford plea to a felony offense under KRS Chapter 510, KRS 529.100 involving commercial sexual activity, KRS 530.020,

530.064(1)(a), 531.310, or 531.320, or who is a violent offender as defined in KRS 439.3401; or

(B) the defendant is found by the court to present a flight risk or to be a danger to others; and

(3) denying a defendant release pursuant to presumptive probation under KRS 218A.135 because the defendant presents a flight risk or is a danger to himself or herself or a danger to others.

HISTORY: Adopted eff. 12–15–11

Section 11   Court's discretion

Nothing in these Guidelines shall be construed to limit the court's discretion as to whether or not to grant pretrial release to a defendant. The court may determine whether to release a defendant on personal recognizance or unsecured appearance bond, release a defendant on one or more conditions, or detain a defendant.

HISTORY: Adopted by Order 2011–12, eff. 12–15–11

Section 12   Uniform bail schedule

The Uniform Bail Schedule, which was implemented as a pilot program in several jurisdictions, shall continue to apply for purposes of allowing a release on a minimal bond prior to a pretrial investigation and presentation of the defendant's case to a judicial officer.

HISTORY: Adopted by Order 2011–12, eff. 12–15–11

Section 13   Constitutionality of underlying statutes

The adoption of these guidelines does not, either expressly or impliedly, reflect on the ultimate constitutionality of the statutes involved.

HISTORY: Adopted by Order 2011–12, eff. 12–15–11

MODEL MEDIATION RULES

Effective February 1, 2000

Rule 1 Preamble and scope

The _____ County Trial Courts find that under some circumstances the process known as mediation may provide an efficient and cost-effective alternative to traditional litigation, and, further, that the wise and judicious use of mediation may benefit litigants.

Mediation is intended to help both litigants and the Courts facilitate the settlement of disputes. Litigants should participate in good faith and in an earnest attempt to resolve their differences.

This Rule refers to mediation. Nothing in this Rule shall prohibit parties from resolving disputes through other methods. However, in any case where one party may pose a risk of harm (such as domestic violence) to another party or family member, mediation should not be used.

Rule 2 Mediation defined

Mediation is an informal process in which a neutral third person(s) called a mediator facilitates the resolution of a dispute between two or more parties. The process is designed to help disputing parties reach an agreement on all or part of the issues in dispute. Decision-making authority remains with the parties, not the mediator. The mediator assists the parties in identifying issues, fostering joint problem-solving, and exploring settlement alternatives.

Rule 3 Referral of cases to mediation

At any time on its own motion or on motion of any party, the Court may refer a case or portion of a case for mediation. In this decision, the court shall consider:

(a) the stage of the litigation, including the need for discovery, and the extent to which it has been conducted;

(b) the nature of the issues to be resolved;

(c) the value to the parties of confidentiality, rapid resolution, or the promotion or maintenance of on-going relationships;

(d) the willingness of the parties to mutually resolve their dispute;

(e) other attempts at dispute resolution; and

(f) the ability of the parties to participate in the mediation process.

Rule 4 No stay of proceedings

Unless otherwise ordered by the Court, mediation shall not stay any other proceedings.

Rule 5 Appointment of mediator

Within fifteen (15) days of referral, the parties shall agree on a mediator or a mediation service. If the parties cannot agree, they shall notify the court, which will select a mediator or a mediation service.

Rule 6 Mediator compensation

The mediator shall be compensated at the rate agreed between the mediator and the parties if the mediator is chosen by agreement. If the mediator is appointed by the Court, the fee for the mediator shall be reasonable and no greater than the mediator's standard rate as a mediator. Unless otherwise agreed by the parties or ordered by the Court, the parties shall equally divide the mediator's professional fees.

Rule 7 Mediation procedure

Following selection of the mediator, the mediator shall set an initial mediation conference within thirty (30) days. The mediation conference shall be held in the county in which the case is pending or at a site agreed upon by the parties. The mediator may meet with the parties or their counsel prior to the mediation conference for the purpose of establishing a procedure for the mediation conference. The mediator may require the parties to submit a confidential statement of the case or other materials that the mediator may reasonably believe appropriate for efficiently conducting the mediation conference.

Rule 8   Attendance at mediation conference

The parties must attend the mediation conference. Counsel shall attend the mediation conference unless otherwise agreed to by the parties and the mediator or ordered by the Court. If a party is a public entity, it shall appear by the physical presence of a representative with full authority to negotiate on behalf of the entity and to recommend settlement to the appropriate decision making body or officer of the entity. If a party is an organization other than a public entity, it shall appear by the physical presence of a representative, other than the party's counsel of record, who has full authority to settle without further consultation. If any party is insured for the claim in dispute, that party shall also be required to have its insurer(s) present by the physical presence of a representative of the insurance carrier(s) who is not that carrier's outside counsel; this representative must have full settlement authority. The foregoing requirements of attendance may be varied only by stipulation of the parties or by order of the Court for good cause shown.

Rule 9   Completion or termination mediation

The mediator may terminate the mediation conference after a settlement is reached or when the mediator determines that continuation of the process would be unproductive. After the initial mediation conference, mediation shall continue only by the agreement of the parties, their counsel and the mediator, or by order of the Court.

Rule 10   Report to the court

The mediator shall report to the court that the mediation has not occurred, has not been completed, or that the mediation has been completed with or without an agreement on any or all issues. With the consent of the parties, the mediator may also identify those matters which, if resolved or completed, would facilitate the possibility of a settlement.

Rule 11   Agreement

If an agreement is reached during the mediation conference, it shall be reduced to writing and signed by the parties. The parties shall be responsible for the drafting of the agreement, although the mediator may assist in the drafting of the agreement with the consent of the parties.

Rule 12   Confidentiality

A.   Mediation sessions shall be closed to all persons other than the parties, their legal representatives, and other persons invited by the mediator with the consent of the parties.

B.   Mediation shall be regarded as settlement negotiations for purposes of K.R.E. 408.

C.   Mediators shall not be subject to process requiring the disclosure of any matter discussed during the mediation, but rather, such matters shall be considered confidential and privileged in nature except on order of the Court for good cause shown. This privilege and immunity reside in the mediator and may not be waived by the parties.

D.   Nothing in this rule shall prohibit the mediator from reporting abuse according to KRS 209.030, KRS 620.030, or other applicable law.

HISTORY: Adopted by Order 99–1, eff. 2–1–00

ADMINISTRATIVE PROCEDURES
OF THE COURT OF JUSTICE

Including Amendments Received Through January 1, 2013

PART I

TRANSITION TO DISTRICT COURT

AP I, Sec. 1   Transfer of lower court dockets to the district court

(1) Each court of limited jurisdiction, or officer or agent of the court, whose actions upon pending cases will have the effect of docketing these cases for hearing, trial or any other proceeding on a date subsequent to January 2, 1978, shall immediately notify the circuit clerk of the style and nature of each case. The circuit clerk may then assign a number to the case to be affixed immediately or at the time the papers are transferred.

(2) On January 2, 1978, all causes and proceedings pending in courts of limited jurisdiction shall stand pending in the district court or circuit court. All papers in these cases along with any exhibits, bail or cash deposits shall be transmitted to the circuit clerk for numbering and docketing. Preference shall be given to cases in which a party is being held in detention.

HISTORY: Adopted eff. 12–1–77

AP I, Sec. 2   Causes and proceedings pending

(1) Causes and proceedings pending in courts of limited jurisdiction shall include only the following:

(a) Civil action in which no judgment has been entered and in which some pretrial step has been taken within the six months previous to January 2, 1978.

(b) Probate actions in which application for the probate of a will, the appointment of an executor, or the appointment of an administrator has been filed but no final settlement has been accepted.

(c) Juvenile actions in which a petition for proceedings concerning a child has been filed but no final disposition has been made.

(d) Criminal actions in which a complaint, citation, summons or warrant has issued but no judgment has been entered. However, in no case pending longer than one year preceding January 2, 1978 shall the papers be transferred to the district court until the warrant or summons is served.

(2) All other cases undisposed filed in expired courts of limited jurisdiction may be transferred to the district court by motion of any party.

HISTORY: Adopted eff. 1–2–78

AP I, Sec. 3   Further disposition of cases transferred from expired courts

(1) If a verdict has been returned or findings of fact and conclusions of law have been filed in a civil case, or a verdict or finding of guilt has been rendered in a criminal case, by a quarterly court, county court, police court, city court, or court of justice of the peace, the district judge may perform all duties in the further disposition of the case. If, however, the judge is satisfied that he cannot perform those duties because

he did not preside at the trial or for any other reason, he may in his discretion grant a new trial.

(2) If the judge does not grant a new trial, appeals from judgments entered pursuant to this rule shall be docketed in the circuit court and tried anew according to the applicable rules of civil or criminal procedure in force prior to January 2, 1978.

HISTORY: Adopted eff. 1–2–78

AP I, Sec. 4   Actions on judgments of expired courts

Actions, except appeals, on judgments of courts of limited jurisdiction rendered prior to January 2, 1978 shall be by motion in the district court. An attested copy of the judgment shall be filed with the motion.

HISTORY: Adopted eff. 1–2–78

AP I, Sec. 5   Cases pending in the circuit court

Cases pending in the circuit court on January 2, 1978 which are within the jurisdiction of the district court shall not be transferred to the district court but shall be decided by the circuit court.

HISTORY: Adopted eff. 1–2–78

AP I, Sec. 6   Accounting

(1) When a case is transferred to the district court the portion of any cash deposit which is in excess of amounts committed for service already rendered shall be transferred to the circuit clerk for deposit with the state treasury. The uniform fees and costs in force on January 2, 1978, shall apply to all cases transferred to the district court and all cases pending in the circuit court on that date. In no case will step costs continue to be assessed. In all these cases filed prior to January 2, 1978, the difference between the amount of cash deposits remitted by the litigants (including step costs paid) and the greater of the uniform filing fees in force on January 2, 1978, or the amount of step costs owing but unpaid shall be assessed and collected by the circuit clerk for deposit with the state treasury.

(2) All fines, fees, forfeitures and costs collected in the Court of Justice on or after January 2, 1978, shall be dispersed in accordance with relevant statutes in force on that date.

HISTORY: Adopted eff. 1–2–78

PART II

JURY SELECTION AND MANAGEMENT

AP II, Sec. 1   Definitions

As used in these sections, unless the context otherwise requires:

(1) "Box" means the receptacle in which are placed the cards with identifying numbers representing the

names of those assigned to a jury panel, from which a grand jury or petit jury shall be chosen.

(2) "Court" means a circuit or district court of this Commonwealth and includes any judge of these courts.

(3) "Identifying number" means the number assigned on the randomized jury list to each name in the jury panel.

(4) "Jury panel" means the group of prospective jurors who are summoned to appear on a stated day and from which a grand jury or petit jury will be chosen.

(5) "Jury period" and "jury period of service" mean the time period for which a group of persons is summoned to jury service.

(6) "Name" includes an identifying number.

(7) "Randomized jury list" means the randomized computer generated list of prospective jurors taken from all county registered voters and all persons over the age of eighteen (18) with valid drivers' licenses issued in the county.

HISTORY: Amended by Order 91–2, eff. 11–15–91; adopted eff. 11–4–77

AP II, Sec. 2　Master list of prospective jurors

(1) A list of persons over the age of eighteen (18) and holding valid drivers' licenses which were issued in the county, and all voter registration lists for the county shall constitute a master list of prospective jurors. The Administrative Office of the Courts shall annually acquire a copy of the drivers' license list from the Transportation Cabinet, and copies of the voter registration lists from the State Board of Elections.

(2) The Transportation Cabinet and the State Board of Elections who have custody, possession, or control of any of the lists required under subsection (1) of this section shall annually furnish a copy of the list to the Administrative Office of the Courts without charge.

HISTORY: Adopted by Order 91–2, eff. 11–15–91

AP II, Sec. 3　Use of computers

The selection of names of prospective jurors shall be accomplished by computer, using the computer in the Administrative Office of the Courts which contains a list of the county registered voters and persons over the age of eighteen (18) and holding valid drivers' licenses which were issued in the county. The Administrative Office of the Courts shall provide a randomized computer list of prospective jurors. The chief circuit judge or his designee shall request said list at least annually. The list shall contain a given number of names as requested by the chief circuit judge or designee.

HISTORY: Amended eff. 10–7–94; adopted eff. 11–15–91

AP II, Sec. 4　Notification of need for jurors

Before the commencement of a jury period of service, each circuit and district judge shall inform the chief circuit judge or designee of the judge's needs for qualified jurors for the next jury period. If any judge anticipates the need for a larger panel than is usually provided, because of a particular nature or notoriety of a pending case, he or she shall so inform the chief circuit judge.

HISTORY: Adopted by Order 91–2, eff. 11–15–91

AP II, Sec. 5　Obtaining names from randomized jury list

(1) The chief circuit judge or designee shall thereupon cause to be taken in sequential order from the randomized jury list as many names as deemed necessary for the impanelling of the number of jurors required. If such names are obtained by the clerk, it shall be done in the presence of the chief circuit judge or of his or her designee.

(2) The names of jurors obtained from the randomized jury list shall be made available to the public.

HISTORY: Adopted by Order 91–2, eff. 11–15–91

AP II, Sec. 6　Juror summons

(1) When the names are obtained from the randomized jury list, the judge thereafter shall cause each person obtained for jury service to be served with a summons requiring that person to report for jury service at a specified time and place, unless otherwise notified by the court, and to be available for jury service for thirty (30) judicial days thereafter. The service of summons may be either made personally by the sheriff or sent by first class mail, addressed to the juror at his or her usual residence, business, or post office address. In either case, notice shall be mailed or served to the juror at least thirty (30) days before required to attend.

(2) The juror qualification form required by § 7 shall be enclosed with summons. If the summons is served by mail, any prospective juror who does not return the juror qualification form within ten (10) days or such other time as may be specified in the summons may be personally served by the sheriff.

HISTORY: Amended by Order 2007–006, eff. 12–20–07; adopted by Order 91–2, eff. 11–15–91

AP II, Sec. 7　Juror qualification forms

(1) The chief circuit judge shall cause to be mailed or delivered with the summons to each juror a juror qualification form accompanied by instructions to fill out and return the form by mail or hand delivery to the clerk within five (5) days after its receipt, or to be completed as otherwise directed. The juror qualification form shall be provided by the Administrative Office of the Courts and subject to approval by the Chief Justice of the Supreme Court.

(2) The juror qualification form shall contain the prospective juror's signed declaration that the responses are true to the best of his or her knowledge and his or her acknowledgment that a willful misrepresentation of a material fact may be punished by a

fine or by imprisonment, or both. Notarization of the juror qualification form shall not be required.

(3) If the prospective juror is unable to fill out the form, another person may do it for the prospective juror and shall indicate that he or she has done so and the reason therefor.

(4) Any prospective juror who fails to return a properly completed juror qualification form as instructed may be directed by the chief circuit judge to appear forthwith to fill out a juror qualification form. A prospective juror who fails to appear as directed by the judge pursuant to this subsection shall be ordered to appear and show cause for failure to appear as directed. If the prospective juror fails to appear pursuant to the judge's order or fails to show good cause for failure to appear as directed by the judge, the prospective juror may be punished for contempt.

(5) On the first day that prospective jurors appear in response to the summons, any prospective juror may be questioned by the judge or designee, but only with regard to responses to questions contained on the form and grounds for his or her excuse of disqualification. Any information thus acquired shall be noted on the juror qualification form.

(6) No person shall willfully misrepresent a material fact on a juror qualification form.

(7) The contents of juror qualification forms shall be made available to the trial judge and to parties or their attorneys of record unless the chief circuit judge or designee determines in any instance in the interest of justice that the information shall be kept confidential or its use limited in whole or in part.

HISTORY: Adopted by Order 91–2, eff. 11–15–91

AP II, Sec. 8   Disqualification for jury service

(1) The chief circuit judge or another judge designated by the chief circuit judge shall determine on the basis of the information provided on the juror qualification form whether the prospective juror is disqualified for jury service for any of the reasons listed in subsection (2) of this section. The judge shall enter this determination in the space provided on the juror qualification form and on the list of names obtained from the randomized jury list. The chief circuit judge shall cause each disqualified juror to be immediately notified of his or her disqualification.

(2) A prospective juror is disqualified to serve on a jury if he or she:

(a) Is under eighteen (18) years of age; or

(b) Is not a citizen of the United States; or

(c) Is not a resident of the county; or

(d) Has insufficient knowledge of the English language; or

(e) Has been previously convicted of a felony and has not been pardoned by the governor or other authorized person of the jurisdiction in which the prospective juror was convicted; or

(f) Is presently under indictment; or

(g) Has served on a jury within the past twelve (12) months.

(3) There shall be no waiver of these disqualifications, except that pursuant to the federal Americans With Disabilities Act of 1990, an individual with a disability shall not be disqualified solely by reason of the disability. For the purposes of this section, "individual with a disability" means a person with a physical or mental impairment that substantially limits one (1) or more of the major life activities of the individual, a record of the impairment, or being regarded as having the impairment.

HISTORY: Amended eff. 10–7–94; adopted eff. 11–15–91

AP II, Sec. 9   Excuses

(1) On the day on which the prospective jurors are summoned to appear, any person not previously excused who desires to be excused shall be heard in a bench conference if he or she so desires. Other persons may be heard in open court or in a bench conference at the discretion of the court.

(2) All the prospective jurors who qualify and are not excused shall be called to report each day by the identifying numbers assigned on the randomized jury list instead of by name. The same numbers shall be used in selecting a grand jury or petit jury from a jury panel under the provision of § 10.

(3) The chief circuit judge shall regulate the random assignment of jurors for use in circuit and district courts. Any petit juror assigned to a judge of circuit or district court may be used by any other judge of any other division of circuit or district court when jurors are needed.

(4) When possible, trials shall be scheduled for the day on which jurors are summoned to appear, in order to maximize their day of service.

(5) All who appear when summoned except those who are excused from service, shall be paid for a day of service in accordance with KRS 29A.170.

HISTORY: Adopted by Order 91–2, eff. 11–15–91

AP II, Sec. 10   Selection of petit and grand jury

(1) To select a grand jury from a jury panel, the judge or designee shall:

(a) Take identifying numbers from those assigned on the randomized jury list;

(b) Deposit in a box numbered cards bearing the same numbers as those assigned to the panel;

(c) Draw the required number of cards, dependent on the number of jurors to be chosen, from the box and record the number of each card as it is drawn.

(2) The persons whose numbers have been drawn shall constitute the grand jury or petit jury as the case may be, unless excused or removed by challenge.

(3) As prospective jurors are excused or challenged, additional cards shall be drawn, one for each juror required, until all of the cards have been exhausted.

(4) If a court does not possess a suitable box, the clerk shall, upon court order, thoroughly mix or shuffle the cards and then take the required number of cards from the top of the set.

(5) In the event that all of the cards are exhausted before a jury is chosen, the judge shall ascertain whether jurors who have been assigned to another courtroom are available. Jurors assigned to any district or circuit court may be used in any other division of district or circuit court when jurors are needed.

(6) Jurors who are not selected for a jury shall be directed to report to the clerk's office (or other central location) to receive another assignment or be dismissed for the day. In those counties using a telephone answering service for daily messages to jurors, all jurors should be reminded to continue to call the telephone answering service for further assignments.

(7) When there is an unanticipated shortage of available jurors obtained from a randomized jury list, the chief circuit judge may require the sheriff to summon a sufficient number of jurors selected sequentially by the judge from the randomized jury list beginning with the first name following the last name previously selected. Jurors summoned in this way need not be given the notice provided in § 6.

(8) Except as provided in subsection (7) of this section, only persons duly summoned and qualified under these procedures shall serve as jurors.

(9) The names of jurors selected as grand and petit jurors shall be made available to the public unless the Chief Circuit Judge, or his designee, determines that in the interest of justice, the names shall be kept confidential.

HISTORY: Amended eff. 4–20–95; adopted eff. 11–15–91

AP II, Sec. 11   Automatic exemptions prohibited

There shall be no automatic exemptions from jury service.

HISTORY: Adopted by Order 91–2, eff. 11–15–91

AP II, Sec. 12   Postponement of service or excusing of juror

(1) Upon the request of a prospective juror prior to his or her assignment to a trial court, the chief circuit judge, or after his or her assignment to a trial court, the trial judge may excuse such juror upon a showing of undue hardship, extreme inconvenience or public necessity.

(2) In his or her discretion the judge may excuse a juror from service entirely or may postpone the ju-

ror's service temporarily, either to a later part of the jury period, or to another jury period. Whenever possible the judge shall favor temporary postponement of service over permanent excuse. When excusing a juror, the judge shall record the juror's name, as provided in § 8, and the reasons for granting the excuse.

HISTORY: Adopted by Order 91–2, eff. 11–15–91

AP II, Sec. 13   Disclosure of records or papers used in selection process

The contents of any records or papers used by the clerk in connection with the selection process and not required to be made public under this chapter shall not be disclosed, except in connection with the preparation or presentation of a motion under the Rules of Civil Procedure or the Rules of Criminal Procedure.

HISTORY: Adopted by Order 91–2, eff. 11–15–91

AP II, Sec. 14   Preservation of records and papers compiled in selection process

After the randomized jury list has been exhausted and all persons selected to serve as jurors have been discharged, all records and papers compiled in the selection process shall be destroyed.

HISTORY: Adopted by Order 91–2, eff. 11–15–91

AP II, Sec. 15   Limitation on jury service within twelve month period

In any twelve (12) month period, a person shall not be required to:

(1) Serve or attend court for prospective service as a petit juror more than thirty (30) court days except when necessary to complete service in a particular case; or

(2) Serve on more than one grand jury; or

(3) Serve as both a grand and petit juror except as provided in § 23 and § 26.

HISTORY: Adopted by Order 91–2, eff. 11–15–91

AP II, Sec. 16   Discharge of juror

At the conclusion of a period of service as required by this chapter, each juror shall be discharged.

HISTORY: Adopted by Order 91–2, eff. 11–15–91

AP II, Sec. 17   Contempt; failure to perform jury service

(1) A person summoned for jury service who fails to appear as directed shall be ordered by the court to appear forthwith and show cause for failure to comply with the summons. If the person summoned fails to show good cause for noncompliance with the summons, he or she may be punished for contempt.

(2) A juror who fails to give attention at court, or who leaves the courthouse while the court is in ses-

sion, or who otherwise fails to complete jury service, without leave of the court, may be punished for contempt.

HISTORY: Adopted by Order 91–2, eff. 11–15–91

AP II, Sec. 18 Responsibility for needs of jurors sequestered, transportation to view scene, security personnel, equipment and services

(1) The sheriff, city police or city marshal, as appropriate under KRS 23A.090 and 24A.140, shall be responsible for meals, housing, and other incidental needs of grand jurors and petit jurors in circuit court and in district court when the jurors are kept overnight or otherwise sequestered when ordered to do so by the judge of the court for which the jurors were summoned. The expenses for these services shall be borne by the Finance and Administration Cabinet and the officer shall be reimbursed in accordance with administrative regulations issued by the Finance and Administration Cabinet, pursuant to KRS Chapter 13A.

(2) The sheriff, city police or city marshal, as appropriate under KRS 23A.090 and 24A.140, shall be responsible for the transportation of jurors and other authorized persons to views of the scene or other locations authorized by the court pursuant to Section 31. In criminal cases the expenses for these services shall be borne by the Finance and Administration Cabinet and the sheriff shall be reimbursed in accordance with administrative regulations issued by the Finance and Administration Cabinet, pursuant to KRS Chapter 13A. Excepting views conducted under the Eminent Domain Act of Kentucky, in civil cases these expenses shall be paid by the party requesting the viewing.

(3) The sheriff, city police or city marshal, as appropriate under KRS 23A.090 and 24A.140, shall be responsible for providing any specialized security personnel, equipment, and services which the judge, with the consent of the chief justice, shall deem necessary for the conduct of a trial in which the judge believes that special security precautions are necessary or desirable. The expenses for these services shall be borne by the Finance and Administration Cabinet and such officer shall be reimbursed in accordance with administrative regulations issued by the Finance and Administration Cabinet, pursuant to KRS Chapter 13A. In such cases the judge may also request the chief justice to provide the services of the Kentucky State Police to ensure proper security precautions relating to the case.

HISTORY: Amended eff. 10–7–94; adopted eff. 11–15–91

AP II, Sec. 19 Adjournment of juries

The court may adjourn the whole or part of the petit jury to any day of their required periods of service, but they shall not be paid for the time they stand adjourned. The grand jury may be adjourned in like manner without pay.

HISTORY: Adopted by Order 91–2, eff. 11–15–91

AP II, Sec. 20 Number of grand jurors; number required to find indictment

A grand jury shall consist of twelve (12) persons, nine (9) of whom concurring, may find an indictment.

HISTORY: Adopted by Order 91–2, eff. 11–15–91

AP II, Sec. 21 Summoning and convening of regular grand juries; sessions

(1) A regular grand jury shall be summoned upon the order of the chief circuit judge. The grand jury shall be convened at least once every four (4) months at such time as may be designated by the circuit court. The court may require the grand jury to convene more often if the ends of justice or the needs of the county so require. The court may require the grand jury to convene if the Commonwealth's or county attorney certifies to the court that there are defendants who have been bound over to the grand jury and that there is a need for the grand jury to consider the return of any indictments.

(2) The Chief Justice may authorize any chief circuit judge to impanel an additional regular grand jury upon a showing that a single grand jury cannot handle the volume of business before the court.

(3) A regular grand jury shall remain in session until discharged by the court but shall not remain in session longer than twenty (20) days of actual court attendance except when necessary to complete work on a single case in which testimony has already been taken.

HISTORY: Adopted by Order 91–2, eff. 11–15–91

AP II, Sec. 22 Special grand juries; sessions; extensions of sessions

(1) Any chief circuit judge may summon for cause a special grand jury to deal with a situation requiring lengthy investigation which cannot be adequately handled during the term of the regular grand jury.

(2) A special grand jury shall remain in session until discharged by the court, but shall not remain in session longer than ninety (90) days, provided, however, that a special grand jury may be extended for additional ninety (90) day periods on the written order of the chief circuit judge.

HISTORY: Adopted by Order 91–2, eff. 11–15–91

AP II, Sec. 23 Release of juror from grand jury service and retention as petit juror

If a juror selected is incapable of serving as a grand juror but capable of serving as a petit juror, the judge may, for good cause shown, release the juror from grand jury service and retain that juror as a petit juror.

HISTORY: Adopted by Order 91–2, eff. 11–15–91

AP II, Sec. 24   Oath to grand jury

The court shall swear the grand jury, using substantially the following oath:

"Do you swear or affirm that you will hear and weigh carefully all the evidence presented to you, and that you will do your duty as prescribed by law, and that you will carry out carefully any investigations which you are requested to make?"

HISTORY: Adopted by Order 91–2, eff. 11–15–91

AP II, Sec. 25   Foreman of grand jury; oath to witness

The foreman of the grand jury shall be selected as provided by RCr 5.04. The foreman shall administer an oath to each witness who testifies before the grand jury, substantially as follows:

"Do you swear or affirm that you will tell the truth, the whole truth, and nothing but the truth?"

HISTORY: Adopted by Order 91–2, eff. 11–15–91

AP II, Sec. 26   Replacement of grand juror who is excused

At any time for cause shown, the court may excuse a grand juror either temporarily or permanently and may swear another grand juror from a current jury panel in place of the one excused. The discharge of any such grand juror shall in no way or manner affect any indictment found by the grand jury as it was composed either before or after such discharge. If it is impossible to fill the vacancy on the grand jury from a current jury panel, the chief circuit judge may summon, using the procedure in § 10(7), such number of prospective jurors as deemed necessary for the purpose.

HISTORY: Adopted by Order 91–2, eff. 11–15–91

AP II, Sec. 27   Number of jurors in circuit and district courts; number required for verdict

(1) Juries for all trials in circuit court shall be composed of twelve (12) persons. Juries for all trials in district court shall be composed of six (6) persons.

(2) A unanimous verdict is required in all criminal trials by jury. The agreement of at least three-fourths (3/4) of the jurors is required for a verdict in all civil trials by jury in circuit court. The agreement of at least five-sixths (5/6) of the jurors is required for a verdict in all civil trials by jury in district court.

(3) The parties may stipulate that the jury shall consist of any number less than provided by law or that a verdict or a finding of a stated majority of the jurors shall be taken as the verdict or finding of the jury.

HISTORY: Adopted by Order 91–2, eff. 11–15–91

AP II, Sec. 28   Challenge to panel

A motion raising an irregularity in the selection or summons of the jurors or formation of the jury must precede the examination of the jurors.

HISTORY: Adopted by Order 91–2, eff. 11–15–91

AP II, Sec. 29   Peremptory challenges in civil cases

(1) In civil cases, each opposing side shall have three peremptory challenges, but co-parties having antagonistic interests shall each have three peremptory challenges.

(2) If one or two additional jurors are called, the number of peremptory challenges allowed each side shall be increased by one.

HISTORY: Adopted by Order 91–2, eff. 11–15–91

AP II, Sec. 30   Oath to petit jury

The court, or the clerk if the court so orders, shall swear the petit jurors, using substantially the following oath:

"Do you swear or affirm that you will impartially try the case between the parties and give a true verdict according to the evidence and the law, unless dismissed by the court?"

HISTORY: Adopted by Order 91–2, eff. 11–15–91

AP II, Sec. 31   Admonition to jury upon separation; view of property or place

(1) If the jury is permitted to separate, either during the trial or after the case is submitted to them, they shall be admonished by the court that it is their duty not to converse with, nor allow themselves to be addressed by, any other person on any subject of the trial; and that, during the trial, it is their duty not to form or express an opinion thereon, until the case is finally submitted to them.

(2) No officer, party, or witness to an action pending, or that person's attorney or attorneys shall, without leave of the court, converse with the jury or any member thereof upon any subject after they have been sworn.

(3) When necessary the judge may authorize the jury to view the real property which is the subject of the litigation, or the place in which any material fact occurred, or the place in which the offense is charged to have been committed.

HISTORY: Adopted by Order 91–2, eff. 11–15–91

AP II, Sec. 32 Duty of jury and officer after submission; causes for discharge of jury; procedure for rendering verdict

(1) When the case is finally submitted to the jury, they shall retire for deliberation. When they retire, they shall be kept together in some convenient place, under the charge of an officer, until they agree upon a verdict or are discharged by the court, subject to the Supreme Court rules permitting them to separate temporarily at night and for their meals. The officer having them under his or her charge shall not allow any communications to be made to them, nor make any communications to them, except to ask them if they have agreed upon their verdict, unless by order of the court; and the officer shall not before their verdict is rendered, communicate to any person the state of their deliberations, or the verdict agreed upon.

(2)(a) The jury may be discharged by the court on account of the sickness of a juror, or other accident, calamity or circumstances requiring their discharge; or by consent of both parties; or, after they have been kept together until it satisfactorily appears that there is no probability of their agreeing.

(b) Cases in which the jury is discharged without making a verdict shall be tried again at such time as the court may direct.

(3) The procedure for rendering the verdict shall be:

(a) When the jurors have agreed on their verdict, the verdict shall be written and signed by the foreman.

(b) When a verdict is rendered by less than the whole jury, it shall be signed by all the jurors who agree to it.

(c) The foreman shall hand the verdict to the judge who shall read the verdict and then make inquiry of the jury as to whether it is their verdict.

(d) When the verdict is announced either party may require that the jury be polled, which is done by the judge asking each juror if it is his or her verdict.

(e) If more than the number of jurors required by § 27 answers in the negative, the jury must be sent out for further deliberation.

(f) If no disagreement is expressed or, in an appropriate case, an insufficient number disagree, the verdict is complete and the jury shall be discharged from the case.

HISTORY: Adopted by Order 91–2, eff. 11–15–91

AP II, Sec. 33 Jury fee

(1) As provided in KRS 23A.200 and 24A.170, the jury fee for civil cases in circuit court is $25 for a jury of more than six persons, and $12.50 for a jury of six persons. The jury fee for civil cases in district court is $12.50.

(2) The jury fee in civil cases shall be paid at the time the request for a jury trial is made, and shall be paid by the party making the request. If two or more cases are consolidated and tried together, the clerk shall collect only one jury fee. A party who is proceeding in forma pauperis shall not be liable for a jury fee.

(3) The clerk shall place the jury fee in an escrow account. If the request for a jury trial is withdrawn or the case is disposed of at least two court days prior to the date set for trial, the amount of the jury fee shall be refunded to the person paying it. Otherwise, it shall be placed in the general fund of the state treasury, in the same manner as the filing fee.

(4) Unless the jury fee has been refunded as provided in subsection (3), the amount of the jury fee shall be assessed as costs against the unsuccessful party upon judgment or dismissal of the action.

HISTORY: Adopted by Order 91–2, eff. 11–15–91

AP II, Sec. 34 Duty of jury and officer after submission; causes for discharge of jury; procedure for rendering verdict—Abolished

HISTORY: Abolished by Order 91–2, eff. 11–15–91

AP II, Sec. 35 Jury fee—Abolished

HISTORY: Abolished by Order 91–2, eff. 11–15–91

PART III
PERSONNEL POLICIES

Publisher's Note: Administrative procedures relating to personnel policies have not been released for publication inasmuch as their application is limited to officers and employees of the Court of Justice.

PART IV
MASTER COMMISSIONERS OF THE CIRCUIT COURT

AP IV, Sec. 1 Appointment of master commissioner and deputies; qualifications

(1) A master commissioner may be appointed for each county within a judicial circuit.

(a) In a single-judge circuit the appointment shall be made by the Circuit Judge.

(b) In judicial circuits with more than one judge the master commissioner shall be chosen by a majority of the circuit judges. In the event of a tie, the chief circuit judge shall choose from those receiving the tie vote. The chief circuit judge shall enter an order appointing the master commissioner for the term of office and shall file a copy of the Order of Appointment with the Clerk of the Supreme Court.

(2) The master commissioner shall serve at the pleasure of the judge(s) of the circuit court, but in no case shall his or her term exceed four years without reappointment.

(a) In a single-judge circuit the term of the master commissioner shall automatically terminate following the death, resignation, or permanent replacement of the circuit judge who appointed the master commissioner.

(b) In a judicial circuit with more than one judge the master commissioner may be removed at any time by a majority of the circuit judges. In the event of a tie, the final decision shall be made by the chief circuit judge.

(3) The master commissioner shall be compensated by fees as provided in Sections 6 and 7 herein. The circuit court may allow the master commissioner a reasonable fee for acting as receiver of the court, for executing documents pursuant to court order, for performing such other functions as ordered by the court, and for performing judicial type functions in actions where the master commissioner does not execute a judicial sale.

(4) The master commissioner shall maintain his or her office at such locations and during such hours as the chief circuit judge shall direct.

(5) The master commissioner shall perform such functions, including those of a receiver, as may be directed by an appropriate order of the court.

(6) Upon the express written authority of the Administrative Office of the Courts on behalf of the Chief Justice, the master commissioner may have such deputies and clerical staff as are necessary to perform the functions of his or her office.

(7) A master commissioner or deputy master commissioner shall hold no other public office of the Court of Justice except that of trial commissioner for the district court pursuant to SCR 5.010, or domestic relations commissioner as approved by the Chief Justice.

(8) Master commissioners and deputy master commissioners shall be qualified as attorneys licensed in the Commonwealth.

(9) The Administrative Office of the Courts shall have the authority to establish audit and accounting standards, prescribe bookkeeping and accounting practices and procedures, and otherwise perform audits and oversee the financial accounts of master commissioners. A copy of any audit shall be submitted by the Administrative Office of the Courts to the chief judge of the circuit. In the event that the audit

reveals an accounting or other irregularity, a copy shall also be submitted to the Chief Justice.

(10) A non-refundable judicial sale administrative fee of $200 shall be added to all cases referred to the master commissioner for judicial sale. The circuit court clerk shall collect the administrative fee at the time the referral is made, prior to processing the motion for judgment and distributing the order of sale. The fee shall be collected prior to the master commissioner undertaking the order of sale. The circuit court clerk shall promptly remit all fee monies collected to the Administrative Office of the Courts. Judicial sale administrative fee money is to be placed in a special account designated to cover the administrative costs of the master commissioner program. These costs include, but are not limited to, all necessary bonding of master commissioners and the employment of sufficient staff to conduct audits of master commissioner offices statewide. To whatever extent total judicial sale administrative fees collected do not fully cover these expenses, funds may be deducted from the excess fees master commissioners submit to the Administrative Office of the Courts with their mandatory annual accounting report.

HISTORY: Amended by Order 2011–08, eff. 1–1–12; prior amendments eff. 1–1–11 (Order 2010–10), 7–1–06 (Order 2006-07), 3–1–06 (Order 2006-04), 7–1–04 (Order 2004–2); adopted by Order 2003–5, eff. 1–1–04

AP IV, Sec. 2　Powers of the master commissioner

An order of reference to the master commissioner or local rules of court may specify or limit powers, and may direct a report only upon particular issues, or to perform particular acts, or to receive and report evidence only. The order of reference may fix the time and place for beginning and closing the acts or issues referenced, and for the filing of the master commissioner's report. The master commissioner shall exercise the power to regulate all proceedings and to take all measures necessary for the efficient performance of his or her duties, subject to the specifications and limitations stated in the order or local rules of court. The master commissioner may require the production of evidence upon matters included in the order of reference, such as the production of all books, papers, vouchers, documents, and writings. The master commissioner may rule upon the admissibility of evidence, unless otherwise directed by the order of reference, and has the authority to put witnesses and parties under oath and examine same. The master commissioner shall make a record of the evidence offered and excluded in the same manner and subject to the same limitations as may be provided in applicable Rules of Civil Procedure and/or Rules of Evidence for a court sitting without a jury.

HISTORY: Amended by Order 2011–08, eff. 1–1–12; prior amendments eff. 1–1–11 (Order 2010–10), 7–1–06 (Order 2006–07), 3–1–06 (Order 2006–04), 7–1–04 (Order 2004–2); adopted by Order 2003–5, eff. 1–1–04

AP IV, Sec. 3   Judicial sales; settlements; receiverships

(1) Pursuant to the circuit court's order and in conformity with AP Part IV, Section 2, judicial sales may be executed, and accounts of estates may be settled, by a master commissioner. The terms and conditions of the judicial sale or estate settlement shall be established by the circuit court either in its order or rule, and in conformity with the Kentucky Revised Statutes.

(2) A master commissioner shall draft and execute documents necessary to complete any responsibility, including a report of any settlement, sale, or receivership. Further, an order of referral shall be entered by the circuit court referring the case to the master commissioner. Such documents shall be filed with the circuit court clerk of the county, which shall be entered into the case management system of the circuit court.

(3) The judgment and order of sale directing the master commissioner to sell property shall be served upon every party who is not in default for failure to appear.

(4) Civil matters pertaining to the discovery of assets of judgment debtors may be referred to a master commissioner.

HISTORY: Amended by Order 2011–08, eff. 1–1–12; prior amendments eff. 1–1–11 (Order 2010–10), 7–1–06 (Order 2006–07), 3–1–06 (Order 2006–04), 7–1–04 (Order 2004–2); adopted by Order 2003–5, eff. 1–1–04

AP IV, Sec. 4   Special proceedings of the master commissioner

(1) References.

References to master commissioners for special proceedings shall be warranted only in special cases and in cases where such reference is mandated by statute or rule of court. Cases may be regarded as special due to complexity of issues, damages which are difficult to calculate, a multiplicity of claims the priority of which must be established, matters of accounting involving complex or numerous transactions, or similar exceptional circumstances.

(2) Meetings.

When an order of reference is made the clerk shall forthwith furnish the master commissioner and all parties not in default with a copy of the order of reference. Upon receipt, the master commissioner shall forthwith set a time and place for the first meeting of the parties or their attorneys to be held within 20 days after the date of the order of reference and shall provide notice. It is the duty of the commissioner to proceed with reasonable diligence. Either party, on notice to the parties and master commissioner, may apply to the court for an order requiring the commissioner to speed the proceedings and to make his or her report. If a party fails to appear at the time and place appointed, the master commissioner may proceed ex parte or adjourn the proceedings to a future day, giving notice to the absent party of the adjournment.

(3) Witnesses.

In special proceedings, the parties may procure the attendance of witnesses before the master commissioner by the issuance and service of subpoenas as provided in CR 45. If, without good cause shown, a witness fails to appear or give evidence, he or she may be held in contempt and be subject to the provisions of CR 37 and CR 45.

(4) Statement of Accounts.

When matters of accounting are in issue before the master commissioner, he or she may prescribe the form in which the accounts shall be submitted. Upon objection of a party to any accounting, the master commissioner may require a different form of statement to be furnished, or take testimony, or receive written interrogatories.

HISTORY: Amended by Order 2011–08, eff. 1–1–12; prior amendments eff. 1–1–11 (Order 2010–10), 7–1–06 (Order 2006–07), 3–1–06 (Order 2006–04), 7–1–04 (Order 2004–2); adopted by Order 2003–5, eff. 1–1–04

AP IV, Sec. 5   Master commissioner's report in special proceedings

(1) Contents and filing of reporting in special proceedings or other mandated referrals.

The master commissioner shall prepare a report to the court upon the matters submitted by the order of reference or local rules of court and shall file the report and sufficient copies for all parties with the clerk of the court. The clerk shall forthwith serve the report and notice of the filing upon all parties. A transcript of reported proceedings may be ordered by any party at that party's expense. If special proceedings or other mandated referrals are recorded on videotape, the untranscribed videotape shall constitute the official record.

(2) Action on report in special proceedings.

In special proceedings, within 10 days after being served with the notice of the filing of the report any party may serve written objections thereto upon the other parties. Application to the court for action upon the report and upon objections thereto shall be by motion and upon notice as prescribed in CR 6.04. The court after hearing may adopt the report, modify it, reject it in whole or in part, receive further evidence, or recommit it with instructions.

(3) Stipulation as to findings in special proceedings.

The effect of a master commissioner's report is the same whether or not the parties have consented to the order of reference, but, when the parties stipulate that a master commissioner's report shall be final, only questions of law arising upon the report shall thereafter be considered.

(4) Draft report of special proceedings.

Before filing the report, a master commissioner may submit a draft thereof to counsel for all parties for the purpose of receiving their comments.

(5) Report as security in special proceedings.

The master commissioner shall not retain the report as security for compensation. If the party ordered to pay the compensation does not pay it after notice and within the time prescribed by the court, the master commissioner is entitled to a writ of execution.

HISTORY: Amended by Order 2011–08, eff. 1–1–12; prior amendments eff. 1–1–11 (Order 2010–10), 7–1–06 (Order 2006–07), 3–1–06 (Order 2006-04), 7–1–04 (Order 2004–2); adopted by Order 2003–5, eff. 1–1–04

AP IV, Sec. 6   Compensation of master commissioners, deputies, and clerical staff

(1) Master commissioners shall be compensated by fee charged upon the parties or paid out of any fund of an action in the circuit court. Deputies, clerical staff and office expenses, as authorized in AP Part IV, Section 8, shall be paid from the excess fees of the office. Salaries of clerical staff shall be set in accordance with the pay schedule established by the judicial personnel system.

(2) The fee for each judicial sale shall be calculated as follows:

(a) 5% of the first $5,000 of the final bid, or if the sale involves multiple indivisible lots sold at the same time under the same judgment, 5% of the first $5,000 of the aggregate of the final bids; 2% of the next $20,000 of the final bid or bids; 1 1/2% of the next $175,000 of the final bid or bids; and 1/2% of the excess over $200,000 of the final bid or bids. The fee based on the foregoing calculation shall be no less than $400 and shall not exceed $5,000.

(b) If the sale involves more than one property, parcel, or judgment, a fee of $650 per additional property, parcel, or judgment (e.g., the second, third, and subsequent) shall be allowed in addition to the fee calculated under subsection (2)(a) of this section.

(c) If the sale is withdrawn, a fee of not more than 50% of what the sale fee would have been as calculated under subsections (2)(a) and (b) of this section based upon the appraisal value of the property, or $400, whichever is greater, shall be allowed by the circuit court.

(d) If the sale is not confirmed through no fault of the master commissioner, a fee of no more than the sale fee as calculated under subsections (2)(a) and (b) of this section shall be allowed by the circuit court.

(3) In addition to the fee authorized in subsection (2), above, the master commissioner may also recover necessary direct expenses attributable to the case referred for judicial sale including the cost of postage, copies, faxes, long distance telephone, advertising, appraisers, and the cost of the care of the property in his or her possession, and shall recover the administrative

fee prescribed in Section 1 (9). Upon good cause shown, agreement of the parties, and the approval of the judge, a qualified auctioneer may be authorized to conduct the sale at a fee to be set by the court. Upon good cause shown, the circuit court may require a deposit sufficient in amount to pay the direct cost of sale.

(4) A fee of $50 shall be charged for each report and recommendation(s) prepared on tendered foreclosure judgments in uncontested cases for enforcement of a mortgage or other lien. Additionally, a fee of $50 shall be charged for drafting any necessary deed or title and executing same.

(5) For receiving and paying out money Under court order, except as otherwise provided in subsection (2), and for settling the accounts of estates the fee shall be 3% of the first $2,000; 2 1/2% for the next $3,000; and, 1 1/2% for the excess over $5,000. For settlement of accounts of insolvent estates this computation shall exclude any amounts exempt from creditors. In no case shall the fee exceed $5,000.

HISTORY: Amended by Order 2011–08, eff. 1–1–12; prior amendments eff. 1–1–11 (Order 2010–10), 7–1–06 (Order 2006–07), 3–1–06 (Order 2006–04), 7–1–04 (Order 2004–2); adopted by Order 2003–5, eff. 1–1–04

AP IV, Sec. 7   Limit on compensation of master commissioners, deputies, and clerical staff

(1) The office of master commissioner shall be limited in total personal compensation derived from fees to not more than $48,000 per annum, unless otherwise approved by written order of the Chief Justice. Said limitation on compensation shall be prorated on a monthly basis where the master commissioner serves less than the entire year. Where a master commissioner also acts as a domestic relations commissioner, the fees generated by the office of master commissioner shall not be co-mingled with the fees generated by the office of domestic relations commissioner.

(2) Each deputy master commissioner shall be limited in his or her total personal compensation derived from fees to not more than $38,400 per annum. Said limitation on compensation shall be prorated on a monthly basis where the deputy commissioner serves less than the entire year. Salaries of clerical staff shall be set in accordance with the pay schedule established by the judicial personnel system. Any increase in personal compensation for clerical staff shall be in accordance with the allowed Court of Justice annual increment.

(3) Fees in excess of the personal compensation of the master commissioner, less authorized expenses, shall be remitted as provided in Section 8(4) of these Rules; however, anticipated three months expenses, excluding the master commissioner salary, may be retained. Computation of anticipated three months expenses shall be supported by adequate records and documentary evidence which shall also be submitted with the annual accounting report tendered to the

Administrative Office of the Courts, Division of Auditing Services.

HISTORY: Amended by Order 2011–08, eff. 1–1–12; prior amendments eff. 1–1–11 (Order 2010–10), 7–1–06 (Order 2006–07), 3–1–06 (Order 2006–04), 7–1–04 (Order 2004–2); adopted by Order 2003–5, eff. 1–1–04

AP IV, Sec. 8 Accounting of master commissioners

(1) Individual Case Report. Each master commissioner shall account to the circuit judge under whose direction he or she is acting for all amounts received and distributed, for all proceeds of sales disbursed, for all fees collected, and for all expenses deducted. These accounts shall be in the manner directed by the circuit judge who shall approve the accounts by his or her signature. The master commissioner shall file the approved accounts with the circuit clerk who shall record the approved accounts in the case management system and file in the applicable case. Each master commissioner shall maintain a current account kept in the office of the circuit clerk or in the office of the master commissioner if the chief circuit judge so directs, of each case in which a fee has been received.

(2) Annual Accounting Report. Each master commissioner shall provide to the Administrative Office of the Courts, on or before March 1 st of each year, a complete accounting of the prior calendar year for all fees collected and for all expenses deducted. The accounting shall be reported on a form prescribed by the Administrative Office of the Courts. The report shall contain, at a minimum, the following information:

(a) Name (printed);

(b) Address;

(c) County and Circuit;

(d) Total income received (fees, commissions and other income including interest);

(e) Fees retained from previous year for three months estimated expense;

(f) Expenses as provided in Subsection (3) herein below;

(g) Master commissioner salary cap;

(h) Notarized signature of master commissioner;

(i) Signature of approving circuit judge.

(3) Expenses.

(a) Adequate records and documentary evidence shall be maintained to support each element of an expense. See IRS Publication 463 and 535 Sections 62, 162, and 274 of the Internal Revenue Code for additional information.

(b) Only salaries, bonding expenses, and other expenses authorized for employees in accordance with Section 1 (9) which are directly related to the office of master commissioner, check printing charges, and the cost incurred for the purchase of accounting/bookkeeping software mandated by the Administrative Of-

fice of the Courts auditing standards may be deducted from any fees in excess of the personal compensation of the master commissioner. Salaries are to be itemized per employee.

(c) Notwithstanding any provision to the contrary herein, a master commissioner authorized by the Chief Justice to operate a full-time master commissioner's office and who does not engage in any private business enterprise in the master commissioner's office may deduct business expenses directly related and necessary to the operation of the master commissioner's office as established by the Administrative Office of the Courts auditing standards.

(4) Excess fees referred to in Section 7 shall be remitted with the annual accounting report to the Administrative Office of the Courts, Division of Auditing Services in accordance with Section 1(9).

HISTORY: Amended by Order 2011–08, eff. 1–1–12; prior amendments eff. 1–1–11 (Order 2010–10), 7–1–06 (Order 2006–07), 3–1–06 (Order 2006–4), 7–1–04 (Order 2004–2); adopted by Order 2003–5, eff. 1–1–04

AP IV, Sec. 9 Escrow accounts of master commissioners

Master commissioners shall maintain one or more separate interest bearing escrow accounts for all proceeds received and disbursed and shall maintain an itemized accounting of same. Proceeds relating to the office of the master commissioner shall not be comingled with any other accounts or funds held by the master commissioner in his personal or other professional capacity. Interest earned on the account shall be remitted to the Administrative Office of the Courts with the annual accounting report in accordance with Section 1(9). The account shall be subject to periodic audits, but no less than annual audits, by the Administrative Office of the Courts.

HISTORY: Amended by Order 2011–08, eff. 1–1–12; prior amendments eff. 1–1–11 (Order 2010–10), 7–1–06 (Order 2006–07), 3–1–06 (Order 2006–04), 7–1–04 (Order 2004–2); adopted by Order 2003–5, eff. 1–1–04

AP IV, Sec. 10 Transfer of office; use of proof and performance of duties of predecessor

(1) Upon the death, termination or removal of a master commissioner, all books, papers, account information, case files and other documents related to the office of master commissioner shall be immediately transferred to the circuit judge for whom the master commissioner served and immediate notice shall be given to the Administrative Office of the Courts, Division of Auditing Services. In a single-judge circuit, if termination is due to the death, resignation, or permanent replacement of the circuit judge who appointed the master commissioner, said documents shall be transferred pursuant to the order of the chief regional circuit judge.

(2) The master commissioner or receiver may use any proof reduced to writing and signed by his or her predecessor, and may execute any order or judgment which it was the duty of the predecessor to have executed, and which remains unexecuted.

HISTORY: Amended by Order 2011–08, eff. 1–1–12; prior amendments eff. 1–1–11 (Order 2010–10), 7–1–06 (Order 2006–07), 3–1–06 (Order 2006–04), 7–1–04 (Order 2004–2); adopted by Order 2003–5, eff. 1–1–04

AP IV, Sec. 11 Disqualification of master commissioner; special commissioners

(1) For the purposes of this section the following words or phrases shall have the meaning indicated:

(a) "Fiduciary" includes such relationships as executor, administrator, conservator, trustee, and guardian;

(b) "Financial interest" means ownership of a legal or equitable interest, however small, or a relationship as director, advisor, or other active participant in the affairs of a party, except that:

    1. Ownership in a mutual or common investment fund that holds securities, or a proprietary interest of a policyholder in a mutual insurance company, of a depositor in a mutual savings association, or a similar proprietary interest, or ownership of government securities is a "financial interest" only if the outcome of the proceeding could substantially affect the value of the interest;

    2. An office in an educational, religious, charitable, fraternal, or civic organization is not a "financial interest" in securities held by the organization.

(2) When performing judicial functions, any master commissioner shall disqualify him/herself in any case:

(a) Where he or she has a personal bias or prejudice concerning a party, or personal knowledge of disputed evidentiary facts concerning the case or has expressed an opinion concerning the merits of same;

(b) Where in private practice or government service he or she served as a lawyer or rendered a legal opinion in the matter in controversy, or a lawyer with whom he previously practiced law served during such association as a lawyer concerning the matter in controversy, or the master commissioner or such lawyer has been a material witness concerning the matter in controversy;

(c) Where he or she knows, individually or as fiduciary, or a spouse or minor child residing in his or her household, has a pecuniary or proprietary interest in the subject matter in controversy or in a party to the proceeding;

(d) Where the master commissioner or the spouse, or a person within the third degree of relationship to either of them, or the spouse of such a person:

    1. Is a party to the proceeding, or an officer, director, or trustee of a party;

    2. Is acting as a lawyer in the proceeding and the disqualification is not waived by stipulation of counsel in the proceeding filed therein;

    3. Is known by the master commissioner to have an interest that could be substantially affected by the outcome of the proceeding;

    4. Is to the knowledge of the master commissioner likely to be a material witness in the proceeding.

(e) Where he or she has knowledge of any other circumstances in which his or her impartiality might reasonably be questioned.

(3) Any master commissioner disqualified under the provisions of this section or unable to discharge the duties of his or her office for any other reason shall be replaced by a special commissioner who shall be appointed by the judge of the court before whom the action is pending. The special commissioner shall meet the same qualifications as a master commissioner and shall take an oath, execute a bond in an amount to be set by the chief circuit judge based upon the estimated sum to be derived from the proceedings, and be subject to the same rules as the regular commissioner.

HISTORY: Amended by Order 2011–08, eff. 1–1–12; prior amendments eff. 1–1–11 (Order 2010–10), 7–1–06 (Order 2006–07), 3–1–06 (Order 2006–04), 7–1–04 (Order 2004–2); adopted by Order 2003–5, eff. 1–1–04

AP IV, Sec. 12 Bond; special bond of master commissioners

(1) The Administrative Office of the Courts shall execute a blanket bond on behalf of master commissioners.

(2) The master commissioner shall execute a special bond when circumstances warrant as required by the court and no action shall be maintained on the blanket bond for matters covered by a special bond. A special bond shall be recorded in the office of the circuit court clerk and a copy shall be submitted to the Administrative Office of the Courts, Division of Auditing Services, with the annual accounting report.

(3) The master commissioner shall procure a surety bond on any employee who has access to the funds received and disbursed by the master commissioner. The surety bond shall be recorded in the office of the circuit court clerk and a copy shall be submitted to the Administrative Office of the Courts, Division of Auditing Services, with the annual accounting report.

HISTORY: Amended by Order 2011–08, eff. 1–1–12; prior amendments eff. 1–1–11 (Order 2010–10), 7–1–06 (Order 2006–07), 3–1–06 (Order 2006–04), 7–1–04 (Order 2004–2); adopted by Order 2003–5, eff. 1–1–04

AP IV, Sec. 13 Compensation of special master commissioners

Fees earned by a master commissioner for service as a Special Master Commissioner in another county(ies) shall be treated as follows:

(1) The first $5,000 earned annually from service as a Special Master Commissioner shall not count toward the master commissioner's salary cap, and should not be reported on the Annual Report of Master Commissioner.

(2) Any fees in excess of $5,000 earned annually from service as a Special Master Commissioner shall count toward the master commissioner's salary cap, and shall be reported on the Annual Report of Master Commissioner.

HISTORY: Amended by Order 2011–08, eff. 1–1–12; adopted by Order 2010–10, eff. 1–1–11

AP IV, Sec. 14 Oath

The master commissioner shall take an oath that he or she will faithfully and honestly discharge the duties of the office. The oath shall be administered by the circuit judge and a copy shall be filed in the office of the circuit court clerk.

HISTORY: Amended by Order 2011–08, eff. 1–1–12; amended and renumbered by Order 2010–10, eff. 1–1–11; prior amendments eff. 7–1–06 (Order 2006–07), 3–1–06 (Order 2006–04), 7–1–04 (Order 2004–2); adopted by Order 2003–5, eff. 1–1–04

AP IV, Sec. 15 Receivers; persons not to be appointed receivers

(1) Receivers, except as provided in subsection (2) of this section, may be appointed under the same terms and conditions as a master commissioner except the receiver need not be an attorney.

(2) Except for personal representatives, guardians, curators, and committees for persons of unsound mind, neither a parry to an action, nor his attorney, nor any person interested therein, shall be appointed as a receiver unless by agreement of the parties.

HISTORY: Amended by Order 2011–08, eff. 1–1–12; amended and renumbered by Order 2010–10, eff. 1–1–11; prior amendments eff. 7–1–06 (Order 2006–07), 3–1–06 (Order 2006–04), 7–1–04 (Order 2004–2); adopted by Order 2003–5, eff. 1–1–04

AP IV, Sec. 16 Hearing fees

For any hearing, the master commissioner shall receive a fee of $60 per hour, assessed at a rate of $15 for each quarter hour or part thereof. Such fees shall be paid through the office of circuit court clerk to the commissioner and shall be due on the fifth working day following the conclusion of the hearing. No more than $600 shall be assessed in any case regardless of the number and length of hearings unless recommended by the circuit judge and approved by the Chief Justice for extraordinary circumstances shown.

If a case is reopened additional fees totaling not more than $200 may be assessed.

HISTORY: Amended by Order 2011–08, eff. 1–1–12; amended and renumbered by Order 2010–10, eff. 1–1–11; prior amendments eff. 7–1–06 (Order 2006–07), 3–1–06 (Order 2006–04), 7–1–04 (Order 2004–2); adopted by Order 2003–5, eff. 1–1–04

PART V
REAL PROPERTY LEASES

Publisher's Note: Administrative procedures relating to real property leases of the Court of Justice have not been released for publication as they do not affect the practice of law.

PART VI
PROCEDURES FOR COURT REPORTING

AP VI, Sec. 1 Applicability of the personnel policies to reporters—Deleted

HISTORY: Deleted eff. 4–20–95; adopted eff. 7–23–80

AP VI, Sec. 2 Custody of notes and exhibits—Deleted

HISTORY: Deleted eff. 4–20–95; prior amendment eff. 1–1–85; adopted eff. 7–23–80

AP VI, Sec. 3 Free–lance reporting—Deleted

HISTORY: Deleted eff. 4–20–95; adopted eff. 7–23–80

AP VI, Sec. 4 Transcription fees—Deleted

HISTORY: Deleted eff. 4–20–95; adopted eff. 7–23–80

AP VI, Sec. 5 Transcripts

AP VI, Sec. 5.01 Compensation for transcription—Deleted

HISTORY: Deleted eff. 4–20–95; adopted eff. 7–23–80

AP VI, Sec. 5.02 Procedures for filing claims—Deleted

HISTORY: Deleted eff. 4–20–95; adopted eff. 7–23–80

AP VI, Sec. 5.03 Procedure for processing claims—Deleted

HISTORY: Deleted eff. 4–20–95; adopted eff. 7–23–80

AP VI, Sec. 6   Substitute court reporters

AP VI, Sec. 6.01   Per diem—Deleted
HISTORY: Deleted eff. 4–20–95; adopted eff. 7–23–80

AP VI, Sec. 6.02   Procedures for appointment and compensation of substitute reporters—Deleted
HISTORY: Deleted eff. 4–20–95; adopted eff. 7–23–80

AP VI, Sec. 7   Recording court proceedings—Deleted
HISTORY: Deleted eff. 4–20–95; prior amendment eff. 1–1–89; adopted eff. 7–23–80

AP VI, Sec. 8   Policies and procedures for transcribing district court tapes—Deleted
HISTORY: Deleted eff. 4–20–95; adopted eff. 7–23–80

AP VI, Sec. 9   Circuits with two or more court reporters—Deleted
HISTORY: Deleted eff. 4–20–95; adopted eff. 11–17–80

PART VII
REIMBURSEMENT FOR OFFICIAL TRAVEL

Publisher's Note: Administrative procedures relating to reimbursement for official travel have not been released for publication as their application is limited to personnel of the Court of Justice.

PART VIII
STATE TRAFFIC SCHOOL

AP VIII, Sec. 1

Any person convicted of any violation of traffic codes as set forth in KRS Chapters 177, 186 or 189 and who is otherwise eligible under these rules may, in the sole discretion of the trial judge, be sentenced to attend the State Traffic School and upon payment of the registration fee and upon completion of the school, such sentence shall be in lieu of any other penalty.

HISTORY: Adopted eff. 12–11–80

AP VIII, Sec. 2

No person shall be eligible to attend the State Traffic School who has been cited for any violation of KRS Chapters 177, 186 and 189, which has as a penalty for such violation a mandatory revocation or suspension of their driver's license.

HISTORY: Adopted eff. 12–11–80

AP VIII, Sec. 3

No person shall be eligible to attend the State Traffic School for any violation when at the time of that violation, the person did not have a driver's license, or their driver's license had been suspended or had been revoked by the department of transportation.

HISTORY: Adopted eff. 12–11–80

AP VIII, Sec. 4

No person shall be eligible to attend State Traffic School more than once in any one-year period.

HISTORY: Amended eff. 8–7–00; adopted eff. 12–11–80

AP VIII, Sec. 5

Any defendant who has been sentenced to attend the State Traffic School will be required to attend and the department of transportation shall notify the sentencing court when a person ordered to attend the State Traffic School is ineligible to attend under the provisions of these rules or for any other reason. Upon notification to the trial court that a person failed to attend, or is ineligible to attend, then the clerk of that court may cause the case to be returned to an active calendar for a hearing on a day certain and a summons shall issue to that defendant to appear and show cause, if any, why an alternative sentence should not be imposed.

HISTORY: Adopted eff. 12–11–80

PART IX
PROCEDURES FOR APPOINTMENT
OF INTERPRETERS

AP IX, Sec. 1   Statement of purpose

Pursuant to KRS 30A.405(2), the Supreme Court is required to prescribe standards for the appointment, qualifications, duties, and other matters relating to interpreters.

HISTORY: Amended by Order 2011–03, eff. 3–15–11; prior amendments eff. 5–12–09 (Order 2009–06), 12–1–04 (Order 2004–3), 10–1–04; adopted eff. 2–17–95

AP IX, Sec. 2   Definitions

As used throughout this Rule, the following definitions will apply:

(1) "AOC" means the Administrative Office of the Courts.

(2) "Appointing/Requesting authority" means the Judge, Chief Judge, Circuit Court Clerk, Supreme Court Clerk, Clerk of the Court of Appeals, AOC Director, or designee, who appoints or requests an interpreter to provide interpreting services in a court proceeding or for direct services to the Court of Justice.

(3) "AOC Interpreter Directory" means the listing of licensed freelance interpreters and staff interpreters for the deaf and hard of hearing and certified and registered spoken language freelance interpreters and staff interpreters who have been approved by the AOC for interpreting in a court proceeding and providing direct services to the Court of Justice. Requirements for approval and entry in the Directory are contained in these rules.

(4) "Certified spoken language interpreter" means an interpreter listed in the AOC Interpreter Directory who has met the requirements set forth in the Kentucky Court of Justice Certification Policy.

(5) "Code of Professional Responsibility" means the Code of Professional Responsibility for Interpreters adopted by Order of the Kentucky Supreme Court, containing Canons of professional conduct which are binding upon all persons, agencies, and organizations that administer, supervise, or deliver interpreting services to the judiciary.

(6) "Contact person" means the individual designated in each county by the Chief Circuit Judge or Chief District Judge of the county who is responsible for scheduling interpreters for court proceedings or direct services, and for notifying the AOC Court Interpreting Services Division when scheduling interpreters for trials or grand jury proceedings, or when there is difficulty scheduling an interpreter. The "contact person" may be a judge's secretary, court administrator, or other Court of Justice employee designated by the judge.

(7) "Court proceeding" means a civil, criminal, domestic relations, juvenile, traffic or other in-court proceeding, whether before a judge, trial commissioner, master commissioner, or domestic relations commissioner; or, a court-ordered proceeding in which court officials or Court of Justice personnel are directly involved.

(8) "Court of Justice" means the Kentucky Court of Justice.

(9) "Court of Justice entity" means any office, operation, or program under the purview of the Judicial Branch.

(10) "Criminal background check" means the KY-CourtNet disposition report provided by the AOC.

(11) "Direct services" means out-of-court services provided by a Court of Justice entity which enables the entity to carry out its duties and responsibilities as directed by statute and/or rule of court.

(12) "Favorable criminal background check" means a criminal background check showing no conviction of any felony or of a misdemeanor involving moral turpitude, dishonesty, false statements, or fraud.

(13) "Freelance interpreter" means a contract interpreter who is not employed by the Court of Justice as an interpreter. A freelance interpreter must meet the qualification criteria as required by these rules.

(14) "Interpreter for the deaf and hard of hearing" means an interpreter who is licensed pursuant to KRS Chapter 309 and other applicable Kentucky law and who has met additional requirements set forth in the Kentucky Court of Justice Certification Policy for Visual Language Interpreters.

(15) "Lapse of certification" means the failure to maintain the continuing education units and court observation hours required by these rules.

(16) "Provisional spoken language interpreter" means an interpreter not listed in the AOC Interpreter Directory but who has met certain minimum requirements set forth in the Kentucky Court of Justice Certification Policy.

(17) "Qualified interpreter" means a staff interpreter or freelance interpreter who has met the licensing, certification, and/or other requirements set out in the Kentucky Court of Justice Policies for Spoken Language and Visual Language Interpreters and in Sections 8 and 9 of these rules.

(18) "Registered spoken language interpreter" means an interpreter listed in the AOC Interpreter Directory who has met the requirements set forth in the Kentucky Court of Justice Certification Policy.

(19) "Remote interpreting services" means the provision of telephone, videoconference, web-based, or other available remote interpreting equipment as approved by the AOC.

(20) "Staff interpreter" means an interpreter who is employed by the Court of Justice to provide interpreting services in court proceedings and for direct services. A staff interpreter must meet the qualification criteria required by these rules.

(21) "Uniform Payment Rate" means the hourly pay rate and travel rate given to freelance interpreters for services rendered while interpreting for the Court of Justice. This rate will be set by the AOC Director.

HISTORY: Amended by Order 2011–03, eff. 3–15–11; prior amendments eff. 5–12–09 (Order 2009–06), 12–1–04 (Order 2004–3), 10–1–04; adopted eff. 2–17–95

AP IX, Sec. 3   Oath

(1) Before accepting assignment as a freelance interpreter in a court proceeding, or at the time of employment as a staff interpreter, an individual must have read the Code of Professional Responsibility for Interpreters and KRE 604, and taken the oath as set forth in Section 3(2). A provisional interpreter or an interpreter provided by an agency other than the AOC must be administered the oath by the judge or chief judge prior to each court proceeding. A copy of the oath must be signed by the freelance interpreter or stall interpreter and kept on file at the AOC Court Interpreting Services Division.

(2) The following oath must be administered to all freelance interpreters and staff interpreters in accordance with the provisions of this section:

Do you solemnly swear or affirm you have the knowledge, skills, experience, and/or education to interpret this proceeding, and you will interpret accurately, completely and impartially, using your best skill and judgment in accordance with the standards prescribed by law, any Code of Ethics under which you have been certified, and the Code of Professional Responsibility for Interpreters, and will make a true translation pursuant to KRE 604.

HISTORY: Amended by Order 2011–03, eff. 3–15–11; prior amendments eff. 5–12–09 (Order 2009–06), 12–1–04 (Order 2004–3), 10–1–04; adopted eff. 2–17–95

AP IX, Sec. 4   Appointment of and requests for interpreters

(1) Party, Juror, Witness, or Non–Party. Pursuant to KRS 30A.410 to 30A.435 and other applicable state and federal law and regulations, in any court proceeding the court will appoint a qualified interpreter for a party, juror, witness, or "non-party" as defined below in subsection (1)(d) of this section:

(a) Who is deaf or hard of hearing, and

(i) Uses sign language such as pidgin, signed English, American Sign Language, or gestures; or

(ii) Is oral/aural and uses interpreters and assistive technology as his or her primary mode of communication;

(b) Who cannot communicate in English; or

(c) Who has, in the opinion of the court, another type of disability which will prevent said person from properly understanding the nature of the proceedings or will substantially prejudice his or her rights.

(d) A non-party is a person;

(i) Whose presence or participation in a court matter is necessary or appropriate, including but not limited to a parent or guardian of a juvenile and any of his or her family members involved in a juvenile proceeding, or a victim of crime or parent or guardian of a minor victim of crime; or

(ii) Who is a family member, friend, or associate of a party or person participating in a court proceeding, who, along with the party or person, is an appropriate individual with whom the court should communicate.

(2) Attorney. The court will appoint a qualified interpreter in any court proceeding for an attorney who is deaf or hard of hearing as described above in subsection (1)(a)(i) or (ii) of this section and who is participating in the court proceeding.

(3) Direct Services. Upon the request of any individual identified above in subsections (1) and (2) of this section, the Court of Justice will provide a qualified interpreter for direct services, as defined in Section 2(12) of these rules, or as otherwise appears necessary.

(4) Appointment of Interpreters for Deaf or Hard of Hearing Individuals. The court will appoint an interpreter in a court proceeding for a party, juror, witness, or non-party who is deaf or hard of hearing as described above in subsection (1)(a)(i) or (ii) of this section, or for an attorney who is deaf or hard of hearing pursuant to subsection (2) of this section, as follows. This process will also apply, where indicated, to requests to use assistive technology in lieu of or in addition to the services of an interpreter, pursuant to Section 11(3) of these rules.

(a) A request for interpreting services or assistive technology must be made in writing to the presiding judge on a form designed and designated by the AOC.

(b) The judge may ask that the individual submit supporting documentation, such as written documentation from a licensed health care provider, establishing that the individual is qualified under applicable state and federal law to receive the requested services or assistive technology. Any medical documentation submitted must be sealed by order of the court and filed in the record.

(c) If the individual is qualified as such, the judge or his or her designee may interact with the individual to evaluate the individual's needs and assess whether the requested services or assistive technology can be reasonably provided. The judge must give primary consideration to the specific request made.

(i) "Primary consideration" means that the court will honor the individual's preferred type of requested services or assistive technology unless another means exists of ensuring effective communication, or unless doing so would result in a fundamental alteration in the nature of the proceeding or in undue financial or administrative burden, or unless the request is for a personal device such as a hearing aid.

(ii) The type of services or assistive technology necessary to ensure effective communication will vary in accordance with the method of communication used by the individual; the nature, length, and complexity of the communication involved; and the context in which the communication is taking place.

(d) If the requested service or assistive technology cannot reasonably be provided, the judge will gather sufficient information from the individual, and qualified experts if necessary, to determine what alternative service or assistive technology will, to the maximum extent reasonably possible, ensure effective communication.

(5) Deaf or Hard of Hearing Attorneys. The provisions below apply to deaf or hard of hearing attorneys needing interpreting services:

(a) In accordance with Section 6 of these rules, all efforts will be made to schedule a qualified staff or freelance interpreter. However, the number and availability of qualified interpreters varies and cannot be fully controlled by the Court of Justice. Therefore, an attorney requesting interpreting services should submit his or her request two weeks or more prior to the proceeding for which interpreting services are needed. In the event a qualified interpreter is not available, the presiding judge will work with the attorney to identify alternative services or assistive technology that will, to the maximum extent reasonably possible, ensure effective communication. The court will grant a continuance as may be appropriate or necessary.

(b) Once an attorney has been determined to be qualified to receive interpreting services, he or she will not be required to re-establish his or her qualifications in future court proceedings before the same presiding judge.

HISTORY: Amended by Order 2011–03, eff. 3–15–11; prior amendments eff. 5–12–09 (Order 2009–06), 12–1–04 (Order 2004–3), 10–1–04; adopted eff. 2–17–95

AP IX, Sec. 5 Responsibility for payment for interpreting services

(1) Pursuant to KRS 30A.415, the Court of Justice will be responsible for payment, including ordinary and reasonable expenses, for interpreting services for court proceedings and direct services provided by a Court of Justice entity. In cases in which the interpreter is providing services out of court, other than direct services, even though that service relates to a pending court case, the person or agency requiring the services of the interpreter will be responsible for payment.

(2) The AOC will not pay for interpreting services provided to or for a non-Court of Justice entity, even when a party is ordered by the Court, or referred by a Court of Justice entity, to obtain services or assistance from the non-Court of Justice entity.

(3) The AOC may seek reimbursement from the "employer," as that term is defined in Title I of the Americans With Disabilities Act, 42 U.S.C. § 12111 et seq., of an attorney for whom the court has appointed an interpreter pursuant to Section 4(1) (c) for the costs of providing interpreting services.

HISTORY: Amended by Order 2011–03, eff. 3–15–11; prior amendments eff. 5–12–09 (Order 2009–06), 12–1–04 (Order 2004–3), 10–1–04; adopted eff. 2–17–95

AP IX, Sec. 6 Responsibility for obtaining and scheduling an interpreter

(1) A contact person must be designated in each county who will be responsible for scheduling a staff interpreter or freelance interpreter for court proceedings or direct services. The contact person may be a judge's secretary, court administrator, or other Court of Justice employee designated by the Chief Circuit Judge or Chief District Judge.

(2) Each Court of Justice entity must notify the contact person or the AOC Court Interpreting Services Division of the need for scheduling interpreters as necessary for direct services.

(3) When scheduling, the Court or Court of Justice entity must make efforts to determine if a conflict exists for an interpreter by providing the interpreter with the name, county, case type, and charge(s) and charge(s) date(s), if any, of the party or person requesting the interpreter.

(4) If there is difficulty obtaining and scheduling an interpreter, the contact person must, if possible, notify the AOC Court Interpreting Services Division at least two weeks prior to the need for the interpreting service, and the Interpreting Services Division will assist with obtaining and scheduling an interpreter.

(5) The contact person must, if possible, notify the AOC Court Interpreting Services Division when scheduling interpreters for trials or grand jury proceedings.

(6) All cases requiring interpreters should be called at the end of the court docket or at another appropriate time during the docket when they can be called as a group in an effort to reduce the cost of the interpreting service and ensure the interpreter is not unduly fatigued.

(7) In an effort to promote judicial economy and enhance the judicial process for interpreting services, each county or judicial district must generate a local or regional protocol with the assistance of the AOC Court Interpreting Services Division, for efficient use of the interpreting services, or an interpreting docket where all such cases may be heard. Staff interpreters and freelance interpreters should not wait more than thirty minutes to interpret.

(8) All efforts will be made to schedule a staff interpreter for court proceedings and direct services. If a staff interpreter is not available, then a certified freelance interpreter may be scheduled. If no certified freelance interpreter is available, then a registered freelance interpreter may be scheduled. If no registered freelance interpreter is available, then a provisional freelance interpreter may be scheduled.

(9) For trials and grand jury proceedings, all efforts should be made to schedule a staff interpreter. If a staff interpreter is not reasonably available, then a certified freelance interpreter will be scheduled.

(10) Absent a showing of extraordinary circumstances, no person who is a family member or friend of the person needing interpreting services will be appointed/obtained to provide said services.

(11) Each Court of Justice entity must, when practical, inform the contact person of the need for interpreting services at a court proceeding.

HISTORY: Amended by Order 2011–03, eff. 3–15–11; prior amendments eff. 5–12–09 (Order 2009–06), 12–1–04 (Order 2004-3), 10–1–04; adopted eff. 2–17–95

AP IX, Sec. 7   Team interpreting requirements

(1) When interpretation for two or more hours is required without breaks, a team of two interpreters should be appointed, except in trials and grand jury proceedings, in which case a team of two interpreters is required and will be appointed. Additional two-person teams may be required if more than one person requires services at the same time.

(2) Team members should rotate every thirty minutes to enhance accuracy and prevent fatigue.

HISTORY: Amended by Order 2011–03, eff. 3–15–11; prior amendments eff. 5–12–09 (Order 2009–06), 12–1–04 (Order 2004-3); adopted by Order 2004-3, eff. 10–1–04

AP IX, Sec. 8   Interpreters for the Deaf and Hard of Hearing

(1) Pursuant to KRS 30A.405, any person appointed/obtained as a staff interpreter or freelance interpreter must be qualified in accordance with these rules to interpret effectively, accurately, and impartially, both receptively and expressively, using any necessary specialized vocabulary.

(2) In order to be designated a qualified interpreter for the Court of Justice and be listed in the AOC Interpreter Directory, each interpreter for the deaf

and hard of hearing must meet the following qualifications:

(a) Staff interpreters and freelance interpreters must be licensed in accordance with KRS 309.301 to 309.319 and 201 KAR 39:030 and must possess all certifications required therein. Additionally, they must:

(b) Have a favorable criminal background check;

(c) Attend the AOC orientation workshop;

(d) Obtain the hours of court observation or work as required by the AOC; and

(e) Read the Code of Professional Responsibility and KRE 604, and take the oath in accordance with Section 3 of these rules.

(3) In order to maintain his or her status as a qualified interpreter for the Court of Justice and continue to be listed in the AOC Interpreter Directory, each interpreter for the deaf and hard of hearing must meet the following requirements:

(a) Maintain a valid license in accordance with the requirements of KRS 309.300 to 309.319 and 201 KAR 39:030;

(b) Comply with the continuing education requirements established by the AOC Court Interpreting Services Division;

(c) Obtain the hours of court observation or work as required by the AOC Court Interpreting Services Division: and

(d) Comply with the Code of Professional Responsibility.

(e) Additionally, a freelance interpreter must annually update his or her personal information on file with the AOC. Personal information must be submitted every year on or before July 1. A sixty day grace period will be allowed after July 1, during which Lime individuals may continue to interpret for the Court of Justice pending submission of the necessary documentation.

(f) Failure by a freelance interpreter to comply with the above-listed requirements, including those relevant to state licensing law, may result in either temporary or permanent removal from the AOC Interpreter Directory.

(4) The AOC will conduct annually a criminal background check on all interpreters listed in the AOC Interpreter Directory.

(5) A licensed freelance interpreter must, upon request by the contact person or appointing/requesting authority, present his or her license for the purpose of determining whether the license is currently valid.

(6) If the person who is deaf or hard of hearing also has minimal language competency, a secondary disability, and/or extensive use of his/her own gestural system such that a qualified interpreter is unfamiliar with the uniqueness of the communication, the court will appoint a certified relay interpreter, e.g., a Certi-

fied Deaf Interpreter ("CDI"), a Certified Deaf Interpreter Provisional ("CDI–P"), or a Reverse Skills Certified Interpreter ("RSC"), to assist the qualified interpreter in providing interpretation.

(7) Proof of compliance with the continuing education units and the required court observation hours must be submitted to the AOC Court Interpreting Services Division bi-annually on or before July 1. A sixty day grace period will be allowed after July 1, during which time individuals may continue to interpret for the Court of Justice pending submission of the necessary documentation.

(8) Pursuant to KRS 30A.400(3), if the eligibility of the person to receive the services of an interpreter is challenged, the judge may, for good cause shown, hold a hearing to determine the bona fide need for interpreting services. If it is determined that the person is not entitled to interpreting services, then no portion of these rules will apply to said person.

(9) When a person does not request an interpreter, but appeal's to be deaf or hard of hearing, the court will conduct a brief voir dire in order to evaluate the person's needs and determine whether or not an interpreter or, alternatively, assistive technology is needed.

(10) When the appointed interpreter and the person receiving interpreting services appear to have difficulties communicating with one another, the appointing/requesting authority should make reasonable efforts on the record to determine that there is sufficient communication between the interpreter and the person receiving interpreting services.

HISTORY: Amended by Order 2011–03, eff. 3–15–11; prior amendments eff. 5–12–09 (Order 2009–06), 12–1–04 (Order 2004–3); adopted by Order 2004–3, eff. 10–1–04

AP IX, Sec. 9 Spoken language interpreters

(1) Pursuant to KRS 30A.405, any person appointed/obtained as a staff interpreter or freelance interpreter must be qualified in accordance with these rules to interpret effectively, accurately, and impartially, both receptively and expressively, using any necessary specialized vocabulary.

(2) The AOC Court Interpreting Services Division will have the authority to establish policies and procedures for time limits and scoring standards for the qualification process.

(3) In order to be designated as a certified or registered interpreter for the Court of Justice and be listed in the AOC Interpreter Directory, each spoken language interpreter must meet the following qualifications:

(a) Have a favorable criminal background check;

(b) Pass the requisite examinations administered by the AOC (the interpreter will be designated as either certified or registered based upon the interpreter's test scores);

(c) Attend the AOC orientation workshop;

(d) Obtain the hours of court observation or work as required by the AOC Court Interpreting Services Division; and

(e) Read the Code of Professional Responsibility and KRE 604, and take the oath in accordance with Section 3 of these rules.

(4) In order to maintain his or her designated status and continue to be listed in the AOC Interpreter Directory, each certified and registered interpreter must:

(a) Comply with the continuing education requirements established by the AOC Court Interpreting Services Division;

(b) Obtain the hours of court observation or work as required by the AOC Interpreting Services Division; and

(c) Comply with the Code of Professional Responsibility.

(d) Additionally, a freelance interpreter must annually update his or her personal information on file with the AOC. Personal information must be submitted every year on or before July 1. A sixty (60) day grace period will be allowed after July 1, during which time individuals may continue to interpret for the Court of Justice pending submission of the necessary documentation.

(e) Failure by a freelance interpreter to comply with the above-listed requirements may result in either temporary removal from the AOC Interpreter Directory, or lapse of certification and permanent removal from the AOC Interpreter Directory.

(5) The AOC will conduct annually a criminal background check on all interpreters listed in the AOC Interpreter Directory.

(6) It is the responsibility of the staff and freelance interpreter to renew his or her certification or designated status. Renewal forms may be obtained at the AOC and should be submitted at least thirty days prior to expiration of certification to avoid a lapse in certification.

(7) Proof of compliance with the continuing education units and the required court observation hours must be submitted to the AOC Court Interpreting Services Division bi-annually on or before July 1. A sixty day grace period will be allowed after July 1, during which time individuals may continue to interpret for the Court: of Justice pending submission of the necessary documentation.

(8) Lapsed Certification, Freelance Interpreters:

(a) Failure to comply with the continuing education units and court observation requirements will result in a lapsed certification and the interpreter may be removed from the AOC Interpreter Directory based on the recommendation of the AOC Court Interpreting Services Division. An interpreter with a lapsed certification will not be permitted to interpret for the Court of Justice.

(b) A lapsed certification may be renewed. The AOC may require that a person applying for renewal of the certification and to be re-listed in the AOC Interpreting Directory show evidence of completion of the required continuing education units and court observation hours as described in the AOC's Spoken Language Certification Policy.

(9) Pursuant to KRS 30A.400(3), if the eligibility of the person to receive the services of an interpreter is challenged, the judge may, for good cause shown, hold a hearing to determine the bona fide need for interpreting services. If it is determined that the person is not entitled to interpreting services, then no portion of these rules will apply to said person.

(10) When a person does not request an interpreter but appears to have limited ability to communicate in English, the court will conduct a brief voir dire in order to evaluate the extent to which the person speaks and understands English and determine whether or not an interpreter is needed.

(11) When the appointed interpreter and the person receiving interpreting services appear to have difficulties communicating with one another, the appointing/requesting authority should make reasonable efforts on the record to determine that there is sufficient communication between the interpreter and the person receiving interpreting services.

HISTORY: Amended by Order 2011–03, eff. 3–15–11; prior amendments eff. 5–12–09 (Order 2009–06), 12–1–04 (Order 2004–3); adopted by Order 2004-3, eff. 10–1–04

AP IX, Sec. 10   AOC Interpreter Directory

(1) The AOC Court Interpreting Services Division will maintain a Directory of licensed freelance interpreters and staff interpreters for the deaf and hard of hearing and certified and registered spoken language freelance and staff interpreters who have satisfied the requirements set out in Sections 8 and 9 herein, including the requirements for maintaining certification/qualification status.

(2) The Director of the AOC will have the authority to remove a freelance interpreter from the AOC Interpreter Directory for good cause which may include, but is not limited to, the following misconduct:

(a) Knowingly and willfully making false interpretation while serving in an official capacity;

(b) Knowingly and willfully disclosing confidential or privileged information obtained while serving in an official capacity;

(c) Failing to follow other standards prescribed by law and the Code of Professional Responsibility for Interpreters;

(d) Failing to appear as scheduled without good cause;

(e) Failing to accept and adhere to the Kentucky Certification Policy for Spoken Language Interpreters;

(f) Failing to accept and adhere to the Uniform Payment Rate; and

(g) Requesting payment for services to the Court of Justice from the person for whom the interpreter is appointed.

(3) Any allegation of a misconduct found in this section will be reported to the AOC Director or designee, for purposes of review. For the duration of the review a freelance interpreter may be temporarily removed from the AOC Interpreter Directory.

(4) Freelance interpreters may be permanently removed from the AOC Directory by the AOC Director, The interpreter must be given notice by certified mail, return receipt requested, of the Director's action taken and must be given an opportunity to request reconsideration within ten days of receipt of the notice.

HISTORY: Amended by Order 2011–03, eff. 3–15–11; prior amendments eff. 5–12–09 (Order 2009–06), 12–1–04 (Order 2004–3); adopted by Order 2004-3, eff. 10–1–04

AP IX, Sec. 11   Use of assistive technology

(1) Pursuant to KRS 30A.435, in the performance of his or her duties for the Court of Justice, the interpreter may utilize electronic recording, foreign language translation, remote videoconference equipment, web-based remote interpreting service equipment, and any other appropriate equipment.

(2) Remote interpreting services may be used for brief non-evidentiary proceedings, including pretrial interviews, initial appearances, arraignments, and direct services for the Court of Justice when necessary.

(3) A person who is deaf, hard of hearing, or speech impaired may elect to use assistive technology in lieu of or in addition to the services of an interpreter. Any request to use assistive technology in a court proceeding must be made in accordance with Section 4[4] of these rules.

(4) Remote interpreting services may be obtained for persons with Limited English Proficiency when there is a time-sensitive matter that requires interpretation and no other resources are available.

(5) Remote interpretation may also be appropriate for non-immediate matters that are scheduled in advance, when the interpretation of these matters cannot be handled in-person by staff or freelance interpreters in a fiscally responsible or timely manner, and the quality of interpretation is not in question.

(6) If the equipment sought to be used is of the type approved by the AOC, or a judicial official, no further approval is required.

(7) If the equipment is of a type for which no approval has been issued by the AOC, the use of the equipment must be approved in writing and in ad-

vance by the Director of the AOC or his/her designee or by the judge making the appointment.

(8) If the equipment is of a type which has been disapproved by the AOC, it will not be used.

(9) All equipment utilized must be in proper mechanical and working order and must be fit for its intended use.

(a) The appointing/requesting authority must ensure the non-English speaking party hears all statements made by the participants if utilizing remote interpreting equipment. If telephone equipment is unavailable for simultaneous interpreting, the appointing/requesting authority must allow consecutive interpretation of each sentence.

(b) When remote interpreting equipment is utilized to translate a written document, the document must be read aloud to allow full oral translation of the material by the remote interpreter.

(c) The appointing authority must ensure that the remote interpreting equipment used for the deaf and hard of hearing is in proper mechanical and working order, and fit for its intended use.

(d) The AOC must provide the Court of Justice with instructions necessary for obtaining and using remote interpreting equipment and services. Only remote interpreting services contracted by the AOC will be used.

HISTORY: Amended by Order 2011–03, eff. 3-15-11; prior amendments eff. 5–12–09 (Order 2009–06), 12–1–04 (Order 2004–3); adopted by Order 2004–3, eff. 10–1–04

AP IX, Sec. 12 Removal of staff interpreter and freelance interpreter from case

(1) Pursuant to KRS 30A.410(2), upon request of the person for whom the interpreter is appointed or on the court's own motion, an interpreter may be removed for inability to communicate with the person, or if for reasonable cause another interpreter is desired by the person for whom the interpreter is appointed, or because the services of an interpreter are not desired by the person.

(2) Removal for Good Cause. Additionally, a judge may remove an interpreter from his or her interpreting duties for good cause, which may include, but is not limited to:

(a) Inability to interpret adequately, including where the interpreter or person for whom the interpreter is appointed reports such inability;

(b) Knowingly and willfully making false interpretation while serving in an official capacity;

(c) Knowingly and willfully disclosing confidential or privileged information obtained while serving in an official capacity;

(d) Failing to follow other standards prescribed by law and the Code of Professional Responsibility for Interpreters; and

(e) Failing to appear as scheduled without good cause.

HISTORY: Amended by Order 2011–03, eff. 3-15-11; prior amendments eff. 5–12–09 (Order 2009–06), 12–1–04 (Order 2004–3); adopted by Order 2004–3, eff. 10–1–04

AP IX, Sec. 13 Disciplinary action—Staff interpreters

(1) The Personnel Policies of the Court of Justice will apply to all staff interpreters. Staff interpreters may be disciplined for misconduct which may include but is not limited to, the following:

(a) Knowingly and willfully making false interpretation while serving in an official capacity;

(b) Knowingly and willfully disclosing confidential or privileged information obtained while serving in an official capacity;

(c) Failing to follow other standards prescribed by law and the Code of Professional Responsibility;

(d) Failing to accept and adhere to the Kentucky Certification Policy for Spoken Language Interpreters;

(e) Failing to appear as scheduled without good cause; and

(f) Requesting payment for services to the Court of Justice from the person for whom the interpreter is appointed.

HISTORY: Amended by Order 2011–03, eff. 3-15-11; prior amendments eff. 5–12–09 (Order 2009–06), 12–1–04 (Order 2004–3); adopted by Order 2004–3, eff. 10–1–04

AP IX, Sec. 14 Compensation of interpreters by the Court of Justice

(1) Court of Justice compensation for freelance interpreters' services will be established by the Director of the AOC as a statewide Uniform Payment Rate. Refusal to accept and adhere to the Uniform Payment Rate will be grounds for removal from the AOC Interpreter Directory.

(2) For payment as authorized under these rules, the freelance interpreter must provide to the AOC form AOC–INT–1, Statement for Interpreting Services. The invoice must be signed by the appointing/requesting authority and by the freelance interpreter, and must be submitted to the AOC no later than seven days after the service has been provided.

(a) For purposes of compensation of the freelance interpreter, the AOC will limit hourly rates to begin no more than fifteen minutes prior to the scheduled time in which interpreting services are being rendered. Hourly rates will end upon the completion of the assigned interpreting service(s). Further, payment will be made for time spent interpreting and waiting to interpret in court proceedings or direct services. If the interpreter provides services for multiple cases on the same docket, all cases must be reported on the same AOC Statement for Interpreting Services form. The AOC will round any "less than one-quarter hour increment" up to the next quarter hour.

(b) Compensation for travel of freelance interpreters will be established by the AOC Director as part of the Uniform Payment Rate.

(c) Cancellation and no—show policies will be established by the AOC Director as part of the Uniform Payment Rate.

(d) Compensation will not be made to a freelance interpreter for time spent in preparation for scheduled interpreting services for a court proceeding or a direct service, except under extraordinary circumstances as determined and approved in advance and in writing by the AOC Director or designee.

(e) Staff interpreters will receive salaries and benefits according to the Court of Justice Personnel Policies, and travel will be compensated according to the Court of Justice Travel Regulations.

HISTORY: Amended by Order 2011–03, eff. 3–15–11; prior amendments eff. 5–12–09 (Order 2009–06), 12–1–04 (Order 2004–3); adopted by Order 2004–3, eff. 10–1–04

AP IX, Sec. 15   AOC authority to implement Court Interpreting Services Division

The AOC will have the authority to establish additional internal policies or procedures relating to the administration of the Court of Justice interpreting services as authorized and established by the AOC Director. The AOC will have the authority to hire staff interpreters to be employed by the AOC.

HISTORY: Amended by Order 2011–03, eff. 3–15–11; prior amendments eff. 5–12–09 (Order 2009–06), 12–1–04 (Order 2004–3); adopted by Order 2004–3, eff. 10–1–04

PART X
CAPITAL CONSTRUCTION PROGRAM

Pursuant to Sections 110(5)(b) and 116 of the Constitution of Kentucky, court facilities construction program development, criteria, and design and construction rules and standards for the Court of Justice shall henceforth be governed in accordance with the Rules of Administrative Procedures of the Court of Justice, Part X, Court of Justice Real Property Management, consisting of three (3) Sections: Construction Program Development; Court Facilities Criteria; and Court Facilities Design and Construction, which is attached hereto. Beginning with the Capital Construction Projects authorized by the 2005 General Assembly, all previous rules and orders regarding court facilities real property management are hereby amended in their entirety. This order is effective June 1, 2007.

HISTORY: Amended by Order 2012–04, eff. 6–1–12; prior amendments eff. 6–1–07 (Order 2007–03), 8–5–05 (Order 2005–05), 9–20–02, adopted eff. 1–2–00

Historical and Statutory Notes

Publisher's Note: This rule was originally ordered Part X by the Supreme Court of Kentucky in an undesignated and unpublished order in 2000. In 2001, Order 2001–1 created another Part X, Electronic Access by the Bar. In 2002, an undesignated and unpublished order corrected the situation with the two rules and ordered that Court of Justice Real Property Management Guide remain as Part X and Electronic Access by the Bar would be Part XI.

In 2012, Order 2014–04, renamed Part X as Capital Construction Program, and amended Section 1 in its entirety. All Kentucky Court of Justice Capital Construction Projects authorized after June 1, 2012, are governed by AP Part X, Section I, Construction Program Development. Sections II and III of AP Part X, which were authorized by Supreme Court Order 2007–03, remain in effect until further order of this Court.

PART XI
ELECTRONIC ACCESS BY THE BAR

AP XI, Sec. 1   Electronic access by the bar

(1) Members are authorized to access Kentucky Court of Justice electronic records and computers by means authorized for use by the general public.

(2) Members are authorized to access Kentucky Court of Justice electronic records and computers by means authorized for members of the bar for the purpose of accessing cases involving members' clients.

(3) Electronic records and computers of the Kentucky Court of Justice not available to the general public shall be accessed only in accordance with the written authorization of the Kentucky Court of Justice

pursuant to terms of use and access approved by the Chief Justice.

(4) Members shall not intentionally access Kentucky Court of Justice electronic records or computers without authorization.

(5) Members shall not access Kentucky Court of Justice electronic records or computers and intentionally exceed authorized access and thereby view, obtain or alter information contained in Kentucky Court of Justice records.

(6) "Member" has the same definition as SCR 3.010.

HISTORY: Amended eff. 9–20–02; adopted by Order 2001–1, eff. 1–1–02

PART XII
MEDIATION GUIDELINES FOR COURT OF JUSTICE MEDIATORS

AP XII, Sec. 1   Statement of purpose

The following Guidelines concern suggested minimum standards for training, experience, education, and ethical conduct for mediators practicing in courts of the Commonwealth of Kentucky. They are intended to promote public confidence in the mediation process. Judges and the public are encouraged to refer to the Administrative Office of the Court's (AOC) website for the roster of mediators who voluntarily agree to comply with these Guidelines. Additional information and related forms are available at *Guidelines for Basic Mediation Training* at www. kycourts.net.

HISTORY: Adopted by Order 2005–02, eff. 4–15–05

AP XII, Sec. 2   Training and experience

(1) **General civil mediator.** A mediator who offers to provide general civil mediation services should have the following minimum training and experience:

(a) Forty hours of training by a mediation training provider covering communication skills; conflict resolution theory and practice; mediation theory, practice, and techniques; the court process; and

(b) Fifteen hours of mediation experience with parties in actual disputes, representing at least three cases, where the mediator is a participating mediator under the guidance of a mediator qualified under these Guidelines or a mediation training center.

(2) **Family mediator.** A mediator who offers to provide family mediation services should have the following minimum training and experience:

(a) Forty hours of training by a mediation training provider including conflict resolution, the mediation process, communication skills, the psychological aspects of divorce on families, domestic violence, substance abuse, financial and property issues, paternity, family law, and family or circuit court procedures. Family mediators are strongly encouraged to take general mediation training prior to this training.

(b) Fifteen hours of mediation experience with parties in actual family disputes, representing at least three cases, where the mediator is a participating mediator under the guidance of a family mediator qualified under these Guidelines, or a mediation training center.

(3) **Special provision for mediators in practice prior to adoption of the guidelines.** Any mediator may be deemed qualified under these Guidelines if the mediator has engaged in a mediation practice prior to the adoption of these Guidelines and submits to the Mediation Division of the Administrative Office of the Courts a written statement describing equivalent training and experience. A form is available at www. kycourts.net.

HISTORY: Adopted by Order 2005–02, eff. 4–15–05

AP XII, Sec. 3   Ethical guidelines

(1) **Mediation defined.** Mediation is an informal process in which a neutral third person, called a mediator, facilitates the resolution of a dispute between two or more parties. The process is designed to help disputing parties reach an agreement on all or part of the issues in dispute. Decision-making authority remains with the parties, not the mediator. The mediator assists the parties in identifying issues, fostering joint problem solving, and exploring settlement alternatives. Parties should comply with orders of the court requiring participants in mediation to have settlement authority. See Kentucky Farm Bureau Mut. Ins. Co. v. Wright, 136 S.W.3d 455 (Ky. 2004).

Comment. A mediator's obligation is to assist the parties in reaching a voluntary outcome. The mediator should not coerce a party in any way. A mediator may make suggestions, but the parties make all settlement decisions voluntarily.

(2) **Mediator conduct.** A mediator's duty to protect the integrity and confidentiality of the mediation process commences with the first communication with a party, is continuous in nature, and does not terminate upon the conclusion of the mediation.

Comment (a). A mediator should not use information obtained during the mediation for personal gain or advantage.

Comment (b). The interests of the parties should always be placed above the personal interest of the mediator.

Comment (c). A mediator should not accept mediations that cannot be completed in a timely manner, or as directed by the court.

Comment (d). Although a mediator may advertise the mediator's qualifications and availability to mediate, the mediator should not solicit a specific case to mediate.

Comment (e). A mediator should not mediate a dispute when the mediator has knowledge that another mediator was appointed or selected without first consulting with the other mediator or the parties. If the previous mediation has been concluded, consultation is not necessary.

(3) **Mediation costs.** As early as practicable, and before the mediation session begins, a mediator should explain all fees and other expenses to be charged for the mediation. A mediator should not charge a con-

tingent fee or base a fee upon the outcome of the mediation. In appropriate cases, a mediator should perform mediation services on a sliding scale, at a reduced fee, or without compensation, based on the parties' ability to pay.

Comment (a). In court mediations, a mediator should avoid the appearance of impropriety regarding the amount of the mediator's fee. The fee should be reasonable and no greater than the mediator's standard rate as a mediator.

Comment (b). If a party and the mediator have a dispute that cannot be resolved before commencement of the mediation as to the mediator's fee, the mediator should decline to serve so that the parties may obtain another mediator.

(4) **Disclosure of possible conflicts.** Prior to commencing the mediation, the mediator should make full disclosure of any known relationships with the parties or their counsel that may affect, or give the appearance of affecting, the mediator's neutrality. A mediator should not serve in the matter if a party makes an objection to the mediator based upon a conflict or perceived conflict.

Comment (a). A mediator should withdraw from mediation if it is inappropriate to serve.

Comment (b). If, after commencement of the mediation, the mediator discovers that such a relationship exists, the mediator should make full disclosure as soon as practicable.

(5) **Mediator qualifications.** A mediator should inform the participants of the mediator's qualifications and experience.

Comment. A mediator's qualifications and experience constitute the foundation upon which the mediation process depends; therefore, if there is any objection to the mediator's qualifications to mediate the dispute, the mediator should withdraw from the mediation. Likewise, the mediator should decline to serve if the mediator feels unqualified to do so.

(6) **The mediation process.** The mediator should inform and discuss with the participants the rules and procedures pertaining to the mediation process.

Comment (a). A mediator should inform the parties about the mediation process no later than the opening session.

Comment (b). At a minimum, the mediator should inform the parties of the following:

(i) The mediation is private. Unless otherwise agreed by the participants, only the mediator, the parties and their representatives are allowed to attend;

(ii) The mediation is informal. There are no court reporters present; no record is made of the proceedings; no subpoena or other service of process is allowed; and no rulings are made on the issues or the merits of the case;

(iii) The mediation is confidential;

(iv) Any outcome rests with the parties; and

(v) The mediator does not render legal advice or represent any party.

(7) **Convening the mediation.** Unless the parties agree otherwise, the mediator should not convene a mediation session unless all parties and their representatives ordered by the court are present, corporate parties are represented by officers or agents who have demonstrated to the mediator that they possess adequate authority to negotiate a settlement, and an adequate amount of time has been reserved by all parties to the mediation to allow the mediation process to be productive.

(8) **Confidentiality.**

(a) Mediation sessions should be closed to all persons other than the parties, their legal representatives, and other persons invited by the mediator with the consent of the parties.

(b) Mediation should be regarded as settlement negotiations for purposes of Kentucky Rule of Evidence 408.

(c) Mediators should not be subject to process requiring the disclosure of any matter discussed during the mediation, but rather, such matters are considered confidential and privileged in nature except on order of the Court for good cause shown. This privilege and immunity reside in the mediator and may not be waived by the parties.

(d) Nothing in this rule prohibits the mediator from reporting abuse according to K.R.S. 209.030, K.R.S. 620.030, or other applicable law.

Comment. A mediator should not permit recordings or transcripts to be made of mediation proceedings. A mediator should maintain confidentiality in the storage and disposal of records and render anonymous all identifying information when materials are used for research, educational or other informational purposes.

(9) **Report to court.** The mediator reports to the court that the mediation has not occurred, has not been completed, or that the mediation has been completed with or without an agreement on any or all issues. With the consent of the parties, the mediator may also identify those matters, which, if resolved or completed, would facilitate the possibility of a settlement.

(10) **Impartiality.** A mediator should be impartial toward all parties.

Comment. If a mediator or the parties find that the mediator's impartiality has been compromised, the mediator should offer to withdraw from the mediation process. Impartiality means freedom from favoritism or bias in word, action, and appearance; it implies a commitment to aid all parties in reaching a settlement.

(11) Disclosure and exchange of information. A mediator should encourage the disclosure of information and should assist the parties in considering the benefits, risks, and the alternatives available to them.

(12) Professional advice. A mediator should not give legal or other professional advice to the parties except as provided in Section 3(17)(b) infra re: Evaluative Mediation.

Comment (a). In appropriate circumstances, a mediator should encourage the parties to seek legal, financial, tax or other professional advice before, during, or after the mediation process.

Comment (b). A mediator should not convene the mediation if the mediator has reason to believe that a pro se party fails to understand that the mediator is not providing legal representation for the pro se party.

(13) No judicial action taken. A person serving as a mediator should not subsequently serve as a judge, master commissioner, guardian ad litem, or in any other judicial or quasi-judicial capacity in matters that are the subject of the mediation, unless the parties otherwise agree.

Comment. It is generally inappropriate for a mediator to serve in a judicial or quasi-judicial capacity in a matter in which the mediator had communications with one or more parties without all other parties present. For example, an attorney-mediator who has served as a mediator in a pending litigation should not subsequently serve in the same case as a special master, guardian ad litem, or in any other judicial or quasi-judicial capacity with binding decision-making authority. Notwithstanding the foregoing, where an impasse has been declared at the conclusion of a mediation, the mediator, if requested and agreed to by all parties, may serve as the arbitrator in a binding arbitration of the dispute, or as a third-party neutral in any other alternative dispute proceeding, so long as the mediator believed nothing learned during private conferences with any party to the mediation will bias the mediator or will unfairly influence the mediator's decisions while acting in the mediator's subsequent capacity.

(14) Termination of mediation session. A mediator should postpone, recess, or terminate the mediation process if it is apparent to the mediator that continuation of the process is unproductive.

(15) Agreement in writing. If an agreement is reached during the mediation conference, it is reduced to writing and signed by the parties. The parties are responsible for the drafting of the agreement, although the mediator may assist in the drafting of the agreement with the consent of the parties.

(16) Mediator's relationship with the judiciary. A mediator should avoid the appearance of impropriety in the mediator's relationship with a member of the judiciary or the court staff with regard to appointments or referrals to mediation.

(17) Mediation styles

(a) **Facilitative mediation.** The facilitative mediator structures a process to assist the parties in reaching a mutually agreeable outcome. The mediator asks questions; validates and normalizes parties' points of view; searches for interests underneath the positions taken by parties; and assists the parties in finding and analyzing options for resolution. The facilitative mediator does not make recommendations to the parties, give his or her own advice or opinion as to the outcomes of the case, or predict what a court would do in the case. The mediator is in charge of the process, while the parties are in charge of the outcome. Facilitative mediators want to ensure that parties come to agreements based on information and understanding. They hold joint sessions with all parties present so that the parties can hear each other's points of view, and hold confidential sessions with individual parties. They want the parties to have the major influence on decisions made.

(b) **Evaluative mediation.** Evaluative mediation is modeled after settlement conferences held by judges. The evaluative mediator assists the parties in reaching resolution by pointing out the weaknesses of their case. An evaluative mediator might make formal or informal recommendation to the parties as to the outcome of the issues. The evaluative mediator is more concerned with the legal rights of the parties, rather than the parties' needs and interests, and evaluation is based on legal concepts of fairness. The evaluative mediator meets most often in separate meetings with the parties and their attorneys, practicing "shuttle diplomacy." He/she helps the parties and their attorneys evaluate their legal position and the costs versus the benefits of settling in mediation rather than pursuing litigation. The evaluative mediator structures the process and directly influences the outcome of mediation.

Comment (a). Providing information. Consistent with standards of impartiality and preserving party self-determination, a mediator may provide information that he/she is qualified to provide by virtue of training or experience.

Comment (b). Independent legal advice. When a mediator believes a party does not understand or appreciate how an agreement may adversely affect legal rights or obligations, the mediator should advise the party of the right to seek independent legal counsel.

Comment (c). Personal or professional opinions. A mediator should not offer a personal or professional opinion intended to coerce the parties, decide the dispute, or direct a resolution of any issue. Consistent with standards of impartiality and preserving party self-determination, however, a mediator may point out possible outcomes of the case and discuss merits of a claim or defense. A mediator should not offer a personal or professional opinion as to how the court in which the case has been filed will resolve the dispute.

(c) **Transformative mediation.** Transformative mediation is based on the values of "empowerment" and "recognition." The potential for transformative mediation is that any or all parties, or their relationships, may be transformed during the mediation. In these ways, the values of transformative mediation mirror those of facilitative mediation. In transformative mediation, the parties structure the process, with the mediator following their lead, and individual caucus sessions are rarely used.

(18) **Responsibilities to the profession and the public**

(a) **Community service.** A mediator is encouraged to provide at least twenty hours per year of mediation services in the community for nominal or no fee.

(b) **Training.** A mediator should acquire substantive knowledge and procedural skills in her/his specialized area of practice.

(c) **Continuing education.** A mediator should participate in continuing mediation education and be personally responsible for ongoing professional growth. A mediator is encouraged to join with other mediators and members of related professions to promote mutual professional development. A mediator should obtain at least four hours of continuing education every two years.

The following are *some* ways to obtain continuing education:

(i) Attending, lecturing, or teaching at a live lecture or seminar on a topic related to the practice of mediation;

(ii) Listening or viewing audio, video, or web based presentations on a topic related to mediation;

(iii) Co-mediating or supervising trainees as part of the trainee's mentorship requirements;

(iv) Participating as a trainer or coach in general or family mediation trainings;

(v) Authoring or editing written materials submitted for publication that have significant intellectual or practical content directly related to the practice of mediation.

(d) **Promotion of mediation.** A mediator should promote the advancement of mediation by providing and supporting efforts to educate the public and members of other professions, and by encouraging and participating in research and publication of accurate information about mediation.

(e) **Advertising.** A mediator should make only accurate statements about the mediation process, its cost and benefits, and about the mediator's qualifications.

HISTORY: Adopted by Order 2005–02, eff. 4–15–05

AP XII, Sec. 4　Roster of mediators

AOC will maintain a Roster of Mediators who agree to comply with these guidelines. Any mediator who wishes to be included on this roster should make application to the AOC. See form on www.kycourts.net.

HISTORY: Adopted by Order 2005–02, eff. 4–15–05

PART XIII
PROCEDURES FOR DRUG COURT

AP XIII, Sec. 1　Definitions

As used in these sections, unless the context otherwise requires:

(1) "Administrative discharge" means the discharge of a participant from drug court due to the participant's inability to complete drug court through no fault of his/her own.

(2) "Aftercare" means the time period following successful completion of Phase III of the drug court requirements, during which the participant shall demonstrate the ability to maintain a drug-free, alcohol-free and crime-free lifestyle and may continue to receive treatment and other supportive services. For felony drug courts, aftercare is 180 days and for misdemeanor drug courts, a minimum of 90 days.

(3) "Agreement of Participation" means the written agreement required to be signed by all potential drug court participants prior to the determination of eligibility for drug court.

(4) "AOC Drug Court Executive Officer" means the AOC employee appointed by the AOC Director to support drug court and administer and oversee its funding.

(5) "AOC" means the Administrative Office of the Courts, the agency authorized by the Kentucky Supreme Court to support drug court and administer and oversee its funding.

(6) "Approved local diversion procedures" means pretrial diversion procedures authorized by the Kentucky Supreme Court within each judicial circuit.

(7) "COJ" means the Court of Justice.

(8) "Drug court graduation" means the public ceremony acknowledging the successful completion of Phases I, II and III of drug court. Aftercare may be required in some drug courts prior to graduation.

(9) "Drug court judge" means a judge who, in addition to his/her regular judicial duties, conducts drug court sessions and staffings, monitors and reviews the participant's progress in the drug court program,

imposes sanctions and incentives, and facilitates other components of the drug court program.

(10) "Drug court program" means any program authorized and administered by the Kentucky Supreme Court which provides an alternative to incarceration in cases which stem from substance abuse or dependence. A drug court shall combine supervision, drug testing, case management, judicial interaction and treatment for drug court participants.

(11) "Drug court staff" means personnel hired and employed by the AOC Drug Court Department who perform the daily operations of drug court, including but not limited to, conducting eligibility assessments, providing case management for participants, attending drug court staffings and sessions, and coordinating drug testing.

(12) "Drug court team" means the non-adversarial group that promotes public safety while acting in the best interest of the public and the participant, and determines the appropriate responses for a participant's compliance or non-compliance with drug court requirements. While the drug court team determines appropriate responses for participant compliance or non-compliance, the drug court judge has the ultimate decision making authority. For adult drug courts, the drug court team shall be comprised of the drug court judge, and drug court staff, and should include law enforcement, prosecutor(s), defense counsel, and treatment provider(s). Optional members with each drug court may be representatives from the office of probation and parole, the circuit court clerk's office, the community, and other ancillary agencies.

(13) "Eligibility Assessment" means a tool used by drug court staff to evaluate drug use history, legal/criminal history, mental/physical health history, family history, and educational/employment history, for purposes of determining whether a defendant will be considered for admission into drug court.

(14) "Eligible offenses" means drug or drug-related offenses, excluding violent offenses and sexual offenses.

(15) "Home visit" means the on-site appearance of drug court staff who are accompanied by a law enforcement or probation and parole officer at the participant's home for the purposes of verifying stable, drug-free housing and curfews, among other verifiers.

(16) "Incentives" means tangible or intangible rewards earned by participants for positive steps taken toward attaining a drug-free, crime-free lifestyle, and may include, but are not limited to, promotion to the next phase, certificates and tokens, decreased supervision, increased privileges and responsibilities, praise from the drug court judge and team, extended curfews, and other individual incentives approved by the drug court team.

(17) "Involuntary termination" means the termination of a participant from drug court by the drug court judge due to the participant's non-compliance with drug court's requirements, rules, or conditions.

(18) "Justice system case processing" means the manner in which a case is processed within the Kentucky COJ, as reflected in KyCourts II or the current COJ case management system.

(19) "Notice of Defendant Referral Status" means the document provided to the sentencing judge following the defendant's assessment wherein a determination of eligibility or ineligibility for admission to drug court has been made.

(20) "Non–AOC support personnel" means interns and volunteers, including but not limited to, other staff supplied by a city or county office or official not employed by the AOC Drug Court Department who work with the drug court.

(21) "Phase" means a set of minimum and distinct criteria required of a drug court participant.

(22) "Recovery program" means a long-term residential program for participants seeking recovery from alcohol or other drugs, which provides a setting for non-medical detoxification and utilizes peer-counseling and other counseling techniques.

(23) "Referring judge" means the judge who refers a defendant to drug court.

(24) "Sanctions" means the range of consequences imposed for the participant's failure to comply with the requirements or other conditions of drug court, which are appropriate, consistent and immediately applied. Sanctions may include, but are not limited to, admonishments from the judge, residential drug treatment, community service, phase demotion, increased group sessions, home incarceration, imprisonment in a detention facility, or termination from drug court.

(25) "Sentencing judge" means the judge who sentences the defendant in the underlying criminal case; he/she may also be the referring judge.

(26) "Session" means the scheduled appearance of the participant before the drug court judge, during which the progress of the participant is reviewed and incentives may be granted or sanctions imposed.

(27) "Staffing" means meetings held by the drug court team prior to a drug court program session, for the purpose of discussing the participants' progress.

(28) "Suspension" means a temporary stay of participation in the drug court program imposed by the drug court judge, during which time no credit is earned toward the completion of the three drug court phases.

(29) "Temporary inactive" means the status of a participant in drug court who is unable to meet drug court requirements on a short-term basis, excluding reasons of inpatient treatment or incarceration. The participant is temporarily released from drug court supervision pursuant to a judge's order and shall

resume participation and supervision when the circumstance is resolved.

(30) "Transfer for all further proceedings" means a transfer of the underlying criminal case to the drug court judge for both drug court proceedings and all further criminal proceedings.

(31) "Treatment provider" means an individual or agency licensed or certified to provide treatment and counseling to drug court participants as specified by the AOC Drug Court Department.

(32) "Violent Offender" as defined by federal regulation 28 C.F.R 93.3 means an offender who either is currently charged with or convicted of an offense during the course of which: 1) The person carried, possessed, or used a firearm or other dangerous weapon; or there occurred the use of force against the person of another; or there occurred the death of or serious bodily injury to any person; with or without regard to whether proof of any of the elements described herein is required to convict; or 2) has previously been convicted of a felony crime of violence involving the use or attempted use of force against a person with the intent to cause death or serious bodily harm.

(33) "Voluntary termination" means the termination by the drug court judge of a participant from drug court at the participant's request, but only after a determination has been made that the request was knowingly and voluntarily made.

HISTORY: Amended by Order 2010–05, eff. 3–23–10; prior amendments eff. 7–30–09 (Order 2009–07); adopted by Order 2006–01, eff. 1–9–06.

AP XIII, Sec. 2   Key components of drug court

All drug court programs shall include the following key components as defined and required by the U. S. Department of Justice, Office of Justice Programs:

(1) Drug courts integrate alcohol and other drug treatment services with justice system case processing;

(2) Prosecution and defense counsel, in a non-adversarial manner, promote public safety while protecting participants' due process rights;

(3) Eligible participants are identified early and promptly placed in the drug court program;

(4) Drug courts provide a continuum of alcohol, drug, and other treatment and rehabilitative services;

(5) Abstinence is monitored by frequent alcohol and other drug testing;

(6) A coordinated strategy governs drug court responses to participants' compliance;

(7) Ongoing judicial interaction with each drug court participant is essential;

(8) Monitoring and evaluation of the drug court program measure the achievement of program goals and gauge effectiveness;

(9) Continuing interdisciplinary education promotes effective drug court planning, implementation, and operations; and,

(10) Forging partnerships among drug courts, public agencies, and community-based organizations generates local support and enhances drug court program effectiveness.

HISTORY: Amended by Order 2010–5, eff. 3–23–10; prior amendment eff. 7–30–09 (Order 2009–07); adopted by Order 2006–01, eff. 1–9–06

AP XIII, Sec. 3   Mission statement

Kentucky Drug Court's mission is to restore lives and reduce recidivism through judicial oversight and behavior modification.

HISTORY: Amended by Order 2010–05, eff. 3–23–10; prior amendments eff. 7–30–09 (Order 2009–07); adopted by Order 2006–01, eff. 1–9–06

AP XIII, Sec. 4   Administrative office of the courts to oversee drug court

The AOC shall support drug courts statewide, and administer and oversee its funding. The AOC shall also be authorized to establish further policies and procedures relating to drug court.

HISTORY: Amended by Order 2010–05, eff. 3– 23–10; prior amendment eff. 7–30–09 (Order 2009–07); adopted by Order 2006–01, eff. 1–9–06

AP XIII, Sec. 5   Drug court referral process

In those jurisdictions having a drug court, a defendant shall be referred to drug court through one of the following procedures:

(1) A referral to drug court may be made at any time during probation, including a referral in lieu of revocation. A defendant who is referred to drug court by an order of probation shall have entered a guilty plea or been found guilty of an eligible offense(s). The sentencing judge, upon request of the attorney for the defendant or another interested party, or, alternatively, sua sponte, may order a defendant to be referred to drug court for a determination of the defendant's eligibility.

(2) A referral to drug court may be made utilizing approved local diversion procedures.

(3) Any judge may refer a person charged with contempt of court to drug court in lieu of being incarcerated on the contempt charge, but only after an order of contempt has been entered.

HISTORY: Amended by Order 2010–05, eff. 3–23–10; prior amendment eff. 7–30–09 (Order 2009–07); adopted by Order 2006–01, eff. 1–9–06

AP XIII, Sec. 6   Eligibility and assessment

(1) Upon receipt of a written order of referral from a judge, drug court staff shall determine whether a defendant meets the following criteria:

(a) The defendant was referred pursuant to Section 5 of these rules;

(b) The defendant never successfully completed or was terminated from a Kentucky adult drug court;

(c) The defendant is not a "sex offender" as defined by KRS 17.550;

(d) The defendant is not a "violent offender" as defined by federal regulation, 28 C.F.R. 93.3

(2) If a defendant does not meet the criteria set forth in subsection (1) above, drug court staff shall inform the referring judge in writing using AOC form #DC–7.

(3) If a defendant does meet the criteria set forth in subsection (1) above, drug court staff shall thoroughly explain the drug court process and the Agreement of Participation to the defendant. The defendant shall be required to sign the Agreement of Participation with or without the presence of his/her attorney. If a defendant refuses to sign the Agreement of Participation, drug court staff shall notify the referring judge by utilizing AOC form # DC–7. Refusal by the defendant to sign the Agreement of Participation shall render him/her ineligible for participation in drug court.

(4) Upon execution of the Agreement of Participation, drug court staff shall complete an eligibility assessment. After completing the eligibility assessment, drug court staff shall complete AOC form # DC–7. The eligibility assessment, AOC form # DC–7 and any other pertinent information regarding the defendant shall be completed and submitted to the drug court team prior to the defendant's next scheduled court appearance.

HISTORY: Amended by Order 2010–05, eff. 3–23–10; prior amendment eff. 7–30–09 (Order 2009–07); adopted by Order 2006–01, eff. 1–9–06

AP XIII, Sec. 7 Acceptance of defendant into drug court

Upon receipt of the eligibility assessment, AOC form # DC–7 and other pertinent information regarding the defendant, the drug court team shall provide input into the decision for acceptance; however, the drug court judge shall have the final decision-making authority concerning acceptance of an eligible person into drug court. To determine acceptance, the drug court judge and team shall evaluate the following:

(1) Current criminal charge(s)/conviction(s);

(2) Past criminal conviction(s), if any;

(3) Results of the eligibility assessment;

(4) Information regarding the victim(s), if any;

(5) Defendant's willingness to participate; and,

(6) Other relevant information as identified by the drug court judge and team.

HISTORY: Amended by Order 2010–05, eff. 3–23–10; prior amendment eff. 7–30–09 (Order 2009–07,); adopted by Order 2006–01, eff. 1–9–06

AP XIII, Sec. 8 Admission of defendant into drug court

Upon an offer of admission to drug court and upon the defendant's acceptance of the offer to enter drug court, the referring judge shall complete AOC form #DC–8 (Order of Admission to Drug Court). The case shall remain with or be assigned to a judge who conducts drug court in the circuit or district where the defendant's underlying criminal case is pending. The Order will require the defendant to report to the drug court judge. Cases may only be transferred to a different circuit or district pursuant to Section 9 of these rules.

HISTORY: Amended by Order 2010–05, eff. 3–23–10; prior amendment eff. 7–30–09 (Order 2009–07); adopted by Order 2006–01, eff. 1–9–06

AP XIII, Sec. 9 Transfer of cases between drug courts

A defendant may request a transfer to a drug court program outside of the circuit or district where his or her criminal case is pending, either at the time of referral to the drug court program or after entry into a drug court program. A defendant/participant who has requested and been granted an order transferring venue of his or her case will be allowed to transfer under the following conditions:

(a) The drug court team in the county where the defendant requests to transfer must first agree to accept the defendant.

(b) If accepted, the defendant must complete a Motion for Transfer (AOC Form #55A), which shall be docketed before the circuit or district judge with jurisdiction over the defendant's underlying criminal case.

(c) If the judge grants the defendant's Motion, the judge shall complete AOC Form #DC–55B (Order Transferring), which will transfer venue of the defendant's case for all further criminal proceedings. The defendant's case will be assigned to a circuit or district judge who conducts drug court in the county to which the case has been transferred.

HISTORY: Amended by Order 2010–05, eff. 3–23–10; prior amendment eff. 7–30–09 (Order 2009–07); adopted by Order 2006–01, eff. 1–9–06

AP XIII, Sec. 10 Drug court participant requirements

(1) A Drug Court shall consist of three phases as follows:

a. Phase I—stabilization phase;

b. Phase II—education phase; and,

c. Phase III—self-motivation phase.

Aftercare shall be required upon a drug court participant's completion of all three phases. The three phases shall take a minimum of twelve months to complete. Drug court, including the aftercare component, can be completed in a minimum of eighteen months for felony defendants and fifteen months for misdemeanor defendants.

(2) Drug court participants shall adhere to the following minimum requirements during each phase as follows:

(a) For Phase I, the participant shall:

i. Provide at least three (3) random urine drug/alcohol screens per week;

ii. Attend at least three (3) contact hours per week;

iii. Attend one court session per week;

iv. Obtain and/or maintain court-approved full-time employment, training or education;

v. Obtain and/or maintain court-approved housing;

vi. Make arrangements for payments of court obligations;

vii. Make at least one (1) weekly individual contact with drug court staff;

viii. Indicate an initial understanding of substance abuse treatment;

ix. Attend a self-help program, such as a 12–step program; and,

x. Remain drug-free for at least 30 consecutive days before consideration for promotion to the next phase.

(b) For Phase II, the participant shall:

i. Provide at least two random urine drug/alcohol screens per week;

ii. Attend two (2) contact hours per week;

iii. Attend one (1) court session every two weeks;

iv. Maintain court-approved full-time employment, training or education;

v. Maintain court-approved housing;

vi. Continue paying court obligations;

vii. Make at least one individual contact with drug court staff per week;

viii. Indicate an appropriate understanding of recovery principles;

ix. Continue to attend self-help programs, such as a 12–step program; and,

x. Remain drug-free for the final 90 consecutive days of this Phase before consideration for promotion to the next Phase.

(c) For Phase III, the participant shall:

i. Provide at least one random urine/drug screen per week;

ii. Attend one (1) contact hour per week;

iii. Attend one (1) court session every three weeks;

iv. Maintain court-approved full-time employment, training or education;

v. Maintain court-approved housing;

vi. Continue paying court obligations;

vii. Make at least one (1) individual contact with drug court staff per week;

viii. Indicate an appropriate understanding of a recovery lifestyle;

ix. Continue to attend self-help programs, such as a 12–step program; and,

x. Remain drug-free for 90 consecutive days, for a total of 180 consecutive days for both Phases II and III before being considered for Aftercare.

(3) Each drug court shall establish an aftercare component, taking into account the availability of resources and the requirements of the drug court team. Each proposed aftercare component shall be submitted to the AOC Drug Court Executive Officer for approval no later than 180 days following implementation of drug court in a circuit or district. Within 30 days following the adoption of these Rules of Administrative Procedures, the aftercare components currently in effect in a circuit or district shall be submitted to the AOC Drug Court Executive Officer for review and approval.

(4) Drug court participants may be ordered to comply with additional requirements, which include, but are not limited to, the following:

(a) Employment, school, and/or home visits by drug court staff (drug court staff shall be accompanied by a law enforcement officer or a probation and parole officer for any home visit);

(b) Domestic violence counseling with a certified domestic violence treatment provider, or other types of counseling, as referred by drug court;

(c) Curfews as established by drug court; and,

(d) Medical and/or mental health referrals and subsequent treatment recommendations.

(5) In the event a situation arises in which it becomes impracticable for a participant to be supervised by drug court staff, the drug court judge shall issue an order placing the defendant on temporary inactive status and releasing drug court staff from supervision responsibilities, on AOC form # DC–66 (Order Designating Temporary Inactive Status). Examples of impracticability may include, but are not limited to: contagious or infectious disease, short-term medical care for a family member, or any other reason that would cause a temporary inability to meet drug court

requirements. Once the defendant has the ability to resume participation in the drug court program, the drug court judge shall enter an order resuming active status and returning the participant to drug court supervision, on AOC form # DC–67 (Order Resuming Active Status).

HISTORY: Amended by Order 2010–05, eff. 3–23–10; prior amendment eff. 7–30–09 (Order 2009–07); adopted by Order 2006–01, eff. 1–9–06

AP XIII, Sec. 11   Incentives

Incentives may be provided during drug court sessions and may include, but are not limited to, promotion to the next phase, certificates and tokens, decreased supervision, increased privileges and responsibilities, praise from the drug court judge and team, extended curfews, and other individual incentives approved by the drug court team.

HISTORY: Amended Order 2010–05, eff. 3–23–10; prior amendment eff. 7–30–09 (Order 2009–07); adopted by Order 2006–01, eff. 1–9–06

AP XIII, Sec. 12   Sanctions for non-compliance with drug court requirements

Each participant shall comply with the requirements and other conditions established by drug court. Failure to comply may result in the imposition of sanctions upon the participant by the drug court judge. Sanctions may include, but are not limited to, admonishments from the drug court judge, community service, phase demotion, increased program requirements, home incarceration, imprisonment in a detention facility, and termination from drug court. Graduated sanctions may be utilized for continuous noncompliance. When considering appropriate sanctions, drug court teams shall consider alternatives to incarceration.

HISTORY: Amended by Order 2010–05, eff. 3–23–10; prior amendment eff. 7–30–09 (Order 2009–09); adopted by Order 2006–01, eff. 1–9–06

AP XIII, Sec. 13   Suspension

In the event that standard drug court participation, as defined in Section 10, is impracticable due to inpatient treatment, incarceration, or similar circumstances in which the participant is being monitored by an authorized third party, the participant shall be placed in suspended status. Upon release from the authorized third party, the participant shall resume standard drug court participation. During the time in which the participant is suspended, no credit shall be earned toward the completion of the three drug court phases.

HISTORY: Amended by Order 2010–05, eff. 3–23–10; prior amendment eff. 7–30–09 (Order 2009–07); adopted by Order 2006–01, eff. 1–9–06

AP XIII, Sec. 14   Administrative discharge

(1) If a drug court participant cannot complete drug court through no fault of his/her own, he/she may be administratively discharged. If the drug court team determines that administrative discharge is appropriate, the drug court staff shall complete a Request for Voluntary Termination to provide to the drug court judge, and the drug court judge shall grant or deny the request. If granted, the Notice of Administrative Discharge shall be filed in the official court record and the case referred back to the appropriate circuit or district court.

(2) An administrative discharge does not preclude eligibility for drug court at a later date.

HISTORY: Amended by Order 2010–05, eff. 3–23–10; prior amendment eff. 7–30–09 (Order 2009–07); adopted by Order 2006–01, eff. 1–9–06

AP XIII, Sec. 15   Voluntary termination

(1) Participants may request voluntary termination from drug court utilizing a Request for Voluntary Termination. If the drug court judge determines that the request is knowingly and voluntarily made, the drug court judge shall grant the request.

(2) Upon voluntary termination, the participant shall be ineligible for further participation in any Kentucky adult criminal drug court.

HISTORY: Amended by Order 2010–05, eff. 3–23–10; prior amendment eff. 7–30–09 (Order 2009–07); adopted by Order 2006–01, eff. 1–9–06

AP XIII, Sec. 16   Involuntary termination from drug court

(1) The drug court staff or team may make a recommendation to the drug court judge that a participant be terminated from drug court due to the participant's non-compliance with drug court requirements or conditions. If the drug court judge agrees with the recommendation of termination, drug court staff shall complete a Notification of Violations and Termination requesting the judge to terminate the participant from drug court. The participant shall be notified of the termination in the drug court session, unless the participant has absconded. Upon signature of the Notification of Violations and Termination by the drug court judge, the case shall be referred back to the appropriate circuit or district court for further proceedings. The Notification of Violations and Termination shall be filed in the official record by the circuit court clerk.

(2) In the case of a participant who has absconded for a period of at least ten working days, drug court staff shall complete a Notification of Violations and Termination. Upon signature of the Notification of Violations and Termination by the drug court judge, the case shall be referred back to the appropriate circuit or district court for further proceedings. The

Notification of Violations and Termination shall be filed in the official record.

(3) Upon involuntary termination, a participant shall be ineligible for further participation in any Kentucky adult criminal drug court.

HISTORY: Amended by Order 2010–05, eff. 3–23–10; prior amendment eff. 7–30–09 (Order 2009–07); adopted by Order 2006–01, eff. 1–9–06

AP XIII, Sec. 17 Successful completion of drug court

(1) A participant shall be determined to have successfully completed drug court after:

(a) Completing all three drug court phases;

(b) Completing aftercare;

(c) Paying all restitution owed; if the participant is unable to pay restitution in full while in drug court, the drug court team may require a reasonable amount be paid to comply with this provision; and

(d) Paying all costs, fines or fees.

(2) Successful completion requires that no criminal charges be pending against the participant.

(3) Upon successful completion of drug court, the drug court judge may:

(a) Dismiss the underlying charge(s), if the participant was on diversion, but only when restitution, if any, has been paid in full; or

(b) Modify probation to be conditionally discharged if the participant was on probation or found in contempt of court, but only when restitution, if any, has been paid in full.

(4) A drug court graduation should be held for an eligible participant within 90 days of successful completion of Phase III of drug court as outlined above, but in no event shall a drug court graduation be held later than 210 days after successful completion of Phase III.

HISTORY: Amended by Order 2010–05, eff. 3–23–10; prior amendment eff. 7–30–09 (Order 2009–07); adopted by Order 2006–01, eff. 1–9–06

AP XIII, Sec. 18 Drug court staffing

(1) The drug court judge and drug court staff shall attend staffing prior to drug court sessions. The prosecutor, defense attorney, and other drug court team members are encouraged to attend these staffings. Drug court staffings shall be confidential and non-team members shall not attend absent extraordinary circumstances. If there is an extraordinary need for a non-team member to attend, upon approval by the drug court judge, the non-team member shall be allowed to attend the staffing, but only after signing a confidentiality agreement.

(2) At drug court staffings, the drug court team shall discuss the following:

(a) Whether to admit potential participants into drug court;

(b) Appropriate sanctions for violations by current participants;

(c) Achievements and phase advancement of participants who will appear at the drug court session; and

(d) Other pertinent issues relating to drug court participants.

HISTORY: Amended by Order 2010–05, eff. 3–23–10; Amended eff. 7–30–09 (Order 2009–07); adopted by Order 2006–01, eff. 1–9–06

AP XIII, Sec. 19 Drug court sessions

A drug court judge shall conduct a drug court session as follows:

(1) In a single-county circuit or district, one drug court session shall be conducted per week.

(2) In a multi-county circuit or district, one drug court session should be held per week; however, if weekly sessions are not possible, a drug court judge shall conduct at least two drug court sessions per month. If drug court sessions are not held every week, drug court staff shall meet with participants at the same time that drug court regularly meets.

HISTORY: Amended by Order 2010–05, eff. 3–23–10; prior amendment eff. 7–30–09 (Order 2009–07); adopted by Order 2006–01, eff. 1–9–06

AP XIII, Sec. 20 Confidentiality

(1) Drug court proceedings shall be confidential and all proceedings shall be closed unless otherwise authorized by the drug court judge.

(2) Documents contained in a participant's drug court case file shall be confidential and shall not be released other than those documents specified in Section 21 of these rules.

(3) In accordance with federal regulations regarding substance abuse treatment programs, drug court team members shall sign a confidentiality agreement.

(4) Drug court team members shall comply with state and federal confidentiality laws regarding treatment information.

HISTORY: Amended by Order 2010–05, eff. 3–23–10; prior amendment eff. 7–30–09 (Order 2009–07); adopted by Order 2006–01, eff. 1–9–06

AP XIII, Sec. 21 Filing of drug court documents

Upon utilization of any of the following documents, the document(s) shall be filed by the drug court staff with the appropriate court clerk for inclusion in the court record of the underlying criminal offense:

(1) Order Referring to Drug Court;

(2) Drug Court Notice of Defendant Referral Status;

(3) Order of Admission;

(4) Motion for Transfer

(5) Order Transferring;

(6) Order Designating Temporary Inactive Status;

(7) Order Resuming Active Status;

(8) Notice of Voluntary Termination;

(9) Notice of Violations and Termination; and

(10) Acknowledgement of Successful Completion, or Notice of Administrative Discharge.

HISTORY: Amended by Order 2010–05, eff. 3–23–10; prior amendment eff. 7–30–09 (Order 2009–07); adopted by Order 2006–01, eff. 1–9–06

AP XIII, Sec. 22   Collection of fees

(1) A reimbursement fee may be imposed by drug court for treatment services, the cost of a laboratory confirmation of a positive drug test, or other required services.

(2) Reimbursement fees shall be in the form of certified checks, cashier's checks or money orders, each of which shall be made payable to the Kentucky State Treasurer. At no time shall drug court staff accept cash from a participant.

(3) No judge or drug court staff shall collect monies for use for drug court through forfeiture, plea agreements, sanctions, fees, fines or other costs, other than those referred to herein.

HISTORY: Amended by Order 2010–05, eff. 3–23–10; prior amendment eff. 7–30–09 (Order 2009–07); adopted by Order 2006–01, eff. 1–9–06

AP XIII, Sec. 23   Drug testing

(1) Drug testing shall be administered to all drug court participants on a frequent and random basis. Phase I participants shall be tested at least three times per week; Phase II participants shall be tested at least two times per week; and Phase III participants shall be tested at least one time per week.

(2) Drug tests performed pursuant to subsection (1) by individuals other than the drug court staff, the drug court team, or the AOC authorized drug testing vendor, shall not be admissible in drug court.

(3) All drug court participants shall be required to make daily telephone contact, utilizing a toll-free telephone number, wherein a recording announces phase(s) and times for specimen collections for each individual drug court.

(4) Instant, laboratory, and other drug tests supplied by drug court shall be utilized for drug court participants only. Inventory of supplies shall be audited on a random basis.

(5) Medically supervised detoxification or treatment that will affect drug testing on a temporary basis may be authorized by the drug court judge. However, medically supervised detoxification or treatment that will affect drug testing beyond a 6–month period shall not be authorized and shall preclude a participant from initiating or continuing participation in drug court.

HISTORY: Amended by Order 2010–05, eff. 3–23–10; prior amendment eff. 7–30–09 (Order 2009–07); adopted by Order 2006–01, eff. 1–9–06

PART XIV
PRETRIAL SERVICES

AP XIV, Sec. 1   Administering oath on affidavit of indigency

A pretrial officer may administer an oath to an affiant on an affidavit of indigency completed pursuant to KRS Chapter 31, KRS 431.515, and Rule of Criminal Procedure 4.06.

HISTORY: Adopted by Order 2009–02, eff. 1–12–09

AP XIV, Sec. 2

1. Within twenty-four hours of a defendant's incarceration on a bailable offense, Pretrial Services must provide the judge or trial commissioner with information to assist the determination of pretrial release and supervision, including an assessment of risks posed by the defendant and recommendations for responding to

the risks through use of appropriate conditions of release.

2. Information provided to the judge or trial commissioner will be obtained through Pretrial Services' investigation, including the interview of the defendant and the risk assessment.

3. Failure by Pretrial Services to present this information to the judge or trial commissioner within twenty-four hours of a defendant's incarceration will not result in the automatic release of a defendant.

4. The twenty-four hour time period referenced in this rule will revert to a twelve-hour time period on June 30, 2013, absent further orders of the Court.

HISTORY: Adopted by Order 2012–13, eff. 10–21–12

PART XV
DOMESTIC VIOLENCE

Under KRS 403.761(9)(c), the Supreme Court of Kentucky hereby establishes the following sliding scale of indigency as a guideline for judges to use in determining the amount a respondent must pay for a global positioning monitoring system in a domestic violence case:

Federal Poverty Guidelines	Percentage Respondent is to Pay
200%	100%
175%	75%
150%	50%
125%	25%
100%	0%

The Federal Poverty Guidelines are established annually by the U.S. Department of Health and Human Services. The 2010 Poverty Guidelines for the 48 Contiguous States may be located in the *Federal Register*, Vol. 75, No. 148, August 3, 2010, pp. 45628–45629, or as set forth below:

2010 Federal Poverty Guidelines for the 48 Contiguous States	
Persons in family	Poverty guideline
1	$10,830
2	$14,570
3	$18,310
4	$22,050
5	$25,790
6	$29,530
7	$33,270
8	$37,010

For families with more than 8 persons, add $3,740 for each additional person.

If a judge finds that the fee would impose an undue burden on the respondent, the judge may reduce or waive the fee. The sliding scale is intended only as a guideline for judges, who are encouraged to use discretion in applying the factors listed on Form AOC–275.14 when making an indigency determination for purposes of the global positioning monitoring system.

The sliding scale will be updated annually to reflect the most current Federal Poverty Guidelines.

HISTORY: Adopted by Order 2010–08, eff. 9–15–10

PART XVI
CIRCUIT COURT CLERKS CONDUCT COMMISSION

Circuit court clerks play a key role in the administration of justice. From maintaining official records to collecting fees, fines, and costs, circuit court clerks perform a variety of duties prescribed by Kentucky's constitution, statutes, rules, and administrative procedures that are integral to Court of Justice operations. Therefore, it is essential that circuit court clerks uphold high standards of integrity, impartiality, and independence in order to promote public confidence in the judicial system.

As elected officials, circuit court clerks are ultimately accountable to the voters in their counties for their conduct in office. However, pursuant to KRS 30A.010, circuit court clerks are also state officers who are subject to the administrative control of the Chief Justice.

These rules and the Circuit Court Clerks Conduct Commission created herein are intended to assist the Chief Justice in determining whether disciplinary action and/or remedial measures against a circuit court clerk for alleged official misconduct or otherwise improper conduct is warranted. These rules shall govern the handling of complaints against circuit court clerks alleged to have engaged in such conduct.

HISTORY: Adopted by Order 2013–01, eff. 1–1–13

AP XVI, Sec. 2 Definitions

For the purpose of these rules, unless the context or subject matter otherwise requires:

(1) "AOC" means the Administrative Office of the Courts.

(2) "Chairperson" and "Vice Chairperson" refer to members of the Circuit Court Clerks Conduct Commission who have been elected to these offices by vote of the Committee. Whenever used herein, the word "Chairperson" shall include, in the absence of the Chairperson, the Vice Chairperson or other member acting as Chairperson.

(3) "Chief Justice" means the Chief Justice of the Commonwealth of Kentucky.

(4) "Clerk" means anyone currently serving in the position of Circuit Court Clerk for the Commonwealth of Kentucky, whether elected or appointed, and whether serving in a permanent or temporary capacity.

(5) "Committee" means the Circuit Court Clerks Conduct Commission.

(6) "Complainant" means an individual, organization, or entity who has communicated to the Circuit Court Clerks Conduct Commission a complaint against a clerk.

(7) "Complaint" means a written statement from an individual, organization, or entity, to the Circuit Court Clerks Conduct Commission, alleging facts that might constitute official misconduct or otherwise improper conduct as identified in Section 6, pursuant to Kentucky's constitution, statutes, rules, and administrative procedures.

(8) "Disciplinary actions" means actions intended to be punitive in nature. Disciplinary actions shall consist of those sanctions and penalties set out in Section 6(1).

(9) "Final disposition" of an investigation conducted pursuant to these rules means all final disciplinary action(s) taken and/or remedial measure(s) imposed by the Chief Justice after reviewing the Committee's findings and recommendations.

(10) "Remedial measures" means actions intended to be corrective in nature and to serve, where relevant and appropriate under the circumstances, as alternatives or in addition to those disciplinary actions set out in Section 6(1). Remedial measures may include, but shall be not be limited to, those measures set out in Section 6(2).

(11) "Secretary" refers to a member of the Circuit Court Clerks Conduct Commission who has been elected to this office by vote of the Committee.

(12) "Special Investigator" means an investigator designated by the Circuit Court Clerks Conduct Commission to assist it in the investigation of a complaint against a clerk, and to take any other action related thereto which the Committee may direct.

(13) "Supreme Court" means the Supreme Court of Kentucky.

HISTORY: Adopted by Order 2013–01, eff. 1–1–13

AP XVI, Sec. 3 Composition of committee

(1) The Committee shall consist of seven members, to include four clerks, one sitting or retired judge appointed by the Chief Justice, one lawyer in good-standing with the Kentucky Bar Association appointed by the Chief Justice, and one citizen member appointed by the Kentucky Association of Circuit Court Clerks.

(2) For purposes of appointment of the clerk members, the President of the Kentucky Association of Circuit Court Clerks will submit a list of ten names to the Chief Justice to be considered for appointment. The Chief Justice will appoint four members from the list.

(3) An alternate member for each member of the Committee will be designated at the time of appointment in the same manner as delineated in Sections 3(1) and 3(2) of these Administrative Procedures.

(4) Each member and alternate member will serve a three-year term from the time of appointment.

(5) A member of the Committee will not participate in any investigation in which he or she has an interest, relationship or bias, such that his or her impartiality might reasonably be questioned. Disqualification pursuant to this subsection will be by majority vote of the Committee members present.

(6) If a Committee member cannot participate in a particular investigation by reason of temporary disqualification or inability to serve for any reason, one or more alternate members may serve to maintain the same membership composition of the Committee.

(7) If a Committee member ceases to be qualified for membership, resigns or becomes permanently unable to serve for any reason, either the Chief Justice or the Kentucky Association of Circuit Court Clerks will fill the vacancy for the duration of the unexpired term in the same manner as delineated in Sections 3(1) and 3(2) of these Administrative Procedures.

HISTORY: Adopted by Order 2013–01, eff. 1–1–13

AP XVI, Sec. 4 Organization of committee

(1) A Chairperson, Vice–Chairperson, and Secretary will be elected annually by the members of the Committee.

(2) Meetings of the Committee will be held upon the call of the Chairperson or the written request of at least two members of the Committee. Meetings will not be held on less than two days' notice, unless otherwise agreed upon by all Committee members. The Chairperson shall preside at meetings of the Committee. The Vice Chairperson shall act in the absence or disqualification of the Chairperson. In the absence or disqualification of both the Chairperson

and the Vice Chairperson, the members shall select one among them as acting Chairperson.

(3) A quorum of the Committee shall consist of five (5) members, including at least two members who are clerks. A majority vote of the Committee members present is required to make recommendations to the Chief Justice regarding a disciplinary action and/or remedial measure. A meeting may be held and a vote may be taken by telephone or video conference unless any member objects.

HISTORY: Adopted by Order 2013–01, eff. 1–1–13

AP XVI, Sec. 5 Special investigator

At any stage of the investigation, and upon approval by the Chief Justice, the Committee may designate a special investigator to gather and present evidence before the Committee, and to take any other action related to the investigation as the Committee may direct.

HISTORY: Adopted by Order 2013–01, eff. 1–1–13

AP XVI, Sec. 6 Authority of the committee

The Committee will have authority to recommend to the Chief Justice the following disciplinary action(s) and/or remedial measure(s). Remedial measures may be used, where relevant and appropriate under the circumstances, as alternatives or in addition to those disciplinary actions set out below in subsection (1).

(1) Disciplinary actions:

(a) Temporary suspension of a clerk from the performance of his or her duties, without affecting his or her pay status, when: (i) there is pending in any state or federal court of the United States an indictment or information charging him or her with a crime punishable as a felony; or (ii) it would be in the best interest of the public that he or she be suspended from acting in his or her official capacity as a clerk until final disposition of an investigation.

(b) Sanctions, separately or collectively, of public or private reprimand, suspension with pay, or institution of removal proceedings before the Supreme Court, when the Committee finds sufficient evidence of any one or more of the following:

(i) Misconduct in office.

(ii) Any willful refusal or persistent failure to perform the duties and obligations as set forth in the Constitution of Kentucky, Kentucky Revised Statutes, Kentucky Supreme Court Rules, including the Kentucky Rules of Civil and Criminal Procedure, and applicable portions of the Administrative Procedures of the Court of Justice, Part III.

(iii) Professional incompetence.

(iv) Habitual intemperance.

(v) Any willful refusal or persistent failure to conform to official policies and directives adopted by the Supreme Court or issued by the Chief Justice in his constitutional capacity as Chief Executive Officer of the Court of Justice.

(vi) Conviction of a crime.

(c) Institution of removal proceedings before the Supreme Court of Kentucky against a clerk whom it finds to lack the qualifications for the office of Kentucky Circuit Court Clerk pursuant to the Constitution of Kentucky, Kentucky Revised Statutes, and Rules of the Supreme Court of Kentucky.

(2) Remedial measures may include but shall not be limited to:

(a) Training, education, and/or development.

(b) Counseling or support groups.

(c) Implementation of a plan addressing the misconduct.

(d) Monitoring the clerk's conduct.

(e) Mentoring.

(f) Referral to relevant policies.

HISTORY: Adopted by Order 2013–01, eff. 1–1–13

AP XVI, Sec. 7 Confidentiality

(1) Except as otherwise provided in these rules, information regarding the existence and details of a complaint, any and all information related to an investigation conducted pursuant thereto, and all other records, files, and reports of the Committee must be kept confidential and will not be disclosed, except as follows:

(a) Upon inquiry by a state or federal agency conducting a criminal investigation, but only information relevant to the investigation will be provided;

(b) Upon order of a court of competent jurisdiction for good cause shown; or

(c) As otherwise required by law.

(2) Except as provided in subsection (1) above, the Committee shall only be authorized to release, upon receiving written request, final disciplinary action(s) taken and/or remedial measure(s) imposed by the Chief Justice against a clerk, and the date of such action(s). The Committee shall provide written notice to a clerk of all such third party requests.

(3) Breach of confidentiality may be deemed grounds for removal of a Committee member and for discharge of any of its agents. Any member so removed, or agent so discharged, shall not be eligible thereafter to serve on the Committee or at its direction.

(4) If, in the course of its proceedings, the Committee becomes aware of credible evidence that any person has committed a crime, the Committee may report such evidence to the appropriate law enforcement agency.

(5) Nothing in this section shall preclude the Committee from taking such action(s) as may be necessary

to conduct inquiries and investigations in accordance with Section 8.

HISTORY: Adopted by Order 2013–01, eff. 1–1–13

AP XVI, Sec. 8   Complaint/preliminary inquiry/investigation

(1) All complaints must be in writing; include the complainant's name, address, and telephone number; be signed by the complainant; and allege specific facts demonstrating why the complainant believes that official misconduct or otherwise improper conduct has occurred. The complaint may be on the form provided by the Administrative Office of the Courts. The complaint may be initiated by the Committee itself or by any individual, organization, or entity.

(2) Upon receiving a written complaint concerning a clerk, the Committee shall determine whether the complaint states facts which, if true, would constitute official misconduct or otherwise improper conduct for which the clerk may be subject to disciplinary action(s) and/or remedial measure(s) under Section 6. If it appears to the Committee that no such conduct has occurred even if the alleged facts are true, no further inquiry shall be made, and the Committee shall report same to the Chief Justice.

(3) If it appears to the Committee that the complaint states facts which, if true, would constitute official misconduct or otherwise improper conduct for which the clerk may be subject to disciplinary action(s) and/or remedial measures under Section 6, it shall make preliminary inquiry as follows: Notice of the complaint shall be given to the clerk by certified mail, return receipt requested, and will be marked "Personal and Confidential." The notice shall:

(a) include the name of the complainant and a written statement that no retaliation shall be taken against the complainant;

(b) include a copy of the complaint;

(c) instruct the clerk that he or she shall provide a written response to the complaint, to be postmarked no later than twenty days after receipt of the notice;

(d) instruct the clerk to include in the response the names of persons who may have relevant information pertaining to the allegations contained in the complaint; and

(e) instruct the clerk that he or she has the right to retain legal counsel at his or her own expense.

(4) If, after reviewing the clerk's response, the Committee determines there is not good cause to proceed with an investigation, it shall report same to the Chief Justice. If, however, the Committee determines there is good cause to proceed with an investigation, or in the event the clerk fails to timely provide the response required in subsection (3) above, the Committee shall commence an investigation to determine whether disciplinary action(s) and/or remedial

measure(s) should be recommended. In either event, the clerk shall be notified in writing.

(5) At any stage of the investigation, the Committee or its special investigator may conduct interviews or take statements, whether or not taken under oath. Interviews should include all relevant persons, including but not limited to, the complainant, the clerk, and witnesses.

(6) Upon conclusion of its investigation, the Committee shall submit written findings of fact and recommendation(s) to the Chief Justice. The Chief Justice shall be entitled to view the file of the matter if he so desires.

(7) The Committee shall make its recommendation(s) to the Chief Justice within ninety days of the commencement of the investigation. An investigation is "commenced" upon the Committee's determination that there is good cause to proceed with an investigation. The Committee may request in writing an extension of time not to exceed thirty days, which extension may be granted by the Chief Justice for good cause shown.

(8) Final action(s) taken by the Chief Justice shall be placed in the Committee's file of the matter.

HISTORY: Adopted by Order 2013–01, eff. 1–1–13

AP XVI, Sec. 9   General provisions

(1) Members and agents of the Committee, including the special investigator, shall be absolutely immune from suit for all conduct in the course of their official duties. A complaint submitted to the Committee, and communications related thereto, shall be absolutely privileged, and no civil action predicated on the complaint or on such communications may be instituted against any complainant or witness or their counsel; provided, however, such immunity from suit shall apply only to communications to the Committee and shall not apply to public disclosure of information contained in or relating to the complaint.

(2) In the event that a clerk under investigation resigns, the Committee may, upon a finding that the integrity of the judicial branch and the interest of the administration of justice would be served, continue its investigation in order to make recommendation(s) to the Chief Justice.

(3) Members of the Committee shall not be compensated but shall be reimbursed for actual expenses incurred by them in attending Committee meetings and conducting investigations, in accordance with the current travel regulations of the Court of Justice.

(4) The Committee shall keep a file of all complaints and investigations concerning a clerk. All such files shall be maintained in the AOC's Office of General Counsel. No person, including the clerk, shall have access to such files except as provided in Section 7 above.

HISTORY: Adopted by Order 2013–01, eff. 1–1–13

AP XVI, Sec. 10   Powers of chief justice

(1) Nothing in these rules shall limit the administrative powers of the Chief Justice under Section 110(5)(b) of the Constitution of Kentucky and KRS 30A.010(2).

(2) Recommendations made by the Committee pursuant to Section 8 herein shall not be binding upon the Chief Justice, nor shall any such recommendations raise a presumption in any proceeding before any court of the Commonwealth.

HISTORY: Adopted by Order 2013–01, eff. 1–1–13

BY-LAWS OF THE KENTUCKY BAR ASSOCIATION

Including Amendments Received Through January 1, 2013

Section 1 Definitions

The definitions embodied in SCR 3.010 are hereby adopted as a part of these By-laws.

HISTORY: Amended by Order 96–1, eff. 1–1–97; approved eff. 11–11–69

Section 2 Honorary memberships

During the term of office of each Justice or Judge of the Court of Justice and each United States Judge in or who is appointed from or maintains a residence in Kentucky they shall be an honorary member of the Association and shall pay to the Treasurer, under SCR 3.040, dues in such sum as may be fixed by the Supreme Court. The Board may by resolution designate members 75 years of age, 50 year members, and other members of the Association as honorary members in recognition of outstanding professional achievement, either for life or for some other designated period of time, who shall not be required to pay dues.

HISTORY: Amended by Order 96–1, eff. 1–1–97; prior amendments eff. 9–30–83, 1–11–78; approved eff. 11–11–69

Section 3 Annual and midyear conventions of the Association

(a) An annual convention of the Association, open to all members in good standing shall be held at such time, during the months of May or June, and at such place, as the Board may designate.

(b) A midyear convention of the Association shall be held at such time and such place as the Board may designate.

The President and/or Executive Director of the Association shall, as soon as possible after the fixing of said dates, notify each presiding Circuit Judge of the dates of said conventions for the purpose of encouraging the Circuit Judge to arrange the trial schedule of the Court so as not to interfere with the dates of said conventions.

HISTORY: Amended by Order 96–1, eff. 1–1–97; prior amendment eff. 9–30–83; approved eff. 11–11–69

Section 4 The Board of Governors

(a) The term of office of each Governor shall commence on July 1 next following their election and shall be for a period of two years and/or until their successor is elected and qualified.

(b) Any member of the Association in good standing shall be eligible for nomination and election to the Board of Governors from the Supreme Court District in which the member resides.

(c) Nomination of a candidate for the Board shall be by written petition signed by not less than twenty members in good standing who are residents of that Supreme Court District. All nominating petitions shall be received by the Executive Director at the Kentucky Bar Center prior to 5:00 p.m., Eastern Time, of the last regular business day of the month of October. If only one candidate is nominated in a District, he/she shall be declared elected to that office and the Executive Director shall at once so certify to the Board and the candidate. Where two or more candidates are nominated, an election shall be held as provided in Section 9.

(d) Any vacancy on the Board or in the office of President–Elect or Vice President shall be filled for the remainder of the term by appointment by the President, subject to the written approval of a majority of the Board of Governors. However, upon a vote of a majority of the Board a special election may be called for filling such vacancy.

(e) The Board shall hold regular meetings at such place and at such time as it may from time to time direct during the months of January, March, May, July, September and November, and immediately preceding the first day of the annual convention of the Association. It shall hold special meetings on the call of the President at such time and place as the President may designate. Special meetings may be called by the President whenever necessary, and shall be called by the President upon the written request of four or more members of the Board. Any of these meetings may be cancelled upon vote of the majority of the Board of Governors.

(f) Eleven members of the Board shall constitute a quorum. Except as otherwise provided in the Rules, the vote of a majority of those present and voting shall be necessary to take action.

HISTORY: Amended eff. 10–14–10; prior amendments eff. 2–3–00 (Order 99–1), 2–1–00, 1–1–97 (Order 96–1); approved eff. 11–11–69

Section 5　Officers

The officers of the Association and of the Board, their duties, tenure, and manner of selection shall be:

(a) The President.

The President shall be the chief executive officer, and preside at all meetings of the Association and of the Board. The President shall be a member of the Board with full power to vote on all matters which it may consider. The President shall perform all duties imposed by the Rules and by these By–Laws. The President's term of office shall be for one year and shall commence on July 1 in the second calendar year next succeeding election as President–Elect.

(b) The President–Elect.

The President–Elect shall be nominated and elected as hereinafter provided and shall hold such office until he/she assumes the office of President. The President–Elect shall endeavor to thoroughly familiarize himself/herself with the duties of the President and the work of the Association and of the Board.

(c) The President and President–Elect shall, during their tenure and for a period of four years thereafter be ineligible to serve as elected members of the Board.

(d) The Vice President.

The Vice President shall be nominated and elected as hereinafter provided. The Vice President's term of office shall commence on July 1 next succeeding his/her election and shall continue for one year. The Vice President shall perform the duties of the President during the absence or disability of the President. If a vacancy shall exist in the office of President, the Vice President shall succeed to that office for the remainder of the term.

(e) The Executive Director.

The Executive Director shall be appointed by the Board and shall hold office at its pleasure. The Executive Director shall maintain an office at such place in Kentucky as may be directed by the Board. The Executive Director shall be the custodian of all records, charges, complaints, transcripts and other documents filed in his/her office or with the Board or any committee, or made by the Board, or certified to him/her by the Recording Secretary of the House. The Executive Director shall keep a record of the proceedings of the Board; provided, that the Board may order any part of its records expunged. In the absence or disability of the Executive Director a member of the Board shall be appointed Acting Executive Director by the Board. The Board may appoint an assistant or assistants to the Executive Director who shall also perform such other duties as are required by the Board.

(f) The Registrar and Deputy Registrar.

The Registrar and Deputy Registrar shall be appointed by and hold office at the pleasure of the Chief Justice. They shall maintain their offices at the Association's headquarters in accordance with the provisions of SCR 3.100. They shall be the custodian of all accounting records, the roster of members and such other information pertaining to Association membership as required by SCR 3.060 or as may be prescribed either by the Court or by the Board. The Registrar's office shall constitute the principal office of the Association, and all transfer files of the Board of Governors, House of Delegates, President and Treasurer, except current files in active cases, shall be deposited with the Registrar and shall be available at all times to the Court and the Board.

(g) The Treasurer.

The Treasurer and Assistant Treasurer shall be appointed by the Board and hold office at its pleasure. The Treasurer shall be the fiscal officer of the Association and of the Board. It shall be the Treasurer's duty to collect all funds due to the Association and the Board, and to receive and disburse funds for the Association under direction of the Board. The Treasurer shall keep accurate books and records of accounts, and at least quarterly (and at more frequent intervals when required by the Board) shall make a written report showing the then-current financial position of the Association, and all receipts and disbursements since the date of his/her last report. In the absence or disability of the Treasurer, a member of the Board shall be named by the President to perform the duties of the Treasurer.

(h) Any vacancy in the offices of President–Elect and Vice President shall be filled for the remainder of the term by appointment by the President subject to the written approval of a majority of the members of the Board.

(i) Executive Committee.

An Executive Committee of the Board of Governors shall consist of the following officers of the Bar: The President, who shall serve as Chair of the Executive Committee, the Immediate Past President, the President-Elect, the Vice-President, Chair of the Young Lawyers Section, and the Executive Director. The Executive Committee shall advise the President on matters concerning the operations of the Bar and provide a forum for discussion and recommendation to the Board of Governors including matters of long range planning. The Executive Committee may also act on matters of an emergency nature that may affect the Bar. When the Executive Director becomes aware of any matter that may require Executive Committee action the Executive Director shall immediately advise the President. The President shall advise the Board of any action taken or any recommendation made by the Executive Committee at the next Board meeting. The Executive Committee shall meet at such times as may be called by the President.

HISTORY: Amended eff. 10–14–10; prior amendments eff. 1–1–06 (Order 2005–10), 1–1–97 (Order 96–1), 4–19–85, 12–30–74; approved eff. 11–11–69

Section 6   Nomination of officers

(a) Nomination to the offices of Vice-President and President-Elect shall be made by written petition as herein provided. All candidates for office shall be members of the Association in good standing.

(b) Nominations for the offices of Vice-President and President-Elect shall be made by written petition signed by not less than one hundred members of the Association in good standing, with not less than ten signatures on the written petition being from each Supreme Court District. Only one candidate may be nominated on a single petition and any number of petitions may be filed for a candidate.

(c) All nominating petitions for the office of Vice-President and President-Elect shall be filed with the Executive Director between October 15 and November 15 in each year. Where only one candidate has been duly nominated for an office that candidate shall be declared elected and the Executive Director shall so certify to the Board and the nominee on or before December 15 in that year.

HISTORY: Amended by Order 2005–10, eff. 1–1–06; prior amendment eff. 1–1–97 (Order 96–1); approved eff. 11–11–69

Section 7   House of Delegates—Deleted

HISTORY: Deleted by Order 2005–10, eff. 1–1–06; prior amendment eff. 1–1–97 (Order 96–1); approved eff. 11–11–69

Section 8   Officers of the House—duties, tenure and manner of selection—Deleted

HISTORY: Deleted by Order 2005–10, eff. 1–1–06; prior amendments eff. 1–1–97 (Order 96–1), 12–30–74; approved eff. 11–11–69

Section 9   Elections

Ballots for the offices of President-Elect, Vice-President, members of the Board of Governors for which there will be an election will be prepared by the Executive Director and will be mailed on December 15 with return envelopes as hereinafter provided, to each member of the Association in good standing entitled to vote in that election. Names of candidates shall be listed on the ballots in alphabetical order with each position being voted upon.

The ballot shall be sealed by the member in an unmarked inner return envelope, which, in turn shall be sealed in an outer return envelope containing the words: "Official Ballot–Not to be opened until January 16" and lines for the signature and county address of the attorney casting the ballot.

All ballots must be received not later than January 15 by the Clerk who shall keep all such ballots in a locked box. Such box shall be opened only at the meeting of the canvassing board to tabulate the votes. Not later than January 20 the canvassing board, appointed by the President, shall meet in the office of the Clerk, or at such other place as may be designated by the President, and canvass the votes. Each candidate for a position shall be entitled to have present at the meeting of the canvassing board an official observer under a written and signed designation by such candidate. No candidate may be present at the meeting of the canvassing board.

A plurality of all votes cast for each position shall be sufficient to elect. The canvassing board shall make and file with the Clerk a written certification of each election, with a copy thereof to the Executive Director who shall promptly notify each candidate of the results of the election.

HISTORY: Amended by Order 2005–10, eff. 1–1–06; prior amendment eff. 1–1–97 (Order 96–1); approved eff. 11–11–69

Section 10   District bar programs

There shall be held each year at least one district bar program in each Supreme Court District as provided in SCR 3.651.

HISTORY: Amended by Order 96–1, eff. 1–1–97; approved eff. 11–11–69

Section 11   Sections

(a) **Sections.** There are created the following sections within the Kentucky Bar Association:

(1) Business Law.

(2) Criminal Law.

(3) Family Law.

(4) Civil Litigation.

(5) Labor and Employment Law.

(6) Probate and Trust Law.

(7) Taxation.

(8) Young Lawyers.

(9) Public Interest Law.

(10) Corporate House Counsel.

(11) Environment, Energy & Natural Resources Law.

(12) Local Government Law.

(13) Workers' Compensation Law.

(14) Real Property Law.

(15) Bankruptcy Law.

(16) Senior Lawyers.

(17) Equine Law.

(18) Education Law.

(19) Construction and Public Contract Law.

(20) Small Firm Practice & Management.

(21) Health Care Law.

(22) Alternative Dispute Resolution.

(23) Appellate Advocacy.

(b) Eligibility. All members in good standing of the Kentucky Bar Association shall be eligible for membership in any one or more of the Sections of the Kentucky Bar Association and may become members by paying the respective dues as designated by each Section.

(c) Officers. Officers for each Section shall include, but need not be limited to, a Chair, a Chair–Elect, and a Vice–Chair, who shall be elected for a term of one or two years, from and by its own membership present and voting at the required annual Section meeting, which shall take place during the annual meeting of the Association or as scheduled by the Section prior to the end of the current fiscal year ending June 30th. Each section shall specify the term of office in the Section by-laws which term may be of either one year or two years in duration. No individual may serve in any one of the required offices of the Section for a period of greater than two years. If a Section fails to fill the required offices at their annual meeting, the Board of Governors, following a petition from the Section, may appoint an interim officer to fill the remainder of the term.

(d) Dues. A majority of the members of the Section in attendance at the annual meeting of the Section may fix dues for the Section. The dues shall be paid to the Treasurer (of the KBA) and disbursed by the Treasurer for programs of each Section as approved by the Executive Director.

(e) By–Laws. Every Section shall have a set of by-laws, which shall include a Section mission statement, describing the purpose of their existence. A majority of the members of the Section in attendance of the annual meeting of the Section shall adopt the by-laws which shall be subject to the approval of the Board of Governors and the Supreme Court, pursuant to the provisions of SCR 3.090.

(f) Annual Report. Each section shall annually file with the Board, on or before the annual meeting, a report of Section activities which shall outline the activities and expenditures of the Section for the current fiscal year ending June 30th.

(g) Forecast Report. Every Section's incoming chair shall submit to the Board on or before the August 1st following their election as chair, an outline of the Section's proposed activities, expenditures and meetings for the ensuing fiscal year.

(h) Approval of Activities and Projects. All Section programs projects, expenditures (excluding routine in-state travel in support of Section activities, programs or projects) and meetings shall be preapproved in writing by the Executive Director.

(i) New Sections. A new Section of the Kentucky Bar Association may be created upon the Board's approval following the submission of an application and petition by a current Kentucky Bar Association member, which shall include the following:

(1) a description of the area(s) of practice the Section will cover;

(2) statement of need and purpose;

(3) signatures of a minimum of one hundred (100) current Kentucky Bar Association members who are interested in seeing the formation of the proposed Section.

Establishment of the Section shall become effective at the start of the following fiscal year following the Court's approval.

(j) Abolition. Upon notice by mail to all current members of a Section, the Board of Governors may abolish a Section, which would take effect at the end of the fiscal year in which notice was given.

HISTORY: Amended eff. 10–14–10; prior amendments eff. 9–1–07, 1–1–06 (Order 2005–10), 1–1–02 (Order 2001–2), 4–16–97, 1–1–97, 2–26–96, 4–19–93, 9–8–92, 9–25–91, 5–18–90, 8–25–89, 6–23–87, 2–15–84, 1–14–83, 10–6–82, 6–8–81, 10–6–80; approved eff. 11–11–69

Section 12   Committees

(a) The Association shall have such committees as may be designated by the Supreme Court.

(b) The Association shall have such standing committees and special committees as the Board may from time to time authorize.

(c) Standing Committees shall include:

(1) Ethics Committee

(2) Unauthorized Practice of Law Committee

(3) Communications & Publications Committee

(4) Diversity in the Profession Committee

(d) Membership and Term of Service. Unless otherwise provided by Rule the following shall apply for membership and terms of service for committees. Each committee shall have at least one member from each Supreme Court District. Each year the President shall appoint a Chair for each committee and one or more members of the Board shall be appointed to each committee whose terms will be for one (1) year. Beginning July 1, 1997, terms of service for all other committee members shall be staggered with one-third appointed for three-year terms, one-third appointed for two-year terms and one-third appointed for one-year terms. A member may be reappointed to a committee but in no event shall a member serve on a committee longer than six (6) consecutive years without a break in service of at least two (2) years. The Board, by majority vote, may modify limits on terms of committees.

(e) Meetings. Each committee shall meet at least one time during the months of June, July or August, and shall meet at such other times as designated by the committee chair or the President.

HISTORY: Amended eff. 10–22–09; prior amendments eff. 10–13–08, 1–1–06 (Order 2005–10), 3–1–98 (Order 97–3), 1–1–97, 7–18–92, 9–18–85; approved eff. 11–11–69

Section 13   Committees of the House—Deleted

HISTORY: Deleted by Order 2005–10, eff. 1–1–06; prior amendment eff. 1–1–97 (Order 96–1); approved eff. 10–22–85

Section 14   Board to promote educational publications

The Board from time to time, pursuant to the authority vested in it by SCR 3.090, shall promote or maintain the printing and distribution of reports, legal pamphlets and other publications, including the sponsoring and production of radio and television programs, which are designed to educate or inform the bar and the public; it shall also conduct continuing legal education programs, seminars and institutes calculated to advance the interests of the bench and bar and promote and improve the administration of justice in Kentucky, and it may appropriate funds necessary to defray the expense thereof.

HISTORY: Amended by Order 96–1, eff. 1–1–97; approved eff. 11–11–69

Section 15   Amendments

These By–Laws may be amended at any regular or special meeting of the Board by a majority vote of the Governors present and voting, and may be amended between meetings of the Board upon written consent of a majority of all the Governors then holding office; provided, that no amendment shall be effective until approved by the Supreme Court pursuant to the provisions of SCR 3.090.

HISTORY: Amended by Order 96–1, eff. 1–1–97; approved eff. 11–11–69

Section 16   Law Student Division —Deleted

HISTORY: Deleted eff. 11–8–10; prior amendments eff. 1–1–97 (Order 96–1), 8–18–78, 1–4–74; approved eff. 11–11–69

Section 17   Removal for Cause

(a) A KBA Board of Governors member, KBA officer, or member of a KBA committee may be removed from the Board, his or her office, or the committee, for cause, as hereinafter defined, on the two-thirds affirmative vote of a quorum of the Board of Governors present at a regular meeting or a meeting called for that purpose. Members of the Board may be present by telephone. For purposes of this Bylaw, the term "cause" shall mean any of the following:

(i) physical or mental impairment rendering him/her incapable of performing duties to the Association for a period of more than three consecutive meetings;

(ii) absence of the Board member or officer at two consecutive Board meetings or absence of a committee member from two consecutive meetings of that committee without cause deemed adequate by the Board;

(iii) continued neglect or failure, after written demand, to discharge his/her duties or to obey a specific written direction from the Board;

(iv) a conflict that renders him/her incapable of fulfilling his/her duties to the Association;

(v) misconduct that is injurious to the Association;

(vi) conviction of a misdemeanor involving dishonesty or immoral conduct; or

(vii) conduct that impairs his/her ability to perform his/her duties to the Association or would impair the reputation of the Association.

A KBA member who is convicted of a felony, which automatically results in suspension under SCR 3.166, or any member who is suspended or disbarred from the practice of law by Order of the Kentucky Supreme Court, is removed effective the date of such conviction, suspension, or disbarment, inasmuch as he/she would be ineligible to serve.

(b) Removal proceedings shall be commenced upon a written request to the KBA President by four or more members of the Board. The proceedings shall be conducted as follows:

(i) All Board members, officers, and any affected committee member shall receive at least thirty (30) days' notice in writing of the meeting at which the Board will consider proposed removal, and the written notice shall set forth the grounds for the proposed removal;

(ii) A written response to the grounds for removal may be presented to the KBA no later than ten (10) days before the meeting;

(iii) At the meeting the member and/or his or her counsel may present oral argument, if oral argument is requested in the written response filed as provided in (b)(ii); and

(iv) At the meeting the Board shall consider the matter and vote in executive session.

(c) In the event of removal, the position shall be filled pursuant to SCR 3.080.

HISTORY: Approved, eff. 9–10–09

SUPREME COURT ORDER IN RE: KENTUCKY BAR ASSOCIATION ANNUAL DUES STRUCTURE

Effective July 1, 2012

The Board of Governors of the Kentucky Bar Association (KBA) unanimously recommended an increase in the annual dues for membership in the KBA to a rate of $350.00 for those members who have been admitted to the practice of law for five years and $220.00 for those members who have been admitted to the practice of law less than five years. The Board also recommended that the Court eliminate the category of dues that allows members of the judiciary to pay a decreased membership fee.

The Court rejected the Board's recommendations, but the majority agreed that an increase in membership dues is necessary to sustain the operating budget of the KBA. Accordingly, under Section 116 of the Constitution of the Commonwealth of Kentucky and Supreme Court Rules (SCR) 3.040, the Court ORDERS:

1) Effective July 1, 2012, the annual dues to be charged for membership in the KBA will be as follows: $310.00 for those members who have been admitted to the practice of law for five years or more; $220.00 for those members who have been admitted to the practice of law less than five years; and $150.00 for members of the judiciary, as set forth in paragraph 8 of this Order;

2) $155.50 from the annual dues of each member who has been admitted less than five years and $233.00 from the annual dues of each member who has been admitted five years or more shall be allocated to the KBA's General Fund. These funds will include an assessment of $10.00 per member for salaries and expenses of the KBA's Lawyers Assistance Program, as set forth in SCR 3.900–SCR 3.995;

3) $40.00 from the annual dues of each member who has been admitted less than five years and $48.00 from the annual dues of each member who has been admitted five years or more shall be allocated to the KBA's Continuing Legal Education Fund for the operation of the mandatory continuing legal education program established under SCR 3.600–SCR 3.690;

4) $17.50 from the annual dues of each member who has been admitted less than five years and $20.00 from the annual dues of each member who has been admitted five years or more shall be allocated for the Bar Center Fund, which has been merged with the Bar Center Construction Fund for the general operations of the Kentucky Bar Center;

5) $2.00 from the annual dues of each member who has been admitted five years or more shall be allocated to the Association's Donated Legal Services (Pro Bono) Development Fund;

6) $7.00 from the annual dues of each member who has been admitted less than five years and $7.00 from the annual dues of each member who has been admitted five years or more shall be allocated to the Clients' Security Fund for the purposes set forth in SCR 3.820;

7) Those members who have been made Honorary Members by order of the Board of Governors shall not be required to pay annual dues;

8) The above paragraphs notwithstanding, the annual dues shall be $150.00 for members of the KBA who hold one of the following listed judicial offices on a full-time basis:

   a) Justice of the Supreme Court of Kentucky;

   b) Judge of the Kentucky Court of Appeals;

   c) Judge of a Kentucky Circuit Court;

   d) Judge of a Kentucky District Court;

   e) Judge of the United States District Court for the Eastern District of Kentucky;

   f) Judge of the United States District Court for the Western District of Kentucky;

   g) Judge of the United States Court of Appeals for the Sixth Circuit;

   h) United States Magistrate for the Eastern or Western District of Kentucky;

   i) Judge of the United States Bankruptcy Court for the Eastern or Western District of Kentucky; and

   j) Retired members of the judiciary who have held one or more of the above-enumerated offices on a full-time basis and who do not engage in the practice of law.

The $150,00 annual dues for the members of the KBA who hold the above-listed offices on a full-time basis shall be apportioned as follows: $118.00 to the KBA General Fund, $21.00 to the Continuing Legal Education Fund, $1.00 to the Donated Legal Services (Pro Bono) Development Fund, $4.00 to the Bar Center Fund, and $6.00 to the Clients' Security Fund. These funds will include an assessment of $10.00 per member for salaries and expenses of the KBA's Lawyers Assistance Program, as set forth in SCR 3.900–SCR 3.995;

9) The annual membership dues for the first fiscal year of membership in the Kentucky Bar Association shall be prorated from the annual rate of $220.00 per year for members who have been admitted less than five years. First-year members will pay $18.33 per month, including the first month of admission, based on a July 1 to June 30 fiscal year;

10) The Board of Governors shall notify the Court of any lack of funds in the Clients' Security Fund reserves that would cause the inability of claims to be paid from either interest income or reserves of the Fund; and

11) The Board of Governors has authority to transfer money as needed among the funds listed in this Order upon majority vote of Board members and notice to the Court.

All sitting. Minton, C.J.; Abramson, Cunningham, Noble, and Venters, JJ. , concur. Scott, J., concurs, in part, and dissents, in part, and states; I dissent from any increase in the dues for attorneys and judicial members of the Kentucky Bar, except for my own, on which I join and will gladly pay. Schroder, J., dissents by separate opinion.

SCHRODER, J., DISSENTING: I vehemently oppose any dues increase in this economy. KBA members engaged in both private and governmental practice are facing budget cuts that are unprecedented, in recent history. In contrast, having reviewed the KBA's proposed budget, it appears that there are no cuts in any programs or expenses, and, over the past few years, I have noticed and warned the KBA that it has been increasing its base salaries at a faster pace than either the private or government sectors. KBA members, as well as the rest of everyday Kentuckians, *have had to cut costs* to sustain themselves in this economy, *while the KBA's approach is to simply increase dues*. I find it very disturbing that the Kentucky Bar Association is trying to immunize itself from the economic downturn by increasing the financial burden on its members, rather than cutting costs.

The KBA also proposed raising the judges' and justices' dues to equal the dues paid by non-judge members. I agreed with this proposal, but the majority did not. With respect to the judges' and justices' dues, I find it morally offensive that we should be treated as a privileged class—*paying less than half of what non-judge lawyers pay.*[1] We are all lawyers and members of the same bar association. There was a period in history when public service was foremost on judges' minds, to the extent that they usually were paid less than their counterparts in private practice. Indeed, this discrepancy in pay between the judiciary and their private-sector counterparts provided a rational basis for giving these judges a break with lower bar dues.

Now the tables have turned. According to the report of the KBA's Task Force on Dues Structure Evaluation, lawyers all across Kentucky make *less* than members of the judiciary. Since I have been on the bench (over 28 years), judges' salaries have increased to become commensurate with private practice. With the recent economic downturn, judges' salaries have been frozen, while the private practice has actually suffered a *decline* in income. As of March, 2011, lawyers in the areas of Louisville, Lexington, Henderson, Owensboro, Bowling Green, and Hopkinsville were earning in the range of $85,000 to $105,000 per year on average. Lawyers in extreme Western Kentucky were earning in the range of $65,000 to $85,000 per year on average. Lawyers in extreme Eastern Kentucky were earning in the range of $125,000 to $145,000 per year on average. Lawyers in Southern Kentucky appear to be earning the least, earning on average in the range of $40,820 to $.65,000 per year.[2]

In contrast, Kentucky state court judges' salaries for Fiscal Year 2012 are as follows (regardless of location):

Supreme Court	
Chief Justice	$140,508
Justice	$135,502
Court of Appeals	
Chief Judge	$133,044
Judge	$130,044
Circuit/Family Court	
Chief Regional Circuit Judge	$125,616
Circuit/Family Judge	$124,620
District Court	
Chief Regional District Judge	$113,664
District Judge	$112,668

As the Justice from the Sixth Supreme Court District, I received a number of comments from my fellow judges arguing that judges should not be required to pay the same amount as other lawyers, because the bar does not provide them with any services—as we have our own CLE, discipline, and etcetera. Nevertheless, I must remind my fellow judges that we are lawyers first, and not every member of the bar association utilizes the same level of benefits. Granted, some judges do volunteer to provide CLE and other services to the bar association at no cost; however, the lawyers provide far more *pro bono* hours as officers of the court, than the judges provide to the KBA.

The majority of our Court approved a $40 increase for both the judiciary and lawyers who have practiced five years or more—choosing to preserve the status quo and leave the judiciary paying less than half of what non-judge lawyers pay. Under a "fair share" proposal, which I support, the judiciary would pay the same amount as other bar members. Fellow judges and justices, in light of the above salary disparity, I believe we should pay our fair share. We should be treated equally with other members of our bar association and not as a privileged class.

This Order shall become effective July 1, 2012.

HISTORY: Adopted eff. 7–1–012

1. Currently, judges and justices pay $110 per year. KBA members with five or more years of practice pay $270, and members under five years of practice pay $220. Under the new schedule, judges and justices will pay $150, KBA members with five or more years of practice will pay $310, and members with under five years remain at $220.

2. W. Douglas Myers, Chairman, *Report of Task Force on Dues Structure Evaluation*, August 21, 2011, pp. 3–4 (Appendix to the Bar Budget).

KENTUCKY BAR ASSOCIATION CODE OF PROFESSIONAL COURTESY

Adopted Effective September 1, 1993

Attorneys are required to strive to make the system of justice work fairly and efficiently. In carrying out that responsibility, attorneys are expected to comply with the letter and spirit of the applicable Code of Professional Responsibility adopted by the Supreme Court of Kentucky.

The following Code of Professional Courtesy is intended as a guideline for lawyers in their dealings with their clients, opposing parties and their counsel, the courts and the general public. This Code is *not* intended as a disciplinary code nor is it to be construed as a legal standard of care in providing professional services. Rather, it has an aspirational purpose and is intended to serve as the Kentucky Bar Association's statement of principles and goals for professionalism among lawyers.

1. A lawyer should avoid taking action adverse to the interests of a litigant known to be represented without timely notice to opposing counsel unless ex parte proceedings are allowed.

2. A lawyer should promptly return telephone calls and correspondence from other lawyers.

3. A lawyer should respect opposing counsel's schedule by seeking agreement on deposition dates and court appearances (other than routine motions) rather than merely serving notice.

4. A lawyer should avoid making ill-considered accusations of unethical conduct toward an opponent.

5. A lawyer should not engage in intentionally discourteous behavior.

6. A lawyer should not intentionally embarrass another attorney and should avoid personal criticism of other counsel.

7. A lawyer should not seek sanctions against or disqualification of another attorney unless necessary for the protection of a client and fully justified by the circumstances, not for the mere purpose of obtaining tactical advantage.

8. A lawyer should strive to maintain a courteous tone in correspondence, pleadings and other written communications.

9. A lawyer should not intentionally mislead or deceive an adversary and should honor promises or commitments made.

10. A lawyer should recognize that the conflicts within a legal matter are professional and not personal and should endeavor to maintain a friendly and professional relationship with other attorneys in the matter—"leave the matter in the courtroom."

11. A lawyer should express professional courtesy to the Court and has the right to expect professional courtesy from the Court.

HISTORY: Adopted by Order 93–1, eff. 9–1–93

PROBATE FORMS

Current with Amendments Received Through January 1, 2013

AOC–740   Petition to Determine if Disabled

AOC-740 Rev. 5-04 11/13/2010 02:44 pm Page 1 of 2 Ver. 1.01 Commonwealth of Kentucky Court of Justice www.kycourts.net KRS 387.530	Doc. Code: PDD **PETITION TO DETERMINE IF DISABLED**	Case No. _____ Court _____ County _____

COMMONWEALTH OF KENTUCKY   PETITIONER

VS.

                                                                  RESPONDENT

_____ has reasonable grounds or knowledge to lead him/her to believe Respondent appears to be unable to provide for his/her physical health and safety and/or manage his/her financial resources effectively and submits to the Court the following facts upon which he/she supports this belief:

1. **Name of Petitioner:** _____

    Address: _____

    _____

    _____

    Telephone Number: _____

    Petitioner's relationship to Respondent: _____

2. **Name of Respondent:** _____

    Address: _____

    _____

    _____

    Respondent's Date of Birth (if known): _____

3. **The nature of Respondent's disability** and the facts or reasons supporting the need for determination of disability are:

    _____

    _____

    _____

    _____

4. Respondent owns the following estate, including government benefits, insurance entitlements, and anticipated yearly income (state none or unknown):

ESTATE	VALUE
Real Property	$_____
Personal Property	$_____
Yearly Income	$_____
Source of Yearly Income	_____

    _____

5. **Name of Person having custody of Respondent:** _____

    Address: _____

    _____

    _____

[Print]   [Reset Form]

6. Respondent's ☐ **Durable Power of Attorney** OR ☐ **Health Care Surrogate** is:
    Name: _____
    Address _____
    _____
    _____

7. Respondent's next of kin:
    Name: _____
    Address _____
    _____
    _____

    Relationship to Respondent: _____
    Name: _____
    Address _____
    _____
    _____

    Relationship to Respondent: _____

    WHEREFORE, Petitioner requests the Court inquire into Respondent's ability to care for himself/herself and to manage his/her financial resources. Petitioner attaches an **Application for Appointment of Fiduciary and further requests:**
    1. Trial by jury;
    2. Counsel to represent the Respondent; and
    3. Court appointment of a physician, psychologist and social worker to evaluate Respondent as provided by law unless the evaluation report is filed with this Petition.

Date: _____, 2_____   _____
                                                          Signature of Petitioner

Subscribed and before me on _____, 2_____ My commission expires: _____, 2_____   _____   Name/Title

To be completed if Applicant is represented by counsel.

Attorney's Name _____
Address _____
_____
_____
_____

Telephone Number _____

_____
Attorney Signature

[Print]   [Reset Form]

AOC–745   Application for Appointment of Fiduciary for Disabled Persons

AOC-745 Doc. Code: AAF Rev. 3-03 Page 1 of 2 Commonwealth of Kentucky Court of Justice www.kycourts.net KRS 387.530(2); 387.720; 395.130	**APPLICATION FOR APPOINTMENT OF FIDUCIARY FOR DISABLED PERSONS**	Case No. _____ Court ____ District ____ County _____

COMMONWEALTH OF KENTUCKY   PETITIONER

VS.

                                                               RESPONDENT

· · · · · · · · ·

1. Comes now _____ , Applicant herein,
    and requests to be appointed as _____ for Respondent.
2. Applicant states his/her relationship to Respondent is _____ .
3. Applicant states his/her qualifications for appointment are as follows: _____
    _____
    _____
    _____
    _____
    _____

4. Applicant offers as surety on his/her bond the following: _____
    _____
    _____

5. Respondent owns the following estate, including government benefits, insurance entitlements, and anticipated yearly
    income (state if none or unknown):

ESTATE	VALUE
Real Property	$ _____
Personal Property	_____
Yearly Income	_____
Source of yearly Income	_____

6. Applicant states that all statements in the foregoing are true.

Applicant's Name: _____   _____

Address: _____
_____
_____

Telephone Number: _____

Date: _____ , 2____ .   _____
                                                       Applicant's Signature

---

Subscribed and sworn to before me on _____ , 2____ . My commission expires _____ ,
2____ .

                                                       _____
                                                       Name/Title

AOC-745
Rev. 3-03
Page 2 of 2

Case No._____

**WAIVER OF NOTICE AND REQUEST
FOR APPOINTMENT OF FIDUCIARY**

The undersigned hereby waive notice of hearing and the right to appointment and request the Court to make the appointment herein applied for:

_____   _____
_____   _____
_____   _____
_____   _____

To be completed if Applicant is represented by counsel:

Attorney's Name _____

Address _____
_____
_____

Telephone Number_____

_____
                                                    Attorney Signature

AOC–747 Petition/Application for Emergency Appointment of Fiduciary for Disabled Persons

AOC-747 Doc. Code: PEF		Case No. _____
Rev. 7-03		
Page 1 of 2	**PETITION / APPLICATION FOR**	Court District
Commonwealth of Kentucky	**EMERGENCY APPOINTMENT**	
Court of Justice *www.kycourts.net*	**OF FIDUCIARY FOR DISABLED PERSONS**	County _____
KRS 387.740; 387.720; 395.130		

COMMONWEALTH OF KENTUCKY ex rel

_____ PETITIONER

VS.

_____ RESPONDENT

1. Comes Petitioner and requests appointment as **emergency limited** [   ] **guardian** OR [   ] **conservator** for
    Respondent for the purpose of: _____
    _____
    _____
    _____
    _____

2. Petitioner states his/her relationship to Respondent is: _____
    and his/her qualifications for appointment are: _____
    _____
    _____
    _____

3. Petitioner offers as surety on his/her bond the following: _____
    _____
    _____

4. Respondent is _____ years of age and resides at: _____
    _____
    _____

5. The person or facility having custody of the Respondent is *(name and address)*:
    _____
    _____
    _____

6. A petition for a Determination of Disability was filed on _____, 2_____ .

7. Respondent's [   ] **Durable Power of Attorney** OR [   ] **Health Care Surrogate** is:
    Name: _____ _____
    Address: _____
    _____

**8.   Affidavit(s) are attached setting forth facts, including any danger alleged as imminent, and reasons
necessitating such appointment.**

AOC-747
Rev. 7-03
Page 2 of 2

9.   Respondent's next of kin is/are:

Name: _____

Address: _____

_____

_____

Relationship: _____

Name: _____

Address: _____

_____

_____

Relationship: _____

WHEREFORE, Petitioner respectfully **requests** that a **hearing be held** within one (1) week of the filing of this Application.

Petitioner's Name: _____

Address: _____

_____

_____

Telephone Number: _____   **Social Security No.** _____

Date: _____   _____
                                                    Petitioner's Signature

Subscribed and sworn to before me this _____ day of _____, 2_____. My Commission expires:
_____, 2_____.   _____
                                                        Name/Title

WAIVER OF NOTICE AND REQUEST FOR APPOINTMENT OF FIDUCIARY
    The undersigned hereby waive notice of hearing and the right to appointment and request the Court to make the appointment herein requested.

_____   _____

_____   _____

_____   _____

To be completed if Petitioner is represented by counsel:

Petitioner's Attorney: _____

Address: _____

_____

Telephone No. _____   _____
                                                          Attorney's Signature

Distribution: Petitioner/Attorney   County Attorney   Respondent/Attorney

AOC–765 Report of Interdisciplinary Evaluation Team

| AOC-765 Doc. Code: RIET
Rev. 10-10
Page 1 of 3
Commonwealth of Kentucky
Court of Justice www.courts.ky.gov
KRS 387.540 | REPORT OF INTERDISCIPLINARY
EVALUATION TEAM | Case No. _____
Court _____
County _____ |

COMMONWEALTH OF KENTUCKY   )
              Petitioner   )
VS.   )
)
)
          Respondent   )

* * * * * * * * * * * *

We, the undersigned, hereby report to the court as follows:

1.   That the nature and extent of the Respondent's disabilities may be described as follows:

_____

_____

_____

_____

2.   That the evaluations ordered regarding the Respondent are current and were performed and signed by the following individuals:

Evaluation:	Name	Title	Date Performed
Intellectual:			
Physical:			
Educational:			
Adaptive Behavior:			
Social Skills:			

AOC-765
Rev. 10-10
Page 2 of 3

Doc Code: RIET

3.   That guardianship:

☐   Is needed for the following reason:

_____

_____

☐   Is not needed for the following reason:

_____

_____

4.   That the recommendation(s) of the type, scope, and duration of guardianship for the Respondent is/are as follows:

_____

_____

5.   The conservatorship:

☐   Is needed for the following reason:

_____

_____

☐   Is not needed for the following reason:

_____

_____

6.   That the recommendation(s) of the type, scope, and duration of conservatorship for the Respondent is/are as follows:

_____

_____

7.   That the social, educational, medical, and rehabilitative services currently being provided to the Respondent are as follows:

_____

_____

_____

8.   That appropriate alternatives to guardianship/conservatorship:

☐   Are available   (explain):

_____

_____

☐   Are not available   (explain):

_____

_____

9.   That the recommendations and reasons as to the most appropriate treatment or rehabilitation plan and living arrangement for the Respondent are as follows:

_____

_____

_____

AOC-765
Rev. 10-10
Page 3 of 3

Doc Code: RIET

10. That for the Respondent to attend the hearing on the Petition filed herein:

☐ Would subject him/her to serious risk of harm.

☐ Would not subject him/her to serious risk of harm.

11. That appended hereto is a list of all medications currently being given to the Respondent on a continuous basis, the dosage of the medication, and a description of its impact upon the Respondent's mental and physical condition and behavior.

12. That any dissenting opinions or other comments are as follows:

_____

_____

_____

_____   _____
Date   Signature of Licensed Physician

                                 _____
                                 Signature of Licensed/Certified Psychologist

                                 _____
                                 Signature of Licensed/Certified Social Worker

                                 _____
                                 Signature of Other

_____
Name of Facility or Agency

_____
Address

_____
Telephone Number

[Print]   [Reset Form]

AOC–777 Verified Petition for the Voluntary Appointment of Guardian or Conservator, etc.

AOC-777 Doc. Code: PVA & OAG		Case No. _____

AOC-777   Doc. Code: PVA & OAG
Rev. 8-03   Or OCON
Page 1 of 2

Commonwealth of Kentucky
Court of Justice *www.kycourts.net*

KRS 387.330

VERIFIED PETITION FOR THE VOLUNTARY APPOINTMENT OF A GUARDIAN OR CONSERVATOR AND STANDBY GUARDIAN AND ORDER

Case No. _____

Court _____

County _____

IN RE: _____
_____ Petitioner's Full Name

Social Security No. _____

Date of Birth / Age _____

_____
Address

Pursuant to KRS 387.330, the above-named petitioner hereby requests this Court to appoint

_____   _____
(Name)   (Address)

_____, as [ ] guardian [ ] conservator of my property. Upon the death,
(Telephone Number)

resignation, removal, or incapacity of the appointed guardian or conservator, I nominate _____,
(Name)

_____, _____
(Address)   (Telephone Number)

as standby guardian. Petitioner requests that the appointment be made [ ] without bond or [ ] with bond to be fixed in the

amount of $_____.

The Petitioner's [ ] Durable Power of Attorney [ ] Health Care Surrogate is:

_____
Name

_____
Address

_____

This petition is to be acted upon by the Court only upon one of the following conditions:

a.   Occurrence of the following event:

_____

The occurrence of the above event shall be established by:

_____

b.   Existence of the following condition of the petitioner's mental or physical health:

_____

The existence of the above condition shall be established by:

AOC-777   Doc. Code: PVA & OAG
Rev. 8-03   Or OCON
Page 2 of 2

     Additionally, this petition is to be acted upon by the Court only if accompanied by an affidavit from a licensed physician indicating that the above-named petitioner is disabled as defined in KRS 387.510. That affidavit [   ] is attached [   ] will be filed later.

     The proposed ward is hereby advised that a guardian's powers are defined in KHS 387.065 and consist of the support, care and education of the ward while not being personally liable for the ward's expenses or to third parties. Specifically, a guardian has the power to take custody of the ward, establishing the ward's place of abode within the Commonwealth, and to take reasonable care of the ward's personal effects and finances. The proposed ward is also advised that a conservator's powers are defined in KRS 387.137 and unlike the guardian's powers, consist only of managing the ward's finances and assets.

_____   _____
          Date   Signature of Petitioner

SUBSCRIBED AND SWORN TO before me this _____ day of _____, 2_____.

                                _____
                                     Name / Title

                                _____
                                   County, Kentucky

                * * *   * * *   * * *   * * *   * * *

ORDER

     Having fully reviewed the above petition, and being otherwise sufficiently advised,

     IT IS HEREBY ORDERED that _____ _____ [   ] is [   ] is not

competent and fit to be appointed as guardian or conservator. It is further ordered that _____

[   ] is [   ] is not competent and fit to be appointed as standby guardian. Therefore, the Court appoints

_____, as [   ] guardian, [   ] conservator and _____ _____,

as standby guardian.

_____   _____
          Date   Judge

AOC–790   Annual Report of Guardian

AOC-790 Doc. Code: RGD Rev. 12-03 Page 1 of 3 Commonwealth of Kentucky Court of Justice *www.kycourts.net* <u>KRS 387.670</u>	**ANNUAL REPORT** **OF GUARDIAN**	Case No._____ Court_____ County_____

COMMONWEALTH OF KENTUCKY   )
)
)
VS.   )
)
)
_____)
           RESPONDENT   )

* * * * * * * * * * * *

    I, the undersigned, state that I am the ❑ Guardian ❑ Limited Guardian of the above-named Respondent, and report to the Court as follows:

1.   Present age of Ward:_____.

2.   Date of birth:_____.

3.   Current address of Ward:_____.

4.   Ward's present living arrangment is:

    ❑ Own home   ❑ Nursing home

    ❑ Guardian's home   ❑ Skilled care

    ❑ Hospital   ❑ Intermediate care

    ❑ Relative's home   ❑ Personal care

    _____
        Relationship

    ❑
Other:_____

5.   Ward has been at present residence since_____.
    If Ward has lived elsewhere during the reporting period, list description and address of each residence and the length of stay at each.

_____

_____

_____

AOC-790   Doc. Code: RGD
Rev. 12-03
Page 2 of 3

6.   During this reporting period, the Ward's mental condition has:

    ❑ Remained about the same.

    ❑ Improved. Describe: _____

        _____

    ❑ Deteriorated. Describe: _____

        _____

7.   During this reporting period, the Ward's physical health has:

    ❑ Remained about the same.

    ❑ Improved. Describe: _____

        _____

    ❑ Deteriorated. Describe: _____

        _____

8.   During this reporting period, the Ward's social condition has:

    ❑ Remained about the same.

    ❑ Improved. Describe: _____

        _____

    ❑ Deteriorated. Describe: _____

        _____

9.   During this reporting period, the Ward has received the following services:

    Medical: _____

    Educational: _____

    Social: _____

    Vocational: _____

    Other: _____

10. My visits and activities on behalf of the Ward were:

    _____

    _____

    _____

AOC-790
Rev. 12-03
Page 3 of 3   Doc. Code: RGD

11. The guardian ❑ should   ❑ should not be continued or modified for the following reasons:

_____

_____

12. I ❑ do ❑ do not have responsibility for managing the Ward's estate. If so, an accounting of the estate ❑ is attached ❑ was filed last year.

13. A standby guardian ❑ has ❑ has not been appointed.

_____   _____
             Date   Guardian

_____
    Guardian's Phone Number

_____   _____
    Guardian's Social Security Number   Address

* * * * * * * * * * * *

SUBSCRIBED and SWORN to before me this_____day of_____, _____.

My Commission expires:_____.

_____
                        Notary Public

* * * * * * * * * * * *

To be signed by Standby Guardian if one is appointed.

     I, the undersigned, state that I am the Standby Guardian of the above-named Respondent and continue to be willing to serve in the event of the death, resignation, removal or incapacity of the Guardian.

_____   _____
             Date   Signature of Standby Guardian

_____
    Standby Guardian's Phone Number

_____   _____
    Standby Guardian's Social Security Number   Address

AOC–795   Petition for Relief, Modification or Termination

| AOC-795
Doc. Code: PRMT
Rev. 7-11
Page 1 of 2

Commonwealth of Kentucky
Court of Justice   www.courts.ky.gov
KRS 387.620 | **PETITION FOR RELIEF,
MODIFICATION OR TERMINATION** | Case No. _____

Court _____ DISTRICT _____

County _____ |

COMMONWEALTH OF KENTUCKY   PETITIONER

VS.

_____   RESPONDENT

*   *   *   *   *   *   *   *   *   *   *

Comes the Petitioner and requests the Court to ☐ terminate ☐ modify as follows:

☐   The order of ☐ partial disability ☐ disability entered on _____ be
☐ terminated ☐ modified as follows: _____

_____

☐   To remove the present fiduciary and replace with _____ .
☐   To renew the appointment of the present fiduciary for a period of _____ .

In support of this request, Petitioner states:

1.   The Respondent's address: _____
    In custody of: _____

2.   Respondent's present fiduciary: _____
    Address: _____
    Appointed on: _____

    As: ☐ Limited Guardian   ☐ Limited Conservator
           ☐ Guardian   ☐ Conservator

3.   The Respondent's ☐ Durable Power of Attorney ☐ Health Care Surrogate is:

    _____   _____
           Name   Address

                                     _____

4.   Respondent's next of kin are:

           Name   Address   Relationship

_____   _____   _____

_____   _____   _____

_____   _____   _____

5.   The facts and reasons supporting this request:

_____

_____

_____

AOC-795   Doc. Code: PRMT
Rev. 7-11
Page 2 of 2

WHEREFORE, the Petitioner requests that this court conduct a hearing within thirty (30) days of the filing of this petition.

If the foregoing petition is for a renewal of the appointment of a limited guardian or conservator, it shall be accompanied by verified affidavits of a physician, a psychologist, or a social worker in support of same pursuant to KRS 387.610.

_____
Petitioner

_____
Address

_____
Relationship to Respondent

SUBSCRIBED and SWORN to before me this _____ day of _____, _____.

_____
Name/Title

_____
County, Kentucky

To be completed if Petitioner is represented by counsel:

_____
Signature of Attorney

_____
Address of Attorney

_____
Telephone Number

An attested copy of this Petition was mailed this date to the Respondent, the attorney of record, the county attorney and all persons named in the Petition.

_____   _____
Date   Signature

| Print | | Reset Form |

AOC–805   Petition

AOC-805 Doc. Code: PPW		Case No._____
Rev. 10-05 or PWF		Court_____ District/Probate
Page 1 of 3		County_____
Commonwealth of Kentucky		
Court of Justice www.courts.ky.gov	PETITION	
KRS 394.145, KRS 395.015		

IN RE: Estate of _____

Decedent's Information: SSN: _____ Birthdate: _____ Date of Death: _____

Last Address: _____

_____

_____

Decedent died: ☐ Intestate (without a Will)   ☐ Testate (with a Will)

PETITION FOR

☐ **PROBATE OF WILL**
☐ **APPOINTMENT OF ADMINISTRATOR/ADMINISTRATRIX**
☐ **APPOINTMENT OF EXECUTOR/EXECUTRIX**

Petitioner states there has been no previous administration in the Decedent's estate in Kentucky or elsewhere. Further, Petitioner states that the statements in the caption are true, and that the names of the surviving spouse, heirs at law and next of kin known to Petitioner are as follows (use additional paper if necessary):

Name: _____ Relation:_____ Age:_____
Address: _____
_____
_____

Name: _____ Relation:_____ Age:_____
Address: _____
_____
_____

Name: _____ Relation:_____ Age:_____
Address: _____
_____
_____

Decedent owned/had interest in the following **real estate** with estimated market values as noted:

_____

_____

_____ **Estimated Total: $**_____

Print		Reset Form

Case No._____

Decedent owned/had interest in the following **personal property** with estimated market values as noted:

_____

_____

_____ **Estimated Total: $** _____

Petitioner is indebted to or owes Decedent $_____.

☐   Petitioner applies for probate of Decedent's Will, filed herewith, which is his/her Last Will and Testament.

☐   Petitioner prays _____, whose address is

_____

_____

be appointed ☐ Executor/Executrix ☐ Administrator/Administratrix of said estate and who offers as surety on the bond

the following: _____. **All the foregoing statements are true.**

Petitioner's Signature:_____ Phone No. : _____

Petitioner's Name (Printed): _____

Petitioner's Address:_____

_____   _____

_____

Subscribed and sworn before me by Petitioner on _____, 2_____. My commission will expire:

_____, 2_____. _____

                                                    Name/Title

This certifies this Petition was prepared or subscribed by the undersigned in accordance with the meaning and tenor of Kentucky Civil Rule No. 11. **(Attorney must prepare and present separate Order of Probate or complete Order on Page 3 of this Petition). (To be filled in duplicate).**

Attorney's Signature:_____ Phone No.:_____

Attorney's Name (Printed): _____

Address:_____

_____

_____

WAIVER

We, the undersigned, surviving spouse and next of kin of the above-named Decedent, resident of _____

_____ County, Kentucky, hereby waive notice of the hearing of the Petition and if applicable, the presentation of said Decedent's Will for probate and/or appointment of fiduciary, and request the Court to appoint _____

_____ as ☐ Executor/Executrix ☐ Administrator/Administratrix.

_____   _____

_____   _____

_____   _____

[Print]   [Reset Form]

AOC-805
Rev. 10-05
Page 3 of 3

Case No._____

IN RE: Estate of_____

ORDER

[ ]   Petition filed this _____ day of _____, 2_____.

[ ]   Will tendered this _____ day of _____, 2_____.

Upon hearing, the Will offered was proven by _____

and **ORDERED PROBATED** as the Last Will and Testament of Decedent this _____ day of _____, 2_____.

The Court appoints: _____as

[ ] Executor/Executrix OR [ ] Administrator/Administratrix of said estate and fixes bond in the sum of

$_____ [ ] with surety OR [ ] without surety.

Date: _____, 2_____.   _____
                                                                                   Judge's Signature

Distribution:
        Case File
        Revenue Cabinet

Print   Reset Form

AOC–806   Order Probating Will and Appointing Executor/Executrix

AOC - 806 Doc. Code: OWF Rev. 12-03 Page 1 of 1 Commonwealth of Kentucky Court of Justice *www.kycourts.net* KRS Chapters 394 and 395	ORDER PROBATING WILL AND APPOINTING EXECUTOR/EXECUTRIX	Case No. _____ Court District Probate County_____

IN RE: Estate of _____

Decedent's Date of Death: _____   SSN: _____

        The Petition for probate of the Will of the above-named Decedent and for appointment of an Executor/Executrix

came on for hearing on _____, 2___. The Will was produced in open court and was [ ] self-proved

under KRS 394.225 **OR** [ ] proved by _____.

        IT IS THEREFORE ORDERED that the Will be, and it is, hereby admitted to probate as the Last Will and Testament

of the Decedent. **IT IS FURTHER ORDERED** that _____,

with an address of _____

_____

_____,

be and is, hereby appointed Executor/Executrix of said estate. The Court fixes bond in the sum of $ _____.

        WHEREUPON said Executor/Executrix took the oath prescribed by law and entered into and acknowledged the

above-mentioned bond with [ ] approved Surety **OR** [ ] Surety having been waived.

Date: _____, 2____.   _____ **Judge**

NOTICE OF ENTRY WAIVED:

_____
    Petitioner's OR Attorney's Signature

CERTIFICATION

    I, _____, Clerk of the _____ District
Court, do certify this constitutes a true and correct copy of the Order Admitting Will to Probate and Appointing
Executor/Executrix, as recorded in my office.

Date: _____, 2____.   _____ **Clerk**

                    By: _____, **D.C.**

Distribution:
        Original - Court File *(with certified copy of Will)*
        Copies - Executor/Executrix
                    Revenue Cabinet *(Inheritance Tax Section)*
        Certified Copy - County Clerk *(with original of Will); Petitioner is responsible for recording fee.*

AOC–807   Certificate of Qualification

AOC-807 Doc. Code: CQ Rev. 6-10 Page 1 of 1 Commonwealth of Kentucky Court of Justice www.courts.ky.gov	**CERTIFICATE** **OF QUALIFICATION**	Case No. _____ Court _____ District _____ County _____

IN Re: Estate of _____

    Proper petition having been filed and the Court having appointed _____

_____ as _____

_____

of the above estate on the _____ day of _____, 2____, and the fiduciary having

filed in Court bond in the sum of $_____, the amount fixed, with _____

_____ as surety,

which was approved by the Court, said fiduciary was thereupon duly sworn as required by law and thus qualified on the

above date.

    The above Order and Qualification is in full force and effect this _____

                                                     (Date)

Attest: _____ Clerk

By: _____

                   Deputy Clerk

[Print]   [Reset Form]

AOC-820 Petition for Appointment of Trustee Under Will

| AOC-820 Doc. Code: PAT & OAT
Rev. 8-11
Page 1 of 2

Commonwealth of Kentucky
Court of Justice www.courts.ky.gov

KRS Chapter 386 | PETITION FOR APPOINTMENT
OF TRUSTEE UNDER WILL | Case No. _____

Court _____

County _____ |

IN RE: Estate of _____

Residence: _____, Kentucky

Social Security Number: _____ Date of Death: _____, _____

The will was probated in _____ County on _____, _____, of
which the original or an accurate copy is submitted herewith to the Court for examination.

Petitioner, _____, says that
the statements in the caption are true, and the names of the life tenant and remaindermen of the instant
trust are as follows (*Write name, interest, age and address of each remainderman*):

Petitioner states that the Trust, created under item _____ of the Will, consist of the following assets:

Personal Estate $_____   Annual Income from Personal Estate $_____

Real Estate $_____   Annual Rents of Real Estate $_____

Petitioner states that the applicant is indebted to or owes decedent _____.

Petitioner prays the Court that _____ be
appointed as Trustee under said will, and _____
is offered as surety.

Petitioner says that all statements in the foregoing petition are true.

Date: _____, 2_____   _____
                                      Petitioner's Signature

Petitioner's Address: _____
                      _____
                      _____

Petitioner's Social Security Number: _____

Subscribed and sworn to before me by petitioner on _____, 2_____. My commission will expire_____, 2_____.
_____   _____ Notary Public   County, Kentucky

This certifies that the within petition was prepared or subscribed by the undersigned in accordance with the
meaning and tenor of CR 11.

_____   _____
Attorney's Signature   Address/Phone Number

AOC-820   Doc. Code: PAT & OAT
Rev. 8-11
Page 2 of 2

IN RE: Estate of _____, a decedent

ORDER

Petition filed in open Court on _____, _____, Upon hearing,
the Court appoints _____,
Trustee of said estate, and fixes bond in the sum of $_____.

Date: _____, 2_____   _____
                                                              Judge's Signature

WAIVER OF NOTICE

The undersigned hereby waive notice of hearing and the right to appoint and request the court to make
the appointment herein applied for:

_____   _____

_____   _____

AFFIDAVIT OF SURETY

Affiant, _____,
states that affiant is a resident of _____ County of the Commonwealth of Kentucky, and
that affiant has fee simple to and beyond amount of liens or encumbrances and homestead exemptions and subject
to execution, real estate of value of $_____ located at _____
in affiant's own name. Value of Property: $_____ Encumbrances and $_____ Homestead.

_____   _____
      Surety's Signature   Phone Number

Surety's Address: _____

_____

Subscribed and sworn to before me by above-named affiant on _____, 2_____.

_____ Clerk

| Print | Reset Form | By:_____ D.C. |

AOC–825   Fiduciary Bond

AOC-825   Doc. Code: BF
Rev. 8-12
Page 1 of 2
Commonwealth of Kentucky
Court of Justice   www.courts.ky.gov
KRS 62.060, 395.130, 395.140,
454.180 -.185

FIDUCIARY BOND

Case No. _____

Court _____

County _____

IN RE: Estate of _____

Address: _____

_____

_____

The Fiduciary named below having been appointed to act as _____ by the order
of _____ Court on _____, 2_____, states the Fiduciary and Surety do hereby covenant
to and with the Commonwealth of Kentucky in the sum of $_____ for the use and benefit of all parties
of interest herein, and the Fiduciary will faithfully perform and discharge all duties of the aforesaid trust according to law.

Name of Fiduciary: _____

Signature of Fiduciary: _____

Address: _____

_____

_____

Name of Surety: _____

Signature of Surety: _____

Address: _____

_____

_____

Name of Surety: _____

Signature of Surety: _____

Address: _____

_____

_____

(Each individual Surety other than licensed surety companies, banks and trust companies must complete the Affidavit of Surety on page 2 of this form)

Taken and subscribed before me on this _____ day of _____, 2_____.

_____ Clerk

By: _____ D.C.

Attorney's Signature: _____   Phone No.: _____

Attorney's Name (Printed): _____

Address: _____

_____

_____

Date: _____, 2_____.   **Approved:** _____ Judge

AOC-825
Rev. 8-12
Page 2 of 2

Case No. _____

Each individual Surety other than licensed surety companies, banks and trust companies must complete the Affidavit of Surety.

AFFIDAVIT OF SURETY

I swear (or affirm) I am a resident of _____ County, Kentucky; I own property worth double the amount

to be secured by this bond beyond the amount of my debts; and, I own property in Kentucky subject to execution equal to

the amount of this bond. Real estate (if any) is located in _____ County. If property is jointly owned,

all owners must sign this affidavit.

_____
Surety's Signature

_____
Surety's Signature

Subscribed and sworn before me on _____, 2____.   _____ Clerk

By: _____ D.C.

426

AOC–830   Petition/Order to Dispense with Administration (Surviving Spouse/Children/Preferred Creditor)

| AOC-830   Doc. Code: PDA & ODA
Rev. 7-12
Page 1 of 2
Commonwealth of Kentucky
Court of Justice   www.courts.ky.gov
KRS 391.030; 394.145; 395.455;
396.095 | **PETITION/ORDER TO DISPENSE
WITH ADMINISTRATION**
(Surviving Spouse/
Children/Preferred Creditor) | Case No._____

Court   District/Probate_____

County_____ |

IN RE: Estate of _____

                                                   (Name of Decedent)

Address: _____

                _____

                _____

Date of Death: _____   Social Security Number: _____

Date of Birth: _____

PETITION

Comes the Petitioner, being first duly sworn, and states as follows:

1. Decedent died ☐ testate ☐ intestate with residence at the above listed address and on the above date.

2. At the time of death, decedent left no estate to be administered with the exception of the following assets (include value for each asset listed):

3. In relation to the above named decedent, I am the *(check all that apply)* ☐ surviving spouse ☐ only surviving child ☐ surviving child whose surviving siblings have signed a waiver herein or attached a waiver ☐ preferred creditor ☐ preferred creditor of the decedent whose surviving spouse has signed a waiver herein or attached a waiver ☐ assignee of the preferred creditor.

4. ☐ *(check if applicable)* Petitioner applies for Probate of Decedent's Will, filed herewith, which is his/her Last Will and Testament.

5. As a preferred creditor/assignee of decedent, I have paid the following claim(s) against the estate in the following order (attach receipts):

Claim	Payee	Amount
a. Cost and Expenses of Administration	_____	_____
b. Funeral expenses	_____	_____
c. Debts and taxes with preference under federal and Kentucky Law	_____	_____
d. Other	_____	_____

6. I certify that there has been no previous administration of decedent's estate within Kentucky or elsewhere.

AOC-830   Doc. Code: PDA & ODA
Rev. 7-12
Page 2 of 2

Case Number _____

Because the exemption given to the above surviving spouse/child(ren) and/or claim(s) of the above preferred creditor/assignee equals or exceeds the value of the above estate asset(s), I ask this Court to dispense with the administration of the above estate and to transfer the above personal property to me or my designee, _____.

_____ _____ _____
Name of Surviving Spouse Waiving Preference   Age   Signature of Surviving Spouse Waiving Preference
(Please Print)   (If Petitioner is not Decedent's Spouse)

Address/P.O. Box Address: _____

_____

_____

_____   _____
Signature of Surviving Child Waiving Preference   Signature of Surviving Child Waiving Preference

_____
Petitioner's Signature

Address: _____

_____

Phone Number: _____

+--+
| Subscribed and sworn before me by petitioner on _____, 2_____. |
| |
| My commission expires _____. |
| |
| _____ |
| Name/Title |
+--+

ORDER

[ ] Upon hearing, the Will offerred was proven by _____ and ORDERED PROBATED as the Last Will and Testament of Decedent this _____ day of _____, 2_____. The Will shall be probated only and no letters of administration shall be issued.

Upon verified petition of the above petitioner, IT IS HEREBY ORDERED that the petition be granted to dispense with the administration of the estate of the above decedent, and the above personal property is transferred to petitioner or his/her designee, _____.

_____, 2_____   _____
Date   Judge's Signature

CERTIFICATE

I certify that this petition and order were prepared in accordance with CR 11.

_____   _____
Attorney for Petitioner   Address and Phone Number

Distribution: Court File   Petitioner

AOC–841 Inventory and Appraisement of Estate

| AOC-841 Doc. Code: INV
Rev. 7-12
Page 1 of 2

Commonwealth of Kentucky
Court of Justice www.courts.ky.gov
KRS 395.250 | **INVENTORY AND APPRAISEMENT
OF ESTATE** | Case No. _____

Court ____ District Probate ____

County _____ |

IN RE: Estate of _____

Decedent's Date of Death: _____   Decedent's SSN: _____

Description of Assets	Estimated Value

AOC-841
Rev. 7-12
Page 2 of 2   Case No. _____

Description of Assets	Estimated Value

Total Estimated Value: $ _____

I submit the foregoing as the Inventory of the above-named Decedent's estate; which Inventory was made on

_____, 2_____.

Signature of Executor / Executrix or Administrator / Administratrix

Subscribed and sworn before me on _____, 2_____. My commission expires: _____, 2_____.

_____
Name/Title

Attorney's Signature: _____ Phone No.: _____

Attorney Name (Printed): _____

Address: _____

_____

_____

CLERK'S CERTIFICATE

The foregoing Inventory having been returned to me in duplicate, the original is now filed in my office and the

duplicate mailed to the Commissioner of Revenue, Commonwealth of Kentucky this on _____, 2_____.

_____ Clerk

By: _____ D.C.

Distribution: Court File (original)   Revenue Cabinet

AOC–846 Settlement

AOC-846 Doc. Code: SET		Case No. _____
Rev. 3-00		Court_____
Page 1 of 2		County_____
Commonwealth of Kentucky		Division_____
Court of Justice *www.kycourts.net*		
KRS 395.600 - .657		

_____ SETTLEMENT of _____ as _____

of the _____

Date		Voucher No.	Receipts	Disbursements

AOC-846   Doc. Code: SET
Rev. 3-00
Page 2 of 2

Date		Voucher No.	Receipts	Disbursements
Total Receipts and Disbursements				

To The Judge of The_____District
Court:

    I hereby certify that the foregoing is a true and correct statement of the amounts received and paid out by me as

_____of the_____

_____from_____to this date.

_____

    Subscribed in my presence, and sworn to before me by

the said_____this the_____day of

_____in the year _____.

_____

    Notary Public,_____

County, _____. My commission as

Notary Public will expire_____

_____
        Attorney Name & Address (If any)

    It is now ordered that this Settlement be filed in the Clerk's office; advertised in accordance with statutory regulations; and continued for exceptions.

_____Judge

Noted of record, and filed therein, this_____

_____

_____Clerk

By_____, D.C.

Having been appropriately advertised on_____

_____, and no exceptions having been filed, this Settlement is now approved; ordered recorded; the estate now closed; the personal representative discharged; and the surety relieved effective this date.

_____Judge

432

AOC–850   Informal Final Settlement: Affidavit, Motion, and Order

AOC-850 Doc. Code: AFF & SETI Rev. 11-10 Page 1 of 2 Commonwealth of Kentucky Court of Justice *www.courts.ky.gov* KRS 395.605	*(seal)* **INFORMAL FINAL SETTLEMENT: AFFIDAVIT, MOTION, AND ORDER**	Case No._____ Court_____ District/Probate_____ County_____

IN RE: Estate of _____

Date of Death _____   Social Security Number _____
                                   (month, day, year)

AFFIDAVIT/MOTION

Comes the affiant, being first duly sworn, and states as follows:

1.   Six months have passed since my appointment as fiduciary to the above estate.

2.   (   ) I am sole beneficiary.

        (   ) I am not sole beneficiary, but I have attached a verified waiver from each beneficiary (AOC-851). (No verified waiver is required of the "nonresiduary legatee," a beneficiary who has received and receipted for his/her share pursuant to a specific will provision. The cancelled check or signed receipt is attached as evidence of satisfaction.)

3.   The estate is solvent.

4.   (   ) All legal claims and debts have been paid.

        (   ) All legal claims and debts have not been paid, but have been provided for in the following manner:

_____.

5.   All inheritance, estate or similar death taxes have been paid. A duplicate or photocopy of such tax releases is attached, if available.

6.   All court costs have been paid.

7.   (   ) My attorney's fee is _____. His/her name and address:

        Name: _____

        Address: _____

        _____

        _____

        (   ) I do not have an attorney.

8.   Each beneficiary has received his/her share.

AOC-850   Doc. Code: AFF & SETI
Rev. 11-10
Page 2 of 2

I ask this Court to dispense with the requirements of KRS Chapter 395 regarding settlement of fiduciaries' accounts and dispense with the requirements of a surety for the fiduciary and accept this informal settlement as final settlement.

_____
Affiant

_____
Address

_____

_____

_____
Phone Number

Subscribed and sworn to before me this _____ , _____ .
                                          (month)   (day)   (year)

_____
Name/Title

ORDER

Upon the affidavit/motion of the above affiant/fiduciary,

IT IS HEREBY ORDERED that the requirements of KRS Chapter 395 regarding settlement of fiduciaries' accounts and the requirements of a surety for the fiduciary are waived, the informal settlement is filed, and the fiduciary (and surety, if any) is discharged.

_____   _____
              Date   Judge

NOTICE TO CLERK AND JUDGE: When a settlement is effected in the informal manner, no notice to any person shall be required (for example, NO ADVERTISEMENT IS REQUIRED) nor shall the court be compelled to inquire into detailed items of income or disbursements. KRS 395.605(1).

Distribution:
     Original - Court File
     Copy - Affiant / Attorney

AOC–851   Affidavit of Waiver of Formal Settlement

AOC-851	Doc. Code: WFS		Case No. _____
Rev. 1-02			
Page 1 of 1			Court District Probate
Commonwealth of Kentucky			
Court of Justice		**AFFIDAVIT OF WAIVER OF**	County_____
KRS 395.605(2)		**FORMAL SETTLEMENT**	

NOTICE: To be used with **AOC- 850, Informal Final Settlement: Affidavit, Motion and Order**, when there is more than one (1) beneficiary.

IN RE: Estate of _____

     We, the undersigned beneficiaries of the above estate, being under no legal disability unless noted, state under oath that we consent to the Informal Settlement of the estate, hereby waiving requirements of KRS Chapter 395 regarding settlement of fiduciaries' accounts.

_____   _____
_____   _____
_____   _____
_____   _____
_____   _____
_____   _____
_____   _____
_____   _____

Subscribed and sworn to before me by beneficiaries whose names are _____

_____

on _____, 2____. My commission expires: _____.

_____
Name/Title

NOTICE TO JUDGE: If one or more beneficiaries is under a disability, you may allow the filing of an Informal Settlement if you are of the opinion the best interests of the person under the disability would be served. KRS 395.605(3). You may require Fiduciary to execute bond with or without Surety to insure application of estate assets to debts of Decedent. KRS 395.605(2).

AOC–852   Petition for Appointment of Guardian/Conservator for Minor

AOC-852 Doc. Code: PGM or Rev. 10-10 PCM Page 1 of 2 Commonwealth of Kentucky Court of Justice www.courts.ky.gov KRS 387.025, KRS 395.016	**Petition For Appointment Of Guardian/Conservator For Minor**	Case No. _____ Court _____ County _____

SS# or EIN# (If any) _____
Voluntary

NOTE TO PETITIONER: A verified application for appointment as guardian/limited guardian/conservator must accompany this form. AOC 853 may be used.

In re estate of _____, a minor under the age of 18.

Petitioner, _____, petitions this Court for appointment of a (choose one):

☐ guardian (individual, agency, or corporation having care, custody, and control of minor and managing minor's financial resources); or

☐ limited guardian (individual, agency, or corporation having care, custody, and control of minor without managing minor's financial resources); or

☐ conservator (individual, agency, or corporation managing minor's financial resources) for the above named minor.

In support of this petition, petitioner states as follows:

1.   Minor's address is _____.

2.   Minor's date of birth is _____.

3.   Name and address of minor's spouse is _____

4.   Name(s) and address(es) of minor's living parent(s) is (are) _____

5.   If no living parent(s), name(s) and address(es) of minor's adult next of kin is (are) _____

6.   Name and address of individual or facility having custody of minor is _____

7.   Facts and reasons supporting need for appointment are: _____

8.   Description and value of estate:

	Description	Value
a. Real Property	_____	$ _____
b. Personal Property	_____	$ _____
c. Other Financial Resources:		
(1) Government Benefits	_____	$ _____
(2) Insurance Entitlement	_____	$ _____

AOC-852
Rev. 10-10
Page 2 of 2

(3) Anticipated Yearly
Income _____ $ _____

(4) Other _____ $ _____

9. Petitioner's address is _____

10. Name and address of petitioner's attorney is _____

_____

11. Name and address of person/entity desiring appointment is _____

_____

Based on the above, petitioner prays that the above named person/entity be appointed as ☐ guardian, ☐ limited guardian, or ☐ conservator. A verified application for appointment as guardian/limited guardian/conservator for minor completed by the above named person/entity is attached.

_____
Petitioner

SUBSCRIBED AND SWORN to before me on this date, _____, _____.

_____
Name/Title

_____
Attorney Name & Address (If any)

Choice of Guardian
by Minor age 14 or older

(This choice must be made in the presence of the Court.)

The undersigned, being a minor aged 14 or older, nominates as ☐ guardian, ☐ limited guardian, or ☐ conservator:

_____   _____
Name   Address

                                     _____
                                     Minor

Copy Distribution:
Minor (If 14 or older)
/ Entity Named in Petition

[Print]   [Reset Form]

AOC–853 Application for Appointment as Guardian/Conservator for Minor

AOC-853 Doc. Code: AAM		Case No. _____
Rev. 5-04		Court _____
Page 1 of 1	**APPLICATION FOR APPOINTMENT AS**	County _____
Commonwealth of Kentucky	**GUARDIAN/CONSERVATOR FOR MINOR**	
Court of Justice *www.kycourts.net*		
KRS 387.025		

In Re: estate of _____, a unmarried minor under the age of 18.

Comes now the applicant, _____, affiant herein, and applies to be appointed as [ ] guardian, [ ] limited guardian, or [ ] conservator of the above-named minor. In support of this application, applicant states as follows:

1. My address is _____

_____

_____.

2. My birthdate is _____.

3. My relationship to minor, if any, is _____.

4. I [ ] have/ [ ] have not been convicted of a crime.

If yes, please explain _____.

5. My qualifications for this appointment are _____

_____.

6. Applicant [ ] waives [ ] does not waive notice of appointment hearing. If waived, applicant has completed waiver at the bottom of form.

Applicant states that all the statements above are true and correct.

_____, 2_____
Date   Applicant's Signature

Subscribed and sworn to before me on this date _____, 2_____.

_____
Name/Title

_____
Attorney Name and Address (if any)

WAIVER OF NOTICE AND
REQUEST FOR APPOINTMENT OF GUARDIAN

The undersigned, being under no legal disability, hereby waive notice of hearing on the appointment of guardian/limited guardian/conservator and request the court to make the requested appointment. A minor age 14 or older may waive notice if present in person at hearing on application. Court may dispense with notice requirements if gross amount of estate is less than $5,000. KRS 387.025; KRS 395.016.

_____   _____

_____   _____

_____   _____

AOC–855   60 Day Inventory or Supplemental Inventory

AOC 855 Doc. Code: INV		Case No. _____
Rev. 10-12		
Page 1 of 2		Court _____ District
Commonwealth of Kentucky	**60 DAY INVENTORY OR**	
Court of Justice www.courts.ky.gov	**SUPPLEMENTAL INVENTORY**	County _____
KRS 387.100	[ ] MINOR [ ] DISABLED PERSON	

NOTICE TO GUARDIAN/CONSERVATOR: FILE THIS INVENTORY WITHIN **60 DAYS** OF APPOINTMENT. IF OTHER PROPERTY LATER COMES TO YOUR KNOWLEDGE, A SUPPLEMENTAL INVENTORY MUST BE FILED WITHIN 60 DAYS OF OBTAINING SUCH KNOWLEDGE.

IN RE: Estate of _____, a [ ] Minor under 18   [ ] Disabled Person.

_____ states that as [ ] guardian [ ] conservator, the following is a full, true and complete Inventory of the Estate which has come into his/her hands or the existence of which he/she has knowledge:

1. **Real Property:** (Include description, address, probable value and probable   **Value**
                        value of rent.)

    _____ $ _____

    _____ $ _____

    _____ $ _____

    _____ $ _____

2. **Personal Property:**

    a. Motor Vehicles (Autos, Trucks, Farm Equipment)   **Value**

        _____ $ _____

        _____ $ _____

        _____ $ _____

        _____ $ _____

    b. Household Appliances and Jewelry   **Value**

        _____ $ _____

        _____ $ _____

        _____ $ _____

        _____ $ _____

3. **List all monies owed for** any item under 1 and 2:

    _____

    _____

AOC 855   Doc. Code: INV
Rev. 10-12
Page 2 of 2   Case No. _____

4.   **Monies or Cash on Hand:**

       a.   Monthly Government Benefits and Pensions, Social Security, SSI   **Value**

                 _____ $ _____

                 _____ $ _____

                 _____ $ _____

                 _____ $ _____

       b.   Savings, Checking Accounts and Certificates of Deposit: **Value**

                 _____ $ _____

                 _____ $ _____

                 _____ $ _____

                 _____ $ _____

5.   **Claims against** the Ward: **Value**

       _____ $ _____

       _____ $ _____

6.   **Claims by the Ward** against others: **Value**

       _____ $ _____

       _____ $ _____

_____   _____
           Date   **Guardian/Conservator Signature**

_____   _____
   Guardian's Phone Number
                                                _____
                                                            Address

Subscribed and sworn to before me this _____ day of _____, _____.

                                                _____
                                                            Name/Title

AOC–856   Periodic/Final Settlement of Guardian/Conservator for Minor/Disabled Person

AOC-856 Doc. Code: SET Rev. 10-12 Page 1 of 2 Commonwealth of Kentucky Court of Justice www.courts.ky.gov KRS 387.175, 387.670, 387.710 395.610-.657; 395.990	**Periodic/Final Settlement of Guardian/Conservator For [ ] Minor [ ] Disabled Person**	Case No. _____ Court _____ District _____ County _____

Notice to Guardian/Conservator: File this Settlement one (1) year after appointment and annually thereafter. If the net estate is $5,000 or less, file this Settlement every two (2) years after the original report.

IN RE: Estate of _____, a [ ] Minor under 18 [ ] Disabled Person.

Comes _____, appointed as [ ] Guardian [ ] Conservator of the above estate on _____, 2____. This [ ] Periodic [ ] Final Settlement indicates, by itemized statement and supported by receipts and vouchers, the assets received and disbursements made since the Inventory or last Settlement was filed. It is submitted pursuant to:

[ ] KRS 387.710   OR   [ ] KRS 387.175, 395.610 - 395.657 and 395.990

ASSETS & INVESTMENTS

(Include anything of value to the estate including government benefits, Social Security and SSI pension plan benefits, savings and checking accounts, certificates of deposit, all personal property, rents from real estate, and proceeds from the sale of real estate and personal property. Attach additional sheets of paper if necessary).

ITEM _____   **AMOUNT**

_____ $ _____

_____ _____

_____ _____

_____ _____

_____ _____

_____ _____

                         TOTAL ASSETS RECEIVED: $ _____

DISBURSEMENTS   **AMOUNT**

_____ $ _____

_____ _____

_____ _____

_____ _____

_____ _____

_____ _____

_____ _____

                      TOTAL DISBURSEMENTS MADE: $ _____

BALANCE   **ASSETS LESS DISBURSEMENTS:** $ _____

For Periodic Settlements - carry balance forward to next report.
For Final Settlements - indicate to whom balance was paid and attach receipt.

AOC 856   Doc. Code: SET
Rev. 10-12
Page 2 of 2   Case No. _____

IN PERIODIC SETTLEMENTS:

PLAN FOR PRESERVING AND MAINTAINING ESTATE (*not to be filled out if estate has net value of $5,000 or less*)

_____
_____
_____
_____
_____
_____
_____

IN FINAL SETTLEMENTS:

UNPAID CREDITORS - ALLOWED CLAIMS   **AMOUNT**

_____ $ _____
_____   _____
_____   _____
_____   _____
_____   _____
_____   _____

                                        TOTAL $ _____

CREDITORS - DISALLOWED CLAIMS   **AMOUNT**

_____ $ _____
_____   _____
_____   _____
_____   _____
_____   _____
_____   _____

                                        TOTAL $ _____

    Above-named Guardian/Conservator submits this Settlement to the Court, and if a Final Settlement, asks that the Surety be discharged.

_____   _____
            Date   **Guardian/Conservator Signature**

_____   _____
   Guardian's Phone Number

                                        _____
                                                        Address

Subscribed and sworn before me on _____, 2____ My commission expires: _____,
2____ .

                                        _____
                                                       Name/Title

AOC–858   Petition By Crematory to Authorize Cremation of Decedent and Order

AOC-858 Rev. 9-10 Page 1 of 1 Commonwealth of Kentucky Court of Justice www.courts.ky.gov KRS 367.97501	**PETITION BY CREMATORY TO AUTHORIZE** **CREMATION OF DECEDENT AND ORDER**	Case No. Court County

IN RE:
_____ Name of Decedent (please print)

Date of Death:

    Comes the Petitioner, the person in charge of a licensed crematory authority, and moves the Court for a finding that in absence of an authorizing agent as defined in KRS 367.97501, the Court act as the authorizing agent and order the cremation of the decedent named above.

_____   _____
Signature of Petitioner   Date

Crematory:

  Address:

Telephone Number:

ORDER

IN RE:
_____ Decedent's full name (please print)

Petitioner:
_____ Crematory

    IT IS HEREBY ORDERED that the Crematory's request to permit the cremation of the decedent is ☐ granted ☐ denied.

SO ORDERED THIS _____ day of _____.

_____
Judge   Div. _____

Distribution: Petitioner
                Crematory
                File

[Print]   [Reset Form]

GENERAL INDEX

AOC . . . . Probate Forms
AP . . . . Administrative Procedures of the Court of Justice
Bar Bylaws . . . . By-Laws of the Kentucky Bar Association
Const . . . . Constitution of Kentucky
CR . . . . Civil Rules
FCRPP . . . . Family Court Rules of Practice and Procedure
KRE . . . . Kentucky Rules of Evidence
Med . . . . Model Mediation Rules
RCr . . . . Criminal Rules
SCR . . . . Supreme Court Rules

ADMISSIBILITY OF EVIDENCE—Cont'd

Medical bills, offer to pay as proof of liability, **KRE 409**

Negligence, proving, subsequent remedial measures, inadmissible, **KRE 407**

Original writing, record or photograph lost, destroyed or unavailable, other evidence of contents, **KRE 1004**

Pleas, **KRE 410**

Preliminary question, **KRE 104**

Rape victims past behavior, **KRE 412**

Relevancy conditioned on fact, **KRE 104**

Relevant evidence, **KRE 402**

Religious beliefs, **KRE 610**

Settlements, **KRE 408**

Subsequent remedial measures, **KRE 407**

Inadmissible, **KRE 407**

Witnesses, inconsistent statements, **KRE 613, 806**

ADMISSION TO BAR

Admission without examination, **SCR 2.040(6), 2.110**

Advocating overthrow of government, prohibition, **SCR 2.012**

Application, **SCR 2.010 et seq., 2.022**

Admission in other states, **SCR 2.022**

Attorney licensed in another jurisdiction, **SCR 2.022**

Deadline, **SCR 2.022**

Eligibility, decision by character and fitness committee, **SCR 2.060**

Extended late filing, **SCR 2.023**

False statements, **SCR 3.130(8.1)**

Fee, **SCR 2.022**

Filing, **SCR 2.022**

Late filing, **SCR 2.023**

Hearings, **SCR 2.050**

Incomplete, **SCR 2.018**

Information provider, immunity from liability, **SCR 2.009**

Packets, **SCR 2.018**

Reapplication, **SCR 2.024**

Refused by another state, effect, **SCR 2.022**

Attorney licensed in another jurisdiction, application, **SCR 2.022**

Background investigation, **SCR 2.022**

Board of bar examiners, **SCR 2.080 et seq.**

Chair, **SCR 2.020**

Employees, **SCR 2.007**

Expenses, **SCR 2.002**

Members, **SCR 2.020**

Compensation, **SCR 2.007**

Qualifications, **SCR 2.007**

Rules, **SCR 2.000**

Travel expenses, **SCR 2.005**

Certificate of admission, **SCR 2.120**

Approval, **SCR 2.085**

Limited certificate, **SCR 2.111**

Expiration, **SCR 2.111**

Time period for validity, **SCR 2.085**

Character and fitness, **SCR 2.011**

Certification, **SCR 2.022**

Denial, **SCR 2.018**

Recertification, **SCR 2.062**

Confidential information, **SCR 2.008**

Investigative or reporting fees, **SCR 2.011**

Character and fitness committee. Bar Association, this index

Conditional admission, **SCR 2.042**

Disabilities, persons with, special accommodations for bar examination, **SCR 2.082**

Disciplinary action in another state, ineligible, **SCR 2.022**

ADMISSION TO BAR—Cont'd

Education, legal, **SCR 2.014**

Erroneous information, **SCR 2.013**

Examination, **SCR 2.080**

Application, **SCR 2.010 et seq.**

Board of bar examiners, generally, ante

Confidential information, **SCR 2.008**

Educational requirements, **SCR 2.014**

Exemption, **SCR 2.040(6), 2.110**

Certificate of admission, **SCR 2.085**

Failure, **SCR 2.080**

Grading, **SCR 2.080**

Multistate examination, **SCR 2.080**

Professional responsibility, **SCR 2.015**

Reexamination, **SCR 2.080**

Restoration of membership, prerequisite, **SCR 3.500(3)**

Special accommodations, disabilities, persons with, **SCR 2.082**

Withdrawal from, **SCR 2.022**

Fees,

Admission without examination, **SCR 2.110**

Application, **SCR 2.022**

Certificate of admission, **SCR 2.120**

Character and fitness, investigative or reporting fees, **SCR 2.011**

Character and fitness committee costs, **SCR 2.040(7)**

Extended late filing, **SCR 2.023**

Late filing, **SCR 2.023**

Legal education, unaccredited, cost of evaluation, **SCR 2.014**

Limited certificate of admission, **SCR 2.111**

Reinstatement, suspended members, **SCR 3.510**

Fitness, hearings, **SCR 2.050**

Foreign attorneys, **SCR 2.110**

Foreign legal education, **SCR 2.014(3), 2.070(3)**

Hearings, **SCR 2.050**

Ineligible, disciplinary action in another state, **SCR 2.022**

Intention to practice law in commonwealth, **SCR 2.013**

Kentucky office of bar admissions, confidential information, **SCR 2.008**

Legal education, **SCR 2.014, 2.070**

Limited certificate of admission, **SCR 2.111**

Expiration, **SCR 2.111**

Moral character, hearings, **SCR 2.050**

Multistate examination, **SCR 2.080**

Multistate professional responsibility examination, passing as prerequisite to bar examination, **SCR 2.015**

Nonresident,

Examination exemption, **SCR 2.110**

Limited certificate of admission, **SCR 2.111**

Expiration, **SCR 2.111**

Oath, **SCR 2.012, 2.120**

Pro hac vice, **SCR 2.111, 3.030(2)**

Professional responsibility examination, passing as prerequisite to bar examination, **SCR 2.015**

Purpose to obtain admission in another state, **SCR 2.013**

Qualifications, **SCR 2.010 et seq.**

Reciprocity, examination exemption, **SCR 2.110**

Restoration or reinstatement of membership, **SCR 3.500 et seq.**

Conditional reinstatement, **SCR 2.042**

Continuing legal education requirements, **SCR 3.500, 3.675**

Dues, payment, **SCR 3.050**

Suspended member, **SCR 3.510**

Restricted admission, application for, **SCR 2.112**

Rules, **Const § 116**

CONVICTS
Prisoners, generally, this index

CORAM NOBIS
Generally, **RCr 11.42**

CORPORATIONS
Appearance at trial, **RCr 8.28(3)**
Deposition of officer or agent, **CR 30.02(5), 31.01(2)**
    Use in court proceedings, **CR 32.01**
Existence, allegation, **CR 9.01**
Interrogatory, service on, **CR 33.01(1)**
Service of process, **CR 4.04(5), 5.02; RCr 2.10(3)**
    Constructive service, **CR 4.05 et seq.**
Surety, as, **RCr 4.30(1)**
Warning order against, **CR 4.05 et seq.**
    See, also, Constructive Service, generally, this index

CORRECTIONAL FACILITIES
Prisoners, generally, this index

CORRECTIONAL INSTITUTIONS
Deposition of employee or officer, **CR 32.01**
Prisoners, generally, this index

CORRECTIONS DEPARTMENT
    See, also, Administrative Organization, generally, this index
Wardens, assessment center, orders and judgments concerning custody of convicted felons served on, **RCr 11.22(3)**

CORROBORATION
Confession of defendant, **RCr 9.60**

COSTS
Court Costs, generally, this index

COUNSEL, LEGAL
Attorneys, generally, this index

COUNSELORS
College students, law students providing counseling, **SCR 2.540**
Law students providing counseling to college students, **SCR 2.540**

COUNTERCLAIMS
    See, also, Cross-Claims, generally, this index
Generally, **CR 13.01 et seq.**
Absent defendant, **CR 4.14**
Acquiring after pleading, **CR 13.05**
Additional parties for complete relief, **CR 13.08**
Alternative relief, demand for, **CR 8.01**
Amendment of pleadings to establish, **CR 13.06**
Answer, **CR 7.01, 8.03**
    Time for service, **CR 12.01**
Attachment, effect, **CR 13.01**
Avoidance by numerous defendants, **CR 5.04**
Caption, mistaken, effect, **CR 8.03**
Commonwealth, against, **CR 13.01, 13.04**
Compulsory, **CR 13.01**
Constructive service, in actions with, **CR 4.14**
Contents, **CR 8.01**
Controverting by numerous defendants, **CR 5.04**
Damages, **CR 13.03**
Default judgment on, **CR 55.03**
Defendants,
    Addition for complete relief, **CR 13.08**
    After dismissal of actions, **CR 41.01(2)**

COUNTERCLAIMS—Cont'd
Defendants—Cont'd
    Multiple defendants, **CR 5.04**
Demand for relief, **CR 8.01**
Denial by numerous defendants, **CR 5.04**
Dismissal, **CR 41.03**
    Original actions, **CR 41.01(2)**
Exceeding recovery sought by opposing party, **CR 13.03**
Failure to plead does not waive, **CR 13.06**
Form, **CR 8.01**
Governmental agency, against, **CR 13.01, 13.04**
Interpleader of parties by, **CR 22; CR Form 16**
Joinder of claims in, **CR 18.01**
Judgments, **CR 54.02**
    Absent defendant, allowance, **CR 4.14**
    Separate trial, **CR 13.09, 42.02**
    Stay of execution, **CR 62.04**
Leave of court to present, **CR 13.06**
Maturing after pleading, **CR 13.05**
Mistakenly designated as defense, **CR 8.03**
Motions in defense of, **CR 12.02**
Multiple parties,
    Defendants, denial and service between, **CR 5.04**
    Plaintiffs, **CR 13.02**
Omitted, setting up by amendment, **CR 13.06**
Parties, additional, for complete relief, **CR 13.08**
Permissive, **CR 13.02**
Plaintiff may bring in third party, **CR 14.02**
Plaintiffs, several, defendant claim against one, **CR 13.02**
Pleading, **CR 7.01**
Procedure after dismissal of actions, **CR 41.01(2)**
Public official, against, **CR 13.04**
Recovery defeated or diminished by, **CR 13.03**
Relief on, **CR 8.01**
Separate trials, **CR 42.02**
    Judgment, **CR 13.09**
Service, **CR 5.01 et seq.**
    Numerous defendants, between, **CR 5.04**
Service of pleadings, arising after, **CR 13.05**
Set-off, **CR 13.03**
State, against, **CR 13.01, 13.04**
Statement of claim, **CR 8.01**
Stay of separate judgment on, **CR 62.04**
Subject of another pending action, **CR 13.01**
Summary judgment for, **CR 56.01 et seq.**
Summons on, **CR 5.01 et seq.**
Supplemental pleadings, presenting by, **CR 13.05**
Third party, by, **CR 14.01**
Third party brought in by plaintiff, **CR 14.02**
Trial, separate, **CR 42.02**
    Judgment, **CR 13.09**

COUNTIES
Actions by or against, **CR 17.01**
Circuit clerk. Clerk of Circuit Court, generally, this index
Service of summons on, **CR 4.04(7)**

COUNTY CLERKS
Deposit in court, payment from, **CR 67.03**
Liens, recording, bail bond secured by real property, **RCr 4.36**
    Discharge, **RCr 4.44(1)**

COURT, SUPREME
Supreme Court, State, generally, this index

COURT CLERKS
Clerks of Courts, generally, this index

DRUG COURT—Cont'd
Noncompliance, sanctions, **AP XIII § 12**
Notice, involuntary termination, **AP XIII § 16**
Oversight, **AP XIII § 4**
Participants, requirements, **AP XIII § 10**
Probation, orders, **AP XIII § 5**
Referrals, **AP XIII § 5**
Sanctions, noncompliance, **AP XIII § 12**
 Definitions, **AP XIII § 1**
Sessions, **AP XIII § 19**
Staffing, **AP XIII § 18**
Suspension, **AP XIII § 13**
Temporary inactive status, **AP XIII § 10**
 Definitions, **AP XIII § 1**
Termination,
 Involuntary termination, **AP XIII § 16**
 Voluntary termination, **AP XIII § 15**
Transfers, orders, **AP XIII § 9**
Voluntary termination, **AP XIII § 15**
 Definitions, **AP XIII § 1**

DRUG OFFENSES
Drug Court, generally, this index
Guilty pleas, presence of defendant, **RCr 8.28(4)**

DRUG TESTS
Drug court, **AP XIII §§ 10, 23**

DRUNK DRIVING
Guilty pleas, presence of defendant, **RCr 8.28(4)**

DURESS
Attorneys, soliciting clients, **SCR 3.130(7.30)**
Pleading as affirmative defense, **CR 8.03**

DYING DECLARATIONS
Hearsay exception, **KRE 804**

ELECTIONS
Bar association positions, nomination,
 Board of governors, **Bar Bylaws § 4**
 Officers, **Bar Bylaws § 6**
Supreme court justices, **Const § 117**

ELECTRONIC DOCUMENTS
Court of justice records, access by public and bar members, **AP XI**

ELECTRONIC TRANSMISSION
Service of Process, this index

EMERGENCIES AND DISASTERS
Bar association, disaster response plan, **SCR 3.130(7.60)**

EMPLOYERS AND EMPLOYEES
Workers Compensation, generally, this index

ENTRY OF JUDGMENT
Entry. Judgments, this index

EQUITY
Claim, **CR 8.05(2)**
Form of action, **CR 2**

ERRORS
Amendment of pleading curing, **CR 15.02**
Appeals, this index
Arrest warrants, correction, **RCr 2.08**
Averment of mistake, **CR 9.02**
Bail bonds, **RCr 4.56**

ERRORS—Cont'd
Citations, correction, **RCr 2.08**
Clerical,
 Correction, **CR 60.01; RCr 10.10**
 Motion for relief due to, **CR 60.02**
  Time for, **CR 6.02**
Complaints, **RCr 3.13**
Consideration on appeal, **CR 61.01; RCr 10.26**
Correction,
 Amendment of pleading, **CR 15.02**
 Citations, **RCr 2.08**
 Clerical mistake, **CR 60.01; RCr 10.10**
 Motion for, **CR 60.01**
 Notice of order for, **CR 77.04**
 Order for, **CR 60.01**
 Summons, **RCr 2.08**
 Time for correction, **CR 6.02**
Depositions, **CR 32.04**
Disregard of harmless, **CR 61.01**
Harmless Errors, generally, this index
Indictment or Information, this index
Judgments, correction of clerical mistakes, **RCr 10.10**
Motion,
 Correction, for, **CR 60.01**
 Preservation by, **CR 59.06**
 Relief due to, **CR 60.02**
  Time for motion, **CR 6.02**
New trials to consider, **RCr 10.26**
Notice of order for correction, **CR 77.04**
Order for correction, **CR 60.01**
 Notice of entry, **CR 77.04**
Plea of mistake, **CR 9.02**
Preservation for appellate review, **CR 59.06**
Recognizance, **RCr 4.56**
Record on appeal, **CR 75.08**
Relief from judgment,
 Motion for, **CR 60.02**
  Time, **CR 6.02**
 Substantial error, **CR 61.02**
 Time for motion, **CR 6.02**
Review, insufficiently raised or preserved, **CR 61.02**
Substantial, relief granted for, **CR 61.02**
Summons, correction, **RCr 2.08**
Time for correction or relief, **CR 6.02**
Transcripts, correction of clerical mistakes, **RCr 10.10**
Variance in pleading, curing, **CR 15.02**
Writs for review abolished, **CR 60.05**

ESTATES
Settlement. Administration of Estates, this index

ESTOPPEL
Affirmative defense, **CR 8.03**

ETHICS
Conflict of Interest, generally, this index
Judicial ethics committee and opinions, **SCR 4.310**

EVIDENCE
 See, also, Witnesses and Testimony, generally, this index
 Generally, **RCr 7.02 et seq.**
Absence, postponement for, **CR 43.03**
Absent defendant, actions against, **CR 4.13**
Accounting trial, **CR 43.04(1)**
Admissibility of Evidence, generally, this index
Allegations and averments that must be proved, **CR 8.04**
Amendment of pleading to conform to, **CR 15.02**

491

INDEX

PLAINTIFFS—Cont'd
Class actions, **CR 23.01 et seq.**
Death, effect, **CR 25.01**
    Public official, **CR 25.04**
Default judgment, examination, **CR 4.13**
Defendant becoming plaintiff upon refusal of joinder, **CR 19.01**
Dismissal of actions, **CR 41.01 et seq.**
Evidence, production, **CR 43.01, 43.02**
Multiple liability, interpleading required, **CR 22**
Name in which actions must be brought, **CR 17.01**
Real party in interest must be plaintiff, **CR 17.01**
Statement of claim, **CR 43.02**
Substitution of, **CR 25.01 et seq.**
Third party plaintiff,
    Bringing in, on counterclaim, **CR 14.02**
    Defendant as, **CR 14.01**
Warning order, examination, **CR 4.13**

PLEADINGS
    See, also, Allegations and Averments, generally, this index
    Generally, **CR 7.01 et seq.; RCr 1.08, 8.02, 8.08, 8.12**
Address of attorney or party stated on, **CR 11**
Administrative decision, **CR 9.05**
Admissions, generally, this index
Adoption of statement by reference, **CR 10.03**
Affidavits required, **CR 11**
    Attorney, by, **CR 43.13(1)**
Affirmative defenses, **CR 8.03**
    Numerous defendants, **CR 5.04**
Allegations and Averments, generally, this index
Alternative relief may be demanded, **CR 8.01**
Alternative statements of claims or defenses, **CR 8.05(2)**
Amendment of Pleadings, generally, this index
Attorney,
    Liability, **CR 11**
    Signature and address, **CR 11**
Averments. Allegations and Averments, generally, this index
Birth dates, redacting, **CR 7.03**
Capacity to sue or be sued, allegations concerning, **CR 9.01**
Captions, generally, this index
Claims for relief,
    Consistency, **CR 8.05(2)**
    Dismissal, **CR 41.01**
    Failure to state, motion for, **CR 12.02**
    Form, **CR 8.01**
    Joinder of Actions, generally, this index
    Judgment limited to relief prayed for, **CR 54.03**
    Paragraphing, **CR 10.02**
    Separation, **CR 10.02**
Commercial paper, copy as part of, **CR 10.03**
Complaints, generally, this index
Conditions precedent, allegations concerning, **CR 9.03**
Confidential or privileged information, redacting, **CR 7.03**
Consistency of claims or defenses, **CR 8.05(2)**
Construction to do justice, **CR 8.06**
Corporate existence, allegation concerning, **CR 9.01**
Counterclaims, generally, this index
Counts, separation, **CR 10.02**
Cross-Claims, generally, this index
Damages,
    Prayer for, **CR 8.01(2)**
    Proof required for allegations, **CR 8.04**
    Special, pleading, **CR 9.06**
Decision of board, officer, or court, pleading, **CR 9.05**

PLEADINGS—Cont'd
Defenses, generally, this index
Definite, motion for, **CR 12.05**
    Extension of time for answer, **CR 12.01**
    Service of notice of entry, **CR 77.04**
Demand for judgment, **CR 8.01**
    Recovery limitation, **CR 54.03**
Demurrer not allowed, **CR 7.02(3)**
Denials, generally, this index
Disability, pleadings against person under, **CR 8.04**
Dismissal, **CR 41.01 et seq.**
Divorce, proof required for allegations, **CR 8.04**
Endorsement by clerk of court, **CR 5.05(3)**
Equitable and legal claims, joinder of, **CR 8.05(2)**
Exceptions to insufficiency not allowed, **CR 7.02(3)**
Exhibit as part of pleading, **CR 10.03**
Failure to make more definite, **CR 12.05**
Failure to plead, effect, **CR 8.04**
False,
    Prohibition, **CR 11**
    Striking of, **CR 12.06**
Filing, **CR 5.05**
    Hours for, **CR 77.01**
Filing format, **CR 7.02**
Financial account numbers, redacting, **CR 7.03**
Forms, **CR 8.05, 10.01 et seq.**
    Caption, **CR 10.01**
    Claim for relief, **CR 8.01**
    Motion, **CR 7.02**
    Specifications, **CR 7.02**
    Technical, abolished, **CR 8.05(1)**
Hearing on defensive pleading or motion, **CR 12.04**
Hypothetical statement of claims, **CR 8.05(2)**
In forma pauperis, **CR 5.05(4)**
    Certifying record on appeal, time for, **CR 73.08**
Insufficiency of pleading, plea not allowed, **CR 7.02(3)**
Intent, averment, **CR 9.02**
Interpleading, **CR 22**
Intervenor, pleadings by, **CR 24.03**
Issues not raised by, trial, **CR 15.02**
Joinder of Actions, generally, this index
Judgment, pleading, **CR 9.05**
Judgment on the pleadings, **CR 12.03**
Jurisdiction, lack of, **CR 12.02**
Jury trial, demand for, endorsement on pleadings, **CR 38.02, 38.03**
Knowledge, averment, **CR 9.02**
Legal and equitable claims, joinder of, **CR 8.05(2)**
Malice, averment, **CR 9.02**
Mentally ill or defective, allegations against, **CR 8.04**
Mind, condition of, **CR 9.02**
Mistake, averment, **CR 9.02**
Motions, generally, this index
Naming of parties, **CR 10.01**
Nonjoinder, omission, **CR 19.03**
Numerous defendants, dispensing with service, **CR 5.04**
Official document or act, pleading, **CR 9.04**
Orders concerning, service, **CR 77.04**
Paragraphing, **CR 10.02**
Partnership existence, allegation concerning, **CR 9.01**
Party, signature, **CR 11**
Petitions, generally, this index
Prayer for judgment, limitation of recovery, **CR 54.03**
Pretrial conference, concerning, **CR 16**
Prohibited pleas, **CR 7.02(3)**
Proof of allegations, when required, **CR 8.04**
Reference, adoption by, **CR 10.03**

†